History of Physical Anthropology

Garland Reference Library of Social Science (Vol. 677)

History of Physical Anthropology

Volume 2
M-Z

Edited by
Frank Spencer

GARLAND PUBLISHING, INC.
New York & London
1997

Library of Congress Cataloging–in–Publication Data

Spencer, Frank, 1941–
    History of physical anthropology : an encyclopedia / edited by Frank Spencer.
      p.   cm. — (Garland reference library of social science ; vol. 677)
    Includes bibliographical references and index.
    ISBN 0–8153–0490–0 (alk. paper)
    1. Physical anthropology—Encyclopedias.   I. Title.   II. Series:
Garland reference library of social science ; v. 677.
GN50.3.S64   1997
573'.03—dc20   96–34389
                                                        CIP

Cover photo: Neanderthal Man. Reprinted by permission of American Museum of Natural
   History.

Cover design: Lawrence Wolfson Design, New York.

Printed on acid-free, 250-year-life paper
Manufactured in the United States of America

Contents

History of Physical Anthropology

M-Z

McCown, Theodore D(oney) (1908–1969)

Born in Macomb, Illinois, McCown moved with his family to Berkeley, California, in 1914, when his father, Chester Charlton McCown, took the position of dean of the Pacific School of Religion. Later, he lived for several years in Palestine, while his father served as director of the Palestine Exploration Fund. During this period, McCown participated in the excavation of the Jerash site in Transjordan. This early exposure to archeology and his reading of the explorer Henry Stanley's (1841–1904) *In Darkest Africa* (1890) were decisive factors in McCown's choice of career. He shared this interest with his younger brother Donald E(ugene) McCown (1910–1985), who conducted archeological investigations with Ernst Herzfeld (1879–1948) at Persepolis and later at various ancient sites in Iran.

On receiving a B.A. in anthropology (with highest honors) from the University of California, Berkeley, in 1929, McCown spent the following year first as a member of the summer school of the American School of Prehistoric Research (ASPR), and then as a field representative of the ASPR assigned to the British School of Archaeology in Jerusalem (BSAJ), where he assisted Dorothy Garrod (1892–1968) in her ongoing excavations at Mount Carmel. At the close of the 1930 season, McCown began his graduate program in anthropology at Berkeley as a teaching fellow. The following year, he returned to Palestine to work once again with Garrod, and it was during this period that he discovered, on 3 May 1931, the first in a remarkable series of Neandertal skeletons in the Skhūl Cave at Mount Carmel. Following this discovery, McCown was invited to undertake the planning and direction of subsequent excavations at Mount Carmel, which began in 1932 under the auspices of the ASPR and the BSAJ. This work, spanning the period from 1932 through 1937, resulted in the recovery of further Neandertal fossil hominids from the caves of Skhūl and Tabūn. Most of this material was forwarded to the Royal College of Surgeons, London, where between 1933 and 1937 McCown and Arthur Keith (1866–1955) subsequently undertook a collaborative study of it (cf. McCown & Keith 1939). During this time, in England, McCown received support from a Taussig Traveling Fellowship in Anthropology covering the years 1933–1934; an Amy Bowler Johnson Traveling Fellowship, 1934–1935, and a grant from ASPR, 1935–1937.

In 1938, he joined the faculty of the Department of Anthropology at Berkeley as an instructor while completing his doctoral dissertation, *The Natufian Crania from Mount Carmel, Palestine, and Their Interrelationships*. He received his Ph.D. in anthropology in 1939 with the approval of his graduate committee, which was composed of Alfred Kroeber (chairman), Robert Lowie, and G.C. Evans. That same year also saw the publication of *The Stone Age of Mount Carmel II: The Fossil Remains from the Levalloiso-Mousterian*, which he had coauthored with Keith. The remainder of McCown's academic career was spent at Berkeley.

As an assistant professor from 1941 to 1946, McCown conducted archaeological research in 1941–1942 and 1945 at Huamachuco and Cajabamba in the northern highlands of Peru under the auspices of the Institute of Andean Research, later examining (on loan) skeletal remains from Aramburu and other Peruvian sites that Kroeber had collected for the Field Museum in Chicago. Between 1942 and 1945, McCown served in the military and was assigned duty in Graves Registration of the U.S. Army Quartermaster Corps at the San Francisco Presidio. These duties included identification of skeletal remains of war dead, and, for a short time, he was also a cryptographer. Between 1948 and 1950, he was a consultant to the military on protheses research he had begun in 1945. During this same time period, he also held a joint appointment in the Department of Criminology at Berkeley. The practical skills McCown acquired in anatomy and skeletal biology through his earlier association with Keith, and as a military specialist in identification of human remains, provided the background for his lifelong contributions to forensic anthropology and as a consultant on many referrals brought to him by medical-legal clients. Among his most notable cases were (1) the identification of the remains of Juan Bautista de Anza, founder of San Francisco, at Arizpe, Mexico; (2) the identification of the remains of Fra Juniperio Serra at the Franciscan mission at Carmel, California; and (3) the negative identification of remains reputed to be those of Amelia Earhart. Analytical methods in forensic anthropology became an intrinsic feature of the two-semester laboratory course he regularly offered at Berkeley.

As McCown moved through the academic ranks from associate professor (1946–1951) to professor (1951–1969), he continued to study the Mount Carmel Neandertal and Natufian fossils from an ecological perspective (cf. McCown 1950, 1961); from 1948, when he was named curator of physical anthropology in the Anthropology (Lowie/Hearst) Museum, onward, he conducted research on the California Indian skeletal materials that had been collected since the establishment of the Department of Anthropology by Kroeber at the turn of the century. Prehistoric human skeletons from Peru and Baja California were examined in collaboration with his graduate students and were the subjects of doctoral dissertations under his supervision. In 1958, he initiated his first field research in India, which included a survey of Paleolithic sites along a 100-mile stretch of the Narmada Valley, as well as a study of prehistoric human skeletal remains from Langhnaj and other Mesolithic sites in India. McCown was the first American physical anthropologist to conduct research in South Asia for an extended period of time, and in 1964–1965 he returned to India to resume the Narmada Valley survey and to direct excavations at Mahadeo Piparia in collaboration with S.C. Supekar, then a graduate student at Deccan College whose doctoral dissertation was based upon the results of this study of Middle Pleistocene lithic technology of Acheulean tradition and stratigraphic sequences of the Narmada region. Prehistoric lithic materials collected during this survey were sent to Berkeley, where they were used extensively in teaching and research. Further paleoanthropological research in South Asia was in the planning stage at the time of McCown's death on 17 August 1969 while hospitalized in Berkeley for treatment of a heart condition. Some phases of his research program have been continued in India, Pakistan, and Sri Lanka by his former student, K.A.R. Kennedy of Cornell University.

In addition to his scientific work, McCown also made a significant contribution to the advancement of academic physical anthropology in the United States. When he joined the faculty of anthropology at Berkeley in 1938, there were only two other sources for training of graduate students in physical anthropology in the United States: Earnest A. Hooton (1887–1954) at Harvard University and Wilton Marion Krogman (1903–1987) at the University of Pennsylvania. During his thirty-one years at Berkeley, McCown served as chairman of eighteen doctoral committees and as a member of twenty-six others; the majority of his students are practicing physical anthropologists today. Sherwood L. Washburn (1911–) joined the Berkeley department in 1958, twenty years after McCown had created the program in physical anthropology, and together they laid the foundations for the prominence of that field at their university. As documented in a 1979–1980 review of the top ten Departments of Anthropology in the United States in the number of Ph.D.'s produced in physical anthropology, Berkeley is listed as third, with forty (cf. Spencer 1981). McCown's philosophy of teaching allowed his students to develop their own fields of research rather than pursue topics of interest to him. And, in guiding their research programs, he stressed the interface of cultural and physical anthropology but warned that it was the responsibility of followers of the latter discipline to support the concept that "man is a part of 'brute creation,' [and] that the processes which are valid for the processes of organic evolution apply as well to man as other animals. . . ." (McCown 1952:314).

McCown was also a most able administrator, serving as acting chairman (1948–1949), chairman (1950–1955), and vice chairman (1962–1963) of his department, as well as associate dean of his College of Letters and Sciences (1956–1961). These years embraced the turbulent period of student activism at Berkeley, and his grasp of changes in campus and academic life was critical to the resolution of many problems of the 1960s that, at the time, seemed insurmountable. Many of the policies he helped shape continue in force at Berkeley and other major American campuses.

Kenneth A.R. Kennedy

See also Hooton, E(arnest) A(lbert); Israel; Keith, (Sir) Arthur; Krogman, Wilton Marion; Mount Carmel (Israel); Neandertals; Royal College of Surgeons (London), Museums of the; Skhūl (Israel); South Asia (India, Pakistan, Sri Lanka); Tabūn, Mugharet el- (Israel); United States of America; Washburn, Sherwood L.

Bibliography
SELECTED WORKS

Pre-Incaic Huamachuco: Survey and excavation in the region of Huamachuco and Cajabamba. *Publications in American Archaeology and Ethnology, University of California* 39:223–400, 1945; Review of *The Lower Palaeolithic cultures of southern and eastern Asia* by Hallam Movius Jr. *Transactions of the American Philosophical Society* 38:329–420, 1948. Reprinted in *American Anthropologist* 52:260–262, 1950; The antiquity of man in South America: Handbook of South American Indians. Bureau of American Ethnology. Bulletin No. 142. 6:1–9, 1950.

The genus *Palaeoanthropus* and the problem of supraspecific differentiation among the Hominidae. *Cold Spring Harbor Symposia on Quantitative Biology* 15:87–96, 1951; The training and education of the professional physical anthropologist. *American Anthropologist* 54:313–317, 1952; Animals, climate, and Palaeolithic man. *Papers of the Kroeber Anthropological Society* (A.L. Kroeber Memorial Issue) 25:221–234, 1961; (with A. Keith) *The Stone Age of Mount Carmel II: The fossil human remains from the Levalloiso-Mousterian.* Oxford:

Clarendon, 1939; (with K.A.R. Kennedy) *Climbing man's family tree: A collection of major writings on human phylogeny, 1699–1971.* Englewood Cliffs, New Jersey: Prentice-Hall, 1972.

ARCHIVAL SOURCES
T.D. McCown Papers: Department of Anthropology, and Bancroft Library, University of California, Berkeley, California 94720.

SECONDARY SOURCES
S.T. Brooks: Theodore D. McCown, 1908–1969. *American Journal of Physical Anthropology* 32(2):165–166, 1970; E.A. Hammel: Theodore Doney McCown, June 18, 1908–August 17, 1969. *Papers of the Kroeber Anthropological Society* 41:1–7, 1969; K.A.R. Kennedy & S.T. Brooks: Theodore D. McCown: A perspective on a physical anthropologist. *Current Anthropology* 25(1):99–103, 1984; F. Spencer: The rise of academic physical anthropology in the United States, 1880–1980: A historical overview. *American Journal of Physical Anthropology* 56:353–364, 1981.

MacCurdy, George Grant (1863–1947)

Born in Warrensburg, Missouri, George Grant MacCurdy began his professional career as public school teacher. In 1881 he enrolled at the State Normal College at Warrensburg. His progress was initially slow because he was obliged to alternate attendance at college with a series of teaching jobs in order to earn his tuition fees. After graduation in 1887, however, advancement came quickly; two years later the youthful MacCurdy was appointed superintendent of schools in his home town.

A crucial turning point in MacCurdy's career came in 1889, when he attended a YMCA conference at Mt. Hermon, Massachusetts, which gave him his first opportunity to visit Boston and Cambridge; apparently it was this visit that kindled a strong desire to attend Harvard University. Two years later he obtained a scholarship and was admitted to Harvard with advanced standing.

Like his contemporary, the Smithsonian physical anthropologist Aleš Hrdlička (1869–1943), MacCurdy followed a roundabout path to the study of paleoanthropology. His studies at Harvard were mostly in biology and geology, and he received his bachelor's and master's degrees in 1893 and 1894, respectively. Although during his sojourn at Harvard he was encouraged to study anthropology with Frederic Ward Putnam (1839–

1915), who was then director of the Peabody Museum, MacCurdy did not change his career aims in that direction until 1896. It was also during his time at Harvard that MacCurdy established a personal and consequential relationship with the Yale orientalist Edward E. Salisbury (1814–1901). It was largely through Salisbury's influence that MacCurdy subsequently pursued a course of study and travel in Europe from 1895 to 1898. At first he undertook biological studies in Vienna, but in 1896 MacCurdy was among those attending the International Zoological Congress in Leiden when Eugène DuBois (1858–1940) first exhibited his *Pithecanthropus erectus* fossils. From all indications it was the latter experience which led him finally to shift his scholarly focus to the study of human prehistory. Upon his return to the United States in 1898 MacCurdy began his long formal association with Yale University in the fields of anthropology and archeology.

At Yale he became an instructor and acted as curator of the anthropological collections at the Peabody Museum, while continuing his studies for a doctorate in anthropology. On receiving his Ph.D. in 1905, MacCurdy joined the permanent faculty at Yale as a professor of archeology, a position he retained until his retirement in 1931.

Although Paleolithic archeology became his principal research interest, in the years between 1905 and 1920 he also made significant contributions to the study of the archeology and physical anthropology of the Americas. A synthesizer rather than an innovator, MacCurdy maintained a thorough acquaintance with emerging discoveries in paleoanthropology during his career but did not play a prominent role in shaping interpretations within the discipline. Furthermore, as Secretary of the American Anthropological Association from 1903 to 1916 and as its President in 1930, MacCurdy performed valuable organizational service to the then fledgling profession. In addition, he was largely responsible for organizing the international conference on "Early Man" held in 1937 at the Philadelphia Academy of the Natural Sciences which publicized important fossil finds of that decade, such as the australopithecine specimens discovered in South Africa by Robert Broom (1866–1951).

Without underestimating the value of this work, it is generally agreed that it is dwarfed by the magnitude of his service to the study of Paleolithic archeology in the United States, and that he did more than any other American of his generation to promote interest and develop expertise in this field. He was able to accomplish this not only because of his numerous writings on the subject and his long tenure as a teacher at Yale, but also through his leadership of the American School of Prehistoric Research (ASPR).

Founded in the early 1920s, the ASPR's original center of study was Paleolithic sites in France, and its principal mode of operation an eight-to-ten week summer "dig" that gave American graduate (and some undergraduate) students "hands on" experience in archeological methods. In the late 1920s and through the 1930s, however, the ASPR was able to carry on a wider range of activities, principally by engaging in longer-term cooperative excavations with European archeologists. The most significant of these ventures was the joint expedition with the British School of Archeology in Jerusalem that yielded the Mount Carmel population of "Neanderthaloid" skeletons in the early 1930s,

MacCurdy's guidance of the American School was marked by his ability to attract gifted graduate students such as the Berkeley paleoanthropologist Theodore D. McCown (1908–1969), his careful cultivation of interest in its activities among prominent Americans, and his wife's unstinting gift of time and energy, she shared fully in the work of what the MacCurdys came to call "our school." His many contacts with European paleoanthropologists brought in a continual supply of guest lecturers, and much-prized access to European museum collections. By kindling enthusiasm for the subject in those who would later go on to become professional archeologists and anthropologists, MacCurdy contributed significantly to the growth of the academic discipline of prehistoric archeology.

MacCurdy appears to have impressed people with the quality of his personality as much as with the quality of his work. His biographers concur in portraying him as an exceptionally kindly, modest, and tolerant individual. For example, Hugh Hencken (1902–1981), his successor as head of the ASPR, remembered MacCurdy as "so truly kind it actually pained him to believe ill of others," and as a self-effacing man in whose life "scheming and self-advertisement had no part." Similarly, the Harvard anthropologist Earnest A. Hooton (1887–1954) praised MacCurdy as someone who "neither desired nor sought scientific personal distinction and academic preferment," and yet "achieved among all who knew him well a reputation for thorough scholarship and skilled teaching that could be envied by any classroom lecturer on anthropological subjects."

MacCurdy was killed, tragically, on November 15, 1947 near Plainfield, New Jersey. While on an auto journey south with his wife, he had stopped to ask directions; a passing car struck him fatally as he tried to cross the road.

Alfred A. DeSimone

See also Academy of Natural Sciences, Philadelphia; Broom, Robert; Dubois, (Marie) Eugène (François Thomas); Harvard University; Hrdlička, Aleš; Java; McCown, Theodore Doney; Mount Carmel (Israel); Neandertals; Putnam, Frederic Ward.

Bibliography
SELECTED WORKS

The Eolithic problem—evidences of a rude industry antedating the Paleolithic. *American Anthropologist* 7:425–479, 1906; The dawn of art: cave paintings, engravings and sculptures. *Art and Archaeology* 4:71–90, 1916; The first season's work of the American School in France for Prehistoric Studies. *American Anthropologist* 24:61–71, 1922; *Human origins: A manual of prehistory.* 2 vols. New York: Appleton, 1924; Concerning human origins. *American Anthropologist* n.s. 28:308–310, 1926.

Old World prehistory in retrospect and prospect. *Proceedings of the American Philosophical Society* 68:95–106, 1929; Prehistoric man in Palestine. *Proceedings of the American Philosophical Society* 76:524–541, 1936; Recent progress in the field of Old World prehistory. *Annual Report of the Smithsonian Institution for 1930.* Washington D.C.: Government Printing Office, 1931, pp. 495–509; (editor) *Early Man: As depicted by leading authorities at the international symposium, The Academy of Natural Sciences, Philadelphia, March 1937.* Philadelphia: Lippincott, 1937.

ARCHIVAL SOURCES

1. MacCurdy's personal papers comprise a portion of the American School of Prehistoric Research Records. Archives, Peabody Museum of Archaeology and Ethnology, Harvard University, Cambridge, MA 02138. 2. A small collection of letters can also be found in Hrdlička's papers, National Anthropological Archives, National Museum of Natural History, Smithsonian Institution, Washington D.C., 20560.

SECONDARY SOURCES

A.A. DeSimone Jr.: *Ancestors or aberrants: Studies in the history of American paleoanthropology, 1915–1940.* Ph.D. Thesis. University of Massachusetts, 1986; H. Hencken: Obituary. George Grant MacCurdy, 1863–1947. *Science* 107:639–640, 1948; H. Hencken: George Grant MaCurdy, 1863–1947. *Bulletin of the American School of Prehistoric Research* 16:v–xxii, 1948; T.D. McCown: George Grant MacCurdy, 1863–1947. *American Anthropologist* 50:516–524, 1948.

McGregor, James Howard (1872–1954)

Born in Bellaire, Ohio, McGregor graduated in 1894 from Ohio State University, where he remained for a year as an assistant in zoology before beginning graduate studies in zoology at Columbia University under Edmund Beecher Wilson (1856–1939) and Henry Fairfield Osborn (1857–1935). He completed his Ph.D. dissertation in 1899 and spent the remainder of his career teaching at Columbia before retiring in 1943. He was a research associate at the American Museum of Natural History in New York City from 1916 until his death.

McGregor began his research on amphibians and fossil reptiles, but in the 1910s Henry Fairfield Osborn convinced him to become involved in work on human evolution at the American Museum. Although a zoologist by training, McGregor possessed considerable artistic skills, and Osborn enlisted him to develop displays for the museum's new Hall of the Age of Man. In 1915 and 1921, he traveled to Europe to examine all of the then available fossil record, which included such specimens as the Javan *Pithecanthropus* (now known as *Homo erectus*) remains found by the Dutch anatomist-paleontologist Eugène Dubois, Piltdown, Neandertal, and Cro-Magnon; on his return each time, he worked closely with Osborn and William King Gregory (1876–1970) to produce reconstructions of these specimens. McGregor created replicas of their skulls and teeth, but more famous were his full-scale sculptured busts of each species or race. His reconstructions embodied Osborn's interpretation of human evolution, including the portrayal of Neandertal as a slouching, heavy-browed, dull-witted creature. Although McGregor never deviated from this view of Neandertal, he subsequently became an outspoken opponent of Osborn's "Dawn Man" theory, which held that humans and simians had evolved from different ancestors. In 1929, he participated in an American

Museum expedition to Africa, and he later focused his attention on the study of gorillas. McGregor's "racial portraits" became a standard feature in science museums and texts. His lectures on human evolution, which he taught even after retirement, remained popular at Columbia into the early 1950s.

McGregor died on 14 November 1954 in New York City, New York.

Ronald Rainger

See also Dubois, (Marie) Eugène (François Thomas); Gregory, William King; *Homo erectus*; Neandertals; Osborn, Henry Fairfield; Piltdown

Bibliography
SELECTED WORKS

Recent studies on the skull and brain of *Pithecanthropus*. *Natural History* 25: 544–559, 1925; Restoring Neanderthal man. *Natural History* 26:287–293, 1926; Human origins and early man. In: Franz Boas (ed) *General anthropology*. New York: Heath, 1938, pp. 24–94; *Laboratory directions in elementary vertebrate zoology*. Ann Arbor, Michigan: Edwards, 1942; (with W.K. Gregory) A dissenting opinion as to dawn men and ape men. *Natural History* 26: 270–271, 1926.

ARCHIVAL SOURCES

There is a small collection of McGregor correspondence in the H.F. Osborn Papers: Central Archives, Library, American Museum of Natural History, Central Park West at 79th Street, New York, New York 10024-5192.

SECONDARY SOURCES

Anon: James Howard McGregor [obituary]. *New York Times*, 15 November 1954; L.C. Dunn: James Howard McGregor, 1872–1954. *American Philosophical Society Yearbook*, pp. 480–482, 1955; B. Schaeffer: James Howard McGregor, 1872–1954. *News Bulletin, Society of Vertebrate Paleontology* 43:33–34, 1955.

Majer, Józef (1808–1899)

Born in Cracow, Poland, Majer completed his secondary education in 1824, whereupon he began his medical studies at the (Jagiellonian) University of Cracow. On completing his doctorate in medicine in 1831, he remained at the university, where he lectured in anthropology from 1856 to 1873. In collaboration with Izydor Kopernicki (1825–1891), he founded

in Cracow an Anthropological Commission of the Akademia Umiejetności, whose work was directed to the study of the Polish population. The product of this work was published in *Zbiór wiadomości do antropologii krajowei* (Collection of Studies on the Anthropology of our Country)—the first serial publication in anthropology in Poland. The *Collection* was published in eighteen volumes from 1877 to 1896, when the series was renamed *Materiały Antropologiczno-Archeologiczni i Etnograficzne* (Anthropological, Archaeological, and Ethnographic Materials). It was published in thirteen volumes up to the beginning of World War I. Under the auspices of the Anthropological Commission, Majer and Kopernicki organized the first Anthropological Survey of Poland and the surrounding region in 1873.

Janusz Piontek

See also Kopernicki, Izydor; Poland

Bibliography
SELECTED WORKS

Charakterystyka fizyczna Rusinów naddnieprzańskich podana przez p. Czubińskiego porównana z charakterystyką Rusinów galicyjskich [Physical characters of Russians along the Dnieper River]. *Zbiór wiadomości do antropologii krajowei* 3:28–35, 1879; Roczny przyrost ciała u żydów galicyjskich jako jako przyczynek do ich charakterystyki fizycznéj [Yearly growth of Jews in Galacia]. *Zbiór wiadomości do antropologii krajowei* 4:3–22, 1880; (with I. Kopernicki) Charakterystyka fizyczna ludności galicyjskiéj [Physical characteristics of the population of Galacia]. *Zbiór wiadomości do antropologii krajowei* 1:1–181; 9:1–92, 1877–1885. (Summarized in *Archivo per l'Antropologia e la Etnologia* [Firenze] 17:391–505, 1887).

SECONDARY SOURCES

J. Piontek & A. Malinowski: *Teoria i empiria w Polskiej szkole antropologicznej*. Poznań: Uniwersytet im. Adama Mickiewicza, 1985, pp. 36–38; A. Wrzosek: Józefa Majera życie i zaslugi naukowe. *Materiały i Prace Antropologiczne* 31:266, 1957.

Majumdar, Dhirendra Nath (1903–1960)

Born in Patna, India, Majumdar studied anthropology at the University of Calcutta and received his master's degree in 1924. That same year, he received a Premchand Roychand Scholarship, which enabled him to continue his studies and, more particularly, his anthropological fieldwork on the Hos, a Chhota Nagpur tribe. It was while involved in this work that Majumdar came into contact with Sarat Chandra Roy (1871–1942), who is fondly referred to as the father of Indian ethnology. Roy had an important influence on Majumdar.

In 1928, Majumdar joined the Department of Economics at Lucknow University under the leadership of Radhakamal Mukharjee, who was also a Premchand Roychand Scholar. Mukharjee's department was unique in that sociology and primitive economics formed a major part of the program, and, as such, Majumdar, with his anthropological background, fitted perfectly into Mukharjee's department. With the exception of the brief period spent in England (*vide infra*) during the 1930s, the remainder of Majumdar's academic career was to unfold at Lucknow.

In the early 1930s, Majumdar spent a period studying in England, where in 1935, he completed a doctoral dissertation on cultural change in the Hos under Thomas Callan Hodson (d. 1953) at Cambridge University. During this time, he studied physical anthropology with Geoffrey M. Morant (1899–1964) and Reginald R. Gates (1882–1962) at the Galton Laboratory in London. While in London, he also had the opportunity to attend seminars given by the anthropologist Bronislaw Malinowski (1884–1942) at the London School of Economics.

Although his talent and scholarship were recognized at a very early stage of his career, he still had to struggle hard to further the cause of academic anthropology, to which he remained devoted until his last days. It was not until 1950, however, that the University of Lucknow finally acknowledged anthropology as a legitimate and independent discipline. At that time, Majumdar was appointed full professor of anthropology, and a year later the Department of Anthropology was created with him at the helm. Although short of faculty and funds, he nevertheless managed in the space of the next decade to establish the academic reputation of his department as second to none in the country.

Majumdar viewed anthropology as a holistic discipline, placing equal emphasis on the three major subdisciplines in anthropology: archeology and physical and cultural anthropology. And, as such, he actively pursued his researches in physical as well as cultural anthropology. He was an active field anthropologist and collected all of his own data. He traveled extensively to various tribal areas in India, and, at the same time as he collected blood samples and anthropometric measurements, he also made extensive notes on ethnographic details of the communities he visited. He did not separate the biological from the cultural sphere. To him, there was an intricate and dynamic relationship between the two—a view that placed him ahead of his time and that few of his contemporaries in India fully appreciated. This viewpoint is clearly reflected in his book *Races and Cultures of India* (1944), which went through several editions within the short span of sixteen years. This now classic work presents an intricate, well-knit mosaic of the biological and cultural dimensions of the people of India and mirrors the problems attending applied anthropology in India.

Majumdar was a pioneer in many research areas. For example, he was the first Indian anthropologist to utilize sophisticated statistical methods. Specifically, he enlisted the cooperation of the eminent statisticians P.C. Mahalanobis (1893–1972) and C.R. Rao in the analysis of his anthropometric data from Uttar Pradesh and Bengal, which enabled him to make the significant observation that intergroup differences in one geographic region are sometimes less pronounced than the intragroup differences in different environments. Majumdar's collaborative efforts with Mahalanobis and Rao are indicative of a devotion to the cause of science greater than any Indian anthropologist has shown on an individual basis.

Majumdar was an avid researcher, a prolific writer, and possessed with a mission to develop anthropology in India. Through incessant hard work and devotion to this latter cause, he was an inspiration to many of his students and earned a love and respect that is reflected in their publications, individual as well as coedited, in his honor—more than thirty years after his death.

Accepting challenges from fellow academics was Majumdar's second nature. For example, in 1938 when Biraja Sankar Guha (1894–1961) proposed that there was a "Negrito" substratum in the Indian population, Majumdar challenged these observations. Indeed, Guha failed to respond adequately to Majumdar's compelling arguments. Later, he made an extensive series of anthropometric surveys in Uttar Pradesh, Gujarat, and Bengal, which, besides substantiating his earlier stand against Guha, also demonstrated that the environment was a significant variable that should also be considered in the interpretation of somatological data.

He was never discouraged by difficulties, opposition, and criticism. This is indicated by his leadership of the Rupkund Expeditions in May and September 1956. The May expedition did not succeed in its original mission, and the expeditionary team was criticized for having "good times" in the cool Himalayas; this both irritated and invigorated Majumdar. Despite the fact that they were not supplied with appropriate gear, in September Majumdar and his expeditionary team negotiated the treacherous terrain of the Himalayas to reach the lake, at an altitude of 18,000 feet, and collected human skeletal remains to investigate their antiquity, populational complex, and source(s).

Majumdar accumulated many honors during his career, including election as a Fellow of the Royal Anthropological Institute in 1936, Fellow of the National Institute of Sciences in India in 1941, and president of the Anthropology and Archaeology Section of the Indian Science Congress in 1939. In addition, he served as India's representative at the International Symposium on Anthropology held in New York in 1952, as a delegate of the United Nations to the World Conference on Population in Rome in 1954, and as president of the first Indian Sociological Conference, held in Dehra Dun in 1955.

He was also founder of the Ethnographic and Folk Culture Society in 1947, as well as *Eastern Anthropologist*, an international journal, for which he acted as editor until his death. In 1949, he founded *Prachya Manav vaigyanic*, a journal published in Hindi on anthropological issues that is now published under the title *Manava*.

Majumdar died on 31 May 1960 in Lucknow of a cerebral hemorrhage.

Ripu D. Singh

See also South Asia (India, Pakistan, Sri Lanka)

Bibliography
SELECTED WORKS
Racial admixture in the United Provinces. *Man in India* 18:9–18, 1938; Racial affiliations of the Bhils of Gujarat. *Journal of the Gujarat Research Society* 6:172–186, 1944; *A tribe in transition*. London & Calcutta: Longmans, 1937; *The matrix of Indian culture*. Lucknow: Universal, 1947; Growth trends among Aboriginal boys of Kolhan, Singhbhum, Bihar. *Eastern Anthropologist* 2:201–205, 1948–1949; *The affairs of a tribe*. Lucknow: Universal 1950a; *Race realities in cultural Gujarat*. Bombay: Gujarat Research Society, 1950b; Rupkund in oral literature. *Eastern Anthropologist* 9:36–41, 1957; *Caste and communication in an Indian village*. Bombay: Asia Publishing, 1958; *Himalayan polyandry*. Bombay: Asia Publishing, 1960; *Races and cultures of India*. Allahabad: Kitabistan, 1944. 2d ed. Lucknow: Universal, 1951. 3d ed. Bombay: Asia Publishing, 1961.

(with S. Bahadur) ABO blood groups in India. *Eastern Anthropologist* 5:101–122, 1951–1952; (with S. Bahadur) Anthropological study of growth among school children in Lucknow. *Eastern Anthropologist* 5:1–26, 1951–1952; (with K. Kishen) Report on the serological survey of the United Provinces, 1941 census. *Eastern Anthropologist* 1:8–15, 1947; (with K. Kishen) Serological status of castes and tribes of cultural Gujarat. *Eastern Anthropologist* 2:92–97, 1948; (with C.R. Rao) *Race elements in Bengal*. Calcutta: Statistical Publishing Society, 1960; (with D.K. Sen, R.D. Singh, & B.K. Varma) [A preliminary report on the] human skeletons from Rupkund. *National Herald* [Lucknow] October, 1955; (with R.D. Singh) Human skeletal remains (unpublished report submitted to the government of Uttar Pradesh, 1960 [cf. R.D. Singh 1972]).

SECONDARY SOURCES
T.N. Madan: Dhirendra Nath Majumdar, 1903–1960. *American Anthropologist* 63:369–374, 1960; T. Madan & G. Sarana (eds): *Indian anthropology: Essays in memory of D.N. Majumdar*. Bombay, 1962; K.S. Mathur et al.: *Anthropological perspectives: Majumdar memorial volume*. Lucknow: Ethnographic and Folk Culture Society, 1987; R.D. Singh: A study of human skeletal remains from Rupkind. In: K.S. Mathur & S.C. Varma (eds) *Man and society*. Lucknow: Ethnographic and Folk Culture Society, 1972, pp. 153–173.

Makapansgat

Makapansgat is an extensive *Australopithecus*-bearing cave system located in the northern Transvaal, 300 km north of Johannesburg. As is the case with the caves near Krugersdorp (i.e., Sterkfontein, Swartkrans, Kromdraai, Gladysvale, and Drimolen), the Makapansgat caves have been formed of Archaean or pre-Cambrian dolomitic limestone belonging to the Malmani Subgroup of the Transvaal Sequence. Formerly thought to comprise several caverns, it is now known that virtually the whole of the Makapansgat Limeworks exposures fill one vast cave, 200 m in length and 150 m in breadth. The bone preservation in the deposit is excellent, and some of the least distorted and most intact of the South African Late Pliocene fossils come from this site.

After the publicity that attended the publication of Raymond A. Dart's (1893–1988) paper on *Australopithecus africanus* from Taung in February 1925 (Dart 1925a), Wilfred I. Eitzman, a schoolteacher from the city of Pietersburg some miles to the north, sent Dart a box of fossil bones embedded in breccia that he had collected at the Makapansgat Limeworks. Some of these bones were black in color, and the fragments of breccia tested positive for free carbon. This led Dart to conclude that the bones had been deliberately burnt and that the site represented an ancient midden deposit that had been accumulated by the activities of fire-using fossil humans (cf. Dart 1925b). However, the blackening was later attributed to manganese in the dolomite, while the free carbon had probably resulted from blasting activities by limeworkers. During the late 1930s and early 1940s, stone implements were recovered from the Cave of Hearths and the Rainbow Cave in the vicinity by C. Van Riet Lowe and B.D. Malan of the Archaeological Survey of the Union of South Africa, but it remained unclear whether Eitzman's bones had come from the same caves. In 1945, a group of Witwatersrand University students led by Phillip V. Tobias determined that the site from which the blackened bones had come was the Makapansgat Limeworks, about a mile from the Cave of Hearths and the Rainbow Cave. From the Limeworks the students recovered baboon fossils, one of which was at first mistakenly interpreted by Dart as part of a hominid cranium. Mindful of his earlier inference about the signs of fire in the deposit, Dart proposed to assign the supposed hominid specimen to a new species *Australopithecus prometheus*. Timeously, Lawrence H. Wells (1908–1980) pointed out that the specimen in question was the cranium of a baboon and Dart's note intended for publication in *Nature* was hurriedly withdrawn (Tobias 1988).

The result of Tobias' expedition aroused much interest and drew Dart back into paleoanthropology after a long absence (cf. Dart & Craig 1959). As a result, investigation of the site was set in motion. Three further student expeditions followed in 1945–1946, and Dart sent James Kitching, of the newly formed Bernard Price Foundation for Palaeontological Research at the University of the Witwatersrand, to scour the massive dumps of breccia that the limeworkers had left behind.

In September 1947, the first australopithecine specimen, the parieto-occipital part of a braincase, was recovered by Kitching from the Makapansgat Limeworks deposit (MLD 1). For the next twelve years, Alun R. Hughes of Dart's Anatomy Department spent a period every year at the Limeworks, systematically investigating the breccia dumps and sorting the bone-bearing fragments into groups matching in color and texture the *in situ* strata exposed in the cave system. More than a score of well-preserved australopithecine specimens came to light. These finds included fragments of mandibles representing at least ten individuals, cranial parts representing two adults, two ilia and an ischium from two adolescents, a partial femur, and an infant cranium and isolated teeth.

The specimens were assigned by Dart to *Australopithecus prometheus*, but John T. Robinson reclassified them as *Australopithecus africanus transvaalensis*, the same subspecies as that to which he had assigned the Sterkfontein australopithecines (cf. Robinson 1954). In 1958–1959, James Kitching recovered from *in situ* Member 4 breccia the posterior two-thirds of a superbly preserved *A. africanus* cranium (MLD 37/38), the calvaria of which was filled with heavily consolidated matrix. In 1990, it proved possible for G.C. Conroy, M.W. Vannier, and Tobias to examine the interior of the calvaria by means of computed tomography and to obtain an estimate of the complete cranial capacity (425 cm^3).

Desultory fieldwork was carried out at Makapansgat Limeworks between the 1960s and the 1990s, including a joint South African–U.S. excavation led by Tobias in 1973. In 1993, J.K. McKee embarked upon a new excavation.

Timothy C. Partridge (1979) determined the stratigraphy of the deposits and found that he could recognize five members of the Makapansgat Formation, numbered from below upward. Most of the australopithecines stemmed from Member 3, which, on faunistic grounds, was dated to about 3.0 my—that is, it proved to be somewhat more ancient than Sterkfontein Member 4 (with a dating estimated to lie between 2.8 and 2.6 my). Partridge and his coworkers found evidence of a suite of paleomagnetic reversals in the cave deposits, the sequence of reversals confirming the dating of 3.0 my for Member 3. A few of the Makapansgat hominid fossils were derived from the superjacent Member 4, which was found to have a dating of 2.8 my and less. Like the australopithecine-bearing Member 4 at Sterkfontein, the fauna from Member 3 at Makapansgat bespoke somewhat moister or more mesic conditions than those in the twentieth century. A new, comprehensive faunal analysis of South African Plio-Pleistocene deposits, founded on a computerized data base of identified mammalian families, genera and species, enabled McKee to confirm that Makapansgat Member 3 is the oldest of the faunal deposits and Member 4 the second oldest. Thus, the *A. africanus transvaalensis* remains from Makapansgat Member 3 represented the oldest hominid remains discovered in South Africa by the early 1990s.

Makapansgat Members 3 and 4 yielded hundreds of thousands of specimens of broken bones. Dart's study of these led to another of his innovative and challenging ideas. From the trends and patterns revealed in these broken bones, Dart inferred that they had been deliberately fractured and fashioned for use as implements. As bones, teeth and horn cores appeared to him to have been used, he developed the concept of an "osteodontokeratic culture," the manufacturer and wielder of which he concluded was the only hominid known from Makapansgat, namely *Australopithecus africanus* (cf. Dart 1957). This revolutionary concept of a Bone Age that had preceded the Stone Age has not stood the test of time. Those who poured scorn on Dart's claims were obliged to initiate a series of studies to determine what other agencies could have been responsible for the accumulation of the mountains of broken bones in the deposit. Up to the 1960s, scarcely anything was known about the effects on bones of biotic forces, such as big cats, canids, hyenas, porcupines, and predatory birds, nor about the effects of chemicals or of physical agencies, such as sun, wind, extremes of temperature, and water, whether standing or rushing water. The work of C.K. Brain (1981) was in the main responsible for showing that the patterns of breakage manifest in the Makapansgat assemblages were most probably the result of the actions of big felines, like saber-toothed cats and leopards, and of hyenas, porcupines, and other animals. Thus, although Dart's hypothesis did not gain acceptance, it did have

the unexpected side effect of stimulating a new field of study, which came to be known as taphonomy. Although it cannot be claimed that the response to Dart's theory originated taphonomy, it considerably catalyzed its progress and development.

A popular account of Dart's discoveries and interpretations of the Makapansgat remains may be found in his book, written in collaboration with D. Craig, *Adventures with the Missing Link* (1959). For assessments of Dart's osteodontokeratic hypothesis, see Tobias (1967), Wolberg (1970), and Brain (1981).

Phillip V. Tobias

See also Australopithecines; Dart, Raymond A(rthur); Kromdraai; South Africa; Sterkfontein; Taphonomy

Bibliography
C.K. Brain: *The hunters or the hunted? An introduction to African cave taphonomy.* Chicago: University of Chicago Press, 1981; R.A. Dart: *Australopithecus africanus*: The ape-man of South Africa. *Nature* 115:195–199, 1925a; R.A. Dart: A note on Makapansgat: A site of early human occupation. *South African Journal of Science* 22:454, 1925b; R.A. Dart: The osteodontokeratic culture of *Australopithecus prometheus. Transvaal Museum Memoir* 10, Pretoria, 1957; R.A. Dart & D. Craig: *Adventures with the missing link.* New York: Harper, 1959; T.C. Partridge: Reappraisal of lithostratigraphy of Makapansgat Limeworks hominid site. *Nature* 279:484, 1979.

J.T. Robinson: The genera and species of the Australopithecinae. *American Journal of Physical Anthropology* 12:181–200, 1954; P.V. Tobias: Cultural hominization among the earliest African Pleistocene hominids. *Proceedings of the Prehistoric Society* 33:367–376, 1967; P.V. Tobias: Lawrence Herbert Wells, 1908–1980, and the Wits Anatomy Department with some glimpses of his role in australopithecine unravelling. *Adler Museum Bulletin* 14:11–17, 1988; D. Wolberg: The hypothesized osteodontokeratic culture of the Australopithecinae: A look at the evidence and the opinions. *Current Anthropology* 11:23–30, 1970.

Malagasy Primates

The indigenous primates of the island of Madagascar, commonly known as lemurs, have been known to Western science since the

A B

Fig. 1. Two Malagasy primates. A: Ring-tailed lemur; B: Indris. From W.H. Flower & R. Lydekker's An Introduction to the Study of Mammals Living and Extinct. *London, 1891.*

seventeenth century, when accounts of sailors and merchants were first published by the East India Company of London (cf. Purchas 1625). It was not until the early eighteenth century, however, that the first live lemurs began to reach Europe and to attract the attention of naturalists such as Linnaeus (Carl von Linné) (1701–1778). In the twelfth edition of his *Systema naturae* (1766), Linnaeus described three species of *Lemur* that we still recognize today: *Lemur catta*, *Eulemur mongoz* and *E. macaco* (the latter two are now generally placed within the genus *Eulemur*. Only *Lemur catta* remains within the genus *Lemur*). The literature of lemur studies thereafter grew apace as systematists such as Etienne Geoffroy Saint-Hilaire (1772–1844) and John Edward Gray (1800–1875) did a brisk business in naming and describing new lemur species (cf. Tattersall 1982). However, despite the manifest interest of missionaries and others in the behavior of lemurs in their natural habitat, our knowledge of lemur behavior and ecology remained strictly at the anecdotal level until after the twentieth century had passed its midpoint.

In the late 1950s, the French naturalist Jean-Jacques Petter (1962) undertook a survey of Madagascar's primate fauna in which he included brief observations of the ecology and social groupings of a variety of lemurs made at sites in different areas of the island. Alison Jolly (1966) of Princeton University followed shortly afterward with a more detailed study of the diet and social behavior of ringtailed lemurs (*Lemur catta*) and Verreaux's sifakas (*Propithecus verreauxi verreauxi*) at the

now famous site of Berenty in Madagascar's far south. Between them, these pioneering studies ushered in a new era of research into lemur ecology and behavior, which has spilled over in later years into an intensive concern for the study and conservation of these unique animals.

Several notable studies of lemur behavior and ecology were undertaken in the late 1960s and early 1970s, prior to a hiatus imposed by political events of the mid-1970s. These included the first detailed study of the sportive lemur, *Lepilemur,* by French biologists Pierre Charles-Dominique and Marcel Hladik (1971); of the mouse lemur, *Microcebus,* by R.D. Martin (1972); and the pioneering rainforest study of the babakoto, *Indri indri,* at Périnet by Jon Pollock (1975). This was also a time of innovative comparative studies: of *Propithecus verreauxi* at sites in the northwest and south of Madagascar by Alison Richard (1978) and of sympatric *Lemur catta* and *Eulemur fulvus rufus,* the red-fronted lemur, in southwestern Madagascar by Bob Sussman (1974). During this period, the first studies were also made of lemurs living in the Comoro Islands: of the mongoose lemur, *Eulemur mongoz,* on Mohéli and Anjouan (Tattersall 1976) and of the Mayotte brown lemur, *Eulemur fulvus mayottensis* (= *Eulemur f. fulvus*), on Mayotte (Tattersall 1977).

Field activity waned in the aftermath of Madagascar's revolution of 1973, but since the early 1980s field studies of the lemurs have resumed with a new vigor, due in part to the renewed involvement with Madagascar of the Duke University Primate Center under the direction of Elwyn Simons. A notable result of this was the establishment, through the efforts of Pat Wright, of a research base and reserve at Ranomafana in the eastern rain forest. Since the mid-1980s, studies on rain-forest lemurs at Ranomafana by Wright and her colleagues have proliferated. Subjects have included the diademed sifaka *Propithecus diadema* (Wright et al. 1987); the red-bellied lemur, *Eulemur rubriventer*, and the eastern red-fronted lemur, *Eulemur fulvus rufus* (Overdorff 1992); the eastern wooly lemur, *Avahi laniger laniger* (Harcourt 1991); and the first report of the previously undescribed golden bamboo lemur, *Hapalemur aureus* (Meier et al. 1987). Another rain-forest primate that has received detailed attention for the first time during this period is the ruffed lemur, *Varecia variegata* (e.g., Morland 1992).

A notable base for studies of lemurs of the southwestern deciduous and spiny forests was established at Beza Mahafaly in 1978, as the result of a collaboration between the University of Antananarivo, Madagascar, and Washington and Yale Universities in the United States. Unusually detailed demographic records of *Propithecus verreauxi verreauxi* (Richard et al. 1991) and of *Lemur catta* (e.g., Sussman 1991) have been permitted by the comprehensive identification of all individuals in the main part of this reserve. Individual identification of animals has also enabled researchers to study life-history patterns and relationships between such things as ecology and social organization (e.g., Sauther 1992).

In the northwest, Jörg Ganzhorn and others (Ganzhorn & Abraham 1991) have renewed research interest in the Ankarafantsika Reserve. To the north of this, near Maromandia, L. Koenders, Y. Rumpler, and J. Ratsirarson (1985) were able to confirm the separate identity of Sclater's black lemur, *Eulemur macaco flavifrons*. Meyers et al. (1989) have since documented the geographical relationship between this subspecies and the black lemur, *Eulemur macaco macaco*, which is itself the subject of several ongoing studies. Yet farther north, the Ankarana Massif has at last begun to attract the attention it deserves from zoologists and ecologists (Hawkins et al. 1990) as well as from paleontologists (Simons et al. 1990). It was on the Ankarana that J.M. Wilson and colleagues (1989) undertook the first field study of the crowned lemur, *Eulemur coronatus*, more recently studied in detail on the Mt. d'Ambre by B.Z. Freed (1995). Close to the northern tip of Madagascar, D.M. Meyers (1993) completed a detailed field

study of the golden-crowned sifaka, *Propithecus tattersalli*. Perhaps the most elusive of all lemurs, the aye-aye, *Daubentonia*, has recently been the subject of a pioneering study by E.J. Sterling (1994).

This brief listing of major field studies on Madagascar's lemurs is not meant to be comprehensive (for a more complete review, see Tattersall 1982 and Harcourt 1990). However, it does point up how the burgeoning of Madagascar's relationship with the West since the mid-1980s has resulted in an ongoing proliferation of lemur field research. However, much remains to be learned about the primate communities of Madagascar. Few species have been studied in a variety of habitats, and a number have not been studied at all. Furthermore, between 1987 and 1994, three new species have been discovered with more doubtless in the offing. It is not unreasonable to hope that by the end of the first decade of the twenty-first century our knowledge of the unique primates of Madagascar will have been transformed—provided, of course, that these fascinating animals survive to become the objects of continuing scrutiny.

Ian Tattersall

See also African and Asian Prosimian Field Studies; Geoffroy Saint-Hilaire, Etienne; Linnaeus, Carolus; Primate Field Studies

Bibliography
P. Charles-Dominique & M. Hladick: *Le Lepilemur du sud de Madagascar: Ecologie, alimentation, et vie sociale. Terre et Vie* 25:3–66, 1971; B.Z. Freed: *Co-occurrence in free-ranging Lemur coronatus and L. fulvus sanfordi in Madagascar*. Ph.D. Thesis. Washington University, St. Louis, 1995; J.W. Ganzhorn & J.-P. Abraham: Possible role of plantations for lemur conservation in Madagascar: Food for folivorous species. *Folia Primatologia* 56:171–176, 1991; J.E. Gray: *Catalogue of monkeys, lemurs, and fruit-eating bats in the collections of the British Museum*. London: British Museum (Natural History), 1870; C. Harcourt: *Lemurs of Madagascar and the Comoros: The IUCN red data book*. Cambridge, England: IUCN, 1990; C. Harcourt: A Study of the diet and behavior of a nocturnal lemur, *Avahi laniger*, in the wild. *Journal of Zoology* 223:667–674, 1991.

A.F.A. Hawkins et al.: Vertebrate conservation in Ankarana Special Reserve, northern Madagascar. *Biological Conservation* 6:83–110. 1990; A. Jolly: *Lemur behavior*.

Chicago: University of Chicago Press, 1966; L. Koenders, Y. Rumpler, & J. Ratsirarson: *Lemur macaco flavifrons* (Gray, 1867): A rediscovered species of Primates. *Folia Primatologica* 44:210–215, 1985; C. Linnaeus: *Systema naturae*. 12th ed. Stockholm, 1766; R.D. Martin: A preliminary field study of the lesser mouse lemur (*Microcebus murinus*, J.F. Miller, 1777). *Zeitschrift für Komparativ Ethologie* 9:43–89, 1972; B. Meier et al.: A new species of *Hapalemur* (Primates) from southeast Madagascar. *Folia Primatologica* 48:211–215, 1987; D.M. Meyers: *The effects of resource seasonality on the behavior and reproduction of the golden-crowned sifaka (P. tattersalli Simons, 1988) in three Malagasy forests*. Ph.D. Thesis, Duke University, 1993.

D.M. Meyers et al. Distribution and conservation of Sclater's lemur: Implications of a morphological cline. *Primate Conservation* 10:77–81, 1989; H.S. Morland: *Social organization and ecology of black and white ruffed lemurs (Varecia variegata variegata) in lowland rain forest: Nosy Mangabé, Madagascar*. Ph.D. Thesis. Yale University, 1992; D.J. Overdorff: Differential patterns in flower feeding by *Eulemur fulvus rufus* and *Eulemur rubriventer* in Madagascar. *American Journal of Primatology* 13:191–203, 1992; J-J. Petter: Recherches sur l'ecologie et l'ethologie des lemuriens malgaches. *Mémoires du Muséum National d'Histoire Naturelle* (Paris) 27:1–146, 1962; J. Pollock: *The social behavior and ecology of Indri indri*. Ph.D. Thesis. London University, 1975.

S. Purchas: *Hakluytus posthumus; or, Purchas his pilgrimes*. 5 vols. London: Fetherston, 1625; A. Richard: *Behavioral variation: Case study of a Malagasy lemur*. Lewisburg, Pennsylvania: Bucknell University Press, 1978; Richard et al.: Demography of *Propithecus verrauxi* at Beza Mahafaly, Madagascar: Sex ratio, survival, and fertility, 1984–1988. *American Journal of Physical Anthropology* 84:307–322, 1991; M.L. Sauther: *The effect of reproductive state, social rank, and group size, on resource use among free-ranging ringtailed lemurs (Lemur catta) of Madagascar*. Ph.D. Thesis. Washington University, St. Louis, 1992; E.L. Simons et al.: Discovery of new giant subfossil lemurs in the Ankarana Mountains of northern Madagascar. *Journal of Human Evolution* 19:311–319, 1990.

E.J. Sterling: *Ecology and behavior of the aye-aye, Duabentonia madagascariensis on Nosy-Bé, Madagascar*. Ph.D. Thesis. Yale University, 1994; R.W. Sussman: Ecological distinctions in sympatric species of *Lemur*. In: R.D. Martin et al. (eds) *Prosimian biology*. London: Duckworth, 1974, pp. 75–108; R.W. Sussman: Demography and social organization of free-ranging *Lemur catta* in Beza Mahafaly Reserve, Madgascar. *American Journal of Physical Anthropology* 84:43–58, 1991; I.M. Tattersall: Group structure and activity rhythm in *Lemur mongoz* (Primates, Lemuriformes) on Anjouan and Mohéli Islands, Comoro, Archipelago. *Anthropological Papers of the American Museum of Natural History* 53:367–380, 1976.

I.M. Tattersall: Ecology and behavior of *Lemur fulvus mayottensis* (Primates, Lemuriformes). *Anthropological Papers of the American Museum of Natural History* 54:421–482, 1977; I.M. Tattersall: *The Primates of Madagascar*. New York: Columbia University Press, 1982; J.M. Wilson et al.: Ecology and conservation of the crowned lemur, *Lemur coronatus*, at Ankarana, N. Madagascar: With notes on Sanford's lemur, other sympatrics, and subfossil lemurs. *Folia Primatologica* 52:1–26, 1989; P.C. Wright et al.: A census and study of *Hapalemur* and *Propithecus* in southeastern Madagascar. *Primate Conservation* 8:84–86, 1987.

Malarnaud

The Malarnaud mandible was discovered at a cave site in the valley of the Arize northeast of St.-Girons, Ariège, France, in 1888 by F. Regnault and M. Bourett. The site and the circumstances of the find were described by Regnault (1889). Based on the associated remains of Cave Bear and other Pleistocene fauna, Regnault dated the site to the *la première époque quaternaire*. The mandible was described in 1889 by Henri Filhol (1844–1902), who noted that its general conformation resembled that of La Naulette, and also that the specimen had been found in similar circumstances. As this suggests, Filhol concluded that the specimen belonged to a Neandertal—a view endorsed by Marcellin Boule (1861–1942) in his 1889 review of the find.

The mandible is low, but very thick at the level of the receding symphysis. Only one molar (M 1) is present. The third molar(s) had not erupted. The alveoli of M 1 and M 2 are approximately the same size. The estimated width–height ratio of the condyles was identical to that of Spy and La Naulette. The specimen is believed to have belonged to a fourteen-year-old individual.

As Paul Topinard (1830–1911) noted in his comments to Filhol's presentation to the Société Philomathique in Paris, the site was destroyed, thereby preventing further exploration (cf. Filhol 1889).

Ursula Zängl-Kumpf

See also Boule, Marcellin; Filhol, (Antoine-Pierre) Henri; Naulette, La; Neandertals; Spy; Topinard, Paul

Bibliography
M. Boule: La Caverne de Malarnaud.
Bulletin de Société Philomathique (Paris) 1 (8th ser.):1889; H. Filhol: Note sur une machoire humaine, trouvée dans la caverne de Malarnaud. *Bulletin de Société Philomathique* (Paris) 1 (8th ser.):1889; F. Regnault: La Grotte de Malarnaud (canton de La-Bastide-de-Seron, Ariège), découverte d'une mâchoire humaine dans les dépôts de la première époque quaternaire. *Revue Pyrénées* 1:3–5, 1889.

Malthus, (Reverend) Thomas Robert (1766–1834)

Born near Dorking, Surrey, England, Malthus was educated privately before entering Jesus College, Cambridge, in 1784. There he studied a wide range of subjects and won several prizes for his declamations in Latin and Greek. In 1788, he graduated with a first in the mathematics tripos. In 1791, he received his master's degree, and two years later he was elected a fellow of Jesus College. In 1797, he took Holy Orders. The following year, Malthus published the first edition of his *An Essay on the Principle of Population*. Five years later, in 1803, he published a second and significantly revised edition of his *Essay*.

A direct result of the second edition was his appointment, in 1805, as professor of history and political economy at the newly created East India Company's College at Haileybury in Hertfordshire, where he spent the remainder of his life. During his tenure at Haileybury, Malthus continued to do his research and publish, including four more expanded editions of the *Essay* (1806, 1807, 1817, 1826), plus a condensation of this work titled *A Summary View of the Principle of Population* (1830).

He received many honors during his lifetime, including being named a Fellow of the Royal Society in 1819 and being elected to the French Académie des Sciences Morales et Politiques in 1833 and the Royal Academy of Berlin, also in 1833.

As indicated by the subtitle of the first edition of Malthus' *Essay*, this work was written in response to the popular and utopian views of the Marquis de Condorcet (1743–1794) and William Godwin (1756–1836). In his now classic work *Esquisse d'un tableau historique des progrès de l'ésprit humain* (1794), Condorcet had endeavored to demonstrate that progress was a vital law underwriting human history, which he viewed optimistically as the increasing perfectability of the human condition. As Godwin's *Enquiry Concerning Political Justice* (1793) suggests, he, too, was an optimist. Like Condorcet, he envisioned the eventual emergence of a society of social and economic justice. Malthus, however, harbored a more pessimistic view of the human condition. To him, poverty and disease were unavoidable social realities. In a nutshell, he argued that where human populations increase in geometric progression, their means of subsistence increase only in arithmetic progression. Accordingly, population size, he claimed, is "necessarily limited by the means of subsistence. . . [and that it will continue to expand to the limit of its subsistence base] unless prevented by some powerful and obvious checks [such as famine, war, and disease]" (cf. Malthus 1798:4–9). Clearly anxious to preserve the status quo, Malthus ignored the possibility of improving food production. Likewise, he considered contraception a "vice." Thus, "misery" and "self-restraint" were seen to be the inescapable fate of the poor and working masses. This pessimistic message endorsed laissez-faire politics of the period. However, Malthus' now classic exposition of the principles of population growth also had a later, far-reaching influence on the development of the Darwinian evolutionary theory.

Malthus died at Haileybury on 23 December 1834.

Frank Spencer

See also Darwin, Charles Robert; Demography; Evolutionary Theory

Bibliography
SELECTED WORKS
An essay on the principle of population; as it affects the future improvement of society; with remarks on the speculation of Mr. Godwin, M. Condorcet, and other writers. London, Johnson, 1798; *An essay on the principle of population; or, A view of its past and present effects on*

human happiness; with an inquiry into our prospects respecting the future removal or mitigation of the evils which it occasions. London: Johnson, 1803, 1806, 1807. 5th ed.: London: Murray, 1817, 6th ed.: London: Murray, 1826; *Principles of political economy considered with a view to their practical application.* London: Murray, 1820; *A summary view of the principle of population.* London: Murray, 1830.

PRIMARY AND SECONDARY SOURCES

J. Bonar: *Malthus and his work.* London: Allen & Unwin, 1885; M.J.A.N.C. Marquis de Condorcet: *Equisse d'un tableau historique des progrès de l'espirit humain.* Paris: Didot, 1794; A. Flew: The structure of Malthus' population theory. *Australian Journal of Philosophy* 35:1–20, 1957; A. Flew (ed): Introduction. In: *Thomas Malthus: An essay on the principle of population.* London: Penguin, 1970, pp. 7–56; W. Godwin: *An enquiry concerning political justice, and its influence on general virtue and happiness.* London: Robinson, 1793; G.F. McCleary, *The Malthusian population theory.* London: Allen & Unwin, 1953.

Malý, Jiří (1899–1950)

Born in Mělnik, 50 km north of Prague (now in the Czech Republic), Malý became interested in anthropology through Jindřich Matiegka's (1862–1941) protracted study of a local ossuary (dating from the fourteenth to sixteenth centuries). At Matiegka's urging, Malý enrolled as a medical student at Universita Karlova v Praze (Charles University in Prague), subsequently specializing in pediatrics. In 1924, he joined the Anthropologický Ústav Universit Karlovy (Institute of Anthropology at Charles University) where he became Matiegka's assistant. At this juncture, Malý began working on his doctoral research, which was a study of a series of artificially deformed crania from Bolivia that had been donated to the Institute by Aleš Hrdlička (1869–1943). Between 1924 and 1929, in addition to successfully defending his doctoral thesis (Malý 1926), he also completed a number of other studies, including the growth of children in Carpatho-Russia (cf. Malý 1930).

In 1929, he spent a year studying in the United States. During this visit, Malý was invited by Hrdlička to accompany him on a field trip to Alaska, where together they studied Eskimo and Indian groups located along the Yukon River, between Fort Yukon and Nome. He also studied, during his sojourn in the United States, the influence of the American environment on the physical characteristics of Czech and Slovak immigrants (cf. Malý 1933).

On returning to Prague, he became co-editor of *Anthropologie*, the journal founded by Matiegka in the early 1920s, and in 1932 he succeeded his mentor as head of the Institute of Anthropology at Charles University. Two years later, he was elevated from the rank of associate professor to *professor ordinarius*.

In the early 1930s, troubled by Adolf Hitler's rise to power in Germany, President Tomás G. Masaryk (1850–1937) invited Czech scientists to express their concern about the racist policies being enacted by the Nazis in a book entitled *The Equality of the European Races*, edited by Karel Weigner (1879–1937) and published in 1934. Malý was the youngest of nine contributors to this volume.

Malý's work during the decade preceding World War II was wide ranging. For example, in the mid-1930s the Viennese ethnologist of Czech origin Pavel Šebesta (1887–1971) donated to the Museum of Man in Prague (which was officially opened in 1937) a collection of pygmy skeletons he had made from the Ituri River region in Zaire. Malý made a study of this collection, which was published in 1938. This was followed by an invitation from Karel Absolon (1887–1960) of Brno to describe two human calottes recovered from the mammoth hunter's site of Dolni Vêstonice (Malý 1939). But perhaps more indicative of his range of interest is his identification and study of the remains of the Czech Romantic poet Karel H. Mácha (1810–1836). Malý was able to confirm the identity of the poet by a scar on the skull that corresponded to an earlier episode in Mácha's life (Malý 1940).

During World War II, all the universities and institutions of higher education in Czechoslovakia were closed by the German occupation forces. The Institute of Anthropology, however, was transformed into the Institut für Rassen-biologie and run exclusively by German officials. As a consequence, Malý spent the war period working in Prague as a pediatrician.

In 1945, the institute was restored and Malý returned to resume his role as teacher and researcher. In addition to his normal teaching responsibilities at the university, he was also instrumental in developing a course in child biology for teachers in Česke Budějovice (in southern Bohemia). He was also responsible for initiating the first course offered at Charles University in forensic anthropology. As for his research, he had harbored the ambition of conducting a nationwide child-growth survey, which was subsequently realized by his successor at the institute, Vojtěch Fetter (1905–1971). Another facet of his work was the practical application of anthropometric data in the industrial design of tools, clothing, and the like; his collaborative efforts with relevant industrial manufacturers were further developed by his successors at the institute.

Malý died at the age of fifty-one on 7 July 1950 in the midst of work in his laboratory.

Miroslav Prokopec

See also Czech and Slovak Republics; Fetter, Vojtěch; Hrdlička, Aleš; Matiegka, Jindřich

Bibliography
SELECTED WORKS

Staropražské lebky a kosti [Skulls and bones of Old Prague]. *Anthropologie* 3:156–176, 1925; Uměle deformované lebky z Tiahuanaco v Bolívii [Artificially deformed skulls from Tihuanaco, Bolivia]. *Anthropologie* 4:251–348, 1926; Vrůst dětí na Podkarpatské Rusi [Growth of children in Carpatho-Russia]. *Anthropologie* 8:149–173, 1930; Čechoslováci zahraniční zvláště severoameričtí [Czechoslovaks living in foreign countries, especially in North America]. In: *Československá vlastivěda II: Člověk* [Czechoslovak national history II: Man]. Praha: SFINK, 1933, pp. 260–269; The equality of physical traits in human races. In: K. Weigner (ed) *The equality of the European races.* (In Czech). Prague: Czech Academy of Sciences & Arts, 1934, pp. 47–59; Kostry středoafrických Pygmejů z poříčí Ituri [Skeletons of Middle African pygmies from Ituri River Basin]. *Anthropologie* 16:1–60, 1938; Lebky fosilního člověk z Dolních Věstonic [Skulls of the fossil man from Dolní Věstonice]. *Anthropologie* 17:171–192, 1939; Ostatky K.H. Máchy a jeho tělesný zjev [Skeletal remains of K.H. Mácha and his physical appearance]. *Anthropologie* 18:36–53, 1940.

SECONDARY SOURCES

F. Škaloud: Vzpomínka na profesora MUDr. Jiřího Malého k výročí nedožitých 75 narozenin [Recollections of Professor Jiří Malý, M.D., at the anniversary of his seventy-fifth birthday]. *Zprávy Československé společnosti antropologické při ČSAV* 27: 1974.

Manouvrier, Léonce-Pierre (1850–1927)

Born in Gueret (Creuse), a small village in central France, Manouvrier received his medical training in Paris, where he came under the influence of the anthropologist Paul Broca (1824–1880). In 1878, he became an unpaid preparator at the École d'Anthropologie (EA), and he continued working there while completing his doctoral research on the morphological variation of the cerebral convolutions. Prior to Manouvrier receiving his doctorate in 1882, Mathias Duval (1844–1907), then director of the Laboratoire d'Anthropologie of the École Pratique des Hautes Études (LA-EPHE), recommended him for the post of demonstrator in 1880. In 1900, Manouvrier succeeded Paul Topinard (1830–1911) as *sous-directeur* of the LA-EPHE, and in 1902, when Duval stepped down, he became director—a position he held until his death. At the same time, Manouvrier was also associated with the laboratory of the experimental physiologist Etienne J. Marey (1830–1904), located in the Bois de Boulogne. Following Marey's death, Manouvrier was made assistant director of this research station—a position he also held until his death in 1927. In addition to these responsibilities, Manouvrier held the posts of secretary-general of the Société d'Anthropologie de Paris (SAP) and editor in chief of the SAP's *Bulletins* and *Mémoires*.

Although Manouvrier began his career under Broca, who unquestionably had an important influence upon him, it was largely through his interaction with Marey that he acquired a functional and nonvitalistic approach to anatomy, and from Duval that he imbibed the essence of the Darwinian thesis. Hence, in marked contrast to his mentor Broca, who had conceded only a minimal influence of the environment, Manouvrier favored a greater role for social factors in the production of biological phenomena. Accordingly, he was a vigorous opponent of the Italian psychiatrist Cesare Lombroso's (1835–1909) criminal anthropology (which claimed that criminals were a fixed and discrete class of individuals), and he was an outspoken critic of the *Anthroposociologie* movement of the French anthropologist Georges Vacher de Lapouge (1854–1936) that had flourished in France between the late 1880s and World War I. Furthermore, he found through his neuroanatomical studies (*contra* Broca) that there was no significant difference in brain size between males and females. The differences alluded to by Broca and earlier investigators were clearly a function of differences in body size. Based on this finding, Manouvrier argued strongly on the rights of women to pursue a higher education at a time when they were routinely refused access to the medical profession, among other fields.

While it is not possible to do full justice here to the entire range of Manouvrier's scientific output, there are several notable and enduring contributions. For example, his studies on the anatomical variations of long bones were particularly influential. His platycnemic index (femur) and platymeric index (tibia) (cf. Manouvrier 1888, 1891) are still widely used. Also influential was his work on the estimation of stature (1893a) and his explanation of tibial retroversion (1893b), first observed by René Collignon (1856–1932) in the Spy fossils. In each case, these studies serve to underscore Manouvrier's commitment to the influence of the environment, behavior, and body size on skeletal anatomy. Although his stature tables were later superseded, they were nevertheless widely used during the first decades of the twentieth century, as seen from Aleš Hrdlička's (1869–1943) Anthropometry (1920) and Rudolf Martin's (1864–1925) Lehrbuch der Anthropologie (1914). Manouvrier is further distinguished as being one of the main supporters in France of Eugène Dubois' (1858–1940) case for the evolutionary significance of the remains he had found at Trinil in Java in the early 1890s. Although Manouvrier initially harbored doubts about the association of the Trinil femur and calotte, as many of Dubois' critics did, a closer study of the remains (originals and casts) led him inexorably to Dubois' synthesis and to conclude that they belonged to a single individual and that this form represented an early "anthropomorphic form" that forged a link between the "lowest living races and the race of Spy" and the "anthropoid apes." Among Manouvrier's colleagues who shared this view were René Verneau (1852–1938), Emile Houzé (1848–1921), and Paul Topinard.

Among the many students who trained under him at the EA and the LA-EPHE was the Czech-American physical anthropologist Hrdlička, on whom he left a deep and lasting impression. In fact, much of Hrdlička's subsequent career embodies Manouvrier's own aspirations for the development of anthropology as a rational and remedial science.

Manouvrier died in Paris on 18 January 1927.

Frank Spencer

See also Anthroposociology; Broca, Paul (Pierre); Collignon, René; Dubois, (Marie) Eugène (François Thomas); France; Hrdlička, Aleš; Lombroso, Cesare; Martin, Rudolf; Société d'Anthropologie de Paris; Spy; Topinard, Paul; Verneau, René (Pierre)

Bibliography
SELECTED WORKS
Mémoire sur la platycnèmie chez l'homme et chez les anthropoides. *Mémoires de la Société d'Anthropologie de Paris* 3 (2d ser.):469–548, 1888; La platymérie. *Comptes-rendus du Congrès International d'Anthropologie et d'Archéologie Préhistoriques* (Paris, France, 1889). Paris: Leroux, 1891, pp. 363–381; La détermination de la taille d'après les grands os de mémbres. *Mémoires de la Société d'Anthropologie de Paris* 4 (2d ser.): 347–402, 1893a; Etude sur la rétroversion de la tête du tibia et l'attitude humaine à l'époque quaternaire. *Mémoires de la Société d'Anthropologie de Paris* 4 (2d ser.):219–264, 1893b.

Etudes sur les variations du corps du fémur dans l'espèce humaine. *Bulletins de la Société d'Anthropologie de Paris* 4 (2d ser.):111–144, 1893c; Discussion du *Pithecanthropus erectus* comme précurseur présumé de l'homme. *Bulletins de la Société d'Anthropologie de Paris* 6 (4th ser.):12–47, 1895a; Le *Pithecanthropus erectus* et la théorie transformiste. *Revue Scientifique* 7 (5th ser.):289–299, 1895b; Etude sur les rapports anthropométriques en général et sur les principales proportions du corps. *Mémoires de la Société d'Anthropologie de Paris* 2 (3d ser.):98–135, 1902.

SECONDARY SOURCES
R. Anthony et al.: Discours prononcés aux obsèques de M.L. Manouvrier, le 20 janvier 1927. *Bulletins et Mémoires de la Société d'Anthropologie de Paris* 8 (7th ser.):2–13, 1927; R. Verneau: Nécrologie: Léonce-Pierre Manouvrier. *L'Anthropologie* 37:220–222, 1927.

Mantegazza, Paolo (1831–1910)

Born in Monza in the province of Milan, Italy, Mantegazza studied medicine at the Universities of Pisa (1848–1849) and Pavia (1849–1853), receiving his medical degree from the latter in 1853. In 1855, he left for Argentina, where for the next three years he traveled and practiced medicine. It was this brief sojourn in South America that resulted in Mantegazza's lifelong commitment to anthropology. On returning to Italy, he was appointed in 1859 to the Chair of General Pathology at the University of Pavia, where he founded the Laboratory of General Pathology—the first of its kind in Europe.

In 1865, following the war that unified Italy, Florence became the provisional capital of the Kingdom of Italy, and Mantegazza held political office as a representative to Parliament until 1876, when he was made senator. It was in this context that Mantegazza's aspirations for anthropology were essentially realized. In 1869, following a suggestion from his secretary, Pasquale Villari (1827–1917), a successful proposal was made endowing a Chair of Anthropology in the Istituto di Studi Superiori Pratici e di Perfezionamento at the University of Florence, and provisions were made for an anthropological museum. Thus, in addition to occupying the first Italian Chair of Anthropology, Mantegazza also became director of the Museo Nazionale di Antropologia (MNA). Two years later, together with several of his students, Mantegazza founded the Società Italiana di Antropologia ed Etnologia (SIAE), along with its organ, the *Archivio per l'Antropologia e la Etnologia*. This society and its journal became the premier forum for scholarly discussion and exchange of anthropological ideas in Italy during the remaining decades of the nineteenth century. In 1878, the title of the SIAE was expanded to include *Psicologia comparata* (comparative psychology), which reflects Mantegazza's developing interest in this field of inquiry and the subsequent founding by him of the Museo Psicologico in 1899. This museum no longer exists. Its collections have since been relocated to other museums in Florence.

In 1871, Mantegazza was named *professor ordinarius* of anthropology in the Faculty of Philosophy and Letters of the Istituto di Studi Superiori. Soon thereafter, however, he requested that his chair be transferred to the Faculty of Natural Sciences, a move that greatly enhanced his aims for physical anthropology as a legitimate and naturalistic science in Italy. In addition to his academic duties, he also directed the MNA, which he enriched with many items of anthropological and ethnological interest—some of which were the product of field trips he made. Two of his most noted excursions were to Scandinavia in 1878 and to India in 1882.

Mantegazza was among the first in Italy to embrace Charles Darwin's evolutionary thesis. But while he defined himself as *un darwinista con benefizio d'inventario*, he was not an orthodox Darwinist. As an anthropologist, his interests were eclectic, and clearly he favored a complex approach to the discipline. He conceived of general anthropology as the "natural history of man," which embraced not only the biological, but also the cultural and psychological spheres of human activity in both the past and the present.

During his career, Mantegazza published over 1,400 scientific papers and monographs whose topics range from the study of superstitions in Italy to the manifestation of sex and age characteristics in the human cranium. Through these works and his public lectures, Mantegazza did much to popularize anthropology and its relevance to Italian society.

After his death on 26 August 1910 in San Terenzio in the province of La Spezia, his assistant and successor, Aldobrandino Mochi (1874–1931), noted: "The master produced scholars, but not a true school." Be that as it may, the sum of his work has justly earned him the title of "The Father of Anthropology in Italy."

Brunetto Chiarelli
Giuseppe D'Amore

See also Argentina; Italy; Mochi, Aldobrandino

Bibliography
SELECTED WORKS
Rio de la Plata e Tenerife; viaggi e studi. Milan: Brigola, 1867 (see also: *Viajes por el Rio de la Plata y el interior de la Confederación Argentina.* Buenos Aires: Universidad de Tucuman Publicaciones, 1916); L'elezioni sessuali e la neogenesi: Lettera a C. Darwin. *Archivio per l'Antropologia e la Etnologia* 1:306–325, 1871a; *Quadri della natura umana: Feste ed ebbrezze.* 2 vols. Milan: Brigola, 1871b; L'uomo e gli uomini: Saggio di una etnologia naturale. *Archivio per l'antroplogia e la Etnologia* 6:30–46, 1876; La riforma craniologica. *Archivio per l'Antropologia e la Etnologia* 10:117–137, 1880a; *Un viaggio in Lapponia con l'amico Sommier.* Milan: Brigola, 1880b; *Un giorno a Madera; una pagina dell'Igiene dell'amore.* Milan: Brigola, 1881.

Studi sull'etnologia dell'India. *Archivio per l'Antropologia e la Etnologia* 13:63–96, 14:161–301, 1883–1884; Die hygiene der klimate. Königsberg: Matz, 1889; *Physiognomy and expression.* London: Scott, 1890; *Leggende dei fiori.* Milan: Dumolard, 1890. English translation by A. Kennedy: *The legends of flowers.* London: Laurie, 1930; Trent'anni di storia della Società Italiana di

Antropologia, Etnologia e Psicologia comparata. *Archivio per l'Antropologia e la Etnologia* 30:1–7, 1901.

ARCHIVAL SOURCES

P. Mantegazza Papers: Museo di Antropologia ed Etnologia di Firenze, Palazzo Nonfinito, Via del Proconsolo 12, 50122 Firenze, Italy.

SECONDARY SOURCES

B. Chiarelli (ed): AAVV: Paolo Mantegazza e il suo tempo: L'origine e lo sviluppo delle Scienze antropologiche in Italia. *Antropologia Contemporanea* 8:3–94, 1985; B. Chiarelli: Lezioni di Antropologia, 1870–1910, di Paolo Mantegazza. *Archivio per l'Antropologia e la Etnologia* 120:3–91, 1989; E. Ehrenfreund: Bibliografia degli scritti di P. Mantegazza. *Archivio per l'Antropologia e la Etnologia* 56:11–176, 1926; G. Landucci: *Darwinismo a Firenze: tra scienza e ideologia, 1860–1900*. Firenze: Olschlei 1977; S. Puccini: Evoluzionismo e positivismo nell'antropologia italiana, 1869–1911. In: P. Clemento et al. (eds) *L'Antropologia italiana: Un secolo di storia*. Bari, 1985, pp. 97–148.

Marro, Giovanni (1875–1952)

Born in Limone Piemonte in the province of Cuneo, Italy, Marro obtained a degree in medicine from the University of Turin in 1900 and subsequently took courses in anatomy and physiology at various institutions in Switzerland, France, and Germany. Following this postgraduate study, Marro worked as a physician in the Psychiatric Hospital at Collegno in the province of Turin. In 1911, he took part, as an anthropologist, in the Italian Archeological Expedition to Egypt led by the Egyptologist Ernesto Schiaparelli (1856–1928). He began teaching anthropology at the University of Turin (UT) in 1923, and in 1940 he was elected titular professor of the Chair of Anthropology at the UT.

In 1926, Marro founded at the UT the Istituto e Museo di Antropologia ed Etnografia. The materials he had collected while in Egypt provided the nucleus of this museum's collections, which included not only extensive ethnographic items but also more than 1,000 crania, 300 skeletons, and mummies dating from eneolithic times through the Dynastic period. In 1929, he began the systematic exploration of Val Camonica in northern Italy (cf. Marro 1929, 1932). This work resulted in the discovery of complex prehistoric rock carvings. Marro also studied the religious systems of the ancient indigenous populations of Val Camonica and found that their alphabet was, perhaps, the oldest in Italy.

Marro's publications include more than 230 items, ranging from his research on the comparison of ancient Egyptian populations to those of the present, to the anthropology of the contemporary Italian population, to his Val Camonica work.

Marro died in Turin on 20 July 1952.

Brunetto Chiarelli
Giuseppe D'Amore

See also Italy

Bibliography
SELECTED WORKS

Osservazioni morfologiche ed osteometriche sopra lo scheletro degli Egiziani antichi (Necropoli di Assiut, 2500–3000 B.C.). *Rivista di Antropologia* 16:63–109, 1913a; Sul profilo della faccia. *Rivista di Antropologia* 18:383–412, 1913b; Microcefalia e Diplegia. *Rivista di Antropologia* 24:215–240, 1921; Dell'arte quaternaria e dell'arte alpestre-rurale. *Rivista di Antropologia* 28:237–270, 1929; Arte rupestre zoomorfica in Val Camonica. *Rivista di Antropologia* 29:209–243, 1932.

ARCHIVAL SOURCES

G. Marro Papers: Istituto e Museo di Antropologia ed Etnologia di Torino, Via Accademia Albertina 17, 10123 Turin, Italy.

SECONDARY SOURCES

S. Fumagalli: *Necrologio: Giovanni Marro*. Borgo Madonnina, Pinerolo: Tipografia Vescovile dei P.P. Giuseppini, 1953.

Martin, Rudolf (1864–1925)

Born in Zurich, Switzerland, Martin initially intended to study the law, but he later switched to philosophy, which he read at the Universities of Freiburg and Leipzig. He graduated from Leipzig in 1892, whereupon he became a privatdocent before securing an associate professorship in anthropology at the University of Zurich in 1899. His inaugural address, "Anthropology As a Science and a Branch of Study," succinctly outlines the tasks and goals he envisioned. It was due to him that a number of new professorships and institutes of anthropology were established in

Germany at the turn of the century. In 1911, he was obliged to quit his academic position on account of his health. It was at this juncture that Martin began writing his now classic textbook *Lehrbuch der Anthropologie*, which was first published in 1914. This work went through several editions during Martin's lifetime, and it was subsequently revised by his former student Karl Saller (1902–1969) after World War II (a new edition is being prepared that will retain its original title).

In 1917, Martin returned to academia, filling the position formerly occupied by Johannes Ranke (1836–1916) at the University of Munich. At the same time, he also became director of the University's Anthropological–Prehistoric Art Collection. In 1924, he founded the *Anthropologischer Anzeiger* (Anthropological Gazette), which he edited until his death. The journal survived World War II; it is one of the most prominent anthropological serial publications in Germany and, since the reunification of Germany in 1990, the journal of the reorganized German Anthropological Society.

Martin's primary research interest was anthropometry. During the early 1920s, concerned with the deficient physical development of Munich schoolchildren, he initiated a protracted somatological study at the University of Munich (1921–1924) (cf. Martin 1924). In 1921–1922, he set up at the university a facility for the anthropological and medical study of human growth and development. In 1923, his anthropometric methods were applied at the Thirteenth German Athletic Games, which resulted in the measurement of 5,000 participants.

Ursula Zängl-Kumpf

See also Germany; Ranke, Johannes; Saller, Karl

Bibliography
SELECTED WORKS
Anthropometrisches Instrumentarium. *Correspondenz-Blatt der Deutschen Gesellschaft für Anthropologie* 30:130–132, 1899; *Anthropologie als Wissenschaft und Lehrfach: Eine akademische Antrittsrede.* Jena: Fischer, 1901; Über einige neuere Instrumentz und Hilfsmittel für den anthropologischen Unterricht. *Correspondenz-Blatt der Deutschen Gesellschaft für Anthropologie* 34:127–132, 1903; Zur Frage der anthropometrischen Prinzipien und Methoden. *Globus* 90:31–33, 1906; *Lehrbuch der Anthropologie in systematischer Darstellung: Mit besonderer Berücksichtigung der anthropologischen*

Methoden: Für Studierende, Ärzte, und Forschungreisende. Jena: Fischer, 1914.
    Anthropometrische und ärztliche Üntersuchungen an Münchener Studierenden. *Münchener Medizinische Wochenschrift* 71:321–325, 1924a; Die Körperentwicklung Münchener Volksschulkinder in den Jahren 1921, 1922, 1923. *Anthropologischer Anzeiger* 1:76–95, 1924a; Die Körperentwicklung der Volksschulkinder im Jahre 1924. *Anthropologischer Anzeiger* 2:59–68, 1924b; *Richtlinien für Körpermessungen und deren statistische Verarbeitung mit Besonderer Berücksichtigung von Schülermessungen.* Munich: Lehmann, 1924d.

SECONDARY SOURCES
    E. Fischer: Rudolf Martin. *Anatomischer Anzeiger* 60:442–448, 1925–1926; K. Saller: Rudolf Martin. *Münchener Medizinische Wochenschrift* 72:1343–1344, 1925; W. Gieseler: Die Anthropologie in München, 1918–1948. *Anthropologischer Anzeiger* 27:258–261, 1965; K. Saller: Die Anthropologie nach dem 2. Weltkrieg in München. *Anthropologischer Anzeiger* 27:262–267, 1965; O. Schlaginhaufen: Aus Rudolf Martins Züricher Zeit. *Anthropologischer Anzeiger* 27:243–246, 1965.

Matiegka, Jindřich (1862–1941)

Born in Benešov, near Prague (now in the Czech Republic), Matiegka studied medicine at Charles University, where he graduated M.D. in 1887. After graduation, he entered private medical practice in Litoměřice and later Mělník, his wife's birthplace. The environs of Mělník are well known as a region with many prehistoric sites that are rich in human skeletal remains. Although manifesting an active interest in this prehistoric legacy (cf. Matiegka 1891), as well as being attracted by the famous charnel house in Mělník, one of the biggest in Europe, in the early 1890s, Matiegka was primarily interested in advancing his medical career. As a consequence, he returned to Prague, where he was appointed public-health inspector in 1891. It was there that he became acquainted with Lubor Niederle (1865–1944), who had recently been appointed lecturer in archeology and anthropology at Charles University in Prague and was an active researcher in anthropology. This friendship was a turning point in Matiegka's career, which moved progressively toward a full-time commitment to anthropology.

    During the next six years, with mounting intensity, Matiegka applied himself to the discipline of physical anthropology and demography at Charles University (CU). In 1897, he was appointed docent at CU. His inaugural dissertation was a study of the "Stature, Development, Physical Properties, and State of Health of the Youth of Prague" (cf. Matiegka 1897). However, he continued working as well in the public-health service until his appointment as extraordinary professor in the newly created Department of Anthropology and Demography (Ústav pro anthropologii a demografii) at CU in 1908. Ten years later, he was promoted to full professor, a position he retained until his retirement in 1932.

Throughout his subsequent career, he was awarded several academic offices and honors, including dean of the Faculty of Sciences (1921–1922) and rector (i.e., chancellor) of Charles University (1929–1930); in 1932, he received an honorary degree for his outstanding contributions to the development of Czech anthropology.

Matiegka published more than 200 scientific papers and monographs. Although his interests traversed the entire spectrum of anthropology, it is possible to distinguish within this body of work three main areas of interest: (1) prehistoric and historical anthropology, (2) human biology (growth and development), and (3) ethnic anthropology.

His studies in the first category embrace the description and analysis of the skeletal remains from a number of early Slavonic burial sites, as well as the physical characteristics of the Czech kings and several outstanding personalities of Czech culture, science, and history. He also made a number of important osteological studies on the cross-sided asymmetry of the long bones in man, variation in the hard palate, and the *os malare bipartitum*, to mention but a few. But perhaps the work for which he is best remembered in this area is his monumental monograph on the human fossil remains from Předmostí near Přerov, Moravia (cf. Matiegka 1934–1938).

From the outset of his career, Matiegka devoted considerable effort to the study of the physical character of the Czech nation, especially its children and youth. These studies became the foundation of all future studies in this area of inquiry. Due largely to Matiegka's efforts, Bohemia and Moravia have the most complete data in Europe on the physical development of children and youth from the nineteenth century to the end of the twentieth. His methodological studies of youth maturation, skeletal age, dental age, and body composition were models at the time of publication (1918–1928), and they are still frequently cited in the literature. A synthesis of Matiegka's work in this field can be found in his monograph *Somatologie školní mládeže* (Somatology of School Children), published in 1927.

In the field of ethnic anthropology, Matiegka contributed substantially to the subject of the ethnogenesis of Slavs and to the knowledge of the racial composition of the Czech and Slovak populations. He also gave attention to the anthropology of national minorites in Czechoslovakia, and he made several important contributions to the anthropology of non-European races: "Anthropology of the Central-African Pygmies" (1935–1936) and (in collaboration with P. Šebesta) "Anthropology of Children of East Asian Negritoes" (1940). A synthesis of Matiegka's thinking in ethnic anthropology can be found in his book *General Theory of the Human Races* (1929).

In addition to his research, Matiegka also contributed significantly to the institutional development of Czech anthropology. Besides founding and organizing the Department of Anthropology in the Faculty of Sciences at Charles University, he was also responsible for launching, with financial assistance from the Czech-American physical anthropologist Aleš Hrdlička (1869–1943), the international journal *Anthropologie* (Prague), which began publication in 1923 and continued to the beginning of World War II. Within the framework of Charles University, Matiegka was also instrumental in the development of its Museum of Man and one of the founders, in 1910, of the Pedological Institute in Prague, which was created specifically to study all aspects of childhood. Finally, and perhaps more lasting, he educated a generation of Czech as well as foreign anthropologists who acquitted themselves with credit at other newly founded universities in Czechoslovakia and abroad.

Matiegka died in Mělnik (Czechoslovakia) on 4 August 1941.

Milan Dokládal

See also Czech and Slovak Republics; Hrdlička, Aleš; Předmostí

Bibliography
SELECTED WORKS
   Crania Bohemica. Prague: Haerpfer,

1891; Vzůrst vývin tělesné vlastnosti a zdravotní poměry mládeže Královského hlavního města Prahy. *Rozpravy České akademie pro vědy, slovesnost a uměná*. No. 17. Prague: Česke akademie, 1897; *The origin and the beginning of the Czechoslovak nation*. Washington, D.C.: Government Printing Office, 1921; Remains of Jan Žižka of Trocnov. (In Czech). *Anthropologie* (Prague) 1:255–283, 1923; *Somatologie školní mládeže* [Somatology of the school children]. Prague: Česká Akademie věd a umění, 1927; *Všeobecná nauka o plemenech* [General theory of the human races]. Prague: Bursík a Kohout, 1929.
Filosofie somatickoanthropologická [Somatoanthropological philosophy]. Prague: Bursík a Kohout, 1932a; *Tělesné pozůstatky českých králů* [Skeletal remains of Czech kings]. Prague: Česká Akademie věd a umění, 1932b; *Homo předmostensis: Fosilní člověk z Předmostí na Moravě*. Vol 1. *Homo předmostensis: Ostatní části kostrové*. Vol. 2. Prague: Česká Akademie věd a umění, 1934–1938; Anthropologie středoafrických Pygmejů [Anthropology of central African pygmies]. *Anthropologie* (Prague) 13:3–26, 1935–1936; (with P. Šebesta) Anthropologie dětí východoasijských negritů [Anthropology of children of East Asian Negritoes]. *Anthropologie* (Prague) 18:147–177, 1940.

ARCHIVAL SOURCES
1. J. Matiegka Papers: Archives and Library, Department of Anthropology, Faculty of Sciences, Charles University, Prague, CS-120 00, Praha-2, Viničná, Czech Republic. 2. A. Hrdlička Papers: National Anthropological Archives, National Museum of Natural History, Smithsonian Institution, Washington, D.C. 20560.

SECONDARY SOURCES
M. Dokládal & J. Brožek: Physical anthropology in Czechoslovakia: Recent developments. *Current Anthropology* 2:455–477, 1961; V. Fetter: Sto let od narození Jindřicha Matiegky [One hundred years from the birth of Jindřich Matiegka]. *Zpravodaj Čs. společnosti anthropolog.* 15:1–2, 1962; J. Malý: *Jindřich Matiegka*. (In Czech). Prague: Česká Akademie věd a umění, 1949; M. Prokopec: Das 110-jahrige Geburts-jubiläum Univ.-Prof. Dr. J. Matiegka's. *Anthropologie* (Brno) 10:151–152, 1972.

Matsumura, Akira (1880–1936)

Born in Tokyo, Japan, Matsumura studied anthropology at the University of Tokyo (UT), from which he graduated in 1907. In 1924, he received a Ph.D. in science, and the following year he became an associate professor of anatomy at UT.

Between 1907 and 1911, he traveled widely in Japan, with a view to inaugurating a comprehensive somatological study of the Japanese population—a project that proved to be too ambitious and that was never done. However, in 1911, he began an extensive anthropometric study of male and female students at UT. In addition to his various anthropometric studies of Japanese populations, Matsumura also conducted ethnological fieldwork in Micronesia (cf. Matsumura 1918) and archeological excavations on the Ryūkyū Islands.

Matsumura died in Tokyo on 21 May 1936.

Bin Yamaguchi

See also Japan

Bibliography
SELECTED WORKS
A gazetter of ethnology. (In Japanese). Tokyo: Maruzan, 1908; Contributions to the ethnography of Micronesia. (In Japanese). *Journal of the Faculty of Science, Imperial University of Tokyo* 40:1–174, 1918; On cephalic index and stature of the Japanese and their local differences. *Journal of the Faculty of Science, Imperial University of Tokyo* 1:1–312, 1925; *People of Japan*. (In Japanese). Tokyo: Iwanami-Shoten, 1935.

SECONDARY SOURCES
A. Suda: Matsumura Akira Sensei den ryakuki. *Journal of the Anthropological Society of Tokyo* 51:357–373, 1936.

Matthew, William Diller (1871–1930)

Born in Saint John, New Brunswick, Canada, Matthew was the son of George Frederick Matthew and Katherine Diller. His father was a fine amateur geologist and invertebrate paleontologist, and from an early age Matthew embraced his father's interest in science and fieldwork. Encouraged by his father, he attended the University of Halifax, and then on graduating in 1892 he moved to the United States to pursue graduate work at Columbia University School of Mines. Matthew's early studies focused on geology, mineralogy, and invertebrate paleontology. In 1894, however, he took a course in vertebrate paleontology with Henry Fairfield Osborn (1857–1935), and after completing his Ph.D. in 1895, he was hired as one of Osborn's assistants in the Department of Vertebrate Paleontology of the American Museum of Natural History in New York City. He spent over thirty years in that department, eventually becoming curator, before leaving in 1927 to become professor of paleontology at the University of California, Berkeley.

Matthew was first and foremost a vertebrate paleontologist, and his work in physical anthropology derived from his studies of the fossil record. His research encompassed virtually all families of fossil mammals, and he was generally considered the leading paleomammalogist of his time. Although Matthew published little on paleoanthropology or human evolution per se, his few papers on the subject had considerable influence. In 1904, he extended earlier interpretations to maintain that placental mammals as well as marsupials had an arboreal ancestry. Studies done in the 1910s by Matthew and his American Museum colleague Walter Granger (1872–1941) considerably extended the knowledge of the Eocene primates in North America and helped substantiate the interpretation that humans belong to the Primate order (cf. Matthew & Granger 1915). Their discovery in 1912 of the remains of the Eocene lemur *Notharctus* in the Bridger Basin of Wyoming had an important impact in leading their close associate William King Gregory (1876–1970) to focus his efforts on the study of paleoprimates. Matthew later made a detailed examination of the Piltdown remains, and despite considerable skepticism, he eventually maintained that the association of jaw and skull was highly probable. A committed Darwinian, Matthew interpreted the evolution of primates and other mammals in terms of the natural selection of random variations. He adopted Gregory's interpretation of *Dryopithecus* as the ancestor of simians and hominids, and along with Gregory, he believed that humans had evolved from organisms similar to anthropoid apes. Matthew was also well known for his views on the geographical distribution of mammals, including humans. In his most famous work, "Climate and Evolution" (1915), he argued that all mammals had originated in the Holarctic region of northern Asia and had subsequently migrated to other areas of the world. For over a generation, this interpretation was widely accepted among students of fossil and recent

vertebrates. It also reinforced the views of Osborn, and together their work served as the basis for the museum's Central Asiatic Expeditions, a series of explorations in the 1920s that were led by Roy Chapman Andrews (1884–1960) in an attempt to recover evidence for human origins in the Gobi Desert of Mongolia. Although cognizant of Raymond A. Dart's (1893–1988) 1924 discovery of the South African fossil *Australopithecus*, Matthew dismissed it as a progressive species of chimpanzee and continued to support the idea that central Asia was the birthplace of humans. Matthew, along with Gregory and James Howard McGregor (1872–1954), was a staunch opponent of the Fundamentalist antievolutionary posture and of Osborn's effort to separate simian and hominid evolution. The human fossil record, he maintained, indicated that several races or species of humans had existed in the early Pleistocene, but that only one, the modern species, had survived and branched into several distinct races inhabiting different parts of the globe. His views reinforced those of Gregory, and together their work had a powerful impact on a younger generation of paleoanthropologists, anthropologists, and zoologists.

Matthew died on 24 September 1930 in Berkeley, California.

Ronald Rainger

See also Andrews, Roy Chapman; Australopithecines; Biogeography; Dart, Raymond A(rthur); Gregory, William King; McGregor, James Howard; Osborn, Henry Fairfield; Paleoprimatology; Piltdown

Bibliography
SELECTED WORKS
The arboreal ancestry of the Mammalia. *American Naturalist* 38:811–818, 1904; Climate and evolution. *Annals of the New York Academy of Sciences* 24:171–318, 1915; The dentition of *Notharctus*. *Bulletin of the American Museum of Natural History* 37:831–839, 1917; *Outline and general principles of the history of life.* Berkeley: University of California Press, 1930; (with W. Granger) A revision of the Lower Eocene Wasatch and Wind River faunas. IV. Entelonychia, Primates, and Insectivora. *Bulletin of the American Museum of Natural History* 34:429–483, 1915.

ARCHIVAL SOURCES
1. W.D. Matthew Papers: Department of Vertebrate Paleontology, American

Museum of Natural History, Central Park West at 79th Street, New York, New York 10024–5192; 2. W.D. Matthew Papers: Bancroft Library, University of California, Berkeley, California 94720; 3. Small collection of correspondence in Witmer Stone Papers: Library, Academy of Natural Sciences, 1900 Benjamin Franklin Parkway, Philadelphia, Pennyslvania 19103–1195.

SECONDARY SOURCES

E.H. Colbert: *William Diller Matthew, paleontologist: The splendid drama observed.* New York: Columbia University Press, 1992; W.K. Gregory: A review of William Diller Matthew's contribution to mammalian paleontology. *American Museum Novitates* 473:1–23, 1931; H.F. Osborn: Memorial of William Diller Matthew. *Bulletin of the Geological Society of America* 42:55–95, 1931; R. Rainger: *An agenda for antiquity: Henry Fairfield Osborn and vertebrate paleontology at the American Museum of Natural History, 1890–1935.* Tuscaloosa: University of Alabama Press, 1991.

Mayr, Ernst (1904–)

Born in Kempten, Bavaria (now Germany), Mayr earned his Ph.D. in biology at the University of Berlin (UB) in 1926. Two years later, as a member of the university's museum, he led the first of three field expeditions (1928–1930) to New Guinea and the Solomon Islands. It was largely this experience that deepened his interest in the question of speciation and geographic distribution of animal species. In 1931, Mayr left Germany for the United States, where he continued his studies at the American Museum of Natural History in New York City as curator of birds—a position he held until 1953. At that time, he moved to Harvard University, where he was installed as the Alexander Agassiz Professor of Zoology; in 1961, he became director of the Agassiz Museum of Comparative Zoology—a position he retained until retiring in 1970. Since then he has been emeritus professor of zoology at Harvard.

Among those who influenced the direction of Mayr's work was Erwin Stresemann (1889–1972), his adviser at UB, who had defended the idea that morphological divergence is independent of physiological divergence (implying that reproductive isolation is the decisive species criterion), and the biologist Bernhard Rensch (1900–), who revived the idea of a correlation between geographic variation of characters and climatic conditions.

In 1942, Mayr published his now classic work *Systematics and the Origin of Species,* a book that made an important contribution to the modern evolutionary synthesis. Specifically, this book is largely devoted to the implications of the biological-species concept from the viewpoint of evolutionary theory and systematics. Mayr stressed that species are inherently variable groups of semi-isolated populations (polytypic species), and that the origin of higher categories can be explained by extrapolation from speciation and intraspecific variation. The biological-species concept required a shift from typological to population thinking (and all that this implied), as well as the adoption of a species definition based on a reproductive gap rather than morphological or ecological differences. Mayr defined species as "actually or potentially interbreeding natural populations, which are reproductively isolated from other such groups." This latter proposition posed the problem of isolation and the process by which the diversity and discontinuity between species is obtained. On this issue, Mayr proposed the idea of geographic or allopatric speciation—that is, "a new species develops if a population which has become geographically isolated from its parental species acquires during this period of isolation characters which promote or guarantee reproductive isolation when the external barriers break down."

Having stressed the polytypic nature of species, Mayr (1954) went on to note and explain the surprising morphological uniformity of most widespread species. Prior to this time, evolution had traditionally been defined as a simple change in gene frequencies. Mayr, however, contended that there was a difference between genetic adjustments in local populations and significant changes during macroevolutionary phenomena, even though all macroevolutionary events can be explained by intraspecific variation (microevolution). These ideas are developed and presented in his *Animal Species and Evolution* (1963a) and the abridged edition, *Populations, Species, and Evolution* (1970).

Mayr's particular contribution to anthropology rests largely with his application of the new systematics to human evolution. In 1950, at the symposium on the "Origin and Evolution of Man" held at Cold Spring Harbor, Long Island, New York, he addressed the issue of the bewildering diversity of names attributed to the fossil hominid remains, arguing for their reduction to a single genus, *Homo.* He also contributed to the movement for the acceptance of the then controversial South African australopithecines as hominids.

At the species level, and in accordance with its polytypic nature, Mayr recognized the considerable geographic variation among hominid populations, but he defended the view that "never more than one species of man existed on the earth at any one time." He also proposed a unilinear scheme for all ape-like and man-like fossils in human evolution. Succinctly, his views (1) contributed significantly to the integration of a previously typologically oriented field within the new evolutionary synthesis, and (2) launched a taxonomic trend toward lumping rather than splitting.

Richard Delisle

See also Evolutionary Theory; Neo-Darwinism; Paleoanthropology Theory; Systematics (1960–1990s)

Bibliography
SELECTED WORKS
Systematics and the Origin of Species. New York: Columbia University Press, 1942; Speciation and systematics. In: G.L. Jepsen, E. Mayr, & G.G. Simpson (eds) *Genetics, paleontology, and evolution.* Princeton, New Jersey: Princeton University Press, 1949, pp. 281–298; Taxonomic categories in fossil hominids. *Cold Spring Harbor Symposia on Quantitative Biology* 15:109–118, 1950; Change of genetic environment and evolution. In: J. Huxley, A.C. Hardy, & E.B. Ford (eds) *Evolution as a process.* London: Allen & Unwin, 1954; *Animal species and evolution.* Cambridge, Massachusetts: Harvard University Press, 1963a; The taxonomic evaluation of fossil hominids. In: S.L. Washburn (ed) *Classification and human evolution.* Chicago: Aldine, 1963b, pp. 332–346; *Principles of systematic zoology.* New York: McGraw-Hill, 1969.
Populations, species, and evolution. Cambridge, Massachusetts: Harvard University Press, 1970; *The growth of biological thought.* Cambridge, Massachusetts: Harvard University Press, 1982a; Reflections on human paleontology. In: F. Spencer (ed) *A history of American physical anthropology, 1930–1980.* New York: Academic Press, 1982b, pp. 231–237; *Toward a new philosophy of biology.* Cambridge, Massachusetts: Harvard University Press, 1988; *One long argument.* Cambridge, Massachusetts: Harvard University Press, 1991; (with P.D. Ashlock) *Principles of systematic zoology.* 2d ed. New York: McGraw-Hill, 1991; (with E.G. Linsley & R.L. Usinger) *Methods and principles of systematic zoology.* New York: McGraw-Hill, 1953; (with W.B. Provine [eds]): *The Evolutionary synthesis.* Cambridge, Massachusetts: Harvard University Press, 1980.

SECONDARY SOURCES
R.G. Delisle: *La structure du programme de recherche en paléontologie humaine: Une historie de 1950 à 1990.* M.A. Thesis. Université de Montréal, 1992; N. Eldredge: Introduction to the reprint of Ernst Mayr, 1942, *Systematics and the Origin of Species.* New York: Columbia University Press, 1982; N. Eldredge: *Unfinished synthesis.* Oxford: Oxford University Press, 1985.

Mendel, Gregor Johann (1822–1884)

Born in Heizendorf (Hyncice) in the province of Moravia (now in the Czech Republic), Mendel began his education at the Gymnasium in Troppau (Opava). In 1840, he enrolled in the philosophy courses at the Philosophical Institute at Olmütz (Olomouc) in preparation for entering the University of Vienna. At the Olmütz institute, he became acquainted with the elements of philosophy, physics, and mathematics. He intended to continue his studies, but his parents were unable to support him. Thus, in 1843, he entered the Augustinian monastery in Brno, where he took the name Gregor. He was ordained in 1847. From 1849 to 1851, he was a teacher of Greek and mathematics in a secondary school at Znaim (Znojmo). Between 1851 and 1853, he attended the University of Vienna, where he took courses in mathematics, physics, chemistry, botany, and zoology. On returning to Brno he taught natural sciences at a secondary school from 1854 to 1868—though he never succeeded in passing the examination for a teacher's license. In 1868, he retired from teaching when he was made abbot of his monastery—a position he retained until his death on 6 January 1884.

The work that led Mendel to the discovery of the basic principle of heredity was the outcome of ten years of laborious experiments with growing and crossing varieties of garden peas (what he called "plant hybridization") in the monastery garden at Brno. According to Mendel, his interest in this subject had been aroused by the desire to produce new colors in his flowers. Artificial fertilization led to surprising results that could not be accounted for in the literature. As such, Mendel decided to investigate the problem himself, and he was evidently quite unaware that his work was pioneering a new field of scientific inquiry.

In his initial experiments, Mendel crossed varieties of garden peas that manifested constant and sharply contrasting morphological traits, such as tallness and dwarfishness, the presence or absence of color in the blossoms, and differences in seed shape, and found that in all cases the progeny of the first generation (F_1) resembled one of the initial parent types. These parental F_1 characteristics, he called *dominant*, and those which had disappeared he called *recessive*. The next stage of his experiments involved the self-fertilization of the F_1 generations. Here Mendel found that the resultant F_2 generation manifested a mixture of dominant and recessive characters, and, more particularly, that the recessive characters reemerged in the ratio of 3:1. Although Charles Darwin (1809–1882) had also noted that the hybrid divided 3:1, he did not pursue this revealing observation. Mendel, on the other hand, correctly concluded that characters of generations are controlled by pairs of inherited factors (now called genes) that separate from one another and that are recombined in definite proportions during fertilization. This explanation is known as Mendel's Law of Segregation. Following from this, Mendel then showed how the heredity units sort themselves, arriving in consequence at a variety of combinations. In fact, by crossing the F_1 generation, Mendel found the ratio of 9:3:3:1 is characteristic of the second generation of a cross of two contrasting heredity units (i.e., pairs of genes). From this experimental series, Mendel postulated that each pair of factors undergoing segregation did so independently of all other pairs of factors. This subsequently became known as Mendel's Law of Independent Assortment.

Mendel presented his findings to the Brünn Society for the Study of Natural Science in 1865. The following year, his paper was published in the transactions of the society under the title: "Versuche über Pflanzenhybriden" (Experiments with Plant Hybrids). Contrary to expectations, the paper went unnoticed. Indeed, even the eminent Swiss botanist Karl Wilhlem von Nägeli (1817–1891), with whom Mendel corresponded, failed to grasp the relevance and significance of the work. In fact, it was not until 1900, when Hugo de Vries (1843–1935), followed by Karl Erich Correns (1864–1933) and Erich Tschermak von Seysenegg (1871–1962), independently reproduced Mendel's results and, in searching the literature, found that both the data and the theory of heredity had been published thirty-four years earlier by an obscure Moravian monk!

Although Mendel is known to have read Charles Darwin's books, his reaction to them went unrecorded. As such, we can do no more than speculate on his understanding of the theory of descent by modification and to what extent, if any, he recognized the relevance of his own work to that of Darwin's.

Mendel died in Brno on 6 January 1884.

Vítěrslav Orel

See also Darwin, Charles Robert; Genetics (Mendelian)

Bibliography
SELECTED WORKS
Versuche über Pflanzenhybriden. *Verhandlungen des Naturforschenden Vereines in Brünn* 4:3–47, 1866; Ueber einige aus Künstlichen Befruchtung gewonnen Hieracium-Bastarde. *Verhandlungen des Naturforschenden Vereines in Brünn* 8:26–31, 1870.

ARCHIVAL SOURCES
1. G.J. Mendel Papers: Mendelianum, Mendelovo nám. 1 Brno, CZ-60200, Czech Republic; 2. C. Stern & E.R. Sherwood (eds): *The origin of genetics: A Mendel source book*. San Francisco: Freeman, 1966. This work contains English translations of Mendel's papers of 1865 and 1869 and his correspondence (1866–1873) with the Swiss botanist Karl Wilhelm von Nägeli.

SECONDARY SOURCES
L.C. Dunn: Mendel, his work, and his place in history. *Proceedings of the American Philosophical Society* (Philadelphia) 109:189–198, 1965; H. Iltis: *Gregor Johann Mendel. Leben Werk und Wirkung*. Berlin: Springer, 1924. English translation by E. & C. Paul: *Life of Mendel*. New York: Norton, 1932; J. Kříženecký: *Gregor Johann Mendel, 1822–1844: Texte und Quellen zu seinem Wirken und Leben*. Leipzig: Barth, 1965; V. Orel: *Mendel*. London: Oxford University Press, 1984.

Mexico

It is possible to distinguish four stages of development in the history of Mexican physical anthropology. The first, or preformative stage embraces events prior to the restoration of the Mexican Republic in 1867. The second, or formative period dates from the third quarter of the nineteenth century to the late 1920s. The third, or early modern stage, during which the modern institutional framework of the discipline was established, embraces the period from the 1930s through the late 1950s. The fourth, or modern period documents the continuing internal development of a completely professionalized discipline.

The Preformative Period: Before 1867

Although Mexico has, since the early sixteenth century, been a focus of European anthropologists, these early investigators, such as Francisco López de Gómara (1510–1560) and José de Acosta (1539–1600), were operative in a colonial setting until the nineteenth century—and thus more accurately identified as visitors rather than as Mexican investigators.

To a large extent, the ethos of this preformative period is captured in the agenda of the Société d'Anthropologie de Paris founded by Paul Broca (1824–1880) in 1859. One of the primary aims of this society was to promote the study and collection of anthropological data from different regions of the world. Accordingly, various documents were prepared, such as the *Instructions Ethnologiques pour le Mexique*, to inform travelers, missionaries, colonial administrators, and others how to collect material of potential anthropological interest. These *Instructions* were published in the *Bulletins et Mémoires de la Société d'Anthropologie de Paris* in 1862 (cf. Comas 1962), and among the topics listed as being of importance were: physical characteristics of indigenous groups, results of research on racial mixtures, endogamy and consanguinuity, acclimatization of Europeans in tropical regions, and the collection and study of skeletal material of indigenous ancient people.

In 1864, as part of the French military expedition to Mexico, a Commission Scientifique du Mexique was established. The Committee on Natural and Medical Sciences (CNMS) was one of four committees established by this commission; it was responsible for developing, among other things, a program of anthropological research to be undertaken by the French expeditionary forces. The instructions for the latter were prepared by Armand de Quatrefages (1810–1892) at the Muséum National d'Histoire Naturelle in Paris and published in 1865 in the *Archives de la Commission Scientifique du Mexique*.

Although the activities of the CNMS were short lived, this committee provided both the thematic and the institutional infra-

structure of anthropology that was to emerge later with the restoration of the Mexican Republic in the 1870s.

Another important work falling into this category (though produced much later) is the *Anthropologie du Mexique* (1884), a study made by Théodore Hamy (1842–1908) in the 1880s, based on materials and collected data on the Aboriginal population of Mexico that were sent to the anthropological institutions in Paris.

The Formative Period: 1870s–late 1920s

Intellectually, the formative period is characterized by the pervasive influence of the French school of anthropology, in particular, the ideas of Broca. As such, many of the racial aspects of this Eurocentric school of thought are reflected in the work of Mexican scientists of this period. Another characteristic of this period, particularly throughout the remainder of the nineteenth century, was the largely individualistic and uncoordinated research activity.

A number of the physicians who had been involved in the initial work of the previously mentioned CNMS not only kept the Medical Section alive, which subsequently led to its transformation into the National Academy of Medicine, but also continued to promote anthropology. It was largely through this support, along with the spirit of José Porfírio Díaz's presidency (1876–1911), that physical anthropology found an increasingly prominent place in Mexico's most prestigious institution, the Museo Nacional.

Founded in 1825, the Museo Nacional de México (MNM), opened a Sección de Antropología Física in 1887 under the direction of Francisco Martínez Calleja. At that time, the MNM was directed by Jesús Sánchez (1849–1911), author of several works on physical anthropology. However, it was not until the turn of the century and the arrival of Nicolás León (1859–1929) that physical anthropology began to assume a more highly visible posture in the MNM's agenda. Prior to his appointment at the MNM, León had been director of the Museo Michoacano (founded in 1886), where he had specialized in the study of the anthropology of the P'urhépecha. In 1892, he resigned his position there. Eight years later, he was appointed head of the Sección de Antropología Física in the Museo Nacional, and in the following year, 1901, he was installed in the museum's Chair of Anthropology and Ethnology. It was around this time that he established a close scientific relationship with the Czech-American physical anthropologist Aleš Hrdlička (1869–1943). During the late 1890s and early in the 1900s, Hrdlička had conducted a series of pioneering studies in northern Mexico, and in 1903 he was appointed to head the Division of Physical Anthropology at the Smithsonian Institution in Washington D.C.—the first full-time position created in physical anthropology in the United States. In addition to sharing a common professional position, both men also had a common goal: the promotion of physical anthropology in their respective countries.

In Léon's case, this goal was achieved on several fronts. In addition to promoting fieldwork, which was conducted primarily by his students, he also engaged in a vigorous program of rescuing and preserving Mexican antiquities, as well as integrating the MNM's osteological collections. His published works are numerous and cover not only physical anthropology but also ethnology, linguistics, archeology, and medical history (for a complete listing of his works from 1874 to 1925, see Léon 1925).

Léon's death in 1929 essentially marks the end of this formative period.

Early-Modern Period: 1930s–1950s

In many respects, the early-modern period reflects the ethos of Lázaro Cárdenas' presidency, which involved the modernization of the Mexican economy, which, in turn, impacted on the sociocultural fabric of the country. Closely linked with these complex changes was the gradual professionalization of Mexican anthropology—a process that was essentially achieved via the creation of the Instituto Nacional de Antropología e Historia (INAH: National Institute of Anthropology and History) and the Escuela Nacional de Antropología e Historia (ENAH: National School of Anthropology and History) in the late 1930s. Both institutions placed a particular stress on the study of contemporary indigenous groups as well as on the pre-Hispanic past, in accordance with the nationalistic ideology of Cárdenas' administration. At the same time, the anthropological community received an important influx of scholars from Europe. Most notable among these European émigrés were Ada d'Aloja (1900–) from Italy in 1936 and Juan Comas (1900–1979) from Spain and Switzerland in 1940. Their achievements in the fields of research and teaching had a considerable influence on the subsequent development of Mexican physical anthropology.

The culmination of this period of professionalization was achieved in 1959 with the founding of the first doctoral program headed by Juan Comas at the Facultad de Filosofía y Letras of the Universidad Nacional Autónoma de Mexico.

Modern Period: 1960s–1990s

The modern period is marked by questioning the influence of state ideology exerted on the practice of physical anthropology in the framework of political and theoretical premises, and a corresponding (ongoing) revision of the theoretical foundations of the discipline and its application to the realities of modern Mexico. This introspection has provided an impulse for a thematic diversification of research, as well as an interdisciplinary convergence that has led to a more open attitude toward an international exchange within the academic framework. In this developing context, anthropological studies have not only become less descriptive and more analytical but they have also acquired a more applied biosocial approach. Bioanthropological research has also been extended to other institutions, among them the Universidad Nacional Autónoma de México (UNAM), with its Instituto de Investigacions Anthropológicas. This institute was created in 1973, based on the former Sección de Antropología of the Instituto de Investigaciones Históricas founded by Comas in 1963. Research at the UNAM institute is concerned primarily with the study of contemporary populations, and since the late 1970s this work has been developed within a growing framework of interinstitutional relationship with other biomedical facilities, whereas research on ancient populations is carried out mainly at the INAH (Dirección de Antropología Física), which is the legal depository of the skeletal remains recovered from archeological sites within Mexico.

Since the 1980s, the introspection alluded to above and a concern for the future and relevancy of the discipline have been fostered by the Asociación Mexicana de Antropología Biológica (AMAB), which was founded in 1981 and since has published a number of works on historical analysis in *Estudios de Antropología Biológica* (the offical organ of the AMAB). Also, in 1987 the Colegio Mexicano de Antropólogos A.C. analyzed the professional practices of the discipline, and in 1988 the Sociedad Mexicana de Antropología (SMA) organized a meeting to discuss the present and future of physical anthropology in Mexico (cf. López, Lagunas, & Serrano 1988).

Within this brief sketch on the development of physical anthropology in Mexico, only those elements regarded as the most significant have been mentioned; for a more detailed account of its history, see León (1919), Comas (1970), Villanueva (1982), Lopez, Serrano, and Lagunas (1993); Villanueva, Serrano, and Vera (in press).

Carlos Serrano
María Villanueva

See also Acosta, José de; Broca, Paul (Pierre); Comas, Juan; Hamy, Jules Ernest Théodore; Hrdlička, Aleš; Quatrefages (de Breau), Jean Louis Armand de; Société d'Anthropologie de Paris

Bibliography
J. Comas: *Las primeras instrucciones para la investigacion antropological en México, 1862.* Cuadernos del Instituto de Historia, ser. antropologica 16. Mexico D.F.: UNAM, 1962; J. Comas: La antropología física en México, 1943–1964. *Cuadernos del Instituto de Investigaciones Historica, ser. antropologica* 17. Mexico, D.F.: UNAM, 1964; J. Comas: History of physical anthropology in Middle America. In: T.D. Stewart (ed) *Handbook of Middle American Indians*. Vol. 9. Austin: University of Texas, 1970, pp. 3–21; J. Faulhaber: Anthropometry of living Indians. In: T.D. Stewart (ed) *Handbook of Middle American Indians*. Vol. 9. Austin: University of Texas, 1970, pp. 82–104; J. Faulhaber: Estudios de poblaciones vivas de México desde el punto de vista de la somatometria y somatotipia. *XIII Mesa Redonda de la Sociedad Mexicana de Antropología*, 15–30, 1973.
E.T. Hamy: *Anthropologie du Mexique; mission scientifique au Mexique dans l'Amérique Centrale.* Paris: Imprimerie Nationale, 1884; A. Hrdlička: *Physiological and medical observations among the Indians of the southwestern United States and northern Mexico.* Bureau of Ethnology No. 34. Washington, D.C.: Smithsonian Institution, 1908; N. León: Historia de la antropología física en México. *American Journal of Physical Anthropology* 2:229–264, 1919; N. Léon: *Noticia de sus escritos originales, impresos e inédito . . . 1874 a 1925.* Mexico, D.F.: Imprenta Manuel León Sanchez, 1925; S. López, Z. Lagunas & C. Serrano: La antropología física en México: Una prospección. *XX Mesa Redonda de la Sociedad Mexicana de Antropología.* México, 1980.
S. López, C. Serrano, & Z. Lagunas: Bosquejo histórico de la antropología física en México. *Balance de la antropología en América Latina y el Caribe.* Mexico, D.F.: UNAM, 1993, pp. 113–131; C.G. Mora: *La antropología en México: Panorama Histórico.* 15 vols. Mexico: INAH, 1988; A. Romano: Balance y proyecciones de los estudios de poblaciones desaparecidas en Mesoamérica y norte de México. *XIII Mesa Redonda de la Sociedad Mexicana de Antropología*, pp. 1–14; Mexico, D.F.: UNAM, 1973; J. Romero (ed): *Antropología física: Epoca prehispánica.* Serie México: Panorama histórico y cultural, 3. Mexico: INAH, 1974.
J. Romero (ed): *Antropología física: Epoca moderna y contemporánea.* Serie México: Panorama histórico y cultual, 10, Mexico: INAH, 1976; L.A. Vargas: La antropología física. In: *Las humaninades en México: 1950–1975.* Mexico, D.F.: UNAM, 1978, pp. 645–666; M. Villanueva: La antropología física de los antropologos fisicos en México. Inventario bibliográfico, 1930–1979. *Estudios de antropología biológica* 1:75–124, 1982; M. Villanueva, C. Serrano, & J.L. Vera: Cien años de antropología física en México. Mexico, D.F.: UNAM, in press.

Mingazzini, Giovanni (1859–1929)

Born in Ancora, Italy, Mingazzini obtained his medical degree from the University of Rome in 1883. Following his graduation, he worked in the laboratory of Giuseppe Sergi (1841–1936), where he continued his neurological research. He obtained his license to teach human anatomy in 1888 and psychiatry in 1894. In 1906, he was appointed director of the Mental Institution of Santa Maria della Pietà in Rome. It was there that he established his famous anatomicopathological laboratory. In 1920, he became director of the Clinica delle Malattie Nervose e Mentali at the University of Rome. He was a founding member, in 1893, of the Società Romana di Antropologia and served as its president in 1905 and 1906.

Mingazzini's research interest was the central nervous system, with particular reference to the brain and especially the lenticular nucleus.

Brunetto Chiarelli
Giuseppe D'Amore

See also Italy; Sergi, Giuseppe

Bibliography
SELECTED WORKS

    *Manuale di Anatomia degli organi nervosi
centrali dell'uomo.* Rome: Piccolo, 1889; *Il
cervello in relazione con i fenomeni psichici.*
Torino: Bocca, 1895; *Anatomia clinica dei
centri nervosi.* Rome: Piccolo, 1908–1913;
Nouvelles études sur le siège de l'aphasie motrice.
Turin: Bona, 1911; *Anatomia clinica dei centri
nervosi.* Turin: U.T.E.T., 1912.

SECONDARY SOURCES

    S. Sergi: Necrologia di Giovanni
Mingazzini. *Rivista di Antropologia* 28:672–
674, 1928–1929.

Mitchell, John (1711–1768)

Born in Lancaster County, Virginia, Mitchell
is believed to have been tutored either "by a
local clergyman or [to have] attended some
small local private school" (Berkeley & Berkeley 1974:7) before being sent to Edinburgh,
Scotland, in the early 1720s to complete his
education. In Edinburgh, Mitchell also acquired a lifelong interest in natural history, in
particular, botany. On receiving his M.A. in
1729, he entered the university's medical
school. Three years later, he graduated M.D.,
and soon thereafter he returned to his native
Virginia. Between 1732 and 1734, he apparently lived on his father's estate, in Lancaster
County, before moving to Urbana, Virginia,
where he established a medical practice. He
remained in Urbana until 1748, when ill
health led him to seek a more congenial environment in London, England, where he
spent the remainder of his life.

By the time of his arrival in London,
Mitchell had acquired a scientific reputation
for his contributions not only to botany (cf.
Mitchell 1748), but also to the study of yellow fever (cf. Packard 1938). In addition to
continuing his botanizing in England,
Mitchell produced a map of North America
that served as a model until the close of the
eighteenth century.

His place in the history of physical anthropology is founded on "An Essay upon the
Causes of the Different Colours of People in
Different Climates," published in the *Philosophical Transactions of the Royal Society of London* in 1744–1745. From all accounts, his
interest in this subject had originally been
stimulated by a competition devised by the
Academy of Bordeaux in the early 1740s that
offered an annual prize for the best paper presented in this field of inquiry. But as he explained in a letter (appended to his published

paper) dated 12 April 1743 to his colleague and
Fellow of the Royal Society Peter Collinson
(1694–1768), a London merchant and botanist,
by the time he had completed his study the
Bordeaux competition had been disbanded.
Collingwood transmitted Mitchell's paper to
the Royal Society where it was subsequently
read in 1744.

What distinguishes Mitchell's essay from
that of other contemporary works on this subject is that his opinions were grounded in his
own observations and experiments, which
contradicted conventional wisdom of the period. From a comparative study of the structure of skin in Blacks and Whites, he rejected
the earlier claim made by the Italian anatomist Marcello Malpighi (1628–1694) in his
Opera omnia (1687, Vol. 2:204) that the skin
color of Africans was caused by a black fluid
lying beneath the epidermis (in the "*rete
mucosum*"). The only difference Mitchell could
detect was that the "Skins of Negroes are of a
thicker Substance, and denser Texture, than
those of white people." It was this apparent
difference in skin thickness that led him to
propose (employing Newtonian "optiks") that
the color of skin was an indirect measure of
the skin's ability to transmit light. As the
thickness increased, so the skin appeared proportionally darker. In the case of the African
Negro, he claimed their skin's "transmit no
Colour thro' them." He also rejected the popular notion that the "primitive and original
Complexion of Mankind" had been white and
that being nonwhite was symptomatic of a
degenerative process. Rather, it appeared to
Mitchell that the original skin color had been
brown and that black and white represented
two extreme states, whose expression was
mediated by the natural and cultural environment. In all cases, he concluded, the resulting complexion of a people was undoubtedly
one best suited "to the Climate where they
resided."

Contrary to expectations, neither
Mitchell's findings nor his general synthesis
had any discernible impact. Although the
Göttingen anatomist Johann Friedrich Blumenbach (1752–1840) mentions Mitchell's
work (without any in-text discussion) in a
footnote of the first edition of his celebrated
thesis *De generis humani varietate nativa* (1775,
in Bendyshe 1865:111)—this footnote appears to have been dropped in subsequent
editions. In this regard it is interesting to note
that a brief survey of other major works from
the late eighteenth and early nineteenth centuries failed to uncover any reference to

Mitchell's thesis. Indeed, most surprising is the apparent failure of the Princeton theologian-philosopher Samuel Stanhope Smith (1750–1819) to use Mitchell's work to support the doctrine of monogenesis in his *An Essay on the Causes of the Variety of Complexion and Figure in the Human Species* (1787).

Frank Spencer

See also Barton, Benjamin Smith; Polygenism; Skin Color; Smith, Samuel Stanhope

Bibliography
SELECTED WORKS

An essay upon the causes of the different colours of people in different climates. *Philosophical Transactions of the Royal Society of London* 43(474):102–150, 1744–1745; Dissertatio brevis de principiis botanicorum et zoologorum, deque novo stabiliendo naturae rerum congruo, cum appendice aliquot generum plantarum recens conditorum. *Acta physico-medica* [Deutsch adademie der naturforscher; a.k.a. Academia naturae curiosorum; and Caesareo-Leopoldina naturae curiosorum] VIII:169–224, 1748; *The contest in America between Great Britain and France, with its consequences and importance.* London: Millar, 1757; *The present state of Great Britain and North America.* London: Becket, 1767.

PRIMARY AND SECONDARY SOURCES

E. Berkeley & D.S. Berkeley: *Dr. John Mitchell: The man who made the map of North America.* Chapel Hill: University of North Carolina Press, 1974; J.F. Blumenbach: *De generis humani varietate nativa.* Göttingen: Rosenbuschii, 1775. English translation by T. Bendyshe in: *The anthropological treatises of Johann Friedrich Blumenbach.* London: Longman, Green, Longman, Roberts & Green, 1865, pp. 69–143; M. Malpighi: *Opera omnia.* 2 vols.: Lugduni Batavorum, 1687; F.R. Packard: The manuscript of Dr. John Mitchell's account of the yellow fever in Virginia in 1741–42. Written in 1748. *Proceedings of the Charaka Club* 9:45–46, 1938; S.S. Smith: *An essay on the causes of the variety of complexion and figure in the human species. To which are added strictures on Lord Kaimes {sic} Discourse on the original diversity of mankind.* Philadelphia: Aitken, 1787; H. Thatcher: Dr. Mitchell, M.D., F.R.S., of Virginia. *Virginia Magazine of History and Biography* 39:126–135, 206–220 (1931), 40:48–62, 97–110, 268–279, 335–346 (1932), 41:59–70, 144–156 (1933).

Mivart, St. George Jackson (1827–1900)

Born in London, England, Mivart was the son of a successful hotelier with broad intellectual interests that included the developing natural sciences and friendship with those who were their practitioners. Young Mivart developed an early avocational interest in zoology, which was tolerated as well as encouraged by the few professionals in the field who were friends of his father. Having converted to Catholicism in 1844, he was prohibited from attending Oxford or Cambridge and, instead, prepared himself for the practice of law by attendance at Lincoln's Inn, from where he was called to the Bar on 30 January 1881. He did not practice, however, choosing instead to follow his scientific interests through a self-developed program—first in anatomy and then in comparative anatomy and systematic zoology. From his father's associates, he learned the elements of natural science. Undisciplined as his early training was, it was probably more rounded and more conservative than that of the majority of his contemporaries. Of particular value and continuing influence was his early association with Richard Owen (1804–1892), then the doyen of natural sciences in Britain. Owen's conciliatory views concerning the relationship between religion and science were of great importance to Mivart's subsequent work in science, religion, and philosophy. He thoroughly absorbed Owen's concept of homology, which provided him with an organizing and unifying principle. Although it allowed for secular change, this concept supported the idea of some underlying extramaterial creative force upon which the structured system of nature appeared to be based. In his conversion to Catholicism, he found the source of that force in a God seemingly gentler and more flexible than that of the doctrines then held by the dominant religious establishment; in pursuing his God and the dictates of his conscience beyond those of his church, Mivart was excommunicated six weeks before his death in 1900.

Mivart was not a major figure in Victorian natural science. He was, however, an active participant in the scientific community. He became a Fellow of the Zoological Society in 1858, of the Linnean Society in 1862, and, following his important contributions to the anatomy and systematics of the Primates, of the Royal Society in 1869. From 1862, when he was first appointed with the support of both Owen and Thomas Henry Huxley (1825–1895), until 1884, he was professor of comparative anatomy at London's St. Mary's

Hospital Medical School. During the 1860s, when he produced the most important of his conributions to comparative anatomy and zoology, although he maintained his relationship with Owen he was also a friend and considered himself a student of Huxley's, whose lectures he attended. Although he wrote more during the succeeding decades, at no later period was his competence as a researcher so apparent. From 1864, when his first article appeared, through 1870, Mivart published alone or with a collaborator (e.g., James Murie) twenty-three separate articles of technical content for the professional journals (e.g., Mivart 1864, 1866, 1867). All of these displayed his skill as a comparative anatomist and his intelligence as a systematist, and, following the path laid out by Huxley as a consequence of the importance of the "man problem" raised by Charles Darwin's *On the Origin of Species* (1859) and Huxley's dispute with Owen on man's place in nature, most of them dealt with the then important problem of the Primate order.

Brief as it was, the series of papers and memoirs he published, particularly on the little-known Lemuroidea, whose affinities he delineated (cf. Mivart 1873a), represents the most complete and comprehensive study of the osteology of the Primates for most of the century. It established Mivart's reputation as one of the few authorities of his generation on the stuctural relationships within the whole of that troublesome order. The result of his work was the classical definition of the order. Apart from the recognized importance of the precise data, carefully observed and described, which characterized the whole of the series, particular importance lay with those data that dealt with the then barely known lemuroids, whose distinctive features led him to construct a suborder for their systematic definition. Although subsequently modified somewhat by a wider range of subjects, it still retains its validity.

As one of the younger group of naturalists excited by Darwin's work and led by Huxley, he was sympathetic to the new theory of organic change and considered himself one of its supporters. However, as it had been for others, the breaking point came with the clear realization that the human species, too, even with or despite its unique moral characters that, supported its traditional claims to preeminence, was itself the product of the same process that had produced the least of nature's world. By the end of the decade, under the influence of Owen's theistically based

progressionism and the doctrines of his church, he became one of the most persuasive critics of the Darwinian position, arguing against what seemed to him to be a mindless materialism that had serious moral implications for the human society. Mivart argued, against the vehement criticism of Huxley, who had become his antagonist, that, properly understood, there was no essential incompatibility between Catholicism and evolution. For the metaphoric tree growing from a single root, he substituted a bush to explain the melange of similarities and differences between evolutionary-distanced forms. It was an argument that he presented in *On the Genesis of Species* (1871) and *Man and Apes* (1873b). Both books, despite a common failure to grasp the important conceptual foundation upon which Darwinian evolution rested, raised important questions about the efficacy of the theory that were later addressed by the concepts of parallelism and convergence. As with his later difficulties with ecclesiastical authority, Mivart's apparent apostasy and the vigor of his argument led to his virtual excommunication from the new science that grew up in the wake of the Darwinian success.

Mivart died in London on 1 April 1900.

Jacob W. Gruber

See also Huxley, Thomas Henry; Owen, (Sir) Richard

Bibliography
SELECTED WORKS
For a complete listing, see J.W. Gruber: *A conscience in conflict: The life of St. George Mivart.* New York: Columbia University Press, 1960, pp. 250–258; Notes on the crania and dentition of the Lemuridae. *Proceedings of the Zoological Society of London* 32:611–648, 1864; Contributions towards a more complex knowledge of the skeleton of Primates: Part I: The appendicular skeleton of Simia. *Transactions of the Linnean Society of London* 6:175–225, 1866; Additional notes on the osteology of the Lemuridae. *Proceedings of the Zoological Society of London* 35:960–975, 1867; (Anonymous) Difficulties of the theory of natural selection. *The Month* 11:35–53, 134–153, 274–289, 1869; *On the genesis of species.* London: Macmillan, 1871.

Evolution and its consequences: A reply to Professor Huxley. *Contemporary Review* 19:168–197, 1872; *Lessons in elementary anatomy*. London: Macmillan,

1873a; Man and apes. *Popular Science Monthly* 12:113–137, 243–264, 1873b; On Lepilemur and Cheirogaleus and on the zoological rank of the Lemuroidea. *Proceedings of the Zoological Society of London* 41:484–510, 1873c; *Lessons from nature as manifested in mind and matter*. London: Murray, 1876; The geography of living creatures. *Contemporary Review* 37:275–299, 1880; On the development of the individual and of the species as forms of instinctive action. *Proceedings of the Zoological Society of London* 52:462–474, 1884; On the possible dual origin of the mammals. *Proceedings of the Royal Society of London* 43:372–379, 1888; *The origin of human reason*. London: Kegan Paul, Tench, 1889; Beginning and end of life: Review of Weismann. *Quarterly Review* 170:370–393, 1890; The evolution of evolution. *American Catholic Quarterly Review* 20:673–697, 1895.

ARCHIVAL SOURCES

1. T.H. Huxley Papers: Archives, Imperial College of Science and Technology, London SW7 2AZ, England; 2. R. Owen Papers: Archives, Natural History Museum, Cromwell Road, London SW7 5BD, England; 3. Miscellaneous Correspondence: Library, Linnean Society of London, Burlington House, Piccadilly, London WIV 0LQ, England.

SECONDARY SOURCES

J.W. Gruber: *A conscience in conflict: The life of St. George Mivart*. New York: Columbia University Press, 1960.

Mladeč

The site of Mladeč consists of a large, complex main cave and a small side cave, both of which formed as solution caverns in the limestone of Třesín Hill on the outskirts of the village of Mladeč in central Moravia (Czech Republic). The main cave was first discovered in 1828 during mining operations. Initial reports on the cave in 1829 claim that bones from large humans were recovered, but no information on these survives. Since the region was then part of Austro-Hungary, the site is often referred to by its German name, *Lautsch*. The local Czech name for the caves is *Bočkova dírá* (Boček's Cave), after a legendary local highwayman.

The first systematic excavations at Mladeč took place in 1881 under the direction of Josef Szombathy (1853–1943) of the Natural History Museum in Vienna. Excavat-

ing in chamber D of the main cave, he recovered the cranium of a young adult female (Mladeč 1), a femoral shaft (Mladeč 27), and animal bones. During the same year, Szombathy recovered numerous other incomplete human and animal remains from other localities in the main cave. Continuing this work in 1882, Szombathy recovered a few other human fragments, lithic artifacts, bone points (now referred to as Mladeč points), and a collection of perforated animal teeth. Szombathy referred to the cave as Fürst-Johanns-Höhle, since the entrance was on the property owned by Prince Johann of Lichtenstein.

Later excavations were carried out in other parts of the cave by Jan Knies, a local schoolteacher, from 1903 until 1911, and by Knies and Jan Smyčka in a second cave (known as the Side, or Quarry, Cave), in 1904. The 1904, excavations yielded the more robust male crania Mladeč 5 and 6. Additional excavations and collections of material in the cave occurred between 1912 and 1922. In total, these excavations recovered at least 137 human bones. Systematic excavations by the Moravian Museum in Brno (1958–1962) suggest that the human skeletal remains are associated with the Aurignacian and date to an early interstadial during the last major glaciation.

The Mladeč remains received little attention initially, in part because the prominent prehistorians Karel Maška and Josef Bayer doubted their Aurignacian age. The skeletal material remained virtually unknown until Szombathy (1925) described some of it. Most specimens remained undescribed and were ultimately destroyed in 1945 at Mikulov Castle on the Czech-Austrian border. Only the remains recovered in the 1881–1882 excavations (curated in Vienna), Mladeč 5 (which miraculously survived Mikulov), and a few fragments kept by Knies have survived.

Most considerations of the Mladeč remains from the 1920s through the 1960s focused on specimens preserved in Vienna. Generally, they were represented, if discussed at all, as eastern European variants of the so-called "Cro-Magnon race" (e.g., Szombathy [1900] 1902). The importance of the Mladeč sample was reemphasized by Jan Jelinek of the Moravian Museum in the 1960s. Jelinek and others have noted the variation in the sample and the Neandertal-reminiscent morphology of the cranial remains, particularly the male Mladeč 5 and 6 crania (Frayer 1986; Smith 1982). In the 1970s, 1980s, and 1990s, the

Mladeč remains have been critical to the argument for regional continuity between European Neandertals and the earliest modern Europeans (e.g., Wolpoff 1980).

Fred H. Smith

See also Cro-Magnon; Czech and Slovak Republics; Předmostí

Bibliography
D. Frayer: Cranial variation at Mladeč and the relationship between Mousterian and Upper Paleolithic hominids. *Anthropos* 23:243–256, 1986; J. Jelinek: Neanderthal man and *Homo sapiens* in central and eastern Europe. *Currrent Anthropology* 10:475–503, 1969; J. Jelinek: The Mladeč finds and their evolutionary importance. *Anthropologie* (Brno) 21:57–64, 1983; F.H. Smith: Upper Pleistocene hominid evolution in south-central Europe: A review of the evidence and analysis of trends. *Current Anthropology* 23:667–703, 1982; J. Szombathy: Un crâne de la race de Cro-Magnon trouvé en Moravie [Mladeč 1]. *XII International Congrès d'Anthropologie et d'Archéologie préhistorique.* (Paris, France, 1900). Paris: Masson & Cie, 1902, pp. 133–140; J. Szombathy: Die diluvialen Menschenreste aus der Fürst-Johanns-Höhle bei Lautsch in Mähren. *Die Eiszeit* 2:1–34, 73–95, 1925; M.H. Wolpoff: *Paleoanthropology.* New York: Knopf, 1980.

Mochi, Aldobrandino (1874–1931)

Born in Florence, Italy, Mochi obtained his degree in the natural sciences at the University of Florence in 1899. After graduating, he remained in Florence, where he became an assistant to Paolo Mantegazza (1831–1910), who held the Chair of Anthropology. In 1904, he received his license to teach anthropology. After the death of Mantegazza in 1910, Mochi was placed in charge of the teaching of anthropology at the University of Florence, and subsequently, in 1924, he became titular professor of anthropology, ethnology, and paleoanthropology. In 1913, in cooperation with Gian Alberto Blanc (1879–1966) and Ettore Regalia (1842–1914), he founded in Florence the Comitato per Ricerche di Paleontologia Umana (CRPU), whose aim was to promote research on Fossil Man and his environment and life conditions in Italy through the methods of the natural sciences. The CRPU later became the Istituto Italiano di Paleontologia Umana (IIPU), which was ultimately established in

Rome in 1953, when the IIPU organized the Fourth International Congress on the Quaternary (INQUA). Mochi held the office of president in the Società Italiana di Antropologia ed Etnologia from 1929 to 1931, and he was editor of the journal *Archivio per l'Antropologia e la Etnologia* from 1910 to 1931.

Mochi's scientific interests included intensive studies of Ethiopian populations and the daily objects used by recent and archaic Italian populations. Subsequently, his studies focused specifically on physical anthropology. He carried out research on the encephalorachidian index (relationship between cranial capacity and the area of the occipital foramen), the relationship between intellectual development and cranial morphology (for which he found that dimensions of the brain are related only in part with the level of intelligence and that they are influenced by other factors), frontal curvature and the temporal squama. He made craniological observations on several populations, and a critical examination of cranial forms according to the system of classification developed by Giuseppe Sergi (1841–1936). Taking this method as a starting point, Mochi developed an integration between the morphological and the metric methods. He was also responsible for mounting several field expeditions in Eritrea (1905–1906), Uganda and Somaliland (1927–1931), and Tibet (1930).

Mochi supported the idea of removing the study of human evolution from the restrictive realm of prehistoric archeology to the more holistic approach of ecology. He held that biological phenomena relevant to paleoanthropology should be studied in relation to all of the environmental factors that influence it.

Throughout his thirty years in academia, Mochi devoted considerable effort to enriching and organizing the Museo di Antropologia ed Etnologia at the Palazzo Nonfinito in Florence whose collections stand as a monument to his memory.

Mochi died in Florence on 20 May 1931.

Brunetto Chiarelli
Giuseppe D'Amore

See also Blanc, Gian Alberto; Italy; Mantegazza, Paolo; Sergi, Giuseppi.

Bibliography
SELECTED WORKS
Indice encefalorachidiano. *Archivio per*

l'Antropologia e la Etnologia 29:107–160, 1899; Sui rapporti tra lo sviluppo intellettuale e la morfologia craniense. *Archivio per l'Antropologia e la Etnologia* 34:82–142, 1904; L'indice di curvatura del frontale. *Archivio per l'Antropologia e la Etnologia* 37:439–445, 1907; Appunti sulla paleoantropologia argentina. *Archivio per l'Antropologia e la Etnologia* 40:203–254, 1910a; Nota preventiva sul *Diprothomo platensis*, Ameghino. *Revista del Museo de La Plata* 17:69–70, 1910b.

ARCHIVAL SOURCES

Museo di Antropologia ed Etnologia di Firenze, Palazzo Nonfinito, Via del Proconsolo 12, 50122 Florence, Italy.

SECONDARY SOURCES

A. Blanc: Commemorazione di Aldobrandino Mochi. *Archivio per l'Antropologia e la Etnologia* 60–61:15–20, 1930–1931; N. Puccioni: Commemorazione di Aldobrandino Mochi. *Archivio per l'Antropologia e la Etnologia* 60–61:11–15, 1930–1931; S. Sergi: Aldobrandino Mochi. *Rivista di Antropologia* 29:676–677, 1930–1932.

Modern Human Origins

Questions regarding the beginnings of modern people have long been inexorably linked to explanations for the geographically based variation exhibited by recent human populations. Speculations on the meaning of human variation extend back to the ancient world but became prominent in Western thought between the fifteenth and the seventeenth centuries. During this "Age of Exploration," the extent of human biological and cultural variation became increasingly evident to Europeans. As with most other scientific discoveries of this period, the initial explanations for these observations were largely tied to religion.

Races and the Nature of Creation
Biblical literalism required that all modern humans were descendants of Adam and Eve, but it soon became obvious that, in order to conform to the biblical account, human "races" would have had to develop their "unique" features in a very short period of time. Johann Friedrich Blumenbach (1752–1840) of the University of Göttingen (Germany) suggested that this was possible if human differences were viewed as adaptive responses to differing environments. This "monogenist" view was supported by, among

others, the American Samuel Stanhope Smith (1750–1819), who based it on environmental arguments similar to Blumenbach's. Such stances were, in part, responses to the heretical notion that human races represented separate acts of divine creation. Lord Kames (also known as Henry Home) (1696–1782) had argued that the differences between human "races" were too great to be explained by climate, especially given the short time since Creation. He postulated instead that there had been several separate creations of humans to fit various geographic and climatic surroundings. This "polygenist," or multiple-creation, perspective was supported by a chorus of early American workers such as Samuel George Morton (1799–1851), Josiah Clark Nott (1804–1873), and George R. Gliddon (1809–1857), and it survived the emergence of Darwinism in the anti-Darwinian work of individuals like Paul Broca (1824–1880) in France, James Hunt (1833–1869) in England, and the Swiss zoologist Louis Agassiz (1807–1873), who emigrated to the United States in the early 1850s. It is interesting to note that Agassiz's conversion to polygenism was largely a product of his encounters with African-Americans in the New World.

The polygenist view regarded the "colored races" as inherently inferior and sought to emphasize the gaps separating "primitive" races from "advanced" ones. One way to do this was to argue that races represented distinctly separate lines extending far back into antiquity. Initially, of course, these ideas were far from evolutionary in nature. For example, Broca's student Paul Topinard (1830–1911) rejected strict polygenism but continued to stress that the origin of races was, in Peter Bowler's words, ". . . too remote for serious investigation" (1986:56). Topinard (1885) argued further that "pure racial types" were the products of an unspecified process in remote antiquity that was no longer in operation. As C. Loring Brace (1982) and others have shown, this acceptance of extensive antiquity for human races was used as an excuse to ignore considerations of their evolutionary origins.

Race and the Emerging Fossil Record
As authentic fossil remains of humans began to accumulate in the late nineteenth century, much effort was focused on their "racial classification," and many explanations for the evolutionary changes documented by these specimens evoked migrations of different races (Bowler 1986; Brace 1981; Stocking 1968).

Although versions of it were often overtly "evolutionary" in perspective, this racial-succession paradigm skirted issues of evolutionary mechanisms and meaningful phylogeny, and became particularly influential in assessments of the European record. Though certainly not explicitly polygenist, these perspectives still stressed the "separateness" and "distinctiveness" of the various prehistoric and modern races recognized. This is perhaps best exemplified by the polytypic theory of the German anatomist Hermann Klaatsch (1863–1916). In his model (see Fig. 1a), some "races" are seen as totally distinct all the way back to *Pithecanthropus* and as being more closely related to various great apes than to many other

human groups. Other similar theories were somewhat less extreme. For example, Harvard University's Earnest A. Hooton (1887–1954) also promoted a polytypic theory. Hooton traced the divergence of human races all the way back to the beginnings of the Pleistocene but correctly realized that all apes diverged much earlier (see Fig. 1b).

During the late nineteenth century and much of the twentieth, discussions of modern human origins based on fossil human material were almost exclusively focused on Europe. Largely, this was because there was virtually nothing in the way of a pertinent fossil record outside of Europe and because scholars interested in such issues were generally Europeans.

Fig. 1. Polytypic theories of modern human origins. (a) Hermann Klaatsch's version traces major racial lines back to Pithecanthropus (Homo erectus) *and represents them as totally independent lineages (from Klaatsch 1920). (b) E.A. Hooton's representation presents the branching of modern Asian, African/Australian, and European "races" back to the early Pleistocene (from Hooton 1931).*

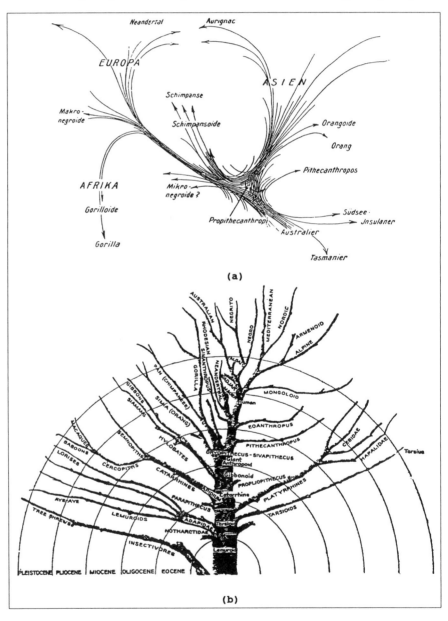

(a)

(b)

Thus, the history of investigation of the origin of modern humans and their biological variations during this period is closely tied to the "Neandertal problem" (Bowler 1986; Brace 1964; Trinkaus & Shipman 1993). As discoveries in Asia and Africa of pertinent post–*Homo erectus* fossil human remains came to light in the 1920s and 1930s, paleontologically based ideas about the roles of these continents in modern human origins began to emerge. Theoretical and speculative ideas, of course, had long focused on the role of Asia in modern human origins, as is well emphasized by the Aryan-migration hypothesis of the Swedish anthropologist Anders Adolf Retzius (1796–1860). But although the fossil record outside Europe was steadily improving, debate on the role of Neandertals continued to dominate ideas on modern human origin throughout most of the twentieth century. Fortunately, the 1970s onward have witnessed much broader, less Eurocentric, discussions of the beginnings of people like us.

Beyond Europe: Keith, Leakey, and Weidenreich
By the second decade of the twentieth century, several prominent scholars based arguments for the antiquity of modern humans directly on human fossil remains. In France, Marcellin Boule (1861–1942) argued that the Grotte des Enfants remains from Grimaldi established the presence of modern people contemporaneously with Neandertals in Europe; while in Britain, Arthur Keith (1866–1955) held that the British remains from Galley Hill pushed modern humans back even further (Keith 1915). Thus, both Boule and Keith were early proponents of the Pre-sapiens hypothesis, which viewed modern humans as a separate evolutionary line from Neandertals and their kin. In those years, the Pre-sapiens lineage was seen as a primarily European phenomenon, although Boule's recognition of "Negroid" affinities for some of the Grimaldi specimens suggests that he may have seen an African influence in the emergence of modern Europeans. Interestingly, a European contemporary of Boule, the Italian Giuseppe Sergi (1841–1936) went even further. He supported the notion that the primitive races of Europe (such as the Neandertals) were displaced by an influx of "brown peoples" from Africa who were the ancestors of the Mediterranean and Nordic varieties of Europeans (Sergi 1901). In 1932, human fossil remains were discovered at Kanam and Kanjera in East Africa (*vide infra*) that gave further credence to the belief of an early appearance of modern humans in Africa.

The discovery of the Broken Hill remains in 1921 in what was then Rhodesia demonstrated the presence of Neandertal-like humans in Africa. In 1932, the Kenyan paleoanthropologist L.S.B. Leakey (1903–1972) recovered early Pleistocene mandibular fragments from Kanam and the somewhat more recent partial crania from Kanjera, both in Kenya. Based on these fragmentary remains, Leakey argued for the presence of a Pre-sapiens lineage in Africa. Leakey believed that Neandertals, the Broken Hill remains, *Pithecanthropus*, *Sinanthropus*, and Mauer represented a separate *family* (the Palaeoanthropidae) that diverged from the family of modern humans (the Neoanthropidae) in the Miocene (Leakey 1934). Interestingly, he included only Piltdown and *Homo kanamensis* among the Neoanthropidae. Leakey's perspective was the most compelling case during these years for a Pre-sapiens lineage outside Europe.

Between 1929 and 1934, excavations at the Wadi el-Mughara, on Mount Carmel in Palestine (now Israel), produced an impressive series of human remains, the ages of which were estimated to be 100 ky BP. These remains were described by Keith and the American paleoanthropologist Theodore D. McCown (1908–1969), who wrote that the combination of Neandertal-like and more-modern specimens, from Tabūn and Skhūl, respectively, reflected a population "in the throes of evolution" (McCown & Keith 1939). Specifically, they believed that the Mount Carmel people were in the process of evolving into modern humans and that, since they were earlier than European Neandertals, they represented the source for the first modern Europeans, the Cro-Magnons (see Fig. 2). Keith had already voiced doubts regarding his previous belief in the great antiquity of the modern human form, particularly in Europe, so that the interpretation of the Mount Carmel skeletons completed a fundamental shift in Keith's perspective on modern human origins. Though he never abandoned his belief in the extinction of European Neandertals, Keith's interpretation, along with McCown, of Skhūl and Tabūn provided the first compelling statement of the Pre-neandertal hypothesis to be rooted in the fossil record itself. This view, that modern humans had passed through a Neandertal-like phase outside of Europe, became the explanation of choice for modern human origins, particularly with the gradual demise of the Pre-sapiens hypothesis in the 1950s and 1960s (cf. Spencer 1984).

The discoveries of *Homo erectus* remains in

Java and China focused paleoanthropological attention on East Asia beginning in the 1890s, but it was the work of Franz Weidenreich (1873–1948) that initially carved out a role for the Far East in the debate on modern human origins. Weidenreich's studies of the remains from Zhoukoudian, Ngandong, Sangiran, and elsewhere convinced him that certain "racial" features could be documented to extend from modern Asian peoples back to at least the Middle Pleistocene. Furthermore, Weidenreich (1946) argued that even within Asia, separate lines could be traced back to *Sinanthropus* and *Pithecanthropus* in China and Southeast Asia, respectively. Based on these studies of Asian remains and his earlier support for the Neandertal-phase hypothesis in Europe, Weidenreich argued that modern humans had originated somewhat separately in different parts of the Old World. In this context, he extended the Neandertal-phase concept to Africa and Asia, arguing that the Broken Hill and Ngandong specimens were African and Asian (or "tropical") Neandertals, respectively, and that they represented regional ancestral stages between *Homo erectus* and moderns in these different regions. Some scholars criticized Weidenreich's model as smacking of orthogenesis or even as suggestive of a type of polygenism. However, Weidenreich was careful to note that these regional lineages did not evolve in total isolation from each other but were always interconnected by varying levels of gene flow. Thus, far from seeing the pattern of the evolving regional lines as like a "candelabra," he saw it distinctly as like a trellis (see Fig. 3). Furthermore, Weidenreich (1941) believed that the general similarity of cranial form shared by modern humans from different regions was the inevitable result of universal selection for increasing encephalization in humans and thus could have evolved independently in those regions.

Weidenreich's views represent the first serious examination of modern human origins across the entire Old World. His was the first attempt to argue that the polytypic nature of the human species had a significant antiquity and that humans had evolved as a polytypic species since *Homo erectus* times. As such, Weidenreich's ideas serve as a bridge between the earlier Neandertal-phase hypothesis, which essentially saw modern humans as arising in Europe only, and certain more recent perspectives, such as multiregional evolution (cf. Wolpoff 1989).

The Battle of the 1960s: Coon, Brace, and Howells

By the early 1960s, Weidenreich's views formed the basis of two very different perspectives on the role of "race" in modern human origins. In 1962, the American paleoanthropologist Carleton S. Coon (1904–1981) published his seminal work, *The Origin of Races*, which elaborated on Weidenreich's trellis model of modern human origins, specifically stressing the polytypic nature of extant human populations and their ancestors. Coon argued that races were, in fact, older than species and that individual human races had crossed the threshold to *Homo sapiens* at different times. Unfortunately, he went on to propose that the earliest races to cross the *sapiens* threshold had evolved the most and that ". . . the levels of civilization attained by some of their populations may be related phenomena" (Coon 1962:x). Coon held that the northern races, the Caucasoids and Mongoloids, were the first to become *sapiens*, implying that these groups were more advanced evolutionarily than the so-called southern geographic races. It is essentially this perspective (and the implications arising from it) that led to the claims of racism against Coon (cf. Shipman 1994) and probably led many to overlook the more useful aspects of his work on the fossil record.

It has often been stated that Coon viewed the major geographic races as evolving virtually in isolation from one another. Certainly Coon often stated that they evolved in a "parallel fashion," and such statements have obviously influenced the perception of many workers that Coon's model was out of step with current biological theory. However, like Weidenreich, he recognized that significant gene flow occurred between populations of these "races," particularly at their margins. On the other hand, Coon thought that adaptations to differing regional conditions would largely overshadow many effects of gene flow. For example, he stated that:

. . . There has been enough gene flow over the last half million years to have homogenized us all had that been the evolutionary scheme of things, and had it not been advantageous to each of the geographic races for it to retain, for the most part, the adaptive elements in its genetic status quo (Coon 1968:663).

Furthermore, in discussing the evolution of polytypic species, Coon argued that the component populations evolve as a *unit* but ". . . cannot do so simultaneously since it takes time for a mutation to spread from one population to another" (1968:29). Thus, while Coon's understanding of biological processes might be suspect, it is clear that he recognized the significance of *gene flow* as well as adaptation to variable local conditions to the origin of modern humans and their biological variation. Whatever one's feelings might be regarding "racism" in Coon's thinking, his contributions to the emergence of current perspectives on modern human origins cannot be dismissed.

During the 1960s, another approach to the study of modern human origins was promoted by the American physical anthropologist C. Loring Brace (1930–). This approach grew out of the earlier Neandertal-phase hypothesis, but it is more directly derived from Weidenreich's worldwide perspectives. Like

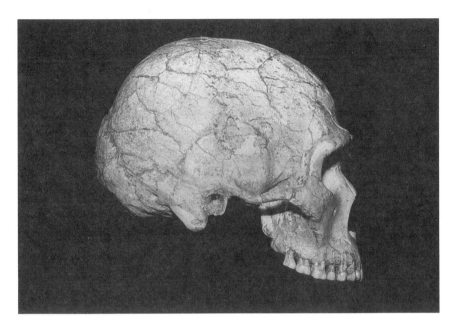

Fig. 2. Early modern human crania: (a) Skhūl 5 from Israel and (b) Cro-Magnon 1 from France. The Skhūl specimens have long been considered logical ancestors of the earliest modern Europeans.

a

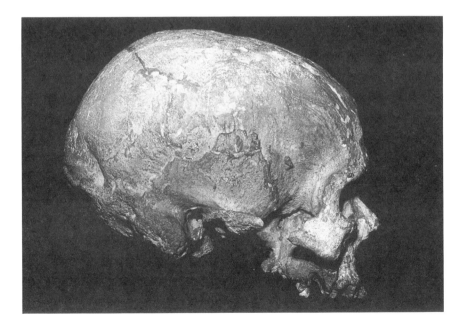

b

Fig. 3. Weidenreich's trellis model of human evolution. The solid lines indicate interconnections (from Weidenreich 1946).

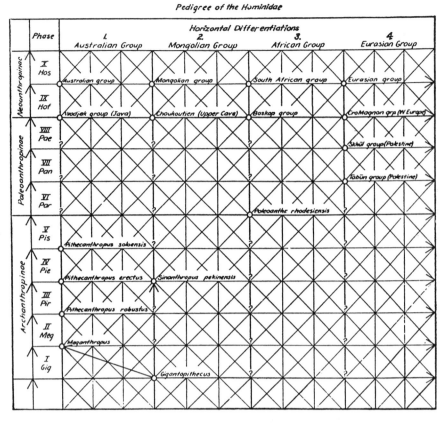

Fig. 3. Weidenreich's trellis model of human evolution. The solid lines indicate interconnections (from Weidenreich 1946).

Weidenreich, Brace suggested that modern humans appeared roughly simultaneously throughout the Old World and that they passed through regional Neandertal phases just prior to their emergence. For Brace, the driving force that produced modern humans was relaxed selection, also called the probable mutation effect. Brace believed that once the selective forces that produced and maintained the distinctive Neandertal cranial form and robust physique were reduced, accumulation of mutations would lead to their reduction and transformation into the modern human form. Brace cited general technological sophistication as the mechanism that promoted the relaxing of selection on the Neandertal anatomical form and that thus ultimately led to the emergence of the modern human anatomical pattern.

With respect to considerations of human variation, Brace held that the concept of "race" was a typological construct and that races, as such, did not really exist. To a much greater extent than Coon, Brace stressed the interconnection of human populations throughout the world. Along with his University of Michigan colleague Frank B. Livingstone (1928–) and others, Brace emphasized the arbitrariness of standard racial groupings and deemphasized

the discussion of "regional" features in considerations of modern human origins.

The contrasting view to the Old World-wide appearance of modern humans, as presented in the 1960s, is best illustrated by the writings of the Harvard physical anthropologist William W. Howells (1908–). In a series of publications, Howells argued for a monocentric origin of modern humans. Like many others, his primary concern was the expulsion of Neandertals from human ancestry, but he also stressed that a single area of origin for modern humans made more sense in terms of the synthetic theory of evolution. In his highly influential book *Mankind in the Making*, Howells (1959) hints that Asia is that source. He also suggests that modern humans evolved from a Pre-Neandertal form and probably hybridized with Neandertals and other archaic humans as they spread throughout the Old World.

Howell's view of the emergence of modern human variation differs considerably from that of both Brace and especially Coon. For Howells, the beginning of current human racial variation was a relatively recent phenomenon, probably extending back less than 40.0 ky BP and certainly not traceable to *Homo erectus* or Neandertals. He wrote: "We can be sure of this: races have become different from one another since the time when the species *sapiens* took shape and came to occupy different regions" (Howells 1967:265).

Howells' views are basically consistent with the Pre-Neandertal hypothesis, which was very popular at the time. His views as expressed in such publications as *Mankind in the Making*, combined with his later pioneering work on recent human cranial variation (cf. Howells 1973) and his efforts to use recent human genetic variation to interpret the history of *Homo sapiens* (Howells 1976), are

clearly at the root of recent monocentric views on modern human origins.

Out of Africa

The Pre-Neandertal model, as supported by the American paleoanthropologist F.C. Howell (1925–), Howells, and others, implied, if not explicitly promoted, a basically monocentric perspective on modern human origins, although its supporters were necessarily vague regarding the exact location of that center. In 1976, Howells succinctly marshaled the evidence available at that time for

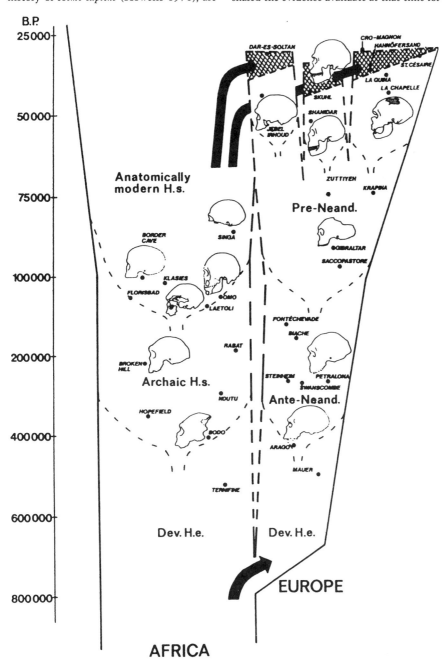

Fig. 4. The Afro-European Sapiens hypothesis as represented by Günter Bräuer in 1984.

a recent, single origin of modern humans, stressing both morphological evidence and data from genetic polymorphisms in living populations. Such views carried over into the initial work of the British paleoanthropologist Chris B. Stringer of the Natural History Museum—British Museum (Natural History)—in England and others during the 1970s and early 1980s (cf. Stringer 1994) and thus strongly influenced the emergence of African-origins models for modern human origins.

In the early 1980s, Günter Bräuer (1949–) at the University of Hamburg focused on Africa as the logical source for modern humans. Though not the first to stress the importance of the African Middle and Late Pleistocene human fossil record in this context (the American paleoanthropologist G. Philip Rightmire and, to a much lesser extent, R.R.R. Protsch at the University of Frankfurt had done so previously), Bräuer was the first to argue unequivocally for an early transition to modern *Homo sapiens* in Africa and their subsequent spread into Europe and Asia (Bräuer 1984). He based his model, termed the Afro-European sapiens hypothesis (AES), on careful studies of recent African skeletal samples and the pertinent fossil record. Bräuer's AES did not recognize modern humans as a distinct biological species. Rather, it was based on the assumption that, while Eurasian archaic humans, like the Neandertals, were replaced by incoming modern populations (see Fig. 4), some archaic genes were assimilated into the modern gene pool. Bräuer described his perspective as "replacement with hybridization" but clearly regarded the "hybridization" as playing only a minor role in the formation of modern Eurasian gene pools. In the mid-1980s, Stringer also endorsed Africa as the center of origin for the modern human radiation, based on the fossil record.

One of the major factors that influenced both Bräuer and Stringer during this period was chronology. In the 1970s, there was no compelling evidence that modern humans were older than ca. 40.0 ky BP anywhere in the world. However, during the 1980s, the application of thermoluminescence (TL) and electron spin resonance (ESR) dating, as well as radiocarbon dating in some cases, to pertinent fossil human localities suggested an age in excess of 100 ky BP for modern humans at the sites of Border Cave, Omo-Kibish, and the Klasies River Mouth caves in Africa, and an age of perhaps slightly less for the modern human remains from Skhūl and Qafzeh in the Near East (cf. Grün & Stringer 1991; Smith,

Follsetti, & Donnelly 1989 for reviews). These dates were older than those for early-modern Europeans and many Neandertals and implied a south-to-north "cline" in the appearance of modern humans.

Additionally, studies of blood groups and other protein-system data in the 1980s seemed also to support a recent African origin for all modern humans (cf. Nei & Roychoudbury 1982). But even more powerful support came from studies of mitochondrial (mt) DNA (deoxyribonucleic acid) in a world-wide series of recent humans by Rebecca Cann, Mark Stoneking, and Allan C. Wilson (1935–1991).

Based on their studies (Cann, Stoneking, & Wilson 1987) and those of others (cf. Cann, Rickards, & Lum 1994 for a review), Cann and her colleagues argued that all recent humans evolved from a single African source within the last 300 ky BP and that the last common ancestor of all non-African populations lived as recently as 90.0 ky BP. Furthermore, they noted that admixture with any archaic humans was highly unlikely. Thus, not only did the genetic studies support a recent African origin for modern humans, but the mtDNA data also implied that the spread of these modern populations into Eurasia involved a total replacement of all archaic human groups (including Neandertals). This primarily mtDNA-based model became widely known as the "Eve theory."

The impact of the genetic studies, particularly the mtDNA analyses, transformed the mainly morphologically based African-origin models into a much more visible and influential perspective on modern human origins. In their seminal paper in *Science*, Stringer and Peter Andrews (1988) refer to this model as the Recent African Evolution model (RAE). In this RAE model, Stringer and Andrews combined the mtDNA data with paleontological indications of an African transition to modern morphology and the absence of such transitions in other areas, along with the absence of morphological continuity between modern and archaic Eurasian peoples, to strongly imply that the replacement of Eurasian archaic humans was essentially total. Based on this, they asserted that modern humans were a distinct species from archaic forms and that the taxon *Homo sapiens* should be reserved only for anatomically modern humans.

The appeal of this model has been widespread, both in professional and public circles. Harvard's Stephen Jay Gould embraced it as a classic example of his perspective on how macroevolution operated—evolution is a "bush not a ladder"—further suggesting that this model underscores the basic unity and brotherhood of all humankind (Gould 1987). Many paleoanthropologists also argued that the branching pattern, and recognition of multiple human species during the Middle and Late Pleistocene, made considerable sense in light of the variation exhibited in the later human fossil record (Rightmire 1990; Tattersall 1986). Finally, virtually every major news and science magazine carried articles focusing on the model's basis and implications, which brought the controversy over modern human origins to the attention of the public.

Although considerable debate still focuses on their accuracy (cf. Aiello 1993; Smith 1994 for reviews), the African-origin models remain popular and, in the eyes of many, robust explanations for the origin of modern humans and their biological variation. In the context of the evolution of these ideas, important attempts have been made to formulate a "marriage" between recent human genetic variation and the fossil record in order to provide a comprehensive perspective on human evolutionary history. Regardless of one's point of view regarding the correctness of these African-origin models, they have fostered a considerable increase in data and analytical studies pertinent to the beginnings of modern people.

Multiregional Evolution

From the theoretical perspective, the African-origin models are children of the Pre-Neandertal hypothesis. The major competing hypothesis, known as Multiregional Evolution (MRE), is usually considered to have its roots in the Neandertal-phase hypothesis. This is somewhat of an oversimplification because many of the early Neandertal-phase models were essentially monocentric, with Europe being the place of origin for modern people. Although generally lumped in this category, Weidenreich's views were not monocentric,

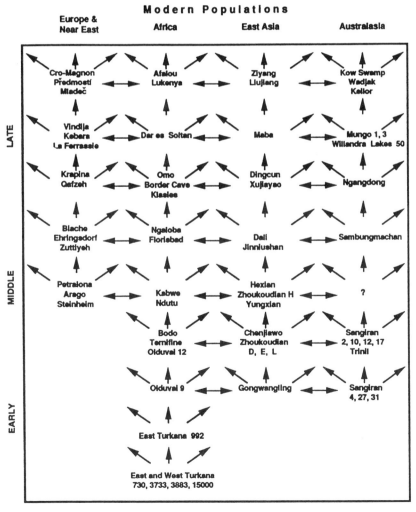

Fig. 5. A schematic representation of the Multiregional evolution model (after Frayer et al. 1993).

and it is specifically his polycentric version of unilinealism, rather than other versions of the Neandertal-phase hypothesis, that underlies modern multiregionalism.

MRE was proposed by Milford H. Wolpoff (1942–), Alan Thorne, and Wu Xin Zhi in 1984, building partly on earlier works by these authors. This model argues that modern humans have existed as an interconnected web of regional lineages extending all the way back to *Homo erectus*. Indeed recently, supporters of this model have argued that *Homo sapiens* includes the specimens traditionally placed in *Homo erectus* and thus has existed as a species since about 1.9 mya (Wolpoff, Thorne, Jelinek, & Yinyum 1994). MRE proponents assert that there are varying degrees of morphological and genetic continuity between local archaic and modern human populations throughout the Old World. The model denies that modern humans exhibit a classical monocentric origin and rejects the suggestion that Neandertals and archaic Asians represent separate species from *Homo sapiens*.

Although sometimes misrepresented as implying parallel regional lines of evolution, MRE embraces Weidenreich's trellis concept (see Fig. 5) and contends that the appearance of modern humans (or, more correctly, modern human anatomical form) in a particular region resulted from the complex interplay of differential amounts of gene flow, the pattern of local selection promoting adaptation to varied environments, and the action of genetic drift in these relatively small populations. Multiregionalism further asserts that: (1) transitional samples bridging archaic-to-modern human populations can be found in Eurasia, not just in Africa; and (2) evidence of morphological continuity is also demonstrable for various regions of Eurasia (cf. Frayer et al. 1993 for a summary of this evidence). Additionally, genetic (including mtDNA) data have also been used to support multiregionalism (Templeton 1993).

MRE has, like the African-origin models, contributed significantly to the refinement of scholarly perspectives on modern human origins. It has promoted detailed studies of the applicable fossil record and modern samples in search of evidence for morphological continuity in various regions of the Old World. MRE has also helped focus primary attention on fossil remains from parts of the world, particularly east Asia and Australia, that had not received much detailed consideration beyond the local level for some time. It has also influenced attempts to determine precisely how modern humans can be defined morphologically.

Both the RAE and the MRE models have themselves evolved since the early 1980s. Stringer, for example, has stated that he does not see replacement as necessarily total, and the strongest evidence in the eyes of supporters of RAE has seemed to shift somewhat from the genetic back to the paleontological data. Similarly, versions of MRE have emerged that view many aspects of modern human morphology as coalescing in a single region and then spreading, but by a process of demic diffusion with selection rather than the systematic migration touted by the African-origins models (cf. Aiello 1993; Smith, Falsetti, & Donnelly 1989).

The issue of what model, if any, is the best explanation for the origin of modern people is not likely to be settled soon. For some, this is very disturbing. These individuals think that, with the amount of information available on the origin of modern humans, a consensus should have emerged. However, in historical science, increasing knowledge allows progressively more-detailed questions to be asked of the pertinent historical record. In the study of modern human origins, the debate in the 1990s centers on much more precise issues than are possible for earlier phases in human evolution. In the future, as these issues are better understood, debate is likely to carry over into even more-detailed aspects of the beginnings of people like us.

Fred H. Smith

See also African Prehistory; Agassiz, (Jean) Louis (Rodolphe); Aryanism; Asian Paleoanthropology; Blumenbach, Johann Friedrich; Boule, Marcellin; Broca, Paul (Pierre); Coon, Carleton S(tevens); Cro-Magnon; Galley Hill; Gobineau, Joseph-Arthur de; Gorjanović-Kramberger, Dragutin (Karl); Grimaldi; *Homo erectus*; Hooton, E(arnest) A(lbert); Howells, William White; Hrdlička, Aleš; Hunt, James; Java; Keith, (Sir) Arthur; Klaatsch, Hermann; Leakey, Louis Seymour Bazett; McCown, Theodore D(oney); Molecular Anthropology; Morton, Samuel George; Mount Carmel (Israel); Neandertal (Feldhofer Grotte); Neandertals; Nott, Josiah Clark; Piltdown; Polygenism; Předmostí; Qafzeh (Jebel) (Israel); Retzius, Anders Adolf; Sergi, Giuseppe; Skhūl (Israel); Smith, Samuel Stanhope; South Africa; Tabūn, Mugharet el- (Israel); Topinard, Paul; Weidenreich, Franz; Zhoukoudian

Bibliography

L. Aiello: The fossil evidence for modern human origins in Africa: A revised view. *American Anthropologist* 95:73–96, 1993; P. Bowler: *Theories of human evolution.* Baltimore: Johns Hopkins University Press, 1986; C.L. Brace: The fate of the "classic" Neanderthals: A consideration of hominid catastrophism. *Current Anthropology* 5:3–43, 1964; C.L. Brace: Tales of the phylogenetic woods: The evolution and significance of evolutionary trees. *American Journal of Physical Anthropology* 56:411–429, 1981; C.L. Brace: The roots of the race concept in American physical anthropology. In: F. Spencer (ed) *A history of American physical anthropology, 1930–1980.* New York: Academic Press, 1982, pp. 11–29.

G. Bräuer: A craniological approach to the origin of anatomically modern *Homo sapiens* in Africa and implications for the appearance of modern humans. In: F.H. Smith & F. Spencer (eds) *The origins of modern humans.* New York: Liss, 1984, pp. 327–410; R. Cann, O. Rickards, & K. Lum: Mitochondrial DNA and human evolution: Our one lucky mother. In: M.H. Nitecki & D.V. Nitecki (eds) *Origins of anatomically modern humans.* New York: Plenum, 1994, pp. 135–148; R. Cann, M. Stoneking, & A. Wilson: Mitochondrial DNA and human evolution. *Nature* 325:31–36, 1987; C.S. Coon: *The origin of races.* New York: Knopf, 1962 (2d ed: 1968); D.W. Frayer, M.H. Wolpoff, A.G. Thorne, F.H. Smith, & G.G. Pope: Theories of modern human origins: The paleontological test. *American Anthropologist* 95:14–50, 1993.

S.J. Gould: Bushes all the way down. *Natural History* 96:12–19, 1987; R. Grün & C.B. Stringer: Electron spin resonance dating and the evolution of modern humus. *Archaeometry* 33:153–199, 1991; E.A. Hooton: *Up from the ape.* New York: Macmillan, 1931; W.W. Howells: *Mankind in the making.* Garden City: Doubleday, 1959. (rev. ed.: 1967); W.W. Howells: Explaining modern man: Evolutionists vs. migrationalists. *Journal of Human Evolution* 5:577–596, 1967; W.W. Howells: *Cranial variation in man.* Papers of the Peabody Museum. Vol. 79. Cambridge, Massachusetts: Harvard University Press, 1973; A. Keith: *The antiquity of man.* London: Williams & Norgate, 1915; H. Klaatsch: *Der Werdegang der Menschheit und die Enstehung der Kultur.* Berlin: Bong, 1920; L. Leakey: *Adam's ancestors.* 3d ed. London: Methuen, 1934.

T. McCown & A. Keith: *The Stone Age of Mount Carmel II: The fossil human remains from the Levalloiso-Mousterian.* Oxford: Clarendon, 1939; M. Nei & A.K. Roychoudbury: Genetic relationship and evolution of human races. *Evolutionary Biology* 14:1–49, 1982; G.P. Rightmire: *The evolution of Homo erectus.* Cambridge: Cambridge University Press, 1990; G. Sergi: *The Mediterranean race: A study of the origin of European peoples.* London: Scott, 1901; P. Shipman: *The evolution of racism.* New York: Simon & Schuster, 1994; F.H. Smith: Samples, species, and speculations in the study of modern human origins. In: M.H. Nitecki & D.V. Nitecki (eds) *Origins of anatomically modern humans.* New York: Plenum, 1994, pp. 227–249; F.H. Smith, A.B. Fallsetti, & S. Donnelly: Modern human origins. *Yearbook of Physical Anthropology* 32:35–68, 1989.

F. Spencer: The Neandertals and their evolutionary significance: A brief historical survey. In: F.H. Smith & F. Spencer (eds) *The origins of modern humans.* New York: Liss, 1984, pp. 1–49; G. Stocking: *Race, culture, and evolution: Essays in the history of anthropology.* New York: Free Press, 1968; C.B. Stringer: Out of Africa: A personal history. In: M.H. Nitecki & D.V. Nitecki (eds) *Origins of anatomically modern humans.* New York: Plenum, 1994, pp. 149–172; C.B. Stringer & P. Andrews: Genetic and fossil evidence for the origin of modern humans. *Science* 239:1263–1268, 1988; I. Tattersall: Species recognition in human paleontology. *Journal of Human Evolution* 15:165–175, 1986; A. Templeton: The "Eve" hypothesis: A genetic critique and analysis. *American Anthropologist* 95:51–72, 1993; P. Topinard: *Elements d'anthropologie générale.* Paris: Delahaye & Lecrosnier, 1885; E. Trinkaus & P. Shipman: *The Neandertals.* New York: Knopf, 1993.

F. Weidenreich: The brain and its role in the phylogenetic transformation of the human skull. *Transactions of the American Philosophical Society* 31(n.s.):34–442, 1941; F. Weidenreich: *Apes, giants, and man.* Chicago: University of Chicago Press, 1946; M.H. Wolpoff: Multiregional evolution: The fossil alternative to Eden. In: P. Mellars & C.B. Stringer (eds) *The human revolution.* Edinburgh: Edinburgh University Press, 1989, pp. 62–108; M.H. Wolpoff, A.G. Thorne, J. Jelinek, & Zhang Yinyum: The case for sinking *Homo erectus:* 100 years of Pithecanthropus is enough! *Courier*

Forschungsinstitut Senckenberg 171:341–361, 1994; M.H. Wolpoff, A. Thorne, & Wu Xin Zhi: Modern *Homo sapiens* origin: A general theory of hominid evolution involving the fossil evidence from East Africa. In: F.H. Smith & F. Spencer (eds) *The origins of modern humans.* New York: Liss, 1984, pp. 411–483.

Molecular Anthropology

Beginning with the study of serology in the first decade of the twentieth century, molecular genetic data have had an ambiguous role in physical anthropology. Though often attractive for their reductionist nature, molecular data have proved frequently difficult to interpret when applied to anthropological questions.

The term "molecular anthropology" was coined by the American chemist, Emile Zuckerkandl, shortly after the elaboration of the structure of DNA and the genetic code. First isolated by Miescher in 1869, deoxyribonucleic acid was thought to be a large, simple biomolecule, not complex enough to encode genetic information. Though a series of well-controlled experiments indicated by the mid-1940s that DNA was indeed identical with the genetic instructions (Avery et al. 1944), it met forceful opposition from the American biochemist Alfred Mirsky (McCarty 1985). A less clear-cut experiment refocused interest a few years later on DNA, rather than on protein, as the substance of which genes are made (Hershey & Chase 1952).

The structure of DNA was established by James D. Watson and Francis H.C. Crick (1953), based on inferences about its composition derived from the chemical analysis of Erwin Chargaff (1950). As described in Watson's lively and candid memoir, *The Double Helix* (1968), Watson and Crick stayed barely a step ahead of the American chemist Linus Pauling (1901–1994) in their elucidation of the structure, relying heavily on unpublished X-ray diffraction photographs taken by an unpopular colleague, Rosalind Franklin (1920–1958).

Blood-Group Serology

Molecular anthropology, however, long antedates the molecular revolution of the 1950s. "Blood" is a strong metaphor for heredity, and hereditary relationships among organisms could apparently be reconstructed from properties of the blood, as demonstrated by George H.F. Nuttall (1862–1937) (1904).

In the first half of the twentieth century,

when the overarching goal of physical anthropology was to establish the number and identity of the fundamental subdivisions of the human species, the blood groups were recruited in the endeavor. Discovered by the German immunologist Karl Landsteiner (1868–1943) in 1900, the ABO system is now known to be governed by three major alleles (A, B, O), resulting in six genotypes (OO, AO, AA, BO, BB, AB) and four blood-group phenotypes (O, A, B, AB). Most populations have all three alleles; what varies is merely the proportion of the alleles within each population (see Table 1). The major source of variation here, then, is polymorphic (within-population variation), and the nature of the variation across populations is clinal (changing gradually with geographical distance).

Early serological studies, however, failed to interpret their findings this way (see Fig. 1). The first surveys during World War I managed to divide the human species into three groups in accordance with their ABO blood groups: European, Intermediate, and Asio-African (Hirschfeld & Hirschfeld 1919). This fell into strong accord with a worldview that separated Europeans racially or constitutionally from the rest of human populations.

Racial invasions of pure A and B peoples superimposing themselves on a primordially O species were invoked to explain the prevalence of polymorphism. Finding little A and virtually no B among Native Americans, serologists interpreted this not as the random loss of alleles due to genetic drift, but rather as evidence that all Old World populations were more closely related to one another than any was to Native American populations (Coca & Diebert 1923). The American geneticist Laurence Snyder (1926) revised the racial analysis of ABO blood groups, identifying seven racial types in the human species, based on their allele frequencies. These were not, however, at all harmonious with the phenotypic clusters identified in the species, leading the American physical anthropologist Earnest A. Hooton (1887–1954) (1931) to doubt the fundamental utility of serology in physical anthropology as focused on "races."

The American immunologist William C. Boyd (1903–1983) refined the use of blood groups in the study of human diversity, but he continued to interpret his results in the context of races. In 1940, when the most useful traits for racial analysis were considered to be *non*adaptive traits, Boyd argued for the superiority of serological data on the basis of

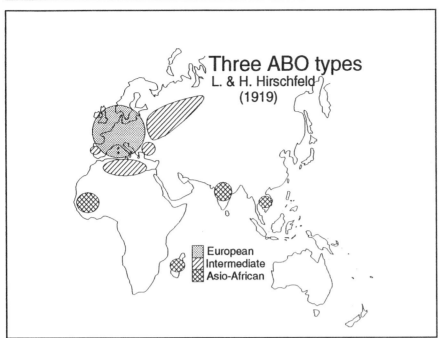

Three ABO types
L. & H. Hirschfeld
(1919)

European
Intermediate
Asio-African

Fig. 1. Geographic samples used by the Hirschfelds (a.k.a Hirszfeld) to separate Europeans from other human populations on the basis of ABO blood group types.

their nonadaptive nature; in 1963, when the optimal racial traits were considered to be *adaptive*, Boyd argued for superiority of serological data on the basis of their adaptive nature. These data, apparently, were the best, no matter what criteria were applied. This reflects not so much the scientific value of genetic data, but the cultural value of hereditarianism—a belief in the simple primacy of genetics.

The Molecular Clock

In 1962, the chemists Zuckerkandl and Pauling analyzed the (sparse) amino-acid sequence data for hemoglobin. Assuming a constant rate of change, they estimated that if humans and horses differed by eighteen amino acids, and shared a common ancestor 100–160 mya, then humans and gorillas diverged about 11.0 mya. An empirical justification for that assumption was given the following year by the biochemist Emanuel Margoliash for cytochrome c. Observing approximately the same number of amino-acid differences between a bird and each of four species of mammals, a fish and each of five species of amniotes, or a yeast and six species of vertebrates, Margoliash inferred that rates of change in different lineages were approximately equal.

With more data available on hemoglobins, Zuckerkandl and Pauling found "an approximate constancy in rate of evolution of different hemoglobin chains" (1965:144) and drew the obvious implication: *"There may thus*

exist a molecular evolutionary clock" (1965:148, emphasis in original). In addition, they noted a great deal of flexibility of structure in relation to protein function and suggested that most amino-acid substitutions had minimal effects on the functional integrity of the protein.

Calculations performed by the Japanese population geneticist Motoo Kimura (1968)

TABLE 1. ABO allele frequencies from representative populations. (From A.E. Mourant, A.C. Kopeć, and K. Domaniewska-Sobczak: *The Distribution of Human Blood Groups and Other Polymorphisms.* 2nd ed. New York, 1976).

Aboriginal population		Allele frequency		
		A	B	O
America	Chippewa	.06	.00	.94
	Kwakiutl	.10	.00	.90
Europe	Denmark	.27	.08	.66
	Bulgaria	.31	.12	.56
	Ukraine	.27	.16	.57
Asia	Kazakhstan	.25	.27	.48
	Pakistan	.20	.25	.55
	Japan	.29	.16	.54
Oceania	Australia	.18	.04	.78
Africa	Efe Pygmies	.26	.21	.53
	Angola	.16	.11	.72
	Sierra Leone	.16	.15	.69

suggested that the high rate of detectable genetic substitutions in proteins might be attributable to the mutations being of roughly equal fitness value, or "neutral." The "neutral theory" gave a theoretical justification for the apparent general constancy of the rate of molecular evolution.

Sequencing proteins, however, was costly and difficult. An estimate of genetic differences between taxa could be made using the vertebrate immune system. The significance of this approach lay in the close association between the immunological reaction and the genetic material itself. A foreign protein can stimulate an immunological reaction in a different species. Vertebrate blood, immunized against a protein derived from a particular species, can distinguish that protein from its homologue in a different species. The immunological reactions could thus measure differences in protein structure, which were a reflection of differences in genetic structure.

Serological Macroevolution and Molecular Systematics

Two major studies in the 1960s brought the application of serological techniques to the forefront of physical anthropology. Nuttall (1904) had shown that the extent of immunological cross-reactions roughly re-create the taxonomic affinities of primate species, though with notable exceptions, such as failing to detect that prosimians are primates. In 1962 the American molecular biologist Morris Goodman (1925–) demonstrated a major taxonomic paradox: Serologically, chimpanzees and gorillas clustered with humans (as an African group) rather than with orangutans (as a "great ape" group). As the serological data were arguably tracking genetic affinities more closely than traditional phenotypic analyses were, the phylogenetic conclusions gained widespread acceptance (Simpson 1963). Goodman further maintained that this necessarily implied a revision of primate classification based on the phylogenetic revision, but most systematists chose to retain the paraphyletic family Pongidae. The school of systematics known as cladism had not yet come into existence; years later, it would provide a retroactive validation for Goodman's viewpoint.

Technical modifications to the immunological studies permitted the results to be quantified by the mid-1960s, and were applied to the primates by the American bioanthropologist Vincent Sarich and New Zealand–born biochemist Allan Wilson (1934–1991) (cf. Sarich & Wilson 1967a, 1967b). The physical anthropologist Sherwood L. Washburn (1911–) had maintained a recent common ancestry of humans and apes, as recent as 1.0 mya (Washburn 1960, 1963). Application of the quantified immunological data to anthropoid evolution showed that immunological differences tended to accumulate in lineages at about the same rate, via the relative-rate test (see Fig. 2). Having estab-

Fig. 2. The relative rate test.

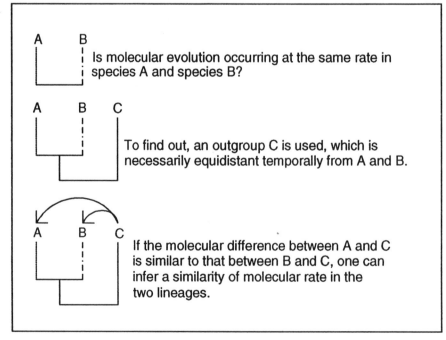

A   B

Is molecular evolution occurring at the same rate in species A and species B?

A   B   C

To find out, an outgroup C is used, which is necessarily equidistant temporally from A and B.

A   B   C

If the molecular difference between A and C is similar to that between B and C, one can infer a similarity of molecular rate in the two lineages.

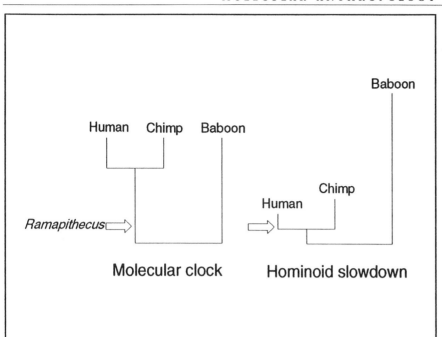

Fig. 3. The rate of molecular evolution could influence the phylogenetic placement of Ramapithecus.

lished this, Sarich and Wilson calculated that, given equal rates of change across lineages, the amount of change that had accumulated between humans and chimpanzees, relative to that which had accumulated between apes and Old World monkeys, implied a divergence date between humans and chimps of about 5.0 mya (Sarich & Wilson 1967a). This was later refined to 3.5 ± 1.5 my (Sarich 1968).

At the same time, however, certain features of the dental anatomy in the fossil genus *Ramapithecus* were being invoked to establish its presence on the unique evolutionary line ending in our species. Since this genus (being synonymized with *Kenyapithecus*) appeared to be present in East Africa 14.0 mya, it implied a human split from the apes prior to that date. The molecular data, in undermining the date, appeared to undermine the hominid allocation of *Ramapithecus* as well. If there was no uniquely human line until 3.5 my, obviously *Ramapithecus* could not have been on it at 14.0 my. Thus, argued Sarich, even given some play in the molecular dating, "one no longer has the option of considering a fossil specimen older than about 8 million years as a hominid *no matter what it looks like*" (Sarich 1970:199, emphasis in original).

Alternatively, it was conceivable that molecular evolution had proceeded at an aberrantly slow rate in the human lineage, such that a relatively long time elapsed with little molecular change (see Fig. 3). This could preserve the hominid allocation of *Ramapithecus*

by retaining an ancient separation for human and chimpanzee, with anomalously little detectable genetic change having occurred since that separation. Such a hominid slowdown, however, was not detectable by the relative-rate test.

Though few genetic regions have been analyzed, studies since the late 1980s have found a slower rate of molecular evolution in the human line, but of insufficient magnitude to have a major effect. And the anatomy of *Ramapithecus* has been reinterpreted, based on subsequent discoveries in Turkey and Pakistan.

The Trichotomy
The widely publicized success of the molecular clock resulted in a period of less critical acceptance of other biochemically generated results. Where earlier molecular studies had found humans, chimpanzees, and gorillas to be genetically so similar as to form a trichotomy, or three-way split, C.G. Sibley and J.E. Ahlquist (1984) claimed to have "resolved the trichotomy" into a human–chimpanzee association, with gorillas a distant third. Again, this appeared to conflict with most interpretations of the anatomy. David Pilbeam (1986), formerly a leading advocate of *Ramapithecus* in opposition to the molecular evidence, now vigorously promoted the new DNA hybridization work. This newfound advocacy, however, was now insufficiently critical of the molecular claims: it was found in short measure that the human–

chimpanzee linkage was not, in fact, sustained by those data, which was subsequently conceded (Marks et al. 1988; Sibley et al. 1990).

DNA studies have revealed considerable ambiguity in the relations of the African apes and humans, due to (1) their very close phylogenetic relationship; (2) the typological nature of these studies, sampling the relict remains of an originally diverse Miocene gene pool and generally reconstructing phylogeny from a single representative of each taxon; and (3) the extensive parallel evolution (homoplasy) that occurs in DNA.

What is clear is that if any pair of human, chimpanzee, and gorilla are closest relatives, the third is very close by. The complex gene pool of the Late Miocene hominoids appears to have been partitioned into three surviving taxa in a manner that is best described as a three-way split, or as two effectively contemporaneous speciation events (Rogers 1993).

Mitochondrial Eve

The pace of change in the determinants of serological specificity—presumably genes—precipitated the conflict over *Ramapithecus*. Cast in terms of the opposition of molecular data to morphological data, only one set was apparently able to yield an accurate phylogenetic inference. The promotion of DNA hybridization was able to capitalize on the newfound faith in molecules over morphology, while maintaining the same antagonism.

A somewhat different approach was taken by Rebecca Cann and her colleagues at Berkeley in a landmark paper (1987). Where two conflicting hypotheses existed in the paleoanthropological literature on the origin of modern humans, molecular data could now be applied to distinguish between them. The first, known as the regional-continuity model, implied deep local ancestries for genetic variation in the human species, while the second, known as the Out-of-Africa model, suggested a shallow ancestry traceable specifically to Africa. Cann and colleagues, analyzing differences in specific DNA marker sequences, found that the patterns of genetic diversity they encountered supported the latter model. Rather than take a hegemonic approach to the traditional avenues of anthropological research, this work was presented as complementary to them—a radical change in style. The precise relationship between patterns of modern genetic variation and the reconstruction of human prehistory is no longer clear, however.

Gene and Genome Structure

The study of physical anthropology is predicated to some extent upon genetics, for evolution is ultimately a genetic process. Little was known about gene structure and function until mid-century, when it was established that genes were composed of DNA, and the structure of DNA was elucidated.

In the phrase "one gene—one enzyme," G.W. Beadle and E.L. Tatum (1941) encapsulated the inference that at the primary level of function, a gene is responsible for the production of a single operational macromolecule. Following the work of Watson and Crick, the cellular role of nucleic acids became the central focus of molecular genetics. In the classic metaphor of the 1960s, the genetic "code" was broken, and the rudiments of transcription (making an RNA copy from a DNA template) and translation (making a protein from the RNA) led to a recognition that the DNA, RNA, and protein molecules were colinear—that is, their polymeric sequences were direct reflections of one another (Judson 1979). The 1970s yielded the recognition that the RNA transcript is extensively modified prior to being translated.

Perhaps the most fundamental revision of molecular genetics in the latter half of the twentieth century, however, has been in our understanding of the structure of the genome, the entire DNA complement of a cell. The pioneering work of the American geneticist Thomas Hunt Morgan (1866–1945) and his coworkers at Columbia University established that genes (i.e., functional hereditary units) were found in a characteristic fixed sequence, each in a specific location on a linear chromosome. The metaphor used to represent the relationship between genes and chromosomes was that the genes were "beads on a string" (Morgan et al. 1915).

By the 1960s, however, it was becoming clear that there was far more DNA in a cell than could be accountable by recourse to genes. In other words, there was a great deal of string linking relatively few beads. Further, there seemed to be a great deal of variation in genome size without apparent relationship to organismal complexity, producing a "C-value paradox," where the C-value is a measure of genome size (Mirsky & Ris 1951; Thomas 1971).

By the late 1960s, satellite DNA (with a slightly different composition than the bulk of genomic DNA, thus appearing as a "satellite" peak on a densitometric tracing) was recognized to be a significant portion of the genome. Satellite DNA consists of simple

DNA sequences tandemly repeated millions of times; it is transcriptionally inactive and localized in its chromosomal distribution. In addition, it appeared to be phylogenetically unstable, for closely related species differed markedly in the proportion of the genome taken by the same class of satellite DNA (Flamm et al. 1967; Britten & Kohne 1968).

But a simple dichotomy of localized "repetitive" DNA, distinct from "unique-sequence" DNA, was undermined by the discovery of a large class of repetitive DNA that was not localized, but rather was interspersed within the "unique-sequence" DNA. The largest class of these interspersed elements is known as *Alu* repeats, and they probably occupy as much of the genome as the informational, coding fraction (Schmid & Jelinek 1982).

It also became apparent that genes themselves were not the solitary isolated entities they had been imagined to be, but were structurally related to other DNA sequences (Ingram 1961). Most genes were found to be members of families, and most gene families exist as localized gene clusters, of which the hemoglobin genes are paradigmatic (see Fig. 4).

Apparently, the genome has a battery of evolutionary modes by which DNA segments of varying lengths can become tandemly duplicated (Ohno 1970). If they happen to contain functional units (i.e., genes), the units are duplicated as well. The duplicate gene can then accumulate degenerative mutations (with no ill effect to the organism, for it still has a functional copy), or acquire a new func-

tion through mutation, or be maintained as a second copy if this is to the organism's advantage. Clearly, all three processes have occurred throughout the evolution of the vertebrate globin genes.

Thus, the dichotomy established between "unique-sequence" and "repetitive" DNA emerged to be false. Virtually all DNA is to some extent repetitive. What varies are the extent and the pattern of the redundancy.

Principles of Molecular Anthropology
Since the genome consists of mostly noncoding DNA, it follows that most genetic change is not expressed as phenotypic change. It also follows that the primary agent directing molecular evolution is genetic drift, a constant stochastic spread of adaptively equivalent variants. Consequently, genetic and phenotypic evolution are now approached in conceptually different ways. A researcher focusing on organismal phenotypes endeavors to explain why two taxa are phenotypically different from each other, and does so by recourse to directional selection. Genotypically, by contrast, two taxa are expected to differ, by virtue of the constant pressure of mutation and drift, and what requires explanation are *similarities*—why two DNA sequences are not as different as they might be, explained by recourse to stabilizing selection. This underlay the initial interest in homeoboxes, regions of DNA strongly conserved between flies and humans, unlike virtually any aspect of the bodies of those organisms.

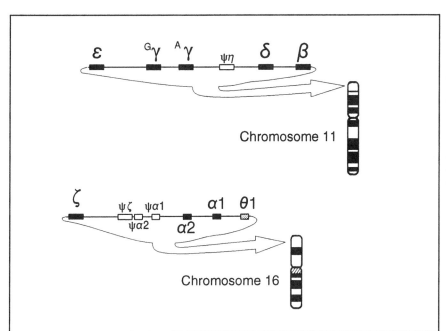

Fig. 4. The β-globin gene cluster, located on chromosome 11, contains an embryonic (ε) globin gene, two fetal (γ) genes, a non-functional "pseudogene" sequence (ψη), a minor adult gene (δ), and the major adult gene (β). On chromosome 16 lie the structurally related α-globin genes: embryonic (ζ), a pseudogene of the embryonic gene (ψζ), two pseudogenes of the adult genes (ψα2 and ψα1), the two adult genes (α2 and α1), and another gene of unknown function (θ1).

Another difficulty in reasoning from molecular to phenotypic evolutionary changes is the fact that they can occur largely independently of one another. The growing organism is both phenotypically plastic and developmentally canalized. As a consequence, except in rare pathological mutations (genetic diseases) it is very difficult to trace specific genetic variations to specific phenotypic variations. Recent conceptions of evolution have, consequently, tended to present changes in DNA or proteins as a basic "level" in an evolutionary hierarchy, in contrast principally to changes in organismal phenotypes (King & Wilson 1975; Gould 1980).

Finally, the most appropriate manner of extracting phylogeny from DNA sequences that has emerged is far from self-evident. DNA sequences are attractive by virtue of their amenability to quantitative treatment. But since there are only four neucleotides, a 25 percent similarity in DNA sequence is random—in contrast to the anatomical comparison, in which comparisons may be more qualitative but there is no obvious limit to how different two organisms may be. Studies of the primates also reveal high levels of parallel evolution (homoplasy) in DNA sequences, which complicates the reconstruction of phylogeny.

In addition to phylogenetic reconstructions, molecular data are now being used to study microevolution, population structure, and demography; paternity diagnosis in nonhuman primate populations with promiscuous matings; and forensics, where DNA can be extracted and amplified not only from crime scenes, but from historic and prehistoric burials as well.

Molecular evolution has become an exciting research area, particularly because technology has outpaced theory. Generating creative explanations for the abundant data being collected will most likely be the source of the major breakthroughs for this field in the next generation.

Jonathan Marks

See also African Apes; Hooton, E(arnest) A(lbert); Landsteiner, Karl; Mutation; Paleoprimatology; *Ramapithecus*; Systematics (1960s–1990s); Washburn, Sherwood L.

Bibliography
PRIMARY SOURCES
O.T. Avery et al.: Studies on the chemical nature of the substance inducing transformation of pneumococcal types: Induction of transformation by a desoxyribonucleic [*sic*] acid fraction isolated from pneumococcus type III. *Journal of Experimental Medicine* 79:137–158, 1944; G.W. Beadle & E.L. Tatum: Genetic control of biochemical reactions in Neurospora. *Proceedings of the National Academy of Sciences* (United States) 27:499–506, 1941; W.C. Boyd: Critique of methods of classifying mankind. *American Journal of Physical Anthropology* 27:333–364, 1940; W.C. Boyd: Genetics and the human race. *Science* 140:1057–1064, 1963.

R.J. Britten & D.E. Kohne: Repeated sequences in DNA. *Science* 161:529–540, 1968; R.L. Cann et al.: Mitochondrial DNA and human evolution. *Nature* 325:31–36, 1987; E. Chargaff: Chemical specificity of nucleic acids and mechanism of their enzymatic degradation. *Experientia* 6:201–209, 1950; A.F. Coca & O. Diebert: A study of the occurrence of the blood groups among the American Indians. *Journal of Immunology* 8:487–491, 1923; W.G. Flamm et al.: Some properties of single strands isolated from the DNA of the nuclear satellite of the mouse (*Mus musculus*). *Journal of Molecular Biology* 40:423–443, 1967.

M. Goodman: Immunochemistry of the primates and primate evolution. *Annals of the New York Academy of Sciences* 102:219–234, 1962; S.J. Gould: Is a new and general theory of evolution emerging? *Paleobiology* 6:119–130, 1980; A. Hershey & M. Chase: Independent functions of viral proteins and nucleic acid in growth of bacteriophage. *Journal of General Physiology* 36:39–56, 1952; L. Hirschfeld & H. Hirschfeld: Serological differences between the blood of different races. *Lancet* (October 18):675–679, 1919; E.A. Hooton: *Up from the ape*. New York: Macmillan, 1931; V. Ingram: Gene evolution and the hemoglobins. *Nature* 189:704–708, 1961; M. Kimura: Evolutionary rate at the molecular level. *Nature* 217:624–626, 1968; M.C. King & A.C. Wilson: Evolution at two levels in humans and chimpanzees. *Science* 188:107–116, 1975.

E. Margoliash: Primary structure and evolution of cytochrome c. *Proceedings of the National Academy of Sciences* (United States) 50:672–679, 1963; J. Marks et al.: DNA hybridization as a guide to phylogeny: Relations of the Hominoidea. *Journal of Human Evolution* 17:769–786, 1988; A.E. Mirsky & H. Ris: The deoxyribonucleic acid content of animal cells and its evolutionary significance. *Journal of Genetics and Physiology* 34:451–462, 1951; T.H. Morgan, A.H. Sturtevant, H.J. Muller, & C.B. Bridges: *The mechanism of Mendelian heredity.* New York: Holt, 1915; G.H.F. Nuttall: *Blood immunity and blood relationship.* Cambridge: Cambridge University Press, 1904; S. Ohno: *Evolution by gene duplication.* Berlin: Springer, 1970; D. Pilbeam: Hominoid evolution and hominoid origins. *American Anthropologist* 88:295–312, 1986.

J. Rogers: The phylogenetic relationships among *Homo, Pan,* and *Gorilla:* A population genetics perspective. *Journal of Human Evolution* 25:201–215, 1993; V.M. Sarich: The origin of the hominids: An immunological approach. In: S.L. Washburn & P.C. Jay (eds) *Perspectives on human evolution.* Vol. 1. New York: Holt, Rinehart & Winston, 1968, pp. 94–121; V.M. Sarich: Primate systematics with special reference to Old World monkeys. In: J.R. Napier & P.H. Napier (eds) *Old World monkeys: Evolution, systematics, and behavior.* New York: Academic Press, 1970, pp. 175–199; V.M. Sarich & A.C. Wilson: Rates of albumin evolution in primates. *Proceedings of the National Academy of Sciences* (United States) 58:143–148, 1967a; V.M. Sarich & A.C. Wilson: Immunological time scale for hominid evolution. *Science* 158:1200–1203, 1967b.

C.W. Schmid & W.R. Jelinek: The Alu family of dispersed repetitive sequences. *Science* 216:1065–1070, 1982; C.G. Sibley & J.E. Ahlquist: The phylogeny of the hominoid primates, as indicated by DNA-DNA hybridization. *Journal of Molecular Evolution* 20:2–15, 1984; C.G. Sibley et al.: DNA hybridization evidence of hominoid phylogeny: A reanalysis of the data. *Journal of Molecular Evolution* 30:202–236, 1990; C.G. Simpson: The meaning of taxonomic statements. In: S.L. Washburn (ed) *Classification and human evolution.* Chicago: Aldine, 1963, pp. 1–31; L. Snyder: Human blood groups: Their inheritance and racial significance. *American Journal of Physical Anthropology* 9:233–263, 1926; C.A. Thomas: The genetic organization of chromosomes. *Annual Review of Genetics* 5:237–256, 1971.

S.L. Washburn: Tools and human evolution. *Scientific American* 203(3):63–75, 1960; S.L. Washburn: Behavior and human evolution. In: S.L. Washburn (ed) *Classification and human evolution.* Chicago: Aldine, 1963, pp. 190–203; J.D. Watson & F.H.C.

Crick: A structure for desoxyribonucleic [*sic*] acids. *Nature* 171:737–738, 1953; E. Zuckerkandl: Perspectives in molecular anthropology. In: S.L. Washburn (ed) *Classification and human evolution.* Chicago: Aldine, 1963, pp. 243–272; E. Zuckerkandl & L. Pauling: Molecular disease, evolution, and genic heterogeneity. In: M. Kasha & B. Pullman (eds) *Horizons in biochemistry.* New York: Academic Press, 1962, pp. 189–225; E. Zuckerkandl & L. Pauling: Evolutionary divergence and convergence in proteins. In: V. Bryson & H.J. Vogel (eds) *Evolving genes and proteins.* New York: Academic Press, 1965, pp. 97–166.

SECONDARY SOURCES

B. Glass: A century of biochemical genetics. *Proceedings of the American Philosophical Society* 109:227–236, 1965; M. Goodman & J.E. Cronin: Molecular anthropology: Its development and current directions. In: F. Spencer (ed) *A history of American physical anthropology, 1930–1980.* New York: Academic Press, 1982, pp. 105–146; R.D. Hotchkiss: The identification of nucleic acids as genetic determinants. *Annals of the New York Academy of Sciences* 325:320–342, 1979; H.F. Judson: *The eighth day of creation.* New York: Simon & Schuster, 1979; M. McCarty: *The transforming principle.* New York: Norton, 1985; V.M. Sarich: Retrospective on hominoid macromolecular systematics. In: R.L. Ciochon & R.S. Corruccini (eds) *New interpretations of ape and human ancestry.* New York: Plenum Press, 1983, pp. 137–150; J.D. Watson: *The double helix.* New York: Atheneum, 1968.

Mollison, Theodor (1874–1952)

Born in Stuttgart, Germany, Mollison studied medicine at the University of Freiburg, where he was a student of the geneticist August Weismann (1834–1914) and the anatomist Robert Wiedersheim (1848–1923). On graduating in 1898, he entered private practice in Frankfurt. From 1902 to 1904, he continued his education in zoology and comparative anatomy at Würzburg University. In 1904, he undertook an independent expedition to East Africa. On his return in 1905, he became Rudolf Martin's (1864–1925) assistant at the Anthropologischen Institut in Zürich. Five years later, he was appointed privatdocent in anthropology at the University of Zürich. The topic of his teaching examination (Mollison 1910) was "Die

Körperproportionen der Primaten" (The Body Proportions of the Primates). This was the first time that exact and, even more important, comparative metric data had been assembled on different primate species. A year later, he was appointed supervisor of the Anthropological Department in the Dresden Museum, and in 1912, he was named curator of the anatomical collections at Heidelberg University. In 1918, he accepted the position formerly occupied by Hermann Klaatsch (1863–1916) at Breslau University (now Wrocław, Poland). Like Klaatsch, Mollison also had an interest paleoanthropology, and during his career he published a number of studies and general review articles on fossil hominids (e.g., Mollison 1924, 1926, 1936b).

Following Rudolf Martin's death in 1925, Mollison was invited to become curator of the State Anthropological Collection in Munich. Subsequently, Mollison served not only as editor of the *Anthropologischer Anzeiger* (1927–1944) but also as a genetic consultant for the forensische anthropologische Vaterschaftsdiagnostik and as chairman of the Munich Society for Racial Hygiene (Münchener Gesellschaft für Rassenhygiene). As this later position indicates, Mollison was a strong supporter of the doctrines of Rassenkunde and Rassenhygiene. Indeed, he had long harbored the ambition of identifying specific protein structures that would enable the definitive separation of the human races (cf. Mollison 1936a).

Although he officially retired in 1939, he was allowed to retain his professorship. After the destruction of the Anthropological Institute of Munich University by Allied bombing in 1944, he moved it to his home until it was reopened in 1948. In 1944, he was awarded the Goethe Medal for Arts and Sciences for his service to anthropology, and he was elected a member of the German Academy of Natural Sciences (Leopoldinisch-Carolinischen Deutschen Akademie der Naturforscher).

Mollison died in Munich on 3 March 1952.

Ursula Zängl-Kumpf

See also Germany; Klaatsch, Hermann; Martin, Rudolf; Poland; Rassenhygiene and Rassenkunde

Bibliography
SELECTED WORKS

Beiträg zur Kraniologie und Osteologie der Maorie. *Zeitschrift für Morphologie und Anthropologie* 11:529–595, 1908; Die Körperproportionen der Primaten. *Morphologisches Jahrbuch* 42:79–304, 1910; Zur Beurteilung des Gehirnreichtums der Primaten nach dem Skelett. *Archiv für Anthropologie* 13:196–388, 1915; Die Abstammung des Menschen. *Naturwissenschaften* 9:128–140, 1921; Technik und Methoden der physischen Anthropologie. In: G. Schwalbe & E. Fischer (eds) *Anthropologie: Kultur der Gegenwart*. Berlin: Teubner, 1923, pp. 12–36.

Neuere Funde und Untersuchungen fossiler Menschenaffen und Menschen. *Ergebnisse der Anatomie und entwicklungsgeschichte* (Munich) 25:696–771, 1924; Fossile Menschenaffen und Menschen. In: W. Salomon: *Grundzüge der Geologie*. Vol. 2. Stuttgart: Schweizerbart, 1926, pp. 517–560; Serologische Verwandtschaftsforschung am Menschen und an anderen Primaten. *Tagungsbericht der Deutschen Anthropologischen Gesellschaft* 45–47:88–91, 1926; Phylogenie des Menschen. In: E. Baur & M. Hartmann (eds): *Handbuch der Vererbungswissenschaften*. Berlin: Borntraeger, 1933.

Rassenkunde und Rassenhygiene. In: E. Rüdin (ed) *Erblehre und Rassenhygiene im völkischen Staat*. München: Lehmann, 1934, pp. 34–48; Die serologischen Beweise für eine chemische Epigenese in der Stammesgeschichte des Menschen. *Archiv für Rassenbiologie* 30: 457–468, 1936a; Zeichen gewaltsamer Verletzungen an den Ofnet-Schädeln. *Anthropologischer Anzeiger* 13:79–88, 1936b; Die Verletzungen am Schädel und den Gliedmaßenknochen des Rhodesiafundes. *Anthropologischer Anzeiger* 14:229–234, 1937; Eine Schausammlung für Anthropologie in München. *Anthropologischer Anzeiger* 15:78–82, 1938.

SECONDARY SOURCES

E. Breitinger: In Memoriam Theodor Mollison, 1874–1952. *Anthropologischer Anzeiger* 20:95–97, 1958; W. Gieseler: Lebensbild Theodor Mollison. *Archiv für Rassenbiologie* 33:187–189, 1939; W. Gieseler: Die Anthropologie in München, 1918–1948. *Anthropologischer Anzeiger* 27:258–261, 1965; P. Kramp: In Memoriam Theodor Mollison, 1874–1952. *Zeitschrift für Morphologie und Anthropologie* 45:416–432, 1953.

Monaco and Geneva Agreements

During the second half of the nineteenth century anthropometric methods proliferated, but the utility of the accumulating data was hampered by a lack of any standardization. Although the Frankfort Agreement adopted by the Deutsche Anthropologische Gesellschaft (cf. Garson 1885) in 1882 was a step in the right direction, the recommended methods and nomenclature embodied therein were not uniformally accepted outside of Germany. Indicative of the growing need for an international agreement was the appeal made by the French anthropologist René Collignon (1856–1932) in 1892 to the Twelfth Congrès International d'Anthropologie et d'Archéologie Préhistoriques (CIAAP) held in Moscow. A result of Collignon's initiative was the appointment of two commissions: the Anthropometric Commission presided over by the Russian anthropologist Anatoly Petrovich Bogdanov (1834–1896), and the Craniometric Commission presided over by the German pathologist-anthropologist Rudolf Virchow (1821–1902). But contrary to expectations, these two commissions failed to reach any appreciable results. However, in 1906 (16–21 April), when the Thirteenth CIAAP met in Monaco, a new commission was appointed, consisting of the German anatomist Wilhelm Waldeyer (1836–1921), president; the Italian anthropologist Giuseppe Sergi (1841–1936), vice president; and the French anthropologist Georges Papillault (1863–1934), secretary. Other members of the commission included: Vincenzo Giuffrida-Ruggeri, Théodore Hamy, Georges Hervé, Felix von Luschan, Eugène Pittard, Samuel Pozzi, and René Verneau. Following Waldeyer's suggestion, the commission limited its activities to recommending standards for the measurements of the skull (craniometric) and the head of living subjects (cephalometric). At the closing session of the Monaco congress, the commission presented its report and recommendations on "craniometric and cephalometric measurements," which was unanimously accepted (a copy of which was printed in L'Anthropologie 17:559–572, 1906; for an English translation see Hrdlička 1920:10–24). At the Fourteenth CIAAP held at Geneva in 1912, the work of the Monaco commission was extended to somatic measurements of the living subject. Presiding over these deliberations were the French anthropologist Léonce-Pierre Manouvrier (1850–1927), Giuseppe Sergi, and the British anatomist Wynfrid Laurence Henry Duckworth (1870–1956). For a complete list of members of this commission, see Hrdlička 1920:26. This commission's report (cf. Duckworth 1914, reprinted in Hrdlička 1920:25–31) was unanimously adopted by the congress at its concluding meeting on 14 September 1912.

Frank Spencer

See also Anthropometry; Bogdanov, Anatoly Petrovich; Collignon, René; Duckworth, Wynfrid Laurence Henry; Frankfort Agreement; Manouvrier, Léonce-Pierre; Sergi, Giuseppe; Virchow, Rudolf

Bibliography
R. Collignon: Projet d'entente internationale au sujet des recherches anthropométriques dans les conseils de revision. *Bulletins de la Société d'Anthropologie de Paris* 13:186–188, 1892; W.L.H. Duckworth: The international agreement for the unification of anthropometric measurements to be made on the living subject. *Comptes rendus Congrès internationale d'Anthropologie et d'Archéologie préhistorique* (Geneva, Switzerland, 1912). Vol. 2. Geneva: Kündig, 1914, pp. 484–490; J.G. Garson: The Frankfort craniometric agreement, with critical remarks thereon. *Journal of the Anthropological Institute of Great Britain and Ireland* 14:64–83, 1885; A. Hrdlička: *Anthropometry*. Philadephia: Wistar Institute, 1920.

Monboddo, Lord (James Burnett) (1714–1799)

Born in Kincardine, Scotland, Monboddo studied law at the Universities of Aberdeen and Edinburgh. In 1767, he was appointed a law lord, or judge, on the Scottish Court of Session. Partly inspired by the Scottish classical scholar Thomas Blackwell's (1701–1757) studies of Homeric myth and the Augustan court, he held classical languages and the valor of the heroic peoples who spoke them in the highest esteem, complaining of the decline of modern man and the prosaic decadence of modern languages in terms similar to Georges-Louis Leclerc Buffon's (1707–1788) conception of the degeneration of flora and fauna in the New World. No prominent thinker of the Scottish Enlightenment was so hostile to the empiricist tendencies of contemporary British philosophy, and Monboddo's attempt to rescue the glorious achievements of ancient science, ethics, and rhetoric by way of a predominantly Aristotelian understanding of the human faculties forms the central thread of his six-volume *Antient Metaphysics*, dating from 1779 to 1799. It also figures prominently in his second and overlapping major work of comparable length, begun even earlier, *Of the Origin and Progress of Language*, completed between 1773 and 1792.

This text embraces an account not only of the wonders of Latin and especially Greek grammars, vocabularies, rhetorical styles, and inflections, but also of the nomenclature of numerous modern and exotic languages, incuding Huron, Carib, Eskimo, and Tahitian, about which Monboddo learned secondhand, through dictionaries and travelers' reports. In tracing the natural history of languages as an expression of both the genealogy of diverse cultures and the universal capacities of the human mind, he believed that our refinement of linguistic skills was a measure of our intellectual accomplishment in general, and along such lines he contributed to the nascent science of etymology and historical linguistics inaugurated at the end of the eighteenth century by Sir William Jones (1746–1789), as well as to the Cartesian and Port-Royal tradition of speculative grammar that this new science had apparently overturned. But if languages developed in and passed through natural histories, their articulation in speech was not of itself natural to human beings, Monboddo contended. This proposition from the Swiss political thinker Jean-Jacques Rousseau's (1712–1778) *Discours sur l'inégalité* (1755) greatly impressed him, and he agreed that language had to be mastered and cultivated through industry and endeavor; it could never have been a gift bestowed upon humanity by nature. For languages to have been invented, it was first necessary that society should be established, as Rousseau had shown, and in pursuing the implications of that claim Monboddo admitted that his own investigations into human origins owed more to Rousseau than to any other thinker. Rousseau had also asserted that language was as indispensable to society as society was to language, leaving in doubt which came first. Monboddo deemed this supposition false, claiming that society was manifestly prior to language, on the grounds that other animal species clearly showed social traits without mastery of language. But in general he followed Rousseau closely and concluded likewise that if language is not natural to human beings, creatures that resemble them but have no command of language are still self-evidently human. The nature of humankind must not be defined in terms of our use of words, since persons whose vocal organs have been damaged or who elect to remain silent, as well as mute wild men in the forest, do not pass out of our species merely on account of their being speechless.

Believing that creatures that partake of our physical characteristics, including our internal organs, remain human even if those organs are not exercised, Monboddo shared Rousseau's belief that orangutans were members of our species. This conclusion stemmed, of course, from the hearsay evidence supplied by other commentators, since neither he nor Rousseau ever set eyes on an orangutan. But Monboddo's credulity about this anthropoid ape's reported behavior drew him, unlike Rousseau, to accept that it lived in society, engaged in hunting and other collective activities, was moved by a sense of justice and modesty, and could express itself in music as it was known to play the harp! Because language does not spring spontaneously from our lips as does sight from our eyes and hearing from our ears, it is a wonder that some of our forebears invented language at all, he argued; but in time, and with proper tuition, he supposed that orangutans might also learn to speak.

This suggestion anticipates the experiments of the Kelloggs in the 1930s and the Hayeses in the 1950s, before the attempt to converse with apes took less articulate forms. But Monboddo's principal contribution to physical anthropology stems from his critique of the supposition of the British anatomist Edward Tyson (1650–1708) and Buffon that human command of language marks an unbridgeable gulf between our species and the rest of animal creation. Although initially ignorant of Tyson's monograph on the *Orang-Outang* (1699) and inattentive to Buffon's views on the animal's subhumanity, Monboddo revised the first volume of his *Origin and Progress of Language* in the light of information supplied to him by friends, and in his work's second edition of 1774 he confronted the Cartesian perspective of Tyson and Buffon by showing that analogical structures in nature characteristically point to homological functions. What purpose were an orangutan's vocal organs intended to serve, he wondered, if not the articulation of speech? Nature must not be presumed so uneconomical as to engage in redundant design.

Many of Monboddo's readers, especially in England and Scotland, found his ideas too strange to merit serious attention. His claim that human beings are often born with vestigial tails and that a teacher from Inverness had successfully concealed his half-foot-long stump all his life prompted one critic to charge that he was just "a Judge *à posteriori*." But his remarks on the humanity of the orangutan did arouse the interest of some commentators, especially on the Continent. The German philosopher Johann G. von Herder (1744–1803) refers to them in his preface to the 1784–1785 German translation of the *Origin and Progress of Language,* and scientific interpreters, including the Dutch anatomist Petrus Camper (1722–1789), the German anatomist Johann Friedrich Blumenbach (1752–1840), and the Scottish physician John Hunter (ca. 1752–1809), addressed them from as early as 1775. Most critics held that Monboddo was mistaken to suppose that orangutans were human, because their anatomical and organic differences from us were sufficient to explain why such animals could not articulate sophisticated sounds. These critics did not resuscitate the perspective of Tyson and Buffon that Monboddo sought to discredit, but rather turned their attention away from speculation about the linguistic boundary between man and ape. Following Blumenbach, physical anthropologists began instead to address the manifest differences between the human races.

Monboddo died in Edinburgh on 26 May 1799.

Robert Wokler

See also African Apes; Aryanism; Asian Apes; Blumenbach, Johann Friedrich; Buffon (Comte) Georges-Louis Leclerc; Camper, Petrus; Rousseau, Jean-Jacques; Tyson, Edward

Bibliography
SELECTED WORKS
Of the origin and progress of language. 6 vols. Edinburgh: Balfour, 1773–1792; *Antient metaphysics; or, The science of universals.* 6 vols. Edinburgh: Balfour, 1779–1799.

ARCHIVAL SOURCES
1. Lord Monboddo Papers (Monboddo Mss. 5738): Department of Manuscripts, National Library of Scotland, George IV Bridge, Edinburgh EH1 1EW, Scotland; 2. Miscellaneous Papers (Dc.6.III; La.II.509; La.III.379/599–605): Department of Manuscripts, Library, University of Edinburgh, George Square, Edinburgh EH8 9LJ, Scotland.

PRIMARY AND SECONDARY SOURCES
E.L. Cloyd: *James Burnett: Lord Monboddo.* Oxford: Clarendon Press, 1972; A.O. Lovejoy: Monboddo and Rousseau. *Modern Philology* 30:275–296, 1932–1933; J.J. Rousseau: *Discours sur l'origine et les fondements de l'inégalité parmi les hommes.* Amsterdam: Rey, 1755; O. Sherwin: A man with a tail: Lord Monboddo. *Journal of the History of Medicine* 23:435–467, 1958; E. Tyson: *Orang-Outang, sive Homo Sylvestris: or, The anatomy of a pygmie compared with that of a monkey, an ape, and a man.* London: Bennet, 1699; R. Wokler: Apes and races in the Scottish Enlightenment: Monboddo and Kames on the nature of man. In: P. Jones (ed) *Philosophy and science in the Scottish Enlightenment.* Edinburgh: John Donald, 1988, pp. 145–168.

Montagu, Ashley (1905–)

Born in London, England, Montagu attended University College (UC), London from 1922 to 1925. His mentor of record there was Grafton Elliot Smith (1871–1937). More influential in his training, however, was Arthur Keith (1866–1955) who was a regular presence in the laboratories for the students at UC even though he had no professorial appointment there. Although Montagu, who is also known as M.F. Ashley-Montagu, went on to become famous for an assessment of the "race" question that was fundamentally at odds with the categorical and hierarchical stance taken by Keith, he has retained a memory of the kindness and support that Keith showed him during his student days in London.

In 1930, Montagu moved to New York and became a graduate student in anthropology under Franz Boas (1858–1942) at Columbia University. As one of the very few Boas students who did not do primary field research, Montagu was awarded his Ph.D. in 1937 for a dissertation on social and physiological maturation in Australian Aborigines (cf. Montagu 1938). Meanwhile, he had been supporting himself and his family by teaching anatomy at the New York University School of Medicine from 1931 to 1938. From 1938 to 1949, he taught anatomy at Hahnemann Medical College in Philadelphia, and he became an American citizen in 1940.

Between 1949 and 1955, he was professor and chairman of the Department of Anthropology at Rutgers University in New Brunswick, New Jersey. Rutgers, however, had not agreed to provide financial support for its anthropology program, and Montagu subsequently left to embark upon a career as a free-lance anthropologist, and he has sustained himself ever since in a more than adequate fashion by his own writings and lecturing. He has had visiting appointments at Harvard and Princeton Universities and the Universities of Delaware and California, but he has never enjoyed the luxury of a permanent faculty position to which he could return.

Early in his career, when he was still teaching anatomy, his technical output was prodigious. He has sustained that same level of productivity without a break, but a change of focus was signaled by his first major book designed to appeal to a wider reading public than only anatomists and anthropologists. This was *Man's Most Dangerous Myth: The Fallacy of Race,* which appeared in 1942 at the peak of the time when that indefensible construct was being used as an excuse to justify the extermination of the millions of victims of Adolf Hitler's Third Reich in Europe. That work has been reprinted frequently in subsequent years and remains arguably the most important contribution from his pen. It was one of the first expositions of the view that "race" has no validity as a biological entity and has served solely as a device for the promotion of human misery.

A decade later, *The Natural Superiority of Women* (1953) served as a further demonstration that Montagu possessed a major talent for presenting biosocial matters in a fashion that was both comprehensible and relevant to the perceptions of the reading public. In all, he has been the author and editor of more than sixty books. His articles number in the many hundreds. The scope of his topics has run from the technical details of human genetics and the anatomical evidence for human evolution, through the dimensions of human physiology and learning capabilities, human sexuality, prenatal and infant development, to a culmination in the consideration of human dignity. Along the way, he has also dealt at length with the cultural dimensions essential for human survival and with aspects of evolution and the history of science.

Throughout that awesome range, there is no faint trace of the superficiality that one might expect from a scholar attempting to exceed the limits of his capabilities. Not only is the supporting research impeccably solid, but his themes are presented in a seamless prose that is seductively easy to read. Those expository gifts are also evident in his performances on the lecture platform, which are delivered in polished fashion without support from written text or notes.

With all of his digressions into peripheral, if actually related, topics, Montagu has never lost the thread of a central concern that an interrelated treatment of both biology and behavior is essential to an understanding of the human condition.

C. Loring Brace

See also Boas, Franz; Keith, (Sir) Arthur; Smith, (Sir) Grafton Eliot; Tyson, Edward; UNESCO Statement on Race

Bibliography
SELECTED WORKS
Coming into being among the Australian Aborigines: A study of the procreative beliefs of the native tribes of Australia. New York: Dutton, 1938; *Man's most dangerous myth: The fallacy of race.* New York: Columbia University Press, 1942; *Edward Tyson, M.D., F.R.S., 1650–1708, and the rise of human and comparative anatomy in England.* Philadelphia: American Philosophical Society, 1943; *An introduction to physical anthropology.* Springfield, Illinois: Thomas, 1945; *Statement on race: An extended discussion in plain language of the UNESCO statement by experts on race problems.* New York: Schuman, 1952.

The natural superiority of women. New York: Macmillan, 1953; *The direction of human development: Biological and social bases.* New York: Harper, 1955; (ed) *Genetic mechanisms in human disease: Chromosomal aberrations.* Springfield, Illinois: Thomas, 1961; *The nature of human aggression.* London: Oxford University Press, 1975a; *Race and IQ.* London: Oxford University Press, 1975b; *The human connection.* New York: McGraw-Hill, 1979; (with C.L. Brace) *Man's evolution.* New York: Macmillan, 1965 (2d ed.: 1977, published as *Human evolution: An introduction to biological anthropology*); (with M. Levitan) *Textbook of human genetics.* 2d ed. London: Oxford University Press, 1977.

ARCHIVAL SOURCES
1. Arrangements have been made to donate Montagu's papers and library to the special collections of the University of California, Los Angeles, California 90024; 2. Correspondence (Montagu-Carmichael) in L. Carmichael (1898–1973) Papers: Library, American Philosophical Society, 104 South Fifth Street, Philadelphia, Pennsylvania 19106-3387.

SECONDARY SOURCES

L. Metzger & J.W. Ross: Montagu, Ashley, 1905– . In: E. Evroy (ed) *Contemporary authors: A biobibliographical guide to current writers*. New Revision Series. Vol. 5. Detroit, Michigan: Gale, 1980, pp. 378–383.

Montané, Luis (1849–1936)

Born in Havana, Cuba, Montané received his medical training in Barcelona and Paris, where he studied under Armand de Quatrefages (1810–1892), Théodore Hamy (1842–1908), and more particularly Paul Broca (1824–1880). His prize-winning doctoral research was conducted under Broca's supervision in his Laboratoire d'Anthropologie de l'École Pratique des Hautes Études. His M.D. thesis, *Étude anatomique du crâne chez microcephales* (1874), resulted in a classification system that was widely attributed to Broca, rather than Montané.

In many respects, Montané was to physical anthropology in Cuba what Earnest A. Hooton (1887–1954) was to the discipline in the United States. Upon his return to Havana in 1874, he began a professional career that quickly led to the development of physical anthropology as a distinct and growing academic enterprise in Cuba. In addition to playing a pivotal role in the founding of the Anthropology Society of Cuba in 1877, Montané was the recipient, in 1899, of the first professorship in anthropology and exercise science at the University of Havana (UH). During his tenure at UH, he established a modest laboratory patterned after Broca's in Paris. From this institutional base, Montané's teaching and research activities influenced two generations of Cuban students and professionals, prior to his retirement from the UH shortly after the end of World War I.

In 1903, Montané was responsible for the founding of an anthropology museum at the UH, which today carries his name (Museo Antropológico Montané). Furthermore, in his honor, the museum periodically hosts an international physical anthropology conference—El Simposio de Antropología Física "Luis Montané." These conferences attract professionals from throughout Latin America, the Caribbean, North America, and Europe.

During his career, Montané was an active participant in international anthropology circles, attending meetings and delivering papers in Europe and throughout the Americas. He served as an official delegate from Cuba to scientific congresses in Monaco and Turin in 1906, and as a corresponding member of several European and American scientific societies. While he published on such diverse subjects as Peruvian natives (among the Jívaro) and captive chimpanzees living in Cuba, much of his research focused on the island's prehistoric Aboriginal populations, with particular reference to the subject of cranial deformation. A good example of such work is his study of a Carib skull, published in 1885. Montané's skeletal-biology research was in keeping with the methods and theory of his time.

In 1899, Montané was a member of a team of Cuban scientists who studied the remains of General Antonio Maceo (1848–1896), who was second in command of the revolutionary forces during much of Cuba's war of independence (1868–1878). Perhaps the best-known and most interesting feature of his work was his discovery of human fossil remains near Sancti Spiritus, in south-central Cuba. This find was displayed at international scientific conventions in Monaco in 1906 and Buenos Aires in 1911. For a time, it was assigned to the taxon *Homo cubensis*, although Montané was not convinced that the remains warranted such a formal status. Ultimately, after considerable international debate and criticism, particularly from the Czech-American physical anthropologist Aleš Hrdlička (1869–1943), the remains were recognized as being of recent prehistoric vintage (i.e., no more than several thousand years old). Montané also devoted considerable energy to the study of Aboriginal biological characteristics manifest in the contemporary Cuban population.

After more than forty-five years of professional activity in Cuba, in the early 1920s Montané returned to Paris, where he spent his remaining years. This departure from Cuba, however, did not signal the end of his professional activities in anthropology. In 1922, he served a term as president of the Société d'Anthropologie de Paris, which his mentor, Broca, had founded in 1859. In recognition of his scientific achievements, the French government named him an Officier de la Légion d'Honneur and a magistrate of public instruction.

Curtis W. Wienker

See also African Apes; Broca, Paul (Pierre); Cuba; Hamy, Jules Ernest Théodore; Hooton, E(arnest) A(lbert); Hrdlička, Aleš; Quatrefages (de Breau), Jean Louis Armand de

Bibliography
SELECTED WORKS

Un Carib Cuban: Estudio craneologico. *Revista Cubana* 2, 1885; L'homme de Sancti Spiritus (Ile de Cuba). In: *Extrait du Comte Rendu au XIII Congrès International d'Anthropologie et d' Archéologie préhistoriques* (Monaco, 1906). Imprimerie de Monaco, 1907–1908; *El Congreso Científico Internacional de Buenos Aires.* Havana: Imprimerie de la Habana, 1911; A Cuban chimpanzee. (Condensed translation of "Notes sobre chimpancé nacido en Cuba," published in the *Memorias Sociedad de historia natural* (Havana) 1:259–269, 1915). *Journal of Animal Behavior* 6:330–333, 1916; L'homme fossile cubain. In: *Proceedings of the Pan American Scientific Congress, 1915–1916.* Vol. 1. Washington, D.C.: Government Printing Office, 1917, pp. 350–355. *Histoire d'une famille de chimpanzés, etude physiologique.* Paris, 1928.

SECONDARY SOURCES

R.A. Alum Jr.: The archaeology and physical anthropology of Cuba, 1972. Unpublished manuscript in possession of author; A.G. Llansó: *Cien años de antropología física en Cuba, 1868–1968.* Translation by J. Riopedrel. Havana: Cuban Academy of Sciences, 1968; A. Mestre: *Montané en nuestra antropología.* Havana: Cuban Academy of Sciences, 1939.

Monte Circeo

The Monte Circeo promontory rises on the Thyrrenian Sea near San Felice Circeo, Latina. On 25 February 1939, A. Guattari, a hotel owner in San Felice Circeo, discovered, during excavations near his hotel, a cave whose entrance appeared to have been closed by a landslide. Inside the cave on the floor of the chamber, he found a virtually complete human cranium and many fossilized bones of Pleistocene fauna. One of his subordinates, Maddalena Palombi, also found a human mandible thought to belong to the cranium. Both fossil remains were retrieved by Alberto Carlo Blanc (1905–1960) (cf. Sergi 1974).

After World War II, Antonio Ascenzi and Giovanni Lacchei, during an excursion to the Guattari Cave, recovered on 30 August 1950 a second mandible with a Mousterian association, from another deposit near the entrance. Another fragmentary mandible and some teeth were found by Blanc and Luigi Cardini (1898–1971) in 1953 and 1954 in the nearby Fossellone Cave. Later excavations in another cave nearby, Grotta Breuil, brought to light a partial parietal and two teeth, discovered between 1986 and 1989.

All of these remains are attributed to Neandertals and have been cataloged as Guattari 1–3, Fossellone 1, and Breuil 1–3, respectively. The recently determined absolute date of approximately 50.0 ky BP for the Guattari 1 Neandertal male cranium has confirmed Blanc's original attribution to Würm II (Piperno & Scichilone 1991).

> *Brunetto Chiarelli*
> *Giuseppe D'Amore*

See also Blanc, Alberto Carlo; Italy; Neandertals; Sergi, Sergio

Bibliography

M. Piperno & G. Scichilone: *The Circeo 1 Neandertal skull: Studies and documentation.* Ministero per i Beni Culturali ed Ambientali. Museo Nazionale Preistorico Etnografico "Luigi Pigorini." Rome: Istituto Poligrafico e Zecca dello Stato, Libreria dello Stato, 1991; S. Sergi: *Il cranio neandertaliano del Monte Circeo (Circeo 1): A cura di A. Ascenzi.* Rome: Accademia Nazionale dei Lincei, 1974.

Moreno, Francisco José Pascacio (1852–1919)

Born in Buenos Aires, Argentina, Moreno was, from early childhood, intensely interested in natural history. Although essentially a self-made scientist, he subsequently received support for his scientific labors from José M. Gutierrez (1809–1878) of the Universidad de Buenos Aires and Hermann Burmeister (1807–1892) of the the Museo Público de Buenos Aires.

In 1873, Moreno began his explorations in Patagonia. During this initial excursion, he collected Aboriginal crania and archeological artifacts that were subsequently studied by Paul Broca (1824–1880) in Paris. Following this, between 1874 and 1880, he traveled extensively in Patagonia, as well as to the province of Entre Rios, to conduct a comparative study of the Tertiary fauna of Patagonia and Paraná.

In 1884, he was appointed director of the newly created Museo de La Plata. During his tenure, he founded two important scientific periodicals published by the museum: the *Revista del Museo de La Plata* (1890) and the *Anales del Museo de La Plata* (1896).

During his later years, he held a number of national offices, including vice president of the National Council of Education. He died in 1919 and was buried on Centinela Island in the province of Rio Negro.

Elvira Inés Baffi
Maria F. Torres

See also Argentina; Broca, Paul (Pierre); Burmeister, Karl Hermann Konrad

Bibliography
SELECTED WORKS
Description des cimitières paraderos préhistoriques de Patagonie. Revue d'Anthropologie 3, 1874a; Noticias sobre antigüedades de los Indios, del tiempo anterior á la conquista descubiertas en la provincia de Buenos Aires. Boletín de la Academia Nacional de Ciencias de Cordova 1:130–149, 1874b; El estudio del hombre sud-americano. Buenos Aires: La Nación, 1878; Exploration in Patagonia. London: Clowes, 1879a; Viaje a la Patagonia austral, emprendido bajo los auspicios del gobierno nacional, 1876–1877. Buenos Aires: La Nación, 1879b; El orígen del hombre sud-americano, razas y civilizaciones de este Continente. Buenos Aires: Coni, 1882; El Museo de la Plata. La Plata: Publicaciones del Museo de La Plata, 1890; Esploración arqueológica de la provincia de Catamarca: Primeros datos sobre su importancia y resultados. Revista del Museo de La Plata 1:199–220, 1890–1891; Catálogo de los pájaros fósiles de la República Argentina conservados en el Museo de La Plata. La Plata: Publicaciones del Museo de La Plata, 1891.

SECONDARY SOURCES
E.V. Moreno: Reminiscences de Francisco P. Moreno. Buenos Aires: Plantie, 1942.

Morselli, Enrico (1852–1929)

Born in Modena, Italy, Morselli obtained his medical degree in 1874 in his native city. Following a short stint in Florence, he was appointed director of psychiatric hospitals in Macerata in 1877 and Turin in 1880. He began his academic career in Turin as a professor of psychiatry at Turin University. From 1889 onward, he was professor of psychiatry and neurology at the University of Genova. In addition to being a founding member in 1893, of the Società Romana di Antropologia, he was also coeditor with Giuseppe Sergi (1841–1936) of the journal Rivista di filosofia scientifica from 1881 to 1891 and cofounder with R. Assagioli of the journal Psiche in 1911.

Morselli's scientific interests ranged across several fields of study, including philosophy, psychiatry, anthropology, legal medicine, and clinical neuropsychiatry. His main contributions to anthropology can be found in his Critica e riforma del metodo in antropologia (1880) and in the two-volume work Antropologia generale (1888–1911). This latter work was the result of an elaboration of his academic lectures in anthropology, in which he stressed the doctrine of evolution as propounded by Charles Darwin (1809–1882) and Ernst Haeckel (1834–1919). His breadth of vision and talent for synthesis have led him to be compared to a humanist of the Renaissance.

Morselli died in Genova on 18 February 1929.

Brunetto Chiarelli
Giuseppe D'Amore

See also Darwin, Charles Robert; Haeckel, Ernst Heinrich Phillip August; Italy; Sergi, Giuseppe

Bibliography
SELECTED WORKS
Critica e riforma del metodo in antropologia fondata sulle leggi statistiche e biologiche dei valori e sull' esperimento. Rome: Botta, 1880; Darwin. Revista analitica 1:613, 1881; Manuale di semeoitica delle malattie mentali. 2 vols. Milan: Vallardi, 1885–1894; Antropologia generale. 2 vols. Turin: U.T.E.T., 1888–1911; Psicologia e spiritismo. Turin: Bocca, 1906; Le neurosi traumatiche. Turin: U.T.E.T., 1913; L'uccisione pietosa. Turin: U.T.E.T., 1925.

SECONDARY SOURCES
U. Cerletti: Enrico Morselli. Riforma Medica 14:1–6, 1929; P. Guarnieri: La psichiatria antropologica di Enrico Morselli. Milan, 1986; L. Rossi: Enrico Morselli e la scienza dell'uomo nell'età del positivismo. Supplement No. 7. Rivista Sperimentale di Freniatria. Reggio-Emilia, 1984.

Mortillet, Gabriel (Louis Laurent) de (1821–1898)

Born in Meylan, Isère, France, Mortillet studied engineering and geology in Paris at the Conservatoire des arts et métiers. His interest in paleoanthropology and archeology dates from 1849, when he was obliged to leave France for his political activities during the Revolution of 1848. While in exile, Mortillet lived and worked in Switzerland and Italy, where he was able to use his engineering and geology skills on various railroad projects. It was during this period that Mortillet became associated with the Swiss geologist Éduoard Desor (1811–1882), and together they were responsible for making the first discovery in Italy (Lake Varese) of a Neolithic settlement. During the early 1860s, he served briefly as editor of the Turin-based *Revue scientifique italienne*. In 1864, he returned to Paris, where he founded the journal *Matériaux pour l'histoire positive et philosophie de l'homme (MHPPH)*, which he edited until 1872, when the editorship passed to Émile Cartailhac (1845–1921). Later, in 1890, this journal was united with the *Revue d'Anthropologie* and the *Revue d'Ethnologie* to form *L'Anthropologie*. His decision to give up the editorship of the *MHPPH* was due in large part to Mortillet's increasing responsibilities at the new Musée des Antiquités Nationales (MAN) at Saint-Germain-en-Laye, which he had joined in 1867, and of which he became director. In addition to his duties at MAN, Mortillet also taught prehistory at the École d'Anthropologie in Paris (*vide infra*).

From the outset of his career, Mortillet was an intellectual and political leader of a group of French intellectuals who saw evolution not only as an exciting new science, but also as a weapon with which to battle for social progress. Essentially, Mortillet and his followers saw nature as an engine of materialist progress, devoid of a Divine hand or Cuvierian catastrophes that destroyed developmental sequences. Using the tautology that whatever was more primitive culturally or morphologically was also older, he produced a ladder-like reconstruction of human physical and cultural evolution as a series of progressive and parallel stages (see *Tableau de la classification* in Mortillet 1881). According to this notion of progressive linear development, the Neandertals were regarded as morphologically more primitive than modern humans, and that their Mousterian culture was primitive, and as such must have existed much earlier in prehistory. And if they existed earlier, they must have been ancestral forms. As this suggests, Mortillet believed there was an intimate relationship between the level of material human culture and biological evolution. Thus, just as the stone implements of the Paleolithic and the Neolithic documented the emergence of modern humans, so, Mortillet believed, the crude stone tools found by workers such as the Abbé Louis Bourgeois (1819–1878) near Thénay on the Loire River represented the biocultural transition of the anthropomorphous apes to man in the European Tertiary. While many investigators of the period tended to reject this evidence as being nothing more than natural objects, Mortillet thought otherwise. To characterize these crude tools and the period to which they belonged, Mortillet coined the term *Eolithique*, or Dawn Stone Age.

Mortillet combined his prehistoric labors with an active political career, and this led to an identification in France between materialist evolution and left-wing political beliefs. He was elected to the Chamber of Deputies, where he sat on the extreme left; and he was also a very controversial representative for a working-class district of Paris. He and his followers sought to stamp out the clerical influence in French education and science. They even founded a Masonic lodge of scientific materialists to carry on their struggles. Of particular interest is their political and scientific alliance with the more moderate Paul Broca (1824–1880) and their involvement with him in the founding of the École d'Anthropologie in 1875—an institution that in the late nineteenth century had the greatest number of courses on evolution of any institution in the world. When Broca retired, they took over the school and freely mixed their linear progressive science with anticlericalism and radical politics. However, this circle was not to survive long into the twentieth century, as scientific discoveries and political changes swept away its members' combative anthropology.

Mortillet died at Saint-Germain-en-Laye on 25 September 1898.

Michael Hammond

See also Cartailhac, Émile (Edouard Phillipe); Paleoanthropology Theory

Bibliography
SELECTED WORKS

L'époque quaternaire dans la valée du Pô. Bulletin de la Société géologique de France 22:138–151, 1864; *Essai d'une classification des cavernes et des stations sous abri-fondeé sur les produits de l'industrie humaine*. Toulouse: Bonnal et Gibrac, 1869; Classification des âges de la pierre. *Comptes rendus de Congrès International d'Anthropologie et Archéologie Préhistorique* (Bruxelles 1872) Brussels: Muquardt, 1873, pp. 432–444; Sur l'homme tertiaire. *Bulletins de la Société d'Anthropologie de Paris* 8:671–684, 1873; *Musée préhistoriques*. Paris: Reinwald, 1881; *Le préhistorique, antiquité de l'homme*. Paris:

Reinwald, 1883 (2d ed.: 1885; 3d ed.: 1990, with A. de Mortillet: *La préhistorique, origine, antiquité de l'humain*).

SECONDARY SOURCES

É. Cartailhac: Gabriel de Mortillet [Nécrologie]. *L'Anthropologie* 9:601–612, 1898; M. Hammond: Anthropology as a weapon of social combat in late-nineteenth-century France. *Journal of the History of the Behavioral Sciences* 16:118–132, 1980.

Morton, Dudley Joy (1884–1960)

Born in Baltimore, Maryland, Morton studied medicine at Hahnemann Medical College, Philadelphia. After graduating M.D. in 1907, he became an assistant in surgery at Johns Hopkins Medical School. From 1910 to 1920, he was instructor in surgery at Hahnemann, and he subsequently taught at Yale Medical School. In 1928, he became professor of surgery at the College of Physicians and Surgeons, Columbia University, a position he retained for the remainder of his career.

Morton's work in anatomy and surgery focused on foot problems, and beginning in the early 1920s he took up the study of the evolution of the human foot. That work brought him into contact with physical anthropologists, particularly William King Gregory (1876–1970), and from 1925 until his death Morton maintained a close working relationship with Gregory at the American Museum of Natural History in New York City. Morton adopted Gregory's interpretation that the human foot had evolved from a generalized gorilloid type. He maintained that changes in habit and function were the principal causes of structural evolution. Although not a neo-Lamarckian, Morton emphasized the importance of use and disuse of parts and claimed that structural characters were invariably associated with a particular manner of use. He explained the evolution of foot structure in terms of mechanics and viewed adaptation and natural selection as compatible with the laws of engineering. In later publications, Morton examined muscles as well as skeletal structure and expanded his research to include the evolution of bodily form and upright posture.

Morton died in New York City on 22 May 1960.

Ronald Rainger

See also Bipedalism; Gregory, William King; Neo-Lamarckism

Bibliography
SELECTED WORKS

Evolution of the human foot. Part 1. *American Journal of Physical Anthropology* 5:305–336, 1922; Evolution of the human foot. Part 2. *American Journal of Physical Anthropology* 7:1–52, 1924; Evolution of man's erect posture. *Journal of Morphology and Physiology* 43:147–179, 1926; Human origin: Correlation of previous studies of primate feet and posture with other morphologic evidence. *American Journal of Physical Anthropology* 10:173–203, 1927; *Human anatomy: Double-dissection method.* New York: Columbia University Press, 1934; *The human foot: Its evolution, physiology, and functional disorders.* New York: Columbia University Press, 1935; (with D.D. Fuller) *Human locomotion and body form.* Baltimore: Williams & Wilkins, 1952.

SECONDARY SOURCES

J.M. Cattell & J. Cattell (eds): *American men of science: A biographical dictionary.* 4th ed. New York: Science Press, 1927, p. 699.

Morton, Samuel George (1799–1851)

Born in Philadelphia, Pennsylvania, Morton was raised as a Quaker. On receiving his M.B. degree from the University of Pennsylvania in 1820, Morton went to Europe, where he attended the University of Edinburgh (1820–1823). While there, he earned an M.D. degree with a thesis entitled *De Corporis Dolore* (On the Pain of the Body). Frank Spencer (1983a) regards this thesis as the probable source of Morton's polygenism. Other early influences on Morton were phrenology, a hereditarian doctrine that was in vogue while he was a medical student, and the views of early polygenist writers such as Charles Caldwell (1772–1853). Indeed, Morton's medical career coincided with the rise of polygenism in Western anthropology.

Morton's early interest in skulls led him to amass what was then one of the world's largest collections of crania of various races (Michael 1988:349; Spencer 1983b). He set out to measure these crania "objectively." His goal was to assess racial differences using the techniques of science rather than deductions from philosophy, politics, and religion, from which the opponents of polygenism (i.e., monogenists) drew much of their strength. Underlying Morton's craniometric work was the assumption, widespread at the time, that differences in skull size and shape cause differences in racial behavior (Gould 1981).

Morton's first major publication was *Crania Americana* (1839). In this landmark work, widely praised as an objective scientific treatise, he used twelve cranial measurements, including a measurement of cranial capacity, to derive a hierarchy of racial types. Morton's hierarchy ranked American Indians (Eskimos excepted) intermediate between Blacks at the bottom and Whites at the top. At the time, his data were cited widely as irrefutable evidence that ranked racial differences are "real." Gould (1978), however, has endeavored to show that Morton's measurements reflected an unconscious racial bias and errors that, if corrected, would make the differences virtually disappear (for an alternative interpretation, see Michael 1988).

Morton followed *Crania Americana* with *Crania Aegyptiaca* (1844), an examination of ancient Egyptian skulls and depictions of skulls brought to his attention by George R. Gliddon (1809–1857), then the U.S. consul in Cairo. In this work, Morton concluded that Blacks and Whites were recognizably distinct as far back as Egypt's first dynasty, almost 2,000 years before the birth of Christ and only 1,000 years after the time ascribed to the Noachian Flood. The implication was that there was not enough time for Blacks and Whites to have diverged from a common ancestor, or that biblical chronologies of human history were unrealistically short.

A vexing problem for polygenists was the time-honored definition of biological species as groups of organisms incapable of producing fertile hybrid offspring. While almost everyone at the time agreed that racial hybrids were "degenerate," nobody could deny that they were fertile. How could races produce fertile hybrids and be different species at the same time? The eventual way out of this dilemma was to abandon the time-honored definition of species in favor of a definition that stressed permanence of racial traits. Morton's work with American and Egyptian crania went a long way toward achieving this end (Morton 1847, 1849).

Monogenists and polygenists alike invoked arguments to support slavery, derived from both the Bible and the "irrefutable evidence" of science. American School polygenists such as Caldwell and Josiah Clark Nott (1804–1873), who lived in the South, gave slavery some of its strongest support. Morton, however, was unwilling to commit himself to a staunch pro-slavery position. Nevertheless, as the proclaimed leader of the American School, he was often bracketed with his pro-slavery associates (Stanton 1960).

Morton's death in 1851 was mourned as a premature loss to science (Gould 1978:503; Meigs 1851). With Morton's passing, the scientific mission of the American School was carried on by Gliddon and Nott, whose book *Types of Mankind* (1854) was dedicated to Morton's memory. On the craniological front, Morton's work was carried forward in America by James A. Meigs (1829–1879), while in Europe he had an important influence on a number of mid-nineteenth-century workers, most notably James Hunt (1833–1869) in England and Paul Broca (1824–1880) in France. The polygenism of the American School survived into the era of the American Civil War and the dawn of the Darwinian age. The craze for measuring skulls, which Morton helped launch, survived even longer. It did not really begin to come to an end until Franz Boas (1858–1942) (1912) showed that head shape is not fixed by heredity and set physical anthropology on a course to overcome its legacy of scientific racism.

Morton died in Philadelphia on 15 May 1851.

Paul A. Erickson

See also American School of Anthropology; Boas, Franz; Broca, Paul (Pierre); Caldwell, Charles; Doornik, Jacob Elisa; Hunt, James; Nott, Josiah Clark; Polygenism

Bibliography
SELECTED WORKS
     Crania Americana; or, A comparative view of the skulls of various Aboriginal nations of North and South America, to which is prefixed an essay on the varieties of the human species. Philadelphia: Dobson, 1839; *Crania Aegyptiaca; or, Observations on Egyptian ethnography, derived from anatomy, history, and the monuments.* Philadelphia: Pennington, 1844; Hybridity in animals considered in reference to the question of the unity of the human species. *American Journal of Science* 3:39–50, 203–212, 1847; *Catalogue of skulls of man and the inferior animals.* Philadelphia: Merrihew & Thompson, 1849.

ARCHIVAL SOURCES
     S.G. Morton Papers: Library, American Philosophical Society, 104 South Fifth Street, Philadelphia, Pennsylvania 19106–3387.

PRIMARY AND SECONDARY SOURCES
     F. Boas: *Changes in bodily form of*

descendants of immigrants. New York: Columbia University Press, 1912; C.L. Brace: The roots of the race concept in American physical anthropology. In: F. Spencer (ed) *A history of American physical anthropology, 1930–1980.* New York: Academic Press, 1982, pp. 17–19; S.J. Gould: Morton's ranking of races by cranial capacity. *Science* 200:503–509, 1978; S.J. Gould: *The mismeasure of man.* New York: Norton, 1981; C.D. Meigs: *A memoir of S.G. Morton.* Philadelphia: Collins, 1851.

J.S. Michael: A new look at Morton's craniological research. *Current Anthropology* 29:349–354, 1988; J.C. Nott & G.R. Gliddon (eds): *Types of Mankind.* Philadelphia: Lippincott, Grambo, 1854; F. Spencer: Samuel George Morton's doctoral thesis on bodily pain: The probable source of Morton's polygenism. *Transactions and Studies of the College of Physicians of Philadelphia* 5:321–328, 1983a; F. Spencer: Jacob Elias Doornik, 1777–1837: Notes on a contributor to Samuel George Morton's cabinet in Philadelphia. *Physical Anthropology News* 2(1):16–17, 1983b; W. Stanton: *The leopard's spots: Scientific attitudes toward race in America, 1815–1859.* Chicago: University of Chicago Press, 1960.

Moulin-Quignon Affair

Although by the early 1860s, the "antediluvian" (Paleolithic) artifacts described by Jacques Boucher de Perthes (1788–1868) and others were widely accepted as the tools of early humans, the identity of "antediluvian man" himself remained a mystery. During the first half of the nineteenth century, a number of human skeletal remains had been found that were considered possible clues. In some instances, this involved material that was much more recent than appreciated at the time. Indeed, throughout the nineteenth century, anatomically modern human remains were considered of great geological age—in some cases, they had been dated to the Pliocene. Examples are the Italian specimens from the marine deposit of Savona (1852) and Castenedolo (1860). By contrast, a number of genuine fossils were misidentified, as was the case with the so-called Red Lady of Paviland found in 1823 in Wales, which had been incorrectly attributed to the Roman period when, in fact, it dates from the early Holocene. Similarly, amidst the Neandertals, the Engis juvenile skull from Belgium (1830) and the Forbes' quarry Gibraltar specimen (1848), were not identified as extinct hominids at the time of their discoveries. The Feldhofer skeleton itself, found in the Neander Valley near Dusseldorf (1856), remained disputed as a fossil human until the mid-1880s.

Finding the remains of the artificer of the tools Boucher de Perthes had recovered from the gravel terraces of the Somme River Valley was thus a crucial scientific issue. Furthermore, such a discovery would also have provided compelling evidence to silence Boucher de Perthes' critics, who had with increasing frequency posed the puzzling question: If human beings had actually manufactured all of the artifacts recovered at Abbeville and elsewhere, where were their mortal remains, and why had only the bones of extinct animals been preserved? Anxious to stem the sarcasm and innuendo of his critics, Boucher de Perthes offered a reward of 200 francs for the first human remains to be recovered from the "diluvium." Soon thereafter, on 23 March 1863, a human tooth and two flint axes were reportedly recovered by Nicolas Halattre, a worker at the Moulin-Quignon quarry (where earlier Boucher de Perthes had found some bony fragments he believed were human). A week later, this was followed by the recovery of a second tooth and the discovery of the right half of a human mandible, which in Boucher de Perthes' estimation differed significantly from the modern form. Although the mandible clearly displays a number of modern features, especially a projecting bony chin, at the time of its discovery there were some aspects of its morphology, such as the great obliquity of the ramus, that were regarded as archaic indicators and evidently served to convince Boucher de Perthes of the specimen's great antiquity.

News of the discovery spread quickly. Among the first of many who visited Abbeville early in April to examine the jaw were the French anthropologist Armand de Quatrefages (1810–1892) and a series of British workers that included Hugh Falconer (1808–1865), William B. Carpenter (1813–1885), Joseph Prestwich (1812–1896), and John Evans (1823–1908).

At the beginning, the reception was enthusiastic. Following Boucher de Perthes' presentation of the fossil to the Société d'Emulation in Abbeville on 16 April, Quatrefages communicated details of his visit (in the company of Falconer) and examination of the find to the Académie des Sciences in Paris on 20 April. In the meantime, while Carpenter had made a similar report to the Royal Society on 16 April and had written an

Fig. 1. The Moulin-Quignon
jaw; s, indicates where Busk
sawed the specimen in half.
B. Stratigraphical profile of
the Moulin-Quignon site;
a,b,c, and d indicate the
original locations of the jaw
and implements. From
Boucher de Perthes (1864).

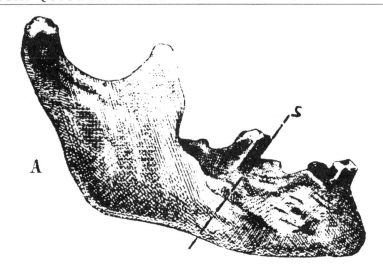

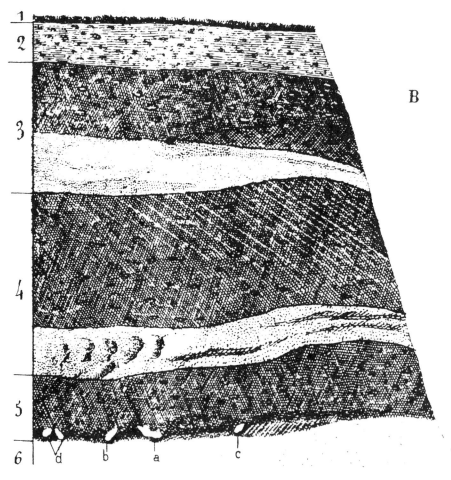

account of the discovery, which was published in the *Athenaeum* (Carpenter 1863), Falconer's earlier conviction regarding the authenticity of the Moulin-Quignon finds was seriously undermined by the discovery made by Prestwich and Evans that some of the stone artifacts from the site were fakes. Falconer furthermore concluded that the isolated tooth given to him by Boucher de Perthes was recent and that the morphology of the mandible entered the range of variation of modern humans. He alerted Boucher de Perthes and

Édouard Lartet (1801–1871) to these findings, but he was too late to prevent Quatrefages from presenting his paper to the Académie in Paris. On 25 April, a letter to the editor by Falconer was published in *The Times* (London), claiming that the whole discovery was a forgery by quarry workers. In the following weeks, the dispute around the mandible rapidly developed into a confrontation between the English and French scientific communities. The original international group, who weeks before had jointly supported the Boucher de Perthes claims, was now torn by conflicting loyalties. In an effort to resolve the controversy, Lartet proposed to Falconer the idea of organizing a scientific committee charged with evaluating the evidence. The resulting committee held its first meeting on 9 May in the Jardin des Plantes, Paris, with the zoologist Henri Milne-Edwards (1800–1885) as moderator. Among the French participants were Louis Bourgeois (1819–1878), Achille Delesse (1817–1881), Jules Desnoyers (1800–1887), Edmond Hébert (1812–1890), Gaudry, Quatrefages, and Lartet. The English contingent included the anatomist George Busk (1807–1886), Prestwich, Carpenter, and Falconer (Evans was unable to make the trip). Essentially, the English favored the view that all of the artifacts were frauds, whereas the French, by and large, argued that the evidence did not support such a negative conclusion. Unable to reach a consensus on this point, the committee then examined the arguments by Falconer against the isolated teeth and jaw. The mandible was sawed into two pieces. The cut surface revealed a rather recent internal aspect of the bone and a filling very different from the Moulin-Quignon sediments, which strongly supported the English viewpoint. Following this dramatic meeting in Paris, the committee moved to Abbeville to examine the Moulin-Quignon layers firsthand. There, under the watchful eye of the committee, the quarry workers unearthed bifaces displaying features similar to those the English said were fakes, and these evidently authentic recoveries clearly mollified Prestwich.

On 13 May, the Moulin-Quignon committee issued its verdict. The mandible was contemporary with the deposits, and for the most part the hand axes were deemed authentic. Although at this juncture Prestwich endorsed this conclusion, Falconer and Busk did not. Full accounts of these proceedings in Abbeville and Paris were published by Milne-Edwards (1863) and by Falconer, Busk, and

Carpenter (1863). For Boucher de Perthes, the verdict was a personal victory, and, on the French side at least, the Moulin-Quignon affair was considered closed.

Although the events in Abbeville had led Prestwich and his English colleagues to reconsider the forgery hypothesis, both Falconer and Busk continued to be troubled by the jaw, whose geological age they seriously doubted. Indeed, on reaching England Falconer once again changed his mind about the Moulin-Quignon bifaces. Eventually, he came to the vexing conclusion that the discovery of artifacts in the presence of the committee had been orchestrated by the quarry workers. Tormented by his doubts, he urged Prestwich and Evans to undertake a new controlled excavation in the Moulin-Quignon quarry. At that point, Falconer could not do any more. In the meantime, Boucher de Perthes, led by a desire for reconciliation with Falconer, made him an honorary member of the Société d'Emulation d'Abbeville, of which he was president.

In England, the Moulin-Quignon case was reopened by Evans with a paper published in the *Athenaeum* (Evans 1863a), in which he noted the initial rarity of hand axes at Moulin-Quignon and the mounting frequency of their discovery at the site, and more especially the recovery of a previously unknown type of flint artifact. Some of these new flints, he suggested, bore the marks made from hammers. He also noted that their surface was covered by a patina that was easily removed by washing. He further charged that the mandible had been fraudulently introduced into the site along with these "new" flint types. With Boucher de Perthes' blessing, Evans sent Henry Keeping, who had been in charge of excavations at the Brixham Cave site, to Abbeville to conduct an investigation. Between 3 and 6 June, Keeping reported that a series of hand axes were discovered at the Moulin-Quignon quarry, which he later argued had been "placed there on purpose for me to find" (Evans 1863b:20). This claim was supported by the discovery of fingerprints on the clay covering the unearthed artifacts. In a letter to the *Athenaeum* dated 4 July, Evans presented a summary of Keeping's findings and emphasized as well the similarity between the Moulin-Quignon mandible and specimens emanating from the local and geologically recent site of Mesnières (where, incidentally, one of the Moulin-Quignon quarry workers had been involved in excavations). From all of this, Evans concluded that the jaw should be "consigned to oblivion: *Requiescat in pace*" (Evans 1863b:20). Soon thereafter, Prestwich concurred by withdrawing his support of the Moulin-Quignon mandible (Prestwich 1863).

In France, some scientists, especially Quatrefages, had been too deeply engaged in support of the Moulin-Quignon discovery to easily renounce the official conclusions of the international committee. As for Boucher de Perthes, who was by this time in his seventy-fifth year, he was not about to relinquish the prize he had long awaited. In the third volume of his *Antiquités* (1864a), while addressing the arguments against the antiquity of the Paleolithic artifacts in general he reviewed this issue against the backdrop of the Moulin-Quignon affair. In that same year, in recognition of the work at Moulin-Quignon he received, along with Quatrefages, the medal of Officier de la Légion d'Honneur.

Although the site continued to yield new remains, most of the time in the presence of highly reliable eyewitnesses (cf. Boucher de Perthes 1864b), the memory of the Moulin-Quignon mandible and its significance was soon eclipsed by new discoveries elsewhere.

Jean-Jacques Hublin

See also Boucher (de Crèvecoeur) de Perthes, Jacques; Brixham Cave; Busk, George; Engis; Falconer, Hugh; Gaudry, Albert Jean; Gibraltar; Lartet, Édouard (Armand Isidore Hippolyte); Neandertal (Feldhofer Grotte); Neandertals; Paviland; Prestwich, (Sir) Joseph; Quatrefages (de Breau), Jean Louis Armand de

Bibliography
ARCHIVAL SOURCES

Hugh Falconer Papers: Archives, Moray District Libraries, Record Office, Forres, Moray, Scotland.

PRIMARY SOURCES

J. Boucher de Perthes: *Antiquités celtiques et antédiluviennes: Mémoire sur l'industrie primitive et les arts à leur origine.* Vol. 3. Paris: Jung-Treuttel, 1864a; J. Boucher de Perthes: *De la mâchoire humaine de Moulin-Quignon: Nouvelles découvertes en 1863 et 1864.* Paris: Jung-Treuttel, 1864b; W.B. Carpenter: Discovery at Abbeville. *Athenaeum* 41:523, 1863; J. Evans: The Abbeville human jaw. *Athenaeum* 41:747–748, 1863a; J. Evans: The human remains at Abbeville. *Athenaeum* 42:19–20, 1863b; H. Falconer, G. Busk, & W.B. Carpenter: An account of the proceedings of the late conference held in France to inquire into the circumstances attending the asserted discovery of a human jaw in the gravel at Moulin-Quignon, near Abbeville, including the *procès verbaux* of the sittings of the conference, with notes thereon. *Natural History Review* 3:423–462, 1863.

H. Milne-Edwards: Note sur les résultats fournis par une enquête relative à l'authenticité de la découverte d'une mâchoire humaine et de haches en silex. *Comptes-rendus hebdomadaires des séances de l'Académie des Sciences* 56:921–933, 1863; J. Prestwich: On the section at Moulin-Quignon, Abbeville, and on the peculiar character of some of the flint implements recently discovered there. *Quarterly Journal of the Geological Society of London* 19:497–505, 1863; A. de Quatrefages: Note sur la mâchoire découverte par M. Boucher de Perthes dans le diluvium d'Abbeville. *Comptes-rendus hebdomadaires des séances de l'Académie des Sciences* 56:782–788, 1863.

SECONDARY SOURCES

P.J. Boylan: The controversy of the Moulin-Quignon jaw: The role of Hugh Falconer. In: L.J. Jordanova & R.S. Porter (eds) *Images of the Earth*. London: British Society for the History of Science, 1979, pp. 171–199; C. Cohen & J.-J. Hublin: *Boucher de Perthes: Les origines romantiques de la préhistoire*. Paris: Belin, 1989, pp.201–221; G.K. Grayson: *The establishment of human antiquity*. New York: Academic Press, 1983, pp. 213–217.

Mount Carmel (Israel)

Mount Carmel is a limestone formation (a barrier reef) running north–south along the northern Mediterranean coast of Israel. It contains a series of caves and shelters, three of which (Mugharet el-Kebara, Mugharet es-Skhūl, and Mugharet et-Tabūn) have yielded important human remains.

The first systematic Paleolithic archeological excavations in the region were carried out in the late 1920s and 1930s by Dorothy A.E. Garrod (1892–1968) and colleagues, under the auspices of the British School of Archaeology in Jerusalem and the American School of Prehistoric Research, at sites in or adjacent to the Wadi el-Mughara (Ronen 1982). Two of these sites, Mugharet es-Skhūl and Mugharet et-Tabūn, yielded important Middle Paleolithic human remains.

In the 1930s, as Theodore D. McCown (1908–1969) worked on the human remains from the sites of Skhūl and Tabūn, he maintained that these samples represented two groups of humans. The former was seen as a more modern human-like sample, whereas the latter was viewed as more Neandertal-like. However, in the final monograph on the human remains (McCown & Keith 1939), it was Arthur Keith's (1866–1955) view—that they represented one variable population—that prevailed. This resulted in Skhūl and Tabūn becoming known jointly as the "Mount Carmel site" and the human remains from them as the "Mount Carmel sample." It has since been recognized, as a result of reanalyses of the Skhūl and Tabūn fossils beginning in the late 1950s (e.g., Boule & Vallois 1957; Howell 1958; Stewart 1960) and continuing through the 1970s (e.g., Howells 1975; Stringer 1974; Trinkaus 1983, 1984; Vandermeersch 1981), that they represented two separate samples. The term "Mount Carmel" is, therefore, now restricted in human paleontology to the geological formation in which these sites and others are located, and the fossil samples are referred to by their specific site names, namely Skhūl and Tabūn.

Erik Trinkaus

See also Israel; Kebara, Mughâret el- (Israel); Keith, (Sir) Arthur; McCown, Theodore D(oney); Neandertals; Skhūl, Mughâret es- (Israel); Tabūn, Mughâret et- (Israel)

Bibliography
M. Boule & H.V. Vallois: *Fossil man.* New York: Dryden Press, 1957; F.C. Howell: Upper Pleistocene men in the southwest Asian Mousterian. In: G.H.R. von Koenigswald (ed) *Hundert Jahre Neanderthaler.* Utrecht: Kemink en Zoon, 1958, pp. 185–198; W.W. Howells: Neanderthal man: Facts and figures. In: R.H. Tuttle (ed): *Paleoanthropology: Morphology and paleoecology.* The Hague: Mouton, 1975, pp. 389–407; T.D. McCown & A. Keith: *The Stone Age of Mount Carmel II: The fossil human remains from the Levalloiso-Mousterian.* Oxford: Clarendon Press, 1939.
A. Ronen: Mt. Carmel caves: The first excavations. In: A. Ronen (ed) The transition from the Lower to Middle Paleolithic and the origin of modern man. *British Archaeological Reports* 151:7–28, 1982; T.D. Stewart: Form of the pubic bone in Neanderthal man. *Science* 131:1437–1438, 1960; C.B. Stringer: Population relationships of Late Pleistocene hominids: A multivariate study of available crania. *Journal of Archaeological Science* 1:327–342, 1974; E. Trinkaus: *The Shanidar Neandertals.* New York: Academic Press, 1983; E. Trinkaus: Western Asia. In: F.H. Smith and F. Spencer (eds) *The origins of modern humans: A world survey of the fossil evidence.* New York: Liss, 1984, pp. 251–293; B. Vandermeersch: *Les hommes fossiles de Qafzeh (Israël).* Paris: CNRS, 1981.

Multidisciplinary Research of Human Biology and Behavior

Early Multidisciplinary Research in Anthropology
Collaborative projects are not unusual in science and have been initiated frequently in anthropology. Expeditions in the nineteenth and early twentieth centuries were often organized with specialists from different areas of expertise. Franz Boas' (1858–1942) first field trip to Baffin Island in 1883–1884 was that kind of expedition (cf. Boas 1884). Other early examples include the Cambridge University Expedition to Torres Straits in 1898–1899 (cf. Haddon 1901–1935) and the investigation of "early man" in Argentina by a team of Smithsonian scientists led by Aleš Hrdlička (1869–1943) in 1910 (cf. Hrdlička et al. 1912). The Asiatic Primate Expedition in 1937, which involved C. Ray Carpenter (1905–1975), Adolph Hans Schultz (1891–1976), and Sherwood L. Washburn (1911–), to study the behavior of gibbons in Siam (Thailand) was also multidisciplinary (Carpenter 1940). However, during the development of anthropology in the first half of the twentieth century, the "single-investigator-who-works-alone" tradition became established in sociocultural anthropology. In archeology, there were different traditions of collaboration, partly because of the nature of the field work. In biological anthropology, anthropologists collaborated with other natural scientists, but studies were often done in the laboratory. At Harvard University, Earnest A. Hooton (1887–1954) initiated many studies by arranging for his students to work closely with scientists in fields outside of anthropology (e.g., Gardner & MacAdam 1934).

Among the first modern and integrated multidisciplinary studies were the !Kung San (Bushman) Project from Harvard that began in 1963 (cf. Lee & DeVore 1976) and the Quechua Indian Project from Pennsylvania State University that was initiated in 1962 (cf. Baker & Little 1976). Both began as anthropological projects that were expanded to be-

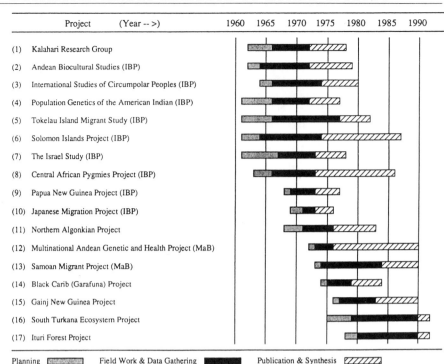

Fig. 1. Multidisciplinary research 1960–1990. A selected list of IBP, MaB, and independent projects.

Planning [   ]   Field Work & Data Gathering [   ]   Publication & Synthesis [//////]

come multidisciplinary in later years. It was also in the early 1960s that the International Council of Scientific Unions (ICSU) began organizing the International Biological Programme (IBP). The program centered on a variety of ecological programs and had three phases: preparation (1964–1967), operation (1967–1972), and synthesis (1972–1976). Human adaptability was identified as the program in which human biological scientists and interested social scientists could participate. However, because of the nature of the research perspectives, more biological than sociocultural anthropologists participated (Weiner 1977). Those sociocultural anthropologists who did conduct research under the IBP were usually oriented toward ecology and demography. Involvement or lack thereof was often the result of the actions of key players in international science.

Multidisciplinary Projects: 1960s–1990s
In the early 1960s, it became apparent to some scientists that many populations whose lifestyles characterized the bulk of human history and prehistory were undergoing dramatic change (Lee and DeVore 1968b; Neel 1968; Weiner 1966). These populations included hunter/gatherer, pastoral, and traditional horticultural and agricultural peoples. Patterns of behavior and biological status of these peoples were being transformed through pro-

cesses of culture change, modernization, assimilation, and, in some cases, physical extinction. It was perceived as urgent, then, to learn as much as possible about these bioculturally endangered populations, particularly since their extinction would mean the loss to modern society of the living populations that most closely resemble human populations during the greater part of our evolutionary past. In addition to the fears about loss of these valuable sources of genetic and cultural information was the growing concern with the impact of civilization on the Earth through increasing population numbers and environmental pollution. This social, intellectual, and emotional environment in the West coincided with the opportunity to initiate multidisciplinary studies of single populations through the IBP.

Before the close of the IBP in 1975, a new international research program was developed by UNESCO (the United Nations Educational, Scientific, and Cultural Organization) called Man and the Biosphere (MaB). The MaB program, as first designed, emphasized interactions between human activities and natural systems and encouraged close research affiliation between social and natural scientists and decision makers. Other hallmarks of the program were the need to transcend national boundaries during the course of research, to employ systems approaches to problem solving, and to encourage training and education to go hand in hand with research efforts. The need for some of these programmatic emphases had arisen during the years of the IBP.

These international programs stimulated the organization of multidisciplinary projects with several different perspectives and orientations. While the concept of adaptation to the environment was central to all projects, there were other theoretical perspectives that played important roles in the formulation of collaborative projects. These included: (1) microevolution, (2) cultural and biobehavioral evolution, (3) systems science and ecology, and (4) health, epidemiology, and environmental change. As these projects were completed, it became clear that multidisciplinary research had led to the achievement of levels of understanding about a population that were not possible with unidisciplinary approaches to science.

Fig. 1 provides a selected list of IBP-associated, MaB-associated, and independent multidisciplinary projects. Fig. 2 gives the location on a map of the world of the populations that were studied.

Adaptation to the Environment
Adaptation to the environment and human adaptability to diverse environments were fundamental themes in many of the multidisciplinary studies of human behavior. Adaptation to extreme environments in the arid tropics was studied by the Kalahari Research Group in Botswana (Lee & DeVore 1976) and the later South Turkana Ecosystem Project in the Kenya savanna (cf. Little et al. 1990). The wet tropics were represented by research on Central African (Cavalli-Sforza 1986) and Ituri (Ellison & Bailey 1989) pygmy populations, as well as several Papua New Guinea populations (Campbell & Wood 1988; Hornabrook 1977). The New Guinea work of D. Carleton Gajdusek (Gajdusek 1977; Gajdusek & Zigas 1957), although conducted in the 1950s, can be cited as a particularly successful collaborative research effort.

Adaptation to high-altitude stress was studied in Peru under the Andean Biocultural Studies Project (Baker & Little 1976) and farther south in the highlands of Chile under the Multinational Andean Project (Schull & Rothhammer 1990). Arctic adaptations were represented by the Eskimo component of the Circumpolar Project, which considered several Eskimo populations in a belt across the United States, Canada, and Greenland (Milan 1980).

Integrated investigations of Algonkian peoples contributed further to our knowledge of Arctic adaptation (Steegmann 1983).

Microevolution
The theme of microevolution and its processes in populations isolates and other groups was applied in a number of projects, some of which began in the 1960s. One of the most successful projects dealt with population genetics in the South American Yanomama, Makiretare, Cayapo, and Xavante Indians (cf. Neel et al. 1977). Language, genes, demography, and phenotypic characteristics of these populations were used to explore selection, drift, other evolutionary processes, and how civilization had changed patterns of interaction between humans, their environment, and evolution from tribal times. Genetic and evolutionary models were also applied in comparisons of several Solomon Islands populations (Friedlaender 1987) and surveys of a number of Central African pygmy groups (Cavalli-Sforza 1977). The Chilean high-altitude research, which involved indigenous Aymara Indians and mestizo populations along an altitudinal gradient, examined how the contrasting environments affected health and whether evidence for genetic adaptation to the high-altitude environment could be detected (Schull & Rothhammer 1977). Also, successful studies of evolution and genetics of the admixed Garifuna or Black Caribs (West African and Carib and Arawak Indians) of Belize, Guatemala, and Honduras demonstrated the value of collaborative research between social and biological scientists (Crawford 1984; González 1969).

Cultural and Biobehavioral Evolution
Several multidisciplinary projects were designed to study modern representatives of hunter/gatherer populations as rough models of Paleolithic societies (Lee & DeVore 1968a). In the same context as the Kalahari Project, collaborative studies of pygmies were identified as important for gaining insights into our Upper Paleolithic prehistory (Bailey 1991; Cavalli-Sforza 1977). Although questions have been raised over whether these remnant populations truly represent Paleolithic peoples, the integrated studies are still considered to have made important contributions to the scientific literature.

Systems Science and Ecology
Systems science and ecosystems ecology became important areas in biology as the result

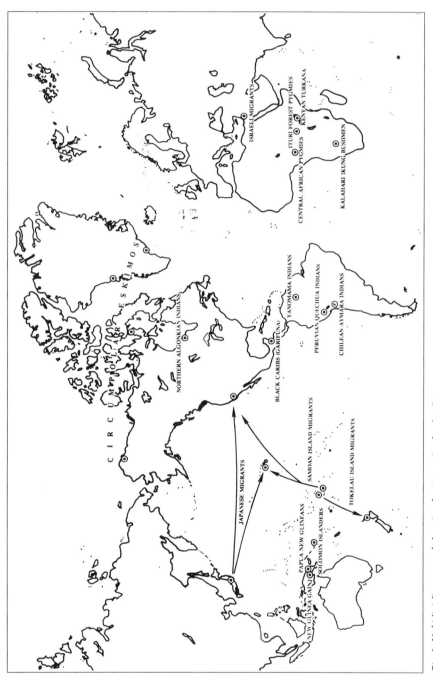

Fig. 2. Multidisciplinary research. Location of various projects listed in Fig 1.

of major integrated projects that dominated IBP research during the 1960s (Worthington 1975). Some of these ideas were incorporated into the multidisciplinary biobehavioral projects because of the IBP influence, but also because ecological anthropology was a popular theoretical research perspective at this time. Thomas' (1976) study of energy flow in the highland Quechua community of Nuñoa, Peru, is a notable example. The most extensive ecological work to date that involved human biobehavioral research was done under the aegis of the South Turkana Ecosystem Project (cf. Leslie et al. 1988; Little et al. 1988).

Health, Epidemiology, and Environmental Change
It became apparent during the years of the IBP that one of the most dramatic effects on human health and adaptability was the rapid transition that many societies were experiencing from an agrarian society to an urbanized "modern" one. The traditional life-styles of, among others, Eskimos, Pacific Islanders, Japanese peasants, and Israeli newcomers were changing through processes of acculturation and modernization. This was occurring either by social change in sedentary populations or by social and environmental change experienced through migration. Issues of health and environmental change figured prominently in the Circumpolar Eskimo study (Milan 1980) and in the projects dealing with migrant peoples. The process of modernization often was experienced most acutely in migrants, who were moving from rural to urban locations with remarkable frequency (Little & Baker 1988). Pacific migrants from Tokelau to New Zealand (Prior et al. 1977) and from Samoa to Hawaii or California (Baker, Hanna & Baker 1986) experience emotional and social stress with concomitant catecholamine changes as well as increases in cardiovascular disease, hypertension, and obesity. These studies of Pacific Island migrants made it clear, also, that specific populations are more prone to develop certain health problems triggered by environmental change.

In these multidisciplinary studies of health and environmental change, the distinction between *applied science* and *basic science* is often blurred. In a sense, all of the multidisciplinary projects described here had applied implications. Furthermore, many of these issues support the need to gather more information about the relationships between human populations and their changing environments to solve some of the most pressing problems facing humanity today.

The Future of Multidisciplinary Research
Considerable progress has been made in the breadth and scope of research into human adaptation and adaptability to the environment. However, many of the problems of conducting multidisciplinary research that were outlined by Baker in 1965 remain. In fact, some of those problems may be unavoidable, simply a concomitant part of large-scale research, at least in the present scientific climate. Be this as it may, the power of multidisciplinary research to solve complex problems is still significant.

A major area for future research concerns the competition between human needs for survival and higher-order biosphere needs for survival. Programs of economic development often carry with them processes that lead to destruction of the environment and losses of both the cultural diversity that enriches human existence and the biological diversity of the environment that is essential for human existence. It is in these very important areas of research that natural and social scientists must engage in multidisciplinary efforts to ensure the survival of our habitat.

Michael A. Little
Paul W. Leslie
Paul T. Baker

See also Adaptation; Baker, Paul Thornell; Boas, Franz; Carpenter, C(larence) Raymond; Damon, Albert; Haddon, A(lfred) C(ort); Hooton, E(arnest) A(lbert); Hrdlička, Aleš; International Biological Programme (Human Adaptability Section); Kuru; Schultz, Adolph Hans; Washburn, Sherwood L.; Weiner, Joseph Sidney

Bibliography
R.C. Bailey: *The behavioral ecology of Efe pygmy men in the Ituri Forest, Zaire.* Anthropological Papers of the Museum of Anthropology. No. 86. Ann Arbor: University of Michigan, 1991; P.T. Baker: Multidisciplinary studies of human adaptability: Theoretical justification and method. In: J.S. Weiner (ed) *International Biological Programme: Guide to the human adaptability proposals.* London: International Council of Scientific Unions, Special Committee for the International Biological Programme, 1965, pp. 63–72; P.T. Baker & M.A. Little (eds): *Man in the Andes: A multidisciplinary study of high-altitude Quechua.* Stroudsburg, Pennsylvania: Dowden, Hutchinson & Ross, 1976; P.T. Baker & J.S. Weiner (eds): *The biology of*

human adaptability. Oxford: Clarendon Press, 1966.

P.T. Baker, J.M. Hanna, & T.S. Baker (eds): *The changing Samoans: Health and behavior in transition*. New York: Oxford University Press, 1986; F. Boas: A journey to Cumberland Sound and on the west shore of Davis Strait in 1883 and 1884. *Journal of the American Geographical Society of New York* 16:242–272, 1884; K.L. Campbell & J.W. Wood: Fertility in traditional societies. In: P. Diggory, M. Potts, & S. Teper (eds) *Natural human fertility: Social and biological determinants*. London: Macmillan, 1988, pp. 39–69; C.R. Carpenter: *A field study in Siam of the behavior and social relations of the gibbon (Hylobates lar)*. Comparative Psychology Monographs 16:1–212, 1940; L.L. Cavalli-Sforza: Biological research on African pygmies. In: G.A. Harrison (ed) *Population structure and human variation*. Cambridge: Cambridge University Press, 1977, pp. 273–284.

L.L. Cavalli-Sforza: *African pygmies*. Orlando: Academic Press, 1986; M.H. Crawford (ed): *Black Caribs: A case study in biocultural adaptation*. Current Developments in Anthropological Genetics. Vol. 3. New York: Plenum Press, 1984; O.G. Edholm & S. Samuelhof: The Israel study: The anatomy of a population study. In: G.A. Harrison (ed) *Population structure and human variation*. Cambridge: Cambridge University Press, 1977, pp. 219–239; P.T. Ellison & R.C. Bailey (organizers): Studies on the ecology and behavior of two forest populations from the Ituri Forest, Zaire. *American Journal of Physical Anthropology* 78:459–545, 1989; J.S. Friedlaender (ed): *The Solomon Islands Project: A long-term study of health, human biology, and culture change*. Oxford: Clarendon Press, 1987.

D.C. Gajdusek: Unconventional viruses and the origin and disappearance of kuru. *Science* 197:943–960, 1977; D.C. Gajdusek & V. Zigas: Degenerative disease of the central nervous system in New Guinea: The endemic occurrence of kuru in the native population. *New England Journal of Medicine* 257:974–978, 1957; B.B. Gardner & D.L. MacAdam: Colorimetric analysis of hair color. *American Journal of Physical Anthropology* 19:187–201, 1934; N.L. González: *Black Carib household structures: A study of migration and modernization*. American Ethnological Society. Seattle: University of Seattle Press, 1969; A.C. Haddon (ed): *Reports of the Cambridge Anthropological Expedition to Torres Straits*. 6 vols. Cambridge: Cambridge University Press, 1901–1935.

R.W. Hornabrook: Human adaptability in Papua New Guinea. In: G.A. Harrison (ed) *Population structure and human variation*. Cambridge: Cambridge University Press, 1977, pp. 285–312; S.M. Horvath et al. (eds): *Comparative studies in human adaptability of Japanese, Caucasian, and Japanese Americans*. Human Adaptability Vol. 1. Japanese International Biological Programme (JIPB) Synthesis. Tokyo: University of Tokyo Press, 1975; A. Hrdlička et al.: *Early man in South America*. Bureau of American Ethnology Bulletin. No. 52. Washington, D.C.: Government Printing Office, 1912; R.B. Lee & I. DeVore (eds): *Man the hunter*. Chicago: Aldine, 1968a; R.B. Lee & I. DeVore: Problems in the study of hunters and gatherers. In: R.B. Lee & I. DeVore (eds) *Man the hunter*. Chicago: Aldine, 1968b, pp. 3–12.

R.B. Lee & I. DeVore (eds): *Kalahari hunters-gatherers: Studies of the !Kung San and their neighbors*. Cambridge, Massachusetts: Harvard University Press, 1976; P.W. Leslie et al.: Biological, behavioral, and ecological influences on fertility in Turkana. In: E.E. Whitehead et al. (eds) *Arid lands today and tomorrow: Proceedings of an international research and development conference*. Boulder: Westview Press, 1988, pp. 705–712; M.A. Little & P.T. Baker: Migration and adaptation. In: C.G. Mascie-Taylor & G.W. Lasker (eds) *Biological aspects of human migration*. Cambridge: Cambridge University Press, 1988, pp. 167–215; M.A. Little, P.W. Leslie, & P.T. Baker: Multidisciplinary studies of human adaptability: Twenty-five years of research. *Journal of the Indian Anthropological Society* 26(1–2):9–29, 1991.

M.A. Little et al.: Resources, biology, and health of pastoralists. In: E.E. Whitehead et al. (eds) *Arid lands today and tomorrow: Proceedings of an international research and development conference*. Boulder: Westview, 1988. pp. 713–726; M.A. Little et al.: Ecosystem approaches in human biology: Their history and a case study of the South Turkana Ecosystem Project. In: E.F. Moran (ed) *The ecosystem approach in anthropology: From concept to practice*. Ann Arbor: University of Michigan Press, 1990, pp. 389–434; F.A. Milan (ed): *The human biology of circumpolar populations*. Cambridge: Cambridge University Press, 1980; J.V. Neel: The American Indian in the International Biological Programme. In: *Biomedical challenges presented by the American Indian.* Scientific Publication No. 165. Washington, D.C.: Pan American Health Organization, 1968, pp. 47–54.

J.V. Neel et al.: Man in the tropics: The Yanomama Indians. In: G.A. Harrison (ed) *Population structure and human variation.* Cambridge: Cambridge University Press, 1977, pp. 109–142; I.A.M. Prior et al.: The Tokelau Island migrant study. In: G.A. Harrison (ed) *Population structure and human variation.* Cambridge: Cambridge University Press, 1977, pp. 165–186; W.J. Schull & F. Rothhammer: A multinational Andean genetic and health program: A study of adaptation to the hypoxia of altitude. In: J.S. Weiner (ed) *Physiological variation and its genetic basis.* London: Taylor & Francis, 1977, pp. 139–169; W.J. Schull & F. Rothhammer (eds) *The Aymara: Strategies in human adaptation to a rigorous environment.* Dordrecht: Kluwer, 1990; A.T. Steegmann Jr. (ed): *Boreal forest adaptations: The northern Algonkians.* New York: Plenum, 1983.

R.B. Thomas: Energy flow at high altitude. In: P.T. Baker & M.A. Little (eds) *Man in the Andes: A multidisciplinary study of high-altitude Quechua.* Stroudsburg, Pennsylvania: Dowden, Hutchinson & Ross, 1976, pp. 379–404; J.S. Weiner (ed): *International Biological Programme: Guide to the human adaptability proposals.* London: International Council of Scientific Unions, Special Committee for the International Biological Programme, 1965; J.S. Weiner: Major problems in human population biology. In: P.T. Baker & J.S. Weiner (eds) *The biology of human adaptability.* Oxford: Clarendon Press, 1966, pp. 1–24; J.S. Weiner: The history of the Human Adaptability Section. In: K.J. Collins & J.S. Weiner (eds) *Human adaptability: A history and compendium of research.* London: Taylor & Francis, 1977, pp. 1–23; J.S. Weiner & J.A. Lourie: *Human biology: A guide to field methods.* IBP Handbook No. 9. Philadelphia: Davis, 1969; E.B. Worthington: *The evolution of the IBP.* Cambridge: Cambridge University Press, 1975.

Muñoa, Juan Ignacio (1925–1960)

Born in Salto, Uruguay, Muñoa had originally intended to pursue a career in medicine, but he did not complete his medical studies. Instead, he quit medical school, and (ca. 1951) went to work at the Museum of Natural History in Montevideo, where he became assistant curator in zoology. He remained in this position until his death in 1960. During this time Muñoa was responsible for organizing the museum's Mammalogy Section.

Although he published only a single work in physical anthropology, "Los Primitivos Pobladores del Este" (1954), it is considered of primary importance because it was the first in-depth study of prehistoric human skeletal remains conducted in Uruguay (cf. Maruca Sosa 1957 for a summary of this work). At the time of his death, Muñoa was working on a sequel, *Los pueblos prehistóricos del territorio uruguayo (The prehistoric peoples of the Uruguayan Territory),* which subsequently was edited and published posthumously by Daniel Vidart (1965). As these two works indicate, Muñoa was influenced considerably by the theoretical views of José Imbelloni (1885–1967). Specifically, Muñoa believed that Uruguay had been peopled by successive waves of immigration that had initially involved the "sambaquis," an admixture of "fuéguidos" and "láguidos"; followed by the "bugres" ("láguidos"), and subsequently the "pámpidos" from the Chaco region, and then Amazon agriculturalists. Unlike Imbelloni and many other South American investigators of the period, Muñoa did not attribute a great time depth to human occupation of the Americas.

Mónica Sans

See also Argentina; Imbelloni, José; Uruguay

Bibliography
SELECTED WORKS
Contribuciones a la Antropología Física del Uruguay, I: Los primitivos pobladores del Este. *Anales del Museo de Historia Natural de Montevideo* 6 (2 ser):1–19, 1954; Los pueblos prehistóricos del territorio uruguayo, y notas de Daniel Vidart. In: P. Rivet & D. Vidart (eds) *Amerindia.* Vol. 3. Montevideo: Centro de Estudios Arqueológicos y Antropológicos, 1965, pp. 9–70.

SECONDARY SOURCES
R. Maruca Sosa: *La Nación Charrúa.* Montevideo, 1957.

Mutation

A mutation is an inherited discontinuity. Though presently applied to strictly genetic phenomena, the term has vacillated in its meaning between what we now call phenotypes and genotypes. The term was originally coined in 1869 by the Austrian paleontologist Wilhelm Waagen (1841–1900) to denote a leap from one stable species morphology to another (the similarity of this to punctuated equilibria has been noted by Niles Eldredge [1979]).

The first application of the term "mutation" to genotypic phenomena was made in 1901 by the Dutch botanist Hugo de Vries (1848–1935), though the distinction between genotype and phenotype was not drawn until the close of the first decade by the Danish botanist Wilhelm Johannsen (1857–1927). Vries' "Mutation Theory" (1901) maintained that a new species was formed in a single generation by a major genetic change, stably inherited. His research centered on the evening primrose, *Oenothera lamarckiana*, later understood to be particularly subject to chromosomal translocation. These specific sorts of genetic changes result in the saltational phenotypic patterns observed by Vries.

Although the English biologist William Bateson (1861–1926) was responsible for giving the name "genetics" to the scientific study of heredity and variation and espoused a theory of evolution that focused on discontinuity, he generally avoided the word "mutation." It was the German geneticist Richard Goldschmidt (1878–1958), later an emigré to the University of California, Berkeley, who revived the theory of saltational evolution in the 1920s and 1930s. By that time, Johannsen's (1909) term "genes" had come into common use for the Mendelian hereditary units; and the spontaneously arising fruit-fly variants analyzed by Thomas Hunt Morgan's (1866–1945) group at Columbia University had come to be regarded as "point mutations," as they involved relatively minor pathological changes to the fly's morphology that could be localized to particular regions of the fruit fly's chromosomes.

Goldschmidt (1937) denied the existence of discrete genes and of spontaneous changes in their nature. Instead, he constructed a model wherein all genetic changes involved chromosomal structure. Point mutations were very minuscule chromosomal changes, and these were not the stuff of transspecific evolution. That was caused, rather, by a scrambling of the genetic architecture, a "chromosomal repatterning" process, whose product would be a macromutation, or a "hopeful monster" (Goldschmidt 1933). In ignoring population processes, and in drawing a direct one-to-one association between genotypic processes and phenotypic patterns, Goldschmidt failed to win many adherents among geneticists.

The discovery in the 1970s that some organisms were far more similar genetically than phenotypically led some workers to revive Goldschmidt's views (Wilson et al. 1975; Gould 1977). Since the kinds of mutations that accounted for the detectable levels of genetic diversity failed to explain the extent of phenotypic diversity, it was suggested that another kind of mutation—namely, regulatory mutation—was at the root of phenotypic change (Wilson et al. 1974). Though there are certainly genes that regulate the activity of other genes, the difficulty of this view lies again in the direct translation of genotypic processes into phenotypic products. Phenotypes actually are emergent properties of genetic systems, often being stably produced in spite of considerable genetic variation, a property called by C.H. Waddington (1957) "buffering" or "canalization." There consequently seems little need to invoke specific classes of mutations as being themselves direct causes of morphological or anatomical evolution.

The American geneticist Hermann Muller (1890–1967) revolutionized experimental genetics with his demonstration in the 1920s that mutations could be induced with certain forms of radiation. Rates of mutation that have been measured in the human species average about 10^{-5} mutations per locus per generation, with a range of about three orders of magnitude. With such breadth, it has proved difficult to distinguish normal mutation rates from aberrant ones. Consequently, it has not been possible to demonstrate a significantly increased incidence of new mutations even in the offspring of survivors of the Hiroshima and Nagasaki atomic bombs, though it almost certainly exists (Schull et al. 1981).

Because mutations are random alterations to a genetic system that has been constructed over eons by natural selection, most individual mutations that affect the phenotype would be expected to affect it adversely. This, however, turns out to be an oversimplification. Since most DNA (deoxyribonucleic acid) is not expressed phenotypically, it follows that most alterations to it are also not expressed phenotypically. Since humans live in structured populations, mutations that are only slightly disadvantageous can spread by genetic drift in spite of their effects.

But more significantly, the view of mutations as being random knocks to a precisely engineered system has often implied the existence of a single optimal homozygous genotype, against which any specific mutation is degenerative. The geneticist Theodosius

Dobzhansky (1900–1975) identified this assumption as Platonic and developed an alternative model, wherein the optimal genotypes are heterozygotes (cf. Dobzhansky 1955). In this "balance model" (as opposed to the "classical model" of Morgan and Muller), a pool of genetic variation is necessary for a population to thrive. Within constraints, therefore, mutations can ultimately be beneficial by making more individuals heterozygous at more loci (Beatty 1987). This also provides the simplest explanation for the well-known phenomena of "inbreeding depression" (inbreeding promotes homozygosity) and "hybrid vigor" (hybridization restores heterozygosity). Although the actual genetic mechanisms are not well understood, this view seems to be borne out by studies of fruit flies in the 1950s and 1960s, by the high level of enzyme polymorphism discovered in the 1960s, and by studies of the immune system in the 1980s.

Modern views of mutation highlight three aspects of its role in evolution. First, the nature of a particular mutation is random with respect to adaptation—that is, a mutation appears regardless of any necessity for it. Second, the physical size of a mutation is generally not correlated with the size of its effect upon the phenotype. The complex phenotype associated with sickle-cell anemia is caused by the smallest kind of genetic change (a nucleotide substitution), while no effect at all may be the result of translocating entire chromosome segments. And third, the molecular basis of mutations appears to be highly heterogeneous.

Jonathan Marks

See also Dobzhansky, Theodosius; Genetics (Mendelian); Molecular Anthropology; Punctuated Equilibria

Bibliography
J. Beatty: Weighing the risks: Stalemate in the classical/balance controversy. *Journal of the History of Biology* 20:289–319, 1987; H. De Vries: Die Mutationstheorie. Leipzig, Veit, 1901. Translation: *The mutation theory*. London: Kegan Paul, 1902; T. Dobzhansky: A review of some fundamental concepts and problems of population genetics. *Cold Spring Harbor Symposia on Quantitative Biology* 20:1–15, 1955; N. Eldredge: Alternative approaches to evolutionary theory. *Bulletin of the Carnegie Museum of Natural History* 13:7–19, 1979; R.B. Goldschmidt: Some aspects of evolution. *Science* 78:539–547, 1933; R.B. Goldschmidt: Spontaneous chromatin rearrangements and the theory of the gene. *Proceedings of the National Academy of Sciences* 23:621–623, 1937; S.J. Gould: The return of hopeful monsters. *Natural History* 86:22–30, 1977; W.L. Johannsen: *Elemente der Exacten Erbichkeitslehre*. Jena: Fischer, 1909; W.L. Johannsen: The genotype conception of heredity. *American Naturalist* 45:129–159, 1911; W.J. Schull et al.: Genetic effects of atomic bombs: A reappraisal. *Science* 213:1120–1227, 1981; C.H. Waddington: *The strategy of the genes*. London: Allen & Unwin, 1957; A.C. Wilson et al.: Two types of molecular evolution: Evidence from studies of interspecific hybridization. *Proceedings of the National Academy of Sciences* 71:2843–2847, 1974; A.C. Wilson et al.: Social structuring of mammalian populations and rate of chromosomal evolution. *Proceedings of the National Academy of Sciences* 72:5061–5065, 1975.

Mydlarski, Jan (1892–1956)

Born in Pilzno, Poland, Mydlarski completed his secondary, undergraduate, and graduate studies at the University of Lvov. He studied anthropology under Jan Czekanowski (1882–1965), completing his doctoral work in 1922. As this work indicates Mydlarski had an early interest in ABO blood groups and the demonstration by Ludwik Hirszfeld (1884–1954) that these blood groups had variable frequencies in different human populations (cf. Hirszfeld 1919).

From 1931 until World War II, he was head of the Department of Anthropology of the Central Institute of Physical Education in Warsaw, which had been founded in 1929. During that period, he pioneered the development of a system of standards for motor fitness for children and adolescents.

From 1945 to 1949, Mydlarski held the Chair of Anthropology at the Maria Curie-Skłodowska University at Lublin. In 1949, he moved to Wrocław in Lower Silesia, where he had been offered the Chair of Anthropology in the newly created university there. From that position, Mydlarski soon emerged as an influential figure in the postwar Polish scientific community. In addition to becoming president of the newly reorganized Zakiad Antropologii Polskiej Akademii Nauk (Institute of Anthropology, Polish Academy of Sciences), he also chaired the Komitet Antropologii Polskiej Akademii Nauk (Anthropological Committee of the Polish Academy) and held the editorship of the country's two anthropological journals: *Przegląd Antropologiczny,* which had been founded prior to World War II; and the newly founded *Materiały i Prace Antropologiczne*. It was largely because of his political clout that the Institute of Anthropology of the Polish Academy of Sciences was founded in 1953 in Wrocław, with Mydlarski as its first director. Indeed, as a direct consequence, Wrocław became and remains the largest anthropological center in Poland. Just prior to his death in 1956, Mydlarski was also instrumental in launching the first major postwar anthropological survey of Poland, which was conducted between 1955 and 1958 under the direction of his longtime assistant, S. Górny. Thus, in addition to making a number of significant contributions to the corpus of anthropological knowledge, he was also the major architect of postwar Polish anthropology.

Janusz Piontek

See also Czekanowksi, Jan; Molecular Anthropology; Poland

Bibliography
SELECTED WORKS
    Recherches seroanthropologiques en Pologne. Paris: 1923; Analiza antropologiczna ludności powiatu pilźnieńskiego. *Archiwum Towarzystwa Naukowego we Lwowie.* 3:1–80, 1924; Sprawozdanie z wojskowego zdjęcia antropologicznego Polski. *Kosmos* 50:530–578, 1925; Zagadnienie miernika w wychowaniu fizycynym. *Sprawozdania Towardzystwa Naukowego Warszawskiego* 27:1–3, 1934; Sprawność fizyczna młodzieży w Polsce. *Przegląd Fizjologii Ruchu* 6:1–109, 403–486, 1934–1935; Anthropological map of the Carpathian populations. *Przegląd Antropologiczny* 16:169–174, 1949.

SECONDARY SOURCES
    L. Hirszfeld: Serological differences between the blood of different races. *Lancet* ii:675–679, 1919; J.Piontek & A. Malinowski: *Teoria w Polskiej Szkole antropologicznej.* Posnaň: Uniwersytet im. Adama Mickiewicza, 1985; W. Stęślicka [-Mydlarska]: Jan Mydlarski jako zoolog. *Przegląd Zoologiczny* 2:97–101, 1957; W. Stęślicka [-Mydlarska]: Prace Jana Mydlarskiego z antropologenezy i genezy ras. *Materiały i Prace Antropologiczne* 76:5–10, 1968.

Napier, John Russell (1917–1987)

Born in Old Windsor, Berkshire, England, Napier trained as a medical doctor at St. Bartholomew's Hospital Medical School, London. After qualifying in 1943, he held a series of medical and teaching posts in London at Hill End Hospital (St. Bartholomew's, 1943–1946), the London School of Medicine for Women (now the Royal Free Hospital School of Medicine, 1946–1949 and 1952–1967) and St. Thomas' Hospital Medical School (1949–1952). He also held a one-year visiting professorship at Iowa State University, Ames. His initial clinical interest in peripheral nerve injuries provided the basis for his primary research focus on the functional anatomy of the hand and foot. Contributions from this period include his well-known classification of human grips as well as papers on the function of the carpometacarpal joint of the thumb, shoe wear, and fibular movement. His interest in the function of the hand also extended to sleight of hand, his talent as a magician leading to the deputy chairmanship of the Council of the Magic Circle in 1954.

On the strength of his anatomical work during the 1950s, Wilfrid Edward Le Gros Clark (1895–1971) invited Napier to become involved in research on African fossil hominoids. In 1959, Napier published his now classic monograph on the forelimb of the early Miocene fossil primate, *Proconsul africanus* (with P.R. Davis). His first paper on hominid fossil hand bones (metacarpals from Swartkrans) was also published in 1959, and his first paper on living primates (hand function) appeared a few years later (cf. Napier 1961).

His developing interest in primate biol-

ogy led to the formation in the early 1960s at the Royal Free Hospital of the Unit of Primatology and Human Evolution, which became the center for primate research in Britain during the 1960s and the mecca for many visiting primatologists. This was also the period of his most productive research. At the invitation of Louis S.B. Leakey (1903–1972), he undertook the analysis of the Olduvai postcranial remains (with M.H. Day and P.R. Davis) that resulted in the coauthorship with Leakey and Phillip V. Tobias of the 1964 paper that established *Homo habilis* as a new species. It was his work on the functional abilities of the Olduvai hand (1962a) that provided the basis for the species name *habilis,* or "handy man." This was also the period of the publication of his widely cited works on brachiation (1963) and the evolution of bipedal walking in the hominids (1964).

In 1967, Napier was invited to establish and direct the Primate Biology Program for the National Museum of Natural History, Smithsonian Institution, Washington, D.C. In 1969, he returned to London to direct a similar unit at Queen Elizabeth College, University of London. In 1973, he accepted a visiting professorship of primate biology at Birbeck College, University of London, a position he held until his retirement in 1976.

Napier's wide interests extended well beyond functional and comparative anatomy, and he has been described as the first primate paleobiologist—emphasizing in his research and teaching that fossils were once living creatures and that to understand them it is necessary to consider their environment as well as their functional morphology and life-history patterns. He was one of the first primate paleontologists to be interested in every aspect of the life and behavior of living primates and to provide an interpretative context for the fossils. His broad interests in behavior, ecology, and taxonomy are evident in his *Handbook of Living Primates* (written with his wife, Prue Napier, in 1967), in his edited volume *Old World Monkeys* (also with Prue Napier, 1970a), and in the broad interests of his research students.

Napier was the founding president of the Primate Society of Great Britain (1967–1970), and through this society he was active in captive husbandry and in the conservation of primates and their habitats. He was also an enthusiastic popularizer of the field through lectures, television and radio broadcasts, and books.

Leslie Aiello

See also Clark, (Sir) Wilfrid Edward Le Gros; *Homo habilis*; Leakey, Louis Seymour Bazett; Olduvai Gorge; Paleoprimatology; Primate Field Studies; Tobias, Phillip V(allentine)

Bibliography
SELECTED WORKS
The form and function of the carpometacarpal joint of the thumb. *Journal of Anatomy* 89:362–369, 1955; The prehensile movements of the human hand. *Journal of Bone and Joint Surgery* 38B:902–913, 1956; Fossil metacarpals from Swartkrans. *Fossil Mammals of Africa* 17:1–18, 1959; Fossil hand bones from Olduvai Gorge. *Nature* 196:409–441, 1962a; Studies of the hand of living primates. *Proceedings of the Zoological Society of London* 134:647–657, 1962b; Brachiation and brachiators. *Symposia of the Zoological Society of London* 10:183–195, 1963; The evolution of bipedal walking in the hominids. *Archives of Biology* (Supplement) 75:673–708, 1964; The evolution of the human hand. *Proceedings of the Royal Institution* 40(187):544–557, 1965.

Paleoecology and catarrhine evolution. In: J.R. Napier & P.H. Napier (eds) *Old World monkeys: Evolution, systematics, and behaviour.* New York: Academic Press, 1970a, pp. 53–95; *The roots of mankind.* Washington, D.C.: Smithsonian Institution Press, 1970b; (with P.R. Davis) The forelimb skeleton and associated remains of *Proconsul africanus. Fossil Mammals of Africa* 16:1–70, 1959; Prehensibility and opposability in the hand of primates.

Symposia of the Zoological Society of London 5: 115–132, 1961; (with L.S.B. Leakey & P.V. Tobias) A new species of the genus *Homo* from Olduvai Gorge. *Nature* 202:7–9, 1964; (with P.H. Napier) *Handbook of living primates.* London: Academic Press, 1967; (with P.H. Napier) *The natural history of the primates.* London: British Museum (Natural History), 1985.

ARCHIVAL SOURCES
J.R. Napier Collection: Department of Anthropology, University College, London, Gower Street, London WC1E 6BT, England.

SECONDARY SOURCES
L.C. Aiello (ed): Primates in Evolution. *Journal of Human Evolution* (John Napier Memorial Issue) 20:239–289, 1992.

Nathan, Hilel (1917–1986)

Nathan was born in Moises Ville, Argentina, where his parents, Russian and Lithuanian immigrants, had settled in a community established in the 1890s by the (Baron Maurice de) Hirsch Jewish Colonization Association. He studied medicine at the medical school of the National University of the Litoral in Argentina, where he received his M.D. degree in 1941. After a decade of practicing medicine in Moises Ville, Nathan immigrated to Israel, where he initially worked as a physician at the Kibbutz Mefalsim, which had been founded in the Negev by a group of Argentinian immigrants. In 1952, he was invited to join the Department of Anatomy of the newly founded Hadassah Medical School in Jerusalem (HMSJ), where he reached the status of associate professor. Shortly after his appointment at the HMSJ, Nathan was the recipient of the Judah Magnes Fellowship, which allowed him to study abroad. Thus, between 1955 and 1956, he studied anatomy and physical anthropology in the United States: in Philadelphia at Jefferson Medical College and the University of Pennsylvania, in Cleveland at the Case Western Reserve University, and in New York at the American Museum of Natural History. Later, beginning in 1962, Nathan spent a sabbatical year working at the Albert Einstein College of Medicine of Yeshiva University in New York. In 1965–1966, the Sackler School of Medicine of Tel Aviv University was opened, and Nathan was invited to establish and head its Department of Anatomy and Anthropology (DAA), where he nurtured an intimate relationship between anatomy and biological anthropology from both a research and an educational point of view.

During his twenty-year tenure as professor and head of the DAA, Nathan pursued wide-ranging research interests, encompassing skeletal biology, paleoanthropology, paleopathology, population genetics, dermatoglyphics, as well as important anatomical-surgical studies, many of which have significant anthropological implications. (For a complete listing of publications of which he was author or coauthor, see Kobyliansky, 1986, which can be obtained through the DAA at Tel Aviv University.)

Nathan died in Ramat-Gan, Israel, on 4 August 1986.

Marcus S. Goldstein

See also Israel

Bibliography
SELECTED WORKS
The skeletal material from Nahal Hever. *Atiquot* 3:165–175, 1961; Osteophytes of the vertebral column: Anatomical study of their development according to age, race, and sex with consideration as to their etiology and significance. *Journal of Bone and Joint Surgery* 44:243–268, 1962; (with B. Arensburg & M.S. Goldstein) The epipalaeolithic (Natufian) population in Israel. *Dos Arquivos de Anatomia e Antropologia* 1:205–221, 1975; (with B. Arensburg et al.) Skeletal remains of Jews from the Hellensitic, Roman, and Byzantine periods in Israel. *Bulletins et Mémoires de la Société d'Anthropologie de Paris* 7:279–295, 1980; (with M.S. Goldstein et al.) Pathology of Bedouin skeletal remains from two sites in Israel. *American Journal of Physical Anthropology* 45:621–640, 1976; (with N. Haas) On the presence of cribra orbitalia in apes and monkeys. *American Journal of Physical Anthropology* 24:351–360, 1966a.

(with N. Haas) Rapport préliminaire sur les squelettes trouves dans un cimitière antique d'Acre. In: *Memorie dell' Istituto Lombardo Accademia di Scienze e Lettere* 29:567–595, 1966b; (with I. Hershkovitz et al.) Mutilation of the uvula among Bedouins of the south Sinai. *Israel Journal of Medical Sciences* 18:774–778, 1982; (with E. Kobyliansky et al.) ABO, MNS, and Rhesus blood-group systems in some Jewish populations of Israel. *Zeitschrift für Morphologie und Anthropologie* 73:97–106, 1982; (with E. Kobyliansky et al.) The

reciprocal influence of the different finger pattern types on their ridge-count value. *Anthropologischer Anzeiger* 41:209–215, 1983; (with H. Weinberg et al.) A simple method of inducing erect posture in baboons. *American Journal of Physical Anthropology* 22:321–327, 1964.

ARCHIVAL SOURCES
N. Hilel Papers: Department of Anatomy and Anthropology, Sackler School of Medicine, Tel Aviv University, Ramat Aviv, Tel Aviv 69978, Israel.

SECONDARY SOURCES
Anonymous: Biography of Professor Hilel Nathan. In: E. Kobyliansky (ed) *Anatomical and anthropological studies with clinical and surgical applications: Collected works.* Tel Aviv: Ramot, 1986.

National Anthropological Archives (USA)

This unit of the Department of Anthropology of the National Museum of Natural History, Smithsonian Institution, Washington, D.C., is devoted to the collection, preservation, and servicing of papers of American anthropologists and records of anthropological organizations.

The National Anthropological Archives (NAA) was founded in 1879 as the archives of the Bureau of American Ethnology. At its inception, it included textual items concerning American Indians that had been collected by the Smithsonian since the 1850s and by several federal Geological Surveys since 1870 (cf. Pilling 1881). To this, the Bureau of American Ethnology added field notes and other documents amassed by its staff and collaborators. By 1950, the archives had also acquired photographic negatives of American Indians made under the auspices of the Geological Surveys, as well as many important collections of photographic prints. When the Bureau of American Ethnology was merged with the Department of Anthropology of the United States National Museum in 1965, the archives gained the department's store of documents, some of which concerned cultures other than those of the American Indians. In 1968, the archives acquired its present name and purpose. That same year, the American Anthropological Association (AAA) recommended that its members who had not made other arrangements for final disposition of their papers consider the National Anthropological Archives as a repository (cf. AAA 1962–1982).

Among the archives' holdings are papers

of physical anthropologists Aleš Hrdlička (1869–1943), Carleton S. Coon (1904–1981), J. Lawrence Angel (1915–1986), Marcus Solomon Goldstein (1906–), Muzaffer Süleyman Şenyürek (1915–1961), and William H. Sheldon (1898–1977). The holdings also include records of the American Association of Physical Anthropologists and the American Dermatoglyphics Society, plus photographic materials and computer printouts of the United States Army Survey of American Male Body Build made in 1946 under the direction of physical anthropologist Francis Eugene Randall (1914–1949) and used by his mentor at Harvard University, Earnest A. Hooton (1887–1954) in producing studies for the U.S. Army during the period 1948–1951. The records of the Randall survey were donated by the U.S. Army, as were the scientific records, captured after World War II, of studies on non-Jewish Poles that were carried out under the auspices of the Institut für Deutsche Östarbeit, which was the cultural and intellectual arm of the Nazi-dominated General Government of Poland during the war.

In addition, there are records concerning the identification of human remains from the Korean War ("Operation Glory"). Smaller amounts of physical-anthropological materials are distributed widely throughout other sets of documents. Relevant administrative records include records of the Department of Anthropology of the National Museum of Natural History, the American Anthropological Association, and the Smithsonian Institution River Basin Survey.

James R. Glenn

See also Angel, J(ohn) Lawrence; Coon, Carleton S(tevens); Hooton, E(arnest), A(lbert); Hrdlička, Aleš; Şenyürek, Muzaffer Süleyman; Sheldon, William H(erbert)

Bibliography
ARCHIVAL SOURCES
Records of the American Anthropological Association (AAA), Resolutions, 1962–1982: National Anthropological Archives, National Museum of Natural History, Smithsonian Institution, Washington, D.C. 20560.

SECONDARY SOURCES
J.R. Glenn: *Guide to the National Anthropological Archives, Smithsonian Institution*. Washington, D.C.: Government Printing Office, 1993; J.C. Pilling: Catalogue of linguistic manuscripts in the library of the Bureau of American Ethnology. In: *First Annual Report of the Bureau of American Ethnology, 1879–1880*. Washington, D.C.: Government Printing Office, 1881, pp. 555–577.

Naulette, La

In this limestone cave 28 m above the Lesse River, on its left bank near Dinant in the province of Namur, Belgium, the paleontologist Édouard François Dupont (1841–1911) discovered, in January 1866, an edentulous human jaw in association with the remains of extinct mammalian bones (Dupont 1866). Based on this associated fauna, he conjectured that the jaw dated from the "Mammoth Age," which according to the chronology established by the French paleontologist Éduoard Lartet (1801–1871) was equivalent to the Lower Quaternary (cf. Lartet 1861). He also suggested that the animal bones were the residue of meals consumed by the human occupants of the cave (Dupont 1867). No artifacts were recovered from the site.

Dupont's discovery aroused great interest, and during the coming decades there was considerable speculation about the jaw's significance. Although later attributed by early-twentieth-century workers to Neandertals, throughout the second half of the nineteenth-century this affinity was obscured by the lack of suitable comparative fossils.

Among the first to debate this specimen was the physician Franz Pruner-Bey (1808–1882) at a meeting of the Société d'Anthropologie in Paris. Like Dupont, he, too, believed the specimen manifested a number of primitive features, and he was clearly struck by the apparent absence of a chin and the size of the dentition inferred from the alveoli, but he stopped short of claiming the specimen had simian features (Pruner-Bey 1866). In marked contrast, the French anthropologist Paul Broca (1824–1880) commented that he believed the jaw's morphology approached the "type of the apes" (Pruner-Bey 1866:594), and he went on to note that it provided the first (tentative) evidence of the probable link between humans and apes. This view was reiterated by Broca's successor in Paris, Paul Topinard (1830–1911), who revisited the La Naulette specimen in 1886. Although the specimen's true identity was still obscured by a paucity of comparative fossil hominid material, Topinard believed the earlier descriptions of the jaw were distortions. From a comparison with modern human jaws, he concluded that the chin of La Naulette, while re-

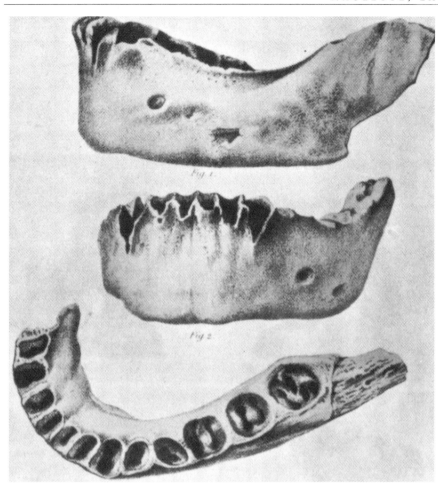

Fig. 1. The Naulette jaw.
After E. Dupont (1866).

ceding, was not entirely absent, merely poorly developed (Topinard 1886). He also corrected a number of other anatomical details, all of which he contended served to support Broca's general thesis. Although the thrust of Topinard's defense of La Naulette as a transitional form was supported by the discoveries later that year at Spy (Belgium), it was not until the beginning of the twentieth century that its Neandertal affinities were essentially recognized (cf. Keith 1915)—and thus it came to represent the first Neandertal mandible to be discovered. (For a more detailed summary of La Naulette's early history, see Trinkaus & Shipman 1993; for a modern assessment, see Twiesselmann 1958.)

Frank Spencer

See also Broca, Paul (Pierre); Neandertals; Spy; Topinard, Paul

Bibliography
É. Dupont: Étude sur les fouilles scientifiques exécutées pendantl'hiver de 1865–1866 dans les cavernes des bords de la Lesse. *Bulletins de l'Académie royale de Belgique* 22:44–45, 1866; É. Dupont: Étude sur cinq cavernes explorées dans la vallée de la Lesse et le ravin de Falmignoul pendant l'été de 1866. *Bulletins de l'Académie royale de Belgique* 23:245–255, 1867; A. Keith: *The antiquity of man.* London: Murray, 1915; E. Lartet: Nouvelles recherches sur la coexistence de l'homme et des grands mammifères fossiles réputés caractéristiques de la dernière epoques géologique. *Annales des Sciences Naturelles* 15 (4th ser.):177–253, 1861; F. Pruner-Bey: Sur la mâchoire de la Naulette (Belgique). *Bulletins de la Société d'Anthropologie de Paris* 1 (2d ser.):584–603, 1866; P. Topinard: Les caractères simiens de la mâchoire de la Naulette. *Revue d'Anthropologie* 1 (3d ser.):385–431, 1886; E. Trinkaus & P. Shipman: *The Neandertals: Changing the image of mankind.* New York: Knopf, 1993; F. Twiesselmann: Les Néanderthaliens découverts en Belgique. In: G.H.R. von Koenigswald (ed) *Hundert Jahre Neanderthaler.* Utrecht: Kemink, 1958, pp. 63–71.

Neandertal (Feldhofer Grotte)

During the first half of the nineteenth century, the romantic and scenic Düssel River Valley and associated gorge, situated 13 km east of Düsseldorf, Germany, had been a favorite rendezvous place for artists and poets. From about 1850, this beautiful area was named "Neanderthal" after the reformed preacher, composer, and poet Joachim Neander (1650–1680), who had lived in Düsseldorf from 1674 to 1679 and had been a frequent vistor to the area. It was around the 1850s that industrial exploitation of the underlying limestone in the valley and gorge began. By the beginning of August 1856, the quarrying activity in the gorge had reached the karst formation known as the "Feldhofer Grotte." This extensive cave (now destroyed), was situated in the cliffs on the south bank of the Düssel, with its entrance 20 m above the bank. From all accounts, it was while the clay sediment covering the cave's floor was being removed (to avoid contamination of the lime) that several human bones were found. Alerted by this discovery, the owner of the quarry, W. Beckershoff, who happened to be passing by, urged the quarrymen to save all of the bones they could find. The quarrymen subsequently salvaged the calvarium (skullcap), the right clavicle and scapula, both humeri, five rib fragments, both ulnae, the right radius, the left hipbone, and two femora. No cultural or faunal remains were recovered.

The skeletal remains were later delivered into the care of Johann C. Fuhlrott (1803–1877), a teacher at nearby Elberfeld, who was known for his interest in fossils. He recognized immediately that they belonged to a human skeleton, which, according to the workers who found it, had been buried 60 cm below the surface with the head pointed toward the cave's entrance. The find was publicized in several newspapers at the beginning of September 1856, and during the winter of 1856–1857 the remains were examined in detail by the anthropologist Hermann Schaaffhausen (1816–1893) of Bonn. Fuhlrott and Schaaffhausen presented details of the find to the Gesellschaft für Natur- und Heilkunde (Natural History Society) in Bonn in 1857. In 1858, the first comprehensive description of the remains was published by Schaaffhausen in the *Verhandlungen des naturhistorischen Vereins der preussischen Rheinlande und Westfalens;* this was followed in 1859 by Fuhlrott's description of the discovery and the geology of the site.

In 1864, the British anatomist William King (1809–1886) assigned the name *Homo neanderthalensis* to the remains. While Fuhlrott and Schaaffhausen both considered the Neandertal skeleton to be of Diluvial (Pleistocene) age, this attribution, along with King's (1864) classification, was generally rejected (cf. King 1863). Among the many who resisted these interpretations was Rudolf Virchow (1821–1902), who was of the opinion that the morphology of the Neandertal skeleton was pathological (cf. Virchow 1872). It was not until after the recovery of the Spy (Belgium) material in 1886 that the significance of the Neander skeleton was finally realized (cf. Fraipont & Lohest 1886; Fraipont 1895). Another two decades were to pass before the works published by Gustav Schwalbe (1844–1916) and Hermann Klaatsch (1863–1916) in 1901 finally refuted Virchow's interpretation, thus proving that the results of Schaaffhausen's earlier research efforts were essentially correct. Schwalbe's study was a detailed reexamination of the calvarium found in 1856, while Klaatsch concerned himself with the postcranial material. Both studies endorsed the observations made by Julien Fraipont (1857–1910) that the Spy material closely resembled the skeleton from the Neander Valley.

In July 1991, an interdisciplinary team of German scholars began a reinvestigation of the skeletal remains (cf. Schmitz & Pieper 1992; Schmitz et al. 1994). These investigations include the use of chemicophysical methods to obtain a more precise dating of the bones; tracking the history of their conservation; and mineralogical, anatomical, prehistoric, and forensic analyses. Prehistoric and forensic investigations are concentrating on the documentation and qualification of the scratches and particularly the cut marks on the bones. Although some of these marks can be attributed to the recovery of the bones in 1856, the cut marks on the calvarium appear to be of a different nature and might well be connected with the burial rites.

The Neandertal skeleton, since the death of Fuhlrott in 1877, has been preserved in the Rheinische Landesmuseum, Bonn.

Ralf W. Schmitz

See also Fraipont, (Jean-Joseph) Julien; Klaatsch, Hermann; Neandertals; Schaaffhausen, Hermann; Schwalbe, Gustav; Spy; Virchow, Rudolf

Bibliography

J. Fraipont: La raçe "imaginaire" de Cannstadt. *Bulletin de la Société d'Anthropologie*

(Bruxelles) 14:32–34, 1895; J. Fraipont &
M. Lohest: La race humaine de Néanderthal
ou de Canstadt en Belgique. *Bulletin de
l'Académie royale de Belgique* 12:741–784
(Bruxelles) 1886; J.C. Fuhlrott: Vortrag
vom 2. Juni über den Fund von
Menschenknochen im Neanderthal.
*Verhandlungen des Naturhistorischen Vereines
der preussischen Rheinlande und Westfalens.*
Korrespondensblatt 50, 1857; J.C. Fuhlrott:
Menschliche Uenerreste aus einer
Felsengrotte des Düsselthals. *Verhandlungen
des Naturhistorischen Vereines der preussischen
Rheinlande und Westfalens* 16:131–153,
1859; W. King: The reputed fossil man of
Neanderthal. *Quarterly Journal of Science*
1:88–97, 1864.

W. King: On the Neanderthal skull.
Anthropological Review 1:393–394, 1863;
H. Klaatsch: Erwiderung auf einen Vortrag
Virchows an 7. August. *Correspondenzblatt
der deutschen Gesellschaft für Anthropologie,
Ethnologie, und Urgeschichte* 10:89 ff, 1901;
H. Schaaffhausen: Vortrag vom 2. Juni zu
den Menschenknochen aus dem Neander-
thal. *Verhandlungen des Naturhistorischen
Vereines der preussischen Rheinlande und
Westfalens* 14:50 ff., 1857; H. Schaaff-
hausen: Zur Kenntniß der ältesten
Rassenschädel. *Müller's Archiv* 5:453–478,
1858; H. Schaaffhausen: *Der Neanderthaler
Fund.* Bonn: Marcus, 1888.

R.-W. Schmitz & P. Pieper:
Schnittspuren und Kratzer. Anthropogene
Veränderungen am Skelett des
Urmenschenfundes aus dem Neandertal-
Vorläufige Befundaufnahme. *Das Rheinische
Landesmuseum Bonn* 2:17–19, 1992; R.-W.
Schmitz et al.: New investigations of the
Homo sapiens neanderthalensis found in 1856.
*Proceedings of the thirteenth meeting of the
International Association of Forensic Sciences,*
1994; G. Schwalbe: Der Neanderthalschädel.
Bonner Jahrbuch 106:1–72, 1901; R.
Virchow: Untersuchung des Neanderthal-
Schädels. *Zeitschrift für Ethnologie* 4:157–
165, 1872; U. Zängl-Kumpf: *Hermann
Schaaffhause, 1816–1893: Die Entwicklung
einer neuen physischen Anthropologie im 19.
Jahrhundert.* Frankfurt: Fischer, 1990.

Editor's Note

Since 1901, when German orthography
was revised, the "h" in Neanderthal has
been omitted in the vernacular name.
However, the name of the species, *Homo
neanderthalensis* (King 1864), according
to the International Code for Zoological
Nomenclature, must continue to be written
with the "h."

Neandertals

The evolutionary significance of the Neandertals has been a continuous point of controversy since the distinctiveness of the original
Neandertal specimen was recognized in 1856.
While several specimens were previously
claimed to represent ancient humans, none
was taken very seriously prior to the
Neandertal skeleton. Thus, the "Neandertal
debate" signals the historical beginnings of
human paleontology.

The original "Neandertaler" posed a series of questions, some of which have been
answered during the intervening years but
many of which remain unanswered. Were
Neandertals an extinct species of human ancestor or simply a "barbaric" race of primitive
Europeans? Alternatively, were they recent
human pathological freaks, suffering from
a unique combination of maladies? If
Neandertals did represent "primitive man,"
what connections to "lower animals," mainly
apes and other primates, were revealed in
their anatomy? And, of course, the ultimate
question: Were they antecedents of modern
humans?

*Race, Progressionism, and Purveyors of Pathology:
1856–1886*

In August 1856, workmen encountered a partial human skeleton during limestone quarrying in the Feldhofer Grotte, located in the
Neander Valley (Tal, in German) near
Düsseldorf, Germany. The bones were entrusted to Johann C. Fuhlrott (1803–1877),
a local teacher and amateur natural historian,
who recognized the potential significance of
the specimen and consulted Hermann
Schaaffhausen (1816–1893), professor of
anatomy at Bonn University. Schaaffhausen,
a pre-Darwinian evolutionist, introduced the
original "Neandertaler" to science early the
next year, arguing that the unique aspects
of its anatomy represented a normal (non-
pathological) condition, typical of the "primitive race" it represented (cf. Schaaffhausen
1858). Schaaffhausen recognized that this
"race" was ape-like in certain morphological
aspects, undoubtedly a contemporary of extinct animals of the Diluvium (Pleistocene),
and thus of some antiquity. But the large brain
of the Feldhofer specimen precluded for
Schaaffhausen its recognition as an ancient
human species.

Schaaffhausen's "primitive race" characterization of Neandertals represents perhaps the most popular interpretation of Neandertals during the third quarter of the nineteenth century. Even the British anatomist and Darwinist Thomas Henry Huxley (1825–1895), who was theoretically disposed to finding transitional species, believed that Neandertals were more akin to a "lower race" of humans than to a missing link between humans and apes (cf. Huxley 1863). As the British historian of science Peter J. Bowler (1986) has shown, most anthropologists and biologists of the period envisioned a racial-succession sequence for Europe during prehistory. Such perspectives were often influenced strongly by Cuverian catastrophism and ideas of cultural/linguistic diffusion and replacement. Thus, they routinely involved denial (or at least avoidance) of an evolutionary explanation for both human biological and cultural change. For others, racial succession was viewed in a neo-Lamarckian framework of purposeful or guided evolution, in which both extinct and extant races (and cultures) were organized along a *scala naturae*, or Chain of Being, from primitive to advanced. In such views, Neandertals were seen as primitive but not qualitatively distinct from living "lower races."

Racial succession is best illustrated by the concepts of the Cannstatt and Aryan races held during the last half of the nineteenth century. In the early 1840s, the Swedish anatomist Anders Adolf Retzius (1796–1860) argued that the indigenous peoples of Europe had been brachycephalic and were replaced by dolichocephalic Aryans from the east, who also introduced Indo-European language into Europe (cf. Retzius 1846). But the recognition, between 1856 and 1886, of dolichocephalic specimens presumably dated to the Pleistocene, including several Neandertals (Feldhofer, Spy, Forbes' quarry) and others (Cro-Magnon, Cannstatt, Eguisheim, Brüx), appeared to establish long-headedness as the indigenous European cranial form. According to this view, these people were later replaced in some areas by more-advanced brachycephalic races. The Cannstatt race was initially defined in 1873 by Armand de Quatrefages (1810–1892) and further developed in collaboration with Théodore Hamy (1842–1908) (cf. Quatrefages & Hamy 1882). As Quatrefages (1873) explained, the "Canstadt [Cannstatt]" race served to designate this indigenous, long-headed primitive European "type," which included the specimens listed above (except Cro-Magnon). The artificial mixture of

Neandertal and more-modern specimens in the Cannstatt race supported the perception that Neandertals were only extreme variants of a primitive race, not a qualitatively separate form of early human.

A second popular, and clearly antievolutionary, explanation for Neandertals during this period is exemplified in the writings of the noted German pathologist and anthropologist Rudolf Virchow (1821–1902). In the 1870s, Virchow argued that the primitive features of the original Neandertaler were the result of pathological alterations brought about by a unique combination of disease and trauma (including rickets and arthritis). Virchow also argued that the advanced age of the individual (based on suture closure) would be attainable only in a sedentary human group, not in hunters and gatherers. Since sedentary living was a recent human development, this invalidated any claim for extensive antiquity for the Feldhofer specimen in Virchow's view (cf. Virchow 1872).

The geological and archeological contexts of the Feldhofer specimen were basically unknown, and its morphology clearly was unique among the known human range. Thus, the possibility that its anatomy was the result of an otherwise unknown combination of pathological conditions was embraced by many individuals with antievolutionary leanings. Even the discoveries of fragmentary (but clearly primitive) mandibles at La Naulette (Belgium) and Šipka (Moravia) in 1866 and 1880, respectively, both in secure association with Mousterian tools and extinct fauna, had little effect on the interpretation of Neandertals. Virchow even suggested that the Šipka remains were also pathological, exhibiting retention of deciduous teeth in an adult mandible, thus "explaining" their primitive appearance (cf. Virchow 1882).

By the 1880s, however, the tide was beginning to turn against both the racial-succession and pathological explanations for Neandertals. This was due in some measure to further discoveries of potential Neandertal skeletal remains from several areas of Europe (cf. Table 1). La Naulette and Šipka suggested that Neandertals were quite ancient, but the remains were just lower jaws and thus not compelling evidence to many. However, the recognition that a strange skull found at Forbes' quarry (Gibraltar) in 1848 was a Neandertal began to cast doubt on the pathological explanation for Feldhofer. It seemed rather unreasonable for two skulls to share this combination of "pathologies" that were un-

TABLE 1. Neandertal Discoveries, 1829–1909

Site/Specimen	Country	Initial Discovery Year	Description
Engis 2	Belgium[a]	1829/1830	cranium of child
Forbes Quarry Neandertal	Gibraltar[a]	1848	cranium with face
Feldhofer Cave	Germany	1856	calotte and partial postcranial skeleton
La Naulette	Belgium	1866	edentulous mandible
Šipka	Czech Republic[b]	1880	mandibular symphasis of child
Spy	Belgium	1886	crania and partial skeletons of 2 adults and 1 child
Bañolas	Spain	1887	mandible
Taubach	Germany	1887	molar teeth
Krapina	Croatia[b]	1899	cranial mandible and postcranial remains of several individuals
Ochoz	Czech Republic[b]	1905	partial mandible
La Chapelle-Aux-Saints	France	1908	cranium, mandible, and partial skeleton
Le Mousteir	France	1908	cranium, mandible, and partial postcranial skeleton of an adolescent[c]
La Quina	France	1908	cranial, mandibular, and postcranial remains of several individuals
La Ferrrassie	France	1909	cranial, mandibular, and partial skeletal remains of several individuals

NOTES: a. Not recognized as a Neandertal until after the discovery of the Spy specimens.

b. Then part of Austro-Hungarian Empire.

c. Postcranial elements lost following World War II.

known in the clinical literature. Despite these hints, little support was given to the suggestion by the British anatomist William King (1809–1886) in 1864 that Neandertals be recognized as an extinct human type and placed in their own species, *Homo neanderthalensis*.

In 1886, two relatively complete human skeletons were recovered from the cave of Spy (Belgium) in clear association with ancient fauna and Mousterian tools. The Belgian anatomist Julien Fraiport (1857–1910) analyzed the skeletons and demonstrated them to be Neandertals. Along with the Belgian archaeologist M. Lohest (1857–1926), Fraipont published his assessment of the Spy skeletons in 1886, which constituted the first systematic description of Neandertals. The Spy specimens confirmed what Šipka, La Naulette, Forbes' quarry, and Feldhofer had previously suggested: Neandertals were clearly ancient and more distinctly separable from "primitive races" than had been commonly recognized. The accumulating number of Neandertal specimens rendered the pathological explanation even more illogical, and it began to fade away. By the end of the century, Neandertals were generally considered to represent an extinct human species.

From Ancestor to Alley-Oop

In a series of publications between 1899 and 1906, the German anatomist Gustav Schwalbe (1844–1916) laid the foundation for the unilineal perspective on human evolution (cf. Schwalbe 1906). Based on his careful comparative analyses of the Feldhofer Neandertal and the Trinil (*Pithecanthropus*) calotte, which had been discovered in Java by the Dutch anatomist Eugène Dubois (1858–1940) in the early 1890s, Schwalbe (1899) argued that Neandertals and the more primitive Trinil *Pithecanthropus* represented logical morphological stages in the ancestry of humans, which bridged to a significant extent the immense structural gap that separated apes and modern humans. A committed Darwinian, Schwalbe also argued that Neandertals were too distinctive to represent only a "primitive race" of *Homo sapiens* and that zoological principles compelled that they be recognized as a separate species from modern people. Schwalbe preferred the taxon *Homo primigenius*—a term used by Ernst Haeckel (1834–1919) in his work *The History of Creation* (1868) to describe the first humans—for Neandertals, rather than King's taxon, *Homo neanderthalensis*. Additionally, Schwalbe's detailed analysis of the Feldhofer Neandertal and his point-by-point refutation of Virchow's arguments resulted in

Fig. 1. Neandertals as a primitive race. Note the divergent hallux on the left foot. From Ludwig Wilser's (1850–1923) Leben und Heimat der Urmenschen. *Leipzig 1910.*

the final dismissal of pathology as a defendable explanation for Neandertal anatomy.

A similar interpretation is reflected in the work of Dragutin Gorjanović-Kramberger (1856–1936), a Croatian paleontologist who directed the excavations at the Hušnjakovo rockshelter near Krapina from 1899 to 1905. Krapina yielded a large series of fragmentary human remains associated with Diluvial (Pleistocene) fauna and Mousterian tools. Gorjanović-Kramberger established that the remains were Neandertals and published the first descriptive/comparative monograph on Neandertals, which of course focused on the Krapina specimens, in 1906. Gorjanović-Kramberger emphasized the variation in the Krapina sample but considered this a reflection of normal variability for Neandertals. He vigorously countered the claim by German anatomist Hermann Klaatsch (1863–1916) that early-modern humans (*Homo aurignaciensis hauseri*) were included in the sample. Gorjanović-Kramberger's extensive writings in both German and Croatian during the first quarter of the twentieth century

strongly supported Neandertals as ancestors of modern humans.

During the first decade of the twentieth century, the unilineal scheme, with Neandertals representing the direct, lineal ancestors of modern humans, seemed entrenched. In France, René Verneau (1852–1938) (cf. Verneau 1924), and in England, Arthur Keith (1866–1955) (cf. Keith 1911) and William Johnson Sollas (1849–1936) (cf. Sollas 1908) accepted the unilineal model, at least during the first decade of the 1900s. Near the end of the decade, however, a discovery was made that ended the short-lived prominence of unilinealism.

In 1908, excavations in the Dordogne region of France yielded a partial Neandertal skeleton from a small cave named La Chapelle-aux-Saints. The specimen was entrusted to Marcellin Boule (1861–1942) of the Muséum National d'Histoire Naturelle in Paris for anatomical study. Boule's analysis, published in a series of articles and a monograph between 1908 and 1913, reaffirmed the distinctiveness of Neandertal morphology and the importance of recognizing Neandertals as a separate species from *Homo sapiens*. Boule placed Neandertals in King's taxon, *Homo neanderthalensis*, and emphasized what he considered to be "simian-like" features of the postcranial skeleton, which among other things would have precluded a totally orthograde (upright) posture. He also noted several primitive cranial features, including the massive supraorbital torus, the absence of the mental eminence, the flattened braincase, and the receding forehead. The form of the braincase, especially the low forehead, offset for Boule the large cranial capacity of the specimen, because it indicated inferior development of the cerebral lobes in Neandertals and, thus, reduced mental abilities compared to later people. Boule's conclusions were that Neandertals were far too primitive and apelike to have given rise to early-modern Europeans (then synonymous with Louis Lartet's [1840–1899] Cro-Magnon skeletons) in the time available, and, consequently, that they should be relegated to a side branch of the human family tree.

Boule's portrayal of Neandertal as stoopshouldered, bent-kneed, divergent big-toed morons has had a lasting effect in scientific and popular images of Neandertals. It has been suggested that Boule was led to this picture of Neandertals in large part because he failed to appreciate the influences of pathology—specifically, degenerative joint dis-

ease—on the specimen. But as Erik Trinkaus (1982) and Michael Hammond (1982) have independently shown, the major factor was certainly his belief, influenced by his mentor Albert Jean Gaudry (1827–1908), that evolution was a branching process, and not a simple lineal one. There should be several extinct branches of the human trunk, and, for Boule, *Homo neanderthalensis* and *Pithecanthropus* (later renamed *Homo erectus*) represented such branches.

Boule's dismissal of Neandertals as reasonable human ancestors occurred at roughly the same time as other candidates for this honor were emerging. Because these "other candidates" provided a better fit with certain prejudices about evolutionary processes prominent at the time, including Boule's passion for branching, the relative abandonment of the unilineal, or Neandertal-phase, model was rapid and relatively widespread.

Ancient Modern Skulls and the Emerging Presapiens Model

At this time, Boule's prime candidates for Cro-Magnon ancestry were the Grimaldi remains, recovered in 1901. Boule considered these anatomically modern specimens to be contemporaries of the Mousterian and Neandertals, thus establishing the existence of a separate lineage for the Cro-Magnons extending back into Mousterian times. Between 1910 and 1912, Arthur Keith (1912) reversed

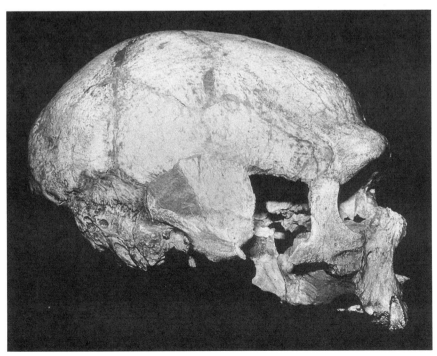

Fig. 2. The Neandertal cranium from La Chapelle-aux-Saints. The projecting supraorbital torus and the relative flat, receding forehead were particularly influential in Marcellin Boule's conception of Neandertals. Courtesy of Musée de l'Homme, Paris.

his support for Schwalbe's model and began to champion specimens from Galley Hill and Ipswich as demonstrating the antiquity of the modern human lineage (cf. Keith 1915). Writing fifty years later, the French paleo-anthropologist Henri Victor Vallois (1889–1981) designated this point of view as the presapiens theory (Vallois 1954).

In 1912, the announced discovery of the Piltdown specimens in England provided evidence that a modern human-like cranial pattern could be traced even further back in prehistory, possibly into the Pliocene. Despite several supposedly primitive features, includ-

ing its very simian-like mandible, the Piltdown cranium generally supported the view held by many influential individuals concerning the early role the emergence of a large brain had played in human evolution. Preeminant among such scholars was the Anglo-Australian anatomist Grafton Elliot Smith (1871–1937), who judged Piltdown's endocast to be primitive and simian-like, but more advanced than that of *Pithecanthropus*. Even Boule, who rejected the other English pre-sapiens specimens (such as Galley Hill and Ipswich), accepted Piltdown's cranium as a reasonable earlier member of the pre-sapiens

Fig. 3. Neandertal Man. An illustration by Kupka, based on Boule's study of La Chapelle-aux-Saints, first published by the French weekly magazine L'Illustration *on 20 February 1909.*

lineage. As Frank Spencer (1990) has documented, Piltdown played well to the preconceptions about human evolution widely held in western Europe during this period and helped to make the pre-sapiens model a powerful and broadly popular explanation for the emergence of modern people.

The Battle between the Wars: 1914–1939
The pre-sapiens model emerged as the most popular explanation for modern human origins during this period. As noted by C. Loring Brace (1964), political issues probably played a role in the model's general appeal. Its scientific popularity was based primarily on the fact that the evolutionary history of other organisms did not seem to show simple lineal progressions, but rather more-complicated, branching phylogenies. Many students of human evolution, Boule in particular, wanted to demonstrate that human evolution also followed a branching pattern and was not biologically "old-fashioned" in its approach.

Suggestions of pre-sapiens specimens outside Europe also came forth at this time. For example, Klaatsch (1910) had argued earlier that modern humans emerged in Asia and then invaded Europe, replacing the Neandertals. But no fossil remains in Asia were known at this time that supported this viewpoint. In the 1930s, the discovery of the Kanam and Kanjera specimens in East Africa by Louis S.B. Leakey (1903–1972) led him to posit the existence of a pre-sapiens lineage in Africa during the Early Pleistocene (cf. Leakey 1953). Despite Leakey's fossils, the major evidence for a pre-sapiens lineage continued to come from Europe.

Not everyone embraced the pre-sapiens model. The Czech-American anthropologist Aleš Hrdlička (1869–1943) believed that modern-human morphology did not have the magnitude of time depth the pre-sapiens supporters claimed. Rather, he believed that earlier humans would have exhibited more-primitive anatomical features, since his perspectives on the evolutionary process precluded long-term stasis, especially in times of environmental change like the Pleistocene. Like Gorjanović-Kramberger before him, he challenged the antiquity of the Piltdown cranium and the association of so "simian" a jaw with it. Also like Gorjanović-Kramberger, Hrdlička (1927) stressed the morphological variability of Neandertals and argued that their morphological overlap with the Aurignacian skeletons from Předmostí and other early-modern specimens demonstrated continuity between Neandertals and early-modern people in Europe.

Hrdlička's views are clearly akin to those of both Schwalbe and Gorjanović-Kramberger, but he accused Schwalbe of having laid the basis of the pre-sapiens model. This curious misinterpretation of Schwalbe probably relates, as Bowler (1986) has indicated, to Hrdlička's misunderstanding of Schwalbe's insistence that Neandertals were a separate species, which he meant in a morphological (or essentialist) sense only. Hrdlička apparently interpreted this as an argument for total morphological discontinuity between Neandertals and modern Euopeans, which was certainly contrary to what Hrdlička saw in the bones.

While Schwalbe and Gorjanović-Kramberger argued for a Neandertal stage in human evolution on the basis of European Neandertals only, discoveries of specimens in Kabwe, Rhodesia, in 1921 and Mount Carmel, Palestine, in the period 1929–1932 expanded the Neandertal range to Africa and Asia. Hrdlička did not argue, however, that modern humans arose from Neandertals throughout their entire range. Rather, he believed that modern humans arose from Neandertals in Europe and then spread into the rest of the world (cf. Spencer & Smith 1981 for further details).

Two other individuals were prominent proponents of a "Neandertal phase" theory at this time. German anthropologists Hans Weinert (1877–1967) (cf. Weinert 1947) and Franz Weidenreich (1873–1948) both supported unilineal models for human evolution, which included a "Neandertal phase of man." However, Weidenreich's (1947) version of the unilineal model was quite different from that of Schwalbe, Gorjanović-Kramberger, and Hrdlička in that he saw the emergence of modern people from regionally differentiated Neandertal groups in Europe, Africa, and Asia. Thus, for Weidenreich, Kabwe was an African Neandertal, and Ngandong was recognized as a Far Eastern, or "tropical," variety. In Weidenreich's view, multiple lineages were evolving toward modern-humankind in several regions of the world, driven by the adaptively related evolution of the brain. These regional lineages preserved regional continuity in terms of morphology but were interconnected enough to prevent speciation. Thus, Weidenreich viewed human evolution as the evolution of a polytypic species stretching all the way back to the initial establishment of regional lineages by *Homo erectus*.

In the pre-sapiens camp, Vallois replaced

Fig. 4. Schematic representation of the role of Neandertals in human evolution. A: Unilineal or Neandertal phase model as presented by René Verneau (1924) and Aleš Hrdlička (1927); B: Presapiens model as depicted by Henri-Victor Vallois (1958); C: Preneandertal model according to Emil Breitinger (1955).

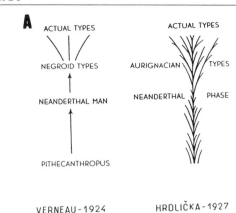

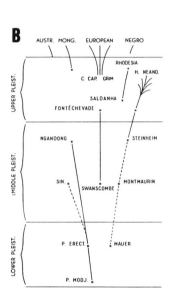

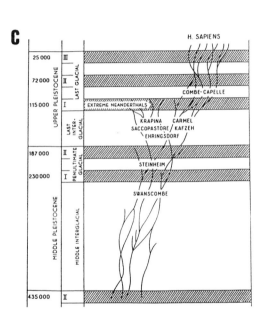

Boule at the Muséum National d'Histoire Naturelle in Paris and as the leading spokesman for the pre-sapiens model in the late 1930s. Many of the earlier pre-sapiens specimens (Grimaldi, Galley Hill, and Ipswich) were demonstrated not to be Neandertal contemporaries, and in 1953 Piltdown was exposed as a fraud. But by the 1950s, Vallois' argument was based on "unequivocal" evidence of the existence of a European lineage distinct from, and more advanced than, Neandertals: the specimens from Swanscombe (England) and the newly excavated site of Fontéchevade (France) (cf. Vallois 1954). These specimens were presumably earlier than Neandertals but purportedly lacked such Neandertal features as a supraorbital torus and an occipital chignon. As Brace (1964) noted, it is interesting that even when its original fossil basis disappeared, the pre-sapiens model persevered by simply substituting new "pre-sapiens" fossils.

Following his analysis of the Mount Carmel skeletons in the 1930s, one prominent pre-sapienist changed his mind. Keith backed away from his previous arguments about the great antiquity of modern humanity and adopted the view that modern humans had, indeed, passed through a stage with some Neandertal features. The suggested 100 ky BP date for the Skhūl hominids also convinced Keith that the earliest modern Europeans, the Cro-Magnons, had migrated from the Near East. Keith's view represents the emergence of the perspective that was to replace the declining pre-sapiens model during the 1950s as the majority opinion on the origin of modern humans. This model is known as the "progressive" Neandertal or pre-Neandertal model.

Adaptive Explanations for Neandertals
In the 1940s and early 1950s, several prominent scholars embraced the idea that modern

humans had evolved from early, or progressive, Neandertals, which had not yet developed the "extreme" morphology characteristic of Würm, or "classic," Neandertals in Europe. The convincing analyses by American paleoanthropologist F. Clark Howell (1925–) in the early 1950s were unquestionably the primary reason for the scientific popularity of this perspective. Howell (1951) argued that the European "classic" Neandertals were the descendents of more-generalized Neandertals but had evolved specialized, cold-adapted morphology during their isolation in Early Würm Europe. Modern people also emerged from generalized (progressive) Neandertals, like those from Mount Carmel, and migrated into Europe during the Middle Würm interstadial. Howell's influence during this period derived from both his thoughtful analyses of the fossil record and his attempts to interpret Neandertals in the context of the neo-Darwinian synthetic theory that characterized this period in biology.

During the early 1960s, C. Loring Brace (1930–) and Carleton S. Coon (1904–1981) also championed adaptive approaches toward deciphering the phylogenetic role of the Neandertals. For Brace, Neandertal morphology was the result of robusticity required by their adaptation to a demanding environment. He particularly focused on anterior dental loading as the factor maintaining Neandertal craniofacial morphology and argued that, with the emergence of more-sophisticated technology, reduced selection would have allowed the establishment of the less robust modern anatomical pattern independently throughout the Old World (Brace 1964, 1967). Coon (1962) believed that Neandertal craniofacial morphology was the result of a cold-adapted nose and mid-face. Additionally, he argued that modern humans arose from regional lineages in several areas of the Old World. Both Coon's and Brace's perspectives served to resurrect the Neandertal-phase, or unilineal, model, using an adaptive framework to explain differences between Neandertals and modern people.

While vestiges of the pre-sapiens model continued to hold on among some French workers until the 1970s, a virtual consensus was reached by the 1960s that some type of Neandertal stage was a part of modern-human ancestry. During this period, Neandertals were considered a worldwide phenomenon, including African and Far Eastern specimens, so the disagreements between supporters of the Neandertal phase and the pre-Neandertal models centered primarily on the phyloge-netic role of European "classic" Neandertals. However, even those who excluded "classic" Neandertals were inclined to consider Neandertals to be members of *Homo sapiens*, perhaps as a distinct subspecies, rather than a separate species.

From the 1950s to the 1970s, the basic biological and behavioral similarities of Neandertals to modern humans were emphasized, and Neandertals were considered once again to be basically an extinct race of *Homo sapiens*. To a considerable extent, this taxonomic view can be traced to the influences of attempts to bring human paleontology into line with the synthetic theory of evolution, which advocated a conservative taxonomy of the hominids. Additionally, the emphasis on the adaptive basis of early human anatomy fostered the belief that morphological changes, like those differentiating Neandertals and modern people, could be brought about relatively quickly as responses to shifts in their natural and cultural environments.

Perspectives Post-1970
The recent history of the Neandertal debate must again be viewed within the context of general trends in biology. The influence of Steven J. Gould and Niles Eldredge's reemphasis on branching (cladogenesis) as the critical process for macroevolution (cf. Eldredge & Gould 1972)—the punctuated equilibrium model, combined with the application of principles of cladistics to the assessment of Middle and late Pleistocene hominids—has resulted in a reemphasis by some paleoanthropologists of the biological and behavioral distinctiveness of Neandertals. The need to demonstrate the existence of branches to the human evolutionary trunk, as well as certain perspectives on how to define species in the fossil record, has also led many scientists (e.g., Rak 1993; Stringer & Gamble 1993) to resurrect *Homo neanderthalensis* as a valid species. These scientists tend to interpret Neandertals as the termination of a lineage of archaic people in Europe and west Asia. For them, this lineage became extinct during the Würm and played at best only a minimal role in the emergence of modern people in that part of the world. Others have tended to stress the inclusion of Neandertals within our species based on evidence of morphological continuity between them and the earliest modern people in Europe and the Near East. This view basically supports a modified version of Weidenreich's conception that polytypism has a long time depth in human biological history.

Supporters of both perspectives have tended to use various techniques to support their points of view. American and British biological anthropologists W.W. Howells (1908–) and C.B. Stringer, respectively, have pioneered the use of multivariate statistical analysis to demonstrate the distinctiveness of Neandertals vis-à-vis recent humans (Howells 1975; Stringer 1974, 1994). Erik Trinkaus (United States), Jean-Jacques Hublin (France), and Yoel Rak (Israel) have used functional morphology to explain the basis of many distinctive features of Neandertal morphology (e.g., Rak 1993; Trinkaus 1983, 1986; see also Trinkaus & Shipman 1992). Anne-Marie Tillier (France) and Nancy Minugh-Purvis (United States) have made considerable strides in unraveling the ontogeny of Neandertals and how it differs from modern people. Recent discoveries of pertinent fossil specimens by Bernard Vandermersch (France) at St. Césaire, the late Mirko Malez (Croatia) at Vindija, and Ofer Bar-Yosef (with Vandermersch) at Kebara, in Israel, have been prominent in arguments concerning the evolutionary role of Neandertals. Finally, proponents of a Neandertal role in our ancestry have identified features and trends that they believe demonstrate a Neandertal contribution to modern Europeans and west Asians (Brose & Wolpoff 1971; Frayer et al. 1993; Smith 1991; Wolpoff 1980). Among those proponents are Milford H. Wolpoff, Fred H. Smith, and David W. Frayer (United States) and Jan Jelinek (Czech Republic).

By the mid-1990s, more was known about Neandertals than any other fossil human group. The fact that paleoanthropologists, even armed with so much information, cannot agree on the interpretation of the Neandertals' role in human evolution is discouraging to many. In a historical science like paleoanthropology, increasing knowledge allows us to ask more detailed and specific questions about the past. In terms of Neandertals, scientists are no longer content with general patterns and broad statements. The recent history of Neandertal studies has been characterized by posing much more precise questions about the biological meaning of their anatomy and their phylogenetic role in human evolution than is possible for any earlier fossil human group.

Fred H. Smith

See also Aryanism; Boule, Marcellin; Cannstatt Skull; Chapelle-Aux-Saints, La; Cro-Magnon; Dubois (Marie) Eugène (François Thomas); Gaudry, Albert Jean; Gibraltar; Gorjanović-Kramberger, Dragutin (Karl); Haeckel, Ernst Heinrich Phillip August; Hamy, Jules Ernest Théodore; Howells, William White; Hrdlička, Aleš; Huxley, Thomas Henry; Keith, (Sir) Arthur; Kebara, Mugharet el- (Israel); Klaatsch, Hermann; Krapina; Leakey, Louis Seymour Bazett; Mount Carmel (Israel); Naulette, La; Neandertal (Feldhofer Grotte); Piltdown; Předmostí; Punctuated Equilibria; Quatrefages (de Breau), Jean Louis Armand de; Retzius, Anders Adolf; Schaaffhausen, Hermann; Schwalbe, Gustav; Šipka; Skhūl (Israel); Smith, (Sir) Grafton Elliot; Sollas, William Johnson; Swanscombe; Systematics; Vallois, Henri Victor; Verneau, René (Pierre); Virchow, Rudolf; Weidenreich, Franz; Weinert, Hans

Bibliography
M. Boule: L'homme fossile de La Chapelle-aux-Saints. *Annales de Paléontologie* 6:111–172, 1911, 7:21–192, 1912, 8:1–70, 1913; P.J. Bowler: *Theories of human evolution: A century of debate, 1844–1944.* Baltimore: Johns Hopkins University Press, 1986; C.L. Brace: The fate of the "classic" Neanderthals: A consideration of hominid catastrophism. *Current Anthropology* 5:3–43, 1964; C.L. Brace: *The stages of human evolution.* Englewood Cliffs, New Jersey: Prentice-Hall, 1967; D.S. Brose & M.H. Wolpoff: Early Upper Paleolithic man and Late Middle Paleolithic tools. *American Anthropologist* 73:1156–1194, 1971; C.S. Coon: *The Origins of races.* New York: Knopf, 1962; N. Eldredge & S.J. Gould: Punctuated equilibria: An alternative to phyletic gradualism. In: T.J.M. Shompf (ed) *Models in paleobiology.* San Francisco: Freeman Cooper, 1972, pp. 82–115.

J. Fraipont & M. Lohest: La race humaine de Néanderthal ou de Canstadt en Belgique. *Bulletin de l'Académie royale de Belgique* 12:741–784, 1886; D.W. Frayer et al.: Theories of modern human origins: The paleontological test. *American Anthropologist* 95:14–50, 1993; D. Gorjanović-Kramberger: *Der diluviale Mensch von Krapina in Kroatien: ein Beitrag zur Paläoanthropologie.* Wiesbaden: Kreidel, 1906; E. Haeckel: *Natürliche Schöpfungsgeschichte.* Berlin: Reimer, 1868; English translation by E. Ray Lankester: *The history of creation.* New York: Appleton, 1868; M. Hammond: The expulsion of the Neandertals from human ancestry: Marcellin Boule and the social context of scientific research. *Social Studies of Science* 12:1–36, 1982; F.C. Howell: The place of

Neanderthal in human evolution. *American Journal of Physical Anthropology* 9:379–416, 1951.

W.W. Howells: Neanderthal man: Facts and figures. In R.H. Tuttle (ed) *Paleoanthropology: Morphology and paleoecology*. The Hague: Mouton, 1975, pp. 389–408; A. Hrdlička: The Neanderthal phase of man. *Journal of the Royal Anthropological Institute of Great Britain and Ireland* 67:249–269, 1927; T.H. Huxley: *Evidence as to man's place in nature*. London: Williams & Norgate, 1863; A. Keith: *Ancient types of men*. New York: Harper, 1911; A. Keith: The Neanderthals' place in nature. *Nature* 88:155, 1912; A. Keith: *The antiquity of man*. London: Williams & Norgate, 1915; W. King: The reputed fossil man of Neanderthal. *Quarterly Journal of Science* 1:88–97, 1864; H. Klaatsch: Die Aurignac-Rasse und ihre Stellung im Stammbau der Menschheit. *Zeitschrift für Ethnologie* 42:513–577, 1910.

L.S.B. Leakey: *Adam's ancestors*. London: Methuen, 1953; A. de Quatrefages: Races humaines fossiles: Race de Canstadt. *Comtes-rendus hebdomadaires des séances de l'Académie des Sciences* 76:1313–1317, 1873; A. de Quatrefages & E.T.J. Hamy: *Crania ethnica: Les crânes des races humaines*. Paris: Baillière, 1882; J. Radovčić: *Gorjanović-Kramberger and Krapina early man*. Zagreb: Školska Knjiga/ Hrvatski Privodoslovni Muzej, 1988; Y. Rak: Morphological variation in *Homo neanderthalensis* and *Homo sapiens* in the Levant: A biogeographic model. In: W.H. Kimbel & L.S. Martin (eds) *Species, species concepts, and primate evolution*. New York: Plenum, 1993. pp. 523–536; A Retzius: Sur la forme du crâne des habitents du Nord. *Annales des sciences naturelles* 6:133–172, 1846.

H. Schaaffhausen: Zur Kentniss der ältesten Rassenschädel. *Archiv für Anatomie* 5:453–488, 1858; G. Schwalbe: Studien über *Pithecanthropus erectus*, Dubois. *Zeitschrift für Morphologie und Anthropologie* 1:1–240, 1899; *Die Vorgeschichte des Menschen*. Braunschweig: Vieweg, 1904; G. Schwalbe: *Studien zu Vorgeschichte des Menschen*. Stuttgart: Schweizerbartsche, 1906; G. Schwalbe and F.H. Smith: The Neandertals: Evolutionary dead ends or ancestors of modern people. *Journal of Anthropological Research* 47:219–238, 1991; W.J. Sollas: On the cranial and facial characters of the Neanderthal race. *Philosophical Transactions of the Royal Society of London* 199:281–

339, 1908; F. Spencer: The Neandertals and their evolutionary significance: A brief historical survey. In: F.H. Smith and F. Spencer (eds) *The origins of modern humans: A world survey of the fossil evidence*. New York: Liss, 1984, pp. 1–50.

F. Spencer: *Piltdown: A scientific forgery*. London: Oxford University Press, 1990; F. Spencer & F.H. Smith: The significance of Aleš Hrdlička's "Neanderthal phase of man": A historical and current assessment. *American Journal of Physical Anthropology* 56:435–459, 1981; C.B. Stringer: Population relationships of later Pleistocene hominids: A multivariate study of available crania. *Journal of Archaeological Science* 1:317–342, 1974; C.B. Stringer: Out of Africa: A personal history. In: M.H. Nitecki & D.V. Nitecki (eds) *Origins of anatomically modern humans*. New York: Plenum, 1994, pp. 149–172; C.B. Stringer & C. Gamble: *In search of the Neanderthals*. London: Thames & Hudson, 1993.

E. Trinkaus: A history of *Homo erectus* and *Homo sapiens* paleontology in America. In: F. Spencer (ed) *A history of American physical anthropology, 1930–1980*. New York: Academic Press, 1982, pp. 261–280; E. Trinkaus: *The Shanidar Neandertals*. New York: Academic Press, 1983; E. Trinkaus: The Neandertals and modern human origins. *Annual Reviews in Anthropology* 15:193–218, 1986; E. Trinkaus & P. Shipman: *The Neandertals: Changing the image of mankind*. New York: Knopf, 1992;

H.V. Vallois: Neandertals and Praesapiens. *Journal of the Royal Anthropological Institute of Great Britain and Ireland* 84:111–130, 1954. H.V. Vallois: L'origine de l'Homo sapiens. In: *La Grotte de Fontéchevade (Anthropologie)*. Paris: Archives de l'Institut de Paléontologie Humaine, 1958. Reprinted in English in: W.W. Howells (ed) *Ideas in human evolution*. New York: Atheneum, 1967, pp. 473–499; R. Verneau: La race de Néanderthal et la race de Grimaldi: Leur rôle dans l'humanité. *Journal of the Royal Anthropological Institute of Great Britain and Ireland* 54:211–230, 1924; R. Virchow: Untersuchung des Neanderthal-Schädel. *Zeitschrift für Ethnologie* 4:157–165, 1872; R. Virchow: Der Kiefer aus der Schipka Höhle und der Kiefer von La Naulette. *Zeitschrift für Ethnologie* 14:277–310, 1882; F. Weidenreich: Facts and speculations concerning the origin of Homo sapiens. *American Anthropologist* 49:187–203, 1947;

H. Weinert: *Menschen der Vorzeit*. 2d ed. Stuttgart: Enke, 1947; M.H. Wolpoff: Paleoanthropology. New York: Knopf, 1980.

Neo-Darwinism

The term "Darwinism" was originally used quite loosely to denote the evolutionary theory inspired by Charles Darwin (1809–1882). Darwin and some of his closest supporters accepted a role for mechanisms other than natural selection. Modern Darwinists, however, insist that natural selection is the sole mechanism of evolution, and by their standards even Darwin was not a true "Darwinian." The term "neo-Darwinism" was first introduced by the biologist George J. Romanes (1848–1894) in the 1890s to denote an evolutionary theory purged of all mechanisms but natural selection. The German biologist August Weismann (1834–1914) in particular insisted that the natural selection of random hereditary variations was the only mechanism of evolution. Weismann's position was at first highly controversial, and biology became polarized between the neo-Darwinians and the neo-Lamarckians, who advocated a role for the inheritance of acquired characteristics, orthogenesis, and other nonselectionist processes.

In modern biology, the term "neo-Darwinism" may conveniently be used to denote the synthesis of the Darwinian selection theory with Mendelian genetics that was created in the 1920s and 1930s and popularized in the 1940s and 1950s. As the 1990s draw toward a close, his theory remains the dominant paradigm within modern biology, although advocates of the various non-Darwinian mechanisms continue to challenge its authority. For its opponents, both inside and outside the biological sciences, neo-Darwinism has become a rigid dogma expressing a radically materialistic worldview in which there is no goal or purpose in the evolutionary process. The neo-Darwinists insist that they alone have gotten rid of the various forms of teleology and progressionism that pervaded early evolutionary thought and held back the recognition of Darwin's most innovative and creative proposals.

Neo-Darwinism is based on the assumption that evolution proceeds via the action of natural selection upon the random genetic variation existing within a population of interbreeding organisms. The variations are random in the sense that the mutations that produce them do not arise in response to the organisms' needs, and generate many different characters within the population. Evolution thus cannot be driven in a particular direction: The population changes because it becomes better adapted to its local environment through the preservation and superior breeding capacity of those organisms whose variant characters allow them to cope better with that environment. Since samples of an original population may migrate to other locations and become isolated from the parent group, evolution must be a multiple-branched process in which each population moves off in its own direction. And since the opportunities for migration and environmental change are basically unpredictable, evolution itself is an unpredictable, open-ended process best represented by a tree or bush-like structure. As the Harvard zoologist Stephen Jay Gould has emphasized, Darwinian evolution is an unrepeatable process: If we could start the world off again, evolution would be most unlikely ever to produce anything like human beings (cf. Gould 1989).

The most obvious contrast between the neo-Darwinian position and that of the various forms of pre- or non-Darwinian evolutionism is that the latter frequently seek to retain a privileged direction or goal for the evolutionary process: Evolution is a ladder rather than a bush, with the human race as its predictable end product. Even theories of multiple-branched evolution can be non-Darwinian if it is assumed that the various branches are driven in parallel in a similar direction. The foundation for this alternative view of evolution often arises from the belief that the development of the individual organism somehow contributed to the evolution of the species—that is, development itself, or purposefully acquired modifications of development, directs the future variation of the species in a preordained direction. For Darwinians, evolution is a process that takes place purely within populations; the individual itself does not evolve or contribute to evolution except by its survival at the expense of rival members of the breeding population.

This insistence that individual development does not direct evolution has been emphasized in modern neo-Darwinism through the synthesis with genetics. The early geneticists rejected natural selection because they were convinced that unit characters must have been created by a discontinuous, or saltative, mechanism of evolution. But they accepted Weismann's view that the "germ plasm"— what became the genetic material of the chromosomes, later identified as DNA (deoxyribonucleic acid)—was isolated from the adult body. The information flow is one way: The parental DNA controls the development of the new organism's body, but the new organism cannot affect the DNA that it inherits and will transmit to its own offspring. Genetics thus destroyed Lamarckism and the other non-Darwiniam mechanisms, and in the 1920s it was gradually recognized that, far from undermining the selection theory, genetics provided a more convincing basis upon which to erect a truly Darwinian theory. Population geneticists such as Ronald A. Fisher (1890–1962) and J.B.S. Haldane (1892–1964) in Britain showed that the population could be seen as a gene pool into which new variations were being fed by mutations (spontaneous changes within existing genes) (cf. Fisher 1930; Haldane 1932). Most large-scale mutations were fatal, so the population generally exhibited a continuous range of variation for each character made up of a number of small genetic differences. Selection acted through the differential reproduction of organisms with slightly different genetic characters: Those best adapted reproduced more and increased the frequency of the favorable gene within the gene pool.

Although Fisher and Haldane emphasized evolution in large populations, the American population geneticist Sewall Wright (1889–1988) saw that selection might work better with small, semi-isolated subpopulations. This allowed the field naturalist Theodosius Dobzhansky (1900–1975) to relate the finding of population genetics to fieldwork that suggested that geographical isolation was critical for the division of one species into many. By the 1940s, fieldworkers such as Julian Huxley (1887–1975) and Ernst Mayr (1904–) had begun to emphasize the superiority of the synthesis of genetics with the selection theory, thus founding the modern form of neo-Darwinism (cf. Huxley 1942; Mayr 1942). George Gaylord Simpson (1902–1984) showed that the evidence from paleontology, once a hotbed of support for Lamarckism, orthogenesis, and parallelism, could be reconciled with the new Darwinism (cf. Simpson 1949).

Some of the early supporters of the synthesis retained the belief that minor nonadaptive changes might be possible, while Julian Huxley retained a form of progressionism. But, gradually, the synthesis "hardened" to eliminate these non-Darwinian ideas (although Michael Ruse [1986] warns that the

rejection of progressionism may be only skin deep). Simpson in particular emphasized the materialism of the neo-Darwinian synthesis. He argued that evolution was undirected and largely unprogressive: There was no purpose in the evolution of life on Earth, and it was ludicrous to suppose that the human race was the goal of evolution. Through the development of sociobiology, neo-Darwinism has greatly extended its ability to explain complex phenomena in terms of the action of natural selection upon the individual and upon genes. The concept of the "selfish gene" (cf. Dawkins 1976) expresses the view that reproductive success is the only thing that makes selection work, and that what is good for the gene may not be good for the organism carrying it.

More-recent proposals, including the theory of punctuated equilibrium, have implied that Darwinian evolution may not be quite the gradualistic process envisaged by the founders of the synthesis. In this theory, only small, isolated populations are able to evolve into new species, while large, widely spread species remain static over vast periods of time until they are replaced quite suddenly by a new species invading from the periphery. The most powerful line of opposition to neo-Darwinism within science comes from those biologists who think that the synthetic theory ignores the role that may be played by developmental factors in limiting the avenue open to evolution. It may no longer be possible to argue that individual development directs evolution along predetermined channels, but mutated genes do not have unlimited capacity to change the phenotype of the organism. Thus, it is possible that only certain kinds of change may be open to a species. In its extreme form, this line of argument leads to epigenetic evolutionism, the belief that minor genetic changes may trigger a cascade of reactions in the developmental process that could produce a radically different phenotype quite abruptly.

Peter J. Bowler

See also Darwin, Charles Robert; Dobzhansky, Theodosius; Evolutionary Theory; Genetics (Mendelian); Mayr, Ernst; Molecular Anthropology; Mutation; Neo-Lamarckism; Punctuated Equilibria; Simpson, George Gaylord; Sociobiology

Bibliography
P.J. Bowler: *Evolution: The history of an idea.* 2d ed. Berkeley: University of California

Press, 1989a; P.J. Bowler: *The Mendelian revolution: The emergence of hereditarian concepts in modern science and society.* London: Athlone/ Baltimore: Johns Hopkins University Press, 1989b; R. Dawkins: *The selfish gene.* Oxford: Oxford University Press, 1976; R. Dawkins: *The blind watchmaker.* Harlow: Longmans Scientific, 1986; T. Dobzhansky: *Genetics and the origin of species.* New York: Columbia University Press, 1937; R.A. Fisher: *The genetical theory of natural selection.* Oxford: Clarendon Press, 1930; Reprint. New York: Dover, 1958.

S.J. Gould: *Wonderful life: The Burgess shale and the nature of history.* London: Hutchinson, 1989; J.B.S. Haldane: *The causes of evolution.* London: Longmans, Green, 1932. Reprint Ithaca, New York: Cornell University Press, 1966; J.S. Huxley: *Evolution: The modern synthesis.* London: Allen & Unwin, 1942; E. Mayr: *Systematics and the origin of species.* New York: Columbia University Press, 1942; E. Mayr: *The growth of biological thought: Evolution, diversity, and inheritance.* Cambridge: Harvard University Press, 1982.

E. Mayr & W.B. Provine: *The evolutionary synthesis: Perspectives on the unification of biology.* Cambridge: Harvard University Press, 1980; W.B. Provine: *The origin of theoretical population genetics.* Chicago: University of Chicago Press, 1971; G.J. Romanes: *Darwin and after Darwin.* 3 vols. London: Longmans, Green, 1892–1897; M. Ruse: *Darwinism defended: A guide to the evolution controversies.* Reading, Massachusetts: Addison-Wesley, 1982; M. Ruse: *Taking Darwin seriously.* Oxford: Basil Blackwell, 1986; G.G. Simpson: *Tempo and mode in evolution.* New York: Columbia University Press, 1944; G.G. Simpson: *The meaning of evolution.* New Haven, Connecticut: Yale University Press, 1949.

Neo-Lamarckism

The neo-Lamarckians of the late nineteenth century set themselves up in a deliberate opposition to the Darwinians by insisting that nonselectionist mechanisms played a major role in evolution. The name derives from the fact that the most important of these mechanisms, the inheritance of acquired characteristics, was thought to have played an important part in the evolutionary theory advanced at the beginning of the century by the French naturalist Jean-Baptiste Lamarck (1744–1829). This mechanism had, in fact, been only a minor part of Lamarck's theory,

and there is thus a sense in which the neo-Lamarckians cannot really be seen as genuine followers of Lamarck. They adapted the nonselectionist ideas to the very different climate of opinion prevailing in the post-Darwinian era.

Lamarck had assumed that living things tend to progress along a linear scale of complexity, generating, in effect, a "Chain of Being" (*scala naturae*). He knew that nature does not exhibit such a linear relationship, and he explained this by supposing that the linear advance is continually distorted by the organisms' need to adapt to an ever changing environment. The inheritance of acquired characteristics was invoked to explain how this secondary, adaptive process would work. In the classic example, when the ancestors of the giraffe were placed in an environment where the best source of food was the leaves on trees, they stretched their necks to reach the leaves, and this constant exercise lengthened their necks. Lamarck assumed that this "acquired character" could be inherited: The next generation was born with slightly longer necks, and continued the stretching process even further. Over many generations, the addition of the successive acquired characters produced the neck of the modern giraffe. This mechanism is also known as "use-inheritance," because it involves the transmission of modifications acquired by the additional use to which an organ is put.

In the period before the emergence of Mendelian genetics in the opening decades of the twentieth century, it was widely assumed that acquired characters could, indeed, be inherited. Charles Darwin (1809–1882) himself accepted this as a legitimate evolutionary mechanism, although he subordinated it to natural selection. Many of the early Darwinians accepted a role for nonselectionist mechanisms. In the later decades of the nineteenth century, evolutionary biology was polarized by the theories of the German biologist August Weismann (1834–1914), who insisted that the mechanism of heredity would not permit the transmission of acquired modifications. For Weismann, the "germ plasm" (precursor of the Mendelian gene and the DNA [deoxyribonucleic acid] of modern molecular biologists) could not be influenced by changes in the adult body: The parents simply transmitted their germ plasm unchanged to the next generation. Many biologists would not accept Weismann's total rejection of use-inheritance, and the neo-Lamarckian movement emerged as a self-conscious school of thought opposed to neo-Darwinism.

For some neo-Lamarckians, the inheritance of acquired characters was simply an alternative mechanism to adaptation, replacing natural selection. In the case of the giraffe, both mechanisms could equally well account for the extension of the length of the neck in conditions in which this was a beneficial modification. Many Lamarckians assumed that their theory could account even better than selectionism for the loss and elimination of organs that were no longer useful. The American neo-Lamarckian Alpheus S. Packard (1839–1905) studied blind cave animals on the assumption that the inherited effects of disuse explained their loss of eyes.

Neo-Lamarckism also became associated with other non-Darwinian processes. Much of the support for the movement came from paleontologists such as the American Edward Drinker Cope (1840–1897). These workers believed that they could detect trends in the fossil record that were too linear to be explained by the selection of random variation. They were exponents of the "recapitulation theory": They believed that the development of the individual repeats the evolutionary history of its species. This arose from their assumption that variation is not random (as Darwin supposed) because it constitutes an addition to, rather than a distortion of, the process of individual development. Usefully acquired characters are one such addition to growth, and they leave the old adult form preserved as an early stage in the developmental process. But Cope and others such as the American zoologist Alpheus Hyatt (1838–1902) also assumed that forces within the developmental process itself might generate variations in a preordained direction. Neo-Lamarckism thus became associated with the theory of "orthogenesis," in which evolution is driven inexorably in certain directions, in some cases forcing the species to develop bizarre nonadaptive characters that lead to extinction.

Both Lamarckism and orthogenesis rest on the assumption that what happens to the individual organism in the course of its development can affect the future evolution of the species. Evolution is, in effect, the summing up of changes affecting successive individuals. This assumption was challenged by Weismann's claim that the germ plasm is transmitted unchanged from one generation to the next. Changes in the developmental process simply cannot feed back into the germ plasm to be transmitted to the next generation. The information flow is strictly one way, and the transmission of characters from one generation to the next is a separate process from that by which those characters are developed in the individual organism. When the geneticists of the early twentieth century adopted this aspect of Weismann's thinking, they, too, became implacably opposed to neo-Lamarckism. The so-called case of the midwife toad was based on the geneticists' exposure of fraud in the Lamarckian experiments of the German biologist Paul Kammerer (1880–1926) in the early 1920s (cf. Koestler 1971).

In more-recent decades, occasional efforts to reinstate a role for the inheritance of acquired characters have been made, even by working biologists. But support for the theory has come mainly from outside science, from thinkers who see neo-Lamarckism as an antidote to the extreme materialism of the Darwinian selection theory. Nineteenth-century Lamarckism drew much of its support from a belief that the selection of random variation was a harsh mechanism that was incompatible with the belief that evolution was instituted by God, and that reduced organisms to the status of puppets controlled by their genetic strings. Writers from Samuel Butler to George Bernard Shaw and Arthur Koestler have insisted that if Lamarckism is valid, there is no need to kill off the unfit in every generation because all of the individuals become fitter through appropriate exercise. Living things can control the destiny of their species by responding purposefully to changes in their environment, and the evolutionary process itself thus retains a teleological character. There can be little doubt that these moral considerations have greatly stimulated support for Lamarckism, although this support has gradually been eroded within the scientific community.

Peter J. Bowler

See also Chain of Being; Genetics (Mendelian); Lamarck, Jean-Baptiste Pierre Antoine de Monet (Chevalier de); Neo-Darwinism

Bibliography
P.J. Bowler: *The eclipse of Darwinism: Anti-Darwinian evolution theories in the decades around 1900*. Baltimore: Johns Hopkins University Press, 1983; P.J. Bowler: *The non-Darwinian revolution: Reinterpreting a historical myth*. Baltimore: Johns Hopkins University Press, 1987; P.J. Bowler: *Evolution: The history of an idea*. 2d ed. Berkeley: University of California Press,

1989a; P.J. Bowler: *The Mendelian revolution: The emergence of hereditarian concepts in modern science and society.* London: Athlone/Baltimore: Johns Hopkins University Press, 1989b; E.D. Cope: *The origin of the fittest.* New York: Macmillan, 1887; A. Hyatt: Evolution of the cephalopods. *Science* 3:122–127, 145–149, 1884; A. Koestler: *The case of the midwife toad.* London: Hutchinson, 1971; E. Mayr: *The growth of biological thought: Evolution, diversity, and inheritance.* Cambridge: Harvard University Press, 1982; A.S. Packard: *Lamarck: The founder of evolution.* New York: Longmans, Green, 1901. A. Weismann: *The evolution theory.* 2 vols. London: Arnold, 1904.

Netherlands, The

Physical anthropology has formally existed in The Netherlands as an independent academic discipline, studied and taught in a specific institute, only from 1960 to 1986, and then again after 1993. Nevertheless Dutch scientists have always manifested an interest in this field of inquiry—be it under that specific name or another. Those activities up to 1938 have been surveyed by A.J. van Bork-Feltkamp (1938). Later, J. Huizinga (1972) and T.S. Constandse-Westermann (1983, in press) supplemented her survey. From these studies, it is clear that in all periods medically trained scientists have been the primary contributors to physical-anthropological research.

Early Developments: Mid-Eighteenth Century–1900
Prior to 1850, the study of skeletal material was one of the main interests of Dutch physical anthropologists. Their investigations focused on cranial diversity, generally involving the study of single exotic specimens, the methodology of skeletal investigation, and evolutionary problems. The evolutionary studies included the examination of somatic features such as skin color. The Leiden anatomist Bernhard Siegfried Albinus (1697–1770) is of particular interest because of his influential atlas of human anatomy, entitled: *Tabulae Sceleti et Musculorum Corporis Humani* (1747). His pupil Petrus Camper (1722–1789) had a similar passionate interest in anatomical illustration. Unlike his mentor, Camper did not favor the use of perspective in medical illustrations as had been the custom since the time of the anatomist Andreas Vesalius (1514–1564). In Camper's view, orthographic projection was not only more accurate but also more informative and scientifically useful. Furthermore, he was in-

ternationally known as the author of influential studies on anthropology in general and evolution and craniology in particular. With regard to the latter, Camper introduced the "facial angle," the first measurable characteristic for identifying the diversity of the human species (Camper 1791). The impulse received from Camper's craniological work led to the emergence of several important crania collections, such as those at Göttingen in Germany and at Leiden in The Netherlands (cf. Sandifort & Sandifort 1827).

Among the most notable Dutch investigators following similar lines of inquiry were Jacob Elisa Doornik (1777–1837), Gerardus Vrolik (1775–1859), and his son Willem Vrolik (1801–1863). The Vrolik collection, consisting for a substantial part of human skeletal material (and crania in particular) and still present at the Amsterdam University, was very influential in its time (cf. Baljet 1990). Another important worker in craniology was the Leiden anatomist J. van der Hoeven (1801–1868). In 1860, he published his *Catalogus Craniorum Diversarum Gentium que Collegit J. van der Hoeven*, which represents a summation of his work in this area. It also reveals the influence of the craniometric methods pioneered by the American physician Samuel George Morton (1799–1851). Physical-anthropological studies were also conducted by the Utrecht ophthalmologist F.C. Donders (1818–1889), who had already touched on many points crucial to Charles Darwin's (1809–1882) evolutionary thesis. However, his views were Lamarckian rather than Darwinian (cf. Vinken 1963).

Human growth and development was another subject studied during this period. The first-known mixed-longitudinal study, of twelve boys, was conducted by J.F. Martinet (1729–1795). He was a master of free arts as well as a doctor of philosophy. Furthermore, he was a member of the Dutch Society of Sciences in Haarlem and served as vicar in the small Dutch town of Zutphen. In his *Katechismus der Natuur* (1778), he published a clearly illustrative drawing and an accurate definition of allometric growth (cf. Roede 1985).

The first investigator to break with the then current approach to craniological problems was P. Harting (1812–1885), who held "modern" views on heredity and was highly critical of the view held by many of his contemporaries that human beings could be classified into groups by the contours and dimensions of their individual crania. He therefore advocated the examination of large series of Dutch crania rather than studying single and exotic specimens. Although his criticism was not immediately appreciated, it eventually led to a better understanding of the extent of human variation and to the application of the analytical methods pioneered by the Belgian Statistician Adolphe Quetelet (1796–1874) and others.

In addition to the gradual appreciation of the utility of increasing the sample size in cranial studies, a widening diversity in the investigated subjects can be observed in the second half of the nineteenth century. To a large extent, these two changes in the attitude of Dutch physical anthropologists are linked with the foundation of two influential research committees within the Koninklijke Nederlandsche Maatschappij tot Bevordering der Geneeskunst (Royal Dutch Medical Association: RDMA). The first of these committees, the Commissie voor Geneeskundige Statistiek in Nederland (Committee for Medical Statistics in The Netherlands), was founded around 1850 to promote the study of the "physiological and pathological status" (Zeeman 1850: 162) of the Dutch population. An immediate result of this development was a series of investigations of the chronological and spatial variability of stature (mostly in nineteen-year-old military recruits) and relating the results to environmental factors. This was followed in 1865 by the foundation of the Commissie voor de Ethnologie (Committee for Ethnology: CE), whose goal was to promote the study of Dutch cranial collections. Later, this committee extended its work to embrace the study of the living (e.g., cephalic index, pigmentation). In many cases, this research was executed by local medical practitioners, and the results of their labors were published as *Rapporten van de Commissie voor de Ethnologie* (Reports of the Committee for Ethnology) in the *Nederlandsch Tijdschrift voor Geneeskunde* (Dutch Journal for Medical Science), the organ of the RDMA. Among the investigators figuring in these endeavors were D. Lubach, A. Folmer and his son H.C. Folmer, J.C. de Man, and A. Sasse and his son J. Sasse. The latter investigator was responsible for initiating the foundation of the Nederlandsche Anthropologische Vereeniging (Dutch Anthropological Association: DAA) in 1898, which more or less replaced the CE as the forum of Dutch anthropology. The foundation of the DAA represented an institutional development that was essential to the emergence of the discipline as a legitimate and

independent science. A variety of subjects were discussed at its first meeting, two of which serve to draw attention to two other future developments. First, there was Herman F.C. ten Kate's (1858–1931) paper on hereditary characteristics, foreshadowing the pending rediscovery of Gregor Johann Mendel's (1822–1884) work. Second, there was a contribution by M.E.F.T. (Eugène) Dubois (1858–1940), who had discovered the remains of his *Pithecanthropus erectus* in Java in the early 1890s. A large number of publications from his hand on these remains and on other evolutionary problems appeared in the decades to follow.

Early Modern Period: 1900–1939

`Any description of physical anthropology in The Netherlands in this period requires a consideration of the work of Lodewijk Bolk (1866–1930). Indeed, he can be considered the founder of modern physical anthropology in The Netherlands. His scientific interests were broad, and in his extremely active professional life he set his stamp on the work of many others. During his lifetime, Bolk was involved in many scientific controversies (cf. Ariëns Kappers 1930; van den Broek 1930; Constandse-Westermann 1991; Mijsberg 1930). One of his best-known theories is that of "retardation." Furthermore, he conducted a large number of population studies, many of which treated the biological diversity of the Dutch population. In 1925, Bolk's efforts led to the foundation of the Anthropologische Commissie (Anthropological Committee). In a letter, he specifically stated its goal was to be a *"commissie voor het physisch anthropologisch onderzoek van de status van de Nederlandsche bevolking"* (committee for the physical-anthropological investigation of the Dutch population), under the auspices of the Koninklijke Nederlandsche Akademie van Wetenschappen (Royal Netherlands Academy of Arts and Sciences). It was the most influential of several bodies established during this period to promote the practice of physical anthropology in The Netherlands.

Bolk's strong influence inspired many investigators to work along similar lines, including A.A.W. Hubrecht and W.A. Mijsberg (evolutionary subjects) and J.A.J. Barge and A.J.P. van den Broek (skeletal and population research). The advancement of archeology further enhanced the execution and publication of skeletal studies. A collection of skeletal dissection material of known age and sex was brought together in Amsterdam between

1883 and 1909. This collection was later described by A. De Froe in his doctoral thesis (1938) and is still frequently used.

Other population studies treated dermatoglyphics (J. Dankmeyer) and the then relatively new field of blood groups (M.A. van Herwerden and H.J.T. Bijlmer). Increasing attention was also given to human genetics. Already at the beginning of the twentieth century, H. de Vries (1848–1935) had made a major contribution to the development of this field. He was, among other things, one of the three scientists who independently rediscovered Mendel's work in the early 1900s. His publications include several papers on human diversity. Other Dutch scientists who were active in this nascent field of inquiry were G.P. Frets and W.C. Keers, who investigated the mode of inheritance of skeletal traits and somatic characteristics such as skin pigmentation. A.L. Hagedoorn and his wife, A.C. Hagedoorn-Vorstheuvel la Brand, recognized already in 1921 the principle of random genetic drift *avant la lettre* (Hagedoorn & Hagedoorn-Vorstheuvel la Brand 1921), which was, in fact, described by R.A. Fisher (1922) as the "Hagedoorn effect."

Modern Period: Post 1945–1990

For much of this modern period, the Instituut voor Antropobiologie (Institute of Human Biology: IHB), founded in 1960 by J. Huizinga at the Utrecht State University, was the primary focus for research, teaching, and training in physical anthropology in The Netherlands. When Huizinga retired in 1986, however, the institute was closed by the university authorities for budgetary reasons, leaving only the Werkgroep Skeletonderzoek (Department of Anthropo-Osteology) intact. Unfortunately, that department, with its limited budget and faculty resources, was unable to fill the vacuum created by the dissolution of the IHB; as a consequence, in 1991 it, too, was closed.

Other university medical departments executing physical-anthropological research are or were those for anatomy and embryology (e.g., at Groningen, Leiden, Maastricht, and Utrecht) and for human genetics and cytogenetics. Nonuniversity institutions were also involved in this research, among them: TNO Voeding at Zeist (TNO Food Research: TNO-FR), the Centraal Laboratorium van de Bloedtransfusiedienst van het Nederlandse Rode Kruis at Amsterdam (Central Laboratory of The Netherlands Red Cross Blood Transfusion Service: CLBT), the Nationaal Natuurhistorisch Museum at Leiden (Na-

tional Museum of Natural History), and the Koninklijk Instituut voor de Tropen at Amsterdam (Royal Tropical Institute). Nationwide growth studies have been conducted at the Nederlands Instituut voor Preventieve Geneeskunde TNO at Leiden (TNO Institute of Preventive Health Care: TNO-IPHC) and later at the Utrecht State University (*vide infra*). However, in all of the latter institutions, only a minor part of the research and/or teaching programs is or was dedicated to subjects that could be combined under the denomination "physical anthropology."

The research undertaken by the above institutions has included the following (NB to avoid arbitrary choices, the reader is referred to Constandse-Westermann [1983, in press] for the names of individual investigators and bibliographic references):

ADAPTATION RESEARCH

Such research was a major priority of the IHB, and it was concentrated on populations living in the West African savanna belt, south of the Sahara. At first, anthropometric and pigmentation studies were a dominant feature of the IHB research agenda. Later, its research goals were expanded to include the collection and study of data on vital capacity, heart rate, work capacity, body composition, and the like. Background information on the subject populations was provided by the study of local archaeology and excavated human skeletal material on the one hand, and of population genetics (blood groups, dermatoglyphics) on the other. Comparative research of subjects from other tropical environments (e.g., eccrine sweat glands in the Surinamese) and of Dutch groups completed the IHB adaptation-research program.

SKELETAL RESEARCH

This type of research was also conducted by the IHB and by investigators in several other Dutch institutions. The IHB was responsible for producing reports on skeletal series from different periods, excavated by, or under the auspices of, the Rijksdienst voor het Oudheidkundig Bodemonderzoek (State Service for Archeological Investigations: SSAI), or by university archeological institutes. Finally, the IHB conducted, in cooperation with the Biologisch Archeologisch Instituut (Biological-Archaeological Institute: BAI) of the Groningen State University, an intensively integrated program of (ethno)-archeological and physical-anthropological research of the Mesolithic period in western Europe. Despite the closing of the IHB in 1986, as of the mid-1990s, this project was being continued by the BAI and the Instituut voor Pre- en Protohistorische Archeologie (Institute for Pre- and Protohistoric Archeology) at the University of Amsterdam.

Other publications in this field by Dutch physical anthropologists have dealt with excavated skeletal material—particularly, dental series (e.g., the earliest [Early Neolithic] well-dated Dutch skeletal material, recovered at Swifterbant)—human skeletal material dredged from the Rhine and Meuse delta, and incidental finds by amateurs. Dutch physical anthropologists have also contributed to the study of hominid skeletal material from Indonesia and the Dutch West Indies.

Theoretical aspects of skeletal research (statistical treatment) continue to be investigated primarily at the Laboratorium voor Anatomie en Embryologie (Laboratory of Anatomy and Embryology) of the Groningen State University. Finally, since ca. 1980, a number of publications has appeared dealing with chemical, histological, microscopic, and paleopathological analyses of recovered bone materials.

GROWTH AND DEVELOPMENT

Nationwide surveys of growth and development have been conducted three times in The Netherlands, in 1955, 1965, and 1980. The first two of these were conducted by the TNO-IPHC, while the Wilhelmina Kinderziekenhuis, Universiteitskliniek voor Kinderen en Jeugdigen (University Hospital for Children and Youth "Het Wilhelmina Kinderziekenhuis") at Utrecht executed the 1980 survey. All three surveys were cross-sectional, and in those from 1965 and 1980 data on infants were also published, along with standards for the developmental stages of secondary sex characteristics. In addition to these nationwide surveys, a comprehensive mixed-longitudinal multidisciplinary survey, incorporating a great number of variables, was carried out by workers at Nijmegen University between 1971 and 1975. Other Dutch investigations in this field have dealt with the problem of secular changes. Furthermore, in 1967 an atlas for somatotyping children was published in The Netherlands (Petersen 1967). The relationships between environmental—specifically, nutritional—factors and anatomical and physiological development (e.g., differences between immigrant groups and the average Dutch population) continue to be studied at TNO-FR.

SOMATIC CHARACTERISTICS OF THE LIVING

These examinations have concerned Dutch as well as Indonesian and other tropical populations. Important in this respect have been studies on dermatoglyphics. A survey of all known data on the (sub)recent Dutch population appeared in 1968. Many studies have been dedicated to the somatic characteristics of sportsmen and sportswomen.

POPULATION GENETICS

Data on Dutch as well as other groups have been published by, or in cooperation with, the CLBT. To begin with, these studies have pertained almost exclusively to the distribution analysis of the ABO and Rh systems. More recently, however, GM allotypes and DNA (deoxyribonucleic acid) polymorphisms have also been investigated. Other population genetic research, such as the study of serum cholinesterase and salivary amylase, has been executed by various university departments of human genetics. Most of this research has involved limited samples and is not directed specifically to the resolution of physical-anthropological problems, but rather serves as a background for the analysis of specific disease-related phenomena.

HUMAN EVOLUTIONARY STUDIES

Until about 1980, these studies pertained mainly to primate behavior. Since then, evolution and the biological differentiation between ethnic groups have been studied, using statistical methods, at Groningen University. Another subject that has received increasing attention is the evolution of the human vocal tract and, consequently, of speech. Those studies have employed computer tomography. Several related studies of a sociobiological nature have also appeared.

Recent Developments

Because the closing of the IHB could be foreseen, and anticipating the reduction of the possibilities for physical-anthropological research in The Netherlands, beginning in the 1980s several initiatives were taken to protect the interests of the discipline and its practitioners. The Nederlandse Vereniging voor Fysische Antropologie (Dutch Society for Physical Anthropology: DSPA) was founded in 1983, with the expressed intention of stimulating and coordinating Dutch physical-anthropological research. Lately, the DSPA has kept a watchful eye on the destination of the collection(s) of human skeletal material and of books and reprints existing primarily at the

IHB at Utrecht. Concurrently with the ongoing efforts of the DSPA, a number of university and other archeological institutions (e.g., the University of Amsterdam and the SSAI) have been trying to create new possibilities for the investigation and analysis of excavated human inhumated and cremated skeletal material. Small-scale teaching programs were created at the Universities of Groningen (skeletal research) and Leiden (physical anthropology), while students in archeology at the University of Amsterdam receive introductory courses to prepare them for the excavation of human skeletal material. Furthermore, some private enterprises have been established, offering identification of excavated human skeletal material on a contract basis, while private individuals have taken initiatives aimed at the research of specific human skeletal collections and/or specific lines of research.

The above joint efforts have resulted in the foundation of the Interuniversitair Centrum voor Fysische Anthropologie (Inter-University Center for Physical Anthropology) at the State University of Leiden. At present this center serves primarily a teaching function and it has only limited financial means for research. It is hoped that in the near future it will be expanded into an adequately equipped and staffed teaching and research institution.

Trinette S. Constandse-Westermann

See also Asian Paleoanthropology; Bolk, Lodewijk; Camper, Petrus; Doornik, Jacob Elisa; Dubois, (Marie) Eugène (François Thomas); Java; Morton, Samuel George; Mutation; Quetelet (Lambert) Adolphe (Jacques); Vesalius, Andreas; Vrolik, Gerardus; Vrolik, Willem

Bibliography
B.S. Albinus: *Tabulae Sceleti et Musculorum Corporis Humani*. Lugdumun Batavorum, 1747; C.U. Ariëns Kappers: In memoriam: L. Bolk. *Psychiatrische en Neurologische Bladen* 1930:1–6, 1930; B. Baljet: Uit de geschiedenis van het Museum Vrolik, de Snijkamer en het Theatrum Anatomicum te Amsterdam. In: B. Baljet (ed) *Gids voor het Museum Vrolik*. Amsterdam: Universiteit van Amsterdam, 1990, pp. 7–24; A.J. van Bork-Feltkamp: Anthropological research in The Netherlands: Historical survey. *Verhandelingen der Koninklijke Nederlandsche Akademie van Wetenschappen sectie 2*, 38:1–166, 1938; A.J.P. van den Broek: In memoriam. Prof. Dr. Louis Bolk. *Nederlandsch Tijdschrift voor Geneeskunde* 74:3078–3081, 1930; P. Camper: *Verhandeling van Petrus Camper, over het Natuurlijk Verschil der Wezenstrekken in Menschen van Onderscheiden Landaart en Ouderdom; over het Schoon in Antyke Beelden en Gesneedene Steenen. Gevolgd door een Voorstel van eene Nieuwe Manier om Hoofden van Allerleye Menschen met Zekerheid te Teekenen*. Utrecht: Adriaan Gilles Camper, 1791.

T.S. Constandse-Westermann: History of physical anthropology in the Netherlands. *International Association of Human Biologists: Occasional Papers*. Vol. 1. No. 3. 1983; T.S. Constandse-Westermann: Bolk, Louis. In: C. Winters (ed) *International dictionary of anthropologists*. New York: Garland, 1991, pp. 72–73; T.S. Constandse-Westermann & M.J. Roede: The history of physical anthropology in the Netherlands. In: D.F. Roberts (ed) *The history and development of biological anthropology*. Cambridge: Cambridge University Press, in press; R.A. Fisher: On the dominance ratio. *Proceedings of the Royal Society of Edinburgh* 42:321–421, 1922.

A. De Froe: *Meetbare Variabelen van den Menschelijken Schedel en hun Onderlinge Correlaties in Verband met Leeftijd en Geslacht*. Ph.D. Thesis. University of Amsterdam, 1938; A.L. Hagedoorn & A.C. Hagedoorn-Vorstheuvel la Brand: *The relative value of the processes causing evolution*. The Hague: Martinus Nijhoff, 1921; J. van der Hoeven: *Catalogus Craniorum Diversarum Gentium que Collegit J. van der Hoeven*. Lugdumun Batavorum, 1860; J. Huizinga: Enseignement et recherche en anthropologie aux Pays Bas. In: A. Leguebe (ed) *Enseignement et recherche en anthropologie*. Brussels: Leguebe, 1972, pp. 99–107.

J.F. Martinet: *Katechismus der Natuur. Deel II*. 5th ed. Amsterdam: Allart, 1778; W.A. Mijsberg: In memoriam: Prof. Dr. L. Bolk. *Geneeskundig Tijdschrift voor Nederlandsch-Indië* 70:737–738, 1930; G. Petersen: *Atlas for somatotyping children*. Assen: Van Gorcum, 1967; M.J. Roede: A Dutch precursor on human biology. *Humanbiologie Budapest* 16:139–151, 1985; E. Sandifort & G. Sandifort: *Museum Anatomicum Academiae Lugduno Batavae*. Leiden: 1827; P.J. Vinken: Donders en Lamarck. *Proceedings of the Koninklijke Nederlandsche Akademie van Wetenschappen Series C* 66:577–586, 1963; J. Zeeman: Programma van wege de Commissie voor Geneeskundige Statistiek in Nederland ter Tweede Algemeene Vergadering der

Maatschappij. *Tijdschrift der Maatschappij* (= *Nederlandsch Tijdschrift voor Geneeskunde*) 1850:61–169, 1850.

Neumann, Georg Karl (1908–1971)

Born in Hamburg, Germany, Neumann moved with his family to Chicago shortly after the end of World War I. He completed his education there, receiving three degrees from the University of Chicago (Ph.B., 1930, M.A., 1936, Ph.D., 1942). Before taking a position at the University of Indiana in 1942, he held a number of research and teaching positions in both archeology and anatomy (Robbins 1972). He remained at Indiana until his untimely death in 1971.

Neumann's eclectic but passionate interest in all fields of knowledge is evident in reviewing the numbers and types of books he purchased for his library; at the time of his death, he possessed more than 12,000 volumes, representing several languages (Robbins 1972:4). Though Neumann's interest was global (he visited many museums worldwide to examine their collections), he was also devoted to the state (Indiana) and the region (midwest United States) where he worked. This commitment is discernible in his forensic work in Indiana and Illinois, in the archeological and osteological projects he conducted in the Midwest, and in his numerous publications in the *Proceedings of the Indiana Academy of Science*.

Four principal themes can be identified in Neumann's career. The first concerns skeletal reconstruction, in the broadest sense of the term. Here his goal was to examine skeletal material and, from it, to reconstruct both a metric and a fleshed-out image of the individual. This skill complemented his work in forensic anthropology and enabled him to provide accurate drawings of individuals whose skeletons had been found.

A second major theme concerns methodology. He is known to have been meticulous in making measurements of skeletal material; a number of his early papers concentrated on the history of standardized measurements of skeletal material (e.g., Neumann 1954).The care he exerted in measuring and recording information and the attention he gave to detail came at the price of slowing his work and reducing his output. Neumann died prior to the era of high-speed computers, and it is interesting to speculate on what he might have accomplished had they been available to him.

A third theme is his study of biological variation in Native American populations. Neumann used data on skeletal populations to build a mode of their origins and migrations. Although Neumann has been called the "last and the best of the typologists," he bridged two paradigms—the typological and the populational. In the years of his training at Chicago, the typological school was dominant. Following World War II, the population revolution swept out of genetics and biology into physical anthropology, replacing a relatively static view of human diversity with a more dynamic one. Race became "an evolutionary episode" rather than a long-term phenomenon that, for example, might leave its mark on Indian tribes thousands of years after migration across the Bering Strait.

In evaluating the relatively short-lived influence of Neumann's postulated varieties of American Indians, it is instructive to look at his variety concept (cf. Neumann 1952). It differed from continental morphological race concepts, which postulate groups such as "American Mongoloid" to refer to all pre-Columbian native peoples, in its use of greater detail and its recognition of unique regional characteristics that in the modern paradigm are considered local populations. Neumann's knowledge of tribal distinctions is well known in the folklore of American physical anthropology, for he is said to have been able to correctly identify the tribe of an individual after examining a skull. While a contemporary physical anthropologist might develop discriminant functions of data on known archeological populations, and use these to help classify unknown skeletal remains, Neumann appeared simply to store the equivalent information in his head and then process the information when an unknown skull was shown to him. One major difference between Neumann's approach and the contemporary approach is the time dimension; today, local populations are regarded as extremely fluid, whereas Neumann saw stability over time in his varieties. Because of the great care with which he described individuals and groups, his work deserves restudy (Long 1966).

A fourth theme that distinguishes Georg Neumann is his holistic view of anthropology. He perceived physical anthropology as a central and integrative discipline that, along with the subdisciplines of archeology, cultural anthropology, and linguistics, had much to contribute to all other fields of the humanities and sciences.

Roberta L. Hall

See also Americas: Paleoanthropology; Race Concept

Bibliography
SELECTED WORKS

Types of artificial cranial deformation in the eastern United States. *American Antiquity* 7:306–310, 1941; Archaeology and race in the American Indian. In: J.B. Griffin (ed) *Archaeology of the eastern United States*. Chicago: University of Chicago Press, 1952, pp. 13–34; Measurements and indices of American Indian varieties. *Yearbook of Physical Anthropology* 8:243–255, 1954; Origins of the Indians of the middle Mississippi area. *Proceedings of the Indiana Academy of Science* 69:66–68, 1960.

A reexamination of the question of the Middle Western origin of the Delaware Indians. *Proceedings of the Indiana Academy of Science* 79:60–61, 1970; (with R.W. Alexander) On the origin of the Tutelo—an eastern Siouan tribe. *Proceedings of the Indiana Academy of Science* 78:88–92, 1969; (with L. Robbins) The origin of the Shawnee Indians. *Proceedings of the Indiana Academy of Science* 78:93–96, 1969; (with C.G. Waldman) Regression formulae for the reconstruction of the stature of Hopewellian and middle Mississippi Amerindian populations. *Proceedings of the Indiana Academy of Science* 77:98–101, 1967.

ARCHIVAL SOURCES

For details of the Neumann Collection (Correspondence, Research Notes, Books, and Skeletal Material) and availability, contact: Department of Anthropology, Oregon State University, Corvallis, Oregon 97331.

SECONDARY SOURCES

J.K. Long: A test of multiple-discriminant analysis as a means of determining evolutionary changes and intergroup relationships in physical anthropology. *American Anthropologist* 68:444–464, 1966; L.M. Robbins: Obituary: Georg Karl Neumann. *American Journal of Physical Anthropology* 36:3–8, 1972.

Neuroanatomy, Comparative

The history of comparative neuroanatomical studies, as they apply to physical anthropology, can be conveniently divided into three broad, though somewhat arbitrary, periods of development: (1) the Premodern, which embraces much of the nineteenth century and the early twentieth century; (2) the Early Modern, which spans the period from the 1920s to the early post–World War II years; and (3) the Modern, from the 1950s to the present.

Premodern Period: ca. 1800–early 1900s

During the first half of the nineteenth century, there was a mounting interest in comparative neurocranial studies. This interest had its origins in the developing concept of organization and the emergence of a functional approach to comparative anatomy at the close of the eighteenth century. The views expressed by the British anatomist William Lawrence (1783–1867) in his *Lectures* (1819) mirror this conceptual shift in the early 1800s. In marked contrast to savants of the 1700s, Lawrence and his contemporaries subscribed to the view that intelligence was inextricably linked with cerebral complexity and the level of somatic organization. Like others, Lawrence was struck by the prodigious development of the human cerebral hemispheres and convolutions compared to all other mammals. Based on his own observations and those of other investigators, Lawrence felt justified in formulating a simple hierarchy of intelligence and cerebral organization beginning with the European brain on through the "lower" human races to the anthropoid apes. At the same time, other investigators, such as German physician Franz Gall (1758–1828) (1810) and his disciple Johann Spurzheim (1766–1832), were forging a relationship between brain structure and behavior, promoting the idea that human intelligence was grounded in innate faculties located in specific organs of the brain, and that these centers had an external influence that was manifest in corresponding locations on the external cranium. Although the school of phrenology had initially gathered considerable support, by the early 1840s the scientific validity of its teachings had been discredited (cf. Flourens 1842), bringing a general retreat from the concept of localization. This latter idea, however, was not completely abandoned; it was resuscitated, thirty years later, by the French surgeon-anthropologist Paul Broca (1824–1880), when he presented evidence suggesting that articulate speech in humans was controlled by a local region in the left cerebral hemisphere (*vide infra*).

Another early pioneer was the Heidelberg anatomist Friedrich Tiedemann (1781–1861), who through his comparative studies endeavored to quantify and thereby understand more clearly the apparent relationship between the size of the cerebrum and intelligence (cf. Tiedemann 1836). His work, along with that of others, such as the Dutch anatomist-zoologist Willem Vrolik (1801–1863), corroborated the earlier observation of the English anatomist Thomas Willis (1621–1675) that the human brain was, indeed, more asymmetrical than that of any other primate species. These later works also confirmed what the British anatomist Edward Tyson (1650–1708) had observed at the end of the seventeenth century—that the neuroanatomical differences between humans and the anthropoid apes are essentially quantitative rather than qualitative ones. However, it was only with the careful work of Louis Pierre Gratiolet (1815–1865) and François Leuret (1797–

1851) in the 1840s and 1850s that realistic illustrations of the convolutions of human and other primate brains emerged (e.g., Gratiolet 1854).

A major event in the mid-nineteenth century was the arrival of the Darwinian synthesis and the resulting reinstatement of Linnaean classification. At the close of the eighteenth century, the German anatomist Johann Friedrich Blumenbach (1752–1840) had presented a compelling case for the separation of human beings (Bimana) from the nonhuman primates (Quadrumana) on the ordinal level (cf. Bendyshe 1865). Blumen-

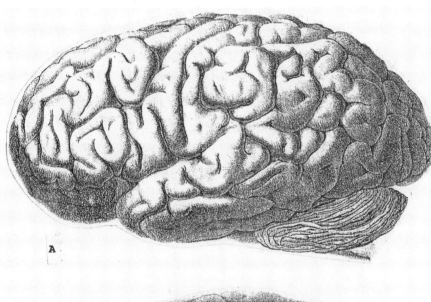

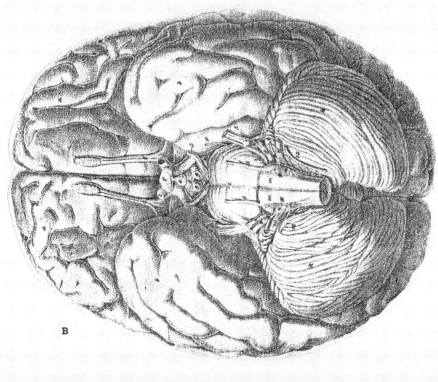

Fig. 1. Drawings of a male Negro brain: A lateral view; B: inferior view. From Tiedemann (1836).

bach's scheme was widely adopted by naturalists during the first half of the nineteenth century, and just prior to the publication of Charles Darwin's (1809–1882) *On the Origin of Species* (1859), the British anatomist Richard Owen (1804–1892) endeavored to push Blumenbach's scheme to its extreme limits. Building on the long-held conviction that the corpus callosum was the "great characteristic" of the mammalian brain, Owen argued not only that mammalia could be differentiated according to the size and conformity of their brains, but also that it was possible, from this perspective, to justify the separation of humans from the anthropoid apes into a subclass of their own (cf. Owen 1857, 1859). Specifically, he contended that the human brain was distinguished by the presence of three unique structures: the posterior lobe of the cerebrum, the hippocampus minor, and the posterior cornu of the lateral ventricle. These characters, as well as Owen's general synthesis, were immediately challenged by the British zoologist Thomas Henry Huxley (1825–1895), who in a series of publications in the early 1860s (culminating with his influential text *Evidence as to Man's Place in Nature* in 1863) not only demonstrated that there was no taxonomic characteristic of ordinal importance to separate humans from the nonhuman primates, but also promoted the Darwinian thesis, which he viewed as an agenda for future research. Indeed, Huxley's work immediately inspired several British anatomists to dissect primate brains to establish the validity of the case against Owen. For example, John Marshall (1818–1891) studied the chimpanzee (1861) and George Rolleston (1829–1881) the orangutan (e.g., 1861), while William Henry Flower (1831–1899) examined the brains of various other primates (e.g., 1861, 1863).

Although the research of the second half of the nineteenth century might simply be dismissed as a consolidation of the Huxley-Darwin viewpoint, this simplification does obscure the development of new techniques to study and preserve neuroanatomical structures, as well as the steady increase in more-detailed neuroanatomical studies. Most prominent in this growing community were German researchers, including, among others, Alexander Ecker (1816–1887) (1873), Theodor Bischoff (1807–1882) (1867), N. Rüdinger (1832–1898) (1882), J.H.F. Kohlbrügge (b. 1865) (cf. 1897), Wilhelm Waldeyer (1836–1921) (1891), and Carl Wernicke (1848–1905) (*vide infra*). Similar

research was also conducted in France by such workers as Théophile Chudziński (1840–1897) (1878–1882), and in Italy by Giovanni Mingazzini (1859–1929) (cf. Mingazzini 1928). The studies were carried into the first decades of the twentieth century. (For bibliographic details of this burgeoning literature, see Connolly 1950.)

From a strictly anthropological perspective, the work of Paul Broca during the third quarter of the nineteenth century is of particular interest. During the 1860s, he made a very specific case for the dominance of the left hemisphere in language (Broca 1863, 1865). It is interesting to note that a similar idea had been proposed by the French physician Gustave Dax in the 1830s (it was later published in 1865)—but from all indications Broca was not aware of this earlier work (cf. Finger 1994). Broca's (and Dax's) argument was subsequently supported by a number of workers, but in particular by Wernicke in his monograph *Der Aphasische Symtomencomplex,* published in 1874.

Given Broca's interest in neuroanatomy, it is not surprising that his Société d'Anthropologie de Paris, founded in 1859, became an important forum for the discussion of racial differences in brain weight and organization. Initially, Broca was of the opinion that there was a connection between brain size and intelligence; he had argued that educated people had bigger brains than the noneducated, and he had criticized Tiedemann for having preconceived views about the equality of brain size in all human races. However, as more comparative data became available on living and fossil populations during the early 1870s, Broca modified these views—though he still believed that racial groups like the Hottentots and the Australian Aborigines were innately inferior because of their comparatively smaller brain capacities. (Further historical details on this issue can be found in Finger 1994.)

In addition to these debates on the truth or fiction of the racial inequality of brain size, the end of the nineteenth century introduced the controversy of the lunate sulcus (simian sulcus, *affenspalte*) and its disposition in apes and humans. The German anatomist Nicholaus Rüdinger was the first to apply this term to a fissure in the human brain in 1882. Among those who initially questioned this observation were the Dublin anatomist John Cunningham (1850–1909) and the Swedish anatomist-anthropologist Magnus Gustaf Retzius (1842–1919). While Cunningham (1892) was plainly skeptical of it being a homologous structure, Retzius (1896) believed the sulcus was a transitory feature rather than a homologue. This controversy was essentially resolved by the Australian anatomist-anthropologist Grafton Elliot Smith (1871–1937). From gross dissections of numerous monkey and ape brains, Smith showed that the stripes of Gennari (named after the Italian anatomist Francesco Gennari [1750–1797] by the German anatomist Heinrich Obersteiner [1847–1922]) characterized the primary visual striate cortex (later known as "area 17 of Brodmann"), which was bounded anteriorly by a deep crescentic (hence "lunate") sulcus. This feature, he contended, was shared by most primates, including humans (cf. Smith 1903, 1904). Among humans, however, the lunate, when and if present, was always in a more posterior position than in apes, signifying that there was a reduction of the relative size of striate cortex and a relative increase in parietal association cortex in humans (cf. Connolly 1950 for an excellent discussion of this structure, along with a review of the similarities and differences between humans and other primates, as well as racial differences in *Homo sapiens*). Although there were some notable workers, such as the American neurologist Frederick Tilney (1870–1951) (1928), who continued to doubt that humans had a homologue of the *Affenspalte*, the vast majority accepted Smith's argument. In the meantime, Smith was so intent in advancing his case for the primacy of the brain in human evolution that he "saw" the lunate sulcus in the endocasts of fossils such as the now infamous and bogus Piltdown remains (Smith 1913), and much later he studied the endocranial cast of "Rhodesian Man" (1928) (cf. Fig. 3).

The study of the brain endocast of the La Chapelle-aux-Saints Neandertal fossil conducted by the French workers Marcellin Boule (1861–1942) and Raoul Anthony (1874–1941) in 1911 was guided by a similar expectation—and these workers also claimed that the La Chapelle brain manifested a primitive disposition of the lunate sulcus (cf. Boule & Anthony 1911). These studies, and in particular Smith's views on the Piltdown endocast, met with a hostile reaction from the Belfast anatomist Johnson Symington (1851–1924) (1916), who vigorously attacked these claims as "highly speculative and fallacious"—arguing that such identifications based simply on endocast material were almost impossible to confirm. Although the lunate sulcus remains a contentious neocortical landmark, the issue is no longer whether it exists but rather *when*

it was in a fully human posterior position—by the time of *Australopithecus* or by the time of early *Homo*? An early posterior migration would indicate that brain evolution was quite early in fossil hominids and preceded the great increase in brain size, thus making the brain one of the first organs, rather than the last, to evolve in human evolution (Holloway 1985).

Early-Modern Period: 1920s–1950

The early-modern period is characterized by the increasing number of research publications that manifest a continuing emphasis on comparative racial neuroanatomy, as well as an increase in paleoneuroanatomical studies. Research in the latter category was fed primarily by the mounting tempo of hominid fossil discoveries in Asia, Africa, and Europe. Following in the wake of the Dutch physician Eugène Dubois' (1858–1940) 1924 study of the endocast of the Javan *Pithecanthropus erectus* calvaria he had found at the close of the nineteenth century was a series of studies on the hominid crania (i.e., *Sinanthropus = Homo erectus*) recovered from the Zhoukoudian site in China in the late 1920s and early 1930s. The Canadian anatomist Davidson Black (1884–1934), who had been largely responsible for these discoveries described the endocast remains of *Sinanthropus pekinensis* in 1933; while the Dutch neuroanatomist C.U. Ariëns Kappers (1877–1946) wrote several papers on both the Chinese and the Javanese pithecanthropine endocasts (Ariëns Kappers 1933; Ariëns Kappers & Bouman 1939). Similarly, the German anatomist-anthropologist Franz Weidenreich (1873–1948), who succeeded Black at Zhoukoudian in the mid-1930s, also made several important contributions to the study of human brain evolution between 1936 and 1947, particularly with regard to *Sinanthropus*.

During this same time period, several new European and African hominid fossils received attention. In France, for example, the details of Anthony's earlier study of the La Quina endocast were published as a part of the French paleoanthropologist Henri Martin's (1864–1936) memoir on *L'homme fossile de La Quina* (cf. Anthony 1923), while in England, Wilfrid Edward Le Gros Clark (1895–1971) described the endocranial cast of the Swanscombe remains (cf. Hinton et al. 1938). The most significant and clearly the most controversial find of the period was the infantile australopithecine skull found in 1924 at Taung in South Africa, which was described by the anatomist Raymond A. Dart (1893–

1988) at the University of the Witwatersrand, Johannesburg. Dart had studied for a while under Grafton Elliot Smith at Manchester University in England and had been influenced by him. In the description of this new hominid genus (which he named), published in 1925, Dart argued that the Taung child showed some modern features in its natural brain endocast. As this and his later work indicate, Dart was a champion of the concept of reorganization in the human brain—an issue

that remains controversial. Dart's assessment of the Taung specimen was vigorously resisted. During the 1930s and 1940s, however, adult representatives of this early hominid were found at other South African sites, which led to the publication of the important monograph in 1946 by Robert Broom (1866–1951) and G.W.H. Schepers on *The South African Fossil Ape-Men: The Australopithecinae*, in which Schepers, an anatomist from the University of the Witwatersrand, contributed sections on

Fig. 2. Brodmann's cyto-architectural map of the brain. The various areas are labeled with different symbols and identified further by figures. (A) is a lateral view of left hemisphere, and (B) is a medial view of right hemisphere.

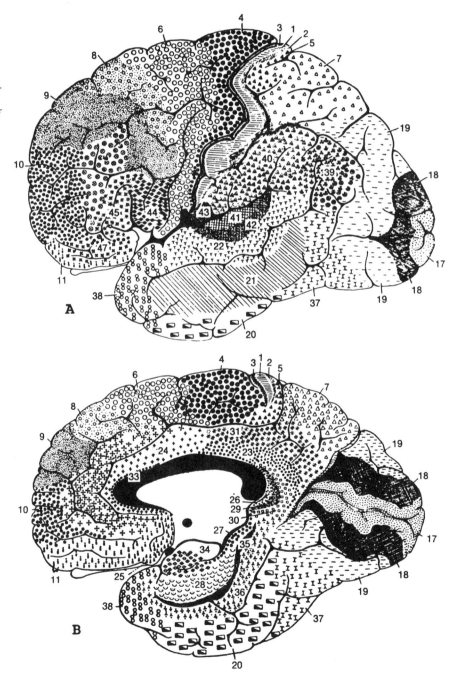

the natural brain endocasts recovered mostly from Sterkfontein (cf. Broom & Schepers 1946: 155–272). Their opinion was similar to that of Dart's that the brain endocasts were from animals more advanced than apes—an opinion that found a more secure foothold in the anthropological community when Clark endorsed it in an article published in the *Journal of Anatomy* in 1947 (cf. Holloway 1985 for a review of this matter).

Racial studies of the human brain were numerous during this time period, and the reader is directed to the excellent bibliography provided by C.J. Connolly (1950) and S. Finger (1994). These studies tend to stress morphological variations that were present or absent in various races and whether some of these patterns were more primitive than others. Reading this literature in the light of modern knowledge is a curious experience. Many of the published descriptions suggest that variation does exist and that it is patterned differently in various geographical areas. Since World War II, the comparative study of morphological and possibly racial neurophysiological variability has been replaced exclusively with concerns and debates regarding either the size of the brain in the sexes and various races or the encephalization quotients applied to our fossil ancestors (*vide infra*).

Building on the foundations laid earlier by the Spanish neurohistologist Santiago Ramón y Cajal (1852–1934), the German neurologist Korbinian Brodmann (1868–1918) (1909) found that areas of the cerebral cortex were distinguished by differences in the arrangement of their six cellular layers, which allowed him to subdivide the human cerebral hemisphere into more than forty discrete areas, the so-called Brodmann areas (see Fig. 2). His numerical system is still used today. It is interesting to note in passing that during this same time period, Smith was able to produce a cortical map based only on gross dissection with a scalpel and magnifying glass (1907).

During the 1930s, detailed cortical maps of human brains were developed—most notably by the American neurosurgeon Wilder G. Penfield (1891–1976) and his coworkers and the German neuroanatomist Gerhardt von Bonin (1890–1979). Important data on the cerebral cortex for nonhuman primates were also gathered at this time—for the gorilla (Fulton 1938), the chimpanzee (Mingazzini 1928; Kreht 1936), the orangutan (Kreht 1936), *Ateles* (Fulton & Dusser de Barenne 1933), and *Macaca* (Dusser de Barenne & McCulloch 1938). These studies remain im-

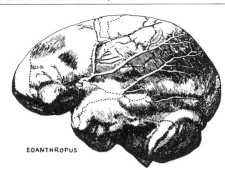

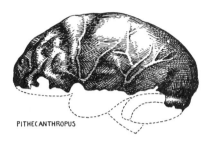

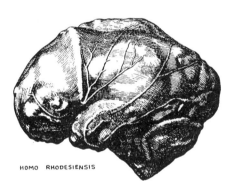

Fig. 3. Endocranial casts studied by Grafton Elliot Smith. From his collection of essays on The Evolution of Man *(1927).*

EOANTHROPUS

PITHECANTHROPUS

HOMO RHODESIENSIS

portant contributions to the understanding of primate variation in cytoarchitectonic cortical studies, which, in concert with C.N. Woolsey's major work on neurophysiology (cf. Woolsey 1958), paved the way for the modern finer-grained understanding of these elements.

During this period, Ariëns Kappers produced two major texts on comparative neuroanatomy, one in 1929 and the other in 1936 (in collaboration with G.C. Huber and E.C. Crosby). These works have since become "bibles" for physical anthropologists and zoologists alike. Several other valuable sources were produced during this time, including Frederick Tilney's two-volume work *The Brain from Ape to Man* (1928) and C.J. Connolly's *The External Morphology of the Primate Brain* (1950). The latter work is extraordinarily valuable not only for its bibliography but also for its breadth and erudition. Another excellent source is the seldom mentioned doctoral dissertation of P. Hirschler, entitled *Anthropoid and Human Endocranial Casts,* which was published in Amsterdam in 1942.

Modern Period: 1950s–1990s

The growth of neuroscience since the late 1950s has been astonishing—indeed, advances have been so rapid that keeping up with the literature has become an increasingly difficult task. Furthermore, without a firm foundation in molecular biology, the nonspecialist will find it difficult to even read the titles of published papers. New techniques such as MRI (magnetic resonance imaging) and PET (positron emission tomography) have added and will continue to add radically to our knowledge regarding where in the brain particular cognitive tasks take place, and their actual process in real time. These studies have already had important impacts on our understanding of motor and receptive aspects of language behavior and the relationship to such traditionally-thought-of regions of the brain as Broca's and Wernicke's areas. In general, the findings indicate that far more of the cortex and subcortex are involved in both simple and complex cognitive tasks. The growing sophistication with which cytoarchitecture of the cortex is now studied, and the complex cortical maps thus far developed for a number of primate species, are producing a tremendous amount of data that will lead to some critical needs for synthesis between the more or less standard areas of the neurosciences, such as neuroanatomy, cell biology, neurophysiology, and neurochemistry, and the newer foci, such as neuroimmunopsychology, neuroimmunoendocrinology, and neurogenetics. However, it should be noted that all of these trends are essentially molecular in nature and, as such, provide no handles with which to deal with the hard fossil evidence regarding the brain. Similarly, these studies have yielded no greater understanding of racial variation or simple within-species variation in humans.

Since the 1960s, there has been a trend among investigators with a direct interest in brain evolution toward the study of brain size and allometry. Although the concepts of scaling and/or allometry extend back into the nineteenth century (e.g., Dareste 1862; Baillarger 1872; Snell 1892; Dubois 1897); and the early twentieth century (Lapique 1912; Count 1947), it was not until the late 1960s and early 1970s that allometry took hold. This trend can be traced in large part to the influence of the American zoologist Harry Jerison and his former student Stephen Jay Gould. Jerison's writings (e.g., Jerison 1963, 1973) and particularly Gould's (1977), which integrated brain–body relationships within an evolutionary framework, have become a driving force in the thinking of many physical anthropologists and zoologists. The arguments have unfortunately taken the force of law, as in Jerison's works and many others. The value of the allometric approach is not that it provides answers to how the brain and behavior coevolved; it is rather that allometric relationships show that there are clearly genetic constraints operating, around which different species vary. Constraint vs. genetic law is a distinction seldom appreciated (cf. Holloway 1979). The American functional morphologist Leonard Radinsky (1937–?1986), who was a major contributing force to the development of paleoneurology during the 1960s and 1970s, was also an open but critical spirit regarding the importance of allometry. He believed that while this approach would offer no solutions to the question of brain organization, it nevertheless could not be ignored (cf. Radinsky 1974).

In addition to a preoccupation with problems of scaling, other quantitative viewpoints have arisen that have taken on a curious life of their own. Two such concepts, "extra cortical neurons" (N_c's) and "encephalization quotients" (E.Q.'s) are popular in physical anthropology into the 1990s. The "Extra Cortical Neurons" concept was developed by Jerison (1963) as a way of quantifying the number of neurons beyond those necessary to operate basic vegetative functions related to body size. Jerison assumed that animals such as shrews had a cortex devoted exclusively to vegetative functioning, and, by using them as a basal standard, he devised an equation based on a double exponentiation of body weight and one of brain weight for other animals. This was based on the assumption that brain–body scaling in mammals was 0.66. With this equation, it became possible to calculate the "extra number of cortical neurons" by simply inserting an animal's brain and body weights into the equation. Despite criticisms leveled at this concept (e.g. Holloway 1966, 1974, 1979), it has remained influential (cf. Tobias 1971, 1987). What is not generally taken into account is that in most mammals' brains, the cerebral cortex is anything but homogeneous. Different cortical regions have very different neural densities, and, at least in primates, there have been some major changes in the distribution of different cytoarchitectural patterns in the cerebral cortex (Holloway 1968).

The whole question of what is "extra" functionally, in the cortex and the corresponding animal behavior, is, to say the least, a thorny one. The upshot is that this has led to undue speculation regarding the number of "extra" cortical neurons in australopithecines vs. habilines based on unknown quantities of brain and body weights that have to be estimated without any final empirical checks.

The E.Q.'s concept, also devised by Jerison (1973), has been championed by many physical anthropologists. This quotient is derived by dividing an animal's actual brain weight by a "basal" allometric equation derived from some set of animal brain and body weights, in which the animal's actual body weight is placed in the equation. Many investigators have introduced their own equations, depending on their perception of what basal animal group is the most appropriate. These are then calculated for fossil hominoids after speculating on their body weights. But what is seldom appreciated is that these E.Q's are entirely relative to the equation chosen, leading to a "relativity" of relative brain weights (cf. Holloway & Post 1982).

Another area of modern concentration has been asymmetries in the brain, particularly the cerebral cortex. As noted earlier, concern with this problem can be traced to the work of Willis in the seventeenth century. Cunningham (1892) had demonstrated asymmetries in the height of the sylvian fissure in a number of primate species' brains. Work along these lines has been carried out by the American anatomist Marjorie LeMay and her colleagues (cf. LeMay 1976; LeMay et al. 1982), as well as the American physical anthropologists Ralph Holloway (Holloway & DeLacoste-Lareymondie 1982; Holloway 1975, 1976, 1983a, b, c; Heilbroner & Holloway 1989) and Dean Falk (e.g., 1978, 1980a, 1980b). It was LeMay's earlier study of the relationship between cerebral petalias and handedness that led Holloway and DeLacoste-Lareymondie (1982) to study the brain endocast collection of both hominids and pongids, and to observe that only hominids had the combined torque-like pattern of a left-occipital petalia combined with a right lateral frontal one. Previously, neuroanatomists had reported brain asymmetries in nonhuman primates (e.g., Yeni-Komshian & Benson 1976), but these were in anatomical structures seldom available in brain endocasts.

A central issue to almost all paleoneuroanatomical studies is the question, When in the evolutionary process did specific reductions or modifications occur? Since the late 1970s, considerable ink has been consumed in a debate regarding the lunate sulcus and its position relative to the occipital pole in the australopithecines. One view is that the shift occurred in early australopithecine times (cf. Holloway 1975, 1983a, 1983b, 1983c; Holloway & Kimbel 1986); the opposing view favors a primitive ape-like retention in australopithecines and a human organization in *Homo habilis* (cf. Falk 1987). This debate, however, like so many others in paleoanthropology, will be resolved only by more fossil discoveries or by other independent assessments of the actual measurements on chimpanzee and australopithecine brain endocasts.

Finally, neuroscientific studies regarding human variation both ethnically and between the sexes have been relatively rare in the latter part of the twentieth century. The overall perception is that differences between the races or sexes with regard to either brain size or organization are not of any scientific value, and, as such, research along those lines has been discouraged. In 1992, however, the journal *Nature* carried a limited exchange between J. Phillipe Rushton and his detractors regarding apparent brain-size differences between "Asians, Blacks, and Whites" (e.g., *Nature* 358:532, 1992). Unfortunately, the fundamental issue of what these differences mean with regard to either behavioral variation or human evolution and adaptation was not addressed. Indeed, these and related questions remain as elusive and unanswered as they were two hundred years ago.

The question of differences in absolute and relative brain weights between females and males is still bandied about, usually with great inaccuracy. Since the 1970s, however, evidence has emerged for minor differences—though of questionable significance—in cognitive behavior between females and males. Similarly, much controversy surrounds issues such as organizational differences between male and female brains. Studies have shown that females have relatively larger corpora callosi compared to males (cf. Holloway et al. 1994 for a review of these questions). There has also been a growing acceptance of the proposition that perhaps males' and females' brains do differ in a number of ways beyond the anterior nucleus of the hypothalamus. Research in the 1990s has been directed to brain differences in gay males and females compared to heterosexuals (cf. Levay 1991, 1993), and with regard to chromosomal evidence as well (Hamer 1994). If these trends can be maintained with judicious and open studies to verify or refute previous studies, neuroscience and anthropology will have close connections. However, if sexual rhetoric wins out, it will ultimately be a loss for all.

Despite the enormous volume of research in primate neuroanatomy during this "modern" period, anthropologists are still unable to provide satisfactory explanations for the qualitative changes that occurred during primate evolution. While this prevailing situation can be blamed in part on the availability of evidence, it is also clear that the profession has, contrary to expectations, failed to muster a concerted research effort in this direction.

Given the central role that the brain has played in human evolution (and surely much of antecedent primate evolution as well), the subject of comparative neuroscience should be a central part of the training of physical anthropologists, but it is not. A careful glance at all of the textbooks devoted to physical anthropology since the Harvard physical anthropologist Earnest A. Hooton's *Up from the Ape* (1946) will quickly show that the brain seldom commands more than a page or two of textual description, and even less for the problems surrounding its evolution (beyond size, with allometry being only a recent concern for such authors) and how the subject might be studied. If nothing else, this might at least equip the physical anthropologist of the twenty-first century to comprehend the anticipated advances in this crucial and exciting field of scientific inquiry.

Ralph L. Holloway

See also Anthony, Raoul; Australopithecines; Black, Davidson; Blumenbach, Johann Friedrich; Broca, Paul (Pierre); Broom, Robert; Chapelle-aux-Saints, La; Chudziński, Théophile (Teofil); Clark, (Sir) Wilfred Edward Le Gros; Dart, Raymond A(rthur); Darwin, Charles Robert; Evolutionary Theory; Flower, (Sir) William Henry; Germany; Gratiolet, Louis Pierre; Huxley, Thomas Henry; Mingazzini, Giovanni; Owen, (Sir) Richard; Paleoanthropology Theory; Phrenology; Piltdown; Retzius, Magnus Gustaf; Smith, (Sir) Grafton Elliot; Taung (formerly Taungs); Tyson, Edward; Weidenreich, Franz

Bibliography
R. Anthony: [On the La Quina brain]. In: H. Martin *L'homme fossile de La Quina.* Paris: Doin, 1923, pp. 108–114; C.U. Ariëns Kappers: *The evolution of the nervous system in invertebrates, vertebrates, and man.* Haarlem: Bohn, 1929; C.U. Ariëns Kappers: The fissuration on the frontal lobe of *Sinathropus pekinensis,* Black, compared with fissuration in Neanderthal men. *Proceedings of the Koninklijke Nederlandsche Akademie van Wetenschappen* 36:802–812, 1933: C.U. Ariëns Kappers & K.H. Bouman: Comparison of the endocranial casts of the *Pithecanthropus erectus* skull found by Dubois and von Koenigswald's *Pithecanthropus* skull. *Proceedings of the Koninklijke Nederlansche Akademie van Wetenschappen* 42:30–40, 1939; C.U. Ariëns Kappers, G.C. Huber, & E.C. Crosby: *The comparative anatomy of the nervous system of vertebrates, including man.* New York: Macmillan, 1936; J.G.F. Baillarger: *Recherches sur l'anatomie, la physiologie et la pathologie du système nerveux.* Paris: Masson, 1872; T. Bendyshe (ed): *The anthropological treatises of J.F. Blumenbach.* London: Longmans, 1865; T.L.W. Bischoff: *Über die Verschiedenheit in der Schädelbildung des Gorilla, Schimpanse, und Orang, vorzüglich nach Geschlect und Alter, nebst einer Bemerkung über die Darwinische Theorie.* München: Verlag der Akademie (G. Franz); 1867.

D. Black: The brain cast of *Sinanthropus*: A review. *Journal of Comparative Neurology* 57:361–367, 1933; M. Boule & R. Anthony: L'encephale de l'homme fossile de la Chapelle-aux-Saints. *L'Anthropologie* 22:129–196, 1911; P. Broca: Localisation des fonctiones cérébrales: Siège de la faculté du langage articulé. *Bulletins de la Société d'Anthropologie de Paris* 4:200–208, 1863; P. Broca: Du siège de la faculté du langage articulé dans l'hémisphère gauche du cerveau. *Bulletins de la Société d'Anthropologie de Paris* 6:377–393, 1865; K. Brodmann: *Vergleichende Lokalisationslehre der Grosshirnrinde in ihren Prinzipenb dargestellt auf Grund des Zellenbaues.* Leipzig: Barth, 1909.

R. Broom & G.W.H. Schepers: *The South African fossil ape-men: The Australopithecinae.* Transvaal Museum Memoirs. No. 2. Pretoria, 1956; T. Chudziński: *Comparative anatomy of the cerebral folds.* In Polish. 2 vols. Paris: Mémoires de la la Société polonaise de Sciences, 1878–1882; W.E. Le Gros Clark: Observations on the anatomy of the fossil Australopithecinae. *Journal of Anatomy* 81:300, 1947; C.J. Connolly: *The external morphology of the primate brain.* Springfield, Illinois: Thomas, 1950; E.W. Count: Brain and body weights in man: Their antecedents in growth and evolution. *Annals of the New York Academy of Science* 46:993–1122, 1947; D.J. Cunningham: *Contributions to the surface anatomy of the cerebral hemispheres*. Royal Irish Academy of Sciences Memoirs. No. 7. Dublin: Royal Irish Academy, 1892.

M.C. Dareste: Sur les rapports de la masse encéphalique avec de développement de l'intelligence. *Bulletins de la Société d'Anthropologie de Paris* 3:26, 1862; R. Dart: *Australopithecus africanus:* The man-ape of South Africa. *Nature* 115:195–199, 1925; G. Dax: Lésion de la moitié gauche de l'encéphale coincidant avec l'oubli des signes de la pensée (Montpellier en 1836). *Gazette hebdomadaires* 2 (2d ser.):259–262, 1865; E. Dubois: Sur la rapport du poids de l'encéphale avec la grandeur du corps chez le mammifères. *Bulletins de la Société d'Anthropologie de Paris* 8:337–376, 1897; E. Dubois: On the principle characters of the cranium and brain, the mandible and the teeth of *Pithecanthropus erectus*. *Proceedings, Koninklijke Akademie van Wetenschappen te Amsterdam* 27:265–278, 1924; J.G. Dusser de Barenne & W.S. McCulloch: Functional organization in the sensory cortex of the monkey (*Macaca mulatta*). *Journal of Neurophysiology* 1:69–85, 1938; A. Ecker: *On the convolutions of the human brain.* English Translation by J.C. Galton. London: Smith 1873.

D. Falk: Brain evolution in Old World monkeys. *American Journal of Physical Anthropology* 48:315–320, 1978; D. Falk: A comparative study of the endocranial casts of New and Old World monkeys. In: R.L. Ciochon & B. Chiarelli (eds) *Evolutionary biology of the New World monkeys and continental drift*. New York: Plenum, 1980a, pp. 275–292; D. Falk: A reanalysis of the South African australopithecine natural endocasts. *American Journal of Physical Anthropology* 53:525–539, 1980b; D. Falk: Hominid paleoneurology. *Annual Review of Anthropology* 16:13–30, 1987; K.M. Figlio: The metaphor of organization: An historiographical perspective on the biomedical sciences of the early nineteenth century. *History of Science* 14:17–53, 1976.

S. Finger: *Origins of neuroscience: A history of explorations into brain function*. New York: Oxford University Press, 1994; P. Flourens: *Examen de la phrénologie*. Paris: Garnier, 1842; W.H. Flower: Observations on the posterior lobes of the cerebrum of the Quadrumana. *Proceedings of the Royal Society of London* 11:376–381, 1861; W.H. Flower: On the brain of the siamang. *Natural History Review* n.s. 2:279–287, 1863; J.F. Fulton: Cytoarchitecture of the gorilla brain. *Science* 88:426–427, 1938; J.F. Fulton & G. Dusser de Barenne: The representation of the tail in the motor cortex of primates, with special reference to spider monkeys. *Journal of Cellular and Comparative Physiology* 2:399–426, 1933; F.J. Gall: *Anatomie et physiologie du système nerveux en générale*. 4 vols. Paris: Schoell, 1810.

S.J. Gould: *Ontogeny and phylogeny*. Cambridge, Massachusetts: Belknap Press, 1977; P. Gratiolet: *Mémoire sur les plis cérébraux de l'homme et des primates*. Paris: Bertrand, 1854; D.H. Hamer et al.: A linkage between DNA markers and the X chromosome and male sexual orientation. *Science* 261:321–327, 1993; P. Heilbroner & R.L. Holloway: Anatomical brain asymmetries in New World and Old World monkeys: Shape of temporal lobe development in primate evolution. *American Journal of Physical Anthropology* 76:39–48, 1988; P. Heilbroner & R.L. Holloway: Anatomical brain asymmetry in monkeys: Frontal, parietal, and limbic cortex in *Macaca*. *American Journal of Physical Anthropology* 80:203–211, 1989; M.A.C. Hinton et al.: Report of the Swanscombe Committee. *Journal of the Royal Anthropological Institute* 68:17–98, 1938.

P. Hirschler: *Anthropoid and human endocranial casts*. Amsterdam: Noord-Hollandsche Uitgeversmaatschappijen, 1942; R.L. Holloway: Cranial capacity and neuron number: Critique and proposal. *American Journal of Physical Anthropology* 25:305–314, 1966; R.L. Holloway: The evaluation of the primate brain: Some aspects of quantitative relationships. *Brain Research* 76:121–172, 1968; R.L. Holloway: The meaning of brain size: Review of Jerison's 1973 *Evolution of the brain and intelligence*. *Science* 184:677–679, 1974; R.L. Holloway: Early hominid endocasts, volumes, morphology, and significance. In: R. Tuttle (ed) *Primate functional morphology and evolution*. The Hague: Mouton, 1975, pp. 393–416; R.L. Holloway: Paleoneurological evidence for language origins. *Annals of the New York Academy of Science* 280:330–348, 1976.

R.L. Holloway: Brain size, allometry, and reorganization: Toward a synthesis. In: M.E. Hahn et al. (eds) *The development and evolution of brain size: Behavioral implications*. New York: Academic Press, 1979, pp. 59–88; R.L. Holloway: Cerebral brain endocast pattern of *A. afarensis* hominid. *Nature* 303:422, 1983a; R.L. Holloway: Human brain evolution: A search for units, models, and synthesis. *Canadian Journal of Anthropology* 3:215–232, 1983b; R.L. Holloway: Human paleontological evidence relevant to language behavior. *Human Neurobiology* 2:105–114, 1983c; R.L. Holloway: The past, present, and future significance of the lunate sulcus in early hominid evolution. In: P.V. Tobias (ed) *Human evolution: Past, present, and future.* New York: Liss, 1985, pp. 47–62.

R.L. Holloway & M.C. DeLacoste-Lareymondie: Brain endocast asymmetry in pongids and hominids: Some preliminary findings on the paleontology of cerebral dominance. *American Journal of Physical Anthropology* 58:101–110, 1982; R.L. Holloway & M.C. DeLacoste: Sexual dimorphism in the corpus callosum: An extension and replication study. *Human Neurobiology* 5:87–91, 1986; R.L. Holloway & W.H. Kimbel: Endocast morphology of Hadar hominid AL 162–28. *Nature* 321:536, 1986; R.L. Holloway & D. Post: The reliability of relative brain measures and hominid evaluation. In: E. Armstrong & D. Falk (eds) *Primate brain evolution.* New York: Plenum, 1982, pp. 59–76; R.L. Holloway et al.: Sexual dimorphism of the human corpus callosum from three independent autopsy samples: Relative size of the corpus callosum. *American Journal of Physical Anthropology* 92:481–498, 1994.

E.A. Hooton: *Up from the Ape.* New York: Macmillan, 1946; T.H. Huxley: *Evidence as to man's place in nature.* London: Williams & Norgate, 1863; H.J. Jerison: Interpreting the evolution of the brain. *Human Biology* 35:263–291, 1963; H.J. Jerison: *Evolution of the brain and intelligence.* New York: Academic Press, 1973; J.H.F. Kohlbrügge: *Muskeln und periphere nerven der primaten, mit besonderer berücksichtigung ihrer anomalien: Eine Vergleichend-anatomische und anthropologische untersuchung.* Amsterdam: Muller, 1897; H. Kreht: Zur Architektonik der Brocaschen Region beim Schimpanzen und Orang-Utan. *Zeitschrift für Anatomische und Entwicklgeschichte* 105:654–677, 1936; L. Lapique: Sur la relation du poids de l'encéphale au poids du corps. *Comptes rendu des séances de la Société de Biologie et de ses Filiales* 50:62–63, 1898; W. Lawrence: *Lectures on comparative anatomy, physiology, zoology, and the natural history of man.* London: Smite, 1819.

M. LeMay: Morphological cerebral asymmetries of modern man, fossil man, and nonhuman primates. *Annals of the New York Academy of Science* 280:349–366, 1976; M. LeMay & A. Culebras: Human brain: Morphological differences in the hemispheres demonstrated by carotid angiography. *New England Journal of Medicine* 287:168–170, 1972; M. LeMay et al.: Asymmetries of the brains and skulls of nonhuman primates. In: E. Armstrong & D. Falk (eds) *Primate brain evolution.* New York: Plenum, 1982, pp. 263–277; S. Levay: A difference in hypothalamic structure between heterosexual and homosexual men. *Science* 253:1034–1037, 1991; S. Levay: *The sexual brain.* Cambridge, Massachusetts: MIT Press, 1993; J. Marshall: On the brain of a young chimpanzee. *Natural History Review* o.s.1:296–315, 1861.

G. Mingazzini: Beitrag zur Morphologie der ausseren Grosshirnhemispharenoberflache bei den Anthropoiden. *Archiv für Psychiatrie und Nervenkrankheiten* 85:1–219, 1928; R. Owen: On the characters, principles of division, and primary groups of the class Mammalia. *Journal of the Proceedings of the Linnean Society* 2:1–37, 1857; R. Owen: *On the classification and geographical distribution of the Mammalia.* London: Parker, 1859; L. Radinsky: The fossil evidence of anthropoid brain evolution. *American Journal of Physical Anthropology* 41:15–28, 1974; G. Retzius: *Das Menschenhirn.* Stockholm: G. Norstedt & Soner, 1896; G. Rolleston: On the affinities and differences between the brain of the orangutan. *Natural History Review* n.s. 1:201–217, 1861.

N. Rüdinger: Ein Beitrag zur Anatomie der Affenspalte und Interparietalfurche beim Menschen nach Race, Geschlecht und Individualität. *Festschrift für J. Henle.* 1882, pp. 186–198; G.E. Smith: The so-called *Affenspalte* in the human (Egyptian) brain. *Anatomischer Anzeiger* 23:75, 1903; G.E. Smith: The morphology of the occipital region of the cerebral hemisphere in man and apes. *Anatomischer Anzeiger* 24:436–451, 1904; G.E. Smith: A new topographical survey of the human cerebral cortex. *Journal of Anatomy* 41:237, 1907; G.E. Smith: Preliminary report on the cranial cast of Piltdown man. *Quarterly Journal of the Geological Society of London* 69:145, 1913.

G.E. Smith: Cranial cast obtained from the Rhodesian skull. In: W.P. Pycraft et al.:

Rhodesian man and associated remains. London: British Museum (Natural History), 1928, pp. 52–58; O. Snell: Die Abhängigbeit des Hirngewichtes von dem Korpergewicht und des Gestigen Fahigbeiten. *Archiv für Psychiatrie* 23:436–446, 1892; J. Symington: Endocranial casts and brain form: A criticism of some recent speculations. *Journal of Anatomy and Physiology* 50:111–130, 1916; F. Tiedemann: On the brain of the Negro compared with that of the European and the Orang-outang. *Philosophical Transactions of the Royal Society of London* 126:497–524, 1836; F. Tilney: *The brain from ape to man.* 2 vols. New York: Hoeber, 1928; P.V. Tobias: *The brain of hominid evolution.* New York: Columbia University Press, 1971; P.V. Tobias: The brain of *Homo habilis:* A new level of organization in cerebral evolution. *Journal of Human Evolution* 16:741–761, 1987.

W. Waldeyer: *Ueber einige neuere Forschungen im Gebiete der anatomie der centralnervensystem.* Leipzig: Thieme, 1891; F. Weidenreich: Observations on the form and proportions of the endocranial casts of *Sinanthropus pekinensis* and the great apes: A comparative study of brain size. *Paleontologia Sinica* 7 (Ser. W):1–50, 1936; F. Weidenreich: Some particulars of skull and brain of early hominids and their bearing on the problem of the relationship between man and anthropoids. *American Journal of Physical Anthropology* 5 (n.s.):387–427, 1947.

C. Wernicke: *Die Aphasische Systomencomplex: Eine psychologische studien auf anatomischer.* Breslau: Cohn & Weigert, 1874; C.N. Woolsey: Organization of somatic sensory and motor areas in the cerebral cortex. In: H. Harlow & C.N. Woolsey (eds) *Biological and biochemical basis of behavior.* Madison: University of Wisconsin Press, 1958, pp. 17–26; G.H. Yeni-Khomshian & D.A. Benson: Anatomical study of cerebral asymmetry in the temporal lobe of humans, chimpanzees, and Rhesus monkeys. *Science* 192:387–389, 1976.

New World Primate Studies

The living nonhuman primates of the Western Hemisphere (Central and South America), commonly known as New World primates, platyrrhine monkeys, or ceboid monkeys, first became known to inhabitants of the Eastern Hemisphere in the early sixteenth century as a result of reports of early European explor-ers. In his now classic tenth edition of *Systema naturae* (1758) the Swedish naturalist Carolus Linnaeus (1707–1778) included all monkeys (both Old and New World) in the same genus, *Simia;* however, he recognized seven species of Neotropical monkeys: *Callithrix jacchus, Saguinus midas, S. oedipus, Ateles paniscus, Cebus apella, C. capucinus,* and *Saimiri sciureus.* By the twelfth edition (1766), he added five additional species. The French naturalist Etienne Geoffroy Saint-Hilaire (1772–1844) was the first to recognize the distinctive nature of the "platyrrhine" (broad) nose of the New World monkeys (cf. Geoffroy Saint-Hilaire 1812). Collectors in the nineteenth century, especially the German naturalist Alexander von Humboldt (1769–1859), added greatly to the knowledge of these primates. The most recent genus described was *Callimico* (Goeldi's monkey) by the British mammologist M.R. Oldfield Thomas (1858–1921) in 1904. New species continue to be found, however, including two in 1992. The evolutionary history of the New World primates is poorly known; however, it is certain they radiated in South America and did not spread to Central America until the "Great Faunal Interchange" of the Pliocene. Fossils are also known from Caribbean Islands.

For the purpose of description, the history of primate field studies in the New World is divided into four phases.

The Carpenter Era: 1931–1937

The first analytical census of any nonhuman primate population was conducted by Clarence Raymond Carpenter (1905–1975) in the early 1930s, working on a postdoctoral fellowship under the psychologist Robert M. Yerkes (1876–1956) at Yale University. At that time, the only previous scientific attempts at studying primates in the wild were by Harold C. Bingham (1888–1958) and Henry Nissen (1901–1958), two other students sent to Africa by Yerkes in 1929 and 1930, respectively. Beginning on Christmas day 1931, Carpenter inaugurated the first field investigation of a Neotropical primate, *Alouatta palliata,* the howler monkey on Barro Colorado Island (BCI). BCI is a 15 km² island created by the flooding of the Chagres River to form Lake Gatun during the building of the Panama Canal. The island became a research reserve of the Smithsonian Institution, Washington, D.C., in 1923.

Over a period of about a year and a half, Carpenter spent about eight months of intensive observation on BCI; in addition, he observed two other subspecies of *A. palliata*, one on mainland Panama and one on Coiba Island, the largest island off the Pacific Coast of Panama. Most of Carpenter's conclusions still stand today (e.g., regarding the centripetal role of the adult female in the group), while others (e.g., "howlers tend to occupy a definite and limited territory" [1934:126]) have been superseded by more-recent work. A year later, Carpenter studied the spider monkey in Panama, which was the first field study of *Ateles* (1935). The howler monkeys on BCI have been studied continuously, except for a hiatus from 1937–1951, ever since 1931 (cf. Eisenberg 1991:132).

The Expansion Era: 1951–1971

With the intervention of World War II, studies of South American primates in their natural habitat came to a halt, and the next field study did not occur until 1951 when D.E.

Fig. 1. Two South American monkeys: (a) black-handed spider monkey (Ateles geoffroyi)*; (b) Humboldt's woolly monkey* (Lagothrix lagotricha)*. From W.H. Flower & R. Lydekker:* An Introduction to the Study of Mammals, Living and Extinct. *London, 1891.*

(a)

(b)

Collias and C.H. Southwick restudied the howlers on BCI (1952). Several studies of howler monkeys followed, but until 1958 only howlers, spider monkeys, and tufted capuchins (Causey et al. 1948; Gilmore 1943) had received any attention. In 1958, M. Moynihan initiated a series of field and captive studies on primates in the Canal Zone (now Panama), yielding data on *Aotus* (Moynihan 1964), *Callicebus* (Moynihan 1966), *Sanguinus* (Moynihan 1970), and others (Moynihan 1967, 1976). Moynihan (1976) also wrote the first book dealing exclusively with New World monkeys. In 1964, the American psychologist William Mason studied *Callicebus moloch ornatus* in Colombia (Mason 1966, 1968). This was only the second study (after Carpenter's) of more than a couple of months' duration on a Neotropical primate, and the first long-term study outside Panama. BCI continued to serve as the major primate field laboratory and was especially noteworthy for the extensive dietary studies of the French biologists A. and C.M. Hladik in the late 1960s (cf. Hladik & Hladik 1969). Toward the end of this phase, the most extensive field study outside of BCI had been conducted in 1967–1968 by the American zoologists Lewis and Dorothy Klein in Colombia. Although the Kleins' primary focus was the spider monkey (1977), the study was especially noteworthy for its synecological comparison of *Ateles*, *Saimiri*, *Alouatta*, and *Cebus* (1975).

Until the late 1960s, BCI was the only study site that had been utilized by more than one researcher for the study of Neotropical primates. BCI, however, was rarely utilized for comparative primate studies. Then an upswing of interest resulted in a number of sites being employed extensively, most of them, unlike BCI, on a comparative ecological basis. These were: La Macarena, Colombia, beginning in 1967 (Klein & Klein 1975, 1977); Hato Masaguaral, Venezuela, in 1969 (cf. Eisenberg 1979); Santa Rosa National Park, Costa Rica, in 1970 (cf. Fedigan et al. 1985); Hacienda La Pacifica, Costa Rica, in 1972 (cf. Glander 1975); Manu National Park, Peru, in 1974 (cf. Terborgh 1983); Mishana, Peru, in 1974 (cf. Kinzey 1977); and Rakighvallen-Voltzberg Nature Reserve, Surinam, in 1974 (cf. Mittermeier & van Roosmalen 1981). In addition, the first field study of the squirrel monkey, *Saimiri*, was conducted by R.W. Thorington (1968) in Colombia. (For an inventory of research conducted at the above sites, see Kinzey 1986; for a more complete list of research facilities, see Castner 1990.)

The Japanese Connection: 1971–1979

In 1971, the Japanese Monkey Centre sponsored the first of many trips by Japanese researchers to South America. This was the first organized effort to study the synecology of many Neotropical primate species. The studies included surveys in Colombia (Izawa 1975, 1976), Bolivia (Izawa 1979; Izawa & Bejarano 1981; Izawa & Yoneda 1981), and Brazil (Nishimura 1979). The Japanese also studied Goeldi's monkey (Masataka 1981, 1982), tamarins (Izawa 1978; Yoneda 1981, 1984), capuchins (Izawa 1979, 1980), woolly monkeys (Nishimura & Izawa 1975), and muriquis (Nishimura 1979). Japanese researchers are continuing their work, in collaboration with local students and colleagues, and they produce two regular series of publications devoted exclusively to studies in the Neotropics.

North American and European primatologists continued to work in Latin America: The first field study of *Aotus*, the only noctural Neotropical primate (and the only nocturnal monkey), in its natural habitat was a two-month study by the American anthropologist P.C. Wright in 1976 (cf. Wright 1978). This was followed by more-extensive studies in Manu National Park and Paraguay (Wright 1989). Wright hypothesized that freedom from interference competition and predation were the two primary benefits of nocturnality. When pressure from diurnal predation and interference competition from large monkeys were removed, *Aotus* became active during daylight as well as at night.

Latin American Nationalism: 1979–1990s

In 1979, the Brazilian Primatological Society (Sociedade Brasileira de Primatologia) was formed, marking the emergence of studies by native Latin Americans. In 1986, the Latin American Primatological Society (Sociedade Latino Americana de Primatologia) was founded, and by the mid-1990s, there were separate primate associations in Mexico, Peru, Venezuela, Colombia, and Costa Rica. As early as September 1967, however, Adelmar Coimbra-Filho had observed *Leontopithecus rosalia* in its natural habitat in the State of Rio de Janeiro, Brazil (Coimbra-Filho 1969). Of all of the Latin American primatologists, Coimbra-Filho probably has had a greater influence than any other, but as a researcher and administrator—he did not have any actual students.

TABLE 1. Summary of Primate Studies by Latin American Researchers 1981–1993

Species	Investigator(s)	Reference
Alouatta fusca	E.C. Da Silva	*Rev. Brasil Biol* 41:897–909, 1981
	S.L. Mendes	M.A. thesis, University of Brasília
Alouatta palliata	A. Estrada & R. Coates-Estrada	*American J. Primatology* 6:77–91, 1984
Alouatta seniculus	M.A. Ybarra Schön	*Folia Primatologica* 46:204–216, 1986
Alouatta caraya	Damián Rumiz	*American J. Primatology* 21:279–294, 1990
Brachyteles arachnoides	G.A.B. Fonseca	In: M. Thiago de Mello (ed) *A Primatologia no Brasil*. Brasilia: Instituto de Ciencias Biologicas, 1986, pp. 177–183
Cacajao calvus	J. Marcio Ayres	*Natural History* (March), 1990, pp. 32–40
Cebus apella	A.D. Brown et al.	In: D.M. Taub & F.A. King (eds) *Current Perspectives in Primate Social Dynamics*. New York: Nostrand Reinhold, 1986, pp. 137–151
Cebus olivaceus	X. Valderrama et al.	*Folia Primatologica* 54:171–176, 1990
Chiropotes albicans	J. Marcio Ayres	Instituto Nacional de Pesquisas da Amazonia, Manaus, Brazil, 1981
Lagothrix flavicauda	Mariella Leo Luna	*International Zoo Yearbook* 22:47–52, 1982
Lagothrix lagotricha	Carlos Peres	*International J. Primatology* 15:233–372, 1994
Leontopithecus chrysopygus	C.T. de Carvalho & C.F. de Carvalho;	*Rev. Brasileira de Zoologia* 6:707–717, 1989
	C.V. Padua	Abst. XIV *Cong Intnl Primatol Soc*, Strasbourg, France, 1992, p. 94
Leontopithecus rosalia	C.A. Peres	*Behavioral Ecology & Sociobiology* 25:227–233, 1989
Pithecia albicans	J.M.S. Oliviera et al.	*Acta Amazônica* 15:249–263, 1985
	Carlos Peres	*American J. Primatology*, in press
Sanguinus mystax	Marleni Ramirez	In: C.J. Saavedra et al. (eds) *La Primatologia en Latinoamerica*. Brasil, 1989, pp. 219–231
General Surveys	M. Neville et al.	*Primates* 17:151–181, 1976

In 1967, the Brazilian zoologist Celio Valle, from Belo Horizonte, Brazil, initiated a long-term study of the rarest of South American monkeys, the muriqui, or woolly spider monkey, at Fazenda Montes Claros, Minas Gerais, Brazil. This site continues its research productivity, largely through the efforts of the American anthropologist Karen Strier (1992), who has been instrumental in training Brazilian students. (See Table 1 for other primate studies conducted by native Latin Americans.)

The prime mover of primatological research in Colombia has been Jorge Hernandez-Camacho (e.g., Hernandez-Camacho & Cooper 1976), who has undertaken a number of studies in collaboration with Japanese primatologists at La Macarena.

In the meantime, other researchers, especially those from the United States, continued to be active. For example, S. Boinski (1989) studied squirrel monkeys in Costa Rica and Peru, P.A. Garber (1993) studied tamarins in Panama and Peru, and C.H. Janson (1986) studied *Cebus* monkeys in Peru and Brazil. For a comprehensive listing of field studies of Neotropical primates through May 1975, see L.A. Baldwin et al. (1977). More-up-to-date listings of field research are available in supplements to *Primate Eye*, the news bulletin of the Primate Society of Great Britain. Since 1980 more than 100 studies on Neotropical primates have been listed there.

The Future

By the mid-1990s, all genera of Neotropical primates had received at least brief study in their natural habitats. The only species that had not been studied or surveyed were *Callithrix geoffroyi* (Rylands & de Faria 1993) and *Ateles fusciceps*. The most difficult species to study, however, seem to be members of the subtribe Pitheciina, especially *Pithecia,* which moves extremely fast and completely silently (Johns 1985), and *Cacajao*, which is largely restricted to flooded Amazonian forests (cf. Robinson et al. 1986).

Over the years, there has been a shift in emphasis from brief, short-term studies to (1) longer studies with more stress on intraspecific variability; (2) studies with more accent on conservation (cf. Mittermeier et al. 1989); and (3) to broad theoretical analyses. For example, the large numbers of prehensile-tailed mammals in the Neotropics is linked to the high occurrence of vines and lianas (Emmons & Gentry 1983), and the paucity of folivores in the Neotropics is linked to the concurrence

of fruiting and leafing (Terborgh & Van Schaik 1987). The largest problem for long-term studies is funding. Researchers conducting short-term studies, especially those dealing with sociobiological questions, seem to have relatively little difficulty in obtaining funds, whereas obtaining funding for the broader ecological issues, and especially the maintenance of research stations, is far more difficult. In the latter case, a small amount of funding would have a major impact.

Warren G. Kinzey

See also Carpenter, C(larence) Raymond; Geoffroy Saint-Hilaire, Etienne; Japanese Primate Studies; Linnaeus, Carolus; Primate Field Studies

Bibliography

R. Aquino & F. Encarnacion: Population densities and geographic distribution of night monkeys (*Aotus nancymai* and *Aotus vociferans*) (Cebidae: Primates) in northeastern Peru. *American Journal of Primatology* 14:375–381, 1988; L.A. Baldwin et al.: Field research on callitrichid and cebid monkeys: An historical, geographical, and bibliographical listing. *Primates* 18:485–507, 1977; S. Boinski: The positional behavior and substrate use of squirrel monkeys: Ecological implications. *Journal of Human Evolution* 18:659–677, 1989; C.R. Carpenter: A field study of the behavior and social relations of howling monkeys. *Comparative Psychology Monographs* 10:1–168, 1934; C.R. Carpenter: Behavior of red spider monkeys in Panama. *Journal of Mammalogy* 16:171–180, 1935.

J.L. Castner: *Rainforests: A guide to research and tourist facilities at selected tropical forest sites in Central and South America.* Gainesville: Feline Press, 1990; O.R. Causey et al.: The home range of Brazilian *Cebus* monkeys in a region of small residual forest. *American Journal of Hygiene* 47:304–314, 1948; A.F. Coimbra-Filho: Mico-leão, *Leontideus rosalia* (Linnaeus 1766), situação atual da espécie no Brasil. *Annaes Academia Brasileira de Ciências* 41:29–52, 1969; N. Collias & C.H. Southwick: A field study of the population density and social organization in howler monkeys. *Proceedings of the American Philosophical Society* 96:144–156, 1952; J.F. Eisenberg: *Vertebrate ecology in the northern Neotropics.* Washington, D.C.: Smithsonian Institution Press, 1979.

J.F. Eisenberg: Mammalian social organizations and the case of *Alouatta*. In:

C. Robinson & L. Tiger (eds) *Man and beast revisited*. Washington, D.C.: Smithsonian Institution Press, 1991, pp. 127–138; L.H. Emmons & A.H. Gentry: Tropical forest structure and the distribution of gliding and prehensile-tailed vertebrates. *American Naturalist* 121:513–524, 1983; L.M. Fedigan et al.: A census of *Alouatta palliata* and *Cebus capucinus* monkeys in Santa Rosa National Park, Costa Rica. *Brenesia* 23:309–322, 1985; P.A. Garber: Feeding ecology and behaviour of the genus *Saguinus*. In: A.B. Rylands (ed) *Marmosets and tamarins: Systematics, behaviour, and ecology*. Oxford: Oxford University Press, 1993, pp. 273–295.

E. Geoffroy Saint-Hilaire: Tableau de quadrumanes, on des animaux composant le premier ordre de la classe des mammiféres. *Annales du Muséum de Histoire Naturelle* (Paris) 19:85–122, 1812; R.M. Gilmore: Mammalogy in an epidemiological study of jungle yellow fever in Brazil. *Journal of Mammalogy* 24:144–162, 1943; K.E. Glander: Habitat description and resource utilization: A preliminary report on mantled howling monkey ecology. In: R. Tuttle (ed) *Socioecology and psychology of primates*. The Hague: Mouton, 1975, pp. 37–57; J. Hernandez-Camacho & R.W. Cooper: The nonhuman primates of Colombia. In: R.W. Thorington Jr. & P.W. Heltne (eds) *Neotropical primates*. Washington, D.C.: National Academy of Sciences, 1976, pp. 35–69; A. Hladik & C.M. Hladik: Rapports trophiques entre vegetation et primates dans la foret de Barro-Colorado (Panama). *Terre et la Vie* 1:25–117, 1969.

K. Izawa: Foods and feeding behavior of monkeys in the Upper Amazon Basin. *Primates* 16:295–316, 1975; K. Izawa: Group sizes and compositions of monkeys in the Upper Amazon Basin. *Primates* 17:367–399, 1976; K. Izawa: A field study of the ecology and behavior of the black-mantled tamarin (*Saguinus nigricollis*) *Primates* 19:241–274; 1978; K. Izawa: Studies on peculiar distribution pattern of *Callimico*. *Kyoto University Overseas Research Reports of New World Monkeys* 1:1–19, 1979; K. Izawa: Social behavior of the wild black-capped capuchin (*Cebus apella*). *Primates* 21:443–467, 1980; K. Izawa & G. Bejarano: Distribution ranges and patterns of nonhuman primates in western Pando, Bolivia. *Kyoto University Overseas Research Reports of New World Monkeys* 2:1–11, 1981.

K. Izawa & M. Yoneda: Habitat utilization of nonhuman primates in a forest of the western Pando, Bolivia. *Kyoto University Overseas Research Reports of New World Monkeys* 2:13–22, 1981; C.H. Janson: The mating system as a determinant of social evolution in capuchin monkeys (*Cebus*). In: J.G. Else & P.C. Lee (eds) *Primate ecology and conservation*. New York: Cambridge University Press, 1986, pp. 169–179; A.D. Johns: First field observations of *Pithecia albicans*. *Primate Eye* 26:17–18, 1975; W.G. Kinzey: Diet and feeding behaviour of *Callicebus torquatus*. In: T.H. Clutton-Brock (ed) *Primate ecology: Studies of feeding and ranging behavior in lemurs, monkeys, and apes*. London: Academic Press, 1977, pp. 127–151.

W.G. Kinzey: New World primate field studies: What's in it for anthropology? *Annual Reviews of Anthropology* 15:121–148, 1986; W.G. Kinzey: *Behavior, ecology, and evolution of Neotropical primates*. New York: Aldine Press, in press; L.L. Klein & D.J. Klein: Social and ecological contrasts between four taxa of Neotropical primates. In: R.H. Tuttle (ed) *Socioecology and psychology of primates*. The Hague: Mouton, 1975, pp. 59–85; L.L. Klein & D.J. Klein: Feeding behavior of the Colombian spider monkey, *Ateles belzebuth*. In: T.H. Clutton-Brock (ed) *Primate ecology: Studies of feeding and ranging behavior in lemurs, monkeys, and apes*. London: Academic Press, 1977, pp. 153–181; C. Linnaeus: *Systema naturae*. 10th ed. Stockholm: Salvi, 1758.

N. Masataka: A field study of the social behavior of Goeldi's monkeys (*Callimico goeldii*) in north Bolivia. I. Group composition, breeding cycle, and infant development. II. Grouping pattern and intragroup relationship. *Kyoto University Overseas Research Reports of New World Monkeys* 2:23–41, 1981; N. Masataka: A field study on the vocalizations of Goeldi's monkeys (*Callimico goeldii*). *Primates* 23:206–219, 1982; W.A. Mason: Social organization of the South American monkey, *Callicebus moloch*, a preliminary report. *Tulane Studies in Zoology* 13:23–28, 1966; W.A. Mason: Use of space by *Callicebus* groups. In: P. Jay (ed) *Primates: Studies in adaptation and variability*. New York: Holt, Rinehart & Winston, 1968, pp. 200–216.

R.A. Mittermeier & M.G.M. van Roosmalen: Preliminary observations on habitat utilization and diet in eight Suriname monkeys. *Folia primatologica* 36:1–

39, 1981; R.A. Mittermeier et al.: Neotropical primate conservation. *Journal of Human Evolution* 18:97–610, 1989; M. Moynihan: Some behavior patterns of platyrrhine monkeys. I: The night monkey (*Aotus trivirgatus*). *Smithsonian Museum Collections* 146:1–84, 1964; M. Moynihan: Communication in *Callicebus*. *Journal of Zoology* (London) 150:77–127, 1966; M. Moynihan: Comparative aspects of communication in New World primates. In: D. Morris (ed) *Primate ethology*. London: Weidenfeld & Nicolson, 1967, pp. 306–342; M. Moynihan: Some behavior patterns of platyrrhine monkeys. II: *Saguinus geoffroyi* and some other tamarins. *Smithsonian Contributions to Zoology* 28:1–77, 1970.

M. Moynihan: *The New World primates*. Princeton, New Jersey: Princeton University Press, 1976; A. Nishimura: In search of woolly spider monkey. *Kyoto University Overseas Research Reports in New World Monkeys* 1:21–37, 1979; A. Nishimura & K. Izawa: The group characteristics of woolly monkeys (*Lagothrix lagotricha*) in the Upper Amazonian Basin. In: S. Kondo, M. Kawai, & A. Ehara (eds) *Contemporary primatology*. Basel: Karger, 1975, pp. 351–357; J.G. Robinson et al.: Monogamous cebids and their relatives: Intergroup calls and spacing. In: D. Cheney et al. (eds) *Primate societies*. Chicago: University of Chicago Press, 1986, pp. 44–53; A.B. Rylands & D.S. de Faria: Habitats, feeding ecology, and home-range size in the genus *Callithrix*. In: A.B. Rylands (ed) *Marmosets and tamarins: Systematics, behaviour, and ecology*. Oxford: Oxford University Press, 1993, pp. 262–272.

E.Z.F. Setz: Feeding ecology of *Pithecia pithecia* (Pithecinae, Cebidae) in a forest fragment. *International Journal of Primatology* 8:543, 1988; C.H. Southwick et al.: Report of the American Society of Primatologists Subcommittee on the Status of Primates in the Wild. *American Journal of Primatology* 10:371–378, 1986; K.B. Strier: *Faces in the forest: The endangered Muriqui monkeys of Brazil*. New York: Oxford University Press, 1992; J. Terborgh: *Five New World primates: A study in comparative ecology*. Princeton, New Jersey: Princeton University Press, 1983; J. Terborgh & C.P. Van Schaik: Convergence vs. nonconvergence in primate communities. In: J.H.R. Gee & P.S. Giller (eds) *Organization of communities past and present*. Oxford: Blackwell, 1987, pp. 205–226; M.R. Oldfield Thomas: New *Callithrix, Midas, Felis, Rhipidomys*, and *Proechimys* from Brazil and Ecuador. *Annual Magazine of Natural History* 14:188–195, 1904.

R.W. Thorington: Observations of squirrel monkeys in a Colombian forest. In: L.A. Rosenblum & R.W. Cooper (eds) *The squirrel monkey*. New York: Academic Press, 1968, pp. 69–85; P.C. Wright: Home range, activity pattern, and agonistic encounters of a group of night monkeys (*Aotus trivirgatus*) in Peru. *Folia Primatologica* 29:43–55, 1978; P.C. Wright: The nocturnal primate niche in the New World. *Journal of Human Evolution* 18:635–658, 1989; P.C. Wright: Night watch on the Amazon. *Natural History* 103:44–51, 1994; M. Yoneda: Ecological studies of *Saguinus fuscicollis* and *Saguinus labiatus* with reference to habitat segregation and height preference. *Kyoto University Overseas Research Reports of New World Monkeys* 2:43–50, 1981; M. Yoneda: Comparative studies on vertical separation, foraging behavior and traveling mode of saddle-back tamarins (*Saguinus fuscicollis*) and red chested moustached tamarins (*Saguinus labiatus*) in northern Bolivia. *Primates* 25:414–442, 1984.

Editor's Note
References cited, but not listed above, may be found in Kinzey (1986), as well as in the extensive bibliography in Kinzey (in press).

New Zealand

The islands of New Zealand were probably the last land masses of significant size to be explored and occupied by human beings, a process that started with the colonizing voyages of Polynesians from central eastern Polynesia (the Cook, Society, and Austral Islands) around A.D. 800. Physical anthropologists were also slow to colonize New Zealand. The first full-time, professional, academic physical anthropologist in the country was hired by the University of Auckland in 1975. In spite of this, however, research into the physical anthropology of the original inhabitants of New Zealand can be traced back to the mid-eighteenth century, when Captain James Cook (1728–1779) and other European explorers first visited the islands. This period of European exploration (1769–1814) was followed by the arrival of missionaries and the first wave of European settlers. In 1840, when the islands officially came under the control of the British Crown, Europeans began to arrive in increasing numbers. As contact between the Polynesian Maori and Europeans increased throughout the nineteenth century, there

Fig. 1. Maori tattooed warriors, from an engraving by Louis de Sainson, 1826–1829. This illustration is from The Zealanders: A Story of Austral Lands by J.S.C. Dumont d'Urville. Translated by Carole Legge. Wellington: Victoria University Press, 1992.

steadily emerged a large body of literature on the culture, language, prehistory, and biology of the Maori.

Emerging Themes in Precolonial and Early Colonial Literature

Although the Dutch explorer Abel Tasman (1603–1659) provided a brief description of the native New Zealanders he encountered in 1642, it was not until the voyages of British and French explorers and naturalists, such as Cook, Joseph Banks, J.R. Forster, and L. de Bougainville, that a more detailed description of the Maori and their culture became available and thereby raised scientific questions regarding the physical nature of New Zealand's indigenous peoples and their origins. Among the first to speculate on these issues was the French explorer Julien-Marie Crozet (1728–1780), who visited New Zealand in 1772. In his journal of his voyage, which was published in 1783 (cf. Booth 1949; Salmond 1991), Crozet conjectured that the Maori represented not one but three distinct races that had evidently peopled the islands at different times. Although this heterogeneous view was widely accepted by European savants at that time, there was not a consensus regarding the number or sequences of occupations. In 1830, the French author Jules Sébastien César Dumont d'Urville (1790–1842), who apparently introduced the Polynesia-Micronesia-Melanesia scheme for dividing the island populations of Oceania (Booth 1949), propounded the view that there were only two races among the Maori: a "yellowish-white" people and the "true negroes."

By the middle of the nineteenth century, however, it was generally accepted that while the extant Maori exhibited considerable physical variation, they were nevertheless a relatively homogeneous group.

Arthur Thomson (1816–1860), a Scottish-born army surgeon who served in New Zealand from 1847 to 1858, termed the Maori a "mixed race." Thomson (1859) was perhaps the first biomedical investigator to examine Maori subjects in detail. He collected anthropometric data, observed disease and deformity in the population, and even did a strength-test study comparing Maori men and Englishmen—in which he noted, with apparent satisfaction, that the English scored

Fig. 2. Moa hunt, a reconstruction. Te Rangi Hiroa {Peter Buck}, left, and two Otago University classmates "stalk" a stuffed moa borrowed from a museum, ca. 1904. Courtesy of the Alexander Turnball Library, Wellington.

higher on many of the tests, thereby disproving the popular notion "that the human race degenerates physically after ages of civilization" (1859:73). Throughout the nineteenth century, however, the idea persisted that New Zealand may have been inhabited by a different race before the Maori, as did the notion that the Maori themselves were the result of admixture between Melanesians and Polynesians.

The New Zealand Institute was founded in Wellington in 1867. It succeeded the New Zealand Society, which had been founded by Governor Sir George Grey (1812–1898) in 1851. For the remainder of the century, the *Transactions and Proceedings of the New Zealand Institute (TPNZI)* was the primary venue for the publication and discussion of scientific matters, including those pertaining to the anthropology of the Maori in Zew Zealand (Sorrenson 1977). The first volume of the *TPNZI* contained a major review article "On the Maori Races in New Zealand" (1868) by William Colenso (1811–1899), a printer and missionary who became a prominent authority on Maori topics and New Zealand natural history. Colenso believed that it was very unlikely that the Maori were the autochthonous race of New Zealand. He thought that a landmass as large as New Zealand must have been settled for some time. He also believed the Moriori of the Chatham Islands were a relic population of the original (i.e., non-Polynesian) New Zealanders. Colenso later became involved in a minor debate concerning the color sense of the Maori (Stack 1879; Colenso 1881).

During the last quarter of the nineteenth century, the major debates in the anthropology of New Zealand involved Maori origins and the identity of the so-called moa-hunters (Anderson 1989; Sorrenson 1992). The origins debate concentrated mostly on Maori linguistics, genealogies, and myths, while the "moa-hunters" debate was concerned primarily with linguistic and archeological data. This latter debate attracted the attention of several major scientific figures: the British zoologist Richard Owen (1804–1892), who was a leading authority on the moas, an extinct ostrich-like flightless bird that he had dubbed *Dinornis*; the French anthropologist and naturalist Armand de Quatrefages (1810–1892); and Julius Haast (1824–1887), a German-born geologist who was arguably New Zealand's most prominent nineteenth-century scientist. Haast was an advocate, along with Colenso and others, of the position that the

moa-hunters were racially and culturally distinct from the Maori (Anderson 1989). In direct opposition to this, Quatrefages and others argued that the Maori had hunted moas and that evidence of such could be found in their oral traditions. Quatrefages (1892) argued further that moas had gone extinct relatively recently, as evidenced by the large amount of dessicated muscle and skin preserved in some moa remains. In New Zealand, physical anthropology did not figure strongly in either of these debates, a fact lamented by the geologist James Coutts Crawford (1887). Crawford argued that racial types were more stable than languages, thus they should be the main source for speculation on Maori origins. Crawford also thought that the Maori connection with the Americas needed to be more fully worked out.

Although Maori origins and the identity of the moa-hunters were dominant issues, they were by no means the only topics of discussion at this time. For example, racial degeneration was of concern to many, including a local physician, A.K. Newman (1849–1924), who during the third quarter of the nineteenth century expounded on the ill effects of the New Zealand environment on the transplanted English race. Assuming a Lamarckian view of evolution, Newman (1876) wrote: "[T]he immigrants' vital capacities diminish, [and] their physical energies deteriorate. . . . [T]hese alterations are more fully developed in their offspring . . . [and] it is very certain that the race would . . . very decidedly deteriorate, were it not for a constant stream of immigrants." He later (Newman 1882) amended these views, which is fortunate, since he later served as president of the New Zealand Rugby Football Union! Newman (1881) was also one of the earliest investigators to discuss the "inevitable" extinction of the Maori race.

The work of the anti-Darwinian polymath Samuel Butler was firmly rooted in New Zealand (Jones 1959). From 1859 to 1864, Butler farmed sheep in New Zealand and was a member of Christchurch's small but active intellectual community. Although initially known to the community as a pro-Darwinian atheist, Butler later rejected the mechanistic and consciousless world he thought Darwinism embodied. In his novel *Erewhon* (1872), Butler combined an account of his New Zealand experience with a critique of Darwinism ("The Book of the Machines").

In 1892, the Polynesian Society was founded, and the *Journal of the Polynesian Society (JPS)* replaced the *TPNZI* as the main outlet for publications on Maori topics. Physical anthropology was rarely represented in the early years of the *JPS* (Sorrenson 1992); however, after 1920, some major articles on Maori physical anthropology did begin to appear (e.g., Te Rangi Hiroa 1922–1923; Shapiro 1940b).

The medical school at the University of Otago (Dunedin) was founded around 1875, and its first dean and professor of anatomy was John Halliday Scott (1851–1914), who published the first comprehensive study of Maori and Moriori crania (1893). In it, Scott argued strongly for the "mixed origin of the Maori race," a position the American physical anthropologist Harry Lionel Shapiro (1902–1990) (1940b:3) attributed to Scott having "absorbed a strong bias from the environment of [then] current theory concerning Maori-Moriori origins." Since Scott's time, physical-anthropological research has continued at the Otago medical school (e.g., Schofield 1959); more recently, Philip Houghton has developed a strong program of research in Polynesian physical anthropology within the Anatomy Department there (e.g., Houghton 1980, 1990).

Subsequent Developments

Te Rangi Hiroa (Sir Peter H. Buck) (1879–1951) is one of the most illustrious graduates of the Otago Medical School. He was a physician and statesman in New Zealand, although he later turned to study Maori and Pacific anthropology (cf. Te Rangi Hiroa 1949), and served concurrently as director of the Bishop Museum in Honolulu and professor of anthropology at Yale University in New Haven, Connecticut, from 1936 to 1951. Te Rangi Hiroa had a long-standing interest in the physical anthropology of the Maori and included some anthropometry in his 1910 M.D. thesis. In 1919, while aboard ship from England to New Zealand, he conducted a major anthropometric survey of more than 800 men of Maori descent with whom he had served in the NZ Maori Battalion during World War I (cf. Te Rangi Hiroa 1922–1923). He received help and instruction for this endeavor from the antomist-anthropologist Arthur Keith (1866–1955) and biometrician Karl Pearson (1857–1936) in England. Te Rangi Hiroa (1924) denied the "inevitable" extinction of the Maori at the hands of a "superior" race as predicted earlier by Newman and others (e.g., Walsh 1908), although he freely acknowledged that admixture would become the norm and hoped that "the best

features of the Maori race will be perpetuated forever" (1924:374). Later, in collaboration with Shapiro, he published an anthropometric survey of Cook Islanders (Shapiro & Buck 1936). As a Maori and a Polynesian, Te Rangi Hiroa brought a unique and invaluable perspective to Pacific anthropology.

Blood-genetics studies of the Maori were published as early as 1931 (Phillips 1931; see also Simmons et al. 1951. For major reviews of this subject, see Shapiro 1940a and Simmons 1962. In dental anthropology, New Zealand was well represented in the work of R.M.S. Taylor (1903–1992). Although primarily a practicing dentist, Taylor nevertheless managed during his lifetime to produce a number of publications on dental variation and health (cf. Taylor 1978). It is also of interest to note that in 1937, Taylor presented a paper (reprinted in Taylor 1978) on the Piltdown dentition, in which he strongly criticized the various reconstructions of the now infamous skull. He later thought that he deserved some credit for anticipating the uncovering of the Piltdown hoax, although this claim is difficult to substantiate based on published versions of the talk.

As noted earlier, physical anthropology in New Zealand is a relatively young academic discipline with a long history. By the mid-1990s, there were physical anthropologists at the Universities of Otago and Auckland. Expatriate New Zealanders who have made contributions to physical anthropology include the evolutionary molecular biologist Allan C. Wilson (1935–1991), the Paleolithic archeologist John W.K. Harris, and the geneticist Richard Ward.

John S. Allen

See also Dental Anthropology; Keith, (Sir) Arthur; Molecular Anthropology; Oceania; Owen (Sir) Richard; Piltdown; Quatrefages (de Breau), Jean Louis Armand de; Shapiro, Henry Lionel; Taylor, Richard Morris Stovin; Te Rangi Hiroa

Bibliography
A. Anderson: *Prodigious birds: Moas and moa-hunting in prehistoric New Zealand.* Cambridge: Cambridge University Press, 1989; J.M. Booth: *A history of New Zealand anthropology during the nineteenth century.* M.A. Thesis. University of Otago, Dunedin, New Zealand, 1949; S. Butler: *Erewhon; or, Over the range.* Auckland: Golden Press, 1872; W. Colenso: On the Maori races of New Zealand. *Transactions and Proceedings of the*

New Zealand Institute 1:1–75, 1868; W. Colenso: On the fine perception of colours possessed by the ancient Maoris. *Transactions and Proceedings of the New Zealand Institute* 14:49–76, 1881; J.C. Crawford: On Maori ancestry. *Transactions and Proceedings of the New Zealand Institute* 20:414–418, 1887.

P. Houghton: *The first New Zealanders*. Auckland: Hodder & Stoughton, 1980; P. Houghton: The adaptive significance of Polynesian body form. *Annals of Human Biology* 17:19–32, 1990; J. Jones: *The cradle of Erewhon: Samuel Butler in New Zealand*. Austin: University of Texas Press, 1959; A.K. Newman: Speculations on the physiological changes obtained in the English race when transplanted to New Zealand. *Transactions and Proceedings of the New Zealand Institute* 9:37–44, 1876; A.K. Newman: A study of the causes leading to the extinction of the Maori. *Transactions and Proceedings of the New Zealand Institute* 14:459–477, 1881; A.K. Newman: Is New Zealand a healthy country? *Transactions and Proceedings of the New Zealand Institute* 15:493–510, 1882.

G. Phillips: The blood of the Maori. *Human Biology* 3:282–287, 1931; A. de Quatrefages: The moa and the moa-hunters. English translation by L. Buller. *Transactions and Proceedings of the New Zealand Institute* 25:17–49, 1892; A. Salmond: *Two worlds: First meetings between Maori and Europeans, 1642–1772*. Auckland: Viking, 1991; G. Schofield: Metric and morphological features of the femur of the New Zealand Maori. *Journal of the Royal Anthropological Institute* 89:89–106, 1959; J.H. Scott: Contributions to the osteology of the Aborigines of New Zealand and of the Chatham Islands. *Transactions of the New Zealand Institute* 24:1–64, 1893; H.L. Shapiro: The distribution of blood groups in Polynesia. *American Journal of Physical Anthropology* 26:409–416, 1940a; H.L. Shapiro: The physical anthropology of the Maori-Moriori. *Journal of the Polynesian Society* 49:1–15, 1940b.

H.L. Shapiro & P.H. Buck (Te Rangi Hiroa): The physical characters of the Cook Islanders. *Memoirs of the Bernice P. Bishop Museum* 12(91):1–35, 1936; R.T. Simmons: Blood groups in Polynesians and comparisons with other Pacific peoples. *Oceania* 32:198–210, 1962; R.T Simmons et al.: Blood, taste, and secretion: A genetical survey in Maoris. *Medical Journal of Australia* 1:425–430, 1951; M.P.K.

Sorrenson: The whence of the Maori: Some nineteenth-century exercises in scientific method. *Journal of the Polynesian Society* 86:449–478, 1977.

M.P.K. Sorrenson: *Manifest duty: The Polynesian Society over one hundred years*. Auckland: Polynesian Society, 1992; J.W. Stack: Notes on the colour sense of the Maori. *Transactions and Proceedings of the New Zealand Institute* 12:153–158, 1879; R.M.S. Taylor: The dentition of the Piltdown fossil man (*Eoanthropus dawsoni*) from a new aspect. (Title Only). Report of the twenty-third meeting of the Australian and New Zealand Association for the Advancement of Science, 1937, pp. 201, 245; R.M.S. Taylor: *Variations in morphology of teeth: Anthropologic and forensic aspects*. Springfield, Illinois: Thomas, 1978; Te Rangi Hiroa (P.H. Buck): *Medicine amongst the Maoris in ancient and modern times*. M.D. Thesis. University of Otago, School of Medicine, Dunedin, New Zealand, 1910.

Te Rangi Hiroa: Maori somatology: Racial averages. *Journal of the Polynesian Society* 37–44, 145–153, 159–170 (1922), 32:21–28, 189–199 (1923); Te Rangi Hiroa: The passing of the Maori. *Transactions and Proceedings of the New Zealand Institute* 55:362–375, 1924; Te Rangi Hiroa: *The coming of the Maori*. Wellington: Whitcombe & Tombs, 1949; A.S. Thomson: *The story of New Zealand, past and present: Savage and civilized*. London: Murray, 1859; A. Walsh: The passing of the Maori. *Transactions and Proceedings of the New Zealand Institute* 40:154–175, 1908.

Niederle, Lubor (1865–1944)

Born in the west Bohemian town of Klatovy, (now in the Czech Republic), Niederle studied classical archeology at the Faculty of Philosophy of Charles University (CU) in Prague. On the basis of his thesis, *On Evolution of Sacred Places and Churches,* he received the degree of doctor of philosophy in 1888. He was a pupil of M. Tyrš, a philosopher and later founder of the SOKOL physical training organization with Tomáš G. Masaryk (1850–1937), who held an academic position in philosophy at CU and later, in 1918, became the first president of Czechoslovakia. It was under Masaryk's influence that Niederle turned his attention to archeology and anthropology, which subsequently led him to become, in 1889, the first curator of anthropology at the National Czech Museum in Prague and, in 1891, the first teacher of anthropology at CU. By way of preparation for these eventual positions, Niederle studied in Munich under Johannes Ranke (1836–1916) and in Paris at the École d'Anthropologie under Paul Topinard (1830–1911), Léonce-Pierre Manouvier (1850–1927), and others. In 1899, Niederle's position at CU was consolidated when he was appointed professor of ethnology and archeology. Later, in 1923, he was instrumental in founding the State Institute of Archeology (Státní ústav archeologický) in Prague, whose primary agenda was the collection and preservation of archeological material, including human skeletons.

Niederle's primary research interests were archeology and the anthropology and ethnogenesis of the Slavs. In 1891, he published an important work, *Contributions to the Anthropology of Czech Lands*. In it, he threw light upon the question of the Slavs arrival in central Europe and determined their physical character. In particular, he rejected the prevailing view of the time that the Old Slavs were characterized by brachycephaly and dark-pigmented skin. In numerous studies of human skeletal remains from different localities in Bohemia and Moravia, he established a solid basis for the mosaic ethnic composition of the ancient populations of the Czech lands.

In addition to *Contributions* (1891), Niederle's most important studies from the pre–World War I period include a study of medieval crania from a charnel house in Žamberk (1892); *Mankind in the Prehistoric Epochs* (1893), which contains comprehensive chapters on the physical anthropology of Slavs; a study of Slavonic skeletons from Staré Město, near Uherské Hradiště in Moravia; *On the Origin of the Slavs* (1896); *Slavic Antiquities* (1902–1928); and the *Handbook of Czech Archaeology* (1910). From this body of work, Niederle established a database and a system for future studies of prehistoric settlements in Bohemia.

In addition to his study of human skeletal remains, Niederle also devoted himself to research on the recent populations of Bohemia, and of fundamental importance in that area is his study on the craniometry of Czech children.

After World War I, Niederle devoted his energies primarily to the completion of *Slavic Antiquities* (1902–1928), his magnum opus, in which he summarized all of the known facts relating to the question of the ethnogenesis of the Slavs. It was the first major synthesis undertaken on this subject and is still regarded as an essential starting point for any-

one interested in Slavic studies.

His last major work, *One of the Tasks of Czech Anthropology*, was published in 1935.
Milan Dokládal

See also Czech and Slovak Republics; Manouvrier, Léonce-Pierre; Ranke, Johannes; Topinard, Paul

Bibliography
SELECTED WORKS
Příspěvky k anthropologii Českých zemí [Contributions to the anthropology of Czech lands]. Prague, 1891; *Lidstvo v době předhistorické* [Mankind in prehistoric epochs]. Prague: Bursík & Kohout, 1893; *O původu Slovanů* [On the origin of the Slavs]. Prague: Burdók & Kohout, 1896; *Slovanské starožitnosti* [Slavic antiquities]. Prague: Bursík & Kohout, 1902–1928; *La race slave, statistique, démographie-anthropologie*. Paris: Alcan, 1911 (2d ed.: 1916); *Handbook of Czech archaeology*. Prague: Bursík & Kohout, 1910; *Moravské Slovensko*. 2 vols. Prague: Národopisná Společnost Českoslovanská, 1922–1923; *Manuel de l'Antiquité Slave*. Paris: Champion, 1923–1926.

ARCHIVAL SOURCES
1. L. Niederle Papers: Archives and Library, Department of Anthropology, Faculty of Sciences, Charles University, CS-120 00-Praha-2, Viničná 7, Czech Republic; 2. L. Niederle Papers: Archives and Library, Archaeological Institute of the Czech Academy of Sciences, CS-120 00-Praha-1, Letenská 4. Czech Republic.

SECONDARY SOURCES
M. Dokládal & J. Brožek: Physical anthropology in Czechoslovakia: Recent Developments. *Current Anthropology*, 2:455–477, 1961; J. Matiegka: L. Niederle. *Anthropologie* (Prague) 3:19–96, 1925; M. Prokopec: Biological anthropology in Czechoslovakia: A historical outline. Part 1. *International Association of Human Biologists: Occasional Papers*. No. 3. Newcastle upon Tyne: IAHB, 1991, pp. 1–56; E. Vlček: Význam Lubora Niederle pro českou antropologii [The importance of Lubor Niederle for the Czech anthropology]. *Anthropologie* (Brno) 4:71–75, 1966.

Norway
Physical anthropology in Norway, as in many other countries, was developed by the desire for a better understanding of national origin

and character. Norway was occupied by foreign powers since 1397, and the country's
political history fostered nationalistic tendencies, especially during the period of the
Napoleonic Wars (1807–1814), when art, literature, and science were strongly influenced
by the attitudes against the occupying foreign
nation. One of the first authors to deal with
such questions in Norway was the Danish
nobleman Peter Frederik Suhm (1728–1798)
in his book *Om de Nordiske Folks ældste
Oprindelse* (On the Origin of the Nordic
People) in 1770. A year later, the historian
Gerhard Schøning (1722–1780) wrote *Norges
Riges Historie* (The History of Norway) which
embodied theories about population movement from the south and east that were in
accordance with the ideas of Swedish scholars
such as Harald Vallerius (1646–1716) and
Carl (von) Linné (Linnaeus) (1707–1778).

During the first half of the nineteenth
century, several Norwegian historians were
preoccupied with the origins of the Norwegian population. Among them was Rudolf
Keyser (1803–1864), who in his book *Norges
Historie* (1866) stated that "well preserved
skeletons, and particularly complete skulls,
are found in graves. Celebrated scientists have
examined these carefully and found that they
could not originate from any other European
group of people, but the Lapps."

In Keyser's time, antiquities from northern Norway were hardly known. The Göta
River (now in Sweden) was regarded as the
border between North and South German
tribes, which could explain the lack of Celtic
Bronze Age finds in Norway. As such, the
Lappic population was thought to have been
driven from the south and forced to settle
along the marginal coasts of northern Norway.

Another historian who participated in
this early debate was Peter Andreas Munch
(1810–1863), the author of the eight-volume
work *Det norske Folks Historie* (1851–1863). In
it, he introduced a racial classification consisting of "North Germans" (the Nordic people),
"Middle Germans" (the Gothic people), and
"South Germans" (the German people). From
the Caucasian Mountains, where Noah was
believed to have built his Ark, these tribes
were thought to have migrated north of the
Baltic and then southward along the coasts of
Norway.

In 1811, when the first University of
Norway was founded in Christiania (now
Oslo), the country was still a Danish colony,
and from 1814 to 1905 it was under Swedish
control. At this juncture, racial discussions
were influenced hardly at all by medical points
of view. The Anatomisk Institutt (Anatomical Institute) was opened in Christiania in
1815, but the first professor of anatomy at the
university in Christiania, Michael Skjelderup
(1769–1852), regarded "anthropology" simply as "anatomy and physiology" and did not
take part in any examination of skull types.
However, he did assemble a private collection
of 148 osteological samples, which he later
donated to the university.

Professor Skjelderup's assistant, Johan
Fritzner Heiberg (1805–1883), was probably
the first to deal with "modern" physical anthropology in Norway. A travel grant in 1835
enabled him to visit Stockholm, Berlin, and
Paris, and it is conjectured that his interest in
anthropology was aroused as a result of this
tour. At the same time, he visited Anders
Adolf Retzius (1796–1860) in Stockholm to
buy a microscope for the university's Anatomical Institute, but instead he returned
with a collection of plaster casts of "national
crania," which still exists in the university
collections in Oslo.

When Skjelderup's successor, Joachim
Andreas Voss (1815–1897), took over in
1850, there was already a small and rather
heterogeneous collection of skulls at the institute, which Voss, with the collaborative
assistance of Norwegian archeologists, subsequently expanded to include skeletal material
from well-defined historical periods. Voss also
established contact with prominent scientists
like Retzius in Stockholm and Paul Broca
(1824–1880) in Paris, and he undertook excursions abroad to study and collect osteo-
anthropological material of various kinds.
When Voss retired in 1875, he established a
foundation to encourage physical anthropological science at the University of Oslo.

Voss was succeeded by Jacob Munch
Heiberg (1843–1888) in 1875. During
Heiberg's time, even Lappic samples were included in the collection. Although anthropology was still regarded by the majority of
Norwegian anatomists as a peripheral concern,
Heiberg presented the first anthropological
paper in Norway, "Lappische Gräber-Schädel"
(1878), which was written in German, then
regarded as the primary language for scientific
publication.

In 1887, Gustav Adolf Guldberg (1854–
1908) was appointed professor of anatomy at
the University of Oslo. As an anatomist he had
already achieved a reputation in Sweden,
where he had worked in Stockholm at the
Karolinska Institute with Magnus Gustaf

Retzius (1842–1919), who is considered to have initiated Guldberg's interest in anthropology. Further studies at foreign universities, particulary in Paris where he studied under Paul Topinard (1830–1911) and Léonce-Pierre Manouvrier (1850–1927), made Guldberg the first trained anthropologist in Norway. He also was the first to make the public at large interested in the anthropological activity at the University, which reached a climax in connection with the famous find, in 1903, of the Viking ship from Oseberg with the skeleton of "Queen Åsa."

By the turn of the century, the anthropological collections of the Anatomical Institute had increased to such an extent that storage space became a problem, which led Guldberg to formulate plans for a new museum building like those he had seen during his study tours in Germany, Austria, Hungary, and Italy. However, the changed political situation in Norway after 1905 and Guldberg's sudden death prevented the realization of this plan.

In the meantime, there had been considerable activity in physical anthropology outside of academia. For example, several army surgeons contributed to the registration and mapping of the Norwegian population, similar to the anthropometric surveys conducted earlier in Sweden and Germany. Among this group, Carl Oscar Eugen Arbo (1837–1906) stands out as being one of the most capable investigators. He was a former student of Broca who wrote his papers in French, and who pioneered works about the different populations of Norway that are noteworthy, even by contemporary standards (*vide infra*). The importance of his work (cf. Arbo 1882, 1887, 1900) lies primarily in the fact that his reports and descriptions define the population at a point just prior to the disruptive influence of industrialization, which dramatically transformed the country and its population.

Also worthy of mention is Halfdan Bryn (1864–1933), who in many respects extended the work of Arbo, and who did pioneering investigations of the Lapps. He also conducted an ambitious anthropological survey of Norway, the results of which can be found in his *Anthropologia Norvegica*, published in 1925. However, his racial theories were much influenced by his contemporaries, and in spite of an imposing scientific production, his works are rarely referenced in the contemporary literature.

The modern era of physical anthropology in Norway begins with Kristian Emil Schreiner (1874–1957), who in 1908 succeeded Guldberg at the Anatomical Institute in Oslo. His original area of specialization had been in cytology and embryology. Several inquiries from army surgeons about anthropological problems, however, alerted him to this gap in his medical education. Subsequent studies at foreign universities gave him more knowledge and a burgeoning interest in physical anthropology, which is reflected in his participation in 1913 in archeological excavations in north Norway as a trained anthropologist. Although the Lapps had attracted the prior attention of foreign investigators, such as Paul Broca, Rudolf Virchow (1821–1902), and Paolo Mantegazza (1831–1910), among others, with the notable exception of Arbo's pioneering work this population had been essentially ignored by Norwegian scientists until Schreiner's visit to north Norway in 1913. Information gathered in the excavations led to the realization that the three northernmost regions of Nordland, Troms, and Finnmark, held a unique position in the racial history of Europe. The anthropology of the Lapps became Schreiner's primary research focus, and when his duties at the Anatomical Institute prevented him from visiting Finnmark, he sent interested and trained medical students in his place to do research work for him. In 1931 and 1935, he published the results of his Lappic investigations in the two-volume monograph *Zur Osteologie der Lappen*, which is still widely regarded as the standard work on Lappic physical anthropology.

With the expansion of the Oslo railway system in the period 1920–1925, resulting excavations led to numerous archeological discoveries that included the recovery of considerable skeletal material (most of it dating from medieval times) that was subsequently absorbed into the collections of the Anatomical Institute. This medieval material formed the basis of Schreiner's major work, *Crania Norvegica* (1939–1946).

His wife, Alette Schreiner (1873–1951), gave up a promising scientific career to support her husband. Although she was never formally attached to the Anatomical Institute, her pioneering investigations on women's physical anthropology, "Anthropologische Studien an norwegischen Frauen" (1924), and several works about the population in north Norway brought her international recognition.

When Kristian Schreiner retired in 1945, he emphasized the importance of continuing anthropological research at the institute, and he did his best to establish a permanent post for an anthropologist there—but financial circumstances in this early postwar period precluded such a luxury. Still, Schreiner's call for continuing anthropological research did not go unheeded. In 1947, Johan Torgersen (1906–1978), who had extensive clinical experience as a medical practitioner and radiologist, became connected with the Anatomical Institute. He had studied in the United States with the somatologist William H. Sheldon (1898–1977) and the geneticist Theodosius Dobzhansky (1900–1975), both of whom increased his interest in fashioning a synthesis of morphological anthropology and genetics. On returning to Norway, he specialized in physical anthropology and consolidated Schreiner's work. Using a combination of radiological and anthropological techniques, Torgersen produced an interesting series of studies ranging from his investigation of sutural patterns in the human skull (1951) to the question of the origin of the Lapps (1968).

In 1952, Torgersen was appointed professor of anatomy and head of the anthropological collections housed in the Anatomical Institute. Like his predecessor, he, too, established working relations with archeologists and endeavored to assist them in identifying and describing skeletal remains they had excavated. Together with Bernhard Getz (1923–1969), who was an associate professor at the Anatomical Institute from 1958 to the time of his death, Torgersen made several investigations, especially on skeletal finds from the Arctic Stone Age. They found that that oldest population in Finnmark had "Nordic" traits, without any "Lappic" features (Torgersen & Getz 1968). Getz, however, is probably best remembered for his study of the hip joint in Lapps and its bearing on the problem of congenital dislocation (1955). In that study, he used physical anthropological methods to show that the high tendency of hip-joint dislocation in the Lappic population is due to a greater antetorsion angle combined with a shallow roof of the hip-joint socket. Both Getz and Torgersen encouraged and supported students interested in anthropological research.

In 1972, Torgersen took the initiative of connecting Schreiner's name to the anthropological collection at the Anatomical Institute. The Schreiner Collection, which comprises 7,500 individual skeletons dating from Neolithic times to the early nineteenth century, is a well-known resource that continually attracts researchers from all over the world. After Torgersen's death, the Schreiner Collection was administered by Ludvig K. Haugen (1930–), who continued the tradition of assisting archeologists and students. As an oral surgeon, he found the collection of great interest, and he subsequently conducted a craniometric study on the normal variations of the facial skeleton that formed the basis of his doctoral thesis (1977; republished with amendments in 1980). His later (1990) investigations of human mandibular tori have given new interpretations to this discrete trait.

The Schreiner Collection is under the curatorial direction of Per Holck (1942–), a medical physician by training who joined the institute in 1989, and since 1993 as a professor. His particular research interest is forensic anthropology and paleopathology as indicated by his monograph *Cremated Bones: A Medical-Anthropological Study*, published in 1986.

Although after 1930 the University of Oslo was no longer the exclusive academic center of Norway, its Anatomical Institute has retained this distinction and continues to be the sole focus for physical anthropological research in the country.

Per Holck

See also Broca, Paul (Pierre); Dobzhansky, Theodosius; Linnaeus, Carolus; Manouvrier, Léonce-Pierre; Mantegazza, Paolo; Retzius, Anders Adolf; Retzius, Magnus Gustaf; Sheldon, William H(erbert); Sweden; Topinard, Paul; Virchow, Rudolf

Bibliography
C.O.E. Arbo: Le première découverte d'ossements humains de l'âge de la pierre en Norvège. *Revue d'anthropologie* 5 (2d ser.):497–505, 1882; C.O.E. Arbo: La carte de l'indice céphalique en Norvège. *Revue d'anthropologie* 2(3d ser.):257–264, 1887; C.O.E. Arbo: Om de somatiske tegn paa to befolkningers optræden i Norge. *Nyt Magazin for Naturvidenskaberne* 37:447, 1900; H. Bryn: *Anthropologia Norvegica* I. Det østenfjeldske Norges antropologi. *Skrifter utgitt av Videnskabsselskabet i Oslo.* No. 6. Oslo: Videnskabsselskabet i Oslo, 1925; H. Bryn: Die Entwicklung der Menschenrassen. *Anthropos* 21:435–461, 1053–1092, 1926.

H. Bryn: *Der Nordische Mensch.* München: Lehmanns, 1929; B. Getz: The hip joint in Lapps, and its bearing on the problem of congenital dislocation. *Acta orthopaedica Scandinavica* (Supplement). No. 18. Copenhagen: Munksgaard, 1955;

B. Getz: Skull thickness in the frontal and parietal regions. *Acta Morphologica Neerlando-Scandinavica* 3:221–228, 1960; G.A. Guldberg: Udsigt over endel fund af gammelnorske kranier. *Nordisk medicinsk arkiv* 8(13):1897; G.A. Guldberg: Die Menschenknochen des Osebergschiffs aus dem jüngeren Eisenalter: Eine anatomisch-anthropologische Untersuchung. *Skrifter udgivne af Det norske Videnskabsselskab.* No. 8. Christiania: Det norske Videnskabsselskab, 1907.

L.K. Haugen: The human upper and middle face. *Acta Morphologica Neerlando-Scandinavica.* No. 15, 1977; L.K. Haugen: The human upper and middle face. *Acta Morphologica Neerlando-Scandinavica.* No. 18, 1980; L.K. Haugen: The tori of the human jaw skeleton: Studies on *Torus palatinus* and *Torus mandibularis*. *Antropologiske Skrifter.* No. 4. Oslo: Anatomisk Institutt, Universitetet i Oslo, 1990; J.M. Heiberg: Lappische Gräber-Schädel. *Archiv for Mathematik og Naturvidenskab,* 1878; J.M. Heiberg: Om de i Gokstadskibet fundne Menneskeben. *Norsk Magazin for Lægevidenskaben* 13:259–260, 1883; P. Holck: Scurvy: A paleopathological problem. Paleopathology Association. V. European Meeting. Siena: Paleopathology Association, 1984, pp. 163–172; P. Holck: Cremated bones: A medical-anthropological study of an archaeological material on cremation burials. *Antropologiske Skrifter.* No. 1. Oslo: Anatomisk Institutt, Universitett i Oslo, 1986.

R. Keyser: *Norges Historie.* Christiania: 1866; P.A. Munch: *Det norske Folks Historie.* 6 vols. Christiania: Tønsberg, 1851–1863; G. Schøning: *Norges Riges Historie.* København, 1771; A. Schreiner: Anthropologische Studien an norwegischen Frauen. *Det norske Videnskabsselskabs skrifter.* No. 9. Kristiania: Det norske Videnskabsselskab, 1924; A. Schreiner: Die Nord-Norweger: Anthropologische Untersuchungen an Soldaten. *Skrifter utgitt av Det norske Videnskabs-Akademi i Oslo.* Oslo: Det norske Videnskabs-Akademi, 1929; K.E. Schreiner: Die Menschenknochen des Osebergschiffs und andere Norwegischen Skelettfunde aus der Eisenzeit. *Osebergfundet* 5:281–307, 1927.

K.E. Schreiner: *Zur Osteologie der Lappen.* 2 vols. Oslo: Instituttet for sammenlignende kulturforskning, 1931–1935; K.E. Schreiner: *Crania Norvegica.* 2 vols. Oslo, 1939–1946; M. Skjelderup: *Anatomisk-Physiologiske Forelæsninger for Anthropologer.* København, 1807; P.F. Suhm: *Om de Nordiske Folks ældste Oprindelse.* København, 1770; J. Torgersen: Hereditary factors in the sutural pattern of the skull. *Acta radiologica* 36:374–382, 1951; J. Torgersen: The origin of the Lapps. In: *Anthropologie und Humangenetik.* Stuttgart: Fischer, 1968, pp. 105–114; J. Torgersen: Rassengeschichte von Skandinavien. In: I. Schwidetsky (ed) *Rassengeschichte der Menschheit: Europa.* Vol. 2, *Ost- und Nordeuropa.* München/Wien: Oldenbourg, 1976, pp. 103–145; J. Torgersen & B. Getz: *Prehistoric man in Finnmark and the origin of the Lapps.* Oslo: Universitetsforlaget, 1968, pp. 59–72.

Nott, Josiah Clark (1804–1873)

Born in Columbia, South Carolina, Nott received his undergraduate education at South Carolina College before entering the University of Pennsylvania, from which he graduated M.D. in 1827. He interned in Philadelphia before returning to Columbia for several years and then moved to Mobile, Alabama. With the exception of another temporary move to New Orleans, Nott remained based in Mobile until after the American Civil War (Erickson 1986; Horsman 1987).

Nott became one of the most prominent doctors in the South. He helped establish the Medical Society of Mobile and the Medical College of Mobile (precursor of the University of Alabama School of Medicine), where he was appointed professor of surgery. Much of his practice was devoted to victims of yellow fever, a disease that ravaged Southern port cities and killed five of his own children. J.C. Nott's Infirmary was designed to treat the special medical problems of Negro slaves. Nott's practice also included many of Mobile's social elite (Erickson 1986).

Nott's medical interests and publications span a wide range of subjects, including gynecology, surgery, and the etiology of yellow fever. He was one of the first scientists to speculate that yellow fever is transmitted by insects (Bean 1974; Carmichael 1948; Downs 1974). In theory and practice, he followed the French clinical approach to medicine, studying diseases in hospital settings and interpreting them in light of a vitalistic physiology (Erickson 1986).

Nott was a prominent member of the American School of Anthropology, a group that espoused racial polygenism, the doctrine that races are separate species with ancient, separate origins. Like other members of the American School he was an anthropologist by avocation only. His anthropological reputation rests mainly on two books, coauthored with George R. Gliddon (1809–1857): *Types of Mankind* (1854) and *Indigenous Races of the Earth* (1857). His ideas in these books began to take root in the early 1840s, inspired by early French polygenists such as Jean Baptiste Bory de Saint Vincent (1778–1846), Louis-Antoine Desmoulins (1794–1828), and Julien Joseph Virey (1775–1846).

Nott's interest in polygenism began with the problem of racial hybridity. Polygenists claimed that races were different species. Species, however, were supposed to be incapable of producing fertile hybrid offspring, while fertile racial hybrids like mulattoes clearly existed. To keep the designation of races as "species" intact, Nott simply redefined the term species, making its essential characteristic not hybrid infertility, but morphological distinctness through time—time longer than could be inferred from the Bible (cf. Nott 1843, 1844).

In a series of publications beginning with *Two Lectures on the Natural History of the Caucasian and Negro Races* (1844), Nott sought to disassociate anthropology from the Bible. His alternative explanation was that races had been separately created before biblical time. His medical experience convinced him that Negroes and Whites possessed different susceptibilities to disease, attributable to innately different "vitalities." Nott argued against monogenist anthropologists, who believed that races had a recent and common origin. His most notable opponent was the Reverend Dr. John Bachman (1790–1874) of his native South Carolina (Nott 1851a).

Nott's comments on race brought him to the attention of other members of the American School, including its proclaimed leader, Samuel George Morton (1799–1851). After Morton's death, George Gliddon, then the U.S. consul in Cairo, persuaded Nott to coauthor a book dedicated to Morton's memory. That book was *Types of Mankind*, followed by *Indigenous Races*. Both books were compilations of contributions by several authors. Gliddon's contribution was to show that Negroes and Whites had been distinct as early as Egypt's first dynasty. Nott's contribution was also intended to demonstrate the antiquity of racial differences, as well as to show that races were immune to major change. Nott was sympathetic to all of the views expressed in the books, but he was displeased

with their editing, which had been done mainly by Gliddon. After 1857, he washed his hands of "scientific" anthropology and never again published at great length on the subject (Erickson 1986).

C. Loring Brace calls Nott " . . . a prototypical Southern racist" (1974:516). This assessment is fair, although offered in hindsight. Nott owned slaves and defended slavery as a Southern partisan, branding Negroes " . . . the lowest point on the scale of human beings . . ." and their interbreeding with Whites " . . . insulting and revolting . . ." (Nott 1851b:330). During the Civil War, he served in the Confederate Army, and after the war he wrote widely circulated diatribes against the Freedman's Bureau (Nott 1866a, 1866b).

In 1867, despairing at the postwar state of affairs in the South, Nott moved to Baltimore and then to New York, where he tried to establish a medical practice to regain some of his lost wealth. Weakened by the effort, he returned to Mobile, where he died in 1873. At the time of his death, the American School of Anthropology, which Nott had helped create, was approaching political and scientific obsolescence.

Paul A. Erickson

See also American School of Anthropology; Morton, Samuel George; Polygenism

Bibliography
SELECTED WORKS
The mulatto a hybrid—probable extermination of the two races if the Whites and Blacks are allowed to marry. *American Journal of the Medical Sciences* 6:252–256, 1843; *Two lectures on the natural history of the Caucasian and Negro races*. Mobile, Alabama: Dade & Thompson, 1844; Diversity of the human race. *DeBow's Southern and Western Review* 10:113–132, 1851a; Nature and destiny of the Negro. *DeBow's Southern and Western Review* 10:329–332, 1851b; The Negro race. *Popular Magazine of Anthropology* 3:102–118, 1866a.

The problem of the Black races. *DeBow's Southern and Western Review* (After the War Series) 1:266–270, 1866b; (with G.R. Gliddon) *Types of mankind; or, Ethnological researches, based upon the ancient monuments, paintings, sculptures, and crania of races, and upon their natural, geographical, philological, and biblical history.* Philadelphia: Lippincott, Grambo, 1854; (with G.R. Gliddon) *Indigenous races of the Earth; or, New chapters of ethnological inquiry; including monographs on special departments of philology, iconography, cranioscopy, palaeontology, pathology, archaeology, comparative geography, and natural history.* Philadelphia: Lippincott, 1857.

ARCHIVAL SOURCES

1. J.C. Nott Correspondence: Academy of Natural Sciences of Philadelphia, 19th & the Parkway, Logan Square, Philadelphia, Pennsylvania 19103; 2. J.C. Nott Correspondence: College of Physicians of Philadelphia, 19 South 22nd Street, Philadelphia, Pennsylvania 19103; 3. J.C. Nott Papers: Library Company of Philadelphia, 1314 Locust Street, Philadelphia, Pennsylvania 19107; 4. J.C. Nott Correspondence: National Library of Medicine, History of Medicine Division, 8600 Rockville Pike, Bethesda, Maryland 20894; 5. J.C. Nott Correspondence (Special Collections, Drawer S): University of Alabama Library, Tuscaloosa, Alabama 35486; 6. J.C. Nott Correspondence: Library, Manuscripts Department & Southern Historical Collection, University of North Carolina, Chapel Hill, North Carolina 27514.

SECONDARY SOURCES

W. Bean: Josiah Clark Nott, a Southern physician. *Bulletin of the New York Academy of Medicine* 50:529–535, 1974; C.L. Brace: The "ethnology" of Josiah Clark Nott. *Bulletin of the New York Academy of Medicine* 50:509–528, 1974; E.B. Carmichael: Josiah Clark Nott. *Bulletin of the History of Medicine* 22:249–262, 1948; W. Downs: Yellow fever and Josiah Clark Nott. *Bulletin of the New York Academy of Medicine* 50:499–508, 1974; P.A. Erickson: The anthropology of Josiah Clark Nott. *Kroeber Anthropological Society Papers* 55–56:103–120, 1986; R. Horsman: *Josiah Clark Nott of Mobile: Southerner, physician, and racial theorist.* Baton Rouge: Louisiana State University Press, 1987.

Oakley, Kenneth Page (1911–1981)

Born in Amersham, Buckingham, England, Oakley entered University College, London, in 1930 to read geology and anthropology. He received a B.Sc. (with first-class honors) in 1933 and a Ph.D. in 1938. In 1934, he joined the Geological Survey, and a year later he transferred to the Geology (Palaeontology) Department of the Natural History Museum (also known as the British Museum [Natural History]) in South Kensington, London, as an assistant keeper in paleontology. During World War II, he was assigned to the Geological Survey. On returning to the museum in 1947, he was promoted to the rank of principal scientific officer; in 1954, the Anthropological Sections of the Departments of Geology and Zoology were placed under his direction; and in 1955, he was elevated to the rank of senior principal scientific officer. Soon thereafter, the museum's Anthropological Sections were consolidated into the Subdepartment of Anthropology and, in 1959, attached to the Department of Palaeontology, which Oakley continued to steward until 1969 when ill health forced him into early retirement.

Essentially, Oakley's fame as a research scientist was founded on his pioneering work in the development of reliable relative-dating techniques and their application to the human fossil record. Apparently, while attached to the Geological Survey during World War II and investigating sources of phosphate for use as a fertilizer, he came across the neglected mineralogical work of James Middleton (d. 1875) (1844) and Marie-Adolphe Carnot (1839–1920) (1893), both of whom had drawn attention to the value of estimating the

fluorine content of bone as a general indicator of age. It was not, however, until after the war that Oakley was provided with an opportunity to test the potential of the Middleton-Carnot methodology. While attending the first Pan-African Congress on Prehistory in Nairobi, Kenya, in January 1947, Oakley heard about the ongoing debate regarding the antiquity of the Kanam-Kanjera materials, and he approached the Kenyan paleoanthropologist Louis S.B. Leakey (1903–1972) about the possibility of applying the fluorine technique to this case. In August of that year, Oakley reported to the Dundee meeting of the British Association for the Advancement of Science that technical problems relating to the high background-fluorine content in the Kenyan material had led to disappointing and inconclusive results, but he remained convinced of the method's value. Soon thereafter, he used it to compare the much disputed Galley Hill remains with those of Swanscombe, both of which had been found in the same vicinity in East Kent, England. The results of this investigation were stunning. Reporting on these findings to the Brighton meeting of the British Association in 1948, Oakley said there was little question that the Galley Hill skeleton was not of great antiquity, as previously supposed, but in all probability was an intrusive burial dating from the early Holocene. Bolstered by this success, Oakley received permission to extend his investigations to the controversial Piltdown remains. From the outset, scientific opinion had been divided over the association of the Piltdown jaw and skull. Oakley had hoped to resolve this issue, but the results of his initial investigations were inconclusive (cf. Oakley & Hoskins 1950). Although he continued, like most of his contemporaries, to be puzzled by the Piltdown enigma, it was not until 1953, when the Oxford physical anthropologist Joseph Sidney Weiner (1915–1982) presented his argument for the jaw being a forgery, that the Piltdown problem was finally resolved. An improved methodology detected significant differences in the fluorine content of the jaw and cranial remains, which, along with other findings, served to confirm Weiner's hypothesis (cf. Weiner, Oakley, & Clark 1953). In addition to rocketing Oakley into the scientific lime-light, the 1953–1955 Piltdown investigations also contributed to the movement leading to the development of reliable relative and ab-solute dating techniques (cf. Oakley, Weiner et al. 1955). Oakley was among the leaders in this movement, and his book *Frameworks for Dating Fossil Man* (1964) is generally regarded as a significant milestone in the modern his-tory of the discipline.

Although ill health forced him into early retirement, Oakley managed to continue with his writing. Among the 100 or more works that he produced during his career are several notable volumes, including the three-volume *Catalogue of Fossil Hominids* (1967–1977), compiled in collaboration with Bernard Campbell and Theya Molleson, and his *Frame-works for Dating Fossil Man* (2d ed.: 1969) mentioned above, which is still a valuable ref-erence work. Another is *Man the Tool Maker.* Widely regarded as a classic work, it received worldwide distribution, and since its first appearance in 1949 it has been translated into several languages.

In recognition of his scientific contribu-tions, Oakley received many awards, includ-ing the prestigous Wollaston Fund Award in 1941 and the Prestwich Medal of the Geologi-cal Society of London in 1963. He was also named a Fellow of the British Academy in 1957, and he was president of the Anthropo-logical Section of the British Association for the Advancement of Science in 1961.

Oakley died on 2 November 1981.

Frank Spencer

See also Clark, (Sir) Wilfrid Edward Le Gros; Galley Hill; Piltdown; Swanscombe; United Kingdom; Weiner, Joseph Sidney

Bibliography

SELECTED WORKS

The succession of life through geological time. London: British Museum (Natural History), 1948 (7th ed.:1967); *Man the tool maker.* London: British Museum (Natural History), 1949 (6th ed.: Chicago: University of Chicago Press, 1976); The fluorine-dating method. *Yearbook of Physical Anthropology* 5:44–52, 1951; The problem of man's antiquity: An historical survey. *Bulletin of the British Museum (Natural History)* 9(5):83–155, 1964; *Frameworks for dating fossil man.* Chicago: Aldine, 1964 (2d ed.: 1966, 3d ed.: London: Weidenfeld & Nicolson, 1969); *Decorative and symbolic uses of vertebrate fossils.* London: Oxford University Press, 1975.

(With B.C. Campbell & T.I. Molleson [eds]) *Catalogue of fossil hominids.* Vol. 1, *Africa*; Vol. 2, *Europe*; Vol. 3, *Americas, Asia, Australasia.* London: British Museum (Natural History), 1967–1975; (with C.R. Hoskins) New evidence on the antiquity of Piltdown man. *Nature* 165:379–382, 1950; (with M.F.A. Montagu) A reconsideration of the Galley Hill skeleton. *Bulletin of the British Museum (Natural History)* 1:25–48, 1949; (with J.S. Weiner & W.E. Le Gros Clark) The solution to the Piltdown problem. *Bulletin of the British Museum (Natural History)* 2:141–146, 1953; (with J.S. Weiner et al.) Further contributions to the solution of the Piltdown problem. *Bulletin of the British Museum (Natural History)* 2:225–287, 1955.

ARCHIVAL SOURCES

K.P. Oakley Papers (P. MSS KPO) and Piltdown Papers: Library of Palaeontology, Natural History Museum, Cromwell Road, London SW7 5BD, England.

PRIMARY SOURCES

A. Carnot: Recherches sur la composi-tion générale et la teneur en fluor des os modernes et des os fossiles de différents âges. *Annales de Mineralogie* (Paris) 3:155–195, 1893; J. Middleton: On fluorine in bones, its source, and its application to the determination of the geological age of fossil bones. *Proceedings of the Geological Society of London* 4:25–52, 1844.

SECONDARY SOURCES

Who's Who. 126th ed. London: St. Martin's, 1974.

Oceania

Oceania, with its island geography, and with its varied peoples and cultures more sharply segregated than those of the continents, has been particularly inviting to hypothetical reconstructions of history. True prehistory, in the form of dates and dirt archeology, did not exist for some time. Physical and cultural anthropologists and linguists, with only frail practical methodologies, at first shared a paradigm of attempting to distill coherent "races" or culture entities that entered the Pacific in succession, subsequently moving about and interacting to produce the historic picture.

Early Reconstructions

THE PERSPECTIVE FROM CULTURE. Cultural anthropologists, usually deeply informed as to the actual data, constructed many detailed hypotheses of supposed past events. An early example was the German *Kulturkreis* school of Fritz Graebner (1877–1934) and Wilhelm Schmidt (1868–1954), which postulated a series of distinct culture complexes spreading outward (cf. Graebner 1905; Schmidt 1913). While first traced out in Oceania, these "waves" were eventually plotted worldwide. One version of Graebner's waves denoted the complexes as Tasmanian, Old Australian, Totemic, Moiety, Melanesian Bow, and Polynesian. In England, the Cambridge psychologist-anthropologist W.H.R. Rivers (1864–1922) followed suit, defining a succession of Aboriginals, Sitting Interment People, Kava People, Betel People, and Cremation People—in migrations that he theorized reached parts of Melanesia and Polynesia differentially (Rivers 1914). Many such diffusionists' hypotheses were reviewed in detail by the British student of Polynesian culture Robert W. Williamson (1856–1932), who had his own version (cf. Williamson 1924, 1939). Such reconstructions rested primarily on museum study. The Polynesians themselves abetted the effort, with their voyaging traditions, their formal genealogies, and their legends of the Ari'i arriving and conquering the primitive Manahune; more was made of these things than should have been.

This general view of culture history was rebutted by the experienced Roland Dixon (1875–1934), Harvard University's great ethnographer, on evidential grounds, and punctured by the grimly ahistorical Functionalist school of social anthropology (cf. Piddington, in Williamson 1939), which argued that culture has its own rules of integration and change. In modern times, there has been a rehabilitation of work on cultural prehistory (cf. Kirch & Green 1987).

THE ROLE OF CRANIOLOGY. The physical anthropology of the day reflected the same model of immigrant racial types essentially modified only by mixing *in situ*. The first material to be addressed was cranial. Collecting began in the nineteenth century; at least as early as the 1860s the great Hamburg trading house of Godeffroy had agents in the Pacific who were instructed to acquire anthropological materials, including skulls, for the Godeffroy Museum (Spoehr 1963). Unfortunately, several such collections were lost at sea before reaching Hamburg, and much cranial material was destroyed in World War II in Germany, as well as in the Royal College of Surgeons in London. Oceanic crania are not a renewable resource, so there has been a permanent diminution since the early twentieth century.

Nevertheless, substantial collections survive, especially from Melanesia and New Guinea. The large body of Tolai skulls from New Britain, collected for the German anthropologist Felix von Luschan (1854–1924) by Richard Parkinson (1844–1909) and originally housed in the Königliche Museum für Völkerkunde in Berlin, were subsequently acquired by the American Museum of Natural History in New York and the Field Museum in Chicago, though the history of these acquisitions is unclear (Howells 1989:98). Otto Schlaginhaufen (1879–1973) amassed an important collection from several parts of New Ireland and its barrier islands (Schlaginhaufen 1965) that, along with other materials, is believed to survive in Berlin, still unpacked since the last war. Eastern Melanesia (Vanuatu, New Caledonia) is represented by considerable numbers, especially in Paris. For Polynesia, Easter Island has been the great source at all times, with an early collection by Alphonse Pinart (1852–1911) for the Musée de l'Homme in Paris. Another valuable Hawaiian series, in the Bernice P. Bishop Museum in Honolulu, was excavated in the Mokapu Peninsula on Oahu between 1938 and 1940 by Kenneth Emory and Gordon T. Bowles (1904–1991) and has been studied in detail (cf. Snow 1974; Howells 1989). This material was recently returned for reburial. For New Zealand, the amount of material is somewhat scattered, but the Moriori of the Chatham Islands are well represented. Micronesia is poorly represented, with the museums in Hamburg being the primary locus both for collections (Schmeltz & Krause 1881) and loss. Altogether, though, surviving material is still substantial in spite of World War II. Michael Pietrusewsky (1986) of the University of Hawaii has compiled a valuable, if necessarily incomplete, inventory of existing Oceanic crania.

Measurement of skulls was anthropology's earliest practice and was well established as to definitions and techniques by the late nineteenth century. Records of measurements were published in some quantity, especially in the *Archiv für Anthropologie* in Germany and in *Biometrika* in England—the last mostly by workers in the Biometric Laboratory under Karl Pearson (1857–1936) (*vide infra*).

ANTHROPOMETRIC ANALYSIS. Anthropometric records on the living began about the turn of the century, aided especially by the German colonization of New Guinea and the western Solomons. The search for racial elements and migrations was on. Roland Dixon was the most explicit. In *The Racial History of Man* (1923), he decomposed series of heads or crania into their proportions of opposite forms of head length (long vs. broad), head height (high vs. low), and nose breadth (narrow vs. broad). Combining these categories allowed eight types into which individuals could fall ($2 \times 2 \times 2$). Although Dixon stressed the experimental nature of his procedure, the types became reified, for him, as primal races, coming into being at times not known and in parts of the Old World judged only from their apparent out-migrations. Here is a sample of his analysis: For the Hawaiians Island, in Kauai "the Palae-Alpine type [round, high, broad] is in the majority, followed in order by the Proto-Negroid [long, high, broad], and Caspian [long, high, narrow]; in Hawaii, at the southeastern or nearer end, the Alpine type [round, high, narrow] is dominant, followed by the Palae-Alpine, Proto-Negroid and Caspian. It seems possible, therefore, that we may regard the Kauai population as representing an older stratum . . . and that there has since entered from the southward an immigration of Alpine peoples. . . " (1923).

With similar analyses of the rest of Polynesia, Oceania, and, in fact, the world, the task of reconstructing hypothetical migrations to Polynesia was not easy. For Dixon, it came down to three basic waves, already mixed themselves, which also had some implied cultural differences and native traditions. Dixon was, in fact, a cultural anthropologist, and as conservative (antidiffusionist) in that field (1928) as he was venturesome in the other.

A major effort at data collection for western and central Polynesia (and Hawaii) was reported in monographs of the Bishop Museum in a joint effort with the American Museum of Natural History. Measurements taken by on-the-scene anthropologists were analyzed and reported on by Louis R. Sullivan (1892–1925) and, after Sullivan's death, by Clark Wissler (1870–1947) and Harry Lionel Shapiro (1902–1990). As Sullivan wrote at the outset: "The determination of the physical characters and of the racial affinities of the Polynesians is an essential part of the Bayard Dominick Expedition" (1921). The result, however, was the publication of individual records and seriations for a number of measurements, largely of the head, valuable but not revealing of the above objectives.

For this whole period, the essential problem was a lack of objective methods of analysis. Although Dixon's effort was badly flawed theoretically, it does serve to suggest the technical and ideological difficulties of the day. By his time, large quantities of measurements on the living and skulls had already been reported, but this was then rather intractable material for comprehension and analysis, and Dixon's was an attempt, however flawed, to improve matters. The existing alternative was the subjective recognition of "types," and this was a usual recourse.

Even if that approach was rejected in favor of simply studying and comparing measurements of the many samples, the result was always the attempt to define "racial elements" for Oceania. This typically suggested a set of immigrants consisting of Australoids, Negritoes, Melanesians of two or more kinds (including a "Papuan"), and Poly/Micronesians (Howells 1934). But there was no proof of objectivity, and no dates at all to suggest actual events. It may be said that, even now, an impressionistic division of peoples would have a somewhat similar outcome. But today no worker would deal in "types" or plunge directly into broad reconstructions of the past. Efforts are more modest and manageable, and controlled somewhat by dates and archeology.

In any event, older studies were in decline before World War II. This early phase might fairly be called the "prescientific." Change came after mid-century, mainly for two reasons: genetics and statistical analysis. We will examine their contributions to prehistory after looking at, first, some basic findings from archeology and linguistic studies, and, second, major problems remaining, to which present and future work in physical anthropology is addressed.

Post–World War II Developments

NEW INFORMATION. In addition to that from physical anthropology, described below, firmer evidence appeared from language and from archeology and dating.

New Guinea and perhaps the western Solomons were reached very early, possibly coeval with arrivals in Australia about 55 ky BP. The Papuan or non-Austronesian languages are so diverse—no area of the world is comparable—as to suggest an antiquity of 10.0 ky or more. They occupy New Guinea except portions of the coast, and extend into parts of the Bismarck Archipelago and the Solomons, as far as Savo Island off Guadalcanal. Except for a disputed case in the Santa Cruz group just beyond the Solomons, these languages are not detectable as an element anywhere to the east.

The Austronesian languages of all of the rest of Oceania (including Indonesia and Taiwan) are estimated, from internal evidence, to have a common source at about 4000 B.C. Those of Melanesia are relatively diverse; those of Polynesia are much more cohesive, suggesting a single later origin. Languages of Micronesia are more varied.

Archeology has increasingly traced a varying Lapita culture complex, marked especially by a specific pottery style and some other elements. It spread rapidly from about 2000 B.C. to 1500 B.C., apparently starting in the Bismarck Archipelago, occupying coastal settlements (not the Melanesian interiors) and being established in Fiji and western Polynesia by perhaps 1500 B.C., before the voyages to eastern Polynesia began about A.D. 0.

CURRENT PROBLEMS. Before considering the impact of physical anthropology it might be well to suggest some problems to be addressed. These are strangely evocative of the *Kulturkreis* era and the search for "racial elements": the succession of arrivals in the Pacific.

Australians and Melanesians are together generally distinguished from other world populations. Are they mutually distinguishable? J.H. Greenberg (1971) sees a remote kinship among Andamanese, Tasmanian, and Papuan (non-Austronesian) languages, which would suggest a community persisting well after the very early first arrival. In agreement with this, there is an emerging hypothesis, from craniometrics, archeology, and genetics, that sees a first southern Asiatic migration of moderns out of Africa at some 60.0 ky BP, as the source for eastern Negritoes, Australians, and Melanesians (cf. especially Lahr, in press). Did such a single immigration enter this area and get at least as far as Bougainville in the Solomons, differentiating later? Did it get farther? In northern New Caledonia, in southeast Melanesia, there are people strongly suggesting Australians in outward appearance.

How complex were the "Lapita" phenomenon and movements through Melanesia? For some, Austronesian = Lapita = Polynesians. According to these writers, Polynesians arose by genetic processes on Melanesia's eastern border and have no connections farther west. Likewise, Austronesian languages made only a single entry. This would be the simplest possible interpretation.

Or were all elements in the above equation multiplex? Polynesian languages are closely related, while the Austronesian languages of Melanesia are much more diverse: still linguists believe this Melanesian diversification could have been local and rapid, and there is much agreement that the whole branch of Remote Oceanic Austronesian has an age probably no greater than 2000 B.C. Lapita pottery is distinctive, but it has been suggested that some elements of the Lapita complex, along with root crops, as well as more capable ocean travel, might be a sort of earlier layer. And the physical distinction of Polynesians from Melanesians (*vide infra*) makes their simple emergence on the border of Melanesia too much for physical anthropologists to swallow.

Polynesians are seen by many as the living embodiment of the Lapita (pottery) travelers, and as having traversed Melanesia in a few centuries without heavy contact with the Melanesian indigenes. This would derive Polynesians from a hearth closer to Asia. But the hearth remains undetected, whether in southeast Asia or farther north.

STUDY OF GENETIC POLYMORPHISMS. Genetic knowledge brought understanding of variation and the possibility of microevolution, coupled with the introduction of blood-antigen studies. This supplied a new objective for study. The American immunochemist William C. Boyd (1903–1983) entered anthropology with a solid understanding of population genetics and had a major impact in his work and writing (e.g., Boyd 1950), showing that intrapopulation variation lay not in mixtures among integrated types but in gene proportions. In 1963, he published a list of blood-group "races" on such a basis (cf. Table 2 for a streamlined summary).

Such work proliferated as many new blood polymorphisms were discovered. For the Pacific, Roy T. Simmons (1906–1975) in Australia was particularly vigorous, publishing early general summaries (see Table 3 for a few comparative figures). These results and large amounts of other data have not, however, made commensurate contributions to prehistory or carried matters effectively beyond Boyd's early effort in broad suggestions; they have been more useful in the kind of comparisons seen in Table 1 than in fine-grained analyses. Multivariate methods (*vide infra*) have, for some time, been applied to blood genetic data, but mostly on a global scale, for which they are well suited, rather than within particular regions. Results, in concert with linguistic studies (also a realm of development of quantitative methods), especially at the hands of researchers such as the Italian geneticist L. Cavalli-Sforza (e.g., 1991) at Stanford University and the American biologist Robert Sokal (e.g., 1988), have been strikingly suggestive when carried out over worldwide samples, but the methods have not been applied on a fine scale to Oceania.

GENETIC DRIFT. Blood-group studies, however, have been illuminating as to microevolution—especially concerning genetic drift and the founder effect, for which Oceania, with its geographically more isolated populations (and an emerging time scale), is especially suited. It is now known that peoples in the west have been there a relatively long time—ca. 40.0 ky BP in the Bismarck Archipelago and longer in Australia—but a relatively short time in Polynesia.

There are several examples of apparent extreme effects of drift. On Bentinck Island off northern Australia, there is a small population of Aboriginals who have only the B and O genes of the ABO system and who in other polymorphisms differ radically from continental groups, being unlike any people anywhere. These people may have been isolated for a very long time. On the other hand, the populations of Rennell and Bellona Islands lying south of the central Solomons, are clearly settlers coming west from Polynesia whose arrival must date within the last 2,000 years. These people, totally unlike other Polynesians (cf. Table 3), have almost none of the A gene, are high in B, and are exceptionally high in the M gene.

Here are striking examples of what can be ascribed only to accidental drift. Within both of the above parent areas, Australia and Polynesia, small populations are in mutual contact but have evidently also been affected overall by drift, which, in the absence of some force like selection, normally acts toward eliminating the least-common common gene—in this case, gene B. For Polynesia in

TABLE 1. Summary of Linguistic and Archeological Research Post-World War II
- New Guinea and perhaps the western Solomons were reached very early, possibly coeval with arrivals in Australia about 55 ky BP.
- The diversity of Papuan or Non-Austronesian languages (no area of the world is comparable) suggest an antiquity of >10 ky BP. They occupy New Guinea except portions of the coast, and extend into parts of the Bismarck Archipelago and the Solomons, as far as Savo Island off Guadalcanal. Except for a disputed case in the Santa Cruz group just beyond the Solomons, these languages are not detectable as an element anywhere to the east.
- The Austronesian languages of Oceania (including Indonesia and Taiwan) are estimated, from internal evidence, to have a common source at about 4000 B.C. Those of Melanesia are relatively diverse; whereas those of Polynesia are much more cohesive, suggesting a single later diversification. The languages of Micronesia are more varied.
- Archeology has increasingly traced a varying Lapita culture complex, marked especially by a specific pottery style and some other elements. It spread rapidly from about 2000 B.C. to about 150 B.C., apparently starting in the Bismarck Archipelago, occupying coastal settlements (not the Melanesian interiors) and being established in Fiji and western Polynesia by perhaps 1500 B.C., before the voyages to Eastern Polynesia began about A.D. 0.

TABLE 2. Summary of W.C. Boyd's Oceanic Data (1963)
Indonesian race
High values of the A and B genes in the ABO system; gene M medium in the MN system; R^1 dominant in the Rh system.
Melanesian race
A and B higher than Indonesia; M low in frequency; R^1 high.
Polynesian race
B almost absent; M above normal; $R^1 = R^2$.
Australian race
A high, B absent; M. low; R^2 at highest.

Note: The short-hand R^1 and R^2 are equivalent to CDE and cde using the Fisher-Race nomenclature.

TABLE 3. Summary of Blood Group Frequencies for Pacific and Other Peoples

Location	Blood Group					
	A	B	M	R^1	R^2	Fy^a
Western Polynesia						
Tonga	0.28	0.06	0.59	0.69	0.24	0.88
Samoa (U.S.)	.10	.12				
Samoa, Western	.24	.10				
Tavala (Ellice)	.19	.14	.62	.76	.13	.68
Tokalu	.23	.03	.44	.72	.22	.74
Outliers						
Kapingamarangi	.25	.00	.71	.75	.24	
Ontong Java	.29	.06	.45	.80	.13	
Rennell	.01	.35	.70	.54	.42	
Bellona	.01	.34	.69	.79	.18	
Central Polynesia						
Southern Cooks	.47	.04	.51	.49	.45	.32
Northern Cooks	.30	.04	.58	.53	.41	.40
Tahiti	.37	.03	.58	.54	.33	.62
Marquesas, Tuamotus, Tubuai	.33	.00	.49	.51	.48	.64
Marginal Polynesia						
Hawaii	.38	.01				
Easter	.42	.01	.37	.37	.57	.67
New Zealand, North Island	.33	.00	.53	.46	.54	.46
Micronesia						
Gilbert Islands	.47	.16	.37	.78	.17	.89
Marshall Islands	.13	.10	.22	.95	.04	.07
Truk	.32	.20	.34	.83	.12	
Guam	.18	.12	.49	.67	.13	.88
Yap	.13	.10	.24	.79	.08	
Palau	.14	.10	.34	.94	.03	
Melanesia and elsewhere						
Fiji	.34	.06	.35	.82	.14	.97
Island Melanesia	.18	.11	.18	.88	.09	.93
Ainu	.28	.21	.40	.56	.21	.92
Haida, North America	.13	.01	.82	.33	.53	.81
South America	.00	.00	.72	.41	.54	.73

particular, these changes would have been intensified by the "founder effect": Repeated colonization of new islands, by nonrandom samples leaving the islands of origin, would have a strong biasing effect on the populations of the new colonies.

The genetic work has been highly successful in illuminating matters of process, while also certifying the relative local isolation of Oceanic populations as compared to those on the Eurasian landmass. However, the very processes just described tend to frustrate hopes of reading long-term prehistory from blood traits on a local scale, and in recent years such efforts have subsided somewhat.

THE GM SYSTEM. Instead of single genes making up a set of alleles at one locus, this complex system comprises strings of genes linked to form haplotypes; these determine linked se-

ries of antigens in the immunoglobulin of the immune system. In an early landmark study, Eugene Giles at the University of Illinois, Urbana, and his coworkers (1965) found striking differences between speakers of Austronesian and non-Austronesian languages over a number of tribes in New Guinea and Bougainville of the Solomons, suggesting possible separate migrations. At that time, relatively few of the Gm antigens, or factors, were known.

More recently, Kevin Kelly of Southern Methodist University and Jeffrey Clark of North Dakota State University (Kelly 1990; Clark & Kelly 1993) have reported Gm associations both with language and with endemicity of malaria in Melanesia. In brief, they found a common antigen (here G1 for short) that has morbid effects (enlarged spleen) in the presence of malaria; it is frequent in non-Austronesian-speaking dwellers in the highlands, who have little exposure to malaria. Another antigen (B3) affords protection against malaria and is very frequent in inhabitants of malarial coastal Melanesia, mainly Austronesian-speakers. In this argument, coastal swampy areas were thus largely left free of indigenous speakers of non-Austronesian languages for easy settlement by arriving Austronesian-speakers, whom the authors would equate with Lapita-using migrants.

This is a thumbnail presentation of a complicated and suggestive argument, and much more will obviously develop in the future. It supports at least two immigrations of Melanesians, and, in fact, the figures allow distinctions among three possible Melanesian populations.

DNA ANALYSIS. DNA (deoxyribonucleic acid) analysis is a new field still being explored but holding much promise. It is known that a deletion of nine base pairs from a specific segment of mitochondrial (mt) DNA occurs in from 10 percent to 40 percent of Asians from Japan to Indonesia, in coastal New Guinea, and in parts of Melanesia, but is found in 100 percent of all living Polynesians (probably a fixation resulting from the founder effect). E. Hagelberg and J.B. Clegg (1993) at Oxford University have used mtDNA from prehistoric bone. In their bone samples, eighteen Polynesians of recent centuries had the deletion. But in early samples from Samoa and Tonga (one each) and from Fiji and the Lapita site of Watom Island, New Britain, dating from near the beginning of the Christian era to about 500 B.C., no example of the deletion was found. This seems puzzling, suggesting to the authors that the original bearers of the Lapita complex were Melanesians, not Polynesians deriving more directly from Asia. Actually, the results may not be startling. The earlier specimens probably represent a period before fixation of the deletion in recent Polynesians. And among these earlier cases, the Fijian specimens (Sigatoka) can well represent not Polynesian ancestors but rather post-Lapita Melanesians coming to Fiji after its first colonization by original Polynesians. This is the likely historical event. Certainly, DNA from the living and from bone may tell much more in the future. The above deletion is entirely missing from interior Bougainville in the Solomons. In this same area there is a different, twelve-base-pair deletion, which has a frequency as high as .27 in some populations; it is present in declining frequencies eastward in the Solomons, but occurs nowhere

else. Possibly this bespeaks an isolation of these populations of some antiquity (cf. Friedlaender 1995).

HUMAN LEUCOCYTE ANTIGEN (HLA) SYSTEM. The HLA system, scarcely less complex than the Gm system and detectable especially on the white blood cells, has at least five loci, closely linked, with many alleles at each. These have already given striking evidence for events in Oceania (cf. Serjeantson 1985). The system is specific enough to provide clear indications of existing problems. Some of these are: The Australians are clearly set off, by their relatively limited number of antigens, as a long-isolated population, whereas New Guineans share certain features with Australians, but the interior non-Austronesian speakers of the island have evidently lost an important gene, A2, probably swamped by entering NAN-speakers in the intermediate past. This same gene later reentered coastal New Guinea and Melanesia, where it is accompanied by some different markers, apparently signaling an arrival of Austronesian-speakers. The Lapita potters, early Polynesians, had other combinations, suggestive of Asiatic populations and of a lack of connection with the previous Austronesian (AN)-speakers, thus marking a separate movement.

ADVANCES IN STATISTICS. The second postwar development was advanced statistical analysis, methods subsumed under the term multivariate analysis and made possible for the first time by computers. Earlier, under Karl Pearson at the Biometric Laboratory at the University of London, various associates had employed the Coefficient of Racial Likeness (CRL) in cranial studies, which was Pearson's attempt to arrive at a numerical statement of group differences. One of Pearson's associates, P.C. Mahalanobis (1893–1972), pointed out the defects of the CRL and introduced D^2, or Generalized Distance (cf. Mahalanobis, Majumdar, & Rao 1949), the basic statistic in present work. In allowing the handling of large masses of numerical or discrete data on an objective basis, this development saw a reversion to anthropometry and craniometry.

ANTHROPOMETRIC ANALYSIS. A simple application in anthropometry is summarized in Fig. 1. This used the means for seven measurements (stature plus six diameters of head, face, and nose) as recorded in the past for 151 Pacific groups. The analysis produced seven principal components, of which three seemed

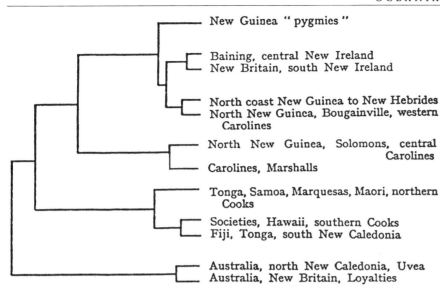

Fig. 1. A summary of anthropometric grouping analysis of Pacific peoples (see text).

New Guinea " pygmies "

Baining, central New Ireland
New Britain, south New Ireland

North coast New Guinea to New Hebrides
North New Guinea, Bougainville, western Carolines

North New Guinea, Solomons, central Carolines
Carolines, Marshalls

Tonga, Samoa, Marquesas, Maori, northern Cooks

Societies, Hawaii, southern Cooks
Fiji, Tonga, south New Caledonia

Australia, north New Caledonia, Uvea
Australia, New Britain, Loyalties

significant: The first registered size, principally in stature and face size; the second, mainly broad noses and relatively long heads (dolichocephaly). Scores allowed clustering by least distance, and Fig. 1 shows the resultant groupings at a high level.

This result is, not unexpectedly, something like the subjective groupings of the past, but it is mechanical and objective. All Australian samples (twenty-eight) form one major group, containing also a few Melanesians. All Polynesians, with Fiji and some outliers, form another; and samples from New Caledonia appear in both main stems—again, affiliations suspected in the past. Melanesians in general form a broader spread, interdigitating somewhat with Micronesia, which does not affiliate with Polynesia.

CRANIOMETRIC STUDIES. The above is not prehistory, only an arrangement of data suggesting questions. Numerous craniometric studies, especially by Michael Pietrusewsky of the University of Hawaii, go further. A general one (1990a) covers fifty-four cranial samples with twenty-eight measurements all made by that author. With canonical variates (which use all of the individuals, not simply means), Pietrusewsky arrived at a clustering, with the major groupings shown in Fig. 2. This offers some small, useful hints. One is separation of the Chatham Islanders from Maori, supporting long isolation from New Zealand or independent settlement from central Polynesia. Another is separation of Marianas from the rest of Micronesia, as well as some ambivalence as to general Micronesian affiliations. Here, Fiji is not connected with

Polynesia. These results are broadly confirmed in a second analysis (Pietrusewsky et al. 1992), giving more attention to Asia: Three sub-branches comprise, respectively, Japan/China, Southeast Asia, and Polynesia/Micronesia; the last is presumed to be a late dispersal, probably from Southeast Asia.

In still another study, Pietrusewsky (1990b) got more detail from the meager Micronesian material, including a Marshalls-Gilberts likeness and an east–west difference (but not an essential heterogeneity), all in general agreement with linguistics and archaeology.

C. Loring Brace of the University of Michigan has also collected much cranial data and done similar analyses, with somewhat fewer and more special measurements and a wider range of samples (Brace et al. 1993). This led him to various conclusions, principally the existence of a general Jōmon-Pacific stem, suggesting that Micronesia and Polynesia were settled ultimately from Japan

TABLE 4. Summary of Christy B. Turner II's dental studies

A general Polynesian-East Malaysian wing, from Easter Island to Java-Sumatra.

A Micronesian wing associated with early Borneo (Niah Cave!).

A wing of northern Indonesian (Philippines, Taiwan) associated with early Sulawesi.

Most remote, an Australo-Melanesian grouping of Australia and Melanesia, including a seemingly tight group of East Melanesians (Santa Cruz, Loyalty Is., Fiji, Rotuma—possible Polynesian connections have previously been suggested for all of these).

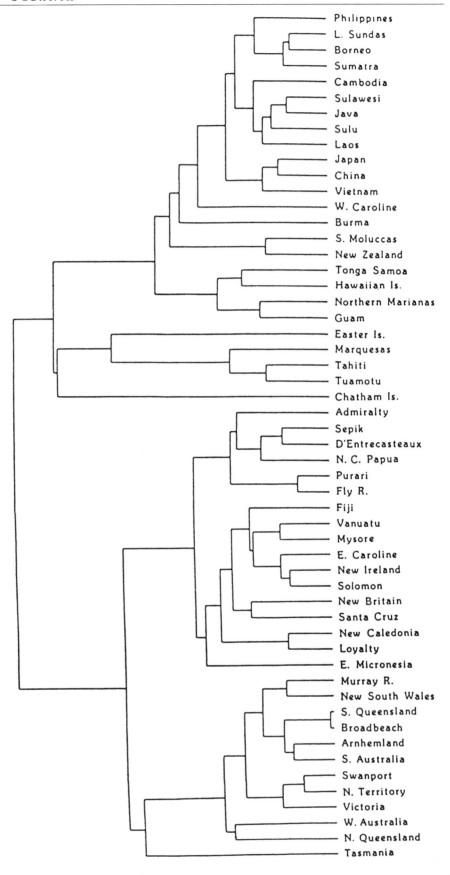

Fig. 2. Clustering analysis from cranial measurements of 54 Australasian male samples (from Pietrusewsky 1990).

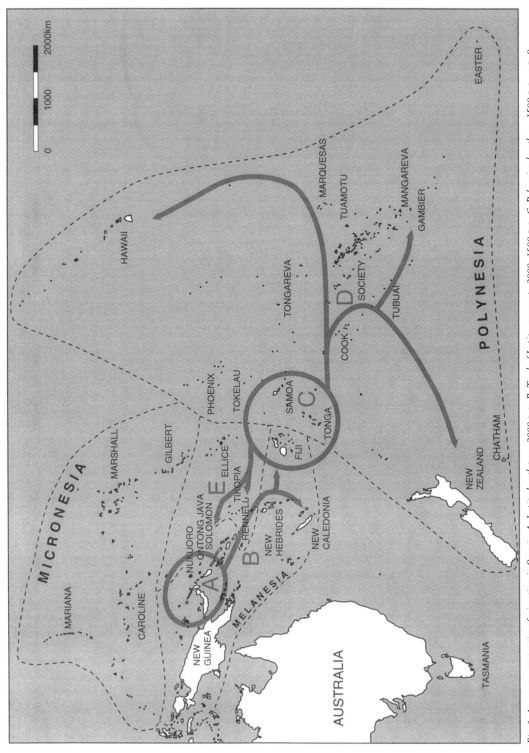

Fig. 3. A current reconstruction of migrations in Oceania. A: Lapita hearth to ca. 2000 B.C.; B: Track of Lapita movements, 2000–1500 B.C.; C: Polynesian hearth, ca. 1500 B.C.– A.D. 0;
D: Post-Lapita movements in Polynesia, from A.D. 0; E: Back migrations to "Polynesian outliers," from A.D. 0.

in Jōmon times (which ended by about the first century A.D.). This connection is not apparent in any work by Pietrusewsky or Howells; the point at issue, of course, is whether Polynesians are to be derived from north Asia rather than Southeast Asia. Brace, Pietrusewsky, and Howells agree in flatly rejecting the suggestion of some writers that the physical Polynesians arose locally in Melanesia.

These methods are not fixed like an archeological profile, since they are subject to the effects of the actual procedure applied and of the material put in. Nevertheless, the pursuit of prehistory has been advanced by their recent use, and their considerable further development may be expected. The methods are also applicable to other materials.

CHARACTERS OF DENTITION. In many papers, Christy G. Turner II of Arizona State University has applied the same methods to worldwide samples, using discrete or quasi-continuous characters of the teeth. For Oceania, some of his findings point to the distinctiveness of Australian-Tasmanian populations from all others, and a general approximation of Micronesia (Guam being somewhat isolated) to Polynesia and distinction from Melanesia (contra Howells). Polynesia, especially Easter Island, however, appears to be connected primarily with Southeast Asia (contra Brace). The weight of Turner's (1990) evidence, on material that is independent in its nature from craniometrics, is impressive (see Table 4 for a summary of his later compilations). In a broader paper, Turner (1992) found distances of various large groups from early Southeast Asia to be, in increasing order, recent Southeast Asia, Polynesia, Taiwan, and Micronesia—all distinctly closer than Jōmon teeth from Japan, which are neither the closest nor the farthest.

DERMATOGLYPHICS
Oceania has also been analyzed as has no other region for dermatoglyphics, especially palm prints, through the work of Jeffery Froehlich of the University of New Mexico (e.g., 1987; Froehlich & Giles 1981a, 1981b). In bivariate (some trivariate) plots, he combines different pairs of traits or counts. Fig. 4 shows an example, not the most complex, that is astonishing for the segregation of significant population sets, specifically Polynesians and Micronesians, as well as separation of Austronesian-speaking Melanesians from non-Austronesians (Papuan-speakers) and of Papuan-speakers in New

Guinea on the one hand and in the Solomons (Bougainville) on the other. This one chart by itself supports all of the arguments for the separation of Polynesians and Micronesians (by separate immigrations) and distinctions among Melanesians (by length of separate residence in the areas found).

OTHER STUDIES IN PHYSICAL ANTHROPOLOGY
Outside of prehistory there are many possibilities for study, which have hardly been explored. In addition to microevolution, the role of selection has been considered. Gadjusek (1970) suggested that the small and wiry body of New Guinea pygmoids is not an original racial trait but is selectively advantageous in energy expenditure in climbing and burden-carrying in tropical mountains. Houghton (1990) proposed that the large bodies of Polynesians were not brought all the way from Asia but evolved for heat conservation in the inescapable breezes of smaller islands. These are reasonable suggestions, however, not investigations. A general attack on biomedical questions was mounted, from 1966 to 1972, by the Harvard Solomon Islands Expedition (Friedlaender 1987), in which anthropology (in many aspects), epidemiology, cardiology, and odontology were all investigated on sixteen different peoples in contrasting environments ranging from groups in mountainous upland regions to shore and atoll dwellers, and each under different conditions of rapid acculturation.

SUMMARY REMARKS
Prehistory, however, has remained at the center of interest. The situation in the closing decade of the twentieth century can be epitomized by paraphrasing some of the considered findings of Friedlaender (1987) following the Harvard study, but resting on his own work and that of others:

1. There is extraordinary Melanesian biological heterogeneity, over relatively short distances, along with emerging natural groupings over large areas.
2. Dynamics of migration and dispersion are seen to be the proximate determinants of patterns of physical diversity suggested by linguistic and biogeographical models.
3. In Bougainville, and, to a lesser degree, in neighboring Solomon Islands, there is a very distinctive biological population; the pattern suggests that the pre-Austronesian settlements in Island Melanesia are very old, and possibly are

Fig. 4. Pacific populations (males) plotted by the mean thenar pattern (including vestiges) and the digital pattern intensity index. (From Froehlich, unpublished, by permission.)

KEY to language groupings: ● is Polynesian; ● is Micronesian; ▲ is Melanesian; ■ is Bougainville Papuan; ▼ is New Guinea Papuan.

the result of a major early migration or migrations followed by local isolation of populations and differentiation of lesser magnitude.

4. The traditional traits of skin color and hair form are just as indicative of these people's distinctiveness.

5. Austronesian-speaking populations in Melanesia tend to show biological similarities in spite of their strong resemblances to immediately neighboring groups.

6. The dispersion of Polynesian groups, from a common population of 2.0 to 4.0 ky BP, is likely to be the best human example of genetic differentiation through discrete branching and subsequent isolation over a well-defined period of time.

7. Natural selection has not been a major determinant of summary population relationships in recent times.

There is little to add to or modify in the above as a statement of the recent position. The contrasting datings of Polynesian arrivals to a very short time of only about 3.5 ky BP, and of that of the Melanesians to something equivalent to that of the Australians at over 50.0 ky BP, are important markers for visible differentiation. Events within Melanesia have remained the least understood.

William W. Howells

See also Bowles, Gordon T(ownsend); Damon, Albert; Dental Anthropology; Dermatoglyphics; Genetic Drift; Harvard University; Japan; Luschan, Felix (Ritter Edler) von; Molecular Anthropology; Royal College of Surgeons (London), Museums of the; Schlaginhaufen, Otto; Shapiro, Harry Lionel

Bibliography
W.C. Boyd: *Genetics and the races of man: An introduction to modern physical anthropology.* Boston: Little, Brown, 1950; W.C. Boyd: Genetics and the human race. *Science* 140:1057–1064, 1963; C.L. Brace et al.: Micronesians, Asians, Thais, and relations: A craniofacial and odontometric perspective. *Micronesia* 2:323–348, 1990; L.L. Cavalli-Sforza: Genes, people, and languages. *Scientific American* 104–110, 1991; J.T. Clark & K.M. Kelly: Human genetics, paleoenvironments, and malaria: Relationships and implications from the settlement of Oceania. *American Anthropologist* 95:614–630, 1993; R.B. Dixon: *The racial history of man.* New York: Scribner's, 1923; R.B. Dixon: *The building of cultures.* New York: Scribner's, 1928.

J.S. Friedlaender (ed): *The Solomon Islands Project: A long-term study of the health, human biology, and culture change.* Oxford: Clarendon Press, 1987; J.S. Friedlaender: Conclusion. In: J.S. Friedlaender (ed) *The Solomon Islands Project: A long-term study of* health, human biology, and culture change. Oxford: Clarendon Press, 1987, pp. 351–362; J.S. Friedlaender et al. New indications of Bougainville genetic distinctiveness. (Abstract). *American Journal of Physical Anthropology* (Supplement) 20:93, 1995; J.W. Froehlich: Fingerprints as phylogenetic markers in the Solomon Islands. In: J.S. Friedlaender (ed) *The Solomon Islands Project: A long-term study of health, human biology, and culture change*. Oxford: Clarendon Press, 1987, pp. 175–214.

J.W. Froehlich & E. Giles: A multivariate approach to fingerprint variation in Papua, New Guinea: Implications for prehistory. *American Journal of Physical Anthropology* 54:73–91, 1981a; J.W. Froehlich & E. Giles: A multivariate approach to fingerprint variation in Papua, New Guinea: Perspective on evolutionary stability of dermatoglyphic markers. *American Journal of Physical Anthropology* 54:93–106, 1981b; D.C. Gadjusek: Psychological characteristics of Stone Age man. *Engineering and Science* 33:26–52, 1970; E. Giles et al.: Gamma-globulin factors (Gm and Inv) in New Guinea: Anthropological significance. *Science* 150:1158–1160, 1965; F. Graebner: Kulturkreise und Kulturschichten in Ozeanien. *Zeitschrift für Ethnologie* 37:28–53, 1905.

J.H. Greenberg: The Indo-Pacific hypothesis. In: T.A. Sebeok (ed) *Linguistics in Oceania*. The Hague: Mouton, 1971, pp. 808–871; E. Hagelberg & J.B. Clegg: Genetic polymorphisms in prehistoric Pacific Islanders determined by analysis of ancient bone DNA. *Proceedings of the Royal Society of London* B 252:163–170, 1993; P. Houghton: Adaptive significance of Polynesian body form. *Annals of Human Biology* 17:19–32, 1990; W.W. Howells: The peopling of Melanesia as indicated by cranial evidence from the Bismarck Archipelago. Ph.D. Thesis. Harvard University, 1934; W.W. Howells: Anthropometric grouping analysis of Pacific peoples. *Archaeology and Physical Anthropology in Oceania* 5:192–217, 1970.

W.W. Howells: Skull shapes and the map. *Papers of the Peabody Museum of Harvard University* 79:1–189, 1989; K.M. Kelly: Gm polymorphisms, linguistic affinities, and natural selection in Melanesia. *Current Anthropology* 31:201–219, 1990; P.V. Kirch & R.C. Green: History, phylogeny, and evolution in Polynesia. *Current Anthropology* 28:431–456, 1987; M.M. Lahr: *The evolution of modern human cranial diversity*. Cambridge: Cambridge University Press, in press; P.C. Mahalanobis, D.M. Majumdar, & C. Rao: Anthropometric survey of the United Provinces, 1941: A statistical study. Appendix 1: Historical note on the statistic D^2. *Sankhya: Indian Journal of Statistics* 9:237–240, 1949.

M. Pietrusewsky: Human cranial collections from the Pacific and Asia preserved in Dresden, Berlin, and Leipzig and information on collections outside the German Democratic Republic. *Abhandlungen und Berichte des Staatlichen Museums für Völkerkunde Dresden* 42:21–52, 1986; M. Pietrusewsky: Craniofacial variation in Australian and Pacific populations. *American Journal of Physical Anthropology* 82:319–340, 1990a; M. Pietrusewsky: Craniometric variations in Micronesia and the Pacific: A multivariate study. *Micronesia* (Supplement) 2:373–402, 1990b; M. Pietrusewsky et al.: Modern and near modern populations of Asia and the Pacific: A multivariate craniometric comparison. In: T. Akazawa et al. (eds) *The evolution and dispersal of modern humans in Asia*. Tokyo: Kenichi Aoki, 1992, pp. 531–558; W.H.R. Rivers: *The history of Melanesian society*. Cambridge: Cambridge University Press, 1914.

O. Schlaginhaufen: *Anthropologie von Neuirland (Neumecklenburg) in der melanesischen Südsee*. Zurich: Füssli, 1965; J.D.E. Schmeltz & R. Krause: *Die Ethnographisch-anthropologische Abteilung des Museum Godeffroy in Hamburg: Eine Beitrag zur Kunde der Südsee-Völker*. Hamburg: Friederischen, 1881; W. Schmidt: Kulturkriese und Kulturschichten in Südamerika. *Zeitschrift für Ethnologie* 45:1014–1124, 1913; S.W. Serjeantson: Migration and admixture in the Pacific: Insights provided by human leucocyte antigens. In: R. Kirk & E. Szathmary (eds) *Out of Asia: Peopling of the Americas and the Pacific*. Canberra: Journal of Pacific History, 1985, pp. 133–145.

R.T. Simmons: Blood-group genes in Polynesia and comparisons with other Pacific peoples. *Oceania* 32:198–210, 1962; R.T. Simmons & J. Graydon: A blood-group genetical study in eastern and central Polynesias. *American Journal of American Anthropology* 15:357–366, 1957; C.E. Snow: *Early Hawaiians: An initial study of skeletal remains from Mokapu, Oahu*. Lexington: University of Kentucky Press, 1974; R.R. Sokal: Genetic, geographic, and linguistic distances in Europe. *Proceedings of the National Academy of Sciences* (United States) 85:1722–1726, 1988.

F.M. Spoehr: White Falcon. In: *The House of Godeffroy and its commercial and scientific role in the Pacific.* Palo Alto, California: Pacific Books, 1963; L.R. Sullivan: *A contribution to Samoan somatology, based on the field studies of E.W. Gifford and W.C. McKern.* Honolulu, Hawaii: Bishop Museum Press, 1921; C.G. Turner II: Origin and affinity of the people of Guam: A dental anthropological assessment. *Micronesia* (Supplement) 2:403–416, 1990; C.G. Turner II: Microevolution of East Asian and European populations. In: T. Akazawa et al. (eds) *The evolution and dispersal of modern humans in Asia.* Tokyo: Kenichi Aoki, 1992, pp. 415–438; R.W. Williamson: *The social and political systems of central Polynesia.* Cambridge: The University Press, 1924; R.W. Williamson: *Essays in Polynesian ethnology.* Edited by R. Piddington. Cambridge: The University Press, 1939.

Olduvai Gorge

Olduvai Gorge, the famous site of early hominid skeletal and cultural remains, is located 650 km southwest of Nairobi, Kenya. Olduvai is an erosion gorge about 40 km long cut into the southeastern corner of the Serengeti Plain of northern Tanzania. The gorge opens into the Olbalbal depression, part of the Great Rift Valley that stretches for over 6,400 km from Mozambique to the Jordan Valley. The strata exposed in the gorge comprise silts, clays, sands, and tuffs (volcanic ashes), the lowest of which rest on a sheet of lava. The layers are classified into four main beds, numbered I to IV from the bottom up; and three more units above Bed IV, from the oldest to youngest, are named the Masek, the Ndutu, and the Naisiusiu Beds. The sequence reflects fluctuations in the activity of neighboring (now inactive) volcanoes, such as Ngorongoro, as well as climatic changes and tectonic events such as "faulting" of the beds, which have accompanied earth movements associated probably with stages in the formation of the Rift Valley.

The volcanic materials in the strata have made possible dating by the potassium-argon method (cf. L.S.B. Leakey, Evernden, & Curtis 1961) and by other dating procedures. Results have shown that the lowest part of Bed I is 2.1–2.0 my old—that is, Late Pliocene. Bed II is dated from about 1.7 my at its base to 1.15 my at the top. Based on stratigraphical and geochronological analyses, Bed II is thus of the Lower Pleistocene. Bed III is dated 1.15–0.80 my, and hence it also falls in the Lower Pleistocene. Bed IV is dated to between 0.8 and 0.6 my; it thus straddles the boundary recognized up to the early 1990s between the Lower and the Middle Pleistocene (0.7 my). The Masek Bed, at 0.6–0.4 my, is Middle Pleistocene. The Ndutu Bed carries the sequence from 0.4 my in the Middle Pleistocene to 32.0 ky BP in the Upper Pleistocene, while the Naisiusiu Bed is as recent as 22.0–15.0 ky BP.

The potential of Olduvai as a paleoanthropological site was discovered in 1911 by the German naturalist Wilhelm Kattwinkel (1866–1935). On its erosion slopes, he collected a number of fossil bones. These were subsequently identified in Berlin and included remains of the extinct three-toed horse *Hipparion.* The interest aroused by Kattwinkel's discovery led in 1913 to an expedition organized by the Berlin geologist Hans Reck (1886–1937). Although this expedition collected many fossils, including a nearly complete human skeleton, it failed to recognize any stone implements. Further expeditions were planned, but the outbreak of World War I prevented Reck's immediate return to East Africa. After the war, the Kenyan paleontologist and anthropologist Louis S.B. Leakey (1903–1972) became actively involved in paleontological and archeological research in East Africa. In addition to being a member of the British Museum's East African Expedition to Tanganyika in 1924, he also led the East African Archaeological Research Expeditions of 1926–1927, 1928–1929, 1931–1932, and 1934–1935. It was in connection with these later expeditions that Leakey visited Reck in Berlin (first in 1925, then in 1927 and again in 1929), where he had an opportunity to examine the human skeleton found earlier at Olduvai. Emerging from these visits was an invitation from Leakey for Reck to accompany him on the third of his East African expeditions (1931–1932). During the two months spent at Olduvai, Reck, whose health no longer permitted strenuous fieldwork, formally ceded to Leakey the scientific rights to work in the gorge. During the next thirty years, Leakey and his second wife, Mary, made many further expeditions to Olduvai. The tempo of the Leakeys' work in the gorge, however, greatly increased following a series of spectacular discoveries made by Leakey and his wife, their sons, and coworkers in the late 1950s and early 1960s.

From 1959, excavations at Olduvai uncovered thousands of vertebrate and some invertebrate fossils. To study and describe the many different faunal species, Leakey enlisted the help of an international group of specialists, including J.J. Jaeger, R. Lavocat, R.F. Ewer, G. Petter, and S.C. Savage. The task of studying and describing all of the hominid remains was entrusted to Phillip V. Tobias (1925–) of the University of the Witwatersrand, Johannesburg; the study of the postcranial bones was subsequently assigned to John Russell Napier (1917–1987), then to Michael H. Day, and ultimately to Bernard A. Wood and Leslie Aiello.

Between 1913 and 1987, the Olduvai Gorge yielded no fewer than sixty-two hominid specimens, fifteen of which were found between 1959 and 1963. At least three hominid species have been identified from Beds I and II. The first was originally named *Zinjanthropus boisei* (L.S.B. Leakey 1959). This specimen, O(lduvai) H(ominid) 5, was shown by Tobias to be a distinct form, though related to the South African australopithecines from Swartkrans and Kromdraai known as *Australopithecus (Paranthropus) robustus*. He renamed it *A. (Zinjanthropus) boisei* (Tobias 1967), thus relegating the term "Zinjanthropus" to the status of a subgenus. Later, some investigators tended to reassign the species to "Paranthropus," either as a subgenus *A. (Paranthropus) boisei* or as a genus *Paranthropus boisei*, while many disregarded the subgeneric label and designated it simply as *A. boisei*. A second hominid species, contemporary with *A. boisei*, was more closely approximated to human anatomical structure in some respects and was believed to have been the artificer of the Oldowan stone culture found in Bed I. Louis Leakey, together with Tobias and Napier (1964), assigned this second group of specimens to the earliest species of the genus *Homo* as a new taxon, *Homo habilis*. It was described and its evolutionary status appraised by Tobias (1991). The third kind of hominid (represented *inter alia* by OH 9), whose remains were first discovered in 1960, occurred in the upper half of Bed II and in Bed IV. It has been classified as *Homo erectus*. Since the discovery of the OH 9 calvaria, other remains of *Homo erectus* have been recovered from Olduvai (cf. M.D. Leakey 1971a; Rightmire 1980).

For many years after she discovered the first cranium of *A. boisei* in July 1959, Mary Leakey continued searching and systematically excavating the extensive Olduvai deposits. After she retired from leading the Olduvai

excavations, D.C. Johanson of the United States and an international team of collaborators conducted excavations at Olduvai in the late 1980s. Their efforts were rewarded in 1987 with the recovery of a partial skeleton of a hominid (OH 62) attributed to *H. habilis*. It proved to have a rather long upper limb in relation to the estimated length of its lower limb (Johanson et al. 1987).

On the other hand, the human skeleton exhumed by Hans Reck in 1913 turned out to be a comparatively recent burial specimen.

Phillip V. Tobias

See also Australopithecines; *Homo erectus*; *Homo habilis*; Kromdraai; Leakey, Louis Seymour Bazett; Napier, John Russell; Tobias, Phillip V(allentine)

Bibliography
R.L. Hay: *Geology of the Olduvai Gorge*. Berkeley: University of California Press, 1976; D.C. Johanson et al.: New partial skeleton of *Homo habilis* from Olduvai Gorge, Tanzania. *Nature* 327:205–209, 1987; L.S.B. Leakey: A new fossil skull from Olduvai (*Zinjanthropus boisei*). *Nature* 184:491–493, 1959; L.S.B. Leakey: *Olduvai Gorge, 1951–1961*. Vol. 1, *A preliminary report on the geology and fauna*. Cambridge: Cambridge University Press, 1965; L.S.B. Leakey, J.F. Evernden, & G.H. Curtis: Age of Bed I, Olduvai Gorge, Tanganyika. *Nature* 191:478–479, 1961; L.S.B. Leakey, P.V. Tobias, & J.R. Napier: A new species of the genus *Homo* from Olduvai Gorge. *Nature* 202:7–9, 1964; M.D. Leakey: Discovery of postcranial remains of *Homo erectus* and associated artefacts in Bed IV at Olduvai Gorge, Tanzania. *Nature* 232:380–383, 1971a.

M.D. Leakey: *Olduvai Gorge*. Vol. 3, *Excavation in Beds I and II, 1960–1963*. Cambridge: Cambridge University Press, 1971b; H. Reck: *Oldoway, die Schlücht des Ürmenschen; die Entdeckung des altsteinzeitlichen Menschen in Deutsch-Ostafrika*. Leipzig: Brockhaus, 1933; H. Reck: *Wissenschaftliche Ergebnisse der Oldoway-Expedition, 1913*. Berlin: Reimer, 1937; G.P. Rightmire: Middle Pleistocene hominids from Olduvai Gorge, Northern Tanzania. *American Journal of Physical Anthropology* 53:225–241, 1980; P.V. Tobias: *Olduvai Gorge*. Vol. 2, *The cranium of Australopithecus (Zinjanthropus) boisei*. Cambridge: Cambridge University Press, 1967; P.V. Tobias: *Olduvai Gorge*. Vols. 4A–4B, *The skulls, endocasts, and teeth of Homo habilis*. Cambridge: Cambridge University Press, 1991.

Omo

The Omo is the major river of southern Ethiopia, draining the Ethiopian highlands west of the Main Ethiopian Rift. The river runs westward, then from north to south, constituting the main water source for Lake Turkana (formerly Lake Rudolf). This river and lake system was responsible for the deposition of a great thickness of sedimentary rocks, known as the Omo Group, during Pliocene and Pleistocene times.

Early Exploration

The explorers Sámuel Teleki (1845–1916) and Lt. Ludwig von Höhnel (b. 1852) traveled into the lower Omo River Basin in 1888 immediately following their discovery of Lake Rudolf (cf. Teleki 1890), in what is now Kenya. In 1896, the Italian geographer Maurizio Sacchi (1804–1897) noted sediments exposed in the north of the Omo delta (Vannutelli & Citerni 1899). The Bourg de Bozas Trans-Africa Expedition (1900–1903) visited the region in 1902 (cf. Bourg de Bozas 1906). The naturalist on the expedition, Émile Brumpt (1877–1951), discovered the first vertebrate fossils from tilted strata below those noted in 1896. The fossil primate *Theropithecus brumpti* is among the species named for him. Emile Haug (1861–1927), professor of geology at the University of Paris from 1917 to 1927, described fish, crocodile, artiodactyl, and proboscidian remains from the Bourg de Bozas collections.

The lower Omo region had several other Western visitors around the turn of the century, but it was not until the Mission Scientifique de l'Omo (1932–1933), that the paleontological potential of the area began to be seriously exploited. The French paleontologist Camille Arambourg (1885–1969) conducted paleontological and geological studies of the lower Omo during this expedition and later published detailed monographs describing his discoveries. During World War II, Louis S.B. Leakey (1903–1972), then curator of what is now the National Museum of Kenya, sent his collector, Heselon Mukiri, into the lower Omo region to procure fossils. The fossils collected by Mukiri, like most of those found by Arambourg, unfortunately lacked precise stratigraphic provenance. No fossil hominids were found by any of these investigators.

The International Omo Research Expedition

In the summer of 1959, F. Clark Howell (1925–), then of the University of Chicago, visited the lower Omo on a monthlong reconnaissance trip. Howell recognized the potential significance of the "Omo Beds" deposits from which Arambourg had collected so many vertebrate fossils.

Arambourg had greatly underestimated both the thickness of the deposits and the complexity of the succession. He had not appreciated that the "fauna" he was describing sampled a long period of Plio-Pleistocene time. Howell met with Arambourg in 1961, and they agreed to pursue jointly further research in this area of southern Ethiopia. Shortly thereafter, Louis Leakey spoke with Emperor Haile Selassie of Ethiopia about the need for an international research program into the prehistory of the lower Omo deposits. The emperor subsequently provided authorization for such research, and in 1966 the International Omo Research Expedition was formed. Arambourg (with assistance from Jean Chavaillon and Yves Coppens) would lead a French contingent, while Howell and Leakey (with the assistance of his son Richard) would lead American and Kenyan contingents, respectively. This venture began with a geological reconnaissance undertaken by Francis H. Brown (then a graduate student at the University of California, Berkeley) in late 1966, and it led to the recognition of the protracted nature of the Omo succession, as well as the presence of datable volcanic products—a series of interbedded tephra.

In 1967, the Omo Research Expedition began the first of eight annual field seasons. This research, the most complex of any paleoanthropological project yet undertaken in Africa, was funded from many sources, including the National Science Foundation (United States), the Wenner-Gren Foundation for Anthropological Research, and the National Geographic Society. In the initial season, Howell's team discovered and worked the Usno Formation outcrops and found the first Pliocene hominids at two localities. The Kenyans, led by Richard Leakey and Kamoya Kimeu, worked in the northernmost sector, exploring Pliocene and Pleistocene sediments. They recovered fossilized remains of Late Pleistocene hominids from the Kibish Formation of the Lake Turkana Group and discovered the Mursi Formation. It was during this early Omo work that Richard Leakey's aerial reconnaissance prompted him to abandon his efforts in Ethiopia and begin, in 1968, a research project in northern Kenya at Koobi Fora.

The French and American teams divided the outcrops of the lower Omo, with French paleontology teams working in the southern sector of the 6.5 km north-to-south outcrop of the Shungura Formation. The entire dated fossiliferous sequence of the Omo became the yardstick of Plio-Pleistocene mammalian evolution in Africa. By the mid-1970s, it became pivotal in providing the framework for hominid evolution in Africa. Geology was conducted in both lower Omo collection areas primarily by Jean de Heinzelin (then at the Laboratorium voor Paleontologie, Geologisch Instituut, Rijksuniversiteit Gent), Paul Haesaerts (Department Paleontologie, Koninklijk Belgisch Instituut voor Natuurwetenschappen, Brussels), and Francis H. Brown (University of Utah), with additional contributions by Karl Butzer (University of Chicago), who investigated the Kibish Formation and the history of the Omo delta and its environs. The geological formations were divided into the older Omo Group and the unconformably superimposed Lake Turkana Group. Of the six formations in the Omo Group, only the Usno and the Shungura Formations yielded fossil hominid remains. The Usno Formation is geographically isolated from, but chronologically correlated to, the bottom of the 766-m-thick Shungura Formation. Over 40,000 vertebrate fossils belonging to about 150 species were collected from the Shungura Formation, a long sequence that spans the time range from ca. 3.5 to ca. 0.9 my. The Shungura Formation was divided into thirteen members named according to the letter designation of the associated interbedded tuffaceous volcanic strata (oldest to youngest, from A through L). Many of these strata were radiometrically dated and their paleomagnetic record deciphered.

As Plio-Pleistocene hominids were recovered from the Shungura Formation in the late 1960s and early 1970s, the large samples from Koobi Fora, Laetoli, and Hadar were not available for comparison. As a result, the initial interpretive framework in which Howell and Coppens deliberated their Omo discoveries was set by the South African and Olduvai (mostly unpublished) fossils. The earliest Omo Group fossil hominids, all isolated teeth dating to >2.95 my (Usno, Member B) were first attributed to *Australopithecus* cf. *africanus* or *A*. aff. *africanus*. This systematic caution proved warranted when primitive characters of these teeth were later recognized by Howell to match those seen in the teeth of *A. afarensis* recovered from Laetoli and Hadar.

Hominid teeth and a jaw from the ca. 2.5 my strata of the Shungura Formation (Member C) share some characters with later *A. boisei*, and one of these specimens, Omo 18–18, was the recipient of new genus and species names, *Paraustralopithecus aethiopicus* (Arambourg & Coppens 1967). The subsequent discovery of a fossil hominid cranium from nearby West Turkana (KNM WT-17000) in the 1980s validated the recognition of this species as a precursor of *A. boisei*. This lineage of robust *Australopithecus* is well represented by teeth, jaws, fragmentary crania, and possibly postcranial fossils in overlying Members D through G of the Omo succession. The contemporary hominid lineage (or, perhaps, lineages) is (are) also represented by similarly incomplete specimens usually assigned to *Homo* sp., or *Homo habilis*, in deposits earlier than ca. 1.7 my, and to *Homo erectus* in later members. Archeological occurrences are known from ca. 2.4 my in the Shungara Formation.

The last fieldwork conducted by the International Omo Research Expedition took place in the mid-1970s, just when a long-standing dispute about the dating of the nearby Koobi Fora deposits was being resolved by biochronological and radiometric analyses. The fossils and rocks of the Omo Shungura Formation played a critical role in the resolution of this and other major controversies in human evolutionary studies. The Omo region has provided the keystone for the chronology now available for deposits at Ileret, Koobi Fora, and Kubi Algi east of Lake Turkana, and for other fossiliferous localities subsequently discovered in the basin west of Lake Turkana and at Fejej to the east. It is certain that the lower Omo region has much more to reveal about mammalian, including hominid, evolution. The fossil and archeological remains from the lower Omo Basin are housed at the National Museum of Ethiopia in Addis Ababa.

Tim D. White

See also Afar Triangle; Arambourg, Camille; Australopithecines; Brumpt, Émile; Koobi Fora; Laetoli; Leakey, Louis Seymour Bazett

Bibliography
C. Arambourg: *Mission scientifique de l'Omo, 1932–1933. Géologie-Anthropologie-Paléontologie*: Paris: Muséum National d'Historie Naturelle, 1935–1947. Part 1 (1935), pp. 1–59, Part 2 (1943), pp. 60–230, Part 3 (1947), pp. 231–562; C. Arambourg & Y. Coppens: Sur la découverte dans le Pléistocène inférieur de la vallée de

l'Omo (Ethiopie) d'un mandibule d'australopithecien. *Comptes-rendus hebdomadaires des séances* de *l'Académie des Sciences* (Paris) 265D:589–590, 1967.

R. Bourg de Bozas: *Mission scientifiques du Bourg de Bozas de la Mer Rouge à l'Atlantique à travers l'Afrique tropicale, Octobre 1900–Mars 1903.* Paris: Rudeval, 1906; C.S. Feibel, F.H. Brown, & I. McDougall: Stratigraphic context of fossil hominids from the Omo Group deposits: Northern Turkana Basin, Kenya, and Ethiopia. *American Journal of Physical Anthropology* 78:595–622, 1989; J. de Heinzelin (ed): The Omo Group: Stratigraphic and related earth sciences studies in the lower Omo Basin, southern Ethiopia. *Annales Sciences Géologiques.* No. 85, 1983.

F.C. Howell & Y. Coppens: Inventory of remains of Hominidae from Pliocene/Pleistocene Formations of the lower Omo Basin, Ethiopia, 1967–1972. *American Journal of Physical Anthropology* 40:1–16, 1974; F.C. Howell, P. Haesaerts, & J. de Heinzelin: Depositional environments, archeological occurrences, and hominids from Members E and F of the Shungura Formation (Omo Basin, Ethiopia). *Journal of Human Evolution* 16:665–700, 1987; S. Teleki: *Ostäquatorial-Afrika zwischen Pangani und dem neudentdeckten Rudolf-see: Ergebnisse der graf S. Telekischen expedition, 1887–1888.* Gotha: Petken, 1890; L. Vannutelli & C. Citerni: *L'Omo: Viaggio di esplorazione nell'Africa orientale.* Milan: Hoepli, 1899.

Osborn, Henry Fairfield (1857–1935)

Osborn was born in New York City, the son of William Henry Osborn, a businessman, and Virginia Reed Sturges. In line with his family's Scottish Presbyterian interests, Osborn attended Princeton University from 1873 to 1877. Although his father hoped he would enter the family's railroad business, Osborn, influenced by Princeton President James McCosh (1811–1894), became interested in pursuing a career in science. Following a fossil-hunting expedition to the western United States in 1877, Osborn spent a year studying the specimens acquired. Subsequently, he did additional course work in England, studying comparative anatomy with Thomas Henry Huxley (1825–1895) and embryology with Francis Maitland Balfour (1851–1882). In 1880, Osborn returned to Princeton to write a dissertation on fossil mammals, and in 1881, after completing his

Sc.D., he was hired to teach comparative anatomy and embryology at Princeton.

Osborn taught at Princeton for ten years but left in 1891 for Columbia University and the American Museum of Natural History (AMNH), both in New York City. At Columbia, he organized the Department of Biology and continued to teach there until 1909. More significant, however, was his role at the American Museum, where he became curator of the new Department in Vertebrate Paleontology in 1891. Under Osborn's direction, and with financial assistance from a wide circle of associates, this department became the leading one of its kind in the world. Beginning with explorations for fossil mammals in the western United States, the program eventually undertook expeditions for extinct vertebrates throughout the world. The specimens collected served as the basis for a series of innovative displays, including paintings and mountings. The department also became a research center where Osborn's Columbia students and other research associates helped lay the foundations for early-twentieth-century vertebrate paleontology. The success of this program, and Osborn's close connections to the AMNH trustees, enabled him to rise rapidly through the museum ranks. In 1908, he became museum president—a position he held for twenty-five years; during that time, the AMNH developed as an extension of Osborn's views and interests.

Osborn also published prolifically. Throughout his career, he had an interest in studying the causal mechanisms and descriptive patterns of evolution. In the 1880s, he explained evolution in neo-Lamarckian terms—as a result of the use and disuse of parts and the inheritance of acquired characteristics. He later developed an orthogenetic interpretation that explained evolution as a gradual unfolding of characters that proceeded in determinate, linear directions. Osborn applied his ideas to mammalian remains and described the evolution of horses, elephants, and titanotheres in terms of a series of multiple, parallel lines of descent.

Beginning in 1910, Osborn turned his attention to the study of human evolution. In this field, as in paleomammalogy, he emphasized the difference among organisms. With help from his AMNH assistants, especially the archeologist Nels C. Nelson (1875–1964), he analyzed Paleolithic and Neolithic artifacts. He also examined, among others, the skeletal fragments of the Heidelberg, Piltdown, and Cro-Magnon specimens. In line with his already established views, Osborn explained human evolution not as a branching, diverging tree of life, but as a series of separate evolutionary histories and replacements. According to Osborn, Paleolithic and Neolithic hominids were not the ancestors of modern humans, but rather different species that had evolved to extinction.

Osborn's views were influenced not only by scientific study, but also by social and political developments. As part of a New York Protestant élite, he had serious concerns about the contemporary immigration of millions of southern and eastern Europeans to the United States. For Osborn, such immigration constituted a biological and social threat to the members of his social and ethnic group. Claiming that immigration produced racial mixing that could lead to degeneration, he called for immmigration restriction as well as birth selection. These concerns also shaped his interpretation of human evolution. According to Osborn, the various races had not mixed during the Paleolithic period; they had remained pure and distinct and had progressed as a consequence of their nomadic life-styles that necessitated a struggle for existence. However, the development of civilization increasingly separated humans from nature and the struggle for existence, produced racial mixing, and resulted in a decline from the height of cultural achievement represented by the Cro-Magnon race. Osborn's *Men of the Old Stone Age* (1915) was more than a study in archeology and physical anthropology; it was an interpretation of human evolution that embodied social and political lessons for modern *Homo sapiens*.

Social and political concerns also influenced the interpretation of human evolution advanced in the 1920s by Osborn, who, having already defined human evolution in polyphyletic terms, now expressed his views on the relationship between humans and primates. In 1925, he presented a theory that humans had evolved from a hypothetical "Dawn Man," an Eocene ancestor that had lived on the plains of northern Asia. Osborn maintained that the evolution of humans from that ancestral form was distinctly separate from any line of simian evolution, and he pointed to morphological, physiological, and behavioral characteristics to separate humans from other primates and "remove the bogey of man's ape ancestry." Osborn's theory drew upon his interpretation of the fossil and artifactual evidence, particularly the East Anglian eoliths discovered by the amateur British archeologist J. Reid Moir

(1879–1944) during the first and second decades of the twentieth century and the now infamous Piltdown remains found in Surrey, England, in 1912–1915 (cf. Osborn 1921a, 1921b). But he also fashioned a theory to offset William Jennings Bryan's (1860–1925) fundamentalist attack on evolution.

Osborn's work on physical anthropology, particularly his "Dawn Man" theory, however, had little scientific influence. While most scientists of the period tended to ignore his anthropological interpretations, his close research associate William King Gregory (1876–1970) became a vociferous critic. Gregory, along with others, also rejected Osborn's view of evolution and inheritance. Yet Osborn's work had an influence at the AMNH because of his administrative position. His interest in physical anthropology led to the construction of a Hall of the Age of Man, an exhibit that included specimen casts and reconstructed busts of extinct humans. Based on his evolutionary interpretations, the museum sponsored expeditions to Asia and Africa. Gregory, whose research originally focused on fossil reptiles, took up physical anthropology as a result of Osborn's influence and enthusiasm for the subject. While his theoretical views were largely rejected, Osborn helped make the AMNH a major center for research on physical anthropology in the 1920s and 1930s.

Osborn died at Garrison, New York, on 6 November 1935.

Ronald Rainger

See also Andrews, Roy Chapman; Cro-Magnon; Gregory, William King; Huxley, Thomas Henry; Neandertals; Neo-Lamarckism; Paleoanthropology Theory; Piltdown

Bibliography
SELECTED WORKS

From the Greeks to Darwin: An outline of the idea of evolution. New York: Macmillan, 1894; *The age of mammals in Europe, Asia, and North America*. New York: Macmillan, 1910; *Men of the Old Stone Age: Their environment, life, and art*. New York: Scribner's, 1915; Review of the Pleistocene of Europe, Asia, and northern Africa. *Annals of the New York Academy of Science* 26:215–315, 1916; *The Hall of the Age of Man in the American Museum*. New York: American Museum of Natural History, 1920; The Dawn Man of Piltdown. *Natural History* 21:565–576, 1921a; The Pliocene Man of Foxhall in East Anglia. *Natural History*

21:577–590, 1921b; *The Earth speaks to Bryan*. New York: Scribner's, 1925; The evolution of human races. *Natural History* 26:3–13, 1926.

Fundamental discoveries of the last decade in human evolution. *Bulletin of the New York Academy of Medicine* 3 (2d ser.):513–521, 1927a; *Man rises to Parnassus: Critical epochs in the prehistory of man.* Princeton, New Jersey: Princeton University Press, 1927b; Recent discoveries relating to the origin and antiquity of man. *Science* 65:481–488, 1927c; The plateau habitat of the pre-Dawn Man. *Science* 65: 570–571, 1928; Is the ape-man a myth? *Human Biology* 1:2–16, 1929a; *The titanotheres of ancient Wyoming, Dakota, and Nebraska.* 2 vols. Washington, D.C.: Government Printing Office, 1929b; The discovery of Tertiary Man. *Science* 71:1–7, 1930; *Proboscidea: A monograph of the discovery, evolution, migration, and extinction of the elephants and mastodonts of the world.* New York: American Museum Press, 1936 (2d ed.: 1942).

ARCHIVAL SOURCES

1. H.F. Osborn Papers: Central Archives, Library, and Department of Vertebrate Paleontology, American Museum of Natural History, Central Park West at 79th Street, New York, New York 10024; 2. H.F. Osborn Papers: New York Historical Society, 170 Central Park West, New York, New York 10024–5194.

SECONDARY SOURCES

W.K. Gregory: Henry Fairfield Osborn. *National Academy of Sciences Biographical Memoirs* 19:53–119, 1938; R. Rainger: *An agenda for antiquity: Henry Fairfield Osborn and vertebrate paleontology at the American Museum of Natural History, 1890–1935.* Tuscaloosa: University of Alabama Press, 1991; G.G. Simpson: Osborn, Henry Fairfield. *Dictionary of American biography.* Supplement 1. New York: Scribner's, 1944, pp. 584–87.

Owen, (Sir) Richard (1804–1892)

Born in Lancaster, England, the son of a wool merchant, Owen began his scientific career at the University of Edinburgh in 1824. He studied there under John Barclay (1758–1826) before going to London, where he became assistant to the surgeon John Abernathy (1764–1831) at St. Bartholomew's Hospital. In 1827, with Abernathy's help, Owen landed an appointment as assistant to William Clift (1775–1849), conservator of the Museum of the Royal College of Surgeons. In 1836, he was appointed Hunterian Professor at the college, and in 1842 he succeeded Clift as conservator. By the early 1850s, Owen was at the zenith of his career and influence, and was widely known as the "British Cuvier." In 1856, he moved from the Royal College to the British Museum in Bloomsbury to become superintendent of the Departments of Natural History. Soon after receiving this appointment, Owen began agitating for a new building to house the collections of the Natural History Departments. In 1871, work began on the new Natural History Museum in South Kensington, and between 1880 and 1883 he supervised the relocation to this new facility. Owen retired in December 1883, and the following year he was knighted.

Owen's reputation was built largely on his description and cataloging of the animal specimens in the Museum of the Royal College of Surgeons collections, and he often used his descriptions to make general points on broader questions. He also described many fossil vertebrates. His opposition to Lamarckian (and later Darwinian) evolutionism and his ability to adapt the latest Continental ideas to the more conservative taste of the British medical and social establishment gave him considerable influence.

Owen has been treated badly by popular histories of science because he rejected Darwinism. In fact, he was a prolific researcher who had a considerable influence on the biology of his time, nor was his position as conservative as many now imagine. Strongly influenced by German idealist thought, Owen sought to demonstrate the underlying unity beneath the diversity of biological forms. In his *On the Archetype and homologies of the vertebrate skeleton* (1848a), he introduced the concept of the "archetype" as the ground plan of the vertebrate type, treating all of the various species as adaptive modifications of this basic pattern. He was also responsible for coining the term "homology" to indicate the underlying identity of structures adapted to different purposes in different species (human arm, horse foreleg, bat wing). This he distinguished from "analogy," in which dissimilar structures served the same purposes (wing of bat or insect) (cf. Owen 1843:374).

Owen was the first to use the term "dinosaur" in his 1841 report on fossil reptiles to the British Association for the Advancement of Science. He visualized the dinosaurs as very early, yet highly developed reptiles, thus disproving the linear progressionism of the Lamarckians. In the 1850s, he noted that earliest members of a class were usually unspecialized types, with the later fossil record revealing a number of distinct lines of specialization radiating out from these generalized forms. He compared this with the Estonian embryologist Karl Ernst von Baer's (1792–1876) Law of Embryological Development by Specialization.

By the 1860s, Owen's fossil work was revealing trends that were compatible with evolutionism, and he may even have toyed with an evolutionary explanation himself. But he could not accept Charles Darwin's (1809–1882) theory of natural selection, with its emphasis on unpredictable change brought about solely by environmental pressure. Far from being an antievolutionist at this stage of his career, however, Owen began to develop an anti-Darwinian evolutionism that would substantiate his belief that the history of life unfolded gradually through Divinely implanted laws of development. He stressed evolutionary parallelism in order to disprove the branching-tree image of the history of life promoted by the Darwinians. His work at this stage still had positive value; he pioneered efforts to reconstruct the life-style of many fossil species and was the first to recognize the significance of the mammal-like reptiles of South Africa.

From the outset of his career, Owen spent a great deal of time dissecting dead animals from the London Zoological Gardens—the results of which contributed greatly to the development of his views on Mammalia. Primates were of particular and lasting interest to him, and he published extensively on the comparative anatomy of the nonhuman primates, including a series he began in the 1840s on the natural history of the anthropoid apes (cf. Owen 1848b, 1853, 1857b, 1862). Initially, Owen's classification of the order Primates followed that of the German anatomist Johann Friedrich Blumenbach (1752–1840) and the French naturalist Georges Cuvier (1769–1832), which recognized two suborders: Bimana (humans) and Quadrumana (anthropoid apes and monkeys). Although Owen continually stressed the anatomical similarities between apes and humans, it evidently became increasingly difficult for him to reconcile biology with theology—in particular, the dogmatic belief in the uniqueness of the human species—as his comparative osteological and neuroanatomical studies pro-

gressed, for ultimately, in 1857, this work led him to not only separate humans from the hominoid apes into a subclass of their own, but also to propose a reclassification of all mammals based on the size and conformity of their brains (cf. Owen 1857b, 1860). Accordingly, Owen envisioned four subclasses of Mammalia that graded imperceptibly one into the other: Lyencephala (unconnected or partially connected hemispheres, e.g., marsupials), Lissencephala ("smooth brains," e.g., rodents, bats, edentates), Gyrencephala ("folded brain," e.g., cetaceans, ungulates, unguiculates, and nonhuman primates), and Archencephala ("overruling brain," exclusively *Homo sapiens*). Specifically, Owen claimed that what separated humans from the hominoid apes and the rest of Mammalia was the manifestation in the former of an anterior and posterior extension of the cerebral hemispheres and the presence of a *hippocampus minor*. This declaration, however, was vigorously challenged in the early 1860s by the anatomist Thomas Henry Huxley (1825–1895), who regarded Owen as an arch-conservative and an obstacle to his own mission to professionalize biology. Although Huxley was to triumph in this celebrated confrontation, it should be noted that there were many workers, such as the biologist St. George Jackson Mivart (1827–1900), who shared Owen's opinion that the relationship between apes and humans was more complex than the Darwinians pretended.

Owen died at Richmond Park, London, on 18 December 1892.

Peter J. Bowler

See also Baer, Karl Ernst von; Blumenbach, Johann Friedrich; Cuvier, Georges Léopold Chrétien Fréderic Dagobert (Baron); Darwin, Charles Robert; Evolutionary Theory; Huxley, Thomas Henry; Mivart, St. George Jackson; Royal College of Surgeons (London), Museums of the

Bibliography
SELECTED WORKS

Report on British fossil reptiles. Part 2. *Report of the British Association for the Advancement of Science*, 1841, pp. 60–204; *Lectures on the comparative anatomy and physiology of the invertebrate animals*. London: Longman, Brown, Green & Longmans, 1843; *On the archetype and homologies of the vertebrate skeleton*. London: Van Voorst, 1848a; Osteological contributions to the natural history of the chimpanzees (*Troglo-*

dytes, Geoffroy). *Transactions of the Zoological Society of London* 3: 381–422, 1848b; *On the nature of limbs*. London: Van Voorst, 1849; Osteological contributions to the natural history of the chimpanzee (*Troglodytes*) and orangs (*Pithecus*). Part 4. *Transactions of the Zoological Society of London* 4:75–88, 1853.

The principal forms of the skeleton and teeth as the basis for a system of natural history and comparative anatomy. London: Orr, 1855; On the characters, principles of division, and primary groups of the class Mammalia. *Journal and Proceedings of the Linnean Society* (London) 2:1–37, 1857a; Osteological contributions to the natural history of the chimpanzee (*Troglodytes*) and orangs (*Pithecus*). Part 5. *Transactions of the Zoological Society of London* 4:89–115, 1857b; *On the classification and geographical distribution of Mammalia*. London: Parker, 1859; On the cerebral system of classification of the Mammalia. *Proceedings of the Royal Institute* 13:174–189, 1860; Osteological contributions to the natural history of the anthropoid apes. Part 7. *Transactions of the Zoological Society of London* 5:1–32, 1862; *On the anatomy of vertebrates*. 3 vols. London: Longman, Green, 1866–1868.

ARCHIVAL SOURCES

1. (Sir) R. Owen Papers: British Library, Reference Division, Department of Manuscripts, Great Russell Street, London WC1B 3DG, England; 2. (Sir) R. Owen Papers: Museum Archives, Natural History Museum, Cromwell Road, London SW7 5BD, England; 3. (Sir) R. Owen Collection: Library, Royal College of Surgeons of England, 35–43 Lincoln's Inn Fields, London WC2A 3PN, England. For further information on available archival materials relating to Owen, see *The manuscript papers of British scientists, 1600–1940*. London: Her Majesty's Stationary Office, 1982.

SECONDARY SOURCES

P.J. Bowler: *Fossils and progress: Paleontology and the ideas of progressive evolution in the nineteenth century*. New York: Science History Publications, 1976; A. Desmond: *Archetypes and ancestors: Palaeontology in Victorian London, 1850–1875*. London: Blond & Briggs, 1982; A. Desmond: *The politics of evolution: Morphology, medicine, and reform in radical London*. Chicago: University of Chicago Press, 1989; (Reverend) R. Owen: *Life of Richard Owen*. 2 vols. London: Murray, 1894; E.S. Russell:

Form and function: A contribution to the history of animal morphology. London: Murray, 1916.

Oyhenart-Perera, Martín (1947–1986)

Born in Uruguay, Oyhenart-Perera received his undergraduate training in biology at the School of Humanities and Sciences in the University of the Republic, Montevideo, and a doctorate in physical anthropology from the Universidad Central de Barcelona, Spain. Prior to his sojourn in Spain, he worked with Renée Kolski as an assistant in Genetics at the School of Humanities and Science, as well as in the School of Veterinarian Science. In Spain, he worked under the direction of José Egocheaga from 1976 to 1986, and his doctoral thesis was on the dermatoglyphics of southwest Spaniards—namely, those groups from the Extremadura and Andalucia regions (1985a). He remained in Spain until 1986, when the military rule in Uruguay was replaced by a democratic form of government. On returning to Uruguay, Oyhenart-Perera shifted his interests increasingly to human (clinical and anthropological) genetics and, in particular, to the study of dermatoglyphic patterns in Uruguayan populations. Unfortunately, his promising career in anthropology was cut short by his sudden death in 1986.

Mónica Sans

See also Spain; Uruguay

Bibliography
SELECTED WORKS

Contribución al estudio de los dermatoglíficos digitales de la población de Montevideo (Uruguay). I. Caracteres cualitativos. *Revista de Biología del Uruguay* 4:45–51, 1976a; Los estudios dermatoglíficos en el Uruguay. *Revista Uruguaya de Patalogía Clínica y Microbiología* 14:10–23, 1976b; Contribución al estudio de los dermatoglíficos digitales de la población de Montevideo (Uruguay) II. Caracteres cuantitativos. *Revista de Biología del Uruguay* 7:65–76, 1979; Variación mensual del número de nacimientos en la población de Montevideo (Uruguay). *Revista Española de Pediatría* 36:309–310, 1980; Las mujeres ginecotrópicas. I. Caracteres físicos. Informaciones Psiquiátricas 85; Los hombres androtrópicos: Estudio dermatoglífico digitopalmar. *Revista del Departmento de Psiquiatría de la Facultad de Medicina de Barcelona* 8:377–394, 1981.

Asociación entre fecundidad y algunas variables climáticas en una muestra de la población de Montevideo (Uruguay). *Revista Española de Obstetricia y Ginecología* 42:488–492, 1983a; Dermatoglíficos en gallegos. I. Caracteres de apreciación cualitativa. *III Congreso de Antropología Biológica de España, Actas y Communicaciones*, 1983b, pp. 386–399; *Aproximación a la descripción dermatoglífica de los españoles del sudoeste: Extremeños y andaluces béticos*. Ph.D. Thesis. Universidad Central de Barcelona, Facultad de Biología, 1985a; Somatología de montevideanos. I. Entrecruzamiento de dedos y brazos; cruzamiento de piernas. *Acta IV Congreso Español de Antropología Biológica* (Barcelona), 1985b, pp. 321–330; New cases of orangoid hand: Carpopetal main lines of the palm. *International Journal of Anthropology* 2:167–170, 1987.

SECONDARY SOURCES

Anon. [Obituary]. Dermatoglyphics (Bulletin of the International Dermatoglyphic Association) 15: 1987.

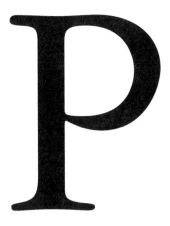

Paleoanthropology Theory

There could be no paleoanthropological theories in the modern sense until scientists became convinced that the human race was older than the biblical creation story implied. The breakthrough that converted archeologists to a belief in the extreme antiquity of the human race did not come until the 1860s, and by that time it was inevitable that theorizing on human origins would be affected by the introduction of evolution theory. Efforts to interpret the gradually increasing number of ancient human remains and hominid fossils also impacted on the theoretical debates. Since the late nineteenth century, there have been many changes in the way that we interpret the origin and early history of hominids, reflecting developments in both scientific theories and cultural values.

Although paleoanthropologists themselves have always had an interest in the history of their discipline, there have been remarkably few studies of this area by professional historians of science. Considering the amount of attention devoted to the debate over "man's place in nature" in the Darwinian revolution, historians of evolution theory have been reluctant to follow through into later episodes in the development of paleoanthropology. Where historical studies have been written, they have often focused on the discovery and interpretation of hominid fossils, which attract great public interest but seem to deflect attention away from the theoretical positions used to interpret the fossils. It has sometimes been claimed that paleoanthropological theory has developed almost in isolation from general evolution theory, but this probably reflects ignorance of the extent to which early evolutionists adopted non-Darwinian ideas that seem bizarre by modern standards.

One of the greatest theoretical divisions in the field has been that between the linear and the multibranch models of hominid evolution. Modern Darwinists may assume that a linear model (in which all known fossil hominids fit onto a line leading toward *Homo sapiens*) is a relic of old-fashioned goal-directed progressionism. But the early twentieth century exponents of a multi-branch model were certainly not Darwinians; they assumed that several different branches of hominid evolution were being driven independently in the same direction. The most enduring character of the multi-branch model, still apparent in its modern manifestations, is its emphasis on the extinction, often through violent conflict, of the less successful branches.

There can be little doubt that scientific thinking on the question of human origin and development has been influenced by wider cultural values. The ideas of progress, degeneration, migration, and extermination, which dominated the field in the period 1860–1930, all carry overtones reflecting the values of Western culture on the age of industrialization and imperialism. Many theories were framed in a way that would allow them to support the prevailing racism of the (invariably White) scientists at the time. In the 1980s, much excitement was generated by the American physical-anthropologist Misia Landau's suggestion that theories of human origins parallel the creation myths and folk tales of primitive cultures (cf. Landau 1991).

The fact that some theories of human origins have a narrative structure should not, in itself, be surprising: Darwinism requires us to create adaptive scenarios to explain the origin of any particular family, and such historical narratives will inevitably have a story-like character. The important point is be to aware of the cultural values embedded in the various theories, whether they can be analyzed as narrative or not.

The Nineteenth Century

By the early decades of the nineteenth century, geologists had rejected the biblical story of the Earth's creation and had greatly expanded the time scale of Earth history. As yet, however, the assumption that the human race itself had been created only a few thousands of years ago remained unchallenged. It was widely accepted on the authority of the French paleontologist Georges Cuvier (1769–1832) that there were no human fossils. The traditional assumptions that the human race had been endowed with civilization and culture from the start, and that the center of cultural activity lay to the east of Europe, remained intact. The archeologists who pioneered the study of stone, bronze, and iron technologies in Europe (the "three-age system") at first assumed that the Stone Age inhabitants had been degenerates conquered by later waves of more-civilized invaders from the east. This assumption was also built into the studies of philologists such as the Anglo-German scholar Max Müller (1862–1919), who explained the development of Indo-European languages in terms of successive invasions by different branches of the Aryan race, originating from central Asia.

Against this conservative, almost biblical, notion of a prehistory dominated by the rise and fall of successive cultures stood a more liberal tradition that interpreted human history in terms of a steady progress brought about by the cumulative efforts of generations of inventive individuals, each seeking their own self-interest. The philosophical historians of the eighteenth-century Enlightenment, including the Marquis de Condorcet in France (1743–1794) and Adam Smith (1723–1790) in Britain, postulated a steady progress from a primitive hunting culture through agriculture to modern commercial and industrial civilization. Modern "primitives" were thought to have been prevented from ascending the ladder of progress by local environmental conditions—they had not been exposed to the same stimulus as the Europe-ans. As yet, however, the limited time span allotted to the human race prevented most scholars from taking this progression theory seriously.

Claims that human remains had been found alongside those of extinct animals were made throughout the early nineteenth century but were almost universally rejected. The amateur archeologist Jacques Boucher de Perthes (1788–1868) unearthed stone tools from the Somme Valley in France, but his discoveries were dismissed. The breakthrough only came in the late 1850s, when a group of British geologists became convinced that the stone tools did, indeed, indicate that the human race had an antiquity stretching back into the later geological periods. Charles Lyell's (1797–1875) *Geological Evidences of the Antiquity of Man* (1863) summed up the new interpretation, while John Lubbock's (1834–1913) *Prehistoric Times* (1865) introduced the terms "Neolithic" and "Palaeolithic" to denote the distinction between the more recent polished stone tools and the chipped flints of the earlier humans.

Lubbock made common cause with anthropologists such as E.B. Tylor (1832–1917), who used the new interpretation of human antiquity to establish the linear model of cultural progress and the dominant paradigm in the field. Low-technology cultures such as the Australian Aborigines were interpreted as relics of the human race's Paleolithic ancestry, preserved into the present by geographical isolation. All of the various human societies represented merely different stages in a single ladder of cultural evolution leading toward Western civilization. The historical sequence of tool-making cultures established by the French archeologist Gabriel de Mortillet (1821–1898) summarized the logic of this linear-development model.

This progressionist message was inevitably linked into the debate over human origins sparked by Darwinism. Although Charles Darwin (1809–1882) did not discuss human evolution in *On the Origin of Species* (1859), it was immediately apparent that his theory implied an animal ancestry of humankind. Thomas Henry Huxley's (1825–1895) *Evidence as to Man's Place in Nature* (1863) summed up the evidence of a link to the great apes, although Huxley said nothing about the mode of evolution. When Darwin himself came to discuss the question in his *Descent of Man* (1871), he adopted many of the progressionist assumptions of his time, but he also made unique suggestions that would not be taken seriously for several decades. Unlike many of his contemporaries, Darwin thought that the human species would have originated in Africa, not central Asia. He also postulated an adaptive scenario to explain why the ancestors of humans had developed in a different direction from that of apes. Our ancestors had left the trees for the open plains, where they had adopted bipedalism as a means of locomotion in the new environment. This freed their hands for tool making, which in turn stimulated the development of intelligence. For Darwin, the upright posture predated the expansion of the brain.

Darwin's insights were inspired by his overall view of evolution as a branching process in which changes were essentially unpredictable. The majority of his contemporaries preferred to see evolution as the inevitable ascent of a developmental hierarchy toward humankind. The main task of the evolutionist was to construct the hypothetical sequence of development, after which it was simply assumed that progress along the hierarchy was inevitable. The physiologist George J. Romanes (1848–1894) explained mental evolution in animals and humans by simply constructing the sequence by which new mental faculties were added in the course of development. It was almost universally assumed that the increase of intelligence, and hence the increase in the size of the brain, was the main driving force of evolution. It was the increase in the size of the brain to a level that allowed the use of language that marked the transition to the nonbiological forms of evolution characteristic of humankind. The acquisition of bipedalism and the transition to a plains environment were secondary consequences of the inevitable increase in intelligence. This view of human origins was summed up by the Australian anatomist-anthropologist Grafton Elliot Smith (1871–1937) in an address to the British Association for the Advancement of Science as late as 1912.

The assumption that there must be a simple sequence leading from apes to humans was used to interpret the oldest human remains. Huxley had noted the ape-like features of the original Neandertal skull (discovered in 1857) but had insisted that its large brain meant that it could not be the "missing link." When more Neandertal remains were discovered later in the century, there was strong pressure to regard them as ape–human intermediates. The discovery of *Pithecanthropus* (the Java *Homo erectus*) in 1891–1892 was thought to provide evidence of an even earlier stage in the process. The German evolutionist Ernst Haeckel (1834–1919) had long promoted a linear model of evolution, and he and his disciple Gustav Schwalbe (1844–1916) constructed a neat developmental sequence from the great apes through *Pithecanthropus* and the Neandertals to modern humans, concentrating on the expansion of the brain. They presented this as the course of development that must have been followed by progressive evolution. The fact that *Pithecanthropus* walked upright, thus confirming Darwin's prediction, was largely ignored.

This linear model of progressive evolution was challenged by those who concentrated on the bewildering variety of late Paleolithic and Neolithic human remains now being unearthed. It was easy to depict the prehistory of Europe as a complex sequence of interaction between different racial types, each of vast antiquity. This kind of evidence was seized upon by those who favored the discontinuous model of social evolution, with the biological origins of the racial types being pushed so far back in time that the question was of no interest to the anthropologist. The British geologist William Boyd Dawkins (1837–1929), however, assumed that the center of the origin lay to the east, in central Asia, and that the marginalized races of modern Europe had been swept aside by successive invasions of higher types radiating out from this center. A model of human prehistory based on successive invasions by higher races was popularized by the Oxford geologist William Johnson Sollas (1849–1936) in his *Ancient Hunters* (1911). Sollas accepted that modern "primitives" were relics of the past, but instead of regarding them as having been preserved *in situ* by isolation and stagnation, he saw them as marginalized remnants of once-dominant races. The stage was now set for the emergence of a theory in which the various fossil hominids were dismissed as dead ends in a multibranch model of human evolution.

The Early Twentieth Century

Sollas' book marks an important transition in attitudes toward paleoanthropology that was typical of the early years of the new century. The linear-development model established by the first generation of evolutionists was now increasingly rejected in favor of a discontinuous model of development that stressed the antiquity of racial types, parallel evolution, and the replacement of one type by another in the course of history. This was not, as has sometimes been alleged, a nonevolutionary model of prehistory: There was plenty of encouragement from paleontologists who now saw evolution in general as a process in which each family branched into many parallel lines soon after its origin, the lines then being driven in roughly the same direction by inherent developmental forces.

The clearest sign of this changing attitude was the emergence of what has become known as the "pre-sapiens theory." Where once *Pithecanthropus* and the Neandertals had been seen as steps on the way from the apes toward modern humans, now they were dismissed as side branches in the human family trees, only distantly related to ourselves. The true human line must thus extend much further back in time, so that we might expect to find evidence of our "pre-sapiens" ancestor alongside the ancient types already discovered. One reason for the initial popularity of the spurious Piltdown remains was that *Eoanthropus* seemed to comfirm the existence of an early non-Neandertal line of human evolution.

The expulsion of the Neandertals from human ancestry was pioneered by the French paleoanthropologist Marcellin Boule (1861–1942), who interpreted the La Chapelle-aux-Saints specimen as too ape-like to have been transformed into the modern human species. The British anatomist-anthropologist Arthur Keith's (1866–1955) *Antiquity of Man* (1915) treated the Neandertals as a distinct hominid species or even a distinct genus, with its own peculiar specializations marking it off from the pre-sapiens line. Keith and many others thought that the archeological record confirmed a rapid replacement of Neandertals by modern humans in Europe, suggesting that the less-human Neandertals had been wiped out by an invasion of the pre-sapiens people. There is clear evidence that ideological factors played a role in the popularization of the pre-sapiens theory. Boule was opposed to the socialist principles that Mortillet had linked to linear progressionism, while Keith advocated an extreme antiquity for the racial divisions within modern humanity and openly compared the extinction of the Neandertals with the disappearance of "lower" races such as the Australian Aborigines when confronted with the invading Whites. When the Canadian anatomist Davidson Black (1884–1934) described *Sinanthropus* (the Chinese *Homo erectus* remains) in the 1930s, he saw this as yet another branch of the hominid family marginalized by higher species radiating out of central Asia.

The belief that central Asia was the source of human evolution persisted into the 1930s. One of its chief advocates was the American paleontologist Henry Fairfield Osborn (1857–1935), who was also a strong exponent of parallelism and orthogenesis (internally directed development) in mammalian evolution. Osborn linked this belief to an extreme version of the pre-sapiens theory in which the human line was extended so far back in time that even the apes were not our ancestors. He argued that the human type had become distinct from the apes in the stimulating environment of central Asia at a very early stage in primate evolution. By distancing us from the apes, he hoped to undermine one of the chief emotional symbols being used by the creationists who opposed evolution. In Britain, the anatomist Frederic Wood Jones (1879–1954) had also argued that humans and apes were unrelated, the human line having been separated from the rest of the primates since the appearance of the tarsiers. These attempts to push the ancestry of the human line further back in time were not antievolutionary: Osborn and Wood Jones were simply expanding upon the anti-Darwinian evolutionary models (orthogenesis and Lamarckism) still popular among anatomists and paleontologists.

In the 1920s, the Czech-American anthropologist Aleš Hrdlička (1869–1943) attempted to revive the view that the Neandertals were ancestral to modern humans, which now became known as the "Neanderthal phase of man" theory. In the following decades, the German anatomist Franz Weidenreich (1873–1948) argued strongly for a theory in which the sequence *Homo erectus*–Neandertal–modern defined stages of development that human populations in all parts of the world had passed through independently. There were Mongoloid features, for instance, in the Chinese versions of *Homo erectus,* indicating a continuity of racial evolution. Here was another manifestation of parallelism, but now confined to different populations within the same species and thus consistent with the linear model of development. In the 1950s, this interpretation was advocated by the American anthropologist Carleton S. Coon (1904–1981), who tried to adapt it to modern views by supposing that more-advanced genes appearing in one racial population would eventually "leak across" to elevate others to the same level. He was accused of arguing that the White race had become fully human before all of the others.

Later Developments

The popularity of the central Asian thesis, and the assumption that the brain led the way in human evolution, had deflected attention away from the Australian-born anatomist Raymond A. Dart's (1893–1988) interpretation of the South African *Australopithecus* discovered in 1924. By the late 1930s, more australopithecine specimens were being unearthed by the paleontologist Robert Broom (1866–1951), and these discoveries helped precipitate a major revolution in paleoanthropological thinking in the 1950s. It appeared Darwin had been right to pick Africa as the center of human origins and to suppose that the earliest hominids had stood upright before they got big brains. At the same time, there had been a major revolution in evolutionary theory. The modern neo-Darwinian synthesis had undermined support for the old non-Darwinian ideas that had sustained paleoanthropologists' belief in parallel evolution and, hence, in the pre-sapiens theory. The living races of humankind now had to be seen as closely related in genetic and, hence, in evolutionary terms. The idea that all of the known hominid fossils could be treated as side branches in the human family tree was no longer respectable, allowing *Homo erectus* (now seen as a single species in all of its geographical variants) to appear as the successor to the australopithecines that had first established the hominid line distinct from the apes. *Homo erectus* was thus the logical candidate for the ancestor of *Homo sapiens*.

The advent of Darwinism also highlighted the need to explain why the separation between the apes and the early hominids had occurred, since the old ideas of internally directed evolution were no longer acceptable. Efforts to establish an adaptive scenario to explain the separation now became fashionable, and it was obvious that a change of environment to the open plains offered a way of accounting for the origins of bipedalism. Led by the American physical anthropologist Sherwood L. Washburn (1911–), many paleoanthropologists sought to explain the success of the early hominids in terms of their adopting a hunting life-style. Since the late 1970s, the model of "man the hunter" has been criticized, especially by feminist scientists, as an attempt to use masculine values to define what made us truly human. The image of "woman the gatherer" has been created to provide an alternative explanation of the successful life-style of the earliest hominids. The true nature of the relationship between the various australopithecines, and between them and the earliest members of the genus *Homo*, also remains controversial despite the discovery of an ever expanding array of fossils. Even the advocates of a linear model of evolution within the genus *Homo* have been forced to admit that the later australopithecines represent an independent side branch.

Controversies have also continued over the nature of the Neandertals and their relationship to modern humans. In the 1960s, the image of the brutal Neandertal was replaced by a more pacific one that had a suspicious similarity to the "flower children" of the hippie decade. Many authorities in the 1950s and 1960s accepted the Neandertals as members of the species *Homo sapiens*. Even so, opinions remained divided as to whether the Neandertals constituted a phase in the evolution of modern Europeans or a specialized racial side branch that disappeared without a trace. By the mid-1990s, many had returned to the view that Neandertals were a distinct species, thus reinstating the multibranch model of human evolution. Based on studies of mitochondrial DNA (deoxyribonucleic acid), efforts have been made to argue that the modern human race is derived solely from a single population expanding out of Africa, displacing all earlier human types. This has been countered by claims that the evidence reveals continuity of racial evolution in the different continents. Thus, debates that have plagued paleoanthropology throughout its history continue to resurface in modernized forms. Although some of the more extreme theories advocated in the early twentieth century have been forgotten, the basic issues of linearity versus divergence, and continuity versus displacement, remain.

Peter J. Bowler

See also Aryanism; Asian Paleoanthropology; Australopithecines; Bipedalism; Boucher (de Crévecoeur) de Perthes, Jacques; Boule, Marcellin; Brixham Cave; Broom, Robert; Chapelle-aux-Saints, La; Coon, Carleton S(tevens); Cuvier, Georges Léopold Chrétien Fréderic Dagobert (Baron); Dart, Raymond A(rthur); Darwin, Charles; Dawkins, (Sir) William Boyd; Evolutionary Theory; Haeckel, Ernst Heinrich Phillip August; *Homo erectus*; Hrdlička, Aleš; Hunting Hypothesis of Human Origins; Keith, (Sir) Arthur; Lubbock, (Sir) John; Lyell, (Sir) Charles; Molecular Anthropology; Mortillet, Gabriel (Louis Laurent) de; Neandertals; Neo-Darwinism; Osborn,

Henry Fairfield; Piltdown; Schwalbe, Gustav; Smith (Sir) Grafton Elliot; Sollas, William Johnson; United Kingdom; Weidenreich, Franz

Bibliography
P.J. Bowler: *Theories of human evolution: A century of debate, 1844–1944.* Baltimore: Johns Hopkins University Press/Oxford: Blackwell, 1986; P.J. Bowler: *The invention of progress: The Victorians and the past.* Oxford: Blackwell, 1989; C.L. Brace: The fate of the "classic" Neanderthals: A consideration of hominid catastrophism. *Current Anthropology* 5:3–43, 1964; M.H. Brown: *The search for Eve.* New York: Harper & Row, 1990; C.R. Darwin: *The descent of man and selection in relation to sex.* 2 vols. London: Murray, 1871; D.K. Grayson: *The establishment of human antiquity.* New York: Academic Press, 1983.

J. Gribben & J. Charfas: *The monkey puzzle: A family tree.* London: Triad/Granada, 1983; M. Hammond: The expulsion of the Neanderthals from human ancestry: Marcellin Boule and the social context of scientific research. *Social Studies of Science* 12:1–36, 1982; D. Haraway: *Primate visions: Gender, race, and nature in the world of modern science.* New York: Routledge, 1989; T.H. Huxley: *Evidence as to man's place in nature.* London: Williams & Norgate, 1863; D.C. Johannsen & M.A. Edey: *Lucy: The beginnings of humankind.* New York: Simon & Schuster, 1981; A. Keith: *The antiquity of man.* London: Williams & Norgate, 1915 (2d ed.: 1925).

M. Landau: *Narratives of human evolution.* New Haven, Connecticut: Yale University Press, 1991; R. Lewin: *Bones of contention: Controversies in the search for human origins.* New York: Simon & Schuster, 1987; J. Lubbock: *Prehistoric times: As illustrated by ancient remains and the manners and customs of modern savages.* London: Williams & Norgate, 1865; C. Lyell: *Geological evidences of the antiquity of man, with remarks on the theories of the origin of species by variation.* London: Murray, 1863; J. Reader: *Missing links: The hunt for earliest man.* London: Collins, 1981; G.E. Smith: Presidential address [British Association for the Advancement of Science]. *Nature* 92:118–126, 1912; W.J. Sollas: *Ancient hunters and their modern representatives.* London: Macmillan, 1911 (2d ed.: 1915, 3d ed.: 1924); G.W. Stocking: *Victorian anthropology.* New York: Free Press, 1987.

Paleopathology

Paleopathology is the study of disease in ancient and prehistoric populations. By examining cultural remains such as artifacts and art (e.g., Dequeker 1991), documentary evidence (e.g., Andersen 1991), biological remains such as skeletons (e.g., Steinbock 1976; Ortner & Putschar 1981), mummies (Cockburn & Cockburn 1980), and even coprolites (Wilke & Hall 1975), the pattern of disease in a population can be discerned. The information gained from such studies can be used to establish the existence of disease within a group. This information is the basis for developing a history of specific diseases. Since the prevalence and pattern of disease are a reflection of the lifeways of a society, they shed light on the adaptation of the population.

While publications span the last two centuries, only in the last quarter of the twentieth century has paleopathology begun to have an impact on other sciences. Most of the earliest paleopathologists were physicans, and the discipline clearly had its beginning in medicine. Even in the modern era, paleopathology has been called "the doctor's hobby" (Eckert n.d.). A recent synthesis (Ortner & Aufderheide 1991) clearly allies paleopathology with biomedicine rather than with anthropology and its biocultural perspective. Although historically these two distinctive viewpoints, medicine and anthropology, have driven this field of inquiry, during the last quarter of the twentieth century anthropology has had a major impact on the field, with its links between biology and culture giving it a unique identity.

The Emergence: Pre-1890 Inquiries

The birth of paleopathology can be marked by the publication of Johann Friedrich Esper's (1732–1781) *Ausführliche Nachricht von neuendeckten Zoolithen unbekannter vierfüsiger tiere* (Description of the Newly Discovered Zooliths of Unknown Quadrupeds) (1774), describing remains recovered from a cave in the vicinity of Bayreuth, Germany. In this work, Esper gave an account of a sarcoma in the bones of a cave bear—though the pathology was most certainly a misdiagnosed callus of a healed fracture. In the century from the 1770s to the 1890s, publications were characteristically single-case studies of pathological conditions found in the bones of humans and animals. The objective of these early studies was primarily diagnosis. These early paleopathologists showed remarkable diagnostic skills in identifying many pathologi-

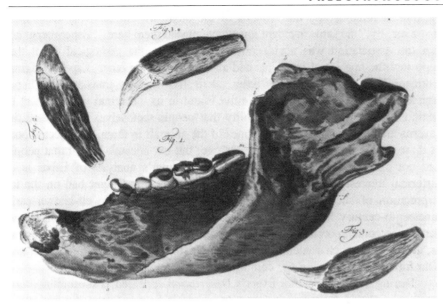

Fig. 1. Cave bear mandible illustrated by Esper (1774).

cal conditions. For example, researchers performed autopsies on mummies as early as 1825, and in the 1850s the Bohemian (Czech) physiologist Johann Neopomuk Czermak (1828–1873) used histological techniques to reveal arteriosclerosis in a large artery of a mummy (cf. Strouhal & Vyhnanek 1979). However, the emphasis on diagnosis became an end in itself, and, as such, throughout this period paleopathology remained essentially a descriptive enterprise. A notable exception, however, was Harrison Allen (1841–1897), a former student of Joseph Leidy (1823–1891) at the University of Pennsylvania. Allen's studies transcended mere description and sought to understand the processes involved in pathogenesis.

The Formative Period: 1890s–1920s
The formative period is characterized by two emerging themes: (1) the determination of the history or geography of a specific disease, and (2) the application of advanced medical technology. While the former theme served to sharpen the focus of paleopathology during this period, the application of the latter, unfortunately, became the standard by which progress in the fledgling discipline was measured—and again this became an end in itself.

Although the diagnosis of infectious disease is always problematical, researchers at the beginning of the twentieth century were able to successfully develop methods to differentially identify skeletal lesions that were caused by communicable diseases. Differential diagnosis of infectious disease is a difficult task

since some pathogens such as viruses often do not leave distinctive lesions on the skin or bones. In addition, bone is surprisingly limited in its ability to respond to stressors (factors that can cause physiological disruption). Bone can resorb or deposit tissue or alternate these processes. Fortunately, this pattern often results in a "signature" that is characteristic of the pathogen that causes the physiological disruption and is a diagnostic feature (the pattern of skeletal involvement) that provides indisputable evidence of specific diseases such as syphilis, leprosy, and tuberculosis. Hence, during this period there were a number of significant attempts to unravel the natural history of specific diseases such as syphilis (e.g., Ashmead 1895a, 1895b), poliomyelitis (Mitchell 1900), tuberculosis (Maher 1929), and leprosy (e.g., Lehmann-Nitsche 1898; Raymond 1921) and to uncover evidence of medical practices (Finlayson 1893).

This concern for infectious disease is not surprising since it represented one of the most significant medical problems of the period. But while the historical perspective consumed the attention of investigators, and although they were accumulating considerable data, there were still few attempts to generalize and synthesize findings.

With regard to the technological theme, undoubtedly the most significant development during this period was the application of radiography to paleopathological investigations. In fact soon after the German physicist Wilhelm Roentgen (1845–1923) discovered the X-ray in 1895, mummies were being radiographed. One of the first to employ this technique was the English Egyptologist William Flinders Petrie (1853–1942) in 1897 (Flinders Petrie 1898), followed by an Australian investigator, F.J. Clendinnen (1898), who identified an abnormal bone in the hand of a mummy.

One of the most impressive researches in paleopathology was undertaken during this period by the British physician (Sir) Marc Armand Ruffer (1859–1917), who played a key role in defining and developing the histological analysis of mummified tissue. Ruffer and his coworkers found evidence of schistosomiasis (cf. Ruffer 1910), Pott's disease (tuberculosis), pneumonia, arteriosclerosis, and variola (cf. Ruffer 1914).

In Egypt, a cottage industry of paleopathology arose with the work not only of Ruffer, but also of the Australian anatomist Grafton Elliot Smith (1871–1937) and his cohorts. In particular, Smith studied the process of mummification and became interested in the similarities in the process used by Egyptians and Australians, which he used as evidence of cultural diffusion from Egypt to that part of the world. As paleopathologists, Smith and his coworkers used innovative research techniques to diagnose pathology in ancient remains. Evidence of gallstones, scrotal hernias, carcinoma, leprosy, tuberculosis, and smallpox were discovered in Egyptian and Nubian material.

Two other workers worthy of note, and whose work serves to further characterize this period, are the Czech-American physical anthropologist Aleš Hrdlička (1869–1943) (e.g., Hrdlička 1914) and the American paleopathologist Roy L. Moodie (1880–1934) (cf. Moodie 1923).

The Modern Era

The 1930s are usually heralded as the beginning of the modern era of paleopathology, and Earnest A. Hooton's (1887–1954) *The Indians of Pecos Pueblo* (1930) is often described as the pivotal publication of the era. In this monograph, Hooton introduced the paleoepidemiological approach that considers the relationship among the host, the pathogen, and the environment. But while Hooton is often cited as initiating the modern era, in actuality his work had little impact during the 1930s, 1940s, and 1950s. Hooton's major contribution was his use of simple frequency statistics in presenting data. Few publications at the time provided this information. For example, the major publications of the archeology survey of Nubia report on more than

10,000 burials but seldom provide information on the frequency of pathology found in the population.

METHODOLOGICAL AND THEORETICAL ISSUES. Three major objectives of modern paleopathology guide its research. The first is historical and geographical: Defining the chronology and spatial distribution of a disease remains one of the primary objectives of most paleopathology research. The second objective is determining the biocultural interactions that occur as a population adapts to its environment, with disease as an index of the success or failure of adaptation. The third objective is concern for understanding the processes (production of change) involved in prehistoric disease. In living organisms, we can study the biological system as it is undergoing a transformation, unraveling the underlying process, while in extinct populations understanding such process is much more difficult. The factors that bring about change are deduced by the examination of many individuals at various stages of a transformation.

The success of any of these objectives requires a reliable diagnosis of pathology in prehistory. While strides have been made in diagnosing various pathological conditions (cf. Steinbock 1976; Ortner & Putschar 1981), there remains a lack of standards for differential diagnosis. Donald J. Ortner (1992:6) contends that there are too many inconsistencies in diagnosis and that there is seldom sufficient information on the characteristics of the lesion or their distribution. Without this information, one is unable to offer a "second opinion." In light of this problem, D.J. Ortner of the Smithsonian Institution has suggested that we suspend any hypothesis testing until acceptable protocols can be developed. However, the American physical anthropologist Jane Buikstra and her coworkers (Buikstra et al. 1993) have demonstrated that it is possible to establish protocols for differential diagnosis and to test hypotheses with their study of disease in ancient Egypt.

The development of modern paleopathology has been enhanced by the use of multiple indicators of pathology (e.g., Goodman et al. 1984; Gilbert & Mielke 1985; Martin et al. 1985). Rather than focus on a single pathology, researchers examine a number of pathological conditions in a systematic fashion. For example, periosteal lesion (an indication of systemic infection), porotic hyperostosis (an indication of iron-deficiency anemia), long-bone lengths and widths, evidence of trace-mineral deficiencies, and enamel hypoplasia may be used to interpret diet and disease in the population.

Some of the stress indicators, such as enamel hypoplasia, have become essential tools for the paleopathologist. For example, the chronology for enamel development is well understood, and the age at which a defect occurs can be determined (Goodman & Armelagos 1985). If a tooth takes six years to mineralize from the crown to the junction with the dentin, the location of an enamel defect actually "times" it to the stage at which it developed. The enamel acts as if it were a kymograph. In this sense, enamel hypoplasia provides a "window into the past," so that fetal and childhood stress can be measured in children and adults who have survived it.

The analysis of pathology in prehistoric populations often follows a deductive methodology in which the researcher attempts to reconstruct the factors that cause the skeletal lesions. In this view, the paleopathologist is much like the detective who has to reconstruct the crime from the evidence long after the criminals have left the scene. The paleopathologist has to reconstruct the lifeways of the population after they lived and died. While the deductive approach has been useful, it has certain inherent limitations. It is usually not possible to select from alternative conclusions.

There is, however, a methodology that can systematically falsify or exclude alternative hypothesis. In 1964, the American scientist J.R. Platt proposed the use of an inductive approach that he calls "strong inference," the roots of which derive from the Baconian approach to experimentation using a multiple hypothesis testing. Although inductive inference has been known for years, only in the latter part of the twentieth century has it penetrated the methodology of paleopathology, providing the means for transforming the discipline into a science. There are four stages in an analysis using the approach of strong inference (Platt 1964:347): (1) formulation of alternative hypotheses; (2) design of experiments that exclude or falsify one or more of the hypotheses; (3) development of experiments to get "clean results"; and (4) recycling of the procedure by repeating the process.

While strong inference is most effectively applied to sciences with experimental possibilities, it can be useful in nonexperimental sciences such as paleopathology—but there is obviously a need to modify the methods. The researcher must rely on comparative analysis for "natural experiments." It is possible to select samples that highlight difference in the biotic or cultural environment and the biology of the group. Thus, application of the inductive approach to paleopathology requires the selection of an appropriate sample. The sampling of skeletal populations remains one of the most difficult problems facing a paleopathologist. Does the cemetery represent a sample of the population that lived there? The American demographer J.W. Wood et al. (1992) claim researchers are unable to control such sampling and thus are restricted in their ability to determine the prevalence or incidence of disease. They further claim that cemetery samples include those who have died at a specific age and do not include all individuals who were at risk. This would lead to overestimations of pathology prevalence. Pathologists using autopsy data face a similar problem. Wood and his coworkers also suggest that paleopathology can tell us little about individual genetic frailty and its relationship to mortality. Paleopathologists can determine the cause of mortality in just a small percentage of all the deaths. There is significant evidence that individual frailty (the genetic or constitutional contribution to mortality) is overridden by socioeconomic factors. The American skeletal biologist A.H. Goodman (1993) has cogently responded to these issues.

These theoretical and methodological issues, however, should not obscure the contributions that paleopathology has made to understanding disease of the past and the impact this has had on understanding disease in the present. For example, criticism of technology-driven paleopathology should not be interpreted as an argument for rejecting technological advances. The technology should be appropriate for the problem to be solved or the question asked. For example, Noreen Tuross (1991) has extracted serum protein from bone in a method that could resolve the issues about the origin and evolution of infectious diseases such as tuberculosis and syphilis.

HISTORY, GEOGRAPHY, BIOLOGY, CULTURE, AND PROCESS. The contribution of paleopathology to the past and to the present can be presented in the context of the three objectives of paleopathology. Recent research suggests that successful studies meet more than one of the objectives. For example, the British researcher Keith Manchester (1984), in his analysis of tuberculosis and leprosy in ancient Britain, considers history, geography, and process. Evidence indicates that leprosy and tuberculosis coexisted in Britain. Eventually, leprosy declined and disappeared in the Middle Ages. Tuberculosis and leprosy are closely related, and cross immunization is possible. Manchester suggests that individuals who have been initially exposed contract *Mycobacterium tuberculosis* and then exposed to *M. leprae* experience a relatively noninfective tuberculoid leprosy. He further speculates that changes in population size and density in the Middle Ages created the ecology for the pulmonary transmission of tuberculosis, spreading the infection to many individuals and creating a reservoir of tubercle-infected individuals who contract a leprosy infection that is transmitted to others.

The collaboration between physical anthropologists and paleopathologists since the 1950s has promoted a biocultural perspective and research agenda. Examples include Jane E. Buikstra's study of the lower Illinois Valley (1976), Ted A. Rathbun et al.'s (1980) study of disease patterns in prehistoric South Carolina, and Douglas H. Ubelaker's work in Ecuador (1980, 1981). From these and similar studies, it appears that with the onset of sedentism there was an increase in infectious disease, whether or not the population was involved in primary food production. Similarly, at Dickson Mounds, Illinois, where the transition to agriculture occurred rapidly (ca. A.D. 950–1350), there was a demonstrable increase in infectious and nutritional diseases. The impact of agriculture on the health of Mississippian populations in the eastern United States has been summarized by M. Cassandra Hill and George J. Armelagos (1990). Mississippian populations from the lower Illinois River Valley, the middle Illinois River Valley (Dickson Mounds), the central Ohio River Valley, the central and lower Mississippi Valley, and Georgia and Alabama were included in their survey. While it was difficult to determine overall trend, there were some interesting patterns. While none of the other cases presented showed the distinct trends noted at Dickson, sedentism and nucleation nevertheless appear to be keys to the increase in infectious disease. The intensification of agriculture did not decrease health in all situations, and there is evidence for a difference in disease patterns for those populations in the core area and those on the periphery, suggesting the possibility of exploitation by population centers at the core. Another issue that has emerged from the

historical geography of disease is whether cancer occurred in prehistory or is a "disease of civilization." Studies, such as that of the Czech physical anthropologist E. Strouhal (1978), have shown that cancer existed in prehistory but at a much lower frequency. The extension of longevity, increase in carcinogenic agents, and changes in patterns of fertility appear to be implicated in the increase in tumors in contemporary populations.

As the above implies, the modern era of paleopathology began in the 1960s. This is evidenced by the content of articles published in a leading biological-anthropology journal. Of the 1,367 articles published in the *American Journal of Physical Anthropology* from 1930 to 1970, 40 percent dealt with osteology (Lovejoy et al. 1982). In the 1930s, 11.5 percent of the osteology articles dealt with pathology. In the 1940s that figure dropped to 7.4 percent; in the 1950s, to 4.1 percent. In the 1960s, the proportion of pathology articles rose to 10.8 percent. However, it was a symposium on human paleopathology organized by the American paleopathologist Saul Jarcho (1966), the publication of a popular book on paleopathology, *Bones, Bodies, and Disease* (Wells 1964), and a compendium titled *Diseases in Antiquity* by D.R. Brothwell and A.T. Sandison (1967) that were the most influential factors in the resurrection of paleopathology. In 1973, one of the strongest forces in the rejuvination of paleopathology was the organization of the Paleopathology Association in Detroit, Michigan, spearheaded by Aiden Cockburn (1912–1981), an authority on the evolution of disease (Cockburn & Cockburn 1980) who effectively brought physician and anthropologist together. The motto of the Paleopathology Association is *mortui viventes docent* (the dead are our teacher), which neatly summarizes this brief review by reminding us that the remains of our ancestors have much to teach us and that we continue to learn from them.

George J. Armelagos

See also Allen, Harrison; Health and Disease; Hooton, E(arnest) A(lbert); Hrdlička, Aleš; Lehmann-Nitsche, Robert; Leidy, Joseph; Skeletal biology; Smith, Grafton Elliot

Bibliography
J.S. Andersen: The diagnosis of leprosy. In: D.J. Ortner & A.C. Aufderheide (eds): *Human paleopathology: Current syntheses and future options.* Washington, D.C.: Smithsonian Institution Press, 1991, pp.

205–208; G.J. Armelagos et al.: *Bibliography of human paleopathology*. Amherst, Massachusetts: Department of Anthropology, University of Massachusetts, 1971; A.S. Ashmead: Pre-Columbian syphilis in Yucatan. *American Anthropologist* 9:106–109, 1895a; A.S. Ashmead: Some facts of interest in connection with the question of the existence of syphilis or leprosy in Peru. *Charlotte Medical Journal* 7:325ff. 1895b; D.R. Brothwell & A.T. Sandison (eds): *Diseases in antiquity*. Springfield, Illinois: Thomas, 1967; J.E. Buikstra: *Hopewell in the lower Illinois Valley*. Archaeological Program Scientific Papers. No. 2. Evanston, Illinois: Northwestern University Press, 1976.

J.E. Buikstra et al.: What diseases plagued ancient Egyptians? A century of controversy considered. In: W.V. Davies & R. Walker (eds) *Biological anthropology and the study of ancient Egypt*. London: British Museum, 1993, pp. 24–53; F.J. Clendinnen: Skiagram of the hand of an Egyptian mummy, showing abnormal sesmoid bones. *Intercolonial Medical Journal of Australia* 3:106–109, 1898; T.A. Cockburn & E. Cockburn (eds): *Mummies, diseases, and ancient culture*. Cambridge: Cambridge University Press, 1980; J.B. Crain: *Human paleopathology: A bibliographic list*. Sacramento State University Anthropology Society Papers. No. 12. Sacramento, California: Sacramento Anthropological Society, 1971.

J. Dequeker: Paleopathology of rheumatism in paintings. In: D.J. Ortner & A.S. Aufderheide (eds) *Human paleopathology: Current syntheses and future options*. Washington, D.C.: Smithsonian Institution Press, 1991, pp. 216–221; W. Eckert: *International references on paleopathology*. Wichita, Kansas: International Reference Organization in Forensic Medicine, n.d.; J.E. Esper: *Ausfürliche Nachricht von neuendeckten Zoolithen unbekannter vierfüsiger tiere*. Nuremberg: Knorr, 1774; J. Finlayson: Ancient Egyptian medicine. *British Medical Journal* 1:748–762, 1014–1016, 1160–1164, 1893; W.M. Flinders Petrie: Veshasheh. In: *Memoirs, Egypt Exploration Fund*. No. 50. London: Egypt Exploration Fund, 1898; R.I. Gilbert & J.H. Mielke (eds): *The analysis of prehistoric diets*. Orlando, Florida: Academic Press, 1985.

A.H. Goodman: On the interpretation of health from skeletal material. *Current Anthropology* 34:282–288, 1993; A.H. Goodman & G.J. Armelagos: The chrono-logical distribution of enamel hypoplasia in human permanent incisor and canine teeth. *Archives of Oral Biology* 30:503–507, 1985; A.H. Goodman & G.J. Armelagos: Childhood stress and decreased longevity in adulthood. *American Anthropologist* 90:936–944, 1988; A. Goodman et al. Induction of stress from bone and teeth. In: M. Cohen & G.J. Armelagos (eds) *Paleopathology at the origin of agriculture*. Orlando, Florida: Academic Press, 1984, pp. 13–49; M.S. Hill & G.J. Armelagos: An evaluation of the biocultural consequences of the Mississippian transformation. In: D.H. Dye & S.A. Cox (eds) *Towns and Temples along the Mississippi*. Tuscaloosa: University of Alabama Press, 1990, pp. 16–37.

E.A. Hooton: *The Indians of Pecos Pueblo*. New Haven, Connecticut: Yale University Press, 1930; A. Hrdlička: Anthropological work in Peru in 1913, with notes on the pathology of the ancient Peruvians. *Smithsonian Miscellaneous Collections* 61:54–61, 1914; S. Jarcho (ed): *Human paleopathology*. New Haven, Connecticut: Yale University Press, 1966; R. Lehmann-Nitsche: Lepra precolombiana. Ensayo critico. *Revista del Museo de La Plata* 3:337–371, 1898 (also published separately under the title *Lepra precolombiana* in La Plata: Talleres de publicaciones de Museo de La Plata, 1898); C.O. Lovejoy et al.: Five decades of skeletal biology as reflected in pages of the *American Journal of Physical Anthropology*. In: F. Spencer (ed) *A history of American physical anthropology, 1930–1980*. New York: Academic Press, 1982, pp. 305–328.

S.J. Maher: Tuberculosis among the American Indians. *American Review of Tuberculosis* 19:407, 1929; K. Manchester: Tuberculosis and leprosy in antiquity: An interpretation. *Medical History* 28:162–173, 1984; D.L. Martin et al.: Skeletal pathologies as indicators of quality and quantity of diet. In: R. Gilbert and J.H. Mielke (eds) *The analysis of prehistoric diets*. Orlando, Florida: Academic Press, 1985; R.L. Miller et al.: Predynastic schistosomiasis. In: W.V. Davies & R. Walker (eds) *Biological anthropology and the study of ancient Egypt*. London: British Museum, 1993, pp.54–60; J.K. Mitchell: Study of a mummy affected with anterior poliomyelitis. *Transactions of the Association of American Physicians* 15:134–136, 1900.

R.L. Moodie: *Paleopathology: An introduction to the study of ancient evidences of disease.* Urbana: University of Illinois Press, 1923; D.J. Ortner: Skeletal pathology: Probabilities, possibilities, and impossibilities. In: J.W. Verano & D.H. Ubelaker (eds) *Disease and demography in the Americas.* Washington, D.C.: Smithsonian Institution Press, 1992, pp. 5–13; D.J. Ortner & A.C. Aufderheide (eds): *Human paleopathology: Current syntheses and future options.* Washington, D.C.: Smithsonian Institution Press, 1991; D.J. Ortner & W.G.J. Putschar: *Identification of pathological conditions in human skeletal remains.* Washington, D.C.: Smithsonian Institution Press, 1981; J.R. Platt: Strong inference. *Science* 146:347–353, 1964; T.A. Rathbun et al.: Disease patterns in a formative period South Carolina coastal population. *Tennessee Anthropological Association Miscellaneous Papers* 5:52–74, 1980.

P. Raymond: *Remarques sur la lepre et la syphilis en France au moyen-age.* Congrès d'International Histoire de la Medecine, 1921; M.A. Ruffer: Note on the presence of *Bilharzia haematobia* in Egyptian mummies of the twentieth dynasty. *British Medical Journal* 1:16, 1910; M.A. Ruffer: Studies in palaeopathology: Note on the diseases of the Sudan and Nubia in ancient times. *Mitteilungen zur Geschichte der Medizin und der Naturwissenschaften* 13:453–460, 1914; R.T. Steinbock: *Pathological diagnosis and interpretations: Bone disease in ancient human populations.* Springfield, Illinois: Thomas, 1976; E. Strouhal: Ancient Egyptian case of carcinoma. *Bulletin of the New York Academy of Medicine* 54:290–302, 1978; E. Strouhal & L. Vyhnanek: Egyptian mummies. *Czechoslovak Collections, Acta Musei Nationalis Pragae* 35B:1–212, 1979.

N. Tuross: Recovery of bone and serum proteins from human skeletal tissue: IgG, osteonectin, and albumin. In: D.J. Ortner & A.C. Auferheide (eds) *Human paleopathology: Current syntheses and future options.* Washington, D.C.: Smithsonian Institution Press, 1991, pp. 51–54; D.H. Ubelaker: Prehistoric remains from the Cotocollao site on the Sta. Elena Peninsula, coastal Ecuador. *Journal of the Washington Academy of Sciences* 70:3–24, 1980; D.H. Ubelaker: *The Ayalan Cemetery: A late Integration Period burial site on the south coast of Ecuador.* Smithsonian Contributions to Anthropology. No. 29. Washington, D.C.: Smithsonian Institution, 1981.

D.H. Ubelaker: The development of American paleopathology. In: F. Spencer (ed) *A history of American physical anthropology, 1930–1980.* New York: Academic Press, 1982, pp. 337–356; C. Wells: *Bones, bodies, and disease.* London: Thames & Hudson, 1964; P.J. Wilke & H.J. Hall: *Analysis of ancient feces: A discussion and annotated bibliography.* Berkeley: Department of Anthropology, University of California Press, 1975; J.W. Wood et al. The osteological paradox. Problems of inferring prehistoric health from skeletal samples. *Current Anthropology* 33:343–370, 1992.

Author's Note

For a more detailed review of the discipline's history, see Brothwell and Sandison (1967), Jarcho (1966), Ortner and Aufterheide (1991), Ubelaker (1982), and Wells (1964). See also Armelagos et al. (1971) and Crain (1971) for bibliographic history, as well as the *International Bibliography of Human Paleopathology and Related Subjects* (being prepared by the Museum of Man, San Diego, California), a more recent effort to list publications in human paleopathology. Approximately 40 percent of the entries listed in this latter publication date from the last decade.

Paleoprimatology

The study of fossil primates began rather abruptly in the late 1830s, when, within a few months, fossilized remains of nonhuman primates were described for the first time from three continents: Asia, Europe, and South America. Although at least two fossil primates had been recovered prior to these (the Eppelsheim femur [?*Pliopithecus*] in 1820 and *Adapis* by the French naturalist Georges Cuvier [1769–1832] in 1821), they were not recognized as such.

The earliest published announcement of a fossil primate is credited to W.E. Baker (1808–1881) and H.M. Durand (1812–1871), two British army engineers, who in 1836 reported the maxilla of a fossil monkey from the Siwalik Hills of what is now Pakistan and India, in the *Journal of the Asiatic Society* in Bengal. They noted that the maxilla was much larger than that of the Indian langur, *Presbytis entellus*, but they did not name it. These authors suggested that the paucity of fossil monkeys is not surprising in light of the arboreal habits of these animals, which would make them less susceptible than other animals to floods and other catastrophes. In May of the following year, Hugh Falconer (1808–1865) and Proby Thomas Cautley

Sub Himalayan fossil Remains

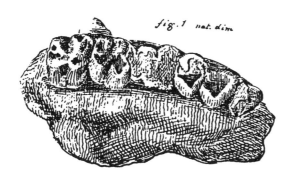

fig. 1 nat. dim.

Quadrumana

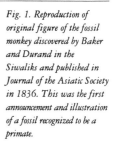

Fig. 1. Reproduction of
original figure of the fossil
monkey discovered by Baker
and Durand in the
Siwaliks and published in
Journal of the Asiatic Society
in 1836. This was the first
announcement and illustration
of a fossil recognized to be a
primate.

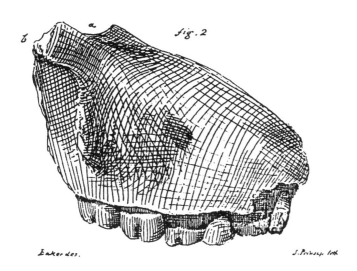

fig. 2

Baker des. *J. Prinsep lith*

(1802–1871) described a monkey astragalus they had recovered earlier (but not described) and some recently recovered monkey jaws that they thought documented the presence of several species. Discussing these finds, Falconer and Cautley (1838:358) noted "the interest attaching to the first discovery in the fossil state of animals so nearly approaching man in their organization . . . ," as well as the fact that the monkeys seemed to come from fossil beds containing some animals that are contemporary with humans today and others that were "characteristic of the oldest Tertiary beds of Europe."

Peter Wilhelm Lund (1801–1880), a Danish naturalist working in Pleistocene caves in Brazil, was the first scientist to name a species of fossil primate. From the cave system of Lagoa Santa in eastern Brazil, he recovered

numerous remains of primates, which he mostly attributed to species living in the same area. In 1836 he discovered a remarkable exception, in the form of a very robust femur and humerus much larger than any living New World monkey. In a letter written in November 1837, and published the following year, he described it as the first antediluvian evidence of primates, and so named it *Protopithecus* (Lund 1838).

The distinction of describing the first fossil ape belongs to Édouard Lartet (1801–1871), a French lawyer and paleontologist, who, in January 1837, described a lower jaw of a small ape similar to the living gibbon. The fossil was named *Pithecus antiquus* by the French zoologist Henri de Blainville (1777–1850) in 1839 and subsequently was given its

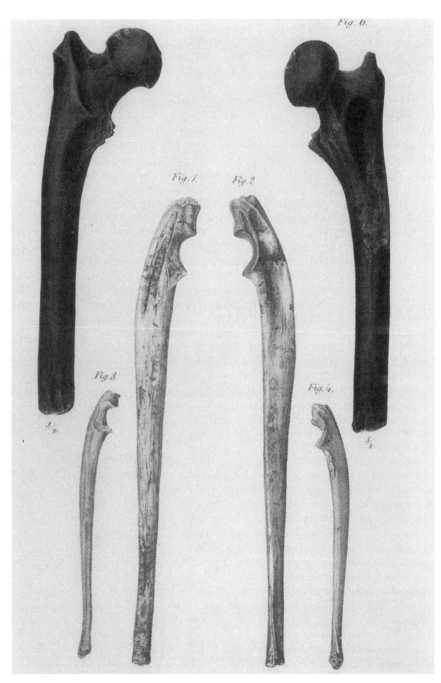

own genus, *Pliopithecus*, by another French zoologist-paleontologist, Paul Gervais (1816–1879), in 1849. Like his contemporaries, Lartet remarked upon finding a fossil ape associated with other mammals that were long thought to be the most ancient mammals of Europe, and thus that primates were not as novel as generally thought.

While the early finds from South America and Asia remained isolated discoveries for many decades, Lartet's description was followed shortly in time by descriptions of other fossil higher primates from all parts of Europe. The fossil colobine *Mesopithecus pentelici* from Pikermi in Greece was named by the German zoologist Andreas Wagner (1797–1861) in 1839. In the next few decades, many additional species and excellent specimens of fossil monkeys were described from other parts of Europe by many distinguished paleontologists, including Lartet, Gervais, and the French paleontologist Albert Jean Gaudry (1827–1908). The British anatomist Richard Owen (1804–1892) described

Fig. 2. The proximal femur in the upper left and right of this illustration was discovered in 1836 and belongs to Protopithecus, the first fossil primate specimen to be formally named. From a lithograph plate in Lund (1838).

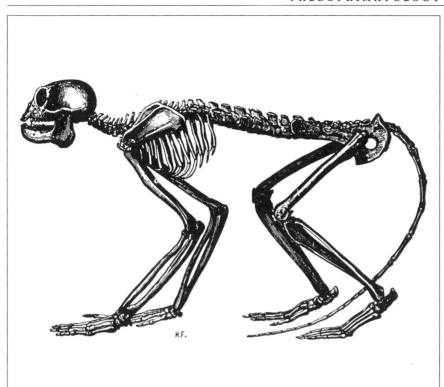

Fig. 3. Mesopithecus pentelici *Wagner 1839. A nearly complete fossil colobine from Greece, discovered in the wake of Lartet's 1837 discovery of* Pliopithecus *in France.*

fossil macaques from England (incorrectly in 1839, correctly in 1845 and 1846), and Gervais described a fossil macaque from France in 1859. However, the European fossil primate from these years that received the most attention in subsequent decades was the fossil ape *Dryopithecus fontani* from Saint Gaudens in southern France, which Lartet described in 1856. The discovery of *Dryopithecus* preceded, by just a few years, the theoretical breakthrough that put the fossil record of primates and all other organisms in a very different light.

Building a Record
With the publication of *On the Origin of Species* by Charles Darwin (1809–1882) in 1859 and its inescapable implication that living and fossil species are linked by a common phylogeny, the primate fossils took on a new significance for documenting human genealogy in earlier epochs. However, the few remains of fossil primates known at the time were clearly inadequate for the task. As a result, for Darwin and his able protagonist, the biologist Thomas Henry Huxley (1825–1895), the primate fossil record was at best irrelevant and at worst a considerable embarassment to the argument that humans were derived from a primate ancestry. Thus, in the *Descent of Man* (1871), Darwin laments that although living

humans are most similar to African apes and one might expect their common ancestor on that continent, the presence of a great ape such as *Dryopithecus* in the Miocene of France shows that there is ample likelihood of large-scale migrations since then. He then goes on to remind the reader that the discovery of fossils is a slow and fortuitous process and that, moreover, Africa had yet to be searched by geologists. In citing the inadequacy of the fossil record in demonstrating a progressive sequence of change, Darwin was following the arguments that his close friend, the geologist Charles Lyell (1797–1875), had been using for many years as evidence against evolutionary change through time. Thus, in the 1860s and 1870s, the fossil record of primates was only a potential source of evidence relevant to the theory of evolution.

Tremendous advances in the discovery of new primate species in North America and Europe followed during the later decades of the nineteenth century. The first recognized fossil prosimian was named *Caenopithecus* by the German anatomist Ludwig Rütimeyer (1825–1895) in 1862, followed a decade later by the French paleontologist Henri Filhol's (1844–1902) identification of *Necrolemur* from the Eocene Quercy phosphorites (cf. Filhol 1873). The affinities of *Adapis* remained unclear; some (Gaudry, Gervais) thought it was a lemur, while others (Filhol) followed Cuvier's original designation of this genus as a pachyderm (ungulate). Recovery of remains of European fossil primates (including *Oreopithecus* named by Gervais in 1872) continued during the last half of the nineteenth century. New remains of fossil apes from both France (by Gaudry in 1890) and Germany were also described, and discussion continued over the earlier discoveries.

The exploration of the American West yielded an extraordinary wealth of fossils, including prosimian primates, which were described by Joseph Leidy (1823–1891) and the paleontological warlords Edward Drinker Cope (1840–1897) and Othniel Charles Marsh (1831–1899). Turning out volume after volume of descriptions of new animals based on fragmentary remains, these early American workers made copious errors both in assigning new names to every new jaw (thus creating a maze of dozens of invalid names) and in misinterpreting the likely affinities of many taxa, usually because of the fragmentary or misassociated nature of the remains.

Compared with Europe and North America, other parts of the world yielded very little in the way of fossil primates until the turn of the twentieth century. Lund's early discovery in Brazil would be the only fossil New World monkey discovered until the Argentine paleontologist Florentino Ameghino (1854–1911) (*vide infra*) described *Homunculus patagonicus* and several other (probably invalid) taxa from Patagonian Argentina in the 1890s. Likewise, following Falconer and Cautley, the next discovery of a fossil primate from Asia was the description in 1879 by the British paleontologist Richard Lydekker (1849–1915) of a complete maxilla of a fossil ape, which he named *Paleopithecus sivalensis*. *Pithecanthropus erectus* was also discovered and described during this time by the Dutch physician Eugène Dubois (1858–1940), and considered by some, including Dubois, to be a fossil ape. The only fossil primate from Africa in this period was a baboon from Algeria. The last decade of the nineteenth century also saw the first descriptions of

giant subfossil lemurs from Madagascar.

While many accounts of fossil primates from this time were descriptions of new fossils or lists of taxa characteristic of different faunas, a number of issues turned up repeatedly in discussions. One was the endless debate of the primate or "pachyderm" affinities of many fossil prosimians from both Europe and North America that had begun with Cuvier's original identification of *Adapis* as a pachyderm. Were these early discoveries fossil primates or ungulates? Did these two groups of mammals share common ancestry in the Eocene? Fossil anthropoids were not subject to as much debate over identification. The Old World monkeys were relatively simple to allocate; *Pliopithecus* appeared to clearly be a gibbon and was even placed in the genus *Hylobates*; the affinity of *Dryopithecus* was more topical, but by consensus it was a great ape as was Lydekker's *Paleopithecus* (*Sivapithecus*). More debated was the Eppelsheim femur (*Paidopithex*), considered by most nineteenth-century commentators to be a fossil gibbon, despite the lack of any comparable remains of *Pliopithecus*.

Real syntheses of the primate fossil record were rare in the later part of the nineteenth century. Broader works on evolution largely ignored the fossils as being too fragmentary to yield much information about the relationships or origins of modern taxa. A notable exception was the work of the German paleontologist Max Schlosser (1854–1932), whose review of fossil primates in his treatise on fossil mammals (1887) is both thorough and insightful. Unlike the reference works of the previous generation, Schlosser provided revised descriptions of the fossil remains of most taxa, synonymies of the invalid names, and even phylogenetic diagrams that interposed known fossil forms (at that time, eight anthropoid genera) into phylogenies of living genera. Nevertheless, by the end of the century, there were still very few fossil primates to be considered in such a review. It was only in the early decades of the twentieth century that the primate fossil record and interpretations of it began to grow exponentially.

Fig. 4. The first phylogenetic tree of fossil primates and their hypothesized modern descendants, from Schlosser (1887).

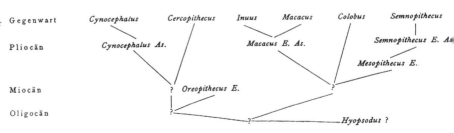

TABLE 1.

New World prosimians	Old World prosimians	Early anthropoids
1990–		
Hesperolemur Gunnell, 1995	*Aframonius* Simons et al., 1995	*Tabelia* Godinot and Mahboubi, 1994
Sphacorhysis Gunnell, 1995	*Wailekia* Ducroq et al., 1995	*Eosimias* Beard, 1994
Wyomomys Gunnell, 1995	*Barnesia* Thalman, 1994	*Omandodon* Gheerbrant et al., 1993
Ageitodendron Gunnell, 1995	*Rencunius* Gingerich et al., 1994	*Shirazodon* Gheerbrank et al., 1993
Tatmanius Bown and Rose, 1991	*Adapoides* Beard et al., 1994	*Algeripithecus* Godinot and Mahboubi, 1992
Yaquius Mason, 1990	*Djebelemur* Hartenberger and Marandat, 1992	*Serapia* Simons, 1992
	Plesiopithecus Simons, 1992	*Arsinoea* Simons, 1992
	Asiomomys Beard and Wang, 1991	*Plesiopithecus* Simons, 1992
	Babakotia Godfrey et al., 1991	
1980–1990		
Jemezius Beard, 1987	*Buxella* Godinot, 1988	*Catopithecus* Simons, 1989
Steinius Bown and Rose, 1984	*Sinoadapis* Wu and Pan, 1985	*Biretia* de Bonis et al., 1988
	Afrotarsius Simons and Bown, 1985	*Qatrania* Simons and Kay, 1983
	Cryptadapis Godinot, 1984	
	Nycticeboides Jacobs, 1981	
	Kohatius Russell and Gingerich, 1980	
1970–1980		
Arapahovius Savage and Waters, 1978	*Sivaladapis* Gingerich and Sahni, 1979	
Copelemur Gingerich and Simons, 1977	*Altanius* Dashzeveg and McKenna, 1977	
Mahgarita Wilson and Szalay, 1976	*Donrussellia* Szalay, 1976	
Mckennamorphus Szalay, 1976	*Cercamonius* Gingerich, 1975	
Pseudotetonius Bown, 1974	*Azibius* Sudre, 1975	
Aycrossia Bown, 1974	*Huerzeleris* Szalay, 1974	
Strigorhysis Bown, 1974	*Microadapis* Szalay, 1974	
Gazinius Bown, 1974	*Agerinia* Crusafont–Pairo and Golpe–Posse, 1973	
1960–1970		
Rooneyia Wilson, 1966	*Komba* Simpson, 1967	*Aegyptopithecus* Simons, 1965
Ekgmowechashala MacDonald, 1963	*Mioeuoticus* Leakey, 1962	*Oligopithecus* Simons, 1962
Tetonoides Gazin, 1962	*Lushius* Chow, 1961	
Cantius Simons, 1962		
1950–1960		
Chlororhysis Gazin, 1958		
Anemorhysis Gazin, 1958		
Ourayia Gazin, 1958		
Utahia Gazin, 1958		
Stockia Gazin, 1958		
1940–1950		
Macrotarsius Clark, 1941	*Pachylemur* Lamberton, 1948	
Loveina Simpson, 1940	*Progalago* MacInnes, 1943	
	Teilhardina Simpson, 1940	
1930–1940		
Dyseolemur Stock, 1934	*Europolemur* Weigelt, 1933	*Amphipithecus* Colbert, 1937
Chumashius Stock, 1933	*Indraloris* Lewis, 1933	
	Hoanghonius Zdansky, 1930	
1920–1930		
		Pondaungia Pilgrim, 1927

New World prosimians	Old World prosimians	Early anthropoids
1910–1920		
Tetonius Matthew, 1915	*Anchomomys* Stehlin, 1916	*Parapithecus* Schlosser, 1910
Absarokius Matthew, 1915	*Periconodon* Stehlin, 1916	*Propliopithecus* Schlosser, 1910
Uintanius Matthew, 1915	*Nannopithex* Stehlin, 1916	
	Pseudoloris Stehlin, 1916	
1900–1910		
Shoshonius Granger, 1910	*Archaeoindris* Standing, 1908	*Apidium* Osborn, 1908
Trogolemur Matthew, 1909	*Mesopropithecus* Standing, 1905	
Smilodectes Wortman, 1903	*Pronycticebus* Grandidier, 1904	
1890–1900		
	Hadropithecus Lorenz, 1899	
	Paleopropithecus Grandidier, 1899	
	Archaeolemur Filhol, 1895	
	Megaladapis Major, 1894	
1880–1889		
1870–1879		
Pelycodus Cope, 1875	*Protoadapis* Lemoine, 1878	
Washakius Leidy, 1873	*Leptadapis* Gervais, 1876	
Anaptomorphus Cope, 1872	*Necrolemur* Filhol, 1873	
Hemiacodon Marsh, 1872		
1860–1870		
Notharctus Leidy, 1870	*Caenopithecus* Rutimeyer, 1862	
Omomys Leidy, 1869		
1850–1860		
	Adapis Cuvier, 1821	
1840–1850		
	Microchoerus Wood, 1846	
1836–1840		

New World monkeys	Old World monkeys	Hominoids
1990–		
Patasola Kay and Meldrum, 1996		*Kamoyapithecus* Leakey et al., 1995
Caipora Cartelle and Hartwig, 1996		*Otavipithecus* Conroy et al., 1992
Antillothrix MacPhee et al., 1995		
Chilecebus Flynn et al., 1995		
Lagonamico Kay, 1994		
Szalatavus Rosenberger et al., 1991		
Laventiana Rosenberger et al., 1991		
Paralouatta Rivero and Arredondo, 1991		
Carlocebus Fleagle, 1990		
1980–1990		
Soriacebus Fleagle et al., 1987	*Microcolobus* Benefit and Pickford, 1986	*Kalepithecus* Harrison, 1988
Mohanamico Luchterhand et al., 1986	*Rhinocolobus* Leakey, 1982	*Lufengpithecus* Wu, 1987
		Simiolus Leakey and Leakey, 1987
Aotus dindensis, Rosenberger		*Nyanzapithecus* Harrison, 1987
and Setoguchi, 1987		*Afropithecus* Leakey and Leakey,
Micodon Setoguchi and Rosenberger, 1985		1986
		Turkanapithecus Leakey and Leakey,
		1986

New World monkeys	Old World monkeys	Hominoids
		Laccopithecus Wu and Pan, 1984
		Platydontopithecus Guand Lin, 1983
		Crouzelia Ginsburg and Mein, 1980
1970–1980		
Tremacebus Hershkovitz, 1974		*Dionysopithecus* Li, 1978
Stirtonia Hershkovitz, 1970		*Micropithecus* Fleagle and Simons, 1978
		Dendropithecus Andrews and Simons, 1977
		Rangwapithecus Andrews, 1977
		Ouranopithecus de Bonis and Melentis, 1977
		Anapithecus Kretzoi, 1975
1960–1970		
Branisella Hoffstetter, 1969	*Paracolobus* R. Leakey, 1969	*Kenyapithecus* L. Leakey, 1962
	Victoriapithecus von Koenigswald, 1969	*Plesiopliopithecus* Zapfe, 1961
	Paradolichopithecus Necrasov et al., 1961	
1950–1960		
Xenothrix Williams and Koopman, 1952		
Cebupithecia Stirton and Savage, 1951		
Neosaimiri Stirton, 1951		
Dolichocebus Kraglievich, 1951		
1940–1950		
	Gorgopithecus Broom and Robinson, 1949	
	Cercopithecoides Mollett, 1947	
1930–1940		
	Dinopithecus Broom, 1937	*Gigantopithecus* von Koenigswald, 1935
	Parapapio Jones, 1937	*Proconsul* Hopwood, 1933
		Limnopithecus Hopwood, 1933
1920–1930		
	Procynocephalus Schlosser, 1924	
1910–1920		
	Prohylobates Fourtau, 1918	*Sivapithecus* Pilgrim, 1910
	Libypithecus Stromer, 1913	
1900–1910		
	Griphopithecus Abel, 1902	
1890–1900		
Homunculus Ameghino, 1891		
1880–1890		
	Dolichopithecus Deperet, 1889	
1870–1880		
		Oreopithecus Gervais, 1872
1860–1870		
1850–1860		
		Dryopithecus Lartet, 1856
1840–1850		
		Pliopithecus Gervais, 1849
1836–1840		
Protopithecus Lund, 1838	*Mesopithecus* Wagner, 1839	

Early Syntheses

The first decades of the twentieth century saw extraordinary new finds from many parts of the world and masterful syntheses of this growing wealth of material (see Table 1). In Asia, the British geologist-paleontologist Guy Ellock Pilgrim (1875–1943) described new remains from Burma and from the Siwaliks, and in later decades additional fossil primates from that region were recovered by Barnum Brown of the American Museum of Natural History in New York City and G. Edward Lewis of Yale University. The fossil apes from India were described and compared with those from Europe in a series of papers by Pilgrim, and the American paleontologists William King Gregory (1876–1970), Milo Hellman (1872–1947), and Lewis. Initially, there was a great proliferation of taxa, with each new specimen assigned to a new species, and considerable debate concerning the relationship of these fossil apes from Asia to the European *Dryopithecus* and their relative affinities to African apes and the Asian orangutan. However, through comprehensive and insightful reviews by Lewis in 1937, and Gregory, Hellman, and Lewis the following year, the number of taxa was reduced considerably, and it was generally agreed that the Siwalik apes formed a closely related group, most of whom showed affinities with the orangutan.

In 1935, the German paleontologist G.H.R. von Koenigswald (1902–1982) described *Gigantopithecus* from the Pleistocene of China, based on isolated teeth purchased in drugstores. Asian prosimians were limited to *Hoanghonius* from China, and *Indraloris* described by Lewis in 1933. The supposed early anthropoid *Pondaungia*, from the Eocene of Burma, described by Pilgrim in 1927, was joined by the aptly named *Amphipithecus*, described by Edwin Colbert in 1937 from the same deposits.

The first important fossil primates of Africa appeared in the early part of the century, when in 1911 Schlosser described the early anthropoids *Parapithecus, Propliopithecus,* and *Moeripithecus* from the Eocene/Oligocene Fayum of Egypt. Later, Miocene primates were described from Wadi Moghara (*Prohylobates*) and Wadi Natrun (*Libypithecus*) (cf. Forteau 1918). In 1933, the British paleontologist Arthur Tindall Hopwood (1897–1969) described the first fossil apes (*Proconsul* and *Limnopithecus*) from Kenya and noted more undescribed finds by Louis S.B. Leakey (1903–1972). In 1916, C.W. Andrews described the first fossil monkey from sub-Saharan Africa, which he called *Simopithecus* (=*Theropithecus*). The well-documented history of the *Australopithecus* discovery (by Raymond A. Dart in 1925) begins here as well; its type specimen was considered by many to be a fossil ape.

The European fossil record was augmented by additional remains of *Dryopithecus* and other fossil apes from Germany and Spain, described by the German paleontologist Othenio Abel (1857–1946) and the British paleontologist Arthur Smith Woodward (1864–1944), respectively; the entire record was reviewed by the German anatomist Adolf Remane (b. 1898) in 1921 and by Abel in 1931. Many fossil prosimians (or supposed prosimians) were described from Europe during the early part of the twentieth century, with major reviews of the European prosimian material by Schlosser in 1907, H.G. Stehlin in 1912, and Abel in 1931.

In North America the fossil record of early prosimians continued to proliferate and was the subject of numerous descriptions and reviews by American paleontologists such as Henry Fairfield Osborn (1857–1935) in the early years of the century, followed by Gregory in 1916, 1920, and 1922 and by Glenn L. Jepsen (1903–1974) and George Gaylord Simpson (1902–1984) in the 1930s. Gregory's monograph on *Notharctus* (1920) remains one of the most complete descriptions of a fossil prosimian ever published, and his reviews of 1916 and 1922 remain definitive summaries of primate evolution as a whole. In his major review of 1940, Simpson summarized the consensus of the time for fossil prosimians from both North America and Europe. Most Eocene taxa could be readily placed in either the adapids, which were related to lemurs, or the anaptomorphids (=omomyids), which were related to tarsiers. The predominantly Paleocene plesiadapids, carpolestids, and apatemyids were more distantly related to other primate groups. From this broad foundation came the later syntheses by Simpson.

Only in South America did paleontological work fail to yield extensive new records of fossil primates (see Table 1). Although Florentino Ameghino described more than a dozen fossil primates from the Tertiary of Argentina, by the early decades of the twentieth century the number of actual primates numbered only half a dozen remains, all placed in a single genus, *Homunculus*, by Swiss anatomist and embryologist Hans Bluntschli (1877–ca. 1946), who reviewed the material in 1931. Other Pleistocene or Recent fossil platyrrhines such as *Protopithecus* from Brazil were either forgotten or dismissed as living forms. Despite the lack of a significant fossil record, the origin of platyrrhines was a much debated issue. While many, such as Gregory, favored an origin from North American adapids, others favored some type of Africa origin.

By the early part of the twentieth century, the record of fossil primates was substantial enough to play an important role in discussions of human evolution. This was also a time in which primate comparative anatomy and embryology were flourishing through the works of several British researchers such as Arthur Keith (1866–1955), Grafton Elliot Smith (1871–1937), Frederic Wood Jones (1879–1954), J.P. Hill (1873–1954), and Wilfrid Edward Le Gros Clark (1895–1971). The great syntheses of the time, such as Gregory's *Origin and Evolution of the Human Dentition* (1922), Abel's *Die Stellung des Menschen im Rahmen der Wirbeltiere* (1931), and Clark's *Early Forerunners of Man* (1934) are impressive works drawing on information from a wide range of sources to put the fossil record in a broad comparative perspective for re-creating overall scenarios of primate evolution. There were primate fossils in considerable numbers from all major continental areas, although the record from Africa was limited and that from Asia was largely limited to northern India. The broad outline of the distribution of fossil primates by time and continental area and their relationships to living families seemed clear. The Paleocene plesiadapids and relatives were odd early offshoots of a basal primate (either lemuroid or tarsioid) stock. The Holarctic Eocene adapids were related to lemurs, and the anaptomorphids to tarsiers. The earliest anthropoids were from the Eocene/Oligocene of Africa, and there were broad radiations of monkeys and apes in the Miocene of Europe and Asia, with a few apes from Africa.

Nevertheless, there were many phylogenetic and biogeographical questions that neither the fossil record nor the evidence from comparative anatomy was adequate to resolve. The contentious issues of 1940 are all too familiar: What is the place of *Tarsius* in primate evolution? Where did higher primates come from? What is the origin of platyrrhines? From which fossil (or living) apes did the hominid lineage arise?

Post–World War II Developments

In the decades since World War II, the study of fossil primates, like most branches of science, expanded dramatically, and the nature of the discipline became strikingly different from that of earlier decades (see Table 1). As in earlier periods, there have been continued new discoveries from all time periods and major continental areas. In addition, the nature of the science has also changed. In the 1960s and 1970s, largely due to the efforts of Elwyn Simons and Louis Leakey, paleoprimatology moved from being a discipline largely concerned with debate over details of jaws and teeth in the rather esoteric ambiance of museum and technical journals, to an area of science whose latest finds are regularly reported in the pages of newspapers and magazines.

In earlier periods, scientists working on primate evolution were usually vertebrate paleontologists, less often anatomists who also worked on the paleontology and comparative anatomy of other groups of mammals. Since the 1960s, the field has become more specialized, with researchers specializing on just primates or, more frequently, just one group of primates or one part of the body. The places where fossil primates are studied have changed as well. In earlier periods, the study of fossil primates was largely confined to major museums and a few universities where there were likely to be collections of fossils and the necessary comparative material. Increasing use of air travel and the advent of epoxy casting during the 1970s greatly increased access to fossil material; consequently, increasing numbers of researchers in this area are found all over the globe.

No single individual has had a greater influence on the development of primate paleontology as we know it today than Elwyn Simons of Yale and Duke Universities. His reviews of the primate fossil record in the early 1960s revived the discipline from the relative doldrums of the 1950s, and they were justifiably authoritative because he was the first scientist in the history of the field to actually see almost all of the original primate fossils then known. He essentially established paleoprimatology as an international discipline and defined the major issues for over two decades. Between 1960 and 1972, he wrote definitive reviews of virtually every major group of primates known from the fossil record, except New World monkeys. In addition, either directly or indirectly, he is responsible for training the vast majority of workers in the field since the 1960s.

Fieldwork and Phylogenies

Conceptually, the study of fossil primates has largely followed the practice and trends in the paleontology of other mammals, despite conventional wisdom otherwise. Research in the 1950s and 1960s was particularly concerned with problems of populations and individual variation, and there was a strong tendency toward lumping of taxa, the most prominent example being Simons and David Pilbeam's revision of fossil apes in 1965. Likewise, the renaissance of functional anatomy in the 1970s and the Hennigian revolution have had a major impact on fossil primate research in recent decades. Despite all of these changes in interpretive focus, it is still true that major breakthroughs in our understanding of primate evolution since the 1950s, as in previous periods, have come predominantly through the recovery of new fossils.

AFRICA. The most striking new discoveries have been the numerous genera and species of fossil monkeys, apes, and prosimians from the Eocene/Oligocene through Pleistocene of Africa (see Table 1). W.E. Le Gros Clark and Louis Leakey initially revised the Miocene hominoids from Kenya and described several new taxa shortly after World War II (cf. Clark & Leakey 1951). Discovery and analysis of fossil apes from East Africa have been continued by the British anatomist John Russell Napier (1917–1987) and others such as Peter Andrews, Richard Leakey, Meave Leakey, Terry Harrison, Martin Pickford, Alan Walker, and Mark Teaford. In the early 1990s, the American paleoprimatologist Glenn Conroy and colleagues discovered the first evidence of Miocene apes from southern Africa. The number of Miocene apes from Africa has increased from *Proconsul* and *Limnopithecus* described by Hopwood in 1933, to over a dozen genera in the mid-1990s. Conceptually, our understanding of evolutionary relationships within this group has gone from a rather naive and static framework in which individual Miocene genera were seen as separately ancestral to individual modern ape genera, to a more complex and bushy phylogeny characterized by a succession of adaptive radiations of increasingly modern taxa through time.

The record of fossil monkeys from Africa has similarly burgeoned since the 1950s (see Table 1). Major reviews of the fossil monkeys of Africa are those of the anatomist Leonard Freedman in the late 1950s and early 1960s, by Simons (1972), and by Simons and primate evolution scholar Eric Delson (1978). The fossil record of lorisids and galagos from the Miocene and Pliocene of Africa has increased slowly over the decades (see Table), with major reviews by Simpson (1967), and Alan Walker (1978).

A gap of fifty years separated Schlosser's initial description of early anthropoids from the Eocene/Oligocene deposits in the Fayum of Egypt and any subsequent new discoveries from this critical time period. A review of this material by J. Kälin in 1961 coincided with Simon's initiation of paleontological work in the Fayum. Continuing for over thirty years, Simons' research has yielded a remarkable record of early anthropoid evolution that continues to grow. The material has been reviewed at frequent intervals by Simons and fellow American students of primate evolution: Richard Kay, John Fleagle, and Tab Rasmussen. Recent expansion of paleontological fieldwork in this time period in northern Africa has resulted in the recovery of other early anthropoid primates.

ASIA. Following the major reviews by Lewis (1937) and Gregory, Hellman, and Lewis (1938), the fossil primate record of Asia saw very little in the way of new fossils for many decades (excepting the discovery of additional remains of *Gigantopithecus* from China in the early 1960s). However, the attention focused on *Ramapithecus* because of its putative hominid status in the 1960s and early 1970s and increased paleontological research in China since the 1970s have led to many new discoveries and analyses of Asian primates. Important recent discoveries include localities in Turkey, India, Pakistan, and China.

Fossil apes from the Siwaliks have been discussed and reviewed by many workers. By the 1980s, new localities in China were producing exciting new remains of Miocene apes, and the Miocene record from that region continues to increase dramatically. The record of fossil monkeys from Asia has received relatively little attention.

SOUTH AMERICA. The explosion in the recovery and study of fossil platyrrhines since the 1950s certainly outpaces that of any other area, if only because the early work was so meager (see Table 1). In the early 1950s, Ruben Stirton (1901–1966) and Donald Savage of the University of California recovered fossil monkeys from Miocene deposits in Colombia (*Cebupithecia, Neosaimiri*). As the names imply, they were interpreted to be quite similar to modern genera. At about the same time, the Argentinian paleontologist Jorge Lucas Kraglievich (1951) described a fossil monkey from Argentina as *Dolichocebus*, and the mammalogists Earnest Williams and Karl Koopman (1952) described a strange fossil monkey from Jamaica.

Following this burst of activity, there was a gap of nearly twenty years until the French mammalogist Robert Hoffstetter (1969) described what is still the earliest known platyrrhine, from the Oligocene of Bolivia (*Branisella*), and the American mammalogist Phillip Hershkovitz's (1970) review of fossil platyrrhines led him to raise some species names to the generic level. Hershkovitz's revision and Lavocat's and Hoffstetter's theory of an African, trans-Atlantic origin of platyrrhines spurred an interest in fossil New World monkeys that continues unabated. Over a dozen new taxa have been or are being described from virtually all time periods from Oligocene through Pleistocene, from southern Argentina to the Caribbean.

EUROPE. Compared with other continents, the fossil record of higher primates in Europe has not increased as dramatically in recent decades, partly because it was relatively well known from the nineteenth century. However, a number of provocative finds have greatly modified views on primate evolution. While *Oreopithecus* had been known for nearly 100 years, it was the spectacular discovery in 1948 of a nearly complete skeleton and its subsequent description and analysis by the Swiss paleontologist Johannes Hürzeler (b. 1908) in the late 1940s and early 1950s that first made this fossil from the Pliocene of Italy a focus of debate (cf. Hürzeler 1949, 1952). While Hürzeler viewed *Oreopithecus* as a European hominid, its exact position in hominoid phylogeny is still not clear despite numerous reviews, by the American anatomist William Straus thirty years ago and more recently by the primate paleontologist Terry Harrison (1986) and others. Likewise, although *Pliopithecus* was among the first fossil primates described in the 1830s, anatomist Helmuth Zapfe's description of several nearly complete skeletons in 1960 made this one of the best-known higher primates and caused considerable debate about its long-standing place as a gibbon ancestor.

More recent discoveries of relatively complete remains of fossil apes from Hungary, Greece, and Spain have brought Europe back in the spotlight for the study of ape evolution.

This is particularly true since phylogenetic studies suggest that the European apes are closer to the human-ape divergence than are either the early Miocene apes from East Africa or the Siwalik apes. Except for the work of Eric Delson, the extensive record of Old World monkey evolution that dominated the fossil record of Europe in the late nineteenth century has received relatively little attention in the twentieth century.

Paleoprimatology: 1975–1995
In addition to the reviews of particular groups, there have been a number of overall reviews of primate evolution. French anatomist Jean Piveteau's volume on primates in the *Traité de Paléontologie* (1957) is an impressive review of the literature through the middle of the twentieth century. Elwyn Simons' *Primate Evolution* (1972) summarizes his views and much of his original research from the previous decade. Fred Szalay and Eric Delson's *Evolutionary History of the Primates* (1979) provides a detailed synopsis of all fossil primate taxa together with synonymies and diagnoses, the scale of which is not likely to be repeated. More-recent general texts include John Fleagle's *Primate Adaptation and Evolution* (1988), Glenn Conroy's *Primate Evolution* (1990), and Robert Martin's *Primate Origins and Evolution* (1990).

While the fossil record certainly still commands tremendous excitement, since the mid-1970s its premier position as the only key to reconstructing evolutionary history has been damped to some degree through two developments. One has been the increased importance of phylogenetic systematics as an analytical tool for reconstructing phylogeny, which has brought about a renewed interest in comparative anatomy.

The second challenge to the role of fossils as the key to primate evolution has come from the development of molecular systematics as a method for reconstructing both phylogenetic relationships and the timetable of evolutionary divergences. For many physical anthropologists, the debate in the late 1960s and early 1970s over whether *Ramapithecus* from the Middle Miocene of northern India was an early hominid or an ape involved molecular phylogeny (which argued for a recent divergence of apes and humans) and paleontology (which argued that *Ramapithecus* was a hominid). Even though the conclusive evidence that brought down *Ramapithecus* as an early hominid was the recovery of new fossils that showed striking similarities to the orangutan, the molecular timetable nevertheless won the battle, and molecular systematics holds a very influential position in studies of phylogeny of all groups of organisms today.

While gains have been made in documenting the fossil record of every major primate group, a matrix of fossil localities by geography and time period would still show a few dense concentrations (Fayum, Wyoming, northern and western Kenya, Siwaliks, La Venta) and a scattering of isolated finds. Some geographic regions, such as the modern tropics, remain unsampled or poorly sampled regardless of the time period. Similarly, some time periods remain poorly sampled in regions that are otherwise abundant with primate fossils, such as the pre-Pleistocene of Madagascar. The binding force of paleontology, the essence of discovery, has not played itself out in the twentieth century, nor is it likely to in the twenty-first.

John Fleagle
Walter C. Hartwig

Authors' Note
The authors thank John Polk for diligent research.

See also Ameghino, Florentino; Argentina; Brazil; Cautley, (Sir) Proby Thomas; Clark, (Sir) Wilfrid Edward Le Gros; Cuvier, Georges Léopold Chrétien Fréderic Dagobert (Baron); Darwin, Charles Robert; Dubois, Eugène; Falconer, Hugh; Filhol, (Antoine-Pierre) Henri; Gaudry, Albert Jean; Gervais, (François-Louis) Paul; Greece; Gregory, William King; Huxley, Thomas Henry; Koenigswald (Gustav Heinrich) Ralph von; Lagoa Santa; Lartet, Édouard (Armand Isidore Hippolyte); Leidy, Joseph; Lyell, (Sir) Charles; Lund, Peter Wilhelm; Molecular Anthropology; Osborn, Henry Fairfield; Owen, (Sir) Richard; Pilgrim, Guy Ellock; *Ramapithecus*; Siwaliks; Smith, (Sir) Grafton Elliot; Systematics (1960s–1990s); Woodward, Arthur (Smith)

Bibliography
O. Abel: *Die Stellung des Menschen in Rahmen der Wirbeltiere.* Jena Fischer, 1931; C.W. Andrews: Note on a new baboon (*Simopithecus oswaldi*) from the Pliocene of British East Africa. *Annual Magazine of Natural History* 18:410–419, 1916; W.E. Baker & H.N. Durand: Sub–Himalayan fossil remains of the Dadoopoor collection. *Journal of the Asiatic Society* 5:739–741, 1836; H. de Blainville: *Ostéographie ou description iconographique comparée du squelette et du systéme dentaires de mammifrères.* Paris: Baillière, 1839; H. Bluntschli: *Homunculus patagonicus* und die ihm zugereihten fossilfunde aus den Santa-Cruz-Schichten Patagoniens. *Gegenbaurs Morphologisches Jahrbuch* 67:811–982, 1931.

P.T. Cautley & H. Falconer: Notice on the remains of a fossil monkey from the Tertiary strata of the Siwalik Hills in the north Hindoostan. *Transactions of the Geological Society of London* 5:499–504, 1837; W.E. Le Gros Clark: *Early forerunners of man.* London: Baillière, 1934; W.E. Le Gros Clark & L.S.B. Leakey: *The Miocene Hominoidea of East Africa. Fossil mammals of Africa.* No.1. London: British Museum (Natural History), 1951; E.H. Colbert: A new primate from the upper Eocene Pondaung Formation of Burma. *American Museum Novitates* 951:1–18, 1937; G.C. Conroy: *Primate evolution.* New York: Norton, 1990; C. Darwin: *On the origin of species by means of natural selection, or the preservation of favoured races in the struggle for life.* London: Murray, 1859.

C. Darwin: *The descent of man and selection in relation to sex.* London: Murray, 1871; H. Falconer & P.C. Cautley: On additional fossil species of the order Quadrumana from the Siwalik Hills. *Journal of the Asiatic Society* 6:354–361, 1838; H. Filhol: Sur un nouveau genre de lémurien fossile, recemment découvert dans les gisements de phosphorite de chaux du Quercy. *Comptes-rendus hebdomadaires des séances de l'Académie des Sciences* 77:111–112, 1873; J.G. Fleagle: *Primate adaptation and evolution.* San Diego: Academic Press, 1988; J.G. Fleagle & W.L. Jungers: Fifty years of higher primate phylogeny. In: F. Spencer (ed) *A history of American physical anthropology, 1930–1980.* New York: Academic Press, 1982, pp. 187–230; R. Forteau: *Contribution à l'étude des vertébrès miocènes de l'Egypte.* Cairo: Survey Department, Ministry of Finance, 1918.

L. Freedman: The fossil Cercopithecoidea of South Africa. *Annals of the Transvaal Museum* (Pretoria) 23:121–262, 1957; P. Gervais: *Zoologie et paléontologie françaises.* 2 vols. Paris: Bertrand, 1849. 2d ed.: 1859; P. Gervais: Sur un singe fossile, d'un espèces non encore décrite, qui a été découverte au monte Bamboli. *Comptes-rendus hebdomadaires des séances de l'Académie des Sciences* 74:1217, 1872; W.K. Gregory: Studies on the evolution of Primates. *Bulletin of the American Museum of Natural*

History 35:239–355, 1916; W.K. Gregory: On the structure and relations of *Notharctus,* an American Eocene primate. *Memoirs of the American Museum of Natural History* 3:49–243, 1920; W.K. Gregory: *Origin and evolution of the human dentition.* Baltimore: Williams & Wilkins, 1922.

W.K. Gregory, M. Hellman, & G.E. Lewis: Fossil anthropoids of the Yale–Cambridge India Expedition of 1935. *Carnegie Institution of Washington Publications* 495:1–27, 1938; T. Harrison: New fossil anthropoids from the Middle Miocene of East Africa and their bearing on the origin of the Oreopithecidae. *American Journal of Physical Anthropology* 71:265–284, 1986; P. Hershkovitz: Notes on Tertiary platyrrhine monkeys and descriptions of a new genus from the late Miocene of Columbia. *Folia Primatologica* 12:1–37, 1970; R.M. Hoffstetter: Un primate de l'Oligocène inférieur sud Américain: *Branisella boliviana* gen. et sp. nov. *Comptes-rendus hebdomadaires des séances de l'Académie des Sciences* 269:434–437, 1969; A.T. Hopwood: Miocene primates from British East Africa. *Journal of the Linnean Society* (Zoology) 38:437–464, 1933.

J. Hürzeler: Neubeschreibung von *Oreopithecus bambolii* Gervais. *Schweizerische paläontologische Abhandlungen* (Basel) 66:1–20, 1949; J. Hürzeler: Contribution à l'étude de la dentition de lait d'*Oreopithecus bambolii* Gervais. *Eclogae geologicae Helvetiae* (Lausanne) 44:404–411, 1952; J. Kälin: Sur les primates de l'Oligocène inférieur d'Egypte. *Annales de Paléontologie* 47:1–48, 1961; G.H.R. von Koenigswald: Eine fossile Säugetier-fauna mit Simia, aus Südchina. *Proceedings, Koninklijke Nederlandsche Akademie van Wetenschappen* 38:872–879, 1935; J.L. Kraglievich: Contribuciones al concimiento de los primates fosiles de la Patagonia. 1. Diagnosis previa de un nuevo primate fosil del Oligoceno superior. Comm. Inst. Nac. Invest. Cien Nat Cien Zool 2:57–81–82, 1951.

E. Lartet: Note sur un grand singe fossile qui de rattache au groupe des singes supérieures. *Comptes-rendus hebdomadaires des séances de l'Académie des Sciences* 43:219–223, 1856; G.E. Lewis: Preliminary notice of a new genus of lemuroid from the Siwaliks. *American Journal of Science* 26:134–138, 1933; G.E. Lewis: Taxonomic syllabus of Siwalik fossil hominids. *American Journal of Science* 31:139–147, 1937; P.W. Lund: Blik

paa Brasiliens dyreverden for sidste jordom-vaeltning. Anden afhandling: Pattedyrene (Lagoa Santa, 16 November 1837). *Det Kongelige Danske Videnskabernes Selskabs naturvidenskabelige og Mathematiske Afhandlinger* 8:61–144, 1838; R. Lydekker: Further notices of Siwalik mammalia. *Records of the Geological Survey of India* 12:35–52, 1879.

R. Owen: Notice sur la découverte, faite en Angleterre, de restes fossiles d'un quadrumane du genre Macaque, dans une formation d'eau douce appartenent au nouveau pliocène. *Comptes-rendus hebdomadaires des séances de l'Académie des Sciences* 21:573–575, 1845; R. Owen: *A history of British fossil mammals and birds.* London: Voorst, 1846; G.E. Pilgrim: A new Sivapithecus palate, and other primate fossils from India. *Memoirs of the Geological Survey of India* (Palaeontology) 14:1–26, 1927; J. Piveteau: Primates. *Traité de paléontologie.* Vol. 7. Paris: Masson et Cie, 1957; A. Remane: Zur Beurteiling der fossilen anthropoiden. *Zentralblatt, Mineralogie, Geologie, und Paläontologie Jahrbuch* 1921:335–339, 1921.

L. Rütimeyer: Eocäene Säugethiere aus dem Gebiet des schweizerischen Jura. *Allgemeine Schweizerische gesellschaft für die gesammten naturwissenschaften neue denkschriften* 19:1–98, 1862; M. Schlosser: Die affen, lemuren, chiropteren, insectivoren, marsupialier, creodonten, und carnivoren des Europaischen Tertiärs un deren beziehungen zu ihren lebenden und fossilen aussereuropaischen verwandten. *Beitrage zur Paläontologie Oesterreich-Ungarns Orients* 6:1–162, 1887; M. Schlosser: Beitrag zue Osteologie und systematischen Stellung der Gattung Necrolemur, sowie sue Stammesgeschichte der Primaten uberhaupt. *Neues Jahrbuch: Mineralogie, Geologie, Paläontologie Festband,* 1907, pp. 197–226.

M. Schlosser: Beitrage zur Kenntniss der Oligozänen Landsägetiere aus dem Fayum, Agypten. *Beitrag sur Paläontologie Oesterreich-Ungarns und Orients* 24:151–167, 1911; E.L. Simons: *Primate evolution.* New York: Macmillan, 1972; E.L. Simons & E. Delson: Cercopithecidae and Parapithecidae. In: V.J. Maglio & H.B.S. Cooke (eds) *Evolution of African mammals.* Cambridge, Massachusetts: Harvard University Press, 1978, pp. 100–119; E.L. Simons & D. Pilbeam: Preliminary revisions of the Dryopithecinae (Pongidae, Anthropoidea).

Folia Primatologica 3:81–152, 1965; G.G. Simpson: Studies on the earliest primates. *Bulletin of the American Museum of Natural History* 77:185–212, 1940.

G.G. Simpson: The Tertiary lorisiform primates of Africa. *Bulletin of the Museum of Comparative Zoology* (Harvard) 136:39–62, 1967; H.G. Stehlin: Die Säugethiere des schweizerischen Eocäens. *Abhandlungen der Schweizerischen Paläontologischen Gesellschaft* 38:1165–1238, 1912; F.S. Szalay & E. Delson: *Evolutionary history of the Primates.* New York: Academic Press, 1979; A. Wagner: Fossile überreste von einem affenschädel und andern Säugethieren aus Griechland. *Gelehrte Anzeigen Bayerische Akademie Wissenschaften* (Munich) 38:301–312, 1839; A. Walker: Prosimian primates. In: V.J. Maglio & H.B.S. Cooke (eds) *Evolution of African mammals.* Cambridge, Massachusetts: Harvard University Press, 1978, pp. 90–99; E.E. Williams & K.E. Koopman: West Indian fossil monkeys. *American Museum Novitates* 1546:1–16, 1952; H. Zapfe: The skeleton of Pliopithecus (*Epipliopithecus vindobonensis*). *American Journal of Physical Anthropology* 16:441–458, 1958.

Editor's Note

The papers listed above are some of the key references and early articles mentioned in the text. Most others can be found in Szalay and Delson (1979) or Fleagle (1988). For additional historical overview, readers might wish to consult Fleagle and Jungers (1982).

Paviland

The Paviland Cave, also known as Goat's Hole, is situated on the rugged Gower Peninsula, 24 km west of Swansea in Glamorganshire, Wales. This site was first excavated by the Oxford geologist William Buckland (1784–1856) between December 1822 and January 1823. During the course of this work, Buckland recovered a partial (extended) human skeleton (Paviland 1). The skull, vertebrae, and most of the right extremities of the skeleton were missing—probably lost through erosion. The remains were covered with red ochre and accompanied by a mammoth skull and tusk, plus a number of bone and ivory artifacts (cf. Fig. 1). Based on these associated artifacts, Buckland assumed, incorrectly, that the remains belonged to a female—hence, the popular name "Red Lady of Paviland." In 1913, William Johnson Sollas (1849–1936), the Oxford geologist and paleontologist, showed that it was, in fact, a male (cf. Sollas 1913). Also during his work at the Paviland Cave in 1912, Sollas recovered the remains of a second individual (Paviland 2), represented by a right metatarsal and left humeral fragment.

Given Buckland's allegiance to the theory of catastrophism, and his understandable caution when it came to interpreting cave deposits (which could be confused by periodic flooding), it is hardly surprising that he was unwilling on this occasion to acknowledge the high antiquity of the "Red Lady of Paviland." Instead of assigning the remains to a probable diluvian age, he endeavored to show that they either predated, or were contemporary with, the Roman occupation of Britain (Buckland

Fig. 1. Buckland's depiction of Paviland Cave (1823). Note the proximity of the human skeleton ("Red Lady") to the remains of a mammoth (E).

1823:88–90). Sollas, however, concluded that the remains dated to the Aurignacian.

In the light of modern dating of the human skeletal remains (ca. 18.5 ky BP) and the bones of associated fauna (ca. 27.5 ky BP) (cf. Oakley 1968), some doubt has been expressed about the contemporaneity of the hominid remains with the archeological artifacts recovered from Paviland (cf. Molleson 1976; Jacobi 1980). Nevertheless, these remains constitute the oldest examples of anatomically modern *Homo sapiens* recovered in the British Isles.

Frank Spencer

See also Buckland, William; Catastrophism; Sollas, William Johnson; United Kingdom

Bibliography
W. Buckland: *Reliquiae diluvianae*. London: Murray, 1823; R.M. Jacobi: The Upper Palaeolithic of Britain with special reference to Wales. In: J.A. Taylor (ed) *Culture and environment in prehistoric Wales*. London: Oxford University Press, 1980, pp. 15–100; T.I. Molleson: Remains of Pleistocene man in Paviland and Pontnewydd Caves, Wales. *Transactions of the British Cave Research Association* 3:112–116, 1976; F.J. North: Paviland Cave, the "Red Lady," the Deluge, and William Buckland. *American Scientist* 5:91–128, 1942; K.P. Oakley: The date of the "Red Lady" of Paviland. *Antiquity* 42:306–307, 1968; W.J. Sollas: Paviland Cave: An Aurignacian station in Wales. *Journal of the Royal Anthropological Institute* 43:337–364, 1913.

Pearl, Raymond (1879–1940)

Born in Farmington, New Hampshire, Pearl graduated in 1899 from Dartmouth College in Hanover, New Hampshire. From there he went to the University of Michigan, where he did graduate work in zoology; in 1902, he received his Ph.D. for a dissertation on the behavior of the flatworm. The most important influence in his development as a biologist was his thesis supervisor, zoologist Herbert Spencer Jennings (1868–1947). After three years of teaching at the University of Michigan, Pearl studied biometric methods with Karl Pearson (1857–1936) in 1905–1906 at the University of London, and, following Pearson's lead, he became an advocate of eugenics and the use of mathematical methods in biology. Pearson's *The Grammar of Science* (1900) had a profound effect on Pearl's views of scientific method and the central place of science in modern society.

On returning to the United States, Pearl worked at the Maine Agricultural Experiment Station from 1907 to 1918, and, as did many other American biologists at that time, he became increasingly interested in Mendelian genetics. In 1910, he was involved in a dispute with Pearson over a Mendelian interpretation of the inheritance of fecundity. Around that time, he also began research on the Danish botanist and geneticist Wilhelm Ludwig Johannsen's (1857–1927) "pure line theory" of inheritance, a line of research aimed at clarification of some of the ambiguous concepts of Mendelian research. Pearl and Jennings, both working on similar research, became the chief advocates of Johannsen's theories in the United States until the mid-1910s (Provine 1971). Pearl's book *Modes of Research in Genetics* (1915) provided a critical study of the then current methods in genetics. In 1916, he was elected to the National Academy of Sciences.

From 1917 to 1919, Pearl was chief of the Statistical Division of Herbert Hoover's Food Administration Program. His experience during World War I reinforced his belief that warfare was caused by the pressure of population on the means of subsistence. The severity of the wartime food shortages in Europe made him aware of the need to compile statistical data on contemporary populations. When he left the Food Administration, he joined the faculty of Johns Hopkins University as professor of biometry and vital statistics in the School of Hygiene and Public Health. Between 1925 and 1930, Pearl directed an Institute for Biological Research, an independent division within the university funded by the Rockefeller Foundation.

As the institute was about to close in 1929, Pearl was considered by Harvard University to direct a new program in human biology being planned there. Because of opposition among certain Harvard faculty, who lacked confidence in Pearl's scientific work, the appointment fell through and Pearl remained at Johns Hopkins. Among the Harvard faculty, his chief supporters in this controversy were the biochemist Lawrence J. Henderson (1878–1942) and the zoologist William Morton Wheeler (1865–1937), both loyal friends. In 1930, following the closing of his institute, Pearl became professor of biology in the School of Hygiene and Public Health—a position he retained until his death in 1940.

During his years at Johns Hopkins, Pearl moved away from genetics into population biology, especially statistical studies of population growth and the causes of human longevity. Many of his studies were published in two journals he founded: the *Quarterly Review of Biology* (1926) and *Human Biology* (1929). He became an enthusiastic advocate of the development of human biology as an interdisciplinary branch of biology (for an overview of human biology, see Cowdry 1930). Pearl was a prolific writer and published many books and articles on population biology and other subjects for a general audience.

Pearl's studies on population growth were controversial, particularly his claim that he had uncovered the law of population growth in the S-shaped curve known as the "logistic curve." At the same time that he developed the field of population studies in the 1920s, he began to criticize the eugenics movement, focusing especially on its class bias (Kevles 1986; Allen 1991). Some of Pearl's criticisms were published in H.L. Mencken's (1880–1956) journal, the *American Mercury* (Pearl 1927). He was one of the first American biologists to openly attack the methods and assumptions of eugenics, and his criticisms, in turn, drew attacks from eugenicists (Paterson & Williamson 1929). His criticisms of eugenics were probably responsible for the breach of friendship between himself and Edward Murray East (1879–1938), a eugenicist and geneticist at Harvard who, until the mid-1920s, had been an enthusiastic supporter of Pearl's work on population growth and the logistic curve.

As part of his advocacy of human biology, Pearl pursued statistical studies on a variety of subjects, in general exploring the causes of human longevity and mortality. His articles dealt with diseases such as tuberculosis, influenza, pneumonia, cancer, and encephalitis. He published a controversial study of alcohol consumption, arguing that moderate consumption did not have deleterious effects on health (Pearl 1926). His work on vital statistics brought him into conflict with Edwin Bidwell Wilson (1879–1964), a Harvard physicist and statistician who was instrumental in blocking Pearl's appointment to the faculty in 1929 (*vide ante*). Pearl (1938) was also one of the first to connect tobacco to cancer and to argue that even small quantities of tobacco were harmful. Pearl was interested also in human reproduction and the effect of contraception in controlling population growth. Initially, he believed that birth control was not responsible for the slowing of the growth rate in human populations, but he later reassessed the data and argued that birth

control was, indeed, an important cause of the decline of the growth rate (Pearl 1934).

Pearl was a larger-than-life figure whose enthusiasms were seen by his colleagues as verging on the propagandistic. Yet, he was also a bold critic of what he saw as humbug in science, especially in the eugenics movement. His wide interests in human biology brought him into contact with leading scientists in a range of disciplines dealing with human behavior, as well as with public figures like Margaret Sanger (1883–1966), a leader in the birth-control movement; and the controversial Baltimore journalist Mencken. This latter friendship was particularly important. As a member of Mencken's inner circle, Pearl developed a reputation as an iconoclast that some of his colleagues viewed with suspicion. Through Pearl, one can examine how human biology developed as a professional field and how biologists, anthropologists, demographers, and other social scientists both cooperated and competed with one another for authority in this field. However, an assessment of Pearl's influence in developing the field of human biology must take into account the negative effects of the several controversies in which he became embroiled.

Pearl died in Hershey, Pennsylvania, on 17 November 1940.

Sharon E. Kingsland

See also Demography; Eugenics; Genetics (Mendelian); Health and Disease

Bibliography
SELECTED WORKS
        For a complete bibliography of Pearl's scientific and popular writings, see H.S. Jennings: Raymond Pearl, 1879–1940. *Biographical Memoirs of the National Academy of Sciences of the USA* 22:296–347, 1942; *Modes of research in genetics*. New York: Macmillan, 1915; *The biology of death: Being a series of lectures delivered at the Lowell Institute in Boston in December 1920*. Philadelphia and London: Lippincott, 1922; *Introduction to medical biometry and statistics*. Philadelphia: Saunders, 1923; *Studies in human biology*. Baltimore: Williams & Wilkins, 1924; *The biology of population growth*. New York: Knopf, 1925; *Alcohol and longevity*. New York: Knopf, 1926; The biology of superiority. *American Mercury* 12:257–266, 1927; Second progress report on a study of family limitation. *Milbank Memorial Fund Quarterly* 12:248–269, 1934; Tobacco smoking and longevity. *Science*

87:216–217, 1938; *The natural history of population*. London: Oxford University Press, 1939.

ARCHIVAL SOURCES

1. (a) R. Pearl Papers, (b) C.B. Davenport Papers: Library, American Philosophical Society, 104 South Fifth Street, Philadelphia, Pennsylvania 19106–3387; 2. A. Hrdlička Papers: National Anthropological Archives, American Museum of Natural History, Smithsonian Institution, Washington, D.C. 20560.

SECONDARY SOURCES

G.E. Allen: Old wine in new bottles: From eugenics to population control in the work of Raymond Pearl. In: K.R. Benson, J. Maineschein & R. Rainger (eds) *The expansion of American biology*. New Brunswick, New Jersey: Rutgers University Press, 1991, pp. 231–261; E.V. Cowdry: *Human biology and racial welfare*. New York: Hoeber, 1930; E. Fee: *Disease and discovery: A history of the Johns Hopkins School of Hygiene and Public Health, 1916–1939*. Baltimore: Johns Hopkins University Press, 1987; D.J. Kevles: *In the name of eugenics: Genetics and the uses of human heredity*. Berkeley: University of California Press, 1986; S.E. Kingsland: *Modeling nature: Episodes in the history of population ecology*. Chicago: University of Chicago Press, 1985; D.G. Paterson & E.G. Williamson: Raymond Pearl on the doctrine of "like produces like." *American Naturalist* 63:265–273, 1929; K. Pearson: *The grammar of science*. 2d ed. London: A. & C. Black, 1900; W.B. Provine: *The origin of theoretical population genetics*. Chicago: University of Chicago, 1971.

Pei Wenzhong (1904–1982)

Chinese paleoanthropologist and archeologist Pei (also known as Pei Wenchung) studied geology at Peking (Beijing) University, from which he graduated in 1927. The following year, he joined the excavation at Zhoukoudian (then known as Choukoutien) under the auspices of the Geological Survey of China (GSC), and in 1929 he found the first complete skull of *Sinanthropus pekinensis* (*Homo erectus*). In 1930, he began a protracted study of the cultural artifacts recovered from Locality 1 at the Zhoukoudian site. Under his leadership, further cultural relics (including evidence of fire) were extracted from the

Upper Cave at Zhoukoudian and from Localities 13 and 15. In addition to these finds, three complete human fossil crania and some postcranial bones were discovered in the Upper Cave.

In 1935, Pei left China for France, where he studied prehistoric archeology under Henri Breuil (1877–1961) in Paris. While there, he also received a doctorate in archeology from the University of Paris in 1937. On returning to Beijing, he continued to work at the GSC. From 1941 to 1945, Pei's research efforts were seriously curtailed as a result of the Japanese occupation, though he did manage during that period to publish a few papers.

With the founding of the People's Republic in 1949, Pei became one of the leading organizers of prehistoric archeology in China. Between 1949 and 1953, he was attached to the Ministry of Culture, where he worked in the Administrative Bureau of Socio-Cultural Affairs, and from 1954 until his death in 1982, he worked in the Institute of Vertebrate Palaeontology and Palaeoanthropology (IVPP), Academia Sinica, in Beijing.

During his tenure at the IVPP, Pei was responsible for directing research at a number of important paleontological sites, many of which produced significant finds. For example, in 1954, Pei began excavating a series of Paleolithic sites in the Dingcun Region, followed by the systematic excavation of the Guanyindong site. On the basis of the stone artifacts recovered from Dingcun and Guanyindong, Pei was able to demonstrate the hitherto unsuspected variety of the Chinese Paleolithic. In addition to these studies, Pei made the first record of Mesolithic artifacts found in China, and he discovered numerous Neolithic sites in northern China. He also made a significant study of the microlithic tradition and the Yangshao culture.

From his study of fossil mammalian fauna, Pei identified several stratigraphic sequences in the Chinese Pleistocene, such as the *Gigantopithecus* section of the Early Pleistocene at Guangxi and the Dingcun section of the early stages of the Upper Pleistocene. Similarly, from the perspective of zoogeographical divisions of Quaternary mammalian faunas, he recognized two regional subdivisions: those of the North China Region and the South China Region. These two regions were separated by a transitional region named Huaihe. This work also involved him in the problem of identifying the boundary between the Tertiary and the Quaternary (as well as Pleistocene chronology) in north China. It was while engaged in the study of Quaternary geology that he observed the solifluction phenomena at Huangshan, near Harbin, and in the Chalainor district, near Manzhouli, Inner Mongolia.

Zhang Senshui

See also China; *Gigantopithecus*; Teilhard de Chardin, Pierre; Zhoukoudian

Bibliography
SELECTED WORKS
An account of the discovery of an adult *Sinanthropus* skull in the Chou Kou Tien deposit. *Bulletin of the Geological Survey of China* 8:203–205, 1929; Notice of the discovery of quartz and other stone artifacts in the Lower Pleistocene hominid-bearing sediments of the Choukoutien cave deposit. *Bulletin of the Geological Survey of China* 11:109–146, 1931; On the Carnivora from Locality 1 of Choukoutien. *Palaeontologia Sinica* (Ser. C)8:1–159, 1934; On a mesolithic (?) industry of the caves of Kwangsi. *Bulletin of the Geological Survey of China* 14:393–412, 1935; Le rôle des phénomènes naturels dans l'eclatement et façonnement des roches dures utilisées par l'homme préhistorique. *Revue de Géographie Physique et de Géologie Dynamique* 9:1–78, 1936.

A preliminary study of a new Palaeolithic station known as Locality 15 within the Choukoutien region. *Bulletin of the Geological Survey of China* 19:147–187, 1939a; The Upper Cave Industry of Choukoutien. *Palaeontologia Sinica* (n.s. D) 9:1–41, 1939b; Archaeological reconnaissance in Kansu Corridor and in Kokonor Region in northwest China. *Contributions from the Institute of Geology* 8:89–117, 1948a; *The study of Chinese prehistory*. Beijing: Commercial Press, 1948b.

Discovery of *Gigantopithecus* mandibles and other material in the Liu-Cheng district of central Kwangsi in south China. *Vertebrata Palasiatica* 1:56–72, 1957a; Discovery of lower jaws on a giant ape in Kwangsi, south China. *Science Record* 1:49–52, 1957b; Observations on the solifluxion phenomena at Huangshan, near Harbin, and in the Chalainor district. *Science Record* 1:61–65, 1957c; The zoogeographical divisions of Quaternary mammalian faunas in China. *Vertebrata Palasiatica* 1:9–24, 1957d.

Excavation of Liuchueng *Gigantopithecus* Cave and exploration of other caves in Kwangsi. *Memoirs of the Institute of Vertebrate Palaeontology and Palaeoanthropology* 7:1–54, 1965; (with D. Black, P. Teilhard de Chardin, & C.C. Young [Yang Zhongjian]) Fossil man in China: The Choukoutien cave deposits with a synopsis of our present knowledge. *Memoirs of the Geological Survey of China* (Ser. A)11:1–166, 1933; (with Woo Ju-kang [Wu Rukang] et al.) Report on the excavation of palaeolithic sites at Tingtsun, Hsiangfenshsien, Shansi Province, China. *Memoirs of the Institute of Vertebrate Palaeontology, Academia Sinica* 2:1–111, 1958; (with P. Teilhard de Chardin) The lithic industry of the *Sinanthropus* deposits in Choukoutien. *Bulletin of the Geological Survey of China* 11:317–358, 1932.

SECONDARY SOURCES
IVPP: Obituary notice of Pei Wenzhong. *Acta Anthropologia Sinica* 1(2):1–2, 1982.

Pennant, Thomas (1726–1798)

Born in Downing, Flintshire, England, Pennant matriculated at Queen's College, Oxford, in 1744 but did not go on to take a degree. It was while at Oxford that Pennant became interested in natural history, which prompted a series of excursions throughout the British Isles and subsequently to the Continent. In addition to becoming a popular writer of travel books, Pennant also wrote a number of influential books on natural history. He also maintained a lively correspondence with many of the leading naturalists of his day. Among his most notable correspondents were Carolus Linnaeus (1707–1778), Georges Louis Leclerc Buffon (1707–1788), and Peter Pallas (1741–1811).

In 1761, he began the work for which he is perhaps best remembered, *British Zoology.* First published in 1766, this treatise was subsequently expanded in new editions between 1768 and 1812. Of particular interest to anthropology, however, is his *History of Quadrupeds* (1781), which is an enlarged version of his *Synopsis of Quadrupeds* published in 1771. As this work reveals, Pennant endorsed the "greater division of animals into hoofed and digitated," proposed by the naturalist John Ray (1627–1705), but strongly opposed the Linnean classification. "My vanity," he wrote,"will not suffer me to rank mankind with apes, monkeys, maucaucos, and bats, the companions Linnaeus has allotted us. . . ," (Pennant 1771:v). Thus, excluding *Homo sapiens*, Pennant classified the nonhuman primates as "Digitated Quadrupeds," whom, he contended, approached the human form with regard to the use of "their feet, which serve the uses of hands in eating, climbing, or carrying; to the flatness of the nails, in many species; and to some, resemblance of their actions, resulting from the structure of their parts only [and] not from any superior sagacity to that of most others of the brute creation" (Pennant 1771:178–226). Pennant did, however, share Linnaeus' views on the immutability of species.

In many respects, Pennant's work assisted in setting the stage for Johann Friedrich Blumenbach's (1752–1840) reclassification of the human species at the close of the eighteenth century.

Pennant died at Downing on 16 December 1798.

Frank Spencer

See also Blumenbach, Johann Friedrich; Buffon, (Comte) Georges-Louis Leclerc; Linnaeus, Carolus

Bibliography
SELECTED WORKS
British zoology, Class I: Quadrupeds, {Class} II: Birds. Published under the inspection of the Cymmrodorion Society. London: March, 1766. 2d ed. 4 vols. London: White, 1768–1770, 3d ed. 4 vols. London: White, 1776–1777, 4th ed. 4 vols. London: Wilkse & Robinson, 1812; *Indian Zoology.* London: Hughes, 1769; *Synopsis of quadrupeds.* Chester: Monk, 1771; *History of quadrupeds.* 2 vols. London: White, 1781; *Arctic zoology.* 2 vols. London: Hughes, 1784; *Of the patagonians.* Darlington: Allen, 1788; *The literary life of the late Thomas Pennant. By himself.* London: White & Faulder, 1793; *Outlines of the globe.* 4 vols. London: Hughes, 1798–1800.

ARCHIVAL SOURCES
1. T. Pennant Papers: Department of Manuscripts and Records, National Library of Wales, Aberywstwyth, Wales; 2. T. Pennant Papers: British Library, Reference Division, Department of Manuscripts, Great Russell Street, London WC1B 3DG, England; 3. T. Pennant Correspondence: Archives, University of Manchester, John Rylands University Library, Oxford Road, Manchester M13 9PP, England.

SECONDARY SOURCES
G. Cuvier: Thomas Pennant, *Biographie universelle.* Paris, 1823. Vol. 33, pp. 315–318; W. Wroth: Thomas Pennant. *Dictionary of National Biography* 49:320–323, 1895.

Pennsylvania, University of

The study of anthropology began at the University of Pennsylvania (UP) with the appointment of Daniel Garrison Brinton (1837–1899) as professor of archeology and linguistics in 1886 and the founding of the University Museum of Archaeology and Anthropology in 1887. The appointment of Frank Speck (1881–1950) in 1908 marked the beginning of the academic Department of Anthropology at UP. Although Speck, a former student of Franz Boas (1858–1942), was primarily a cultural anthropologist, he included instruction in physical anthropology. In 1915, Earnest William Hawkes was awarded, for his dissertation on Eskimo crania, the first doctorate in physical anthropology at the UP—but it was not until after World War II, when the department was reorganized and experienced a vigorous growth in all areas of the discipline, that physical anthropology became established as such.

In 1946, Wilton Marion Krogman (1903–1987) was appointed professor of physical anthropology in the Graduate School of Medicine. Soon thereafter, he established the Philadelphia Center for Research in Child Growth at Children's Hospital with a major program in longitudinal research to establish norms of skeletal growth. In 1947, Loren C. Eiseley (1907–1977) was appointed chair of the reorganized department, adding instruction in human evolution and human paleontology. A year later, Carleton S. Coon (1904–1981) was appointed curator of general anthropology in the University Museum and offered instruction in race and evolution. Coon and Krogman both had secondary appointments in the department's faculty.

Doctoral degrees in the history of evolutionary theory were awarded to Jacob Gruber in 1952 and Gerald Henderson in 1958. Doctorates in physical and biomedical anthropology soon followed in increasing numbers: Daris Swindler earned the first such degree in 1959, and by 1992 the number had reached forty-five.

The number of physical and medical anthropologists and the range of their research interests began to grow with the appointment in the department of Francis Johnston (biomedical anthropology) in 1962, followed by Alan Mann (human paleontology) in 1969,

Robert Harding (primate behavior) in 1973, and Rebecca Huss-Ashmore (biomedical and nutritional anthropology) in 1984. The program at UP was further supplemented by faculty from other schools and departments within the university, including the Nobel laureate Baruch Blumberg (biomedical anthropology), Solomon Katz (biomedical anthropology), Dorothy Cheney (primate behavior), Michael Zimmerman (paleopathology), Setha Lowe (medical anthropology), Robert Seyfarth (primate behavior), and Morrie Kricun (paleopathology and skeletal biology)—which more than offset in number the death of Eiseley in 1977 and the retirement of Coon in 1963 and Krogman in 1971. In 1992, Phillip V. Tobias (human paleontology) of the University of Witwatersrand, Johannesburg, South Africa, joined the faculty with a visiting appointment to teach in the fall term for three years.

The Philadelphia Center for Research in Child Growth, with Krogman as director and Johnston (from 1962 to 1968) as associate director, in collaboration with the Department of Anthropology, received a grant from the National Institute of Dental Research for a Ph.D. Training Program in Physical Anthropology. The first two students, Robert Malina and Solomon Katz, were admitted in 1963, and the last of three Ph.D.'s funded by the program was received by Ted Rothstein in 1971. Three other students under separate funding (Robert Biggerstaff, Elizabeth Watts, and Keith Herzog) also received doctorates in association with this program. This degree was in "physical anthropology" rather than "anthropology," the trainees being expected to receive broad anthropological training without being formally examined in archeology and cultural anthropology, as was required of other graduate students in anthropology. It was explicitly aimed at broadening the scope of dental researchers and attracting people to dental research who had been trained in basic science. The program significantly increased the visibility of UP's Anthropology Department among biomedical scientists. Since Krogman's retirement, the center, renamed the Krogman Center for Research in Child Growth and Development and thereafter directly associated with the University of Pennsylvania, has continued under the direction of Solomon Katz.

Recognizing that many topics for research involve more than one subdiscipline of anthropology, it is departmental policy to require of its doctoral students a broad train-

ing in the several subdisciplines of anthropology. In this way, the department has sought to develop an awareness in students of the contributions other subdisciplines can make to their research and to encourage them to get the necessary training in other disciplines in order to do justice to their research. This policy has produced dissertation projects that have combined research in osteology and archeology, blood serology and ethnography, blood pressure and ethnography, and medical anthropology and ethnography, among others. Dissertation committees have frequently included archeologists and cultural anthropologists together with physical anthropologists.

After the death of Frank O. Barlow (1880–1951) of the Natural History Museum—formerly the British Museum (Natural History)—in London, Loren Eiseley helped negotiate the acquisition of Barlow's master casts of fossil hominids through the Wenner-Gren Foundation for Anthropological Research in 1952. The Casting Department of the University Museum held the Barlow molds as the foundation's agent from 1952 to 1964. They were then returned to the Wenner-Gren Foundation, which built a larger collection of about 1,500 molds and operated its own casting program from 1962 to 1976. As this program was phased out by the foundation, Alan Mann began a casting program in UP's Anthropology Department, and the department acquired from the Wenner-Gren Foundation all of its molds, including the Barlow molds. Under grants from the National Science Foundation, Mann added more molds (now over 3,000) and made epoxy replicas of them. The casting program, under the management of Janet Monge, keeper of physical anthropology in the University Museum, has developed methods for producing the most accurate replicas possible and has made them available at cost or exchange to anthropology departments and museums worldwide. The money generated from the casting program has provided support for students and travel expenses for people from other countries to learn molding and to attend conferences. It has also underwritten many colloquia in physical anthropology.

In addition to the foregoing activities, research was being actively conducted as of 1994 in biomedical anthropology in Central America, Africa, and Papua New Guinea, in primate behavior in Venezuela and Africa, in human paleontology in Africa, and in physical growth and development in Philadelphia.

Ward H. Goodenough

See also Boas, Franz; Brinton, Daniel Garrison; Child-Growth Studies; Coon, Carleton S(tevens); Eiseley, Loren C(orey); Krogman, Wilton Marion; United States of America

Bibliography
R. Darnell: *The development of American anthropology, 1879–1920: From the Bureau of American Ethnology to Franz Boas.* Ph.D. Thesis. University of Pennsylvania, 1969; R. Darnell: The emergence of academic anthropology at the University of Pennsylvania. *Journal of the History of the Behavioral Sciences* 6:80–92, 1970.

Phrenology

Phrenology was a doctrine that paralleled, fostered, and in some ways caricatured the rise of hereditarianism in nineteenth-century anthropology. Phrenologists believed the brain to be the material instrument of the mind, comprised of numerous regions with specialized cerebral functions thought to determine the mental characteristics of individuals and groups. They also believed that these regions could be measured on the outside of the skull. Some phrenologists devised whole moral systems based on the configuration of bumps on people's heads.

Phrenology was developed by the German physicians Franz Gall (1738–1828) and Joseph Spurzheim (1776–1832), and the Scottish lawyer George Combe (1788–1858). While studying medicine in Strasbourg, Gall observed that students with outstanding memories were not necessarily of exceptional overall intelligence, but they had heads of the same shape. He went on to observe that other special talents and dispositions were associated with particular head shapes, visiting schools, prisons, and insane asylums to measure the correlations. When he performed dissections, he discovered that the shape of the brain conformed to the external shape of the head, and this led him to the theory of the localization of cerebral function.

Gall invented "cranioscopy" to embody and illustrate his findings. He argued that inborn mental functions depend on cerebral structures and that the brain comprises numerous "organs" impressed on the interior surface of the skull and measurable on the outside. For example, the "organ of Destructiveness" appeared large on the head of a medical student who enjoyed torturing animals; the "organ of Love of Approbation" appeared large on the head of a lunatic who thought she was the Queen of France; and the "organ of Adhesiveness" appeared enlarged on the head of an acquaintance whom Gall considered to be a model friend. Each organ was identified in this way and then illustrated by more cases in which personality and head shape matched. Once the system was established, cranioscopists began to diagnose personality on the basis of external examination of the head. (One diagnostic scheme appears in Fig. 1.)

Because cranioscopy was materialistic, it was opposed by religious leaders. Facing religious opposition, Gall began to lecture in Vienna, where in 1804 he was joined by Spurzheim, also trained in medicine. With religious opposition intensifying, Gall and Spurzheim left Vienna to tour Europe, and they eventually settled in Paris, where Gall established a lucrative medical practice. He continued to lecture and write about cranioscopy and published his major work, *Anatomie et Physiologie du Système Nerveaux en Générale et du Cerveau en Particulière* (1810). Spurzheim helped him write the book, then left Paris to popularize "phrenology," a term he introduced as a substitute for cranioscopy.

In Edinburgh, one of Spurzheim's lectures was attended by Combe. Initially skeptical, Combe converted to phrenology and soon became its most prominent promoter. Under his leadership, local societies and journals sprang up, and literati, social reformers, and medical men joined the movement.

The heyday of phrenology was in the 1820s and 1830s. Then, in the 1840s, the movement began to decline. Religious opposition was now joined by increasing scientific criticism. Phrenologists grew smug and insufficiently self-critical. They quarreled about materialism, with the result that orthodox Christians deserted the movement while others tried to make its materialism more extreme. "Serious" phrenologists suffered from the reputation of popularizers who linked phrenology to mesmerism, animal magnetism, and other spiritualist phenomena. When Gall, Spurzheim, and Combe died, no new generation of leaders took their place.

At the time phrenology was most popular, anthropologists were engaged in a vigorous debate about the origin of races. Monogenists believed that human races were derived from a recent common source, while polygenists believed that the human races were distinct species with ancient separate origins. Numerous scholars (Bowles 1974; Comas 1960; Davis 1971; Erickson 1977, 1979; Harris 1968; Hoyme 1953; Kottler 1974; Reigel 1930; Shapiro 1959; Sheldon 1963; Stanton 1960; Tether 1970; Topinard 1885; Warren 1921) have established a link between phrenology and polygenism, then on the rise. Phrenologists and polygenists shared a hereditarian outlook, a belief in a fixed hierarchy of race and class, as well as a preoccupation with skulls.

Besides these parallels, there were tangible connections between phrenology and anthropology. The constituency of phrenology included a sizable minority of medical men with anthropological interests. One-fourth to one-half of the members of the most respectable phrenological societies were physicians and surgeons, and so were one-third of the authors of phrenological publications. Like anthropologists, phrenologists collected skulls, which they displayed in museums and reproduced for sale. The largest collections were in London, Edinburgh, and Paris. One London collection boasted 1,400 specimens, including 500 crania of "different nations." To phrenologists and polygenists alike, these

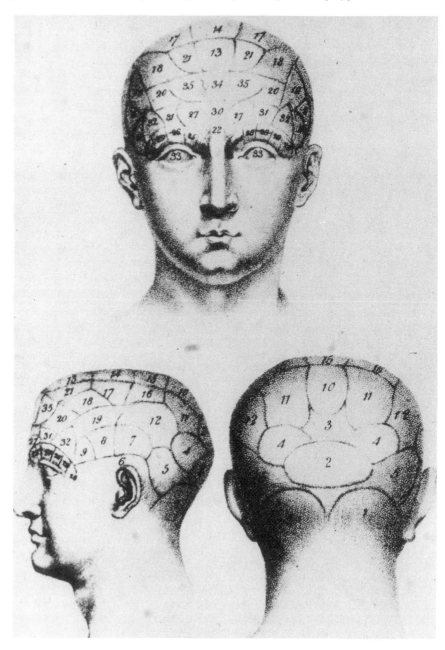

Fig. 1. Phrenological map. From Spurzheim's Précis de Phrénologie (1825).

Fig. 2. "The Phrenologist," an early 19th-century French caricature.

skulls showed that natural character and crania correspond (Erickson 1977, 1979).

Polygenists' support for phrenology was broad but not always deep. The American craniologist Samuel George Morton (1799–1851) asked Combe to study his large collection of American Indian crania and published phrenological data in his book *Crania Americana* (1839). Morton agreed that there was a correspondence between mental and craniological characteristics of Indians, but he rejected phrenology's more exaggerated claims. After Morton's time, the influence of phrenology on anthropology began to fade, leaving behind traces in books such as *Indigenous Races of the Earth* (Nott & Gliddon 1857) and *Crania Britannica* (Davis & Thurnam 1865).

Phrenology's enduring legacy to anthropology was the tenet that the human brain is the material instrument of the mind. Without this tenet, anthropologists had little reason to study skulls as much as they did. The corollary that differently shaped brains correspond to differently shaped skulls and differ-ent mental traits was eventually rejected, beginning in the late nineteenth century. Until then, phrenology and anthropology shared the same hereditarian tradition, the former being a caricature of the latter.

Paul A. Erickson

See also Broca, Paul (Pierre); Combe, George; Flourens, (Marie Jean) Pierre; Morton, Samuel George; Neuroanatomy, Comparative

Bibliography
PRIMARY SOURCES

J.B. Davis & J. Thurnam: *Crania Britannica: Delineations and descriptions of the skulls of the Aboriginal and early inhabitants of the British Islands, with notes of their other remains.* 2 vols. London: printed for subscribers, 1865; J.F. Gall: *Anatomie et physiologie du Système nerveaux en générale, et du cerveau en particulière avec des observations sur la possibilité de reconnoitre plusiers dispositions intellectuelles et morales de l'homme et des animaux par la configuration de leurs têtes.* 4 vols. Paris: Schoell, 1810; S.G.

Morton: *Crania Americana; or, A comparative view of the skulls of various Aboriginal nations of North and South America*. Philadelphia: Dobson, 1839; J.C. Nott & G.R. Gliddon: *Indigenous races of the Earth; or, New chapters in ethnological inquiry*. London: Trubner, 1857.

SECONDARY SOURCES

F.B. Bowles: Measurement and instrumentation in physical anthropology. *Yearbook of Physical Anthropology* 18:174–190, 1974; J. Comas: *Manual of physical anthropology*. Springfield, Illinois: Thomas, 1960; J.D. Davis: *Phrenology: Fad and science*. London: Archon, 1971; P.A. Erickson: Phrenology and physical anthropology: The George Combe connection. *Current Anthropology* 18:92–93, 1977; P.A. Erickson: *Phrenology and physical anthropology: The George Combe connection*. Occasional Papers in Anthropology. No. 6. Halifax: Department of Anthropology, Saint Mary's University, 1979; M. Harris: *The rise of anthropological theory: A history of theories of culture*. New York: Crowell, 1968; L. St. Hoyme: Physical anthropology and its instruments: A historical study. *Southwestern Journal of Anthropology* 9:408–430, 1953.

M.J. Kottler: Alfred Russel Wallace, the origin of man, and spiritualism. *Isis* 65:145–192, 1974; R.E. Reigel: Early phrenology in the United States. *Medical Life* 37:361–376, 1930; H.L. Shapiro: The history and development of physical anthropology. *American Anthropologist* 61:371–379, 1959; W.H. Sheldon: *The varieties of human physique*. New York: Hafner, 1963; W. Stanton: *The leopard's spots: Scientific attitudes toward race in America, 1815–1859*. Chicago: University of Chicago Press, 1960; J.E. Tether: Brain. *Encyclopedia Americana* 4:419–432, 1970; P. Topinard: *Elements d'anthropologie générale*. Paris: Delhaye et Lecrosnier, 1885; J.C. Warren: The collection of the Boston Phrenological Society: A retrospect. *Annals of Medical History* 3:1–11, 1921.

Pilgrim, Guy Ellock (1875–1943)

Born in Upton, near Didcot, Berkshire, England, Pilgrim was educated at Harrison College, Barbados, before entering University College, London, in 1894; he received his B.Sc. in 1901 and his D.Sc. in 1908. From 1902 to 1930, Pilgrim worked for the Geological Survey of India (GSI). After his retirement from the GSI, he returned to his birthplace; until his death, he was a member of the supernumerary staff of the Department of Geology, British Museum (Natural History), now the Natural History Museum.

During his tenure with the GSI, Pilgrim functioned as both a geologist and a vertebrate paleontologist. In the former capacity, he was responsible for several important stratigraphical surveys in the Persian Gulf, the Siwaliks, and other Tertiary and Quaternary deposits in northwestern India and the Simla Hills. Of particular interest is his work on the Siwalik Formation, which prior to his time had been divided simply into a lower (unfossiliferous) and an upper (fossiliferous) section. Pilgrim subsequently showed that there are three separate fossiliferous divisions to the Siwaliks, each characterized by a distinct suite of vertebrate fossils (cf. Pilgrim 1910), which he endeavored to correlate with equivalent strata in Europe (Pilgrim 1913, 1944). Having defined the faunal sequences characterizing the Siwalik Formation, Pilgrim's efforts shifted to the study of the fossil collections he had made. The result of this work was a steady stream of publications that include a series of major monographs on the fossil Giraffidae, Suidae (1926), Carnivora (1932), and Primates (1915, 1927) of India. Among the latter, Pilgrim (1915) identified two Miocene apes: *Dryopithecus punjabicus* and *Sivapithecus indicus*. In his evaluation of these fossils, he conjectured that the former was an Asian relative of the European dryopithecines and that it was more closely related to the hominoid apes, while the latter was a possible progenitor of Eugène Dubois' (1858–1940) *Pithecanthropus erectus* (now *Homo erectus*). Like most of his contemporaries, however, Pilgrim rejected the idea of the Javan form being on the main line of human evolution. Later, G. Edward Lewis (1937) of Yale University lumped these fossils into the genus *Ramapithecus*.

The pioneering efforts of Pilgrim (and Lewis in the 1930s) in the Siwaliks were later extended by David Pilbeam of Yale, who in the early 1970s began his protracted study of this region in collaboration with the Geological Survey of Pakistan.

Frank Spencer

See also Dubois, (Marie) Eugène (François Thomas); Falconer, Hugh; Gregory, William King; *Homo erectus*; Paleoprimatology; *Ramapithecus*; Siwaliks

Bibliography
SELECTED WORKS
The geology of the Persian Gulf and

the adjoining portions of Persia and Arabia. *Memoirs of the Geological Survey of India* 34:1–177, 1908; Notices of new mammalian genera and species from the Tertiaries of India. *Records of the Geological Survey of India* 40:63–71, 1910; The correlation of the Siwaliks with the mammalian horizons of Europe. *Records of the Geological Survey of India* 43:264–326, 1913; New Siwalik primates and their bearing on the question of the evolution of man and the Anthropoidea. *Records of the Geological Survey of India* 45:1–74, 1915.

The fossil Suidae of India. *Palaeontologia Indica* 13:1–65, 1926; A *Sivapithecus* palate and other primate fossils from India. *Palaeontologia Indica* 14:1–24, 1927; The fossil Carnivora of India. *Palaeontologia Indica* 18:1–232, 1932; The fossil Bovidae of India. *Palaeontologia Indica* 26:1–356, 1939; The application of the European time scale to the Upper Tertiary of North America. *Geological Magazine* (London) 77:1–27, 1940; The lower limit of the Pleistocene in Europe and Asia. *Geological Magazine* (London) 81:28–38, 1944.

ARCHIVAL SOURCES

Some of Pilgrim's Manuscripts and Notes are located in the archives of the Natural History Museum, Cromwell Road, London SW7 5BD, England.

PRIMARY AND SECONDARY SOURCES

L.L. Fermor, C. Forster-Cooper, & A.T. Hopwood: Guy Ellock Pilgrim, 1875–1943. *Obituary Notices of Fellows of the Royal Society* 4:577–590, 1944; G.E. Lewis: Taxonomic syllabus of Siwalik fossil anthropoids. *American Journal of Science* 31 (ser. 5):139–147, 1937.

Piltdown

The so-called Piltdown skull and associated remains that were reportedly recovered from a gravel deposit in East Sussex, England, between 1912 and 1915 constitute one of the most famous forgeries in the history of science. During the forty years that this forgery went undetected, these bogus finds created considerable confusion. In particular, the Piltdown skull provided support for the preeminence of the brain in human evolution and advancement of the pre-sapiens hypothesis and thereby, among other things, delayed acceptance of the South African australopithecines as valid early hominids.

Recovered from a gravel deposit located on a small plateau near Piltdown Common in the parish of Fletching in East Sussex (see Fig. 1), the Piltdown skull was unveiled before a meeting of the Geological Society of London, at Burlington House on 18 December 1912, by the principal discoverers, Charles Dawson (1846–1916), a Sussex solicitor and amateur geologist, and Arthur Smith Woodward (1864–1944), keeper of paleontology at the Natural History Museum, South Kensington, London. According to the story Dawson recounted to the Geological Society (cf. Spencer 1990a, 1990b), his interest had been aroused when he found (ca. 1910) a fragment of a human cranium that had been tossed up by laborers excavating a gravel deposit (for road metal) located on the estate of Barkham Manor, of which he was steward. Following this, Dawson reported that in 1911 he discovered another, larger fragment of the same skull, and that, impressed by its general thickness, he took the fragments to Woodward. Excited by what he was shown, Woodward agreed to assist Dawson in the excavation of the site.

During the summer of 1912, Dawson and Woodward, assisted occasionally by a few trusted associates, such as the French paleontologist Pierre Teilhard de Chardin (1881–1955), conducted a systematic search for further remains. Their labors yielded a further seven fragments of the skull, which when fitted together made up the greater part of the left side and a portion of the right mid section of a thick, but essentially modern-looking, human braincase (see Fig. 2). They also found the (incomplete) right half of a seemingly apelike jaw with two molar teeth (with worn crowns), plus an assortment of fossil animal bones and "eoliths" (supposed primitive stone tools). The stratigraphical circumstances in which many of these remains reportedly had been found supported Woodward's subsequent argument of association and his unwavering conviction that the braincase and the jaw belonged together.

Although in retrospect the welding of these two specimens created a bizarre amalgam, at the time it was viewed as a perfectly acceptable form, and one that met all of the then current theoretical expectations of what an early human ancestor would look like. To accomodate this creature (see Fig. 2), Woodward created a new genus and species, *Eoanthropus dawsoni* ("Dawson's Dawn Man").

In accordance with the notion that the Piltdown skull represented an early hominid,

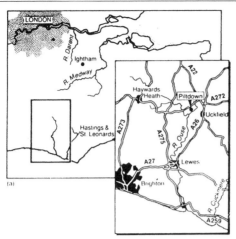 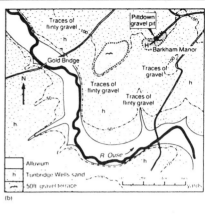

Woodward assigned to his reconstruction a relatively small cranial capacity of 1070 cm³. Likewise, the neuroanatomist Grafton Elliot Smith (1871–1937), from his examination of the endocranial cast, found evidence for declaring it "the most primitive and most simian human brain so far recorded" (cf. Smith, in Dawson & Woodward 1913:147). But because the skull had been broken in such a way as to preclude a definitive reconstruction, the anatomist-anthropologist Arthur Keith (1866–1955) of the Royal College of Surgeons, was able to argue for an alternative assembly (see Fig. 3) and to raise the cranial capacity of *Eoanthropus* upward to around 1400 cm³ and thereby to promote his particular version of the pre-sapiens theory of human evolution. Although Woodward's general reconstruction was subsequently "vindicated" by Teilhard's fortuitous find of a canine tooth in 1913, this did not prevent Keith from continuing to advocate his reconstruction (cf. Keith 1915, 1925).

In the meantime, resistance was building against the monistic interpretation of the Piltdown remains. Except for the passing remark made by the American paleontologist William King Gregory (1876–1970) that the remains "might represent a deliberate hoax" (1914:190–191), no one seemed to have questioned their validity. Most critics appeared to favor the view promoted by Gerrit S. Miller (1869–1956) (1915), then curator of mammals at the National Museum of Natural History in Washington, D.C., that the jaw was that of a fossil ape, which, by chance, had become associated with an ancient human cranium in the gravel deposit at Piltdown. This and similar arguments, however, were dismissed by Woodward and his supporters as most improbable, particularly given the fact

that no fossil apes later than the Early Pliocene had been found in England or Europe.

In 1917, the dualistic movement suffered a further setback when Woodward announced, shortly after the death of Dawson, the discovery of Piltdown II. These remains, consisting of two cranial fragments and a molar tooth (plus a fragment of a fossil rhinoceros molar), had reportedly been found by Dawson in 1915 in a field situated in Sheffield Park, near Piltdown. It is interesting to note that the exact location of this second site was never discovered, despite considerable efforts by Woodward and later by others.

Although the years between the two World Wars witnessed the discovery in South Africa of fossil hominid remains that seriously challenged the Piltdown synthesis, it was not until the late 1940s and early 1950s that the significance of these new finds began to be generally appreciated. Meanwhile, the failure to recover further evidence in England or elsewhere in Europe of fossils that remotely resembled *Eoanthropus*, compounded with the discovery in 1936 of the (morphologically different) Swanscombe skull in geological circumstances akin to those at Piltdown, served to revive interest in the dualist argument (which continued to be circular and nonproductive).

In 1948, Kenneth Page Oakley (1911–1981) of the Natural History Museum, applied the newly developed fluorine-dating technique to a comparative study of the Swanscombe and the contentious Galley Hill remains—both of which had been reportedly found in similar geological circumstances. Furthermore, the Galley Hill specimen had long been used by Keith and others to support the pre-sapiens hypothesis. The results of the fluorine tests showed unequivocally that

Galley Hill, unlike Swanscombe, was a comparatively recent specimen. Bolstered by this success, Oakley extended the fluorine tests to the Piltdown skull in an effort to resolve the dualist-monist debate, but contrary to expectations, these tests were inconclusive (Oakley & Hoskins 1950). It was not until 1953, when Joseph Sidney Weiner (1915–1982), then a reader in physical anthropology at Oxford University, presented a case for the Piltdown jaw being a forgery (cf. Weiner 1955:47; Spencer 1990b:196–197) that this issue was finally resolved.

From all accounts, while attending a Wenner-Gren Foundation conference in London in the early summer of 1953, Weiner had an opportunity to view the celebrated remains and was astounded by the conflicting opinions the specimen elicited from other conferees. On returning to Oxford, he continued to ruminate on the issue and the enigmatic jaw in particular. Divorcing the jaw from the braincase, in Weiner's mind, created another problem: Why, if it in fact belonged to an ape, did its dentition not match any known living or fossil ape? It was along this line of reasoning that Weiner ultimately entertained the prospect that the jaw had been deliberately remodeled. His subsequent experiments on chimpanzee molars revealed how relatively easy it was to file and stain these teeth to approximate those of Piltdown. Later that summer, armed with this experimental evidence, Weiner took his forgery hypothesis to his boss, Wilfrid Edward Le Gros Clark (1895–1971), who in turn relayed it to Oakley in London, who agreed that the Piltdown remains should be retested using a more sensitive fluorine methodology (cf. Harrison 1983). The results of this new test revealed that the cranium and the jaw contained significantly different amounts of fluorine and other elements—thereby providing evidence for the first time that the cranium and jaw were not contemporaneous specimens. On 21 November 1953, a preliminary report was published in which the Piltdown jaw was identified as a modern ape that had been deliberately remodeled and stained to match the Piltdown I cranial fragments (Weiner et al. 1953). Much later, it was shown that the jaw was, in fact, that of an orangutan (Lowenstein et al. 1982). In 1953–1954, an exhaustive reexamination of the entire Piltdown assemblage was made, using a wide range of techniques. In a sec-

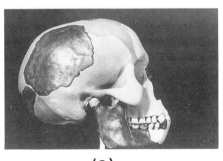

(a)

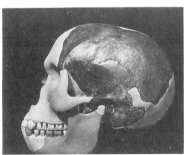

(b)

(c)

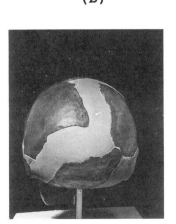

(d)

Fig. 2. Reconstruction (Woodward) of the Piltdown skull (1914). White areas reconstructed. Dark areas indicate original bone. (a) Right lateral view; (b) left lateral view; (c) frontal view (d) occipital view. Courtesy of the Trustees of the Natural History Museum.

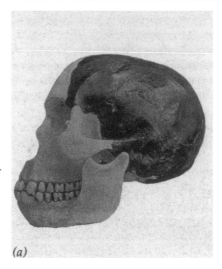

(a)

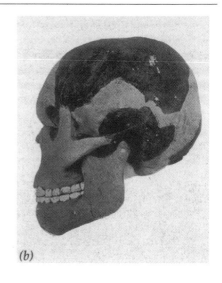

(b)

ond report, issued on 21 January 1955, it was revealed that the entire Piltdown assemblage was bogus (Weiner et al. 1955).

While these investigations provided a solution to the Piltdown puzzle and set the stage for a progressive retreat from the pre-sapiens hypothesis, they did not uncover the identity of the person or persons who had been responsible for the forgery—and since 1953 there have been numerous attempts to solve this remaining mystery. At one time or another, all of the major personalities in the Piltdown affair have been implicated, along with several peripheral figures: Dawson with an unknown accomplice (Weiner 1955), Grafton Elliot Smith (Millar 1972), William Johnson Sollas (Halstead 1978), Pierre Teilhard de Chardin (Gould 1980), Arthur Conan Doyle (Winslow & Meyer 1983), Samuel Woodhead (Costello 1985), W.J. Lewis Abbott (Blinderman 1986), Arthur Keith and Dawson (Langham and Spencer in Spencer 1990a; Tobias 1992), Martin A.C. Hinton (cf. Spencer 1990a:175–178), and Arthur Smith Woodward and Dawson (Drawhorn 1994). (For a detailed survey of the entire episode and suspects, see Spencer 1990a, 1990b.)

Frank Spencer

See also Australopithecines; Clark, (Sir) Wilfrid Edwin Le Gros; Galley Hill; Gregory, William King; Keith, (Sir) Arthur; Lankester, (Sir) Edwin Ray; Modern Human Origins; Neandertals; Oakley, Kenneth Page; Paleoanthropology Theory; Smith, (Sir) Grafton Elliot; Swanscombe; Teilhard de Chardin, Pierre; Weiner, Joseph Sidney; Wenner-Gren Foundation; Woodward, Arthur (Smith)

Bibliography
PRIMARY SOURCES
C. Dawson & A.S. Woodward: On the discovery of a Palaeolithic human skull and mandible in a flint-bearing gravel overlying the Wealden (Hastings Beds) at Piltdown, Fletching (Sussex). *Quarterly Journal of the Geological Society of London* 69:117–151, 1913; C. Dawson & A.S. Woodward: Supplementary note on the discovery of a Palaeolithic human skull and mandible at Piltdown (Sussex). *Quarterly Journal of the Geological Society of London* 70:82–90, 1914; C. Dawson & A.S. Woodward: On a bone implement from Piltdown (Sussex). *Quarterly Journal of the Geological Society of London* 71:144–149, 1915; W.K. Gregory: The dawn man of Piltdown. *American Museum Journal* 14:189–200, 1914; A. Keith: *The antiquity of man.* London: Williams & Norgate, 1915 (2d ed., 2 vols.: 1925).

J.M. Lowenstein et al.: Piltdown jaw confirmed as orang. *Nature* 299:294, 1982; G.S. Miller: The jaw of the Piltdown man. *Smithsonian Miscellaneous Collections* 65:1–31, 1915; K.P. Oakley & C.R. Hoskins: New evidence on the antiquity of Piltdown man. *Nature* 165:379–382, 1950; J.S. Weiner et al.: The solution to the Piltdown problem. *Bulletin of the British Museum (Natural History)* 2:141–146, 1953; J.S. Weiner et al.: Further contributions to the solution of the Piltdown problem. *Bulletin of the British Museum (Natural History)* 2:225–187, 1955; A.S. Woodward: Fourth note on the Piltdown gravel with evidence of a second skull of *Eoanthropus dawsoni. Quarterly Journal of the Geological Society of London* 73:1–10, 1917.

SECONDARY SOURCES

C. Blinderman: *The Piltdown inquest*. New York: Prometheus, 1986; P. Costello: The Piltdown hoax reconsidered. *Antiquity* 59:167–171, 1985; J.M. Drawhorn: Piltdown: Evidence for Smith Woodward's complicity. (Abstract). *American Journal of Physical Anthropology* (Supplement) 18:82, 1994; S.J. Gould: The Piltdown conspiracy. *Natural History* (New York) 89:8–28, 1980; L.B. Halstead: New light on the Piltdown hoax. *Nature* 276:11–13, 1978; G.A. Harrison: J.S. Weiner and the exposure of the Piltdown forgery. *Antiquity* 57:46–48, 1983.

I. Langham: The Langham brief. In: F. Spencer: *Piltdown: A scientific forgery*. London: Oxford University Press, 1990, pp. 188–198; R. Millar: The Piltdown man. New York: Ballantine, 1972; F. Spencer: *Piltdown: A scientific forgery*. London: Oxford University Press, 1990a; F. Spencer: *The Piltdown papers, 1908–1955: The correspondence and other documents relating to the Piltdown forgery*. London: Oxford University Press, 1990b; P.V. Tobias: Piltdown: An apprasial of the case against Sir Arthur Keith. *Current Anthropology* 33:243–293, 1992; J.S. Weiner: *The Piltdown forgery*. London: Oxford University Press, 1955; J. Winslow & A. Meyer: The perpetrator at Piltdown. *Science* 83(4):32–43, 1983.

Pöch, Rudolf (1870–1921)

Born in Tarnopol, Galicia, Pöch studied medicine in Vienna, graduating M.D. in 1895. In 1896, he became assistant physician at the clinic for internal medicine at the General Hospital in Vienna. From February to May 1897, he worked in Bombay, India, as an assistant physician with a German commission for the study of plague. On returning to Vienna, three members of the team contracted pneumonic plague, and Pöch, risking his own life, volunteered to take care of them until they died. In recognition of this and for controlling the epidemic in Vienna, he was given high honors. For further details of his work as a physician in Vienna controlling the spread of the plague, see his contribution to the volume *Special Pathology and Therapy* (1898), edited by H. Nothnagel and Pöch & Müller (1900). In 1903, he published the results of a study of malaria he conducted in 1902 partly in West Africa and partly at the Tropical Institute in Hamburg.

Stimulated by his earlier experiences in India and his sojourn in Africa, Pöch studied anthropology and ethnography under Felix von Luschan (1854–1924) at the University in Berlin. He also worked at the Afrikanisch-ozeanischen Abteilung des Museums für Völkerkunde in Berlin. From 1904 to 1906, he conducted an independent expedition to New Guinea, the Bismarck Archipelago, and New South Wales, Australia (e.g., see, Pöch 1915). This field trip provided an opportunity to study various Papuan tribes and to conduct the first study of the pygmy people of the Kai (Pöch 1905), plus study Australian Aboriginal groups. This was followed by a commission from the Akademie der Wissenschaften (Academy of Science) in Vienna to conduct an expedition from 1907 to 1909 to South Africa and the Kalahari, where he studied several groups of San Bushmen and the Khoi-khoi (Hottentots) (Pöch 1911).

In 1910, Pöch was made an assistant professor of anthropology and ethnology at the University of Vienna. His inaugural dissertation was based on his earlier travels to New Guinea. In 1913, he was promoted to the rank of associate professor. With the outbreak of World War I, he was drafted to serve as a doctor at the hospital for the casualties of war at the University of Vienna (1914–1916). In the meantime, he received a Ph.D. from Munich University for his dissertation, *Studien an Eingeborenen von Neu-Südwales und an australischen Schädeln* (1915). During the remainder of the war period, he was commissioned by the Austrian Academy of Science to conduct an extensive ethnological survey of prisoner-of-war camps.

After the war, in 1919, he was made a regular professor and director of the newly founded Institute for Anthropology and Ethnology and a corresponding member of the Austrian Academy of Science.

During the course of his fieldwork, Pöch made important collections of ethnographic materials that included skeletal remains, anthropometric data, photographic and cinematographic recordings, reports about illnesses, phonographic recordings of languages, songs, and musical instruments, works of art, and numerous zoological and botanical objects (eg. Pöch 1917). Many of these items are preserved at the Naturhistorischen Museum and the Museum für Völkerkunde in Vienna. A detailed scientific evaluation of this material, which he was unable to complete because of his early death on 4 March 1921, was published in the twelve-volume *Rudolf Pöchs Nachlaß* by the Austrian Academy of Science between 1927 and 1962.

G. Ziegelmayer

See also Khoisan; Luschan, Felix Ritter Edler von; Oceania

Bibliography

SELECTED WORKS

Die Pest. In: H. Nathnagel (ed) *Spezielle Pathologie und Therapie* [Special Pathology and Therapy]. Wien: Hölder, 1898; Ergebnisse einer Reise längs der Küste von Senegambien und Oberguinea. *Archiv für Schiffs- und Tropenhygiene* 7, 1903; Fälle von Zwergwuchs unter den Kai (Deutsch-Neu-Guinea). *Mitteilungen der Anthropologischen Gesellschaft in Wein* 35:40–42, 1905; Die Stellung der Buschmannrasse unter den übrigen Menschenrassen. *Korrespondenzblatt der Deutsche Gesellschaft für Anthropologie, Ethnologie, und Urgeschichte* 42:8–12, 1911; *Studien an Eingeborenen von Neu-Südwales und an australischen Schädeln*. Wien: Anthropologische Gesellschaft, 1915; Ein Tasmanierschädel im k.k. naturhistorischen Hofmuseum: Die anthropologische und ethnographische Stellung der Tasmanier. *Mitteilungen der Anthropologischen Gesellschaft in Wien* 46:31–91, 1916; *Technik und wert des sammelns phonographischen sprachproben auf expeditionen*. Wien: Hölder, 1917; (with H.F. Müller) *Die Pest*. Wien: Hölder, 1900.

SECONDARY SOURCES

E. Oberhummer: Rudolf Pöch (gestorben am 4 März 1921). *Mittheilungen der Anthropologischen Gesellschaft in Wien* 51:95–104, 1921; J. Szilvássy, P. Spindler, & H. Kritscher: Rudolf Pöch: Arzt, Anthropologe, und Ethnograph. *Annalen, Naturhistoriches Museum Wien* 83:7434–762, 1980; M. Weninger: Rudolf Pöch zum 40. Jahrestag seines Todes, 1870–1921. *Mittheilungen der Anthropologischen Gesellschaft in Wien* 51:142–143, 1921.

Podbaba Skull

Although the Podbaba skull has since become a footnote in the history of European paleoanthropology, at the time of its discovery it provoked considerable interest and in particular contributed to the nascent debate on the significance of the human remains recovered from the Neander Valley in Germany in 1856. The remains of the Podbaba skull (frontal and left parietal bones, plus fragments of the mastoid process) were discovered on 30 November 1883 at Podbaba, near Prague. Among the first to comment on this find was the German anatomist Hermann Schaaffhausen (1816–1893), who noted that the skull was clearly dolichocephalic. In addition, the specimen manifested a receding forehead, a prominent supraorbital torus, and other resemblances to the Neander Valley skull. Based on these characteristics, Schaaffhausen believed the specimen could be chronologically aligned with those of Cro-Magnon. This conclusion, however, was rejected by the French prehistorian Gabriel de Mortillet (1821–1898), who believed it to be a recent specimen manifesting atavistic elements.

Ursula Zängl-Kumpf

See also Cro-Magnon; Mortillet, Gabriel (Louis Laurent) de; Neandertal (Feldhofer Grotte); Neandertals; Schaaffhausen, Hermann

Bibliography

G. de Mortillet *Le Préhistorique: Antiquité de l'homme*. Paris: Reinwald, 1885, p. 253; H. Schaaffhausen: [On the Podbaba skull]. *Verhandlungen des naturhistorischen Vereins der preussischen Rheinlande und Westfalens* 41:77–78, 1884; H. Schaaffhausen: Die Schädel aus dem Löss von Podbaba und Winaric in Böhmen. *Verhandlungen des naturhistorischen Vereins der preussischen Rheinlande und Westfalens* 41:364–379, 1884.

Poland

Although the roots of physical anthropology in Poland can be traced to the sixteenth century, when scholars such as Szymon of Łowicz (d. 1538) produced texts with a distinctly anthropological character, it was not until the late eighteenth and early nineteenth centuries that the foundations of the modern discipline were established. The subsequent history of Polish physical anthropology can be divided into three arbitrary stages of development: (1) the formative period: early 1800s into the 1890s; (2) the early-modern period: ca. 1900s through to World War II; and (3) the modern period: 1945 through the mid-1990s.

Formative Period

It is possible to identify a mounting interest in anthropology during the first half of the nineteenth century. Among the first to publish in this still nascent field was Jędrzej Śniadecki (1768–1838), a naturalist and former professor at Vilnius University, who published two important anthropological texts during the first decade of the century: *On Physical Education of Children* (1805–1806) and *Theory of Organic Beings* (1811). In the latter work, Śniadecki defined anthropology in much the same way the Vilno botanist Józef Jundziłł (1784–1877) had in 1807, namely, as the science embracing not only human biology (at all stages of development) but also a characterization of the biocultural milieu in which the human organism operates. Another early anthropologist from this period, who also hailed from the province of Vilnius, was Józef Jasiński (d. 1833). In 1810, this worker published the first Polish handbook of anthropology, titled *Anthropology: On the Physical and Moral Properties of Man*. But perhaps the most significant work of the early formative period was that of Wawrzyniec Surowiecki (1768–1827), a professor of linguistics at the University of Warsaw, who in 1824 published his book *Śledzenie początków narodów słowiańskich* (The Search for the Origins of Slavic Nations). It represented the first major description of the physical characteristics and geographic variation of the Slavic-speaking peoples, and it employed an approach that anticipated the cartographical method utilized with increasing frequency by anthropologists during the second half of the nineteenth century.

During the third quarter of the nineteenth century, the primary center for anthropological research was the Jagiellonian University (JU) in Cracow, where the first steps toward the institutionalization of the discipline were taken by the physiologist Józef Majer (1808–1899), who began lecturing on anthropology at the university in 1856 (cf. Majer 1876). In 1873, Majer was succeeded at the JU by his associate Izydor Kopernicki (1825–1891), who was officially installed in the first Chair of Physical Anthropology created at a Polish university. Coinciding with this event was the establishment of an anthropological commission, sponsored by the Akademia Umiejętności (Academy of Sciences) in Cracow and headed by Majer and Kopernicki. This commission was responsible for the collection of anthropometric data on the various ethnic groups located in the regions of Galicia (a region of southeastern Poland and the western Ukraine). The results of this protracted survey, which continued through into the late 1880s, were published in a serial publication called *Zbiór wiadomości do antropologii krajowej* (Collection of Studies on Anthropology of our Country), which was launched in 1877 and represents the first scientific Polish periodical devoted exclusively to anthropology. The *Collection* was published continuously from 1877 to 1896, whereupon it was transformed into *Anthropological, Archaeological, and Ethnographic Materials*, which was published in thirteen volumes until the outbreak of World War I.

In spite of this academic focus in Cracow, most Polish investigators during this and the following period continued to receive their training in other European centers such as France and Germany. And some, because of the political climate in Poland, became émigrés, as was the case with Théophile Chudziński (1840–1897), who subsequently settled in Paris, where he worked with Paul Broca (1824–1880) and Paul Topinard (1830–1911) and was a faculty member of the renowned École d'Anthropologie. Essentially, the closing phases of this period can be conveniently marked by the death of Kopernicki in 1891.

Early-Modern Period

The early-modern period witnessed the emergence of four important centers for physical anthropology in Poland: Cracow, Warsaw, Lvov, and Poznań.

After Kopernicki's death, the Chair of Physical Anthropology at the JU in Cracow was suspended by the Austrian authorities until 1908, whereupon a Department of Anthropology was founded at the university under the direction of Julian Talko-Hryncewicz (1850–1936), who had a broad vision of the discipline (cf. Talko-Hryncewicz 1910, 1913). Prior to his appointment at Cracow, Talko-Hryncewicz had spent several years working as a physician in the Trans-Baikal region (cf. Talko-Hryncewicz 1899). Under his guidance, the first longitudinal studies were initiated in Poland (cf. Stołyhwo 1938). In the meantime, Kazimierz Stołyhwo (1880–1966) had organized an anthropological laboratory at the Museum of Industry and Agriculture in Warsaw, which in 1920 (when Poland regained its independence) developed into the Instytut Nauk Antropologicznych (Institute of Anthropological Sciences) under the aegis of the Towarzystwo Naukowe Warszawskie (Warsaw Scientific Society). Stołyhwo's research interests were wide ranging (e.g., Stołyhwo 1912; 1932), but he had a particular sustained interest in paleoanthropology (cf. Stołyhwo 1910). Indeed, it was this manifest interest that brought him the commission from the Smithsonian Institution's physical anthropologist Aleš Hrdlička (1869–1943) to conduct prehistoric excavations in the Ukraine in 1912 and in Siberia in 1913 with a view to securing material for an elaborate exhibit Hrdlička was planning for the Panama-California Exposition that was to be staged in San Diego in 1915 (cf. Spencer 1979, Vol. 2:456–457, 463–465). After World War I,

Stołyhwo was involved in further institutional developments in Warsaw (*vide ante*), and later he succeeded Talko-Hrynecwicz at Cracow.

In 1913, a new Chair of Anthropology was established at the Jan Kazimierz University (JKU) in Lvov and occupied by Jan Czekanowski (1882–1965), one of several notable Polish anthropologists from this period who received their training under the German anthropologist Rudolf Martin (1864–1925) in Zurich. Prior to accepting the position at JKU, Czekanowski had worked in Berlin as a member of the Prussian Museum Service, and between 1907 and 1909 he participated in an expedition to central Africa led by Prince Adolf Frederick Mecklenburg (1848–1914). The department founded by Czekanowski at JKU subsequently became a converging point for a number of Polish workers, including: Stanisław Klimek, Salamon Czortkower, Jan Mydlarski, Boleslaw Rosiński, Konstanty Tobolski, Karol Stojanowski, Jan Bryk, Rościslaw Jendyk, Slanisław Żejmo-Żejmis, Adam Wanke, Franciszek Wokroj, Józef Grajek, and Adam Krechowiecki. At JKU, Czekanowski, together with these workers, produced the first studies in Poland aimed at reconstructing ethnic history and, as such, pioneered a number of original typological methods grounded in biometrical principles (cf. Czekanowski 1913, 1928, 1934). During the 1920s and 1930s, this emerging school of anthropology (sometimes referred to as the Czekanowski School, the Lvov School, or the Polish Anthropological School) gained an international reputation. In addition to the JU and JKU foci, there were during the interwar years a number of other significant developments elsewhere in the country.

In Warsaw, Edward Loth (1884–1944), another of Rudolf Martin's Polish protégés, had been working since 1905 in the Department of Anatomy at Warsaw University, where he had pioneered the comparative study of the soft tissues. His book *L'Anthropologie des Parties Molles* (1931) attracted international attention. Also in Warsaw, Stołyhwo was responsible for founding the Division of Military Anthropology (DMA) at the Military Technical Institute in 1921, and it was from the DMA that the first major anthropological survey of the Polish population was launched in the autumn of 1921 under the direction of Jan Mydlarski (1892–1956). This survey involved the anthropometric examination of 80,310 Polish soldiers, including the determination of each soldier's ABO blood group. This was one of the first anthropological studies to include tests for the ABO blood groups—which is hardly surprising given that it was the Polish immunologist Ludwik Hirszfeld (1884–1954) who first documented the existence of ethnic differences in the ABO blood-group frequencies (cf. Hirszfeld & Hirszfeld 1919). The preliminary summary of this survey's results was published in 1925 by Mydlarski, who in 1930 became head of the Department of Biometry in the newly established Central Institute of Physical Education in Warsaw. There Mydlarski and his cohorts conducted significant studies on the influence of physical exercise on a child's physical development.

Following in the wake of World War I, two additional academic Departments of Anthropology were founded, one at the University of Vilnius (UV) and the other at the University of Poznań (UP). After World War II, in 1956, the UP was renamed Adam Mickiewicz University. Founded in 1919, the UV department was originally organized by Talko-Hryncewicz, but it failed to flourish. A few years later, Michał Reicher (1888–1973), who was head of the Anatomy Department at the UV, resuscitated an interest in anthropology when he established an anthropological laboratory (cf. Reicher 1923). Since then, workers associated with this laboratory have conducted research on the ethnic composition of the surrounding Baltic region. The department at the UP was founded by Adam Wrzosek (1875–1905), who was also instrumental in establishing the Polskie Towarzystwo Antropologiczne (Polish Anthropological Association) and its official journal, the *Przegląd Antropologiczny,* in 1925. Under Wrzosek's energetic leadership, Poznań developed into a thriving research center, with particular emphasis on physiological anthropology, skeletal biology, paleopathology, and child growth and development.

In September 1939, World War II began—and by the end of the month, Poland found itself partitioned between Germany and Soviet Russia. This tragic event serves to set the stage for the commencement of the next stage of development.

Modern Period

The impact of World War II on Poland was considerable. First, it resulted in the death of many young and outstanding Polish investigators. For example, Stanisław Klimek (1903–1939) was killed in action at

Umiastów on the outskirts of Warsaw; Salamon Czortkower (1903–1943) was murdered by Ukranian fascists in the Lvov ghetto; Stanisław Poniatowski (1884–1945) and Stanisław Żejmo-Żejmis (1903–1942) both perished in German concentration camps; while Edward Loth was killed during the Warsaw Uprising in August 1944. Second, the war also led to a reshaping of the map of Poland and a subsequent reshuffling of the anthropological community. For example, Lvov became part of the Soviet Ukraine, while Vilnius University found itself part of Soviet Lithuania. As a consequence of this, Czekanowski moved from Lvov to Poznań, while other investigators from this once thriving research center in the east were dispersed throughout the country. Another immediate consequence of the war was the establishment of two new foci of anthropology at Lublin in southeast Poland: One was at the Catholic University in 1945; the other, at the Maria Curie-Skłodowska University in 1948. During this same time period, anthropology emerged at the University of Łódź. Then, in 1949, a new university was established in Wrocław (formerly Breslau) in southwestern Poland along with a Department of Anthropology, which was headed by Mydlarski.

During the next decade, under Mydlarski's influence Wrocław was to emerge as the primary institutional focus of Polish anthropological research. In addition to stewarding his own department at Wrocław, Mydlarski subsequently became, among other things, chairman of the Komitet Antropologii Polskiej Akademii Nauk (Anthropological Committee of the Polish Academy of Sciences), which was responsible for coordinating and supervising all research and teaching conducted within the country, and editor in chief of *Przegląd Antropologiczny* and the newly founded (in 1953) journal *Materiały i Prace Antropologiczne*. Also in 1953, he was instrumental in the founding of a new Institute of Anthropology (IA) of the Polish Academy of Sciences in Wrocław, which he directed until his death in 1956. Following Mydlarski's death, the directors of the IA have been Adam Wanke (1956–1965), Halina Milicer (1965–1970), and Tadeusz Bielicki (1970–).

During the 1960s, more new Departments of Anthropology were created at Copernicus University in Toruń and at several Academies of Physical Education—in Cracow, Poznań, Warsaw, and Wrocław.

By the mid-1990s, the Polish anthropological community consisted of 183 active investigators employed in a variety of institutional settings (see Table 1 for a general overview). The largest center of anthropology was Wrocław, followed by Warsaw, Poznań, and Cracow. The primary training centers are located at the universities in Cracow, Poznań, and Wrocław.

TABLE 1. The Present Institutional Landscape of Polish Anthropology

Institutions	Directors/Professors
Universities	
ŁÓDŹ	
Department of Anthropology	A. Malinowski
CRACOW	
Department of Anthropology	K. Kaczanowski
POZNAŃ	
Institute of Anthropology:	
Department of Biology of Human Development	J. Cieślik
Department of Human Evolutionary Biology	J. Pointek
Department of Human Populational Ecology	J. Strzałko
Museum and Osteological Laboratory	E. Milosz
TORUŃ	
Department of Anthropology	G. Kriesel
WROCŁAW	
Department of Anthropology	T. Krupiński
WARSAW	
Department of Historical Anthropology	A. Wierciński
Institute of Anthropology of the Polish Academy of Science	
WROCŁAW	T. Bielicki
Anthropology Departments in Academies of Physical Education	
WARSAW	J. Charzewski
CRACOW	S. Panek, Z. Bocheń, S. Gołab, J. Szopa
WROCŁAW	A. Janusz
POZNAŃ	Z. Drozdowski, B. Marecki
GDAŃSK	J. Gładykowska Rzeczycka, D. Gerard-Białko

Note: In addition to the above there are also active anthropological laboratories in medical school departments of anatomy in Białystok, Poznań, Wrocław, and Szczecin. The discipline is also represented in varying degrees in the Institute of Pediatrics in Lublin, Cracow, Łódź, and Warsaw; and in the Institute of Orthodontics in Poznań, Wrocław, and Cracow.

The research undertaken by the institutions listed in Table 1 has included the following (to avoid arbitrary choices, the reader is referred to Bielicki, Krupiński, and Strzałko 1985 and Piontek and Malinowski 1985 for more complete details and representative bibliographic references):

HUMAN EVOLUTION

Unlike other neighboring European countries, Poland's human fossil record is almost nonexistent, and what few specimens have been recovered are all restricted to the Upper Paleolithic or later. However, in spite of this, craniological and odontological studies of primates and fossil man have been a perennial feature of Polish anthropology, as indicated by the work of K. Stołyhwo et al. One recent development worthy of note is the establishment in 1983 of an informal interdisciplinary study group, organized and chaired by A. Wierciński of Warsaw University and A. Wiercińska of the State Archeological Museum, Warsaw. (For further details on this development, see Piontek and Wierciński 1991.)

SKELETAL BIOLOGY

During the 1960s and 1970s, the subject of brachycephalization and the problem of microevolutionary changes in cranial morphology in the Holocene attracted the attention of a number of Polish investigators. Extensive work has been done in the field of paleopathology and ethnogenesis of the Slavic people. Considerable attention has also been devoted to methods of reconstructing the demographic characteristics of prehistoric and early-historic populations, including a refinement of techniques for determining sex and age at death. Included among those prominent in these fields of inquiry are A. Wierciński, A. Wiercińska, T. Bielicki, Z. Welon, M. Henneberg, J. Piontek, and J. Strzałko.

HUMAN ECOLOGY

Human ecology has long been the domain of a group headed by N. Wolański of the Department of Human Ecology, Academy of Sciences, Warsaw, whose work embraces virtually the whole field of human biology. Many of Wolański's studies and those of his associates have been published in international journals and the Polish journal *Studies in Human Ecology*. This area has also been the domain of research groups in Departments of Anthropology at Poznań, Wrocław, and Cracow.

AUXOLOGY

Individual Variation in Growth Studies. Auxological research constitutes a traditional research interest in Polish anthropology, and, as such, developmental studies have been conducted at one time or another in all academic centers. Most of these studies have been concerned with the development of somatic characters observed in either longitudinal or cross-sectional studies of schoolchildren (cf. Bielicki, Krupiński, & Strzałko 1985).

Biosocial Stratification and Secular Trends. Auxologic studies directed along these lines have been principally conducted by T. Bielicki and his group at the Institute of Anthropology of the Academy of Science in Wrocław. This group has studied, among other things: (1) the effects of urbanization on growth; (2) the impact urbanization and parental education have had on stature in both children and conscripts; and (3) secular trends in growth and maturation. The results of these and related studies have been published in international journals and in the Polish publications *Studies in Physical Anthropology*; *Materiały i Prace Antropologiczne*; *Monographs of the Institute of Anthropology* (Polish Academy of Sciences, Wrocław); and *Przegląd Antropologiczny*.

Longitudinal Studies of Twins. In the 1960s, there were two independent studies initiated on monozygotic and dizygotic twins: one by M. Skład at the Academy of Physical Education in Warsaw, and the other by Z. Orczkowska at the Institute of Anthropology in Wrocław. The Warsaw project involved 100 pairs of twins, 50 of which are being examined longitudinally; the Wrocław study, however, was terminated with growth curves covering a period of ten to eleven years. An analysis of the available data to date has been published in *Materiały i Prace Antropologiczne* (cf. vol. 110, 1990). Both projects represent a classical analysis of intrapair differences in body dimensions, menarcheal age, skeletal and sexual maturity, fatness, and somatotype.

Kinesiology. Since World War II, anthropological researchers have made significant contributions to Kinesiology (cf. Table 1). Specifically, the research focus has been on factors influencing body build and their role as determinants of motor fitness; the influence of physical exercise on growth and body composition; and the effects of maturity status and physique on working capacity.

Applied Anthropometry. Applied anthropometry has been an important line of activity in the postwar period. Work has proceeded in two directions: the application of anthropometry in cloth design, and the use of static and functional anthropometry in the design of human workspace.

Janusz Piontek

See also Auxology; Beddoe, John; Broca, Paul (Pierre); Chudiński, Théophile (Teofil); Czekanowski, Jan; Czortkower, Salomon; France; Growth Studies; Hrdlička, Aleš; Kopernicki, Izydor; Loth, Edward; Majer, Jósef; Martin, Rudolf; Molecular Anthropology; Mydlarski, Jan; San Diego Museum of Man; Topinard, Paul

Bibliography
PRIMARY SOURCES
    J. Czekanowski: *Zarys metod statystycznych w zastosowaniu do antropologii.* Warsaw: Wendego, 1913; J. Czekanowski: Das Typen-frequenzgesetz. *Anthropologischer Anzeiger* 5:335–359, 1928; J. Czekanowski: *Człowiek w czasie i przestrzeni.* Warsaw: Trzaska Evert i Michalski, 1934; L. Hirszfeld & H. Hirszfeld: Serological differences between the blood of different races. *Lancet* 2:675–679, 1919; E. Loth: *Anthropologie des parties molles.* (Muscles, intestins, vaisseaux, nerfs périphériques). Paris: Masson, 1931; J. Majer: *Charakterystyka fizyczna ludności galicyjskiej, na podstawie spostrzeżeń dokonanych, za staraniem Komisji Antropologicznej Akademii Umiejętności w Krakowie.* Cracow: Univ. Jagiellońskiego, 1876.
    J. Mydlarski: Sprawozdanie z wojskowego zdjęcia antropologicznego Polski. *Kosmos* 50:530–578, 1925; M. Reicher: *Rozwój wzrostu i proporcji ciała płodów ludzkich* [On the growth of human fetuses]. English summary, pp. 83–87. Archiwum nauk antropologicznych. No. 2. Warsaw: Ksiaznica polska towarzystwa naczyciels szkól wyzszych, 1923; J.T. Śniadecki: *Teoria jestestw organicznych.* Wilno: Rafłowicz, 1811; K. Stołyhwo: W sprawie czlowieka kopalnego i jego poprzedników w Argentynie. *Sprawozdania z posiedzeń Towarzystwa Naukowego Warszawskiego* 4:21–41, 1910; K. Stołyhwo: Sur Frage einer neuen polygenistischen Theorie der Abtsammung des Menschen. *Zeitschrift für Ethnologie* 44:97–104, 1912.
    K. Stołyhwo: Körpergrösse ihre Verebung und Abhägigkeit von dem neuen milieu bei polnischen emigranten in Paraña (Brasilien). *Gesellschaft für Physische Anthropologie* 6:94–106, 1932; K. Stoływho: Szlaki imigracyjne czlowieka na kontynent Ameryki. *Przegląd Antropologiczny* 16:300–311, 1949; K. Stoływho: The antiquity of man in the Argentine and survival of South American fossil mammals until contemporary times. In: S. Tax (ed) *Indian Tribes of Aboriginal America.* New York: 1952; J. Stołyhwowa: Recherches sur la differentiation raciale de longeur de la période de la femme. *Przegląd Antropologiczny* 12:1–22, 1938.
    W. Surowiecki: *Śledzenie początków narodów słowiańskich.* Warsaw, 1824; J. Talko-Hryncewicz: *Notes sur l'anthropologie des Chinois du Nord: Les Chinois de Maimatchen, de Kiakhta, et d'Ourga.* Moscow, 1899; J. Talko-Hryncewicz: *Materyaly do etnologii i antropologii ludów Azyji środkowej, mongolowie, buriaci i tungusi.* Cracow: Nakładem Akademii umiejetnosci, 1910; J. Talko-Hryncewicz: *Człowiek na Ziemiach Naszych.* Cracow: Mortkowicza, 1913; J. Talko-Hryncewicz: *Materijaly k antropologii i etnografii tsentral'noi Azii.* Cracow: Nakładem Akademii umiejetnosci, 1926.

SECONDARY SOURCES
    T. Bielicki, T. Krupiński & J. Strzałko: History of physical anthropology in Poland. *International Association of Human Biologists: Occasional Papers.* Vol 1. No. 6. Newcastle upon Tyne: IAHB, 1985; J. Czekanowski: The theoretical assumptions of Polish anthropology and the morphological facts. *Current Anthropology* 3:481–494, 1962; A. Malinowski & A. Wolański: Anthropology in Poland. In: J. Piontek & A. Malinowski (eds) *Teoria i empiria w Polskiej Szkole Antropologicznej.* Seria antropologa. No. 11. Poznań: Wydawnictwo Naukowe UAM, 1985; J. Piontek & A. Malinowski (eds) *Teoria i emperia w Polskiej Szkole Antropologicznej.* Seria antropologa. No. 11. Poznań: Wydawnictwo Naukowe UAM, 1985; J. Piontek & A. Wierciński (eds) *The peculiarity of man: Sociobiological perspective and other approaches.* Poznań: Adam Mickiewicz University Press, 1991; F. Spencer: *Aleš Hrdlička, M.D., 1869–1943: The life and work of an American physical anthropologist.* 2 vols. Ann Arbor, Michigan & London: University Microfilms, 1979.

Polygenism

Physical anthropologists have always debated the topic of race origins. In the pre-Darwinian period, especially the eighteenth and early nineteenth centuries, the debate took place between two schools of thought called monogenism and polygenism. Monogenists believed the human races represented a single species with a recent common origin, while polygenists believed them to be separate species with ancient separate origins. In the past, almost every anthropologist took a position on these two extremes.

Because monogenism stressed human commonality, it was compatible with orthodox Christianity and developed in tandem with the theologies of Saint Augustine (354–430) and Saint Thomas Aquinas (1225–1275). But the postmedieval era of European geographical expansion called monogenism into question. Many scholars thought that newly discovered aboriginal peoples were too different from Europeans to belong to the same human species. American "Indians" appeared extremely different. In the sixteenth century, Spanish theologians such as José de Acosta (1539–1600) and Bartolome de Las Casas (1475–1566) were forced to interpret scriptures so that Indians could be declared potentially fully human. Otherwise, missionaries would have been unable to save their souls.

Other scholars doubted that the newly discovered range of racial variation could be accommodated by the monogenist view. They became the forerunners of polygenism (Bendyshe 1863). One such scholar was the Frenchman Isaac La Peyrère (1596–1676), who argued that scriptures applied to races descended from Adam and Eve but not to races he called "pre-Adamites." For 200 years, La Peyrère's and others' radical interpretations of scriptures remained a minority position. The majority of scholars were bound by the apparent support for monogenism derived from a literal interpretation of the Bible.

The eighteenth century, sometimes referred to as the Age of Enlightenment, bolstered the monogenist position with arguments that were less theological and more philosophical and social scientific. Heterodox philosophers could scarcely have been expected to abide by the story of Adam and Eve. Instead, they preached the gospel of human commonality by citing examples of racial "improvement" and the ability of one race to acquire traits of another. The anthropological principles of enculturation and acculturation were underpinnings of the Enlightenment's faith in human reason, progress, and perfectibility. Meanwhile, the doctrine of polygenism lay in abeyance, ready to take center stage when the Age of Enlightenment was over.

The heyday of polygenism was in the first half of the nineteenth century. The rising popularity of polygenism has been linked to an emerging Romantic and extreme hereditarian outlook (e.g. Brace 1982; Count 1946; Erickson 1974a; Haller 1970; Lyons 1974; Spencer 1986; Stepan 1982). As the pendulum of opinion about race swung from "nurture" to "nature," it became fashionable to think about races as immutable Romantic "essences." Accordingly, anthropologists began to abandon biblical and philosophical ideas that called attention to racial similarities in favor of scientific evidence that served to separate and stress racial differences. A host of anthropometric measurements, especially those of the skull, were used to establish a fixed racial hierarchy.

In the United States, this approach was pioneered by a group of polygenists known as the American School of Anthropology. The proclaimed leader of this school was Samuel George Morton (1799–1851), whose main works were *Crania Americana* (1839) and *Crania Aegyptiaca* (1844). Other members of the school were Charles Caldwell (1772–1853), Ephraim George Squier (1821–1888), George P. Gliddon (1809–1851), and Josiah Clark Nott (1804–1873). By sidestepping contradictions with scripture, the American School provided tacit support for slavery in the Bible-reading antebellum South (cf. Stanton 1960).

The emerging popularity of polygenism was not restricted to the United States. As scientific anthropology came of age, polygenism emerged as a doctrine of choice in France, England, and Germany, where the American School was held in high regard.

France had its own homegrown version of polygenism pioneered by Jean Baptiste Bory de Saint Vincent (1778–1846), Louis-Antoine Desmoulins (1794–1828), and Julien Joseph Virey (1775–1846). The most influential French polygenist was Paul Broca (1824–1880), founder of the Société d'Anthropologie de Paris in 1859. In Broca's time, different species were supposed to be incapable of producing fertile offspring. For this reason, accumulating evidence of racial interfertility posed a serious problem for polygenists. Drawing on a long line of research, Broca sought to demonstrate that, because different animal species could interbreed, human races could interbreed and be different species at the same time (Broca 1864).

Broca's counterpart in England was James Hunt (1833–1869), founder of the Anthropological Society of London in 1863. His closest counterpart in Germany was Rudolf Virchow (1821–1902). Both of these eminent anthropologists were polygenists (cf. Ackerknecht 1953; Hunt 1863–1864). The widespread popularity of polygenism is one reason historians call nineteenth-century anthropology "racist" (Harris 1968; Poliakov 1977).

Polygenism reached its peak of popularity in the years immediately preceding the publication of Charles Darwin's (1809–1882) *On the Origin of Species* (1859). Technically, Darwin's theory of evolution rendered the monogenist–polygenist debate redundant: Races could not be both different species and change at the same time. But few anthropologists really understood evolution and its relevance to anthropology, and thus many continued to find polygenism attractive. Polygenism persisted into the post-Darwinian period (Bowler 1988; Haller 1971; Spencer 1986; Stocking 1968). Thinking typologically (Brace 1982), "evolutionary polygenists" (Erickson 1974b) maintained that races had long, separate evolutionary histories and were just as distinct as if their origins had been separate. The attitudes behind polygenism did not really begin to change until after 1900, when Franz Boas (1858–1942) showed that key racial characteristics are not fixed by heredity (Boas 1912). Boas and his followers helped push the pendulum of scientific opinion about race from "nature" back to "nurture," which ushered in a new chapter in the history of anthropology (Allen 1989).

Paul A. Erickson

See also Acosta, José de; American School of Anthropology; Boas, Franz; Broca, Paul (Pierre); Caldwell, Charles; Darwin, Charles; Desmoulins, Louis-Antoine; Hunt, James; La Peyrère, Isaac; Morton, Samuel George; Nott, Josiah Clark; Squier, Ephraim George; Virchow, Rudolf

Bibliography
PRIMARY SOURCES
F. Boas: *Changes in bodily form of descendants of immigrants.* New York: Columbia University Press, 1912; P. Broca: *On the phenomenon of hybridity in the genus Homo.* London: Longman, Green, Longman & Roberts, 1864; J. Hunt: On the Negro's place in nature. *Memoirs of the Anthropological Society of London* 1:1–63, 1863–1864; S.G. Morton: *Crania Americana; or, A comparative view of the skulls of various Aboriginal nations of North and South America.* Philadelphia: Dobson, 1839; S.G. Morton: *Crania Aegyptiaca; or, Observations on Egyptian ethnography, derived from anatomy, history, and the monuments.* Philadelphia: Pennington, 1844.

SECONDARY SOURCES
E.H. Ackerknecht: *Rudolph Virchow: Doctor, statesman, anthropologist.* Madison: University of Wisconsin Press, 1953; J.S. Allen: Franz Boas' physical anthropology: The critique of racial formalism revisited. *Current Anthropology* 30:79–84, 1989; T. Bendyshe: The history of anthropology. *Memoirs of the Anthropological Society of London* 1:335–360, 1863; P.J. Bowler: *The non-Darwinian revolution: Reinterpreting a historical myth.* Baltimore: Johns Hopkins University Press, 1988; C.L. Brace: The roots of the race concept in American physical anthropology. In: F. Spencer (ed) *A history of American physical anthropology, 1930–1980.* New York: Academic Press, 1982, pp. 11–29.

E.W. Count: The evolution of the race idea in modern Western culture during the period of the pre-Darwinian nineteenth century. *Transactions of the New York Academy of Science* 8:139–165, 1946; C.R. Darwin: *On the origin of species by means of natural selection or the preservation of favoured races in the struggle for life.* London: Murray, 1859; P.A. Erickson: *The origins of physical anthropology.* Ph.D. Thesis. University of Connecticut, 1974a; P.A. Erickson: Racial determinism and Nineteenth-century anthropology. *Man* 9:489–491, 1974b; J.S. Haller Jr.: The species problem: Nineteenth-century concepts of racial inferiority in the origin of man controversy. *American Anthropologist* 72:1319–1329, 1970; J.S. Haller Jr.: *Outcasts from evolution: Scientific attitudes of racial inferiority, 1859–1900.* Urbana: University of Illinois Press, 1971.

M. Harris: *The rise of anthropological theory: A history of theories of culture.* New York: Crowell, 1968; A. Lyons: *The question of race in anthropology from the time of J.F. Blumenbach to that of Franz Boas.* Ph.D. Thesis. Oxford University, 1974; L. Poliakov: *The Aryan myth: A history of racist and nationalist ideas in Europe*. New York: New American Library, 1977; F. Spencer: *Ecce Homo: An annotated bibliographic history of physical anthropology*. New York: Greenwood, 1986, pp. 124–128; W.D. Stanton: *The leopard's spots: Scientific attitudes toward race in America, 1815–1859*. Chicago: University of Chicago Press, 1960; N. Stepan: *The idea of race in science: Great Britain, 1800–1960*. Hamden, Connecticut: Shoestring Press, 1982; G.W. Stocking Jr.: *Race, culture, and evolution: Essays in the history of anthropology*. New York: Free Press, 1968, pp. 42–68.

Portugal

Physical anthropology in Portugal began in the mid-nineteenth century, initially with strong influence from France. Research and some teaching in physical anthropology were instituted in three cities: Lisbon, Coimbra, and Porto. While there are differences in context among these three centers, there are overall similarities that are distinctively Portuguese. Perhaps the most unique aspect of Portuguese physical anthropology has been the amassing of very large and meticulously documented collections of modern human skeletons coupled with the excavation and conservation of some of the largest collections of prehistoric human skeletal remains in Europe.

Lisbon

In 1857, the Comissão de Trabalhos Geológicos was founded in Lisbon, with Carlos Ribeiro (1813–1882) as director, assisted (and later succeeded) by F.A. Pereira da Costa (1809–1889) and J.F. Nery Delgado (1835–1908), three men described by A. Xavier da Cunha (1982:7) as *"les premiers anthropologistes portugais."* Collectively and individually, they were responsible for the initial investigations of the Mesolithic middens at Muge (e.g., Costa 1865; Oliviera 1888) and for excavations at Neolithic ossuary caves such as Casa de Moura (Delgado 1867). Heavily influenced by contemporary French science, Delgado's excavations were models for their time, and although subsequent conditions of conservation have been less than ideal, the enormous human skeletal collections recovered remain of great interest and utility for modern investigators. They certainly were such for nineteenth-century European anthropologists such as Émile Cartailhac (1845–1921), who devoted most of a chapter in his *Les Âges Préhistoriques de l'Espagne et Portugal* (1886) to a description of the Lisbon collections written by F. Paula e Oliviera (1888).

While the interest of early physical anthropologists in Lisbon was primarily paleontological, there was also an early development of interest in modern human variation, initially focused on osteological variability. F. Ferraz de Macedo (1845–1907) established a major collection of modern skeletal remains in the Museu Bocage of the Faculty of Sciences at Lisbon, which, although partly destroyed by fire in the 1970s, has been a prime resource for studies of modern skeletal age changes by both Portuguese and non-Portuguese anthropologists (MacLaughlin 1990; Masset & Almeida 1990).

Coimbra

The focus on modern human variation was also pursued at Coimbra by Bernadino Machado (1851–1944), who was appointed to the Chair of Anthropology, Human Paleoanthropology, and Prehistoric Archeology at the University of Coimbra in 1885 and founded the teaching of anthropology in Portugal (Houart et al. 1985). Bernadino was succeeded in 1907 by Eusébio Tamagnini (b. 1880), who continued a program of teaching and research on both modern and archeological human populations until 1950. This included, as with Macedo in Lisbon, the establishment of a very large collection of human skeletons from individuals of known age, sex, occupation, place of birth, and the like (e.g., Bocquet et al. 1978; Bocquet-Appel 1984; Cunha 1995, Cunha & van Vark 1990; Fernandes 1985).

Tamagnini was originally trained as a biologist and had a strong interest in statistics. He brought to Coimbra the statistician W.L. Stevens, a student of the British statistician and geneticist Ronald A. Fisher (1890–1962), who, in the 1940s, produced a number of publications in Portuguese (cf. Cunha 1982 for references). At the same time, Tamagnini with his students and colleagues published a series of monographs (in *Contribuições para o Estudo da Antropología Portuguesa*) on modern human variation based on both osteological (e.g., Queiroz Lopes & Serra 1944; Serra 1938; Tamagnini & Vieira de Campos 1949) and nonosteological (e.g., Tamagnini 1936, 1947) data. These multifaceted researches were continued by his successor, A. Xavier da Cunha, who has written (1982) a very useful history of the development of physical anthropology in Portugal. As of the mid-1990s, physical anthropology as such was taught only at the

University of Coimbra, where the journal *Antropología Portuguesa* was being published as the successor to the *Contribuições*.

Porto

In Porto, anthropology was made a part of the curriculum at the Polytechnic Academy in the 1880s. However, it was not until the appointment in 1912 (the year following the establishment of the University of Porto) of A.A. Mendes Corrêa (1888–1959) to the Chair of Anthropology, that the discipline became well established there. Originally trained in medicine, and a powerful politician for much of his life, Corrêa continued the tradition of teaching and research in both paleoanthropology and modern human variation (e.g. 1915, 1924, 1932) and added to these such topics as forensic anthropology (1931), race (1940), and human biology (1951). He established an Institute of Anthropology at the University of Porto to which Portuguese and non-Portuguese reseachers came, and many of the human remains excavated at the Muge sites in the twentieth century were housed there (although a fire in the 1970s resulted in the loss, and loss of identification, of a number of specimens). His interests, and those of his students, were broad, encompassing all aspects of anthropology both in Portugal and its overseas colonies, and he was active internationally as, for example, in his role as organizer of the 1930 meetings of the International Congress of Anthropology and Prehistoric Archaeology. His student and successor J.R. Santos Júnior continued his academic interests, as did the subsequent successor, J.A. Machado Cruz.

Foreign Interest and Influences

Anthropological research on Portuguese skeletal material has been undertaken by non-Portuguese since the 1920s. French influence has been paramount, with the work of Henri Breuil (1877–1961) and his students (1920, 1942) eliciting an anthropological study by Henri Victor Vallois (1889–1981) in 1930 of skeletons from the Mesolithic sites at Muge. The archeological work on those sites, begun in the nineteenth century, was continued by J. Roche (1972), leading to a detailed study of the human material by Denise Ferembach (1974), with an emphasis on the typological approach characteristic of French anthropology of the period. A similar approach has been used for later material by Bubner (1986).

French dental researchers with an interest in anthropology have contributed extensively to knowledge of the Portuguese Mesolithic (Fléchier et al. 1976; Lefèvre 1973; see also Sueiro & Frazão 1959). A full understanding of Portuguese Mesolithic and Neolithic dentitions has proved elusive (Jackes & Lubell 1996) but has been set within the broad context of dietary change through time (Lubell et al. 1994), with attention to problems of interpretation of new dates, bone chemistry and faunal analyses.

Recently, more-general studies by non-Portuguese anthropologists based on Portuguese skeletal materials have been characterized by research into methodological problems initially identified using large Iroquoian and French Neolithic ossuary samples: Masset and Almeida (1990), J.-P. Bocquet-Appel et al. (1978), and M. Jackes (1992) have discussed modern and Neolithic Portuguese collections in the context of adult age assessment, paleodemography, and preservation bias. This distinctive approach is shaping Portuguese analyses (Duarte 1993), and research by Portuguese nationals will no doubt continue in this vein, especially in view of the extremely careful work of modern Portuguese excavators of Neolithic sites (Zilhão 1992). However, the restructuring of academic life since the 1974 revolution had not, by the mid-1990s, led to a solid renaissance in anthropology after the long period of dictatorship.

Forensic sciences have a long history in Portugal (Cunha 1982:30–31; Tavares da Rocha 1985), but it appears likely that Portugese research of most interest to human biologists, apart from osteological work, is based on genetic studies. Portugese work on thalassemia, sickling, and Machado-Joseph disease, for example, is readily available in international publications. Although research in general human biology is also being published outside Portugal (e.g., Sobral 1990), numerous Portuguese journals publish articles relevant to physical anthropology: *Antropología Portuguesa* (Instituto de Antropología, Universidade de Coimbra), *Arqueologia* (Grupo de Estudos Argueológicos, Porto), *O Arqueólogo Português* (Museu Nacional, Lisbon), *Trabalhos de Antropología e Etnologia* (Sociedade Portuguesa de Antropología e Etnologia, Porto), *Communicações dos Serviços Geológicos de Portugal* (Lisbon). As well, the institutes at Porto and Coimbra each publish a monograph series, as does the Departamento de Arqueologia of the Instituto Português do Património Arquítectónico e Arqueológico (*Trabalhos de Arqueologia*).

David Lubell
Mary Jackes

See also Cartailhac, Émil; Forensic Anthropology; France; Vallois, Henri Victor

Bibliography
J.-P. Bocquet et al.: Estimation de l'âge au décès des squelettes adultes par régressions multiples. *Contribuições para o Estudo da Antropología Portuguesa* 10(3):107–167, 1978; J.-P. Bocquet-Appel: Biological evolution and history in nineteenth-century Portugal. In: G.N. van Vark & W.W. Howells (ed) *Multivariate statistical methods in physical anthropology*. Dordrecht: Reidel, 1984, pp. 289–321; H. Breuil: La station paléolithique ancienne d'Arronches (Portalègre). *O Arqueólogo Português* 24:47–55, 1920; H. Breuil & G. Zbyszewski: Contribution à l'étude des industries paléolithiques du Portugal et de leurs rapports avec la géologie du Quaternaire. *Communicações Serviços Geológicos de Portugal* 23:1–394, 1942; T. Bubner: Restos humanos de Carenque. O Arqueólogo Português 4 (sér 4):91–148, 1986; E. Cartailhac: *Les âges préhistoriques de l'Espagne et Portugal*. Paris: Reinwald, 1886.

A.A. Mendes Corrêa: Contribuição para o estudo antropológicas da população da Beira Alta. *Anales da Academia Polytécnica do Porto* 10:153–169, 1915; A.A. Mendes Corrêa: *Os povos primitivos da Lusitânia*. Porto: Instituto de Antropología, 1924; A.A. Mendes Corrêa: *A nova antropología criminal*. Porto: Imprensa Portuguesa, 1931; A.A. Mendes Corrêa: Questions du mésolithique portugais. *Proceedings of the First International Congress of Prehistoric and Protohistoric Sciences* (London) 1:1–2, 1932; A.A. Mendes Corrêa: *Da raça e do espirito*. Porto: Instituto de Antropología, 1940; A.A. Mendes Corrêa: *A alimentação do povo português*. Lisbon: Publicação do Dentro de Estudos Demográficos, 1951; F.A. Perreira da Costa: *Da existência do homem em épocas remotas no vale do Tejo, 1.º opúsculo: Notícia sobre os esqueletos humanos descobertos no cabeço da Arruda*. Lisbon: Serviços Geológicos de Portugal, 1865.

A. Xavier da Cunha: Contribution à l'histoire de l'anthropologie physique au Portugal. *Contribuições para o Estudo da Antropología Portugesa* 11:5–56, 1982; Cunha: Testing identification records: Evidence from the Coimbra identified skeletal collections (nineteenth and twentieth centuries). In: S.R. Saunders & A. Herring (eds) *Grave reflections: Portraying the past through cemetery studies*. Toronto: Canadian Scholars' Press, 1995, pp. 179–198; Cuhna & G.N. van Vark: Càlculo de funções discriminantes para a diagnose sexual do crânio. *Antropología Portuguesa* 8:17–37, 1990; J.F. Nery Delgado: *Da existência provável do homem no nosso solo em tempos mui remotos provada pelo estudo das cavernas. Vol. 1, Notícia acerca das grutas da Cesareda*. Lisbon: Estudos Geologicos, Commissão Geológica de Portugal, 1867; C.M.P. Duarte: *Analysis of wear and pathological conditions in human teeth from the Neolithic site of Grutas Artificias do Tojal de Vila Chã, Carenque (Estremadura, Portugal)*. M.A. Thesis. University of Alberta, 1993.

D. Ferembach: *Le gisement mésolithique de Moita do Sebastião. Muge. Portugal. Vol. 2, Anthropologie*. Lisbon: Direcção-Geral do Assuntos Culturais, 1974; M.T.M. Fernandes: Colecções osteológicas. In: J. Houart et al. (eds) *Cem anos de antropología em Coimbra*. Coimbra: Museu e Laboratório Antropológico, Universidade de Coimbra, 1985, pp. 77–81; J.-P. Fléchier et al.: Mensurations dentaires des hommes de Muge. *Bulletins et Mémoires de la Société d'Anthropologie de Paris* 13 (13th ser.):147–164, 1976; J. Houart et al.: *Cem anos de antropología em Coimbra*. Coimbra: Museu e Laboratório Antropológico, Universidade de Coimbra, 1985; M. Jackes: Paleodemography: Problems and techniques. In: S.R. Saunders & M.A. Katzenberg (eds) *Skeletal biology of past peoples: Research methods*. New York: Wiley-Liss, 1992, pp. 189–224.

M. Jackes & D. Lubell: Dental pathology and diet: Second thoughts. In: M. Otte (ed) *Nature et Culture*. Actes du Colloque International de Liège, 13–17 decembre 1993. Liège: Études et Recherches Archéologiques de l'Université de Liège. No. 68. 1996, pp.457–480; J. Lefèvre: Étude odontologique des hommes de Muge. *Bulletins et Mémoires de la Société de Paris* 10:301–333, 1973; D. Lubell et al.: The Mesolithic–Neolithic transition in Portugal: Isotopic and dental evidence of diet. *Journal of Archaeological Science* 21:201–216, 1994; S.M. MacLaughlin: Epiphyseal fusion at the sternal end of the clavicle in a modern Portugese sample. *Antropología Portuguesa* 8:59–68, 1990; Cl. Masset & M.E. de Castro Almeida: Âge et sutures crâniennes. *Atti della Accademia Mediterranea delle Scienze*. Anno V. Vol. 1. No. 2, 1990; F. Paula e Oliviera: Notes sur les ossements humains existants dans le Musée de la

Commission des travaux géologiques. *Communicações da Comissão dos Trabalhos Geológicos de Portugal* 2:1–13, 1888.

A. Queiroz Lopes & J.A. Serra: Correlações entre a estatura e alguns caracteres osteométricos. *Contribuições para o Estudo da Antropología Portuguesa* 4:313–358, 1944; J. Roche: *Le gisement Mésolithique de Moita do Sebastião. Muge, Portugal.* Vol. 1, *Archéologie.* Lisbon: Instituto de Alta Cultura, 1972; J.A. Serra: A pelve nos Portugueses: Morfologia de pelve no homem. *Contribuições para o Estudo da Antropología Portuguesa* 3:1–174, 1938; F. Sobral: Secular changes in stature in southern Portugal between 1930 and 1980, according to conscript data. *Human Biology* 62:491–504, 1990; M.B.B. Sueiro & J.V. Frazão: Lesões dentárias no homem do Mesolíticos Português: Nota de paleopatologia. *Arquivos de Anatomica e Antropología* 30:197–209, 1959.

E. Tamagnini: A pigmentação dos portugueses: A cor dos olhos e dos cabelos. *Contribuições para o Estudo da Antropología Portuguesa* 1:127–198, 1936; E. Tamagnini: Os grupos sanguíneos dos portugueses. *Contribuições para o Estudo da Antropología Portuguesa* 3:179–347, 1947; E. Tamagnini & D.S. Vieira de Campos: O fémur português. *Contribuições para o Estuda da Antropología Portuguesa* 2:5–69, 1949; M.A. Tavares da Rocha: Antropología criminal. In: J. Houart et al.: *Cem anos de antropología em Coimbra.* Coimbra: Museu e Laboratorio Antropológico, Universidade de Coimbra, 1985, pp. 83–107; H.V. Vallois: Recherches sur les ossements mésolithiques de Mugem. *L'Anthropologie* 40:337–389, 1930; J. Zilhão: *Gruta do Caldeirão: O Neolítico Antigo.* Trabalhos de Arqueologia. No. 6. Lisbon: Instituto Portugês do Património Cultural, 1992.

Předmostí

Located in northeastern Moravia (Czech Republic), Předmostí is one of the largest and most famous open-air Upper Paleolithic occupation sites on the loess plains of central Europe. The first systematic excavations were carried out there in 1880 by the Czech scientist Jindřich Wankel (1812–1897), but as early as 1571 there are records of the discovery of "giant bones" from the site. Wankel discovered the first human specimen, a mandible (Předmostí 24), in 1884, lying under a mammoth femur. But from the standpoint of human paleontology, the most significant discovery at Předmostí was the 1894 discovery of a communal grave in Chromček's garden. The grave was a 4 × 2.5 m elliptical pit containing the remains of eighteen individuals (Předmostí 1–18) of various ages and sexes, most with their heads oriented to the north. The grave was covered with limestone slabs and mammoth bones (principally scapulae)—a burial style characteristic of the Pavlovian (eastern Gravettian) in the region.

The communal grave at Předmostí was discovered by Karel Maška (1851–1916), a middle-school teacher and director of the Realschule in Telč, whom many credit as the father of paleolithic archeology in Moravia. Maška excavated in Šipka Cave, discovering the juvenile Neandertal Šipka mandible in 1880. He began excavations at Předmostí in 1882.

Excavations at Předmostí by Wankel, Maška, Jan Knies, and Martin Kříž (1841–1916), and in the 1920s by Karel Absolon (1887–1960) resulted in a total of twenty-nine human specimens and a tremendous assemblage of cultural remains. The main cultural level covered more than 10,000 m² and contained several thousand lithic artifacts, a rich bone and antler industry, and numerous art and decorative items. Extensive faunal remains, including the remains of an estimated 500–1,000 mammoth, were also present. Many of the famous artworks from Předmostí are crafted in mammoth bone and ivory. This level was assigned to the Pavlovian, and the later work by the Czech prehistorian Bohuslav Klíma has established the contemporaneity of cultural remains with the grave (cf. Absolon & Klíma 1978).

The Předmostí skeletons were described in two detailed monographs by Jindřich Matiegka (1862–1941), in 1934 and 1938. Maška had previously named the Předmostí people *Homo předmostensis*, and it had been suggested that their prominent brow ridges and occipital chignons reflected an intermediate status between Neandertals and other early-modern Europeans. Matiegka retained Maška's taxonomic name but argued that the Předmostí skeletons, although variable and tending toward robustness, represented an eastern variant of the "Cro-Magnon race."

At the beginning of the twentieth century, the remains from Předmostí, as well as those from Brno (the Brno II specimen found in 1891), Brüx (found in 1871), and sometimes Galley Hill, were considered to represent a distinct dolichocephalic people who lived primarily in central Europe. Within the racial successionist paradigm common to this period, this Předmostí race—also known as the Brünn (German for Brno) race—was generally compared with the supposedly more advanced Cro-Magnon race from France. Other races, such as the Grimaldi (Negroid) race, and the German anatomist Hermann Klaatsch's (1863–1916) Aurignacian race were also recognized by various scholars.

The Předmostí race was considered to be of a "lower type" than Cro-Magnon, and it was generally held by scholars such as Arthur Keith (1866–1955) in England, and Gustav Schwalbe (1844–1916) and Carl Toldt (1840–1920) in Germany, that its members bridged the gap, to some extent, between Neandertals and recent Europeans. There was a difference of opinion, however, as to how Neandertal-like the Předmostí race was. Toldt, for example, emphasized the "flat, retreating forehead and heavy brow ridges" of the Předmostí males as distinct Neandertal features. While recognizing the Neandertal connections in this morphology, Schwalbe, on the other hand, showed that their total anatomical pattern placed them within modern *Homo sapiens* and not Neandertals.

Following Schwalbe, the Czech-American physical anthropologist Aleš Hrdlička (1869–1943) also argued that the morphology of the Předmostí people clearly indicated that they were derived from Neandertals. The specimens from Předmostí and other members of their "race" became important to Hrdlička's argument that Neandertals were ancestral to the earliest modern people. And since the late 1960s, these remains have formed an essential part of a similar argument, specifically that the earliest modern Europeans reflect some degree of Neandertal ancestry. These views are held by proponents of the multiregional model for modern human origins.

It is fortunate that Matiegka carried out his detailed studies of the Předmostí remains, because the skeletons were later destroyed. During the German occupation of Moravia in World War II, many famous Paleolithic artworks and skeletal remains were designated Reichsschätze, or treasures of the Reich, and duly confiscated. In many cases, museum curators were able to substitute casts for artworks but not the skeletons. In 1945, these were being stored at Mikulov Castle on the Czech–Austrian border. As the local Axis collaborators withdrew in the face of the Allied advance, the castle was burned, along with virtually all of the "treasures" stored there. Among the human fossil remains destroyed

were the Šipka mandible, all the Předmostí skeletons, virtually all of the Mladeč specimens excavated after 1882, and several specimens from Dolní Věstonice.

Fred H. Smith

See also Brno; Brüx; Galley Hill; Grimaldi; Hrdlička, Aleš; Keith, (Sir) Arthur; Klaatsch, Hermann; Matiegka, Jindřich; Mladeč; Modern Human Origins; Neandertals; Schwalbe, Gustav; Šipka

Bibliography
K. Absolon & B. Klíma: *Předmostí: Ein Mammutjägerplatz in Mähren*. Brno: Archeologický Ústav ČSAV v Brne, 1978; J. Jelinek: Neanderthal man and *Homo sapiens* in central and eastern Europe. *Current Anthropology* 10:475–503, 1969; J. Matiegka: *Homo předmostensis: Folilní Člověk z Předmostí na Moravě. I. Lebky*. (French summary). Prague: Česká Akademie Věd i Umění, 1934; J. Matiegka: *Homo předmostensis. Fosilní Člověk z Předmostí na Moravě. II. Ostatni Časti Kostrové*. (French summary). Prague: Česká Akademie Věd i Umění, 1938; H.F. Osborn: *Men of the Old Stone Age*. New York: Scribner's, 1925; F.H. Smith: Upper Pleistocene hominid evolution in south-central Europe: A review of the evidence and analysis of trends. *Current Anthropology* 23:667–603, 1982.

Prestwich, (Sir) Joseph (1812–1896)

Born in Clapham, London, England, the son of a successful wine merchant, Prestwich was educated at private schools in London and Paris before entering University College, London, in 1829, where he had intended to read chemistry. The following year, however, he was obliged to withdraw and assist in the running of his father's business. Although he became a conscientious businessman, he nevertheless remained devoted to his scientific interests, which during the next decade shifted from chemistry to the study of geology. Being both cautious and practical by nature, he was naturally drawn to the highly fact-oriented aspect of this fledgling science, and in particular to stratigraphical analysis.

Prestwich's subsequent scientific career can be conveniently separated into two distinct periods. The first embraces the years between the publication of his first paper "On the Geology of Coalbrookdale" (1840) and his retirement from business in 1870; the second covers the period from 1874, when he succeeded John Phillips (1800–1874) to the

Chair of Geology at Oxford (1874–1888), until his death in 1896.

Essentially, his reputation as a geologist was founded on a series of papers published between the mid-1840s and 1850s elucidating the stratigraphy of the Tertiary beds lying between the Chalk and the London Clay in southeast England and correlated with the corresponding beds across the Channel in northwest France and Belgium (e.g., Prestwich 1847a, 1847b, 1852, 1855). In fact, by the mid-1850s he was not only widely acknowledged as a leading authority on Tertiary and Quaternary geology, but also firmly ensconced in an elite circle of scientists that then ruled British geology.

Based in part on his standing in the geological community and the fact that he was then treasurer of the Geological Society of London, in 1858 he was made treasurer and secretary of the committee established to oversee the excavation of Brixham Cave. During the summer of 1858, this cave yielded compelling evidence supporting the thesis of the coexistence of human beings with extinct mammalian fauna. But while some of the committee members, such as William Pengelly (1812–1894) and Hugh Falconer (1808–1865), were convinced by the evidence, there were others like Charles Lyell (1797–1875) and Richard Owen (1804–1892) who shared Prestwich's reservations—which were grounded in the long-recognized problem that caves were subject to periodic flooding that could result in the mixing of deposits. As such, Prestwich had informed Pengelly, who was supervising the excavations, that "cave evidence alone was not sufficient" to extablish a *prima facie* case for human antiquity. This led Falconer to visit Jacques Boucher de Perthes (1788–1868) in Abbeville to examine the evidence he had found in the Somme River Valley. Although Boucher de Perthes' (1847) work was well known, it was not then generally accepted. Impressed by what he saw, Falconer challenged his skeptical colleague to cross the Channel and examine the evidence himself (cf. G.A. Prestwich 1899:119–120), which Prestwich did in April 1859. As a result of this visit, Prestwich became the first scientific authority to confirm Boucher de Perthes' evidence for human antiquity (Prestwich 1860, 1861). It also initiated a comparative study of river-valley systems in northwest France and southeast England, from which emerged his system of comparing the relative age of river terraces (1863). In this regard, he noted that, without

exception, the flint-implement-bearing gravels at Abbeville and at other sites in the Somme River Valley (as well as those like Hoxne in England) were found in "high-level gravels"—namely, at elevations between 50 and 100 feet above the present valley floor. This system of relative dating was widely used into the twentieth century, and it is interesting to note that it was first applied to the celebrated Moulin-Quignon jaw (cf. Carpenter 1863; see Hinton & Kennard 1905 for a more recent elaboration of the system).

Although Prestwich's initial estimates of the age of the human remains found at Brixham and elsewhere were modest, he subsequently adopted a less conservative posture, advocating that "our present chronology with respect to the first appearance of Man must be greatly extended" (1863:52). Indeed, he later spearheaded the eolithic movement in Britain during the 1880s and early 1890s (cf. Prestwich 1887, 1889, 1892, 1895; Spencer 1990:14–19). Much of this latter work was done after he vacated his professorship at Oxford (being succeeded by Alexander Green [1833–1896]). Among his most notable works produced during this second period is his two-volume *Geology* (1886–1888).

Prestwich was elected a Fellow of the Geological Society in 1833 and of the Royal Society in 1853. He was the recipient of several notable prizes, including the Wollaston Medal in 1849 and a Royal Medal in 1865. He was knighted in 1896.

He died at his home in Shoreham, Kent, on 23 June 1896.

Frank Spencer

See also Boucher (de Crèvecoeur) de Perthes, Jacques; Brixham Cave; Buckland, William; Eolithic Theory; Falconer, Hugh; Lankester, (Sir) Edwin Ray; Lyell, (Sir) Charles; Moulin-Quignon Affair; Owen, (Sir) Richard

Bibliography
SELECTED WORKS
    On the geology of Coalbrookdale. *Transactions of the Geological Society of London* 5:413–493, 1840; On the main points of structure and the probable age of the Bagshot Sands, and their presumed equivalents in Hampshire and France. *Quarterly Journal of the Geological Society of London* 3:378–409, 1847a; On the probable age of the London Clay, and its relations to the Hampshire and Paris Tertiary systems. *Quarterly Journal of the Geological Society of London* 3:354–377, 1847b; On the

correlation of the Lower Tertiaries of England with those of France and Belgium. *Quarterly Journal of the Geological Society of London* 10:206–246, 1852; On the correlation of the Eocene Tertiaries of England, France, and Belgium. *Quarterly Journal of the Geological Society of London* 13:89–134, 1855.

On the occurrence of flint implements, associated with the remains of animals of extinct mammalia, in undisturbed beds of a late geological period. *Proceedings of the Royal Society of London* 10:50–59, 1860; On the occurrence of flint implements, associated with the remains of extinct mammalia, in undisturbed beds of a late geological period, in France at Amiens and Abbeville, and in England at Hoxne. *Philosophical Transactions of the Royal Society of London* 150:277–317, 1861; Theoretical considerations on the conditions under which the drift deposits containing the remains of extinct mammalia and flint implements were accumulated, and their geological age. *Proceedings of the Royal Society of London* 12:38–52, 1863.

Geology: Chemical, physical, and stratigraphical. 2 vols. Oxford: Oxford University Press, 1886–1888; Considerations on the date, duration, and conditions of the glacial period, with reference to the antiquity of man. *Quarterly Journal of Geological Society of London* 43:393–410, 1887; On the occurrence of Paleolithic flint implements in the neighbourhood of Ightham, Kent: Their distribution and probable age. *Quarterly Journal of the Geological Society of London* 45:270–297, 1889; On the primitive characters of the flint implements of the chalk plateau of Kent. *Journal of the Anthropological Institute* 21:246–276, 1892; The greater antiquity of man. *Nineteenth Century Magazine* 37:617–628, 1895.

PRIMARY SOURCES

J. Boucher de Perthes: *Antiquités celtiques et anté-diluviennes: Mémoire sur l'industrie primitive et les arts à leur origine.* Paris: Treuttel et Wurtz, 1847; W.B. Carpenter: Discovery at Abbeville. *Athenaeum* 41:523, 1863; M.A.C. Hinton & A.S. Kennard: The relative ages of the stone implements of the lower Thames Valley. *Proceedings of the Geological Association* 19:76–100, 1905.

SECONDARY SOURCES

J. Challinor: Joseph Prestwich. In: C.C.

Gillespie (ed) *Dictionary of scientific biography.* Vol. 11. New York: Scribner's, 1970, pp. 130–131; G.A. Prestwich: *Life and letters of Sir Joseph Prestwich.* Edinburgh: Blackwood, 1899; F. Spencer: *Piltdown: A scientific forgery.* London: Oxford University Press, 1990; F. Spencer: The Brixham ark. In: *Fallen Idols: Case studies in the history of paleoanthropology.* In preparation.

Prichard, James Cowles (1786–1848)

Born at Ross, Herefordshire, England, to Quaker parents, Prichard received his preliminary training in medicine at hospitals in Bristol and London in the years 1802–1806 before going to Edinburgh University, from which he graduated M.D. in 1808 with an anthropological thesis entitled *De generis humani varietate (vide infra).* On completing his medical studies, he spent a year at Trinity College, Cambridge, during which time he evidently converted to the Church of England, and a term at St. John's College, Oxford, before settling in Bristol in 1810 (Stocking 1973: xviii). There he established a practice and managed to continue his study of anthropology while expanding his medical commitments. In 1811, he was elected physician to St. Peter's Hospital in Bristol, and in 1814 he was elected to the same post at the Bristol Infirmary.

It was largely his experiences at the former institution that led him to write *A Treatise on Diseases of the Nervous System* (1822), which was followed by *A Treatise on Insanity* (1833) and *A Treatise on Insanity, and Other Disorders Affecting the Mind* (1835). In this latter work, Prichard presented his controversial concept of moral insanity, which he defined as "a morbid perversion of the natural feelings, affections, inclinations, temper, habits, moral dispositions, and natural impulses, without any remarkable disorder or defect of the intellect or knowing and reasoning faculties, and particularly without any insane illusion or hallucination" (1835:6). He later explored the legal ramifications of this new doctrine in a book entitled *On the Different Forms of Insanity* (1842). This body of work resulted in his appointment in 1845 as a commissioner of lunacy. Since his duties involved the inspection of asylums, he had to quit his Bristol position and relocate to London, where he remained until his death in 1848 (*vide infra*).

Prichard's contributions to anthropology were also influential. As he noted in the preface to his now classic *Researches into the Physical History of Man (RPHM)* (1813: ii–iii), his initial interest in anthropology had been aroused at Edinburgh by the lectures of the moral philosopher Dugald Stewart (1753–1828), and evidently one of his remarks had stimulated Prichard to devote his doctoral dissertation to the subject of human variation, which he later expanded into the *RPHM*.

At the core of the *RPHM* is the issue of human diversity, which at this juncture in the history of anthropological thought, was in the midst of a general retreat from orthodox monogenism. The extent to which the burgeoning polygenist movement at the turn of the century had eroded confidence in the traditional environmental explanations of human diversity is revealed in the first edition of the *RPHM*. As Prichard (1813:ii) remarks there: "Most of the theories concerning the effects of climate and other modifying causes are in great part hypothetical and irreconcilable with facts that cannot be disputed." He believed the process of civilization was a more plausible explanatory mechanism, noting that "domestication" was a powerful cause of variation in animals and plants—an idea derived from the London anatomist John Hunter's (1728–1793) *Observations on Certain Parts of the Animal Oeconomy* (1786). Following this line of thinking, Prichard posited that the primal color of humankind had not been white, as had long been supposed, but black, and that it was via the "transmutation of the characters of the Negro" that the European and all other varieties of the human species were derived (Prichard 1813:233). In subsequent editions, however (evidently taking a defensive posture against the mounting popularity of the polygenist viewpoint), he abandoned this idea, along with the notion that civilization had been a formative force, and replaced it with a less specific environmental argument (climate). And in the third edition, he skirted the entire issue, focusing instead on the task of demonstrating through historical and linguistic analysis the probable connections between the racial groups of humankind, thereby revealing the underlying unity of the species. The seeds of this approach can be found in his early treatises: *An Analysis of the Egyptian Mythology* (1819) and *The Eastern Origin of the Celtic Nations* (1831). As the title of this latter work indicates, he was a supporter of the Indo-European character of the Celtic languages and thus an early contributor to the "Aryan controversy." (For a more detailed analysis of Prichard's anthropology, see Stocking 1973). Midway through the last edition of the *RPHM*, Prichard published the

equally influential volume *The Natural History of Man* (1843). This title, however, is misleading, since the work is, as Prichard noted himself, more archeological and historical than biological—which is the essence of his vision of the anthropological endeavor (cf. Stocking 1973).

Although he had supported his friend and medical colleague Thomas Hodgkin (1798–1866) in his efforts to establish the Ethnological Society of London (ESL) in 1844 and its parent organization, the Aborigines' Protection Society in 1837, Prichard's involvement in these developments had been rather peripheral. However, following his move to London in 1845, he took an active role in the affairs of the ESL, over which he presided in 1847–1848. It was in this context that he made a case for the scientific importance of ethnology, arguing vainly at the time for its representation in a separate Section of the British Association for the Advancement of Science.

He died in London on 23 December 1848.

Frank Spencer

See also Aryanism; Hodgkin, Thomas; Hunt, James; Polygenism; Skin Color; United Kingdom

Bibliography
SELECTED WORKS

De generis humani varietate. Edinburgh: Abernethy & Walker, 1808; *Researches into the physical history of man*. London: Arch, 1813 (2d ed., 2 vols.: 1826; 3d ed., 5 vols.: London: Sherwood, Gilbert & Piper, 1836–1847); *An analysis of Egyptian mythology*. London: Arch, 1819; *A treatise on diseases of the nervous system*. Part 1: *Comprising convulsive and maniacal affections*. London: Underwood, 1822; *The eastern origin of the Celtic nations proved by a comparison of their dialects with the Sanskrit, Greek, Latin, and Teutonic languages*. London: Arch, 1831 (2d ed.: edited by Robert G. Latham [1812–1888]. London: Houston, 1857); *A treatise on insanity*. London: Marchant, 1833.

A treatise on insanity, and other disorders affecting the mind. London: Sherwood, 1835; *On the different forms of insanity, in relation to jurisprudence. Designed for the use of persons concerned in legal questions regarding unsoundness of mind*. London: Baillière, 1842 (2d ed.: 1847); *The natural history of man: Comprising inquiries into the modifying influence of physical and moral agencies on the different tribes of the human family*. London: Baillière, 1843 (2d ed.: 1845; 3d ed.: 1848; 4th ed.: edited by E. Norris. 2 vols., 1855); On the relations of ethnology to other branches of knowledge. *Journal of the Ethnological Society of London* 1:301–329, 1847.

ARCHIVAL SOURCES

There appears to be no primary repository of either Prichard's manuscripts or his correspondence. However, some correspondence is preserved in the following collections: 1. James C. Prichard (in files of incoming letters), Library, Royal Geographical Society, Kensington, London SW7 2AR, England; 2. Thomas Hodgkin Papers: (Rhodes House Library), Bodleian Library, Oxford OX1 3BG, England.

PRIMARY AND SECONDARY SOURCES

T. Hodgkin: Obituary: Dr. Prichard. *Lancet* i:18–19, 1849; T. Hodgkin: Obituary. *Journal of the Ethnological Society of London* 2:182–207, 1850; J. Hunter: *Observations on certain parts of the animal oeconomy*. London: Nicol, 1786; D. Leigh: James Cowles Prichard, M.D., 1786–1848. *Proceedings of the Royal Society of Medicine* 48:586–590, 1955; G.W. Stocking: From chronology to ethnology: James Cowles Prichard and British anthropology, 1800–1850. In: G.W. Stocking (ed) *James Cowles Prichard: Researches into the physical history of man*. London: Arch, 1813. Reprint. Chicago: University of Chicago Press, 1973, pp. ix–cxviii.

Primate Field Studies

Nineteenth-Century Roots

It might be said that scientific interest in the natural behavior of primates began with an argument at the annual meeting of the British Association for the Advancement of Science in 1860 at Oxford. It was at this meeting that Thomas Henry Huxley (1825–1895) defended the evolutionary thesis of Charles Darwin (1809–1882) against the bishop of Oxford, Samuel ("Soapy Sam") Wilberforce (1805–1873). After a long-winded criticism of Darwin's theory of natural selection, the bishop is reported to have turned to Huxley, and begged to know: "Was it through his grandfather or his grandmother that he claimed descent from a monkey?" To which Huxley replied: "If the question is put to me would I rather have a miserable ape for a grandfather or a man highly endowed by nature and possessing great means and influence

for the mere purpose of introducing ridicule into a grave scientific discussion—I unhesitatingly affirm my preference for the ape" (cited in Montagu 1959:2–3).

Soon thereafter, in 1863, Huxley's *Evidence as to Man's Place in Nature* was published. In this book, he put human and nonhuman primates into Darwin's evolutionary narrative and compiled what could be thought of as the first "textbook" in biological anthropology. The book was organized into three sections: One section dealt with comparative anatomy, illustrating the anatomical likeness of humans to other animals; another included a summation of the human fossil remains known at that time. In the first section of the book, Huxley wrote the first systematic review of what was known about primates in their natural habitat, though as this review indicates much of the information was simply anecdotal.

Contrary to expectations, this book did not promote an immediate exodus of scientists into the field to study the natural behavior of the primates. Indeed, there appear to have been only a few scientists interested in venturing into the forests to observe wild-living primates. By and large, most researchers during the second half of the nineteenth century confined their inquiries to either captive animals or the examination of skeletal material. There were, however, some notable exceptions. For example, between 1889 and 1892 the British anatomist Arthur Keith (1866–1955) visited Siam, where he observed the behavior of gibbons and related his findings to anatomical dissections of these animals.

Another was Richard L. Garner (1848–1920), an American zoologist and collector, who in the 1890s went to Gabon, West Africa, to collect great apes and decided to observe them in the wild. Because it was commonly thought that gorillas were bold and violent, Garner armed himself and built a protective cage to sit in while waiting for the animals to come by. This he did for much of the day and night for 112 successive days. A few individual animals approached and quickly wandered off. Needless to say, little was learned about the behavior of gorillas and chimpanzees by Garner's venture.

Tentative Foundations: 1920s–1940s

In 1929, the Yale psychologist Robert Mearns Yerkes (1876–1956), and his wife, Ada, published *The Great Apes*, a compilation of current knowledge about primates. Since there was no field research to report, this volume

Fig. 1. R.L. Garner and the cage in which he spent over 100 days waiting for gorillas and chimpanzees to pass in the 1890s.

concentrated principally on summarizing knowledge gleaned from observations and experiments performed on captive animals. Coinciding with this publication was the establishment by Yerkes of a great-ape breeding facility in Orange Park, Florida, as an extension of the Yale Primate Laboratory, which had been founded five years earlier. Later, the Orange Park facility became the Yerkes Regional Primate Center of Emory University, Georgia. Cognizant of the paucity of comparative observations of the behavior of apes in their natural habitat, Yerkes sponsored two pioneering expeditions to Africa. In 1929, Harold C. Bingham (1888–1958) set off for the Congo to conduct research on gorillas, and a year later, Henry Nissen (1901–1958) went

to French Guinea, West Africa, to collect and study chimpanzees.

Yerkes, Bingham, and Nissen were psychologists, and their research on great apes was motivated mainly by an interest in the study of the evolution of intelligence. Yerkes and Bingham had both scientific and political influence. They were leaders in the eugenics movement in the United States during the decades preceding world War II and were major proponents of the use of intelligence testing to restrict immigration into the United States, and their work was often used to support and rationalize other forms of racial prejudice.

Nissen's expedition was fairly successful. He was able to observe chimpanzees on forty-nine of sixty-four days in the field, thereby dispelling a number of widely believed but fictitious ideas about these animals. His research was published as a monograph, the earliest on primate field behavior (Nissen 1931). Bingham had little more success in his study of gorillas than did Garner before him. Believing anecdotal accounts of the gorilla's ferocity, he thought it necessary to track the animals with a large entourage of guides, gun bearers, and porters. Bingham armed himself with a rifle and his wife with a pistol. After about two weeks in the field, his party inadvertently surprised a group of feeding gorillas and were threatened by a large male. Bingham shot the animal and returned home a month later, learning very little about the natural behavior of gorillas (Bingham 1932).

At about the same time that Nissen and Bingham were attempting to study great apes in West and Central Africa, the South African medical doctor and anatomist Solly Zuckerman (1904–1993) was studying a captive colony of baboons in Regent's Park Zoo, London. In 1930, he returned to his native South Africa to add some information on natural populations of these animals. He spent only nine days, however, observing chacma baboons in the field. His monograph *The Social Life of Monkeys and Apes* (1932) focused on the importance of the social behavior of primates and emphasized the fact that higher primates lived in permanent social groups. Zuckerman theorized that sex was the major reason for group life in primates, and, although his theory is no longer accepted, the factors underlying social organization in primates are still being debated.

Although Zuckerman is frequently credited as being the first to study baboons in the wild, there was, in fact, one earlier study by the South African journalist, lawyer, and naturalist Eugene Marais (1871–1936). Sometime around 1907, shortly after the Boer War, Marais retreated to Waterburg, a remote area of the Transvaal. There, he and a young colleague studied a troop of habituated chacma baboons for three years, essentially from his backyard. It is interesting to note that Marais was worried during his observations because he "had no libraries and no means of checking what work had already been accomplished in this field" (Marais 1968:63). Little did he know that there had been no previous studies of this sort. However, until his unfinished monograph *The Soul of the Ape* appeared in 1968, long after his death, the primate fieldwork of Marais remained relatively unknown (though Zuckerman did make passing reference to Marais' work in his 1932 volume).

Thus, although some field studies had been done during this early period, none of the individuals involved were interested in dedicating their lives to the study of primates in remote habitats and none contributed to field primatology in any permanent way. However, C. Raymond Carpenter (1905–1975) was an exception. After earning his Ph.D. from Stanford University in psychology (1932) for his dissertation on the sexual behavior of birds, Carpenter was granted a postdoctoral fellowship to work with Yerkes at Yale. It was Yerkes, along with the ornithologist Frank M. Chapman, who convinced him to study monkeys at Chapman's field site on Barro Colorado Island (BCI), Panama. Thus began the

Fig. 2. An early encounter with a gorilla. An illustration from Paul Du Chaillu (1831–1903): Explorations and Adventures in Equatorial Africa *(1861), in which the gorilla was depicted as ferocious, a myth that lasted well into the 20th century.*

first long-term involvement of a scientist in field primatology or, as Carpenter called it, studying "the naturalistic behavior of nonhuman primates" (Teleki 1981:384). Carpenter spent a number of months studying howler monkeys, and recording with some peripheral observation on spider monkeys, on BCI between 1931 and 1935 (Carpenter 1934, 1935). He focused mainly on social organization, social interactions, and group censuses.

In 1937, Carpenter was invited to collect the behavioral data on a multidisciplinary expedition to study gibbons in Thailand (then Siam) initiated by Harold J. Coolidge Jr., who, during the early 1930s, had made a number of field trips to Africa studying the distribution of the pygmy chimpanzee and the gorilla (cf. Coolidge 1936). The Asian Expedition was sponsored by Harvard, Columbia, and Johns Hopkins Universities and included two physical anthropologists who were to become very important to primatology, namely, Adolph Hans Schultz (1891–1976) and Sherwood L. Washburn (1911–). Carpenter spent four months in the field studying white-handed gibbons, which led to his now classic monograph on this species (cf. Carpenter 1940). A year later, Carpenter was instrumental in exporting 450–500 rhesus monkeys from India and releasing them on Cayo Santiago, an island off the coast of Puerto Rico. This began the first long-term research on semicaptive primate populations. The Cayo Santiago colony is now part of the Caribbean Primate Research Center, which embraces similar primate colonies on the islands of Guayacan, La Cueva, and Tesecheo.

Post–World War II Developments
Although it is obvious from the activities of Carpenter and others in the 1930s that the natural behavior of primates was beginning to attract the interest of scientists, it was not until after World War II, more specifically the early 1960s, that the subdiscipline of field primatology became solidly established.

Field research on primates during the 1950s stemmed mainly from four different areas: (1) The epidemiological study of yellow fever which during World War II had spread in many tropical areas involving both human and nonhuman primate populations. Some studies of free-ranging primates were carried out in relation to the epidemiology of this disease, such as that done by the Virus Research Institute in Entebbe, Uganda (e.g., Haddow 1952). (2) Following Carpenter's lead, the American zoologist Nicholas Collias and his then graduate student Charles Southwick recensused the howler monkeys on BCI (Collias & Southwick 1952). This was followed by another American zoologist, Stuart Altmann, who studied the social behavior of the BCI howlers (S.A. Altmann 1959). Both Southwick and Altmann became major contributors to primate field studies during the next decade and were still very active in the field into the mid-1990s. (3) A few animal ethologists and mammalogists teaching and residing in tropical countries did studies of primates as part of more-general research on local fauna. For example, Niels Bolwig of the University of the Witwatersrand in Johannesburg, South Africa, studied baboons in South Africa (Bolwig 1959), and Angus Booth of University College, Ghana, did sophisticated studies of synecology of West African primate communities (e.g., Booth 1956). It is conjectured that Booth would have had a major influence on primate field research had he not died tragically in 1959 at the age of thirty. (4) Under the lead of Kinji Imanishi in 1948, a number of Japanese animal behaviorists from Kyoto University began studying the indigenous Japanese macaques (e.g., Imanishi 1957; Kawamura 1959). These were the first long-term studies of identified individuals of known kinship in natural primate populations, and the beginning of what has turned out to be one of the most active centers of primate research. This Japanese group of researchers founded the first journal in primatology, *Primates*, which was first published in English in 1959.

It was not, however, until the next decade that field primatology finally emerged as an identifiable subdiscipline. It appears that two developments in the 1950s were crucial to the enormous growth of the subdiscipline in the 1960s. The first was the exchange of ideas and concepts between population biologists and anthropologists, especially concerning evolution. This is exemplified by the Cold Spring Harbor Symposium on the "Origin and Evolution of Man" in June 1950. This meeting was attended by 129 of the most influential biologists and anthropologists in the world. The proceedings were published in 1951 and contained a number of papers calling for a more detailed look at primate behavior in interpreting nonhuman and human primate fossils (Warren 1951). In 1953, a paper was published in the *American Anthropologist*, coauthored by a biologist, George Bartholomew Jr. and an American anthropologist, Joseph Birdsell (who had attended the Cold Spring Harbor Symposium), titled "Ecology and the Protohominids." This paper developed a method for reconstructing the behavior of early hominids by extrapolating from the behavior of extant primates and other mammals. The second stimulus was the discovery, in the early 1950s, that the highly controversial but pivotal Piltdown remains were fake, and the concomitant acceptance of the South African australopithecines as true ancestors of humans. These two events ended any idea that there was a major evolutionary hiatus between human and nonhuman primates and emphasized the continuity between ourselves and our ancestors.

Stimulated by these events, biologists, especially biological anthropologists, began to think seriously about the behavior and ecology of early humans and to see living primates as potential windows into the study of the evolution of human behavior. By the mid-1950s and 1960s, many conferences and books focused on the relationship between primate behavior and human evolution. For example, in 1953, a symposium was presented at the annual meetings of the American Association for the Advancement of Science titled "The Nonhuman Primates and Human Evolution." The proceedings of this meeting (cf. Gavan 1955) were dedicated to Earnest A. Hooton (1887–1954), the Harvard physical anthropologist who had been calling for primate field studies since his classic book *Man's Poor Relations* (1942). He delivered a paper at this conference, shortly before his death, titled "The Importance of Primate Studies in Anthropology" (Hooton 1954). Other volumes to appear were *The Evolution of Man* (Tax 1960), *Social Life of Early Man* (Washburn 1961), *Ideas on Human Evolution* (Howells 1962), *Classification and Human Evolution* (Washburn 1963), and *African Ecology and Human Evolution* (Howell & Bourlière 1963).

Except for the volume edited by Howells, each of these books developed out of international conferences. One of the prime movers for this interchange was Washburn, an anthropologist and functional anatomist who had been a student of Hooton and, as noted earlier, a member of the Asian Expedition with Carpenter. As a graduate student, he had spent a semester in 1936 at Oxford, where he had attended the lectures of the anatomist-primatologist Wilfrid Edward Le Gros Clark (1895–1971), whose book *Early Forerunners of Man* (1934) had stressed the anatomical relationship between structure and function. While at Oxford, Washburn also took care of

some of Zuckerman's monkeys (DeVore 1992). Papers by Washburn, stressing the need for primate field research, appeared in each of these volumes, including the now classic papers by Washburn and his student Irven DeVore, on baboon and early human ecology and social behavior (e.g., Washburn & DeVore 1961; Washburn 1962, 1963; DeVore & Washburn 1963).

These works stimulated students to study primates in their natural habitats, and by the early 1960s a number of conferences on free-ranging primates were held, and related books began to appear. The first two of these volumes to appear were based based on international conferences held in 1962 in New York (Buettner-Janusch 1962) and London (Napier & Barnicot 1963). Other early collections were edited by Southwick (1963), DeVore (1965), P.C. Jay (1968), and S.A. Altmann (1967). The latter three volumes were based on meetings held between 1962 and 1965. The international journal *Folia Primatologica* was founded in 1963.

Washburn was again a major catalyst for many of the meetings in the 1960s, and his influence on primate field biology cannot be overemphasized. In fact, the first eight dissertations in primatology after 1960, and fifteen of the first nineteen, were stimulated by Washburn and, as stated by H.A. Gilmore, Washburn and his students "have probably produced more than half of the present number of anthropological primatologists" (1981:388). This statement was still true in the mid-1990s.

The research in field primatology during the late 1950s and early 1960s was mainly descriptive natural history, with few comparative and quantitative, or problem-oriented, studies. However, by the 1970s and 1980s, field primatology moved into a problem-oriented phase (cf. Sussman 1979; Smuts et al. 1987). S.A. Altmann (1965) and K.R.L. Hall (1917–1965) (1962, 1965) were the first to collect quantitative data on free-ranging primate populations. Hall urged the use of quantitative methods and, at his suggestion, two of his colleagues in the Psychology Department at Bristol University in England, John Crook and Pelham Aldrich-Blake (1968), were the first to use the now common "scan sampling" method in a primate ecology field study. In 1974, Jeanne Altmann, whose Ph.D. was earned in 1979 from the University of Chicago, Committee on Human Development, published a paper describing various methods of collecting quantitative data on free-ranging primates; it remains one of the most referenced papers by field primatologists.

Problem-oriented studies, focused mainly on determining relationships between behavior and morphology on the one hand and ecology and social structure on the other, were an important component of field primatology during the 1970s and 1980s. Since the early 1970s, many field primatologists have attempted to formulate and test theories that have developed out of classical sociobiology, such as those related to kin selection, reciprocal altruism, dominance and reproductive success, and the relationship of sexual selection to social organization and infanticide. In many cases, the theories and studies are elegant and elaborate, but the supporting data are meager (e.g., Bartlett et al. 1994 on problems with the general acceptance of sexual selection as a major explanation of infant killing).

The American philosopher of science F.S.C. Northrop (1965) has suggested that any healthy scientific discipline goes through three stages during its development: The first stage involves the analysis of the problem, the second is a descriptive natural-history phase, and the third stage involves postulationally prescribed theory, in which fundamental theories are tested. Although field primatology has been moving toward this final stage of inquiry, even by the mid-1990s many primate species have not been studied in detail, and the most-studied species normally are known from only a few localities. The range of variation in the behavior and ecology of most free-ranging primates is still unknown, and basic natural history remains a necessary component of the subdiscipline. As stated by Northrup:

In fact, if one proceeds immediately to the deductively formulated type of scientific theory which is appropriate to the third stage of inquiry, before one has passed through the natural history type of science with its inductive Baconian method appropriate to the second stage, the result inevitably is immature, half-baked, dogmatic and for the most part worthless theory. (1965:37–38)

These cautions should be borne in mind when developing theories concerning primate ecology and social behavior.

Robert W. Sussman

See also African and Asian Prosimian Field Studies; African Apes; African Monkeys; Asian Monkeys; Australopithecines; Buettner-Janusch, John; Carpenter, C(larence) Raymond; Clark, Wilfrid LeGros; Hall, Kenneth Ronald Lambert; Hooton, E(arnest) A(lbert); Japanese Primate Studies; Keith, (Sir) Arthur; Malagasy Primates; New World Primate Studies; Russian Primate Studies; Schultz, Adolph Hans; Washburn, Sherwood L.; Zuckerman, Solly (Lord)

Bibliography
J. Altmann: Observational study of behavior: Sampling methods. *Behaviour* 49:227–267, 1974; S.A. Altmann: Field observations on a howling monkey society. *Journal of Mammalogy* 40:317–330, 1959; S.A. Altmann: Sociobiology of rhesus monkeys. II. Stochastics of social communication. *Journal of Theoretical Biology* 8:490–522, 1965; S.A. Altmann (ed): *Social communication among primates.* Chicago: University of Chicago Press, 1967; G.A. Bartholomew Jr. & J.B. Birdsell: Ecology and the protohominids. *American Anthropologist* 55:481–498, 1953; T.Q. Bartlett et al.: Infant killing in primates: A review of observed cases with specific reference to the sexual selection hypothesis. *American Anthropologist* 95:958–990, 1994.

H.C. Bingham: Gorillas in a native habitat. *Carnegie Institution Publications.* No. 426, 1932; N. Bolwig: A study of the behavior of the chacma baboon. *Behaviour* 14:136–163, 1959; A.H. Booth: The distribution of primates in the Gold Coast. *Journal of the West African Science Association* 2:122–133, 1956; J. Buettner-Janusch (ed): The relatives of man: Modern studies on the relation of the evolution of nonhuman primates to human evolution. *Annals of the New York Academy of Sciences* 102:181–514, 1962; C.R. Carpenter: A field study of the behavior and social relations of howling monkeys (*Alouatta palliata*). *Comparative Psychology Monographs* 10:1–168, 1934; C.R. Carpenter: Behavior of the red spider monkey (*Ateles geoffroyi*) in Panama. *Journal of Mammalogy* 16:171–180, 1935.

C.R. Carpenter: A field study in Siam of the behavior and social relations of the gibbon (*Hylobates lar*). *Comparative Psychology Monographs* 16:1–212, 1940; W.E. Le Gros Clark: *Early forerunners of man.* London: Baillière, 1934; N. Collias & C. Southwick: A field study of population density and social organization in howling monkeys. *Proceedings of the American Philosophical Society* 96:143–156, 1952; H.J. Coolidge Jr.: Zoological results of the George Vanderbilt African Expedition of 1934. IV. Notes on four gorillas from the Sanga River region.

Proceedings of the Academy of Natural Sciences (Philadelphia) 88:479–501, 1936; J.H. Crook & P. Aldrich-Blake: Ecological and behavioral contrasts between sympatric ground dwelling primates in Ethiopia. *Folia Primatologica* 8:192–227, 1968; I. DeVore: *Primate behavior: Field studies of monkeys and apes.* New York: Holt, Rinehart & Winston, 1965.

I. DeVore: An interview with Sherwood Washburn. *Current Anthropology* 33:411–423, 1992; I. DeVore & S.L. Washburn: Baboon ecology and human evolution. In: F.C. Howell & F. Bourlière (eds) *African ecology and human evolution.* Chicago: Aldine, 1963, pp. 335–367; J.A. Gavan (ed): *The nonhuman primates and human evolution.* Detroit: Wayne State University Press, 1955; H.A. Gilmore: From Radcliffe-Brown to sociobiology: Some aspects of the rise of primatology within physical anthropology. *American Journal of Physical Anthropology* 56:387–392, 1981; A.J. Haddow: Field and laboratory studies on an African monkey, *Cercopithecus ascanius schmidti Matschie. Proceedings of the Zoological Society of London* 122:297–394, 1952.

K.R.L. Hall: Numerical data, maintenance activities, and locomotion of the wild chacma baboon. *Proceedings of the Zoological Society of London* 139:181–220, 1962; K.R.L. Hall: Experiment and quantification in the study of baboon behavior in its natural habitat. In: H. Vagtborg (ed) *The baboon in medical research.* San Antonio: University of Texas Press, 1965, pp. 43–61; E.A. Hooton: *Man's poor relations.* New York: Doubleday, 1942; E.A. Hooton: The importance of primate studies to anthropology. *Human Biology* 26:179–188, 1954; F.C. Howell & F. Bourlière (eds): *African ecology and human evolution.* Chicago: Aldine, 1963; W.W. Howells (ed): *Ideas on human evolution: Selected essays, 1949–1961.* Cambridge: Harvard University Press, 1962.

T.H. Huxley: *Evidence as to man's place in nature.* London: Williams & Norgate, 1863. Reprint. Ann Arbor: University of Michigan Press, 1959; K. Imanishi: Social behavior in Japanese monkeys (*Macaca fuscata*). *Psychologia* 1:47–54, 1957; P.C. Jay (ed): *Primates: Studies in adaptation and variability.* New York: Holt, Rinehart & Winston, 1968; S. Kawamura: The process of subculture propagation among Japanese macaques. *Journal of Primatology* 2:43–60, 1959; E. Marais: *The soul of the ape.* New

York: Atheneum, 1968; A. Montagu: Introduction to the Ann Arbor Paperbacks edition of Thomas H. Huxley: *Man's place in nature.* Ann Arbor, Michigan: University of Michigan Press, 1959, pp. 1–5; J.R. Napier & N.A. Barnicot (eds): *The primates.* Symposium of the London Zoological Society. No 10. London: Zoological Society of London, 1963; H.W. Nissen: A field study of the chimpanzee. *Comparative Pyschology Monographs* 8:1–122, 1931.

F.S.C. Northrup: *The logic of the sciences and humanities.* Cleveland: Meridian, 1965; B.B. Smuts et al. (eds): *Primate societies.* Chicago: University of Chicago Press, 1987; C.H. Southwick (ed): *Primate social behavior.* New York: Van Nostrand Reinhold, 1963; R.W. Sussman (ed): *Primate ecology: Problem-oriented field studies.* New York: Wiley, 1979; S. Tax (ed): *The evolution of man.* Chicago: University of Chicago Press, 1960; G. Teleki: C. Raymond Carpenter, 1905–1975. *American Journal of Physical Anthropology* 56:383–386, 1981; K.B. Warren (ed): *Origin and evolution of man.* Cold Spring Harbor Symposia on Quantitative Biology. Vol. 15. Cold Spring Harbor, New York: The Biological Laboratory, 1951.

S.L. Washburn (ed): *Social life of early man.* Chicago: Aldine, 1961; S.L. Washburn: The analysis of primate evolution with particular reference to the origin of man. In: W.W. Howells (ed) *Ideas on human evolution: Selected essays, 1949–1961.* Cambridge, Massachusetts: Harvard University Press, 1962, pp. 154–171; S.L. Washburn (ed): *Classification and human evolution.* Chicago: Aldine, 1963; S.L. Washburn & I. DeVore: *Social behavior of baboons and early man.* In: S.L. Washburn (ed) Social life of early man. Chicago: Aldine, 1961, pp. 94–105; R.M. Yerkes & A.W. Yerkes: *The great apes.* New Haven, Connecticut: Yale University Press, 1929; S. Zuckerman: *The social life of monkeys and apes.* London: Routledge & Kegan Paul, 1932.

Puccioni, Nello (1881–1937)

Born in Florence, Italy, Puccioni studied medicine for three years and natural sciences for two, receiving his degree in the natural sciences from the University of Florence in 1904. That same year, he became a voluntary assistant to Paolo Mantegazza (1831–1910) at the Institute of Anthropology. In 1912, he obtained his license to teach anthropology. The following year, he became assistant to

Mantagazza's successor, Aldobrandino Mochi (1874–1931). From 1926 to 1931, he taught anthropology at the University of Pavia; from 1931 to 1937, at the University of Florence.

Puccioni's primary research interests were comparative morphology and anthropometry. He carried out anthropometric observations in Somaliland (cf. Puccioni 1931, 1937), and made interesting observations on anthropological and ethnological characteristics of the populations he encountered. His observations were developed into several publications. He traveled widely through the Italian Peninsula investigating the traces of prehistoric Italian populations.

Puccioni died in Florence on 30 May 1937.

Brunetto Chiarelli

See also Italy; Mantegazza, Paolo; Mochi, Aldobrandino

Bibliography
SELECTED WORKS

Di alcune omologie fra le ossa dello scheletro cefalico e viscerale dell'uomo e dei cranioti inferiori. Firenze: Landi, 1908; Appunti intorno al frammento mandibolare fossile di Piltdown (Sussex). *Archivio per l'Antropologia e la Etnologia* 43:167–175, 1913; Morphologie du maxillaire inférieur. *L'Anthropologie* 23:291–321, 1914; *Antroplogia e etnografia delle genti della Somalia.* Bologna: Zanichelli, 1931; *Antropometria delle genti della Cirenaica.* Firenze: Monnier, 1934; *Le popolazioni indigene della Somalia italiana.* Bologna: Capelli, 1937.

Punctuated Equilibria

Punctuated equilibria, propounded and named by the American paleontologists Niles Eldredge and Stephen J. Gould (Eldredge & Gould 1972; cf. Eldredge 1971), is a proposition about evolutionary stasis and change at the species level. In its simplest formulation, punctuated equilibria claims that morphological stasis is the common rule, rather than the exception, during the history of most species. Stasis is defined as the relative stability of species—with only minor changes, commonly oscillatory in nature, accruing through often considerable segments of time. Marine invertebrate species, for example, tend to persist with little or no conspicuous evolutionary change for 5 million to 10 million years and, in some instances, even longer. Morphological change is associated primarily with

cladogenesis, interpreted as allopatric speciation events. Thus, the essence of punctuated equilibria is the application of speciation theory to patterns of morphological stasis and change as seen especially in the fossil record. Eldredge (1985) gives a general account, and history, of the concept of punctuated equilibria. Punctuated equilibria is contrasted especially with phyletic gradualism—the notion, going back to Charles Darwin (1809–1882), that evolution is primarily a matter of the wholesale transformation of entire species lineages. Stasis was well known as an empirical generalization to mid-nineteenth-century paleontologists. Indeed, Darwin acknowledged stasis in the sixth edition of his *On the Origin of Species* (1872), but he persisted in his original position that the lack of examples of phyletic gradualism was due in greatest part to the overall poor quality of the fossil record itself. In general, stasis was ignored as an empirical phenomenon because it seemed to contradict Darwinian expectations of gradual phyletic evolutionary change.

The immediate intellectual antecedents of punctuated equilibria lie in two disparate facets of the "modern synthesis" as developed especially by geneticist Theodosius Dobzhansky (1900–1975), systematist Ernst Mayr (1904–), and paleontologist George Gaylord Simpson (1902–1984). On the one hand, Dobzhansky (1937) and Mayr (1942) were concerned with discontinuity—a theme Dobzhansky claimed had been ignored in the Darwinian tradition, which stresses the evolution of (morphological) diversity through natural selection. Dobzhansky and Mayr developed the "biological species concept," which holds that species are groups of interbreeding individual organisms. Gaps between species arise naturally in the evolutionary process through the formation of descendant reproductive communities by a process of fission. Dobzhansky and Mayr further held that geographic isolation is the usual forerunner to such "reproductive isolation"—their theory of "allopatric speciation."

On the other hand, Simpson (1944) maintained, in the Darwinian tradition, that species are not the sort of discrete entities that Mayr and Dobzhansky claimed them to be; to Simpson, species and genera evolve in the phyletic manner as Darwin originally maintained. Simpson further agreed with Darwin that lack of good "insensibly graded series" (Darwin's phrase) demonstrating phyletic evolution at the species level is due to gaps in the fossil record.

But Simpson did suggest that large-scale evolutionary tranformations as seen in the fossil record could not possibly conform to the original Darwinian expectation of slow, gradual change. For example, the derivation of bats and whales from terrestrial placental mammalian ancestors seemed to Simpson to suggest that such evolutionary transitions occur extremely rapidly when compared with the more moderate rates of evolution typically seen once a group is established. Bats and whales first appear in the Eocene. The oldest known fossils of each group, while somewhat primitive in form, have the fundamental features ("synapomorphies") that stamp each group. Some of the oldest known bats, for example, have the complex anatomical features of the ear used in echolocation.

Simpson realized that the rates of observed evolutionary change from the Eocene to the Recent, if extrapolated *back* in time to account for the origin of the earliest known bats and whales, would place their origin far further back in time than the date of origin of the first placental mammals—an absurd result. Therefore, he reasoned, major adaptive shifts associated with the origins of higher taxa must take place relatively rapidly when compared with subsequent, much longer periods of slower evolutionary change and diversification within established lineages.

Simpson showed that evolutionary patterns of the fossil record are directly relevant to evolutionary theory, and, indeed, such patterns may well be at variance with the standard models based on simple extrapolation of short-term phenomena (as seen in animal breeding and, later, laboratory experiments in genetics) in the Darwinian tradition of phyletic evolutionary models. Punctuated equilibria embraces Simpson's appreciation of the importance of paleontological pattern, but it sees the pattern as especially relevant at the species level, and it applies the Dobzhansky-Mayr notion of allopatric speciation to explain such patterns.

There are many ramifications to punctuated equilibria. Species under punctuated equilibria emerge as spatiotemporally discrete, bounded historical entities—often themselves called "individuals." Species are seen to have births, histories, and deaths. Because most evolutionary changes seem to occur *between* species, associated in some fashion (still debated) with the process of speciation itself, punctuated equilibria raises the issue of how evolutionary trends might accrue. Early discussion of trends led to notions of "species selection" (e.g., Stanley 1975), later more generally termed "special sorting" (cf. Vrba 1984).

Challenges to punctuated equilibria include denial (by paleontologists and others) of the generality of stasis and the assertion that punctuated equilibria is a form of saltationism associated especially with the writings of the German geneticist Richard Goldschmidt (1878–1958) and the German paleontologist Otto Schindewolf (1896–1971). Insofar as the latter change is concerned, proponents of punctuated equilibria have always linked evolutionary patterns with speciation—claiming the suddenness of evolutionary change as seen in the fossil record is relative only: Most transitions take thousands of years, brief only in comparison with the much longer intervals of ensuing species stability. No proponent of punctuated equilibria has linked such patterns with the "macromutations," for example, of Goldschmidt.

The phenomenon of stasis is now generally accepted as an unanticipated evolutionary phenomenon of great general importance. Debate on the cause(s) of stasis persists. However, most analysts seem to be converging on the idea that stasis is the natural result of stabilizing selection in the face of environmental change—a result wholly unexpected in traditional Darwinian circles, in which evolution was held to be the result of directional natural selection modifying organismic phenotypic properties in response to changing environments. However, it is now widely recognized that environmental change causes shifts in distribution of basic habitat types. Apparently, so long as a species can find "recognizable" habitat in the face of climatic and other forms of environmental change, that species will tend to persist unchanged.

Thus, in its most general form, punctuated equilibria is no longer generally viewed as a radical proposal fundamentally outside Darwinian evolutionary biology. Some of its broader implications—such as species sorting, the association of cladogenesis and morphological change, and more-general issues pertaining to the hierarchical organization of the biological world—remain points of active contention and further research.

Niles Eldredge

See also Darwin, Charles Robert; Dobzhansky, Theodosius; Evolutionary Theory; Mayr, Ernst; Mutation; Simpson, George Gaylord

Bibliography
T. Dobzhansky: *Genetics and the origin of species*. New York: Columbia University Press, 1937; N. Eldredge: The allopatric model and phylogeny in Paleozoic invertebrates. *Evolution* 25:156–167, 1971; N. Eldredge: *Time frames*. New York: Simon & Schuster, 1985; N. Eldredge & S.J. Gould: Punctuated equilibria: An alternative to phyletic gradualism. In: T.J.M. Schopf (ed) *Models in paleobiology*. San Francisco: Freeman, Cooper, 1972, pp. 82–115; E. Mayr: *Systematics and the origin of species*. New York: Columbia University Press, 1942. Reprint. New York: Columbia University Press, 1982; G.G. Simpson: *Tempo and mode in evolution*. New York: Columbia University Press, 1944; S.M. Stanley: A theory of evolution above the species level. *Proceedings of the National Academy of Science* 72:646–650, 1975; E.S. Vrba: What is species selection? *Systematic Zoology* 33:318–328, 1984.

Purkyně (Purkinje), Jan Evangelista (1787–1869)

Born in Libochovice, northern Bohemia (now Czech Republic), Purkyně entered the Piarist Gymnasium at Mikulov in 1798 with the intention of entering the Piarist order. But at the age of twenty, he decided against that and left to study philosophy in Prague. He soon became interested in *Naturphilosophie* and finally decided to become a naturalist. To this end, he began studying medicine at Charles University in 1813. The records of the Prague Medical Faculty show that Purkyně studied so effectively that in all of his subjects he was graded "excellent." He completed his medical studies in 1818 with a dissertation on the *Subjective Contributions to the Knowledge of Vision*. Following graduation, he worked as an assistant in anatomy and physiology at the Prague Medical Faculty until 1823, when he was named to the Chair of Physiology and Pathology at Breslau University (now Wrocław, Poland). His inaugural dissertation was *Commentatio de examine physiologico organi visus et systematis cutanei*, which is considered one of his most pioneering works, particularly with regard to anthropology. Among other things, he was the first to distinguish and classify the variety of dermatoglyphic patterning of the fingers.

During his career, Purkyně made a number of fundamental discoveries, and he is generally regarded as the founder of experimental physiology. For example, in 1837, during a lecture in Prague, he provided a description of somatic cells and their nuclei and thereby anticipated the cell theory of Theodor Schwann (1810–1882) by two years. He was also the first to use the term "protoplasm," and a number of his discoveries now bear his name, such as "Purkinje's" germinal vesicles, heart fibres, the cell of the cerebellum cortex, and many others.

In 1849, he resigned his position in Breslau and returned to Charles University in Prague, where he was offered the Chair of Physiology. In 1862, he founded the Society of Czech Physicians (Spolek lékařů českých) and the *Czech Medical Journal* (Časopis lékařů českých).

Committed to raising the level of scientific education, he worked tirelessly to that end. He also did much to popularize science through his public lectures and articles (such as those that appeared in the journal *Živa*, of which he was editor). As for anthropology, he was convinced of its importance and relevance, particularly to a medical education. His commitment is clearly revealed in his inaugural address at the opening of the Department of Physiology in Prague in 1851, in which he noted:

> . . . {W}e should use {anthropology} as an introduction to physiological knowledge in order that the student can first of all become acquainted with man himself, as he appears to him at first sight without studying him. What is said here of man applies equally to every organism, no matter what its nature. The natural history of the plant and animal world follows the same lines as anthropology . . .

Like many others in the nineteenth century, Purkyně was greatly interested in craniology, and in the 1850s he conducted the first craniological study in Bohemia. He also designed a number of craniometric instruments, such as his goniometer. Purkyně's interest in craniology and anthropology was continued by his former assistant Eduard Grégr (1827–1907).

Purkyně died in Libochovice on 28 July 1869.

Jaroslav Slípka

See also Czech and Slovak Republics; Dermatoglyphics; Poland

Bibliography
SELECTED WORKS
    For a complete listing of Purkyně's publications, see *Sebrane spisy* [Opera

omnia]. 13 vols. Prague: Zdravotnické,
1918–1985.

SECONDARY SOURCES
    E. Grégr: On human skulls in general
and Slav ones in particular. (In Czech). *Živa*
9:10, 1858; J. Haubelt: *Jan Evangelista
Purkyně*. (In Czech). Prague: Horizont,
1987; H.J. John: *Jan Evangelista Purkyně:
Czech scientist and patriot*. Philadelphia:
American Philosophical Society, 1959; J.
Malý: Jean Evariste Purkyně anthropologue.
Anthropologie 6: 11–16, 1928; F.K.
Studnička: Aus der Vorgeschichte der
Zellentheorie. *Anatomischer Anzeiger*
73:390–416, 1932; F.K. Studnička: Joh.
Ev. Purkynjes histologische Arbeiten.
Anatomischer Anzeiger 82:41–66, 1936.

Putnam, Frederic Ward (1839–1915)

Born in Salem, Massachusetts, Putnam, after
early training under Henry Wheatland
(1812–1893) at the Essex Institute in Salem,
studied with Louis Agassiz (1807–1873) and
Asa Gray (1810–1888) at Harvard University.
After the revolt of Agassiz's students in 1863,
Putnam returned to Salem, where he founded
and published the *American Naturalist*, directed the new (1868) Peabody Academy of
Science, and pursued a career in ichthyology
and herpetology. Upon the death of the anatomist Jeffries Wyman (1814–1874) in 1874,
he returned to Cambridge as director and curator of the Peabody Museum of Archaeology
and Ethnology at Harvard. He became
Peabody Professor of Anthropology as well in
1887, and he held all three positions until his
retirement in 1909. He served as permanent
secretary of the American Association for the
Advancement of Science (AAAS) from 1873
to 1898 and as president of the AAAS in
1898–1899. He was a founding member of
the Archaeological Institute of America in
1879 and largely responsible for its early work
in the Western Hemisphere. From 1891 to
1894, he served as chief of the Department of
Ethnology of the World's Columbian Exposition in Chicago, directing the anthropological work of Franz Boas (1858–1942),
Alice C. Fletcher (1838–1923), Zelia Nuttall
(1857–1933), Marshall H. Saville (1867–
1935), George Byron Gordon (1870–1972),
George A. Dorsey (1868–1931), Warren K.
Moorehead (1866–1939), and many others.
From 1894 to 1903, he served as curator of
anthropology at the American Museum of
Natural History in New York City. He
brought Boas to New York, and together they
supervised the Jesup North Pacific Expedition
and the Hyde Expeditions to the American
Southwest. In 1903, he founded the Department of Anthropology at University of California, Berkeley, and he served as professor of
anthropology and director of the Anthropological Museum there until 1909. He was
elected to the National Academy of Sciences
in 1884.

    Putnam was a major institution builder
in early American anthropology. His significance derived primarily from his organizational abilities; his support for, and influence
on, younger men and women (especially Boas
and Alfred M. Tozzer [1877–1954]); his pioneering work in preserving Serpent Mound in
southern Ohio and other sites; and his popularization of North American archeology. He
and Boas jointly trained the next generation
of anthropologists in the four-field tradition
by dividing the labor: archeology at Harvard,
linguistics and ethnography at Columbia
University, and physical (biological) anthropology at both. His own archeological fieldwork of the 1880s in southern Ohio
(preceded by explorations in Kentucky and
Tennessee and followed a decade later by
work in California) established field methods on a new plane, with emphasis on pay-
ing attention to the context (spatial,
stratigraphic) of specimens, careful recording of the excavation process, viewing each
site as a complex unit for purposes of study,
and employing conservative excavation techniques. Deeply embroiled in the controversies of his generation over "ancient man" in
North America, Putnam supported the
claims of Charles Conrad Abbott (1843–
1919) and others for a presence of 10,000 or
more years. Permanently influenced by his
early zoological training under Agassiz,
Putnam evinced always a preference for close
description of the artifactual base and a reluctance to make broader generalizations.

    He died in Cambridge, Massachusetts,
on 14 August 1915.

Curtis M. Hinsley

See also Abbott, Charles Conrad; Agassiz, (Jean)
Louis (Rodolphe); American Anthropological
Association; Americas: Paleoanthropology;
Boas, Franz; Harvard University; Hrdlička,
Aleš; Wyman, Jeffries

Bibliography
SELECTED WORKS
    Archaeological explorations in
Tennessee. *Peabody Museum Annual Report*

11:305–360, 1880; Sketch of Hon. Lewis H. Morgan. *Proceedings of the American Academy of Arts and Sciences* 27:249–236, 1882; The altar mounds of the Turner Group in Ohio. *Peabody Museum Annual Report* 17:554–562, 1886; The proper method of exploring and earthwork. *Ohio Archaeological and Historical Quarterly* 1:60–62, 1887; Paleolithic man in eastern and central North America. *Proceedings of the Boston Society for Natural History* 23:421–449, 1888; The Serpent Mound of Ohio. *Century Illustrated Monthly Magazine* 39:871–888, 1890; Archaeological and ethnological research in the United States. *Proceedings of the American Antiquarian Society* 24:461–470, 1902; (with A.S. Packard): *The Mammoth Cave and its inhabitants.* Salem, Massachusetts, 1879.

ARCHIVAL SOURCES

F.W. Putnam Papers: 1. Peabody Museum Archives, Peabody Museum, Harvard University, 11 Divinity Avenue, Cambridge, Massachusetts 02138; 2. Harvard University Archives, Pusey Library, Harvard University, Cambridge, Massachetts 02138.

SECONDARY SOURCES

F. Boas (ed): *Putnam anniversary volume: Anthropological essays presented to Frederic Ward Putnam in honor of his seventieth birthday.* New York: Stechert, 1909; F. Boas: Frederic Ward Putnam. *Science* 42:330–332, 1915; R.W. Dexter: The Putnam-Abbott correspondence on Palaeolithic man in North America. *Twelfth International Congress of the History of Sciences* 9:17–21, 1971; R.W. Dexter: The role of F.W. Putnam in developing anthropology at the American Museum of Natural History. *Curator* 9:303–310, 1976; C.M. Hinsley: From shell heaps to stelae: Early anthropology at the Peabody Museum. In: G.W. Stocking (ed) *Objects and others: Essays on museums and material culture.* Madison: University of Wisconsin Press, 1985, pp. 49–74; A.L. Kroeber: Frederic Ward Putnam. *American Anthropologist* 17:712–718, 1915; E.S. Morse: Frederic Ward Putnam, 1839–1915. *National Academy of Sciences Biographical Memoirs* 16:125–153, 1935.

Qafzeh (Jebel) (Israel)

The cave of Qafzeh (also known as Kafzeh, Qafza, or Kafze) and its associated terrace is located just above the opening of a small wadi 2.5 km outside the city of Nazareth in northern Israel. The cave is a karstic chamber in the limestone hill that contains a long sequence of Middle and Upper Paleolithic deposits. The adjacent terrace deposits contain an equally rich sequence of Middle Paleolithic deposits. Both portions of the site have yielded a spectacular series of especially Middle Paleolithic hominid partial skeletons.

The cave was originally excavated by René Neuville, the French consul in Jerusalem, and Moshe Stekelis (1898–1967) of Hebrew University in 1933 and 1935. During these excavations within the cave, Neuville documented a rich Middle to Upper Paleolithic stratigraphic sequence (cf. Neuville 1951); in addition, in 1934 he unearthed the remains of two individuals from the Upper Paleolithic (Qafzeh 1 and 2) and of four individuals (Qafzeh 3 to 6) from the Middle Paleolithic. A seventh individual was found in 1935.

These remains from Qafzeh were stored in the Institut de Paléontologie Humaine in Paris, where they remained largely ignored until the 1950s. The only comments concerning them are a mention by the French paleoanthropologist Henri Victor Vallois (1889–1981) (cf. Boule & Vallois 1957) noting their similarity to the Skhūl sample and statements subsequent to his occasional use of them as part of a comparative sample (e.g., Vallois 1958), plus the explicit recognition by the American paleoanthropologist F. Clark

Howell (1958) of their affinities to the remains from Skhūl. Howell, in particular, noted that "one finds here all of the important morphological requirements of an ancestral, proto-Cro-Magnon human group" (1958:191).

In 1965, the French paleoanthropologist Bernard Vandermeersch reopened excavations at Qafzeh, working primarily on the Middle Paleolithic terrace deposits adjacent to the cave-entrance deposits excavated by Neuville, and he continued that work through 1979. During his excavations, he discovered eight individuals in the Middle Paleolithic levels, six immature and two mature associated partial skeletons, plus isolated teeth. As a result, the Qafzeh sample came to represent one of the largest known Middle Paleolithic human skeletal samples, including one largely complete skeleton (Qafzeh 9), a largely complete adult cranium (Qafzeh 6), and the quite complete remains of neonates and children, especially Qafzeh 11 (Vandermeersch 1981).

There has been little doubt that the Qafzeh Middle Paleolithic hominid sample, especially once the description of the adults appeared (Vandermeersch 1981) and as descriptions of the immature remains are completed (e.g., Tillier 1984), consists of craniofacial robust early modern humans with close morphological affinities to the sample from Mugharet es-Skhūl. This was repeatedly confirmed during the 1980s as aspects of their cranial, dentognathic, and especially postcranial anatomy were integrated into the greater later Pleistocene human sample. This interpretation led Vandermeersch (1981) to reaffirm Howell's appellation of them as "proto-Cro-Magnon," even though the British researcher D.R. Brothwell (1961) had pointed out the difficulty inherent in deriving only the European Upper Paleolithic populations from this Levantine group.

Since the early 1980s, debates have focused on the geological age of the Qafzeh Middle Paleolithic deposits and the age of the hominid remains relative to others from the Middle Paleolithic of the Near East. Neuville (1951) assigned the Middle Paleolithic of Qafzeh, based on evidence for a relatively wet climate at the time of its deposition, to a pluvial phase contemporary with the early last glacial, or Early Würm. This general date was challenged in 1981 by the Israeli archeologist Ofer Bar-Yosef and Vandermeersch, who noted that a major erosional event at the top of the Qafzeh Middle Paleolithic may well correspond with a similar erosional event between the Middle Paleolithic layers D and C in Mugharet et-Tabūn. This was supported by the presence at Qafzeh of two species of rats, *Arvicanthis etcos* and *Rattus (Mastomys) batei*, which are present in Late Acheulean and initial Mousterian sites in the Levant but are apparently absent from more recent Middle Paleolithic levels (Bar-Yosef 1989). The implication was that the Qafzeh early-modern humans were geologically older than the late archaic humans from Tabūn C and possibly other sites. If so, this would make a simple unilineal phylogenetic sequence from late archaic to early modern humans in the Levant untenable.

The age of Qafzeh was actively debated through the mid-1980s, with the American archeologist A.J. Jelinek in particular arguing, on the basis of technological comparisons to the Tabūn Middle Paleolithic sequence, that the Qafzeh Middle Paleolithic should be more recent than the levels at Tabūn (Jelinek 1982a, 1982b). The question remained largely open until a series of thermoluminescence (TL) determinations from the Qafzeh terrace deposits became available, which placed them in the vicinity of 90.0 ky BP (cf. Valladas et al. 1988). Shortly thereafter, this was followed by age determinations from the related electron spin resonance (ESR) technique, which provided similar mid-Last Interglacial dates for the Qafzeh terrace deposits and their hominid remains (Schwarcz et al. 1988). Although these dates and the whole relative chronology of Levantine Middle Paleolithic levels continues to be modified and debated (e.g., Jelinek 1992), it appears most likely that the Qafzeh remains do, indeed,

derive from the middle of the last interglacial, making them among the oldest, and reasonably well dated, early modern humans in the Old World.

Erik Trinkaus

See also Cro-Magnon; Israel; Modern Human Origins; Mount Carmel (Israel); Skhūl (Israel); Tabūn, Mugharet et- (Israel); Vallois, Henri Victor

Bibliography
O. Bar-Yosef: Upper Pleistocene cultural stratigraphy in southwest Asia. In: E. Trinkaus (ed) *The emergence of modern humans.* Cambridge: Cambridge University Press, 1989, pp. 154–180; O. Bar-Yosef & B. Vandermeersch: Notes concerning the possible age of the Mousterian layers in Qafzeh Cave. In: P. Sanlaville & J. Cauvin (eds) *Préhistoire du Levant.* Paris: CNRS, 1981, pp. 281–285; M. Boule & H.V. Vallois: *Fossil man.* New York: Dryden Press, 1957; D.R. Brothwell: The people of Mount Carmel: A reconsideration of the position in human evolution. *Proceedings of the Prehistoric Society* 6:155–159, 1961; F.C. Howell: Upper Pleistocene men of the southwest Asian Mousterian. In: G.H.R. von Koenigswald (ed) *Hundert Jahre Neanderthaler.* Utrecht: Kemink, 1958, pp. 185–198.

A.J. Jelinek: The Middle Paleolithic in the southern Levant, with comments on the appearance of modern *Homo sapiens.* In: A. Ronen (ed) The transition from the Lower to Middle Paleolithic and the origin of modern man. *British Archaeological Reports* 151:57–104, 1982a; A.J. Jelinek: The Tabūn Cave and Paleolithic man in the Levant. *Science* 216:1369–1375, 1982b; A.J. Jelinek: Problems in the chronology of the Middle Paleolithic and the first appearance of early-modern *Homo sapiens* in Southeast Asia. In: T. Akazawa et al (eds) *The evolution and dispersal of modern humans in Asia.* Tokyo: Hokusen-sha, 1992, pp. 253–275.

R. Neuville: Le Paléolithique et le mésolithique du désert de Judée. *Archives de l'Institut de Paléontologie Humaine* 24:1–271, 1951; H.P. Schwarcz et al.: ESR dates for the hominid burial site of Qafzeh in Israel. *Journal of Human Evolution* 17:733–737, 1988; A.M. Tillier: L'enfant Homo 11 de Qafzeh (Israël) et son apport à la compréhension des modalités de la croissance des squelettes moustériens. *Paléorient* 10:7–48, 1984; H. Valladas et al.:

Thermoluminescence dating of Mousterian "proto-Cro-Magnon" remains from Israel and the origin of modern man. *Nature* 331:614–616, 1988; H.V. Vallois: La Grotte de Fontéchevade. II. Anthropologie. *Archives de l'Institut de Paléontologie* 29:5–164, 1958; B. Vandermeersch: *Les hommes fossiles de Qafzeh (Israël)*. Paris: CNRS, 1981.

Quatrefages (de Breau), Jean Louis Armand de (1810–1892)

Born at Berthezéne, near Valleraugue (Gard), France, Quatrefages attended (1822–1826) the Collège Royal, Tournon, before going on to the University of Strasbourg[1] to study medicine. On receiving his M.D. in 1833, he established a medical practice in Toulouse, where he remained until 1840, when he moved to Paris.

During his first years in Paris, Quatrefages earned his living as a scientific illustrator and writer of popular scientific articles. It was through his talent as a draftsman that he became associated with the zoologist Henri Milne-Edwards (1800–1885) at the Muséum National d'Histoire Naturelle (MNHN), who at that time was preparing a new edition of Georges Cuvier's (1769–1832) *Le régne animal*. This association developed into a lasting friendship. Between 1840 and 1855, with the support of Milne-Edwards, Quatrefages published extensively on invertebrate biology and classification. During this same time period, he also participated in a series of scientific expeditions, details of which can be found in his two-volume *Souvenirs d'un naturaliste* (1854).

In 1850, he was appointed to the Chair of Natural History at the Lycée Henri IV; in 1855, with Milne-Edwards' backing, he was appointed to the vacant Chair of Anthropology (formerly the Chair of Anatomy and Human Natural History) at the MNHN. Although he continued to work and publish in zoology, after his appointment at the MNHN his interests assumed an increasingly anthropological focus.

As indicated by his book *Darwin et ses précurseurs français* (1870), an anthology of articles published during the 1860s, Quatrefages was strongly opposed to Darwinian theory. He also vigorously resisted the proposition advanced by the British biologist Thomas Henry Huxley (1825–1895) in 1863 for the simian origins of the human genus, and he defended the concept of *Homo* as a distinct and separate entity from the rest of the animal kingdom. He was, however, an ardent monogenist, and in several publications, such as *Unité de l'espèce humaine* (1861) and *Rapport sur les progrès de l'anthropologie* (1867), he argued forcefully against the doctrine of polygenism. In a nutshell, Quatrefages was a conservative, and, not surprisingly, this posture placed him in direct opposition to the more liberal and materialistic wing of French anthropology, which during the third quarter of the nineteenth century was led by Paul Broca (1824–1880).

Although resolute in his opposition to the evolutionary thesis, Quatrefages was an early convert to the idea of human antiquity and, as such, had supported Jacques Boucher de Perthes' (1788–1868) claims for the controversial Moulin-Quignon jaw (1863a, 1863b, 1863c, 1863d, 1864). This growing conviction led him to undertake with his assistant Théodore Hamy (1842–1908) a collaborative study of the crania of the living and ancient "races" of Europe, which culminated in the publication of their highly influential book *Crania ethnica* (1882). One of the primary contributions of this work was the recognition of the so-called race de Canstadt [Cannstatt], which, in retrospect, is seen to have been an important step leading to the eventual recognition of the Neandertals as a discrete group of hominids of the European Upper Pleistocene. The "race de Canstadt [Cannstatt]" had been fabricated from a number of fossil hominids that included the Feldhofer remains from the Neander Valley, Gibraltar, Cannstatt, and La Naulette, which Quatrefages and Hamy characterized as the "oldest in Europe" and the first in a succession of "racial" types leading to the modern European population. Much of the credit for this hypothetical construct and the implicit argument for the precedence of dolichocephaly in the Quaternary embodied therein, must go to Hamy (cf. Hamy's *Précis de paléontologie humaine*, 1870).

Quatrefages died in Paris on 12 January 1892.

Frank Spencer

Editor's Note
Following the Franco-Prussian War of 1870–1871, the French provinces of Alsace and Lorraine became part of Germany and remained so until 1919 when the territory was returned to France. During this time Strasbourg became Strassburg.

See also Broca, Paul (Pierre); Cannstatt Skull; Cuvier, Georges Léopold Chrétien Fréderic

Dagobert (Baron); Gibraltar; Hamy, Jules Ernest Théodore; Huxley, Thomas Henry; Moulin-Quignon Affair; Naulette, La; Neandertals; Polygenism

Bibliography
SELECTED WORKS

Souvenirs d'un naturaliste. Paris: Masson, 1854; *Unité de l'espèce humaine*. Paris: Hachette, 1861; Deuxième note sur la mâchoire d'Abbeville. *Comptes-rendus hebdomadaires des séances de l'Académie des Sciences* 56:809–816, 1863a; Mâchoire de Moulin-Quignon. *Comptes-rendus hebdomadaires des séances de l'Académie des Sciences* 56:933–935, 1863b; Note sur la mâchoire humaine découverte par M. Boucher de Perthes dans le diluvium d'Abbeville. *Comptes-rendus hebdomadaires des séances de l'Académie des Sciences* 56:782–788, 1863c; On the Abbeville jaw. *Anthropological Review* 1:312–335, 1863d; Nouveau ossements humains découverts par M. Boucher de Perthes à Moulin-Quignon. *Comptes-rendus hebdomadaires des séances de l'Académie des Sciences* 59:107–111, 1864; *Rapport sur les progrès de l'anthropologie*. Paris: Hachette, 1867; *Histoire de l'homme*. 5 vols. Paris: Hachette, 1867–1868.

Darwin et ses précurseurs français; étude sur le transformisme. Paris: Baillière, 1870 (2d ed., 1892); *La race prussienne*. Paris: Hachette, 1871. English translation by I. Innes: *The Prussian race, ethnologically considered*. London: Virtue, 1872; *Races humaines fossiles: Race de Canstadt*. *Comptes-rendus hebdomadaires des séances de l'Académie des Sciences* 76:1313–1317, 1873; *L'espèce humain*. Paris: Baillière, 1879. English translation: *The human species*. New York: Appleton, 1879; *Hommes fossiles et hommes sauvages: Etudes d'anthropologie*. Paris: Baillière, 1884; *Histoire générale des races humaines*. Paris: Hennuyer, 1887; *Les émules de Darwin*. 2 vols. Paris: Alcan, 1894; (with E.T. Hamy) *Crania ethnica: Les crânes des races humaines*. Paris: Baillière, 1882.

ARCHIVAL SOURCES
A. de Quatrefages: Archives, Muséum National d'Histoire Naturelle, 57 rue Cuvier, 75281 Paris, France.

PRIMARY AND SECONDARY SOURCES
E.T. Hamy: *Précis de paléontologie humaine*. Paris: Baillière, 1870; G. Hervé & L. de Quatrefages: Armand de Quatrefages. *Bulletin de la Société française d'histoire de la médecine* 20:309–330 (1926), 21:17–35, 200–231 (1927); T.H. Huxley: *Evidence as to man's place in nature*. London: Williams & Norgate, 1863; A.G. Malard: Liste des ouvrages et mémoires publieés de 1822 à 1891 par A. de Quatrefages. *Nouvelles Archives du Muséum d'Histoire Naturelle* 4 (3d ser.):1–49, 1892.

Quetelet, (Lambert) Adolphe (Jacques) (1796–1874)

Born in Ghent, Belgium, Quetelet studied mathematics at the local Lycée and in 1819 received his doctorate in mathematics from the newly established University of Ghent. That same year, he was appointed to the Chair of Mathematics at the Athenaeum in Brussels. In 1828, he founded the Royal Observatory in Brussels, of which he became director. From 1834 to 1874, he was permanent secretary of the Brussels Académie Royale des Sciences, which after 1845 became the Belgian Académie Royale des Sciences, des Lettres, et de Beaux-Arts. He also played a central role in the creation of a Statistical Section of the British Association for the Advancement of Science, at its third annual meeting at Cambridge in 1833, and was responsible for organizing the first international statistical congress held in Brussels in September 1853 (see *Comptes rendus des travaux du Congrès général de Statistique*. Brussels: Hayez, 1854).

From all accounts, it was while developing his astronomical research that Quetelet became involved with statistics and the theory of probability, which, through the encouragement of the French epidemiologist Louis-René Villermé (1782–1863), he subsequently applied to social phenomena. In the early 1830s, he conducted the first in a series of anthropometric surveys (reported to the Académie Royale des Sciences in Brussels in 1831 and 1833), the product of which formed the basis of his first major publication: *Sur l'homme et le développement des ses facultés* (1835). This work was well received and was promptly (1838) translated into German, followed by an English translation (1842) made by Robert Knox (1791–1862). In 1846, Quetelet applied his theory of probability to "moral and political science," which was equally well received, particularly in Britain where its merits were lauded by the astronomer Sir John Herschel (1792–1871) in the pages of the *Edinburgh Review*. Later, Quetelet dedicated his last work *Anthropométrie* (1870) to Herschel.

At the core of Quetelet's work is the concept to which his name is forever linked: *l'homme moyen*, or average man. As his measurements of stature and other anthropometric data revealed, there was an average size to which around 70 percent of humans approximated, with 15 percent falling on either side of the median, or average, forming a frequency distribution curve (or what Quetelet referred to as the "Law of Deviation from the Average"). But where English biometrician Francis Galton (1822–1911) later viewed this average as embracing "mediocrity," Quetelet saw it as a "type of perfection" and said that ". . . everything differing from his proportions would constitute deformity and disease . . ." (1842:99). Although this concept provoked debate, Quetelet's methodology nevertheless led the way to similar anthropometric surveys throughout Europe and the United States and to the introduction into the anthropological arena of the perspective of populational thinking—though it was another century before that approach became fully integrated into anthropology.

In spite of the stroke he suffered in 1855, he continued to work with the assistance of a secretary, though he did relinquish his directorship of the Royal Observatory that year. He died in Brussels on 17 February 1874.

Frank Spencer

See also Demography; Galton, (Sir) Francis; Growth Studies

Bibliography
SELECTED WORKS

Instructions populaires sur le calcul des probabilités. Bruxelles: Tarlier et Hayez, 1828; Recherches sur le poids de l'homme aux différents âges. *Mémoires de l'Académie Royale de Bruxelles* 7:1–44, 1833; *Sur l'homme et le développement des ses facultés; ou, Essai de physique sociale*. Paris: Bachelier, 1835. English translation by R. Knox: *A treatise on man and the development of his faculties*. Edinburgh: Chambers, 1842; *Lettre à SAR le duc régnant de Saxe-Coburg et Gotha, sur la théorie des probabilités appliquée aux sciences morales et politiques*. Bruxelles: Hayez, 1846; *Physique sociale; ou, Essai sur le développement des facultés de l'homme*. Bruxelles: Muquardt, 1869; *Anthropométrie; ou, Mésure des différentes facultés de l'homme*. Bruxelles: Muquardt, 1870.

SECONDARY SOURCES

J.M. Joly & P. Dagnelie: Adolphe Quetelet, 1796–1874. In: C. Olby (ed) *Early-nineteenth-century European scientists*. London: Oxford University Press, 1967, pp. 153–179; E. Mailly: Essai sur la vie et les ouvrages de L.A.J. Quetelet. *Annulaire de l'Académie royale de Belgique* 41:109–297, 1875; J.M. Tanner: *A history of the study of human growth*. London: Cambridge University Press, 1981, pp. 121–141.

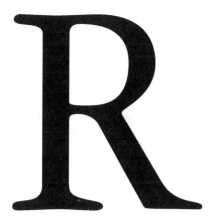

Race Concept

Prior to the conquest of the Western Hemisphere by Europeans, there was no general term for "race," and, indeed, there was no concept that implied anything of its equivalent. Neither the term nor its conceptual counterpart appears in Judeo-Christian sacred writings. The casual use of the term in some of the renditions of the English Bible can mean the descendants of a particular figure or region—the race of David or of Judah or whatever. But the concept as it is pervasively assumed today is completely absent.

The concept and a term that could be used to denote it are also absent from the first systematic efforts to record history and geography. The first formal European historical account, the *Histories* of Herodotus in the fifth century B.C., uses neither the term nor the concept, although Herodotus traveled widely. His travels took him throughout the area of the Persian Empire and beyond, ranging from Greece through southern Russia, the shores of the Black Sea, Turkey, Syria, Iran (Babylonia), Egypt as far up the Nile as Aswan, and Libya (cf. Herodotus 1954).

The medieval Italian (Venetian) traveler Marco Polo (1254–1324) went all the way across central Asia to China, then back via Southeast Asia and India before recounting his experiences (Polo 1968). His travels were surpassed by those of the Islamic geographer from Morocco, Ibn Batutah (1304–1377), who also visited the Balkans, the Black Sea and southern Russia, the Middle East, North and East Africa, India, Southeast Asia, and China. He further visited the western Mediterranean as far as Gibraltar and Spain, and he made a trek across the Sahara to Timbuktu and West Africa before settling in Fez to write his memoirs (Dunn 1986).

The concept of "race" is significantly absent from the writings of these two travelers, and they used no term that could be employed to represent it. Although, like Herodotus, they regularly recorded the skin color and appearance of the people they encountered on their voyages, the only kinds of categorizing words that they used were more in the nature of cultural or religious designations such as "idolators" and "infidels."

The Peasant Perspective

Throughout much of recorded history, the normal range of human experience was limited to what could be seen in that segment of the world lying within a radius of little more than 25 miles from the place of one's birth. Roads were rudimentary, mere paths in many instances. There was no such thing as "public" transportation, "horse and buggy" travel was for the prosperous few, and books could be read and were owned only by the educated well-to-do. Even phenomena like the family Bible or its equivalents and that recent urban luxury, the newspaper, were possible only after the invention of the printing press in the middle of the fifteenth century.

Throughout the Old World, it is still true that human appearance is essentially the same between adjacent 25-mile circles. What differences are perceived tend to relate to customs and dress and traditions of behavior and speech. Variations in accent and even different languages can be encountered in adjacent districts in many parts of the world, but discernible differences in appearance just do not occur.

The reason that Herodotus, Marco Polo, Ibn Batutah, and other such travelers of yesteryear never perceived human differences in categorical fashion is that they got from place to place largely over land—25-mile segment by 25-mile segment—and the gradation of one human group into another is so continuous that no boundaries are discernible. If the printing press marked a quantum change in the speed with which information could be disseminated, it was another Renaissance development—long-distance ocean-going transport—that changed the way direct perception of human differences took place. The little ships that allowed Columbus to cross the Atlantic and Vasco da Gama to circumnavigate Africa late in the fifteenth century meant that travel from Europe to the equator had ceased to be an overland tramp. One could board ship in Oslo, Norway, and arrive next in Nigeria with few if any stops in between. No longer was one's perception of the spectrum of human difference a composite of one 25-mile segment followed by another. The overwhelming impression was the categorical distinction of the physical differences between northwest Europeans and equatorial Africans.

The traditional peasants'-eye view of the world that had conditioned all previous perceptions of human difference from one part of the world to another was now shattered for good, especially for those responsible for molding general opinion.

"Race" in the Enlightenment

It is no accident that the picture of human biological variation that emerged in the Enlightenment of the late seventeenth and eighteenth centuries following the Renaissance was based on descriptions of human form as it was found at the end points of the ocean-going trade network dominated by a mercantile western Europe. The stereotypic image of the native inhabitants of the Western Hemisphere was provided by the Amerindians encountered on the Eastern Coast of North America. The African stereotype was based on people encountered on the Gold Coast, Ivory Coast, and "Slave" Coast of West Africa. First impressions of the Far East were of the people met in Indonesia—Sumatra, Java, and the Malay Peninsula. Only later when trade extended to Canton on the China Coast and up to Japan was the basis provided for the establishment of a variant to the East Asian stereotype.

The Enlightenment naturalist and synthesizer, the Swedish botanist Carolus Linnaeus (Carl von Linné) (1707–1778), described human biological form as divided into four subspecies: *Homo sapiens europaeus* based in northwest Europe; *H. sapiens afer* based in West Africa; *H. sapiens asiaticus* based in Indonesia; and *H. sapiens americanus* based in northeast North America. These were the human varieties he listed in the tenth edition of his *Systema naturae* (1758), which was his formal appraisal of the living world as a totality. Later in the eighteenth century, the person who is widely regarded as the founder of biological anthropology, Johann Friedrich Blumenbach (1752–1840) in Germany, expanded on Linnaeus' view of four human varieties with the recognition of the distinction between the people of Southeast and Northeast Asia (cf. Bendyshe 1865:264–265).

Linnaeus' division of the human spectrum into four varieties or subspecies was based in part on the traditional flat-Earth view of a world described by its four cardinal directions—north, south, east, and west. Of course, he was well aware that the Earth was a sphere, but the pragmatic value of describing a world in terms of four quarters was so useful that he did it that way simply as a matter of convenience. He went further and ascribed one of the four "humors" of the pre-Christian Greco-Roman physician Galen to each of his four subspecies. He identified the Asiatic "race" with the "melancholic" humor, the American with the "choleric," the African with the "bilious," and the European with the "sanguine" humor (Stocking 1988:5).

Blumenbach, for his part, accepted the basic rationale of Linnaeus' scheme with the pragmatic addition of a northeast Asian component. Although this tactic perpetuated the categorical and discrete picture of the nature of human biological variation, Blumenbach was well aware of the fact that there were no boundaries among the five "varieties" that he recognized. He explicitly mentioned the fact that gradation is continuous and that the named divisions were purely arbitrary. The continuum could be cut up into any number of named components, none of which had any greater justification than any other such formulation. The scheme he presented was chosen as a matter of convenience and familiarity since it corresponded with the commonly verbalized treatment of Linnaeus and other less formally established accounts (cf. Bendyshe 1865:264).

It should be noted here that Linnaeus' pragmatic use of the major blocks of the world—Europe, Africa, Asia, and America—corresponds to one of the basic expectations of evolutionary biology, although this is not the way he thought of it in the middle of the eighteenth century. That expectation is that the long-term inhabitants of any given area are more likely to resemble their ancestors in that area, simply because of genetic continuity, than they are likely to resemble people in another part of the world. On the other hand, the fact that traits that are of adaptive significance will be distributed as clines according to the graded intensity of their relative selective forces instead of regional or populational boundaries was not suspected by Linnaeus and could not be illustrated by his system.

"Racial" Origins in Biblical Perspective

The use of the term "Caucasoid" dates directly to the account of Blumenbach late in the eighteenth century. Blumenbach was not the first to focus his attention on human biological variation, but he was the first to specialize in such a study to the exclusion of other lines of investigation. In the course of his researches at the University of Göttingen, he assembled a collection of human skulls representing the different manifestations of human form visible in the world with which he had contact. In his judgment, the most perfectly formed specimen came from that mountainous stretch of land at the eastern edge of the Black Sea where Russia meets Turkey and Iran, a region dominated by the Caucasus Mountains. That whole stretch of land dividing the Black Sea on the west from the Caspian Sea on the east is referred to colloquially as "the Caucasus," and Blumenbach thought that the skulls in his collection from that area represented the most perfectly formed and "beautiful" of human beings (Bendyshe 1865:269). This is the source of the stereotypic word "Caucasian" with its attendant emotional baggage of implicit perfection and consequent superiority in comparison to other differing human forms.

The Caucasus is close enough to where the Judeo-Christian Garden of Eden was presumed to have been located, and, according to their sacred writings, Noah's Ark, bearing the ancestors of all living humans and animals, landed at Mount Ararat in Turkish Armenia at the southwestern edge of the Caucasus. From a biblical perspective, then, "Caucasians" could be regarded as the direct and unmodified descendants of original human form. Blumenbach clearly assumed that this was the case.

Although defense of a literal biblical view was not Blumenbach's primary motivation, it did not hurt the credibility of his scheme that it could be made compatible with the standard Christian outlook. The non-"Caucasoid" peoples of the world, then, could be regarded as having departed from the place of origin and having acquired an appearance that differed in proportion to the distance of their removal. Blumenbach attributed this difference in appearance to a process of "degeneration" from original "Caucasian" perfection, partially by the influence of the various differing conditions of climate and environment, and partially by the effects of different social circumstances and ways of life.

Implicit in Blumenbach's scheme, then, was the idea of a hierarchy of worth. The concept of hierarchy was widely assumed in the eighteenth century. God, representing ultimate perfection, had created "man"—"a little lower than the angels," in the words of the biblical psalm—and human form was arranged from its most perfect "Caucasian" manifestation down to those whose level of "degeneration" was measured by their difference from the "Caucasoid" standard.

It requires little reflection to realize that his was a completely subjective view of the meaning of human biological difference. With hierarchical assumptions built into it, the ensuing depiction of named human "races" contained the clear-cut implication that differences in appearance denoted differences in worth. If there were nothing else wrong with the scheme, that alone would be reason enough to abandon it. As can be seen in an examination of the actual nature of human biological variation, there is much more wrong with it than that. Not only has it proven to be next to impossible to show that configurations that cluster in given regions have any adaptive significance, but it is evident that traits that are under demonstrable selective-force control follow those forces across regional and populational boundaries in clinal fashion without break (Livingstone 1962; Brace 1996). Unfortunately, the neoplatonic legacy inherited from the Middle Ages encouraged a worldview in which reality was constituted of typological essences, and any scheme that promoted an essentialist interpretation of human variation was hugely influential and popular. That is what underlies virtually all "racial" classification right up to the present day.

The Genesis of the American Perspective

Blumenbach's American contemporary, Samuel Stanhope Smith (1750–1819), professor of moral philosophy and later president of the institution that became Princeton University, independently produced his *An Essay on the Causes of the Variety of Complexion and Figure in the Human Species* (1797). The approach was strikingly similar to that taken by Blumenbach, and, by the time he prepared his second edition (1810), Smith had become aware of his German counterpart's contribution and included copious references to it (cf. Jordan 1965b).

Unlike Blumenbach, Smith's primary loyalty was to the literal truth of the account of human origins in the Christian Bible. The descent of all living people from a biblical Adam and Eve was taken for granted. Departure from the original created form—assumed to be represented by living Europeans—was the result of the circumstances of living in various different parts of the world at which the descendants of the refugees from Eden had eventually arrived. This view led Smith to expect that people of African origin would come to look like Europeans in a century or two after living in the North Temperate Zone (Jordan 1965a). Smith had nowhere near the impact on the perceptions of the world enjoyed by Blumenbach, but his book clearly shows "how very much more immediate the problem of human physical and cultural diversity had become for transplanted Europeans who lived with it than for those who sat reading about it in the comfortable home of civilization" (Jordan 1965b:xli).

In the America that produced the concerns that stimulated the writing of Smith's *Essay*, there was no counterpart to the peasant perspective that had shaped the perceptions of the Old World for so long. The Native Americans, confronted by the invading Europeans, had spread over the entire Western Hemisphere after the end of the Pleistocene less than 12.0 ky BP, and time had not been sufficient to generate anything even beginning to resemble the graded variation characteristic of those parts of the world that have been continuously occupied for 100 ky or more. The transplanted Europeans, then, perceived an indigenous population that looked much the same throughout the entire hemisphere. In addition, they added quantities of unwilling imports from restricted parts of Africa. As a consequence, America had become the scene of confrontation among three distinct groups, each derived from a different and restricted part of the world, uprooted and thrown together with no indication of what their differences signified and no guide that specified the appropriate behavior of each toward the others.

The European element in that confrontation was composed largely of Protestants who assumed the literal accuracy of the biblical account, but who also assumed that it could not be contradicted by the findings of scientific inquiry. If there were unanswered questions or apparent discrepancies, it was presumed that these would be properly resolved by further investigation. One of those unresolved questions was whether the ancestors of Africans and Native Americans also were descendants of Adam and Eve. If they were, then how had they come to look so different from Europeans, and what was the significance of that difference in appearance? And if they were not of the same origin, what did this imply for the nature of their origins?

A Trinity of "Races"

During the eighteenth century also, those who dealt with the evidence for human biological variation came to the general realization that the native populations of North and South America probably represented an offshoot of the inhabitants of eastern Asia who had moved into a previously uninhabited Western Hemisphere some time in the not-too-remote past. If the Amerindians were a subdivision of the peoples of Asia, then Linnaeus' four-part scheme could be simplified and rendered in tripartite form. This was done by the French naturalist Georges Cuvier (1769–1832) early in the nineteenth century (Cuvier 1817, Vol. 1:94) and gained wide public recognition.

The number three has a strong emotional appeal to those brought up in the context of Occidental culture and society. The Western outlook traditionally divides things into three parts—right, left, and center; early, middle, and late; high, medium, and low—and this kind of approach receives powerful support from the overtones of sanctity that derive from its representation in Christian religious formulations. It was emotionally satisfying, then, to conceive of human variation as being represented in terms of three assumed entities whether or not that is an effective representation of reality.

Since Western traditions also led to the belief that there is some sort of "essence" underlying such divisions, the names for these divisions tended to suggest some of that essence rather than being names that simply denote geography. So the major geographic divisions of Europe, Africa, and Asia are commonly thought of as being inhabited by people referred to as "White," "Black," and "Yellow," or "Caucasoid," "Negroid," and "Mongoloid."

The Nineteenth Century and the End of Enlightenment

As the Enlightenment world of Linnaeus and Blumenbach gave way to the succeeding nineteenth century and its temporal offspring, the modern era, the demise of the old peasant perspective was vitually complete. In America, there was a major retreat from the faith that science could resolve the apparent discrepancies between the biblical account of human origins and the perceptions of categorical "racial" distinctions that were reinforced by daily contact. It was the insistent and unavoidable aspect of this situation that led to the first fully developed depiction to be published in English of human "races" as categorically distinct and possibly unrelated to each other. This was *Crania Americana* (1839) by the Philadelphia anatomist Samuel George Morton (1799–1851).

Morton gave full credit to the emerging polygenism in France—as fashioned by Julien Joseph Virey (1775–1846) and Jean Baptiste Geneviève Marcellin Baron Bory de Saint Vincent (1780–1846) (Erickson 1986; Blanckaert 1988; Léonard 1988)—and rooted his scheme in the five "varieties" of Blumenbach, which he preferred to call "races" to avoid the question of whether they were all really members of the same species (1839:5). Morton further divided these into twenty-two "families" (1839:4). The groups Morton identified have been used as the starting point for the construction of virtually every subsequent "racial" classification.

Although Morton's scheme underlies all subsequent manifestations of the concept of "race," he never produced a satisfactory or consistent definition of the concept himself. He repeatedly declared his faith in "the doctrine of *primeval diversities* among men" (1839:3, 1844:37, 1847:40), and the essence of that faith has continued to the present time, along with an equivalent inability to offer a satisfactory definition—for example, "Races there are; how to delimit them, how to draw the line between them is not only difficult, it is impossible" (Mayr 1968:103).

After Morton's death in 1851, some of his self-declared disciples offered his scheme to the American South in an attempt to jus-

tify the institution of slavery (Nott & Gliddon 1854). The almost simultaneous occurrences of the publication of Charles Darwin's *On the Origin of Species* (1859) and the outbreak of the American Civil War (1861), followed by the abolition of slavery that accompanied the defeat of the South, removed some of the principal factors that had operated to support Morton's "anthropology" in the English-speaking world, but neither the American domestic situation nor the dynamics of Darwinian evolution had much impact on the European continent.

Morton's assumptions concerning the nature of "races" and the techniques he used in pursuing his comparative studies—in sum, his "anthropology"—were adopted in detail and built upon by the French physician-anthropologist Paul Broca (1824–1880) in Paris (Brace 1982:18–19). Like Morton, Broca thought that "races" were "primordial" (Broca 1862:283), but, like his disciple Paul Topinard (1830–1911), he warned against reifying "racial types" (Broca 1859:602; Topinard 1879:657). Despite this warning, the concept of "race" that was identified with Broca's school late in the nineteenth century reflected the essence of Romantic-period transcendentalism. Curiously, it was an American economist, William Z. Ripley (1867–1941), who attributed the following verbalization to Topinard, although the latter never articulated it in quite this fashion: "Race in the present state of things is an abstract conception, a notion of continuity in discontinuity, of unity in diversity. It is the rehabilitation of a real but directly unattainable thing" (Ripley 1899:111–112).

That description of the concept of "race" was not used when Carleton S. Coon (1904–1981) was asked to produce a revised version of Ripley's *The Races of Europe* just before the outbreak of World War II (Coon 1939), but, after the war was over, it appeared again when the anthropological profession regrouped and collaborated in a compendium designed to display the state of the art as it was presumed to be in a world supposedly once more at peace (Vallois 1953:151). Once again, although Topinard was given the credit for that view, Henri Victor Vallois (1889–1981) used the words that Ripley had attributed to Topinard at the end of the last century. It was a perception, derived from America's own artificial situation, articulated in the framework of typological essentialism that secular French scholarship had inherited from the medieval Church, and presented in the phraseology of transcendentalism that had become particularly popular in the literary world as the era of Enlightenment was supplanted by the outlook of Romanticism (Lovejoy 1936:11–12). The concept of "race" that this produced was a creation of a world of preconceptions, feelings, and emotions and was not the product of scientific investigations.

Yet, however much anthropologists may decry the facile racial terminology that has attained a universal usage, it is still obvious that people differ in appearance from one part of the world to another, and the query is continually thrown back at us: What shall we call "them"? The answer is this: We should use geographical terms rather than names that purport to convey descriptive aspects of the people in question. If people are referred to in terms of the landmass of their origin, this can neutralize at least some of the baggage that invariably accompanies the old racial terminology. Regional labels can be modified by directional adjectives specifying "southern," "northwestern," "central," or whatever other desired indicator might be added.

The "race" concept itself "is a social construct derived mainly from perceptions conditioned by the events of recorded history, and it has no basic biological reality" (Brace, 1996:106). Although "... the concept is a sociological fact and should be studied in this context as long as people believe in race," it cannot help us in the investigation and understanding of the biological variation present in the living representatives of *Homo sapiens* (Scott 1968:67).

C. Loring Brace

See also Blumenbach, Johann Friedrich; Broca, Paul (Pierre); Chain of Being; Coon, Carleton S(tevens); Cuvier, Georges Léopold Chrétien Fréderic Dagobert (Baron); Linnaeus' Anthropology; Morton, Samuel George; Polygenism; Smith, Samuel Stanhope; Topinard, Paul

Bibliography
T. Bendyshe (ed): *The anthropological treatises of Johann Friedrich Blumenbach*. London: Longman, Green, Longman, Roberts & Green, 1865; C. Blanckaert: On the origins of French ethnology: William Edwards and the doctrine of race. In: G.W. Stocking (ed) *Bones, bodies, behavior: Essays on biological anthropology*. Madison: University of Wisconsin Press, 1988, pp. 18–55; C.L. Brace: The roots of the race concept in American physical anthropology. In: F. Spencer (ed) *A history of American physical anthropology, 1930–1980*. New York: Academic Press, 1982, pp. 11–29; C.L. Brace: A four-letter word called "race." In: L.J. Reynolds & L. Lieberman (eds) *Race and other misadventures: Papers in honor of Ashley Montagu*. Dix Hills, New York: General Hall, 1996, pp. 106–141; P. Broca: Des phénomènes d'hybridité dans le genre humain. *Journal de la Physiologie de l'Homme et des Animaux* 2:601–625, 1859.

P. Broca: La linguistique et l'anthropologie. *Bulletins de la Société d'Anthropologie de Paris* 3:264–319, 1862; C.S. Coon: *The races of Europe*. New York: Macmillan, 1939; G. Cuvier: *Le règne animal distribué d'après son organisation, pour servir de base à l'histoire naturelle des animaux et d'introduction à l'anatomie comparée.* Vol. 1. Paris: Deterville, 1817; C. Darwin: *On the origin of species by means of natural selection; or, the preservation of favoured races in the struggle of life.* London: Murray, 1859; R.E. Dunn: *The adventures of Ibn Batutah: A Muslim traveler of the fourteenth century.* London: Croom Helm, 1986; P.A. Erickson: The anthropology of Josiah Clark Nott. *Kroeber Anthropological Society Papers* 65–66:103–120, 1986; Herodotus: *Herodotus: The histories.* English translation by Aubrey de Selincourt. Harmondsworth, England: Penguin, 1954.

W.D. Jordan (ed): *An essay on the causes of the variety of complexion and figure in the human species, by Samuel Stanhope Smith.* Cambridge, Massachusetts: Belknap Press, 1965a; W.D. Jordan: Introduction. In: W.D. Jordan (ed) *An essay on the causes of the variety of complexion and figure in the human species, by Samuel Stanhope Smith.* Cambridge, Massachusetts, Belknap Press, 1965b, pp. vii–lvii; J. Léonard: Pour situer Virey. In: C. Bénichou & C. Blanckaert (eds) *Julien-Joseph Virey: Naturaliste et anthropologue.* Paris: Vrin, 1988, pp. 17–22; C. Linnaeus: *Caroli Linnaei Systema naturae regnum animale.* Holmiat: Salvi, 1758. Facsimile of 10th ed. Vol. 1. London: British Museum (Natural History), 1956; F.B. Livingstone: On the nonexistence of human races. *Current Anthropology* 3:279, 1962.

A.O. Lovejoy: *The great chain of being: A study of the history of an idea.* Cambridge, Massachusetts: Harvard University Press, 1936; E. Mayr: Biological aspects of race in man. In: M. Mead et al. (eds) *Science and the concept of race.* New York: Columbia University Press, 1968, pp. 103–105; S.G. Morton: *Crania Americana; or, A comparative view of the skulls of various Aboriginal nations of North and South America; to which is prefixed an essay on the varieties of the human species.* Philadelphia: Dobson, 1839; S.G. Morton: *Crania Aegyptiaca.* Philadelphia: Pennington, 1844; S.G. Morton: Hybridity in animals considered in reference to the question of the unity of the human species. *American Journal of Science* 3:39–50, 203–212, 1847; J.C. Nott & G.R. Gliddon (eds): *Types of mankind.* Philadelphia: Lippincott, Grambo, 1854.

M. Polo: *The travels of Marco Polo, the Venetian.* The translation by [William] Marsden, revised with a selection of his notes, edited by Thomas Wright. London: Bohm, 1854. Reprint. New York: AMS Press, 1968; W.Z. Ripley: *The races of Europe: A sociological study.* New York: Appleton, 1899; J.P. Scott: Race as a concept. In: M. Mead et al. (eds) *Science and the concept of race.* New York: Columbia University Press, 1968, pp. 59–68; G.W. Stocking Jr.: Bones, bodies, behavior. In: G.W. Stocking Jr. (ed) *Bones, bodies, behavior: Essays on biological anthropology.* Madison: University of Wisconsin Press, 1988, pp. 3–17; P. Topinard: De la notion de race en anthropologie. *Revue d'Anthropologie* 2 (2d ser.):589–660, 1879; H.V. Vallois: Race. In: A.L. Kroeber (ed) *Anthropology today: An encyclopedic inventory.* Chicago: University of Chicago Press, 1953, pp. 145–162.

Rakshit, Hirendra Kishor (1927–1992)

Born in Dacca (now Bangladesh), Rakshit received his master's degree in physical anthropology from the University of Calcutta in 1951. Between 1951 and 1956, he held a number of temporary teaching positions at the Universities of Calcutta and Banaras and at the School of Archeology at Andhra University. During this time, he was also a research scholar in the Department of Anthropology at the University of Calcutta. His particular research interests embraced anthropometry, microdemography, population genetics, and ethnology of Indian castes and tribes.

In 1957, his experience and wide interests attracted the attention of the Nutrition Research Laboratory at Coonoor, where he was appointed an assistant research officer. Rakshit, however, was not totally satisfied with the facilities and remained there only from February to October 1957, whereupon he secured a tenure-track position with the Anthropological Survey of India (ASI). There his research needs were amply satisfied, and

he remained at the ASI, rising to the rank of director, until ill health forced his premature retirement in 1982. He died in Calcutta on 2 July 1992.

Although overburdened from the outset by administrative responsibilities at the ASI, he remained an enthusiastic and dedicated researcher. Besides his many micro-level studies, he also initiated a number of important macro-level projects, including the All India Anthropometric Survey: South Zone (1960–1963) and the All India Bioanthropological Survey (1972–1980), which involved data collection on demography, marriage practices, body measurements, morbidity, and food habits. He was very methodical and planned his projects to represent various regions and communities thoroughly.

Soft spoken and mild mannered, Rakshit always supported his colleagues who worked with him. However, his polite and friendly approach in dealing with personnel working under him at times did not help him to effect administrative policies and discharge his responsibilities as head of a regional office. But, as director, he discharged his responsibilities well and adhered to rules and regulations meticulously. His inflexbility in this regard, and his inability to constructively handle academic criticism, pitched him against many at various administrative levels. Nonetheless, Rakshit maintained his calm composure—remaining an ardent researcher—and never embraced the aura of a bureaucrat.

His numerous publications appeared in journals published in India and abroad. He undertook the editorial responsibilities of the journal *Man in India* and of the *Journal of the Indian Anthropological Society*, and he remained an active member of the Indian Science Congress Association, the Indian Anthropological Society, and the Ethnographic and Folk Culture Society.

S.H. Ahmad
Ripu D. Singh

See also India, Anthropological Survey of; South Asia (India, Pakistan, Sri Lanka)

Bibliography

SELECTED WORKS

The Mongolian element in Indian population: Real and alleged. *Anthropos* 50:49–64, 1965; The Brahmans of India: An anthropometric study: Language, culture, and race in south India. *Journal of the Indian Anthropological Society* 5:205–232, 1970; Anthropometry of the Bastar tribes.

Man in India 54:101–128, 1974; (ed):
Bioanthropological research in India. Proceedings of a seminar in physical anthropology
and allied disciplines. Calcutta: Anthropological Survey of India, 1975; (ed): *Directory
of anthropologists in India.* Calcutta: Anthropological Survey of India, 1981; (with R.D.
Singh et al.): *Anthropology in India: All
Indian anthropometric survey.* South zone
(basic data). Calcutta: Anthropological
Survey of India, 1988.

SECONDARY SOURCES
       S. Roy (ed): *Anthropologists in India.*
New Delhi: Indian Anthropological
Association, 1970.

Ramapithecus

The genus *Ramapithecus* (now defunct) was
originally based on two isolated maxillas collected in 1932 by a Yale University expedition to the Siwaliks in north India. G. Edward
Lewis, then a doctoral student at Yale, announced the new material in 1934, describing two separate species: *Ramapithecus
brevirostris* and *Ramapithecus hariensis.* The fragmentary right palate (Y[ale] P[eabody]
M[useum]) 13799 served as the holotype for
brevirostris, and the even more incomplete
maxilla YPM 13807 was the holotype for
hariensis. Minor morphological differences
separated the two species, but according to
Lewis (1934:167), *hariensis* was more primitive in that it possessed a longer face (as
judged by the extent of interproximal wear
facets) and was found "some 2,000 feet below"
the YPM 13799 maxilla. Given that the
hariensis maxillary fragment contained only

two fragmentary teeth (M1 and M2) and very
little maxillary bone, little support was generated for recognizing it as a valid species.
Ramapithecus brevirostris (Rama's short-faced
ape) was identified by Lewis (1934) as a hominid based on its small canine (represented only
by a socket), absence of a diastema, short
(nonprognathous) face with homomorphic,
vertically implanted upper incisors, divergent
(i.e., parabolic) dental arch, and other "progressive" molar and premolar features. Until
the American paleoprimatologist Elwyn
Simons resurrected the taxon in 1961, very
little importance was placed on the specimen
or its identification as an early hominid. This
was probably largely due to a review of the
YPM 13799 maxilla by the Smithsonian
physical anthropologist Aleš Hrdlička (1869–
1943) in 1935. Among other things, Hrdlička
argued that the palate shape could not be accurately determined due to the fragmentary
nature of the specimen, and that the maxilla
showed considerable subnasal prognathism,
plus every indication that the canine was not
especially small. Even though this tooth was
missing, Hrdlička (1935:35) argued that the
specimen was probably a female (based on
overall size of the maxilla) and that, if correc-
tions were made for the inwardly crushed la-
bial face of the canine socket, the tooth could
"not [have been] small in relation to the jaw
or the rest of the teeth" (1935:35). Based on
his examination of the original specimen,
Hrdlička concluded YPM 13799 was
"pithecoid."
       Elwyn Simons' brief 1961 article in the
journal *Postilla* initiated almost two decades
of complete and generally uncritical acceptance of *Ramapithecus* as a hominid ancestor.
In this article, Simons basically reiterated
Lewis' points concerning the type specimen,
YPM 13799. In subsequent publications,
Simons (1963) added another maxilla and a
number of fragmentary mandibles (1964),
which were previously allocated to other taxa.
Then, in collaboration with the Anglo-American paleoanthropologist David Pilbeam in
1965, he published their influential "Preliminary Revision of the Dryopithecinae," in
which the *Ramapithecus* sample was expanded
to include even more material (Simons &
Pilbeam 1965). At this juncture, the species
name was changed from *brevirostris* to
punjabicus. This was required since two mandible fragments (G[eological] S[urvey] [of]
I[ndia] D-118/119) originally designated by
the British geologist Guy Ellock Pilgrim
(1875–1943) (1910) as *Dryopithecus punjabicus*

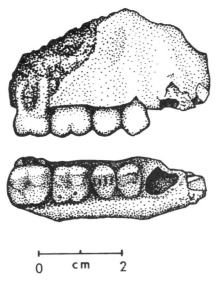

Fig. 1. The type specimen for
Ramapithecus *(YPM–
13799) shown in lateral
(top) and occlusal (bottom)
view. Note the absence of
anterior teeth and fractured
and depressed canine socket.
The specimen is drawn from
a cast.*

0   c m   2

were included by Simons and Pilbeam in *Ramapithecus*, and *punjabicus* had nomenclatural priority. In their 1965 revision, Simons and Pilbeam also sunk Louis S. B. Leakey's (1903–1972) *Kenyapithecus wickeri* material (FT 1271/2) from Fort Ternan, Kenya, and *Dryopithecus keiyuanensis* from south China into *Ramapithecus punjabicus*. While all specimens still represented only a handful of rather fragmentary material, *Ramapithecus* was almost universally accepted as hominid precursor. Moreover, since dates from Fort Ternan were estimated at about 14.0 mya, the split between hominids and pongids was considered to have had a great antiquity. Besides the taxonomic revisions, it was suggested that *Ramapithecus* was probably a tool-using biped. In short order, Leakey identified "probable" tools from Fort Ternan (cf. Leakey 1968). While Leakey maintained substantial interpretative differences with Simons and Pilbeam and never accepted the sinking of *Kenyapithecus* into *Ramapithecus*, both sides agreed that this African and Asian material represented an indisputable hominid ancestor. By the end of the decade, the tabulation of hominid features for *Ramapithecus* grew from the original features listed by Lewis to include absence of simian shelf, homomorphic lower premolars, differential tooth wear (signaling delayed maturation), a deeply arched palate, thickened enamel, and short, broad mandibles. Some of these characteristics were inferred. For example, neither a symphysis nor lower third premolars were known for *Ramapithecus*, yet these structures were presumed to be like hominids. Moreover, the facial fragments were very incomplete and no postcranial remains were known, so questions concerning facial prognathism and mode of locomotion, although inferred as hominid-like and often repeated in the professional literature and textbooks, remained guesses.

Questions about the hominid nature of *Ramapithecus* arose in 1971 when the British paleontologist Peter Andrews determined that the Fort Ternan (FT) *wickeri* maxilla was associated with a lower jaw (FT 45) that had been previously described as a fossil ape. The FT 45 jaw possessed a sectorial lower third premolar and a simian shelf—neither of which was found in hominids nor were thought to occur in *Ramapithecus*. Later, the Anglo-American paleoanthropologist Alan Walker and Andrews (1973) determined that the dental arcade of FT 45 was V-shaped, not parabolic. Beyond these problems with the African fossils attributed to *Ramapithecus*, molecular

geneticists predicted a much more recent date for the ape-hominid split (Sarich & Wilson 1967), and the American physical anthropologist Vincent Sarich argued from the perspective of his immunological dates that "one no longer had the option of considering a fossil specimen older than about eight million years as a hominid *no matter what it looks like*" (1971:76, his italics). In addition, several others questioned the validity of most of the hominid features ascribed to *Ramapithecus* (e.g., Eckhardt 1975; Frayer 1974, 1975; Greenfield 1974, 1975, 1978, 1979; Vogel 1975; Yulish 1970), but until the discovery of new Siwalik material in the late 1970s these criticisms were mostly ignored (cf. Lewin 1987:102). With the discovery of new Siwalik material (Pilbeam 1979), especially the G[eological] S[urvey] [of] P[akistan] 15000 face (Pilbeam 1982), it became clear to Pilbeam and Simons that the *Ramapithecus* was more likely an orang than a hominid ancestor. This position was anticipated by Leonard Greenfield, in his "late-divergence hypothesis" (1980) which was in press before the GSP 15000 face was discovered in 1979. In that paper, Greenfield sank *Ramapithecus* into *Sivapithecus*. Following the description of the GSP 15000 face, the taxon *Ramapithecus punjabicus* was abandoned, and the fossils were reallocated back to *Sivapithecus* as Greenfield had earlier proposed. Today, *Ramapithecus* is no longer considered a valid taxon nor a hominid ancestor. (For further details, see Kay 1982; Lewin 1987; Tattersall 1975; Wolpoff 1982.)

Location of Original Specimens
1. YPM 13799 & 13807: Peabody Museum of Natural History, Yale University, Box 6666, New Haven, Connecticut 06511; 2. FT 1271/2 and FT 45: National Museum of Kenya, Nairobi, Kenya; 3. GSI D-118/119: Geological Survey of India, 27 Chowringhee Road, Calcutta 13, India; 4. GSP 15000: Geological Survey of Pakistan, Quetta, Pakistan.
David W. Frayer

See also Gigantopithecus; Hrdlička, Aleš; Leakey, Louis Seymour Bazett; Molecular Anthropology; Paleoprimatology; Pilgrim, Guy Ellock; Siwaliks

Bibliography
P. Andrews: *Ramapithecus wickeri* mandible from Fort Ternan, Kenya. *Nature* 231:192–194, 1971; R.B. Eckhardt: *Gigantopithecus* as a hominid. In: R.H. Tuttle (ed)

Paleoanthropology, morphology, and paleoecology.
The Hague: Mouton, 1975, pp. 105–130;
D.W. Frayer: A reappraisal of *Ramapithecus.*
Yearbook of Physical Anthropology 18:19–30,
1974; D.W. Frayer: The taxonomic status of
Ramapithecus. In: M. Malez (ed) *Krapinskii
procovjek i evolucija hominida. Zagreb:*
Jugoslavenska Akademija Znanosti i
Umjetnosti, 1975, pp. 255–268; L.O.
Greenfield: Taxonomic reassessment of two
Ramapithecus specimens. *Folia Primatologica*
22:97–115, 1974; L.O. Greenfield: A
comment of relative molar breadth in
Ramapithecus. Journal of Human Evolution
4:267–273, 1975a; L.O. Greenfield:
Taxonomic reassessment of two *Ramapithecus*
specimens. *Folia Primatologica* 22:97–115,
1975b; L.O. Greenfield: On the dental
arcade reconstructions of *Ramapithecus.*
Journal of Human Evolution 7:345–359,
1978.

L.O. Greenfield: On the adaptive
pattern of *Ramapithecus. American Journal of
Physical Anthropology* 50:527–548, 1979;
L.O. Greenfield: A late-divergence
hypothesis. *American Journal of Physical
Anthropology* 52:351–365, 1980; A.
Hrdlička: The Yale fossils of anthropoid
apes. *American Journal of Science* 29:34–40,
1935; R.F. Kay: *Sivapithecus simonsi*, a new
species of Miocene hominoid, with special
comments on the phylogenetic status of the
Ramapithecinae. *International Journal of
Primatology* 3:113–173, 1982; L.S.B.
Leakey: Bone smashing by Late Miocene
Hominidae. *Nature* 218: 528–530, 1968; R.
Lewin: *Bones of contention.* New York: Simon
& Schuster, 1987; G.E. Lewis: Preliminary
notice of new man-like apes from India.
American Journal of Science 27:161–179,
1934.

D.R. Pilbeam: Rearranging our family
tree. *Human Nature*: 38–45, 1968; D.R.
Pilbeam: Recent finds and interpretations of
Miocene hominoids. *Annual Review of
Anthropology* 8:333–353, 1979; D.R.
Pilbeam: New hominid skull material from
the Miocene of Pakistan. *Nature* 295:232–
234, 1982; G.E. Pilgrim: Notice of new
mammalian genera and species from the
Tertiary of India. *Records of the Geological
Survey of India* 45:1–74, 1910; V. Sarich: A
molecular approach to the question of
hominid origins. In: P. Dolhinow & V.
Sarich (eds) *Background for man.* New York:
Little, Brown, 1971, pp. 60–81; V. Sarich &
A.C. Wilson: Immunological time scale for
hominid evolution. *Science* 158:1200–1203,

1967; E.L. Simons: The phyletic position of
Ramapithecus. Postilla 57:1–9, 1961; E.L.
Simons: Some fallacies in the study of
hominid phylogeny. *Science* 141:879–889,
1963.

E.L. Simons: On the mandibles of
*Ramapithecus. Proceedings of the National
Academy of Sciences* 51:528–525, 1964; E.L.
Simons: A source of dental comparison of
Ramapithecus with *Australopithecus* and *Homo.*
South African Journal of Science 64:92–112,
1968; E.L. Simons: *Ramapithecus. Scientific
American* 263(5):28–36, 1977; E.L. Simons
& D.R. Pilbeam: Preliminary revision of the
Dryopithecinae (Pongidae, Anthropoidea).
Folia Primatologica 3:81–152, 1965; I.
Tattersall: *The evolutionary significance of
Ramapithecus.* Minneapolis: Burgess, 1975;
C. Vogel: Remarks on the reconstruction of
the dental arcade of *Ramapithecus.* In: R.H.
Tuttle (ed) *Paleoanthropology, morphology, and
paleoecology.* The Hague: Mouton, 1975, pp.
87–98; A. Walker & P. Andrews: Reconstruction of the dental arcades of
Ramapithecus wickeri. Nature 224:313–314,
1973; M.H. Wolpoff: *Ramapithecus* and
hominid origins. *Current Anthropology*
25:501–522, 1982; S.M. Yulish: Anterior
tooth reductions in *Ramapithecus. Primates*
11:255–263, 1970.

Ranke, Johannes (1836–1916)

Born in Thurnau, Oberfranken, Germany,
Ranke studied medicine at the Universities of
Munich, Tübingen, Berlin, and Paris. His interest in anthropology emerged during his
student years, during which time he was significantly influenced by the pathologist-
anthropologist Rudolf Virchow (1821–1902).
In 1861, he graduated from the University
of Munich, and in 1863 he was appointed a
lecturer in physiology there. In 1869, he was
promoted to the rank of associate professor
in general natural history. In 1882, he received an honorary doctorate of philosophy,
and in 1886 he was given the first formal
teaching position for anthropology established in Germany. In 1885 at the University of Munich, he founded a prehistoric
collection, which was transformed in 1889
into a Konservatorium.

Ranke played an integral role in 1870 in
the founding of the Munich Anthropological
Society (Münchener Anthropologische Gesellschaft), which later joined the German
Anthropological Society (Deutsche Anthropologische Gesellschaft: DAG). He served as
the first secretary and chairman of the Munich

Society, and as secretary of the DAG. In 1875, a decision was made to start a scientific journal, the *Beiträge zur Anthropologie und Urgeschichte Bayerns*, which Ranke edited at first in cooperation with the anatomist Nicolaus Rüdinger (ca. 1832–1896) and later alone. From 1877, he was editor of the *Berichte der Allgemeinen Versammlungen* [Report of General Conventions] *der Deutschen Anthropologischen Gesellschaft*. At first he acted as an editorial assistant to Julius Kollmann (1834–1918), but when Kollmann moved to Basel, Ranke assumed full responsibility for editing the newsletter.

Ranke worked chiefly on the craniology of Bavaria. Among his many publications, probably the most important is his book *Der Mensch* (1886), which went through three editions. Virchow described this as a "great work" (cf. Ziegelmayer 1987). In addition, it was largely through Ranke's support that the Frankfort Agreement, a standardized method of cranial measurement, was agreed upon in 1882.

Ursula Zängl-Kumpf

See also Deutsche Anthropologische Gesellschaft; Frankfort Agreement; Virchow, Rudolf

Bibliography
SELECTED WORKS
Die Schädel der altbayerischen Landbevölkerung: Zur Physiologie des Schädels und Gehirns. *Beiträge zur Anthropologie und Urgeschichte Bayerns* 1:227–285, 1877; Beiträge zur Craniologie der Bayern und ihrer Nachbarstämme. *Correspondenz-Blatt der Deutschen Gesellschaft für Anthropologie* 10:123–15, 1878; *Grundzüge der Physiologie des Menschen mit Rücksicht auf Gesundheitsapflege*. Leipzig: Engelmann, 1881; Zur Methodik der Kraniometrie und über die in Bayern vorkommenden Schädelformen. *Correspondenz-Blatt der Deutschen Gesellschaft für Anthropologie* 9:136–142, 1883.
Die Schädel der Altbayerischen Landbevölkerung. Ethnologische Kraniologie der Bayern. *Beiträge zur Anthropologie und Urgeschichte Bayerns* 3:108–205 (1882), 5:53–248 (1884); *Der Mensch*. Leipzig: Bibliographisches Institut, 1886 (3d ed., 2 vols.: 1911–1912); Beiträge zur physischen Anthropologie der Altbayern. Munich: Literarisch-Artistische Anstalt, 1878. (2d ed., 2 vols.: Munich: Reidel, 1883–1892); Die Körperproportionen des Bayerischen Volkes. *Beiträge zur Anthropologie und Urgeschichte Bayerns* 8:49–92, 1889; Die somatisch-anthropologische Abteilung der anthropologisch-prähistorischen Staatssammlung. *Sitzungsbericht der Bayerischen Akademie der Wissenschaften*. 1912.

SECONDARY SOURCES
F. Birkner: Johannes Ranke. *Correspondenz-Blatt der Deutschen Gesellschaft für Anthropologie* 47:35–40, 1916; G. Ziegelmayer: 100 Jahre Anthropologie in München. *Würzburger medizin-historische Mitteilungen* 5:245–269, 1987.

Rassenhygiene and Rassenkunde

Athough the origin of these two movements can be traced to the closing decades of the nineteenth century, it was not until the decade immediately following the World War I Versailles Peace Conference in 1919 that their separate missions merged, forming a scientific coalition that was to provide, after the collapse of the Weimar Republic in 1933, both the theoretical and the practical tools for the subsequent implementation of the Third Reich's eugenic and racial laws.

Unlike Rassenhygiene, which is invariably translated as "race hygiene" or "eugenics," the term "Rassenkunde" does not have an exact English equivalent, though "racial lore" seems to capture the essence of its meaning in German. While this latter term was first introduced in the early 1900s (cf. Gumplowicz 1909:ix), the first major treatise to appear with Rassenkunde in its title was the anthropologist Hans F.K. Günther's (1891–1968) *Kleine Rassenkunde der deutschen Volkes* (1922), which went through a dozen editions during the 1920s (Proctor 1988). Following the appearance of Günther's book, there was a mounting tide of other works in this genre, which collectively mirror a radical shift in the perceived mission of physical anthropology in Germany during the late Weimar and subsequent Nazi periods.

A major preoccupation of Rassenkunde was the problem of racial classification. Building on a taxonomic tradition established in the eighteenth century, German scholars endeavored to develop even finer racial delineations. At the core of this movement was Aryanism, which extolled the virtues of the Teutonic (or Nordic) genius. During the late 1800s and early 1900s, Aryanism, found increasing expression in the rhetoric of burgeoning nationalism throughout Europe as well as the United States (cf. Day 1993; Poliakov 1971). In 1902, the German physician Ludwig Woltmann (1871–1907) founded the *Politisch-anthropologische Revue*, a journal that was to become the flagship of the Nordic suprema-cist movement in Germany prior to the Weimar period. Like his French counterpart, Georges Vacher de Lapouge (1854–1936), who had founded the ultraconservative move-ment of *anthroposociologie* in France, Woltmann made singular use of the Aryan debate to pro-mote his ill-starred political message. Draw-ing on Lapouge's *L'Aryen: Son rôle sociale* (1899), as well as the French writer Arthur de Gobineau's (1816–1882) *Essai sur l'inégalité des races humaines* (1853–1855), Woltmann claimed that competition between the races had been a prime mover in human history, and that all that was good in the world could be attributed to the innately superior "Nordics," the blond dolichocephalic race. He also ar-gued, like Lapouge, that miscegenation was a social evil and the root of many of the prob-lems then manifest in German society, and that unless steps were taken to preserve the purity of "Aryan blood" the productive Germano-Aryan race would experience even-tual extinction.

This pessimistic theme in Woltmann's message was complemented by the emergence of the international eugenics movement at the close of the nineteenth century, which was concerned with the study of human heredity and the improvement of the human condition by genetic control.

In Germany, the eugenics movement was founded by the physician Alfred Ploetz (1860–1940), who gave it the name "Rassen-hygiene," and whose popular book *Die Tüchtigkeit unserer Rasse und der Schutz der Schwachen* (1895) provided a theoretical basis for subsequent efforts to "improve the race" in Germany. Subsequently, in 1905, Ploetz founded the journal *Archiv für Rassen- und Gesellschaftsbiologie* and the Deutsche Gesell-schaft für Rassenhygiene, which attracted to its ranks a number of leading German anthro-pologists, such as Ernst Haeckel (1834–1919), Felix von Luschan (1854–1924), and Johannes Ranke (1836–1916).

At this juncture, however, genetics was still very much in its infancy, and the first attempt by a German anthropologist to ap-ply Mendelian principles to humans was made by Eugen Fischer (1874–1964), then sta-tioned at the University of Freiburg. In 1908, he had traveled to German South-West Africa (now Namibia) to study the Rehobothers, a group descended largely from the union of

Nama (Khoikhoi) women with Afrikaner trekboers who had moved from the Cape Colony in the 1860s and settled in the region of Rehoboth. Published in 1913, Fischer's *Rehobother Basters* was immediately received at home and abroad as a major contribution to anthropology. While he dispelled a number of misconceptions regarding the question of miscegenation, such as the popular notion that half-breeds were either genetically or morally inferior, he later went on to assert that it was highly probable that crosses between genetically distant races produced offspring inferior to those resulting from the mating of genetically similar races. Fischer believed that behavioral traits were controlled by dominant alleles and inherited in much the same way as physical traits—according to Mendelian laws of inheritance. The fact that these racial alleles continued to be expressed after repeated crossings provided evidence, so Fischer be-lieved, for concluding that populations do mix without blending, which convinced him that genetics was going to be an invaluable tool in the study of race and racial issues (Proctor 1988).

By the mid-1920s, Fischer's expectations were realized, as can be seen from the book *Allgemeine Rassenkunde* (1925) written by the University of Hamburg anthropologist Walter Scheidt (1895–1976). There, as in other anthropological publications, genetics was portrayed as a theoretical and practical bridge unifying the hitherto separate endeav-ors of cultural and physical anthropology. Spe-cifically, Scheidt postulated not only how specific physical and cultural traits might be explained within the rubric of human genet-ics, but also how physical and cultural anthro-pologists might solve social as well as biological problems plaguing German society using methods advocated by racial hygienists.

The emerging introspective nature of German anthropology and its apparent obses-sion with the concept of race and racial pu-rity, can in large part be viewed, at least during the early Weimar period (1919–1933), as a product of the political and socioeconomic turmoil in Germany after World War I. Its economy was in ruins, and its government in disarray, and, as conditions worsened, many commentators predicted an eventual collapse of German society. It was in this initially cha-otic and pessimistic context that anthropol-ogy in the early Weimar period acquired what the American social historian Robert Proctor has called a "therapeutic impulse" (Proctor 1988) that was consciously directed to combating a wide range of biosocial problems (cf. Scheidt 1925). Among the earliest attempts along this line was a series of elaborate anthropometric surveys conducted by the physical anthropologist Rudolf Martin (1864–1925) on Munich schoolchildren that endeavored to show, among other things, that physical exercise could help reverse the negative effects of war on a child's health (cf. Oetteking 1926:416). It was this "therapeutic mission" that also prompted the proposal in 1922 by the Preussischer Landesgesundheitsrat für Rassenhygiene (Prussian Council for Racial Hygiene) for the establishment of what eventually became the Kaiser Wilhelm Institut für Anthropologie, menschliche Erblehre und Eugenik. It was established in 1927 in Berlin to study and combat the "physical and mental degeneration of the German people"—investigating, among other things, the effects of alcohol and venereal disease on the German germplasm (Proctor 1988).

Between 1922 and the opening of the Kaiser Wilhelm Institut, several other events transpired that served to seal the fate of traditional physical anthropological research in Germany and thereby secured the ultimate missions of the Rassenkunde and Rassenhygiene movements to sanitize the German *volk* (people). First, there was the organization of the Deutsche Gesellschaft für Physische Anthropologie (DGPA), which held its inaugural meeting at Freiburg in 1926. Among the leading participants at this meeting were Otto Aichel (b. 1871), Egon von Eickstedt (1892–1965), Wilhelm Gieseler (1900–1976), Theodor Mollison (1874–1952), Karl Saller (1902–1969), Walter Scheidt, Otto Schlaginhaufen (1879–1973), Hans Weinert (1887–1967), and Eugen Fischer, who subsequently became a dominant force in the new DGPA (Proctor 1988). Later, in 1937, the DGPA changed its name to Deutsche Gesellschaft für Rassenforschung (Society for Racial Research: SRR), which further reinforced its seemingly intended mission. In 1941, due to the disruption of the war, the SSR became inactive and did not survive. During the fifteen years of its existence, the DGPA-SRR superseded the Deutsche Anthropologische Gesellschaft as Germany's premier anthropological society.

Although the founding of the DGPA can be viewed simply as a natural step in the professionalization of German physical anthropology, it also marks the beginning of the end of physical anthropology as practiced in the tradition of Rudolf Martin, who had died the year preceding the first DGPA meeting. This movement was further enhanced by the death in 1924 of Felix von Luschan, who had also exerted a significant influence on the development of German physical anthropology. His vacated Chair of Anthropology at the University of Berlin passed to Eugen Fischer, whose power was further increased by his installation in 1927 as director of the newly

Fig. 1. Berlin 1933. The "plastometer" depicted in the window was a device designed by R. Burger-Villingen (see Fig 2) to determine the racial identity of the human skull. From R. Vishniac: A Vanished World. New York: Farrar, Straus & Giroux, 1983.

Fig. 2. *The Plastometer (see Fig. 1) and its designer R. Burger-Villingen.*

founded Kaiser Wilhelm Institut. Fischer's appointment at the University of Berlin and as director of Germany's then most prestigious anthropological institute guaranteed that the new alliance of anthropology, genetics, and eugenics would constitute the primary focus of anthropological research in Germany.

In January 1933, when the National Socialists seized power, the events of the preceding Weimar period took on a new and heightened significance. Soon thereafter, the Kaiser Wilhelm Institut was transformed into a major training center for SS (Schutzstaffel: "defense echelons" or "black shirts," which embraced the Gestapo) physicians who were responsible for administering the eugenic and racial policies of the Third Reich (Proctor 1988). At the same time, many of the most prominent workers associated with the Rassenkunde and Rassenhygiene movements were quickly absorbed into the Nazi hierarchy, where their expertise was suitably employed. For example, among his many other duties, Fischer served as a judge in Berlin's Erbgesundheitsobergericht (Appellate Genetic Health Court). The purpose of such courts, which were established throughout Germany, was to determine who should be sterilized according to the provisions of the new Eugenics Law (Erbgesundheitsrecht) passed in July 1933 that had been designed to eradicate the threat of "genetically diseased offspring" (cf. Proctor 1988). Among those targeted for sterilization were the mentally retarded, the mentally ill, and chronic alcoholics. When the Third Reich collapsed in

1945, records revealed that close to two million Germans had been forcibly sterilized under this law (Chase 1975). It is of more than passing interest to note that this pernicious piece of legislation was based on a model Eugenical Sterilization Law written during the 1920s by an American, Harry Hamilton Laughlin (1880–1943), who was then superintendent of the Eugenics Record Office at Cold Spring Harbor, Long Island, New York. (For further details on Laughlin's views on sterilization, see Laughlin 1922.)

Along with Fischer there were many others, such as Hans Günther, whose careers benefited directly from the Nazis' rise to power. In Günther's case, he joined the Nazi Party in 1932, the same year he was appointed Germany's first professor of Rassenkunde at the University of Jena, and in 1935 he was installed as director of the Anstalt für Rassenkunde at the University of Berlin. A year later, he received the coveted Rudolf Virchow Medal for his contributions to anthropology (cf. Proctor). Another beneficiary was the geneticist Fritz Lenz (1887–1976). A former student of Ploetz, Lenz was editor of his mentor's *Archiv für Rassen- und Gesellschaftsbiologie* between 1913 and 1933. In 1923, he was appointed to the first professorship of Rassenhygiene established in Germany, at the University of Munich. In the early 1920s, he and Fischer (along with E. Baur) had coauthored the highly influential text *Grundriss der menschlichen Erblichkeitslehre* (Foundations of the Theory of Human Heredity) (1923). In 1933, he moved to the University of Berlin, where he was made professor of eugenics, as well as head of the Department of Rassenhygiene at the Kaiser Wilhelm Institut. In this latter position, Lenz played a significant role in the development of the Nazis' eugenic policies.

Two years later, coinciding with the annual Congress of the Nationalsozialistische Deutsche Arbeitpartei: NSDAP (the National Socialist German Workers' Party, otherwise known as the Nazi Party) held in Nuremberg (Nürnberg) in September 1935, the Nationalist Socialist government passed two additional eugenic laws: the Law to Protect German Blood and Honor (Gesetz zum Schutze des deutschen Blutes und der deutscher Ehre), and the Reich Citizenship Law (Reichsbürgergesetz)—collectively known as the Nuremberg Laws. These laws transformed the xenophobic fantasies of the Rassenkunde movement into reality. Although later extended to embrace Gypsies and Negroes, among others, the primary target of this legislation was German Jewry. The Nuremberg Laws not only prohibited marriage and sexual relations between Jews and other German citizens, but also severely restricted their civil rights. In 1938, further restrictive laws (again aimed primarily at the Jews) were passed, which included the confiscation of their property.

While all of these measures led to a significant emigration of Jews from Germany, the level was considerably less than had been anticipated. Hence, in 1939, on the eve of World War II, the Reich Central Office for Jewish Emigration was established to solve the Jewish question through compulsory deportation. Between 1939 and 1941, several evacuation plans were entertained, such as the idea of deporting German and other European Jews to Madagascar. But ultimately all of these schemes were rejected in favor of the deportation of Jews to the eastern territories and, finally, into extermination camps.

Although there were condemnations of the Nazis' eugenic policies prior to World War II, they were surprisingly few and did little to promote an international censure of the National Socialist government in Germany. For example, the American geneticist Leslie C. Dunn (1893–1974), following a visit to Germany in 1935, condemned the abuses being perpetrated under the guise of eugenics in Germany in a letter to the paleontologist John C. Merriam (1869–1945), then president of the Carnegie Institution of Washington (cf. Archives of Eugenic Record Office: Library, American Philosophical Society, 104 South Fifth Street, Philadelphia, Pennsylvania 19106-3387). Another example was the condemnation issued by the Seventh International Genetics Congress held in Edinburgh in 1939 (Ludmerer 1972). (For further details on this period and the general reception of the eugenics movement in Britain and the United States, see Barkan 1992:279–340.)

It was not until after the collapse of the Third Reich in 1945 that the international community was finally confronted with the obscene evidence of what had transpired under the banner of Rassenhygiene and Rassenkunde in Nazi-occupied Europe. These terrible revelations, compounded with the emerging synthetic theory of evolution and the resulting retreat from typological thinking, provided the context for the early postwar movement that led to an international statement on race issued in 1950 by UNESCO (United Nations Educational, Scientific, and Cultural Organization) that rejected the doctrine of pure races and racial hierarchies and condemned the use of science for racial discrimination.

Frank Spencer

See also Anthropometry; Anthroposociology; Aryanism; Deutsche Anthropologische Gesellschaft; Eugenics; Fischer, Eugen; Gieseler, Wilhelm; Germany; Genetics (Mendelian); Gobineau, Joseph-Arthur de; Haeckel, Ernst Heinrich Phillip August; Khoisan; Luschan, Felix Ritter Edler von; Martin, Rudolf; Mollison, Theodor; Ranke, Johannes; Saller, Karl; Scheidt, Walter; Schlaginhaufen, Otto; UNESCO Statement on Race; Weinert, Hans

Bibliography
E. Barkan: *The retreat of scientific racism: Changing concepts of race in Britain and the United States between the World Wars.* New York: Cambridge University Press, 1992; A. Béjin: Le sang, le sens et le travail: Georges Vacher de Lapouge, darwiniste social, fondateur de l'anthroposociologie. *Cahiers International de Sociologie* 73:323–343, 1982; A. Chase: *The legacy of Malthus: The social costs of the new scientific racism.* New York: Knopf, 1975; J. Day: *The Aryan race: Proto-Indo-Europeans and the concept of race in nineteenth-century scholarship.* M.A. Thesis. University of Edinburgh, 1993; E. Fischer: *Die Rehobother Bastards und das Bastardierungsproblem beim Menschen; anthropologische und ethnographische Studien am*

Rehobother Bastardvolk in Deutsch Südwest-Afrika. Berlin: Fischer, 1913.

E. Fischer: Anthropologischer Nomenklaturfragen. *Verhandlungen der Deutsche Gesellschaft für Physische Anthropologie* 1:70–72, 1926; E. Fischer, F. Lenz, & E. Baur: *Grundriss der menschlichen Erblichkeitslehre und Rassenhygiene*. Munich: Lehmann, 1923; E. Fischer & M.W. Hauschild: *Grundriss der Anthropologie*. Berlin: Gebrüder Borntraeger, 1926; A. de Gobineau: *Essai sur l'inégalité des races humaines*. 4 vols. Paris: Didot, 1853–1855; L. Gumplowicz: *Der Rassenkampf: Sociologische Untersuchungen*. 2d ed. Innsbruck: Wagner, 1909; H.F.K. Günther: *Kleine Rassenkunde der deutschen Volkes*. Munchen: Lehmann, 1922; G.V. de Lapouge: *L'Aryen: Son rôle sociale*. Paris: Fontemoing, 1899; H.H. Laughlin: *Eugenical sterilization in the United States*. Chicago: Psychopathic Laboratory of the Municipal Court of Chicago, 1922. Rev. ed., New Haven: American Eugenics Society, 1926.

K.M. Ludmerer: *Genetics and American society: A historical appraisal*. Baltimore: Johns Hopkins University Press, 1972; B. Oetteking: Rudolf Martin. *American Anthropologist* 28:414–417, 1926; A. Ploetz: *Die Tüchtigkeit unsurer Rasse und der Schutz der Schwachen. Ein versuch über rassenhygiene und ihr verhältniss zu den humanen idealen, besonders zum socialismus*. Berlin: Fischer, 1895; L. Poliakov: *The Aryan myth: A history of racist and nationalist ideas in Europe*. New York: Basic Books, 1971; R. Proctor: From Anthropologie to Rassenkunde in the German anthropological tradition. In: G.W. Stocking Jr. (ed) *Bone, bodies, behavior: Essays on biological anthropology*. Madison: University of Wisconsin Press, 1988, pp. 138–179; W. Scheidt: *Allgemeine Rassenkunde als Einführung in das Studium der Menschenrassen*. Munich: Lehmann, 1925.

Ray, John (1627–1705)

Born at Black Notley, near Braintree, Essex, England, Ray entered Trinity College, Cambridge, in 1644 and became interested in natural history, particularly botany. He graduated with a B.A. in 1647, and an M.A. in 1651. Following his appointment as lecturer in Greek, he rose rapidly in his college, becoming junior dean in 1658 and finally steward in 1660. In 1662, however, Ray, who was a Puritan, became a casualty of the Restoration. Unwilling to take the oath prescribed by the Act of Uniformity, he was dismissed from his position at Cambridge. Although now denied the security of an academic position, Ray was able to continue his career in natural history largely through the patronage of a former student, Francis Willughby (1635–1672). Between 1663 and 1666, he accompanied Willughby and a small party of friends on a tour of the Continent, which greatly extended his knowledge of European flora and fauna. On returning to England, Ray took up residence at Willughby's home at Middleton Hall in Warwickshire, where he remained until 1676. He spent his remaining years at Falkbourne Hall in Witham, Essex, where it is believed he had an appointment as a tutor.

During Ray's early years at Middleton Hall, he produced, with the assistance of Willughby, a systematic description of British flora, the *Catalogus plantarum Angliae* (1670). With Willughby's death in 1672, Ray was left an annuity, which, supplemented by his earnings as a tutor, enabled him to continue his research and writing.

Ray's first independent systematic work on plants, *Methodus plantarum nova* (1682), formed the basis of his masterwork, the three-volume *Historia plantarum* (1686–1704). Prior to completion of this work, he embarked on an ambitious review of the natural world, which resulted in a series of synopses. The *Synopsis methodica animalium quadrupedum et Serpentini generis* (1693) is widely regarded as the first major classification of animals based on scientific principles and clearly set the scene for the Swedish naturalist Carolus Linnaeus' *Systema naturae* (1735).

For a diagrammatic summary of Ray's classificatory scheme, see Fig. 1. Of particular interest is his treatment of the *quadrupedia vivipara*, which he divided into *terrestria* and *aquatica* (whales). In the former, he recognized two major divisions: *ungulata* (hoofed animals) and *unguiculata* (clawed animals). Among the clawed animals, he identified a group with "separate" digits, which included the *Anthropomorpha* (*vide infra*), but, unlike Linnaeus some years later, Ray refrained from placing human beings in this scheme.

From all indications, Ray's classification of the nonhuman primates is an elaboration of an earlier scheme produced by Willughby (1668). Specifically, Ray characterized two general groups composing the *Anthropomorpha*: (1) those that had either a short tail or no tail—the Baboon ("Drill") and the Ape ("Jackanapes"); and (2) those with long tails—the Monkey ("Marmosit") and the Sloth

ANIMALIA

Fig. 1. A summary of Ray's system of classification (1693).

```
                        ANIMALIA
              ┌─────────────┴─────────────┐
          Sanguinary                  Ex-Sanguinary
      ┌───────┴───────┐                    │
Gill Breathers   Lung Breathers        Mollusks
                      │                 Crustacea
          ┌───────────┴───────────┐
Heart with single ventricle   Heart with two ventricles
          │                ┌────────┴────────┐
       Reptilia         Ovipara          Viviparia
                           │          ┌──────┴──────┐
                         birds    Terrestrial    Aquatic
                              ┌──────┴──────┐        │
                          Ungulates   Unguiculates  Whales
                              │            ┊
                           Cattle          ┊
                                    Anthropomorpha
```

(which at that time was still regarded, incorrectly, as a primate).

Another interesting aspect was Ray's involvement in the emerging debate on the Earth's natural history. Like his contemporaries John Woodward (1665–1708) and William Whiston (1667–1752), Ray supported the reality of the universal Noachian Flood. Ray believed that the source of the flood water had come from subterranean reservoirs and that through some cataclysmic event, the Earth's crust had been ruptured, allowing this water to rush to the surface. As for the organic origin of fossils, however, Ray was plainly cautious in his endorsement of this idea (1692).

As in the work of contemporaries such as the anatomist Edward Tyson (1650–1708) and the physicist Isaac Newton (1642–1727), Ray believed that his scientific endeavors demonstrated the Divine plan of an omniscient Creator—a view neatly encapsulated in his most popular book, *The Wisdom of God Manifested in the Works of the Creation*, which went through multiple editions following its appearance in 1691.

Ray died at Black Notley on 17 January 1705.

Frank Spencer

See also Anthropomorpha; Linnaeus, Carolus; Tyson, Edward

Bibliography
SELECTED WORKS

Catalogus plantarum Angliae. London: Martyn, 1670 (2d ed.: 1677); *Methodus plantarum nova.* London: Faithorne & Kersey, 1682 (2d ed.: 1703); *Historia plantarum.* 3 vols. London: Faithorne, 1686–1704; *Synopsis methodica stirpium Britannicarum.* London: Smith, 1690 (2d ed.: 1696); *The wisdom of God manifested in the works of the creation.* London: Smith, 1691 (2d ed.: 1692, 3d ed.: 1701, 4th ed.: 1704, 5th ed.: 1709. . . . 12th ed.: 1759); *Miscellaneous discourses concerning the dissolution and changes of the world.* London: Smith, 1692. Subsequently recast as: *Three physicotheological discourses.* London: Innys, 1713. Reprint. New York: Arno, 1977; *Synopsis methodica animalium quadrupedum et serpentini generis.* London: Smith & Walford, 1693.

ARCHIVAL SOURCES

1. J. Ray Correspondence: Library, Natural History Museum, Cromwell Road, London SW7 5BD, England; 2. Miscellaneous Letters: Library, Royal Society of London, 6 Carlton House Terrace, London SW1Y 5AG, England; 3. John Aubrey (1626–1697) Correspondence and Edward Lhwyd (1660–1709) Correspondence: Bodleian Library, University of Oxford, Oxford OX1 3BG, England.

PRIMARY SOURCES

F. Willughby: Of animals. In: J. Wilkins (ed) *An essay towards a real character, and a philosophical language*. London: Gellibrand, 1668, pp. 121–168.

SECONDARY SOURCES

G.S. Boulger: Ray, John. *Dictionary of national biography*. Vol. 16. London: Oxford University Press, 1922, pp. 782–787; C.E. Raven: *John Ray, naturalist: His life and work*. London: Cambridge University Press, 1942.

Retzius, Anders Adolf (1796–1860)

Born in Lund, Sweden, Retzius was introduced to natural history by his father, Anders Jahan Retzius (1742–1821), who was professor of natural history at the University of Lund. In 1816, Retzius spent a year at the University of Copenhagen studying under the Danish anatomist Ludvig Jacobsson (1783–1843); in 1917, he returned to Sweden, where he completed his medical studies at the University of Lund in 1819 with an M.D. thesis on the anatomy of cartilaginous fish, *Observationes in anatomium chondropterygium praecipue squali et rajae generum*. In 1821, he was appointed lecturer at the Veterinary Institute in Stockholm; in 1824, he was named professor of anatomy at the Institute. In the meantime, in 1823 he had also become professor of anatomy at the Karolinska Institute (Karolinska Medico-Kirurgiska Institutet). This arrangement continued until 1840, when he resigned his position at the Veterinary Institute and devoted himself exclusively to his work at the Karolinska Institute. During these years, he conducted studies on the hagfish *Myxine*, among the lowest vertebrates, which provided clues to the primitive formation of the chondrocranium, brain, and cranial nerves. He studied ossification centers in the jugal arch of birds and variations within the human vertebral column.

In 1828, he participated in a meeting of natural scientists in Berlin, where he met, and made lasting friendships with, several famous anatomists of the period, such as Karl Ernst von Baer (1792–1876). A research trip in 1833 to England, France, Germany, and Austria sparked an interest in microscopy, and in 1835 he managed to secure a microscope for the Karolinska Institute. A year later, in 1836, he published a monograph dealing with the microscopy of teeth. He discovered, contemporaneously with the Czech anatomist Jan Evangelista Purkyně (1787–1869), canals in the dentine, in addition to the so-called Retzius' parallel striae, and demonstrated as well the existence of cement between the enamel prisms.

During his career, he traveled widely in Europe and was visited in Stockholm by several internationally renowned scientists. He was a prodigious writer, with 350 publications to his credit. Although the majority are written in Swedish, he also published a number in Latin, German, and French. Thirty-five of these papers were published in international journals during the period 1826–1858. A collection of his ethnological papers was published in German posthumously in 1864 by his son Magnus Gustaf Retzius under the title *Ethnologische Schriften von Anders Retzius, nach dem Tode des Verfassers gesammelt*.

He was a member and honorary member of a large number of national and international scientific societies throughout Europe, South America, and the United States. It was largely through his inspired teaching and research that the Karolinska Institute was the first Medical Faculty in Sweden to acquire the designation "Recognized School" by the Royal College of Surgeons (London), testifying to its quality as both a teaching and a research facility.

Retzius' craniological studies began about 1840. His major contribution to physical anthropology consists of his attempt to classify the human race. This classification was influenced by the Swedish zoologist Sven Nilsson (1787–1883), who made one of the first studies of human crania from prehistoric graves—though the ongoing phrenological debate may also have inspired Retzius to inquire into the differences in skull form.

The cranial index devised by Retzius was originally expressed as the skull length:skull width = 1000:X. Solving this with respect to X gives the solution 1000.(skull width)/(skull length), in which the skull width is expressed in per mille of the skull length. This original relationship explains the German name for the cranial index, *Längen-Breiten-Index* (length-width index), an expression that has puzzled some modern researchers ignorant of the original definition. Originally, the length and the width of the skull were measured in cm, and not in mm, though this did not affect the index. Later, however, the factor of 1000 was changed to 100, thus expressing the skull width as a percentage of the length.

Employing the cranial index, Retzius devised a classification system in which the human species was divided into two major groups: dolichocephalae (long-headed) and brachycephalae (short-headed). The first term, though actually relating to the head, originally designated a skull with a length one-fourth or more longer than the width. The second term related to a skull with a length one-seventh or one-eighth longer than the width. This description indicates the emphasis was on the length, not the width, of the skull. Each of these two major groups, were further subdivided into orthognathae and prognathae. The former was characterized by a fairly straight and vertical facial skeleton, while the latter embraced those with jaws that tended to protrude in front of the braincase. In spite of later criticisms—for example, the loss of information about details of form derived from the value of the cranial index—at the time, Retzius' system served to reveal that skin color and other traditional physical traits such as hair color and structure were not enough to classify the human species. There was much more variation than had been previously recognized, and explanations for this variation were not straightforward. Though Retzius' classification system may now be of only historical interest, it provided further impetus to the development of a new branch of research within physical anthropology: craniometry.

Anders Retzius died in Stockholm on 18 April 1860.

Torstein Sjøvold

See also Baer, Karl Ernst von; Purkyně, Jan Evangelista; Retzius, Magnus Gustaf; Sweden

Bibliography

SELECTED WORKS

Mikroskopiska undersökningar öfver tändernes, särdeles tundbenets struktur. Stockholm: Norstedt, 1837; Om formen af nordboernes cranier. *Förhandlingar vid de Skandinaviska naturforskarnas 3. Möte i Stockholm* 3:157–201, 1843 (cf. Mémoire sur les formes du crâne des habitants du Nord. *Annales des sciences naturelles* 6:133–172, 1846, and Ueber die Schädelformen der Nordbewohner. *Archiv für Anatomie, Physiologie, und wissenschaftliche Medizin* 84–129, 1845); *Om formen af hufvudets benstomme hos olika folkslag.* Christiana: Gröndahl, 1847.

Phrenologien bedömd från en anatomisk ståndpunkt. *Förhandlingar ved de Skandinaviske naturforskeres 5. møte i København*: 5:178ff., 1848 (cf. Beurtheilung der Phrenologie vom Stanpunkte der Anatomie aus. *Archiv für Anatomie, Physiologie, und wissenschaftliche Medezin.* p. 263ff., 1848); Blick öfver fördelningen af huvudskålformerna hos folkslagen i de fem verldsdelarne. *Förhandlingar ved de Skandinaviske naturforskeres 7. møte i Christiana*: 68–121, 1856; The present state of ethnology in relation to the form of the human skull. *Smithsonian Institution Report* 7:251–270, 1859.

ARCHIVAL SOURCES

A.A. Retzius Papers: 1. Karolinska Institute, Library, Doktorsringen 21D, Box 200, S-171, 77 Solna, Sweden; 2. Karolinska Institute, Department of Anatomy, S-171, 77 Solna, Sweden.

SECONDARY SOURCES

A.J. Bruzelius: Anders Adolf Retzius. In: A.H. Wistrand, A.J. Bruzelius, & C. Edling (eds) *Sveriges Läkare-Historia: Ifrån Konung Gustav den I: till Närvarande Tid.* Stockholm: Norstedt, 1873, pp. 623–638; O. Larsell: Anders Adolf Retzius, 1796–1860. *Annals of Medical History* 6:16–24, 1924; E. Müller: Anatomiska institutionen i Stockholm, 1756–1910. In: *Karolinska Medico-Kirurgiska Institutets Historia.* Vol. 3. Stockholm: Marcus, 1910, pp. 94–122; S. Severin: Porträtt och biografiska uppgifter till Karolinska Medico-Kirurgiska Institutets Historia: Anders Adolf Retzius. In: *Karolinska Medico-Kirurgiska Institutet Historia.* Vol. 3. Stockholm: Marcus, 1910, p. 20.

Retzius, Magnus Gustaf (1842–1919)

Born in Stockholm, Sweden, the son of Anders Adolf Retzius (1796–1860), Retzius studied medicine first in Uppsala and later in Stockholm; he received his doctorate from the University of Lund in 1871. Since his father died when Retzius was seventeen years old, there was hardly any direct, personal influence of the father on the son's scientific career—though it is clear that young Retzius certainly perceived the impact of his father's achievements in anatomy and physical anthropology. Further, during his early years Retzius not only traveled throughout Europe with his father, but also had the opportunity to meet some of his father's colleagues, many of whom were distinguished scholars of the period—and these early experiences unquestionably influenced his determination to follow in his father's footsteps.

On receipt of his doctorate, Retzius obtained a position as an assistant in the Department of Pathology at the Karolinska Institute. Together with Axel Key (1832–1901), then professor of pathology, he conducted advanced research on the brain and the anatomy of the central nervous system, the results of which were initially circulated in the form of preprints and later published in a two-volume work (1875–1876). Subsequently, Retzius developed an interest in the comparative anatomy of the auditory organ, which resulted in the publication of two monographs, in 1881 (fishes and amphibians) and 1884 (reptiles, birds, and mammals). He also became an eminent histologist, and in 1877 he was given a personal professorship in histology at the Karolinska Institute with special funding from the government.

Although the examples of his research mentioned above pertain to his well-known studies in comparative anatomy, he was at the same time becoming actively involved in anthropological research. In 1864, he published a collection of his father's ethnological works. About the same time, he became interested in photography, which was still very much in its infancy, and made a photographic record of the skulls his father had employed in his racial classification (cf. A.A. Retzius 1843). In 1873, he founded the Antropologiska sällskapet i Stockholm (Stockholm Anthropological Society). His first major anthropological work was a study conducted in Finland in 1873, published under the title *Finska kranier* (1878). During the late 1870s and into the 1880s, he participated as an anthropologist in several archeological excavations, in particular those connected with the megalithic tombs in central-southern Sweden (Västergötland). The results of these activities were summarized in a large volume entitled *Crania suecica antiqua* (1899), in which he further developed his interest in the scientific application of photography. He illustrated this volume with life-size photographic plates of the skulls described. Although these natural-size portraits were presented as accurate facsimiles of the originals, in retrospect it is evident that their scientific utility is marred by the unforeseen problem of parallax. Using a lens-to-object distance that was too short resulted in a slight distortion of the images. But be that as it may, it does not detract from the book's importance as a valuable source on Swedish craniology at the end the nineteenth century.

Between 1884 and 1887, Retzius' scientific work was interrupted after he accepted the position of general editor of the Swedish liberal newspaper *Aftonbladet*, which had been founded by his father-in-law, Lars Johan Hierta (1801–1872). He took the post because he was concerned with the newspaper's editorial policies. Still in existence, it is one of Sweden's four largest newspapers.

In 1887, Retzius returned to scientific activities. In 1899, he was offered and accepted the Chair of Anatomy—a post he held until 1909 when he resigned to devote himself exclusively to scientific research. By then, he was financially independent, which made it possible for him to fund most of his major publications without having to seek outside assistance.

In addition to his monumental *Crania suecica antiqua*, another major contribution in the field of physical anthropology was his evaluation of anthropometric data collected on 45,000 conscripts. The resulting major work, *Anthropologia suecica*, written in collaboration with the Swedish anatomist Carl Magnus Fürst (1854–1935) was published in German in 1902.

During the period from 1890 to 1914, Retzius published eighteen volumes under the collective title *Biologische Untersuchungen* (Biological Studies), comprising more than 17,000 pages and 450 plates in foliate. In 1909, he was the recipient of the Huxley Medal and was invited to give the Huxley Memorial Lecture in London, which was published under the title "The So-Called North European Race of Mankind."

At the outbreak of World War I, Retzius ceased scientific publication. According to Fürst, a longtime friend and collaborator, the war had a profound impact on Retzius, who saw many of the liberal ideals he had so long defended being swept away in the European conflict.

During his career, Retzius' contributions to science were widely recognized, and he was awarded honorary doctoral degrees at several international universities, including Harvard in 1893 and Cambridge in 1904.

Gustaf Retzius died in Stockholm on 21 July 1919.

Torstein Sjøvold

See also Finland; Retzius, Anders Adolf; Sweden

Bibliography
SELECTED WORKS

Studien in der Anatomie des Nervensystems und des Bindegewebes. 2 vols. Stockholm, 1875–1876; Matériaux pour servir à la connaissance des caractères ethniques des races finnoises. *Compte rendu Congrès International d'Anthropologie et d'Archéologie Préhistoriques* (Stockholm 1874). Vol. 2. Stockholm: Imprimerie centrale, 1876, pp. 741–765; *Finska kranier jämte några natur- och litteraturstudier inom andra områden af finsk antropologi.* Stockholm: Aftonbladet, 1878; *Crania suecica antiqua, beskrifning af svenska mennisko-kranier från stenåldern, bronsåldern och järnåldern jämte en blick på forskningen öfver de europeiska folkens ras- karaktärer.* Stockholm: Aftonbladet, 1899; *Cerebra simiarum illustrata, Das Affenhirn in bildlicher Darstellung.* Stockholm: Centraldruckerei, 1906; (with C.M. Fürst) *Anthropologia suecica: Beiträge zur Anthropologie der Schweden.* Stockholm: Aftonbladet, 1902.

ARCHIVAL SOURCES

M.G. Retzius Papers: 1. Karolinska Institute, Library, Doktorsringen 21D, Box 200, S-171, 77 Solna, Sweden; 2. Karolinska Institute, Department of Anatomy, S-171, 77 Solna, Sweden.

SECONDARY SOURCES

C.M. Fürst: [Obituary notice]. *Mannus* 11–12:433–435, 1920; C.M. Fürst: Inhaltverzeichnis der Biologischen Untersuchungen I–II und der Biologischen Untersuchungen Neue Folge I–XIX nebst Verzeichnis der sämtlichen wissenschaftlichen Werke von Gustaf Retzius. (Contains complete bibliography). *Biologische Untersuchungen.* 19:1–20, 1923; E. Müller: Anatomiska institutionem i Stockholm, 1756–1910. In: *Karolinska Medico-Kirurgiska Institutets Historia.* Vol. 3. Stockholm: Marcus, 1910, pp. 94–122; S. Severin: Porträtt och biografiska uppgifter till Karolinska Medico-Kirurgiska Institutets Historia: Magnus Gustaf Retzius. In: *Karolinska Medico-Kirurgiska Institutets Historia.* Vol. 3. Stockholm: Marcus, 1910, p. 21; R. Tigerstedt: [Obituary notice]. *Finska läkaresällskapets handlingar* 41:3–14, 1919.

Rivet, Paul (1876–1958)

Born in Wasigny, Ardennes, northern France, Rivet was trained as a military doctor, graduating in 1897. In 1901, he went to Ecuador as part of a French geographic expedition; fascinated by the country and its people, he remained there studying and collecting anthropological data. On returning to France in 1906, he became associated with the

Muséum National d'Histoire Naturelle (MNHN) in Paris. From 1909, when René Verneau (1852–1938) was installed at the MNHN as Professor of the Natural History of Man (a position previously occupied by Théodore Hamy [1842–1908]), Rivet served as his assistant until 1928. From all indications, Rivet was groomed to be Verneau's successor, but after World War I his activities shifted more and more to the Sorbonne, where, in collaboration with the sociologist Lucien Lévy-Bruhl (1857–1939), he founded an Institut d'Ethnologie in 1925. Hence, when Verneau finally stepped down in 1927, he had serious reservations about Rivet replacing him. In spite of this reluctance, Rivet was ultimately elected to the chair and immediately changed its title to the Chair of Ethnology of Present and Fossil Man. Soon thereafter, in 1929, he was made director of the Musée d'Ethnographie du Trocadéro. With the help of Georges Rivière (1897–1985), whom Rivet recruited as *sous-directeur,* this museum was systematically reorganized and ultimately transformed into the Musée de l'Homme in 1937. During this same time period, Rivet also became actively involved in politics and was associated with the *Front populaire.* Because of his early activities in the Resistance, he was later forced to flee the country and spend most of World War II living in South America. After the war, he returned to Paris, where he resuscitated his political career.

As for Rivet's many contributions to anthropology, he is perhaps best remembered for his opposition to the traditional monogenetic thesis, which held that the original and exclusive source of the Amerindians had been northeastern Asia. In direct contrast to the proponents of this thesis, such as the Smithsonian anthropologist Aleš Hrdlička (1869–1943), who tended to regard the Amerindians as an essentially homogenous racial group, Rivet (1925) thought that the indigenous (pre-Columbian) population of the Americas was markedly heterogenous as the result of a series of racial migrations. Specifically, he argued that the original occupants of the New World had come from Asia. He characterized them as Mongolian and Eskimo elements, who, following their entry via the Bering Strait land bridge, had spread slowly southward into South America. Later, this basal group in South America was compounded with the arrival of Melanesoid (Malayan-Polynesian) and Australoid groups. The former group, Rivet identified with the Paleo-

Amerindian, or Lagoa Santa type—which he believed had entered South America via a trans-Pacific route. To support this thesis, he noted the similarity between the Lagoa Santa crania and those from the Pacific Islands of Fiji and New Caledonia (cf. Rivet 1908, 1925). As for the Australoid element, he believed that the somatometric characters of the Patagonians confirmed this connection. Although he was unsure of how these Australians had entered the continent, the Portugese anthropologist A.A. Mendes Corrêa (1888–1959) (1926) supplied him with an ingenious solution, proposing that, similar to the Bering Strait in the north, a land bridge had also existed in the south connecting Australia, Tasmania, Antarctica, and

Tierra del Fuego (see Fig. 1).

Although Rivet's thesis was vigorously rejected by scholars such as Hrdlička (1928, 1935), the race-succession paradigm became very popular in South America, where its most influential proponent was the Italian-born Argentinian anthropologist José Imbelloni (1885–1967).

Rivet died in Paris on 21 March 1958.

Frank Spencer

See also Americas: Paleoanthropology; Boule, Marcellin; France; Hamy, Jules Ernest Théodore; Hrdlička, Aleš; Imbelloni, José; Lagoa Santa; Oceania; Vallois, Henri Victor; Verneau, René

Fig. 1. Mendes Corrêa's hypothesis (1925) on the peopling of South America via Antartica.

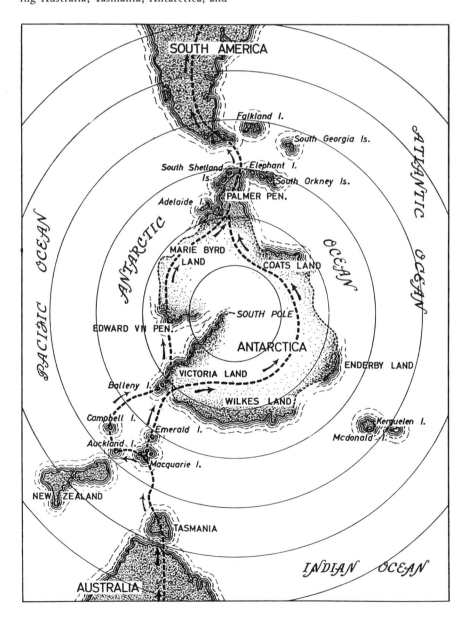

Bibliography
SELECTED WORKS
    La race de Lagoa-Santa chez
les populations précolumbiennes de
l'équateur. *Bulletins et Mémoires de la Société
d'Anthropologie de Paris* 9:209–223, 1908;
L'origine de l'homme. Paris: Poinat, 1914; Les
origines de l'homme américain.
L'Anthropologie 35:283–319, 1925; Les
Mélano-Polynésiens et les Australiens en
Amérique. *Anthropos* 20:51–54, 1926; Le
peuplement de l'Amérique précolumbienne.
Scientia 40:89–100, 1926; Les donnés de
l'anthropologie. In: G. Dumas (ed) *Nouveau
traité de psychologie*. Paris: Alcan, 1930, pp.
55–100; *Les origines de l'homme américain*.
Mexico City: Cuadernos americanos, 1943;
(with G.H. Rivière) La réorganisation du
Musée d'ethnographie du Tracadéro.
*Bulletin du Muséum national d'Histoire
Naturelle* 2 (2d ser.):478–487, 1930; (with
R. Verneau) *Ethnographie ancienne de
l'Équateur*. 2 Vols. Paris: Gauthier-Villars,
1912–1922.

PRIMARY SOURCES
    A.A. Mendes-Corrêa: Nouvelle
hypothèse sur le peuplement primitif de
l'Amérique du Sud. *Comptes-rendus XXII
International Congrès d'Américanistes* (Rome)
1:97–118, 1926.

SECONDARY SOURCES
    R. d'Harcourt: Paul Rivet, 1876–
1958. *Journal de la Société des Américanistes*
47:7–11, 1958; J. Jamin: Le Musée
d'ethnographie en 1930: l'ethnologie
comme science et comme politique. In:
G.H. Rivière (ed) *La muséologie*. Paris: 1988,
pp. 110–121.

Robinson, John Talbot (1923–)

Born in Elliot, South Africa, Robinson received his academic training at the University
of Cape Town, where he earned a B.Sc. in
1943, an M.Sc. in 1945, and a D.Sc. in 1955
in the field of zoology. In 1947, he joined the
Transvaal Museum in Pretoria and worked in
the Department of Palaeontology and Physical Anthropology (DPPA) with Robert Broom
(1866–1951). He and Broom carried out the
first extensive excavations at the australopithecine sites of Sterkfontein, Swartkrans, and
Kromdraai in South Africa. When Broom
died in 1951, Robinson remained with the
Transvaal Museum as head of the DPPA, and
he continued excavations of the australopithecine sites and analysis of the fossils. In 1960,

he also assumed the position of assistant director of the Transvaal Museum. One of his
major contributions to australopithecine research was to recognize that there were two
major hominid lineages: *Paranthropus* and
Australopithecus. Robinson contended that the
morphological differences between these two
genera could be explained by differences in
dietary adaptation. This became known as the
"dietary hypothesis" (cf. Robinson 1954),
which has since become a model applied to
subsequent fossil hominid finds from other
parts of Africa. In the same paper, he provided
a much needed reassessment of australopithecine taxonomy based on all of the material
known at that time.

    In 1963, because of his dissatisfaction
with the political system in South Africa,
Robinson resigned his position in Pretoria and
moved to Madison, Wisconsin, where he accepted a joint appointment in the Departments of Zoology and Anthropology at the
University of Wisconsin. He spent only a few
years in the Anthropology Department before
becoming a full-time member of the Zoology Faculty. This initiated a new period in his
life, as he took on the task of teacher as well
as researcher. Although he had had a part-time
lectureship at the University of the Witwatersrand, Johannesburg, his position at the
University of Wisconsin required him to teach
courses in human evolution on a regular basis. He developed a reputation as an excellent
teacher, and his classes were always full. He
was highly respected by graduate students and
supervised a number of students through their
doctoral studies. Although he retired from
teaching in 1985 because of poor health, he
has maintained a position with the university's
Zoology Museum.

Becky A. Sigmon

See also Australopithecines; Broom, Robert;
Kromdraai; Sterkfontein

SELECTED WORKS
    The evolutionary significance of the
australopithecines. *Yearbook of Physical
Anthropology:* 33–41, 1950; *Telanthropus
capensis* and zoological nomenclature.
American Journal of Physical Anthropology
10:1–4, 1952; *Meganthropus*, australopithecines, and hominids. *American Journal of
Physical Anthropology* 11:1–38, 1953a;
Telanthropus and its phylogenetic significance. *American Journal of Physical Anthropology* 11:445–502, 1953b; The genera and
species of the Australopithecinae. *American*

Journal of Physical Anthropology 12:181–200, 1954; Further remarks on the relationship between *Meganthropus* and australopithecines. *American Journal of Physical Anthropology* 13:429–445, 1955; The dentition of the Australopithecinae. *Transvaal Museum Memoir* 9:1–179, 1956; Cranial cresting patterns and their significance in the Hominoidea. *American Journal of Physical Anthropology* 16:397–428, 1958.

The australopithecines and their bearing on the origin of man and of stone-tool making. *South African Journal of Science* 57:3–13, 1961; The origin and adaptive radiation of the australopithecines. In: G. Kurth (ed) *Evolution and hominization*. Stuttgart: Fischer, 1962, pp. 120–140; Adaptive radiation in the australopithecines and the origin of man. In: F.C. Howell & F. Boulière (eds) *African ecology and human evolution*. Chicago: Aldine, 1963, pp. 385–416; *Early hominid locomotion and posture*. Chicago: University of Chicago Press, 1972; (with R. Broom) A new type of fossil man. *Nature* 164:322, 1949; (with R. Broom) Man contemporaneous with the Swartkrans ape-man. *American Journal of Physical Anthropology* 8:151–156, 1950; (with R. Broom & G.W.H. Schepers) Sterkfontein ape-man *Plesianthropus. Transvaal Museum Memoir* 4:1–117, 1950.

ARCHIVAL SOURCES

J.T. Robinson Papers (Notebooks and Other Materials Associated with his Australopithecine Research): Zoology Museum, University of Wisconsin, Madison, Wisconsin 53706.

SECONDARY SOURCES

B.A. Sigmon: *J.T. Robinson: A biography* (work in progress); B.A. Sigmon (ed): Papers in honor of J.T. Robinson (Festschrift), in press.

Romer, Alfred Sherwood (1894–1973)

Born in White Plains, New York, Romer received a liberal arts education at Amherst College (1913–1917). After serving in the U.S. Army from 1917 to 1919, he entered Columbia University as a doctoral student in the Department of Zoology. In two years, he not only made up for his deficiency in scientific preparation (he had none of the standard prerequisite courses, in fact, not a single laboratory course in any science), but also earned his Ph.D. in 1921 under William King Gregory (1876–1970) of the Department of Ver-

tebrate Paleontology of the American Museum of Natural History. He immediately published his thesis as a monograph, "The Locomotor Apparatus of Certain Primitive Mammal-Like Reptiles" (1922).

After two years as instructor in the Anatomy Department of New York University's Bellevue Medical College, he was catapulted into the rank of associate professor of vertebrate paleontology at the University of Chicago. In his eleven years at Chicago (1923–1934), Romer laid the groundwork for his extraordinarily productive career. His detailed researches centered on reconstructing the musculature and functional anatomy of the locomotor apparatus of pelycosaurs and therapsid reptiles and the parallel story of the embryonic development of muscle matrices in the chick and lizard. This work presaged his long devotion to the study of the great transitions in vertebrate evolution: fish to amphibian, amphibian to reptile, and reptile to mammal. Throughout his lifetime, he vigorously pursued the fossil evidence in the Red Beds of the southwestern United States and in related beds in the Gaspé, South Africa, and Argentina. A constant companion and fellow worker in all of these labors was his wife, Ruth Hibbard Romer.

At the same time, he was entering fully into the intellectual life of the young, rapidly expanding University of Chicago. He worked with sixteen colleagues in the planning of a course in general education for nonscientists, epitomized in the title of their seminal text *The Nature of the World and Man*, published in 1926 (cf. Romer 1926). He soon expanded his chapter into his two famous textbooks, *Man and the Vertebrates* and *Vertebrate Paleontology*, both published in 1933. These were joined in 1949 by his classic textbook on comparative anatomy, *The Vertebrate Body*, all of which were periodically revised during his lifetime, and the latter two by his students after his death.

In 1934, he moved to Harvard University as professor of zoology in the newly amalgamated Department of Biology and as curator of vertebrate paleontology in the Agassiz Museum of Comparative Zoology (MCZ). His nearly forty years at Harvard were highly productive. He regularly taught courses on comparative anatomy and vertebrate paleontology and supervised the graduate careers of twenty-six Ph.D. candidates. Progressively, the MCZ became the center of his intellectual life, and his fifteen-year tenure as director (1946–1961) saw a large expansion and reorganization of his and other departments' collections and brought the entire administration from the patronage system of his predecessor, Thomas Barbour (1884–1946), to a fully integrated element in the university—with a tenfold increase in its budget. He soon developed into the universally recognized doyen of vertebrate paleontologists and played a major role in the development of the field. He founded and became the first president of the Society of Vertebrate Paleontology in 1941 and led the move of the comparative anatomists from their place in the backwaters of the American Association of Anatomists to a renewed vigor as a separate Division of Vertebrate Morphology in the American Society of Zoologists. In 1947, he began bringing to Harvard a series of Alexander Agassiz Research Professors (his was the first appointment) that included George Gaylord Simpson, Ernst Mayr, Bryan Patterson, D.M.S. Watson, and T.S. Westoll.

His extensive travels won him a broad and intimate experience in the worldwide paleontological scene. An early typical example of his sure, direct grasp and style can be seen in the report he fired off to *Science* in 1930 after seeing the Taungs skull (Romer 1930). Although clearly unsure of its hominid affinities, Romer was convinced it could not be classified as either a gorilla or a chimpanzee, as some had claimed.

His large, detailed monographs on key Paleozoic and Permian types were informed by broad, general perspectives on the significance of anatomical features. Among the provocative concepts developed in his various publications were those on (1) cartilage as an embryonic adaptation; (2) on the nature and history of bone; (3) the role and fate of the notochord; (4) the importance of freshwater environments in early vertebrate evolution; (5) the pervasive significance in vertebrae morphology of the concept of seven functional components in the nervous system and the related concept of adult vertebrae as the product of visceral and somatic components amalgamated in the ancient pedomorphic protochordate; (6) the growing certainty of the phenomenon of continental drift; and (7) the significance of the contribution of vertebrate paleontology both to the general theory and to our conceptions of Gondwanaland. These broadly relevant biological concepts were first announced in clear, persuasive papers and gradually integrated into his books and reviews.

In the later decades of his career, honors poured steadily on him. He was elected to membership in the triumvirate of prime honorific societies in America: the National Academy of Sciences, the American Philosophical Society, and the American Academy of Arts and Science. In addition, he was elected to the presidency of those societies relevant to his field: the Society of Vertebrate Paleontology (1941), the Paleontological Society (1950), the American Society of Zoologists (1951), the Society for Systematic Zoology (1952), the Society for the Study of Evolution (1953), and the American Association for the Advancement of Science (1966). He was also the recipient of five honorary degrees and a dozen honorary medals.

He died on 5 November 1973.

G.E. Erikson

See also Australopithecines; Gregory, William King; Harvard University

Bibliography
SELECTED WORKS

The locomotor apparatus of certain primitive mammal-like reptiles. *Bulletin of the American Museum of Natural History* 46:517–606, 1922; Evolution of the vertebrates. In: H.H. Newman (ed) *The nature of the world and man*. Chicago: University of Chicago, 1926; *Australopithecus* not a chimpanzee. *Science* 71:482–483, 1930; *Man and the vertebrates*. Chicago: University of Chicago Press, 1933a (2d ed.:1937, 3d ed.:1941); *The vertebrate body*. Philadelphia: Saunders, 1949; *Vertebrate paleontology*. Chicago: University of Chicago Press, 1933b (2d ed.: 1945, 3d ed.: 1966).

SECONDARY SOURCES

E.H. Colbert: Alfred Sherwood Romer. *Biographical Memoirs, National Academy of Sciences* 53:264–294, 1982; G.E. Erickson: Alfred Sherwood Romer, 1894–1973. *Anatomical Record* 189:314–324, 1977.

Romero, Javier (1910–1986)

Born in Mexico City, Romero began studying medicine in 1928 but abandoned it in 1930. In 1931, he started working in the Department of Physical Anthropology of the Museo Nacional de Antropología (MNA) under Daniel Rubín de la Borbolla (1907–1990), who had just returned to Mexico after a visit to anthropological institutions in the United States. From 1936 to 1953, Romero was the head of this department. During this period, several important developments took place in Mexico. The Escuela Nacional de Antropología e Historia (ENAH) (National School of Anthropology and History) started its program in 1938, and at about the same time, a number of scholars arrived from war-torn Europe. Among these European émigrés were Ada d'Aloja (1900–) from Italy and the distinguished Spanish physical anthropologist Juan Comas (1900–1979). Although by this time Romero already had considerable experience as a physical anthropologist, both in the field and the laboratory, he nevertheless decided to enroll at the ENAH and became a student of d'Aloja and Comas, who were under his authority at the MNA. This was an unusual situation, and it serves to exemplify his intellectual and moral integrity. With his experience and rank at the MNA, he could have easily become a teacher at this school (*vide infra*). He graduated from the ENAH in 1946; his dissertation reported on the pre-Hispanic population of Tilantongo, Oaxaca.

Romero's first professional years at the MNA were devoted to the study of skeletal remains found at Cholula, Mexico City, Monte Albán, Monte Negro, Sierra Azul in Tamaulipas, and several other sites. His international reputation, however, was secured primarily through his collaborative study (1949) with Helmuth de Terra (1900–1981) and T. Dale Stewart (1901–) of the human remains discovered at Tepexpan in 1947. Later, in the early 1950s, he was a member of a group of investigators who reported on the human remains found at Ixateopan, which had been attributed to Cuauhtémoc, the last Aztec emperor. Romero and the Mexican physical anthropologist Eusebio Dávalos-Hurtado (1909–1968) were responsible for the description and analysis of these remains. Contrary to popular belief, Romero and Dávalos-Hurtado showed that the remains could not be those of this historical figure. It was at this time that Romero became deeply interested in the cultural practices that modify skeletal morphology, such as cranial deformation, tooth mutilation, and trephination. This research interest led to a number of significant articles and monographs published between the late 1950s and early 1970s (Romero 1958, 1960, 1965, 1970). Indeed, his monograph on the classification of tooth mutilation (Romero 1958) is considered a classic work.

Romero had a broad view of physical anthropology. He promoted and conducted a large series of anthropometric surveys on contemporary groups, among them schoolchildren; students in physical education and at the Colegio Militar, Mexico's national military school; and various Mexican Indian groups. However, it is evident even from his early studies that he was not interested simply in collecting traditional anthropometrical measurements, but rather in combining them with a variety of physiological variables, such as blood pressure, physical fitness, and several psychological tests. Romero did some pioneering studies using standardized photographs of the whole body proposed by American somatologists. His work at the Colegio Militar is still considered the most comprehensive ever undertaken in Mexico. Romero's interest in combining physical anthropology and psychology led him to create the Direction of Anthropological Research, where he had a good laboratory to study psychomotor functions, which led to a considerable number of articles on the subject.

As a teacher, Romero had a significant influence in Mexico. On graduating in 1946 from the ENAH, he became a professor there—a position he retained until his retirement in 1979. He preferred giving seminars to advanced students, who appreciated his great knowledge and human qualities. He was director of the ENAH from 1974 to 1979. From 1960 to 1970, he was the general subdirector of the Instituto Nacional de Antropología e Historia, and from 1971 to 1976 he served as the head of the institute's editorial department.

Romero's merits were recognized during his lifetime. He was emeritus researcher at the Instituto Nacional de Antropología e Historia, and a collection of papers in his honor was published in 1982 (*vide infra*).

Romero died in Mexico City on 10 February 1986.

Luis Alberto Vargas

See also Comas, Juan; Dávalos-Hurtado, Eusebio; Mexico; Stewart, T(homas) D(ale).

Bibliography
SELECTED WORKS
Mutilaciones dentarias, prehispánicas de México y América en general. Mexico: Instituto Nacional de Antropología e Historia, Series investigaciones. No. 3. 1958; Ultimos hallazgos de mutilaciones dentarias en México. *Anales Instituto Nacional de Antropología e Historia* 12:151–215, 1960; Recientes adiciones a la colección de dientes mutilados. *Anales Instituto Nacional de Antropología e Historia* 17:199–256, 1965; Dental mutilation,

trephination, and cranial deformation [in Middle America]. In: T.D. Stewart (ed) *Handbook of Middle American Indians*. Vol. 9. Austin: University of Texas Press, 1970, pp. 50–67; *Antropología física: Época prehispánica*. Vol. 3. México, panorama histórico y cultural series. Mexico: Instituto Nacional de Antropología e Historia, 1974; *Antropología física: Época moderna y contemporánea*. Vol. 10. México, panorama histórico y cultural series. Mexico: Instituto Nacional de Antropología e Historia, 1976; (with H. de Terra & T.D. Stewart) *Tepexpan man*. Viking Fund, Viking Fund Publication. No. 11. New York: Viking Fund, 1949.

SECONDARY SOURCES

Hombre: Tiempo y conocimiento. Homenaje al antropólogo Javier Romero Molina. (Festschrift). Mexico: Escuela Nacional de Antropología e Historia, Instituto Nacional de Antropología e Historia, 1982; J. Faulhaber: Javier Romero Molina. In: L. Odena-Güemez & C.G. Mora (eds) *La antropología en México: Panorama histórico*. Vol. 2, *Los protagonistas*. México: Instituto Nacional de Antropología e Historia, Colección Biblioteca del Instituto Nacional de Antropología e Historia, 1988, pp. 353–371 (contains Romero's complete bibliography).

Rousseau, Jean-Jacques (1712–1778)

Born in Geneva, Switzerland, of an artisan, republican, and Calvinist background, Rousseau was to exercise a profound influence upon late-eighteenth-century European political thought. Initially a friend of the *philosophes* and a contributor to the *Encyclopédie*, from the mid-1750s he distanced himself from the leading figures of the Enlightenment, whose faith in civilization rather than Providence he came to deplore. In turning away from their cosmopolitan culture, he was drawn instead to the more vigorous but austere temper of the republics of antiquity. In his various writings, he was to prove his century's preeminent philosopher of nature and a pioneer of Romanticism. Following the banning of his *Social Contract* (1762a) and *Emile* (1762b) on account of their affront to orthodox Christianity, he spent most of the remaining years of his life at bay, averting both real and imaginary persecutors. After his death, his doctrine of popular sovereignty was to make him a hero of the French Revolution.

Described by the French anthropologist Claude Lévi-Strauss in the 1960s as the founder of anthropology, Rousseau contributed to the discipline in both its physical and cultural dimensions, largely by way of his philosophical abstraction of human nature from the accretions and institutions of civilization. His first *Discours sur les sciences et les arts* (1750) formed a critique of such civilization, winning him great notoriety. In his second *Discours sur l'inégalité* (1755) he speculated on the original traits of our savage ancestors before their passage into civil society. More than any other thinker of his day, Rousseau believed that humankind's prevalent psychological attributes must have been acquired characteristics. Contrary to the English philosopher Thomas Hobbes (1588–1679), he contended that masterless savages would have no cause for belligerence; only in society, where persons live outside themselves and seek self-esteem in the eyes of their neighbors, do strangers become enemies, he supposed. Contrary to the German philosopher Samuel Pufendorf (1632–1694), he perceived primitive man as self-reliant and robust, with scant need for company apart from the intermittent and purely physical promptings of sex. The first societies, he contended, would have arisen not by choice but by chance, perhaps on islands formed by natural catastrophes whose inhabitants would have confronted each other with greater frequency than on the mainland. Contrary to the English philosopher John Locke (1632–1704), he claimed that in their original solitary condition our ancestors could have had no family ties and no notion of right and duty, and hence no conception of property, whose establishment must, in fact, have marked the beginnings of civil society and later have given rise to war.

Illustrating such propositions in the light of explorers' and missionaries' testimony that he culled mainly from the Abbé (Antoine François) Prévost's (1697–1763) *Histoire générale des voyages* (1746–1789), Rousseau attempted to show that Hottentots, Turks, Guineans, Mongols, and other savage peoples were evidently closer to our uncouth progenitors than were Europeans—their sharper senses, greater spontaneity, and relatively unrefined cultures being little scarred by the effete sophistication of Western societies. Unlike the French naturalist Georges-Louis Leclerc Buffon (1707–1788), who thought that primeval man must have been White, with darker races degenerating from that original stock, Rousseau saw the modern European as being more disfigured and debilitated. His apparent respect for men of color won him admirers, not least the English poet

Thomas Day (1748–1789), who dedicated the 1775 third edition of his *The Dying Negro* to Rousseau.

No one in the eighteenth century was more convinced that our ancestral nature must have been closer to that of animals than to civilized man's. Like animals, human beings in their primitive state would have been motivated by both benign self-love and compassion for other members of their species, he supposed, relying on doubtful evidence. Unlike animals, however, human nature is malleable, as witnessed by the fact that we can, for instance, choose and change our diet and are thus innately neither herbivorous nor carnivorous. This freedom of choice had made human history possible, he argued, whereas for all other species each phenotype is destined to repeat the life cycle of its ancestors: For humankind alone, in effect, ontogeny does not recapitulate phylogeny. Cumulative change—that is, the cultural transmission of acquired characteristics—was embraced by Rousseau's ascription to humankind of the faculty of "perfectibility," a term he coined in the *Discours sur l'inégalité*. While that trait might have made the moral advance of civilization possible, its abuse had, in fact, led to the decrepitude of the human species and our degradation to a self-inflicted state far worse than that of animals.

Among the features of social life that Rousseau claimed could not be natural was language, whose intelligible articulation required shared meanings possible only in a preexistent society. On the other hand, since society itself is unnatural and depends upon an agreed vocabulary of signs, he found he could not establish whether society or language must have come first. From certain features of his conjectural history of the origins of language springs his principal contribution to physical anthropology. Buffon, like the British anatomist Edward Tyson (1650–1708) before him, contended that our command of language showed that nature had established an unbridgeable gulf between the human and animal realms, ensuring our superiority over all other creatures, including the orangutan or chimpanzee, which closely resembled us physically but was spiritually unable to animate its organs of speech. Rousseau took issue with this claim, and in his *Discours sur l'inégalité*, further embellished by his 1756 "Lettre à Philopolis" (to the naturalist Charles Bonnet [1720–1793] who had criticized Rousseau's portrait of savage man), he put forward an alternative account of the orangutan and another explanation of its apparent linguistic ineptitude.

The orangutan's human countenance suggested at least a *prima facie* case for its humanity, he contended, in the light of the sixteenth- and seventeenth-century testimony of the African voyages of Andrew Battel, Olfert Dapper, and Girolamo Merolla. Since dramatic metamorphoses even of the human body could be ascribed to climate and diet, as Buffon had shown, there was no reason to doubt the evolution of our mental faculties, including our mastery of language, as well. If language was not natural to human beings, then the languages of civilized peoples comprised no greater proof of human nature than did other complex traits of social behavior. Reason and speech were just "virtual faculties" that must have passed through an evolutionary history, and their presence among the most familiar members of our species was no mark of the subhumanity of wild and mute creatures that otherwise bore the outward and physical traits of humankind. Accepting Buffon's definition of a viable species—that sexual unions must produce fecund offspring—Rousseau insisted that we could establish only by experiment whether orangutans were human.

Rousseau never saw a real orangutan (of which there were no live specimens in Europe until the 1770s), and it was not until around 1778, the year of his death, that the animal came to be reliably distinguished from the chimpanzee, with which he and so many others had confused it. But the originality of his views on the humanity of this Asian ape was widely recognized in the late eighteenth century, inspiring (James Burnett) Lord Monboddo's (1714–1799) more elaborate but essentially similar speculations, and inviting the criticisms of Bonnet, the German philosopher J.G. von Herder (1744–1803), the German anatomist Johann Friedrich Blumenbach (1752–1840), and the Dutch anatomist Petrus Camper (1722–1789), who sought to explain the linguistic backwardness of apes in terms of either mental or physiological factors rather than their lack of civilization. In that regard, Rousseau's remarks form one of the earliest and boldest conjectures about possible human descent from apes, contradicting the view, which might appear more in keeping with Buffon's ideas, that apes could even be degenerate humans. As presented in the *Discours sur l'inégalité*, and notwithstanding his assumption that our savage ancestors must have walked upright and been marked by roughly the same external characteristics as ourselves, they suggest that the moral and physical transformations comprising the last link in the Chain of Being—that is, the relation between apes and humans—might be one of genetic continuity.

This, of course, is no full-fledged theory of human evolution. Rousseau was too much persuaded of the overarching immutability of the natural order created by an intelligent and beneficent God to allow for the unforeseen genesis of new species, as distinct from varieties, produced either naturally over time or artificially through selective breeding, such as of domestic animals. He believed that orangutans and humans in all of their diversity were unrelated to other species, and that monkeys could not possibly be counted among our progenitors because they lacked the attribute of perfectibility, apparently a characteristic of the highest primates alone. He assumed that modern humans, moreover, could have developed out of a certain creature still plainly extant in the contemporary world, rather than from any ancestral prototype of the hominoid superfamily. Our roots could thus not be traced to so distant a source in the Earth's history nor to so low a place in the *scala naturae* as evolutionists and physical anthropologists later came to perceive, and his main point about orangutans was to stress that since articulate languages have to be learned in appropriate settings, we should not place too much emphasis upon their absence from creatures otherwise like us.

His portrait of the orangutan as a kind of speechless savage in a state of nature coincidentally happens to have been drawn with greater accuracy than any description of that animal's behavior for at least the next 200 years. From the fieldwork since the 1960s of the primatologists John MacKinnon, Peter Rodman, and Biruté Galdikas, it now appears that earlier firsthand observers—not least Alfred Russel Wallace (1823–1913)—had been grossly mistaken in their portraits of the animal's predatory nature, sexual appetite, and disposition to violence, and that Rousseau had been correct in his conjectures about the creature's diet of fruit, nomadic existence, infrequent sexual relations, and, for the most part, solitary and indolent life.

Robert Wokler

See also Asian Apes; Blumenbach, Johann Friedrich; Buffon, (Comte) Georges-Louis Leclerc; Camper, Petrus; Chain of Being; Khoisan; Monboddo, Lord (James Burnett); Tyson, Edward; Wallace, Alfred Russel

Bibliography
SELECTED WORKS

Discours sur les sciences et les arts. Geneva: Barillot, 1750; *Discours sur l'inégalité et les fondements l'inégalité parmi les hommes*. Amsterdam: Rey, 1755. English translation: *Discourse on the origin and foundations of inequality among men*. London: Dodsley, 1761; *Du contrat social*. Amsterdam: Rey, 1762a. Translated and edited by M. Cranston: *The social contract*. London: Penguin, 1969; *Emile; ou, De l'éducation*. Amsterdam and Paris: Néaulme, 1762b. English translation by A. Bloom: *Emile, or, On Education*. New York: Basic Books, 1979; *Essai sur l'origine des langues*. Geneva, 1781. All of the above can be found in: *Oeuvres complètes de J.-J. Rousseau*. Geneva: Société typographique, 1780–1789; Translated and edited by V. Gourevitch: *The first and second discourses, together with the replies to critics and "Essay on the origin of languages."* New York: Harper, Row, 1986; *Les rêveries du promeneur solitaire*. Geneva: Société typographique, 1782. English translation by P. France: *Reveries of the solitary walker*. London: Penguin, 1979.

ARCHIVAL SOURCES

1. Bibliothèque de la Ville de Neuchâtel, 3 place Numa-roz, Neuchâtel, Switzerland. This archive includes correspondence, the manuscript and drafts of Rousseau's second major work in anthropology, *Essai sur l'origine des langues* (published posthumously in 1781), and a few fragments of the *Discours sur l'inégalité* (the original manuscript is lost); 2. Bibliothèque publique et universitaire de Genève, Promenade des Bastions, 1211 Genève, Switzerland. This archive houses substantial manuscript collections of correspondence and other writings; 3. Other notable manuscripts can be found in the (a) Bibliothèque Nationale, 58 rue Richlieu, 75084 Paris, France; and (b) Bibliothèque de l'Assemblée Nationale, Palais Bourbon, 75007 Paris, France.

PRIMARY AND SECONDARY SOURCES

T. Day: *The dying Negro*. 3d ed. London: Flexney, 1775; M. Duchet: *Anthropologie et histoire au siècle des lumières*. Paris: Maspero, 1971; V. Gourevitch: Rousseau's pure state of nature. *Interpretation* 16:23–59, 1988; F. Moran III: Natural man in the *Second Discourse. Journal of the History of Ideas* 54:37–58, 1993; A.F. Prévost: *Histoire générale des voyages.* Paris: Didot, 1746–1789; F. Tinland: *L'homme sauvage: Homo ferus et homo sylvestris, de l'animal à l'homme.* Paris: Payot, 1968; R. Wokler: Perfectible apes in decadent cultures: Rousseau's anthropology revisited. *Daedalus* (Proceedings of the American Academy of Arts and Sciences) 107:107–134, 1978.

Royal College of Surgeons (London), Museums of the

Originally, the Royal College of Surgeons of England (RCS) housed a single large museum: the Museum of the Royal College of Surgeons of England (MRCS). After World War II, the parts of the collections that survived the bombing in 1941 were distributed among four museums: the Hunterian Museum, the Odontological Museum, the Wellcome Museums of Anatomy and Pathology, and the Natural History Museum (South Kensington, London).

The Museum of the Royal College of Surgeons of England: 1800–1945

In the latter part of the eighteenth century, the eminent surgeon John Hunter (1728–1793), in the course of his anatomical studies, assembled an extraordinary collection of 17,000 preparations of human, animal, and plant material. In 1799, six years after his death, Hunter's collection was purchased by the government and entrusted to the Com-

TABLE 1. Conservators of the Museum of the Royal College of Surgeons, 1800–1945

Conservators

William Home Clift	1800
Richard Owen	1842
John Thomas Quekett	1856
William Henry Flower	1861
Charles Stewart	1884
Arthur Keith*	1908
John Beattie	1934

Assistant Conservators

William Home Clift	1824
Richard Owen	1832
John Thomas Quekett	1843
Richard H. Burne	1908
Alexander James Edward Cave**	1935

*From 1933 to 1955, Keith served as master of Buckstone-Browne Research Station of the Royal College of Surgeons, at Downe, near Farnborough, Kent. **Cave was responsible for the administration of the museum from 1941 to 1944.

pany of Surgeons, which became the Royal College of Surgeons in London in 1800. Later, in 1843, the name was formally changed to the Royal College of Surgeons of England. (For further details on the institutional history of the college, see Cope 1959.) The RCS used Hunter's collection as the nucleus of its new museum (MRCS), which was officially opened in 1813. Although named the Museum of the Royal College of Surgeons, it is often referred to as the Hunterian Museum.

From the outset, the MRCS was placed under the care of a conservator. The first to be appointed was Willam Clift (1774–1849), who had been the assistant in Hunter's museum and who held the MRCS position for forty years. (See Table 1 for a list of all of the conservators from Clift's appointment to the present.) Among the post-Clift conservators are a number who made significant contributions to the development of not only the anthropological collections of the MRCS and also to the profession at large, in particular, Richard Owen (1804–1892), William Henry Flower (1831–1899), Arthur Keith (1866–1955), and Frederic Wood Jones (1879–1954). They embodied in their work the "Hunterian tradition"—among other things, the recognition of the indivisibility of the study of biology and the understanding of human anatomy, physiology, and pathology.

When founded, the MRCS had 113 human osteological specimens (cf. Flower & Stewart 1907), which included the articulated skeleton of the famous "Irish Giant," Charles Byrne (plus his enormous leather boots) all of which are still on display. The museum collections grew steadily, largely through donations from private collectors, colonial administrators, and explorers, as well as through the acquisition of particular collections such as that of the craniologist Joseph Barnard Davis (1801–1881). This notable collection, purchased in November 1879 for £1000, comprised nearly 1,800 human crania and a few skeletons from many different parts of the world, including a large number of archeological specimens, and was accompanied by a magnificently illustrated catalog (Davis 1867, 1875). (For a detailed inventory of the museum's osteological collection, excluding the Davis Collection, see Flower & Stewart 1907.)

Throughout the nineteenth and early twentieth centuries British archeologists made significant contributions to the MRCS skeletal collections. For example, the Egyptologist William Flinders Petrie (1853–1942) donated fourteen skeletons and twelve crania recovered from tombs of the fourth Dynasty in Egypt. A mummy from the twenty-eighth Dynasty at Thebes was ceremoniously unwrapped before being presented to the RCS by the Duke of Sutherland in 1875. Later, in 1907, another important Egyptian skeletal collection from the Aswan region was acquired by the MRCS; it had been made by the anatomist-anthropologist Grafton Elliot Smith (1871–1937) with the assistance of Frederic Wood Jones, who later became a conservator. This collection, now in the Natural History Museum, is of particular interest since it offers excellent research possibilities in paleopathology and other medical-related problems (cf. Smith & Jones 1910). A more recent sample acquisition along these lines is the collection of sixteen crania made by (Charles) Leonard Woolley (1880–1960) during his excavations of the fourth-millennium site of Al Ubeid in Mesopotamia, which was presented to the MRCS by the British Museum (cf. Keith 1927). In 1931, this collection was further supplemented by the finds of Woolley's excavations of the Royal Cemetery at Ur (cf. Keith 1934; Woolley 1934).

While archeological material formed a significant part of the MRCS collections, most of its Paleolithic specimens were casts supplied from elsewhere; important exceptions are the Neandertal Gibraltar skull presented to the museum by the surgeon George Busk (1807–1886) in 1868 (cf. Flower 1879; Wood 1979) and transferred to the collections of the

Natural History Museum in 1948, along with the Middle Paleolithic skeletons from the Mount Carmel caves in Palestine (*vide infra*).

Some other notable individual specimens and collections acquired by the MRCS include: (1) "Caroline Crachami, the Sicilian dwarf," which was donated by Sir Everard Home (1756–1832), John Hunter's brother-in-law, who plagiarized and then destroyed most of Hunter's papers. Her skeleton and related materials are still on display. (2) A skull and femur belonging to (Lord) Henry Stewart Darnley (1545–1567), father of King James I (James VI of Scotland). This femur was inscribed: "Thigh bone of Lord Darnley, husband of Mary Queen of Scots, murdered and blown up Feb. 10th, 1567" (cf. Pearson 1928). (3) The skulls of twenty Africans who had died of cholera while awaiting transportation as slaves. This collection was made by the renowned explorers Richard Francis Burton (1821–1890) and John Hanning Speke (1827–1864), who originally presented it to the Royal Geographical Society in 1859. (4) Burton also presented to the museum, in 1879, 100 Egyptian skulls he had collected in the vicinity of Giza—the exact provenance of most of these crania, however, is lacking. (5) The Nicolucci Collection, purchased in 1870, which consisted of 166 crania and skeletons from Italy and Greece, some ancient and some modern. (6) The Hutchinson Collection, which consisted of 100 crania recovered from burial grounds in Peru was presented to the

Fig. 1. Royal College of Surgeons of England. Damage to the Museum following a German bombing raid on 11 May 1941. Courtesy of the Royal College of Surgeons of England.

museum by the (Royal) Anthropological Institute in 1873 (cf. Busk 1874). Also, during the mid-nineteenth century, the museum received a large collection of skeletal material from the Andaman Islands, which was subsequently described by Owen (1861, 1863) and later used by Flower in his Hunterian Lectures in 1879 (cf. Flower 1880a, 1880b).

By 1907, the museum's human osteological collections had grown to well over 2,000 specimens, excluding the material in the Davis Collection, and, during the next three decades, it continued to grow.

Among the most important anthropological material to come to the MRCS were the Mount Carmel skeletons excavated by Dorothy Garrod (1892–1968) and Theodore D. McCown (1908–1969) in the 1930s. It took McCown and Keith, who had by then retired as conservator, about four years to complete their study of this material. The skeletons had been excavated in blocks of breccia, each weighing a ton or more, which arrived at the MRCS in 1931. The extraction was carried out at the RCS; the restoration, examination, comparison, drawing, and photography, at the college's research station at Downe, near Farnborough, Kent, where Keith was master (cf. McCown & Keith 1939). After World War II, the Mount Carmel material was divided between the Natural History Museum in London and the Rockefeller Museum in Jerusalem.

On 11 May 1941, the collections of the museum were decimated during a German bombing raid (cf. Fig. 1). Commenting on this event, Keith wrote: "All that my predecessors and I had laboured to bring about had been wiped out in a night" (1950: 673). (For a comprehensive account of the damage sustained in this air raid, see Cave 1941.)

The Museum of the Royal College of Surgeons since 1945

After World War II, the MRCS was divided into two: the Pathological Museum and the Anatomical Museum (which included all that survived of the Anatomical Series, the Hunterian Collection, the Odontological Series, and the Historical Instrument Collection). The Anatomical Series was used as the basis of the new Wellcome Museum of Anatomy; the Odontological Series became the Odontological Museum; and the Hunterian Collection, augmented by a large number of non-Hunterian specimens, formed the new Hunterian Museum. (For a more complete history of the museum during and after

TABLE 2. Conservators of the Museums of the Royal College of Surgeons, 1945–1983*

Anatomical Conservators

Frederic Wood Jones**	1945
Gilbert Causey	1952
Robert McMinn	1970

Pathological Conservators

Rupert Alan Willis	1945
Geoffrey Hadfield	1948
George J. Cunningham	1955
John Turk*	1970

*From 1945 to 1984, the anatomical and pathological conservators were in joint charge of the Hunterian Museum, as well as the Anatomical and Pathological Museums. John Turk was sole conservator of all of the museums of the Royal College of Surgeons from 1984–1994. Caroline Grigson is the principal curator of the College Museums. Elizabeth Allen has been curator of the Hunterian Museum since 1971.

**Jones was honorary curator of the Hunterian Collection from 1952 to 1954.

the war, see the annual *Scientific Reports of the Royal College of Surgeons of England.*)

As well as being conservators of their own museums, the professors of anatomy and pathology were also joint conservators of the Hunterian Collection (cf. Table 2). However, since 1984 the museums of the RCS have gradually reunited under a single conservator.

Almost all of the surviving anthropological material was transferred to the Natural History Museum, although a small quantity went to Cambridge University—namely, the Duckworth Laboratory, which is now part of the Department of Anthropology—and a few crania were retained and subsequently relocated in the new Odontological Museum.

The RCS library has an extensive collection of papers relating to John Hunter, the Hunterian Collection, and the work of conservators of the museum, as well as an important collection of the professional and private correspondence of Keith and Jones.

Hunterian Museum (HM)

The HM, which was opened in 1963, contains the Hunterian Collection of about 3,500 specimens, augmented by 2,500 non-Hunterian specimens added since 1813, which are arranged in the same manner as John Hunter's original museum. About one-third of the specimens are human anatomical, pathological, or histological preparations, including a very few crania. It is here that the skeletons of the "Irish Giant" and of Caroline Crachami are on display.

The HM has an extensive collection of papers and early catalogs relating to the history of the MRCS and its collections.

The Odontological Museum (OM)
The OM was founded in 1859 by the dental surgeon John Tomes (1815–1895) and others as the Museum of the Odontological Society of Great Britain. Originally housed in the Royal Dental Hospital, it was moved in 1902 to Hanover Square. In 1907, the society merged with the Royal Society of Medicine and became the latter's Odontological Section. Two years later, after negotiations initiated by Keith, arrangements were made for the OM to be housed and cared for by the RCS. Although this was on a temporary basis, the OM was integrated with the MRCS and, with some items already there, became the Odontological Series of the Museum of the Royal College of Surgeons of England.

Unlike the remainder of the MRCS, the Odontological Series escaped almost unscathed in the 1941 bombing raid, and in 1943 the part owned by the Royal Society of Medicine was given permanently to the RCS. After several moves, the collection was rearranged and opened in 1959 as the OM in the RCS. (For further details on the history of the OM, see Colyer 1943 and Miles 1964.)

As of 1994, the OM contained about 260 human crania and about 3,000 preparations of human jaws and teeth, including a large number of dental casts. The collection also includes a series of human crania from the Anglo-Saxon cemeteries of Breedon-on-the-Hill, Leicestershire, and Polhill, Kent.

The Wellcome Museum of Anatomy (WMA)
The Anatomical Series, comprising many new and a few old specimens, became the WMA in 1953 and was opened in 1954. As of 1994 it housed 800 human preparations, many of soft tissues, as well as many fine corrosion casts prepared by D.H. Tompsett. Most notable among the displays is a large collection of human skeletons of known age, particularly of children and fetuses, mostly assembled during Flower's term as conservator.

The Wellcome Museum of Pathology (WMP)
About 20 percent of the RCS approximately 15,000 pathological specimens survived the bomb damage in 1941; about 1,500 of these were reassembled to form the basis of the collection of the Pathological Museum, which became the WMP in 1951 and was opened in 1954. As of 1994, the WMP housed about 2,500 preparations of human pathological material, much of it obtained and prepared since 1941.

Current Anthropological Research at the RCS
Physical anthropological research at the RCS is largely confined to visitors using the various collections of the above museums, with the notable exception of A.E.W. Miles, who was honorary curator of the OM from 1954 to 1989, and has been emeritus honorary curator since 1989. Miles has accomplished a significant body of research, which includes his forensic work on the Christie murders (cf. Miles & Fearnhead 1953) and, during his tenure at the RCS, his studies of age changes in human dentitions (e.g., Miles 1958, 1962, 1978). Since the late 1980s, he has been studying the human skeletal remains he has excavated from a sixteenth- to seventeenth-century cemetery located on the island of Ensay in the Outer Hebrides (cf. Miles 1989). The principal curator of the museums, Caroline Grigson, and the curator of the Hunterian Museum, Elizabeth Allen, are both engaged in research into the history of the RCS collections (cf. Grigson 1990).

Caroline Grigson

See also Busk, George; Flower, (Sir) William Henry; Jones, Frederic Wood; Keith, (Sir) Arthur; McCown, Theodore D(oney); Mount Carmel (Israel); Owen (Sir) Richard; Paleopathology; Smith, (Sir) Grafton Elliot

Bibliography
G. Busk: Remarks on a collection of 150 ancient Peruvian skulls presented to the Anthropological Institute by T.J. Hutchinson. *Journal of the Anthropological Institute* 3:86–94, 1874; A.J.E. Cave: Museum. *Scientific Reports of the Royal College of Surgeons of England: 1940–1941*. London: Royal College of Surgeons, 1941, pp. 3–16; F. Colyer: The history of the Odontological Museum. *British Dental Journal* 75:1–7, 31–34, 1943; Z. Cope: *The Royal College of Surgeons of England: A history*. London: Blond, 1959; J.B. Davis: *Thesaurus craniorum: Catalogue of skulls of the various races of man in the collection of Joseph Barnard Davis* (1867), *Supplement* (1875). London: privately printed; W.H. Flower: *Catalogue of specimens illustrating the osteology and dentition of vertebrated animals, recent and extinct, contained in the Museum of the Royal College of Surgeons of England*. Part 1, *Man*. London: Printed for the College by D. Bogue, 1879.

W.H. Flower: On the osteology and affinities of the natives of the Andaman Islands. *Journal of the Anthropological Institute* 9:108–135, 1880a; W.H. Flower: On the stature of the Andamanese. *Journal of the Anthropological Institute* 10:124, 1880b; W.H. Flower & C. Stewart: *Catalogue of specimens illustrating the osteology and dentition of vertebrated animals, recent and extinct, contained in the Museum of the Royal College of Surgeons of England.* Part 1, Man. 2d ed. London: 1907; C. Grigson: Missing links in the Piltdown fraud. *New Scientist* 1699:55–58, 1990; A. Keith: A report on the Galilee skull. In: F.A.J. Turville-Petre (ed) *Researches in prehistoric Galilee.* London: British School of Archaeology in Jerusalem, 1927, pp. 1–52; A. Keith: Report on the human remains. In: C.L. Woolley (ed) *Ur excavations.* Vol. 2, *The cemetery.* London: Benn, 1934, pp. 400–410.

A. Keith: *An autobiography.* London: Watts, 1950; T.D. McCown & A. Keith: *The Stone Age of Mount Carmel II: The fossil human remains from the Levalloiso-Mousterian.* Oxford: Clarendon, 1939; A.E.W. Miles: The assessment of age from dentition. *Proceedings of the Royal Society of Medicine* 51:1057–1060, 1958; A.E.W. Miles: Assessment of the ages of a population of Anglo-Saxons from their dentitions. *Proceedings of the Royal Society of Medicine* 55:17–22, 1962; A.E.W. Miles: The Odontological Museum. *Annals of the Royal College of Surgeons of England* 34:50–58, 1964; A.E.W. Miles: Teeth as an indicator of age in man. In: P.M. Butler & K.A. Joysey (eds) *Development, function, and evolution of teeth.* London: Academic Press, 1978, pp. 455–464; A.E.W. Miles: *An early Christian chapel and burial ground on the Isle of Ensay, Outer Hebrides, Scotland, with a study of the skeletal remains.* Oxford: British Archaeological Reports, British Series. No. 212. 1989.

A.E.W. Miles & R.W. Fearnhead: Examination of the teeth and jaws. In: F.E. Camps (ed) *Medical and scientific investigations in the Christie case.* London: Medical Publications, 1953, pp. 100–124; R. Owen: On psychical and physical characters of the Micopies, or natives of the Andaman Islands, and on the relations thereby indicated to other races of mankind. *Report of the British Association for the Advancement of Science 1861,* pp. 241–249, 1861; R. Owen: On the osteology and dentition of the Aborigines of the Andaman Islands and the relations thereby indicated.

Transactions of the Ethnographical Society 2:34–49, 1863; K. Pearson: The skull and portraits of Henry Stewart, Lord Darnley. *Biometrika* 20B:1–104, 1928; G.E. Smith & F.W. Jones: Report on the human remains. *The archaeological survey of Nubia: Report for 1807–1908.* Vol. 2. Cairo: National Printing Department, 1910; B.A. Wood: The "Neanderthalers" of the Royal College of Surgeons. *Annals of the Royal College of Surgeons of England* 61:385–389, 1979.

Ruggeri

See Giuffrida Ruggeri, Vincenzo

Russell, Frank (1867–1903)

Originally trained as a zoologist at the University of Iowa (*Variation of Animals in a State of Nature* was the title of his M.A. thesis in 1891), Russell became interested in anthropology while on an expedition to northern Canada and Alaska in 1891–1892. During the expedition, the purpose of which was to secure a series of musk ox specimen, Russell collected various ethnological materials as well.

Through this new interest, Russell came into contact with Frederic Ward Putnam (1839–1915), then director of the Peabody Museum and professor of anthropology at Harvard University. Putnam invited Russell to come to Harvard and study anthropology. After completing his M.A. in zoology at the University of Iowa, Russell enrolled at Harvard, and in 1896 he received a second B.A. under Putnam in anthropology. A year later, Russell completed his M.A., also under Putnam's tutelage.

In the interest of expanding the capabilities of the fledgling Department of Anthropology at Harvard, Putnam encouraged Russell to study geology and anatomy and to attend human-dissection courses at the Harvard Medical School. Russell completed his Ph.D. in anthropology in 1898, the first person to be awarded that degree specializing in physical anthropology at Harvard. That same academic year, he was appointed instructor of anthropology—a position he held until shortly before his death.

During 1898, under the auspices of the Bureau of American Ethnology, Russell spent a year studying Pima Indians in Arizona. From his studies among the Pima, Russell published several essays and one book-length report on Piman folklore, subsistence patterns, and record keeping, and the formulation of a new constitution of the Pima reservation

(Russell 1903a, 1903b, 1909).

Back at Harvard, Russell specialized in somatology and was the first person to teach that course in the Anthropology Department. When Russell fell ill with tuberculosis in 1902, Putnam took on William Curtis Farabee (1865–1939) to replace Russell as instructor in anthropology.

Russell died in 1903.

Kalman Applbaum

See also Farabee, William Curtis; Harvard University; Putnam, Frederic Ward

Bibliography
SELECTED WORKS
An Apache medicine dance. *American Anthropologist* 11:367–372, 1898a; Gauging cranial capacity with water. *American Anthropologist* 11:52–53, 1898b; Myths of the Jicarilla Apaches. *Journal of American Folklore* 11:253–272, 1898c; Human remains from the Trenton gravels. *American Naturalist* 33:143–153, 1899; Athabascan myths. *Journal of American Folklore* 13:11–18, 1900a; Studies in cranial variation. *American Naturalist* 34:50–56, 1900b; Laboratory outlines in somatology. *American Anthropologist* 3:28–50, 1901; Know, then, thyself. *Journal of American Folklore* 15:1–15, 1902; Pima annals. *American Anthropologist* 5:76–80, 1903a; Piman constitution. *Journal of American Folklore* 16:222–228, 1903b; Pima nursery tales. *Out West* 31:890–895, 1909; (with H.M. Huxley) A comparative study of the physical structure of the Labrador Eskimos and the New England Indians. *Proceedings of the American Association for the Advancement of Science,* pp. 365–379, 1899.

ARCHIVAL SOURCES
Frank Russell Papers: 1. Accession files, Peabody Museum of Archaeology and Ethnology, Harvard University, 11 Divinity Avenue Cambridge, Massachusetts 02138; 2. Harvard College Library, Harvard University, Cambridge, Massachusetts 02138.

SECONDARY SOURCES
J.O. Brew: *Early days of the Peabody Museum at Harvard University.* Cambridge, Massachusetts: Harvard University Press, 1966; C.M. Hinsley: The museum origins of Harvard anthropology, 1866–1915. In: C.A. Elliott & M.M. Rossiter (eds) *Science at Harvard University: Historical perspectives.*
Bethlehem, Pennsylvania: Lehigh University Press, 1992; C.C. Nutting: [Obituary]. *Iowa Alumnus* 28 Nov. 1903.

Russia
Physical Anthropology in Prerevolutionary Russia
The roots of physical anthropology in Russia can be traced to the eighteenth century, when a number of scholars concerned themselves with the natural history of the human species and its relationship to the rest of the animal world. For example, Afanasy Kawersniew (ca. 1748–ca. 1812), in his doctoral thesis *Von der Abartung der Thiere* (The Transmutation of Animals), written and published in Leipzig in 1775, endorsed the Swedish naturalist Carolus Linnaeus' (1707–1778) classification of human beings with the anthropoid apes and the monogenetic perspective that humankind constituted a single biological family in which all of its members were able to interbreed. Similarly, the writer Aleksandr N. Radishchev (1749–1802) endeavored in his thesis, *On Man, His Mortality, and Immortality,* which he wrote during his 1792–1796 exile in Siberia and was published in 1809, to demonstrate the close biological link between human beings and the rest of animate nature. Like his contemporary the German anatomist Johann Friedrich Blumenbach (1752–1840), he placed great stress on our species' unique features, namely, the mode of locomotion and the faculty of speech. Accordingly, Radischev argued that "the hands were man's guide to reason."

It was not, however, until the nineteenth century and the arrival of Karl Ernst von Baer (1792–1876) that physical anthropology in Russia acquired a more substantial foundation. Prior to his appointment as professor of zoology at the Academy of Sciences in St. Petersburg (ASSP) in 1834, von Baer had worked at the University of Königsberg, where he established a reputation as an embryologist and anthropologist. During his tenure of well over three decades at the ASSP, he assembled and organized an important crania collection, which, along with his numerous publications in the fields of craniology and human variation, contributed significantly to the development of physical anthropology as a legitimate and independent discipline in Russia.

Indicative of this trend is the Society of the Friends of Natural Science, Anthropology, and Ethnography (SFNSAE) (Obshchestvo liubitelei estestvoznaniiā, antropologii i ètnografii), which was founded at the University of Moscow in 1863. A year later, the Department of Anthropology was established in the same institution and placed under the control of Anatoly P. Bogdanov (1834–1896), a devoted Darwinist whose role in the development of the new discipline in Russia cannot be underestimated. His numerous works include a fundamental study of medieval Slavic crania (1867), the first monograph in physical anthropology written by a Russian national. Also supporting the development of the discipline were the 1879 Anthropological Exhibition in Moscow, which was organized by Bogdanov and attended by such notable delegates as the French anthropologists Paul Broca (1824–1880) and Armand de Quatrefages (1810–1892), and the subsequent decision to hold the eleventh meeting of the International Congress of Anthropology and Prehistoric Archaeology in Moscow in 1892.

Among Bogdanov's most notable students was Dmitrii N. Anuchin (1843–1923), who subsequently went on to teach at the University of Moscow and to preside over the SFNSAE. As revealed by the journals he assisted in founding, Anuchin's research interests ranged over the entire anthropological spectrum. These journals included the *Etnograficheskoe obozrienie* (1889–1916), *Zemlevedenie* (1894–1938), and *Russkiĭ antropologicheskiĭ Zhurnal*, which was also known as the *Journal russe d'anthropologie* (1900–1930). Later, in 1932, this latter journal was reorganized by Arkady Isaakovich Yarkho (1903–1935) and Mark Plisetzky under the new title *Antropologicheskiĭ Zhurnal* and published until 1937.

Another notable worker from this period with a specific research interest in physical anthropology was Nikolay N. Miklukho-Maklay (1846–1888), the brother of the geologist Mikhail N. Miklukho-Maklay (1857–1927), a naturalist who received his scientific training in Germany under Karl Gegenbaur (1826–1903) and Ernst Haeckel (1834–1919). Between 1870 and 1883, Miklukho-Maklay made several trips to New Guinea, where he spent a total of almost three years, plus excursions to Australia, Melanesia, Micronesia, the Philippines, Malacoa, and Indonesia. During the course of these field trips, he conducted a number of anthropometric studies of indigenous peoples that he used to correct erroneous racial classifications to refute racist interpretations.

Efim Chepurkovsky (1871–1950) is another prominent worker of the late prerevolutionary period; he introduced a geographical

method of analyzing racial variation that later became very popular among Soviet scholars. Chepurkovsky was greatly influenced by the British biometric school. After the revolution, he emigrated to Manchuria and then to the United States, where he spent the remainder of his life.

The Founders of Modern Soviet Physical Anthropology
During the years immediately following the revolution of 1917, it is possible to identify four major figures in the new Soviet anthropology. The first, and arguably the most influential of this group, was Viktor V. Bunak (1891–1979). As a disciple of Anuchin, Bunak endeavored to link the scholarly tradition of the prerevolutionary era with the new Soviet philosophy of science. Like Anuchin, his research interests covered virtually every major area of the discipline, including paleoanthropology, population genetics, origin of speech, and human growth and development (cf. Bunak 1980). Bunak began his academic career at the University of Moscow, where he was named a lecturer in 1919 and a full professor in 1925. In 1923, he succeeded Anuchin as director of the Moscow Institute of Anthropology (MIA)—a position he held until 1930.

The Soviet school of physical anthropology and human population biology is largely the product of Bunak's efforts, and most specialists in these disciplines working in the former USSR in the mid-1990s were either directly or indirectly his pupils.

A second, and possibly equally influential, figure during this period was Georgy F. Debetz (1905–1969), who received his initial scientific training at Irkutsk University. On graduating in 1925, Debetz moved to Moscow, where he initially became a researcher at the MIA. Later, in 1944, he worked at the Institute of Ethnography of the Academy of Sciences (Moscow). His primary research focus was racial variation, particularly in the USSR, where his studies took him from the Caucasus to Chukotka and from north Siberia to Afghanistan. And like Bunak, Debetz was responsible for training numerous students who served to foster his anthropological perspective throughout the Soviet Union. Representing different traditions though, it is not surprising to learn that Debetz and Bunak were professional rivals (*vide infra*).

The tradition to which Debetz belonged was initiated by Arkady Yarkho (*vide ante*), a theorist by inclination whose approach to the study of human variation was a kind of protocladistic analysis (involving a hierarchical ordering of physical traits) that had a profound impact upon an entire generation of Soviet physical anthropologists.

A fourth dominant force during this nascent period was Yakov Roginsky (1895–1986), who spent his entire career at the University of Moscow. His principle area of research was in paleoanthropology. While his publications are not as numerous as those of Bunak and Debetz, his work is nevertheless distinguished by its attention to detail and exceptional insights. For example, the theory of "broad monocentrism" that Roginsky developed after the 1940s endeavored to reconcile the idea of the monocentric origin of modern humans with evidence favoring a regional continuity model, and thereby anticipated some of the issues that were to surface in paleoanthropology during the last quarter of the twentieth century.

Other notable figures belonging to this period include the paleoanthropologist Vsevolod Yakimov (1912–1982), the ethnographer and physical anthropologist Nikolai N. Cheboksarov (1907–1980), and Mikhail M. Gerasimov (1907–1970), who is best remembered for his work in forensic anthropology and, in particular, his development of methods for reconstructing facial soft parts on the skull of unknown individuals.

As implied above, during the 1920s Bunak and his pupils endeavored to link their research with modern principles of population genetics at the Moscow Institute of Anthropology. The MIA, initially headed by Anuchin, was founded in 1922 at the University of Moscow (cf. Zalkind 1973). From 1923 to 1930, it was headed by Bunak. However, the prevailing political climate worked against the efforts of Bunak and his followers to modernize Soviet physical-anthropological research, and this situation continued to deteriorate in the 1930s and 1940s. In 1937, publication of the *Russian Journal of Anthropology* (Russkiï antropologicheskiï Zhurnal), the only anthropological journal to survive the revolution, was stopped. Soon thereafter, Bunak was forced from his position at the MIA. After 1948, he worked at the Institute of Ethnography of the Soviet Academy of Sciences in Moscow.

Post-Stalin Developments: 1953–1990s
The four decades following the death of Soviet leader Joseph Stalin in 1953 have seen the gradual collapse of the Soviet political system. The story of this demise and its progressive impact on the mechanics of Russian society are very involved and beyond the scope of this review, but these complex events also had a profound impact on the Russian academic community. While it is not possible to do justice to these events insofar as they relate to what was happening in physical anthropology during this period, some ad hoc observations are offered here as a starting point for some future historian of science interested in the development of physical anthropology in post-Stalin Russia.

In 1957, a new journal, *Voprosy antropologii* (Problems of Anthropology), was founded at the University of Moscow; still published, its contents provide some insights into what has been happening in the discipline from 1957 on.

A review of the literature from 1957 to 1990 reveals there has been a distinct shift away from the traditional research concerns of physical anthropologists, such as comparative anatomy, skeletal biology, primatology, and paleoanthropology, and an increasing trend toward studies embracing anthropometry, physiology, genetics, adaptation, growth and development, and body composition. Another palpable feature of this trend, and in direct contradistinction to more traditional studies, is that, more often than not, these human biology projects have been orchestrated by a team of workers rather than by an individual researcher. However, contrary to expectation, this trend has not led to the elimination of the more traditional research pursuits or concerns of physical anthropologists. Rather it appears that after an initial period of rapid development (1957–1975), the newer research focus has reached a fluctuating plateau that is probably indicative that a process of normalization is underway.

It is conjectured that this dramatic shift in research emphasis reflects the influence of Bunak's program at the University of Moscow, which, in contrast to Debetz's at the Institute of Ethnography, placed a greater emphasis on biology. This institute, which as noted earlier is connected with the Academy of Sciences, formerly had two branches, one in Moscow, and the other in St. Petersburg (the latter is now independent). In contrast to Bunak's original program at the University of Moscow, the curriculum at Debetz's institute placed a greater emphasis on ethnic and racial studies, which followed, by and large, his interest in such questions as racial origins and population history. Although many provincial anthropological centers have been controlled by

Debetz's former students, even in them there has been a general shift away from these traditional concerns. Specifically, there has been a discernible increase in the number of studies from these centers dealing with population genetics, dermatoglyphics, and dental anthropology.

As of the mid-1990s, it appears that Russian physical anthropology has reached a temporary and harmonious balance between the rival agendas of Bunak and Debetz, but, with increasing contact and exchange with the world's community of anthropological scientists, further changes are undoubtedly forthcoming.

Alexander G. Kozintsev

Editor's Note
For further details on the history of Russian physical anthropology, see L. Godina et al. (1993) and Kozintsev (1993).

See also Anuchin, Dimitrii Nikolaevich; Baer, Karl Ernst von; Blumenbach, Johann Friedrich; Bogdanov, Anatoly Petrovich; Broca, Paul (Pierre); Bunak, Victor Valerianovich; Debetz, Georgy Frantsevich; Haeckel, Ernst Heinrich Phillip August; Linnaeus, Carolus; Quatrefages (de Breau), Jean Louis Armand de; Russian Primate Studies; Yarkho, Arkady Isaakovich

Bibliography
V.P. Alexeev: Anthropological investigations in the USSR. *Sovetskaya etnografiya* 4:40–67, 1964; V.P. Alexeev: Anthropology in the USSR: Some results and prospects. *Sovetskaya etnografiya* 5:17–31, 1987; A.P. Bogdanov: Materials on the anthropology of the Kurgan period in the government province of Moscow. [In Russian]. Résumé in German: *Archiv für Anthropologie* 11:295–300, 1867; V.V. Bunak: *Rod Homo ego vozniknovenie i posle duiushchaia evoliutssia.* Moscow: Nauka, 1980; T.D. Gladkova, M.I. Uryson, & V.Z. Yurovskaya: Anthropology at the Moscow University. *Voprosy antropologii* 64:3–22, 1980; L. Godina, M.L. Butovskaya, & A.G. Kozintsev: *History of biological anthropology in Russia and the former Soviet Union.* International Association of Human Biologists. Occasional Papers Vol. 3. No. 5. Newcastle upon Tyne: IHAB, 1993; B.H. Heath: Impressions of current anthropology in the Soviet Union. *Yearbook of Physical Anthropology* 15:280–304, 1969; A. Hrdlička: An anthropologist in Russia. *Scientific Monthly* March–May, 1942; A. Kawersniew: *Von der Abartung der Thiere.* Leipzig: Sommer, 1775.

A.G. Kozintsev: Physical anthropology in the Soviet Union. In: B.A. Sigmon (ed) *Before the wall fell: The science of man in socialist Europe.* Toronto: Canadian Scholars' Press, 1993, pp.19–37; M.G. Levin: *Essays on the history of anthropology in Russia.* Moscow: Nauka, 1960; B.A. Nikityuk: Soviet medical anthropology over seventy years. *Arkhiv anatomii, embriologii, i gistologii* 93:27–36, 1987; A.N. Radishchev: On man, his mortality, and immortality. In: *A collection of unpublished works of the late A.N. Radishchev.* Parts 1–2. Moscow: Beketov, 1809; Y. Roginsky: Racial studies in the USSR over fifty years, 1917–1967. *Voprosy antropologii,* 28:21–35, 1968; I. Schwidezky, B. Chiarelli, & O. Necrasov (eds): *Physical anthropology of European populations.* The Hague: Mouton, 1980, pp.1–55, 391–426; C.G. Turner II: Physical anthropology in the USSR today. *Quarterly Review of Archaeology,* June:11–14; Fall:4–6, 1987; N.G. Zalkind: Fifty years of the Institute of Anthropology. *Voprosy antropologii* 43:25–40, 1973; N.G. Zalkind: *The Moscow school of anthropologists.* Moscow: Nauka, 1974.

Russian Primate Studies

The beginnings of primatology in Russia can be traced to the first decade of the twentieth century. It is possible to differentiate four distinct periods in the development of primate research according to the theoretical bias, sphere of interest, and basic objective of such investigations. As indicated in Table 1, the first three periods are dominated by workers primarily interested in comparative psychology, whereas the fourth period reflects an emerging interest in ethological studies grounded in an evolutionary framework.

Period 1: 1911–1940s
The founder of primate studies in Russia was Nadejda Ladygina-Kots (1889–1963), who was trained as a biologist and a psychologist at the Moscow State University. As a student, she was inspired by the ideas of prominent Russian psychologist Vladimir Bekhterev (1857–1927) and became increasingly interested in the subject of the evolutionary development of human consciousness. In 1911, she began working at the State Darwin Museum, where she conducted detailed observations on ontogenetic development of chimpanzee behavior (Ladygina-Kots 1923). Later, she extended these observations to the study of the

TABLE 1. Main Stages of Development in Russian Primate Studies

Theoretical orientation	Sphere of Interest	Discipline	Investigators
1917–1947			
			N. Ladygina-Kots[a]
	Cognitive abilities of apes	Psychology	N. Tih[b]
			P. Denisov[c]
Darwinian Theory			E. Vatsuro[d]
			I. Pavlov[e]
	Modeling of human diseases	Medicine	N. Voitonis[f]
1948–1964			
			N. Ladygina-Kots
	Sensory mechanisms,		G. Roginski[g]
Lamarckism;	communication,	Comparative Psychology	I. Pavlov
Pavlov's	intelligence, etc.		L. Alexeeva[h]
Theory of			N. Tih
Conditioned			L. Firsov[i]
Reflexes	Modeling of human disease	Medicine	B. Lapin[j]
1965–1977			
	Intelligence,		N. Tih
	communication,	Comparative Psychology	L. Alexeeva
	social structure		S. Novoselova[k]
Darwinian			
Theory;	Behavior, physiology,	Social Psychology	A. Stchastny[l]
Mendelian	adaptation		L. Firsov
Genetics;	Brain structure		
Pavlovian Theory	Modeling of human disease	Medicine	B. Lapin
			V. Startsev[m]
			E. Djikidze
1978–present			
	Social structure,		L. Firsov
	communication, locomotion,	Primate Ethology	M. Deriagina[n]
Modern Evolutionary	comparative behavior	Social Psychology	M. Butovskaya[o]
Synthesis			V. Chalian[p]
			N. Meishvili
	Behavioral parameters of		B. Lapin
	stress, psychopharmacology	Medicine	V. Startsev
			E. Djikidze

Sample References

(a) Ladygina-Kots 1923, 1935; (b) cf. Tih 1970; (c) Denisov 1958; (d) Vatsuro 1949; (e) Pavlov 1949; (f) Voitonis 1949; (g) Roginski 1948; (h) Alexeeva 1977; (i) Firsov 1977; (j) Lapin & Jakovleva 1963, Lapin et al. 1987; (k) Novoselova 1965; (l) Stchastny 1972; (m) Startsev 1971; (n) Deriagina 1986, Deriagina et al. 1984; (o) Butovskaya & Ladygina 1989, Butovskaya & Fainberg 1993; (p) Chalian & Meishvili 1989.

human child (using her own son) compared with that of the chimpanzee infant (cf. Ladygina-Kots 1935). It was under her guidance that a new generation of Soviet primatologists was formed (e.g., S. Novoselova, V. Mychina, and K. Fabri). Furthermore, her ideas greatly influenced the scientific work of other Russian primatologists, such as Grigory Roginski, Eduard Vatsuro, Nina Tih, and A. Katz.

In the period 1925–1927, coinciding with the creation of the Yerkes Primate Center in Florida, the first Russian Primate Research Station (now Center) was founded at Suhumi (SPC), located on the coast of the Black Sea. This was followed in 1933 by the organization of another primatological center at Koltushi, on the outskirts of Leningrad, by Ivan Pavlov (1849–1936). The aim of this center was the comparative investigation of behavioral physiology, primate intelligence, and manipulatory abilities. At that time, under the guidance of Pavlov, a large research team was assembled at Koltushi, which included, among others, A. Dolin and G. Roginski.

It was during this period that the biological sciences in Russia became increasingly influenced by the ideas of Trofim Denisovich Lysenko (1898–1976). The impact of "Lysenkoism" became manifest in the following period.

Period 2: 1940s–1964

By the second period, Darwinian evolutionary theory and Mendelian genetics had been officially discredited under Joseph Stalin's regime and superceded by a primitive version of Lamarckian theory developed by Lysenko and his followers. All findings that contradicted Marxist dogma about the leading role of labor in human origins were strictly forbidden. Pavlov's theory of conditioned reflexes became the only acceptable way of interpreting behavioral phenomena.

During this "destructive" period, the two most prominent workers in Soviet primatology were Nina Tih (1905–1983) and Ludmila Alexeeva (1918–1984). Tih received her Ph.D. in 1935 from the Institute of Psychology (Moscow), and from 1936 to 1948 she worked in the Laboratory of Comparative Psychology at Suhumi. As indicated in Table 1, Tih used a comparative physiological approach in her research and focused on the study of the manipulatory abilities of animals in social groups. In 1948, she moved to Leningrad, where she worked in the Department of Psychology of Leningrad State University. Alexeeva completed her graduate studies in the Department of Anthropology of Moscow State University in 1945 and was greatly influenced by the ideas of Jakov Roginski and Mikhail Nesturkh, both specialists in the field of human evolution. Thus, it is not surprising that Alexeeva's work at the SPC, from 1946 to 1972, was initially oriented to the analysis of correlations between behavioral and morphological patterns. In 1972, she moved to Puschino (the biological center located 120 km from Moscow), where she worked in the Institute of Biophysics of the USSR Academy of Science.

Period 3: 1965–1977

The commencement of the third period is marked by the fall of Soviet leader Nikita Khrushchev and the subsequent erosion of the influence of Lysenko in the biological sciences

in Soviet Russia—though it was not until the late 1970s that the full impact of this shift was felt. However, this transitional period did witness a number of notable events. One was the establishment in the Pskovski region of a project designed to study the ape's adaptive ability (cf. Firsov 1977). In 1971, a similar "acclimation" project was initiated under the auspices of the SPC, which involved the study of a troop of wild hamadryas baboons that was released on the Black Sea coast near Tuapse. Later, in 1974, another group was released in the Gumista Reserve.

Another important development was the publication of Tih's book *Prehistory of Society* in 1970. In this work, Tih stressed the importance of competition and cooperation in primate societies and concluded that sexual bonding was not the primary cause of primates living in groups. She also noted the importance of long-lasting mother–infant relationships, as well as individual orientations toward contacts and cooperation with conspecifics—members of the same species.

Period 4: 1977–1995

Essentially, the fourth period is marked by an ongoing readjustment to the changing political climate in Russia. This changing situation has involved a number of changes in the course of primate studies. First is the recognition that all previous studies in comparative psychology, ontogenetic development, and physiology of behavior of nonhuman primates had been developed in isolation and without any practical or intellectual contact with Western science. Second, despite the rapid development of ethological and socioecological approaches in the West, by the end of the third period, the ethological studies of primate behavior were still absent in Russia. Third, until the end of the third period, all investigations of primate behavior were essentially descriptive and directed to medico-psychological problems rather than anthropological ones. Any kind of quantitative assessment of behavior was absent. Fourth, until the third period, there were no Russian universities offering specialized courses of lectures or training in primatological methods and theory.

In 1978–1979, a group of specialists from the Department of Anthropology at Moscow State University and from the SPC began ethological investigations of primates (Deriagina et al. 1984). Manipulatory and tool-using abilities and communications in representatives of different primate taxa were examined by Margarita Deriagina's group.

General and species-specific peculiarities of aggression and friendly behavior in groups of sixteen primate species were investigated by Marina L. Butovskaya. Kin effects in distribution of social bonds were tested, and the role of personal sympathies and antipathies in the development of the social structure of groups of macaques was demonstrated (Butovskaya & Ladygina 1989).

The "acclimation" study of hamadryas baboons at Tuapse has continued with observations on demography and ecology, territorial behavior, harem formation, and infanticide, among other things (Chalian & Meishwili 1989).

At the beginning of the 1980s, two Suhumi satellite centers were established in Adler (100 km to the west) and Tamish (40 km to the east), both on the Black Sea coast. As this suggests, this was a period of rapid development of primatology in Russia, with the SPC becoming one of the largest centers in the world. By the late 1980s, the SPC had 6,000 primates in its charge, respresenting more than fifteen species, including, *Papio hamadryas*, *Papio anubis*, *Macaca mulatta*, *Macaca fascicularis*, *Macaca nemestrina*, and *Cercopithecus aethiops*. Unfortunately, in August 1991, when Georgia and Russia became independent states, the Suhumi Primate Research Center was divided into two independent centers. The part located in Suhumi has been reorganized as the Georgian Primatological Center, and the part located in Tamish was destroyed in the civil war in the early 1990s.

Since 1991, the Russian Primate Center and the Institute for Medical Primatology have developed an active research program, headed by Professor Boris Lapin, near Adler on the Black Sea coast (south of Tuapse). Futhermore, as a consequence of the political changes in the early 1990s, Russian primatologists have at last a real opportunity for international cooperation and exchange of scientific data.

Marina Butovskaya

See also African Apes; African Monkeys; Primate Field Studies

Bibliography

L.V. Alexeeva: *Polycyclicity of reproduction in primates and anthropogenesis*. Moscow: Nauka, 1977; M.L. Butovskaya & L.A. Fainberg: *At the origin of human society*. Moscow: Nauka, 1993; M.L. Butovskaya & O.N. Ladygina: Support and cooperation in agonistic encounters of stumptail macaques (*Macaca arctoides*). *Anthropologie* 27:73–81, 1989; V.G. Chalian & N.B. Meishwili: Behaviour and reproductive states in hamadryas baboons as the model of gender relationships in early hominids. In: V.P. Alexeev & M.L. Butoskaya (eds) *Biological prerequisites of human evolution*. Moscow: Institute of Ethnography Press, 1989, pp. 81–97; P.K. Denisov: Analyzator and synthetic functions of cerebral hemispheres in chimpanzee. *Journal of High Brain Activity* 8:845–854, 1958.

M.A. Deriagina: *Manipulatory activity in primates*. Moscow: Nauka, 1986; M.A. Deriagina et al.: The application of ethological methods in studies of primate behaviour. *Voprosy Antropologii* 73:128–135, 1984; L.A. Firsov: *The behaviour of apes in natural habitats*. Leningrad: Nauka, 1977; N.N. Ladygina-Kots: *The investigation of the cognitive abilities of chimpanzees*. Moscow: Petrograd State Press, 1923; N.N. Ladygina-Kots: *Chimpanzee infant and human child*. Moscow: State Darwin Museum Publications, 1935; B.A. Lapin & L.A. Jakovleva: *Comparative pathology in monkeys*. Springfield, Illinois: Thomas, 1963; B.A. Lapin et al.: *Guidance on medical primatology*. Moscow: Medicine Publishers, 1987; S.L. Novoselova: Comparative analysis of mediated activity in primates by means of independent experience and imitation. In: A.D. Sionim (ed) *Biological bases of imitative activity and social forms of behaviour*. Moscow: Leningrad Soviet Science Press, 1965, pp. 70–81.

I.P. Pavlov: *Pavlovskije sredy*. Moscow: Leningrad Soviet Science Press, 1949; G.Z. Roginski: *Habits and premises of intellectual actions in apes (chimpanzees)*. Leningrad: Academic Publishers, 1948; V.B. Startsev: *Modelling of neurogenic diseases of man in experiments on monkeys*. Moscow: Medicine Publishers, 1971; A.I. Stchastny: *The complex forms of ape behaviour: Psychological investigations of "spontaneous" activity of chimpanzees*. Leningrad: Nauka, 1972; N.A. Tih: *Prehistory of society*. Leningrad: Leningrad State University Publishers, 1970; E.G. Vatsuro: *Investigations of high neural activity of an anthropoid ape (chimpanzee)*. Moscow: Leningrad Soviet Science Press, 1948; N.U. Voitonis: *The prehistory of intelligence and the problem of anthropogenesis*. Moscow: Leningrad Soviet Science Press, 1949.

Rutot, Aimé Louis (1847–1922)

Born in Mons in the province of Hainaut, Belgium, Rutot was trained as a mining engineer and geologist at the Université de Liège. In 1880, he joined the Musée d'Histoire naturelle in Brussels as a conservationist, collaborating in the preparation of a detailed geological map of Belgium. He was largely responsible for identifying and surveying the Belgian Tertiary and Quaternary formations. In 1906, he was made a member of the Académie royale Belgique (ARB). He was president of the ARB in 1926.

During the last decade of the nineteenth century, Rutot became increasingly interested in the subject of human prehistory and an energetic proponent of the French prehistorian Gabriel de Mortillet's (1821–1898) eolithic theory. Although from the outset this movement was embroiled in controversy, there were many who were persuaded by Rutot's arguments—indeed, for a while he was considered by some, such as the British anatomist-anthropologist Arthur Keith (1866–1955), as one of Europe's leading authorities on Plio-Pleistocene geology and anthropology.

From the various stone artifacts he collected in Belgium and France, Rutot defined a series of discrete eolithic industries that he believed documented the genesis of human culture in the Pliocene through the emergence of the Lower Paleolithic in the basal strata of the Quaternary. This cultural sequence comprised the "Reutélien," "Mafflien," and "Mesvinien." To these and the later Paleolithic industries (i.e., the Pre-Chellean, Chellean, and Acheulean), Rutot associated specific hominid types. Based on recovered human paleontological material in Europe and elsewhere, he commissioned the sculptor Louis Mascré (1871–1929) to make models of his reconstructions of these hominid remains. For example, the "Tertiary Forerunner" was based on his reconstruction of the *Pithecanthropus erectus* (now *Homo erectus*) remains found by the Dutch physician Eugène Dubois (1858–1940) in Java in the early 1890s. This project entailed fifteen reconstructions tracing the different stages of human evolution from *Pithecanthropus* to Neandertal to Cro-Magnon and so forth. Although in retrospect these models appear little more than scientific fantasies, at the time they attracted considerable attention—indeed, the American physical anthropologist Aleš Hrdlička (1869–1943) purchased ten of these reconstructions for the anthropological exhibit he had organized at

the Panama–California Exposition at San Diego in 1915.

After his retirement in 1919, Rutot dedicated his remaining years to spiritualism and metapsychical studies.

He died in Brussels on 6 August 1933.

André Leguebe

See also Dubois, (Marie) Eugène (François Thomas); Keith, (Sir) Arthur; Mortillet, Gabriel (Louis Laurent) de; San Diego Museum of Man

Bibliography
SELECTED WORKS

Nouvelles observations sur la Quaternaire de la Belgique: Echelle stratigraphique et projet de légende des terrains quaternaires. *Bulletin de la Société belge de Géologie* 15:97–107, 1901; Equisse d'une comparaison des couches pliocènes et quaternaires de la Belgique avec celles du sud-est de l'Angleterre. *Bulletin de la Société belge de Géologie* 17:57–100, 1903a; L'état actuel de la question de l'antiquité de l'homme. *Bulletin de la Société belge de Géologie* 17:425–438, 1903b; *Un essai de reconstitution plastique des races humaines primitives.* Bruxelles: Hayez, 1919a; *La préhistoire: Introduction à l'étude de la préhistoire de la Belgique.* Bruxelles: Hayez, 1919b.

ARCHIVAL SOURCES

A.L. Rutot Papers: Library, Institut royal des Sciences naturelles de Belgique, rue Vautier 29 B-1040 Bruxelles, Belgium.

PRIMARY AND SECONDARY SOURCES

M. Boule: Aimé Louis Rutot. *L'Anthropologie* 43:633–635, 1933; J. de Heinzelin: Déclassement de la collection Dethise. *Bulletin de l'Institut royal des Sciences naturelles de Belgique* 35: 1959; J. de Heinzelin: Fagnien, Flénusien, Mafflien, Mesvinien, Omalien, Reutélien, Spiennien, Strepyen. In: *Lexique stratigraphique international.* Vol. 1. Part 4b: France, Belgique, Pays-Bas, Luxembourg: Quaternary. Paris: Centre international de la Recherche scientifique, 1957, p. 31 (Fagnien), 32 (Flénusien), 50 (Mafflien), 63–64 (Mesvinien), 88 (Omalien), 152 (Reutélien), 160–161 (Spiennien), 161 (Strepyen); A. Hrdlička: Preparation of exhibits illustrating the natural history of man. *Smithsonian Miscellaneous Collections* 65:52–62, 1915; F. Stockmans: Notice sur Aimé Louis Rutot. *Annuaire de l'Académie Royale de Belgique* 132:1–123, 1966.

Saatçioğlu, Armağan (1944–1985)

Born in Konya, Turkey, Saatçioğlu studied physical anthropology as an undergraduate at the Faculty of Languages, History, and Geography (D.T.C.F.) at Ankara University, graduating in 1965. She devoted the next five years to research for her doctoral dissertation, a biometric study among Turks of three anthropometric characters (height, cephalic index, and chest circumference) according to socioeconomic status (cf. Saatçioğlu 1975). Following the receipt of a doctorate in 1970, Saatçioğlu spent a sabbatical year (1971–1972) at Oxford University, where she collaborated with Geoffrey Ainsworth Harrison in a study of psychometric and anthropometric variation in Oxfordshire. She returned to the D.T.C.F. at Ankara University to replace Seniha Tunakan (1908–), who was scheduled to retire in 1973. The work Saatçioğlu (e.g., 1978, 1979, 1980) did in population genetics during the next decade led to her promotion to the rank of docent (associate professor) in 1981. A year later, the passage of a new University Act resulted in Saatçioğlu's resignation and the closing of the academic program in physical anthropology. Soon thereafter she died of cancer at the age of forty-one.

Aygen Erdentuğ

See also Tunakan, Seniha; Turkey

Bibliography
SELECTED WORKS
Türk kadınları ve Türk erkeklerinin boy uzunlukları ile başlarının en büyük uzunluğu ve en büyük genişliği arasındaki korelasyonun biyometrik izahı [A biometric analysis of the correlation between two head measurements, namely, the M.L.G. and M.W.G., and the stature of Turkish males and females]. *Antropoloji* 3:163–194, 1965; A biometrical investigation on three anthropometric characters and their changes according to their socioeconomic groups in Turkey. *Antropoloji* 7:175–199, 1975; *ABO Genleri Yönünden Türkiye'nin Yeri Ve Bu Ülkedeki Gensel Çeşitlilik Üzerine Biyometrik Bir İnceleme* [The ABO genes in Turkey and a biometric analysis of the gene frequencies in the country]. Ankara: A.ü.D.T.C.F., 1978; An analysis of the ABO gene frequencies in Turkey. *Journal of Human Evolution* 8:367–373, 1979; Instrument for measuring the angles of the living body. *Anthropologischer Anzeiger* 38:220–223, 1980; A survey on the racial types of Anatolian skeletal remains. A.ü.D.T.C.F. *Dergisi* 30:193–209, 1982.

SECONDARY SOURCES
A. Erdentuğ: A.ü.D.T.C.F. antropoloji bibliografyasi, 1935–1983 [Bibliography of anthropology, D.T.C.F., Ankara University, 1935–1983]. *Antropoloji* 12:488–489, 1985.

Saccopastore

Saccopastore is a site on the third and lowest terrace of the left bank of the River Aniene, a tributary of the Tiber, situated 3 km from the Porta Pia, Rome. In April 1929, during gravel- and breccia-quarrying work, a fossilized human cranium was found in the gravel of a fluvio-lacustrine layer. This virtually complete cranium was given to the paleoanthropologist

Sergio Sergi (1878–1972) of the University of Rome, who immediately recognized its overall Neandertal morphology (Sergi 1929). Later, on 16 July 1935, Alberto Carlo Blanc (1905–1960) and Henri Breuil (1877–1961), during a visit to the exhausted quarry, discovered a second encrusted skull a few meters above the point where the first cranium had been found. It was in fragmentary condition and less complete than the 1929 find (Blanc 1948). Four years were needed for Sergi to complete the cleaning and reconstruction of this latter specimen.

Saccopastore 1 and 2 crania were described by Sergi as female and male individuals of a Mediterranean variety of Neandertals. Their chronological attribution is to the Riss-Würm Interglacial, ca. 125 ky BP. These fossils have recently been restudied (cf. Condemi 1992).

Brunetto Chiarelli
Giuseppe D'Amore

See also Blanc, Alberto Carlo; Breuil, Henri (Éduoard Prosper); Italy; Neandertals; Sergi, Sergio

Bibliography
A.C. Blanc: Notizie sui ritrovamenti e sul giacimento di Saccopastore e sulla sua posizione nel Pleistocene laziale. *Paleontographia Italica* 42:3–23, 1948; S. Condemi: *Les Hommes fossiles de Saccopastore et leurs position philogénétique*. Paris: CNRS, 1992; S. Sergi: La scoperta di un cranio del tipo di Neandertal presso Roma. *Rivista di Antropologia* 28:457–462, 1929; S. Sergi: Il cranio del secondo paleantropo di Saccopastore. *Paleontographia Italica* 42:25–164, 1948; S. Sergi: Die Neandertalischen Paleanthropen in Italien. In: G.H.R. von Koenigswald (ed) *Hundert Jahre Neanderthaler*. Utrecht: Kemink, 1958, pp. 38–51.

Sahabi

Fossils were first found in the 1920s at a site, now known to cover an area of 150 km², by Italian soldiers stationed at the historic desert fortress of Qasr as-Sahabi, Libya. This fort was largely destroyed during World War II. The fossil deposits at Sahabi first received professional attention when Italian geologist Ardito Desio visited the site in 1930 (Desio 1935). Paleontological survey and excavation were undertaken from 1934 to 1939 by Desio's protégé, Carlo Petrocchi, a professor at the University of Tripoli Medical School. Petrocchi is best known for his discovery at Sahabi of a complete skeleton of the previously unknown four-tusked proboscidean *Stegotetrabelodon syrticus*. Many other large fossil vertebrates were discovered at the site (Petrocchi 1952). Fieldwork was halted by World War II, and work was not reinitiated because of the presence of many landmines in the area.

In 1975, the American physical anthropologist Noel T. Boaz visited Sahabi at the invitation of the Faculty of Science of Al-Fateh University in Tripoli and then organized the multidisciplinary International Sahabi Research Project (ISRP), codirected by paleontologist Abdel Wahid Gaziry of the Department of Earth Sciences at Garyounis University, Benghazi. The geological investigation of Sahabi was directed by Jean de Heinzelin of the University of Gent, Belgium, and Ali El-Arnauti of Garyounis University. The ISRP discovered the first primates from Sahabi in 1978, a cercopithecid mandible ascribed to *Libypithecus cf. markgrafi*. Subsequently, the presence of *Macaca cf. lybica* was also documented at the site. Vertebrate taxa added to the faunal list from Sahabi included several species of micromammals, including the new gerbil species *Protatera yardangi*, a new species of shovel-tusked proboscidean *Amebelodon cyrenaicus*, the ursid *Agriotherium*, four taxa of hyenids, the anthracothere *Merycopotamus petrochii*, and the sirenian *Metaxytherium serresii*, among others. The fauna share taxa with sub-Saharan Africa and with Eurasia, but there are clear differences of a unique character. Most striking is the abundance at Sahabi of the large anthracothere, a group of animals that was extinct in eastern Africa after the Early Miocene. In this respect, Sahabi documents a unique paleozoogeographic zone in North Africa during the Late Neogene.

On the basis of the Sahabi discoveries, the Belgian paleoxylologist (fossil wood expert) Roger Dechamps has suggested an environment of "open galley forests along river courses fringed by drier biotopes." In the monograph *Neogene Paleontology and Geology of Sahabi, Libya* (Boaz et al. 1987), the site was accorded a basal Pliocene age of ca. 5.0 my. This was based on the stratigraphic position of the fossiliferous levels above massive gypsiferous deposits ascribed to the Messinian Event, separating the Miocene from the Pliocene Epochs, and on biostratigraphic studies of the vertebrate fauna from Sahabi. No geological levels appropriate for geochronological dating were discovered. Some paleontologists have questioned the basal Pliocene date of Sahabi and believe instead that it represents a latest Miocene age, a position that is still in the minority.

Three specimens from Sahabi have been attributed to Hominoidea. One of these, a putative clavicle, was contested by T.D. White et al. (1983) and instead interpreted as a posterior rib of a small cetacean. Despite Boaz's rejection of this claim in 1987, the bone's identity remains obscure. A primate right parietal bone from a subadult individual (21P21A) evinces a size and curvature that is somewhat gibbon-like, and was ascribed to Hominoidea gen et. sp. indet. (indeterminate genus and species) by Boaz. A left distal fibula (114P33A) was also ascribed to Hominoidea gen et sp. indet. These remains are the first reputed hominoid fossils from the North African Pliocene but must await further fieldwork and comparative study to clarify their true significance.

Noel T. Boaz

See also African Prehistory

Bibliography

N.T. Boaz et al. (eds): Results from the International Sahabi Research Project (Geology and Paleontology). *Garyounis. University Scientific Bulletin.* Special Issue No. 4. Benghazi: Garyounis University Research Center, 1982; N.T. Boaz et al. (eds): *Neogene paleontology and geology of Sahabi, Libya.* New York: Liss, 1987; A. Desio: Appunti geologici sui dintorni di Sahabi (Sirtica). *Rendiconti del Reale Istituto di Lettere, Roma* 68 (2d ser.):137–144, 1935; C. Petrocchi: Paleontologia di Sahabi (Cirenaica). I. Notizie generali sul giacimento fossilifero di Sahabi: Storia degli scavi e risultati. *Rendiconti dell'Accademia Nazionale dei Quaranta (Roma)* 3 (4th ser.):9–33, 1952; T.D. White et al.: "Hominoid clavicle" from Sahabi is actually a fragment of cetacean rib. *American Journal of Physical Anthropology* 61:239–244, 1983.

Saint-Hilaire, Isidore Geoffroy
See Geoffroy Saint-Hilaire, Etienne

Saller, Karl (1902–1969)
Born in Kempten/Allgäu, Germany, Saller studied medicine and anthropology under Rudolf Martin (1864–1925) at the University of Munich. His doctoral examination, conducted by Martin in 1924, was on hair pigmentation in mixed populations. In 1926, he passed the state examination and graduated

M.D. with a thesis dealing with the relationship of gonad function and skeletal morphology. At this juncture, Saller became an assistant at the Anthropological Institute in Kiel University, where he became a lecturer in anthropology to the Medical Faculty. In 1929, he joined the Institute of Anatomy at Göttingen University. However, in 1934 he was dismissed from his position as privatdocent at Göttingen by the Office of Racial Policies of the NSDAP (the National Socialists Workers' Party of Germany, the ruling Nazi party) with the explanation that he was "falsifying" the doctrines of the new state, and misusing his academic position for the purposes of political antipropaganda. Saller championed the view that the human races are not fixed typologies, but rather biological units that are constantly changing as a consequence of the constant interaction of their genetic heritage with the environment. His books were banned in 1935, and, as a consequence of these rulings, he entered private medical practice, founding his own sanatorium at Badenweiler in 1936. Between 1939 and 1945, he served as a doctor in the military. After the war, he became director of the Robert Bosch-Krankenhaus in Stuttgart. Although in 1946 he was reinstated at Göttingen University, Saller accepted the position of professor in the Medical Faculty at the University of Munich, where he taught anatomy as well as anthropology. Two years later, he was offered a position in anthropology and human genetics at the University of Munich—a position formerly occupied by Rudolf Martin and Theodor Mollison (1874–1952). Thus, in the spring of 1948, he began teaching courses in both anthropology and anatomy. For the former, he used several of his own publications, including *Grundlagen der Anthropologie* (Fundamentals of Anthropology) (1949b), *Art- und Rassenlehre des Menschen* (Kinds and Races of Man) (1949a), and *Angewandte Anthropologie* (Applied Anthropology) (1951).

In addition to his academic duties, Saller also ran a private clinical hospital near Munich and was president of the Federal Association of German Doctors for Natural Healing (Bundesverbandes Deutscher Ärzte für Naturheilverfahren).

During the last decade of his life, he received a number of awards and honors, including an honorary doctorate from the Friedrich Schiller University at Jena in 1962, the Humboldt Medal from the University of Berlin in 1959, and, shortly before his death, the Hrdlička Medal in 1963.

In the late 1950s, Saller undertook the task of producing a third edition of his former mentor's influential *Lehrbuch der Anthropologie*, in which he endeavored to redefine the scope of the discipline. Indeed, through this and his other works, Saller greatly assisted anthropology in regaining its respectability in Germany after the war. In his last years, he began working on a multivolume work with a tentative title of "History of Human Races," of which only the first volume was realized.

He died on 15 October 1969.

Ursula Zängl-Kumpf

See also Martin, Rudolf; Mollison, Theodor; Rassenhygiene and Rassenkunde

Bibliography
SELECTED WORKS

Die Cromagnonrasse. *Anthropologischer Anzeiger* 2:176–181, 1925; Anthropologie, Konstitutionsforschung und Eugenik in ihren gegenseitigen Beziehungen. *Archiv für Soziale Hygiene und Demographie* 5:514–516, 1930a; Ein neuer Meßkoffer für anthropologische Reisen. *Zeitschrift für Morphologie und Anthropologie* 27:492–496, 1930b; Eine neue Augenfarbentafel. *Zeitschrift für Konstitutionslehre* 15:674–678, 1930c; *Leitfaden der Anthropologie*. Berlin: Springer 1930d; *Lehrbuch der Anthropologie*. Hamburg: Hermes, 1948; *Art- und Rassenlehre des Menschen*. Stuttgart: Schwab, 1949a; *Grundlagen der Anthropologie*. Stuttgart: Schwab, 1949b.

Der Begriff der Anthropologie. In: H. Grüneberg & S.W. Ulrich (eds) *Moderne Biologie: Festschrift zum 60 Geburtstag von Hans Nachtsheim*. Berlin, 1950, pp. 205–214; *Angewandte Anthropologie*. Stuttgart: Schwab, 1951; Der Rassebegriff in der modernen Anthropologie. In: *Rassenfrage heute*. München: Pflaum, 1955; *Lehrbuch der Anthropologie in systematischer Darstellung. Begründet von Rudolf Martin*. 3d ed. Stuttgart: Fischer, 1957–1966. *Die Rassenlehre des Nationalzozialismus in Wissenschaft und propaganda*. Darmstadt: Progress-Verlag, 1961; *Leitfaden der Anthropologie*. Stuttgart: Fischer, 1964; Die Anthropologie nach dem 2. Weltkrieg in München. *Anthropologischer Anzeiger* 28:262–267, 1965.

SECONDARY SOURCES

G. Glowatzki: Karl Saller zum 65. Geburtstag. *Medizinische Klinik: Die Wochenschrift für Klinik und Praxis* 62:1368, 1967; M. Günther: *Die Institutionalisierung der Rassenhygiene an den deutschen Hochschulen vor 1933*. M.D. Thesis. University of Mainz, 1982; K. Hennig: *Personalbibliographien der Professoren und Dozenten des Anthropologischen Institutes an der Naturwissenschaftlichen Fakultät der Ludwig-Maximilians Universität zu München im Zeitraum von 1865–1970*. Inaugural Dissertation. Medical Faculty, Erlangen-Nürnberg, 1972; G. Ziegelmayer & F. Schwarzfischer: In Memoriam Karl Saller, 1902–1969. *Anthropologischer Anzeiger* 32:287–288, 1969.

San Diego Museum of Man

With the construction of the Panama Canal nearing completion in 1912, it was decided to commemorate this approaching historic event with two large expositions in California, one to be staged in San Francisco and the other in San Diego. Like the World's Columbian Exposition in Chicago in 1893, the Panama–Pacific International Exposition at San Francisco was to be an elaborate but temporary extravaganza designed to stagger the imagination and demonstrate America's progress in arts and industry. By contrast, however, the organizers of the San Diego exposition envisioned their event being not merely a temporary showcase of the commercial resources of Southern California, but rather something more permanent that would be a "tangible expression" of the "collective soul of the [American] Southwest" (Brinton 1916). To this end, the civic leaders of San Diego decided to transform a 1,400-acre exposition site at the heart of the city into a permanent cultural and recreational center (now Balboa Park).

Edgar Lee Hewett (1865–1946), director of the Museum of New Mexico and professor of anthropology at the University of New Mexico, was appointed to develop the plans for the educational exhibits, while the cooperation of the Smithsonian physical anthropologist Aleš Hrdlička (1869–1943) was secured to provide a comprehensive exhibit illustrating the "progress of man from earliest prehistoric times to the present day"—which was later to form the nucleus of a permanent anthropological museum in San Diego.

Hrdlička saw this commission as a "magnificient opportunity" to promote his ambitions for American physical anthropology. Accordingly, he demanded that his exhibit should cover the entire range of the discipline and consist entirely of "original" and "newly collected material" from different parts of the world. This was, he told Hewett, fundamental if the collections of the anticipated San Diego Museum were to be of "permanent scientific value" (Spencer 1979, Vol. 1:363).

With funds provided by the Panama–California Exposition Corporation, Hrdlička organized an unprecedented program of research and collection that called for expeditions to Alaska, the Philippines, Siberia, Mongolia, Europe, Africa, Australia, and Peru. Although not all of this work was completed, due in large part to the outbreak of World War I, Hrdlička was clearly satisfied by the results of his labors and of those he had employed, saying later that, "[while not] complete and perfect" as it might have been, "it

Fig. 1. Panama–California Exposition 1915, Science of Man Building. A: Interior of room with busts for age cycle and racial variation series, viewed from the right of the room. B: View of room containing busts and masks for racial variation series.

[is] safe to say that in richness, instructiveness, and harmony [the exhibit] surpassed considerably anything attempted before in this line" (Hrdlička 1915:407–410).

One of the most exciting sections of Hrdlička's exhibit was the Hall of Human Evolution. This included a series of displays portraying the evolution of modern humankind through a number of prehistoric races illustrated in sculptured busts produced by Louis Mascré, a prominent Belgian sculptor. Most of these busts were consistent in detail with the anthropological knowledge of the period—though a notable exception was the now infamous Piltdown reconstruction.

From this hall, which formed the entrance to the main exhibit, the visitor passed through a series of connected sections that dealt in logical progression with other aspects of the discipline. For example, to illustrate the range of human variation and the "development of the human head in the three principal races in America," the Czech-American sculptor Frank Mička, who later worked with Gortzon Borglum on the Mt. Rushmore monument, was commissioned at great expense to prepare thirty busts (fifteen male and fifteen female) of each race at different stages of development, commencing with the fetal stage and proceeding at intervals from birth to seventy-five years.

The most complete and original of the exhibits, however, was the one on human paleopathology, the study of diseases and the healing arts from prehistoric to recent times. Much of the material displayed in this section was derived from the expedition Hrdlička himself conducted in Peru during the spring of 1913. Of the more than 1,000 skulls recovered during this expedition, many showed traces of trephination, the opening of a hole in the cranial vault by cutting or scraping. Hrdlička wrote extensive field notes and diagnoses for all of the specimens, which have made the collection invaluable for study in both anthropological and medical investigations. In 1980, in recognition of this collection's importance, the museum published a *Catalogue of the Hrdlička Paleopathology Collection*, edited by Rose A. Tyson and Elizabeth S. Dyer Alcauskas of the museum staff. This catalog includes many photographs and diagnostic descriptions of the specimens, plus a detailed index. Descriptions were reviewed and when necessary revised by the physical anthropologist Charles F. Merbs, a specialist in human osteology and paleopathology.

Cultural anthropology was also well represented in the displays of the exposition. Members of the scientific staff of the National Museum of Natural History in Washington, D.C., were drawn into this work and subsequently provided, among other things, a series of scale models of American Indian dwelling structures, ranging from skin tepees of the Plains to stone temples of the Maya. A series of full-scale clay-figure groups were modeled in plaster to illustrate the mining of copper, fishing through holes in the ice, and carving inscriptions on stone blocks. The tremendous task of assembling, mounting, and labeling all of these materials for exhibit was being carried out while the buildings were being constructed and the ground landscaped. Ground was broken for construction as planned on 19 July 1911, and the exposition opened for visitors on 1 January 1915.

Following the closure of the Panama-California Exposition at the end of 1916, the Board of Trustees decided to proceed with its original intention of founding the San Diego Museum, an institution for the purpose of collecting, preserving, and interpreting ancient bones and artifacts as a service to the community. As such, the museum was founded as a nonprofit corporation, which assumed its duties in 1917.

Despite the political and economic pressures of World War I, the San Diego Museum (SDM) continued in its role of preserving the collections assembled for the exposition, with a gradual increase in the number of items through occasional personal gifts and fieldwork. The most impressive and valuable of these were anthropological, but there were also numerous art items in the form of paintings, drawings, and ceramics.

However, action was subsequently taken by the Board of Trustees to limit the scope of the SDM to Aboriginal materials originating in North or South America. With this decision, the name of the museum was changed to the San Diego Museum of Man (SDMM), giving emphasis to the anthropological facilities and functions of the museum. This emphasis has continued, except in areas such as human paleontology in which the finds on other continents are vital to the presentation.

The SDMM has two serial publications: (1) *Discovery*, a monthly bulletin devoted mainly to events and activities of the SDMM for the use of members and others interested in the description and scheduling of lectures, exhibits, and workshops; and (2) *Papers*, which includes occasional technical monographs that generally deal with items represented in the museum collections.

Spencer L. Rogers

See also Hrdlička, Aleš; Paleopathology; Rutot, Aimé Louis

Bibliography
C. Brinton: *Impressions of the art at the Panama-Pacific Exposition.* New York: Lane, 1916; A. Hrdlička: *Descriptive catalogue of the section on physical anthropology, Panama-California Exposition.* San Diego, 1914; A. Hrdlička: An exhibit in physical anthropology. *Proceedings of the National Academy of Sciences* 1:407–410, 1915; F. Spencer: *Aleš Hrdlička M.D., 1869–1943: A chronicle of the life and work of an American physical anthropologist.* 2 vols. Ann Arbor, Michigan: University Microfilms, 1979. See particularly Vol. 1:381–391; Vol. 2:454–467; R.A. Tyson & E.S. Dyer Alcauskas (eds): *Catalogue of the Hrdlička paleopathology collection.* San Diego: San Diego Museum of Man, 1980.

Schaaffhausen, Hermann (1816–1893)

Born in Koblenz, Germany, Schaaffhausen studied medicine at Bonn and Berlin Universities. He received his medical degree in 1839 from Berlin University, where he had studied under Johannes Müller (1801–1858), with a dissertation titled *De vitae viribus.* On completing the state examination in 1840, he spent nine months abroad in Paris and London, during which time he studied local anthropological and archeological collections. In 1844, he qualified to become an unsalaried lecturer. His dissertation subject was: *About Progress of the Natural Sciences, Especially of Physiology.* In 1844–1845, he lectured on anatomy at Bonn University; after 1845, on anthropology. His lectures were among the most frequented at the university, and in 1855 he was named an associate professor. He was the cofounder, in 1866, of *Archiv für Anthropologie,* the first anthropological periodical published in Germany. Later, he repeatedly served as chairman of the Deutsche Anthropologische Gesellschaft (DAG) (German Anthropological Society), which was founded in 1869.

During his lifetime, Schaaffhausen received numerous honors, the most important of which were the Order of the Swedish Northstar and the Portuguese Order of St. Jacob. Both were civil decorations bestowed mostly for outstanding scientific merit. Not only had he gained high respect in private life in the Rheinland, he also earned a national and international reputation. Kaiser Wilhelm was a frequent visitor to Schaaffhausen's country home at Bad Honnef. This residence has been preserved and is now known as the Villa Schaaffhausen. When Schaaffhausen died, he was buried in the Old Cemetery in Bonn, which is still used to bury important personages. His funeral was a social event that was attended not only by the faculty of Bonn University, but also by Kaiser Wilhelm II, the Queen of Sweden, the Princess of Wied, and Duke Albrecht Johann von Mecklenburg-Schwerin.

Schaaffhausen is regarded as one of the founders of modern physical anthropology in Germany. He made important intellectual contributions to the discipline, particularly to paleoanthropology, and also influenced the institutionalization of the science through his activities at Bonn University and with the DAG.

With regard to Schaaffhausen's intellectual contributions, he is perhaps best remembered for his description and evaluation of the fossilized skeletal remains recovered from the Neander Valley, near Düsseldorf, in 1856, whose antiquity and evolutionary significance he defended against the fierce opposition of the pathologist-anthropologist Rudolf Virchow (1821–1902) and his supporters. Largely through Schaaffhausen's efforts, the celebrated and important Neandertal remains were preserved in Germany—had it not been for his purchase, they probably would have gone to England (cf. Zängl-Kumpf 1990). In addition to his work on the Düsseldorf Neandertal, Schaaffhausen also supplied the first description of the Šipka hominid remains (Schaaffhausen 1880), which, again over Virchow's objections, he likened to the Neandertal remains. In the Spy find, he saw further proof for his theory about the transformation of the fossil hominid form to modern human beings (cf. Schaaffhausen 1887). As this indicates he was an avid evolutionist; indeed, Charles Darwin (1809–1882) acknowledged his intellectual debt to Schaaffhausen in his *Descent of Man* (1872).

Schaaffhausen also took a decisive part in the efforts to standardize national and international anthropometry. Within the DAG, he headed a commission that was responsible for cataloging all skeletal material found in Germany. The work required uniformity in how the measurements were taken, and Schaaffhausen was at pains to achieve this (cf. Zängl-Kumpf 1990). Indeed, it was these efforts that finally led to the Frankfort Agreement, reached in 1881, which, among other things, introduced and fixed the position of the ear-eye plane as a guiding horizontal. Like the anatomist-anthropologist Paul Broca (1824–1880) in Paris, Schaaffhausen was acutely interested in the problems associated with the determination of the cranial capacity, and again he made efforts to establish an international standard methodology. The vast amount of data that the DAG commission accumulated is in every way comparable to modern data banks, although the information was compiled laboriously by hand. This work involved meticulously listing all of the objects of various collections and recording associated anthropometric data. Schaaffhausen constantly re-edited the resulting catalogs in an effort to have them conform to individual agreements (cf. Zängl-Kumpf 1990).

Schaaffhausen had membership or honorary membership in a number of national and international societies, including the (Royal) Anthropological Society (London), the Imperial Leopold-Charles German Academy for Naturalists, the anthropological societies of Florence, Washington, Brussels, and Vienna, and the Société d'Anthropologie de Paris.

Although Schaaffhausen had pushed for a full professorship in anthropology at Bonn University ever since he was appointed associate professor in 1855, he was constantly turned down. However, in 1889, three years before he died, a full honorary professorship was bestowed on him—but it did not raise his standing within the university: He still continued to receive the salary for his regular professorship, and there was neither a chair nor an institute connected with the honorary title. The reasons for this appear to be largely linked to the general disapproval within the university's Medical Faculty (as well as the medical profession at large) of his views on human evolution.

Schaaffhausen died of myocarditis in Bonn on 26 January 1893.

Ursula Zängl-Kumpf

See also *Archiv für Anthropologie;* Broca, Paul (Pierre); Deutsche Anthropologische Gesellschaft; Frankfort Agreement; Neandertal (Feldhofer Grotte); Neandertals; Spy; Virchow, Rudolf

Bibliography
SELECTED WORKS
Übersetzung der Dissertatio inauguralis:
De vitae viribus. M.D. Thesis. University of
Berlin, 1839; Ueber die Beständigkeit und Umwandlung der Arten. *Verhandlungen des naturhistorischen Vereins der preussischen Rheinlande und Westfalens* 10:420–451, 1853; Zur Kenntniß der ältesten Rassenschädel. *Jahrbücher und Jahresbericht des Vereins für mecklenburgische Geschichte und Alterthumskunde* 24:167–188, 1859; On the crania of the most ancient races of man, with remarks and original figures taken from a cast of the Neanderthal cranium. English translation by G. Busk. *Natural History Revue* I:155–174, 1861; Ueber die Urform des menschlichen Schädels. *Die Niederrheinische Gesellschaft für Natur- und Heilkunde.* (Festschrift). 59–84, 1868.

L'Anthropologie préhistorique. *Extrait du Compte rendus du Congrès International d'Anthropologie et d'Archéologie préhistorique* (Sixth session, Brussels, Belgium, 1872). Brussels: Muquardt, 1873, pp. 538–548; Dr. Carl Fuhlrott: Nekrolog. *Correspondenz-Blatt der Deutschen Anthropologischen Gesellschaft* 7:27–29, 1878a; Der Neanderthaler Fund. *Correspondenz-Blatt der Deutschen Anthropologischen Gesellschaft* 7:116–120, 1878b; Die kraniologischen Sammlungen Deutschlands. *Correspondenz-Blatt der Deutschen Anthropologischen Gesellschaft* 9:97–103, 1879a; Ueber die Höhlenfunde in der Wildscheuer und dem Wildhaus bei Steeten an der Lahn. *Annalen des Vereins für nassauische Alterthumskunde und Geschichtsforschung* (Wiesbaden) 15:305–322, 1879b.

Funde in der Schipkahöhle in Mähren. *Verhandlungen des naturhistorischen Vereins der preussischen Rheinlande und Westfalens* 37:260–264, 1880; Ein pithecoider Unterkiefer aus der Schipka-Höhle. *Correspondenz-Blatt der Deutschen Anthropologischen Gesellschaft* 1:2–4, 1881; Charles Robert Darwin: Ein Nachruf. *Archiv für Anthropologie* 14:251–256, 1883a; Ueber den menschlichen Kiefer aus der Schipka-Höhle bei Stramberg in Mähren. *Verhandlungen des naturhistorischen Vereins der preussischen Rheinlande und Westfalens* 40:1–297, 1883b.

Die Schädel aus dem Löss von Podbaba und Winaric in Böhmen. *Verhandlungen des naturhistorischen Vereins der preussischen Rheinlande und Westfalens* 41:364–379, 1884; Ueber die Fortschritte der Naturwissenschaften, insbesondere der Physiologie. Habilitationsrede, gehalten in Bonn am Nov. 19.11. 1844. In: *Anthropologische Studien.* Bonn: Marcus,

1885, pp. 20–35; Ueber den Fund von Spy. *Verhandlungen des naturhistorischen Vereins der preussischen Rheinlande und Westfalens* 44:75–76, 1887; *Der Neanderthaler Fund*. Bonn: Marcus, 1888a; Die vorgeschichtliche Ansiedelung in Andernach. *Bonner Jahrbücher. Jahrbücher des Vereins von Alterthumsfreunden im Rheinland*. 89:1ff, 1888b.

SECONDARY SOURCES

H. Fremerey-Dohna: Hermann Schaaffhausen: Materialien zu einer zukünftigen Biographie. In: O. Wenig (ed) *Wege zur Buchwissenschaft*. Bonn: Bouvier, 1966, pp. 97–149; J. Ranke: Nachruf auf Hermann Schaaffhausen. *Bonner Jahrbücher. Jahrbücher des Vereins von Alterthumsfreunden im Rheinland* 94:1–27, 1893; U. Zängl-Kumpf: *Hermann Schaaffhausen, 1816–1893: Die Entwicklung einer neuen physischen Anthropologie im 19. Jahrhundert*. Frankfurt/Main: Fischer, 1990.

Scheidt, Walter (1895–1976)

Born in Weiler-Allgäu, Germany, Scheidt studied medicine and the natural sciences at the University of Munich, where his mentor had been Rudolf Martin (1864–1925). After graduating M.D. in 1923, he obtained a teaching position in anthropology at the University of Munich. A year later, he was installed as director of the Anthropological Division of the Museum für Völkerkunde, Hamburg, and in 1928 he became an associate professor there. In 1933, he became a regular professor and director of the newly established Rassenbiologischen Institut der Universität Hamburg—which in 1945 was converted to the present Anthropological Institute—where he remained until his retirement.

The results of his scientific activity include several books and 200 scientific articles. Although his initial output was in the area of paleoanthropology (1923a, 1924) and anthropometry, his research interests shifted increasingly to the study of racial biology. However, he repeatedly rejected the notion frequently encountered in the Rassenhygiene and Rassenkunde literature that pure races existed, and he considered all attempts to evaluate racial differences from that perspective as fallacious. He also reacted against attempts to misuse the results of the biological study of races for political, religious, moral, or social ends (1923b, 1925).

At the beginning of his Hamburg period, Scheidt conducted nationwide inquiries, which were later reflected in several volumes of the serial publication *Deutschen Rassenkunde*, published under the editorship of the physical anthropologist Eugen Fischer (1874–1964) between 1929 and 1936. In his *Kulturbiologie* (1930), he tried to combine the results of genetic research with medical psychology and ethnology. The goal of his research activity in the following decades was to make a "scientific inquiry into the processes of mental life" and the "corporal and mental development of humans." These were also the central topics of his *Lehrbuch der Anthropologie* (1948)—which he later revised in its third edition under the title *Die menschlichen Inbilder* (Images of Humans) (1954)—and *Der Mensch, Naturgeschichte seines Verhaltens* (History of Human Behavior) (1966).

He died in Lindenberg, near Lindau, on 9 August 1976.

G. Ziegelmayer

See also Fischer, Eugen; Martin, Rudolf; Rassenhygience and Rassenkunde

Bibliography
SELECTED WORKS

Die eiszeitlichen Schädelfunde aus der grossen Ofnet-Höhle und vom Kaufertsberg bei Nördlingen. München: Lehmann, 1923a; *Einführung in die naturwissenschaftliche Familienkunde*. München: Lehmann, 1923b; *Die Rassen der jüngeren Steinzeit in Europa*. München: Lehmann, 1924; *Allgemeine Rassenkunde*. München: Lehmann, 1925; *Rassenforschung: Eine einführung in rassenkundliche Methoden*. Leipzig: Thieme, 1927; *Kulturbiologie: Vorlesungen für Studierende aller Wissensgebiete*. Jena: Fischer, 1930; *Grundlagen einer Neurologischen Psychologie*. Jena: Fischer, 1937; *Aufbau einer Neurologischen Psychologie*. Jena: Fischer, 1938; *Lehrbuch der Anthropologie*. Hamburg: Hermes, 1948; *Die menschlichen Inbilder*. München: Schwarzenberg, 1954; *Der Mensch, Naturgeschichte seines Verhaltens*. München/Berlin/Wien: Schwarzenberg, 1966.

SECONDARY SOURCES

K. Hennig: *Personalbibliographien der Professoren und Dozenten des Anthropologischen Instituts an der Naturwissenschaftlichen Fakultät der Ludwig-Maximilians Universität zu München im Zeitraum von 1865–1970*. Inaugural Dissertation. Medical Faculty Erlangen-Nürnberg, 1972; A. Vogl: In Memoriam: Walter

Scheidt, 1895–1976. *Anthropologischer Anzeiger* 37:59, 1979.

Schlaginhaufen, Otto (1879–1973)

Born in St. Gallen, Switzerland, Schlaginhaufen studied anthropology at the University of Zürich under Rudolf Martin (1864–1925) and graduated in 1905 with a dissertation titled *Das Hautleistensystem der Primatenplanta*. From 1901 to 1905, he served as Martin's assistant at the Anthropological Institute. After a short appointment at the Museum für Völkerkunde in Berlin, he served as an assistant in anthropology at the Zoologisch-Anthropologisch-Ethnographischen Museum des Zwingers in Dresden from 1906 to 1911. While in that position he participated, in 1907, in a scientific expedition to Melanesia (New Guinea, New Ireland), which resulted in a number of publications. In 1911, he became an associate professor of anthropology at the University of Zürich, succeeding his mentor, Martin, and from 1927 to 1951, he was professor and director of the Anthropological Institute in Zürich.

In addition to his contributions to the methodology of anthropometry and to his individual works in human genetics, Schlaginhaufen focused his research on prehistoric anthropology and the biology of the Recent peoples of Switzerland. This latter research is summarized in his four-volume work *Anthropologia Helvetica* (1946–1959). During the course of his career, he published 161 papers and monographs.

Together with Fritz Sarasin (1859–1942) and Eugène Pittard (1867–1962), he was one of the founders of the Schweizer Gesellschaft für Anthropologie und Ethnologie and its annual *Bulletin* in 1920.

He earned special merits for the research in general heredity in Switzerland and was one of the founders of the Julius Klaus-Stiftung für Vererbungaforschung, Sozialanthropologie, und Rassenhygiene, of which he was president and one of the editors of its journal, *Archiv der Julius Klaus-Stiftung,* from 1925 to 1967.

G. Ziegelmayer

See also Martin, Rudolf; Rassenhygiene and Rassenkunde

Bibliography
SELECTED WORKS

Das Hautleistensystem der Primatenplanta unter Mitberücksichtigung der Palma. *Morphologisches Jahrbuch* 33:577–671 (1904), 34:1–125 (1905); Über eine Schädelserie von den Marianen. *Jahrbuch St. Galler Naturwissenschaft* 1905; pp. 656–707 Untersuchungen über den Sagittalumfang und seine Komponenten an 100 Schädeln aus Melanesien. *Mitteilungen des Vereins für Erdkunde in Dresden* 5:10–40, 1907; Über Siedlungsverhältnisse in Süd-Neu-Mecklenburg. *Zeitschrift für Ethnologie* 42:822–829, 1910; Reisewege und Aufenthalte in Melanesien. *Verhandlungen der Schweizerische Naturforschende Gesellschaft* 94. Jahresversein in Solothurn 1:172–191, 1911.

Anthropologische Untersuchungen an Eingeborenen in Deutsch-Neuguinea. *Abhandlungen und Berichte des Zoologisch-Anthropologisch-Ethnographischen Museums Dresden* 14(5), 1914; Pygmäenrassen und Pygmäenfrage. *Vierteljahresschrift der Naturforschenden Gesellschaft Zürich* 61:249–276, 1916; Die menschlichen Knochen aus der Höhle Freudenthal im Schaffhauser Jura. *Archiv Suisses d'Anthropologie général* 3(2–4):275–299, 1919; Die anthropologischen Funde aus den Pfahlbauten der Schweiz. *Mitteilungen der Antiquarischen Gesellschaft Zürich* 29:221–241, 1924.

Die menschlichen Skelettreste aus der Steinzeit des Wauwilersees im Kanton Luzern und ihre Stellung zu andern anthropologischen Funden aus der Steinzeit. Erlenbach/Zurich: Rensch, 1925; Zur Anthropologie der mikronesischen Inselgruppe Kapingamarangi (Greenwich-Inseln). *Archiv der Julius Klaus-Stiftung* 4:219–287, 1929; *Anthropologia Helvetica: Die Anthropologie der Eidgenossenschaft.* Vol.1. Zurich: Füssli, 1946; Der Mensch: Die Anthropologie der Steinzeit der Schweiz. In: O. Tschumi (ed) *Urgeschichte der Schweiz.* Vol. 1. Frauenfeld: Huber, 1949, pp. 369–405; *Anthropologia Helvetica: Die Anthropologie der Kantone und der natürlichen Landschaften.* Vol. 2. Zurich: Füssli, 1959.

SECONDARY SOURCES

A. Ernst (ed): Festgabe für Prof. Dr. Otto Schlaginhaufen zum 70. Geburtstag. *Archiv der Julius Klaus-Stiftung* 24, 1949; W. Scheffrahn: Prof. Dr. Otto Schlaginhaufen. *Archiv für Genetik* 48:1–2, 1975; A.H. Schultz: Otto Schlaginhaufen zum 80. Geburtstag. *Anthropologischer Anzeiger* 23:239–240, 1959.

Schmerling, Phillipe-Charles (1790¹–1836)

Born in Delft, western Netherlands, Schmerling studied medicine in The Netherlands before moving to Liège, Belgium, where he completed his studies in 1825. From all accounts, Schmerling's interest in paleontology was prompted by one of his patients, a quarryman who presented him with some fossils he had found near the village of Chokier, near Liège (Grayson 1983:108). Schmerling initiated a systematic search of the numerous caves located in the region, including Engis and Engihoul, along with that of Chokier. The discoveries he made in these caves are recounted in his *Recherches sur les ossemens fossiles* (1833–1834). In several of these caves, most notably Engis, Engihoul, Chokier, and Fond-de-Forêt, Schmerling recovered evidence that convinced him that at some remote period human beings had coexisted with now extinct mammals—contrary to the then current scientific wisdom. Although his discoveries attracted considerable attention, prompting visits from such notable researchers as the geologist Charles Lyell (1797–1875) from London, Schmerling's case for human antiquity did not prevail. Although Lyell had been impressed by Schmerling's collections as well as his arguments, like most other scientists of the period he harbored insurmountable reservations about the reliability of cave data—due primarily to the fact that such sites were subject to periodic flooding, which could cause shifting of the sediment layers and artifacts within. It was not until 1859, when British scientists confirmed the validity of similar finds made by the French savant Jacques Boucher de Perthes (1788–1868) in the Somme River valley, that Schmerling's claims were finally vindicated.

Schmerling died in Liège on 6 November 1836.

Frank Spencer

Editor's Note

It has long been assumed that Schmerling's birth date was 29 February 1791, but this has been shown by Henderickx (1994) to be in error. The correct date is 2 March 1790. See L. Henderickx: Philippe Charles Schmerling. *Actes 4ᵉ Congrès de l'Association des Cercles Francophones d'Histoire et d'Archéologie de Belgique*. pp.576–594, 1994.

See also Boucher (de Crèvecoeur) de Perthes, Jacques; Brixham Cave; Engis; Lyell, (Sir) Charles

Bibliography
SELECTED WORKS

Recherches sur les ossemens fossiles découverts dans les cavernes de la province de Liège. 2 vols. Liège: Collardin, 1833–1834; Annonce de la découverte faité dans deux grottes de deux os fossiles façonnés, et de fragmentes de silex taillés. *Bulletin de la Société Géologique de France* 6:170–173, 1835.

SECONDARY SOURCES

D.K. Grayson: *The establishment of human antiquity*. New York: Academic Press, 1983, pp. 108–112; A. Legeube: Importance des découvertes de Néandertaliens en Belgique pour le développement de la paléontologie humaine. *Bulletin de la Société royale belge d'Anthropologie et de Préhistoire* 97:13–31, 1986; C. Morren: Notice dur la vie et les travaux de P.C. Schmerling. *Annuaire de l'Académie royale de Bruxelles* 4:130–150, 1838.

Schreider, Eugène (1901–1978)

Born in St. Petersburg, Russia, Schreider emigrated with his parents from Russia to Rome, Italy, in 1918. While in Italy (1919–1922), Schreider studied law and medicine for two years at the University of Rome. It was there that he became interested in the study of constitutional types. In 1922, he moved to Berlin for a year before going to Prague, where his interest turned to social anthropology. After a year in Prague, he went back to Paris, but he returned to Prague again in 1925 and stayed for the next three years as a scientific worker in sociology. Finally, in 1928, he returned to Paris permanently.

In Paris, Schreider studied biology and psychology, and in 1932 he received his diploma from the Institut de Pyschologie and began working on his thesis, *Les mobiles affectifs du travail salarié*. From 1932 to 1940, he worked as a research associate in the Laboratoire de physiologie du travail du Conservatoire National des Arts et Métiers, studied anthropology, and began research in physiological anthropology at the Laboratoire d'Anthropologie physique de L'École pratique des Hautes Études (LAP-EPHE), at that time under the directorship of Georges Papillault (1863–1934). There he began researching aspects of the relationship between somatic and psychological variations, which provided the basis of his publication "Les facteurs physiologiques de la prédisposition aux accidents" (1934). During this period, Schreider spent the summer of 1936 in Mexico studying the Otomi and Nahuatl Indians and their adaptation to work in a textile industry. In 1939, he was placed in charge of a course dealing with *travaux pratiques d'anthropologie physiologique* at the Institut d'Ethnologie de l'Université de Paris.

With the outbreak of World War II, Schreider, because of his Russian Jewish background, was in jeopardy and left Paris. He first went to Bordeaux, from where he was sent to work in Henri Vallois' (1889–1981) Laboratoire d'Anthropologie physique in Toulouse. Shortly after arriving in Toulouse, Schreider received an invitation from the American biometrician Raymond Pearl (1879–1940) to come to work in the United States, but he declined on the grounds that he wanted to work for the French resistance movement. To that end, he finally reached London, where he remained from 1941 to 1946 working for the British Broadcasting Corporation (BBC). During this period, he also participated in research on the acclimation of servicemen posted to tropical countries.

Schreider returned to Paris in 1946, and three years later he secured a permanent post as assistant director of the LA-EPHE. In 1961, when Vallois retired from the directorship of this laboratory, Schreider was chosen to replace him—a position he retained until his retirement in 1971. Also in 1961, he succeeded H. Laugier (1888–1973) as director of the Laboratoire de Biométrie Humaine du Centre National de la recherche Scientifíque (CNRS). Although this post was unsalaried, it allowed him to receive financial support and technicians. This support continued until 1973.

Schreider's primary research interest was human evolution, which he approached from a biometrical perspective. One of his earlier studies had been on thermoregulation and its impact on human morphology. He assembled a considerable body of data on this subject, which enabled him to demonstrate the general validity of the application of the Bergman and Allen laws to human beings. Throughout his career, he applied himself to defining those factors that influence biological characters, including social and cultural factors, climate, altitude, morphology, physiology, consanguinity, and hybridization.

Schreider was a member of the Société d'Anthropologie de Paris and was elected its president in 1956. At the Société de Biotypologie, which changed its name to the Société de Biométrie humaine in 1966, he served as general secretary from 1962–1975.

Schreider died in Paris on 24 March 1978.

Denise Ferembach

See also Adaptation; France; Pearl, Raymond; Vallois, Henri Victor

Bibliography
SELECTED WORKS

Facteurs physiologiques et psychologiques de la prédisposition aux accidents. *Le Travail humain* (ser. A) 2:1–60, 1934; *Les types humaines.* 3 vols. Paris: Hermann, 1937; Quelques problèmes préalables à toute recherche de biométrie physiologique. Variations intra-individuelles instabilité des milieux intérieurs. Corrélations faibles et nulles. *Biotypologie* 13:20–61, 1952; Recherches anthropologiques sur les Otomis de la region d'Ixmiquiljan (Méxique). *L'Anthropologie* 57:453–489 (1953), 59:253–296 (1955).

Règles écologiques, régulation thermique et différentiation humaine. *Biotypologie* 18:168–183, 1957; Variations et corrélations intra-individuelles de quelques caractères physiologiques et biochimiques chez l'homme. *Biotypologie* 19:99–107, 1958; *La biologie humaine.* Paris: Presses Universitaires de France, 1967; L'influence de l'hétérosis sur les variations staturales. *L'Anthropologie* 72:279–296, 1968a; Variations du cerveau chez les deux sexes d'après les registres de Paul Broca. *Biometrie humaine* 3:162–173, 1968b.

Hérédité des caractères à variation continue et planification des recherches biométriques et anthropologiques. *Bulletins et Mémoires de la Société d'Anthropologie de Paris* 7 (12th ser.):115–119, 1971; Influences sociales et culturelles sur le développement biologique. *Bulletin du Musée d'Anthropologie Préhistorique de Monaco* 19:161–180, 1973; (with R. Kherumian) Répartition départementale de la stature, du poids et de la circonférence thoracique en France métropolitaine. *Biotypologie* 24:1–27, 1963; (with L.C. Soula) Etude de l'interdépendence de quelques caractères anatomiques, physiologiques et biochimiques. Evolution des corrélations avec l'âge. *Biotypologie* 12:19–32, 1951.

ARCHIVAL SOURCES

E. Schreider Papers: 1. Société de Biométrie humaine, Faculté de Médecine, Laboratoire d'Anatomie, 45 rue des Saints-Pères, 75007 Paris, France; 2. Musée de l'Homme, Laboratoire d'Anthropologie, 17 Place du Trocadéro, 75116 Paris, France.

SECONDARY SOURCES

D. Ferembach: Eugène Schreider, 21 Mars 1901–24 Mars 1978. *Bulletins et*

Mémoires de la Société d'Anthropologie de Paris 2:89–98, 1978.

Schultz, Adolph Hans (1891–1976)

Born in Stuttgart, Germany, Schultz began his studies of the natural sciences in 1909 at the University of Zürich, which at that time was one of the leading centers for the study of comparative vertebrate anatomy. Its Anatomy Institute possessed a large collection of primate skeletons as well as living specimens. Among those at Zürich who had a lasting influence on Schultz were the zoologists Arnold Lang (1855–1914) and Karl Hescheler, the anatomist O. Ruge, and the anthropologist Otto Schlaginhaufen (1879–1973). In 1916 Schultz was awarded a Ph.D. in comparative anatomy for his dissertation on the base of the skull in various human races (cf. Schultz 1917). At this juncture, he moved to the United States and became a research associate at the Carnegie Institution's Embryology Research Laboratory (ERL) in Baltimore, Maryland, where he continued his work on racial variability. Using human fetal material, Schultz was able to show that racial differences and individual variability were established *in utero* (1919). During his tenure at the ERL (1918–1925), Schultz studied such subjects as prenatal sexual behavior, cranial anomalies, and the description of primate fetuses. In 1925, he was invited to become professor of anthropology at the Johns Hopkins University in Baltimore—a position he retained until 1951. During this period, he published over seventy works, which served to establish his international reputation as an authority in primate comparative anatomy and biology. This body of work includes fundamental studies on growth, variability, and pathology in the nonhuman primates (e.g., 1933, 1937, 1940, 1941). He also collected much of his own material during field trips to Nicaragua, Panama, Siam, and Borneo. These materials formed the basis of the Schultz Collection, which is preserved in the Anthropology Institute, Zürich. In 1951, he returned to Zürich, having accepted an invitation to succeed his mentor Schlaginhaufen, and during the next twenty years he transformed the Anthropology Institute into one of the leading research centers for primatology in Europe.

In cooperation with the anatomist D. Starck (1908–) of Frankfurt/Main and the zoologist H. Hofer (1912–) of Giessen, he was cofounder and editor of the monographic series Bibliotheca Primatologica and the journal *Folia Primatologica* and an associate editor of the *American Journal of Physical Anthropology* (1925–1942) and *Human Biology* (1929–1952).

In recognition of his contributions to science, he was inducted into the National Academy of Sciences (United States) in 1938 and the American Philosophical Society in 1973, and was awarded the (Wenner-Gren) Viking Fund Medal in Anthropology in 1948. He also served a term as president (1932–1934) of the American Association of Physical Anthropologists. In 1957, he was made an honorary member of the British Zoological Society and the Anatomical Society of Great Britain and Ireland; and, in 1962, he was named *doctor honoris causa* at the University of Basel.

He died in Zürich on 16 May 1976.

G. Ziegelmayer

See also African Apes; Primate Field Studies; Schlaginhaufen, Otto: Wenner-Gren Foundation for Anthropological Research

Bibliography
SELECTED WORKS

Anthropologische Untersuchungen an der Schädelbasis. *Archiv für Anthropologie* 16:1–103, 1917; The development of the external nose in Whites and Negroes. *Carnegie Institution of Washington Publication* 272:173–190, 1919; Growth studies on primates bearing upon man's evolution. *American Journal of Physical Anthropology* 7:149–164, 1924; Variations in man and their evolutionary significance. *American Naturalist* 60:297–323, 1926; Observations on the growth, classification, and evolutionary specializations of gibbons and siamangs. *Human Biology* 5:212–255, 385–428, 1933; Fetal growth and development of the rhesus monkey. *Carnegie Institution of Washington Publication* 479:71–98, 1937.

Growth and development of the chimpanzee. *Carnegie Institution of Washington Publication* 518:1–63, 1940; Growth and development of the orangutan. *Carnegie Institution of Washington Publication* 525:57–110, 1941; Primatology and its relation to anthropology. *Yearbook of Anthropology,* pp. 47–60, 1955; Age changes and variability in the skulls and teeth of the Central American monkeys *Alouatta, Cebus,* and *Ateles. Proceedings of the Zoological Society of London* 133:337–390, 1960; Die rezenten Hominoiden. In: G. Heberer (ed) *Menschliche Abstammungslehre.* Stuttgart: Fischer, 1965, pp. 56–102; *The life of primates.* London: Weidenfeld & Nicolson,

1969; *Die Primaten*. Lausanne: Editions Recontre, 1972.

SECONDARY SOURCES

J. Biegert (ed): Festschrift Adolph Hans Schultz zum 70. Geburtstag. *Bibliotheca Primatologica*. Basel/New York: Karger, 1962, pp. iii–xiv; J. Biegert: Adolph H. Schultz, 1891–1976: Zum Tod des Züricher Anthropologen. *Folia Primatologica* 26(1):2–4, 18–23, 1976; G.E. Erikson: Adolph Hans Schultz, 1891–1976. *American Journal of Physical Anthropology* 56:365–371, 1981; W.W. Howells: Adolph Schultz. *American Journal of Physical Anthropology* 46:189–196, 1977; T.D. Stewart: Adolph H. Schultz, 1891–1976. *Biographical Memoirs of the National Academy of Sciences* (U.S.A.) 54:325–349, 1983.

Schwalbe, Gustav (1844–1916)

Born in Quedlinburg, Germany, Schwalbe earned his M.D. degree at the University of Berlin in 1866, but, though he passed his medical boards the following year, his efforts quickly turned toward research. His early work was primarily in general histology and physiology—disciplines to which he made several significant contributions, such as the discovery of the existence of taste buds and pioneering work on the lymphatic system. Apart from his paleoanthropological writings, his most influential works were his textbooks on neurology (1881) and the anatomy of sense organs (1883). He held posts at several academic institutes (Bonn, Amsterdam, Halle, Freiburg, Leipzig, Jena, and Königsburg) before becoming, in 1883, professor of anatomy at the University of Strassburg[1]—a post he retained until his retirement in 1914.

Throughout his writings, Schwalbe emphasized the critical importance of methodologically precise comparative morphological studies to the assessment of evolutionary relationships among organisms. During the late 1880s and early 1890s, he began to focus application of this methodology to problems of human phylogeny. Specifically, he initiated comparative studies of variation of living human races, studies that he considered critical to unraveling human evolutionary history.

As he delved into physical anthropology, Schwalbe clearly saw the need to improve its methodological precision and theoretical focus. In 1899, he founded the *Zeitschrift für Morphologie und Anthropologie* with the expressed purpose of bringing detailed comparative anatomical and developmental studies to bear on human evolution. His dedication to this goal is reflected in the fact that, after 1899, he published almost exclusively on this topic.

At the same time, to facilitate precise methodology in human evolutionary studies, Schwalbe developed a basically metrical method for comparative study of fossil hominids, which involved calculations of several angles and indices on the cranial vault. He referred to this approach as *formanalyse* (the analysis of form or shape) and based its use on concepts that today we would call taxonomic relevance and total morphological pattern.

Using the methodology of *formanalyse*, Schwalbe contributed to several significant paleoanthropological controversies around the turn of the century. For example, he argued that the so-called Cannstatt race, established by the French anthropologists Armand de Quatrefages (1810–1892) and Théodore Hamy (1842–1908), was an artificial mixture of true Neandertals—or, as he referred to them, *Homo primigenius*—and a robust, but otherwise modern cranial series, which included such specimens as Cannstatt, Brüx (Most), Podkumak, and Brno II, among others. The former group, Schwalbe argued, hailed from the Early Diluvium (Pleistocene), while the latter was restricted to the Late Diluvium. However, Schwalbe repeatedly claimed that these robust, Late Pleistocene forms were structurally intermediate between Neandertals and the Australian Aborigines, who were then regarded as the most primitive of extant humans. This implied that Neandertals were reasonable ancestors of recent humans.

While many of his contemporaries, such as Quatrefages, Hamy, Julien Fraipont (1857–1910), and Gabriel de Mortillet (1821–1898), considered the Neandertals to be nothing more than a primitive race of *Homo sapiens*, Schwalbe believed Neandertals and modern humans were different enough morphologically that the rules of systematic zoology compelled their placement in separate species (if not genera). This, more than any other single point, became Schwalbe's *cause célèbre*, and he regarded recognition of this fact as inexorably tied to transforming paleoanthropology into a true science, characterized by the same stringent and objective methodology employed in other sciences. It is in this context that Schwalbe's attack on Rudolf Virchow's (1821–1902) assessment of the original Neandertal (Feldhofer Grotte) skeleton must be viewed. Schwalbe set out to demonstrate that its morphology could not be related to pathology or to advanced age in a member of a primitive race, as Virchow had argued. Rather, the original Neandertal's basic morphology made sense only as a normal representative of an anatomically primitive species, occupying a morphological position near, but not in, *H. sapiens*.

A third controversy to which Schwalbe contributed dealt with the existence of a pre-sapiens lineage in Europe. Schwalbe systematically argued against this perspective, noting that no specimen with a modern human morphology could be unequivocally attributed to a time period earlier than, or contemporary with, the Neandertals. He presented detailed objections to the major candidates for representatives of this lineage put forth during the early twentieth century, including Galley Hill, Ipswich, and Piltdown. In the same vein, he dismissed the Argentine paleontologist Florentino Ameghino's (1854–1911) arguments for the existence of humans from the Pliocene of Argentina.

Yet a fourth controversy concerned the evolutionary connection between living humans and apes. A committed Darwinian and a devotee of the German biologist Ernst Haeckel (1834–1919), Schwalbe believed that anatomical similarities in extant forms supported a close phylogenetic relationship between great apes and humans. Furthermore, based on his comparative analyses, he argued that *H. primigenius* and the Dutch anatomist Eugène Dubois' (1858–1940) *Pithecanthropus* (now *H. erectus*) bridged significantly the still immense structural gap that separated apes and humans. Because *Pithecanthropus* had a smaller brain and more ape-like cranial features, Schwalbe viewed it as more primitive than Neandertals. But in recognizing a structural series from ape, through *Pithecanthropus* and Neandertal, to modern humans, he made it clear that this was not necessarily a phylo-

genetic or geneaological series. He stated his position succinctly in what is perhaps his most comprehensive paleoanthropological work, *Studien zur Vorgeschichte des Menschen* (1906). There he wrote:

As previously stated, I lay little value on a decision whether the fossil skulls under consideration {Pithecanthropus and Neandertals} belong to the direct ancestral lineage of humans or represent side branches of the ancestral lineage. For in the latter case also, the ancestors must have looked similar to the preserved remains of Pithecanthropus and Homo primigenius. In a pure zoological sense Homo primigenius is an intermediate between Homo sapiens and Pithecanthropus erectus. (1906:14)

Because of his views on the role of *Pithecanthropus* and Neandertals, Schwalbe is often cited as the initial architect of the unilineal interpretation of human evolution. Certainly, several later unilinealists acknowledge Schwalbe's perspectives as foundations of their own views, including the German paleoanthropologist Hans Weinert (1877–1967); Schwalbe's best-known student, Franz Weidenreich (1873–1948); and, more recently, scholars such as the American physical anthropologist C. Loring Brace (1930–).

Interestingly, Czech-American physical anthropologist Aleš Hrdlička (1869–1943) accused Schwalbe of being a prime contributor to pre-sapiens ideas—a misconception partly derived from Hrdlička's misunderstanding of Schwalbe's arguments that Neandertals were a separate species from recent humans. It may also be that Schwalbe's support of the assessment of the La Chapelle-aux-Saints Neandertal skeleton by the French paleoanthropologist Marcellin Boule (1861–1942) further misled Hrdlička into thinking that Schwalbe had become a pre-sapienist.

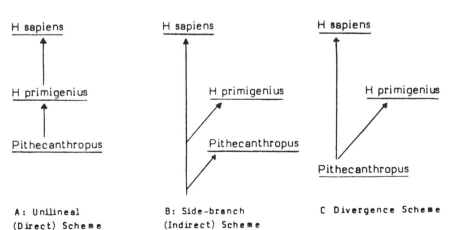

Fig. 1. Schematic representations of Schwalbe's views on human phylogeny. (a) and (b) are from his 1906 monograph; (c) is from his posthumous 1923 paper.

Schwalbe's (1913) review of Boule's La Chapelle monograph was one of the last things he published; in it, he applauds Boule's recognition that Neandertals were clearly a distinct species from *H. sapiens*, and suggests that the Neandertals were likely on a sideline rather than a direct ancestral form (see Fig. 1). Schwalbe, however, accepted that either (a) or (b) in Fig. 1 was possible. From the above quotation, it is clear that he did not regard these alternatives as significantly different from each other. Furthermore, it is clear from his review of Boule and his final paper (published posthumously in 1923), that he never accepted anything like (c) in Fig. 1 (which would certainly be a pre-sapiens phylogeny), nor did he see any fossil evidence demonstrating the existence of a pre-sapiens lineage. Thus, his shift to favoring (b) rather than (a) was not, from Schwalbe's perspective, a fundamental one, and it was not a shift away from a basically unilineal perspective on human evolution.

While Schwalbe's "flexibility" regarding (a) and (b) may seem confusing and contradictory, it is necessary to understand that, despite his Darwinian convictions, he adhered to a somewhat essentialist interpretation of a species. Species, for him, could be defined on morphological grounds alone and were separated by distinct morphological gaps. Despite his allusions to the significance of heredity to evolution, Schwalbe obviously had little conception of how it operated and no real feeling for the biological basis of a species in the modern sense. Thus, in spite of his firm conviction that ancient species were ancestral to extant forms, his writings reveal that he could deal with this relationship only in strictly structural or typological terms. As Ernst Mayr (1904–) has noted, such a species concept dominated scientific thinking well into the first half of the twentieth century—and, obviously in this case, Schwalbe is one of the majority.

Fred H. Smith

Editor's Note

1. Prior to the Franco-Prussian War of 1870–71, the provinces of Alsace and Lorraine had been French territory. In 1871 these provinces became part of Germany until 1919, when they were returned to France. Thereafter Strassburg became Strasbourg—as it had been before 1871.

See also Ameghino, Florentino; Boule, Marcellin; Brno; Brüx; Cannstatt Skull; Chapelle-aux-Saints, La; Dubois, (Marie)

Eugène (François Thomas); Fraiport, Julien; Galley Hill; Haeckel, Ernst Heinrich Phillip August; Hamy, Jules Ernest Théodore; *Homo erectus*; Hrdlička, Aleš; Mortillet, Gabriel (Louis Laurent) de; Neandertals; Piltdown; Quatrefages (de Breau), Jean Louis Armand de; Virchow, Rudolf; Weidenreich, Franz; Weinert, Hans

Bibliography

SELECTED WORKS

Lehrbuch der Neurologie. Erlangen: Besold, 1881; *Lehrbuch der Anatomie der Sinnesorgane.* Erlangen: Besold, 1883; Über die Schädelformen der ältesten Menschrassen mit besonderer Berücksichtigung des Schädels von Eguisheim. *Mittheilungen der Philomathischen Gesellschaft in Elsass-Lothringen* 3:72–85, 1897; Studien über *Pithecanthropus erectus* Dubois. *Zeitschrift für Morphologie und Anthropologie* 1:1–240, 1899; Der Neanderthalschädel. *Bonner Jahrbücher.* No. 106:1–72, 1901a; Über die specifischen Merkmale des Neanderthalschädels. *Verhandlungen der Anatomischen Gesellschaft: Ergänzungsheft zur Anatomische Anzeiger* 19:44–61, 1901b.

Die Vorgeschichte des Menschen. Braunschweig: Vieweg, 1904; *Studien zur Vorgeschichte des Menschen.* Stuttgart: Schweizerbartsche Buchhandlung, 1906; The descent of man. In: A.C. Stewart (ed) *Darwin and modern science.* London: Cambridge University Press, 1910, pp. 112–136; Kritische Besprechung von Boule's Werk: "L'homme fossile de la Chapelle-aux-Saints" mit eigenen Untersuchungen. *Zeitschrift für Morphologie und Anthropologie* 16:527–610, 1913; Die Abstammung des Menschen und die Ältesten Menschenformen. In: P. Hinneburg (ed) *Die Kultur der Gegenwart.* Leipzig/Berlin: Teubner, 1923.

SECONDARY SOURCES

P.J. Bowler: *Theories of human evolution: A century of debate, 1844–1944.* Baltimore: Johns Hopkins University Press, 1986; F. Keibel: Gustav Albert Schwalbe. *Anatomischer Anzeiger* 49:210–221, 1916; F.H. Smith: Gustav Schwalbe: Neandertal morphology and systematics, 1899–1916. *PAN: Physical Anthropology News* 6:1–5, 1987.

Schwidetzky, Ilse (1907–)

Born in Lissa (Prussia), Germany, Schwidetzky studied anthropology under Egon von Eickstedt (1892–1965) at Breslau University (now Wrocław, Poland). After World War II, she followed von Eickstedt to Mainz, where they set up an Institute of Anthropology at the newly formed University of Mainz. In 1946, she became a privatdocent at Mainz; in 1949, an associate professor; and in 1961, a regular professor. She retired (emerita) in 1975.

Schwidetzky's main area of research is the Neolithic, and she has conducted regional research in Schlesia, Westfalia, and Rheinland-Pfalz. She also has published on population biology and on social anthropology with an emphasis on Rassenbiologie. She conducted an intensive study of the prehistoric and contemporary inhabitants of the Canary Islands (cf. Schwidetzky 1963). In addition to her research, since 1956 she has been editor of *Homo* (*Internationale Zeitschrift für die vergeleichende Biologie der Menschen*).

During her career, she has received a number of awards in recognition of her contributions, including the Medal of the Roumanian Academy of Science in 1966 and the Aleš Hrdlička Medal in 1968. She is also an honorary member of the anthropological societies of Austria, Belgium, and Croatia.

Ursula Zängl-Kumpf

See also Germany

Bibliography
SELECTED WORKS
Die Rassenforschung in Polen. *Zeitschrift für Rassenkunde* 1:76–83, 136–204, 289–314, 1935a; Zur Frage der Differentialdiagnose zwischen nordischen und mediterranen Schädeln. *Zeitschrift für Rassenkunde* 1:316–317, 1935b; Anthropologie und Geschichtswissenschaft. *Zeitschrift für Rassenkunde* 4:268–284, 1936; Einige Ergebnisse der Rassenuntersuchung Schlesiens. *Verhandlungen der Deutschen Gesellschaft für Rassenforschung* 8:167–192, 1938; Fragen der anthropologischen Typenanalyse. *Zeitschrift für Rassenkunde* 9:201–237, 1939; Neue Merkmalskarten von Mitteleuropa. *Zeitschrift für Rassenkunde* 14:1–30, 1941; *Grundzüge der Völkerbiologie.* Stuttgart: Enke, 1950; *Das Menschenbild der Biologie: Ergebnisse und Probleme der naturwissenschaftlichen Anthropologie.* Stuttgart: Fischer, 1959.
Die vorspanische Bevölkerung der Kanarischen Inseln. Vol.1, *Beiheft zu Homo.* Göttingen: Musterschmidt, 1963; Anthropologische Untersuchungen auf den Kanarischen Inseln I. (Provinz Teneriffa:

Herkunftskreise und Fingerbeermuster). *Homo* 15:72–96, 1964; *Die neue Rassenkunde.* Stuttgart: Fischer, 1967; *Hauptprobleme der Anthropologie.* Freiburg: Rombuch, 1971; Die vorspanische und die heutige Bevölkerung der Kanarischen Inseln. Kontinuität und Diskontinuität von Bevölkerungsstrukturen. (Anthropologische Untersuchungen auf den Kanarischen Inseln II). *Homo* 22:226–252. 1972; *Grundlagen der Rassensystematik.* Zurich: Bibliographischen Institut, 1974.

SECONDARY SOURCES
W. Mainz: Ilse Schwidetzky zum 65. Geburtstag. *Anthropologischer Anzeiger* 34:86–87, 1973; W.E. Mühlmann: Ilse Schwidetzky zum 65. Geburtstag. *Homo* 23:298–299, 1972.

Semliki

The Semliki Valley of eastern Zaire is part of the African Western Rift Valley. It has early to late Pleistocene fossiliferous deposits in the southern "Upper Semliki" area near Ishango, which were first intensively investigated in the 1950s by the Belgian geologist Jean de Heinzelin (1955, 1957). Fossil deposits dating to Late Miocene and Pliocene times occur in the "Lower Semliki" area near the Sinda and Mohari Rivers and were investigated by de Heinzelin's team for three months in 1960, before political unrest forced the evacuation of the field team.

In 1982, the region was briefly resurveyed by Noel T. Boaz of the International Institute for Human Evolutionary Research at George Washington University, Washington, D.C. The following year, Boaz assembled a multidisciplinary international research team—the Semliki Research Expedition (SRE)—composed of more than fifty scientists and graduate students from ten countries. Jean de Heinzelin of the Institut Royal des Sciences Naurelles, Brussels, and University of Gent, Belgium, directed the geological investigation of the site. Archeological research was directed by J.W.K. Harris of Rutgers University (Plio-Pleistocene), Alison Brooks of George Washington University, and Kanimba Misago of the Institute of Zairean National Museum, Kinshasa. Most of the work of the Semliki Research Expedition was concentrated in the Upper Semliki before renewed political instability in Zaire caused field operations to be halted in 1990.

The most important discoveries of the expedition were the documentation for the first time in the African Western Rift Valley of an early Pleistocene fauna and flora, along with contemporaneous archeological records of hominid presence (Boaz 1990; Boaz et al. 1992; Harris et al. 1987). De Heinzelin's initial discovery of three stone artifacts at Kanyatsi was confirmed, and the presence of several hundred artifacts, mostly quartz, has been documented in the Upper Semliki Lusso Beds in association with a mammalian fauna that correlates to East Rift sites at 2.0 to 2.3 mya. An abundant fossil flora studied by the Belgian paleoxylologist (fossil wood expert) Roger Dechamps documents the nearby presence of dense lowland forest, but the prevailing environment is open woodland and wooded savanna. The fauna are dominated by antelopes and contain other such savanna-adapted taxa as giraffids and equids. Fossil remains of the makers of the Lusso Bed stone tools eluded discovery.

Redating of the uppermost levels of the Upper Semliki and further archeological work by Brooks showed that significant population densities and sophisticated bone harpoon technology had appeared by 20.0 ky BP (cf. Brooks & Smith 1987). At the other end of the age spectrum, preliminary results from the Lower Semliki indicate that these deposits contain a forest-adapted fossil fauna with a high degreee of endemism. A single fossil primate molar referred to *Macaca sp.* is known from Ongolina in the Lower Semliki.

Noel T. Boaz

See also African Prehistory; Multidisciplinary Research of Human Biology and Behavior

Bibliography
N.T. Boaz (ed): *Evolution of environments and Hominidae in the African Western Rift Valley.* Memoir, No. 1. Martinsville, Virginia: Virginia Museum of Natural History, 1990; N.T. Boaz et al.: A new evaluation of the significance of the Late Neogene Lusso Beds, Upper Semliki Valley, Zaire. *Journal of Human Evolution* 22:505–517, 1992; A.S. Brooks & C. Smith: Ishango revisited: New age determinations and cultural interpretations. *African Archeology Review* 5:67–78, 1987; J.W.K. Harris et al.: Late Pliocene hominid occupation in Central Africa: The setting, context, and character of the Senga 5A site, Zaire. *Journal of Human Evolution* 16:701–728, 1987; J. de Heinzelin: *Le fossé tectonique sous le parallèle d'Ishango. Exploration du Parc National Albert, mission J. de Heinzelin de Bracourt (1950).* Vol. 1.

Bruxelles: Institut des Parcs Nationaux du Congo Belge, 1955; J. de Heinzelin: *Les fouilles d'Ishango. Exploration du Parc National Albert, mission J. de Heinzelin de Bracourt (1950).* Vol. 2. Bruxelles: Institut des Parcs Nationaux du Congo Belge, 1957.

Sen, Dilip Kumar (1921–1972)

Born in Dinajpur (now in Bangladesh), Sen received his master's degree in anthropology from Calcutta University in 1947 and a Ph.D. in anthropology from the University of London in 1959. Soon after receiving his initial degree in anthropology he joined the Anthropological Survey of India (ASI) under a training program in which he further specialized in physical anthropology. He left the ASI in 1950 after receiving a teaching appointment at the newly created Department of Anthropology at the University of Lucknow, then under the stewardship of Dhirendra Nath Majumdar (1903–1960). After six years' teaching at Lucknow, he chose to upgrade his academic qualifications by pursuing a doctorate at the University of London. His doctoral research was a study of biological variation in Indians and Pakistanis settled in London. On receiving his doctorate in 1959, he returned to India, where he took over from Majumdar the responsibility of running the Department of Anthropology at Lucknow in 1960.

Sen remained at Lucknow until 1962, when he was appointed deputy director of the ASI in Calcutta; in 1964, he was promoted to director—a position he retained until his untimely death in 1972.

Sen's basic research interests were in the area of population variations, and he chose serology and dermatoglyphics as the focus of his studies. His interest in anthropometry was peripheral, although he did publish on racial characters and anthropometric studies in India. After leaving Lucknow for the ASI, Sen shifted gears in favor of ethnographic studies—with the result that he was largely responsible for redefining the research objectives and activities of the ASI in the areas of social/cultural and physical anthropology, and for emphasizing applied aspects, contemporary relevance, and national significance. To meet the demands of the situation, he increased the number of research personnel and also established the Basic Data Archive, designed to preserve data collected by Indian academics for future reference, research analysis, and, where indicated, publication. In many respects, it was through his efforts that the

ASI became the country's premier research institution.

D. Tyagi
Ripu D. Singh

See also India, Anthropological Survey of; Majumdar, Dhirendra Nath; South Asia (India, Pakistan, Sri Lanka)

Bibliography
SELECTED WORKS
Some notes on the fertility of the Jaunsari women. *Eastern Anthropologist* 10:60–67, 1956; Blood groups and haemoglobin variants in upper castes of Bengal. *Journal of the Royal Anthropological Institute* 90:161–172, 1960; Races of ancient India: A study of methods. Presidential Address. *Proceedings of the Indian Science Congress* (Calcutta 1964). Part 3. Calcutta: Indian Science Congress Association, 1964, pp. 1–23; Racial studies in India. *Journal of the Indian Anthropological Society* 2:1–18, 1967; A review of anthropometry in India. *Bulletin of the Anthropological Survey of India* 20:188–229, 1971.

ARCHIVAL SOURCES
M.K. Bhasin: *Biology of the peoples of Indian region (Bangladesh, Bhutan, India, Maldives, Nepal, Pakistan, Sri Lanka).* Delhi: Raj Enterprises, 1988.

SECONDARY SOURCES
T.N. Madan: Dilip Sen: A personal reminiscence. *Eastern Anthropologist* 26(1):5–7, 1973; K.S. Mathur: Dilip Kumar Sen, 1921–1972. *Eastern Anthropologist* 26(1):1–4, 1973; C.T. Thomas: Reminiscences in the service of the Anthropological Survey of India. In: K.S. Singh (ed) *The history of the Anthropological Survey of India.* Calcutta: ASI, 1991.

Şenyürek, Muzaffer Süleyman (1915–1961)

Born in İzmir (Turkey), Şenyürek studied biological anthropology, on a scholarship from the Turkish government, at Harvard University, where he received his Ph.D. in 1939 for his thesis, *A Metric Approach to the Study of the Evolution of Human Dentition.* His principal adviser at Harvard was Earnest A. Hooton (1887–1954). On returning to Turkey in 1940, Şenyürek began his academic career as a docent (associate professor) in the Faculty of Languages, History, and Geography (D.T.C.F.)

in Ankara. In 1958, he was installed in the newly created Chair of Paleoanthropology, and at the same time promoted to the rank of *professor ordinarius*, a title also held by Şevket Aziz Kansu (1903–1983), the founder of modern anthropology in Turkey. Following in the footsteps of Kansu, he became the second anthropologist to serve as dean of the D.T.C.F. (1959–1960). Then, in 1961, while still in his prime, Şenyürek was killed in a plane crash near Ankara.

In addition to becoming a leading figure in Turkey, Şenyürek was also an internationally recognized authority in his field. His particular area of specialization was the study of the early Anatolians, with particular reference to their dentition and attending pathologies (cf. Şenyürek 1941a, 1947, 1956). Springing from this interest was his collaborative work with İsmail Kılıç Kökten (1904–1974) at Karain (Antalya) and the subsequent recovery of fossil hominid teeth, which Şenyürek identified as Neandertal (cf. Şenyürek 1949a). Shortly before his death, he completed a study of the dentition of the Shanidar infant (1959).

From a historical viewpoint, it is noteworthy that he was among the few workers during the 1940s to endorse the hominid status of the South African australopithecines (cf. Şenyürek 1941b). Also, while at Harvard, he was the first to study and publish on the fossil hominid mandible found near Rabat in Morocco in 1933. Şenyürek believed this specimen displayed morphological affinities to the European Neandertals (cf. Şenyürek 1940). He was also an early proponent of the multidisciplinary approach in paleoanthropology. In all three instances, his viewpoint has prevailed.

Aygen Erdentuğ

See also Australopithecines; Hooton, E(arnest) A(lbert); Kansu, Şevket Aziz; Kökten, İsmail Kılıç; Shanidar (Iraq); Turkey.

Bibliography
SELECTED WORKS
Cranial equilibrium index. *American Journal of Physical Anthropology* 24:23–41, 1938; *Fossil man in Tangier.* [With an introduction by C.S. Coon]. Papers of the Peabody Museum. Vol. 16. No. 3. Cambridge, Massachusetts: Peabody Museum, Harvard University, 1940; A craniological study of the Copper Age and Hittite populations of Anatolia. *Belleten (Türk Tarih Kurumu)* 5:237–253, 1941a; The dentition

of *Plesianthropus* and *Paranthropus*. *Annals of the Transvaal Museum* (Pretoria) 20:203–302, 1941b; A note on the duration of life of the ancient inhabitants of Anatolia. *American Journal of Physical Anthropology* 5 (n.s.): 55–56, 1947; A short preliminary report of the two fossil teeth discovered from the cave at Karain under the auspices of the Turkish Historical Association. *Belleten (Türk Tarih Kurumu)* 13:835–836, 1949a; Taurodontism among the ancient inhabitants of Anatolia. *Belleten (Türk Tarih Kurumu)* 13:221–227, 1949b; A study of the Pontian fauna of Gökdere (Elmadağ) southeast of Ankara. *Belleten (Türk Tarih Kurumu)* 16:449–492, 1952; Order of eruption of the permanent teeth in the Chalcolithic and Copper Age inhabitants of Anatolia. *Belleten (Türk Tarih Kurumu)* 20:1–28, 1956; *A study of the deciduous teeth of the fossil Shanidar infant: A comparative study of the milk teeth of fossil men.* Ankara: Türk Tarih Kurumu Basımevi, 1959.

ARCHIVAL SOURCES

M. Şenyürek Papers: National Anthropological Papers, National Museum of Natural History, Smithsonian Institution, Washington, D.C. 20560.

SECONDARY SOURCES

A. Erdentuğ: A.Ü.D.T.C.F. antropoloji bibliyografyası, 1935–1983 [Bibliography of anthropology, D.T.C.F., Ankara University, 1935–1983]. *Antropoloji* 12:489–496, 1985; A. Sayılı: Ordinaryüs Prof. Dr. Muzaffer Şenyürek, 1915–1961. *Belleten (Türk Tarih Kurumu)* 26:181–200, 1962.

Sera, Gioacchino Leo (1878–1960)

Born in Rome, Italy, Sera was trained in medicine and surgery at the University of Rome. He attended the Institutes of Anthropology of Rome, Florence, and Bologna. In Bologna, he obtained his license to teach anthropology in 1911, and from 1911 to 1925 he taught anthropology at the University of Pavia. In 1913, he founded, at Pavia, the Institute of Anthropology and the *Journal for the Morphology of Man and Primates*, which was the primary outlet for his own work and that of his students. He taught for one year at the University of Milan (1924–1925), whereupon he was appointed professor of anthropology at the University of Naples, where he remained until his retirement.

Sera was primarily concerned with methodological questions. He developed a model for recording cranial indices and also devised a special system of evaluation of the facial form in different races, along with the instruments for this evaluation. He also did research in paleoprimatology and paleoanthropology, expressed original ideas on the nature of the Neandertals and on the origins of human bipedality, and served as editor of the anthropology section of the *Enciclopedia Italiana*.

Sera died in Florence on 7 May 1960.

Brunetto Chiarelli

See also Italy; Neandertals

Bibliography

SELECTED WORKS

Nuove osservazioni ed induzioni sul cranio di Gibraltar. *Archivio per l'Antropologia e la Etnologia* 39:151–212, 1909; Di alcuni caratteri importanti sinora non rivelati nel cranio di Gibraltar. *Atti della Società Romana di Antropologia* 15:197–208, 1910; Un preteso Hominida miocenico *Sivapithecus indicus*. *Natura* 8:149–173, 1917a; La testimonianza dei fossili di antropomorfi per la questione dell'origine dell'uomo. *Atti della Società Italiana di Scienze Naturali* 56:1–156, 1917b; I caratteri morfologici di *Paleopropithecus* e l'adattamento acquatico primitivo dei Mammiferi e dei Primati in particolare. *Archivio Italiano di Anatomia e di Embriologia* 35:229–270, 1935; Alcuni caratteri scheletrici di importanza ecologia e filetica nei Lemuri fossili ed attuali. *Paleontographia Italica* 38:1–112, 1938; Ulteriori osservazioni sui lemuri fossili ed attuali. *Paleontographia Italica* 47:1–113, 1950.

Sergi, Giuseppe (1841–1936)

Born in Messina, Sicily, Sergi originally intended to study law but postponed it in order to follow Giuseppe Garibaldi (1807–1882) in his campaign to unify the Kingdom of Italy. His military action included taking part in the battle of Milazzo (Sicily) in 1860. After the war, he returned to his studies at the University of Messina, focusing on comparative philology and philosophy, but he subsequently was attracted by Charles Darwin's evolutionary thesis. From this and a general biological perspective, Sergi began to concern himself with human psychology viewed from a physiological standpoint, which led him to write a book on the subject, *Elementi di psicologia* (which was translated into French in 1888 under the title *La psychologie physiologique*). Published in two parts in 1873 and 1874, this work was widely acclaimed in and outside of Italy and subsequently brought Sergi to the attention of Francesco De Sanctis (1817–1883), the founder of modern literary criticism in Italy. At the time, De Sanctis was serving in the government, and in 1880 he conferred upon Sergi the responsibility for teaching anthropology in the Faculty of Letters at the University of Bologna. However, in accepting this invitation, Sergi, like his contemporary and colleague Paolo Mantegazza (1831–1910) in Florence (*vide infra*), requested that his professorial position be transferred to the Faculty of Sciences. Although this was finally achieved in 1883, the following year he transferred to the University of Rome, where he was appointed to the Chair of Anthropology in the Faculty of Sciences. Sergi remained at the University of Rome until his retirement in 1916.

In Rome, Sergi continued to study psychology from a physiological point of view, and in 1889 he established there—and directed—the Laboratorio di Psicologia Sperimentale as a new section of the university's Istituto di Antropologia. This was the first laboratory of its kind in Europe and, as such, attracted considerable attention in the scientific community. Sergi was also instrumental in the founding in 1893 of the Società Romana di Antropologia (SRA) and its journal, *Atti della Società Romana di Antropologia*. In 1911, the *Atti* became the *Rivista di Antropologia*, and in 1937 the SRA was renamed the Istituto Italiano di Antropologia, having gained an international reputation.

With his gathering fame, Sergi attracted scores of students to Rome seeking his tutelage. Among them was Vincenzo Giuffrida Ruggeri (1872–1921), who after serving as Sergi's assistant was appointed to the Chair of Anthropology at the University of Naples in 1907. Fabio Frassetto (1876–1953) and Enrico Tedeschi (1860–1931) were two other notable former assistants. Frassetto received the Chair of Anthropology at the University of Bologna in 1908, while Tedeschi, who was also a cofounder of the SRA, received the Chair of Anthropology at the University of Padua in 1903.

Sergi's scientific interests and knowledge were truly phenomenal, embracing history, philosophy, philology, psychology, ethnology, biology, anthropology, and sociology. His published works span a period beginning in 1868 and ending in 1936. From 1879 to 1893, Sergi's view of anthropology was very traditional, particularly with regard to the

employment of craniometry in racial classifications. However, in 1893 he presented a new method of classifying and arranging crania, at the International Congress of Anthropology in Moscow (Sergi 1893). This method focused on the general conformation of the skull. This and his subsequent rejection of earlier racial classifications sparked a controversy in Italian anthropological circles that led Sergi to break away from the Florentine school of thought established by Mantegazza, and to establish the SRA. It was this descriptive method of studying crania that Sergi employed in his equally controversial book on the *Origine e Diffusione della Stirpe Mediterranea* (1895). In it, he presented a general classification of humankind that he used to support a polygenistic scheme for the origin of the human genus. This latter issue was strongly contested, and among those who debated Sergi was his former assistant Giuffrida Ruggeri, who favored monogenist interpretation.

Sergi died in Rome on 17 October 1936.

Brunetto Chiarelli
Giuseppe D'Amore

See also Frassetto, Fabio; Giuffrida Ruggeri, Vincenzo; Italy; Mantegazza, Paolo; Tedeschi, Enrico

Bibliography
SELECTED WORKS

Elementi di psicologia. Milano: Rivara, 1879; *Antropologia fisica della Fuegia*. Roma: Centenari, 1888; *Antropologia e scienze antropologiche*. Messina: Stefano, 1889a; *Le degenerazioni umane*. Milano: Dumolard, 1889b; *Le varietà umane: Principi e metodo di classificazione*. Torino: Bruno, 1893. English translation: *The varieties of the human species and methods of classification*. Washington, D.C.: Smithsonian Institution, 1894; *Origine e diffusione della stirpe mediterranea: Induzioni antropologiche*. Roma: Società-Editrice Dante Alighieri, 1895. Translated and revised by G. Sergi as: *The Mediterranean race: A study of the origin of European peoples*. London: Scott, 1901; *Africa: antropologia della stirpe camitica (specie euroafricana)*. Torino: Bocca, 1897.

Specie e varietà umana: Saggio di una sistematica antropologica. Torino: Bocca, 1900; *L'evoluzione umana individuale e sociale*. Torino: Bocca, 1904; *Europa: l'origine dei popoli europei e loro relazioni coi popoli d'Africa e d'Oceania*. Milano: Bocca, 1908; *L'apologia del mio poligenismo*. *Atti della Società Romana di Antropologia* 15:187–195, 1909;

Paleontologie sud-americaine. *Scientia* 8:465–475, 1910; *Hominidae: L'uomo secondo le origini, l'antichità, le variazioni e la distribuzione geografica: Sistema naturale di classificazione.* Torino: Bocca, 1911; *L'evoluzione organica e le origini umane. Induzioni paleontologiche.* Torino: Bocca, 1914a; La mandibola umana. *Rivista di Antropologia* 19:119–168, 1914b; La testimonianza dei fossili di antropomorfi per la questione dell'origine dell'uomo. *Atti della Società Italiana di Scienze Naturali* 56: 1–156, 1917.

ARCHIVAL SOURCES

G. Sergi Papers: 1. Museo di Antropologia "Sergio Sergi"; 2. Istituto Italiano di Antropologia, Università di Roma, "La Sapienza," Piazzale Aldo Moro 5, 00185 Roma, Italia.

SECONDARY SOURCES

Anon: G. Sergi [Necrologio]. *Rivista di Antropologia* 46:vi–xlvii, 1936; A. Mochi: La discriminazione delle forme craniensi ed il sistema del Sergi. *Archivio per l'Antropologia e l'Etnologia* 37:87–126, 1908; S. Puccini: Sergi, Giuseppe. In: C. Winters (ed) *International dictionary of anthropologists.* New York: Garland, 1991, pp. 631–632; S. Sergi: Opere e memorie di Giuseppe Sergi: Elenco bibliografico, 1868–1936. *Rivista di Antropologia* 31:xi–xxvii, 1935–1937.

Sergi, Sergio (1878–1972)

Born in Messina, Sicily, Sergi, like his father Giuseppe Sergi (1841–1936), was attracted to anthropology—but unlike him he first secured training in medicine at the University of Rome, from which he graduated in 1902. Following graduation, he won a foreign scholarship to study in Berlin, where he studied neuroanatomy and physiology under Wilhelm von Waldeyer (1836–1921) at the University of Berlin's Institute of Anatomy and anthropology under Felix von Luschan (1854–1924) at the Institute of Anthropology. On returning to Rome in 1908, Sergi obtained his teaching license. From 1916 to 1925, he was in charge of teaching anthropology at the Faculty of Science at the University of Rome, and from 1926 to 1951 he was also the director of the university's Institute of Anthropology. In 1925, he was named the titular head of the institute.

Although Sergi's interests in anthropology were broad, his particular specialties were comparative neuroanatomy and myology.

Some of his more noted studies were on the vertebromedullary topography of chimpanzees and the cerebral sulci in different human races. He conducted important studies in skeletal biomechanics from which he determined several planes of physiological orientation for different parts of the skeleton—for example, his work on the determination of the planes of the human skull (1919) and on the correct orientation of the skull and postcranial bones for craniographic and osteographic purposes (1949–1950). He also identified the verticality of the basion-bregma axis of the skull. In addition, he designed several anthropometric instruments, such as the pantagoniostat-cranio-osteophore, which enables an investigator to determine the contours of the skull or other bones on various planes. It also allows for the measurement of several angles of slope of the bone in three dimensions.

In 1934, Sergi participated in the anthropological mission to Fezzan (central Libya), which resulted in a study of the skeletal remains recovered from a necropolis dated from the fifth century B.C. to the fourth century A.D. He also made a number of important studies of Italian fossil hominids, in particular the remains recovered in 1939 and 1950 at San Felice Circeo, as well as those discovered in the gravel quarry of Saccopastore in 1929 and 1934, respectively.

These studies led Sergi to undertake a comprehensive survey of the available European hominid fossil record. He found that in all of the paleoanthropic remains, the occipital foramen had the same position as in modern humans. To him, this was a clear indication of erect posture. His findings also suggested to him (contrary to what most workers believed at that time) that there was a probable genetic connection between some Neandertaloid populations and early-modern *Homo sapiens*—though, in his opinion, the only "true" Neandertals of the Würm glaciation contributed nothing! Using the terms "Palaeanthropi," "Prophaneranthropi," and "Phaneranthropi," Sergi endeavored to explain the phylogenetic history of modern *Homo sapiens.* According to him, the Phaneranthropi, or morphologically modern humans, were derived from the Prophaneranthropi, which had made their appearance during the Early Middle Pleistocene. The Prophaneranthropi, represented by such specimens as Swanscombe, Saccopastore, and Steinheim, were considered by Sergi to be a blend of Palaeanthropi (i.e., Neandertal) and modern *H. sapiens.* In Sergi's opinion, the Prophaneranthropi had been the "common forerunner" of both the more specialized Neandertals and modern humans—though he left unexplained the circumstances leading to the appearance of the Phaneranthropi and "final extinction" of the Palaeanthropi.

Sergi was a member of several scientific societies in Italy and abroad. He held the office of secretary of the Istituto Italiano di Antropologia (IIA) from 1913 to 1943, and again from 1947 to 1967. After the fall of Benito Mussolini's fascist regime in 1944, Sergi was appointed by the new government to be the IIA's commissary for proposing the requirements necessary for its reorganization. He was also asked to prepare a text of new statutes. All of his recommendations were approved.

Sergi died in Rome on 22 June 1972.

Brunetto Chiarelli
Giuseppe D'Amore

See also Italy; Luschan, Felix Ritter Edler von; Modern Human Origins; Neandertals; Neuroanatomy; Saccopastore; Sergi, Giuseppi

Bibliography
SELECTED WORKS

Metodo per la determinazione dei piani del cranio. *Rivista di Antropologia* 23:241–244, 1919; Studi sul midollo spinale dello scimpanze. *Rivista di Antropologia* 24:301–387 (1920–1921), 25:375–372 (1922–1923); La scoperta di un cranio del tipo Neanderthal presso Roma. *Rivista di Antropologia* 28:457–462, 1929; Il cervello nelle razze umane e negli antropomorfi. *Enciclopedia Italiana* 9:845–858, 1931; Sulle variazioni di forma e di posizione dell'osso temporale nell'uomo. *Rivista di Antropologia* 31:373–408, 1935–1937; Der Neanderthaler des Monte Circeo. *Zeitschrift für Rassenkunde* 10:113–119, 1939.

Sulle variazioni di posizione dell'osso zigomatico nell'uomo. *Rivista di Antropologia* 33:287–334, 1942a; La topografia dell'osso zigomatico nell'uomo in relazione ai problemi dell'architettura del cranio e della faccia. *Accademia Nazionale dei Lincei* 7:195–198, 1942b; Sulla morfologia cerebrale del secondo paleantropo di Saccopastore. *Rivista di Antropologia* 34, 1943; Craniometria e craniografia del primo paleantropo di Saccopastore. *Ricerche di Morfologia* 20–21:733–791, 1944; Il secondo paleantropo di Saccopastore. *Rivista di Antropologia* 36:3–95, 1948a; Sulla morfologia della "facies anterior corporis maxillae" nei paleantropi di Saccopastore e del Monte Circeo. *Accademia Nazionale dei Lincei* 8:391–394, 1948b.

The Paleantropi in Italy: The fossil man of Saccopastore and Circeo. *Yearbook of Physical Anthropology* (1948) 57–65, 76–79, 1949; Pantogoniostat-ocranioosteophore and axidiateter. *Rivista di Antropologia* 37:202–218, 1949–1950; I Prophanerantropi di Swanscome e di Fontechévade. *Accademia Nazionale dei Lincei* 15:601–608, 1953; Die neandertalischen Palaeanthropen in Italien. In: G.H.R. von Koenigswald (ed) *Hundert Jahre Neanderthaler*. Utrecht: Kemink en Zoon, 1958, pp. 38–51; I tipi umani piú antichi: Preominidi ed ominidi fossili. In: R. Biasutti (ed) *Razze e popoli della Terra*. 4th ed. Torino: U.T.E.T., 1967, pp. 84–162; (with A. Ascenzi) La mandibola Neanderteliana Circeo III (Mandibola B). *Rivista di Antropologia* 42:337–403, 1955.

ARCHIVAL SOURCES

S. Sergi Papers: 1. Museo di Antropologia "Sergio Sergi"; 2. Istituto Italiano di Antropologia, Università di Roma, "La Sapienza," Piazzale Aldo Moro 5, 00185 Roma, Italia.

SECONDARY SOURCES

V. Correnti: Commemorazione del Prof. Sergio Sergi ed elenco dei suoi scritti. *Rivista di Antropologia* 58:7–34, 1972–1973.

Shanidar (Iraq)

The large cave of Shanidar is located in the Zagros Mountains of Iraqi Kurdistan, northwest of Rowanduz, close to where the borders of Iraq, Iran, and Turkey meet. This region has been occupied for much of the twentieth century by local Kurdish peoples, and it remained largely so during the period from 1951 to 1960 when archeological excavations took place within the cave.

The site was discovered in 1951 by the American archeologist Ralph S. Solecki during an archeological survey of northeastern Iraq that was undertaken with the express purpose of finding a promising cave to excavate. In 1951, Solecki dug a small test pit in the middle of the cave, and later he returned to place a deeper sounding through the deposits. This sounding established the basic stratigraphy, with Layers D to A being sequentially Middle Paleolithic, early Upper Paleolithic (Baradostian), Mesolithic and proto-Neolithic, and Neolithic to modern. Excavations, primarily enlarging the sounding to bedrock (at ca. 14 m below datum), continued in 1953, 1956–1957, and 1960. Political difficulties between the Iraqi government and (sequentially) the Kurds, the Iranians, the allies of Operation Desert Storm in 1992, and again the Kurds have prevented additional excavation at the cave since 1960. However, in the early 1960s and from 1976 to 1980 the human remains in the Iraq Museum, Baghdad, have been restored and analyzed.

During excavations, remains of nine individuals were found in the Middle Paleolithic levels, in addition to a dozen or so individuals from the proto-Neolithic levels (Layer B1). The Middle Paleolithic hominids were associated with two concentrations of cultural debris, one near the top of Layer D (Shanidar 1, 3, and 5) and other near the middle of Layer D (Shanidar 2, 4, 6, 8, and 9).

The first discovered human fossil remains were that of a crushed but largely complete and articulated infant (ca. nine months old) skeleton, first called the "Shanidar child" but later numbered Shanidar 7. It was turned over to Muzaffer Süleyman Şenyürek (1915–1961), a Turkish physical anthropologist trained at Harvard University, who recovered a few of the bones but described the largely complete and unworn deciduous dentition in detail, using its morphology to propose a new subspecies of *Homo sapiens*, *H. sapiens shanidarensis* (Şenyürek 1959). Further analysis of the Shanidar fossils suggests that this subspecies designation is unwarranted.

The 1956–1957 season yielded three adult partial skeletons, Shanidar 1, 2, and 3. Shanidar 1, with most of the postcranial skeleton and a largely complete skull, received most of the attention, with a few comments on the extensively crushed Shanidar 2 remains. In the meantime, Şenyürek was killed in an airplane crash, so the study of the remains was turned over to Solecki's American colleague at the Smithsonian Institution, T. Dale Stewart (1910–). During 1957, Stewart restored most of the Shanidar 1 skeleton and published preliminary reports on it, concentrating initially on the skull (cf. Stewart 1958). The 1960 season was even more productive, yielding more of Shanidar 3; an isolated partial skeleton, Shanidar 5; plus a multiple burial containing an articulated skeleton on top (Shanidar 4), a partially articulated skeleton immediately below (Shanidar 6), and pieces of another adult (Shanidar 8) and an infant (Shanidar 9). Soil samples associated with Shanidar 4, later analyzed by Arlette Leroi-Gourhan (1968), yielded abundant wildflower

pollen; this led to the designation of this burial as the "Flower Burial" (Solecki 1971). This remains a unique case in the Middle Paleolithic that continues to provide fuel for speculation on Middle Paleolithic burial practices.

The Shanidar partial skeletons were stored in the Iraq Museum, with the exception of Shanidar 3, which went to the Smithsonian Institution, Washington, D.C. In 1960 and 1962, Stewart completed restoration of most of Shanidar 2 and much of Shanidar 4 and 6, writing preliminary descriptions of them plus comparative analyses of Neandertal pubic, scapular, and cervical vertebral morphology, using the Shanidar remains as a starting point (cf. Stewart 1961, 1962a, 1962b). Subsequent attention through the late 1960s and early 1970s was focused on the "Flower Burial" and the multiple lesions on the Shanidar 1 skeleton (the latter becoming the prototype for the shaman in Jean M. Auel's novel *Clan of the Cave Bear* published in 1980). In the later 1970s, Stewart completed a summary of his findings on the Shanidar adult fossils (1977), and in 1975, with Solecki's support, he turned the completion of the paleontological analysis of the remains over to the American paleoanthropologist Erik Trinkaus.

Trinkaus and Stewart completed the description of the Shanidar 3 skeleton, and then Trinkaus, in a series of articles culminating in a monograph on the fossils (1983), restored the Shanidar 5 skeleton, completed the reconstruction of the Shanidar 2, 4, 6, and 9 remains, re-sorted the Shanidar 4, 6, and 8 remains (which had been mixed *in situ*), and described all of them in the context of other Near Eastern and European later Pleistocene human remains. Since then, the Shanidar remains have been integrated into the Near Eastern human fossil record and the ongoing debates concerning the relationship between late archaic and early modern humans in that region.

The Shanidar human fossil sample consists of four older adult males (1, 3, 4, and 5), a young adult male (2), two young adult females (6 and 8), and two infants (7 and 9). They derive from two temporal samples, which were initially assigned to the early last glacial. Redating of the early Middle Paleolithic to the late Middle Pleistocene, plus morphological consideration of the earlier Shanidar fossils, suggests that the two samples derive from last interglacial and early last glacial deposits. Their morphology indicates a postcranial pattern characteristic of all known later Pleistocene archaic humans. Their dentitions show size proportions and wear patterns similar to those of Levantine archaic humans and European Neandertals. The earlier sample has faces that are generally archaic, similar to those of many late Middle Pleistocene humans; whereas the later sample exhibits faces very similar to those of European Neandertals. This facial similarity to Neandertals, especially in the more complete Shanidar 1 skull, led to the designation of the sample as "the Shanidar Neanderthals" by Stewart, and then Trinkaus. However, it is now more generally recognized (Trinkaus 1991) that most of the morphology of the Shanidar individuals only identifies them as late archaic humans. The exceptions are the facial configurations of the later Shanidar 1 and 5 individuals, plus some aspects of the temporal region of Shanidar 1, which show clear affinities to European Neandertals. This has been explained as the product of (1) essentially parallel European and Near Eastern evolution of late archaic humans (Trinkaus 1983), (2) migration in the early Last Glacial from Europe (Bar-Yosef 1988), and (3) parallel trends combined with an east–west cline maintained by gene flow between the Near East and Europe (Trinkaus 1991). The last scenario perhaps best explains the currently available data, but it is subject to refinement as more data become available from eastern Europe and Anatolia.

Erik Trinkaus

See also Neandertals; Şenyürek, Muzaffer Süleyman; Stewart, T(homas) Dale; Turkey

Bibliography
J.M. Auel: *The clan of the cave bear.* New York: Crown, 1980; O. Bar-Yosef: The date of southwest Asian Neandertals. In: E Trinkaus (ed): L'Homme de Néandertal 3: L'Anatomie. *Etudes et Recherches Archéologiques de l'Université de Liège.* 30:31–38, 1988; A. Leroi-Gourhan: Le Néanderthalien IV de Shanidar. *Comptes rendus de la Société Préhistorique Française* 65:79–83, 1968; M. Şenyürek: *A study of the deciduous teeth of the fossil Shanidar infant.* Ankara: Türk Tarih Kurumu Basimevi, 1959; R.S. Solecki: *Shanidar: The first flower people.* New York: Knopf, 1971; T.D. Stewart: First view of the restored Shanidar I Neanderthal skeleton in Baghdad, Iraq. *Sumer* 14:90–96, 1958.

T.D. Stewart: The skull of Shanidar II. *Sumer* 17:97–106, 1961; T.D. Stewart: Neanderthal cervical vertebrae with special attention to the Shanidar Neanderthals from Iraq. *Bibliotheca Primatologica* 1:130–154, 1962a; T.D. Stewart: Neanderthal scapulae with special attention to the Shanidar Neanderthals from Iraq. *Anthropos* 57:779–800, 1962b; T.D. Stewart: The Neanderthal skeletal remains from Shanidar Cave, Iraq: A summary of findings to date. *Proceedings of the American Philosophical Society* 121:121–165, 1977; E. Trinkaus: *The Shanidar Neandertals.* New York: Academic Press, 1983; E. Trinkaus: Les Hommes fossiles de la Grotte de Shanidar, Irak: Evolution et continuité parmi les hommes archaïques tardifs du Proche-Orient. *L'Anthropologie* 95:535–572, 1991.

Shapiro, Harry Lionel (1902–1990)

Born in Boston, Massachusetts, Shapiro attended Boston Latin School before entering Harvard University. On graduating magna cum laude in 1923, he stayed on to become Earnest A. Hooton's (1887–1954) first Ph.D. (1926) in physical anthropology. His doctoral thesis was on the hybrid descendants of the *Bounty* mutineers who had migrated from Pitcairn to Norfolk Island (*vide infra*). Following completion of his graduate studies, he was hired by Clark Wissler (1870–1947) in the Department of Anthropology at the American Museum of Natural History (AMNH), New York City, where, except for occasional field expeditions, he remained for the duration of his professional career. From 1942 to 1970 (when he officially retired), he was chairman of the department. After his retirement, he was curator emeritus. In addition to his many museum duties, he was also an adjunct professor of anthropology at Columbia University from 1938 to 1973.

Shapiro's doctoral study of the *Bounty* descendants on Norfolk Island was the beginning of a lifelong interest in the anthropology of Oceania and the Far East in general. Prior to World War II, he was particularly energetic in this arena, and during this period he produced two of his most significant and enduring publications, *The Heritage of the Bounty* (1936) and *Migration and Environment* (1939). In the *Heritage* volume, he revisited his doctoral research from the perspective of his observations and comparisons of populations on Norfolk and Pitcairn Islands made during September 1934 and February 1935. This work enabled him to muster further evidence to refute the claim made by workers such as Charles B. Davenport (1866–1944) and Morris Steggarda (1900–1950) that racial cross-breeding resulted in biologically inferior offspring (cf. Davenport & Steggarda 1929; Davenport 1917). Similarly, the *Migration and Environment* volume assaulted another "dangerous myth" of the period, that hereditary characteristics were stable entities. Although a seminal study of the descendants of immigrants born in the United States made at the close of the first decade of the twentieth century by the Columbia University anthropologist Franz Boas (1858–1942) had clearly undermined this proposition, the results of Boas' study had been widely resisted (cf. Boas 1912). In his *Migration* volume, Shapiro presented evidence supporting the Boasian thesis. Originally, Shapiro had intended to compare two oriental immigrant populations living in Hawaii and their respective relatives in China and Japan. However, for reasons no longer clear, only the Japanese data was published, showing that, on average, the Hawaiian offspring of Japanese migrants were not only distinctly taller than their parents and relatives (living in Japan), but they were also characterized by a number of other anthropometric changes. It is interesting to note that much of the Japanese anthropometric data was collected by Frederick Seymour Hulse (1906–1990), then a graduate student in physical anthropology at Harvard University; while the unpublished Chinese data was collected by the Harvard graduate William A. Lessa (1908–), who later received his Ph.D. in anthropology at the University of Chicago in 1938. Among Shapiro's other books is *Peking Man* (1974), which recounts his involvement in the fruitless efforts to recover the Zhoukoudian materials that were lost during World War II.

During his career, he held offices in several national anthropological organizations: vice president of the American Association of Physical Anthropologists (1941–1942), president of the American Ethnological Society (1942–1943), president of the American Anthropological Association (1948), and president of the American Eugenics Society (1955–1962). He was elected to the National Academy of Sciences in 1949 and a recipient of the Theodore Roosevelt Distinguished Service Medal in 1964 and the T. Dale Stewart Award for Distinguished Service, which was bestowed on him by the American Academy of Forensic Science in 1983.

Shapiro died in New York on 7 January 1990.

Frank Spencer

See also American Association of Physical Anthropologists; Boas, Franz; Davenport, Charles Benedict; Growth Studies; Harvard University; Hooton, E(arnest) A(lbert); Hulse, Frederick Seymour; Zhoukoudian

Bibliography
SELECTED WORKS

The heritage of the Bounty: The story of Pitcairn Island through six generations. London: Simon & Schuster, 1936; *Migration and environment: A study of the physical characteristics of Japanese immigrants to Hawaii and the effects of environment on their descendants.* London: Oxford University Press, 1939; *Aspects of culture.* New Brunswick: 1956a; (ed) *Man, culture, and society.* New York: Oxford University Press, 1956b; *The Jewish people: A biological history.* Paris: UNESCO, 1960; *Peking Man.* New York: Simon & Schuster, 1974.

ARCHIVAL SOURCES

H.L. Shapiro Papers: Library, American Museum of Natural History, Central Park West at 79th Street, New York, New York 10024.

SECONDARY SOURCES

C.B. Davenport: The effects of race intermingling. *Proceedings of the American Philosophical Society* 56:364–368, 1917; C.B. Davenport & M. Steggarda: *Race crossing in Jamaica.* Carnegie Institution of Washington Publication No. 395. Washington, D.C.: Carnegie Institution, 1929; W.W. Howells: Obituary: Harry Lionel Shapiro, 1902–1990. *American Journal of Physical Anthropology* 83:499–500, 1990; F.S. Hulse: Habits, habitats, and heredity: A brief history of studies in human plasticity. *American Journal of Physical Anthropology* 56:495–501, 1981. F. Spencer: Harry Lionel Shapiro 1902–1990. *National Academy of Sciences Biographical Memoirs* 70:3–21, 1996.

Sheldon, William H(erbert) (1898–1977)

Born in Warwick, Rhode Island, Sheldon attended Brown University as an undergraduate, getting his B.S. in 1918. He received a master's in psychology in 1923 from the University of Colorado, and a Ph.D. in psychology in 1925 from the University of Chicago.

As a graduate student, he met and became friends with Italian anthropologist Sante Naccarati (1887–1929), who was working at Columbia University in 1920 on possible relationships between physique and intelligence. Naccarati was himself a student of the Padua school of anthropology, which had been founded about 1885 by Achille di Giovanni (1839–1916), sometimes called the father of modern constitutional research. Giacinto Viola (b. 1870), one of Naccarati's teachers, was the most illustrious proponent of this school, and he had differentiated three morphological types: (1) the "microsplanchnic" (essentially the *habitus phthisicus* set up by Hippocrates [ca. 460–377 B.C.] and the "asthenic" or "leptosome" posited by the German psychiatrist Ernst Kretschmer [1888–1964]); (2) the "macrosplanchnic" (Hippocrates' *habitus apoplecticus* and Kretschmer's "pyknic"; and (3) "normosplanchnic" (an intermediate variation not entirely equivalent to Kretschmer's earlier category, the "athletic").

Sheldon was very much influenced by Naccarati. He planned future collaborations with Naccarati, but these plans were destroyed when Naccarati was killed in an automobile accident in 1929 while in Italy on holiday.

Sheldon entered medical school at the University of Wisconsin in 1929 and graduated in 1933. After completing his internship in 1934, he went to England and the Continent for two years. He met Kretschmer, who by that time had given up a three-way classification and was not tempted to adopt the system Sheldon was in the process of designing. He also met the psychiatrists Sigmund Freud, Alfred Adler, and Carl Jung, but it was primarily Kretschmer's studies of various psychotics and their physical types that had the most profound impact on Sheldon's psychological typology—for example, Kretschmer's findings that manic-depressives are pyknic and schizophrenics predominantly asthenic. (Sheldon's own later work supported these findings only in part).

In England, he met several important intellectuals, including Bertrand Russell, Christopher Isherwood, and the Huxley brothers, Julian and Aldous. His association with Aldous Huxley was particularly important because he accepted Sheldon's scheme and popularized it in his collection of essays, *Ends and Means* (1937) and *The Perennial Philosophy* (1947), in which he discussed its moral and ethical implications.

When he returned to the United States in 1936, Sheldon persuaded several institutions and the Universities of Chicago and Wisconsin to cooperate in the collecting of standardized photographs of the human body. These were to become the basis for his

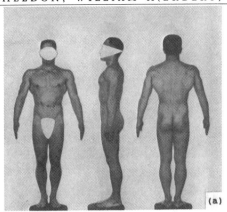

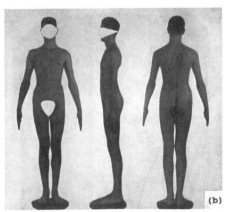

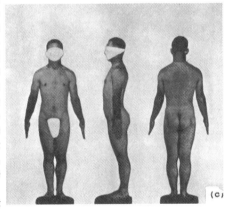

Fig. 1. Examples of Sheldon somatotypes. (a) 1–7–1; (b) 3–1–6; (c) 4–5–1. From Sheldon's Atlas of Men. *New York, 1954.*

somatotyping—a method for determining the overriding morphological structure of an individual according to the strengths of the three primary components Sheldon posited: "endomorphy," "mesomorphy," and "ectomorphy." An individual somatotype was designated in a series of three numbers showing the approximate strength of a component (1 being the lowest, 7 the highest). The numbers in such a series (e.g., 1–4–5 or 3–1–6) were always to refer to the components in the order given above: 1–4–5 would mean a 1 in endomorphy, and so on. Thus, a 1–7–1 would be the most extreme mesomorph. Sheldon developed a rule that the sum of the three component ratings should be no less than 9, no greater than 12 (see Fig. 1).

These components reflected the three-way scheme of Viola as opposed to the many competing two-way schemes. (The armchair psychoanalyst would probably say that being one of three children tipped the scales for Sheldon.) He originally used terms more reminiscent of Kretschmer's classification: "pyknosomic" instead of "endomorphic" (round, fat component) and "leptosomic" instead of "ectomorphic" (slim, linear component). Sheldon's "mesomorphic" (originally "somatosomic") was really new and refers to the muscular component.

The most ambitious part of his scheme was to correlate somatotype with temperament, which he characterized similarly in terms of three components. He dealt with sixty traits that were used in a scale for measuring the relative strength of these components. They were labeled: (1) "viscerotonia" (manifested by relaxation, love of food, sociality—a kind of extroversion), (2) "somatotonia" (bodily assertiveness and desire for muscular activity—another kind of extroversion), and (3) "cerebrotonia" (inhibition, restraint—introversion). Individuals were described with a number series identical in structure to the somatotyping formulas; for example, a 1–5–3 would be low in viscerotonia, highest in somatotonia, with a significant degree of cerebrotonia. Sheldon found it possible to characterize God in the Christian conception as a 7–7–7, and he spoke of "God in three persons—the somatotonic Father, the viscerotonic Son, and the cerebrotonic Holy Ghost" (Sheldon & Stevens 1942:146).

In 1938, he began work with Smith S. Stevens of Harvard, who collaborated with him on Sheldon's two most influential works *The Varieties of Human Physique* (Sheldon, Stevens, & Tucker 1940), and *The Varieties of Temperament* (Sheldon & Stevens 1942). The first of these was dedicated to the Harvard physical anthropologist Earnest A. Hooton (1887–1954), who was initially impressed by Sheldon's work and later modified somatotyping for his own use. Interestingly enough, however, although Sheldon is identified on the title pages of these books as having a Harvard affiliation, he never really held any formal (and salaried) academic position there.

In 1938, he began a study relating delinquency to physical type with his investigation of 200 boys at the Hayden Goodwill

Inn, Boston. World War II made him postpone this study, but he did complete it after his military service and published the results in *Varieties of Delinquent Youth* (Sheldon, Hartl, & McDermott 1949).

After the war, he began a collaboration with Barbara Honeyman Heath (now Roll), who emerged as one of the foremost proponents of somatotyping, though in a modified form. By this time, Sheldon had the general reputation of being "difficult," and earlier supporters such as Hooton had cooled somewhat. Heath herself (cf. Carter & Heath 1990) has noted a number of problems she experienced and has described him as a "racist male chauvinist" who showed contempt for anyone who wasn't of Anglo-Saxon descent. More tellingly, she has stated that he was "a 70-inch (178 cm) 3–3^1/$_2$–5 who saw himself as a 72-inch (183 cm) 2–4–5" (see the previous discussion of constitutional components). She put up with him until, she has said, he asked her to alter some somatotyping photographs to appear in his *Atlas of Men* (1954) to illustrate certain hypothetical somatotypes, namely 1–1–7 and 7–1–1 (apparently an instance of such an altered photograph is No. 1 in the *Atlas*; see Fig. 1). Heath refused, and soon thereafter their collaboration ended. In the 1950s, Sheldon abandoned his original somatotype scheme for a new one: the Trunk Index method, though he published relatively little about it.

Sheldon's contribution to physical anthropology was at least twofold: He introduced standardized photography into the study of physique differences, and he produced the most sophisticated way known at the time of classifying physiques. His terms for physical types—but not personality types—have entered the language. But his own work has been eclipsed by other approaches and concerns. One of the major criticisms had to do with the stability of somatotypes over a lifetime and can be summed up in questions such as, is an emaciated endomorph still an endomorph? Sheldon himself defined the somatotype as "a trajectory or pathway along which the living organism is destined to travel under average conditions of nutrition and in the absence of grossly disturbing pathology" (Sheldon, Dupertuis, & McDermott 1954:337). A somatotype is not a fixed point in time—although the use of somatotype photos may suggest this—but a master plan. One of the best examples of this is what Sheldon called a PPJ ("pyknic practical joke"), a female 4–4–2, who before marriage is extraordinarily slender, but "[a]fter marriage the joke is sprung" (Sheldon, Stevens, & Tucker 1940:199) and she becomes very fat. So Sheldon's answer to the question raised above is: Yes, an emaciated endomorph is an endomorph still. Most scholars were more skeptical.

Still more questionable are Sheldon's correlations of physique with temperament. Most reject them as unproved. Nearly twenty years after his death, Sheldon's work gained renewed notoriety because of the somatotype photographs themselves. An article in the *New York Times Magazine* (13 January 1995) entitled "The Posture Photo Scandal" presented an exposé of what was called the "bizarre ritual" of (formerly) requiring all students at Harvard, Yale, Wellesley, and other colleges and universities to be photographed in the nude by "cunning pseudoscientists" who were in cahoots with Sheldon. Presumably included among these students were George Bush (later U.S. president) and Hillary Rodham (later the wife of U.S. President Bill Clinton). A few weeks after this article appeared, the Smithsonian Institution shredded more than 100 pounds of the photographs and negatives taken at Yale. It is not known how many still exist from other institutions.

Although out of favor today, in their heyday Sheldon's ideas were influential in a number of disciplines, including criminology (his findings supported a form of Lombrosianism). He even seems to have influenced the founders of Alcoholics Anonymous in the 1930s.

Despite his wide appeal, his approach was remarkably narrow. For example, Sheldon seldom, if ever, took cultural factors into consideration. This is true in his discussion of Boris (cf. Sheldon & Stevens 1942), an extreme example of both somatotonia (1–7–1) and mesomorphy (1–6$^1/_2$–2). Boris' sexual life history is described without reference to the fact that his family was not college-educated and that he himself did not finish college: These are crucial variables in Alfred C. Kinsey et al.'s findings in *Sexual Behavior in the Human Male* (1948). Interestingly, Boris fits perfectly with Kinsey's findings—but they were published six years after Sheldon's report.

Sheldon was not one for undervaluing his own theory. For example, he argued that the classic interpretations of both World War I and World War II in terms of economics were shortsighted. "What might have been the story had they sought causes in the differential constitutional endowments of groups of men? . . . Had we been able to define

somatotonia, it is possible that we might have saved Germany from herself and ourselves from Germany" (Sheldon & Stevens 1942:432–433).

He died in 1977 in Cambridge, Massachusetts.

Edgar Gregersen

See also Body-Composition Studies; Growth Studies; Hippocrates; Hooton, E(arnest) A(lbert); Lombroso, Cesare

Bibliography
SELECTED WORKS
Psychology and the promethean will. New York: Harpers, 1936; *Prometheus revisited.* Cambridge, Massachusetts: Schenkman, 1969; (with C.W. Dupertuis & E. McDermott) *Atlas of men: A guide for somatotyping the adult male at all ages.* New York: Gramercy, 1954; (with E.M. Hartl & E. McDermott) *Varieties of delinquent youths: An introduction to constitutional psychiatry.* New York: Harper, 1949; (with D.C. Noland et al.) Psychotic patterns and physical constitution. In: D.V. Siva Sankar (ed) *Schizophrenia: Current concepts and research.* Hicksville, New York: P.J.D. Publications, 1969; (with S.S. Stevens) *The varieties of temperament: A psychology of constitutional differences.* New York: Harper, 1942; (with S.S. Stevens & W.B. Tucker) *The varieties of human physique: An introduction to constitutional psychology.* New York: Harper, 1940.

ARCHIVAL SOURCES
1. W.H. Sheldon Somatotyping Materials: National Anthropological Archives, National Museum of Natural History, Smithsonian Institution, Washington, D.C. 20560; 2. W.H. Sheldon Papers: Harvard University Library, Cambridge, Massachusetts 02138.

PRIMARY AND SECONDARY SOURCES
W.T. Austin: William Herbert Sheldon, 1898–1977. In: R. Martin, R.J. Mutchnick & W.T. Austin (eds): *Criminological thought: Pioneers past and present.* New York: Macmillan, 1990, pp. 119–136. J.E. Carter & B.H. Heath: *Somatotyping: Development and applications.* Cambridge: Cambridge University Press, 1990; R. Osborne: Sheldon. In: D. Sills (ed) *International encyclopedia of social sciences.* Biographical Supplement. New York: Free Press, 1986, p. 716; J.M. Tanner: Growth and

constitution. In: A.L. Kroeber (ed) *Anthropology today: An encyclopedic inventory.* Chicago: University of Chicago Press, 1953, pp. 750–770.

Simpson, George Gaylord (1902–1984)

Born in Chicago, Illinois, Simpson grew up in Denver, where as an undergraduate he studied geology at the University of Colorado (1918–1922). He received his Ph.D. from Yale University in 1926. While studying vertebrate paleontology at Yale, Simpson had the opportunity to learn about zoology. In 1927, he became assistant curator in the Department of Vertebrate Paleontology (DVP) at the American Museum of Natural History in New York; in 1945, he was named chairman of the DVP—a position he held until 1959. During this same time period, he was professor of geology at Columbia University. In 1959, he was appointed Alexander Agassiz Professor at Harvard University, a position he retained until 1970. In that year, he moved to the University of Arizona, where he spent the remainder of his career.

Among those who greatly influenced the direction of Simpson's work were his adviser at Yale, Richard S. Lull (1867–1957); the paleontologist William Diller Matthew (1871–1930) of the American Museum, for whom Simpson did fieldwork in 1924; and the geneticist Theodosius Dobzhansky (1900–1975).

Without question, Simpson's major work is the now classic book *Tempo and Mode in Evolution* (1944), a work that contributed to the modern evolutionary synthesis that began to emerge in the late 1930s and early 1940s (cf. Mayr & Provine 1980). In this context, Simpson attempted a synthesis of paleontology and genetics by assuming that some, if not all, mechanisms involved in paleontology are the same as those found in laboratory organisms, and asserting at the same time that only paleontologists can determine whether laboratory principles are sufficient to explain macroevolutionary phenomena. *Tempo and Mode* is, in a way, a system of loosely linked elements providing generalizations about evolution. Simpson argued that the evolutionary rate (or tempo) among fossil groups varies considerably and that population size is an important determinant for explaining it. By linking evolutionary rate, or tempo, with population size and equivalent selective pressure, he loosely linked the tempo of evolution with the pattern, or mode, of evolution—hence explaining his book's title.

In 1953, Simpson published *The Major Features of Evolution*, which can be regarded as an extension of his *Tempo and Mode* text. The most important difference between these two books is his treatment of the concept of quantum evolution. In its earlier form, it was explained in terms of small populations shifting from one adaptive peak to another through a nonadaptive phase, propelled by genetic drift (a nonselective mechanism). In the 1953 work, quantum evolution is depicted as a special case of phyletic evolution involving selective factors—though Simpson still retained the "conviction that the basic processes are the same at all levels of evolution, from local populations to phyla [and that the]. . .circumstances leading to higher levels are special and the cumulative results of the basic processes are characteristically different at different levels" (Gould 1980; cf. Simpson 1953, 1959b).

As a paleontologist, Simpson's contribution comes not so much from specific propositions about human evolution as from the clarification of evolutionary principles and taxonomic concepts. Among the "clarifications" are those he presented at the Cold Spring Harbor Symposia on Quantitative Biology (Simpson 1950b). There he discussed, among other things, the importance of the time dimension for determining phylogenetic relationships, the principles of morphology correlation, parallelism, convergence, divergence, reversibility, and trends. Later, at the Wenner-Gren conference on "Classification and Human Evolution," held at Burg Wartenstein in Austria in 1962 (cf. Simpson 1963), he stressed the biological meaning of taxonomy and its importance as an unambiguous language for scientific communication. In so doing, he noted the prevailing tendency in human paleontology at that time of naming individual fossils without any reference to a population, and the failure therein to understand the biological meaning of taxonomy.

Simpson died in Tucson, Arizona, on 6 October 1984.

Richard G. Delisle

See also Dobzhansky, Theodosius; Evolutionary Theory; Matthew, William Diller; Neo-Darwinism; Punctuated Equilibrium

Bibliography
SELECTED WORKS

Patterns of phyletic evolution. *Bulletin of the Geological Society of America* 47:303–314, 1937a; Supraspecific variation in nature and in classification. *American Naturalist* 71:236–267, 1937b; *Tempo and mode in evolution.* New York: Columbia University Press, 1944; Principles of classification and classification of mammals. *Bulletin of the American Museum of Natural History* 85:1–350, 1945; *The meaning of evolution.* New Haven, Connecticut: Yale University Press, 1949; Evolutionary determinism and the fossil record. *Scientific Monthly* 71:262–267, 1950a; Some principles of historical biology bearing on human origins. *Cold Spring Harbor Symposia on Quantitative Biology* 15:55–66, 1950b; *The major features of evolution.* New York: Columbia University Press, 1953; Mesozoic mammals and the polyphyletic origin of mammals. *Evolution* 13:405–414, 1959a.

The nature and origin of supraspecific taxa. *Cold Spring Harbor Symposia on Quantitative Biology* 24:255–271, 1959b; The history of life. In: S. Tax (ed) *Evolution after Darwin.* Vol. 1. Chicago: University of Chicago Press, 1960, pp. 117–180; *Principles of animal taxonomy.* New York: Columbia University Press, 1961; The meaning of taxonomic statements. In: S.L. Washburn (ed) *Classification and human evolution.* Chicago: Aldine, 1963, pp. 1–31; *This view of life.* New York: Harcourt, Brace & World, 1964; *Biology and man.* New York: Harcourt, Brace & World, 1969; The evolutionary concept of man. In: B. Campbell (ed) *Sexual selection and the descent of man.* Chicago: Aldine, 1972, pp. 17–39; Recent advances in methods of phylogenetic inference. In: W.P. Luckett and F. Szalay (eds) *Phylogeny of primates.* New York: Plenum, 1975, pp. 3–19.

ARCHIVAL SOURCES

1. G.G. Simpson Papers: Library, American Philosophical Society, 104 South Fifth Street, Philadelphia, Pennsylvania 19106–3387; 2. L.F. Laporte (ed): *Simple curiosity: Letters from George Gaylord Simpson to his family, 1921–1970.* Berkeley: University of California Press, 1987.

SECONDARY SOURCES

R.G. Delisle: Human paleontology and the evolutionary synthesis during the decade 1950–1960. In: R. Corbey & B. Theunissen (eds) *Man and ape: Changing views since 1600.* Proceedings of the *Pithecanthropus* Centennial Congress. Vol. 4. Leiden: Department of Prehistory, Leiden University, 1995; N. Eldredge: *Unfinished synthesis.* Oxford: Oxford University Press, 1985; S.J. Gould: G.G. Simpson, paleontology, and

the modern synthesis. In: E. Mayr & W.B. Provine (eds) *The evolutionary synthesis: Perspectives on the unification of biology.* Cambridge, Massachusetts: Harvard University Press, 1980, pp.153–172; L.F. Laporte: Simpson's *Tempo and mode in evolution* revisited. *Proceedings of the American Philosophical Society* 127:365–417, 1983; L.F. Laporte: George Gaylord Simpson as mentor and apologist for paleoanthropology. *American Journal of Physical Anthropology* 84:1–16, 1991; E. Mayr & W.B. Provine (eds): *The evolutionary synthesis. Perspectives on the unification of biology.* Cambridge, Massachusetts: Harvard University Press, 1980.

Šipka

On 26 August 1880, Karel J. Maška (1851–1916), who is credited by many as a founding force in Czech paleoanthropology and Paleolithic prehistory, recovered a fragment of a human lower jaw near the entrance of Šipka Cave (Schipka-Höhle in German), situated near Štramberk in northern Moravia (Czech Republic). The specimen consisted of the mandibular symphysis of a juvenile with three erupted permanent incisors and three other teeth (the right canine and premolars) still in their crypts. Maška's careful excavation demonstrated a direct association between the human specimen, Mousterian artifacts, Pleistocene animal remains, and traces of hearths. Because the specimen was found during the incipient stages of discussion of the role of Neandertals in human evolution, the Šipka specimen attracted considerable scientific attention.

The first description and assessment of this find was made by the German anatomist-anthropologist Hermann Schaaffhausen (1816–1893) (1880), who, based largely on the robust appearance of the specimen, attributed it to *Homo primigenius* (a term later synonymous with Neandertals). This conclusion was supported by the large size of the anterior teeth and the virtual absence of a mental eminence. However, attribution of the specimen to a Neandertal was immediately rejected by the German pathologist-anthropologist Rudolf Virchow (1821–1902). Virchow (1882) explained the robustness of the specimen by attributing it to an adult modern human characterized by the pathological retention of deciduous canines and molars. Much later, the French paleoanthropologist Marcellin Boule (1861–1942) dismissed it as too fragmentary to be diagnostic (1923:182); whereas his contemporary, the Czech-American physical anthropologist Aleš Hrdlička (1869–1943), noted: "The specimen makes a strong impression of primitiveness, and of a general relationship with the lower jaws of the Neanderthalers" (1930:313).

As this suggests, the morphology of the specimen is difficult to interpret. Part of this is due to its fragmentary status, and part is due to its juvenile age. There are also dating uncertainties, although a Middle Würm interstadial date is probable (Smith 1982). E. Vlček (1969) suggests Neandertal affinities, but with several progressive features. Metrically and morphologically, the specimen could be accommodated in either a late Neandertal or an early modern sample (cf. Smith 1982).

Fred H. Smith

See also Boule, Marcellin; Hrdlička, Aleš; Neandertals; Schaaffhausen, Hermann; Virchow, Rudolf

Bibliography
M. Boule: *Les hommes fossiles*. 2d ed. Paris: Masson, 1923; A. Hrdlička: *The skeletal remains of early man.* Smithsonian Miscellaneous Collections. No. 83. Washington, D.C.: Smithsonian Institution, 1930; J. Jelinek: Neanderthal man and *Homo sapiens* in central and eastern Europe. *Current Anthropology* 10:475–503, 1969; K. Maška: Über den diluvialen Menschen in Stramberg. *Mittheilungen der Anthropologischen Gesellschaft in Wien* 12:32–38, 1882; H. Schaaffhausen: Funde in der Schipkahöhle in Mähren. *Verhandlungen des naturhistorischen Vereins der preussischen Rheinlande und Westfalens* 37:260–264, 1880; F.H. Smith: Upper Pleistocene hominid evolution in south-central Europe: A review of the evidence and analysis of trends. *Current Anthropology* 23:667–703, 1982; R. Virchow: Der Kiefer aus der Schipka-Höhle und der Kiefer von La Naulette. *Zeitschrift für Ethnologie* 14:277–310, 1882; E. Vlček: *Neandertaler der Tsechechoslowakia*. Prague: Academia, 1969.

Siwaliks

The Siwalik Hills, or Siwalik range, form the southernmost belt of the Himalayan foothills that extend for more than 2,000 km across northern Pakistan and India—from the Indus River in the west to the Brahmapunta in the east. The name Siwalik comes from Sanskrit, meaning "belonging to Siva" (the Indian deity of destruction and reproduction), and it was originally restricted to a section of the range that runs from the Ganges River at Hardwār to the Beās River in the northwest. Geologically, the Siwalik range is composed of a thick sequence of sedimentary rocks spanning a period from the early Miocene to the Pleistocene; since the early nineteenth century, these sediments have yielded important collections of fossil fauna that include several important primate genera such as *Sivapithecus*, *Ramapithecus*, and *Gigantopithecus*.

The first major study of the Siwaliks was initiated in the early 1830s by Hugh Falconer (1808–1865), then curator of the botanical gardens at Sahāranpur in northern Uttar Pradesh. In addition to determining their Tertiary age, Falconer, assisted by the military engineer Proby Thomas Cautley (1802–1871), assembled the first major collection of Siwalik fossil fauna (ca. 1831–1840). A summary of this work can be found in their monograph, *Fauna antiqua sivalensis* (1846). Meanwhile, two other members of the British military working in the Siwalik Hills, William Erskine Baker (1808–1881) and Henry M. Durand (1812–1871), published the first description of an Asian fossil primate (Baker & Durand 1836). During this same time period, the English geologist William Vicary (1811–1903) discovered the rich fossiliferous Bugti Bone Beds. Expanding on Vicary's work in the 1880s, William T. Blandford (1832–1905) of the Geological Survey of India, concluded that these formations were the base of the Siwaliks (cf. Blandford 1883; *vide infra*).

The next major collection of Siwalik fossil fauna was made in the 1870s by British geologists William Theobald (1829–1908) and Francis Fedden, working in the Potwar Plateau and Sind (cf. Fedden 1879). The results of their labors were later described by the paleontologist Richard Lydekker (1849–1915) (1884). During this same time period, two members of the Indian Geological Survey, Henry B. Medlicott (1829–1905) and Arthur B. Wynne (1835–1906), demonstrated the correlation between the formations of the Potwar Plateau and the Siwalik Hills.

It was not until the opening decades of the twentieth century that a concerted effort was made to study the stratigraphy of this region. Prior to that time, the Siwalik deposits had been divided simply into a lower (unfossiliferous) and an upper (fossiliferous) section. In 1910, the British geologist and paleontologist Guy Ellock Pilgrim (1875–1943), who was attached to the Geological Survey of India from 1902 to 1930, subdi-

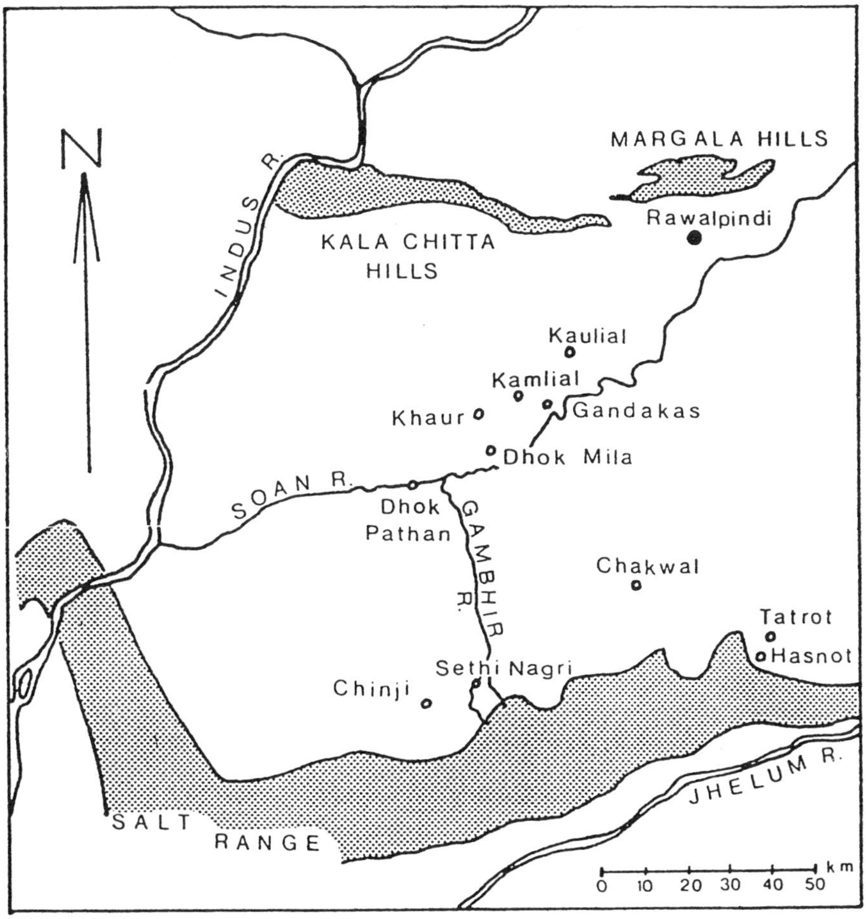

Fig. 1. The Potwar Plateau (Pakistan) showing the main fossiliferous areas. Courtesy of David Pilbeam.

vided the Siwalik deposits on the basis of faunal analysis into three stratigraphical units: Lower, Middle, and Upper (Pilgrim 1910). At the same time, he adopted the Potwar area as the "type" locality for "Indian" continental sediments, noting that beds of probable Lower Siwalik age were found throughout the Potwar Plateau and extended south to the Bugti Hills and Sind, a southeastern province of Pakistan. Elaborating on this simple tripartite scheme, Pilgrim (1913) introduced these stratigraphic terms: Chinji, Nagri, Dhok Pathan, Tatrot, and Pinjor. Based on faunal criteria, these terms were originally intended to identify a sequence of "zones" (oldest to youngest) within the three major divisions (see Fig. 1), which were correlated with what he believed were equivalent stratigraphic zones in Europe. For example, the Chinji was viewed as a Sarmatian equivalent, while the Dhok Pathan faunas were likened to those from Pikermi. Having defined the faunal sequences characterizing the Siwalik Formation, Pilgrim shifted his efforts to the study of the fossil collections he had made. The result of

this work was a steady stream of publications that included the identification of two Miocene apes: *Dryopithecus punjabicus* and *Sivapithecus indicus*. In his evaluation of these fossils, Pilgrim (1915) conjectured that the former was more closely related to the hominoid apes and an Asian relative of the European dryopithecines, whereas the latter was viewed as a possible progenitor of Eugène Dubois' (1858–1940) *Pithecanthropus erectus* (now *Homo erectus*). However, like most of his contemporaries, Pilgrim rejected the idea of the Javan fossil being on the main line of human evolution.

In the 1920s, an expeditionary party from the American Museum of Natural History made a significant collection of fossil fauna from the Potwar Plateau, which was later described by Edwin H. Colbert (1905–) (1935). This was followed by the work (in what is now Pakistan and India) of G. Edward Lewis, then a doctoral student at Yale University, in the early 1930s. Emerging from Lewis' fieldwork was his decision to lump Pilgrim's dryopithecine and sivapithecine fossils into

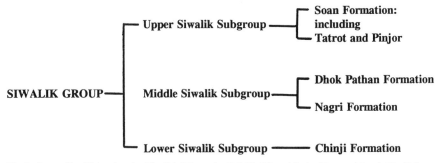

Fig. 2. *Current Siwalik stratigraphy. The Chinji Formation (Middle Miocene) is the oldest, overlying the Kamlial Formation, which was frequently placed in the Siwalik group in the earlier literature (cf. Lewis 1937b). The Dhok Pathan and Nagri Formations are intermediate strata dating to the late Miocene. The Soan Formation includes the Tatrot and Pinjor Formations (Pleistocene). Courtesy of David Pilbeam.*

the single genus *Ramapithecus* (now defunct), which he claimed as a hominid precursor (cf. Lewis 1934, 1937a, 1937b)—a conclusion that was vigorously rejected by the Smithsonian physical anthropologist Aleš Hrdlička (1869–1943) (1935).

Although the German paleontologists G.H.R. von Koenigswald (1902–1982) and Richard Dehm are known to have made modest collections in this region prior to World War II (Pilbeam: personal communication 1994), it was not until the 1950s that research in the Siwaliks slowly gathered momentum. In the late 1950s and early 1960s, several notable collections were made in Pakistan by Dehm and his coworkers (cf. Dehm et al. 1958, 1963) and in the Indian Siwaliks by K.N. Prasad of the Geological Survey of India (1962, 1964) and Elwyn Simons of Yale (cf. Simons & Chopra 1969). These efforts were followed by the establishment of the joint Yale Peabody Museum–Geological Survey of Pakistan (YPM–GSP) Project (cf. Pilbeam & Meyer 1974). Led by David Pilbeam, then of Yale, the YPM–GSP, began its work in the Potwar Plateau, south of Rawalpindi in 1973 (see Fig. 2). Since 1980, when Pilbeam moved to the Harvard Peabody Museum, the project has been directed from there. This ongoing collaborative project has not only contributed significantly to the understanding of the geology and paleoecology of the region (cf. Pilbeam et al. 1977; Badgely & Behrensmeyer 1980), but also greatly expanded the hominoid fossil record (cf. Barry 1986; Pilbeam 1979, 1982, 1986). The Siwalik fossil primates are confined essentially to the Chinji and Nagri Formations, representing a period from ca. 13.0 to 6.0 my (in the absence of suitable rocks on which to make radiometric determinations, these limits are coarse approximations). In addition to the accumulating fossil collections from the Potwar region, other significant collections have been made in India (Haritalyangar) and Kashmir (Ramnagar).

Frank Spencer

See also Cautley, (Sir) Proby Thomas; Dubois, (Marie) Eugène (François Thomas); Falconer, Hugh; *Gigantopithecus;* Hrdlička, Aleš; Koenigswald, (Gustav Heinrich) Ralph von; Lydekker, Richard; Paleoprimatology; Pilgrim, Guy Ellock; *Ramapithecus;* South Asia (India, Pakistan, Sri Lanka)

Bibliography
C. Badgely & A.K. Behrensmeyer: Paleoecology of middle Siwalik sediments and faunas, northern Pakistan. *Palaeogeography, Palaeoclimatology, Palaeoecology* 30:133–155, 1980; W.E. Baker & H.M. Durand: Sub-Himalayan fossil remains of the Dadoopoor collection. *Journal of the Asiatic Society* 5:739–741, 1836; J.C. Barry: A review of the chronology of Siwalik hominids. In: J.G. Else & P.C. Lee (eds) *Primate evolution.* London: Cambridge University Press, 1986, pp. 93–105; W.T. Blandford: Geological notes on the hills in the neighbourhood of the Sind and Punjab frontier between Quetta and Dera Ghazi. *Memoirs of the Indian Geological Survey* 20:105–240, 1883; E.H. Colbert: Siwalik mammals in the American Museum of Natural History. *Transactions of the American Philosophical Society* 26:1–401, 1935.

R. Dehm et al.: Paläontologische und geologische Untersuchungen im Tertiär von Pakistan. *Bayerische Akademie der Wissenschaften Mathematisch-Naturwissenschaftlichen Abhandlungen* 90:1–13, 1958; R. Dehm et al.: Paläontologische und geologische Untersuchungen im Tertiär von Pakistan.

III. Dinotherium in der Chinji-Stufe der Unterun Siwalik-Schichten. *Bayerische Akademie der Wissenschaften Mathematisch-Naturwissenschaftlichen Abhandlungen* 114:1–34, 1963; H. Falconer & P.T. Cautley: *Fauna antiqua sivalensis, being the fossil zoology of the Sewalik {sic} hills, in the north of India.* London: Smith, Elders, 1846; F. Fedden: On the distribution of the fossils . . . in different Tertiary and infra-Tertiary groups of Sind. *Memoirs of the Geological Survey of India* 17:197–210, 1879.

A. Hrdlička: The Yale fossil anthropoid apes. *American Journal of Science* 29:34–40, 1935; G.E. Lewis: Preliminary notice of new man-like apes from India. *American Journal of Science* 22:161–181, 1934; G.E. Lewis: A new Siwalik correlation. *American Journal of Science* 33:191–204, 1937a; G.E. Lewis: Siwalik fossil anthropoids. Ph.D. Thesis, Yale University, 1937b; R. Lydekker: Catalogue of vertebrate fossils from the Siwaliks of India, in the Science and Art Museum, Dublin. *Scientific Transactions of the Royal Society of Dublin* 3:69–86, 1884.

D. Pilbeam: Recent finds and interpretations of Miocene hominoids. *Annual Reviews of Anthropology.* Vol. 8. Palo Alto, California: Annual Reviews Inc., 1979, pp. 333–352; D. Pilbeam: New hominoid skull material from the Miocene of Pakistan. *Nature* 295:232–234, 1982; D. Pilbeam: Hominoid evolution and hominid origins. *American Anthropologist* 88:1–18, 1986; D. Pilbeam & G.E. Meyer: Yale in Kenya and Pakistan: Paleoanthropology in two continents. *Discovery* (Peabody Museum, Yale University): 9:73–81, 1974; D. Pilbeam et al.: Geology and paleontology of Neogene strata of Pakistan. *Nature* 270:684–689, 1977.

G.E. Pilgrim: Notices of new mammalian genera and species from the Tertiaries of India. *Records of the Geological Survey of India* 40:63–71, 1910; G.E. Pilgrim: The correlation of the Siwaliks with mammal horizons of Europe. *Records of the Geological Survey of India* 43:264–326, 1913; G.E. Pilgrim: New Siwalik primates and their bearing on the question of the evolution of man and the anthropoids. *Records of the Geological Survey of India* 55:1–74, 1915; K.N. Prasad: Fossil primates from the Siwalik Beds near Haritalyangar, Himchal Pradesh, India. *Journal of the Geological Society of India* 3:86–96, 1962; K.N. Prasad: Upper Miocene anthropoids from the Siwalik Beds of Haritalyangar, Himchal Pradesh, India. *Palaeontology* 7:123–134, 1964; E.L. Simons

& S.R.K. Chopra: *Gigantopithecus* (Pongidae, Hominoidea): A new species from north India. *Postilla* 138:1–18, 1969.

Skeletal Biology

Skeletal biology is the physical anthropological investigation of human remains recovered from archeological contexts (also known as bioarcheology). Because bones and teeth are more commonly encountered than soft tissues, biological inference is largely limited to skeletal remains. Despite the selectivity of this record as well as other problems characteristic of human death assemblages, skeletal and dental tissues offer a plethora of information due to their sensitivity to the physical environment, reflecting a record of events occurring during an individual's lifetime.

Prior to the 1960s, the field was dominated by descriptive reports on bones and teeth. Since the mid-1970s, there has been a shift to more processually oriented biocultural studies involving understanding of skeletal biology within an evolutionary context (Blakely 1977). Due in large part to these changes in perspective and increased recognition of the value of human remains in anthropological and archeological interpretation, more holistic, integrative approaches involving collaboration between physical anthropologists are being followed (cf. Buikstra 1991). Three key areas of bioarcheological inquiry are highlighted: (1) health, (2) functional morphology and behavioral inference, and (2) biological distance (cf. Larsen 1987).

Health

GENERAL. Imprinted upon the human skeleton is a record or "memory" of various circumstances affecting the hard tissues, especially those conditions arising during the growth period. This record comes under the purview of paleopathology, the study of ancient disease. Much of paleopathology has been devoted to disease diagnosis and description of pathological conditions of individual skeletons. Although great strides have been made in this regard (cf. Ortner & Putschar 1985), recent trends have shown a reorientation of approach involving the impact of diseases on human populations in a biocultural framework (Ubelaker 1982).

INFECTIOUS DISEASE. Bones generally respond to a variety of infections in a similar way, through a process involving both abnormal bony apposition, often apparent as an additional outer layer of reactive bone, and at times, abnormal resorption (e.g. forming a cloaca, or drainage canal for pus). Months or even years are sometimes required for a bony response to an infection to develop. If an individual succumbs to a disease prior to skeletal involvement, or if the disease is one that does not affect the bones, it will not be apparent in prehistoric remains. Therefore, the prevalence of infectious diseases in skeletal series is not an accurate estimate of their frequencies during life.

Most infectious diseases affecting the bones are classified as nonspecific, since the causative organism cannot be identified. Nonspecific infections leading to periosteal reactive bone formation are one of the most commonly represented pathologies in archeological series. In the Eastern Woodlands of the United States, there is a low prevalence of nonspecific infections in foraging populations and higher frequencies in late prehistoric, agricultural populations. The increases are likely due to the effects of increased sedentism and population size, which are prerequisites to the maintenance and spread of infectious disease generally.

Only a few diseases (e.g. leprosy, tuberculosis, and treponemal diseases) may be differentially diagnosed from skeletal material and are known in archaeological skeletons (Ortner & Putschar 1985; Steinbock 1976). Leprosy occurred prehistorically only in the Old World, but the origins of tuberculosis and treponemal diseases have been controversial. Beginning with Joseph Jones' (1833–1896) (1876) attribution of venereal syphilis to bone pathology from late prehistoric skeletons in Tennessee, the presence of pre-Columbian treponematosis in the New World was hotly debated for well over a century. Powell (1988) has suggested that for some regions of the Eastern Woodlands, the pattern of skeletal involvement is most consistent with a nonvenereal, endemic form of treponematosis. Based on a review of available evidence, Baker and Armelagos (1988) argue that treponematosis is a relatively new disease first evolving in tropical and subtropical areas of the New World, where it was contracted by Columbus's crews and thereafter transported to the Old World. Once the disease reached Europe, it rapidly evolved into its present venereal form.

Tuberculosis is present in the Old World in skeletons approaching 6,000 years of age (Manchester 1991). Increasing evidence also exists for the presence of tuberculosis or a tuberculosis-like infection in New World pre-Columbian populations (Buikstra 1981). Like treponematosis, most accounts of tuberculo-sis indicate that the disease was present in prehistoric samples associated with large, sedentary populations.

DIETARY ANALYSES. Recent dietary research is based on the fact that foods have variable quantities of stable isotopes or trace elements and that these elements may be incorporated into the skeletal system in frequencies reflecting their importance in the diet. The trace element strontium, and carbon and nitrogen isotopes have received the most attention from researchers (Aufderheide 1989; DeNiro 1987).

Strontium is discriminated against by animals; its presence in bone reflects the quantity of meat in the diet with carnivores showing lower levels. Carbon isotope ratios ($^{13}C/^{12}C$) vary between plants with different photosynthetic pathways. They are used to assess the amount of maize or marine foods in the diet. Nitrogen isotopes are utilized to determine marine or leguminous components of the diet. Although all of these analyses have problematic aspects, they may be useful, in conjunction with traditional paleopathological studies (Huss-Ashmore, et al. 1982), in ascertaining nutritional health.

IRON DEFICIENCY ANEMIA. During childhood episodes of anemia when skeletal tissues are undergoing very rapid growth, a series of accompanying changes arise as a result of increased demand for red blood cell production. This results in expansion of the diploë of cranial bones and the development of sieve-like perforations that frequently accompany abnormally thick vault bones. Known as porotic hyperostosis (or cribra orbitalia when present on the upper margins of the orbits), these lesions are known from a wide variety of populations worldwide, and have been attributed to hereditary hemolytic anemias, consumption of iron-poor foods, especially cereal grains, or the combined effects of parasitism, infection, and other factors affecting iron metabolism, although diet and parasites are thought to be the most common causes (Stuart-Macadam 1989).

HARRIS LINES. Radiographically visible transverse lines may be observed on the diaphyses of long bones and on the round bones. The lines represent increased mineralization resulting from renewed growth after a period of nutritional deprivation or infectious disease (Martin et al. 1985), as well as from other factors affecting the physiology of bone (Garn et al., 1968). They therefore document recovery from a disruption of normal growth. Although the lines frequently persist into adulthood, they may eventually remodel and no longer be visible, especially those forming at an early age.

ENAMEL DEFECTS. Enamel, the outer covering of the tooth crown, is sensitive to nutritional insufficiencies, disease and other stressors during development (Goodman & Rose 1991). Defects arising from metabolic stress may be observed both macroscopically (hypoplasia and hypocalcification) and microscopically (striae of Retzius, prism defects). Hypoplasias are exhibited as linear furrows, horizontal pits, or lines, reflecting periods of disruption in enamel development. Defects owing to heredity and localized trauma are rare, so that systemic factors, such as nutrition or disease, are responsible for most defects in archaeological samples.

Enamel defects are widely used to elucidate patterning of stress episodes prior to birth through age six (the period during which tooth crowns form). Some evidence suggests that hypoplastic activity peaks between ages two and four years, and may be associated with physiological stress due to weaning, or to local factors relating to susceptability of particular regions of the tooth crown (Goodman & Armelagos, 1985). Relatively wide hypoplasias represent greater duration and/or severity of stress than narrow hypoplasias.

DENTAL DISEASE. A number of disorders affect the dentition and associated structures, with caries, periodontal disease, and dental abcesses being some of the most common (Lukacs 1989). Dental caries are a byproduct of bacterial infection (usually with *Streptococcus mutans*). In the process of breaking down sugar, lactic acid is released, which decalcifies the enamel. Periodontal disease is an inflammation of the gums, which may lead to resorption of the underlying alveolus. Dental abcesses result from exposure and subsequent infection of the pulp cavity, which then spreads through the root into the alveolus. Pulp cavity exposure can be due to a variety of factors, including caries or dental attrition.

Dental disease (and attrition - *vide infra*) is closely tied to diet and food processing techniques. In general, caries rates have increased dramatically over time with the incorporation of more starchy carbohydrates in the diet. Frequently, the shift to agriculture is accompanied by a large rise in caries rates. Dental abcesses do not show a similar trend, since they may be caused by either caries or attri-

tion (which typically declines with the adoption of agriculture or innovations in food processing technology).

BONE GROWTH AND MAINTENANCE. Bone growth and maintenance are governed by a complex set of factors, including diet, age, hormones, and activity levels, among others (Garn 1970). Frequently, cortical thickness is used as an indicator of overall dietary sufficiency. However, since the level of physical activities can also influence cortical area and its distribution, it is crucial to consider mechanical attributes of bones as well (*vide infra*).

PALEODEMOGRAPHY. Demographic inference based on construction of life tables and determination of other statistics (e.g., mean age at death) has held an important place in analysis of skeletal samples. Although most demographic analyses have emphasized mortality, death assemblages often provide more appropriate information about fertility and population growth (Johansson & Horowitz 1986). For example, a skeletal series from a population with high fertility rates will exhibit a much lower mean age at death than a population having low fertility. The mean age at death, in this case, does not reflect differences in health but rather in fertility.

Other factors continue to bedevil accurate interpretation of population profiles based on age structure, including relatively poor preservation of delicate bones of very young and very old individuals, inaccurate age and sex estimates, incomplete sampling due to selective recovery, and culturally–based mortuary variability resulting in underrepresentation of some individuals dying in a population. These and other problems associated with skeletal samples make interpretation of mortality complex at best.

TRAUMATIC INJURY AND VIOLENCE. Evidence of violent behavior and traumatic injury in human remains is usually limited to description. However, at the population level, patterns of trauma may reveal important aspects of community behavior in past societies (Merbs 1989). Fracture patterns, for example, document the ability of past societies to care for individual members of a community and help elucidate activity patterns. The greater extent of violence or warfare in some prehistoric communities indicates high levels of social conflict and stress.

OSTEOARTHRITIS. Osteoarthritis (or degenerative joint disease) may be caused by a variety of factors, but "wear and tear" fostered by physical activities or traumatic injuries is the most common influence. Deterioration of cartilage leads to hypertrophy of bone around the margins of the joint and porosity of joint surfaces. Destruction of cartilage can result in eburnation, where bone has rubbed against bone. Because of its relationship to activities or injuries, osteoarthritis may reveal important information about lifestyle. However, because of the multiplicity of causative factors, including age, it is not always possible to link arthritis directly to either levels or types of physical activities (Bridges 1992; Jurmain 1992).

SURGERY. Trephination, an operation involving the removal of a part of the cranial vault, has been documented in a number of regions of the world. Many known examples are associated with compression fractures, suggesting that the operation was frequently performed in order to relieve intracranial pressures. Prehistoric surgeons were apparently quite adept at the practice, because the survival rates are often high.

Morphology: Shape, Form, and Function
HISTORICAL CONTEXT—TYPOLOGICAL ANALYSIS. In his monumental volume, *Crania Americana*, the Philadelphian anatomist Samuel G. Morton (1799–1851) (1839) provided the first systematically collected data—anthropometric and morphological—on a large sample of American Indian crania. Morton's work was presented at a time when scientists were attempting to document and understand the origins, affinities, and movements of Native Americans prior to the arrival of Europeans.

Soon thereafter, the Swedish anatomist Anders A. Retzius (1796–1860) introduced the cranial index which enabled investigators to broadly classify cranial shapes as either dolichocephalic (long-headed) or brachycephalic (short, round-headed), a dichotomy that appeared to represent a temporal sequence involving an earlier migration of "dolichocephals" preceding a later migration of "brachycephals." Typological in perspective, the idea dominated much of osteological research well into the 1960s (Armelagos et al. 1982; Buikstra 1979). With a greater understanding of bone biology and skeletal remodeling, other perspectives have emerged.

CRANIOFACIAL BIOMECHANICAL ADAPTATION. Although craniofacial morphology is highly heritable (reviewed in Kohn 1991), it is tempered by other factors, such as hardness of food in the diet. When viewed in the context of dietary change, shifts in cranial shape appear to be related not to population migrations but rather to dietary and subsistence technology changes and associated musculoskeletal adaptation. Thus, the trend for broader, shorter crania observed in later prehistoric sites in North America may reflect mechanical adaptations to changes in diet and subsistence technology.

DENTAL WEAR AND FUNCTION. Both the kinds of foods eaten as well as how foods are prepared affect the amount of tooth wear seen in archaeological samples. Hunter-gatherers tend to exhibit evenly distributed, flat wear, and agriculturalists possess highly angled wear planes on the molar teeth. As well, there is a tendency for a reduction in degree of wear in later populations, specifically, when agriculture is adopted. Although the reasons for this trend are unclear, it may reflect the shift to agricultural foods which are oftentimes cooked to soft consistencies.

With the development of scanning electron microscopy during the second half of the twentieth century, it has become possible to analyze minute wear patterns on teeth (Teaford 1991). Even though applications are limited at present, a number of microscopic features may reflect dietary patterns.

POSTCRANIAL BIOMECHANICAL ADAPTATION. The typological perspective is best known from studies of human crania, but it was also applied to cross-section shapes of the major long bones, especially the tibia and femur. More recently, application of an engineering beam model has made it possible to determine mechanical loads reflecting the level of physical activities (Ruff 1992). For example, the increasing circularity of long bones reflects a decline in the level or change in the type of mechanical demand, especially during late prehistory and in modern industrial populations, possibly relating to degree of mobility (Ruff 1987).

OTHER APPROACHES TO BIOMECHANICAL INFERENCE. Other kinds of functional models of biomechanical adaptation have also been applied to the study of skeletal structures. Findings from analysis of histological structure (i.e., osteons) in femora from Pecos Pueblo are consistent with the study of gross geometry of long bones in relation to physically demanding lifestyles (Burr et al. 1990). Both types of analysis show that age-related bone loss (osteoporosis) is at least partially compensated for by mechanical changes in bone, both at the gross and histologic levels.

Biological Distance

Biological distance (or biodistance) is the measurement of population divergence as it is based on polygenic traits (Buikstra et al. 1990). Biological distance studies have proven useful to varying degrees in providing insight into relatedness both within and between populations in the past. Biodistance methods focus on variation in skeletal (primarily cranial) and dental form, including measurement as well as documentation of discrete (a.k.a. non-metrical, epigenetic, or quasi-continuous) traits in bones and teeth. With the development of high-speed computers and sophisticated statistical approaches involving the simultaneous use of a large number of variants, it appeared that a solution to problems of more limited approaches to population history were within grasp. Unfortunately, it has been too often the case that the application of multivariate statistics has simply created newer, more complex typologies without appreciation for some very basic biological issues, such as the developmental basis of traits (cf. Armelagos et al. 1982).

Nonetheless, biodistance studies have an important role in bioarcheology in that they contribute to discussions about evolutionary history in regional context, they provide insight into basic archeological questions such as residence patterns, and they supply useful background for other concerns in bioarcheology where knowledge of population history is an essential backdrop for interpreting other components of biological inquiry, such as disease prevalence in temporal and regional context (cf. Buikstra 1990).

Conclusions

From the time of the publication of Morton's *Crania Americana*, on through to the mid-twentieth century, bioarcheology was dominated by typologically oriented research. This tendency reflected an overriding concern for reconstruction of population history without a broader understanding of the biological processes underlying human variation. In the early 1970s, J. Lawrence Angel (1915–1986) lamented that "study of the process of human evolution at the population level is seldom attempted. It is high time to study an ancient population functionally, [and] to relate it to its physical and cultural environment. . . " (1971:5). Bioarcheology has since taken important strides on a number of fronts, and the foregoing discussion indicates that Angel's call for processual investigation of archeological human remains is beginning to be answered. Especially noteworthy is the development of regionally oriented research programs utilizing collaborative, interdisciplinary teams of scientists who offer various areas of expertise in addressing multifactorial and often complex issues (e.g., references in Cohen & Armelagos 1984).

Throughout the history of bioarcheology, human remains have proved to be an invaluable component of the archeological record, offering a unique source of information about earlier human cultures. Despite the increasing recognition of the value of human remains for addressing a range of issues, the investigation and retention of collections of native skeletons in North America, Australia, and elsewhere are being publically scrutinized (Ubelaker & Grant 1989). The debates both within anthropology and with the public regarding the disposition of human remains have resulted in legislation leading to reburial of at least some native remains now and in the future. In addition to encouraging further scientific development in this field, it will become increasingly important for bioarcheologists and others to convey to the public the importance of human remains for understanding history and culture of earlier societies.

Clark Spencer Larsen
Patricia S. Bridges

See also Angel, J. Lawrence; Anthropometry; Demography; Dental anthropology; Garn, Stanley M.; Health and disease; Jones, Joseph; Morton, Samuel George; Paleopathology; Retzius, Anders A.

Bibliography
J.L. Angel: *The people of Lerna: Analysis of a prehistoric Aegean population*. Washington, D.C.: Smithsonian Institution Press, 1971; G.J. Armelagos et al.: The theoretical foundations and development of skeletal biology. In: F. Spencer (ed) *A history of American physical anthropology, 1930–1980*. New York: Academic Press, 1982, pp. 305–328; A.C. Aufderheide: Chemical analysis of skeletal remains. In: M.Y. İşcan & K.A.R. Kennedy (eds) *Reconstruction of life from the skeleton*. New York: Liss, 1989, pp.237–260.

B.J. Baker & G.J. Armelagos: The origin and antiquity of syphilis. *Current Anthropology* 29:703–737, 1988; R.L. Blakely (ed) *Biocultural adaptation in prehistoric America*. Athens, Georgia: University of Georgia Press, 1977; P.S. Bridges: Prehistoric arthritis in the Americas. *Annual Review of Anthropology*

21:67–91, 1992; J.E. Buikstra: Contributions of physical anthropologists to the concept of Hopewell: A historical perspective. In: D.S. Brose & N. Greber (eds) *Hopewell Archaeology*. Kent, Ohio: Kent State University Press, 1979, pp. 220–233; J.E. Buikstra (ed): Prehistoric tuberculosis in the Americas. Evanston, Illinois: Northwestern University Archaeological Program, 1981; J.E. Buikstra: Out of the appendix and into the dirt: Comments on thirteen years of bioarchaeological research. In: M.L. Powell, P.S. Bridges, & A.M.W. Mires (eds) *What mean these bones? Studies in southeastern bioarchaeology*. Tuscaloosa: University of Alabama Press, 1991, pp. 172–188; J.E. Buikstra et al.: Skeletal biological distance studies in American physical anthropology: Recent trends. *American Journal of Physical Anthropology* 82:1–7, 1990; D.B. Burr et al.: Patterns of skeletal histologic change through time: Comparison of an archaic Native American population with modern populations. *The Anatomical Record* 226:307–313, 1991.

M.N. Cohen & G.J. Armelagos (eds): *Paleopathology at the origins of agriculture*. Orlando, Florida: Academic press, 1984; M.J. DeNiro: Stable isotopy and archaeology. *American Scientist* 75:182–191, 1987; S.M. Garn: *The earlier gain and the later loss of cortical bone*. Springfield, Illinois: Thomas, 1970; S.M. Garn et al.: Lines and bands of increased density. *Medical radiography and photography* 44:58–89, 1968; A. Goodman & G.J. Armelagos: Factors affecting the distribution of enamel hypoplasia within the human permanent dentition. *American Journal of Physical Anthropology* 68:479–493, 1985; A. Goodman & J.C. Rose: Dental enamel hypoplasias as indicators of nutritional stress. In: M.A. Kelley & C.S. Larsen (eds) *Advances in dental anthropology*. New York: Wiley-Liss, 1991, pp. 279–293.

R. Huss-Ashmore et al.: Nutritional inference from paleopathology. *Advances in archaeology method and theory* 5:395–474, 1982; S.R. Johansson & S. Horowitz: Estimating mortality in skeletal populations: Influence of the growth rate on the interpretation of levels and trends during the transition to agriculture. *American Journal of Physical Anthropology* 71:233–250, 1986; J. Jones: Explorations of the aboriginal remains of Tennessee. *Smithsonian Contributions to Knowledge* 22:1–171, 1876; R.D. Jurmain: Degenerative changes in peripheral joints as indicators of mechanical stress: Opportunities and limitations. *International Journal of Osteoarchaeology* 1:247–252, 1992; L.A.P. Kohn: The role of genetics in craniofacial morphology and growth. *Annual Review of Anthropology* 20:261–278, 1991.

C.S. Larsen: Bioarchaeological interpretations of subsistence economy and behavior from human skeletal remains. In: M.B. Schiffer (ed) *Advances in archaeological method and theory*. Vol 10. San Diego, California: Academic Press, 1987, pp. 339–445; J.R. Lukacs: Dental paleopathology: Methods for reconstructing dietary patterns. In: M.Y. İşcan & K.A.R. Kennedy (eds) *Reconstruction of life from the skeleton*. New York: Liss, 1989, pp.261–286; K. Manchester: Tuberculosis and leprosy: Evidence for interaction of disease. In: D.J. Ortner & A.C. Aufderheide (eds) *Human paleopathology: Current syntheses and future options*. Washington, D.C.: Smithsonian Institution Press, 1991, pp.23–35; D.L. Martin et al.: Skeletal pathologies as indicators of quality and quantity of diet. In: R.I. Gilbert Jr. & J.H. Mielke (eds) *The analysis of prehistoric diets*. Orlando, Florida: Academic Press, 1985, pp. 227–279, 1985; C.F. Merbs: Trauma. In: M.Y. İşcan & K.A.R. Kennedy (eds) *Reconstruction of life from the skeleton*. New York: Liss, 1989, pp.161–189; S.G. Morton: *Crania Americana*. Philadelphia: Dobson, 1839.

D.J. Ortner & W.G.J. Putschar: *Identification of pathological conditions in human skeletal remains*. Washington, D.C.: Smithsonian Institution Press, 1985; M.L. Powell: *Status and health in prehistory: A case study of the Moundville chiefdom*. Washington, D.C.: Smithsonian Institution Press, 1988; C.B. Ruff: Sexual dimorphism in human lower limb bone structure: Relationship to subsistence strategy and sexual division of labor. *Journal of Human Evolution* 16:391–416, 1987; C.B. Ruff: Biomechanical analyses of archaeological human skeletal remains. In: S.R. Saunders & M.A. Katzenberg (eds) *The skeletal biology of past peoples: Advances in research methods*. New York: Wiley-Liss, 1992, pp. 37–58; R.T. Steinbock: *Paleopathological diagnosis and interpretation*. Springfield, Illinois: Thomas, 1976; P.L. Stuart-Macadam: Nutritional deficiency diseases: A survey of scurvy, rickets, and iron-deficiency anemia. In: M.Y. İşcan & K.A.R. Kennedy (eds) *Reconstruction of life from the skeleton*. New York: Liss, 1989, pp.201–222.

M.F. Teaford: Dental microwear: What can it tell us about diet and dental function? In: M.A. Kelley & C.S. Larsen (eds) *Advances in dental anthropology*. New York: Wiley-Liss, 1991, pp.342–356; D.H. Ubelaker: The development of American paleopathology. In: F. Spencer (ed) *A history of American physical anthropology, 1930–1980*. New York: Academic Press, 1982, pp. 337–356; D.H. Ubelaker & L.G. Grant: Human skeletal remains: Preservation or reburial? *Yearbook of Physical Anthropology* 32:249–287, 1989.

Skhūl, Mugharet es- (Israel)

From 1929 to 1934, the British archeologist Dorothy A.E. Garrod (1892–1969) organized and ran the Joint Expedition of the British School of Archaeology in Jerusalem and the American School of Prehistoric Research in Palestine, or what is now northwestern Israel. The work concentrated on the excavation of three caves or shelters in, or adjacent to, the Wadi el-Mughara in the southern part of the Mount Carmel range. The least spectacular of these sites was the terrace site of Mugharet es-Skhūl, located on the south side of the Wadi el-Mughara a short distance from its entrance. This modest site yielded one of the largest known samples of human remains from the Middle Paleolithic: the associated skeletons of ten individuals plus sixteen isolated elements (cf. McCown & Keith 1939).

The excavation of the site was directed by the then graduate student Theodore D. McCown (1908–1969), later assisted by another young American archeologist, Hallam L. Movius Jr. (1907–1987). McCown discovered an infant's skeleton, Skhūl 1, in May 1931, and then McCown and Movius recovered the additional remains during the April-to-May 1932 season, all from the Middle Paleolithic Layer B.

The analysis of the human remains from Skhūl was undertaken by McCown, working closely with, and largely under the direction of, the elderly British anatomist-anthropologist Arthur Keith (1866–1955). This cooperative work resulted, in 1939, in one of the now classic monographs in human paleontology (McCown & Keith 1939). Initially, McCown thought that the Tabūn 1 and 2 remains, from the neighboring site of Mugharet et-Tabūn, were significantly different from those he had unearthed at Skhūl, but Keith remained unconvinced that there were two groups represented in these Palestinian fossil humans. The latter's view won out in the fi-

nal monograph, and the remains from Skhūl and Tabūn were described as a variable sample of Middle Paleolithic humans (even though the authors admitted that the Tabūn remains were generally more archaic than those from Skhūl).

Even though McCown and Keith noted that a large percentage of the characters in the Skhūl sample aligned more with "Neanthropic" (i.e., early modern human) people, it was not until the late 1950s that the French paleontologist Henri Vallois (1889–1981) (cf. Boule & Vallois 1957) and the American physical anthropologist F. Clark Howell (1957, 1958) noticed the similarities between the Skhūl and Qafzeh cranial remains and separated them out from the Tabūn and more Neandertal-like fossils from the Near East and Europe. This was followed by a growing series of comments—with respect to pubic morphology (Stewart 1960), craniofacial morphology (Howells 1975; Stringer 1974; Santa Luca 1978), femoral and pubic morphology (Trinkaus 1976a, b), dental proportions (Brace 1979), and other aspects of the postcranial skeleton (e.g., Endo & Kimura 1970; Vandermeersch 1981; Trinkaus 1983)—that characterized the Skhūl sample as craniofacially robust and generally quite muscular but otherwise closely aligned with early modern humans across the Old World.

Consequently, since the late 1970s most paleoanthropologists have viewed the large Skhūl sample as being distinct from the Near Eastern late archaic humans from the sites of Amud, Kebara, Shanidar, and Tabūn, and closely aligned with the remains from Jebel Qafzeh. At the same time, there is a full recognition that they are not fully modern humans, since their craniofacial skeletons in particular fall outside the ranges of variation of Holocene humans (e.g., Corruccini 1992; Kidder et al. 1992). There have been a few recent attempts to embrace all of the Near Eastern Middle Paleolithic hominids in one variable lineage/population (e.g., Arensburg 1991; Frayer et al. 1993), but the morphological evidence remains sufficient to keep them separate.

The accepted geological age of the sample from Skhūl has fluctuated almost as much as its perceived morphological affinities. McCown and Keith (1939) originally accepted a "last interpluvial" (last interglacial) age for the sample, maintaining nonetheless that it must be younger than the Tabūn Layer C remains, given the latter's more archaic morphology. Variants of this view were maintained until E.S. Higgs (1961), on the basis of faunal and sedimentological considerations, assigned the Skhūl remains to a dry-phase early last glacial, considerably younger than the Tabūn C remains. The Skhūl sample thus came to be considered increasingly as relatively late in the Near Eastern Middle Paleolithic sequence, generally assigned an age in the vicinity of 40.0–50.0 ky BP (e.g., Jelinek 1982a, b; Trinkaus 1984).

This view was maintained until ESR (electron spin resonance) dating was applied to bovine teeth from Skhūl, producing age estimates between ca. 80.0 and 100 ky BP (Stringer et al. 1989). These dates place it in the middle of the last interglacial and roughly contemporary with the Qafzeh Middle Paleolithic sample. More recently, TL (thermoluminescence) dates have supported the ESR dates (Mercier et al. 1993), but uranium-series dates have provided two sets of dates for Layer B, one confirming the ESR age of ca. 90.0 ky BP, and the other placing part of Layer B as perhaps as recent as 40.0–70.0 ky BP (McDermott et al. 1993). The problem remains whether the skeletal sample dates to the former or the latter, or whether it represents two chronologically separated samples: one from the last interglacial and the other from the later part of the early last glacial.

Regardless of its chronological position, it is apparent that the human remains from Skhūl are morphologically distinct from the Middle Paleolithic Neandertal-like lineage represented at Amud, Kebara, Shanidar, and Tabūn. This is evident in the shapes of their faces (despite supraorbital tori on most of them), their relatively small front teeth, their long and linear body proportions, their robust pubic bones, the modest development of muscular attachments of the limb bones, and several details of the hand skeletons. All that remains to be determined is whether they were contemporaneous with the Near Eastern Neandertals, hence representing a parallel lineage to them, or were chronological successors, hence possibly early modern human descendants.

Erik Trinkaus

See also Amud Cave (Israel); Kebara, Mugharet el- (Israel); Keith, (Sir) Arthur; McCown, Theodore D(oney); Mount Carmel (Israel); Neandertals; Qafzeh (Jebel) (Israel); Shanidar (Iraq); Tabūn, Mugharet et- (Israel); Vallois, Henri Victor

Bibliography
B. Arensburg: From sapiens to Neandertals: Rethinking the Middle East. Abstract. *American Journal of Physical Anthropology* (Supplement) 12:44, 1991; M. Boule & H.V. Vallois: *Fossil man.* New York: Dryden Press, 1957; C.L. Brace: Krapina, "classic" Neanderthals, and evolution of the European face. *Journal of Human Evolution* 8:527–550, 1979; R.S. Corruccini: Metrical reconsideration in the Skhūl IV and IX and Border Cave 1 crania in the context of modern human origins. *American Journal of Physical Anthropology* 87:433–446, 1992; B. Endo & T. Kimura: Prostcranial skeleton of the Amud man. In: H. Suzuki & F. Takai (eds) *The Amud man and his cave site.* Tokyo: Academic Press, 1970, pp. 231–406.

D.W. Frayer et al.: Theories of modern human origins: The paleontological test. *American Anthropologist* 95:14–50, 1993; E.S. Higgs: Some Pleistocene faunas of the Mediterranean coastal areas. *Proceedings of the Prehistoric Society* 6:144–154, 1961; F.C. Howell: The evolutionary significance of variation and varieties of "Neanderthal" man. *Quarterly Review of Biology* 32:330–347, 1957; F.C. Howell: The Pleistocene men of the southwest Asian Mousterian. In: G.H.R. von Koenigswald (ed) *Hundert Jahre Neanderthaler.* Utrecht: Kemink en Zoon, 1958, pp. 185, 198; W.W. Howells: Neanderthal man: Facts and figures. In: R.H. Tuttle (ed) *Paleoanthropology: Morphology, and Paleoecology.* The Hague: Mouton, 1975, pp. 389–407.

A.J. Jelinek: The Middle Palaeolithic in the southern Levant, with comments on the appearance of modern *Homo sapiens*. In: A. Ronen (ed) The transition from the Lower to Middle Palaeolithic and the origin of modern man. *British Archaeological Report* 151:57–104, 1982a; A.J. Jelinek: The Tabūn Cave and Paleolithic man in the Levant. *Science* 216:1369–1375, 1982b; J.H. Kidder et al.: Defining modern humans: A multivariate approach. In: G. Bräuer & F.H. Smith (eds) *Continuity or replacement: Controversies in Homo sapiens evolution.* Rotterdam: Balkema, 1992, pp. 157–177; T.D. McCown & A. Keith: *The Stone Age of Mount Carmel II: The fossil human remains from the Levalloiso-Mousterian.* Oxford: Clarendon Press, 1939.

F. McDermott et al.: Mass spectrometric U-series dates for Israel Neanderthal/early-modern hominids sites. *Nature* 363:252–255, 1993; N. Mercier et al.: Thermoluminescence date for the Mousterian burial site of Es-Skhūl, Mt. Carmel. *Journal of Archaeological Science* 20:169–174,

1993; A.P. Santa Luca: A reexamination of presumed Neandertal-like fossils. *Journal of Human Evolution* 7:619–636, 1978; T.D. Stewart: Form of the pubic bone in Neanderthal man. *Science* 131:1437–1438, 1960; C.B. Stringer: Population relationships of Late Pleistocene hominids: A multivariate study of available crania. *Journal of Archaeological Science* 1:317–342, 1974.

C.B. Stringer et al.: ESR dates for the hominid burial site of Es-Skhūl in Israel. *Nature* 338:756–758, 1989; E. Trinkaus: The evolution of the hominid femoral diaphysis during the Upper Pleistocene in Europe and the Near East. *Zeitschrift für Morphologie und Anthropologie* 67:44–59, 1976a; E. Trinkaus: The morphology of Europan and southwest Asian Neandertal pubic bones. *American Journal of Physical Anthropology* 44:95–104, 1976b; E. Trinkaus: *The Shanidar Neandertals*. New York: Academic Press, 1983; E. Trinkaus: Western Asia. In: F.H. Smith & F. Spencer (eds) *The origin of modern humans: A world survey of the fossil evidence*. New York: Liss, 1984, pp. 251–293; B. Vandermeersch: *Les hommes fossiles de Qafzeh (Israël)*. Paris: CNRS, 1981.

Skin Color

Skin, the body's largest organ, performs several diverse and important functions that include thermoregulation and protection of the body from physical and chemical injury, as well as from the invasion of microorganisms. Skin pigmentation is intimately bound up with this protective role (*vide infra*). Being one of the most conspicuous of all human polytypic variations, skin color has, perhaps more than any other, attracted the attention of scholars over the centuries, and since the seventeenth century it has served as one of the primary characters in racial classifications (see Table 1). What follows is a brief overview of the development of scientific inquiry into the biology of skin pigmentation, along with changing scientific attitudes on its significance and utility in anthropology.

With the founding of trading settlements on the West African coast and the subsequent development of the slave trade in the sixteenth century, Europeans were brought into firsthand contact with Black Africans, and, as can be seen from Richard Hakluyt's (ca. 1552–1616) popular compendium of *Voiages and Discoveries* (first published in 1589), there was both a growing fascination with the image of Black human beings and a

corresponding need to explain this curious fact. Although during the Renaissance period there had been whisperings that Black Africans may not be of the same "protoplast" as Europeans, throughout much of the sixteenth century the action of the sun's heat[1] was invariably identified as the underlying cause of the differences in the complexion of the European and African Negro.[2]

By the mid-seventeenth century, it had become apparent to many scholars that the traditional environmental hypothesis was at variance with the emerging evidence. To begin with, the supposition that there was a simple relationship between latitude and complexion had been clearly undermined by accumulating ethnographic data: The skin color of the aborigines of North America was neither black nor white, but "olive" (cf. Hakluyt 1589), while in Africa, the differences in complexion were found to range from black to yellow (cf. Ovington 1696). Furthermore, the transportation of Black African slaves to more temperate climes had not, contrary to expectations, led to an appreciable change in their skin color—even after several generations. While many continued to share the optimism of the British scholar Thomas Burnet (1635–1715) (1691) and remained convinced that the anticipated change in complexion was forthcoming, there was a growing number of skeptics, such as the English physician Thomas Browne (1605–1682) (1646), the German physician-anatomist Johann Nicolas Pechlin (1644–1706) (1677), and the French traveler-physician François Bernier (1620–1688) (1684), who were equally convinced that the African's blackness was innate and permanent. The essence of this emerging viewpoint is neatly encapsulated in the following extract from Browne's *Pseudodoxia epidemica* (1646):

If the fervour of the Sun, or intemperate heat of clime did solely occasion this complexion, surely a migration or change thereof might cause a sensible, if not a total mutation; which notwithstanding experience will not admit. {Despite their transplantation, there remains among their descendants} a strong shadow of their Originals: and if they preserve their copulations entire, they still maintain their complexion. . . . {L}ikewise, fair or white people translated in hotter Countries receive not impressions amounting to this complexion." (Browne 1904, Vol. 2:368–380)

In making his case against the environmental hypothesis, Browne also refuted the

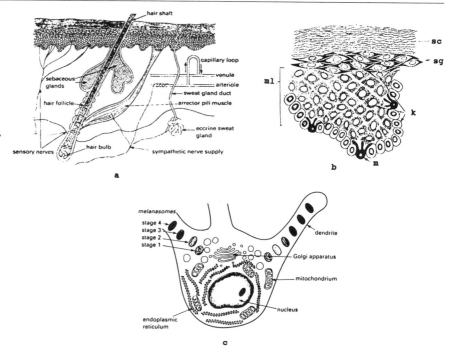

Fig. 1. (a) Human skin, general structure; (b) structure of epidermis showing its four layers: ml: "Malpighian layer" consisting of the basal layer (stratum basale) and the stratum spinosum, sc: stratum corneum, sg: stratum granulosum, k: keratinocytes, m: melanocytes; (c) internal structure of a melanocyte. Note melanosomes, shown in varying stages of development. Adapted from Robins 1991.

biblical thesis that the skin color of the African Negro was a result of Noah's curse on Ham's son Canaan (cf. Genesis 9:20–28). But despite Browne's efforts to dismiss this explanation as a "foolish tale," it continued to attract adherents well into the eighteenth century. In large part, the attraction of this latter theme can be attributed to the continuing need to confirm science with Scripture.

It was during the seventeenth century, however, that the first attempts were made to resolve whether variation in human skin color was due to innate differences in biological structure or simply a transitional response to the sun's heat. Among the first to formally address this issue was the Italian physician-anatomist and former pupil of Galileo, Santorio Santorio (also known as Sanctorius) (1561–1636), who, in his *De statica medicina* (a pioneering treatise on the physiology of metabolism) published in 1614, resuscitated an idea first proposed by the Arabian physician 'Ali al-Tabari in his ninth-century medical compendium *Paradise of Wisdom*[3]—that the skin's complexion was determined by the presence of bile. Toward the end of the century, the Italian anatomist Marcello Malpighi (1628–1694) (1687) added his support to the authority of the bile theory when he presented the first scientific description of the skin's structure. Although employing different terms, he correctly identified the principal structural elements of mammalian skin: (1) the *cutis* (dermis), which contains the blood

vessels and hair follicles and upon which is superimposed a sticky sheath of tissue forming the *rete mucosum* (now known as the Malpighian layer (*vide infra*; see Fig. 1); and (2) the *cuticula* (now known generally as the *stratum corneum*) that forms the horny external surface of the skin. Having determined that the *cuticula* and the *cutis* were colorless in both Blacks and Whites, Malpighi concurred with Sanctorius that the blackness of the African Negro must, therefore, originate in the underlying mucous and reticular body (*rete mucosum*).[4]

During the first half of the eighteenth century, the bile theory was further advanced by a number of scholars, most notably by the Dutch anatomist Bernhard Siegfried Albinus (1697–1770) (1737) and the French physician Pierre Barrère (1690–1755) (1741), both of whom reported that their experimental observations had revealed the presence of black bile in the *rete mucosum*. To many, these studies, particularly that of Barrère, were considered to be a decisive refutation of the environmental hypothesis (cf. Edward Long's [1734–1813] *History of Jamaica*, Vol. 2:351–352, 1774), which in turn lent credence to the earlier cautious speculations of such observers as John Atkins (1658–1757) (1734:23–24) that the European and African Negro had been derived from different "protoplasts."

In the meantime, scholars who were anxious to avoid the polygenistic implications of the bile theory (cf., Feijoo 1736) tended to cite the work of the French surgeon Alexis Littré (1658–1726), whose experiments had evidently failed to demonstrate a black gelatinous bile in the *rete mucosum* of Negroes (cf. Robins 1991:4). In an effort to circumvent objections against the case of the sun's heat being the primary cause of differences in human complexion, many of these same scholars began advocating a more complex view of the environment in which, among other things, they stressed the differential quality of the atmosphere. Grounded in the Hippocratic thesis *De aere, aquis et locis*, this aerobic theory was first enunciated in the eighteenth century by the French Abbé Jean Baptiste Du Bos (1670–1742) in his philosophical treatise *Réflexions* (1719). It was subsequently expanded by such workers as the German philologist Johann Albert Fabricius (1668–1736) (1721), the Scottish physician John Arbuthnot (1667–1735) (1733), and the Spanish cleric-scholar Benito Gerónimo Feijoo (1676–1764) (1736). As seen from Johann Friedrich Blumenbach's (1752–1840) highly influential thesis *De generis humani varietate nativa* (1795), this aerobic theory remained popular well into the opening decades of the nineteenth century.

Among the supporters of the aerobic theory in the mid-eighteenth century was the French physiologist Claude Nicolas Le Cat (1700–1768). From his microscopic studies conducted at the Hôtel-Dieu in Rouen, Le Cat discerned the presence of black deposits, what he called "æthiops," in the nerve tissues of a variety of animals (1765a). It was this apparent connection of æthiops with nerve tissue that led him to reject the bile theory as an explanation of skin color. In his *Traité de la couleur de la peau humaine en général, et de celle des Nègres en particulier* (1765b), he conjectured that these mysterious æthiopic structures might be the basis of the Negro's dark complexion. While at a loss to explain the origin and role of æthiops, he was convinced that there was an intrinsic relation between these structures and the environment, noting that the Negro probably had a greater number of these structures than Europeans did.

Another alternative to the bile theory during the first half of the eighteenth century was what might be called the "optics" theory, which claimed that the differences in human complexion resided in the skin's ability to transmit light. One of the earliest versions of this optics theory was articulated by the French poet-novelist Simon Tyssot de Patot (1655–1738) in 1733. A far more elaborate version was offered a decade later by the American physician John Mitchell (1711–1768), who has the distinction of producing the first major scientific study of ethnic pigmentation in the New World (published by the Royal Society of London in 1744). Through his comparative study of the skin of colonial Whites and African slaves in Virginia, Mitchell concluded that there was no empirical basis for the bile theory. The only structural difference he could find was in the thickness of the skin. This led him to apply the principles of Newtonian optics and to conjecture that the color of the skin was determined by its thickness and ability to transmit light. As the thickness increased, so the skin appeared proportionally darker. In the case of the African Negro, whose skin was claimed to be comparatively thicker, Mitchell concluded that their skin "transmit[ed] no Colour thro' them" (1744:124). Mitchell's thesis is further distinguished by his rejection of the then popular notion (at least among those supporting a monogenetic thesis of human origins) that the "primitive and original Complexion of Mankind" had been white. Mitchell believed that the original skin color had been neither white nor black, but rather something in between, and that Whites and Blacks represented two divergent extremes mediated by the degenerative influence of the environment.

During the eighteenth century, several variations on the theme of the "degeneration of the primordial type" can be found in the literature. For example, the French naturalist Georges-Louis Leclerc Buffon (1707–1788) developed evidence for what he termed the geographical degeneration of human beings. To effect a restoration of the "degenerate races to the purity and vigor of the original type," Buffon contended, would require the transplantation of these peoples to a more temperate zone, plus a change of diet and a long span of time (cf. Buffon 1749:523–530, 1766:314–315). Another version of this degenerative theme was that pigmentation was essentially a pathology precipitated by adverse environmental conditions. An early example of this theme can be found in the writings of the French Jesuit missionary Joseph F. Lafitau (1670–1746) (1724), who lived for a while (1712–1717) among the Canadian Iroquois. Cognizant of the arguments against the environmental hypothesis, and impressed by the reports that the fetuses of African Negroes were already pigmented, he conjectured that this pigmented condition was a congenital malformation. Later, the American physician

Benjamin Rush (1745–1813) claimed that the skin color of the Negro was "derived from the Leprosy" (cf. Rush 1799). According to Rush, the African Negro was suffering from a congenital disease that was so mild in form that excess pigment was essentially its only symptom. Similarly, albinism and other conditions resulting in depigmentation in African Negroes were viewed by many eighteenth-century scholars as evidence of a reversion to the original complexion. A case in point is that of Henry Moss, an African-American from Virginia, whose condition had been used by the American scholar Samuel Stanhope Smith (1750–1819) to support the argument for pigmentation being nothing more than a "universal freckle." Moss' condition, however, was not albinism, but rather what appears to have been bilateral vitiligo, an idiopathic condition (whose etiology is still uncertain) characterized by enlarging patches of depigmented skin that give the individual a piebald appearance. It is interesting to note in passing that in the late nineteenth century, the description of melanin spots, sometimes known as the "Mongolian" or "sacral" spots, aroused a similar interest, and for a while they were considered to be a racial marker. Among the first Western scientists to investigate this condition was the German anatomist Erwin O. Baelz (1849–1913) (1883), followed later by several Japanese workers, most notably Buntaro Adachi (1865–1945) (Adachi 1903; Adachi & Fujisawa 1903). The demonstration of similar spots in the nonhuman primates by Adachi and others led some workers to suggest that these spots were proof of "evolutionary primitivism" (Ratsimamanga 1941).

By the close of the eighteenth century, it was well recognized that there was an inherent connection between the skin's complexion and the color of the hair and the iris of the eye (cf. Blumenbach 1795, in Bendyshe 1865:223–226). Among Europeans with fair and lightly pigmented skins, the color of the eyes ranged from blue to gray, whereas in all other groups the eye color was found to be dark brown or black. It was the same with the coloring of the hair. In those with fair or light skins the hair color was highly variable, whereas among those with pigmented skins the hair color was invariably black. A satisfactory explanation for this apparent conformity, however, continued to elude researchers until well into the twentieth century. In the meantime, hair color and form became an increasingly common feature of racial classifications in the nineteenth century (see Table 1).

In 1860, the German anatomist Heinrich Müller (1820–1864) demonstrated the presence of pigment-forming cells (*ramificirte Pigmentzellen*) in the skin of rats, which was followed soon thereafter by the observation of similar cells in human epithelium by the Swiss zoologist Albert von Kölliker (1817–1905) (1867). Although the terms "Melanian" and "Melanic" (derived from the Greek *melas*: μελαζ meaning black) had been introduced at the beginning of the nineteenth century as synonyms with Negroid (cf. Bory de Saint Vincent 1825; Prichard 1826), it appears that the French physician Charles Robin (1821–1885) was the first to apply the term *mélanique* to describe the pigment-forming cells in animals (cited in Robins 1991). At this juncture, while the underlying causes of skin color continued to mystify researchers, they did not dampen the enthusiasm of anthropologists, who continued to regard them as a primary racial marker (see Table 1). In an effort to objectify and refine classificatory schemes, anthropologists began developing chromatic scales such as the one produced by the French anthropologist Paul Broca (1824–1880) (1865). Broca's scheme recognized thirty-four color tones, which his protégé, Paul Topinard (1830–1911), later simplified, and was widely adopted (cf. Garson & Read 1892). These efforts to objectify the estimation of skin tones continued on into the twentieth century (e.g., Todd et al. 1928; Bowman 1930), leading ultimately to the introduction of reflectance spectrophotometry in the early 1950s (cf. Weiner 1951; Lasker 1954; Garn et al. 1956), which provided the means for the collection of a more reliable body of comparative data for evaluating not only the relationship between pigmentation and solar radiation (e.g., Leguebe 1961; Harrison et al. 1967; Roberts 1972; Frisancho et al. 1981), but also the genetic determinants of skin color variation (*vide infra*).

Meanwhile, in the closing years of the nineteenth century, experimental evidence had revealed that melanization in plants and insects involved an enzyme tyrosinase, which catalyzed the oxidation of the amino acid tyrosine to melanin (cf. Fitzpatrick et al. 1950). Although it was generally assumed that a similar process occurred in mammalian skin, it was not until the middle decades of the twentieth century that this was confirmed. The experiments of the German histochemist Bruno Bloch (1878–1933) (cf. Bloch 1927) demonstrated that sections of human skin incubated in a solution containing dopa (3,4–dihydroxyphenylalanine) formed black granules in cells (which he called "melano-blasts") at the epidermal–dermal junction, whereas in skin incubated in solutions containing either tyrosine or epinephrine, no such deposition occurred. This led Bloch to conclude that the melanoblasts in human skin contained a specific "dopa oxidase." Soon thereafter, a British researcher, Henry Stanley Raper (d. 1951) (1928), established that dopa was, in fact, the first product formed in the enzymatic oxidation of tyrosine to melanin in the tissues of both plants and insects. Later, the American histochemist Thomas B. Fitzpatrick (b. 1917) and his coworkers at Harvard confirmed that a similar pathway was operative in human skin (Fitzpatrick et al. 1950). Coinciding with this was the demonstration that melanin was synthesized exclusively in the cytoplasm of specific dendritic cells (melanocytes) (Billingham 1948) and that these cells originate in the neural crest during the early stages of embryonic life (Rawles 1953).

From this collective work, it was firmly established that the melanocytes reside exclusively in the basal strata of the epidermis, which is composed of four distinct layers (see Fig. 1b). The basal *stratum germinativum* (also called the *stratum basale*) produces the melanocytes, which constitute about 10 percent of

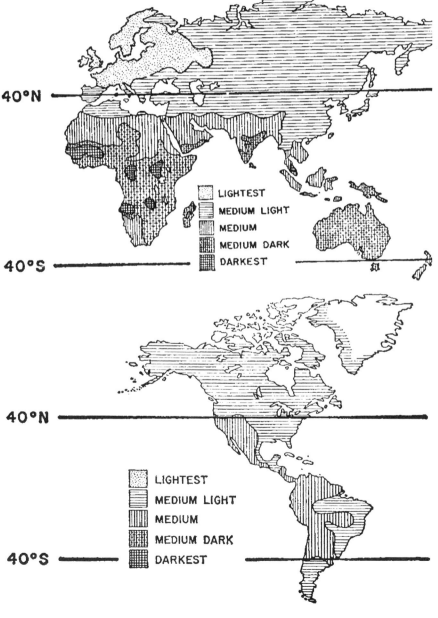

Fig. 2. Geographic distribution of human skin color. From Loomis 1967.

the cells in this relatively thick layer of cells. Resting on this layer of columnar cells is the *stratum spinosum*, which is composed of several layers of irregular polyhedral cells, often called "prickle cells" because their surfaces are covered with short spines that serve to link these cells together. Often the term Malpighian layer is used to refer jointly to the *stratum basale* and the *stratum spinosum*. Sandwiched between this Malpighian layer and the uppermost *stratum corneum* is a quilt of cells known as the *stratum granulosum*. This layer is composed of flattened polyhedral cells, which produce keratin granules (keratinocytes) that ultimately lead to the destruction of the cell's nucleus. These dead, horny, nonnucleated cells form the outer exfoliative layers of the *stratum corneum*. As this suggests, a major function of the Malpighian layer is to provide a continual supply of keratinized cells to the external horny layer. Melanin production is another feature of the protective properties of the epidermis, produced by the melanocytes, which are specialized dendritic cells (see Fig. 1c) located exclusively in the *stratum germinativum*. The melanin-granules (now known as melanosomes) produced in the Malpighian layer are phagocytized by surrounding epidermal cells where they evidently serve to form a protective shield around the resident nucleus. Experimental evidence has shown that melanin is, indeed, an effective shield against the damaging effects of ultraviolet (UV) radiation in sunlight (e.g., Thomson 1955), and there is little doubt that this has been an important contributing factor in the differential melanization of human populations.

While the density of melanocytes is seen to vary according to the region of the body, the total number of melanocytes per surface area in any one part of the body is the same within and between the human races (cf. Robins 1991). There is no correlation between skin complexion and the number of melanocytes present in the epidermis; skin color differences are due primarily to the amount of melanin produced by the melanocytes (*vide infra*). Variation in skin color is dependent not only on melanin, but also on the presence of relative proportions of carotene in the surrounding tissues and hemoglobin in neighboring capillary blood vessels (cf. Robins 1991).

In addition to the protective role of melanin, the results of modern research have shown that there are many other extrinsic as well as intrinsic factors involved in the determination of skin color. Among the latter, it is now known that the skin is the site for the endogenous production of vitamin D. This fat-soluble vitamin stimulates the absorption of calcium and phosphate from the gut, which are essential for maintaining normal bone development. Although vitamin D can be obtained from dietary sources such as fish oils, most is manufactured within the skin of the human body.

While the idea of an intrinsic relationship between vitamin D synthesis and the evolution of the white skin was first suggested in the early 1930s (cf. Murray 1934), this hypothesis went unattended until the mid-1970s, when it was refined and popularized by the American biochemist, W. Farnsworth Loomis. The Loomis version of the so-called vitamin D hypothesis endeavored to provide a comprehensive explanation of the differential development of skin color in human populations.

In a nutshell, Loomis proposed that the rate of vitamin D synthesis in the *stratum granulosum* is governed by the twin (protective) processes of pigmentation and keratinization of the overlying *stratum corneum*, which permit only regulated amounts of UV radiation to penetrate into the deeper layers of the skin, where it is required to convert the endogenous provitamin 7-dehydrocholesterol to vitamin D. Accordingly, racial variation in skin color is viewed as an adaptation that serves to maximize UV transmission in northern latitudes, where UV levels are generally low, and to minimize it in those latitudes closer to the equator, where the levels tend to be higher (see Fig. 2), so that the rate of vitamin D is maintained within normal physiological limits (Loomis 1967:501).

As long suspected, skin color is a hereditary character, whose inheritance is polygenic. Among the first to investigate the genetics of human skin color was the American eugenicist Charles Benedict Davenport (1866–1944), who deduced from his studies that skin color was controlled by two allelic pairs of cumulative factors (Davenport & Danielson 1913). Later, the anthropologist Reginald Ruggles Gates (1882–1962) in 1953 based on his study of the pedigrees of Negro families, concluded that three genes were involved. At the same time, the geneticist Curt Stern (1953), employing color-top data collected by Melville Herskovits (1895–1963) in the late 1920s on African-American populations in Louisiana (cf. Herskovits 1930), estimated that four to six loci are involved. This was followed by a study conducted by the British physical anthropologist Geoffrey Ainsworth Harrison, who estimated that skin color varia-

TABLE 1. Some examples of the Differential Employment of Skin Color in Racial Classification from 1684–1959

Pub. Date	Author	sc	h	n	cf	Notes
1684	François Bernier*	P	S	S		Recognized five *espèces*, though it is clear he does not mean species in the modern sense of the word. His "Nouvelle division de la terre par les différentes espèces ou races d'hommes qui l'habitent," was published in the *Journal des Sçavans*.
1721	Richard Bradley*	P	P			Characterized five major groups. His scheme was presented in a volume titled *A Philosophical Account of the Works of Nature*.
1758	Carolus Linnaeus (Carl v. Linné)*	P	P	S		In the 10th edition of his *Systema naturae*, Linnaeus placed human beings in the order Primates. In addition to his continuing acknowledgement of monstrous races such as Patagonian giants and feral man (*Homo ferus*, also known in the early literature as *H. sylvestris*), Linnaeus recognized four geographical varieties: Americanus, Europaeus, Asiaticus, and Afer. In addition to emphasizing skin color and hair color and type, he also noted that these geographic varieties manifested a suite of psychocultural characteristics.
1795	Johann Friedrich Blumenbach*	P	S	P		In the third edition of *De generis humani varietate nativa*, Blumenbach (contra Linnaeus) advocated the placement of humans in a separate suborder. Although acknowledging that the divisions of humankind were arbitrary, he nevertheless emphasized the utility of skin color and cranial morphology in characterizing the five varieties he identified: Caucasian (Europeans), Mongolian, Ethiopian (African), American, and Malayan (peoples of Oceania).
1801	Julien Joseph Virey	S	S		P	In his *Histoire naturelle du genre humaine*, Virey claimed that humankind consisted of two species that were separated by their facial angles. He further subdivided these two species into six major races. Species 1 (angle > 85°) contained four races: *blanche, jaune, cuivreuse et brune;* and Species 2 (angle 75° à 80°) contained two races: *noire et noirâtre* (e.g., "Hottentots").
1825	Jean-Baptiste Bory de Saint Vincent	S	P			Following in the footsteps of Virey, Bory de Saint Vincent identified fifteen separate human species, which he organized into two subgenera. The latter were characterized by their hair type: those with smooth hair (*Léiotriques à cheveux lisses*) and those with crinkled hair (*Ulotriques à cheveux crépu*). This polygenetic scheme was published in his two-volume work *L'Homme: Essai zoologique sur le genre humain*.
1868	Ernest Haeckel*	S	P		P	In his *Natürliche Schöpfungsgeschichte,* Haeckel proposed that humankind was composed of two divergent branches: the *Ulotrichi* ("woolly haired men") and the *Lisotrichi* ("straight haired men"). Within these two branches he identified twelve distinct races.

TABLE 1. continued	Pub. Date	Author	sc	h	n	cf	Notes
	1870	Thomas Henry Huxley*	P	P		P	Using skin color, hair, and cranial morphology as primary features, Huxley identified four major stocks (a term he preferred to varieties or races): Negroid, Australoid, Mongoloid, and Xanthochroi, which were subdivided into fourteen secondary "modifications." For further details, see Huxley entry, and his original article "On the Geographical Distribution of the Chief Modifications of Mankind." *Journal of the Ethnological Society of London* 2 (n.s.):404–412.
	1885	Paul Topinard*	P	(P)	P		Prior to 1885, Topinard had used hair type to characterize three primary groups that he subdivided into sixteen secondary races. In 1885, however, using nasal morphology and skin color, he identified three primary groups: the White Leptorrhine races, the Yellow Mesorrhine races, and the Black Platyrrhine races, which he subdivided into nineteen secondary races.
	1889	Joseph Deniker	P	P		P	Deniker recognized what he called "natural" groups, which he subdivided into two dozen or more subraces based on skin color, hair type, cranial form, and other physical characteristics. In the 1926 edition of his book *Les races et les peuples de la terre*, his final tally was twenty-nine races.
	1923	Roland Burrage Dixon			P	P	Dixon employed essentially three cranial indices for his racial classification: (1) horizontal cephalic index, (2) length-height index, and (3) nasal index. From these he derived three morphological types, which were then grouped into twenty-seven different combinations. For further details, see his book *Racial History of Man*.
	1925	Alfred Cort Haddon*	S	P	S	S	The principal character in Haddon's classification is hair type, compounded with skin color, nasal index, and cranial morphology. Using hair type, Haddon identified three primary groups: *Ulotrichi* (woolly hair), *Cymotrichi* (smooth wavy hair), and *Leiotrichi* (straight hair), which were subdivided into sixteen subgroups. See his book *The Races of Man and Their Distribution* for further details.
	1948	Henri V. Vallois*	P				Based primarily on skin color, Vallois classified humanity into twenty-seven secondary races, which were sorted into four primary racial groups: Australoid race, Black race, Yellow race, and White race. For details on this scheme, see his book *Les races humaines*.
	1950	Carleton S. Coon* Stanley M. Garn* Joseph B. Birdsell	P	P	P	P	The classification presented by these authors is described as a "tentative" list of thirty "races" that are not based on traditional superficial characters but rather on "morphological-evolutionary" features such as tooth and jaw size, and on somatic characters that appear to be adaptations to environmental factors (e.g., temperature). For further details, see their book *A Study of the Problems of Race Formation in Man* and Garn's sequel, *Human Races*, published a decade later.

Pub.Date	Author	sc	h	n	cf	Notes
1959	Renato Biasutti*	P	P	P	P	In his book *Le Razze ed i Popoli della Terra*, Biasutti proposed and described four subspecies, sixteen primary and fifty-two secondary races. Skin color appears to be the primary character, supplemented by other physical characters.

Note: * Denotes a biographical entry in this volume; sc: skin color; h: hair type/color; n: nasal morphology; cf: cranial form; P: primary; S: secondary.

tion was best explained by four pairs of factors (Harrison & Owen 1964). The American physical anthropologist Frank B. Livingstone (1969) arrived at a similar conclusion. Although it is now generally agreed that only a relatively small number of genes are involved, the exact number and the underlying mechanisms remain unknown (cf. Byard & Lees 1981; Robins 1991).

(For a comprehensive review of modern research on the biology of human pigmentation, see Robins 1991.)

Frank Spencer

Endnotes

1. The plays of William Shakespeare (1564–1616) contain several such references. For example, in the *Merchant of Venice*, Act 2, Scene 1, the Prince of Morocco says to Portia: "Mislike me not for my complexion, / The shadowed livery of the burnished sun, / To whom I am a neighbour and near bred, / Bring me the fairest creature northward born, / Where Phoebus' fire scarce thaws the icicles. . . ." Another popular version of this environmental hypothesis was the story of Phaeton: "The Æthiopians then were white and fayre, / Though by the worlds combustion since made black / When wanton Phaeton overthrew the Sun" (cited in R.W. Ward (ed): *The poetical works of William Basse, 1602–1653*. (London: Ellis & Elvey, 1893).

2. The term "Moor" was widely used in the early literature as a synonym of the more enduring term "Negro." In the early English literature, the term "blackamoor" (derived from "Black Moor") is also frequently encountered. Evidently, this term was introduced to distinguish the Black Negro from the Moors of North Africa, the latter being another general term embracing the Berbers and the Arabs. However, among Continental scholars, the term Moor continued to be used well into the eighteenth century to describe sub-Saharan Black Africans, with resulting confusion.

3. Specifically, 'Ali al-Tabari notes: ". . . When in anyone the light bile predominates, he becomes light-skinned; when dark bile predominates, he becomes dark-skinned" (cited in E. Boyd: *Origins of the study of human growth*. Eugene, Oregon: University of Oregon, 1980, p. 127).

4. Malpighi: "Certum enim est, ipsis cutim albam esse, sicuti & cuticula, unde tota nigredo a subjecto mucoso, & reticulari corpore ortum trahit" (Malpighi 1687, Vol. 2:204, cited in Adelmann 1966, Vol. 1:259).

See also Bernier, François; Blumenbach, Johann Friedrich; Broca, Paul (Pierre); Buffon, (Comte) Georges-Louis Leclerc; Davenport, Charles Benedict; Greco-Roman Anthropology; Haddon, A(lfred) C(ort); Hakluyt, Richard; Koganei, Yoshikiyo; Mitchell, John; Polygenism; Race Concept; Smith, Samuel Stanhope; Topinard, Paul

Bibliography

B. Adachi: Hautpigment beim Menschen und bei den Affen. *Zeitschrift für Morphologie und Anthropologie* 6:1–131, 1903; B. Adachi & K. Fujisawa: Mongolen-Kindefleck bei Europäern. *Zeitschrift für Morphologie und Anthropologie* 6:132–133, 1903; H.B. Adelmann: *Marcello Malpighi and the evolution of embryology*. 5 vols. Ithaca, New York: Cornell University Press, 1966; B.S. Albinus: *De sede et causa coloris Aethiopicum et caeterorum hominum*. Leidae Batavorum: Haak, 1737; J. Arbuthnot: *An essay concerning the effects of the air on human bodies*. London: Towson, 1733; J. Atkins: *The Navy surgeon; or, A practical system of surgery*. London: Ward & Chandler, 1734; E.O. Baelz: *Die körperlichen Eigenschaften der Japaner: Eine anthropologische studie*. Yokohama: "Echo du Japan," 1883.

E.O. Baelz: Menschen-Rassen Ost-Asiens mit specieller Rücksicht auf Japaner. *Zeitschrift für Ethnologie* 33:166–190, 1901; P. Barrère: *Dissertation sur la cause physique de la couleur des Nègres, de la qualité de leurs cheveux et de la dégénération de l'un et de l'autre.* Paris: Simon, 1741; F. Bernier: Nouvelle division de la terre par les différentes espèces ou races d'hommes qui l'habitent. *Journal des Sçavans* 12:148–155, 1684. Reprint in English, translated by T. Bendyshe: The history of anthropology. *Memoirs of the Anthropological Society of London* 1:360–364, 1864; R.E. Billingham: Dendritic cells. *Journal of Anatomy* 82:93–109, 1948; B. Bloch: Das pigment. In: B. Bloch *Handbuch der haut- und geschlectskrankheit.* Vol. 1, *Anatomie der Haut.* Berlin: Springer, 1927, pp. 434–541.

J.F. Blumenbach: *De generis humani varietate nativa.* 3d ed. Göttingen: Vandenhoek & Ruprecht, 1795. Reprint in English, translated by T. Bendyshe (ed) *The anthropological treatises of J.F. Blumenbach.* London: Longman, Green, Longman, Roberts & Green, 1865, pp. 145–276; J.B. Bory de Saint Vincent: *L'homme: Essai zoologique sur le genre humain.* 2 vols. Paris: Gravier, 1825; H.A. Bowman: The color-top method of estimating skin pigmentation. *American Journal of Physical Anthropology* 14:59–72, 1930; P. Broca: Instructions générales pour les recherches et observations anthropologiques. *Mémoires de la Société d'Anthropologie de Paris* 2:113–123, 1865; T. Browne: *Pseudodoxia epidemica.* London: Dod, 1646. Reprinted in C. Sayle (ed): *The works of Sir Thomas Browne.* Vol. 2. London: Richards, 1904.

G. Buffon: Variétés dans l'espèce humaine. In: G. Buffon (ed) *Histoire naturelle, générale et particulière, avec la description du Cabinet du Roi.* Vol. 3. Paris: Imprimerie Royale, 1749; G. Buffon: De la dégénération des animaux. In G. Buffon (ed) *Histoire naturelle, générale et particulière, avec la description du cabinet du Roi.* Vol. 14. Paris; Imprimerie Royale, 1766; T. Burnet: *Sacred theory of the Earth.* London: Norton, 1691; P.J. Byard & F.C. Lees: Estimating the number of loci determining skin colour in a hybrid population. *Annals of Human Biology* 8:49–58, 1981; C.B. Davenport & F.H. Danielson: *Skin color in Negro White crosses.* Carnegie Institution of Washington Publication. No. 188. Washington, D.C.: Carnegie Institution, 1913; J.B. Du Bos: *Réflexions critiques sur la poésie et la peinture.* Paris: Mariette, 1719.

J.A. Fabricius: *Dissertation critica de hominibus orbis incolis.* Hamburgensis, 1721. Reprinted in English, translated by T.

Bendyshe. In: The History of anthropology. *Memoirs of the Anthropological Society of London* I:372–419, 1864; B.J. Feijoo: Color etiopico. In: *Teatro critico universal.* Vol. 3. Madrid: Mojados, 1736; T.B. Fitzpatrick (ed): *Biology of normal and abnormal melanocytes.* Baltimore: University Park Press, 1971; T.B. Fitzpatrick et al.: Tyrosinase in human kin: Demonstration of its presence and of its role in human melanin formation. *Science* 112:223–225, 1950; A.R. Frisancho et al.: Heritability components of phenotypic expression in skin reflectance of Mestizos from the Peruvian lowlands. *American Journal of Physical Anthropology* 55:203–208, 1981.

S.M. Garn et al.: Skin reflectance studies in children and adults. *American Journal of Physical Anthropology* 14:101–117, 1956; S.M. Garn et al.: Skin reflectance studies in children and adults. *American Journal of Physical Anthropology* 14:101–117, 1956; J.G. Garson & C.H. Read: *Notes and queries on anthropology.* 2d ed. London, Anthropological Institute, 1892; R.R. Gates: A new theory of skin-colour inheritance. *International Anthropological and Linguistic Review* 1:15–67, 1953; R. Hakluyt: *The principal navigations: voiages, traffiques and discoveries of the English nation.* London: Bishop & Newberie, 1589; G.A. Harrison & J.J.T. Owen: Studies on the inheritance of human skin color. *Annals of Human Genetics* 28:27–37, 1964; G.A. Harrison et al.: Skin colour in southern Brazilian populations. *Human Biology* 39:21–31, 1967.

M.J. Herskovits: The anthropometry of the American Negro. *Columbia University Contributions in Anthropology* 11:1–283, 1930; A. von Kölliker: *Handbuch der Gewebelehre des Menschens.* Leipzig: Engelmann, 1867; J.F. Lafitau: *Moeurs des sauvages Amériquains comparées aux moeurs des premiers temps.* Paris: Saugrain, 1724; G.W. Lasker: Photoelectric measurement of skin color in a Mexican Mestizo population. *American Journal of Physical Anthropology* 12:115–121, 1954; C.N. Le Cat: *Traite de l'existence, {sic} de la nature et des propriétés du fluide des nerfs, et principalement de son action dans le mouvement musculaire.* Berlin, 1765a; C.N. Le Cat: *Traité de la couleur de la peau humaine en générale, et de celle Nègres en particulier, et de la métamorphose d'une des ses couleurs en l'autre, soit de naissance, soit accidentellement.* Amsterdam, 1765b; A. Leguebe: Contribution à l'étude de la pigmentation chez l'homme. *Bulletin de l'Institut Royale des Sciences Naturelles de Belgique* 37:1–29, 1961.

F.B. Livingstone: Polygenic model for the evolution of human skin color differences. *Human Biology* 41:480–493, 1969; E. Long: *The history of Jamaica; or, A general survey of the antient and modern state of that island.* 3 vols. London: Lowndes, 1774; W.F. Loomis: Skin-pigment regulation of vitamin-D biosynthesis in man. *Science* 157:501–506, 1967; M. Malpighi: *Opera omnia.* 2 vols. Lugduni Batavorum, 1687; J. Mitchell: An essay upon the causes of the different colour of people in different climates. *Philosophical Transactions of the Royal Society of London* 43:102–150, 1744; H. Müller: Bewegungs-Erscheinungen an ramification Pigment-Zellen in der Epidermis. *Würzburger naturwissenschaftlichen Zeitschrift* 1:164–166, 1860.

F.G. Murray: Pigmentation, sunlight and nutritional disease. *American Anthropologist* 36:438–445, 1934; J. Ovington: *A voyage to Surat in the year 1689.* London: Towson, 1696. Reprint, edited by H.G. Rawlinson. London: Oxford University Press, 1929; J.N. Pechlin: *De habitu et colore Æthiopum qui vulgo nigritae.* Kiloni: Reumanni, 1677; J.C. Prichard: *Researches into the physical history of mankind.* 2 vols. London: Arch, 1826; H.S. Raper: Aerobic oxidase. *Physiological Review* 8:245–282, 1928; A.R. Ratsimamanga: Tache pigmentaire héréditaire et origine de Malgaches. *Revue Anthropologique* 50:5–128, 1941; M. Rawles: Origin of mammalian pigment and its role in the pigmentation of hair. In: M. Gordon (ed) *Pigment cell growth.* New York: Academic Press, 1953, pp. 1–15.

D.F. Roberts: Human pigmentation: Its geographical distribution and biological significance. *Journal of the Society of Cosmetic Chemists* 28:329–342, 1972; A.H. Robins: *Biological perspectives on human pigmentation.* Cambridge: Cambridge University Press, 1991; B. Rush: Observations intended to favour a supposition that the black colour (as it is called) of the Negroes is derived from the Leprosy. *Transactions of the American Philosophical Society* 4:289–297, 1799; S. Santorio: *De statica medicina.* Venetiis: Polum, 1614; C. Stern: Model estimates of the frequency of white and near-white segregants in the American Negro. *Acta Genetica* 4:281–298, 1953.

C. Stern: Model estimates of the number of gene pairs involved in pigmentation variability of the Negro-American. *Human Heredity* 20:165–168, 1970; M.L.

Thomson: Relative efficiency of pigment and horny layer thickness in protecting the skin of Europeans and Africans against solar ultraviolet radiation. *Journal of Physiology* 127:236–246, 1955; T.W. Todd et al.: Skin pigmentation: The color-top method of recording. *American Journal of Physical Anthropology* 11:187–204, 1928; S. Tyssot de Patot: *Voyages et avantures de Jacques Massé.* Bordeaux: Aveugle, 1710. Reprinted in translation by S. Whatley. London: Watts, 1733; J.S. Weiner: A spectrophotometer for measurement of skin colour. *Man* 51:152–153, 1951.

Smith, (Sir) Grafton Elliot (1871–1937)

Born in Grafton, New South Wales (Australia), Smith received his medical training at the University of Sydney, where he graduated M.B., Ch.M. in 1893, and M.D. in 1895. The subject of his doctoral dissertation was the *Anatomy and Histology of the Cerebrum of the Nonplacental Mammal.* At this juncture, he received a traveling scholarship from the University of Sydney, which enabled him to further his anatomical research in England, specifically, at the University of Cambridge. While in Cambridge, he was awarded a research scholarship by the British Medical Association in 1898 and elected a Fellow at St. John's College in 1899. During this period, he was invited by Charles Stewart (1840–1907), then conservator at the Royal College of Surgeons (RCS) (London), to undertake the preparation of a new descriptive *Catalogue* of the mammalian and reptilian brains in the RCS collections, which he completed in 1902. In the meantime, in July 1900, he had received and accepted another invitation to become the first occupant of the Chair of Anatomy in the Government School of Medicine in Cairo. Smith held this position from 1900 until 1909 when he returned to England, where he had been appointed to the Chair of Anatomy at Manchester University. He remained there until 1919, when he succeeded George D. Thane (1850–1930) as professor of anatomy at University College, London—a position he retained until his death.

As chair of the newly established Department of Anatomy at the Government School of Medicine in Cairo, he became interested in preserved brains that were recovered from archeological sites at El Amrah. While he retained an interest in neurology (he published forty-two papers on the topic while in Cairo), his preoccupation with paleopathology grew. The recovery of splints in Egypt and their comparison with those found in the Sudan and Abyssinia suggested diffusion. His analysis of what he called "chance and a multitude of arbitrary circumstances" in the process of mummification (1906) supported this contention. His interest in mummification also resulted in a monograph on the royal mummies (1912b) and a review on mummies coauthored with the anatomist Warren R. Dawson (1888–1968) (1924). Smith (1915b) saw similarities in the process of mummification in Egyptian and Australian mummies and concluded that it was further evidence of cultural diffusion. His books *The Migrations of Early Culture* (1915a) and *The Ancient Egyptians and the Origin of Civilization* (1923) summarize his elaborate theory of cultural diffusion.

Smith was the major force in planning and completing the Archaeological Survey of Nubia. In 1902, the Egyptian government completed the great dam at Aswan, and the reservoir that was created in 1903 destroyed many monuments, such as the Temple at Philae, and inundated thousands of burials. The public outrage was extensive, and later when government officials decided to raise the height of the dam a further 7 m, they realized they could not repeat the earlier fiasco. The government decided to record all threatened antiquities and examine, describe, photograph, and recover all burials. The recovery of these skeletal populations represents the largest sample of burials that have ever been excavated from archeological sites. In 1907, more than 6,000 mummies were recovered in one season—Frederic Wood Jones (1879–1954) was called in to help; in all, nearly 10,000 bodies were eventually studied. The analysis by Smith and his coworkers revealed the prevalence of many interesting diseases. For example, the following were diagnosed in mummified remains: appendicular adhesions (Smith & Dawson 1924), gout (Smith & Dawson 1924), scrotal hernia (Smith 1912b), leprosy (Smith & Derry 1910; Smith & Dawson 1924), carcinoma (Smith & Dawson 1924; Smith & Derry 1910), smallpox (Smith 1912b), mastoid infection (Smith & Jones 1910; Smith & Dawson 1924), and tuberculosis (Smith & Jones 1908; Smith & Ruffer 1910). The methods developed during these studies changed the course of paleopathology.

Smith also made substantial contributions in primate evolution. He believed that primate evolution could be characterized by increasing neurological development in those areas associated with sight, touch, and hear-

ing (cf. Smith 1910, 1912a). He also played a role in the interpretation of the now infamous Piltdown skull with his influential assessment of the neurocranial endocast (e.g., Smith 1913a, b).

He accumulated many honors during his career, including a Fellowship of the Royal Society in 1907, a Royal Medal in 1912, a knighthood in 1934, and the decoration of Chevalier de l'Ordre National de la Legion d'Honneur in 1936.

Smith died at Broadstairs, Kent, on 1 January 1937.

George J. Armelagos

See also Jones, Frederic Wood; Neuroanatomy, Comparative; Paleopathology; Piltdown

Bibliography
SELECTED WORKS

The origin of the *Corpus callosum:* A comparative study of the hippocampal region of the cerebrum of Marsupialia and Cheiroptera. *Transactions of the Linnean Society* (London) 7:47–69, 1897; The natural subdivision of the cerebral hemisphere. *Journal of Anatomy and Physiology* 35:431–454, 1901; *Descriptive and illustrated catalogue of the Physiological Series of Comparative Anatomy contained in the Museum of the Royal College of Surgeons of England.* London: Taylor & Francis, 1902; A contribution to the study of mummification in Egypt. *Mémoires présentés à l'Institut Égyptien* 5:1–53, 1906; The causation of the symmetrical thinning of the parietal bone in ancient Egyptians. *Journal of Anatomy and Physiology* 41:232–233, 1907; Arris and Gale Lectures on some problems relating to the evolution of the brain. (Summary). *Nature* 82:349–350, 1910.

Presidential address to the Anthropological Section, British Association for the Advancement of Science meeting in Dundee (Scotland). *Nature* 92:118–126, 1912a; *The royal mummies.* Catalogue général des antiquités Égyptiennes du Musée du Caire. No. 61051–61100. Cairo: Service des Antiquités de l'Égypt, 1912b; The Piltdown skull and brain cast. *Nature* 92:267–268, 318–319, 1913a; Preliminary report on the endocranial cast [of the Piltdown skull]. *Quarterly Journal of the Geological Society of London* 69:145–147, 1913b; *The migrations of early culture.* London: Longmans Green, 1915a; On the significance of the geographical distribution of the practice of mummification: A study of the migrations of peoples and the spread of certain customs and beliefs. *Memoirs and Proceedings of the Manchester Literary and Philosophical Society* 59:1–143, 1915b.

The ancient Egyptians and the origin of civilization. London: Harper, 1923; *The evolution of man: Essays*. London: Milford, 1927; *Human history*. New York: Norton, 1929; (with W.R. Dawson) *Egyptian mummies*. London: Allen & Unwin, 1924; (with D.E. Derry) Anatomical report. *Bulletin of the Archaeological Survey of Nubia* 5:11–25, 1910; (with F.W. Jones): Anatomical report. *Bulletin of the Archaeological Survey of Nubia* 2:29–54, 1908; (with F.W. Jones) Report on human remains. *Archaeological Survey of Nubia: Report for 1907–1908*. Vol. 2. Cairo, 1910; (with M.A. Ruffer) Pott'sche Krankheit in einer ägyptischen Mumie, aus der Zeit der 21 Dynastie (um 1000 vor Chr). In: K. Sudhoff (ed) *Zur historischen Biologie der Krankheitserreger*. Giessen: Topelmann, 1910.

ARCHIVAL SOURCES

1. Correspondence & Manuscripts: British Library, Reference Division, Department of Manuscripts, Great Russell Street, London WC1 3DG, England; 2. Piltdown-Related Correspondence: Library of Palaeontology, Natural History Museum, Cromwell Road, London SW7 5BD, England (cf. Spencer 1990).

SECONDARY SOURCES

A.A. Abbie: Sir Grafton Elliot Smith: Annual postgraduate oration. *Bulletin of the Postgraduate Committee on Medicine* 15:101–150, 1959; W.R. Dawson: *Sir Grafton Elliot Smith: A biographical record by his colleagues*. London: Cape, 1938; F. Spencer: *The Piltdown papers 1908–1955: The correspondence and other documents relating to the Piltdown forgery*. London: Oxford University Press, 1990; T.W. Todd: The scientific influence of Sir Grafton Elliot Smith. *American Anthropologist* 39:523–526, 1937; J.T. Wilson: Sir Grafton Elliot Smith, 1871–1937. *Obituary Notices of Fellows of the Royal Society* 2:323–333, 1936–1938.

Smith, Samuel Stanhope (1750–1819)

Born in Pequea, Lancaster County, Pennsylvania, Smith graduated in 1769 from the College of New Jersey (later renamed Princeton University), where his mentor had been John Witherspoon (1723–1794), who was also

president of the college from 1768 to 1794. After a term of active ministry in Virginia from 1775 to 1779, Smith returned to Princeton, where he was married to Witherspoon's daughter and installed as professor of moral philosophy—a position he held until 1812. He was awarded an honorary doctorate of divinity from Yale University in 1783 and Harvard University in 1810. In 1795, he succeeded to his father-in-law's post, which he held until his resignation in 1812.

Smith's place in the history of anthropology is based solely on two editions of a single treatise he wrote, titled *An Essay on the Causes of the Variety of Complexion and Figure in the Human Species*, which first appeared in 1787. The second edition was issued in 1810. The primary objective of the first edition of Smith's *Essay* had been to correct the "intransigencies" of the Scottish legal scholar Henry Home (1696–1782), otherwise known as Lord Kames. In his book, *Sketches of the History of Man* (1774), Kames had picked up on the growing skepticism concerning the traditional environmental explanation of human variation. Applying "common sense" to this issue, Kames had reasoned that perhaps human diversity was simply a Divine punishment for the presumption of the Tower of Babel, and that when God had scattered humankind from Babel he had divided them into different pairs that were best fitted to their allotted regions of the Earth.

In taking issue with Kames' polygenism, Smith set forth a compelling defense of both the biblical doctrine of monogenism and the environmental hypothesis. With regard to the latter, he identified "climate, state of society, and the manner of living" as the chief causes of the human varieties. In retrospect, what distinguishes Smith's text from others of the period is that he made no attempt to distinguish between groups of humankind, noting that it is "impossible to draw a line precisely between the various races of man, or even to enumerate them with certainty; and that it is in itself a useless labor to attempt it" (Smith 1810:240). But contrary to Smith's expectation, his *Essay* did not stem the advance of polygenism.

The second edition of the *Essay* was issued primarily in response to the thesis of the English physician Charles White (1728–1813) published in 1799. White's *An Account of the Regular Gradation of Man, and in Different Animals and Vegetables; from the Former to the Latter* supported the opinion that the human races formed a natural hierarchy, with the

African Blacks representing an intermediary species between the European Whites and the apes. Although through his reliance on such authorities as the German anatomist Johann Friedrich Blumenbach (1752–1840) Smith was able to muster evidence to counter some of White's arguments regarding the innate inferiority of Blacks, his apparent unwillingness to follow Blumenbach's (1795) rejection of the concept of the Great Chain of Being seriously hampered his counterattack. However, the second edition does provide some important insights into the methodological and theoretical changes that had occurred in anthropology since the publication of the first edition of the *Essay*. (For further details on Smith's anthropology, see Hudnutt 1956 and Jordan 1965, 1968.)

Smith died in Baltimore, Maryland, on 21 August 1819.

Frank Spencer

See also Barton, Benjamin Smith; Blumenbach, Johann Friedrich; Caldwell, Charles; Chain of Being; Polygenism; Skin Color; United States of America

Bibliography
SELECTED WORKS
An essay on the causes of the variety of complexion and figure in the human species. To which are added strictures on Lord Kaimes's [sic] *discourse on the original diversity of mankind.* Philadelphia: Aitken, 1787 (2d ed: *An essay on the causes of the variety of complexion and figure in the human species. To which are added animadversions on certain remarks made on the first edition of this essay by Mr. Charles White, and strictures on Lord Kames's discourse on the original diversity of mankind.* New Brunswick: Simpson, 1810). Reprint, with introduction by W.D. Jordan. Cambridge, Massachusetts: Belknap Press, 1965.

SECONDARY SOURCES
J.F. Blumenbach: *De generis humani varietate nativa.* Göttingae: Vandenhoek & Ruprecht, 1795. Reprinted in translation by T. Bendyshe: *The anthropological treatises of Johann Friedrich Blumenbach.* London: Longman, Green, Longman, Roberts & Green, 1864, pp. 147–276; W.H. Hudnutt III: Samuel Stanhope Smith: Enlightened conservative. *Journal of the History of Ideas* 17:540–552, 1956; W.D. Jordan: Introduction. In reprint of S.S. Smith's *An essay on the causes of the variety of complexion and figure in the human species.* Brunswick: Simpson, 1810. Cambridge, Massachusetts: Belknap Press, 1965; W.D. Jordan: *White over Black: American attitudes toward the Negro, 1550–1812.* Chapel Hill: University of North Carolina Press, 1968; Lord Kames [H. Home]: *Sketches of the history of man.* 4 vols. Edinburgh: Creech, 1774; W.B. Sprague (ed): *Annals of the American pulpit.* Vol. 3. New York, 1861, pp. 335–345; C. White: *An account of the regular gradation of man, and in different animals and vegetables; from the former to the latter.* London: Dilly, 1799.

Snow, Charles Ernest (1910–1967)

Born in Boulder, Colorado, Snow attended the University of Colorado, Boulder, graduating with a B.A. in geology in 1932. He then went on to Harvard University, where he became a student of Earnest A. Hooton (1887–1954) and earned his doctorate in anthropology in 1938 with a dissertation on the *Comparative Growth of Jewish and Non-Jewish Pupils in a Greater Boston Public School.* At this juncture, Snow moved to Birmingham, Alabama, where, following Marshall T. Newman (b. 1911), he supervised analysis of skeletal material from the Works Project Administration–Tennessee Valley Authority Archaeological Project. With the closure of the project in 1941 because of the war, its director, William Snyder Webb (1892–1964), who was simultaneously chairman of the Department of Anthropology at the University of Kentucky (UK), invited Snow to join his department. Snow accepted and spent the remainder of his career at the UK, where he was promoted to the rank of full professor in 1946 and served as chairman of the department from 1952 to 1957.

Although Snow collaborated on a number of projects on skeletal remains from the Eastern Woodlands, his most influential work was on the Indian Knoll skeletons, from a large Archaic shell mound in the Green River Valley of Kentucky (1948b). Snow's later research interests also embraced forensic anthropology. In the late 1940s, he was invited to join a team of specialists being assembled by Francis E. Randall (1914–1949) of the Anthropology Unit, Research and Development Branch of the Office of Quartermaster General, to assist in the identification of the war dead in the Pacific theater. Along with Snow, three other anthropologists were chosen to do this work in the Central Identification Laboratory at Oahu, Hawaii: Wilton Marion Krogman (1903–1987), Harry Lionel Shapiro (1902–1990), and T. Dale Stewart (1901–), and subsequently Mildred Trotter (1899–

1991). Snow spent six months in Hawaii in 1947–1948 (cf. Snow 1948a).

He died in Madison, Wisconsin, on 5 October 1967.

Patricia S. Bridges

See also Forensic Anthropology; Harvard University; Hooton, E(arnest) A(lbert); Krogman, Wilton Marion; Shapiro, Harry Lionel; Stewart, T(homas) Dale; Trotter, Mildred

Bibliography
SELECTED WORKS
Anthropological studies at Moundville. *Papers of the Alabama Museum of Natural History* 15:1–59, 1941; Two prehistoric Indian dwarf skeletons from Moundville. *Papers of the Alabama Museum of Natural History* 21:1–90, 1943; The identification of the unknown war dead. *American Journal of Physical Anthropology* 6:323–328, 1948a; Indian Knoll skeletons of the site Oh2, Ohio County, Kentucky. Part 2. *University of Kentucky Reports in Anthropology* 4:371–554, 1948b; (with B.P. Gatliff & K.R. McWilliams) Reconstruction of the facial features from the skull: An evaluation of its usefulness in forensic anthropology. *American Journal of Physical Anthropology* 33:221–227, 1970; (with F.E. Johnston) The reassessment of the age and sex of the Indian Knoll skeletal population: Demographic and morphological aspects. *American Journal of Physical Anthropology* 19:237–244, 1961; (with D.S. Marshall) An evaluation of Polynesian craniology. *American Journal of Physical Anthropology* 4:405–428, 1956; (with W.S. Webb) The Adena people. *University of Kentucky Reports in Anthropology* 6:1–369, 1945.

ARCHIVAL SOURCES
C.E. Snow Papers: Archives, W.S. Webb Museum, University of Kentucky, Lexington, Kentucky 40506.

SECONDARY SOURCES
W.M. Bass: Charles Ernest Snow, 1910–1967. *American Journal of Physical Anthropology* 28:369–372, 1967; M.O. Smith: Physical anthropology. In: J.K. Johnson (ed) *The development of southeastern archaeology.* Tuscaloosa: University of Alabama Press, 1993, pp. 53–77.

Société d'Anthropologie de Paris

The Société d'Anthropologie de Paris (SAP), the oldest anthropological society in existence, was founded in 1859 by the surgeon-anatomist-anthropologist Paul Broca (1824–1880) to promote free discussion of subjects related to the natural history of the human genus. Prior to this, Broca had encountered considerable difficulty in presenting and publishing his controversial work on *hybridité dans le genre humain*. Between November 1858 and May 1859, Broca managed to assemble a group of nineteen prospective members of the new society. These founding members included professors and teachers in the Parisian medical community (Jules Béclard, Armand de Fleury, François A.E. Follin, and Aristide A.S. Verneuil), professors of the Muséum National d'Histoire Naturelle (Isidore Geoffroy Saint-Hilaire, Louis Pierre Gratiolet and M. Lemercier) and the Collège de France (Charles Brown-Séquard), one hospital doctor (Louis J.F. Delasiauve), a prosector (M. Rambaud), four physicians (Adrien Antelme, Louis Adolphe Bertillon, Gabriel M.C. Dareste, and M. Goddard), one free-professor of anatomy (M. Martin-Magron), and two nonmedical members (Henri de Castelnau, who was editor of the *Moniteur des Hôpitaux*, and Gabriel Grimaud de Caux, a hygienist). As this list indicates, the membership was dominated by members of the medical profession.

The civic authorities, however, were initially suspicious, and only after some difficult negotiation plus the assurance that the society would not engage in the discussion of either religion or politics at its meetings was approval given—and even then it was agreed that a police official would be present at all meetings for the first two years. The SAP was officially founded on 19 May 1859, and the first meeting was held just less than two months later, on 7 July. The SAP's membership grew quickly—by 1860, its numbers were just short of 100—and on 21 July 1864, the SAP was officially recognized.

During the next two decades, the SAP's membership continued to expand, reaching an all-time high of 505 in 1884 (cf. Manouvrier 1902). Thereafter it began to decline. This regression is explained in part by increasing specialization and the subsequent formation of new societies devoted exclusively to special interests (such as ethnology, prehistory, lingusitics, and genetics), which prompted the departure of their representatives from the SAP.

During its heyday, the SAP played a major role in gathering anthropological data from around the world, either via its own members who engaged in international travel, or through its published *Directions* that were utilized by explorers and the military (cf. Quatrefages 1867). In many cases, these *Directions* were written for specific regions, such as Sicily, Mexico, Peru, Chile, Brazil, Senegal, the Sahara and Sudan, and the littoral of the Red Sea. There were also *General Directions*, as well as a questionnaire on the anthropology of France. In addition to stimulating travelers and others to record their observations, these *Directions* also provided a how-to for the preservation of significant collections of skeletal material and other anthropological items that were donated either to the SAP or to Broca's Laboratoire d'Anthropologie at the École pratique des Hautes Études (LA-EPHE). Many of these items were subsequently displayed at the universal exhibitions of 1878 and 1889 in Paris. For his part, Broca wrote two texts for the benefit of workers in the LA-EPHE, one on anthropology and the other on craniology.

Originally, the SAP met regularly twice a month (generally in the late afternoon); later, however, this was reduced to once a month, and since 1974 meetings have been held every two months (with sessions lasting the whole day). As Article 5 of the SAP's Constitution states, the society is directed by a council formed of twenty-five members elected for three years by secret ballot by the general meeting. This council is responsible for choosing among its members, by secret ballot, a board consisting of a president, two vice-presidents, a general secretary, an assistant general secretary, two secretaries of sessions, a treasurer, and an assistant treasurer. With the exception of the general secretary and the treasurer, who serve for three years, the remainder of the appointments to the board are for one year.

The role of the general secretary is an important one, and Broca occupied that position until his death. Initally, he was responsible for organizing sessions and for keeping records of discussion at the meetings, but later he left that task to the session secretaries and instead directed his attention to the equally time-consuming task of editing the SAP's two publications: the *Bulletins*, which was published quarterly, and the *Mémoires*, which initially was published irregularly. The first volume of the *Bulletins* and the *Mémoires* appeared in 1860. In 1900, these two publications were united, becoming the *Bulletins et Mémoires de la Société d'Anthropologie de Paris*. Two cumulative indexes, by author and by subject, have been published, the first covering the period from 1860 to 1899, and the

second embracing the period from 1900 to 1959. In addition, the SAP has also published, as independent volumes, important monographs and anthologies.

Following Broca's death in 1880, the physical anthropologist Paul Topinard (1830–1911) became general secretary, but his efforts to keep the vision of his former mentor alive were stymied by the counterefforts of the prehistorian Gabriel de Mortillet (1821–1898) and his followers. Discouraged by this increasingly powerful opposition, Topinard resigned the secretaryship in 1887. His place was taken by Charles Letourneau (1831–1902), whose interests were primarily in the areas of ethnology and psychology. Letourneau was followed by Léonce-Pierre Manouvrier (1850–1927), who held the position from 1903 until 1927. Unlike Letourneau, Manouvrier was a disciple of Broca, and his entire professional career unfolded essentially within the framework of the LA-EPHE. After Manouvrier, the anatomist Raoul Anthony (1874–1941) held the general secretary post until resigning in 1936, whereupon he was succeeded by the neurologist Octave Crouzon. Crouzon's death a year later led to the 1939 election of the anthropologist Henri Victor Vallois (1889–1981), who occupied the post for the next thirty years. In 1969, Vallois was succeeded by another anthropologist, Georges Olivier, who held the position for only one year. Following his resignation, Denise Ferembach (1924–1994), formerly of the Centre National de la Recherche Scientifique (CNRS), held the office until 1982. She was followed by Jean Dastugue, a former director of an anthropological laboratory in the medical faculty at Caen, who served until 1989. In 1990, the position was taken over by the paleoanthropologist Jean-Jacques Hublin, the director of research at CNRS.

The SAP delivers three biennial prizes. The oldest of these is the Broca Prize, established by Broca's wife in 1881 (cf. Mme. Broca 1881), followed by the Adolphe Bertillon (cf. Bertillon 1885) and Vallois Prizes (cf. Vallois 1982:349–350).

During its long history, the SAP has changed the location of its meeting place and head office several times. After some initial meetings at the EPHE, the SAP enjoyed the hospitality of the Société de Chirurgie, whose premises were located on the rue de l'Abbaye. Later, in 1871, Broca obtained the use of the large loft of the Rèfectoire des Cordeliers, which was remodeled to incorporate a lecture room and a place for collections (cf. Vallois

1960). In 1941, the SAP was obliged to relocate. For some years thereafter, meetings were held at the Sorbonne, followed by the Musée de l'Homme, then the Institut de Paléontologie, where the sessions were held in the Orfila Museum of the Faculty of Medicine. Since 1983, however, the meeting place and head office of the SAP have been located at the Musée de l'Homme.

Denise Ferembach

See also Anthony, Raoul; Broca, Paul (Pierre); France; Manouvrier, Léonce-Pierre; Topinard, Paul; Vallois, Victor Henri

Bibliography
A. Bertillon: Prix Bertillon. *Bulletins de la Société d'Anthropologie de Paris* 8 (3d ser.):511–512, 1885; Mme. Broca: Prix Broca. *Bulletins de la Société d'Anthropologie de Paris* 4 (3d ser.):547–548, 1881; P. Broca: Des phénomènes d'hybridité dans le genre humain. *Journal de la Physiologie de l'Homme et des Animaux* 2:601–625, 1859; P. Broca: Des phénomènes d'hybridité dans le genre humain. *Journal de la Physiologie de l'Homme et des Animaux* 3:392–439; P. Broca: Histoire des travaux de la Société, 1859–1863. *Mémoires de la Société d'Anthropologie de Paris* 2:vii–li, 1865; P. Broca: Compte rendu des travaux de la Société pendant les années 1865–1867. *Mémoires de la Société d'Anthropologie* de Paris 3:i–xxviii, 1868.

P. Broca: Laboratoire d'Anthropologie. *Rapport des Directeurs de Laboratoire et de Conférence de l'École Pratique des Hautes Études, 1868–1877.* Paris: EPHE, 1877, pp. 179–194; D. Ferembach: The Anthropology Society of Paris, 1859– . In: D. Ferembach: History of biological anthropology in France. Part 3. *International Association of Human Biologists: Occasional Papers.* Vol. 2. No. 3. Newcastle upon Tyne, IAHB, 1988, pp. 2–3; L. Manouvrier: L'état de la Société d'Anthropologie de Paris. *Bulletins et Mémoires de la Société d'Anthropologie de Paris* 3 (5th ser.):371–384, 1902.

L. Manouvrier: La Société d'Anthropologie de Paris depuis sa fondation, 1859–1909. *Bulletins et Mémoires de la Société d'Anthropologie de Paris* 10 (5th ser.): 305–328, 1909; A. de Quatrefages: *Rapport sur les progrès de l'Anthropologie.* Paris: Hatchette, 1867; P. Topinard: *A la mémoire de Broca: La Société, L'École, le Laboratoire, et le Musée Broca.* Paris: privately printed, 1890, pp. 1–40; H. Vallois: La Société d'Anthropologie de Paris, 1859–1959. *Bulletins et Mémoires de la Société d'Anthropologie de Paris* 1 (11th ser.):293–312, 1960; H. Vallois: Legs laissé, par M. et Mme. Vallois à la Société d'Anthropologie de Paris. *Bulletins et Mémoires de la Société d'Anthropologie de Paris* 9 (13th ser.):349–350, 1982.

Société des Observateurs de l'Homme (Paris)

Founded in 1799 by the natural historian and geographer Louis-François Jauffret (1770–1850) to pursue the "comparative study of man" (cf. Bouteiller 1956), this society is generally regarded as the first scientific society founded exclusively for the purposes of anthropology. Among its founding members were Georges Cuvier (1769–1832), Etienne Geoffroy Saint-Hilaire (1772–1844), and Jean-Baptiste Lamarck (1744–1829). (For a complete list of the founding members, which included five doctors, fourteen naturalists, and three lawyers, see Kilborne 1982.) However, for reasons linked to the changing political climate in France, the society lasted only a little more than four years. By the end of 1804, it had essentially been disbanded. Although the plan to publish its *Mémoires* was never realized, several rather interesting documents were produced and have survived—in particular, two instructional memoirs, one written by the idéologue Joseph-Marie Degérando (1772–1842) and the other by Cuvier, that were commissioned by Nicolas Baudin (1754–1803) for use in his planned scientific expedition to the Southwest Coast of New Holland (Australia). Degérando provided "Methods to Follow in the Observation of Savage Peoples" (cf. Degérando 1883), and Cuvier contributed an "Instructive Note on the Researches to Be Carried Out Relative to Anatomical Differences between the Diverse Races of Man" (Hervé 1910). While at once intrinsically interesting, these documents also provide insights into French anthropology at the beginning of the nineteenth century. As G.W. Stocking Jr. (1968) has noted, these memoirs were mutually incompatible: While Degérando's piece is grounded in the eighteenth-century universalist tradition (and essentially optimistic in tone), Cuvier's instructions lean heavily in the opposite direction and reflect the emerging diversitarian character of physical anthropology.

It should be noted that Baudin's expedition (consisting of two vessels, the *Géographe* and the *Naturaliste*) was unsuccessful in its venture. When the ships left France in October 1800, there was reportedly considerable dissension among the crew and the scientific contingent. On reaching Mauritius, several members of the scientific contingent disembarked, and a number of sailors deserted their ships. Among the scientists in this expedition was the naturalist Jean-Baptiste Bory de Saint-Vincent (1788–1846), who later distinguished himself with his two-volume work *L'homme: Essai zoologique sur le genre humain* (1825), in which he separated the human genus into two subgenera and fifteen species. Bory apparently left his ship on reaching Madagascar. In spite of these losses, Baudin pressed on. Eventually, however, he was forced to turn back, and like many others on this ill-fated expedition, he died on the return voyage to France. Another interesting footnote to this return voyage is that during a brief stop at Cape Town, South Africa, the two remaining naturalists on the expedition, Charles Lesueur (1778–1846) and François Péron (1775–1810), made one of the first scientific studies of the external anatomy of a Khoisan female.

Frank Spencer

See also Cuvier, Georges Léopold Chrétien Fréderic Dagobert (Baron); France; Geoffroy Saint-Hilaire, Etienne; Khoisan; Lamarck, Jean-Baptiste Pierre Antoine de Monet (Chevalier de)

Bibliography
J.B.G. Bory de Saint Vincent: *Essai zoologique sur le genre humain.* 2 vols. Paris: Gravier, 1825; M. Bouteiller: La Société des Observateurs de l'Homme, ancêtre de la Société d'Anthropologie de Paris. *Bulletins et Mémoires de la Société d'Anthropologie de Paris* 7:448–465, 1956; J-M. Degérando: Considérations sur les méthodes à suivre dans l'observation des peuples sauvages. In: Documents anthropologiques: L'ethnographie en 1800. *Revue d'Anthropologie* 6 (2d ser.):152–181, 1883; G. Hervé: À la recherche d'un manuscrit: Les instructions anthropologiques de G. Cuvier pour le voyage du *Géographe* et du *Naturaliste* aux Terres Australes. *Revue de l'École d'Anthropologie de Paris* 20:289–291, 1910; B. Kilborne: Anthropological thought in the wake of the French Revolution: La Société des Observateurs de l'Homme. *European Journal of Sociology* 23:783–791, 1982; G.W. Stocking Jr.: French anthropology in 1800. In: *Race, culture, and evolution: Essays in the history of anthropology.* New York: Free Press, 1968, pp. 15–41.

Society for the Study of Human Biology

The Society for the Study of Human Biology (SSHB) was founded on the initiative of Joseph Sidney Weiner (1915–1982), then a Reader in physical anthropology at Oxford University in 1957. Although physical anthropology had been recognized as a separate subject in academic studies in the United Kingdom for a long time, it had been so transformed in content, aim, and method that a redefinition of its scope had become necessary. None of the older established societies adequately covered the new concepts, and few of those working in allied disciplines were aware of the new emphases. Weiner convened a symposium at the Ciba Foundation in London on 6 November 1957 to explore the scope of physical anthropology and human population biology, and their place in academic studies. The papers presented there were subsequently published, with the assistance of the Wenner-Gren Foundation for Anthropological Research, New York, as the first of the volumes of the proceedings of symposia of the SSHB (cf. Roberts & Weiner 1958). At that meeting, there was general agreement that there was a pressing need for an association of professional workers whose interests lay primarily in the field of human population biology, and that symposia should be held at regular intervals to facilitate contact among them. The inaugural meeting of the SSHB was held in London on 7 May 1958. The first elected chairman was A.C. Stevenson, Belfast, 1958; followed in succession by J.Z. Young, London, 1960; N.A. Barnicot, London, 1963; J.S. Weiner, Oxford, 1968; G.A. Harrison, Oxford, 1973; J.M. Tanner, London, 1978; D.F. Roberts, Newcastle, 1983; E.J. Clegg, Aberdeen, 1988; and A.J. Boyce, Oxford, 1992.

Though members initially were from the United Kingdom, others soon joined from other countries. There was strong support from the United States and a U.S. branch was subsequently established.

The SSHB publishes a bimonthly journal, the *Annals of Human Biology* founded in 1973. It holds an annual symposium on a chosen theme, and from time to time special symposia in addition. It has held two joint symposia with the American branch, one in Detroit, Michigan, in 1978 and the other in Durham, England, in 1990. It also holds an annual meeting where members present their work. The symposia proceedings are published in the society's symposium series, which by the mid-1990s consisted of more than three dozen volumes. In 1995 the secretary was C.J. Henry of the School of Biological and Molecular Sciences, Oxford Brookes University, Headington, Oxford; and the chairman was A.J. Boyce of the Department of Biological Anthropology, Oxford University.

Derek F. Roberts

See also International Association of Human Biologists; United Kingdom; United States of America; Weiner, Joseph Sidney; Wenner-Gren Foundation for Anthropological Research

Bibliography
D.F. Roberts & J.S. Weiner (eds): *The scope of physical anthropology and its place in academic studies*. London: SSHB and the Wenner-Gren Foundation for Anthropological Research, 1958.

Sociobiology

The term "sociobiology" became widely known following the publication of Edward O. Wilson's *Sociobiology: The New Synthesis* in 1975. A zoologist at Harvard University, Wilson defined sociobiology as the "systematic study of the biological basis of all social behavior" (Wilson 1975:4). By "biological," he meant using evolution as a central theory to understand social behavior; he not only cataloged and compared social behaviors and systems across the entire animal kingdom, he also considered how these behaviors and systems could have evolved under natural and sexual selection. He explained his goal as being to create a unified science, or theory, that would use a common analytical structure to understand variable features of animal societies such as group size, age composition, systems of communication, and the division of labor. He saw kinship as the most important force generating sociality, and the evolution of altruism as the central theoretical problem.

In arguing his case, Wilson used the concept of the "multiplier effect," noting that a small, evolved change in the behavior of individuals can be amplified through a social system to produce profound differences in social structure. In demonstrating how altruism—which by definition reduces personal fitness—can evolve by natural selection, Wilson relied on the concepts of "kin selection" and "reciprocal altruism" (*vide infra*). He also

argued that in some cases interdemic "group selection" may occur.

When Wilson's book appeared, sociobiology was neither a novel concept nor a novel term. Indeed, Wilson had himself spent many years studying social insects, with a focus on ants; an important fruit of this work was his book *The Insect Societies* (1971), which ended with a short chapter entitled "The Prospect for a Unified Sociobiology." In this chapter, he set the stage for his 1975 book, arguing the need to integrate information about insect and vertebrate societies under one theoretical umbrella. As an example of a vertebrate society, Wilson referred specifically to rhesus macaque troops, with which he was familiar through the work of one of his doctoral students, Stuart A. Altmann, who studied the social behavior of rhesus monkeys on Cayo Santiago, Puerto Rico. Altmann used the term "sociobiology" in the title of a 1963 paper describing the results of his doctoral research. Sociobiology and primatology, therefore, had early links.

The basic scientific concepts underlying sociobiological theory, however, have an even more ancient history than the term itself. In *On the Origin of Species* (1859), Charles Darwin (1809–1882) discussed at some length the evolution of animal "instincts" by natural selection, and in his later works *The Descent of Man* (1871) and *The Expression of the Emotions in Man and Animals* (1872), he very clearly extended his evolutionary arguments to social behavior and to humans.

Much of Wilson's reasoning about the evolution of behavior in different animals is based on the comparative method. The same method was employed in the first half of the twentieth century by zoologists such as Charles Otis Whitman (1842–1910), Oskar Heinroth (1871–1945), Konrad Lorenz (1903–1989), and Nikolaas Tinbergen (1907–1988) in their pioneering comparative studies of animal behavior, including social behavior (e.g., Tinbergen 1953). These zoologists focused on "innate" or "instinctive" behaviors and considered, among other things, the phylogeny and adaptive significance of these behaviors. Such work led to the development of a new biological discipline, ethology, which has contributed significantly to sociobiological theory.

The evolution of social behavior in animals was, therefore, a topic receiving considerable attention from ethologists and zoologists long before the publication of Wilson's *Sociobiology*. For instance, in 1962, the

British zoologist V.C. Wynne-Edwards argued in his book *Animal Dispersion in Relation to Social Behavior* that many social behaviors could be understood as having evolved because of the benefit they provide to a group or population. This "group selection" argument was countered by, among others, the American zoologists G.C. Williams (1966) and R.D. Alexander (1974), who contended that group living could best be understood in terms of fitness advantages to individuals.

Both Alexander and Wilson noted the importance of the theoretical contributions to an understanding of sociality made by the evolutionary geneticists Ronald A. Fisher (1890–1962) and William D. Hamilton. Hamilton (1964) showed mathematically how apparently self-sacrificing altruistic behavior can evolve among social animals if there is some hereditary tendency to perform an altruistic act, and if the act is performed by individuals sharing many genes with their neighbors. Hamilton also introduced the concept of "inclusive fitness," which he defined as personal fitness less components due to the individual's general social environment, plus fractions of the quantities of harm and benefit that an individual causes to his neighbors (where the fractions are the coefficients of relationship between the individual and these neighbors).

Further important contributions were made by the evolutionary biologist Robert L. Trivers. Trivers (1972) argued that altruistic behavior patterns can be selected for when they are not normally directed toward close relatives, provided that the benefit of the altruistic act to the recipient is considerably greater than the cost of the act to the donor, and that there is a good chance of the altruism being returned in the future. He termed this system "reciprocal altruism." In another influential contribution, Trivers (1972) drew attention to the potentially important role of "sexual selection" in determining differences in male and female reproductive strategies. He argued that, if members of one parental sex invest more in their young than members of the other, then members of the latter sex will compete among themselves to mate with members of the former, leading to sexual selection for traits that are advantageous in intrasexual competetion. Trivers suggested that infant killing by adult male langur monkeys that have taken over a group might be a behavioral trait that has been favored by sexual selection.

The concept of "social evolution" entered physical anthropology by way of primatology in the early 1960s. It has been noted that only two doctoral degrees in primatology were awarded by American Departments of Anthropology between 1929 and 1959, while 36 were awarded in the years 1960–1969, and 125 in 1970–1979—and that this dramatic increase derived essentially from the influence of the "new physical anthropology" espoused by Sherwood L. Washburn (1911–) during the 1950s and 1960s (Gilmore 1981). Washburn, along with his student Irven DeVore, developed arguments about the adaptiveness of primate social organizations, with extrapolations to humans (cf. Washburn & DeVore 1961; DeVore 1963). Findings from a growing wave of field studies on primates and other mammals were soon incorporated into the popular literature. (See, for example, *The Territorial Imperative* [1966] written by Robert Ardrey [1908–1980] and *The Naked Ape* [1967] by Desmond Morris.) Meanwhile, "sociobiology" became a central focus of much primatological work.

Given the earlier history of sociological concepts, it is legitimate to ask why Wilson's *Sociobiology* produced such a strong reaction, particularly in the anthropological community. Much of the reaction focused on the provocative final chapter. Titled "Man: From Sociobiology to Sociology," it examines human societies in an evolutionary perspective, discussing phenomena such as religious belief and warfare and noting that anthropology and sociology might, from one perspective, be considered as the sociobiology of a single primate species. Wilson further enlarged on these ideas in *On Human Nature* (1978), written for a general audience.

There are probably many factors contributing to the adverse reaction to sociobiology. It could be argued that Wilson's stature, the scope and detail of his book, and its publication by Belknap Press of Harvard University gave his argument more weight than that of earlier authors. In addition, the book appeared in a politically charged period in American academia, soon after the rise of modern intellectual feminism, which had a radical, revolutionary quality (e.g., Germaine Greer's *The Female Eunuch*, published in Britain in 1970 and the United States in 1971). Much of the hostile reaction had a political and, in particular, a socialist flavor. In fact, Wilson's work was characterized by what was to become the "Sociobiology Study Group of Science for the People" as being an example of "biological determinism," from which "powerful countries or ruling groups within them have drawn support for the maintenance or extension of their power" (Allen et al. 1975), and of sexism (Alper et al. 1978). Furthermore, Wilson's book appeared at a time of increasing rift between physical/biological and cultural anthropologists in their theoretical approach to the study of human behavior and societies. From all indications, the ensuing debate precipitated by the book has served to deepen that rift (cf. Lieberman 1989; Hrdy 1990), to the extent that some cultural anthropologists still view biological explanations of human behavior as a "sexist and racist storyline created by Western White men" (J. Collier, cited in Morell 1993).

Contrary to expectation, the term "sociobiology" has not been widely adopted. One possible reason may be that many scientists working on sociobiological problems wish to avoid the political stigma that the term acquired during the early debates. Nevertheless, the theoretical approach developed by Hamilton, Trivers, Alexander, and Wilson is central to much animal-behavior study, as well as many analyses of human social behavior (e.g., Betzig et al. 1988; Diamond 1991). Meanwhile, Wilson has become increasingly concerned with other issues, especially the growing extinction threat facing many of the Earth's species (Wilson 1992).

John F. Oates

See also Ardrey, Robert; Hunting Hypothesis of Human Origins; Primate Field Studies; Washburn, Sherwood L.

Bibliography
R.D. Alexander: The evolution of social behavior. *Annual Reviews of Ecology and Systematics* 5:325–383, 1974; E. Allen et al.: Against "sociobiology." *New York Review of Books* 22: 1975; J. Alper et al.: Sociobiology is a political issue. In: A.L. Caplan (ed) *The sociobiology debate.* New York: Harper, 1978, pp. 476–488; S.A. Altmann: A field study of the sociobiology of rhesus monkeys, *Macaca mulatta. Annals of the New York Academy of Sciences* 102:338–435, 1963; R. Ardrey: *The territorial imperative.* New York: Atheneum, 1966; L.L. Betzig et al.: *Human reproductive behavior: A Darwinian perspective.* Cambridge: Cambridge University Press, 1988; C.R. Darwin: *On the origin of species by means of natural selection, or the preservation of favoured races in the struggle for life.* London: Murray, 1859.

C.R. Darwin: *The descent of man, and selection in relation to sex.* 2 vols. London: Murray, 1871. Reprint with introduction by J.T. Bonner & R. May. Princeton, New Jersey: Princeton University Press, 1981; C.R. Darwin: *The expression of the emotions in man and animals.* London: Murray, 1872. Reprint with a preface by K. Lorenz. Chicago: University of Chicago Press, 1965; I. DeVore: A comparison of the ecology and behavior of monkeys and apes. In: S.L. Washburn (ed) *Classification and human evolution.* Chicago: Aldine, 1963, pp. 301–319; J. Diamond: *The rise and fall of the third chimpanzee.* London: Radius, 1991.

R.A. Fisher: *The genetical theory of natural selection.* Oxford: Clarendon, 1930; H.A. Gilmore: From Radcliffe–Brown to sociobiology: Some aspects of the rise of primatology within physical anthropology. *American Journal of Physical Anthropology* 56:387–392, 1981; G. Greer: *The female eunuch.* London: MacGibbon & Kee, 1970; W.D. Hamilton: The genetical evolution of social behaviour. Parts 1–2. *Journal of Theoretical Biology* 7:1–52, 1964; S.B. Hrdy: Sex bias in nature and in history: A late 1980s reexamination of the "biological origins" argument. *Yearbook of Physical Anthropology* 33:25–37, 1990.

L. Lieberman: A discipline divided: Acceptance of human sociobiological concepts in anthropology. *Current Anthropology* 30:676–682, 1989; V. Morell: Anthropology: Nature-culture battleground. *Science* 261:1798–1802, 1993; D. Morris: *The naked ape.* London: Cape, 1967; N. Tinbergen: *Social behaviour in animals, with special reference to vertebrates.* London: Methuen, 1953; R.L. Trivers: The evolution of reciprocal altruism. *Quarterly Review of Biology* 46:35–57, 1971; R.L. Trivers: Parental investment and sexual selection. In: B. Campbell (ed) *Sexual selection and the descent of man, 1871–1971.* Chicago: Aldine, 1972, pp. 136–179.

S.L. Washburn & I. DeVore: The social life of baboons. *Scientific American* 204:62–71, 1961; G.C. Williams: *Adaptation and natural selection.* Princeton, New Jersey: Princeton University Press, 1966; E.O. Wilson: *The insect societies.* Cambridge, Massachusetts: Belknap Press of Harvard University, 1971; E.O. Wilson: *Sociobiology: The new synthesis.* Cambridge, Massachusetts: Belknap Press of Harvard University, 1975; E.O. Wilson: *On human nature.* Cambridge, Massachusetts: Harvard University Press, 1978; E.O. Wilson: *The diversity of life.*

Cambridge, Massachusetts: Belknap Press of Harvard University, 1992; V.C. Wynne-Edwards: *Animal dispersion in relation to social behaviour*. Edinburgh: Oliver & Boyd, 1962.

Sollas, William Johnson (1849–1936)

Born in Birmingham, England, Sollas began his scientific studies in 1865 under the chemist Edward Frankland (1825–1899) at the Royal College of Chemistry. In 1867, he entered the Royal School of Mines (RSM), where he came under the influence of the geologist Andrew C. Ramsay (1814–1891) and the naturalist Thomas Henry Huxley (1825–1895). On completing his studies at the RSM (ca. 1870), he was awarded a scholarship to St. John's, Cambridge, where his tutor was the petrologist Thomas G. Bonney (1833–1923). It was evidently Bonney who was responsible for persuading Sollas to make geology his principal subject of study. After graduating in 1873 with a first-class degree in the natural sciences tripos (geology), Sollas worked for the next six years as a lecturer in the University Extension Program. Then, in 1879, he received an appointment as professor of geology and zoology at University College, Bristol, where he remained until 1883, when he moved to Trinity College, Dublin, as professor of geology and mineralogy. Finally, in 1897, he returned to England, where he was installed in the Chair of Geology and Paleontology at Oxford—a position formerly occupied by such illustrious personages as John Phillips (1800–1874) and Joseph Prestwich (1812–1896). He remained in this position until his death.

Sollas' research career can be divided into two phases. The first, spanning the period from 1873 to 1897, is devoted almost exclusively to geology. One of his major interests in this period was sponges, which he studied from both a biological and a physicochemical viewpoint, and it is interesting to note that he was responsible for describing the sponges that were collected during the voyage of HMS *Challenger*, an oceanographic survey expedition conducted between 1872 and 1876. Sollas' research on sponges and related forms led him to study the origin of flints in chalk, as well as coral reefs. (For bibliographic details on this research, see Woodward & Watts 1938.) Also worthy of note is his protracted engagement (1904–1924) as editor and translator (assisted by his daughter Hertha B.C. Sollas) of Eduard Suess' (1831–1914) five-volume masterwork *Das Antlitz der Erde*. Suess, an Austrian geologist, was one of the forerunners of the theory of continental drift generally associated with German geologist Alfred Wegener (1880–1930). Specifically, Suess had postulated the existence of Gondwana, a former southern supercontinent that fractured into smaller units during the Early Mesozoic, forming Antarctica, Australia, India, Africa, and South America.

The second phase of Sollas' career, spanning essentially the period from his arrival at Oxford in 1897 to the 1930s, is characterized by a mounting interest in anthropology and archeology. Although his first venture into this field dates from 1880, when he described some bone implements from Greenland, it was not until the early 1900s that this interest became a primary research focus. He began with a still much cited study, "On the Cranial and Facial Characters of the Neandertal Race," published by the Royal Society (1908). Although agreeing with the German anatomist-anthropologist Gustav Schwalbe's (1844–1916) earlier observation that the Neandertals possessed a unique suite of morphological features, Sollas was, at this juncture, still willing to accept them as an antecedant form to modern humans, noting: "[The] Neandertals and *Pithecanthropus* skulls stand like the piers of a ruined bridge which once continuously connected the kingdom of man with the rest of the animal world" (1908:337). During the next decade, however, he abandoned this position, as did many others. In Sollas' case, the shift in opinion was due in large part to the influence of the French paleoanthropologist Marcellin Boule's (1861–1942) work on the La Chapelle-aux-Saints (Neandertal) skeleton. Also linked with this change in perspective is Sollas' acceptance of the Piltdown skull. However, it is important to stress that he did not accept the opinion of some other supporters who claimed it as a Pliocene specimen. Furthermore, as he made clear in the first edition of his book *Ancient Hunters* (1911) which actually appeared in the spring of 1912, he was not predisposed to eolithic theory, which postulated the existence of Tertiary Man. According to this theory, a pre-Pleistocene hominid had been the artificer of a primitive stone tool industry, known as the Eolithic or Dawn Stone Age, that was considered by eolithophiles to have been the forerunner of the Paleolithic. Sollas completely rejected these propositions, and was a major critic of the zoologist Edwin Ray Lankester (1847–1929), who had coined the term "rostro-carinate" (cf. Lankester 1912) to describe the peculiar beak-shaped stone "tools" found near Ipswich, East Suffolk (East

Anglia), between 1909 and 1910 by the amateur archeologist James Reid Moir (1879–1944). Sollas endeavored to show that these stones were, in fact, natural objects. In addition to this protracted controversy, his name is linked with several other historically important studies. The first was his reexamination of the Paviland site and the so-called Red Lady skeleton found there by William Buckland (1784–1856) in the early 1820s. The results of this study formed the basis of his Huxley Memorial Lecture delivered to the Royal Anthropological Institute in 1913. Another was his assessment of the Taung skull (cf. Sollas 1926). In contrast to many of his British associates who had dismissed this skull, Sollas concluded from his comparative study that it was, in fact, more human than pongid, but he also noted that a final decision would have to await the discovery of an adult specimen. The following year, he published a study on the Chancelade skull (1927), in which he supported the earlier observation made by the French anthropologist Léo Testut (1849–1925) in 1890 that this Magdalenian skeleton exhibited "Eskimoid" characters—an idea that harmonized with his views on the race-succession paradigm.

Sollas was elected a Fellow of the Royal Society in 1889 and received a Royal Medal in 1914. He was president of the Geological Society of London (GSL) from 1908 to 1910 and received the GSL's Bigsby Medal in 1893 and its Wollaston Medal in 1905. In addition to receiving the Huxley Medal from the Royal Anthropological Institute in 1913, he was also the recipient of several honorary doctorates.

Sollas died in Oxford on 20 October 1936.

Frank Spencer

See also Boule, Marcellin; Buckland, William; Chapelle-aux-Saints, La; Dawkins, (Sir) William Boyd; Huxley, Thomas Henry; Lankester, (Sir) Edwin Ray; Neandertals; Paviland; Piltdown; Prestwich, (Sir) Joseph; Schwalbe, Gustav; Taung (formerly Taungs); Testut, Léo

Bibliography
SELECTED WORKS

On some Eskimo bone implements from the East Coast of Greenland. *Journal of the Anthropological Institute* 9:329–336, 1880; *Pithecanthropus erectus* and the evolution of the human race. *Nature* 53:150–151, 1895; On the cranial and facial characters of the Neandertal race. *Philosophical Transactions of the Royal Society of*

London B199:281–339, 1908; Palaeolithic races and their modern representatives. *Science Progress* 3:326–353, 1909; On the evolution of man. (Presidential address). *Quarterly Journal of the Geological Society of London* 66:liv–lxxxviii, 1910; *Ancient hunters and their modern representatives*. London: Macmillan, 1911 (2d ed.: 1915, 3d ed.: 1924).

The formation of "rostro-carinate" flints. *Report of the British Association for the Advancement of Science*, pp. 778–790, 1913a; Fractured flints from Selsey. *Nature* 92:452, 1913b; Paviland Cave: An Aurignacian station in Wales. (Huxley Memorial Lecture). *Journal of the Royal Anthropological Institute* 43:325–374, 1913c; On the sagittal sections of the skull of *Australopithecus africanus*. *Quarterly Journal of Geological Society of London* 82:1–11, 1926; The Chancelade skull. *Journal of the Royal Anthropological Institute* 57:89–122, 1927; (with A.C. Haddon & G.A.J. Cole) The geology of the Torres Straits. *Transactions of the Royal Irish Academy* 30:419–476, 1894; (with H.B.C. Sollas) *The face of the earth*. 5 vols. Oxford: Clarendon Press, 1904–1924. English translation of Edward Suess' *Das Antlitz der Erde*. 5 vols. Wien: Tempsky, 1883–1899.

ARCHIVAL SOURCES

1. W.J. Sollas Correspondence (1875–1927): Bodleian Library, Oxford OX1 3BG, England; 2. Sollas Lecture Notes and Miscellaneous Correspondence: Geological Collections, University Museum, Parks Road, Oxford OX1 3PS, England; 3. T.G. Bonney Correspondence: Manuscripts and Rare Books Room, D.M.S. Watson Library, University College, London, Gower Street, London WC1E 6BT, England.

PRIMARY AND SECONDARY SOURCES

E.R. Lankester: On the discovery of a novel type of flint implements below the base of the Red Crag of Suffolk, proving the existence of skilled workers of flint in the Pliocene age. *Philosophical Transactions of the Royal Society of London* B 102:283–336, 1912; L. Testut: Recherches anthropologiques sur le squelette quaternaire de Chancelade, Dordogne. *Bulletin de la Société d'Anthropologie de Lyons* 8:131–246, 1890; A.S. Woodward & W.W. Watts: William Johnson Sollas, 1849–1936. *Obituary Notices of Fellows of the Royal Society of London* 2:265–281, 1938.

Sontag, Lester W. (1901–1991)

Born in Heron Lake, Minnesota, Sontag studied medicine at the University of Minnesota. Soon after his graduation in 1926, he moved to Antioch College, Yellow Springs, Ohio, as the resident physician. In 1929, he was invited to establish the Fels Research Institute in Yellow Springs and to become its first director—a position he held until 1970.

Sontag was extremely active in research until 1947, by which time the institute had enlarged to the extent that most of his time was occupied by administrative tasks. Despite these many duties, he published more than sixty articles in peer-reviewed journals. His personal research interests were wide ranging. Until 1947, they included fetal behavior, especially heart rate and movements and the response of these to the environment. One environmental factor he studied was music (1935a), and another was maternal smoking (1935b). His demonstration that maternal smoking increased the fetal heart rate was one of the first observations that this practice influenced the fetus. He also studied basal metabolic rate, maternal diets, skeletal variations, and the similarity of phenotypes in twins and triplets. Much of his work was methodological: New approaches were needed to address new questions, and there were some intriguing answers. For example, it was shown that fetuses that are active *in utero* have low values for weight and recumbent length at birth. After 1947, Sontag's research interests focused on cognitive development, with an occasional paper on a psychiatric subject. During this period, he produced what may be his most enduring research finding: that IQ scores change during childhood.

Sontag was active in many regional and national professional organizations, including the Society for Research in Child Development, which he served as president from 1951 to 1952.

Sontag died in Dayton, Ohio, on 24 October 1991.

Alex F. Roche

See also Child-Growth Studies; Fels Research Institute; Garn, Stanley M.; Growth Studies

Bibliography
SELECTED WORKS

Mental growth and personality development: A longitudinal study. Society for Research in Child Development Monograph. No. 23. Lafayette, Indiana: Child Development Publications, 1958; (with I.M. Harris) Evidences of disturbed prenatal and neonatal growth in bones of infants aged one month. II. Contributing factors. *American Journal of Diseases of Children* 56:1248–1255, 1938; (with R.F. Wallace) The movement response of human fetus to sound stimuli. *American Journal of Diseases of Children* 51:583–589, 1935a; (with R.F. Wallace) The effect of cigarette smoking during pregnancy upon fetal heart rate. *American Journal of Obstetrics and Gynecology* 29:77–82, 1935b.

ARCHIVAL SOURCES

Lester Sontag Papers: Fordham Health Sciences Library, Wright State University, 3640 Colonel Glenn Highway, Yellow Springs, Ohio 45435.

South Africa

Even before the colonial period in the history of South Africa, flimsy ethnological observations were made and records kept by Persian and Arab chroniclers from the tenth century onward and by Portuguese navigators, explorers, and missionaries from the fifteenth and sixteenth centuries. During the colonial era, sporadic observations on the indigenous peoples were added to the stockpile of knowledge—for example, the work of the German zoologist and traveler Martin Heinrich Lichtenstein (1780–1857) (cf. Lichtenstein 1928–1929). Until the end of the third quarter of the nineteenth century, however, anthropological inquiry was focused mainly on ethnology, linguistics, history, and folklore.

The Configuration of Physical Anthropology: 1877–1920s
While the establishment of the South African Philosophical Society (SAPS) in 1877 has been marked as the birth date of anthropology in South Africa (Tobias 1985), the SAPS did not provide an immediate nucleus for systematic research in physical anthropology. This had to wait until the growth of local institutions of research and teaching in the early twentieth century, at which time physical anthropology found its way into three kinds of establishments: museums, new university medical schools, and medical facilities attached to Native Labour Associations of mining companies.

The first major museum focus was in Cape Town, where, in 1897, a Department of Anthropology was created in the South African Museum (SAM). Under the auspices of this department, Louis Albert Peringuey

(1855–1924), who later served as director of the SAM (1906–1924), initiated a program of gathering skeletons through a network of amateur collectors. By 1923, the SAM collections had expanded to the point that Peringuey was able to loan a series of more than 100 skeletons to Eugène Pittard (1867–1962) for study in Geneva, Switzerland. Furthermore, under the influence of the German anthropologist Felix von Luschan (1854–1924), Peringuey and his assistant James Drury (1875–1962) began making whole-body casts of the Bushman, or San, people. Between 1907 and 1924, seventy casts were made by Drury of individuals thought to be "pure" Bushmen from Botswana, the northern Cape Province, the eastern Transvaal, and the prisons of Cape Town, Windhoek, and Gaberone. The motivation for this particular project was to record what was thought to be a "dying race." Other notable early museum foci from this period include the Port Elizabeth Museum (PEM) and the National Museum at Bloemfontein (NMB). Between 1915 and 1928, the PEM mounted a series of expeditions to caves along the southern Cape coast from which prehistoric skeletal material was recovered. During this period, the NMB began building archeological and anthropological collections resulting from excavations in the western Transvaal, the southern and northern Cape Province, and from the Orange Free State.

The first two South African academic institutions to attain university status were the South African College in Cape Town (cf. Phillips 1993) and Victoria College in Stellenbosch, both in 1918. The Cape Town college was to host the first medical school, and in anticipation it began offering preclinical courses in anatomy and physiology in 1911. Since the majority of Cape Town's medical practitioners in the late nineteenth century had been trained at Edinburgh University in Scotland, it was chosen as the institutional model. The first two anatomists, R.B. Thomson (ca. 1880–1937) (from 1911 as professor) and Matthew A. Drennan (1885–1965) (from 1913 as lecturer), were both trained in Edinburgh. When Thomson resigned because of ill health in 1919, Drennan began his long tenure as department head, which was to last until his own retirement in 1955.

Drennan's anthropological research interests included the origin of southern African peoples. He published widely on this and related subjects and proposed the concepts of pedomorphism and later of gynecomorphism

to explain the distinctive morphology of living Bushman people. He also produced a small volume entitled *A Short Course on Physical Anthropology* (1937), which was the first South African textbook on physical anthropology. Despite his extensive publications and professional activity, Drennan left few students, and for most of his tenure Cape Town was not a major research center. The same can also be said for Stellenbosch, though it is of passing interest to note that from 1903 to 1910, Robert Broom (1866–1951), who would later have a profound impact on the development of human paleontology in South Africa, was professor of zoology and geology at Victoria College. At that time, however, Broom's research interests were focused primarily on mammal-like reptiles.

The choice of Cape Town and Stellenbosch for the new universities was not without some acrimony. Pressure to establish a university in the growing mining city of Johannesburg was strong from the turn of the century (cf. Murray 1982). When official permission was granted to begin planning the "University of Johannesburg" (eventually called the University of the Witwatersrand), the medical faculty was the first to be inaugurated. Edward Philip Stibbe (1884–1943) was hired as the first professor of anatomy in 1919, three years before the university gained its charter. The character of the new medical school was quite different from that of Cape Town. The pattern established in Johannesburg was along the lines of the London teaching hospitals, and the ethos of the university was far less conservative than that of its counterpart in Cape Town. Indeed, during the 1920s and 1930s, the University of the Witwatersrand (Wits) became the center of Johannesburg economic liberalism that embraced many socialist developments and some Black activists.

Johannesburg's liberalism, however, did not extend to sexual matters, as indicated in 1922 when Stibbe was forced to resign because of an extramarital relationship that became public knowledge. His departure led to the appointment of Raymond A. Dart (1893–1988) (Murray 1982; Tobias 1984). Unlike Stibbe (and Drennan in Cape Town), Dart endeavored to be more than just a teacher of anatomy. In addition to initiating separate Bachelor of Science and Honors programs in the Department of Anatomy, which ensured a continual flow of research-oriented students, he also infected his students with his enthusiasm for the subject. Through these efforts, plus the publicity that followed in the wake of his pronouncements on the Taung fossil in 1925, Dart attracted skilled anthropologically oriented faculty, as indicated by the arrival in 1932 of Alexander Galloway (1901–1965) from Aberdeen (via Saskatoon, Canada). Later, when a School of Dentistry was added to the university's faculties, Dart's influence ensured that it, too, would be research oriented. He became a key figure in promoting African studies.

With the development of the diamond and gold mines of Kimberley and Johannesburg in the late nineteenth century, there was a growing need for native labor. The mine owners created a system of mine compounds where this labor force could be concentrated and controlled, which they soon recognized needed careful medical supervision. In 1912, the Chamber of Mines, in conjunction with the government, created the South African Institute for Medical Research (SAIMR) specifically to study diseases that afflicted mine workers of the Witwatersrand, and also to perform routine medical tests on newly arrived laborers. Some of the early data collected (e.g., on stature) have been used to examine secular trends (cf. Tobias 1985). Also worthy of note is the pioneering work on the ABO blood-group types done by J.H. Harvey Pirie in 1921. Later, in 1936, Ronald Elsdon-Dew, also of the SAIMR, took the opportunity of routine screening procedures to elaborate on Pirie's work.

The contrast between the pioneering studies of Pirie and others from the SAIMR and the contemporary writings of Drennan and Dart is revealing. While the former employed hundreds of individual samples, the studies of Drennan and Dart were more often than not confined to the study of a single or a few specimens, whose interpretation was couched in a prevailing typological mold.

The Configuration of Physical Anthropology: 1920s–1950s

Although typology as a method of interpreting human variation was at that time well entrenched and well-nigh universal in anthropological thinking, its appearance on the South African scene can be dated from the first published description of the Boskop skull, by Sidney Henry Haughton (1888–1982) in 1917. This large calvaria, plus part of a mandible and limb-bone fragments of doubtful provenance, was found in 1913. Haughton concluded that the specimen manifested a mosaic of modern and primitive features reminiscent of the Cro-Magnon specimens from Europe. This was followed by a more forceful paper by Broom (1918), in which he declared that the specimen represented a new type of primitive human, which he dubbed *Homo capensis*. Soon thereafter, F.W. FitzSimons (1875–1951), then director of the Port Elizabeth Museum, who had been excavating caves along the southern Cape Coast (FitzSimons 1915), sent Dart skeletal material recovered from the deepest layers of one of these caves. The Boskop-like characters of a few of these skeletons suggested to Dart that a whole population of large-headed "pre-Bushmen" must have existed in prehistoric times, and in a paper published in 1923 he created the Boskop type, or race, to represent that population.

To Dart and his students, the Boskop type was a new race comparable to the living races of South Africa. Alexander Galloway became an early convert to this view. Another enthusiast was Drennan, who identified a modern cadaver from the Cape Town dissection room as a Boskop type. This extension of an extinct race into the present was completed in 1936, when Dart identified the presence of supposed Boskop features in a group of Bushmen from the Kalahari Gemsbok Park, near the northern border of the Cape Province (cf. Dart 1937). Furthermore, Dart believed that this group revealed signs of intermixture from Bantu-speaking Negroid peoples, as well as Mediterranean (Hamitic), Armenoid, and Mongoloid elements. This interpretation reflects Dart's earlier association with the anatomist-anthropologist Grafton Elliot Smith (1871–1937)—in particular, his commitment to Smith's concept of cultural diffusion (cf. Smith 1915). Indeed, during the period from 1924 to 1970, Dart published more than forty papers in which he endeavored to demonstrate the prehistoric connections among South Africa, Egypt, Europe and Asia.

The establishment of the "Boskop race" concept marked the flowering of typology in South African physical anthropology. By this time, Broom was settled as a district medical officer (1918–1929) at Douglas in the northern Cape Province. As noted earlier, his interests had initially been in vertebrate morphology and paleontology. Soon after World War I, when he turned to characterizing human populations (as indicated by his treatment of the Boskop skull), he did so with the same strictly typological methods he had used in his studies of mammal-like reptiles. Like Dart, he recognized "Bush" and "Bantu" ("South African Negro") types, to which

Broom proposed to add another, more ancient, type, that of the Korana. The Korana (or, more correctly, the !Ora), a group of Khoikhoi still living in the region of the middle Orange River when Broom was resident there, were considered by him to possess morphologically robust traits not seen in other African peoples. Broom hypothesized that the Korana were the remnants of a very ancient population akin to the "Australian Aboriginal" type, which was thought to have lived in Africa (and presumably Asia and Australia) in prehistoric times.

During the 1940s and early 1950s, Thomas F. Dreyer (1886–1954), a South African with a Ph.D. in zoology from Halle University in Germany, became interested in anthropology after becoming professor of zoology at Grey University College (later the University of the Orange Free State) in 1912. His excavations at Matjes River Cave from 1929 to 1933 and at Florisbad in 1932 led him to reject the Boskop type in favor of the Bushman as the sole aboriginal race in South Africa. Along with A.J.D. Meiring and A.C. Hoffman of the National Museum, Bloemfontein, Dreyer proposed that the living Khoikhoi were descendants of Hamitic migrants from the north, which they endeavored to prove by excavating a series of graves along the banks of the Orange River near the town of Kakamas (Dreyer & Meiring 1937; Dreyer, Meiring, & Hoffman 1938). The expectation of what this North African Hamitic ancestor should look like was founded on a typologically selected set of five crania recovered from these graves, which became the "Kakamas type." This proposal was accepted by several South African anatomists and physical anthropologists: L.H. Wells from the University of the Witwatersrand, J.A. Keen from the University of Cape Town, and C.S. Grobbelaar from the University of Stellenbosch.

In the meantime, the Eugenics Movement, as elsewhere, enjoyed a brief flowering in South Africa between the two World Wars. In 1920, a Eugenics Committee was established under the chairmanship of H.B. Fantham (1876–1937), a zoologist from Wits; among other things, it advocated the separation of the races (cf. Jenkins 1990). During the 1930s, however, the movement lost momentum when Fantham emigrated to Canada, and it was not until the late 1940s that this theme was revived in the political platform of the National Party.

Unlike the system followed in most American universities, physical anthropology and social (cultural) anthropology were taught in separate departments, and during the 1930s the latter became important vehicles for the expression of antiracist viewpoints. However, by the 1940s, social anthropology in South Africa had divided into two distinct camps: the liberal tradition of British social anthropology at the English-medium universities, and Volkekunde at the Afrikaans-medium universities. Volkekunde was descriptive anthropology based on the German ethnological tradition: the cultural analogue of biological typology. Each *volk* (people) was said to have its own ethos or culture linked to inherited physical and mental characteristics (Sharp 1981). The English-speaking schools fought against these concepts, and many of the social anthropologists joined the ranks of the antisegregationist South African Institute of Race Relations after it was formed in 1929. The election of the National Party in 1948 signaled a major change in the political structure of the country—namely, the implementation of its racial policy of apartheid. No South African physical anthropologists were involved in the planning or implementation of apartheid legislation, nor in the furnishing of the Rassenkunde underpinning of that philosophy (Tobias 1985). Indeed one or two stood out strongly against racism and, especially, the racialistic policies of the Nationalist government after it came to power in 1948. At the same time, it should be appreciated that, worldwide, the theoretical and typological stance of most physical anthropology of the 1930s and 1940s did not provide adequate scientific arguments against the racial preconceptions, racial discrimination, and segregation that underlay the government's new policy. For Dart and Drennan, science was neatly partitioned from politics. Social anthropologists dealt with social issues, while physical anthropologists dealt with facts of biology. But while the old guard said little or nothing publicly about the events unfolding in South Africa, there was a younger generation of physical anthropologists who were not prepared to remain silent. A leading figure in this emerging group was Phillip V. Tobias (1925–). As a student at Wits in the late 1940s, he had been president of the nonracial National Union of South African Students (1948–1951) and a vocal critic of the government's race policies. In 1953, he attacked the Nationalist government's policy of race classification as scientifically unsound. In 1954, he demonstrated the baselessness of some views on "human racial crossing" that had lately been propounded by the German geneticist Fritz Lenz (1887–1973). In *The Meaning of Race*, published by the South African Institute of Race Relations in 1961 and revised and enlarged in 1972, Tobias exposed the racist preconceptions that underlay the apartheid policy and every aspect of South African society. He argued directly against the policies of race classification, discrimination and segregation, the prohibitions against "mixed marriages," the conception of racial superiority and inferiority, and the attribution of temperament, personality, and mental qualities to race.

Meanwhile, in 1958, Ronald Singer (1924–), then at the University of Cape Town, made a strong attack on the surviving remnants of typological thinking in South African physical anthropology.

In many respects, Singer's and Tobias' early careers serve to highlight the changing configuration of physical anthropology after World War II, prompted by the rapid and widespread acceptance of the new evolutionary synthesis among biologists in the late 1940s and its rapid spread to anthropology, and the appearance of populational and adaptational thinking. Tobias' background in genetics enabled him to make this transition with ease; it was further enhanced by his involvement in the multidisciplinary Panhard-Capricorn Expedition to the Kalahari in 1952, which was directed to the study of the Bushmen in their own cultural and bioecological context, and by his leadership of the Kalahari Research Committee from 1956 to 1971. In Singer's case, a similar shift in approach was spurred by his participation during 1954 in an expedition to study the Malagasy people of Madagascar. The closest earlier South African researchers came to this approach was the 1936 Witwatersrand University Expedition to the Kalahari Gemsbok Park, but the Bushman subjects were studied out of the context of their ecocultural environment.

The Panhard-Capricorn Expedition was followed by the creation of the Wits Kalahari Research Committee (KRC) in 1956. Tobias' earlier experience made him a natural choice to head the KRC. Between 1956 and 1971, annual excursions to the Kalahari were organized. With typology excluded as the method of analysis, these field trips produced a wealth of data on biological anthropology, applied physiology, psychology, dentition, serology, and anthropometry. Other similar expeditions were mounted by Singer to study Khoikhoi populations in the Richtersveld and by Lorna Marshall (cf. articles published in the journal *Africa* between 1959 and 1962), Joseph Sidney Weiner, and the Harvard Kalahari Research Group on the San of Botswana (cf. Lee & DeVore 1976). It is interesting to note that the holistic program of the KRC was later used as a model by the Human Adaptability Section of the International Biological Programme that began its work in 1968.

Developments after the 1950s

HUMAN PALEONTOLOGY AND PALEOANTHROPOLOGY. From the 1960s onward, two main centers for paleoanthropological research emerged in South Africa. One was the Wits Department of Anatomy and Human Biology (especially its Palaeo-Anthropological Research Unit), directed by Tobias (assisted by A.R. Hughes and R.J. Clarke). This center also became an important training center of South African and foreign students in paleoanthropology. Among the many research students who have obtained their higher degrees in that department are F.E. Grine, H. de Villiers, P.M. de Beer, D.E. Ricklan, A.G. Morris, J.A. Wallace, G.H. Sperber, M.M. Benade, A. Jacobson, G.T. Nurse, J.A. Kieser, P. Christie, R.J. Clarke, and L.R. Berger. The second center was the Transvaal Museum, Pretoria, where a series of distinguished scholars conducted researches on hominid evolution, including Broom, John Talbot Robinson (1923–), C.K. Brain, and F. Thackeray. These two centers are also major repositories of original fossils bearing on hominid evolution, particularly the early stages.

By the early 1960s, the studies of the anatomist and physical anthropologist Lawrence Herbert Wells (1908–1980), followed by those of Singer, Tobias, and others, had undermined the concept of the Boskop race. Other studies had thrown light on the kind of people who had lived in southern Africa in the Upper Pleistocene (125–120 ky BP). These included studies on the skeleton from Tuinplaas in the Springbok Flats, central Transvaal (Broom 1929); the skeletal material from Border Cave at Ingwavuma on the KwaZulu side of the border with Swaziland found in 1941, 1942, and 1974; and the cranial and mandibular fragments and teeth from Klasies River Mouth Cave, 120 km west of Port Elizabeth (cf. Singer & Smith 1969).

The researches of Hertha de Villiers of Wits and of L.P. Fatti of the National Research Institute for Mathematical Sciences, Pretoria, have indicated that most of these Upper Pleistocene remains were essentially of the form of

Homo sapiens sapiens, and that the remains suggested an early presence of Black (Negro) peoples in Africa. Wells dubbed this kind of early African people *H. sapiens afer,* after Carolus Linnaeus' term (Wells 1969), while Tobias (1972, 1974) regarded them as "proto-negriform," the common ancestral stock of Black Africans and Yellow Khoisan peoples.

A broader role for these smooth-browed Upper Pleistocene African peoples was proposed when newer dating methods revealed that several of them (Border Cave and Klasies River Mouth, as well as Omo-Kibish I from Ethiopia), were estimated to be 100 ky old, which would make them older than what were called "anatomically modern" *H. sapiens* from outside of Africa (cf. Beaumont & Boshier 1972; Rightmire 1979; Klein 1983). While the dating of this material is controversial, in the early 1980s Günter Bräuer of Hamburg University proposed what came to be known as the Afro-European *sapiens* hypothesis—namely, that modern Europeans had originated in Africa (cf. Bräuer 1984a, 1984b). This sparked a major resurgence of interest during the 1980s and 1990s in the origins of living humanity.

An earlier form of humankind of the genus *Homo* first came to light at Kabwe (Broken Hill) in Zambia in 1921 and 1925. After being subject to varied nomenclatural vicissitudes, it became commonly accepted as a subspecies of *H. sapiens,* called *H.s. rhodesiensis.* A South African representative of this population was found in 1953 by Singer and K. Jolly at Hopefield, inland from Saldanha Bay in the Cape Province. This specimen was variously attributed to an "African Neandertal" (e.g., Singer 1954) and a separate species, *H. saldanensis* (Drennan 1955), but most scholars came to accept it as *H.s. rhodesiensis.* To the same subspecies were assigned a mandibular and two radial fragments from the Acheulean horizon in the Cave of Hearths at Makapansgat (Tobias 1971).

The Florisbad cranium found in 1932 by Dreyer (*vide ante*) posed a somewhat more difficult problem. A variety of systematic appellations had been applied to it, ranging from a new subgenus of *Homo* (*Africanthropus*) to a new species (*H. helmei*). The American paleoanthropologist G. Philip Rightmire (1978) concluded that it belonged to *H.s. rhodesiensis*—but to a somewhat later and less archaic phase than that represented by the skulls of Kabwe and Hopefield.

The picture had thus emerged by the 1980s of a Middle Pleistocene population of sub-Saharan Africans classified in the subspecies *H.s. rhodesiensis.* They were seemingly derived from *H. erectus* ancestors, such as had become known from Swartkrans in the Transvaal and from Tanzania, Kenya, and Ethiopia. This fossil evidence, compounded with genetic evidence from living populations, supports the inference that in the Upper Pleistocene the "proto-negriform" population that had remained in Africa branched into two main streams: one leading to the Black (Negro) peoples and the other to the Khoisan populations.

OSTEOLOGY AND POPULATION AFFINITY STUDIES

As noted earlier, the demise of typological thinking was linked to a shift to the population approach, which is clearly expressed in the work of Hertha de Villiers of Wits. De Villiers completed her doctorate as Tobias' student in 1963, having served a typological apprenticeship under Dart. Her thesis, *The Skull of the South African Negro* (published in 1968), was innovative in that it stressed the statistical range of variation of a large and representative sample of South African crania from the Raymond Dart Collection of cadaver-derived skeletons. This collection has since become an important reference source for many studies on normal variation in South African Black populations. Studies have examined the pneumatization of the cranium, the variability of endocranial capacity, dental characteristics and dental health, stature reconstruction, anthropopathology, upper and lower limb-bone variability, and the morphology and developmental anomalies of the vertebral column.

The first study to examine large numbers of prehistoric and protohistoric skeletons as representatives of a single population in the same manner as de Villiers was conducted by Alan G. Morris for his doctoral thesis (1984), again under Tobias. Morris used multivariate analysis to assess population affinities but also went beyond that to include information on the health and life-style in these early historic and prehistoric groups. This latter theme has been continued by Mary Patrick (1989) in restudies of the Oakhurst remains excavated in the 1930s, and by Maryna Steyn (1994), who has restudied the large skeletal series from Mapungubwe.

The topic of diet as reflected in the biochemistry of bone has been the focus of a team under the direction of N.J. van der Merwe, A. Sillen, and J.C. Sealy in the Department of Archaeology at the University of Cape Town.

The results of these investigations have yielded the dietary patterns of prehistoric populations in the western Cape Province.

POPULATION GENETICS. Following on the pioneering ABO surveys of the 1930s and 1940s has been the compilation of serogenetic profiles of South African populations. Initially, these profiles focused on the polymorphisms in the genetics of sickle-cell disease, but since the late 1960s Trefor Jenkins and George Nurse of the SAIMR (along with local and overseas colleagues) have extended them to include a wide range of serum protein polymorphisms. Nonhematological profiles, such as dermatoglyphics and color blindness, have also been gathered. A summary and mean values of these data can be found in Tobias' presidential address to the Royal Society of South Africa in March 1971 (Tobias 1972).

The many immigrants to South Africa, especially those from Europe and Asia, have opened up another area of genetic research. The founder effect in these groups has resulted in a number of clinically significant genetic disorders, and research teams from the Universities of Johannesburg and Cape Town have examined the frequency of albinism, porphyria, skeletal disorders, and Huntington's and Gaucher's diseases, among others.

Research in population genetics continues in South Africa, in Cape Town (E.D. Du Toit, P. Beighton and colleagues), Pretoria (H.W. Hitzeroth), and Johannesburg (T. Jenkins). Recent work by the geneticist Himla Soodyall on mtDNA in Kalahari peoples is a particularly promising line of research.

GROWTH STUDIES. Large-scale cross-sectional growth studies have been a phenomenon since the 1960s, when C.S. Grobbelaar (1963, 1964, 1971) studied White schoolchildren in Bloemfontein and Pretoria, and P.J. Smit (1969) and E. Levine (1969), in their doctoral studies at Wits, extended Grobbelaar's work with a wide range of morphological and developmental data on different groups in Pretoria. Among other things, Smit's study showed that economically and nutritionally less-favored groups manifest significant delays in the onset and duration of puberty. Further studies since the 1960s on growth and skeletal maturation enlarged the earlier cross-sectional data for more populations, including Khoisan groups in the Cape Province and Namibia.

Comparison of cross-sectional data for stature gathered from the long bones of cadavers in Johannesburg has suggested that the worldwide secular trend in stature has been negative or absent, rather than positive, for some groups in South Africa. Although Tobias has stressed in numerous papers that these data indicate a biological response to the unequal distribution of nutrition resources in South Africa, more-recent work on South African Whites suggests that the picture may be more complicated (Henneberg & van den Berg 1990).

The results of the first longitudinal studies in South Africa were published in 1985 and served to stimulate interest in the study of growth (cf. Cameron 1992a). Noel Cameron and his students at Wits have examined rural and urban children in KwaZulu and in the northwestern Transvaal (Cameron 1992b). Their studies have contributed to the debate about the use of growth standards in assessing the health of communities—an issue that will undoubtedly intensify with the reconstruction of health in the post-apartheid South Africa. By the mid-1990s, further longitudinal data were being gathered for other groups by Maciej Henneberg of the University of the Witwatersrand in conjunction with Graham Louw of the University of Cape Town.

Alan G. Morris
Phillip V. Tobias

See also African Prehistory; Australopithecines; Broom, Robert; Dart, Raymond A(rthur); Eugenics; International Biological Programme (Human Adaptability Section); Khoisan; Kromdraai; Makapansgat; Modern Human Origins; Molecular Anthropology; Neo-Darwinism; Primate Field Studies; Robinson, John Talbot; Smith, (Sir) Grafton Elliot; Sterkfontein; Taung (formerly Taungs); Tobias, Phillip V(allentine); Weiner, Joseph Sidney

Bibliography
B.P. Beaumont & A. Boshier: Some comments on recent findings at Border Cave, northern Natal. *South African Journal of Science* 68:22–24, 1972; G. Bräuer: The Afro-European sapiens hypothesis and hominid evolution in east Asia during the Late Middle and Upper Pleistocene. *Courier Forschungsinstitut Senckenburg* 69:145–165, 1984a; G. Bräuer: A craniological approach to the origin of anatomically modern *Homo sapiens* in Africa and implications for the appearance of modern Europeans. In: F.H. Smith & F. Spencer (eds) *The origins of*

modern humans: A world survey of the fossil evidence. New York: Liss, 1984b, pp. 327–410; R. Broom: Evidence afforded by the Boskop skull of a new species of primitive man (Homo capensis). Anthropological Papers of the American Museum of Natural History 23:67–79, 1918,

R. Broom: The Transvaal fossil human skeleton. Nature 123:415–416, 1929; N. Cameron: The monitoring of growth and nutritional status in South Africa. American Journal of Human Biology 4:223–234, 1992a; N. Cameron: The contribution of the pattern of human growth and development to adult morphological diversity in southern Africa. South African Journal of Science 88:262–268, 1992b; R.A. Dart: Boskop remains from the south east African coast. Nature 112:623–625, 1923; R.A. Dart: The physical characters of the ?Auni/Khomani Bushmen. Bantu Studies 11:175–246, 1937; H. de Villiers: The skull of the South African Negro. Johannesburg: University of the Witwatersrand Press, 1968; M.R. Drennan: A short course on physical anthropology. Cape Town: Mercantile, 1937.

M.R. Drennan: The special features and status of the Saldanha skull. American Journal of Physical Anthropology 13:625–634, 1955; T.F. Dreyer & A.J.D. Meiring: A preliminary report on an expedition to collect old Hottentot skulls. Soölogiese Navorsing van die Nasionale Museum (Bloemfontein) 1:81–88, 1927; T.F. Dreyer, A.J.D. Meiring, & A.C. Hoffman: A comparison of the Boskop with other abnormal skulls from South Africa. Zeitschrift für Rassenkunde 7:289–296, 1938; R. Elsdon-Dew: The blood groups of the Bantu of South Africa. Publications of the South African Institute for Medical Research 7:221–300, 1936; F.W. FitzSimons: Palaeolithic man in South Africa. Nature 95:615–616, 1915; C.S. Grobbelaar: Observations on the differences between body measurements in urban and rural European boys of the age ten to eighteen years. South African Journal of Science 59:565–572, 1963.

C.S. Grobbelaar: Suggested norms of physical status for White South African males aged 10–20 years, based on an anthropometric survey. Cape Town: Struik, 1971; C.S. Grobbelaar: Grafieke van die Groei en die Norme van Fisieke Status van Dogters 6–20 Jaar van die Provinsiale Administrasie Skole, Kolleges en Universiteit van die Stad Bloemfontein. Bloemfontein: University of Stellenbosch, 1971; S.H. Haughton: Preliminary note on the ancient human skull remains from the Transvaal. Transactions of the Royal Society of South Africa 6:1–14, 1917; M. Henneberg & E.R. van den Berg: Test of socioeconomic causation of secular trend: Stature changes among favored and oppressed South Africans are parallel. American Journal of Physical Anthropology 83:459–465, 1990.

T. Jenkins: Medical genetics in South Africa. Journal of Medical Genetics 27:760–779, 1990; R.G. Klein: The Stone Age prehistory of southern Africa. Annual Review of Anthropology 12:25–48, 1983; R.B. Lee & I. DeVore (eds) Kalahari hunter-gatherers: Studies of the !Kung San and their neighbors. Cambridge, Massachusetts: Harvard University Press, 1976; E. Levine: A radiological study of hand and wrists ossification in South African children of four population groups. Ph.D. thesis. University of the Witwatersrand, 1969; H. Lichtenstein: Travels in southern Africa in the years 1803, 1804, 1805, and 1806. Cape Town: Van Riebeeck Society, 1928–1929; A.G. Morris: An osteological analysis of the protohistoric populations of the Northern Cape and western Orange Free State, South Africa. Ph.D. Thesis. University of the Witwatersrand, 1984.

B.K. Murray: Wits: The early years. Johannesburg: University of the Witwatersrand Press, 1982; M.K. Patrick: An archaeological, anthropological study of the human skeletal remains from the Oakhurst rockshelter, George, Cape Province, southern Africa. M.A. Thesis. University of Cape Town, 1989; H. Phillips: The University of Cape Town, 1918–1948: The formative years. Cape Town: University of Cape Town Press, 1993; G.P. Rightmire: Florisbad and human population succession in southern Africa. American Journal of Physical Anthropology 48:475–486, 1978; G.P. Rightmire: Implications of Border Cave skeletal remains for later Pleistocene human evolution. Current Anthropology 20:23–35, 1979; J.S. Sharp: The roots and development of Volkekunde in South Africa. Journal of Southern African Studies 8:16–36, 1981; R. Singer: The Saldanha skull from Hopefield, South Africa. American Journal of Physical Anthropology 12:345–362, 1954.

R. Singer: The Boskop "race" problem. Man 58:173–178, 1958; R. Singer & P. Smith: Some human remains associated with the Middle Stone Age deposits at Klasies River, South Africa. American Journal of Physical Anthropology 31:256, 1969; P.J. Smit: *Anthropometric motor performances and physiological studies on South African children involved in a nutritional survey*. Ph.D. Thesis. University of the Witwatersrand, 1969; G.E. Smith: *Migrations of early culture*. London: Longmans Green, 1915; M. Steyn: *A reanalysis of the skeletal remains of Mapungubwe and Bambandyanalo*. Ph.D. Thesis. University of the Witwatersrand, 1994; P.V. Tobias: The problem of race identification: Limiting factors in the investigation of South African races. *Journal of Forensic Medicine* 1:113–123, 1953; P.V. Tobias: On a Bushman-European hybrid family. *Man* 54:179–182, 1954.

P.V. Tobias: Physical anthropology and somatic origins of the Hottentots. *African Studies* 14:1–22, 1955; P.V. Tobias: *The meaning of race*. Johannesburg: South African Institute of Race Relations, 1961; P.V. Tobias: Human skeletal remains from the Cave of Hearths, Makapansgat, northern Transvaal. *American Journal of Physical Anthropology* 34:335–367, 1971; P.V. Tobias: Recent human biological studies in southern Africa, with special reference to Negroes and Khoisans. *Transactions of the Royal Society of South Africa* 40:109–133, 1972; P.V. Tobias: The biology of the southern African negro. In: W.D. Hammond-Tooke (ed) *The Bantu-speaking peoples of southern Africa*. London: Routledge & Kegan Paul, 1974, pp. 3–45; P.V. Tobias: *Dart, Taung and the "Missing Link."* Johannesburg: University of the Witwatersrand Press, 1984; P.V. Tobias: History of physical anthropology in southern Africa. *Yearbook of Physical Anthropology* 28:1–52, 1985; L.H. Wells: *Homo sapiens afer* Linn: Content and earliest representatives. *South African Archaeological Bulletin* 24:172–173, 1969.

South Asia (India, Pakistan, Sri Lanka)

Physical Anthropology in Ancient India

The earliest references to human diversity in the populations of the Indian subcontinent can be traced to Rigvedic literature, the oldest of the *Vedas* traditionally dated to ca. 2000 B.C. The Rigvedic literature of ca. 900–500 B.C. consists of the *Samhitas*, a collection of hymns; *Brahmanas*, instructions for religious rites; and *Aranyakas*, or philosophical speculations. The *Upanishads* developed from these latter Rigvedic texts.

The period covered by this early literature was one of profuse development and diffusion of culture and population movements, when social and cultural norms were being codified. The *Dharma* (the ultimate law of all things) is continually referred to, and its significance emphasized. The *Dharma* of class and stage of life was both self-evident and unimpeachable; it was preserved and enforced by the ruling authorities. The implication of this was that *Dharma* was not the same for all human beings—there was a hierarchy of social class, which determined both an individual's duties and general way of life.

Given this sociocultural context in which the Rigvedic literature emerged, its apparent emphasis on the physical and cultural differences between the "Aryan" and "non-Aryan" populations is hardly surprising. Among the latter, specific reference is made to the *Ayogave, Chandala, Nishada*, and *Paulakasa*—the *Ayogave* being of mixed ethnic origin. References to other groups and their distinctive bodily characteristics abound in the Vedic literature.

Vedic *Samhitas* and *Brahmanas* approach the study of human variation through their treatment of medicine, physique, body proportions, temperamental dispositions, and male and female compatibilities in marriage and sexual relations. A systematic exposition of these is offered in the texts called *Carakasamhita, Susrutasamhita*, and *Astangasangraha* (ca. 600–900 B.C.).

Vatsyayana (fl. A.D. 300), a commentator on the *Sutras*, elaborated the theme of physical compatibilities in mating, which was further developed by Kalyana Malla, the author of the erotic manual *Ananga Ranga* (ca. A.D. 1100).

Another aspect of these early systems of classification was the corpus of texts concerned with normal variations in body proportions through a system of measurements—the *Pramanas*.

Western Physical Anthropology

The development of modern physical anthropology in south Asia has its roots in studies initiated by British colonial administrators. Contemporary approaches were introduced by scholars trained in continental Europe, the United Kingdom, and the United States. Continued contacts with the West have contributed to the shaping of physical anthropology in a distinctive manner that is a combination of both ancient and modern traditions (R.D. Singh 1985).

In 1784, the Orientalist and jurist William Jones (1746–1794) founded the Asiatic Society in Calcutta, India, at the time of the expanding power of the British East India

Company, under Governor-General Warren Hastings (1732–1818). It gained support from civil servants and military personnel. Jones sought to establish an organization modeled along the lines of the Royal Society as a center for discussion and publication of research resulting from systematic explorations of Asian natural history, geography, epigraphy, monuments and antiquities, and native customs and languages. The Museum of the Asiatic Society was established in 1808.

Jones is recognized for discovering the family of Indo-European languages and establishing the first absolute chronological date correlating Indian and European history. His work in comparative linguistics encouraged him to reconstruct the origins of populations and the ancient roots of migrations, hypothesize causes behind cultural diversity, and reconstruct the cultural history of five ethnic groups: Arabians, Persians, Tartars, Chinese, and Indians (Jones 1788). With their expansion into many parts of India, culminating with the First War of Independence (the Sepoy Mutiny) in 1857, the British gained a secure foothold on the subcontinent, and, as a consequence, a new research dimension was added to the study of physical variation in human populations.

Anthropometry

Anthropometry is a methodology employed in the study of human variations that was introduced into India by British administrators such as Herbert H. Risley (1851–1911) and Edgar Thurston (1855–1935) (cf. Risley 1893, 1908, 1909; Thurston 1906). Anthropometric procedures apply to human skeletal remains as well as to living subjects. Measurements are taken by precision instruments according to standardized methods.

The period prior to the international agreements for the unification of anthropometric measurements at Monaco in 1906 and Geneva in 1912 is characterized by populational and/or regional surveys. Despite the enormous wealth of data collected during this period, their applicability to comparative studies is marred by the fact that the anthropometric techniques employed were not standardized, and the investigators were inadequately trained (R.D. Singh 1987).

In direct contrast, the post-Monaco-Geneva Agreements period laid emphasis on standardization of the landmarks, definitions, techniques, methodologies, and the assembly of larger sets of data. A host of studies was undertaken (e.g., Basu 1929; Guha 1935;

Majumdar, 1945, *1949, *1958). While the interpretations of Biraja Sankar Guha (1894–1961), and his predecessors were along traditional lines, Dhirendra Nath Majumdar (1903–1960), in collaboration with the statisticians C.R. Rao and P.C. Mahalanobis, focused attention on inter- and intrapopulational differences in various geographic regions. In 1937–1938, E.W.E. Macfarlane studied the rate of growth of children in Trivandrum (Kerala) (cf. Table 1).

The Indian independence period is characterized by the trend set by Majumdar, which endeavored to study intrapopulational variations under specific environmental conditions—an approach further developed by Irawati Karve (1905–1970) at Deccan College in Poona (e.g., Karve *1948; *1954). Growth studies of single populations as well as comparative samples were also undertaken early in this period. The Indian Council of Medical Research embarked on a growth study of schoolchildren in Uttar Pradesh in the mid-1950s under the stewardship of Majumdar and Profulla Chandra Biswas (1903–1984) with an intent to cover other states later. However, the traditional approach of data collection as an end in itself was not abandoned, and the data on convict populations, university students, and schoolchildren were collected by R.D. Singh and B.K. Varma in the years 1954–1955 (R.D. Singh *1987).

The Anthropological Survey of India (ASI) launched yet another ambitious and comprehensive survey in 1960 in order to include populations throughout India (Rakshit et al. *1988). Publications based on these data have become available in recent years (Sreenath & Ahmad *1989; Sirajuddin et al. *1992).

In contrast to earlier approaches, since the late 1960s the emphasis in Indian anthropometric studies has shifted to applied projects, which include nutrition, growth, and aging (Arora et al. *1963; Agarwal et al. *1983; Prakash *1987), environment, adaptation, and performance (Bharadwaj et al. *1982; Ahluwalia et al. *1987), bone abnormalities and growth (Chatterjee *1968; Chadha & Kapoor *1985), forensic anthropology (Ghosh *1968; Maniar et al. *1974; Jit and Bakshi *1986), space requirements (Verma *1960; Malik et al. *1984), sports (Malhotra et al. *1972; Singh, Sidhu & Malhotra *1987), and other related topics. These sample citations indicate the direction, vigor, and contemporaneity of Indian anthropometry.

*Note: * indicates reference in Table.*

TABLE 1. Human Biological Research in India 1948–1992. Selected References

Year	Principal Investigator	Reference
Anthropometry		
1948	I. Karve	*Deccan College Monograph Series* No. 2.
1949	D.N. Majumdar	*Sankhya* 9:93–110
1954	I. Karve	*Journal of Anthropological Society*, Bombay 8:45–75
1958	D.N. Majumdar	*Race Elements in Bengal*
1987	R.D. Singh	In: K.S. Mathur et al. (eds) *Anthropological Perspectives*, pp. 1–19
1988	H.K. Rakshit et al.	*All India Anthropometric Survey: South Zone* I–VII:1–574
1989	J. Sreenath & S.H. Ahmad	*All India Anthropometric Survey: South Zone: Andhra Pradesh*
1992	S.M. Sirajuddin, S.H. Ahmad, & R.D Singh	*All India Anthropometric Survey: South Zone: Karnataka State* I–XIII:1–234
Nutrition, Growth, and Aging		
1963	S. Arora et al.	*Indian Journal of Child Health* 12:612
1983	K.N. Agarwal et al.	*Indian Journal of Medical Research* 77:839–844
1987	S. Prakash	In: A.K. Kalla & K.S. Singh (eds) *Anthropology, Development, and Nation Building*, pp. 201–210
Environment, Adaptation, and Performance		
1982	H. Bharadwaj et al.	In: A. Basu & K.C. Malhotra (eds) *Human Genetics and Adaptation* 2:70–80
1987	P. Ahluwalia et al.	In: L.S. Sidhu et al. (ed) *Sports Sciences, Health, Fitness, and Performance*, pp. 109–116
Bone Abnormalities and Growth		
1968	K.P. Chatterjee	*Eastern Anthropologist* 21:279–284
1985	N.K. Chadha & A.K. Kapoor	*Spectra of Anthropological Progress* 7:71–76
Forensic		
1968	G.C. Ghosh	*Man in India* 48:364–368
1974	B.H. Maniar et al.	*Indian Pediatrics* 11:203–211
1986	I. Jit & V. Bakshi	*Indian Journal of Medical Research* 83:322–331
Space Requirements		
1960	B.K. Verma	*Eastern Anthropologist* 13:172–184
1984	S.L. Malik et al.	*Indian Anthropologist* 14:41–61
Sport		
1972	M.S. Malhotra et al.	*Indian Journal of Physiology and Pharmacology* 16:55–62, 301–308
1987	S.P. Singh, L.S. Sidhu, & P. Malhotra	In: L.S. Sidhu et al. (ed) *Sports Sciences, Health, Fitness, and Performance*, pp. 55–65
Dermatoglyphics		
1953	D.C. Rife	*American Journal of Human Genetics* 5:389–399
1963	R.D. Singh	*Eastern Anthropologist* 21:28–46
1977	A. Sharma & S.M. Thukral	*Indian Anthropologist* 21:34–40
1978	R.D. Singh	*Human Biology* 50:251–260
1983	S.C. Tewari	*Human Biology—Recent Advances* 2:429–443
1985	A. Basu	*Anthropological Survey of India Memoir* 62
Genetic Demography		
1949	L. Dubey	*Eastern Anthropologist* 2:153–159
1951	K. Davis	*The Population of India and Pakistan.* Princeton University Press
1953	V.M. Dandekar	Gokhale Institute Political and Economic Publication, *Poona* 27:115–187
1954–1955	D.N. Majumdar	*Eastern Anthropologist* 8:161–172
1955	C.T. Hu	*Eastern Anthropologist* 9:4–20
1966	L.D. Sanghvi	*Indian Journal of Genetics* 26:351–365
1976	H.K. Rakshit	*Physical Anthropology ASI* 2:45–60

Year	Principal Investigator	Reference
1978	K.C. Malhotra	*Journal of Indian Anthropological Society* 13:89–94
1978	L.D. Sanghvi	*Medical Genetics in India* 2:113–118
1983	S. Talukdar	*Man in India* 63:151–166
Human Population Biology and Adaptation		
1952	D.N. Majumdar	*Eastern Anthropologist* 5:101–122
1958	N. Kumar	*Indian Anthropologist* 5:42–46
1960	S.S. Sarkar	*Anthropological Survey of India Memoir* 6:71–78
1962	R.L. Kirk	*American Journal of Physical Anthropology* 20:485–497
1973	S.R. Das	*Human Heredity* 23:381–385
1974	S.R. Das	*Human Heredity* 24:24–31
1976	R.S. Negi	Ph.D. Thesis, University of Calcutta
1980	N. Kumar	*Journal of Indian Anthropological Society* 15:211–213
1981	L.D. Sanghavi	*Biology of the People of Tamil Nadu*
1983	R.C. Jain	*Indian Journal of Medical Research* 78:552–555
Non-Human Primate Behavior		
1961	C.H. Southwick	*Ecology* 42:538–547; 698–710
1963	P. Jay	In: *Primate Social Behavior*, Princeton University Press
1965	P.E. Simonds	In: I. DeVore (ed) *Primate Behavior*
1968	F. Poirier	*Primates* 9 (1–2):29–43; *Primates* 9 (1–2):43–68
1974	S.B. Hrdy	*Folia Primatologica* 22:19–58
1982	S.M. Mohnot	*International Journal of Primatology* 3:314
1984	C. Vogel	In: *Infanticide: Comparative and Evolutionary Perspectives*, pp. 237–255
1984	P. Winkler	*Folia Primatologica* 43:1–23

Dermatoglyphics

Although the British biometrician Francis Galton's (1822–1911) seminal treatise *Finger Prints* was published in 1892, it took almost another fifty years for dermatoglyphic studies to appear on the Indian scene. This movement was pioneered by P.C. Biswas, who began publishing in this field in 1936. His work generated an enthusiasm, as indicated by a new generation of investigators such as A. Sharma, S.C. Tewari as his junior colleagues, and J. Mavalavala and M.R. Chakravarty as his students at Delhi (cf. Table 1). A very active publication record by Sharma from 1957 to 1977 and Tewari from 1952 to 1983 covered populational, genetic, and methodological aspects of the field. D.K. Sen set the tone at Lucknow University in the early 1950s, attracting the attention of R.D. Singh and R.P. Srivastava, later joined by B.R.K. Shukla and D. Tyagi. Singh and Srivastava were influenced by D.N. Majumdar's anthropometric orientation to inter- and intracaste variations existing under different environmental conditions. Their studies, beginning in 1959 and 1962, respectively, investigated the regional distribution of dermatoglyphic traits in that regard. Since the beginning of the 1970s B.R.K. Shukla and D. Tyagi have been active primarily in the populational aspects of dermatoglyphics. M.R. Chakravarty

and D.P. Mukherjee have done research in population dermatoglyphics and interested other researchers at the ASI. K.C. Malhotra contributed to the field through his connection with the Indian Statistical Institute (ISI) in Calcutta. Genetic, clinical, methodological, and populational aspects of dermatoglyphics were advanced by these scholars.

The nature of population distribution in India, including the existence of endogamous caste units, caste subsections, and small populations with varying social and geographic environments, has offered a challenging field for study of selective factors. These topics have been addressed by D.C. Rife (*1953), R.D. Singh (*1963, 1978), A. Basu (*1985), and other investigators.

Genetic Demography

Since 1949, there has been a shift away from the study of ethnic origins to the examination of the demographic patterns of genetic traits (cf. Table 1). Although the first serious attempt, apart from census reports, was made by K. Davis (*1951) on populations in India and Pakistan, later demographics of pregnancy and childbirth were reported by L. Dubey (*1949), C.T. Hu (*1955) on Chandanpur, under the supervision of D.N. Majumdar. V.M. Dandekar (*1953) combined fertility and mortality in the Pune district of Maharashtra. Majumdar investigated the polyandrous society among the Khasas of Jaunsar Bawar in Uttar Pradesh (Majumdar *1952; *1954–1955). From wide-scale inbreeding practices in India to localized rural Andhra Pradesh, L.D. Sanghvi examined the genetic consequences of inbreeding, outbreeding, and interbreeding from 1966 to 1978. While K.C. Malahotra (e.g., *1978) and his colleagues mainly concentrated on individual populations, S. Talukdar focused on selection intensity and genetic demography between 1971 and 1983.

Within the context of cultural as well as regional distribution of populations, Hirendra Kishor Rakshit (1927–1992) and his colleagues in the ASI emphasized aspects of natural selection and called their focus "anthropological demography" (Rakshit *1976). The general direction of such studies parallels investigation of the Australian Aboriginal populations by the American anthropologist Joseph B. Birdsell (1908–1994) and his concern for their genetic characters and clinal distributions.

Human Population Biology and Adaptation

The Polish serologist Ludwik Hirzsfeld's (1884–1954) pioneering studies of the ABO blood group distributions in human populations (1919) mark the beginning of human population biology. These studies were carried forward by a number of researchers in India—most notably, R.H. Malone and M.N. Lahiri (1929) on blood-group distributions in certain population and castes and S.R. Pandit on Todas (1934)—while E.W.E. Macfarlane (1937, 1941), Majumdar (1941–1952), and S.S. Sarkar (1937, *1960) centered their attention upon blood-type distributions and population affinities. Significant contributions were made by Narendra Kumar between 1958 and 1980 and his associates (cf. Table 1). Between 1958 and 1985, B.M. Das, in collaboration with others, paid special attention to hemoglobin distributions, and glucose-6-phosphate dehydrogenase deficiencies (cf. Table 1). The data on populational studies continued to be collected until the late 1960s, and occasionally such studies still appear.

Following World War II, the work of R.S. Negi and L.D. Sanghvi deserves special mention. Sanghvi's major contribution has been in the areas of genetic variations and genetic distances between populations (cf. Table 1). Negi focused attention on the distribution of sickle-cell traits in Indian populations and the role of Aboriginal populations in the dispersal of the mutant hemoglobin (cf. Table 1). A further study of sickle-cell genes was done by R.C. Jain and his collaborators in the early 1980s (cf. Table 1). Similarly, H. Kaur and her colleagues studied serum protein polymorphisms, haptoglobin polymorphisms, and breast cancer during the years 1977 to 1986 (cf. Kaur et al. 1986). The study of serum protein and enzyme groups, with special reference to Indian populations, was analyzed by R.L. Kirk in the early 1970s, among others (cf. Table 1). Kirk and his collaborators also studied these genetic variables in Sri Lanka during the early 1960s (cf. Table 1).

Another researcher worthy of special mention is Sudhir Ranjan Das (1909–). During his career, which unfolded initially at the ASI during the years 1948–1968 and then at the Indian Statistical Institute in Calcutta, Das made a number of significant contributions to the various subfields of human genetics, including ABH secretion, sickle-cell, PTC tasting, color blindness, hemoglobin, and genetic variants of lactate dehydrogenase.

Nonhuman Primate Behavior

The earliest studies on macaque and langur behavior were undertaken in the late 1920s and early 1930s by the British naturalist Reginald I. Pocock (1863–1947). He also collected some data on their morphology and habitat. Thereafter, with the exception of Angela Holt's study of the south Indian macaques in 1948, there was a lull until the early 1950s, when the American physical anthropologist Sherwood L. Washburn's (1911–) views on behavioral studies were emphasized in an evolutionary context. Washburn expressed his ideas during a Wenner-Gren Foundation conference on "Early Man in Africa" held in London in 1953. Beginning in the early 1960s, a number of American investigators (cf. Table 1) began working in central and north India, including Washburn's students Phyllis Jay on langurs and Paul Simonds on bonnet macaques; and the American zoologist Charles H. Southwick who studied rhesus monkeys. These pioneering studies were followed by that of the American primatologist Frank Poirier in the mid-1960s on Nilgiri langurs. All of the above studies attracted the attention of Indian scholars. Among many others, P.K. Seth and S.M. Mohnot have significantly contributed to the development of this field in India. Seth has been active in this area since 1960 and has concentrated on the behavior of the rhesus macaque, although his major contribution is the study of variations in genetic characters. Mohnot focused his attention on *Presbytis entellus* from 1971 to 1982.

During the 1970s and 1980s, there were a number of foreign primatologists active in India. For example, in the 1970s Sarah B. Hrdy studied the langurs of Abu, and C. Vogel made similar studies in Rajasthan (cf. Table 1). Following Vogel, P. Winkler during the 1980s contributed to the study of langurs in Rajasthan (cf. Table 1). These studies, too, have generated considerable enthusiasm among Indian and foreign researchers.

Paleoprimatology

The Museum of the Asiatic Society, founded in 1808, received many fossil specimens from the Siwalik Hills, including the first finds of fossil cercopithecid primates from the Himalayan region. Since 1836, when the British paleontologist Hugh Falconer (1808–1865) and military engineer Proby Thomas Cautley (1801–1871) announced the discovery of a fossil ape specimen from this region, paleontological research in the Siwaliks has continued unabated.

The description of the Siwalik primate fossils named *Palaeopithecus sivalensis* by the British paleontologist Richard Lydekker (1849–1915) in 1880 appears to be the first description of an Asian anthropoid ape. Later finds between 1910 and 1915 added another genus, *Ramapithecus*. This was followed by the recovery in the Siwaliks of further dryopithecine and sivapithecine material by the Yale North India Expedition of 1932 (cf. Lewis 1934). In 1968, a Yale-Punjab Universities research team led by Elwyn Simons recovered mandibular and dental remains near Haritalyangar and Hasnot. They were assigned to the taxon *Giganthopithecus bilaspurensis*. Their ascription to the Pliocene Dhok Pathan Formation makes them earlier than *G. blacki* from China (Simons & Chopra 1969). These fossils occupy a position in the pongid ancestry. Subsequently, the Anglo-American paleontologist David Pilbeam extended his work to the Siwalik ranges in Pakistan and discovered cranial and facial parts of *Ramapithecus* clearly indicating pongid features in teeth and mandibular morphology, which had been a subject of debate earlier.

Paleoanthropology

The discoveries of Pleistocene fossil vertebrates in the Narmada valley (cf. Spilsbury 1833) and from Karimkhan on the Yamuna (cf. Princep 1833) in the early 1830s, raised hopes that ancient human remains might be recovered from these localities. However, it was not until 1982 that a Middle Pleistocene fossil hominid was found at Hathnora in the Narmada valley under well-documented circumstances (cf. Sonakia 1984) and later described by the Cornell University American paleoanthropologist Kenneth A.R. Kennedy (cf. Kennedy et al. 1991). The Narmada calvaria provides some idea of cranial morphology of ancient humans in this region, although artifactual evidence from northwestern Pakistan suggests the earlier existence of hominids on the subcontinent ca. 2.2 my ago.

Evidence that prehistoric human populations inhabited the subcontinent was not established until the 1860s, when Robert Bruce Foote (1834–1912) of the Geological Survey of India recognized that quartzite tools he had collected at Palarvaram in Tamil Nadu were comparable to European Acheulean handaxes. This event stimulated the search for prehistoric stone tools in other sectors of the subcontinent.

Until the 1930s, the prehistoric cultures of India were classified as either Paleolithic or Neolithic, and the mysterious megalithic monuments with their burial chambers containing human skeletons and iron artifacts were of uncertain antiquity.

It was with the goal of finding fossil man in India that the Yale-Cambridge Expedition was staged in 1935. Although this expedition failed to recover hominid remains, it did identify a regional non-Acheulean lithic tradition in Kashmir and the Potwar plateau, which was dubbed by the Harvard archeologist, Hallam Movius (1908–1987), as the Soan Culture. While this is no longer accepted as a distinctive lithic tradition by prehistorians, the Soan has persisted into later revisions of the classification of India's prehistoric cultures (e.g., Bendapudi Subbaro's reduction in 1958 of the Indian Stone Age to three classes: Early, Middle, and Late, which favored African over European tool typology). Since the 1970s there has been a trend to return to the European classification of Lower, Middle, and Upper Paleolithic followed by Mesolithic, Neolithic, Chalcolithic/Bronze Age and Iron Age/Megalithic for south Asia.

Paralleling the emergence in the nineteenth century of the scientific study of ancient south Asian peoples by comparative linguistics and the classification of prehistoric artifacts, was the excavation of sites marked on the landscape by orthostatic monuments and stone circles reminiscent of the pre-Christian constructions found at Stonehenge, Carnac, and other places in Europe. These structures were first excavated in 1820 (cf. Babington 1823), and incited some western scholars to conceive of a widespread diffusion of a "Megalithic Culture" based on the assumption that ancient Indians must have had ties with Europe and the Far East. The first anatomical description of a prehistoric south Asian from a megalithic burial was undertaken by the British scholar Meadows Taylor (1808–1876) in the early 1850s (cf. Taylor 1873). During the last quarter of the nineteenth century and the opening decade of the twentieth century careful collections of skeletons from the Iron Age urn field of Aditanallur in Tirunelvelli (formerly Tinnevelly) were made for a number of European museums such as the Königliche Museum für Völkerkunde in Berlin and the Muséum National d'Histoire Naturelle in Paris. Furthermore, the Aditanallur crania excavated between 1889 and 1908 by Alexander Rea for the Government Museum in Madras (cf. Rea 1902–1903a, 1902–1903b) were the subjects of the first attempt to place India's prehistoric inhabitants into the racial typology conceived by Herbert Risley (*vide ante*) for the living populations of south Asia on the basis of the anthropometric survey he had directed for the 1901 census of India. The Aditanallur crania were also the basis for the comparative study made in 1930 by the British anatomist Solly Zuckerman (1904–1993). From this study, Zuckerman concluded that the racial origins of living Indians were to be found among ancient populations to the west of the Indus and that a "Dravidian" race had formed as a result of crossings of the former with an indigenous "Australoid" stock—a view that shaped scientific opinion for the next thirty years concerning not only the physical anthropology of India's megalithic people but also the entire subcontinent.

Along with Zuckerman, B.S. Guha's (1931) scheme, in which he defined seven racial elements in India from both prehistoric and living populations, has also been influential. Indeed Guha's typology, which reflects the influence of his mentor at Harvard University, Roland B. Dixon (1875–1934) (1923), remains the most frequently cited among Indian physical anthropologists.

In the 1960s, a dramatic shift in the physical anthropology of the Iron Age skeleton was precipitated by S.S. Sarkar's (1908–1969) study of human remains from Brahmagiri in Karnataka, a site that the British archeologist Mortimer Wheeler (1890–1973) had dated to the centuries just prior to the Christian era (cf. Wheeler 1947). Sarkar sought to establish the biological affinities of the Brahmagiri people and those represented in the skeletal record of other Indian megalithic sites by means of comparative statistical analyses with various ancient skeletal series from western Asia. It is interesting to note that Sarkar was strongly influenced by the earlier study of an Iranian series of human remains from Tepe Hesar by the Dutch anatomist Cornelius Ubbo Ariëns Kappers (1877–1946) in 1934. Sarkar concluded that the aboriginal racial element in India was what he called "Indo-Caspian" (whereas Kapper's had referred to this basal stock as "Scytho-Iranian").

Included in Guha's (1931) racial classification were skeletal remains from Mohenjodaro, a major urban site of the Indus civilization, which was unknown to archeologists until 1920. Excavations at Mohenjodaro from 1920 to 1931 yielded over forty human skeletons buried in the debris of houses and lanes. These specimens were described by Guha (cf. Sewell & Guha 1931), who identified four racial elements out of the seven in his racial typology—a classification upheld by his successors at the Anthropological Survey of India in Calcutta. In 1962, a study was published of the human skeletons from the Indus site at Harappa (cf. Gupta & Basu 1962), which had been excavated between 1923 and 1947. The Harappa skeletons were from two cemeteries, one of the mature urban period (Cemetery R-37) and the other dated to a period after 1700 B.C. (Cemetery H). Although for some scholars in post-colonial India a unique south Asian racial identity for the architects of the Indus civilization was deemed desirable, others have tended to favor the view that the racial origins for the Indus valley populations had been western Asia and the Mediterranean basin (e.g., Cappieri 1969).

Since the 1960s the skeletal record of prehistoric humans in south Asia has increased, and prehistoric and protohistoric sites yielding human osteological remains have been the subject of systematic reports (see Table 2 for a summary). They mostly represent a period from 200 ky BP to A.D. 50. The prehistoric skeletal record in regard to Mesolithic, Neolithic, and Chalcolithic archeological contexts has improved. With the discoveries at Langhnaj in Gujarat Baghai

TABLE 2. Summary of work on prehistoric and protohistoric sites in India, Pakistan, and Sri Lanka

Location	Principal Investigator	Reference
India		
Narmada (Hathnora)	A. Sonakia	*Records of the Geological Survey of India* 113:159–172, 1984
	K.A.R. Kennedy et al.	*American Journal of Physical Anthropology* 86:475–496, 1991
Aditanallur (Tamilnadu)	B.K. Chatterjee & P. Gupta	Calcutta, ASI, 1963
Brahmagiri (Karnataka)	S.S. Sarkar	*Bulletin of the Department of Anthropology of the Government of India* 9:5–26, 1960
Mohenjodaro Harappa (Punjab)	J. Marshall	*Mohenjodaro and the Indus civilization.* London, 1931
	E.J.H. Mackay	*Further excavations at Mohenjodaro.* New Delhi, 1938
	D.R. Sahni	*Annual Report of the Archaeological Survey of India 1923–1924*
	M.S. Vats	*Excavations at Harappa.* Delhi, 1940
	R.E.M. Wheeler	*Ancient India* 3:58–130, 1947
	P. Gupta et al.	*Mem. ASI* No. 9, 1962
Langhnaj & Lothal (Gujarat)	H.D. Sankalia & I. Karve	*American Anthropologist* 51:28–34, 1949
Bagor (Rajasthan)	V.N. Misra	In: D.P. Agrawal & A. Ghosh (eds) *Radiocarbon and Indian Archaeology.* Bombay, 1973, pp. 58–72
Sarai Nahar Rai	G.R. Sharma	*Proc. Prehist. Society* 39:129–146, 1973
Mahadaha	G.R. Sharma	*Proc. Prehist. Society* 39:129–146, 1973
Damdama	G.R. Sharma	*Proc. Prehist. Society* 39:129–146, 1973
Chandoli Khurd	K.C. Malhotra	In: *Chalcolithic Chandoli.* Pune: Deccan College, 1965, pp. 69–80
Inamgaon	J.R. Lukacs & G.L. Badam	*Journal of the Indian Anthropological Society* 16:59–74, 1981
	J.R. Lukacs & S.R. Walimbe	In: *Excavations at Inamgaon.* Vol. 2. Deccan College, 1986
Nevasa	K.A.R. Kennedy & K.C. Malhotra	Deccan College Building Centenary and Silver Jubilee Ser. 55:1–135, 1966
Pakistan		
Mehrgarh (Baluchistan)	J.-F. Jarrige	In: G. Possehl (ed) *Harappan civilization.* Delhi, 1982, pp. 79–84
	J.-F. Jarrige	*Pakistan Archaeology* 10–22:63–161, 1986
Timargarha (Gandhara)	A.H. Dani	*Ancient Pakistan* 3:1–407, 1967
Sarai Khola (Gandhara)	M.A. Halim	*Pakistan Archaeology* 7:23–89, 1971
	M.A. Halim	*Pakistan Archaeology* 8:3–112, 1972
Sri Lanka		
Batadomba	S.U. Deraniyagala	*Prehistory of Sri Lanka.* 2 vols. 1992
	K.A.R. Kennedy et al.	*American Journal of Physical Anthropology* 72:441–461, 1987
Fa-Hien	S.U. Deraniyagala	*Prehistory of Sri Lanka.* 2 vols. 1992

Khor and Lekhahia in the Kaimur hills of Uttar Pradesh, Sarai Nahar Rai, Mahadaha, and Damdama of the Gangetic plains, and burials at Bagor in Rajasthan, the Mesolithic establishes the continuity of the Paleolithic into the Neolithic in India. The southernmost Sri Lankan extension of anatomically modern *Homo sapiens* dates back to 28.5 ky BP from the cave site of Batadomba in Sri Lanka. An-other site, at Fa-Hien Cave, is a millenium earlier (cf. Kennedy & Deraniyagala 1989; Kennedy et al. 1987). All of these provide the most ancient evidence of anatomically modern *Homo sapiens* in south Asia.

The Neolithic and Chalcolithic remains from Chandoli Khurd, Inamgaon, Nevesa, and Tekkalakota provide a further continuity and presence of modern humans in this region.

The Chalcolithic traditions of the mid-second millenium B.C. were a fusion of regional cultural elements from the Neolithic and the reorganization of Indus culture upon the decline of its urban phase. Timargarha and Sarai Khola in Pakistan represent the period between the end of the Indus civilization and the dawn of the historic period of the Archaeminid invasions in the sixth century B.C.

Paleodemography was pioneered by J.M. Datta (1959, 1962) and B. Subbarao (1959). They related ecology to population structure and process in ancient populations through the data of the archeological and biological records. Employment of paleodemographic data led to researches in paleopathology (e.g., Bannerjee 1941; Lovell & Kennedy 1989). A major vehicle for resolution of a number of significant demographic questions of south Asian physical anthropology has been dental anthropology, an area of inquiry advanced by J.R. Lukacs (e.g., 1976, 1989) and R. Reddy (1986). It sheds light on problems of paleodiet, pathology, and craniofacial stress and employs discrete dental traits in the determination of biological affinities between both early and modern populations; it has also included the dental evolution of contemporary peoples of the subcontinent. Radiographic analysis, so critical to sound dental description, is becoming more widely used in examination of bones, particularly with respect to paleopathology and indicators of interrupted ontological development. Various methods of multivariate analysis have been introduced into the studies of the prehistoric skeletal record (e.g., Datta 1972; Bartel 1979; Kennedy & Levisky 1985; Kennedy et al. 1984) to supplement or replace the former methods of Coefficient of Racial Likeness (Lee & Pearson 1901), Students' T-Test, and Mahalanobis' D^2.

As of the 1990s, human skeletal collections are located in government institutions of the Anthropological Survey of India (incorporating collections formerly housed in the museum of the Asiatic Society, the Geological Survey of India, and the Zoological Survey of India), the Archaeological Survey of Pakistan at Karachi and the Harappa Museum, the Ceylon National Museum centers at Colombo and Ratnapura, as well as the Archaeological Department of the Government of Sri Lanka in Colombo, and at various state government museums affiliated with the Archaeological Survey of India. Other collections are curated at universities: Delhi University, Lucknow University, University of Allahabad, Vikram University, and Deccan College. The Italian Archaeological Mission in Pakistan has collections at Saidu Sharif and Rome, and the French archeologists have collections at Karachi. Permanent and loan study collections are also located at the Natural History Museum in London, the Musée de l'Homme in Paris, the Berlin Museum, the University of Pennsylvania in Philadelphia, the Smithsonian Institution in Washington, D.C., and Cornell University in Ithaca, New York. Because India has been a major source of human skeletons for research purposes through 1990, collections of osteological specimens from historic or nonarcheological sources, such as tribal cemeteries, medical schools, biological supply houses, and nonhuman primate series are widely scattered in south Asia and abroad. Conservation of prehistoric skeletal series in South Asian collections remains an area for concerted scrutiny and improvement by curators.

The Modern Institutional Structure of Indian Anthropology

The role of the Indian Statistical Institute (ISI), which was established in 1931, has been very effective with regard to a vigorous program of applied statistics in relation to physical anthropology, demography, history, and biometry. It has successfully combined the activities of a learned society with a teaching institution, having physical anthropologists on the staff as well.

Anthropology was first introduced into the curriculum of an Indian university in 1918, as a subsidiary subject to ancient history at the University of Calcutta. In 1920, it became an independent subject for the master of arts and master of science degree—an event coinciding with the founding of the first Department of Anthropology in India. The curriculum and the department were organized along the lines of the University of London, with Ashutosh Mukherjee as the department head. The staff included people with local experience as well as those trained abroad. The curriculum was broad and representative of the subfields of anthropology. In 1950, the Universities of Lucknow and of Delhi followed suit, and by 1963 there were eleven university Departments of Anthropology in India. By the mid-1990s, every major province in the country had at least one, and some even had two. The directory of anthropologists in India (cf. Rakshit 1981) listed a total of 552 respondents to a questionnaire, of whom 51 percent called themselves physical anthropologists, with the greatest number identifying research interests in anthropometry, dermatoglyphics, growth and development, and serology and the fewest responses in paleoanthropology, primate studies, and skeletal biology. The distribution reflects the availability of government-sponsored research funding in applied aspects of anthropology over studies of prehistoric populations. Collaborative ventures such as the Yale-Punjab Universities research team in the late 1960s made a number of significant discoveries. The government's emphasis on applied aspects of the science, coupled with financial resources, curtailed research in human paleontology, although a number of foreign investigators have carried on their work using their own resources.

Although anthropology programs exist at Dacca University in Bangladesh, at Quaid-I-Azam University in Islamabad, and at Karachi University in Pakistan, they lack a strong curriculum in physical anthropology. In Sri Lanka, the physical-anthropology program is closely associated with Medical and Biology Departments at Peradeniya and Colombo Universities.

Where physical anthropology is offered in the university curriculum in south Asia, concern over governmental sanctions has threatened the development of highly specialized and individual research, and there is even discussion of redefining physical anthropology in view of specific and immediate social needs of the citizens. The bottom line is the paucity of funds.

Physical anthropology has retained ties with government and university museums—examples are the Asiatic Society and the Indian Museum (founded in 1875), the Madras Government Museum (1868), the Victoria Museum at Karachi (1851), the Pathology Museum of Grant Medical College, Bombay (1854), and the Museum of the Bombay Natural History Society (1883), along with the museums in major cities on the subcontinent. The Colombo Museum (1877) holds the majority of the Sri Lankan finds. The number of museums was increased during the second half of the twentieth century to well over 170.

A number of scientific societies, some with their own organs of publication, represent physical anthropology. The first Indian publication of anthropological research was *Man in India,* established in 1921 by Sarat Chandra Roy (1871–1942). This was followed by the *Eastern Anthropologist* (1947), the *An-*

thropologist (1956), the *Journal of Human Evolution* (1988), and the *Indian Journal of Physical Anthropology and Human Genetics* (1970). Occasional articles in physical anthropology also appear in archeological journals, such as the *Bulletin* of the Deccan College Research Institute (1939), *Man and Environment* (1977), *Puratattva* (1967), and *Ancient India* (1946). In Pakistan, the *Archaeology of Pakistan* (1964) and *Pakistan Archaeology* (1964) periodically publish articles in physical anthropology. Physical anthropology papers in Sri Lanka have appeared in *Spolia Zeylanica* (1903) and *Ancient Ceylon* (1971).

Various summer schools, workshops, and annual society meetings include physical anthropology sessions from time to time. The Indian Science Congress, founded in 1914, has an Anthropology Section in which physical anthropology has its own niche. South Asian physical anthropologists are prominent members of various international congresses, such as the ICAES (International Congress of Anthropological and Ethnological Sciences), the UISPP (International Union of Prehistoric and Protohistoric Sciences), and the IDA (International Dermatoglyphic Association), and frequent contributors to foreign scientific journals in physical anthropology and human biology.

Kenneth A.R. Kennedy
Ripu D. Singh

See also Asian Monkeys; Asian Paleoanthropology; Biswas, Profulla Chandra; Cautley, (Sir) Proby Thomas; Das, Sudhir Ranjan; Demography; Dermatoglyphics; Falconer, Hugh; Galton, (Sir) Francis; Guha, Biraja Sankar; India, Anthropological Survey of; Karve, Irawati; McCown, Theodore D.; Majumdar, Dhirendra Nath; Molecular Anthropology; Monaco and Geneva Agreements; Paleoprimatology Theory; Primate Field Studies; Rakshit, Hirendra Kishor; *Ramapithecus*; Siwaliks; Washburn, Sherwood L; Zuckerman, (Lord) Solly

Bibliography
C.U. Ariëns Kappers: *An introduction to the anthropology of the Near East in ancient and recent times.* Amsterdam: Noord-Hollandsche Uitgevermaatschappijen, 1934; S. Babington: Description of the Pandoo Coolies in Malabar. *Transactions of the Literary Society of Bombay* 3:224–230, 1823; D.N. Bannerjee: Studies in paleopathology. *Journal of the Indian Medical Association* 10:263–267, 1941; B. Bartel: A discrimi-

nant analysis of Harappan civilization human populations. *Journal of Archaeological Science* 6:49–61, 1979; P.C. Basu: The anthropometry of the Bhuiyas of Mayurbhanji. *Journal of the Asiatic Society of Bengal* (n.s.) 25:157–163, 1925; M. Cappieri: *The Mediterranean race in Asia before the Iron Age*. Miami: Field Research Projects, 1969; J.M. Datta: Demography of prehistoric man. *Man in India* 39:257–270, 1959.

J.M. Datta: Demographic notes on Harappa skeletons. *Memoirs of the Anthropological Survey of India* 9:6–12, 1962; P.C. Datta: The Bronze Age Harappans: A reexamination of the skulls in the context of the population concept. *American Journal of Physical Anthropology* 36:391–396, 1972; R.B. Dixon: *The racial history of man*. New York: Scribner's, 1923; H. Falconer & P.T. Cautley: *Sivatherium giganteum*: A new fossil ruminant genus from the valley of the Markanda in the Siwalik branch of the sub-Himalayan Mountains. *Asiatic Researches* 19:1–24, 1836; B.S. Guha: The racial affinities of the people of India. In: *Census of India 1931*. Part 1, 3a. Simla: Government of India, 1935.

P. Gupta & A. Basu: *Human skeletal remains from Harappa*. Calcutta: Anthropological Survey of India, 1962; W. Jones: The third anniversary discourse. *Asiatic Researches* 1:415–4341, 1788; K.A.R. Kennedy & S.U. Deraniyagala: Fossil remains of 28,000-year-old hominids from Sri Lanka. *Current Anthropology* 30:394–399, 1989; K.A.R. Kennedy & J. Levisky: The element of racial biology in Indian megalithism: A multivariate analysis approach. In: V.N. Misra & P. Bellwood (eds) *Recent advances in Indo-Pacific prehistory*. New Delhi: Oxford University Press, 1985, pp. 455–464; K.A.R. Kennedy et al.: Principal-components analysis of prehistoric south Asia crania. *American Journal of Physical Anthropology* 64:105–118, 1984; K.A.R. Kennedy et al.: Upper Pleistocene fossil hominids from Sri Lanka. *American Journal of Physical Anthropology* 72:441–461, 1987.

K.A.R. Kennedy et al.: Is the Narmada hominid an Indian *Homo erectus*? *American Journal of Physical Anthropology* 86:475–496, 1991; R.L. Kirk: Serum protein and enzyme groups in physical anthropology with special reference to Indian populations. In: A.H. Ghosh, S.K. Biswas, & R. Ghosh (eds) *Physical anthropology and its extending horizons*. Calcutta: Orient Longmans, 1973;

A. Lee & K. Pearson: A first study of the correlations of the human skull. *Philosophical Transactions of the Royal Society of London* 196:225–264, 1901; G.E. Lewis: Preliminary notice of new man-like apes from India. *American Journal of Science* 27:161–179, 1934; N.C. Lovell & K.A.R. Kennedy: Society and disease in prehistoric south Asia. In: J.M. Kenoyer (ed) *Old problems and new perspectives in the archaeology of south Asia*. Wisconsin Archaeological Reports. No. 2. Madison: University of Wisconsin, 1989, pp. 89–92.

J.R. Lukacs: Dental anthropology and the biological affinities of an Iron Age population from Pomparippu, Sri Lanka. In: K.A.R. Kennedy & G.L. Possehl (eds) *Ecological backgrounds of south Asia prehistory*. South Asia Occasional Papers and Theses, South Asia Program, Cornell University. No. 4. Ithaca, New York: Cornell University, 1976, 197–215; J.R. Lukacs: Dental paleopathology: Methods of reconstructing health status and dietary patterns in prehistory. In: M.Y. Isçan & K.A.R. Kennedy (eds) *Reconstructing life from the skeleton*. New York: Liss, 1989, pp. 261–286; R. Lydekker: A sketch of the history of the fossil vertebrata of India. *Journal of the Asiatic Society of Bengal* 49:8–40, 1880.

E.W.E. Macfarlane: Eastern Himalayan blood groups. *Man* 37:127–129, 1937; E.W.E. Macfarlane: Rate of growth of non-vegetarian and vegetarian children of Trivandrum, Travancore. *Current Science* 6:148–151, 1938; E.W.E. Macfarlane: Blood groups among Balahis (weavers), Bhils, Korkus, and Mundas, with a note on Pardhis and Aboriginal blood types. *Journal of the Asiatic Society of Bengal* 7(n.s.):15–24, 1941; E.J.H. Mackay: *Further excavations at Mohenjodaro*. New Delhi: Manager of Government Printing, 1938; D.N. Majumdar: Blood groups of criminal tribes. *Science and Culture* 7:334–337, 1941–1942; D.N. Majumdar: *Race elements in Gujarat*. Bombay: Gujarat Research Society, 1945.

R.H. Malone & M.N. Lahiri: The distribution of the blood groups in certain races and castes of India. *Indian Journal of Medical Research* 16:963–972, 1929; J. Marshall: *Mohenjodaro and the Indus civilization*. London: Probsthain, 1931; S.R. Pandit: Blood group distribution in the Todas. *Indian Journal of Medical Research* 21:613–615, 1934; J. Princep: Note on the fossil bones discovered near Jabalpur. *Journal of the Asiatic Society of Bengal* 2:583–588, 1833; A. Rea: Adichanallur excavations. *Annual Report of the Archaeological Survey of Madras and Coorg for the Year 1902–1903.* Madras: Archaeological Survey, 1902–1903a, pp. 9–14; A. Rea: Prehistoric antiquities in the Tinnevelly. *Annual Report of the Archaeological Survey of India* 1 (2):111–140; 1902–1903b; R.R. Reddy: *Dimensions of anthropology: Dentition, pathology, and crown morphology.* 2 vols. New Delhi: B.R. Publishing Corp., 1986; H.H. Risley: Measurement of Cingalese, Moormen, and Tamali taken in Ceylon in November 1892. *Journal of the Asiatic Society of Bengal* 62:33–45, 1893.

H.H. Risley: *Census of India, 1901.* Ethnographic appendices. Calcutta & Simla: Government of India, 1903; H.H. Risley: *The people of India.* Calcutta: Thacker, Spink, 1908; H.H. Risley: *Manual of anthropometry.* Calcutta: Government Press, 1909; D.R. Sahni: *Harappa.* Annual Report, 1923–1924. Calcutta: Archaeological Survey of India, 1925; S.S. Sarkar: Blood group investigations in India with special reference to Santal Parganas. *Transactions of the Bose Research Institute* 12:89–101, 1937; S.S. Sarkar: *Ancient races of Baluchistan, Punjab, and Sind.* Calcutta: Bookland, 1964; R.B.S. Sewell & B.S. Guha: Human remains. In: J. Marshall (ed) *Mohenjodaro and the Indus civilization, being an official account of archaeological excavations carried out by the Government of India between the years 1922 and 1927.* Vol. 2. London: Probsthain, 1931, pp. 599–648.

E.L. Simons & S.R.K. Chopra: *Gigantopithecus* (Pongidae, Hominoidea): A new species from north India. *Postilla* 138:1–8, 1969; R.D. Singh: Physical anthropology in India. I. The roots of the discipline. *PAN: Physical Anthropology News* 4(2):1–4, 1985; R.D. Singh: Physical anthropology in India. II. A modern perspective. *PAN: Physical Anthropology News* 5(1):16–19, 1986; A. Sonakia: The skullcap of early man and associated mammalian fauna from Narmada Valley alluvium, Hoshangabad area, Madhya Pradesh (India). *Records of the Geological Survey of India* 113:159–172, 1984.

C.G. Spilsbury: Account of the fossil bones discovered in the bed of the Omar Nadi near Narsinghpur at Bedarwara in the valley of Nerbudda. *Journal of the Asiatic Society of Bengal* 2:388–395, 1833; B.

Subbarao: *The personality of India: Pre- and proto-historic foundations of India and Pakistan.* 2d ed. Baroda: Sadhana, 1959; P.M. Taylor: Description of cairns, cromlechs, kistvaens, and other Celtic, Druidical, or Scythian monuments in the Dekhan. *Transactions of the Royal Irish Academy* 24:329–362, 1873; E. Thurston: *Castes and tribes of northern India.* Madras: Government Press, 1906; R.E.M. Wheeler: Brahmagiri and Chandravalli, 1947; Megalithic and other cultures in the Chitaldrug District, Mysore State. *Ancient India* 4:180–310, 1947; S. Zuckerman: The Adichanallur skulls. *Bulletin of the Madras Government Museum* 2:1–24, 1930.

Spain

Although it is possible to trace the history of anthropological inquiry in Spain back to Isidore of Seville (ca. 560–636), whose *Etymologiae* contains numerous references to anthropological issues (cf. Lindsay 1911), a more definite beginning can be found in the sixteenth century, when a number of Spanish scholars made an influential contribution to the ethnography and theory related to the natural history of the native populations of the New World. Among those involved in this brief fluorescence were José de Acosta (1539–1600), Fernández de Oviedo (1478–1557), Pedro de Cieza de León (1518–1560), Bartolomé de La Casas (1474–1566), and Bernardino de Sahagún (1499–1590), but, contrary to expectations, this activity was short lived. Because of the prevailing sociopolitical circumstances in Spain through the seventeenth, eighteenth, and early nineteenth centuries, there was a general eclipse of anthropological scholarship. There were some exceptions—for example, in the early eighteenth century with Benito Gerónimo Feijoo y Montenegro (1676–1764), who, in his *Teatro crítico universal* (1736), grappled with the then controversial issue of the cause of differences in human skin color.

For the purpose of description, the subsequent history of physical anthropology in Spain is divided into three arbitrary periods of development: (1) The formative period, which embraces developments during the second and third quarter of the nineteenth century; (2) the early modern period, which spans the period from the last quarter of the nineteenth century to the middle of the twentieth century; and (3) the modern period, which documents developments during the remainder of the twentieth century.

The Formative Period: 1825–1874

In 1833, a book by Vicente Adam entitled *Lecciones de Antropología ético-político-religiosa; es decir, sobre el Hombre considerado como un ser social, religioso, y moral* (Lessons about Ethical-Political-Religious Anthropology; Concerning Man Considered as a Social, Religious, and Moral Being) was published; it represents the first tentative steps toward the modern concept of anthropological inquiry in Spain. At the same time, many Spanish naturalists, physicians, and antiquarians were increasingly adopting the new ideas coming from the other side of the Pyrenees, which formed the basis for developments in the second half of the nineteenth century.

A prominent figure of this early formative period was the anatomist Pedro González de Velasco (1815–1882), who was elected director of the Anatomy Museum of the Universidad Central, Madrid in 1857. This nomination allowed him to visit Paris in order to learn more about that city's museums, and there he met Paul Broca (1824–1880), who aroused in him a deep and lasting interest in anthropology. On his return to Spain, Velasco founded in 1864 (though it was not officially recognized until the following year) the Sociedad Antropológica Española (SAE) for the purpose of studying ". . . the natural history of man and its related sciences" modeling it along the lines of the Société d'Anthropologie de Paris, which Broca had founded in 1859.

The SAE counted among its early membership an array of Spanish intellectuals, many of whom were physicians and naturalists, such as Francisco A. Delgado Jugo (1830–1875), R. Tormes Muñoz, Juan Vilanova y Piera (1821–1893), and Manuel Sales y Ferré (1843–1910). The formation of the SAE contributed significantly to the development of research in physical anthropology, the products of which were published in several newly established journals, including *El Anfiteatro Anatómico Español* (founded in 1873), *Revista de Antropología* (1874), *Museo Antropológico* (1881), and *La Antropología Moderna* (1883). The research contained in the pages of these journals includes, among other things ethnographic descriptions of different human populations, the results of archeological excavations, and anthropometric studies. The SAE also became a forum for the discussion of human evolution and thus played an important role in the initial reception of Darwinian theory in Spain (cf. Glick 1972). Another important feature of the early activities of the SAE were its efforts to preserve anthropological remains, especially historic and modern crania (an emphasis characteristic of the period). This developing collection, along with other ethnographic material, became the nucleus of the Museo Antropológico de Madrid (MAM), founded (and financed) by González de Velasco in 1875, a date that interestingly enough coincided with the discovery of the Altamira Cave. Following the death of González de Velasco in 1882, the MAM was closed for several years before being reopened as the Museo Etnológico Nacional.

In addition to the SAE, the International Congress of Anthropology and Prehistoric Archaeology, which held its first meeting at Neuchâtel, Switzerland, in 1866, provided another important early stimulus to the development of physical anthropology in Spain.

Some other events characterizing this early period include the establishment of the Museo Arqueológico Nacional in 1867, followed by the foundation of two important societies in 1871: the Sociedad Española de Historia Natural (SEHN) and the Sociedad Antropológica de Sevilla. A year later, the SEHN began publishing its *Anales*, which became another important outlet for physical anthropologists.

Early Modern Period: 1875–1944

A central figure in the early modern period is Manuel Antón (1849–1929), who received his scientific training in the natural sciences at the Universidad Central, Madrid. On completing his studies in 1878, he joined the Museo de Historia Natural (MNH) in Madrid. Apparently, his interest in anthropology surfaced during a field trip to Morocco and from reading the works of prominent French anthropologists. In 1883, when a Section of Anthropology was created at the MNH, Antón was chosen to become its first director. A year later, in Paris, he participated in a course given by the French anthropologists Armand de Quatrefages (1810–1892) and René Verneau (1852–1938) at the Muséum National d'Histoire Naturelle. Returning to Spain, he published his now classic study "La Raza de Cro-Magnon en España" (1884) and several other notable works, including his volume on the *Razas y naciones de Europa* (1895). He was also responsible for transferring the private library of González de Velasco to the Section of Anthropology of the MNH.

In 1885, a *càtedra libre* professorship in anthropology was established at the MNH, with Antón as the first recipient. This professorship enabled him to formally train a new generation of anthropologists that included Luis de Hoyos Sáinz (1868–1951), Telesforo de Aranzadi (1860–1945), and Francisco de Las Barras de Aragón (1868–1955). Soon thereafter, in 1892, Antón was installed in the first Chair of Anthropology in a Spanish university, which had been created in the Faculty of Sciences of the Universidad Central.

Another important figure in the early modern period was Federico Olóriz y Aguilera (1855–1912), who had been trained in medicine. As a professor of anatomy at the Universidad Central, Olóriz was able to indulge his interest in anthropology and, more particularly, morphology. He assembled an important collection of human crania from different regions of Spain, as well as skeletons from the San Carlos Hospital, Madrid. He also carried out extensive anthropological research on both cadavers and living populations. Among his many studies are his now classic "Distribución geográfica del índice cefálico en España" (1894) and *La talla humana en España* (1896), both written from a biogeographical viewpoint. He later developed an interest in forensic anthropology and went on to become pioneer in that field in Spain. Olóriz also trained a number of students who went on to have distinguished careers, including Montero, Bernaldo de Quirós, Necochea.

Luis de Hoyos Sáinz, one of Antón's most outstanding students, in the late 1890s produced, in collaboration with Aranzadi, another student of Antón's, an influential text *Lecciones de Antropología* (1899–1900). Hoyos Sáinz's research interests were broad, embracing many aspects of physical anthropology, archeology, ethnology, and folklore. In physical anthropology, he studied living populations, as well as historic and prehistoric samples. He also pioneered the use of serology in Spanish anthropology (Hoyos Sáinz 1947).

Telesforo de Aranzadi was initially trained in pharmacy. On completing those studies, he worked under Antón's direction at the MNH. In addition to his collaborative work with Hoyos Sáinz (*vide ante*), Aranzadi published numerous papers and books. One of the most important was *El pueblo Euskalduna* (1889), the first anthropometric study, in the anthropological sense, published in Spanish. In 1920, he was installed as professor of anthropology at the Universidad de Barcelona, where he carried out important research and trained many anthropologists—in particular, Santiago Alcobé, who, in turn, was responsible for training the paleoanthropologist Miguel Fusté (d. 1966), and José Pons.

Modern Period: 1945–1995

During the first half of the twentieth century, two Chairs of Anthropology were established, in the Faculties of Sciences at Madrid and Barcelona and an informal group of physicians, linked to university Departments of Anatomy, Legal Medicine, and Pediatrics, banded together to exchange ideas. The primary forum for the exchange of ideas was still the SEA, though; in its published proceedings, which ceased publication in 1951, can be found the results of most of the research conducted during much of the early modern period. In 1945, however, a new journal was founded titled *Trabajos del Instituto Bernardino de Sahagún sobre Antropología y Etnología* (Studies of the Bernardino de Sahagún Institute of Anthropology and Ethnology), followed in 1949 by the first publication of the *Revista de Antropología y Etnología*. Both journals were financed by the Consejo Superior de Investigaciones Científicas (Superior Council of Scientific Research) and attached to the Bernardino de Sahagún Institute. However, in 1958 the *Revista* ceased publication. The former journal, which was renamed *Trabajos de Antropología* in 1970, experienced a similar fate in 1989. Although both are defunct, during their time they provided an important outlet for biological anthropologists in Spain, and they essentially document the development of the discipline through much of the second half of the twentieth century. Among the many researchers represented in the pages of these two journals, there is one worthy of special mention, José Pons (1918–), who played an important role in the development of the disicipline through his earlier activities at the Universidad de Oviedo and the Universidad Central, Madrid, and subsequently at the Universidad de Barcelona. Throughout his professional career, Pons developed important research in a variety of areas of anthropology. But especially remarkable is the fact that he was able to organize laboratories of physical anthropology (at Oviedo, Madrid, and Barcelona) and train many students who hold professorships of anthropology in various Spanish universities.

During the First Spanish Congress of Anthropology, held in Barcelona in 1976, the decision was made to found a Section of Biological Anthropology within the Sociedad Española de Historia Natural. José Pons was elected president; María Dolores Garralda, general secretary. Two years later, M.D. Garralda and R.M. Grande organized at the Universidad Complutense de Madrid (formerly the Universidad Central, Madrid) the first Simposio de Antropología Biológica de España (SABE), which was held 28–31 March 1978. The SABE was an important watershed in the history of physical anthropology in Spain because it brought together, for the first time and in an independent way, all of the people interested in the discipline. Furthermore, the enthusiastic participaton of several foreign colleagues provided an additional impulse. The *Proceedings* of the Primer Simposio, edited by M.D. Garralda and R.M. Grande, was published in 1979.

At the formal closing of the SABE in 1978, the Sociedad Española de Antropología Biológica (SEAB) was created. The officers of this new society included J. Pons, president; M.D. Garralda, general secretary; and R.M. Grande, treasurer. Since that time, the SEAB has continued to flourish, as indicated by its biannual congresses (the eighth one was held in September 1993), and the publication of its *Boletín de la Sociedad Española de Antropología Biológica*, as of the mid-1990s the only journal in Spain devoted exclusively to biological anthropology.

As of 1994, biological anthropology was taught in ten Spanish universities in Faculties of Sciences/Biology, a number of which, especially the Universidad Complutense de Madrid and the Universidad de Barcelona, support large graduate and postgraduate programs. Academic and research interests cover the entire spectrum of the discipline, ranging from different aspects of human genetics, to biodemography, human evolution, historical anthropology, growth and development, and kinanthropometry. Many of the ten universities sponsor both multidisciplinary and international teams of research.

María D. Garralda

See also Acosta, José de; Aranzadi, Telesforo de; Broca, Paul (Pierre); Cro-Magnon; Hoyos Sáinz, Luis de; Quatrefages (de Breau), Jean Louis Armand de; Skin Color; Verneau, René

Bibliography

S. Alcobé: Telesforo de Aranzadi. *Trabajos del Instituto Bernardino de Sahagún sobre Antropología y Etnología* 7:7–18, 1949; M. Antón: La raza de Cro-Magnon en España. *Annales de Sociedad Española de Historia Natural* 13: 1884. M. Antón: *Razas y naciones de Europa*. Madrid, 1895; T. de Aranzadi: *El pueblo euskalduna: Estudio de antropología*. San Sebastian: Imp. de la Provincia, 1889; B.J. Feijoo y Montenegro: Color etiopico. In: *Teatro crítico universal*. Vol. 3. Madrid: Mojados, 1736; M.D. Garralda & R.M. Grande: *I Simposio de Antropología Biológica de España*. Madrid: Sociedad Española de Antropología Biológica, 1979; T.F. Glick: Spain. In: T.F. Glick (ed) *The comparative reception of Darwinism*. Austin: University of Texas Press, 1972, pp. 307–345.

L. de Hoyos Sáinz: *Distribución geográfica de los grupos sanguíneos en España: Ensayo de seroantropología*. Madrid: Consejo Superior de Investigaciones Científicos, Instituto Juan Sebastián Elcano, 1947; L. de Hoyos Sáinz & T. de Aranzadi: Un avance á la Antropología de España. *Anales de la Sociedad Española de Historia Natural* 21:31–101, 1892; L. de Hoyos Sáinz & T. de Aranzadi: *Lecciones de antropología*. 2 vols. Madrid: Bravo, 1899–1900; T.W. Lindsay (ed): *Isidori Hispanlensis episcopi Etymologiarum*. 2 vols. London: Oxford University Press, 1911; F. Olóriz y Aguilera: Distribución geográfica del índice cefálico en España. *Boletín de la Sociedad geográfica* 36:389–422, 1894; F. Olóriz y Aguilera: *Distribución geográfica del indice cefalico en España deducida del examen de 8,368 varones adultos*. Madrid: "Memorial de ingenieros," 1894; F. Olóriz y Aguilera: *La talla humana en España*. Madrid, 1896; M.A. Puig-Samper & A. Galera: *La Antropología española del siglo XIX*. Madrid: CSIC, 1983.

Spuhler, J(ames) N(orman) (1917–1992)

Born in Tucumcari, New Mexico, Spuhler began his academic training at the University of New Mexico (UNM), where he received his B.A. in 1940. From there he went on to study anthropology at Harvard University, where he was a recipient of a Cutter Scholarship. At Harvard, he earned his M.A. in 1942 and his Ph.D. in 1946. While at Harvard, he came under the influence of Earnest A. Hooton (1887–1954), who was his dissertation adviser; and Clyde Kluckhohn (1905–1960), with whom he collaborated on the Rimrock Project, a study of the Ramah Navajo.

Like many of his generation, Spuhler had his education interrupted by military service during World War II. At the urging of Serge Elisseff, who was professor of Far Eastern languages at Harvard, he enlisted in the United States Navy and was sent to Boulder, Colorado, to learn Japanese. After completion of an intensive language course, he saw service at Kunming and Chungking in China as a junior naval officer involved in translating Japanese documents. This involvement aroused an interest in the peoples of the Far East that continued throughout his professional career, and upon his retirement from the University of New Mexico in 1984, at the request of the People's Republic of China, he returned on several occasions to teach anthropology and human genetics.

His academic career began at Ohio State Univeristy (OSU), where he accepted a position as an instructor in the Department of Anthropology and Sociology in 1946. He remained at OSU until 1950, when he moved to the University of Michigan (UM) to join the Department of Anthropology and the Institute of Human Biology. At the latter institute, he was reponsible for possibly the first comprehensive effort to document and measure the extent of assortive mating in a small urban American community. When, in 1956, the institute was disbanded, he became a member of the university's newly established Department of Human Genetics, while continuing his appointment in Anthropology. At the UM, he rose rapidly through the academic ranks and served as chairman of the Anthropology Department in the period 1959–1967. In 1967, he returned to the UNM as the first Leslie Spier Professor of Anthropology. He remained there until his retirement.

Spuhler's contributions to physical anthropology were many, but undoubtedly the most important was the furtherance of the relationship between human genetics and physical anthropology long before this became fashionable. Early in his career, he recognized that if physical anthropology was to remain a dynamic discipline it needed to broaden its outlook, its techniques, and its approaches to problem solving, and he saw human genetics as a natural ally. His own interest in genetics had taken form at Harvard, which had a strong tradition in mammalian genetics dating back to William E. Castle (1867–1954) and Laurence H. Snyder (1901–). Spuhler's 1946 doctoral dissertation, one of the first in human genetics submitted to any Department of Anthropology in the United States, was entitled *Some Procedures in Human Genetics: A Methodological Study*. It presaged a lifetime's commitment to human genetics and physical anthropology, and to the encouragement of the merging of these two perspectives that has proved profitable to both areas of endeavor. After his retirement, as an affiliate of the Ge-

netics Group at the Los Alamos National Laboratory, he continued to further this association, now focusing on the Human Genome Project and the molecular developments of interest to his two chosen fields of research.

His writings, particularly his review articles, are models of clarity and exhibit an impressive depth of scholarship. Indeed, his keynote address, titled "Genes, Molecules, Organisms, and Behavior," at a NATO (North Atlantic Treaty Organization) sponsored meeting on behavioral genetics won the 1990 National Academy of Sciences Award for Scientific Reviewing. Recognition of his scientific stature came through frequent invitations to be a visiting professor at various universities or a contributor to compendia. He also held office in the American Association of Physical Anthropologists, which he served as a member of the Executive Committee in 1954 and 1955 and as president from 1975 to 1977; and the American Anthropological Association, serving as a member its Executive Board from 1958 to 1960. He was twice, in 1955–1956 and 1971–1972, a Fellow of the Center for Advanced Study of the Behavioral Sciences in Palo Alto, California, and was also a Research Fellow at Oxford University. In addition, he served on numerous editorial boards, including a stint as editor of the *Southwestern Journal of Anthropology*.

Spuhler died at Sante Fe, New Mexico, on 2 September 1992.

William J. Schull

See also Hooton, E(arnest) A(lbert); United States of America

Bibliography
SELECTED WORKS
Some problems in physical anthropology of the American Southwest. *American Anthropologist* 56:604–625, 1954; The scope of natural selection in man. In: W.J. Schull (ed) *Genetic selection in man*. Ann Arbor: University of Michigan, 1963, pp. 1–11; The maximum opportunity for natural selection in some human populations. In: E. Zubrow (ed) *Demographic anthropology*. Albuquerque: University of New Mexico Press, 1977, pp. 185–226; Genetic distances, trees, and maps of North American Indians. In: W.S. Laughlin & A.B. Harper (eds) *The first Americans: Origins, affinities, and adaptations.* New York: Fischer, 1979, pp. 135–183.

Evolution of mitochondrial DNA in humans and other organisms. (Raymond

Pearl Memorial Lecture 1988). *American Journal of Human Biology* 1:509–528, 1988a; Genes, molecules, organisms, and behavior: Evolution of mitochondrial DNA in monkeys, apes, and humans. *Yearbook of Physical Anthropology* 31:15–48, 1988b; Population genetics and evolution in the genus *Homo* in the last two million years. In: C.F. Sing & L.C. Hanis (eds) *Genetics of cellular, individual, family, and population variability.* New York: Oxford University Press, 1993, pp. 262–297.

SECONDARY SOURCES

W.J. Schull: In Memoriam: James Norman Spuhler (1917–1992). *American Journal of Physical Anthropology* 92:113–116, 1993.

Spy

The Spy cavern (now destroyed), was situated beneath a limestone promontory (known as the Betch-aux-Rotches), overlooking the Orneau Valley in the province of Namur, Belgium. In the mid-1880s, this site yielded critical skeletal and archeological evidence that served to secure an unequivocal association of European Neandertals with extinct Pleistocene mammalian fauna and "primitive" stone tools. These associations demonstrated a considerable antiquity for Neandertals and helped establish them as a distinct group of Pleistocene hominids.

Although earlier investigations of the cavern had yielded archeological artifacts (cf. Rucquoy 1886), it was not until the 1880s that the full potential of the site was realized when Marcel De Puydt (1855–1940), a lawyer and amateur archeologist, and Maximin Lohest (1857–1926), a geologist and paleontologist from the University of Liège, began their excavations. Their work, which spanned two seasons (1885–1886), is distinguished by its attention to precise stratigraphic determination.

Finding that much of the cave's interior had been disturbed by earlier investigators, De Puydt and Lohest decided to concentrate their efforts on a flat terrace at the front of the cave, which appeared to have been untouched. During the first season, commenced in the summer of 1885, a trench was dug into this terrace, to an approximate depth of 1.5 m. At this depth, a fossiliferous layer was found, approximately 40 cm thick, from which were extracted numerous artifacts and fossil remains of extinct mammals. The following year, the trench was extended in length (by 11

m) and depth (ca. 4 m). It was during this operation that De Puydt and Lohest discovered the remains of two largely complete skeletons 10–12 m from the present entrance of the cave, along with associated stone tools and fossil animal bones.

The skeletal remains were subsequently described by Julien Fraipont (1857–1910), a professor of paleontology at the University of Liège. From his study of the two skeletons, designated Spy 1 and 2, Fraipont believed that 1 was an adult female, while 2 was a male. Some workers, such as Paul Topinard (1830–1911), however, believed that 1 was a male. Of greater importance, though, was the result of Fraipoint's comparative study. In particular, he was greatly impressed by the conformation of the Spy crania, which were markedly dolichocephalic with strong, protruding browridges, to the anatomical pattern already known from several other European fossil hominid forms, including the Feldhofer specimen found in the Neander Valley in Germany in 1856 and the Gibraltar specimen described in the early 1860s. From this, Fraipont conjectured that all of these specimens were members of the same group. Furthermore, the similarity between the Spy and the Feldhofer specimens was not confined to cranial features. There were marked similarities in their postcranial skeletons, which served to further dinstinguish this group of hominids from both modern and Neolithic skeletons. In addition to this new and important insight, the carefully controlled excavations of De Puydt and Lohest also established Neandertals as the artificer of the Mousterian stone-tool industry.

Primary details of the excavations at Spy can be found in De Puydt and Lohest (1887) and Fraipont and Lohest (1887), which also embody the results of Fraipont's study and evaluation of the remains. Shortly after these works appeared, Topinard drew Fraipont's attention to an article written by the French anthropologist René Collignon (1856–1932) in the *Revue d'Anthropologie* (1880), in which the particular morphology of the Feldhofer (Neandertal) tibial head was discussed. Specifically, Collignon had noted that while the head of the tibia in modern humans was almost horizontal, in the Feldhofer specimen it was bent backward—thereby preventing the leg from being fully straightened. Following up on this observation, Fraipont (1888) found that the head of the Spy tibia was also retroverted. Extending this study to anthropoid apes, he discovered that they, too, manifested this character, except that they had even higher angles of retroversion.

Tibial retroversion became an important feature for illustrating the semierect posture of Neandertals by the French paleoanthropologist Marcellin Boule (1861–1942) (1921) and others, despite the fact that the Parisian physical anthropologist Léonce-Pierre Manouvrier (1850–1927) had previously demonstrated that this feature in the Spy tibiae related to their activity patterns in life and did not reflect a lack of ability to stand upright (Manouvrier 1893).

During World War I, Lohest hid the Spy fossils in his home. While this may have saved them from being confiscated by the invading Germans, it resulted in the mixing of the two specimens. It is now not possible to determine which postcranial bones go with which skull, and some small pieces are missing.

In the 1920s, the Spy skeletons were studied by the Smithsonian physical anthropologist Aleš Hrdlička (1869–1943), who emphasized the variation exhibited by the Spy specimens and Neandertals in general. Hrdlička (1930) argued that the Spy crania, especially Spy 2, were transitional between other Neandertal and early modern Europeans, like Předmostí. The Spy specimens consequently played a major role in Hrdlička's claim that Neandertals were the ancestors of modern humans.

Apart from Hrdlička's perspective, the Spy skeletons have always been at the heart of discussions of variation in Neandertals. For example, the Croatian paleoanthropologist Dragutin Gorjanović-Kramberger (1856–1936) (1906) recognized two varieties of Neandertals, the Krapina and the Spy varieties. More recently, the transitional nature of the Spy specimens has been both denied (Thoma 1975) and reaffirmed (Wolpoff 1980). For more recent considerations of the Spy remains, see Stringer et al. 1984; Trinkaus & Shipman 1993.

Fred H. Smith

See also Boule, Marcellin; Collignon, René; Cro-Magnon; Fraipont, (Jean-Joseph) Julien; Gibraltar; Gorjanović-Kramberger, Dragutin (Karl); Hrdlička, Aleš; Manouvrier, Léonce-Pierre; Neandertal (Feldhofer Grotte); Neandertals; Předmostí; Topinard, Paul

Bibliography
M. Boule: *Les hommes fossiles: Éléments de paléontologie humaine.* Paris: Masson et Cie, 1921; R. Collignon: Description des ossements fossiles humains trouvés à Bollvillier. *Revue d'Anthropologie* 1880; M. De Puydt & M. Lohest: L'homme contemporain du Mammoth à Spy, province de Namur (Belgique). *Annales de la Fédération archéologique et historique de Belgique* 2:205–240, 1887; J. Fraipont: Le tibia dans la race de Néanderthal: Étude comparative de l'incurvation de la tête du tibia, dans ses rapports avec la station verticale chez l'homme et les anthropoides. *Revue d'Anthropologie* 3 (3d ser.):145–158, 1888.

J. Fraipoint & M. Lohest: La race humaine de Néanderthal ou de Canstadt en Belgique: Recherches ethnographiques sur les ossements humains découverts dans les dépôts quaternaires d'une grotte à Spy et détermination de leur âge géologique. *Archives de Biologie* 7:587–757, 1887; D. Gorjanović-Kramberger: *Der Diluviale Mensch von Krapina in Kroatien: Ein Beitrag zür Paläoanthropologie.* Wiesbaden: Kriedals, 1906; A. Hrdlička: *The skeletal remains of early man.* Smithsonian Miscellaneous Collections. Vol. 83. Washington, D.C.: Smithsonian Institution Press, 1930; L. Manouvrier: Étude sur le rétroversion de la tête du tibia et l'attitude humaine à l'époque quaternaire. *Mémoires de la Société d'Anthropologie de Paris* 4 (4th ser.):219–264, 1893.

M. Rucquoy: Notes sur les fouilles faites en aout 1879 dans la caverne de la Bèche-aux-Roches, près de Spy. *Bulletin de la Société d'Anthropologie de Bruxelles* 5:318–328, 1886; C.B. Stringer et al.: The origin of anatomically modern humans in western Europe. In: F.H. Smith & F. Spencer (eds) *The origins of modern humans: A world survey of the fossil evidence.* New York: Liss, 1984, pp. 51–135; A. Thoma: Were the Spy fossils evolutionary intermediates between classic Neandertal and modern man? *Journal of Human Evolution* 4:387–410, 1975; E. Trinkaus & P. Shipman: *The Neandertals: Changing the image of mankind.* New York: Knopf, 1993; M.H. Wolpoff: *Paleoanthropology.* New York: Knopf, 1980.

Squier, Ephraim George (1821–1888)

Squier was born in Bethlehem, New York, in an era of American expansionism that encouraged adventure and ambition. True to that era, he sought fame and fortune in a variety of enterprises before becoming a journalist. In 1845, he moved to Chillicothe, Ohio, to edit the *Scioto Gazette*, a local newspaper (cf. Tax

1975). Chillicothe was in the vicinity of mysterious earthen mounds that for years had been the subject of a popular "mound-builder myth." According to the myth, the mounds had been built by a vanished race of people who had predated the American Indians and been vastly superior to them. Squier became fascinated by these mounds and, with the help of Edwin Hamilton Davis (1811–1888), a prominent local doctor, sought to solve their mystery by means of archeology. Their coauthored book, *Ancient Monuments of the Mississippi Valley* (1848), was heralded as a landmark work.

Ancient Monuments was published by the Smithsonian Institution as the first volume in its Contributions to Knowledge series. The book bore the stamp of the Smithsonian's first secretary, Joseph Henry, who did his best to purge it of speculation and make the high quality of its descriptions stand out. Henry deserves part of the credit for its critical and financial success.

In *Ancient Monuments*, Squier and Davis combined their own fieldwork with the fieldwork of several assistants to categorize Mississippi and Ohio Valley mounds into several functional types. They concluded (incorrectly) that the mounds had been constructed according to extraordinarily sophisticated principles of mathematics, and that a pattern of interspersed fortifications showed that the mound builders had moved south in the face of another advancing race—presumably Indians. Squier and Davis stressed that the mounds were extremely ancient and that the builders were not immigrants to North America, but indigenous.

Because *Ancient Monuments* was supposed to be objective, Squier and Davis did not address the mound-builder myth at great length, preferring to let readers judge the myth themselves. Astute readers, however, could infer easily that Squier and Davis supported the myth. Squier and Davis maintained that while American Indians did not build the mounds, Indians might be descended from the race that did. This possibility was confirmed by American School anthropologist Samuel George Morton (1799–1851), who identified a skull unearthed by Squier as intermediate between mound-builder and Indian types (Tax 1975:114). Evidence that American races were both ancient and indigenous brought Squier in line with the American School (cf. Stanton 1960).

Personal connections between Squier and the American School were not as strong as personal connections among members of the school itself. Anthropologists such as Morton, George R. Gliddon (1809–1857), and Josiah Clark Nott (1804–1873) supported Squier more enthusiastically than he supported them. Nevertheless, Squier was a polygenist in almost every sense of the word. He was especially pleased that archeology and anthropology refuted chronologies of human history derived from biblical text (Tax 1975:104).

Squier speculated that the North American mound builders were related to the builders of the temples and pyramids in Central and South America (Stansifer 1959). Henry had prevented this speculation from surfacing too much in Squier's book. After *Ancient Monuments* was published, Squier decided to explore this relationship further by doing archeological fieldwork in Central America. To facilitate his fieldwork, he arranged to be appointed Central American *chargé d'affaires*. Squier was able to complete only a small amount of fieldwork in Nicaragua before his appointment was terminated in 1850.

Although brief, Squier's diplomatic appointment in Central America marked a turning point in his life. While there, he became interested in ethnography, particularly the ethnography of Miskito Indians. He published prolifically on this subject for ten years, making it a second anthropological career. Although Squier's ethnography was highly praised, M.D. Olien (1985) has shown that it was inferior to his archeology, politicized and "racist."

Squier's accomplishments are distinguished enough for Thomas Tax (1975:99) to have suggested that he was the premier archeologist of his time. Squier became involved with, and gave support to, a number of professional societies, notably the American Ethnological Society. In 1873, however, personal trauma brought his career to an ignominious close. His wife divorced him and married another man. As a result, he lost his mental health and spent most of the rest of his life in institutions (Tax 1975:120). In that sad state, he was unable to follow the progress of scientific archeology, which he helped launch in America.

Squier died in Brooklyn, New York, on 17 April 1888.

Paul A. Erickson

See also American School of Anthropology; Morton, Samuel George; Nott, Josiah Clark; Polygenism

Bibliography

SELECTED WORKS

American ethnology; being a summary of some of the results which have followed the investigation of this subject. *American Review* 3:385–398, 1849a; Historical and mythological traditions of the Algonquins. *American Review* 3 (n.s.):273–293, 1849b; *Nicaragua: Its people, scenery, monuments, and the proposed interoceanic canal.* 2 vols. London: Longman, Brown, Green & Longman, 1852; Observations on the archaeology of Nicaragua. *Transactions of the American Ethnological Society* 3:85–158, 1853; *Peru: Incidents of travel and exploration in the land of the Incas.* New York: Harper, 1877; (with E.H. Davis) *Ancient monuments of the Mississippi Valley, comprising the results of extensive original surveys and explorations.* Smithsonian Contributions to Knowledge. No. 1. Washington, D.C.: Smithsonian Institution, 1848.

ARCHIVAL SOURCES

1. E.G. Squier Papers: Indiana Historical Society, 315 West Ohio Street, Indianapolis, Indiana 46202; 2. E.G. Squier Papers: Library of Congress, Manuscript Division, James Madison Memorial Building, First Street & Independence Avenue, S.E., Washington, D.C. 20540; 3. E.G. Squier Papers: New York Historical Society, Manuscript Department, 170 Central Park West, New York, New York 10024; 4. J. Henry Collection: Smithsonian Archives, Smithsonian Institution, Washington, D.C. 20560.

SECONDARY SOURCES

T.A. Barnhart: *Of mounds and men: The early anthropological career of Ephraim George Squier.* Ph.D. Thesis. Miami University, 1990; M.D. Olien: E.G. Squier and the Miskito: Anthropological scholarship and political propaganda. *Ethnohistory* 32(2):111–133, 1985; C.L. Stansifer: *The Central American career of E. George Squier.* Ph.D. Thesis. Tulane University, 1959; W. Stanton: *The leopard's spots: Scientific attitudes toward race in America, 1815–1859.* Chicago: University of Chicago Press, 1960; T.G. Tax: E. George Squier and the mounds, 1845–1850. In: T.H.H. Thoresen (ed) *Toward a science of man: Essays in the history of anthropology.* The Hague: Mouton, 1975, pp. 99–124; G.R. Willey & J.A. Sabloff: *A history of American archaeology.* 2d ed. San Francisco: Freeman, 1980.

Starr, Frederick (1858–1933)

Born in Auburn, New York, Starr received his Ph.D. in geology at Lafayette College, Pennyslvania, in 1885. He then joined the faculty of Coe College, Iowa, where he taught the first course in anthropology offered in the state. During his four-year tenure at Coe, Starr was an active member of the Davenport Academy of Sciences and published a number of monographs dealing with the archeology of Iowa. In 1888, he returned to New York, where he held the position of professor of geognosy at the Chautauqua Institute. It was in this position that Starr met, and formed a friendship with, William R. Harper (1856–1906), who later (1892) became the first president of the newly created University of Chicago (Evans 1991). On receiving this appointment, Harper invited Starr to join the faculty as an anthropologist in the Department of Sociology and Anthropology. Starr spent the remainder of his professional career (1892–1923) at Chicago, where he endeavored (unsuccessfully) to establish a separate Department of Anthropology.

Starr's research interests embraced archeology, ethnography, and physical anthropology. With regard to the latter his anthropometric studies are of particular historical interest. Between 1898 and 1902, he conducted what was then the most extensive anthropometric survey of central and southern Mexico. During the four summers he spent in Mexico, he managed to measure 2,875 individuals, representing twenty-three different ethnic groups distributed from Hidalgo (north of Mexico City) to the Yucatan. Later, Starr's work was continued by the Czech-American physical anthropologist Aleš Hrdlička (1869–1943), and, along with data collected by the German-American anthropologist Franz Boas (1858–1942) on the principal Indian groups in the United States and Canada, it provided an early composite picture of the distribution of the American Indian according to stature. From these data, it was shown that the shortest Indians were confined to Central America, while in the north there was a general increase in size, with the Indians of the eastern states and much of the Plains being the tallest among North American Indians.

Following his work in Mexico, Starr spent a short period in northern Japan collecting ethnographic materials that were used in the anthropological exhibit of the St. Louis Exposition, staged in 1904. After this initial trip, Starr was a frequent visitor to Japan; in fact, it was during one of these periodic visits that he contracted pneumonia and died on 14 August 1933.

Frank Spencer

See also Boas, Franz; Hrdlička, Aleš; United States of America

Bibliography
SELECTED WORKS
    Early man in Europe: Syllabus of a course of six lecture-studies in anthropology. Chicago: University of Chicago Press, 1895a; *Some first steps in human progress.* Chautauqua, New York, 1895b; *The pygmies.* London: Macmillan, 1895. Translation of Armand de Quatrefages' *Les pygmées.* Paris: Baillière, 1887; *Indians of southern Mexico.* Chicago, 1899; *Notes upon the ethnography of southern Mexico.* Davenport, Iowa: Putnam Memorial Publication Fund (Davenport Academy of Natural Sciences), 1900; The physical characters of the Indians of southern Mexico. *University of Chicago Decentennial Publications* 4:53–109, 1902; *Bibliography of Congo languages.* Chicago: University of Chicago Press, 1908; *Congo natives: An ethnographic album.* Chicago: Lakeside Press, 1912.

SECONDARY SOURCES
    N.L. Evans: Frederick Starr. In: *International dictionary of anthropologists.* New York: Garland, 1991, pp. 664–665.

Sterkfontein

The important Sterkfontein fossil hominid site is located near the summit of a low hill to the south of the Bloubank River Valley, 9.6 km north-northwest of Krugersdorp, Transvaal. It is near the center of an almost straight line connecting Swartkrans (1.2 km west) and Kromdraai (1.6 km east). These sites, and several others in the vicinity such as Bolt's Farm, Plovers' Lake, and Gladysvale, were formed as a result of karstic solution in Archaean or pre-Cambrian dolomitic limestone belonging to the Malmani Subgroup of the Transvaal Sequence. The main Sterkfontein fossil cave lies at an elevation of 1,486 m. The discovery of the bone-bearing breccias of this site was made in 1896, soon after quarrying for lime in the region began. At that time, Italian-born Guglielmo Martinaglia, who was lessee of the Sterkfontein lime deposits, blasted through from the surface into a maze of underground caves, spectacularly festooned with stalactites and stalagmites. Among the many visitors

attracted by news of this discovery in 1896–1897 were a party of Marist Brothers from the first high school for boys in Johannesburg, South Africa. On their visit, they found fossil bones and later they published an article under the author's sobriquet "Un Frère Mariste," reporting their visit and their find in the now effete French periodical *Cosmos* (1898, Vol. 47, No. 679, pp. 133–135). In the early 1930s, three of Raymond A. Dart's (1893–1988) students, J.H.S. Gear and the Goedvolk brothers, collected fossil bones at Sterkfontein and removed them to the South African Institute for Medical Research in Johannesburg. The subsequent history of the scientific study of this site may be divided into four phases.

Phase 1: 1936–1939

Despite the interest in cave sites following the momentous discovery of the first australopithecine fossil at Taung in 1924, it was not until 1935–1936 that the bone-bearing breccias at Sterkfontein became the focus of a protracted scientific search for hominid fossils. The reason for this apparent neglect probably resides in the fact that Dart had, in the early 1920s, examined a consignment of fossil bones that had been collected at Sterkfontein and sent to him after the announcement of the Taung discovery. From these, Dart considered that the deposit was relatively recent compared with Taung (cf. Dart & Craig 1959).

    In 1935, one of Dart's students, T.R. Trevor-Jones, who afterward became the first professor of general anatomy at the Dental School of the University of the Witwatersrand, Johannesburg, recovered fossil baboon skulls from the Sterkfontein deposit. Two more of Dart's students, G.W.H. Schepers and W. Harding Le Riche, visited Sterkfontein in 1936 and recovered a collection of bones that included more baboons. On Dart's advice, they showed these to Robert Broom (1866–1951), who in 1934 had joined the Transvaal Museum, Pretoria. Broom visited the site with Schepers and Le Riche on 9 August 1936 and alerted G.W. Barlow, the caretaker of the Sterkfontein caves, to be on the lookout for fossils that resembled the Taung skull. On Broom's third visit to the site, on 17 August 1936, Barlow handed him part of the skull and natural endocranial cast of an adult australopithecine—the first discovery of its kind since the child skull was recovered at Taung a dozen years earlier.

    From 1936 to 1939, Broom found a number of additional remains of these fossil hominids, comprising crania, upper and lower jaws, teeth, and some limb bones. Most of these specimens came from the main Sterkfontein lime quarry, an area that was to be called the "type site," and from a stratum that the South African geomorphologist Timothy C. Partridge (1978), who established the stratigraphic sequence of the deposit, later designated Member 4 of the Sterkfontein Formation.

In 1937, Broom was invited to attend the International Symposium on Early Man held at the Academy of Natural Sciences in Philadelphia; he spent six months in the United States before returning to South Africa. Back at Sterkfontein, he found that Barlow had switched operations to a "lower cave" 10 m lower and a short distance east of the type site. This part of the deposit belonged to the same formation as the main quarry, and from it Broom recovered some additional australopithecine specimens.

All of the Sterkfontein fossils found in that period provided a picture of what the adult australopithecines had looked like, and, in broad terms, their morphology confirmed for the adult what Dart had claimed for the Taung child. Broom at first ascribed the Sterkfontein form to the same genus, *Australopithecus*, but to a different species, which initially he designated *Australopithecus transvaalensis* (Broom 1936). Later, however, after he recovered some diagnostic teeth, such as the lower first deciduous molar, Broom came to believe that the Sterkfontein australopithecine represented a genus different from that of the Taung specimen. To accommodate it he proposed to classify the Sterkfontein ape-men as *Plesianthropus transvaalensis* (Broom 1938). However, John Talbot Robinson (1923–), Broom's assistant and eventual successor, lumped the Sterkfontein australopithecines into the same species as Dart had created for the Taung hominid, though as a different subspecies, *Australopithecus africanus transvaalensis* (Robinson 1954). The name *Plesianthropus* became of only historic interest, although a reminder of it persisted in the nickname, "Mrs. Ples," popularly assigned to one of the most complete crania from Sterkfontein (Sts 5).

With the outbreak of World War II, scientific excavation at Sterkfontein was suspended. The first phase of activity culminated in the 1946 publication of a monograph by Broom and Schepers that provided a summary of all australopithecine material found up to that date at Taung, Sterkfontein, and Kromdraai.

Phase 2: 1947–1949

Encouraged by Field Marshal J.C. Smuts, who was South Africa's World War II premier and author of *Holism and Evolution* (1926), Broom, assisted now by Robinson, resumed excavation at Sterkfontein in 1947. They were immediately rewarded by the recovery of a complete cranium of an adult australopithecine (Sts 5— in popular parlance, "Mrs. Ples"). This discovery, along with a number of scientific papers from Dart, Broom, Schepers, and Robinson, served to bolster a growing international interest in the South African hominids. Among the earliest postwar visitors and converts to Dart's viewpoint on the australopithecines was the British anatomist Wilfrid Edward Le Gros Clark (1895–1971), whose meticulous studies of these hominids from 1947 onward did most to turn the tide of scientific opinion toward the acceptance of *Australopithecus* as a hominid (cf. Clark 1947).

Broom and Robinson continued working at Sterkfontein until 1949. This phase yielded a number of important specimens that included a lower jaw, a complete hipbone, an incomplete femur, a few vertebrae, a partial skeleton, and several incomplete crania. In 1949, Broom and Robinson shifted their efforts to the neighboring site of Swartkrans.

Phase 3: 1956–1958

The third phase opened in 1956 when C.K. Brain discovered stone artifacts embedded in the breccia of an upper level (Member 5) of the Sterkfontein deposit. Prior to this, no stone implements had been recovered from any of the australopithecine sites.

The Sterkfontein artifacts came mostly from the West Pit, to the west of the main quarry. This area was at first called the "Extension Site," but the term was misleading since it suggested to some a different cave site from that where the original Sterkfontein discoveries were made. The stone-tool-bearing breccia constituted Member 5 of the Sterkfontein Formation (Partridge 1978).

In 1957, Robinson returned to Sterkfontein, where he excavated a volume of the artifact-bearing breccia. Apart from more stone artifacts, he recovered during 1957–1958 a juvenile upper jaw containing teeth, some isolated teeth, and part of a neck vertebra. These remains he attributed to *Australopithecus africanus*, which had been found in the subjacent Member 4, implying that *A. africanus* was the stone-tool maker. Later, Phillip V. Tobias (1925–), who had been working on *Homo habilis* from Olduvai

Gorge in Tanzania, found that the Sterkfontein Member 5 teeth were morphologically close to those of *H. habilis*, who he proposed was also the Sterkfontein toolmaker (Tobias 1965). The matter was not resolved until finally a skull attributed to *H. habilis* was found in Member 5 in 1976 (*vide infra*).

After his 1957–1958 work at Sterkfontein, Robinson recognized three breccia units at Sterkfontein: a lower breccia, which had proved a rich source of fossils of *A. africanus*, yielding 100 catalogued specimens; the artifact-bearing Middle Breccia; and a thin deposit of more-recent, tool-bearing Upper Breccia immediately under the roof of the original cave. Partridge (1978) labeled these three breccia deposits Members 4, 5, and 6 of the Sterkfontein Formation, respectively, and he identified three still lower deposits, respectively, Members 1, 2, and 3.

Phase 4: 1966–1996
In 1966, several years after Robinson had left South Africa for the University of Wisconsin, Tobias initiated a new long-term excavation at Sterkfontein. From 1966 to 1991, the work was carried out by a full-time team of excavators under Alun R. Hughes (1916–1992), who had for a dozen years conducted excavations for Dart at Makapansgat (cf. Tobias & Hughes 1969). His experience as an excavator of the intractable dolomitic limestone cave breccias was put to excellent use at Sterkfontein, and for a quarter of a century the work continued at the site under his direction—for forty-eight weeks a year. During this period, more than 550 more specimens of hominids were recovered, over and above the 100 that had been recovered by Broom and Robinson. Most of these new specimens stemmed from Member 4 and could be assigned to *A. africanus* (cf. Hughes & Tobias 1977). A smaller number came from Member 5, along with stone tools. Systematic studies on these hominid remains were begun by Tobias, his collaborators, and research students in the 1990s.

On 9 August 1976 and over the ensuing eight days, Hughes recovered from Member 5 a cranium, including palate and maxillary teeth and part of the mandible, of a hominid cheek by jowl with Member 5 stone tools. The skull proved to be close in its morphology to *H. habilis* recovered from Beds I and II of the Olduvai Formation in northern Tanzania. The recognition of *H. habilis*, or a form very closely related to it, in the artifact-bearing Member 5 of Sterkfontein appeared to resolve the problem of the authorship of at least some of the stone tools from Member 5.

After Hughes' health declined in 1991, Tobias placed Ronald J. Clarke in charge of the Sterkfontein excavation. Work commenced on the much older, *in situ* breccia of Member 2 of the Formation, as exposed in the Silberberg Grotto, named after H. Silberberg (who in 1942–1943 had discovered in that grotto a very primitive member of the hyaena family, which had led Broom to revise his conception of the dating of the Sterkfontein deposits). Member 2 proved to be rich in fossil remains, and it was hoped that a hominid appreciably older than *A. africanus* of Member 4, would come to light. In 1994 Clarke recognized four articulating bones of a hominid left foot from Member 2: he and Tobias found that it combined human-like with chimpanzee-like features (Clarke & Tobias 1995). While work on Member 2 breccia continued, Clarke at the same time delved into the implement-bearing Member 5. He and his wife, Kathleen Kuman, an archeologist, found that there were at least two and possibly three culturally distinct horizons within Member 5. The problem of determining which hominid was associated with each cultural phase became an important objective. Moreover, in 1992–1993, the discovery of a few teeth attested the presence of *A. (Paranthropus) robustus* in Member 5, synchronic and sympatric with early *Homo*.

Dating and Ecology
For a long time, there was little secure information on the dating of the Sterkfontein deposits. Despite an assiduous search, Tobias and his associates were unable to find any materials suitable for radioisotope or uranium disequilibrium dating, although attempts to use electron spin resonance were proving encouraging. However, the rich fauna, discovered in good provenance in each Member, enabled H.B.S. Cooke, V. Maglio, E. Delson, E.S. Vrba, and others to make comparisons with the well-dated faunal assemblages from East African localities. From such comparisons, Elisabeth Vrba established that the antelopes of Sterkfontein Member 4 were 2.8–2.3 my old and pointed to somewhat more moist or more mesic conditions than prevail now (Vrba 1974). Other lines of faunal dating, including J.K. McKee's (a paleoanthropologist in Wits Department of Anatomy and Human Biology) computerized analysis of all identified fossil mammals as well as a sequence of paleomagnetic determi-

nations, were in keeping with such an age for Member 4 (cf. McKee, Thackeray, & Berger 1995). Member 5 appeared to be over half a million years more recent than Member 4, Partridge (1978) having reported a disconformity between these two members. Thus, the older part of Member 5 appeared to be 2.0–1.8 my, although this estimate did not allow for the heterogeneity, or at least the archeological duality, of Member 5. It did seem, however, that the fauna and perhaps the pollen pointed to drier conditions in Member 5 times.

Phillip V. Tobias

See also Australopithecines; Broom, Robert; Clark, (Sir) Wilfrid Edward Le Gros; *Homo habilis*; Kromdraai; Makapansgat; Robinson, John Talbot; Taung (formerly Taungs)

Bibliography
C.K. Brain: The Transvaal ape-man-bearing cave deposits. *Transvaal Museum Memoirs.* No. 11. Pretoria, 1958; R. Broom: A new fossil anthropoid skull from South Africa. *Nature* 138:486–488, 1936; R. Broom: The Pleistocene anthropoid apes of South Africa. *Nature* 142:377–379, 1938; R. Broom & G.W.H. Schepers: The South African fossil ape-men, the Australopithecinae. *Transvaal Museum Memoirs.* No. 2. Pretoria, 1946; R. Broom, J.T. Robinson, & G.W.H. Schepers: Sterkfontein ape-man, *Plesianthropu*s. *Transvaal Museum Memoirs,* No. 4, Pretoria, 1950; K.W. Butzer: Another look at the australopithecine cave breccias of the Transvaal. *American Anthropologist* 73:1197–1201, 1971.

W.E. Le Gros Clark: Observations on the anatomy of the fossil Australopithecines. *Journal of Anatomy* (London) 81:300–333, 1947; W.E. Le Gros Clark: *The fossil evidence for human evolution.* 2d ed. Chicago: University of Chicago Press, 1964; R.J. Clarke & P.V. Tobias: Sterkfontein Member 2 foot bones of the oldest South African hominid. *Science* 269:521–524, 1995: R.A. Dart & D. Craig: *Adventures with the missing link.* New York: Harper, 1959; A.R. Hughes & P.V. Tobias: A fossil skull probably of the genus *Homo* from Sterkfontein. *Nature* 265:310–312, 1977; J.K. McKee, J.F. Thackeray, & L.R. Berger: Faunal assemblage seriation of Southern African Pliocene and Pleistocene fossil deposits. *American Journal of Physical Anthropology* 96:235–250, 1995; T.C. Partridge: Reappraisal of lithostratigraphy

of Sterkfontein hominid site. *Nature* 275:282, 1978; J.T. Robinson: The australopithecine-bearing deposits of the Sterkfontein area. *Annals of the Transvaal Museum* 22(1):1–19, 1952.

J.T. Robinson: The genera and species of the Australopithecinae. *American Journal of Physical Anthropology* 12:181–200, 1954; J.T. Robinson: The Sterkfontein tool maker. *Leech* 28:94–100, 1958; J.T. Robinson & R.J. Mason: Occurrence of stone artefacts with *Australopithecus* at Sterkfontein. *Nature* 180:521–524, 1957; J.C. Smuts: *Holism and Evolution.* 1st ed. London: Macmillan, 1926; P.V. Tobias: *Australopithecus, Homo habilis,* tool using and tool making. *South African Archaeological Bulletin* 20:167–192, 1965;. P.V. Tobias & A.R. Hughes: The new Witwatersrand University excavation at Sterkfontein. *South African Archaeological Bulletin* 24:158–169, 1969; E.S. Vrba: Chronological and ecological implications of the fossil Bovidae at the Sterkfontein australopithecine site. *Nature* 250:19–23, 1974.

Stewart, T(homas) Dale (1901–)

Born in Delta, Pennsylvania, Stewart began his long association with the United States National Museum (USNM) (now the National Museum of Natural History) in Washington, D.C., in 1924 as a "temporary" aide to Aleš Hrdlička (1869–1943) in the Division of Physical Anthropology (DPA). With the encouragement of Hrdlička, Stewart followed a premedicine curriculum at George Washington University (GWU) while continuing to work at the USNM. After receiving his A.B. degree from GWU in 1927, he attended medical school at the Johns Hopkins University, receiving his M.D. in 1931. Although while at Johns Hopkins he studied under Adolph Hans Schultz (1891–1976), his primary mentor was Hrdlička. At Johns Hopkins, he studied primates in addition to the usual medical-school curriculum, but he began his primary career interest in studies of the human skeleton through his work with Hrdlička. Upon completion of medical school, he was promoted at the USNM to assistant curator. In 1939, he became associate curator, and in 1942 he succeeded Hrdlička as curator of the DPA. He became head curator in 1961 and served as director of the USNM from 1963 to 1966. Following his term as director, Stewart was given the title senior research scientist until his retirement in 1971.

In 1943, Stewart served as visiting professor of anatomy at Washington University Medical School, St. Louis. In 1945, he taught at the Escuela de Antropología in Mexico City. This was followed by research trips to Guatemala in 1947 and 1949 and to Peru in 1949. From September 1954 to February 1955, he worked with the United States Army Quartermaster Corps in Japan, identifying bodies of American soldiers killed in the Korean conflict. During this time, Stewart also collected data that led to his 1957 classic publication with T.W. McKern, *Skeletal Age Changes in Young American Males*. In 1958, and again in 1960, Stewart visited Iraq, where he studied the Neandertal remains recovered at Shanidar Cave.

From 1942 to 1962, Stewart served as a regular consultant in forensic anthropology to the Federal Bureau of Investigation (FBI) in Washington, D.C. In that capacity, he frequently studied human remains submitted to the FBI and occasionally testified as an expert witness in court. His successor in 1962 was J. Lawrence Angel (1915–1986). Stewart is a member of the National Academy of Sciences (elected in 1962), a member and former president of the Anthropological Society of Washington, former vice president of the Washington Academy of Sciences, former president of the American Institute of Human Paleontology, a Fellow of the American Anthropological Association, and a former member of the Committee on Research and Exploration of the National Geographic Society. Stewart also served as editor of the new series of the *American Journal of Physical Anthropology* from 1942 to 1948. He was president of the American Association of Physical Anthropologists (AAPA) from 1950 to 1952 and AAPA treasurer-secretary during a difficult period from 1960 to 1964.

Stewart is an internationally recognized authority in comparative human osteology, paleopathology, and human identification. He is well known for his careful attention to detail. His works include interpretations of the skeletal remains of pre-Columbian and early post-Columbian populations in the Americas, the Melbourne skull, the Tepexpan skeleton, and studies of the Shanidar Neandertal remains. Through his activities and publications, Stewart led the developing field of forensic anthropology, publishing extensively on new and improved techniques of identification and analysis.

When Stewart retired from the USNM in 1971, his position was filled by Douglas H. Ubelaker, with whom he had worked closely

on various research projects. Since his "retirement," Stewart has continued working at the Smithsonian. In 1992, at the age of 91, he published a monograph on his work at the Patawomeke site in Virginia, where he had excavated between 1935 and 1940. Also in 1993, he received the Charles R. Darwin Lifetime Achievement Award from the AAPA.

Douglas H. Ubelaker

See also American Association of Physical Anthropologists; Angel, J(ohn) Lawrence; Forensic Anthropology; Hrdlička, Aleš; Neandertals; Schultz, Adolph Hans Shanidar (Iraq)

Bibliography
SELECTED WORKS

Spondylolisthesis without a separate neural arch (pseudospondylolisthesis of Junghahns). *Journal of Bone and Joint Surgery* 17:640–648, 1935; The life and writings of Dr. Aleš Hrdlička, 1869–1939. *American Journal of Physical Anthropology* 26 (o.s.):3–40, 1940; Skeletal remains with cultural associations from Chicama, Moche, and Viru Valleys, Peru. *Proceedings of the United States National Museum* 93:153–185, 1943; A reexamination of the fossil human skeletal remains from Melbourne, Florida, with further data on the Vero skull. *Smithsonian Miscellaneous Collections* 106:1–28, 1946; (ed) *Hrdlička's practical anthropometry*. 3d ed. Philadelphia: Wistar, 1947 (4th ed.: 1952); Medico-legal aspects of the skeleton. I. Sex, age, race, and stature. *American Journal of Physical Anthropology* 6 (n.s.):315–321, 1948.

Comparisons between Tepexpan man and other early Americans. In: H. de Terra, J. Romero & T.D. Stewart (eds) *Tepexpan man*. Viking Fund Publications in Anthropology. No. 11. Chicago: Viking Fund, 1949, pp. 139–145; First view of the restored Shanidar I skull. *Sumer* 14:90–96, 1958; A physical anthropologist's view of the peopling of the New World. *Southwestern Journal of Anthropology* 16:259–273, 1960; The skull of Shanidar II. *Sumer* 17:97–106, 1962; Shanidar skeletons IV and VI. *Sumer* 19:8–26, 1965; (ed) *Personal identification in mass disasters*. Washington, D.C.: Smithsonian Institution, 1970; *The people of America*. New York: Scribner's, 1973.

The Neanderthal skeletal remains from Shanidar Cave, Iraq: A summary of findings to date. *Proceedings of the American Philosophical Society* 121:121–165, 1977; *Essentials of forensic anthropology, especially as developed in the United States.* Springfield, Illinois: Thomas, 1979; *Archeological explorations at Patawomeke, the Indian town site (44ST2). Ancestral to the one (44ST1) visited in 1608 by Captain John Smith.* Smithsonian Contributions to Anthropology. No. 36. Washington, D.C.: Smithsonian Institution Press, 1992; (with T.W. McKern) *Skeletal age changes in young American males.* Quartermaster Research and Development Center, Environmental Protection Research Division, Technical Report EP-45, 1957; (with E. Spoehr) Evidence on the paleopathology of yaws. *Bulletin of the History of Medicine* 26:538–553, 1952.

ARCHIVAL SOURCES

T.D. Stewart Papers: National Anthropological Archives, National Museum of Natural History, Smithsonian Institution, Washington, D.C. 20560.

SECONDARY SOURCES

J.L. Angel (ed): Symposium in honor of T. Dale Stewart. *American Journal of Physical Anthropology* 45(3):519–530, 1976; W.L. Straus: Thomas Dale Stewart: Viking Fund medalist for 1953. *American Journal of Physical Anthropology* 12 (n.s.):253–255, 1954.

Suk, Vojtěch (1879–1967)

Born in Prague, Czech Republic, Suk began his studies in anthropology and ethnology at Charles University, which he continued in Zürich principally under the physical anthropologist Rudolph Martin (1864–1925) and later in Bologna with Fabio Frassetto (1876–1953). He was awarded a Ph.D. at Zurich University in 1910. Between 1910 and 1912, he traveled widely in Italy and Dalmatia studying the inhabitants of those countries. In 1912 he received a commission from Aleš Hrdlička (1869–1943) of the National Museum in Washington, D.C., to go to South Africa to examine and collect anthropological data on the "Negro child" in its native environment and to study the Kalahari Bushman. This information Hrdlička planned to use in an ambitious anthropological exhibit he was preparing for the Panama–California Exposition to be staged in San Diego in 1915. Suk left Prague for Durban, South Africa, in the summer of 1913 and worked first in Natal and Zululand (cf. Suk 1927a) before venturing into the Kalahari Desert. Although he completed a major portion of the work re-

quested by Hrdlička before the fateful summer of 1914, when war was declared, he found himself in "enemy territory," and he was interned in a British detention camp on the outskirts of Nairobi for the duration of the war. After the war, he returned to Prague, where he studied medicine at Charles University. He received his M.D. degree in 1920. From 1920 to 1923, he served as Jindřich Matiegka's (1862–1941) assistant in the newly founded Department of Anthropology at Charles University, Prague, before being appointed professor of anthropology and ethnology at the newly established second Czech university: Masaryk University in Brno. There Suk was responsible for founding and building the Department of Anthropology.

Between 1926 and 1927, he visited Labrador, where he studied, among other things, the incidence of tuberculosis and syphilis in the native Eskimos and Indians living on the northern coast (Suk 1927b). From 1920 to 1936, he made a protracted study of the physical characteristics of the Ruthenians in the Sub-Carpathian Ukraine.

As his writings amply demonstrate, Suk was thoroughly imbued with the ideals of humanism. During the 1930s, he was among the first to warn against the ascent of racism and belligerent nationalism in Europe. In all of his papers, he emphasized the equality of all human races and decisively rejected any claim for the innate superiority of one group versus another. During the German occupation of Czechoslovakia in World War II, Suk was persecuted by the Gestapo for his scientific views, and, as a consequence, he was obliged to leave Brno and work for the remainder of the war period as a physician in a provincial hospital. A distillation of his moral and scientific views on race and racism can be found in his last book (published in English) entitled *Race and Racism* (1955).

Together with his former pupil and successor Jindřich A. Valšík (1903–1977), Suk founded the Anthropological Society in Brno, which in 1961 was transformed into the Czechoslovak Anthropological Association.

Milan Dokládal

See also Czech and Slovak Republics; Frassetto, Fabio; Hrdlička, Aleš; Martin, Rudolf; Matiegka, Jindřich; San Diego Museum of Man

Bibliography
SELECTED WORKS
Eruption and decay of permanent teeth

in Whites and Negroes with comparative remarks on the races. *American Journal of Physical Anthropology* 2:351–388, 1920; Anthropological and physiological observations on the Negroes of the Natal and Zululand. *American Journal of Physical Anthropology* 10:31–64, 1927a; Occurrence of syphilis and tuberculosis among Eskimos and mixed breeds of the north coast of Laborador. *Spisy vydávané Přírodovědeckou fakultou Masarykovy University* 84:1–18, 1927b; Blood groups in Czechoslovakia. *Publication of the Faculty of Sciences* (Brno) 188:1–28, 1930; Ethnic pathology: Some new aims and ways of physical anthropology. *Publication of the Faculty of Sciences* (Brno) 141:1–16, 1931; On the question of human races on the basis of precipitin tests and isoagglutinations. *Práce Moravské Přírodovědecké Společnosti* (Brno) 8:1–42, 1933; *Races and racism.* Brno: Czechoslovak Academy of Sciences, 1955.

ARCHIVAL SOURCES

1. V. Suk Papers: Archives and Library, Department of Anthropology, Faculty of Sciences, Masaryk University, Cs-602 00-Brno, Kotlářská 2, Czech Republic. 2. A. Hrdlička Papers: National Anthropological Archives, Smithsonian Institution, Washington, D.C. 20560.

SECONDARY SOURCES

M. Dokládal: Prof. V. Suk v letech 1947–1967 [Professor V. Suk in the years 1947–1967]. *Zprávy Čs. společnosti antropologické* 20:37–38, 1967a; M. Dokládal: Vědecký odkaz profesora V. Suka [The scientific heritage of Professor V. Suk]. *Zprávy Čs. společnosti antropologické* 20:36–37, 1967b; M. Dokládal & J. Brožek: Physical anthropology in Czechoslovakia: Recent developments. *Current Anthropology* 2:455–477, 1961; Editorial: Professor V. Suk, 1879–1949: Seventy years old. *Zprávy Čs. společnosti antropologické* 2:1–2, 2–5, 1949; M. Prokopec: Biological anthropology in Czechoslovakia: An historical outline. *International Association of Human Biologists: Occasional Papers.* Vol. 3. No. 3. Newcastle upon Tyne: IAHB, 1991, pp. 1–54.

Suzuki, Hisashi (1912–)

Born in Hatogaya, Japan, Suzuki graduated in 1936 from the University of Tokyo School of Medicine, where he studied physical anthropology under Professor Emeritus Yoshikiyo Koganei (1859–1944) in the De-

partment of Anatomy. In 1943, he transferred to the Department of Anthropology in the Faculty of Science, becoming the head of the department in 1955.

In 1953, he excavated more than 900 skeletal remains from the medieval mass burial of Zaimokuza in Kamakura that demonstrated brachycephalization in the Japanese people from medieval to modern times (cf. Suzuki & Watanabe et al. 1956). From 1958 to 1960, he investigated the skeletal remains of the Tokugawa *shōguns* and their wives throughout the dynasties and clarified physical characteristics of the peerage in early modern times (cf. Suzuki & Yajima et al. 1967).

After 1957, he expanded his investigations to search for Pleistocene hominid fossils within the Japanese Archipelago. This work resulted in the discoveries and detailed reports on series of hominid remains from Uskikawa, Mikkabi (1962), Hamakita (1966), and Minatogawa (Suzuki & Hanihara et al. 1982).

In 1961, he led an expedition to Israel, where his team excavated Amud Cave in the Lake Tiberias region—the result of which was the discovery of a well-preserved Neandertal skeleton (cf. Suzuki & Takai et al. 1970).

In 1972, Suzuki resigned his position at the University of Tokyo and moved to the National Science Museum, where he became the founding director of the Department of Anthropology.

Bin Yamaguchi

See also Amud Cave (Israel); Israel; Japan; Koganei, Yoshikiyo

Bibliography
SELECTED WORKS

Skeletal remains of Mikkabi man. *Journal of the Anthropological Society of Nippon* 70:1–20, 46–48, 1962; Skeletal remains of Hamakita man. *Journal of the Anthropological Society of Nippon* 74:119–136,172–174, 1966; Pleistocene man in Japan. *Journal of the Anthropological Society of Nippon* (Supplement) 90:11–26, 1982; *Suzuki Hisashi Kokkaku Jinruigaku Ronbunshu* [Selected papers of Hisashi Suzuki on skeletal anthropology]. Tokyo: Terapeia, 1992; (with K. Hanihara et al.) *The Minatogawa man.* Bulletin No. 19. Tokyo: University Museum, University of Tokyo, 1982; (with F. Takai et al.) *The Amud man and his cave site.* Tokyo: University of Tokyo, 1970.

Racial history of the Japanese. In: I. Schwidetsky (ed) *Rassengeschichte der*

Menschheit, Asien I. Vienna: Oldenbourg, 1981; (with H. Watanabe et al.) *Kamakura Zaimokuza Hakken no Chūsei Iseki to Sono Jinkotsu* [Medieval Japanese skeletons from the burial site at Zaimokuza, Kamakura City]. Tokyo: Iwanami-Shoten, 1956; (with K. Yajima et al.) *Zōjōji Tokugawa Shōgunbo to Sono Ihin Itai* [Studies of the graves, coffin contents, and skeletal remains of Tokugawa *shōguns* and their families at the Zōjōji Temple]. Tokyo: University of Tokyo Press, 1967.

ARCHIVAL SOURCES

H. Suzuki Papers: Library, Department of Anthropology, University of Tokyo, 7–3–1 Hongo, Bunkyo-ku, Tokyo, Japan.

SECONDARY SOURCES

H. Suzuki: Watakushi no jinruigaku 50-nen [Fifty years as an anthropologist]. *Shizenkagaku to Hakubutsukan* 43:30–37, 1976; K. Terada: Suzuki Hisashi Sensei no koki o iwatte [A short biography of Professor Hisashi Suzuki in commemoration of his seventieth birthday]. *Journal of the Anthropological Society of Nippon* 90:1–10, 1982.

Swanscombe

The Swanscombe hominid site, located in Barnfield Pit, not far from All Saints Church, Swanscombe, in East Kent, forms a section of the 100-foot terrace of the Thames River Valley. It was there, near the base of the Upper Middle Gravel terrace, that the London dentist Alvan T. Marston (1889–1971) found a human occipital bone on 29 June 1935 and a left parietal on 15 March 1936 (cf. Marston 1935, 1936). These remains were found in association with a series of flint implements of the Acheulean type (synonymous with the Lower Paleolithic) and fossil mammalian fauna. In 1955, a right parietal was found by other workers (cf. Wymer 1955). All three pieces fit together, forming the braincase of a young adult, which, except for its general thickness, looks deceptively similar to that of modern *Homo sapiens (vide infra)*. During the late 1960s and early 1970s, further excavations at the site yielded additional specimens of worked flint and mammalian bones (cf. Waechter 1969–1972).

Prior to the discovery in 1994 of a reportedly 500 ky old tibial fragment at Boxgrove in West Sussex, the Swanscombe skull had the distinction of being the earliest hominid remains found in the British Isles. However, be

this as it may, the Swanscombe skull continues to occupy an important niche in the human paleontological record

Given the date of the first discoveries, it is not surprising that an immediate comparison was made between Swanscombe and the Piltdown skull found in 1912. The initial stance taken by the then principal arbiter in British paleoanthropology, Arthur Keith (1866–1955), was that the Swanscombe skull belonged to *Homo sapiens*, closely resembling Piltdown but of a later form (cf. Marston 1937), while Arthur Smith Woodward (1864–1944), who had been responsible for reconstructing the Piltdown skull in 1912, believed that the Swanscombe remains represented "neither Piltdown nor [an] ordinary Neanderthal." To which he added that the remains indicated yet "another form of human skull in the Lower Pleistocene" (Letter from A.S. Woodward to Dorothea M.A. Bate, Department of Geology, British Museum (Natural History), 28 August 1935, in Spencer 1990a:172). Disappointed by these reactions, Marston approached the neuroanatomist-anthropologist Grafton Elliot Smith (1871–1937), who agreed to examine the Swanscombe endocranial cast. Much to Marston's satisfaction, Smith concluded that Swanscombe skull was decidedly more primitive than that of Piltdown (cf. Marston 1937:374). Then, to complicate matters further, Marston learned through Kenneth Page Oakley (1911–1981), a geologist-anthropologist at the Natural History Museum in South Kensington, London, that a recent geological survey had determined that the Piltdown site was not sitting on a 100-foot terrace as previously supposed but rather a 50-foot one—the implication being that Swanscombe was older than Piltdown (cf. Spencer 1990b:125). Furthermore, through a study he made of the Piltdown mandible in 1936–1937, Marston became convinced that this jaw did not belong with the braincase.

In attempting to disassociate the Piltdown jaw from the braincase, Marston hoped to strengthen his case for the greater antiquity of the Swanscombe skull. Although he was unable to advance this case, his agitations did lead to the formation by the Royal Anthropological Institute of a committee to evaluate his find. In its report issued in 1938, the Swanscombe Committee concluded that the Swanscombe skull was, indeed, "an indigenous fossil of the 100-ft terrace," belonging (probably) to the Middle Pleistocene—though it was undecided about its taxonomic status. Unlike Smith, the Oxford anatomist Wilfrid Edward Le Gros Clark (1895–1971) found nothing, other than its exceptional thickness, in the skull that departed significantly from that of modern crania (cf. Hinton et al. 1938). Geoffrey Morant (1899–1964) of the Galton Laboratory, University College, London, concurred, concluding that it could be a form on either the direct line to *Homo sapiens* or one that was heading to Neandertals, noting that its biasterionic breadth and thickness of the bones resembled that of the Steinheim skull (cf. Hinton et al. 1938). Thus, among pre-sapiensists, the Swanscombe skull was frequently portrayed in the literature of the 1950s and 1960s (particularly after Piltdown was dispatched as a forgery in 1953) as evidence supporting their viewpoint (e.g., Vallois 1954). On the other hand, followers of the Neandertal hypothesis regarded it as an intermediate form between *Homo erectus* and Neandertals (e.g., Weinert 1955; Breitinger 1955). A third group, subscribing to the pre-Neandertal hypothesis, viewed Swanscombe as a kind of intermediary form between *H. erectus* and *H. sapiens*, which was envisioned to have been ancestral to both Neandertals and *H. sapiens* (e.g., Sergi 1953; Howell 1957).

In the early 1960s the Neandertal features of the Swanscombe occipital bone were first noted by the American physical anthropologist T. Dale Stewart (1964). Later, in the early 1970s, two independent studies using multivariate analyses were used to show that Swanscombe was more like Neandertals (cf. Corruccini 1974; Stringer 1974). From the perspective of these and later studies in the 1980s (e.g., Hublin 1978, 1983; Santa Luca 1978), it is now generally held that the morphometrics of Swanscombe neatly fit the lineage leading to the Neandertals. For further discussion of the Swanscombe specimen, see Stringer et al (1984) and Trinkaus & Shipman (1993).

Frank Spencer
Fred H. Smith

See also Clark, (Sir) Wilfrid Edward Le Gros; Keith, (Sir) Arthur; Modern Human Origins; Neandertals; Oakley, Kenneth Page; Piltdown; Smith, (Sir) Grafton Elliot; Woodward, Arthur (Smith)

Bibliography
E. Breitinger: Das Schädelfragmentes von Swanscombe und das "Praesapiens problem." *Mitteilungen der Anthropologischen Gesellschaften in Wien* 84–85:1–45, 1955; R.S. Corruccini: Calvarial shape relationships between fossil hominids. *Yearbook of Physical Anthropology* 18:89–109, 1974; M.A.C. Hinton et al.: Report of the Swanscombe Committee. *Journal of the Royal Anthropological Institute of Great Britain and Ireland* 68:17–98, 1938; F.C. Howell: The evolutionary significance of variation and varieties of Neanderthal man. *Quarterly Review of Biology* 32:330–347, 1957; J.-J. Hublin: *Le torus occipital transverse et les structures associées: Evolution dans le genre Homo.* Doctoral Thesis. University of Paris, 1978.

J.-J. Hublin: Les origines de l'homme de type moderne en Europe. *Pour La Science* 64:62–71, 1983; A.T. Marston: (Note on discovery of the Swanscombe occipital fragment). *Nature* 136:637, 1935; A.T. Marston: Preliminary note on a new fossil human skull from Swanscombe, Kent. *Nature* 138:200–201, 1936; A.T. Marston: The Swanscombe skull. *Journal of the Royal Anthropological Institute of Great Britain and Ireland* 67:339–406, 1937; A.P. Santa Luca: A reexamination of presumed Neanderthal-like fossils. *Journal of Human Evolution* 7:619–636, 1978; S. Sergi: I Profaneranthropi di Swanscombe e di Fontéchevade. *Rivista di Antropologia* (Rome) 40:65–72, 1953.

F. Spencer: *The Piltdown Papers: Correspondence and other documents relating to the Piltdown forgery.* London: Oxford University Press, 1990a; F. Spencer: *Piltdown: A scientific forgery.* London: Oxford University Press, 1990b; T.D. Stewart: A neglected primitive feature of the Swanscombe skull. In: C.D. Ovey (ed) *The Swanscombe skull: A survey of research on a Pleistocene site.* London: Royal Anthropological Institute, 1964, pp. 151–159; C.B. Stringer: Population relationships of later Pleistocene hominids: A multivariate study of available crania. *Journal of Archaeological Science* 1:317–342, 1974; C.B. Stringer et al.: The origin of anatomically modern humans in western Europe. In: F.H. Smith & F. Spencer (eds) *The origin of modern humans: A world survey of the fossil evidence.* New York: Liss, 1984, pp. 51–135; E. Trinkaus & P. Shipman: *The Neandertals: Changing the image of mankind.* New York: Knopf, 1993; H.V. Vallois: Neanderthals and praesapiens. *Journal of the Anthropological Institute of Great Britain and Ireland* 84:111–130, 1954; J.D.'A. Waechter: Swanscombe *Proceedings of the Royal Anthropological Institute of Great Britain and Ireland,* pp. 53–

61 (1969), pp. 87–89 (1970), pp. 43–49 (1971), pp. 73–78 (1972); H. Weinert: Die Neanderthaler-Gruppe und die Praesapiens-Funde. *Forschungen und Fortschritte* 29:297–304, 1955; J. Wymer: A further fragment of the Swanscombe skull. *Nature* 176:426–427, 1955.

Sweden

Among the Nordic countries, Sweden has the longest tradition in physical anthropology. As early as 1705, the Swedish mathematician Harald Vallerius (1646–1716) published his essay *De varia hominum forma externa*, in which he discussed the origin and physical appearance of the human races. In this work, he claimed that food and habits affect the physical appearance of human beings, and he presented one of the first racial classifications. But unlike the French savant François Bernier (1620–1688), who had earlier recognized five major divisions of the human family (cf. Bernier 1684), Vallerius identified only four: (1) Ethiopians, with dark skin color and curled hair; (2) Lapps and Samojeds, with brownish skin color and black wiry hair; (3) Italians, Spaniards, and French, also with black hair but grayish skin color; and (4) "Leuko-Ethiopians," or "white negroes," corresponding to Caucasians with white-colored skin, sleek hair, and "harmonious" stature and appearance.

It is, however, Linnaeus (Carl [von] Linné) (1707–1778) rather than Vallerius who is more often than not associated with the first scientific classification of the human genus, which he presented in his book *Systema naturae*, published in 1735. His classification indicates that he was obviously influenced by Vallerius. In placing human beings under the *Anthropomorpha*, along with the apes and monkeys, Linnaeus noted that in contrast to other animals they were wise, thinking creatures, and hence his designation *Homo sapiens*—which he separated into four groups according to skin color and geographical limitations: *Europeaus albus, Americanus rubescens, Asiaticus fuscus,* and *Africanus niger.* In later editions of the *Systema*, Linnaeus provided more differential information on these four major geographic groups and introduced the taxonomic term Primates.

Following Linnaeus, the next major figure to advance physical anthropology in Sweden was the zoologist, geologist, botanist, and archeologist Sven Nilsson (1787–1883). The first measurements on Lappic skulls had been taken by the anatomist Arvid Henrik Florman (1761–1840) of Lund and presented in his anatomical manual of 1823, *Anatomisk Handbok för Läkare och Zoologer.* As indicated by his employment of the *Angulus facialis,* he was familiar with the work of the Dutch anatomist Petrus Camper (1722–1789). Still, it was Nilsson who was largely responsible for pioneering this field of inquiry in Sweden. In his 1835 book *Skandinavisk Fauna* (Scandinavian Fauna), he advanced the idea of studying the Swedish people who had once used stone tools and animal bones by recovering their skeletal remains—in particular, the skulls. He was also responsible for establishing the proportions of the skull characterizing the Swedish population, and in so doing he introduced a system of classification that was widely used abroad. He further developed his ideas in *Skandinaviska Nordens Ur-Invånare* (Aborigines of the Nordic Scandinavia), which he published in the period 1838–1843. His cranial studies of Swedish Stone Age "Aborigines" led him to suggest that the first inhabitants of Sweden had been Lapps. He was also strongly skeptical of the German physician Franz Gall's (1758–1828) phrenological thesis, and it was this that prompted him to urge his anatomist friend Anders Retzius (1796–1860) to study morphological variation in human crania (cf. A. Retzius 1848).

In 1842, two years after the death of the German anatomist-craniologist Johann Friedrich Blumenbach (1752–1840), Retzius introduced the cranial index upon which he developed a new cranial classificatory system. In this new craniometric system, which was presented to the Academy of Science in Stockholm, he classified crania in two main groups: the brachycephalics (short heads) and dolichocephalics (long heads). These two groups were further divided according to the frontal conformation of skull—that is, whether it tended to the vertical plane or protruded. Those skulls with a less protusive and vertical profile were termed "orthognathic" (after Camper), while protrusive profiles were designated "prognathic."

Like Camper's facial angle, Retzius' cranial index provided investigators with the means of distinguishing cranial forms by a simple mathematical expression that required merely two measurements: the length and breadth of the skull. In retrospect, it is clear that Retzius' innovative system placed craniology on a new scientific footing. Details of his system were published under the title *Om Formen af Nordboernes Cranier* (On the Shape of the Skulls of the Northerners) in 1843, and it immediately attracted the attention of the international scientific community.

The work of Anders Retzius was carried on by his son Magnus Gustaf Retzius (1842–1919), who later became professor of anatomy at the Karolinska Institute in Stockholm. He ultimately quit medicine, however, to devote his energies exclusively to physical anthropology. Like his father, he was an avid craniologist, and he enlarged his father's collection of crania to about 2,200 specimens. His most important work was *Crania suecica antiqua* (1899), a large monograph in which full-size photographs of the skulls were used as illustrations. In this work, Retzius claimed that the autochthones of Sweden had been a tall, light-haired, blue-eyed and dolichocephalic people.

It was largely due to the initiative of Gustaf Retzius that an anthropological society (Antropologiska Sällskapet i Stockholm) was established in 1873. When founded the society had a recorded membership of 758. Four years later, it was reorganized into two separate societies—devoted, respectively, to physical anthropology and geography, and the allied sciences of each. In 1880, however, these two societies were reunited as the Swedish Society for Anthropology and Geography (Svenska Sällskapet för Antropologi och Geografi). Because of the Swedish–Norwegian union in the period 1814–1905, it was decided that Norwegian members of the society should have equal representation. Since its foundation in 1873, the society has published a periodical. Initially named *Tidsskrift för Antropologi och Kulturhistoria*, in 1880 it was renamed *Ymer*. According to Nordic mythology, "Ymer" is the primitive substance of the world, and, as such, the journal captures the essence and objective of the anthropological sciences.

Toward the close of the nineteenth century, Carl Magnus Fürst (1854–1935), professor of anatomy at Lund University and a close colleague of Gustaf Retzius (cf. G. Retzius & Fürst 1902), emerged on the Swedish scene. Although he was initially active in histological research, he shifted his interests progressively during the 1890s to physical anthropology, paleopathology, and medical history. He did much to popularize the anthropological sciences through his writings, as indicated by his book *När de döda vittna* (When the Dead Are Witnesses), published in 1920. He also established an international reputation for his *très indices* method (Fürst 1933), which is a classification of the different skull types, expressed only by a triplet

combination of the numbers 1, 2, and 3.

During the first decades of the twentieth century, investigations on cremated, prehistoric skeletal material were undertaken in Sweden by a number of workers—most notably, the zoologist Ludvig Hedell (1844–1923), who pioneered the examination of bones from the famous grave mounds in Uppsala in 1919. Another was the zoologist Elias Dahr (1896–1983), who contributed to this field of osteological research with the examination of the Uppsala material in 1927.

During the interwar years, racial questions were considered of great importance in Sweden, as well as in the other European countries. Fürst's pupil Gaston Backman (1883–1964), also a professor of anatomy at Lund University from 1933 to 1948, worked on problems related to human growth and variation among different racial groups represented in the Swedish population.

It was through the influence of Fürst and Backman that Carl-Herman Hjortsjö (1914–1978) became interested in physical anthropology. He, too, came from Lund University, and during his years as professor of anatomy there (1948–1978), he demonstrated his capacity and wide-ranging interests in anthropology. He developed further Fürst's index combinations, and with his students and colleagues he established the most important range of subjects within anatomy, medical history, and physical anthropology in Sweden (cf. Hjortsjö 1962, 1967).

Among Hjortsjö's colleagues was the anatomist Ejnar Sjövall (1879–1964). His particular research interests were in forensic medicine and paleopathology (cf. Sjövall 1932). Nordic anthropologists have benefited greatly from the special skills and knowledge he brought to these subjects.

At Uppsala University, Bertil Lundman (1899–), who had a special interest in racial variation and conducted a number of studies on Swedish population, was an associate professor in physical anthropology from 1947 to 1966. Also at Uppsala (and Gothenburg) was the anatomist Bo Erik Ingelmark (1913–1972), who had an active interest in physical anthropology. His research focus was paleopathology, in which he did important work on the medieval skeletons from the Battle of Visby/Gotland (cf. Ingelmark 1939) and the examination of the skeletal remains of the sixteenth-century Wasa family in 1945–1946 (Holck: personal communication with Nils-Gustaf Gejvall, n.d.).

Another important contributor to Swedish physical anthropology was the pathologist and gerontologist Folke Henschen (1881–1977). His renowned work *Kraniets kulturhistoria* (The Cultural History of the Cranium), published in 1965, ranks as the standard work on the subject. He is also remembered for his study of the philosopher Emanuel Swedenborg (1688–1772).

As this brief review reveals, physical anthropology has long been the domain of anatomists in Sweden, as is the case in most other European countries. However, in 1936, this tradition was changed by Nils-Gustaf Gejvall (1911–1991), a zoologist from Lund University who was hired to manage the osteological collections at the Museum of Natural History in Stockholm. In 1964, he established the Osteological Research Laboratory (ORL) at the University of Stockholm with a grant from the Wallenberg Foundation and the generosity of the then King Gustaf VI Adolf of Sweden, whose archeological interests and skills were widely renowned. By offering one of the buildings at Castle Solna outside Stockholm, the king made an instant reality of the ORL, which began its activities in 1967. At the same time, a professorship in physical anthropology (historical osteology) was established for Gejvall at the ORL and connected to the University of Stockholm.

Gejvall's best-known work is his monograph on the medieval Västerhus population, *Westerhus: Medieval Population and Church in the Light of Skeletal Remains* (1960), which is widely regarded as a classic in the anthropological literature. Similarly, his pathbreaking methods of analyzing cremated bones, which he began developing in 1947, and his system of identification have also served to establish his international reputation.

From 1974 to 1990, Gejvall was general editor of the periodical *OSSA*, which is an international forum of human osteology as well as forensic sciences. Shortly before his death, Gejvall published a collection of essays—highlights from his life as an osteologist—*In på bara benen* (1990).

When Gejvall retired in 1978, his work was taken over by the young Norwegian scientist Torstein Sjøvold (1946–), who had been his assistant since 1971. Neither Gejvall nor Sjøvold were medically trained. The fact that anthropology was carried out by investigators other than anatomists, was a new trend in Scandinavia at that time. Sjøvold's specialty is biostatistics, and he has conducted work on nonmetric traits, age grouping, and estimations of stature (e.g., Sjøvold 1976, 1978,

1988, 1990). He is a member of the Norwegian Academy of Science, and since 1979 he has held the only Chair of Osteology in Scandinavia, thus making Sweden one of the leading European nations in physical anthropology. Indicative of this is the invitation that was extended to Sjøvold to lead an international team to examine the preserved remains of a Neolithic male (the "Ice Man") found in the Tyrolean Alps in the early 1990s (cf. Sjøvold et al. 1992).

Among others at the ORL in the mid-1990s were Ebba During, an associate professor who, since 1978, has worked on zoological as well as human osteological material, and Berit Sigvallius, who has further developed the work of Gejvall on cremated bones (cf. Sigvallius 1993, 1994). In addition to the research on skeletal material from archeological sites, work at the ORL has also concentrated on the development of methods in data collection and classification, testing of mechanical stress on bones, and the like.

At the University of Lund, Associate Professor Elisabeth Iregren (e.g., Iregren 1972) is responsible for human and animal osteology, while Caroline Arcini specializes in paleopathology (e.g., During 1991).

Per Holck

See also Bernier, François; Blumenbach, Johann Friedrich; Camper, Petrus; Linnaeus, Carolus; Linnaeus' Anthropology; Phrenology; Retzius, Anders Adolf; Retzius, Magnus Gustaf

Bibliography
G. Backman: *Über die Scaphocephalie.* Wiesbaden: Bergmann, 1908; G. Backman: *Människoraserna och moderna rasproblem.* Stockholm: Bonniers, 1935; G. Backman: *Wachstumszyklen und phylogenetische Entwicklung.* Lunds universitets årsskrift. No. 34. Lund: Gleerup, 1938; F. Bernier (published anonymously): Nouvelle division de la terre par les différentes espèces ou races d'hommes qui l'habitent. *Journal des Sçavans* 12:148–155, 1684; E. During: Mechanical surface analysis of bone: A case study of cut marks and enamel hypoplasia on a Neolithic cranium from Sweden. *American Journal of Physical Anthropology* 84:113–125, 1991; A.H. Florman: *Anatomisk Handbok för Läkare och Zoologer.* Stockholm, 1823; C.M. Fürst: *Zur Kraniologie der Schwedischen Steinzeit.* Kungliga svenska vetenskapsakademiens handlingar. No. 49. Stockholm: Svenska Vetenskapsakademien, 1912.

C.M. Fürst: *När de döda vittna.* Stockholm: Svenska Teknologiföreningens, 1920; C.M. Fürst: Eine Zahlenberechnung für die Kombination der Indices der drei Dimensionen des Schädels. *Anthropologischer Anzeiger* 10:209–214, 1933; N.G. Gejvall: Bestämning av brända ben från forntida gravar. *Fornvännen* (Stockholm) 42:39–47, 1947; N.G. Gejvall: *Westerhus: Medieval population and church in the light of skeletal remains.* Stockholm: Almquist & Wiksell, 1960; N.G. Gejvall: Cremations. In: D.R. Brothwell & E. Higgs (ed) *Science in archaeology.* London: Thames & Hudson, 1965, pp. 380–390; N.G. Gejvall: *In på bara benen: En skelettforskares minnen.* Stockholm: Ohlsson 1990.

F. Henschen. Emanuel Swedenborg's cranium. *Nova acta regiae societatis scientiarum Upsaliensis* IV, 1960; F. Henschen: *Kraniets kulturhistoria.* Stockholm: *Natur och kultur,* 1965; C.H. Hjortsjö (ed): *Erik XIV. Gravöppningen 1958 i Västerås domkyrka.* Stockholm: Norstedts & Söners, 1962; C.H. Hjortsjö: *Drottning Christina: Gravöppningen i Rom 1965.* Lund: Bokförlaget Corona, 1967; B.E. Ingelmark: Skeleton finds from the warrior graves outside Visby. In: B. Thordeman (ed) *Armour from the Battle of Visby 1361.* Uppsala: Anatomisk Institut, Uppsala University, 1939; B.E. Ingelmark: Über die Längenassymetrien der Extremitäten und ihren Zusammenhang mit der Rechts-Links-Händigkeit. *Uppsala Läkarförenings förhandlingar.* No. 52. Uppsala, 1947.

E. Iregren: *Vårby och Vårberg II: Studie av kremerat människo- och djurbensmaterial från jernåldern.* Stockholm, 1972; C.v. Linné (Linnaeus): *Systema naturae, sive regna tria naturae systematice proposita.* Leiden: DeGruot, 1735; B. Lundman: *Jordens Människoraser och Folkstammar i deras etnografiska och geografiska sammanhang.* Uppsala: Nyblooms, 1943; B. Lundman: *Dala-allmogens antropologi.* Uppsala: Almquist & Wiksell, 1945; B. Lundman: *Umriss der Rassenkunde des Menschen in geschichtlicher Zeit.* Copenhagen: Munksgaard, 1952; S. Nilsson: *Skandinavisk fauna.* Stockholm: Gleerup, 1835; S. Nilsson: *Skandinaviska Nordens Ur-invånare, ett försök i komparativa ethnografien och ett bidrag till menniskoslägtets utvecklings historia.* Lund: Berlingska, 1838–1843.

A. Retzius: *Om Formen af Nordboernes Cranier: Förhandlingar vid de Skandinaviska naturforskarnes möte* (Stockholm) 3:157–201, 1843; A. Retzius: *Phrenologien bedömd från en anatomisk ståndpunkt.* Copenhagen, 1848; G. Retzius: *Crania suecica antiqua, beskrifning af svenska mennisko-kranier från stenåldern, bronsåldern och järnåldern jämte en blick på forskningen öfver de europeiska folkens raskaraktärer.* Stockholm: Aftonbladet, 1899; G. Retzius & C.M. Fürst: *Anthropologia suecica: Beiträge zur Anthropologie der Schweden.* Stockholm: Aftonbladet, 1902.

B. Sigvallius: *Funeral pyres, Iron Age cremations in North Spånga.* Theses & papers in Osteology. No. 1. Osteological Research Laboratory, Stockholm University, 1994; E. Sjövall: Die Bedeutung der Skelettanalyse bei Grabuntersuchungen. *Kungliga fysiologiska sällskapet i Lund* 2:113–136, 1932; T. Sjøvold: A method for familial studies based on minor skeletal variants. *Ossa* 3–4:97–107, 1976; T. Sjøvold: Inference concerning the age distribution of skeletal populations and some consequences for paleodemography. *Anthropologiai Közlemények* 22:99–114, 1978.

T. Sjøvold: Geschlechtsdiagnose am Skelett. In: R. Knußmann (ed) *Anthropologie.* Stuttgart/New York: Fischer, 1988; T. Sjøvold: Estimation of stature from long bones utilizing the line of organic correlation. *Human Evolution* 5:431–447, 1990; T. Sjøvold: The Stone Age "Ice Man" from the Alps: The find and the current status of the investigation. *Evolutionary Anthropology* 1:117–124, 1992; T. Sjøvold et al.: Some anthropological aspects of the prehistoric Tyrolean "Ice Man." *Science* 258:455–457, 1992; H. Vallerius: *De varia hominum forma externa.* Uppsala: Ström, 1705.

Systematics (1960s–1990s)

Since the publication of the German entomologist Emil Hans Willi Hennig's (1913–1976) *Phylogenetic Systematics* in 1966, the field of bioanthropological systematics has changed radically. In 1982, the American primatologist Matt Cartmill described the early events of this period as "the collapse of classical primate systematics" (Cartmill 1982:158). The changes that came, though profound, were nourished more by a methodological twist than by a strongly rooted theoretical advance. The intense debate that reverberated among anthropologists echoed the broader field of systematic biology, and the past. As the German-American Ernst Mayr wrote in the early 1980s: "To a surprising extent the current controversies in systematics are the same as those of the post-Darwinian period; indeed, many of them go back to Linnaeus, to the Renaissance botanists, or even to Aristotle" (1982:9).

Some Landmarks

The shift toward a new-era systematics (to borrow an apt phrase from the British biologist Julian S. Huxley [1887–1975]), that began in the 1960s is illustrated in the pages of two important anthologies spanning a pivotal transition period: *Classification and Human Evolution* (Washburn 1963) and *Phylogeny of the Primates* (Luckett & Szalay 1975). Although the objectives of these two edited volumes differed, they reveal a turnover in research foci, methods, and personnel and the makings of a revolution. The titles, for example, suggest a departure from the prevailing view of classification as the principal enterprise of systematic biology—with phylogeny entwined, somehow, in this pursuit. In achieving a new understanding, the new-era systematics dissected the notions of phylogeny and classification in an effort to move the science ahead. Classification was now secondary to phylogeny reconstruction, both conceptually and within a research program.

The jargon that permeates the volume of the evolutionary biologist W. Patrick Luckett and the mammalian systematist Frederick S. Szalay volume reflects a cascade of methodological innovation inspired by Hennig (1966). Terms such as cladogram, character analysis, synapomorphy, plesiomorphy, morphotype, and morphocline polarity were rampant, appearing in papers dealing with fossils, soft tissue, molecules, and behavior. Similarly, the gradistic approach that was so prominent in the volume by Sherwood L. Washburn (1911–)was swept aside by phylogenetic thinking. In the seventeen chapters of the Washburn volume, only the brief theoretical paper by the Oxford bioanthropologists Geoffrey A. Harrison and Joseph Sidney Weiner (1915–1982) anticipated the changes about to come (Harrison & Weiner 1963). In contrast, the article by the American paleontologist George Gaylord Simpson (1902–1984) devoted thirty pages to explaining the semantics of classification and nomenclature, an exercise that, if anything, revealed the hopeless ambiguity of prevailing doctrine (Simpson 1963).

If cladistic analysis was the beacon of bioanthropology's new-era systematics, its lights were the American paleoprimatologist Eric Delson and the British paleontologist Peter Andrews (1975), whose chapter on ca-

tarrhine relationships represented the state of the art in the Luckett and Szalay volume. Their outline of character analysis, the phylogenetic interrogation of traits through the comparative method, has since become a model for scores of contributions in bio- and paleoanthropology. Delson and Andrews, along with colleagues Ian Tattersall (physical anthropologist) and Niles Eldredge (invertebrate paleontologist), encouraged fundamental reversals from the traditional systematics of Simpson (1963), Elwyn Simons (1972), and others. They exhorted, for example, that phylogenists, and even paleontologists, essentially ignore the arrow of time in the quest to discover ancestors. They insisted that phylogenetic studies should be limited essentially to inferring genealogy, the network of sister-group relationships, rather than descent. Hence, in the all-influential visual medium of scientific communication, the flowing phylogenetic tree was replaced by the angular cladogram.

Concern deepened during the 1970s that stratigraphic gaps in the fossil record could not reliably reveal primitive-to-derived evolution. In an ironic tribute to Simpson (cf. Schaeffer et al. 1972), cladistic paleontologists virtually rebuked time. In the new convention, fossils were treated as if they were modern, arranged on the same time line as living species, in forfeit of their unique historical information. This analytical strategy was applied in many subsequent cladistic analyses, in which, for example, comparisons of *Pan, Gorilla, Pongo, Homo,* and *Australopithecus* were implemented in an effort to reconstruct ancestral hominine features with a taxonomic evenness that belies the likelihood of australopithecines bearing primitive traits. Delson and Andrews (1975) did, however, offer a caveat. They allowed temporal information, provisionally, when inferring morphotypes (hypothetical constructs of characters—not taxa—both primitive and derived, found in the last common ancestor of a clade) in cases in which other methods proved ambiguous, and temporal precedence did not present a conflict. Eschewing a more pluralistic phylogenetic approach, Szalay (1977) warned strongly against stripping fossils of their unique contribution to evolutionary biology: age and sequence. The American paleontologist Phillip Gingerich (1976) also fought the atemporal cladistic approach with a "stratophenetic" method, which relied on detailed stratigraphy and phenetic similarity to reveal the trace of descent from rocks. In practice, today, more and more studies tend toward the center, employing the character-analysis methods that emerged from within cladistics but without relegating fossils to background.

Consequences and Trends

The *Phylogeny of the Primates* volume also broadened the taxonomic and comparative viewpoint within the bioanthropology community. Questions of "higher phylogeny" now dominated the agenda: primate origins, affinities among the Archonta (primates, bats, tree shrews, and colugos), the phylogeny of tarsiers, anthropoid origins, and so forth. The shift in focus from classification to phylogeny demanded an expanded knowledge of anatomy and biodiversity, and a welcome attention to detail, in terms of both evidence and hypothesis. Nevertheless, a price was paid as aims changed. The importance given to synthesis of morphology, adaptation, behavior, and ecology was sadly diminished. A new perspective arose. Euphemistically, it dubbed all nongenealogical considerations as "scenarios." The stark, angular precision of the cladogram became the mettle of scientific rigor and the grail of scientific results.

Enthusiasm for higher phylogeny also grew at the expense of research at the species level. Alpha taxonomy, the sorting, description, and identification of species-level taxa was once the keystone of paleoanthropology. Until the 1990s, when Tattersall (1992), Bernard Wood (1992), a British paleoanthropologist, and others began revisiting the question "How many hominid species are there?" this crucial area of evolutionary biology and systematics had become narrowly construed within the community as an argument over the "single-species hypothesis" of the American paleoanthropologists C. Loring Brace and Milford Wolpoff. Now that that is settled, it is expected that anthropologists will turn their attention to a less esoteric cause such as conservation; conservationists are becoming acutely aware that their decisions must be based on sound alpha taxonomy, biogeography, and phylogeny.

Since the mid-1970s, the literature suggests other problematic trends arising from the conceptual simplification of the systematic enterprise that is associated with the rise of cladistics. For example, as an enlarging array of biomedical technologies (strain gauges, telemetered electromyography, computed tomography, and the like) are applied to questions, functional morphology is being defined in increasingly narrow terms—where once it was a part of the whole field of systematic biology (Mayr 1982). Similarly, in deference to fashionable notions of scientific rigor and sampling theory, many systematists have adopted a formalized, reductionistic approach to their data. This is evident in the miraculous growth in the length of trait lists seen in cladistic studies.

Morphology, as cladistic evidence, is becoming atomized and portrayed as a ream of "character states," which often seem like an inchoate amalgam drawn from the index of *Gray's Anatomy*. Where is the biology? Are these minutia variable within species? Are they functionally, developmentally, genetically, or otherwise discrete; or, are they intercorrelated? What is their biological meaning? And so on. Rather than offer solutions to these problems by sharing in them, the diverging interests of systematists and functional morphologists seem to be driving these subdisciplines away from any potential synthesis of method. Ironically, a point has been reached where deeper knowledge of adaptation and function can help, but it is still largely ignored by systematists.

Two other areas rooted in technology—desktop computing and molecular biology—have become the engines of systematics research since the 1960s, thus rendering the traditional low-tech comparative anatomy a threatened and possibly endangered species, despite a brief renaissance in the 1970s. Just as Delson and his colleagues made phylogeny simple via the cladistic recipe, it is suspected that the sheer ease of implementing computer-based phylogeny has undercut scrutiny of form, function, biological role, and homology, once the basic foundation of systematics research. For many, these issues are but an afterthought, noise in the system: the metaphysical stuff of a scenario.

It also appears as if molecular systematics is subsuming the role of anatomical inquiry, at all taxonomic levels (*vide infra*). Clearly, what is saving morphology are the fossils. Still, here also a dramatic new application that enables extraction of ancient DNA (deoxyribonucleic acid) from fossils is challenging morphology's preeminence. There are signs, however, that another emerging technology, computerized three-dimensional visualization, will redress some of the limitations of traditional morphological practice (e.g., Huijismans et al. 1986; Hartwig & Sadler 1993; Vannier & Conroy 1989).

Classification and Taxonomy

Despite the shift from classification to phylogeny-based research, there never seems to be a lack of enthusiasm for toying with classification. With a strident interest in genealogy, neo-Hennigian cladists have argued—in opposition to Hennig's (1966) declared views—that classification should bear a strict resemblance to the nested, monophyletic branchings of a cladogram, to permit a semantic identification of genealogy. This view, which is consistent with the nineteenth-century objective of classifying in "natural groups," has taken hold. However, attempts to radically alter the Linnaean hierarchy in order to express cladistic relationships more precisely have not taken root. The American paleomammologist M.C. McKenna (1975) experimented with this approach and gave us mammals by the Superlegion, Legion, Sublegion; the Magnorder, Superorder, Granorder, and Microrder. Few, however, have followed his lead. Similarly, the intention to employ a nameless and rankless "primitive category," the Plesion, when failing to link one taxon to another, has not gained acceptance.

In spite of these and other efforts to routinize the system since the 1960s, no alternatives have proven more practical than the Linnaean hierarchy, with all of its well-known imperfections. It appears that classification will remain a somewhat subjective exercise even as scientific clarity grows. Thus, while Cartmill (1982) could announce the collapse of classical primate systematics a few years after the appearance of the Luckett and Szalay (1975) volume, its ancient taxonomic battles would still be revisited with no end in sight— for example, the subdivision of the Order Primates into prosimians (including tarsiers) and anthropoids or into strepsirhines (prosimians less tarsiers) and haplorhines (anthropoids plus tarsiers). For hominids, the flux of names and hierarchical conventions has also become extreme. In 1963, the term had one meaning for all of the contributors to Washburn's volume: *Homo* plus *Australopithecus*, but no longer. Alternative definitions of Hominidae abound and vascillate, even among the highly accomplished. Consider three: Homininae, Ponginae, and Hylobatinae (Szalay & Delson 1979); Homininae and Ponginae (Tattersall et al. 1988), and Homininae and Australopithecinae (Martin 1990).

With regard to taxonomy, the one usage that reemerged in the 1970s and 1980s and will probably endure is the rank of tribe, which falls below the family and above the genus. Improved knowledge of phylogeny has meant that new groupings, such as Tribe Papionini (informally papionins) for African baboons and relatives, are likely to become common concepts and parlance. Szalay and Delson (1979), the primate systematist A.L. Rosenberger (1981), and others have shown that the tribe and subtribe ranks (which were used extensively in the nonprimate sections of Simpson's pivotal classification of mammals published in 1945) have real value for communicating about primates.

Reconstructing Phylogeny

The lasting contribution of this new-era systematics for bioanthropology is, undoubtedly, the clarification it brought to the methods of phylogeny reconstruction. This profound advance arose via extensive published debate among three main camps: the phenetic, the cladistic, and the classicist schools. Pheneticists developed an important following during the 1970s as multivariate morphometrics became broadly available through mainframe computers. The British anatomist Charles Oxnard, with both functional and phylogenetic questions in mind, did pioneering work in this field.

Phenetics fell out of favor once Hennig (1966) explained why similarity per se could have little to no direct genealogical significance if the features in question were ancestral rather than derived traits. This dichotomy became the pillar of cladistic analysis. Similarly, although classicists had long been concerned with sorting primitive from so-called advanced traits, this notion was applied loosely until the mid-1960s. Classicists failed to formulate a consistent method for analyzing the primitive-to-derived polarity, for they required no more than a broad brush stroke to paint phylogenetic trees en route to their primary objective, classification. To do this, they often relied on a gradistic view of evolution and a gradistic justification for taxonomic assignments.

Eventually, cladistics offered an executable program for phylogenetic reconstruction that yielded predictions suitable for testing. The value of Hennig's pillar, the rule of shared derived characters, is evident. The synapomorphy principle has thus been adopted by morphologists of classical persuasion and also by those more inclined toward metrics, who might otherwise have become aligned with pheneticists. This was made easier as the original jargon of Hennig, that so miffed competing scholars, became simplified into a few key terms. As a result, the conceptual differences among systematists have been generally blurred by a common language.

Hennig's synapomorphy principle is compelling because of its simplicity: Only shared derived features are valid evidence of phyletic relationships. It should be noted, however, that the edifice supporting Hennig's pillar is an artificially narrow construction of the concept of phylogeny, as Mayr (1969), Szalay (1977), and others have stressed. Cladists interpret evolutionary or phylogenetic relationships as "monophyletic relatedness," joint descent from a single ancestor. This makes it possible to neatly express affinity using the sister-group metaphor—for example, modern humans are the sister-group to modern chimps and gorillas; platyrrhines are the sister-taxon of catarrhines. It also permits dismissal of ancestral characteristics as having no value at all for phylogeny.

However, this narrow view of phylogeny is misplaced. Species transform by speciation and phyletic evolution, so phylogeny means more than propinquity of descent. It is an inquiry into the pattern of descent. Ancestors occur within evolving lineages, and one of the principal ways to discover them comes from studying the primitive features of a clade. It is not enough to simply know that *Australopithecus* is a sister-taxon of *Homo*. We need to know which species, *A. afarensis* or another, is our ancestor, because we also wish to know: What features changed? Why? And how quickly? Cladistics offers no way of doing this.

Hennig and his followers are credited for shifting the paradigm at a time when systematics was still steeped in gradism, and classicists were being challenged on several fronts. But implementing the fundamental protocols of cladistics—the character analysis—turns out not to be straightforward. As Mayr (1982) has noted, these issues have confused generations of systematists. Indeed, in the introduction to his "The Orders of Mammals" (1910), the American paleontologist William King Gregory (1876–1970) wrote:

The greatest stumbling blocks of the phylogenist lie: first in the difficulty of distinguishing between primitive and specialized characters, secondly in the tendency to assume relationships between two given forms on the basis of resemblances that may have been brought about by either parallel or convergent evolution. (1910)

Situation through the Mid-1990s

For the moment, cladistics is firmly entrenched, having greatly benefited from user-friendly computer programs that generate genealogies on the basis of parsimony (e.g., Swofford 1992). Although these programs are seductive for their operational simplicity, the British cladistic theoretician C.P. Groves and the Anglo-Australian primatologist J.D. Paterson (1991), who undertook an exploratory analysis of the PHYLIP software using an extensive data set dealing with hominoids, claimed that without careful selection of traits and solid judgment regarding polarities, they merely affirm ". . . the general rule about the use of computers, the infamous "Garbage in-Garbage Out" or GIGO principle. . . ." (Groves & Paterson 1991:176). A great advantage of the cladistic/parsimony system is that it can be applied to molecules, morphology, or any other data set. One of the acknowledged difficulties concerns the huge number of trees that can potentially arise in multispecies studies and the criteria used to prune the less likely branch clusters. Since the results of parsimony studies are also strongly driven by the characteristics of the out-group, it should be understood that there is a huge chance of error automatically built in: All of the same questions and difficulties concerning homology, analogy, and relationships pertain to the data and selection of out-group species.

Difficulties notwithstanding, the high-tech combination of molecules as material and computer-driven parsimony as an analytical tool has changed the course of bioanthropological systematics. Molecules have largely supplanted anatomy as the system of choice, once investigators learned to use them cladistically. This shift began within phenetics, spearheaded by the American molecular biologist Morris Goodman (1963), who learned from serological study that great apes, an old gradistic grouping, was not monophyletic: Orangutans are more distantly related to African apes than *Pan* and *Gorilla* are to *Homo*.

Thereafter, molecular anthropology developed quickly in the direction of DNA (Kohne 1970), whose sequential structure was more amenable than serum to homology verification via trait-by-trait examination, a prerequisite for character analysis. In the interim, the American physical anthropologist V.M. Sarich and New Zealand molecular biologist A.C. Wilson (1935–1991) (1967), also employing a phenetic approach, gave momentum to nonmorphological approaches and the "molecular clock," an inroad into the domain of paleoanthropology that promised to squeeze time from living tissue. This made it possible, theoretically (but not without suffering the heated disputations of morphologists), to calibrate the timing of hominoid divergence via immunology, and later using DNA–DNA hybridization (Sibley & Ahlquist 1984). Fortunately for the molecular advocates, the crux of the debate over molecules versus morphology hinged for a long while on the systematic status of the Late Miocene ape *Ramapithecus*, which throughout most of the 1960s and 1970s was a genus assembled from a scattering of incomplete fossils, analyzed in much the same vein as Washburn's (1963) authors looked at their data, gradistically. In another alluring result, DNA data also became widely cited as evidence that chimps are more closely related to humans than to gorillas, although this matter is far from a resolution (Marks 1993). As this suggests, molecules and morphology share some of the same weaknesses, and it is difficult to identify the most informative material and the best analytical methods for a particular problem.

Today we know more about primate and human evolution than we did in the 1960s. Not only are there more investigators, but there are more and better fossils, more techniques and questions being curried from other fields, and more awareness of the mistakes of past practice. But as we move into the twenty-first century, flushed with enthusiasm, we should not forget William King Gregory's advice:

In the study of the genetic relations of mammals there are few maxims which are of universally deductive application. Phylogeny is essentially an inductive subject, a reasoning by analogy, which is the shifting sand whereon hypotheses and theories are built. In general, the student must (1) concede nothing more than he is forced to, (2) strive to separate probability from plausibility, (3) test his hypotheses by the principle of negation, and (4) avoid explaining the little known by the less known. Above all (5) he must strive to keep in touch with all the data bearing on the subject, and (6) make constant reviews to see that no pertinent fact has been omitted, and (7) test again and again his basal assumptions. (1910:106)

Alfred L. Rosenberger

See also Gregory, William King; Hennig, Emil Hans Willi; Mayr, Ernst; Molecular Anthropology; Punctuated Equilibria; Simpson, George Gaylord; Washburn, Sherwood L.; Weiner, Joseph Sidney

Bibliography
M. Cartmill: Basic primatology and prosimian evolution. In: F. Spencer (ed) *A history of American physical anthropology, 1930–1980*. New York: Academic Press, 1982, pp. 147–186; E. Delson & P. Andrews: Evolution and interrelationships of the catarrhine primates. In: W.P. Luckett & F.S. Szalay (eds) *Phylogeny of the primates: A multidisciplinary approach*. New York: Plenum, 1975, pp. 405–446; P.D. Gingerich: Paleontology and phylogeny: Patterns of evolution at the species level in early Tertiary mammals. *American Journal of Science* 176:1–28, 1976.

M. Goodman: Man's place in the phylogeny of the primates as reflected in the serum proteins. In: S.L. Washburn (ed) *Classification and human evolution*. Chicago: Aldine, 1963, pp. 204–234; W.K. Gregory: The orders of mammals. *Bulletin of the American Museum of Natural History* 27:3–524, 1910; C.P. Groves & J.D. Paterson: Testing hominoid phylogeny with the PHYLIP programs. *Journal of Human Evolution* 20:167–183, 1991; G.A. Harrison & J.S. Weiner: Some considerations in the formulation of theories of human phylogeny. In: S.L. Washburn (ed) *Classification and human evolution*. Chicago: Aldine, 1963, pp. 75–84; W.C. Hartwig & L.L. Sadler: Visualization and physical anthropology. In: A.J. Almquist & A. Manyak (eds) *Milestones in human evolution*. Prospect Heights, Illinois: Waveland Press, 1993, pp. 183–222.

W. Hennig: *Phylogenetic systematics*. Urbana: University of Illinois Press, 1966; D.P. Huijismans et al.: Toward computerized morphometric facilities: A review of fifty-eight software packages for computer-aided three-dimensional reconstruction, quantification, and picture generation from parallel serial sections. *Anatomical Record* 216: 449–470, 1986; D.E. Kohne: Evolution of higher-organism DNA. *Quarterly Review of Biology* 33:327–375, 1970; W.P. Luckett & F.S. Szalay (eds): *Phylogeny of the primates: A multidisciplinary approach*. New York: Plenum, 1975; J. Marks: Hominoid heterochromatin: Terminal C-bands as a complex genetic trait linking chimpanzees and gorillas. *American Journal of Physical Anthropology* 90:237–246, 1993; R.D. Martin: *Primate origins and evolution*. Princeton, New Jersey: Princeton University Press, 1990.

E. Mayr: *Principles of systematic zoology*. New York: McGraw-Hill, 1969; E. Mayr: *The growth of biological thought*. Cambridge, Massachusetts: Harvard University Press, 1982; M.C. McKenna: Towards a phylogenic classification of Mammalia. In: W.P. Luckett & F.S. Szalay (eds) *Phylogeny of the primates: A multidisciplinary approach*. New York: Plenum, 1975, pp. 21–46; A.L. Rosenberger: Systematics: The higher taxa. In: A.F. Coimbra-Filho & R.A. Mittermeier (eds) *Ecology and behavior of Neotropical primates*. Vol. 1. Rio de Janeiro: Academia Brasiliera de Ciencias, 1981, pp. 160–180; V.M. Sarich & A.C. Wilson: Immunological time scale for hominid evolution. *Science* 158:1200–1204, 1967.

D. Schaeffer et al.: Phylogeny and paleontology. *Evolutionary Biology* 6:31–46, 1972; G.C. Sibley & J.E. Ahlquist: The phylogeny of the hominoid primates, as indicated by DNA–DNA hybridization. *Journal of Molecular Evolution* 20:2–15, 1984; E.L. Simons: *Primate evolution: An introduction to man's place in nature*. New York: Macmillan, 1972; G.G. Simpson: The principles of classification and a classification of the mammals. *Bulletin of the American Museum of Natural History* 85:1–

350, 1945; G.G. Simpson: *Principles of animal taxonomy*. New York: Columbia University Press, 1961; G.G. Simpson: The meaning of taxonomic statements. In: S.L. Washburn (ed) *Classification and human evolution*. Chicago: Aldine, 1963, pp. 1–31; R.R. Skelton et al.: Phylogenetic analysis of early hominids. *Current Anthropology* 27:21–35, 1986.

D.L. Swofford: *PAUP: Phylogenetic analysis using parsimony, Version 3.0*. Champaign: Illinois Natural History Survey, 1992; F.S. Szalay: Constructing primate phylogenies: A search for testable hypotheses with maximal empirical content. *Journal of Human Evolution* 6:3–18, 1977; F.S. Szalay & E. Delson: *Evolutionary history of the primates*. New York: Academic Press, 1979; I. Tattersall: Species concepts and species identification in human evolution. *Journal of Human Evolution* 22:341–349, 1992; I. Tattersall et al. *Encyclopedia of human evolution and prehistory*. New York: Garland, 1988; M.W. Vannier & G.C. Conroy: Imaging workstation for computer-aided primatology. *Folia Primatologica* 53:7–21, 1989; S.L. Washburn (ed): *Classification and human evolution*. Chicago: Aldine, 1963; B. Wood: Early hominid species and speciation. *Journal of Human Evolution* 22:351–366, 1992.

Tabūn, Mugharet et- (Israel)

From 1929 to 1934, the British archeologist Dorothy A.E. Garrod (1892–1969) organized and ran the Joint Expedition of the British School of Archaeology in Jerusalem and the American School of Prehistoric Research in Palestine, or what is now northwestern Israel. The work concentrated on the excavation of three caves or shelters in, or adjacent to, the Wadi el-Mughara in the southern part of the Mount Carmel range. The most spectacular of these, once excavated, was Mugharet et-Tabūn, the most southern of the cave sites. Its stratigraphy of more than 24 m extends from later Acheulean deposits (Layers F and G); through "transitional" Lower-to-Middle Paleolithic assemblages, the Yabrudian and Amudian (Layer E); to a series of Middle Paleolithic deposits (Layers B, C, and D).

The best-known human remains from the site are the largely complete skeleton of a young adult female, Tabūn 1, found along the southern wall of the shelter and generally attributed to Layer C. In addition, several incomplete series of teeth were found in Layer B, a complete mandible (Tabūn 2), a femoral shaft (Tabūn 3), and several wrist and hand bones were found in Layer C, and a femoral shaft plus a molar derive from layer Ea. These remains were included in the original description of the Mount Carmel fossil hominids made by the American physical anthropologist Theodore D. McCown (1908–1969) and the British anatomist-anthropologist Arthur Keith (1866–1955) in 1939, which they characterized as a variable Palestinian Middle Paleolithic human group (McCown & Keith 1939). Yet, even they noted a series of "peculiar" characteristics of the "Tabūn woman," as well as the massiveness of the Tabūn 2 mandible; as a result, they considered them to be the more archaic representatives of the overall sample.

The Tabūn 1 skeleton, although partially crushed and distorted, is clearly aligned with other Near Eastern late archaic humans. This was evident from the shape of its brow region (with prominent and rounded supraorbital tori), its archaic mandible and cranial base morphology (especially of the temporal bone). This interpretation is further reinforced by the form of the pubic bones, femoral shafts, scapulae, and hand remains (Trinkaus 1983). It is nonetheless one of the smallest and most gracile of the known late archaic, or Neandertal, human skeletons.

The only ongoing problem regarding the Tabūn 1 skeleton is its stratigraphic provenance. Garrod originally assigned it to layer C, noting however that it might be intrusive from Layer B (cf. Garrod & Bate 1937). However, it was subsequently noted that the stratigraphic layers at Tabūn curve upward at the site (or, more appropriately, slump down in the middle through post-depositional karstic action), leading to the possibility that Tabūn 1 derives from Layer D (Jelinek 1982, 1992). The American paleoanthropologist Erik Trinkaus (unpublished data) has also noted that the Tabūn 4 and 5 right radii and hamate bones from Layer C almost certainly represent those missing elements from the Tabūn 1 skeleton, associating it again with Layer C.

The Layer B dental remains are impossible to assign with confidence to a late archaic versus early modern human sample; whereas, the Tabūn 3 and Layer Ea femoral shafts clearly represent those of archaic humans. The massive Tabūn 2 mandible, however, has been considered both archaic and early modern. The latter attribution is based on its possession of a modest mental eminence. Yet, its size, robusticity, and overall proportions, as well as the anterior-to-posterior dental proportions, clearly align it with late archaic humans. Consequently, Tabūn Cave has yielded Late Acheulean archaic human remains, a series of Middle Paleolithic archaic human remains (probably all from Layer C), plus some undiagnostic isolated teeth from the Late Middle Paleolithic deposits.

As with other Near Eastern Middle Paleolithic fossils, scientific opinion on the geological age of this assemblage has fluctuated since the fossils were discovered. They were originally considered to be of "last interpluvial" (i.e., the last interglacial) age, based primarily on faunal remains, combined with their more archaic morphology relative to the remains from nearby Mughuret es-Skhūl. A series of radiocarbon dates on Layer C placed it around 50.0 ky BP (Jelinek 1982), which almost certainly reflects the limits of radiocarbon dating rather than the age of the site and, therefore, should be considered only as a minimum age for the site. However, these dates combined with new sedimentological analyses, led the American archeologist Arthur J. Jelinek (1982) to include most of the Tabūn sequence within the last interglacial and early last glacial.

In the early 1990s, the application of electron spin resonance (ESR) dating to teeth from the site (Grün et al. 1991) placed Layers B and C in the earlier last interglacial, and Layer D well back into the Middle Pleistocene. Subsequent thermoluminescence (TL) dating of layers (Mercier 1992) has nearly doubled the calculated ages of the Middle Paleolithic at Tabūn. However, the most recent uranium-series dates for the Tabūn Layers B to Ea (McDermott et al. 1993) place Layers B and C in the later and earlier interglacial, respectively, and appear to confirm the late Middle Pleistocene ages of Layers D and Ea.

From this, it appears most likely that the Tabūn fossil humans from Layer C date to sometime in the last interglacial. If correct, that would make them older than the early last glacial archaic humans from Amud Cave and Kebara, but roughly contemporaneous with the Qafzeh early modern human remains,

as well as the earlier Shanidar archaic human sample, and possibly contemporaneous with the Skhūl sample. However, given the continuing refinement of dating technology, this scheme is likely to be altered in the future. The fossils nonetheless retain their significance as reasonably well-preserved (probably last interglacial) representatives of the Near Eastern late archaic human lineage.

Erik Trinkaus

See also Amud Cave (Israel); Israel; Kebara, Mughuret el- (Israel); Keith, (Sir) Arthur; McCown, Theodore D(oney); Mount Carmel (Israel); Neandertals; Qafzeh (Jebel) (Israel); Shanidar (Iraq)

Bibliography
D.A.E. Garrod & M.A. Bate: *The Stone Age of Mount Carmel I: Excavations at the Wadi el-Mughara.* Oxford: Clarendon Press, 1937; R. Grün et al.: ESR dating of teeth from Garrod's Tabūn Cave collection. *Journal of Human Evolution* 20:231–248, 1991; A.J. Jelinek: The Tabūn Cave and Paleolithic man in the Levant. *Science* 216:1369–1375, 1982; A.J. Jelinek: Problems in the chronology of the Middle Paleolithic and the first appearance of early *Homo sapiens* in southwest Asia. In: T. Akazawa et al. (eds) *The evolution and dispersal of modern humans in Asia.* Tokyo: Hokusen-sha, 1992, pp. 253–275.

T.D. McCown & A. Keith: *The Stone Age of Mount Carmel II: The fossil human remains from the Levalloiso-Mousterian.* Oxford: Clarendon Press, 1939; F. McDermott et al.: Mass spectrometric U-series dates for Israeli Neanderthal/early-modern hominid sites. *Nature* 363:252–255, 1993; N. Mercier: *Rapport des méthodes radiométriques de datation à l'étude du peuplement de l'Europe et du Proche-Orient au cours du Pleistocène moyen et supérieur.* Ph.D. Thesis. Université de Bordeaux I, 1992; E. Trinkaus: *The Shanidar Neandertals.* New York: Academic Press, 1983.

Talgai

The Talgai cranium was discovered in 1884, embedded in the wall of Dalrymple Creek, on Talgai Station in the Darling Downs southwest of Brisbane, Australia. This heavily mineralized and encrusted cranium was eventually brought to the attention of Tannatt W. Edgeworth David (1858–1934), professor of geology at the University of Sydney (Smith 1918). David realized the importance of Talgai to a continent which, at the time, was without fossil evidence of early human occupation. After a photograph of Talgai was shown to the anatomist James T. Wilson (1863–1945) he recommended that it be purchased by the university. David and Wilson then jointly announced Talgai to the British Association for the Advancement of Science (BAAS) in Sydney in August 1914. It was left to the Sydney general practitioner, Stewart Arthur Smith to write the formal decription of the specimen, which was published in 1918.

Unfortunately for Smith, Talgai's vault was crushed and distorted, a difficulty exacerbated by its sagittal and coronal sectioning during preparation. Nevertheless, Smith concluded that the cranium was that of a fourteen- to fifteen-year-old male whose cranial vault was "similar in all respects to the cranium of the Australian of to-day" (1918:382). In the face, palate, and dentition, however, he identified what he considered to be more archaic characteristics. The canine teeth, for example, were interpreted as having a size and morphology consistent with an ape-like canine-premolar cutting complex. In his assessment of Talgai, Smith had been strongly influenced by the apparent similarity of its dentition to that of the celebrated Piltdown specimen—an observation that had been publicly promoted by the anatomist-anthropologist Grafton Elliot Smith (1871–1937), who had attended the BAAS meeting in Sydney and had firsthand experience of both specimens (cf. Langham 1978). And as both S.A. Smith and Elliot Smith appreciated, if Talgai was dated to the Pleistocene, or perhaps earlier, then given the beliefs of the time it should also have had this meld of modern human and ape characteristics.

Smith's assessment of the significance of Talgai's teeth and palate was subsequently refuted by T.D. Campbell (1925), A.N. Burkitt (1928), M. Hellman (1934), and N.W.G. Macintosh (1952). The canine teeth, while large, were within the modern Aboriginal range of variation (Campbell 1925), and the wear facets on the maxillary canines were not consistent with those in hominoid primates (Burkitt 1928). Reconstructions of the palate by Hellman (1934) and Macintosh (1952) also indicated that there was nothing unusual about its shape. While broad, particularly anteriorly, this is a common feature of terminal Pleistocene Australian palates (Brown 1989). Perhaps the only unusual feature of the Talgai's teeth is the relatively extreme molar wear for an individual of fourteen to fifteen years of age (Brown 1992).

Some recent references to Talgai have stressed its size and robustness, particularly for a juvenile cranium. Macintosh (1967) emphasized the connection between Talgai and *Homo erectus,* highlighting "its prognathic face, its low retreating forehead, and its low vault, and huge canine teeth." Certainly, Talgai did possess a receding frontal squama and a low vault, but as is demonstrated by S.A. Smith's (1918) original photographs, this was primarily a result of severe postmortem compression and distortion. The Australian paleoanthropologist Alan Thorne (1977) places Talgai, along with Kow Swamp and Cohuna, in his robust group of Pleistocene Australians, which he distinguished from Lake Mungo and Keilor. More recent research by the Australians Phillip Habgood (1986) and Peter Brown (1987) has found little support for Thorne's dual Pleistocene populations. After several inappropriate attempts at reconstruction, Talgai consists of a number of eroded fragments from which little morphological or metrical information can be obtained. Although not directly dated, the soil horizon from which Talgai may have originated has been dated to ca. 11.65 ky BP (cf. Oakley, Campbell, & Molleson 1975).

Peter Brown

See *also* Australia; Australian Paleoanthropology; Piltdown; Smith, (Sir) Grafton Elliot

Bibliography
P. Brown: Pleistocene homogeneity and Holocene size reduction: The Australian human skeletal evidence. *Archaeology in Oceania* 22:41–71, 1987; P. Brown: *Coobool Creek: Terra Australis 13.* Canberra: Department of Prehistory, Research School of Pacific Studies, Australian National University, 1989; P. Brown: Post-Pleistocene change in Australian Aboriginal tooth size: Dental reduction or relative expansion? In: P. Brown and S. Molnar (eds) *Human craniofacial variation in Pacific populations.* Adelaide: Anthropology and Genetics Laboratory, University of Adelaide, 1992, pp. 33–52.

A.N. Burkitt: Further observations upon the "Talgai" skull, more especially with regard to the teeth. In: *Report of the Nineteenth Meeting of the Australian Association for the Advancement of Science,* pp. 366–371, 1928; T.D. Campbell: *Dentition and palate of the Australian Aboriginal.* Adelaide: Hassell Press, 1925; P.J. Habgood: The origin of the Australians: A multivariate approach. *Archaeology in Oceania* 21:130–137, 1986; M. Hellman: The form of the Talgai palate. *American Journal of Physical Anthropology* 19:1–15, 1934; I. Langham: Talgai and Piltdown: The common context. *Artefact* 3:181–224, 1978; N.W.G. Macintosh: The Talgai teeth and dental arch: Remeasurement and reconstruction. *Oceania* 23:106–109, 1952.

N.W.G. Macintosh: Fossil man in Australia. (Paper presented at the ANZAAS Thirty-ninth Congress, University of Melbourne, Transcript of Australian Broadcasting Commission live broadcast, 1967; K.P. Oakley, B.G. Campbell, & T.I. Molleson: *Catalogue of fossil hominids.* Part 3, *Americas, Asia, Australasia.* London: British Museum of Natural History, 1975; S.A. Smith: The fossil human skull from Talgai, Queensland. *Philosophical Transactions of the Royal Society London* B 208:351–387, 1918; A.G. Thorne: Separation or reconciliation? Biological clues to the development of Australian society. In: J. Allen, J. Golson, & R. Jones (eds) *Sunda and Sahul.* London: Academic Press, 1977, pp. 187–204.

Tanner, James Mourilyan (1920–)

Born in the west country of England, Tanner began his study of medicine at the University of London (UL), continued it at the University of Pennsylvania (M.D. 1944) and Johns Hopkins Hospital, Baltimore, Maryland, under a wartime Rockefeller training scheme, and completed it in London in 1945. He subsequently worked in human anatomy at Oxford University, and was lecturer and senior lecturer in physiology at St. Thomas' Hospital, London. During this time, he earned a Ph.D. in physiology from the UL and later a D.Sc. In 1956, he took a position as lecturer at the Institute of Child Health (UL), where he rose to senior lecturer, reader, and finally professor of child health and growth. He became emeritus in 1985. Since the 1980s, he has spent two months a year as a visiting professor at the University of Texas School of Public Health in Houston. He has received honorary doctorates from the Universities of Madrid and Genoa and from Eotvos University of Budapest. In 1993, he was nominated as a foreign honorary member of the American Academy of Arts and Sciences.

Tanner is best known for his book *Growth at Adolescence.* First published in 1955, it continues to be cited in most papers written on child growth. It was the first comprehensive book on biological aspects of growth. While the first edition was not limited to the adolescent period, the second (1962) more thoroughly deals with the growth process at all ages and through time. Tanner has authored more than 250 scientific papers and ten books. The later growth publications include a general book on growth for nonprofessionals (Tanner & G.A. Harrison et al. 1989); a history of the study of human growth (Tanner 1981), reputedly his own favorite work; a huge *Atlas of Children's Growth,* coauthored with R.H. Whitehouse (1982); and an edited set of three volumes on human growth, in its second edition (cf. Tanner & Falkner 1986). He is also one of the founding editors of the journal *Annals of Human Biology* and a founding member of the International Association of Human Auxology. He was one of the leaders of the International Children's Center (Paris) Project, which carried out and coordinated birth-to-maturity longitudinal studies in many European countries using standard methodologies. Working within the International Biological Programme from 1964 to 1974, he headed the Office of Growth and Physique, stimulating standardization of anthropometric measurements and assisting others with instrumentation and data analysis.

There are five other areas, at least, in which Tanner has made major contributions to anthropology and medicine: (1) methods and standards for assessing skeletal maturation; (2) a rating system for pubertal maturation (although often referred to in the United States as "Tanner's stages," he did not develop them but did refine and publicize them); (3) standards and growth charts for both distance growth and growth velocity in height, weight, sitting height, and other parameters; (4) human-growth-hormone therapy in growth disorders; and (5) physique of Olympic athletes.

Phyllis B. Eveleth

See also Auxology; Child-Growth Studies; Growth Studies

Bibliography
SELECTED WORKS
Some notes on the reporting of growth data. *Human Biology* 23:93–159, 1951; *Growth at adolescence.* 2d ed. Oxford: Blackwell, 1962; *The physique of the Olympic athlete.* London: Allen & Unwin, 1964; *A history of the study of human growth.* Cambridge: Cambridge University Press, 1981, pp. 349–356; (with P.B. Eveleth) *Worldwide variation in human growth.* 2d ed. Cambridge: Cambridge University Press, 1990;

(with F. Falkner [eds]) *Human growth*. 3
vols. 2d ed. New York: Plenum, 1986;
(with G.A. Harrison et al.) *Human biology:
An introduction to human evolution, variation,
growth, and adaptability*. 3d ed. London:
Oxford University Press, 1989; (with R.H.
Whitehouse) *Atlas of children's growth*.
London: Academic Press, 1982; (with R.H
Whitehouse & M. Takaishi) Standards from
birth to maturity for height, weight, height
velocity, and weight velocity: British
children, 1965. *Archives of Disease in
Childhood* 41:454–471, 613–635, 1966;
(with R.H. Whitehouse et al.) Effect of
human growth hormone treatment for one
to seven years on growth of 100 children,
with growth hormone deficiency, low
birthweight, inherited smallness, Turner's
syndrome, and other complaints. *Archives of
Disease of Childhood* 46:745–782, 1971;
(with R.H. Whitehouse et al.) *Assessment of
skeletal maturity and prediction of adult height*.
2d ed. London: Academic Press, 1983.

ARCHIVAL SOURCES

J.M. Tanner Papers: Department of
Anthropology, University of Pennsylvania,
325 University Museum, 33rd & Spruce
Streets, Philadelphia, Pennsylvania 19104-
6398.

Taphonomy

Taphonomy is a branch of paleontology concerned with the laws (*nomos*) of burial (*taphos*);
the term was coined by a Russian paleontologist, J.A. Efremov, who offered the classic
definition:

*The chief problem of this branch of science is the
study of the transition (in all its details) of animal remains from the biosphere into the lithosphere,
i.e., the study of the process in . . . which the organisms pass out of the different parts of the biosphere
and, being fossilized, become part of the lithosphere.
The passage from the biosphere into the lithosphere
occurs as a result of many interlaced geological and
biological phenomena. (1940:85)*

Two important terms derived from
taphonomy are "taphonomic agent"—an organism or process that affects the survival and
preservation of animal remains—and
"taphonomic history"—the sum total of
events that have intervened between the death
of the animals in question and the present. In
some cases, the relevant taphonomic history
of an assemblage of specimens does not stop
with preservation or fossilization and may

include discovery, collection, and curation.
Taphonomic history is one aspect of site formation processes; attempts to trace it ally
taphonomy with archeology as well as physical anthropology.

Taphonomy is more properly considered
an approach to the fossil, or archeological,
record than a discipline. Its fundamental tenet is that the fossil or archeological record
cannot be assumed to be an undistorted representation of the animal community from
which it is drawn; the action of various
taphonomic agents may bias or alter the assemblage. Therefore, tracing the taphonomic
history of an assemblage may yield important
information about the ecosystem from which
it was drawn and about the actions and behaviors of those agents. Although in the context of physical anthropology the focus of
taphonomic studies is usually vertebrate remains (bones, teeth, or fossils of these), there
is also a literature on the taphonomy of invertebrates and plants and on the geological processes that affect preservation.

Typical data used in taphonomic analyses may include: (1) the proportions of different species represented, calculated as
Minimum Number of Individuals (MNI); (2)
their body sizes, state of maturity, and habits; (3) the proportions of various skeletal elements of each species; (4) the extent of
articulation or spatial association of anatomical units; (5) the Number of Specimens per
Individual (NSI); (6) various indicators of the
economic utility of various body parts; (7)
patterns of damage to individual elements,
including weathering, trampling, cut marks,
carnivore tooth marks, traces of abrasion, di-
gestion, or chemical erosion; (8) the distribution of bones within the site; (9) the
orientation and geological dip of bones *in situ*;
and (10) the spatial association of bones or
fossils with other items, such as tools or artifacts. From analyses of such data, the researcher tries to deduce, as fully as possible,
what taphonomic agent was primarily responsible for the collection of the bones into an
assemblage; what criteria or properties of the
bones led to their selection and preservation;
and what agents have damaged or winnowed
the assemblage, distorting the paleoecologi-
cal and behavioral information the assemblage
records.

Historically, a primary concern of taphonomic studies has been to determine whether
an assemblage reflects human or nonhuman
activities. Among the early pioneers of such
research is the English geologist and clergy-

man William Buckland (1784–1856), who in 1823 published *Reliquiae Diluvianae*. A confirmed catastrophist, Buckland summarized evidence for a wide range of sites that, he believed, preserved fossils of animals that had been decimated by a worldwide deluge that he identified as the Noachian Flood. One of the most striking parts of this work involved the description of the fossils from Kirkdale Cave, in Yorkshire, England. The animals preserved included extinct cave hyenas and numerous prey animals; by comparing the damage on the bones with that produced by hyenas at the Exeter Zoo, Buckland concluded that the Kirkdale assemblage was collected and damaged by hyenas who denned in the cave. This was one of the first times any paleontologist had addressed the question, How did these bones get here? in a systematic or comparative way. Buckland's informal studies of the bone-collecting and bone-damaging habits of hyenas and other large carnivores was the first of many to document the resemblances and differences in the ways hominids and carnivores modify the surfaces of bones and alter the patterns of bone distribution on the landscape.

Buckland's work exemplifies both of the two main thrusts of taphonomic studies. One is "actualism" or "actualistic studies": the use of experimental evidence obtained from modern circumstances to derive general principles or criteria for the recognition of similar actions in the past. The logic of actualistic studies is often given as the uniformitarian epigram: "The present is the key to the past."

The other thrust of taphonomy, which developed more fully in the twentieth century, is the detailed consideration of the entire fossil assemblage itself. Traditionally, paleontologists tended to collect and examine only those bones or fossils that were nearly complete or that were of special importance in identifying species (especially crania). Formulating a list of species present at the site and acquiring suitable specimens for display were the major concerns. But, as taphonomy has come to occupy the crossroads of paleontology, ecology, physical anthropology, zooarcheology, and ethnoarcheology (Gifford 1981), the practice of collecting every scrap of bone from the site has become more common, making it possible to conduct valid taphonomic analyses.

After Buckland's study, the next important innovation in taphonomy came in 1949, with Raymond A. Dart's (1893–1988) seminal analysis of the Makapan Cave from South Africa (Dart 1949, 1957), which included remains of the hominid *Australopithecus africanus*. Dart was the first to base an interpretation on the proportions of different species, their skeletal element representation, and the damage to those bones. He concluded that the fossils were the remains of animals hunted and dismembered by australopithecines and that some of the bones were used by them as crude tools, an interpretation based on the patterns of breakage and the apparent suitability of the resultant shapes for various tasks. He conducted experiments using broken bones as tools and gathered evidence suggesting (incorrectly) that hyenas never collect bones and could not, therefore, be responsible for the formation of the assemblage. Although Dart's evangelical style hindered acceptance of his ideas, his work was groundbreaking. From that time onward, taphonomic studies were used to deduce the behavior of extinct hominids.

Many subsequent studies have followed upon Dart's work, developing new means of identifying hominid activities in bone or fossil assemblage (see summaries and bibliographies in Andrews 1990; Behrensmeyer & Hill 1980; Binford 1981; Bonnichsen & Sorg 1989; Brain 1981, Grayson 1984; Koch 1989; Shipman 1981).

During the 1960s and 1970s, a wide range of different taphonomic agents were investigated through experiments or observations in natural settings. M.R. Voorhies, a geologist at the University of Nebraska (1969), was the first to experiment with the behavior of bone assemblages subjected to water currents to derive general rules about the transport of skeletal elements. C.K. Brain, a zoologist and former director of the Transvaal Museum in Pretoria (1967 and other works summarized in 1981), was a leader in observing carnivore activities and carcass decay in the wild as contrasted with the effects of human intervention (followed more recently by, for example, Binford 1981; Hill 1984). Brain also pioneered studies examining the relationship between the density or physical strength of a bone and the probability that it would survive various taphonomic events. Voorhies (1969) and the archeologist R.G. Klein (1978) recognized the importance of the distribution of prey species into age classes (based on physical maturity and tooth wear) in making reconstructions of their paleoecology and mode of death (see more recently Klein & Cruz-Uribe 1984; Haynes 1991).

In the 1970s, taphonomic studies first became common among Africanists, many of whom were friends and colleagues. A similar, but largely independent, group of taphonomists developed among Americanists, especially those interested in the peopling of the continent (cf. Bonnichsen 1979; Morlan 1980). The commonality of their concern, problems, and approaches was demonstrated at the First International Bone Modification Conference held in Carson City, Nevada, in 1984 (Bonnichsen & Sorg 1989), where personal contacts and collaborations were established that unified two geographically based schools. The taphonomic approach has now been applied to sites on all continents (Solomon, Davidson, & Watson 1990).

In the early 1980s, several studies opened up new directions in taphonomy. With the observation that cut marks on fossil bones provided a causal link between the bones and stone tools at a site (Bunn 1981; Potts & Shipman 1981), one major concern of taphonomic research became the documentation and interpretation of patterns of damage on fossil bones. Experimental research focused on the marks or breakage inflicted on bones during the processing of carcasses by hominids and carnivores, as well as the damage caused by trampling hooves, transport by water, sedimentary abrasion, weathering, use of bones as tools, and other such events. Scanning electron microscopy of bone surfaces (reviewed in Olsen 1988) and statistical studies of bone assemblages of known taphonomic history were used to characterize various types of damage. This procedure enabled marks or damage of unknown origin to be diagnosed with reasonable confidence, yielding a taphonomic history for an individual specimen. A similar logic has been used in describing and documenting patterns of bone breakage and destruction due to natural or hominid causes (e.g., Johnson 1985). Thus, taphonomic studies have provided pivotal evidence in a number of scenarios and hypotheses about the behavior and the ecology of ancient and more-recent hominids. Of special interest have been food-procurement strategies, such as hunting or scavenging, and considerations of the economic utility of different strategies for targeting, transporting, and processing prey animals (e.g., Binford 1981; Speth 1983; Lyman 1985).

Surveys of bone assemblages and carcasses in unsettled or sparsely inhabited areas provided another major source of information. These data on death assemblages were compared in frequency, distribution across microhabitats, and ecology with the known, living communities of animals as means of discovering how closely death assemblages reflect the communities from which they are drawn (e.g., Behrensmeyer & Dechant-Boaz 1980; Blumenschine 1986; Haynes 1991; Vrba 1976, 1980). These studies forged important links between paleoecology and taphonomy (Behrensmeyer & Kidwell 1985) and provided guidelines for reconstructing past habitats of extinct species, including hominids.

As new techniques of analysis continue to be developed, the taphonomic approach to fossil and archeological assemblages remains central to attempts to reconstruct ancient biology and behavior.

Pat Shipman

See also Australopithecines; Buckland, William; Dart, Raymond A(rthur)

Bibliography
P. Andrews: *Owls, caves, and fossils: Predation, preservation, and accumulation of small mammal bones in caves, with an analysis of the Pleistocene cave faunas from Westbury-sub-Mendip, Somerset.* Chicago: University of Chicago Press, 1990; A.K. Behrensmeyer & D.E. Dechant-Boaz: The recent bones of Amboseli National Park, Kenya, in relation to East African paleoecology. In: A.K. Behrensmeyer & A.P. Hill (eds) *Fossils in the making.* Chicago: University of Chicago Press, 1980, pp. 72–92; A.K. Behrensmeyer & A.P. Hill (eds) *Fossils in the making.* Chicago: University of Chicago Press, 1980; A.K. Behrensmeyer & S. Kidwell: Taphonomy's contribution to paleobiology. *Paleobiology* 11:105–119, 1985.

L.R. Binford: *Nunamuit ethnoarchaeology.* New York: Academic Press, 1978; L.R. Binford: *Bones: Ancient men and modern myths.* New York: Academic Press, 1981; R.J. Blumenschine: *Early hominid scavenging opportunities: Implications of carcass availability in the Serengeti and Ngorongoro.* International Series. No. 283. Oxford: British Archaeological Reports, 1986; R. Bonnichsen: *Pleistocene bone technology in the Beringian refugium.* Archaeological Survey of Canada Paper. No. 89. Mercury Series. Ottawa: National Museum of Canada, 1979; R. Bonnichsen & M. Sorg (eds): *Bone modification.* Orono, Maine: Center for the Study of the First Americans, 1989; C.K. Brain: Hottentot food remains and their bearing on the interpretation of fossil bone assemblages. *Scientific Papers* (Namib Desert Research Station) 32:1–11, 1967.

C.K. Brain: *The hunters or the hunted? An introduction to African cave taphonomy.* Chicago: University of Chicago Press, 1981; W. Buckland: *Reliquiae diluvianae; or, Observations on the organic remains contained in caves, fissures, and diluvial gravel, and on other geological phenomena, attesting the action of an universal deluge.* London: Murray, 1823; H.T. Bunn: Archaeological evidence for meat-eating by Plio-Pleistocene hominids from Koobi Fora and Olduvai Gorge. *Nature* 291:574–577, 1981; R.A. Dart: The predatory implemental technique of *Australopithecus. American Journal of Physical Anthropology* 6:259–284, 1949; R.A. Dart: *The osteodontokeratic culture of Australopithecus prometheus.* Tranvaal Museum Memoirs. No. 10. Pretoria: Transvaal Museum, 1957; J.A. Efremov: Taphonomy: New branch of paleontology. *Pan-American Geologist* 74:81–93, 1940.

D.P. Gifford: Taphonomy and paleoecology: A critical review of archaeology's sister disciplines. In: M.B. Schiffer (ed) *Advances in archaeological method and theory.* Vol. 4. New York: Academic Press, 1981, pp. 365–443; D.K. Grayson: *Quantitative zooarchaeology: Topics in the analysis of archaeological faunas.* New York: Academic Press, 1984; G. Haynes: *Mammoths, mastodons, and elephants: Biology, behavior, and the fossil record.* Cambridge: Cambridge University Press, 1991; A.P. Hill: Hyaenas and hominids: Taphonomy and hypothesis testing. In: R. Foley (ed) *Hominid evolution and community ecology.* London: Academic Press, 1984, pp. 111–128; E. Johnson: Current developments in bone technology. In: M.B. Schiffer (ed) *Advances in archaeological method and theory.* Vol. 8. New York: Academic Press, 1985, pp. 157–235.

R.G. Klein: Stone Age predation on large African bovids. *Journal of Archaeological Science* 5:195–217, 1978; R.G. Klein & K. Cruz-Uribe: *The analysis of animal bones from archaeological sites.* Chicago: University of Chicago Press, 1984; C. Koch: *Taphonomy: A bibliographic guide to the literature.* Orono, Maine: Center for the Study of the First Americans, 1989; R.L. Lyman: Bone frequencies: Differential transport, *in situ* destruction, and the MGUI. *Journal of Archaeological Science* 12:221–236, 1985; R.E. Morlan: *Taphonomy and archaeology in the Upper Pleistocene of the Northern Yukon Territory: A glimpse of the peopling of the New World.* Archaeological Survey of Canada Paper. No. 94. Mercury Series. Ottawa: National Museum of Man, 1980.

S. Olsen (ed): *Scanning electron microscopy in archaeology.* International Series. No. 442. Oxford, British Archaeological Reports, 1988; R.B. Potts & P. Shipman: Cut marks made by stone tools on bones from Olduvai Gorge, Tanzania. *Nature* 291:557, 580, 1981; P. Shipman: *Life history of a fossil: An introduction to taphonomy and paleoecology.* Cambridge: Harvard University Press, 1981; A Solomon, I. Davidson, & D. Watson (eds): *Problem-solving in taphonomy: Archaeological and palaeontology studies from Europe, Africa, and Oceania.* Queensland, Australia: Anthropology Museum, University of Queensland, 1990.

J.D. Speth: *Bone counts and bison kills.* Chicago: University of Chicago Press, 1983; M.R. Voorhies: *Taphonomy and population dynamics of an Early Pliocene vertebrate fauna, Knox County, Nebraska.* Contributions to Geology. Special Paper. No. 1. Wyoming: University of Wyoming Press, 1969; E.S. Vrba: *The fossil Bovidae of Sterkfontein and Kromdraai.* Transvaal Museum Memoir. No. 21. Pretoria: Transvaal Museum, 1976; E.S. Vrba: The significance of bovid remains as indicators of environment and predation patterns. In: A.K. Behrensmeyer & A.P. Hill (eds) *Fossils in the making.* Chicago: University of Chicago Press, 1980, pp. 247–271.

Taung (formerly Taungs)

Taung, the site of the first discovery of an early hominid, *Australopithecus,* lies in the former Buxton Limeworks, 10 km southwest of the village of Taung and 130 km north of Kimberley in the northern Cape Province, South Africa. To the west is the great elevation of the Ghaapplato Dolomite Formation of the Griqualand West Sequence. At intervals along the escarpment marking the easterly face of the plateau, great masses, or tufas, of surface limestone, travertine, and calcrete have formed. The largest series of tufas occurs at Buxton, near Taung. At many places within the limestone tufas are pinkish or reddish patches of "impure limestone," constituting the filling of caves and fissures within the tufas. Some of these discolored masses constitute bone breccias.

The first reported discovery of fossilized bones at the Taung site was in 1919, when seven or eight small fossil baboon skulls were sent to the South African Museum, Cape

Town. On 20 May 1920, a paper on these fossil baboons was read before the Royal Society of South Africa by Sidney Henry Haughton, later director of the Geological Survey of the Union of South Africa and still later honorary director of the Bernard Price Institute for Palaeontological Research of the University of the Witwatersrand, Johannesburg. In the abstract of his paper, which was published in 1925, Haughton suggested that the extinct baboon "may extend back in point of time to a level contemporaneous with the early and possibly pre-Pleistocene of Europe" (Haughton 1925:68).

In November 1924, M. De Bruyn, a quarryman at Buxton, blasted out of one of the old pink fillings in the limestone at Taung a petrified skull whose exposed endocranial cast struck him as being much larger than those of baboons, of which he had personally recovered a number. According to the Czech-American physical anthropologist Aleš Hrdlička (1869–1943), who visited the site in August 1925, "From what he [De Bruyn] could see he thought it was possibly the skull of a young bushman" (cf. Hrdlička 1925:384). The limeworks manager, A.E. Spiers, saved the specimen, along with further baboon fossils. Robert Burns Young (1874–1949), professor of geology at the University of the Witwatersrand (UW), visited the site a week or two after De Bruyn's discovery, as a consultant to the Northern Lime Company. He had been alerted to the presence of fossil baboons by Raymond A. Dart (1893–1988), professor of anatomy at the UW, who had been shown one such specimen, which had been borrowed by his student Josephine Salmons from the son of E.G. Izod, a director and later chairman of the Northern Lime Company. Young selected the large endocast and related breccia with skull parts in it, as well as some baboon specimens, and brought them back to Johannesburg. He handed them over to Dart on 28 November 1924. (For more complete details of the sequence of events related to the discovery, see Tobias 1984.)

On receiving the specimen, Dart proceeded to disengage the fossilized skull from the hard matrix. It became clear to him the specimen's features comprised a then unprecedented blend of human and ape-like characteristics. He called the species represented by the remains *Australopithecus africanus*—and published an account of it in *Nature* (Dart 1925). There, Dart asserted that the Taung specimen was an ape-like higher primate (hence the name *Australopithecus* rather than

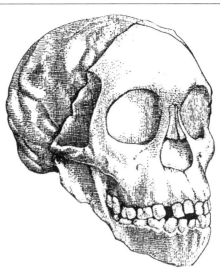

Fig. 1. Drawing of a plaster cast of the face and endocranial cast of the Taung hominid. Drawn by T.L. Poulton, from Grafton Elliot Smith's The Evolution of Man (1927).

Australanthropus), with rudimentary, human-like anatomical features; thus it fulfilled the role of a "missing link" (in an older concept of the Chain of Being). He claimed that it represented a type ancestral to the genus *Homo*. The present-day environment at Taung, the treeless verge of the Kalahari thirstland, and the associated faunal remains led Dart, on the assumption that the environment had not changed much from earlier times, to ascribe to *Australopithecus* a way of life different from that of any extant forest-living ape. Moreover, Dart had the insight and the vision to claim that *Australopithecus* from Taung vindicated Charles Darwin's (1809–1882) prediction in his book *The Descent of Man* (1871) that Africa, and not Asia, would prove to have been the cradleland of human ancestors.

Dart's claims evoked a storm of controversy that was not settled until over twenty-five years later. The reasons for the initial resistance to Dart's claims were complex. For example, while the specimen's juvenile status had undoubtedly been a contributing factor, it is clear also that the morphological pattern shown by the Taung skull—human-like small canine teeth and poise of the skull on the spinal column, with an ape-like small cranial capacity—was at variance with the expected morphological pattern on a widely held paradigm of the time. Furthermore, most workers at that time favored central Asia rather than Africa as the cradle of humankind. With hindsight, we see Taung and *Australopithecus* as an example of what the molecular biologist and philosopher of science Gunther Stent (1972) called a premature discovery. The measure of its prematurity was about twenty-five years; only after 1950, when many new australopithecine specimens had been recovered, thoroughly studied, and compared with much new data on the morphology and variations of the great apes, did Dart and *Australopithecus* gain belated recognition. The swing of opinion to the general acceptance of *Australopithecus* as an ancestral hominid, from about 1950 onward, was further assisted by the replacement of the paradigms of the first quarter of the twentieth century and the uncovering of the Piltdown forgery in 1953–1955.

Dart made no excavations at Taung but, under a U.S. expedition, the American scientist Frank E. Peabody carried out careful and systematic excavations in the area of the original hominid discovery from 1947 to 1950. His work threw much light on the precise whereabouts, the nature, and the stratigraphy of the locality, but no new hominid specimens were recovered. Early in the 1980s, Phillip V. Tobias, director of the Palaeoanthropology Research Unit in the Department of Anatomy at the University of the Witwatersrand, carried out a series of test "digs" to determine the extent of the surviving breccia in the area of the original discovery. As a result, he set in motion a program of annual winter excavations—by Michele Toussaint in 1988 and Jeffrey K. McKee (from 1988 to 1993). McKee's meticulous excavations greatly added to knowledge about the site, its age, stratigraphy, problems of cave formation, and taphonomy (cf. McKee 1993). No new hominid specimen was recovered, and this lack added to the enigma of the Taung child and how it came to be in the Taung cave system. A solution to this taphonomic mystery was suggested by L.R. Berger and R.J. Clarke in 1995. They provided evidence in support of the hypothesis that many of the small animals, whose bones abound in the Taung deposit, and the head of the hominid child itself, had been taken by one of Africa's giant raptors such as the crowned eagle.

The fauna that were described from Taung included insectivores, at least two of which were extinct forms; a bat similar to a living species; several kinds of baboons of the extinct genus *Parapapio* as well as extinct species of the genus *Papio*; a number of rodents; two extinct species of hyrax; an extinct warthog; and several antelopes. A number of new species were recovered by McKee, and his analysis led him to revise the faunal dating of Taung (*vide infra*).

For many years, Taung was regarded as the oldest of the five main southern African australopithecine sites. Yet the evidence for this view was slender, based on sketchy samples of small mammals. Lawrence H. Wells (1908–1980), a South African anatomist and physical anthropologist, questioned this traditional view and concluded that the Taung fauna was more recent than had been believed (Wells 1969). Taung, he inferred, could have been no older than the youngest of the other four main South African sites (Sterkfontein, Kromdraai, Makapansgat, and Swartkrans). Wells' claim appeared to be supported by the geomorphological work of Timothy C. Partridge (1973), the geological analysis of Karl Butzer (1974), and the uranium disequilibrium studies of John C. Vogel (1985; Vogel & Partridge 1984). After a good sequence of cercopithecoid species and datings had been established in East Africa, it became possible for the American paleoanthropologist Eric Delson to reexamine the cercopithecoid fossils from Taung. In 1984, he concluded that the baboon assemblage from Taung (on the assumption that all specimens were coeval) was about 2.3 myo. That dating was more in keeping with the "hominid dating," as the Taung child and the australopithecine specimens of Sterkfontein were classified in the same species, and *A. africanus* from Sterkfontein was dated at that time faunistically to 2.8–2.3 my.

Later uranium disequilibrium studies on samples from various parts of the Buxton sequence proved that the Taung site was not a "closed system" but an "open system." Therefore, the disequilibrium method was inapplicable for the dating of the deposit. The best estimate of the age of the Taung baboons—and presumably of the hominid—was then the latest faunal dating by Delson (Tobias et al. 1993), although McKee found that his newer faunal results made the dating of the Taung fossil mammals ca. 2.8–2.4 my, about the same age as that of Sterkfontein Member 4. The important point was that *A. africanus* from Taung and from Sterkfontein were seen to be virtually synchronic.

During Peabody's and McKee's excavations, many additional bone-bearing cave deposits were located within the former Buxton Limeworks. These ranged from very old deposits with the most ancient of the tufas, the Thabaseek, to more recent deposits containing stone implements of various cultural horizons. Studies of Berger Cave, Quinney Cave, and Tobias Cave were conducted by McKee and his assistants. Along the escarpment, other tufa flows, such as that at Thoming, were found to be bone-bearing in patches. The subtropical Taung had proved to be the most southerly and until recently the most westerly of the many African sites from which ancient hominids had been recovered.

Phillip V. Tobias

See also Australopithecines; Chain of Being; Dart, Raymond A(rthur); Darwin, Charles Robert; Hrdlička, Aleš; Kromdraai; Makapansgat; Piltdown; Sterkfontein; Tobias, Phillip V(allentine)

Bibliography
K.W. Butzer: Paleoecology of South African australopithecines: Taung revisited. *Current Anthropology* 15:367–382, 1974; R.A. Dart: *Australopithecus africanus*, the ape-man of South Africa. *Nature* 115:195–199, 1925; R.A. Dart: Taungs and its significance. *Natural History* 26:315–327, 1926; E. Delson: Cercopithecid biochronology of the African Plio-Pleistocene: Correlation among eastern and southern hominid-bearing localities. *Courier Forschunginstitut Senckenberg* 69:199–218, 1984; S.H. Haughton: Note on the occurrence of a species of baboon in limestone deposits near Taungs (Abstract). *Transactions of the Royal Society of South Africa* 12:68, 1925.

A. Hrdlička: The Taungs ape. *American Journal of Physical Anthropology* 8:379–392, 1925; J.K. McKee: The faunal age of the Taung hominid fossil deposit. *Journal of Human Evolution* 25:363–376, 1993; T.C. Partridge: Geomorphological dating of cave opening at Makapansgat, Sterkfontein, Swartkrans, and Taung. *Nature* 246:75–79, 1973; G. Stent: Prematurity and uniqueness in scientific discovery. *Scientific American* 227:84–93, 1972; P.V. Tobias: *Dart, Taung, and the "missing link": An essay on the life and work of Emeritus Professor Raymond Dart.* Johannesburg: Witwatersrand University Press, 1984.

P.V. Tobias et al.: New isotopic and sedimentological measurements on the Thabaseek deposits and their bearing on the dating of the Taung hominid. *Quaternary Research* 40:360–367, 1993; J.C. Vogel: Further attempts at dating the Taung tufas. In: P.V. Tobias (ed) *Hominid evolution: Past, present, and future.* New York: Liss, 1985, pp. 189–194; J.C. Vogel & T.C. Partridge: Preliminary radiometric ages for the Taung tufas. In: J.C. Vogel (ed) *Late Cainozoic palaeoclimates of the Southern Hemisphere.* Rotterdam: Balkema, 1984, pp. 507–514; L.H. Wells: Faunal subdivision of the Quaternary in South Africa. *South African Archaeological Bulletin* 24:93–95, 1969.

Taylor, Richard Morris Stovin (1903–1992)

The great-grandson of a pioneer missionary to New Zealand, Taylor was trained as a dentist at the University of Otago, where he received his B.D.S. in 1926 and his D.D.S in 1934. His doctoral thesis was an anthropological study of *The Form and Orientation of the Human Palate,* based on Maori and Moriori skeletal material. Advice and instrumentation for this project were provided by T. Wingate Todd (1885–1938) of Western Reserve University, Cleveland, Ohio. From 1930 to 1948, Taylor worked for the New Zealand Department of Health (NZDH). During his tenure at the NZDH, he published reports on the dental health of the Maori (Taylor & Saunders 1938) and Australian Aborigines (Taylor 1949). In 1948, Taylor entered private practice, where he remained until his retirement in 1964. At the same time, he also held a part-time lecturership in physical anthropology at the University of Auckland (UA). During this period, he conducted a major nonmetrical study of the palate and dentition of Maori and Moriori crania (Taylor 1962, 1963). After retiring, Taylor was made an honorary staff member of the Department of Zoology at the UA, and in 1978 he published *Variation in Morphology of Teeth: Anthropologic and Forensic Aspects,* the culmination of his life's work, for which he was awarded a D.Sc. degree from the UA in 1980. During the 1980s, he worked out of the UA Department of Anatomy and continued an active research program (e.g., Taylor 1986). In 1991, he published a monograph on Maori and Aborigine dentition, for which he was awarded a second D.Sc. in 1992, this time from the University of Otago.

Although Taylor's publications were overwhelmingly descriptive and based on skeletal material, his experience as a dentist, especially in the NZDH, guaranteed that his analyses were strongly informed by the dental requirements and cultural practices of living people. It is also of historical interest to note that, in 1937, Taylor presented a paper on "The Dentition of the Piltdown Fossil Man (*Eoanthropus dawsoni*) from a New Aspect," (reprinted in Taylor 1978:362–370), at the Twenty-Third Annual Meeting of the Australian and New Zealand Association for the Advancement of Science, held in Auckland. Based on an examination of casts of Piltdown, Taylor concluded that the putative lower canine tooth was an upper canine, which lead to a general criticism of the dental aspects of the various reconstructions made of the now infamous skull. Although he later claimed that his report constituted the earliest identification of the Piltdown hoax (Taylor 1992), this claim is difficult to substantiate based on the published version of the talk.

John S. Allen

See also New Zealand; Piltdown; Todd, T(homas) Wingate

Bibliography

SELECTED WORKS

The dentition of the Piltdown fossil man (*Eoanthropus dawsoni*) from a new aspect. Title Only. *In: Report of the Twenty-Third Meeting of the Australian and New Zealand Association for the Advancement of Science*. 1937, pp. 201, 245. Complete article reprinted in Taylor 1978, pp. 362–370; Dental caries in children of Northern Territory, Australia. *Dental Journal of Australia* 21:123–137, 1949; Nonmetrical studies in the human palate and dentition in Moriori and Maori skulls. *Journal of the Polynesian Society* 71:83–100, 167–187, 1962; Cause and effect of wear in teeth. *Acta Anatomica* 53:97–167, 1963.

Variation in morphology of teeth: Anthropologic and forensic aspects. Springfield, Illinois: Thomas, 1978; Nonlever action of the mandible. *American Journal of Physical Anthropology* 70:417–421, 1986; *Anatomy and biology of tooth dislocation in pre-European Maoris and Australian Aborigines.* Auckland: Department of Anatomy, School of Medicine, University of Auckland and the New Zealand Dental Research Foundation, 1991; *Look and see through.* Privately published by the author, 1992; (with J.L. Saunders) The dental condition and diet of the Maoris of Maungapohatu village, Urewara. *New Zealand Dental Journal* 34:92–96, 1938.

SECONDARY SOURCES

F. Spencer: *The Piltdown papers, 1908–1955: The correspondence and other documents relating to the Piltdown forgery.* London: Oxford University Press, 1990, p. 131.

Te Rangi Hiroa (1879–1951)

Born in the Taranaki region of the North Island of New Zealand to a Maori mother and an Irish father, Te Rangi Hiroa spent his childhood in a predominantly Maori community. Peter Henry Buck was his European (Pakeha) name; his Maori name was initially Te Materori, which was later changed by elders in his community to Te Rangihiroa. He changed this spelling to Te Rangi Hiroa, probably to make pronunciation easier for non-Maori. He used Te Rangi Hiroa for most of his publications, and whenever he acted as a part or an observer of a Polynesian community (including his own). In 1896, he was admitted to Te Aute College, a high school for Maori boys that was the training ground for a generation of political and social leaders who began the long process of defining a place for Maori in New Zealand (European) society. From there, he entered the University of Otago, where he studied medicine. On graduating in 1904, he became one of the first New Zealand–trained Maori physicians. Later, in 1910, he received an M.D. from Otago for his thesis *Medicine amongst the Maoris in Ancient and Modern Times*. This thorough and in some ways remarkable work is an example of what would now be called biocultural anthropology. His report of the health status (as defined by Western medicine) of the Maori is balanced by a lengthy and well-informed discussion of traditional definitions of illness and methods of healing. Included in this thesis were also some anthropometric (height and weight) data comparing growth rates of Maori and European children. In 1909, he was selected to one of the four seats reserved for Maori in Parliament, which he held until 1914 when he lost the election for an open seat by only 100 votes. During World War I, he served in both the medical corps and the infantry, first at Gallipoli and then in France, where he eventually rose to the rank of lieutenant-colonel in the New Zealand Maori Battalion.

At war's end, Te Rangi Hiroa consulted with the biometrician Karl Pearson (1857–1936) and the anatomist-anthropologist Arthur Keith (1866–1955), both of whom provided advice and access to instruments, on conducting an anthropometric survey of the Maori Battalion as they returned home to New Zealand aboard ship. A total of 814 men were measured, including 424 "full-blooded Maoris" (Te Rangi Hiroa 1922–1923). Like his thesis, this study goes beyond simply reporting Western scientific measurements (although he included plenty of numbers) by presenting an emic perspective on the Maori body. For example, there are extensive discussions of Maori terms for hair form and attitudes toward nose shape. His craniometric analyses followed the lead of the Harvard anthropologist Roland B. Dixon (1875–1934)

(1923) and Louis Sullivan (1892–1925) of the American Museum of Natural History (New York) (1923); though he later wrote that the former could be "disregarded" and the latter "shelved" (1949:67).

Upon returning to New Zealand after World War I, Te Rangi Hiroa became director of Maori hygiene for the Department of Health. It was during this time that he addressed the "inevitable" extinction of the Maori (1924). He pointed out that the stresses that lead to the initial decline in population were being alleviated, and that the population was making a comeback. He believed that admixture and assimilation were inevitable; however, he hoped this would lead "to the evolution of a future type of New Zealander in which . . . the best features of the Maori race will be perpetuated forever" (1924:374). During this period, his work on anthropometry and material culture drew the attention of the staff at the Bernice P. Bishop Museum in Honolulu, in 1926, and he joined their expedition to the Cook Islands, where he again conducted anthropometric measurements (cf. Shapiro & Buck 1936). In 1927, he joined the Bishop Museum as part of its five-year program of research in Polynesia, which was sponsored primarily by the Rockefeller Foundation. Since the New Zealand government would not grant him leave, he had to resign his position with the Department of Health. In 1932, he became a temporary lecturer at Yale University. Six years later, he was appointed professor of anthropology at Yale and director of the Bishop Museum—concurrent posts he held until his death. He was knighted in 1946.

Although physical anthropology formed only a small part of Te Rangi Hiroa's total research output, those publications constitute an important contribution to the field in Polynesia. Most important, as a Maori and a Polynesian, his "home-made" anthropology (cf. Sorrenson 1982) was imbued with a unique sense of identification with his subject matter. In physical anthropology particularly, this resulted in publications of greater depth and broader perspective than were typical of his time.

John S. Allen

See also Keith, (Sir) Arthur; New Zealand; Oceania; Shapiro, Harry Lionel

Bibliography
SELECTED WORKS
Medicine amongst the Maoris in ancient and modern times. M.D. Thesis. University of

Otago School of Medicine, 1910; Maori somatology: Racial averages. *Journal of the Polynesian Society* 31:37–44, 31:159–170, 32:21–28, 32:189–199, 1922–1923; The passing of the Maori. *Transactions and Proceedings of the New Zealand Institute* 55:362–375, 1924; *Vikings of the sunrise.* New York: Stokes, 1938; Arts and crafts of the Cook Islands. *Bernice P. Bishop Museum Bulletin* (Honolulu) 179:1–533, 1944; *The coming of the Maori.* Wellington: Whitcombe & Tombs, 1949; (with H.L. Shapiro) The physical characters of the Cook Islanders. *Memoirs of the Bernice P. Bishop Museum* 12:3–35, 1936.

ARCHIVAL SOURCES
Peter Buck Papers: Alexander Turnbull Library, National Library of New Zealand, P.O. Box 12-349, Wellington, New Zealand.

SECONDARY SOURCES
J.B. Condliffe: *Te Rangi Hiroa: The life of Sir Peter Buck.* Christchurch: Whitcombe & Tombs, 1971; R.B. Dixon: *The racial history of man.* New York: Scribner's, 1923; G.S. Roydhouse: Te Rangi Hiroa. *Journal of the Polynesian Society* 60:243–254, 1961; M.P.K. Sorrenson: Polynesian corpuscles and Pacific anthropology: The home-made anthropology of Sir Apirana Ngata and Sir Peter Buck. *Journal of the Polynesian Society* 91:7–27, 1982; M.P.K. Sorrenson (ed): *Na To Hoa Aroha: The correspondence of Sir Apirana Ngata and Sir Peter Buck, 1925–1950.* 3 vols. Auckland: Auckland University Press, 1986–1988; L.R. Sullivan: The racial diversity of the Polynesian people. *Journal of the Polynesian Society* 32:79–84, 1923.

Tedeschi, Enrico (1860–1931)

Born in Trieste, Italy, Tedeschi was initially interested in sociology but had his interest in anthropology awakened by Giuseppe Sergi (1841–1936). He was one of the founding members, in 1893, of the Società Romana di Antropologia. In 1899, he began teaching anthropology at the Faculty of Sciences at the University of Padua. In 1903, he was elected titular professor, and in the same year he founded at Padua the Institute of Anthropology and a laboratory of psychophysical techniques.

Tedeschi's principal anthropological interest was craniological research. Due largely to a sort of modesty that led him to produce only original and perfect scientific works, he unfortunately left few publications. Among them, the most important, although incomplete, was his *Sistema di Craniologia* (1906), of which he wrote only the first part. In it, he presented some new principles and methods in craniology. Indeed, he is recognized as the precursor of the movement that led to the orthogonality rule of the German physical anthropologist Hermann Klaatsch (1863–1916), and to Frédéric Falkenburger (b. 1890) and his law of parallelism of the basicranial axis with the parietal chord. Tedeschi himself also conceived and designed several innovative craniological instruments.

He died in Padua on 5 November 1931.

Brunetto Chiarelli
Giuseppe D'Amore

See also Italy; Sergi, Giuseppe

Bibliography
SELECTED WORKS

Studi sulla simmetria del cranio. *Atti della Società Romana di Antropologia* 4:245–279, 1897; Le aree del cranio. *Atti della Società Romana di Antropologia* 6:153–159, 1899–1900; Ricerche morfologiche. *Atti della Società Romana di Antropologia* 7:198–213, 1900–1901; Crani romani moderni. *Atti della Società Romana di Antropologia* 8:297–335, 1901–1902; *Sistema di Craniologia*. Padua: Drucker, 1906; Nuovi probemi di geometria cranica. *Rivista di Antropologia* 20:3–20, 1916.

SECONDARY SOURCES

S. Sergi: Necrologio di Enrico Tedeschi. *Rivista di Antropologia* 29:669–673, 1930–1932.

Teilhard de Chardin, Pierre (1881–1955)

Born near Orcines (situated a few miles west of Clermont-Ferrand), Puy-de-Dôme, in central France, Teilhard began his formal education in 1892 at the Jesuit college of Nôtre-Dame-de-Mongré near Villefranche-sur-Saône. In 1899, he entered the Society of Jesus, serving his novitiate at Aix-en-Provence, near Marseilles. From there, he was moved to Jersey, where he remained until September 1905, whereupon he was sent to Cairo. There he taught chemistry and physics in a secondary school. During the three years he spent in Egypt, he completed a geological study of *The Eocene Strata of the Minieh Region,* which was published in 1909. Then, in 1908, Teilhard was moved to England, to the Jesuit seminary at Ore House near Hastings in Sussex, to complete his theological training. On 24 August 1911 he was ordained into the priesthood, and on 14 July 1912 he formally completed his undergraduate theological studies. It was during this period that he became friends with the geologist-collector Charles Dawson (1864–1916), who is regarded by many as the primary architect of the forgery perpetrated at Piltdown (Sussex) ca. 1912. The basis of their association was a common interest in Wealden fossils, and it was through Dawson that Teilhard's valuable collection of Wealden fossil plants was relayed to the Natural History Museum in London, where the contents were subsequently described and published by the Cambridge botanist Albert C. Seward (1863–1941) in 1913. Although Teilhard's association with Dawson has implicated him in this infamous forgery, the case against him does not withstand scrutiny (Spencer 1990). Teilhard left Hastings in 1912 and spent the next two years in Paris studying paleontology at the Institut Catholique and the Muséum National d'Histoire Naturelle (MNHN). It was in the latter institution that Teilhard established a lifelong relationship with the paleoanthropologist Marcellin Boule (1861–1942) and the archeologist Abbé Henri Breuil (1877–1961).

Teilhard's graduate studies were interrupted by the outbreak of World War I. Throughout the war, he served as a stretcher-bearer with the Second Regiment of North African Zouaves and was frequently mentioned in dispatches for his conspicuous bravery. He received the Croix de Guerre and made Chevalier de la Légion d'honneur for his war service (Cuénot 1965:25).

After demobilization in 1919, he returned to Paris. Between 1920 and 1922 (during which time he successfully completed his doctoral thesis, *Les Mammifères de l'Éocene inférieur français et leurs gisements*), Teilhard served as an adjunct lecturer in geology at the Institut Catholique. After receiving his doctorate in 1922, he became a lecturer in geology at the École des Sciences, where he formed a close relationship with Jean Piveteau (b. 1898). In 1923, Teilhard was sent to China to work for a year with Pére Emile Licent, who had established a Museum of Natural History in the Jesuit mission at Tientsin. This, the first of several visits to China during the next decade, introduced Teilhard to the research potential of Chinese paleoanthropology (cf. Teilhard de Chardin & Licent 1924). His second visit to Tientsin (1926–1927) allowed him not only to continue fieldwork with Licent in Sang-kan-ho and eastern Mongolia, but also to visit Peking (now Beijing) where he met, among others, the Canadian anatomist Davidson Black (1884–1934) at the Peking Union Medical College, and visited Choukoutien (now Zhoukoudian), which at that time was attracting considerable attention following Black's identification of the hominid status of the teeth found there in the early 1920s by the Austrian geologist Otto Zdansky. By the time Teilhard returned to China in 1929, the excavations at Zhoukoudian had revealed that it was a veritable treasure house of hominid remains, but it was not until 1931, when he returned again to Beijing, that he was able to collaborate in the excavations at Zhoukoudian.

In the meantime, he spent the summer of 1929 with the Chinese paleontologist C.C. Young (Yang Zhongjian) (1897–1979) surveying the loess lands of western Shansi and northern Shensi provinces (cf. Teilhard de Chardin & Young 1930), followed by a brief stint with the Citroën Trans-Asia Expedition (October 1929–February 1930). He then returned briefly to France en route to the United States. In February 1931, he left San Francisco for China, where he remained until 1936 (except for a three-month visit to the United States in the summer of 1933). It was during this period that he was associated with the excavations at Zhoukoudian (cf. Teilhard de Chardin & W.C. Pei [Pei Wenzhong] 1932) and conducted surveys elsewhere in the country (cf. Teilhard de Chardin & Young 1932, 1935; Teilhard de Chardin, Young, & Pei 1935).

After an interlude in Paris (during which time he completed the manuscript of his best-known work, *Le Phénomène humain* [The Phenomenon of Man]), in 1939, he returned to Beijing, where he spent the war years. In 1945, he was repatriated. He remained in Paris from 1946 to 1950, then moved to New York, where he was associated with the Wenner-Gren Foundation for Anthropological Research, for which he made two trips to South Africa.

Although he made significant contributions to the geology and paleoanthropology of China, Teilhard is more widely known for his philosophical writings, particularly *The Phenomenon of Man* (published posthumously), in which he endeavored to harmonize evolution with Christian theology. In a nutshell, he viewed the process of hominization of the biosphere in teleological terms, in which biostructure and function were ultimately directed to the emergence of human consciousness (noosphere) and its ultimate union with the Omega (what the British biologist Julian Huxley took to be the equivalent of a "cosmic Christ"). Teilhard's treatise was severely criticized by a number of scientists, most notably the American paleontologist George Gaylord Simpson (1902–1984), who was clearly at odds with its mysticism and use of such dubious principles as Lamarckism and orthogenesis (cf. Simpson 1960). But despite the scientific criticism leveled at it, Teilhard's book, and the scientific-religious worldview it projects, has become a favorite among those anxious to embrace both science and the Christian faith.

Teilhard died in New York on Easter Sunday (10 April), 1955.

Frank Spencer

See also Asian Paleoanthropology; Black, Davidson; Boule, Marcellin; Breuil, Henri; China; Pei Wenzhong; Piltdown; Simpson, George Gaylord; Wenner-Gren Foundation for Anthropological Research; Woodward, (Sir) Arthur Smith; Zhoukoudian

Bibliography
SELECTED WORKS

Le cas de l'homme de Piltdown. *Revue des questions scientifiques* (Bruxelles) 77:149–155, 1920; Early man in China. *Institut de Géo-Biologie* 7:1–99, 1941; *Le phénomènon humain.* Paris: Editions du Seuil, 1959. English translation *The phenomenon of man* by B. Wall. New York: Harper & Row, 1959; (with E. Licent) On the discovery of a Palaeolithic industry in northern China. *Bulletin of the Geological Society of China* 3:45–50, 1924; (with W.C. Pei) The lithic industry of the *Sinanthropus* deposits in Choukoutien. *Bulletin of the Geological Society of China* 11:315–364, 1932; (with C.C. Young) Preliminary observations on the pre-Loessic and post-Pontian Formation in western Shansi and northern Shensi. *Memoirs of the Geological Society of China* 8:1–37, 1930.

(with C.C. Young) On the Neolithic (and possibly Palaeolithic) finds in Mongolia, Sinkiang, and west China. *Bulletin of the Geological Society of China* 12:83–104, 1932; (with C.C. Young) The Cenozoic sequence in the Yangtze Valley. *Bulletin of the Geological Society of China* 14:161–178, 1935; (with C.C. Young & W.C. Pei) On the Cenozoic formations of Kwangsi and Kwangtung. *Bulletin of the*

Geological Society of China 14:179–210, 1935; For a complete listing of Teilhard's publications and unpublished manuscripts, see C. Cuénot: *Teilhard de Chardin: A biographical study*. Baltimore: Helicon, 1965.

ARCHIVAL SOURCES

See C. Cuénot: *Pierre Teilhard de Chardin: Le grandes étapes de son évolution*. Paris: Librairie Plon, 1958. English translation *Teilhard de Chardin: A biographical study* by V. Colimore and edited by R. Hague. Baltimore: Helicon, 1958 for details regarding location of his post–World War I correspondence. For his early letters, see: P. Teilhard de Chardin: *Letters from Hastings, 1908–1912*. New York: Herder, 1968; and *Letters from Paris, 1912–1914*. New York: Herder, 1967.

PRIMARY AND SECONDARY SOURCES

A.C. Seward: A contribution to our knowledge of Wealden floras with special reference to a collection of plants from Sussex. *Quarterly Journal of the Geological Society of London* 69:85–116, 1913; G.C. Simpson: Review of *The phenomenon of man*. *Scientific American* 202:201–207, 1960; F. Spencer: *Piltdown: A scientific forgery*. London: Oxford University Press, 1990.

ten Kate, Herman F.C. (1858–1931)[1]

Born in Amsterdam, The Netherlands, ten Kate entered Leiden University in 1877 and studied medicine, geography, ethnology, and non-Western languages. While at Leiden, he came under the influence of the ethnologist Pieter J. Veth (1814–1895). On completing his studies at Leiden in 1879, ten Kate went to Paris, where he studied for a year under Paul Topinard (1830–1911) at the École d'Anthropologie, and then to Berlin, where for another year he took instruction in ethnology under Adolf Bastian (1826–1905). Following this, he went to the University of Heidelberg, where he received a Ph.D. in zoology for his dissertation *Zur Craniologie der Mongolöiden* (1882). At this juncture, ten Kate embarked on a one-year field trip to the United States commissioned by the Dutch government and the Société d'Anthropologie de Paris. It was during this brief visit that he made several important contacts with American anthropological workers attached to the Bureau of American Ethnology (BAE), in particular Frank H. Cushing (1857–1900). An account of this initial visit can be found in ten Kate's book *Reizen en onderzoekingen in Noord Amerika* (1885a). In the summer of 1885, he accompanied Prince Bonaparte (1858–1924) on a tour of Scandinavia and Lapland, and the following year he accepted the prince's commission to visit Dutch Guiana, where he made an ethnographic study. From there, he returned to Holland via Venezuela.

Through his connections with Cushing at the BAE, ten Kate was invited in 1887 to act as chief physical anthropologist in the Hemenway Southwestern Archaeological Expedition. In this capacity, he spent the next year working in the American Southwest, where he made a number of important studies that included a major anthropometric survey of Indian groups of the region, as well as a collaborative study, with Jacob L. Wortman of the U.S. Army Medical Museum, Washington, D.C., of the hyoid bone in pre-Columbian Pueblo skeletal material (ten Kate & Wortman 1890). It was during this period that ten Kate (1888) took issue with Daniel Garrison Brinton's (1837–1899) pluralistic hypothesis on the origin of the American Indians (cf. Brinton 1888). Ten Kate supported the view that the American Indians had been derived exclusively from Asia.

Between 1890 and 1892, under the auspices of the Dutch government and the Royal Geographical Society, ten Kate explored Indonesia, Australia, and Polynesia. In the winter of 1892, he crossed the Chilean Andes into Argentina, where in 1893 he became a member of the Calchaqui Expedition under Francisco Moreno (1852–1919) of the Museo de La Plata. Following this expedition, he returned to Holland—but not before accepting Moreno's invitation to become curator of physical anthropology at the Museo de Ciencias Naturales de La Plata. In 1895, he returned to Argentina to take up his curator duties, which enabled him to travel extensively throughout the country and neighboring Paraguay. Two years later, he resigned his position at the La Plata Museum and moved to Japan, where he practiced medicine for the next eleven years. During this sojourn in Japan, ten Kate married a Japanese woman, who accompanied him in 1909 to Europe, where they remained until 1913 before returning to Japan.

In 1919, ten Kate lost his wife in the influenza epidemic, and soon thereafter he returned to Europe. Unable to settle there, he finally moved to North Africa, where he died on 5 February 1931. During his last decade, ten Kate's health went into a sharp decline, which greatly reduced his capacity for sustained research and writing. (For further details on ten Kate's anthropological researches in North America, see Hovens 1989.)

Editor's note

1. Since Kate is better known as "ten Kate," he has been listed here rather than with the K entries.

Frank Spencer

See also Argentina; Brinton, Daniel Garrison; Moreno, Francisco José Pascacio; Topinard, Paul

Bibliography
SELECTED WORKS

Zur Craniologie der Mongolöiden: Beobachtungen und Messungen. Berlin: Schumacher, 1882; *Reizen en onderzoekingen in Noord Amerika.* Leiden: Brill, 1885a; Sur les crânes de Lagoa Santa. *Bulletins de la Société d'Anthropologie de Paris* 8:240–244, 1885b; On the alleged Mongolian affinities of the American race: A reply to Dr. Daniel Garrison Brinton. *Science* 12:227–228, 1888; Ethnographische und anthropologische Mitteilungen aus dem amerikanischen Südwesten und aus Mexiko. *Zeitschrift für Ethnologie* 21:664–668, 1889a; The Hemenway Southwestern Archaeological Expedition. *Internationales Archiv für Ethnologie* 2:48–49, 1889b.

Somatological observations on the Indians of the Southwest. *Journal of American Ethnology and Archaeology* 3:119–144, 1892a; Sur la question de la pluralité et de la parenté des races en Amérique. *Comptes rendus du huitième Congrès International des Américanistes* (Paris, France, 1890). Paris: Leroux, 1892b, pp. 288–294; Contribution à l'anthropologie de quelques peuples d'Océanie. *L'Anthropologie* 4:279–300, 1893a; Contribution à la craniologie des Araucans argentins. *Revista del Museo de La Plata* 4:209–220, 1893b; *Anthropologie des anciens habitants de la région calchaquie.* La Plata: Talleres de Publicaciones del Museo de La Plata, 1896.

Description des caractères physiques des Indiens Guayaquis. *Annales del Museo de La Plata* 2:25–38, 1897; Matériaux pour servir à l'anthropologie des Indiens de la République Argentine. *Revista del Museo de La Plata* 12:31–64, 1904; (with J.L. Wortman) On anatomical characteristics of the hyoid bone of the pre-Columbian Pueblo Indians of Arizona. In: *Comptes*

rendus du quatrième Congrès International des Américanistes (Berlin, Germany, 1888). Berlin: Kühl, 1890, pp. 263–270.

ARCHIVAL SOURCES

Unlike his correspondence, ten Kate's private papers have not survived. The primary location of his private and professional correspondence is: Rijksmuseum voor Volkenkunde, Steenstraat 1, P.O. Box 212, NL-2300 AE Leiden, Netherlands. This is essentially a photocopy collection made by Pieter Hovens (personal communication) of ten Kate's surviving correspondence in European and American archives.

SECONDARY SOURCES

D.G. Brinton: On the alleged Mongolian affinities of the American race. *Science* 12:121–123, 1888; J. Heyink & F.W. Hodge: Herman Frederik Carel ten Kate. *American Anthropologist* 33:415–418, 1931; P. Hovens: *Herman F.C. ten Kate Jr., 1858–1931: En de antropologie der Nord-Amerikaanse Indianen.* Meppel: Krips, 1989; P. Hovens: Herman F.C. ten Kate, 1858–1931: Anthropologist and Indianist. *PAN: Physical Anthropology News* 9:1–4, 1990.

Terry, Robert James (1871–1966)

Born in St. Louis, Missouri, Terry spent two years at Cornell University, where he studied under the zoologist-anthropologist Burt G. Wilder (1841–1925) and the comparative anatomist Simon Gage (1851–1944), before going on to the College of Physicians and Surgeons of Columbia University in 1895. However, for largely financial reasons, Terry was obliged to leave New York and complete his M.D. degree at the Missouri Medical College (MMC) in St. Louis (1895). This was followed by a year of postgraduate study under (Sir) William Turner (1832–1916) at the University of Edinburgh, Scotland. It was largely through Turner's influence that Terry acquired a lifelong interest in anthropology (and the idea of establishing a major osteological collection). On returning to St. Louis in 1899, he joined the faculty of the new medical school at Washington University (which had been formed from a merger of the MMC with the existing Medical Department of Washington University). In 1900, Terry was promoted from assistant professor to full professor and head of the department—positions he retained until his retirement in 1941.

From the outset, Terry not only began

offering regular courses in physical anthropology, but also initiated the collection of the skeletons of dissected human cadavers for research purposes. In fact, until the arrival of T. Wingate Todd (1885–1938) at Case Western Reserve University at Cleveland, Ohio, in 1912 and the initiation of his equally famous collection, Terry's accumulating skeletal collection was unique. Additions to the Terry Collection continued until 1965, at which time the entire collection (1,636 skeletons) was transferred to the National Museum of Natural History in Washington, D.C.

Terry's interest in physical anthropology was further enhanced through his friendships with the then fledgling German anthropologist Eugen Fischer (1874–1964), whom he met in Freiberg while on study-leave in 1903, and the Smithsonian anthropologist Aleš Hrdlička (1869–1943). Although Terry's association with Hrdlička appears to date from the late 1890s, when they both joined the American Association of Anatomists, it was not until World War I that their friendship blossomed. Taking advantage of a course in anthropometry and anthropology that Hrdlička offered at that time in his division at the National Museum, Terry sent a number of faculty and students from his department to receive instruction from him. Furthermore, it appears that it was Hrdlička who suggested to Terry the idea of founding the Anthropological Society of St. Louis (now defunct) in 1920. In fact, during the 1920s and 1930s Terry's department emerged as an influential research center. Indicative of this trend was the arrival of Mildred Trotter (1899–1991) in the department and the decision of Raymond A. Dart (1893–1988), one of the first recipients of a Rockefeller Travelling Fellowship granted in 1920–1921, to choose Terry as his mentor and to spend six months working in St. Louis. In addition to serving as an associate editor of Hrdlička's fledgling *American Journal of Physical Anthropology,* Terry also shared Hrdlička's aspirations for development of academic physical anthropology in the United States—and in this regard he played a significant supporting role in the movement that led to Hrdlička's founding of the American Association of Physical Anthropologists in 1930.

Terry died in Weston, Massachusetts, on 18 April 1966.

Robert W. Sussman

See also American Association of Physical Anthropologists; Dart, Raymond A(rthur);

Fischer, Eugen; Hrdlička, Aleš; Todd, T(homas) Wingate

Bibliography
SELECTED WORKS

The nasal skeleton of *Amblystoma punctatus* (Linnaeus). *Transactions of the Academy of Science of St. Louis* 16:95–124, 1906; *The primordial cranium of the cat.* Baltimore: Waverly, 1917; *An introduction to the study of human anatomy.* New York: Macmillan, 1929; Osteology and articulations. In: J. Schaeffer (ed) *Morris' human anatomy.* 10th ed. Sections 3–4. Philadelphia: Blakiston, 1942; Memories of a long life in St. Louis. Part 1. *Missouri Historical Society Bulletin* 11:123–140, 1955.

ARCHIVAL SOURCES

A small collection of letters (ca. 1920–1930s) can be found in A. Hrdlička Papers: National Anthropological Archives, National Museum of Natural History, Smithsonian Institution, Washington, D.C. 20560.

SECONDARY SOURCES

M. Trotter: Robert James Terry, M.D., January 24, 1871–April 18, 1966. *American Journal of Physical Anthropology* 25:97–98, 1966; M. Trotter: Robert J. Terry, 1871–1966. *American Journal of Physical Anthropology* 56:503–508, 1981.

Teshik-Tash (Uzbekistan)

In 1938, during excavations in the cave of Teshik-Tash in the Bajsun-Tau Mountains of southern Uzbekistan, the Russian archeologist A.P. Okladnikov (1908–1982) discovered a partially flexed burial of a juvenile human in the uppermost of the Middle Paleolithic levels of the site (Okladnikov 1940; Gremyatskij & Nesturkh 1949). The partial skeleton was closely associated with horns of wild goats (*Capra sibirica*), and it has long been assumed that those horns represented grave goods as part of the intentional burial of the individual; however, more than 95 percent of the fauna in the site is *Capra sibirica*, making it possible that the association is fortuitous.

The Teshik-Tash 1 partial skeleton, which consists of most of the skull and major (but fragmentary) portions of the postcranial skeleton of a juvenile between eight and ten years old, was originally attributed by Okladinokov (1940) and the anthropologist Georgy Debetz (1905–1969) (1940) to the Neandertals, based primarily on the generally robust and archaic nature of the facial skeleton. This view was challenged in 1945 by the German paleoanthropologist Franz Weidenreich (1873–1948), who maintained that it represented an immature individual of the same group as the Skhūl sample and hence a transitional form between late archaic (or Neandertal-like) population and early modern humans, a view subsequently adopted by Debetz. More recently, a reconstruction of the "adult" form of the Teshik-Tash 1 skull has shown that it most closely resembles the Near Eastern Neandertals Amud 1 and Shanidar 1 (Alexeev 1981). This view has been reinforced by comparisons of the specimens to a non-Neandertal late archaic human (Irhoud 3) (Hublin & Tillier 1981) and a Near Eastern early modern human (Qafzeh 11) (Tillier 1984), and through an analysis of its femur (Ruff, Walker, & Trinkaus 1994) that confirms its robust, archaic shaft morphology.

The Teshik-Tash 1 partial skeleton, therefore, provides a well-preserved late-juvenile partial skeleton with which to analyze patterns of growth and development for the Neandertals. It also documents that a Neandertal craniofacial morphology was present in Middle Paleolithic populations at least as far east as Uzbekistan, presumably through genetic contact ultimately with populations in the region of the Black Sea and the Zagros Mountains.

Erik Trinkaus

See also Debetz, Georgy Frantsevich; Neandertals; Russia; Skhūl Mugharet es- (Israel); Weidenreich, Franz

Bibliography
V.P. Alexeev: Fossil man on the territory of the USSR and related problems. In: D. Ferembach (ed) *Les processus de l'hominisation*. Paris: CNRS, 1981, pp. 183–188; G.F. Debetz: Sur les particularités anthropologiques de la squelette humanine obtenue à la grotte de Teshik-Tach. *Académie des Sciences SSSR Uzbekistan* 1(1):46–71, 1940; M.A. Greymatskij & M.F. Nesturkh (eds): *Teshik-Tash*. (In Russian). Moscow: Moscow State University, 1949; J.-J. Hublin & A.M. Tillier: The Mousterian juvenile mandible from Irhoud (Morocco): A phylogenetic interpretation. In: C.B. Stringer (ed) *Aspects of human evolution*. London: Taylor & Francis, 1981, pp. 167–185.
A.P. Okladnikov: Neanderthal man and his culture in central Asia. *Asia* 40:357–361, 427–429, 1940; C.B. Ruff, A. Walker, & E. Trinkaus: Postcranial robusticity in *Homo*. III. Ontogeny. *American Journal of Physical Anthropology* 93:35–54, 1994; A.M. Tillier: L'enfant *Homo* 11 de Qafzeh (Israël) et son apport à la compréhension des modalités de la croissance des squelettes moustériens. *Paléorient* 10:7–48, 1984; F. Weidenreich: The Paleolithic child from the Teshik-Tash Cave in southern Uzbekistan (central Asia). *American Journal of Physical Anthropology* 3:151–162, 1945.

Testut, Léo (1849–1925)

Born in Saint-Avit-Senieur (Dordogne), France, Testut began his scientific career at the University of Bordeaux, where he received his doctoral degree in anatomy and physiology in 1884. On completing his studies at Bordeaux, Testut spent a brief period at the University of Lille before moving to Lyon, where he was installed as professor of anatomy in 1885. Testut remained in Lyon for the remainder of his career.

Although primarily an anatomist, Testut devoted a significant part of his time to anthropology. His interest in anthropology appears to have emerged while he was studying medicine at Bordeaux, where he participated in the founding of the Anthropological Society of Bordeaux and the Southwest in 1884. In Lyon, his summer vacations were invariably devoted to field excursions and the occasional excavation of archeological sites. He was also a member of the Société d'Anthropologie de Lyon, which had been founded by the archeologist Ernest Chantre (1843–1924) in 1881. Testut became president of this society in 1890.

In 1883, he was admitted to the Société d'Anthropologie de Paris, and soon thereafter he was awarded the Broca Prize for his publication *Les anomalies musculaires chez l'homme expliquées par l'anatomie comparée* (Muscular Anomalies of Man Explained by Comparative Anatomy) (cf. Testut 1884a). By studying normal and abnormal variations of the human body, and comparing these observations with other animals, Testut believed he could find evidence supporting the transformist theory of evolution.

His three-volume *Traité d'Anatomie Humaine* (1889–1894) is considered a masterly work and has been translated into several languages. His major anthropological work, however, is the study of the Chancelade skeleton, which was published in 1890. While many of his propositions regarding this

Magdalenian skeleton are no longer accepted (e.g., the skeleton's Eskimo affinities and the opposability of the great toe), the work itself is still considered a valuable reference source.

On his retirement, Testut moved to Beaumont (Périgord), where he devoted his remaining years to a history of the town and surrounding region.

Denise Ferembach

See also France; Société d'Anthropologie de Paris

Bibliography
SELECTED WORKS
    Les anomalies musculaires chez l'homme expliquées par l'anatomie comparée. Paris: Masson, 1884a; *Contribution à l'anatomie comparée des races nègres.* Memoirs. No. 2 and No. 3. Bordeaux: Bellier, 1884b; *Anatomie anthropologique: Qu'est-ce-que l'homme pour un anatomiste.* [Leçon d'ouverture du cours d'anatomie, faite à la Faculté de médecine de Lyon]. Paris: Bureau des deux revues, 1887; *Traité d'Anatomie Humaine* 3 vols. Paris: Doin, 1889–1894; Recherches anthropologiques sur le squelette quaternaire de Chancelade, Dordogne. *Bulletin de la Société d'Anthropologie de Lyon* 8:131–246, 1890. Reprinted in Lyon: Pitrat, 1889; *Contribution à l'anatomie comparée des races nègres.* Memoir. No. 4. Lyon: Pitrat, 1890.

SECONDARY SOURCES
    P. Bonjean: Le Professeur Léo Testut. *Le mois scientifique bordelais* 12:1–2, 1980; M. Dubreuil-Chambardel: Eloge de M. le Professeur Testut. *Bulletins et Mémoires de la Société d'Anthropologie de Paris* 6:4–5, 1925; D. Ferembach: Léo Testut, 1849–1925. In: History of biological anthropology in France. *International Association of Human Biologists: Occasional Papers.* Part 2. Vol. 2. Newcastle upon Tyne: IAHB, 1987, pp. 1–46; R. Verneau: Le Professeur Léo Testut. *L'Anthropologie* 23:183–186, 1925.

Thailand

Although it is possible to document the activity of foreign investigators in Thailand prior to the twentieth century—such as the British anatomist Arthur Keith (1866–1955), whose anthropological career can be traced to the years he spent as a medical officer in the province of Bangtaphan (1889–1892), it was not until after World War I that physical anthropology became a concern of Thai academics and scientists. This movement originated with the arrival in Bangkok in 1926 of Edgar Davidson Congdon (1879–1965), a Harvard-trained zoologist who had received his doctorate in 1912 for a study of the effect of radium on animals (cf. Congdon 1908–1913). Prior to coming to Thailand, Congdon had been an associate professor at the Peking Union Medical College in China. In Bangkok, he succeeded C.W. Stump (1891–1971) as professor and head of the Anatomy Department in the Faculty of Medicine at Siriraj Hospital of Chulalongkorn University, which had been founded in 1917 by King Rama VI.

During his tenure at Chulalongkorn (1926–1931), Congdon initiated a number of anatomical studies on the Thai population, as well as the study of metrical and nonmetrical characters in adult Thai males (cf. Congdon, Sangvichien, & Vachananda 1987). These studies were undertaken with the assistance of Thai medical students. Among this group were Sood Sangvichien (1909–) and Sangiam Huta Sankas (1899–1939), both of whom were sent to the United States on Rockefeller study scholarships in 1931–1932. Sankas, who had already published an article in the *American Journal of Physical Anthropology* (1930), spent a year in Washington, D.C., working under Aleš Hrdlička (1869–1943) in the Division of Physical Anthropology at the National Museum of Natural History, Smithsonian Institution. Sood Sangvichien studied anatomy and physical anthropology under T. Wingate Todd (1885–1938) at Case Western Reserve University in Cleveland, Ohio.

On their return to Thailand in 1932 both men were employed in the Anatomy Department at Siriraj Hospital. Sangiam Huta Sankas assumed teaching responsibilities in all areas of the medical curriculum, which left him little time to pursue his research interests in physical anthropology. His untimely death in 1939 robbed the discipline of an effective teacher and a promising researcher. Sood Sangvichien was appointed acting head of the department (replacing Congdon, who by that time had returned to the United States)—a position he held until 1944, when he was promoted to the rank of full professor and department head. This promotion coincided with a major reorganization of the medical faculties in Bangkok, with Siriraj Hospital becoming the nucleus of the newly created University of Medical Science. In 1969, it was renamed Mahidol University, after Prince Mahidol (1892–1992), in recognition of his efforts to modernize medical education in Thailand.

TABLE 1. Summary of Thai Dissertations in Physical Anthropology Faculty of Medicine, Siriraj Hospital, Mahidol University 1950s–1990s

Author	Year	Title of Dissertation
*Bachelor (B.Sc.) Dissertations in Medical Science**		
T. Aranyapal		
V. Danasiriraks	1975	Ergonomic anthropometric data on Thai male
Yaovarak Chansilpa & Nalinee D. Vivath	1978	Humerus of the Thai
Masters (M.Sc.) Dissertations in Anatomy		
Sitthi S. Srisopark	1968	A study of the size of permanent teeth, shovel-shaped incisors and paramolar tubercle in Thai skull
Kanda Chaipakdee	1969	A study on Thai and Chinese femora
Kamontip Ratanapairote	1972	Pelvic dimensions among Thai and Chinese
Preecha Dhanvarajorn	1979	The tibiae of Thai and Chinese
Somsiri Ratansasuwan	1984	Sex assessment of femur by discriminant analysis
Chaynit Manoonpol	1992	The cervical vertebrae in Thai
*Doctoral (D.Sc.) Dissertations in Anatomy**		
Dhera Uthayanung	1951	Cranial capacity, cranial module dimensions, and indices in Thai and Chinese
Sanjai Sangvichien	1970	Thai skull: Detailed anthropometric and anthroposcopic study of Thai skulls

*B.Sc. and D.Sc. dissertations are in Thai.

While circumstances prevented both Sood Sangvichien and Sangiam Huta Sankas from engaging in research during the 1930s, this period did witness in 1937 the visit of several American investigators belonging to the Asiatic Primate Expedition, sponsored by Harvard, Columbia, and Johns Hopkins Universities and led by Harold Coolidge Jr. Among the members of this expedition were several notable American scientists, including C. Raymond Carpenter (1905–1975), Adolph Hans Schultz (1891–1976), and Sherwood L. Washburn (1911–). (For further details on this expedition, see Carpenter 1964:145–271.) Another foreign visitor during this same time period was a graduate student of Earnest A. Hooton (1887–1954) at Harvard University, James Andrews, who spent some time in Bangkok and the surrounding region collecting data for his doctoral thesis, *An Anthropometric Survey of Siam* (1939).

During World War II, the previously neglected study of paleoanthropology in Thailand received an unexpected boost with the discovery of archeological artifacts along the banks of the River Kwai in Kanchanaburi Province by the Dutch archeologist H.R. van Heekeren. Because van Heekeren was a Japanese prisoner of war at the time, his discovery went unreported until much later. In 1960, a joint Thai-Danish Archaeological Expedition was mounted to investigate van Heekeren's earlier observations. This two-year project resulted in the recovery of several Mesolithic and Neolithic skeletons and thousands of stone implements and other miscellaneous cultural artifacts. Sood Sangvichien (along with his colleague Patai Sirigaroon) was actively engaged in these excavations, and, on completion of the work in 1962, they were both invited by the Danish surgeon-anthropologist Jørgen Balslev Jørgensen (1923–) to go to Copenhagen, Denmark, to study the skeletal material. This led to the collaborative publication *Ban Kao: Neolithic Cemeteries in the Kanchanaburi Province* (1969), which fueled a mounting research interest in the paleoanthropology of Thailand that has involved both Thai and foreign investigators (cf. Sood Sangvichien 1981). This developing interest was further enhanced by the founding of a museum and laboratory by Sood Sangvichien in his Department of Anatomy at Siriraj Hospital. This facility was formally opened in 1972 by the king and is named the Sood Sangvichien Prehistoric Museum and Laboratory.

In the meantime, Sood Sangvichien had been actively promoting the study of physical anthropology through his teaching and through encouraging his staff to engage in research (e.g., Davivongs 1963a, 1963b; Sanjai Sangvichien et al. 1985) and to study abroad (cf. Table 1 for a summary of Thai dissertations completed from the 1950s to the 1990s). Among those who benefited from overseas study are Smerchai Poolsuman (United States, University of Michigan, 1986–1991), Malee Buranaruk (New Zealand, University of Otago, 1974–1979), M.R. Veerapan Davivongs (Australia, University of Adelaide, 1962–1963), and Sanjai Sangvichien (Denmark, University of Copenhagen, 1967–1968). On completing their study leaves, Smerchai Poolsuman returned to Thammasart University in Bangkok, while Malee Buranaruk went to Khon Kaen University in northeast Thailand. Veerapan Davivongs and Sanjai Sangvichien returned to Mahidol University, where in 1969, the latter succeeded Sood Sangvichien as head of the Anatomy Department. In Bangkok, Veerapan Davivongs was responsible for developing graduate and undergraduate courses in physical anthropology at Mahidol, Silpakorn, and Thammasart Universities. In addition to the above, Chiangma University also offers graduate courses in physical anthropology and supports research faculty.

Finally, since the 1960s, a number of foreign scientists have conducted research in Thailand. For example, the American paleoanthropologist Geoffrey G. Pope has conducted excavations at several Early Paleolithic localities in northern Thailand. He has also followed up on earlier work at Mae Tha and Ban Don Mun and excavated at the new site of Kao Pah Nam. The ongoing work of Pope and others, such as the French paleontologist J.J. Jaeger, has complemented the earlier research of the Dutch paleontologist G.H.R. von Koenigswald (1902–1982) at several Miocene deposits in northeastern and northern Thailand, which have yielded fossil faunas from the Early and Middle Miocene to the Pleistocene. During this same time period, a number of studies have been made on indigenous primates groups, including the gibbon.

Sanjai Sangvichien

See *also* Asian Apes; Asian Paleoanthropology; Carpenter, C(larence) Raymond; Denmark; Harvard University; Hooton, E(arnest) A(lbert); Hrdlička, Aleš; Keith, (Sir) Arthur; Koenigswald, (Gustav Heinrich) Ralph von; Primate Field Studies; Schultz, Adolph Hans; Todd, T(homas) Wingate; Washburn, Sherwood L.

Bibliography

C.R. Carpenter: A field study in Siam of the behavioral and social relations of the gibbon (*Hylobates lar*). In: *Naturalistic behavior of nonhuman primates*. University Park: Pennsylvania State University Press, 1964, pp. 145–271; E.D. Congdon: Effects of

radium on living substances. *Bulletin of the Museum of Comparative Zoology* 53:345–368, 1908–1913; E.D. Congdon, Sood Sangvichien, & B. Vachananda: Anthropometry of Thai male in 1929. [In Thai]. *Siriraj Hospital Gazette* 39:705–709, 1987. Reprinted in English in: *Studies on physical anthropology in Thai subjects*. Bangkok: Faculty of Medicine, Siriraj Hospital, Mahidol University, 1991; V. Davivongs: The femur of the Australian Aborigine. *American Journal of Physical Anthropology* 21:457–467, 1963a.

V. Davivongs: The pelvic girdle of the Australian Aborigine: Sex differences and sex determination. *American Journal of Physical Anthropology* 21:443–455, 1963b; Sood Sangvichien: The study of artifacts and skeletons contained in earthen jars at Haeay Kha Khaeng Forest, Uthai Thani Province, Thailand. *Journal of the National Research Council of Thailand* 13, 1981; Sood Sangvichien, S. Patai, & J.B. Jørgensen: *Ban Kao: Neolithic cemeteries in the Kanchanaburi Province. Part 2, The prehistoric Thai skeletons.* Copenhagen: Munksgaard, 1969; Sanjai Sangvichien et al.: Equation for estimation of stature of Thai and Chinese from the lengths of femur, tibia, and fibula. [In Thai]. *Siriraj Hospital Gazette* 37:215–218, 1985; S.H. Sankas: Relation of cranial module to capacity. *American Journal of Physical Anthropology* 14:306–318, 1930.

Tobias, Phillip V(allentine) (1925–)

Born in Durban, South Africa, Tobias was educated in Johannesburg at the University of the Witwatersrand (UW), to which he has been attached for more than fifty years, and where, as a student, he came under the spell and was the protégé of the anatomist and paleoanthropologist Raymond A. Dart (1893–1988).

He graduated from the UW with a B.Sc. in histology and physiology in 1946, B.Sc. (Hons) in 1947, a medical degree (M.B., B.Ch.) in 1950, and a Ph.D. in 1953 for his thesis, *Chromosomes, Sex Cells, and Evolution of the Gerbil.* During his student years, Tobias played an active and decisive role in student affairs, serving as president of the nonracial National Union of South African Students from 1948 to 1951. He rose to prominence with his opposition to the apartheid policies of the then government of South Africa. His political academic activism for equality of races has prevailed throughout his career.

As a student, in 1945–1946, Tobias led

expeditions to Sterkfontein, Kromdraai, Gladysvale, Mwulu's Cave, Buffalo Cave, and Makapansgat, initiating a lifelong investigation of a series of caves having the most complete record of continuous hominid habitation of approximately three million years' duration. Appointed as lecturer in Dart's Anatomy Department in 1951, and subsequently promoted to senior lecturer, Tobias succeeded Dart in 1959 as professor and chairman—a post he was to occupy for thirty-two years, during which time he also served as dean of medicine from 1980 to 1982.

In 1952, he joined the French Panhard Capricorn Expedition, crossing southern Africa on the Tropic of Capricorn, studying Bushmen and other African tribes of the Kalahari Desert, and carrying out the first archeological survey of Botswana, while also learning some French! This led to his setting up the Kalahari Research Committee in 1956, resulting in the annual multidisciplinary expeditions to the Kalahari until 1971 and culminating in his editing and contributing to *The Bushmen* (1978). Among the various studies he conducted during this fifteen-year period was the first preliminary ecological investigation of the San. Yet, it was genetics that first sparked his serious research interests, revealed in his Ph.D. thesis and his establishment of the first human genetics counseling service in South Africa. These early undertakings established the basis for his interest in evolution.

In 1955, Tobias was awarded a Nuffield Dominion Senior Traveling Fellowship to Cambridge University, England, (which conferred a D.Sc. [Hon. causa] on him thirty-five years later). A Rockefeller Traveling Fellowship awarded in 1956 took him to the Universities of Michigan and Chicago and many other centers in the United States.

On returning to South Africa, he conducted in 1957–1958 an anthropological and genetic study of the Tonga peoples in southern Zambia. Shortly thereafter, having succeeded Dart, Tobias established at the UW the first Somatotype Laboratory for the study of human physique in southern Africa. This led to his publication, in 1972, of the first account of the somatotypes of Black peoples of southern Africa, in which he showed that they were predominantly robust (mesomorphic) and linear (ectomorphic) in average build.

Tobias' reading of a paper on his restudy of the Kanam jaw to participants at the Fourth Pan-African Congress of Prehistory and Quaternary Studies at Kinshasa in 1959 led Louis B. Leakey (1903–1972) and Mary Leakey (1913–) to invite him to describe their find of *Australopithecus* (*Zinjanthropus*) *boisei*. His meticulous analysis (1967) published in the Olduvai Gorge Series (Vol. 2), the first comprehensive monographic study of an African early hominid cranium, and his role in identifying the new hominid taxon *Homo habilis*, culminated in his receiving a D.Sc. from the UW in 1967 and in his establishment as a paleoanthropologist of international stature.

As director of the UW Palaeoanthropology Research Unit (and its predecessors) for more than thirty years, Tobias has been responsible for excavations at such well-known fossil hominid sites as Sterkfontein, Taung, Makapansgat, and Gladysvale. As a result of these digs, more than 550 cataloged hominid specimens, mainly of *A. africanus* and *H. habilis*, have been recovered. The field and laboratory studies under his leadership have led the UW Anatomical Sciences Department to become a major world center of paleoanthropological research and teaching. In 1980, he was the first to claim that *H. habilis* possessed the neurological basis of spoken language. Among his morphological discoveries, he was the first to describe the unusual cranial venous sinus drainage pattern and heart-shaped *foramen magnum* of the robust australopithecines and elucidated their functional and evolutionary relatedness.

Apart from his enormous scholarly output of over 900 publications, Tobias as an administrator has had a profound influence in paleoanthropology and medical education. In 1958, he and his UW colleagues established the Institute for the Study of Man in Africa (ISMA) to perpetuate the work of Raymond Dart. Tobias presided over the ISMA from 1958 to 1968, and again in 1983–1984. He was also the founding president of the Anatomical Society of Southern Africa (1969) and of the Southern African Society for Quaternary Research. He has been a member of the International Anatomical Nomenclature Committee, the Human Biology Council, and the American Society of Naturalists—as well as an officer in a host of learned societies. He is a fellow of the Royal Society (London), and a member of the U.S. National Academy of Sciences and the American Philosophical Society, as well as an Honorary member of the Anatomical Society of Great Britian and Ireland. He is a Fellow of the Linnean Society of London and of the Royal College of Physicians (London) and an Honorary Fellow of the Royal Society of South Africa, of which he is a past president. He is president of the International Association of Human Biologists.

Despite his scholarly research and administrative achievements, it is as an educator that he is most revered. His gift of eloquent exposition has endeared him to generations of students, the more so for his legendary recollection of their names and faces. He has supervised no fewer than forty-eight Ph.D. and M.Sc. students in a diversity of anatomical, anthropological, odontological, and genetic fields.

Honors conferred upon Tobias include the Balzan International Prize in 1987—the first physical anthropologist thus honored; twenty-two medals, prizes, and other awards; and ten honorary degrees from universities in the United States, Britain, Canada, and South Africa. He has been elected an honorary fellow or life member of fifteen international and six South African learned societies, he has thrice been nominated for the Nobel Prize and a recipient of the Huxley Memorial Medal (1996).

Since 1992, he has been a visiting professor in anthropology at the University of Pennsylvania.

Geoffrey H. Sperber

See also Australopithecines; Dart, Raymond A(rthur); *Homo habilis*; Leakey, Louis Seymour Bazett; Makapansgat; Olduvai Gorge; South Africa; Sterkfontein; Taung (formerly Taungs)

Bibliography
SELECTED WORKS
    Chromosomes, sex cells, and evolution in a mammal. London: Lund, Humphries, 1956; *Embryos, fossils, genes, and anatomy.* Johannesburg: Witwatersrand University Press, 1960; *The meaning of race.* Johannesburg: South African Institute of Race Relations, 1961 (2d ed.: 1972); *Olduvai Gorge*. Vol. 2, *The cranium and maxillary dentition of Australopithecus (Zinjanthropus) boisei*. Cambridge: Cambridge University Press, 1967; *Man's past and future*. Johannesburg: Witwatersrand University Press, 1969; *The brain in hominid evolution*. New York: Columbia University Press, 1971.
    Homo erectus. In: *Encyclopaedia Britannica*. 15th ed. Vol 8. Chicago: Helen Hemingway Benton, 1974; *Tobias on the evolution of man*. Washington, D.C.: National Geographic Society, 1975. Film; (ed/contrib) *The Bushmen*. Cape Town: Human & Rousseau, 1978; *The evolution of the human brain, intellect, and spirit.* Adelaide: University of Adelaide Press, 1981; *Dart, Taung, and the "missing link."* Johannesburg: Witwatersrand University Press, 1984; (ed/contrib) *Hominid evolution: Past, present, and future.* New York: Liss, 1985; *Olduvai Gorge.* Vols. 4A–4B, *The skulls, endocasts, and teeth of Homo habilis*. Cambridge: Cambridge University Press, 1991; *Il Bipede Barcollante: Corpo, cervello evoluzione umana*. Torino: Einaudi, 1992a.
    Paleoantropologia. Milan: Jaca Books, 1992b. French translation: *La paléoanthropologie*. Editions Mentha, 1992; (with M. Arnold) *Man's anatomy*. 3 vols. Johannesburg: Witwatersrand University Press, 1963–1964 (2d ed.: 1967, 3d ed.: 1977, 4th ed.: 1988); (with A. Galloway) *The skeletal remains of Bambandyanalo*. Johannesburg: Witwatersrand University Press, 1959; (with L.S.B. Leakey & J.R. Napier) A new species of the genus *Homo* from Olduvai Gorge. Vol. 2, *Nature* 202:7–9, 1964; for a listing of Tobias' publications (1945–1990), see G.H. Sperber (ed): *From apes to angels: Essays in anthropology in honor of Phillip V. Tobias*. New York: Wiley, 1990 and *Images of humanity: The selected writings of Phillip V. Tobias*. Rivonia, South Africa: Ashanti, 1991.

ARCHIVAL SOURCES
    1. P.V. Tobias Papers: University Archives, University of the Witwatersrand, Private Bag. P.O. Wits 2050, Johannesburg, South Africa; 2. P.V. Tobias Papers: Department of Anatomy & Human Biology, University of the Witwatersrand Medical School, 7 York Road, Parktown, Johannesburg 2193, South Africa.

SECONDARY SOURCES
    K. Anderson: Professor Phillip Tobias. In: *And so they talked*. Cape Town: Timmins, 1963, pp. 159–164; P. Shipman: A journey towards human origins: Geneticist Phillip Tobias evolved into a leading light in the study of the beginnings of the human species. *New Scientist* 1791 (October 19):45–47, 1991; B. Wood: An interview with Phillip Tobias. *Current Anthropology* 30:215–224, 1989.

Todd, T(homas) Wingate (1885–1938)

Born in Sheffield, England, Todd received his medical education at the University of Manchester (UM), from which he graduated M.B., Ch.B., with first-class honors in 1907.

From 1907 to 1909, he worked under Alfred Harry Young (d. 1912) in the Department of Anatomy, serving as demonstrator in 1907–1908 and then as senior demonstrator in 1908–1909. In 1909, Young suffered a stroke, and in 1910 he was replaced by Grafton Elliot Smith (1871–1937), who came to the UM direct from Cairo. Todd worked under Smith (holding the position of lecturer) from 1910 to 1912, whereupon he received an invitation to succeed Carl August Hamann (1868–1930) as professor of anatomy at (Case) Western Reserve University (WRU), Cleveland, Ohio. Hamann had vacated the Chair of Anatomy to become dean of the medical school, and, anxious to secure the "best young man in England" as his successor, he had turned to Arthur Keith (1866–1955) at the Royal College of Surgeons in London for a name (Cobb 1959:236). Keith came up with Todd's name. Todd accepted the invitation and began his appointment in December 1912. He remained at WRU until his premature death in 1938.

During World War I, he served as a surgeon with the rank of captain in the Canadian Army Medical Corps. In 1920, he was given the additional title of director of the newly established Hamann Museum of Comparative Anthropology and Anatomy of the School of Medicine (1920), which housed, among other things, Todd's expanding skeletal collection (*vide infra*). To this was added, in 1928, the directorship of the newly created Brush Foundation—an appointment that enabled him to expand medico-anthropological research at WRU on a broader front. On his death, this directorship passed to Walter Greulich (1899–1986), while Normand L. Hoerr (1902–1958) took over as Chair of Anatomy.

During his tenure at WRU, Todd was responsible for establishing a major collection of human skeletons prepared from cadavers dissected in his department (cf. Cobb 1933). What made this skeletal collection such an important resource was that each specimen is fully documented: All unclaimed cadavers brought to Todd's laboratory were first photographed and then carefully measured before commencing dissection. During dissection, all anomalies encountered were recorded and preserved (along with samples of skin and hair); and prior to maceration, additional measurements were recorded on the vertebral column, pelvis, and cranium. The skeletal parts were then stored in boxes for future reference. At the time of Todd's death, this carefully documented collection consisted of 3,000 skeletons

and was rivaled only by the Terry Collection at Washington University, St. Louis (which in the late 1960s was transferred to the National Museum of Natural History, Smithsonian Institution, Washington, D.C.). The Todd Collection is housed in the Cleveland Museum of Natural History.

While the Todd Collection has since become a major research resource, during its assembly it served as the primary basis of Todd's own research agenda, which spanned both physical anthropology and medical anatomy. In the former category, his primary research interest was the study of growth, and during the 1920s and early 1930s he published a series of influential studies on skeletal age changes (epiphyseal union, pubic metamorphosis, and cranial suture closure), facial growth, and cadaver anthropometry. Many of these studies were later extended by his students and colleagues, including Wilton Marion Krogman (1903–1987), Sarah Idell Pyle, Greulich, William Montague Cobb (1904–1990, and W.W. Graves. Among these contributions, perhaps the most notable is his protracted investigation of the metamorphosis of the pubic bone with age. Todd (1920) began this research with a study of the pubic bones of white males, from which he defined ten (age) phases of male pubis metamorphosis. This was followed by studies of the pubic symphyses of white females, American Black-hybrids (cf. Todd 1921a), and other mammals (cf. Todd 1921b). Todd's scheme is still widely used by forensic anthropologists, along with the refinements emerging from the research of Thomas W. McKern (1920–1974) and T. Dale Stewart (1901–) in the mid-1950s (cf. McKern & Stewart 1957). For a comprehensive review of Todd's work on growth and development, along with an accompanying bibliography, see Krogman 1939a.

Todd was a founding member of the American Association of Physical Anthropologists (AAPA) in 1930. From 1930 to 1936 he was a member of the AAPA's Executive Committee, and at the time of his death he was its president.

He died in Cleveland on 28 December 1938.

Frank Spencer

Bibliography
SELECTED WORKS

Age changes in the pubic bone. I. The white male pubis. *American Journal of Physical Anthropology* 3:285–334, 1920; Age changes in the pubic bone. II. The pubis of the male Negro-White hybrid. III. The pubis of the White female. IV. The pubis of the Negro-White hybrid. *American Journal of Physical Anthropology* 4:1–25, 26–39, 40–70, 1921a; Age changes in the pubic bone. V. Mammalian pubic metamorphoses. *American Journal of Physical Anthropology* 4:333–406, 1921b; Age changes in the pubic bone. VIII. Roentgenographic differentiation. *American Journal of Physical Anthropology* 14:255–271, 1930a; The roentgenographic appraisement of skeletal differentiation. *Child Development* 1:298–310, 1930b.

Atlas of skeletal maturation. London: Kimpton, 1932; (with D.W. Lyon Jr.) Cranial suture closure: Its progress and age relationship. *American Journal of Physical Anthropology* 7:325–284 (1924), 8:23–71, 149–168 (1925). Reprinted in: T.D. Stewart & M. Trotter (eds) *Basic readings on the identification of human skeletons: Estimation of age*. New York: Wenner-Gren Foundation, 1954, pp. 265–347; (with A. Lindala) Dimensions of the body: Whites and American Negroes of both sexes. *American Journal of Physical Anthropology* 12:35–119, 1928;

ARCHIVAL SOURCES

T.W. Todd Papers: University Archives, Case Western Reserve University, 10900 Euclid Avenue, Cleveland, Ohio 44106.

PRIMARY SOURCES

W.M. Cobb: Materials in American institutions available for anthropological study. *American Journal of Physical Anthropology* 17:1–45, 1933; T.W. McKern & T.D. Stewart: *Skeletal age changes in young American males. Analyzed from the standpoint of age identification*. United States Army, Environmental Protection Research Division Technical Report, EP-45. Natick, Massachusetts, 1957.

SECONDARY SOURCES

W.M. Cobb: Thomas Wingate Todd, 1885–1938. *Journal of the National Medical Association* 51:233–246, 1959; W.M. Cobb: Thomas Wingate Todd, 1885–1938. *American Journal of Physical Anthropology* 56:517–520, 1981; A. Keith: In memoriam: Thomas Wingate Todd, 1885–1938. *Journal of Anatomy* 73:350–353; W.M. Krogman: Contributions of T. Wingate Todd to anatomy and physical anthropology. *American Journal of Physical Anthropology* 25:145–186, 1939a; W.M. Krogman: Thomas Wingate Todd. *Science* 89:143–144, 1939b; W.M. Krogman: T. Wingate Todd: Catalyst in growth research. *American Journal of Orthodontics* 37:679–687, 1951.

Topinard, Paul (1830–1911)

Born at L'Isle Adam (Seine-et-Oise), France, Topinard spent much of his childhood and early adolescent years in the United States, where his father owned property in the state of New York. In 1848, he returned to Paris, where he registered in the Faculty of Medicine. Promoted to *interne des hôpitaux de Paris* in 1853, he graduated M.D. in 1860.

Although Topinard originally intended a career in medical practice, events led him in another direction. As early as 1860, at the instigation of the anatomist-anthropologist Paul Broca (1824–1880), who had taken an early interest in him, Topinard became a member of the newly founded Société d'Anthropologie de Paris (SAP). The turning point in his career, however, was the Franco-Prussian War (1870–1871), in which he served as a military surgeon. Discouraged by this experience, and on the advice of Broca, he decided to devote all of his energy to anthropology.

In 1872 he was made an assistant in Broca's Laboratoire d'Anthropologie of the École Pratique des Hautes Études (LA-EPHE), and in 1877 he became assistant director—a position he retained until his retirement in 1900. Coinciding with this was his appointment as subeditor of the *Revue d'Anthropologie*,[1] a journal Broca had founded in 1872 for the publication of articles written by the staff of the LA-EPHE. After Broca's death in 1880, Topinard assumed full editorial responsibility of the *Revue* until 1890, when it was amalgamated with two other journals to form *L'Anthropologie*. Following the foundation (again by Broca) of the École d'Anthropologie (EA) in 1874, Topinard was recruited to the Chair of Biological Anthropology (later renamed "general anthropology" in 1882), which he occupied until his removal in 1889 (*vide infra*).

With Broca's death, Topinard's fortunes changed. Although it had been generally expected that he would succeed his mentor as director of the LA-EPHE, Topinard declined the invitation, preferring instead to remain in the position of assistant director. The director's position was thus offered to the anatomist Mathias Duval (1844–1907), who accepted with the provision that Topinard assume responsibility for running the laboratory and that he be permitted to continue his research on embryogenesis—an arrangement Topinard accepted, along with Broca's former duties at the SAP. In 1881 he was elected general secretary of the SAP, but as he later noted in his memoir (1890), the next decade was not a happy one. Harmony within the SAP, as well as in the LA-EPHE and the EA, was increasingly disrupted by a group led by the prehistorian Grabriel de Mortillet (1821–1898), whose views were the antithesis of those of Topinard. After only six years, Topinard resigned his position in the SAP (Topinard 1890), From all accounts, his situation at the LA-EPHE and the EA was no better. Little by little, his authority was eroded, making it increasingly difficult, if not impossible, for him to either teach or advance his own research agenda. Then, in December 1889, he lost his professorial chair at the EA, which signaled Topinard's complete retreat from anthropology. His last publication, *L'Homme dans la nature*, appeared in 1891.

In spite of the difficulties he encountered during the 1880s, Topinard made a number of significant contributions to the discipline. Of particular interest are his attempts to produce a rational classification of humankind based on specific physical traits. Initially, Topinard had followed the British biologist Thomas Henry Huxley (1825–1895) in using hair type as the primary racial marker (cf. Huxley 1870). Accordingly, Topinard recognized three primary racial groups: the "straight-haired races," the "wavy/frizzy-haired races," and the "woolly-haired races." In the mid-1880s, however, he modified this approach employing nasal morphology as the primary racial character. Using this scheme, Topinard identified nineteen distinct races distributed within three primary groups: "White leptorrhine [slender nose] races," "Yellow mesorrhine [an intermediate nasal form] races," and "Black platyrrhine [flattened nose] races" (cf. Topinard 1885).

He also published extensively on craniology, comparative anatomy, evolution, and the history of anthropology, and he developed several new anthropometric techniques and instruments. But he is perhaps best remembered for his book *Eléments d'Anthropologie générale* (1885), which may be regarded as the first anthropological textbook.

Topinard died in Paris on 20 December 1911.

Denise Ferembach

See aslo Broca, Paul (Pierre); France; Huxley, Thomas Henry; Mortillet, Gabriel (Louis Laurent) de

Bibliography
Selected Works
Étude sur les races indigènes de l'Australie (Instructions). Paris: Masson, 1872; De la méthode en craniométrie. *Bulletins de la Société d'Anthropologie de Paris* 8 (2d ser.):851–860, 1873a; Des diverses espèces de prognathisme. *Bulletins de la Société d'Anthropologie de Paris* 8 (2d ser.): 19–48, 1873b; De la morphologie du nez. *Bulletins de la Société d'Anthropologie de Paris* 8 (2d ser.):947–958, 1873c; *L'Anthropologie*. Paris: Reinwald, 1876a; Étude sur la taille considérée suivant l'âge, le sexe, l'individu, les milieux et les races. *Revue d'Anthropologie* 4:34–83, 1876b; *Eléments d'Anthropologie générale*. Paris: Delahaye et Lecrosnier, 1885; Carte de la couleur des yeux et des cheveux en France. *Bulletins de la Société d'Anthropologie de Paris* 9 (3d ser.):590–602, 1886a; Présentation de 4 Boshimans vivants. *Bulletins de la Société d'Anthropologie de Paris* 9 (3d ser.):530–566, 1886b; *La Société, L'École, le Laboratoire et le Musée: A la mémoire de Paul Broca*. Paris: Chamerot, 1890; *L'Homme dans la nature*. Paris: Alcan, 1891.

Secondary Sources
P. Broca: Laboratoire d'Anthropologie. *Rapport des Directeurs de laboratoire et de conférences de l'École Pratique des Hautes Études, 1868–1877*. Paris: EPHE, 1879, pp. 179–194; A. Chervin: Discours prononcé sur la tobe du Dr. Paul Topinard. *Bulletins et Mémoires de la Société d'Anthropologie de Paris* 3 (6th ser.): 2–5, 1912; D. Ferembach: Paul Topinard, 1830–1911. In: D. Ferembach: History of biological anthropology in France. Part 2. *International Association of Human Biologists: Occasional Papers*. Newcastle upon Tyne: IAHB, 1987; M. Sanemeterio Cobo: L'École d'Anthropologie de Paris. *La Nouvelle Revue Anthropologique* 1:12–52, 1979; R. Verneau: Paul Topinard. *L'Anthropologie* 23:111–114, 1912; C. Weisgerber: Annonce du décès de M. Paul Topinard. *Bulletins et Mémoires de la Société d'Anthropologie de Paris* 2 (6th ser.):568, 1911.

Editor's Note

1. Not to be confused with the journal *Revue Anthropologique* (École d'Anthropologie de Paris), which was published from 1891 to 1942. Between 1891 and 1910, its title varied as *Revue de l'École d'Anthropologie de Paris*.

Trotter, Mildred (1899–1991)

Born in a rural area near Monaca, Pennsylvania, Trotter received a bachelor's degree in zoology from Mount Holyoke College in 1920, a master's in 1921 and a Ph.D. in 1924 (both in anatomy) from Washington University, St. Louis, Missouri. In 1925, she spent a year at Oxford University on a National Research Council Fellowship studying skeletal biology under Arthur Thomson (1858–1935). The following year, she returned to Washington University Medical School, where she remained until her retirement. (For further information on her activities at St. Louis, in particular her relationship with the anatomist Robert James Terry (1871–1966), under whom she worked until 1941, see Trotter 1981.)

Trotter's primary research focus was skeletal biology, in which she made a number of significant contributions—in particular, her studies on adult long limb bones in American Blacks and Whites, from which she derived new formulas for stature estimation (cf. Trotter & Gleser 1952). These formulas were effectively utilized by the Smithsonian physical anthropologist T. Dale Stewart (1901–) and his team in their efforts to identify the American dead of the Korean conflict. In addition to these studies, her name is also associated with a comparative study of human hair (cf. Trotter & Duggins 1964), which also found application in forensic anthropology.

During the course of her long career, she held a number of professional offices, including associate editor (1944, 1956–1960, 1968–1972) of the *American Journal of Physical Anthropology*; vice president (1952–1954) of the American Association of Physical Anthropologists; president (1955–1957) of the American Association for the Advancement of Science (Section H: Anthropology); and Executive Committee and member (1969–1973) of the American Association of Anatomists.

Trotter died in St. Louis on 23 August 1991.

Robert W. Sussman

See also Body-Composition Studies; Forensic Anthropology; Stewart, T(homas) Dale; Terry, Robert James

Bibliography

SELECTED WORKS

Robert J. Terry, 1871–1966. *American Journal of Physical Anthropology* 56:503–508, 1981; (with O.H. Duggins) Hairs. In: V.M. Emmel & E.V. Cowdry (eds) *Laboratory techniques in biology and medicine*. 4th ed. Baltimore: Williams & Wilkins, 1964, pp. 195–196; (with G.C. Gleser) The effect of ageing on stature. *American Journal of Physical Anthropology* 9:311–324, 1951; (with G.C. Gleser) Estimation of stature from long bones of American Whites and Negroes. *American Journal of Physical Anthropology* 10:463–514, 1952; (with R.R. Peterson) Ash weight of human skeletons in percent of the dry, fat-free weight. *Anatomical Record* 123:341–368, 1955; (with T.D. Stewart) Role of physical anthropology in the field of human identification. *Science* 122:883–884, 1955.

SECONDARY SOURCES

G. Conroy et al.: Mildred Trotter, Ph.D., Feb. 2, 1899–Aug. 23, 1991. *American Journal of Physical Anthropology* 87:373–374, 1992; T.D. Stewart: *Essentials of forensic anthropology, especially as developed in the United States*. Springfield, Illinois: Thomas, 1979, pp. 201–208.

Tulp, Nicolaas (1593–1674)

Born into a prosperous Protestant Amsterdam merchant family, Tulp received his medical education at Leiden University, where he matriculated in 1611 and from which he graduated M.D. in 1614 after defending twenty-four propositions on *De Cholera Humida*. Among his teachers were Professors Reinier Bontius (1576–1623), Aelius Vorstius (1565–1624), and Pieter Paaw (1564–1617). The latter, a famous botanist and anatomist, was the first to obtain permission to dissect dead criminals in Leiden. His stimulating activities resulted in the construction of the Leiden Anatomical Theatre in 1597.

After the completion of his studies in Leiden, Tulp returned to Amsterdam, where he opened a highly successful practice in surgery and general medicine. Apart from his medical interests, Tulp was intimately involved in the municipal affairs of the city of Amsterdam. In 1662, he was elected to the office of alderman and was one of the thirty-six councilors of the town. He was reelected to this office in 1627, 1634, 1641, and 1642. He later served as one of the city's four burgomasters, in 1654, 1655, 1666, and 1671.

Some of the other civic positions Tulp held include: trustee of the city orphanage in 1649 and 1660; treasurer of the city in 1645, 1654, 1656, 1660, 1668, 1670, and 1672; and curator of the grammar school and Athenaeum in 1666. From 1663 to 1665 and from 1673 to 1674, he served as a member of the Committee Council of the States of Holland and West Frisia concerning Amsterdam.

In 1628, Tulp was appointed *praelector anatomiae* of the Surgeons' Guild—a position he held until 1652. His duties were to lecture in anatomy and surgery to apprentice-surgeons and to deliver the public dissections, of which nine have been recorded. The most famous, held on 31 January 1632, was painted by Rembrandt as *The Anatomy Lesson of Dr. Tulp,* now in the museum Het Mauritshuis in The Hague. During the plague epidemic of 1635, Tulp advocated quarantine as a means to control the spread of the disease. Because of the inefficiency of the local pharmacists, Tulp suggested that they be placed under municipal control, which resulted in the installation of the first local medical authority in The Netherlands, the Collegium Medicum Amstelodamense. Another consequence of Tulp's concerns was the publication of the first Dutch pharma-copoeia, the *Pharmacopoea Amstelaedamensis* (1636), the greater part of which was written by him.

The scientific results of Tulp's medical and anatomical interests are published in his main work, the *Observationum Medicarum* (1641). It contains descriptions of 228 cases, from which we learn that he rediscovered the chyle vessels of the small intestine and that he was the first to describe the ileocecal valve at the junction of the large and small intestines. His outstanding anatomical and surgical capacities are reflected in the descriptions of the ways of removing urethral stones and, in the case of a head trauma, skull fragments that pressed on the brain. Other important observations are the pulsation of the spleen, the significance of the cauda equina, and the first recorded description of a chimpanzee in Europe.

Tulp introduced in 1641 the Javanese word "orangutan" (meaning "man of the woods," synonymous with *Homo sylvestris*) and used it to designate an Angolese chimpanzee in the private menagerie of Frederic Henry, Prince of Orange. The young female chimpanzee he described is depicted in a modest pose with downcast eyes and hands shielding the genital region (See Fig. 1).

Tulp stressed the human character of the chimpanzee's behavior and used the remarkable name "*Satyrus Indicus,*" because he had been informed that in Java real orangutans did show a great interest in local women. This characteristic he also attributed to the animal he had studied, which, in combination with its external features, led him to believe that this "man of the woods" was identical to the satyrs of the classics and, as such, confirmed the Swiss anatomist and botanist Kaspar Bauhin's (1560–1624) earlier contention that "satyrs" described by Greco-Roman scholars were real entities. Tulp's description became very popular, and his illustration was reprinted numerous times until far into the eighteenth century.

Tulp was a great admirer of Hippocrates and consequently opposed the ideas of the iatrochemists like Jean Baptiste van Helmont (1577–1644). This meant, among other things, that he rejected the use of the new medicines, such as antimony, advocated by these workers. Few medical activities of Tulp have been recorded from the later years of his life, when he was mainly concerned with his civic duties.

Tulp died in The Hague on 12 September 1674.

L.C. Palm

Fig. 1. Tulp's Homo sylvestris, Orang-outang *(1641).*

See also African Apes; Asian Apes; Hippocrates; Tyson, Edward

Bibliography
SELECTED WORKS
Pharmacopoea Amstelaedamensis, senatus auctoritate munita. Amsterdam: Elzevirium, 1636; *Observationum medicarum libri tres.* Amsterdam: Elzevirium, 1641. The first description of the chimpanzee appears in the first edition of the *Observationum*: Lib. 3, cap. 56; pp. 274–279. Table 14 appears on p. 275 of the second edition. This work went through six editions (2d ed.: 1652, 3d ed.: 1672, 4th ed.: 1685; 5th ed.: Leiden: Vivié, 1716, 6th ed.: Leiden: Wishoff, 1739). The fifth edition has a biography, and the sixth contains Tulp's funeral oration. The first Dutch translation of the *Observationum* was published in 1650 under the title *De drie Boecken der Medicijnsche aanmerkingen.*

SECONDARY SOURCES
R.M. Goldwyn: Nicolaas Tulp [1593–1674]. *Medical History* 5:270–276, 1961; W.S. Heckscher: *Rembrandt's Anatomy of Dr. Nicolaas Tulp: An iconological study.* New York: New York University Press, 1958; G.A. Lindeboom: Medical aspects of Rembrandt's *Anatomy Lesson of Dr. Tulp. Janus* 64:179–203, 1977; C.D. O'Malley & H.W. Magoun: Early concepts of the Anthropomorpha. *Rivista di Storia delle Scienze mediche & naturali* 4:45–46, 1962; P.W. van der Pas: Nicolaas Tulp. In: C.C. Gillispie (ed) *Dictionary of scientific biography.* Vol. 13. New York: Scribner's, 1976, pp. 490–491; J.C.C. Rupp: Matters of life and death: The social and cultural conditions of the rise of anatomical theatres, with special reference to seventeenth-century Holland. *History of Science* 28:263–287, 1990; R.P.W. Visser: *The zoological work of Petrus Camper, 1722–1789.* Amsterdam: Rodopi, 1985, pp. 34, 36.

Tunakan, Seniha (née Hüsnü) (1908–)
Born in İstanbul, Turkey, Tunakan studied biology at İstanbul University, graduating in 1934. During her postgraduate work in anthropology under Şevket Aziz Kansu (1903–1983), she received a government scholarship on his recommendation to continue her studies in Germany. She received her doctorate in physical anthropology from the Kaiser Wilhelm Institut für Anthropologie, menschliche Erblehre und Eugenik in Berlin in 1941. Returning to Turkey, she was appointed assistant to her mentor, Kansu, who was then chairman of the Anthropology Institute at the Faculty of Languages, History, and Geography (D.T.C.F.) in Ankara. Tunakan remained with the D.T.C.F. until her retirement in 1973.

In addition to her collaborative work with Kansu on the anthropomorphology of the ancient inhabitants of Anatolia (cf. Kansu & Tunakan 1946, 1948), Tunakan's main areas of specialization were dermatoglyphics and population genetics. Of particular interest here is the work she produced that supported Kansu's claim that the Turks were of the Caucasoid race. The series of papers on the Turkish palm prints (cf. Tunakan 1960, 1969) and twin studies (cf. Tunakan 1955) that she produced between the late 1940s and late 1960s were regarded as significant contributions to the demonstration that the Turks were biogenetically affiliated with what were then called the "races of eastern Europe."

Aygen Erdentuğ

See also Germany; Kansu, Şevket Aziz; Turkey

Bibliography
SELECTED WORKS
Memleketimizde ikiz doğumun çoğunluğu üzerinde ilk deneme [A report on the multitude of twin births in Turkey]. *A.Ü.D.T.C.F. Dergisi* 13:17–19, 1955; Türk suçlularında parmak izlerinin karşılaştırmalı incelenmesi [A comparative study on the fingerprints of Turkish convicts]. *A.Ü.D.T.C.F. Dergisi* 18:85–91, 1960; Türk suçlularında el ayasının karşılaştırmalı incelenmesi [A comparative palm study of Turkish convicts]. *Antropoloji* 4:1–26, 1969; (with Ş.A. Kansu) Alacahöyük (1943–1945) kazılarında çıkarılan Kalkolitik, Bakır ve Tunç çağlarına ait halkın antropolojisi [The anthropology of the remains of the peoples of the Chalcolithic, Copper, and Bronze Ages found in the 1943–1945 excavations at Alacahöyük]. *Belleten (Türk Tarih Kurumu)* 10:539–555, 1946; (with Ş.A. Kansu) Karaoğlan höyüğünde çıkarılan Eti, Frig, ve Klasik devir iskeletlerinin antropolojik incelenmesi [An anthropological study of the Hittite, Phrygian, and Classic Period skeletons found in the mound at Karaoğlan]. *Belleten (Türk Tarih Kurumu)* 12:759–778, 1948.

SECONDARY SOURCES
A. Erdentuğ: A.Ü.D.T.C.F. antropoloji bibliyografyası, 1935–1983 [Bibliography

of anthropology, D.T.C.F., Ankara University, 1935–1983]. *Antropoloji* 12:496–498, 1985.

Turkey

Anthropology, and more especially physical anthropology, in Turkey had its formal origin in the nationalist movement that emerged after World War I. In fact, the discipline owes much to Kemal Atatürk (1881–1938), who viewed the quest for the biocultural origins and history of Turks as an integral part of his agenda for sociopolitical reform in the new Turkish Republic founded in 1923. In addition to modernizing the educational system, Atatürk encouraged the adoption of European life-styles, which included raising the status of women. Since then, the history of the discipline can be divided into four arbitrary phases of development.

Phase 1: 1925–1940
The Centre for Anthropological Research in Turkey (CART), which became known as the Anthropology Institute, was established at the University of Istanbul in 1925, and it was one of the first tangible manifestations of anthropology in academia. At the same time, the journal *Türk Antropoloji Mecmuası* was founded to assist in the promotion of the CART's work. The CART and its journal became the primary focus for bioanthropological research in Turkey until 1946 *(vide infra)*.

Among the founding junior faculty of the CART was Şevket Aziz Kansu (1903–1983), who was sent to study anthropology in Paris. On returning to Istanbul in 1929, Kansu was made a doçent (equivalent to the American associate professor or the British reader) in the CART faculty. Following the passage of the University Act of 1933, the CART was reorganized, the result of which was the establishment of a Chair in Anthropology. The first recipient of this new chair was Kansu. Linked with these administrative changes was the transference in 1935 of the CART, together with Kansu, to Ankara, where they formed part of the newly established Dilve Tarih-Coğrafya Fakültesinin (D.T.C.F.) (Faculty of Language, History, and Geography). Until the close of Phase 3 in 1980, the D.T.C.F. in Ankara was the exclusive focus of physical anthropological research and instruction in Turkey. By contrast, the anthropological sciences at the University of İstanbul focused on archeology and prehistory under the auspices of Helmuth Bossert (1889–1961). With the founding of the D.T.C.F., the

government also established forty academic scholarships, which were awarded according to the results of a national competition. Among the first recipients of these D.T.C.F. scholarships was Nermin Erdentuğ (née Aygen), who received the first doctorate awarded at Ankara in 1942. Prior to this time, students such as Muzaffer Süleyman Şenyürek (1915–1961) and Seniha Tunakan (1908–), who were sent abroad to study, were on government scholarships throughout their studies.

Prior to Şenyürek and Tunakan completing their postgraduate studies abroad (in 1940 and 1941, respectively), the burden of instruction in anthropology had fallen on Kansu's shoulders. The curriculum of this period emphasized not only a multidisciplinary approach but also a mixture of predominantly French and German influences. The latter influence was due in large part to an increasing number of courses being taught by German émigrés who were hired as lecturers during World War II. However, it was the French conception of anthropology that was at the core of the curriculum. Indeed, until 1937 when Kansu introduced the first generation of Turkish textbooks, students and faculty relied exclusively on foreign—in particular, French—textbooks and journals.

The major research project directed by Kansu during this formative period was an anthropometric survey of the Turkish population, which involved the measurement of 64,000 men and women—the results of which supported his initial work at the CART that the Turks were of the Caucasoid race. This period also witnessed the first prehistoric excavation, initiated in 1937 by Kansu, at Eti Yokuşu, Ankara (cf. Kansu 1940).

Phase 2: 1941–1960
The foundation of Ankara University, and the annexation of the D.T.C.F., in 1946, resulted not only in autonomy from Istanbul but also important structural changes. Seven research units were established within the D.T.C.F. In the anthropology unit, the old CART, or Anthropology Institute, professorship held by Kansu was renamed the Chair of Anthropology-Ethnology. In 1955, that designation was changed to the Chair of Paleo-Physical Anthropology, Paleoethnography (Prehistory), and Ethnology. Three years later, Şenyürek was installed in the new Chair of Paleoanthropology with a separate curriculum, leaving the Chair of Physical Anthropology, Prehistory, and Ethnology to continue with the old curriculum. Under Şenyürek's influence, the cur-

riculum in anthropology at Ankara assumed an increasingly American bias. The end of this phase is marked by the creation of a Chair of Prehistory, which in 1960 was filled by İsmail Kılıç Kökten (1904–1974), leaving Kansu to retain the Chair of Physical Anthropology until his retirement in 1973.

This second phase of development witnessed the emergence of anthropological research on a broad front—ranging from archeological excavations to the study of population genetics. Initially, Kansu, Tunakan, and Şenyürek were all engaged in the study of the ancient inhabitants of Anatolia. However, during the late 1950s each of these workers began to specialize. While Kansu tended toward prehistory, Tunakan concentrated on human biology and genetics, leaving paleontology and paleoanthropology to Şenyürek. Although Şenyürek was prematurely removed from the scene by a fatal air crash in 1961, his research agenda was continued by two of his former assistants, Enver Yaşar Bostancı (1923–1995) and Refakat Çiner (1929–1974). In 1968, Bostancı was installed in the Chair of Paleoanthropology.

Phase 3: 1961–1981
In 1960, a new University Law was passed that resulted in the creation of a separate Department of Anthropology within the D.T.C.F., which incorporated both the Chair of Physical Anthropology, Prehistory, and Ethnology and the Chair of Paleoanthropology. This period is further characterized by a number of important changes in the D.T.C.F. academic personnel, as well as the hiring of the paleoanthropologist Güven Arsebük (1936–) at İstanbul University in 1970. By this time, Bossert had retired (1960) and Halet Çambel (1916–) had gone on to found the Institute of Prehistory at the University of İstanbul, where she had been director and full professor since 1964. Also worthy of note is Metin Özbek (1948–), who received his doctorate in biological anthropology from the University of Bordeaux in 1976 and an appointment the following year in the Department of Social Anthropology at Hacettepe University (Ankara).

Between 1965 and 1975, four junior appointments were made to the D.T.C.F. faculty: Berna Alpagut (1946–), E. Güleç (1950–), Armağan Saatçioğlu (1944–1985), and Işın Yalçınkaya (1943–)—all graduates of the D.T.C.F. programs in anthropological sciences. In each case, these appointments served to replace the gaps created by the re-

tirements of Kansu in 1973, Tunakan in 1973, and Kökten in 1974, and the sudden death of Refakat Çiner early in 1974. The remainder of Phase 3 at this institution may be characterized as a period of adjustment to these events.

The end of Phase 3 is marked by the coup d'etat of 1980, which resulted in a major restructuring of higher education in 1982. Specifically, the Turkish Council of Higher Education (Yükseköğretim Kurulu: YÖK) adopted a modified version of the American academic system, limiting Departments of Anthropology to the Chairs of Social Anthropology, Paleoanthropology, and Physical Anthropology, and annexing prehistory to the Department of Archeology and History of Art.

Phase 4: 1982–1996
While the ultimate fate of the system inaugurated in 1982 has yet to be determined, it is already clear that physical anthropology as envisioned by Kansu and his students is no longer operative in Turkey. For example, the strictures imposed by the YÖK in 1982 resulted in Armağan Saatçioğlu's resignation in 1983 and the closing of the D.T.C.F.'s physical anthropology program. Although the program was reopened in 1987, nominally, with Güleç assuming responsibility, it was subsequently annexed in 1992 to the Department of Paleoanthropology, when Berna Alpagut found herself head of an independent department following her succession to the chair of the department the year before.

To a large extent, the current plight of traditional physical anthropology in Turkey is frustrated by a lack of government support for this kind of research endeavor. By contrast, paleoanthropology and prehistory have managed to find a haven in state excavation policies and the increasing demand for international cooperation. The D.T.C.F.'s original curriculum has undergone a downgrading in academic status due to imposed limitations on its content and lack of personnel. At Hacettepe University, Özbek, with his particular research interest in paleontology and prehistory, has survived these changes, becoming full professor in 1988, and head of the Department of Anthropology in 1991.

Aygen Erdentuğ
Nermin Erdentuğ

See also Bostancı, Enver Yaşar; Çiner, Refakat; Hooton, E(arnest) A(lbert); Kansu, Şevket Aziz; Kökten, İsmail Kılıç; Saatçioğlu,

Armağan; Şenyürek, Muzaffer Süleyman; Tunakan, Seniha (née Hüsnü)

Bibliography
M. Çadırcı & A. Süslü: *Ankara Üniversitesi Gelişim Tarihi* [*The development of Ankara University*]. Ankara: Basımevi, 1982; A. Erdentuğ: A.Ü.D.T.C.F. antropoloji bibliyografyası, 1935–1983 [Bibliography of anthropology, D.T.C.F., Ankara University, 1935–1983]. *Antropoloji* 12:451–504, 1985; Ş.A. Kansu: *Türk Antropoloji Enstitüsü Tarihçesi* [*History of the Turkish Anthropology Institute*]. İstanbul: Maarif Matbaası, 1940; P.J. Magnarella & O. Türkdoğan: The development of Turkish social anthropology. *Current Anthropology* 17:263–273, 1976; A. Süslü: *Dil ve Tarih-Coğrafya Fakültesinin 50 Yıllık Tarihi* [*The Faculty of Languages, History, and Geography in its Fiftieth Year*]. Ankara: A.Ü. Basımevi, 1986.

Twiesselmann, François-Ernest (1910–)

Born in Bouillon, a province of Luxembourg, Belgium, Twiesselmann received his M.D. degree from the Free University of Brussels in 1936. Soon thereafter, Victor Van Straelen (1889–1964), then director of the Musée d'Histoire naturelle—which was renamed Institut royal des Sciences naturelles de Belgique (IRSNB) in 1947—in Brussels, placed him in charge of organizing a Section of Anthropology to complement the Section of Prehistory. The remainder of his career unfolded at the IRSNB. In 1938, and again in 1939, Twiesselmann visited Henri Victor Vallois (1889–1981) at the Institut des Hautes Etudes in Toulouse to receive instruction in anthropological methodology.

With the outbreak of World War II, Twiesselmann tailored his research agenda to fit the prevailing circumstances. His concerns at this time were: (1) studies in classical anthropology, notably the study of cranial thickness (1941); (2) the application of heredity and the principles of genetics to the study of normal human characteristics (1947); and (3) the study of pubertal growth (1949). After the war, recognizing the importance of biometry, he secured the assistance of the mathematician Elisabeth Defrise-Gussenhoven (1912–) to develop biostatistical methods for use in paleontology and human growth studies.

In 1954, in his *Propos sur l'Anthropologie*, he presented a synthesis of his ideas regarding the interrelatedness of anthropology with the other biological sciences, in which he underlined the primary importance of genetics.

He also believed that the phenotypic analyses of traditional anthropology provided a foundation upon which the new methodologies of biology could be based. In brief, the individuals that are the subject of anthropological observations are the vectors of hereditary potentialities, whose comparative study constitutes the basis of the evolutionary perspective of the discipline. The later works of Twiesselmann seek to illustrate the richness of this viewpoint, and therein demonstrate the connections between extant and fossil human populations. This work can be separated under three headings: paleontology, growth studies, and population genetics.

In human paleontology, he studied, among other things, the Mesolithic remains from Ishango (1958), the Neandertal femur from Fond-de-Forêt (1961), and the evolution of the human jaw and teeth (1972). In the area of human growth, most notable is his study of Black school-children in Léopoldville (1957), school-children in Brussels (1969), and the craniofacial anatomy of Belgian-Congolese half-castes (1982). His various studies in human genetics include a study of the rate of consanguinity in Belgium and the demographic factors likely to explain this (Twiesselmann, Moreau, & François 1962).

Twiesselmann continued to direct the Section of Anthropology and Prehistory at the IRSNB until 1975. During his tenure at the IRSNB, he also taught human genetics and anthropology at the Université de Bruxelles. In his role as researcher and teacher, he did much to revitalize the discipline in Belgium while at the same time contributing to the development of European anthropology.

André Leguebe

See also Belgium; Neandertals; Vallois, Henri Victor

Bibliography
SELECTED WORKS
Méthode pour l'évaluation de l'épaisseur des parois crâniennes. *Bulletin du Musée royal d'Histoire naturelle de Belgique* 17(48):1–33, 1941; *L'Hérédité. Buts et méthodes de la génétique humaine.* Bruxelles: Office de publicité, 1947; Contribution à l'étude de la croissance pubertaire chez l'homme. *Mémoires de l'Institut royal des Sciences naturelles de Belgique* 35 (2d ser.):1–88, 1949; *Propos sur l'anthropologie. Volume jubilaire V. Van Straelen, 1925–1954.* Vol. 2. Bruxelles: Institut royal des Sciences naturelles de Belgique, 1954, pp. 1065–

1069; De la croissance des écoliers noirs de Léopoldville entre la sixième et la dix-septième année d'âge. *Mémoires de l'Académie royale des Sciences coloniales* 6(7):1–64, 1957; Les ossements mésolithiques du site d'Ishango. *Explorations du Parc national Albert: Mission J. de Heinzelin, 1950.* Vol. 5. Bruxelles: 1958.

Le fémur néanderthalien de Fond-de-Forêt. *Mémoires de l'Institut royal des Sciences naturelles de Belgique* 148:1–164, 1961; *Développement biométrique de l'enfant à l'adulte.* Bruxelles: Presses universitaires de Bruxelles, 1969; *Élements de génétique médicale.* Bruxelles: Presses universitaires de Bruxelles, 1970; Evolution des dimensions et de la forme de la mandibule et des dents de l'homme. *Archives de Paléontologie* 59:173–277, 1972; Populations préhistoriques, historiques et actuelles de la Belgique et du Grand-Duché de Luxembourg. In: I. Schwidetzky (ed) *Rassengeschichte der Menschheit.* Vol. 7. München: Oldenbourg, 1979, pp. 103–146; Croissance des dimensions cranio-faciales de métis belgo-zaïrois. *Bulletins et Mémoires de la Société d'Anthropologie de Paris* 9 (13th ser.):163–175, 1982; (with P. Moreau & J. François) Evolution du taux de consanguinité en Belgique de 1918 à 1959. *Population* 17:241–266, 1962.

Tyson, Edward (1650–1708)

Born in Clevedon, Somerset, England, Tyson matriculated at Magdalen College, Oxford, in 1667, graduating with a B.A. in 1670 and an M.A. in 1673. He studied medicine at Cambridge, where he received his M.D. in 1680; in 1683, he was elected a Fellow of the College of Physicians. From 1684 to 1699, he lived in London, where he was physician to Bridewell and Bethlehem Hospitals, as well as Ventera Reader in Anatomy at Chirurgeon's Hall. He was elected a Fellow of the Royal Society in 1679.

Along with Marcello Malpighi (1628–1694), Anton van Leeuwenhoek (1632–1723), and Jan Swammerdam (1637–1680), Tyson was one of the preeminent comparative anatomists of the late seventeenth century. He had already won wide acclaim for his documented dissections of dolphins (1680), rattlesnakes (1682–1683), lumpfish, and opossums (1698)—the earliest descriptive anatomy of a marsupial—before turning his attention, in 1698, to the first recorded anthropoid ape imported into England, a male chimpanzee. Tyson had long been interested in exotic ani-mals, including species that most resembled man. His *Orang-Outang; or, The Anatomy of a Pygmie* (1699) is in part a dissertation on the history of previous portrayals of similar creatures, including the unnamed beast in Bernhard von Breydenbach's (d. 1497) *Peregrination in terram sanctum* (1486), the fabulous *cercopitheci* of Konrad von Gesner's (1516–1565) *Historiae animalium* (1551), the "orangutan" (also a chimpanzee) of Nicolaas Tulp's (1593–1674) *Observationum medicarum* (1641), and the freely illustrated true orangutan of Jacob Bontius' (1592–1631) *Historiae naturalis* (1658). Since Tyson's specimen had been nearly dead when he set eyes on it, he was occasionally mistaken in some of the behavioral inferences that he drew from its anatomy, and his inaccurate depiction of the animal as a club-footed biped, upright in its gait, and assisted by a crutch, was unreliably indebted to a number of these earlier portraits. But in most respects, his meticulous description of its external features and internal organs was so exact that *Orang-Outang* is still regarded by comparative anatomists as among the finest studies of a nonhuman primate ever published. Although Tyson doubted whether previous accounts had been of the same animal, he accepted the name *orang-outang* given to it by Tulp, which is of Malay origin meaning "man of the woods." This term, currently applied exclusively to the red ape of Southeast Asia, survived as a generic name for all of the great apes until the late nineteenth century.

The main purpose of Tyson's work was to provide an exact comparative anatomy of the chimpanzee with man, as a possible explanation of ancient mythology, recounted by Homer, Herodotus, Aristotle, and others, that there really were several species of humankind in the world. Such tales of "cynocephali," "satyrs," "sphinges," and "pygmies," Tyson claimed, were, at best, descriptions of apes, monkeys, and orangutans. He accordingly termed the orangutan a pygmie as well, but concluded that its anatomical features resembled those of man even more than of apes or monkeys, so that, coming nearest to humankind, the creature might in consequence be thought "the nexus of the animal and rational." In the great *scala naturae,* or Chain of Being, the last hitherto apparently missing link, according to Tyson (1699), was thus taxonomically filled by the anthropoid ape he had studied.

For some natural historians and other scientists in the eighteenth century, that proposition was to give rise to evolutionary implications, sometimes even to the claim, recognized as contrary to both reason and revelation, that human beings might have ascended from such an ape, or the ape descended from man. Most Enlightenment thinkers who adhered to the idea, however, generally inferred that the creature was really a degenerate person, of human countenance and appearance, which others had confused for a species of monkey merely on account of its mute condition. Tyson's own comparative anatomy of the chimpanzee and man was principally designed to show that the last link in the Chain of Being must be qualitatively distinct from all of the others, since the animal's stupidity and lack of speech proved that its organs were not animated by the spiritual principle that enabled humankind alone to make use of its manifestly similar features. The "nobler faculties in the mind of man," he contended, could never be due to mere "matter organized," for, in that case, anatomical homologies, not only of the chimpanzee but of other animals as well, "would be too near akin to us."

Following René Descartes' (1596–1650) *Traité de l'homme* (1664) and especially Claude Perrault's (1613–1688) *Suite des mémoires pour servir à l'histoire des animaux* (1676), Tyson supposed that all animals were just bodies without souls, and that their brain, larynx, pharynx, and other vocal organs, including those of the chimpanzee, were merely pipes and vessels not intended by God to be exercised as instruments of rational discourse. The greater the physical resemblance of these creatures to man, he imagined, the more such resemblance confirmed the spirituality of the human soul and hence our disjunction from the rest of nature. In his 1766 discussion of orangutans in the *Histoire naturelle, générale, et particulière*, Georges Buffon (1707–1788) refined similar arguments with reference to more species, even while correcting some of Tyson's comparative anatomy and allowing, among other things, that the creature was more probably a quadruped rather than a biped. He was entirely persuaded, however, by Tyson's central thesis about the discontinuity between orangutans and human beings in the *scala naturae*. In support of it, Buffon further asserted that since it was impossible for humans and apes to procreate fecund offspring, and that since human racial differences were due to climatically induced degeneration from a single stock, it was inconceivable that mankind was descended from an orangutan.

Other Enlightenment thinkers were nev-

Fig. 1. Edward Tyson's Homo sylvestris *(chimpanzee). From his monograph,* Orang-Outang, sive Homo Sylvestris . . . etc. *(1699).*

ertheless to take issue with Tyson's perspective of an unbridgeable gulf between man and ape. Some objected to his ascription of reason and a command of language to human nature in general, since infants do not speak at birth, and language, which can be mastered only in society, was not a necessary manifestation of intelligence. Such propositions were adopted by Jean-Jacques Rousseau (1712–1778) and Lord Monboddo (James Burnett) (1714–1799) in particular. Others followed Johann Friedrich Blumenbach (1752–1840) in claiming that apes are subhuman not only because they lack reason but also because their vocal organs are not, as Tyson supposed, so arranged as to make possible their articulation of the modulated tones required for speech.

More elaborately formulated questions—but still fundamentally the same as those Tyson raised about comparative anatomy and language—inform the experiments of the psychologists John and Beatrix Gardner in the late 1960s and Herbert Terrace in the 1970s, and of the primatologists David Premack also in the 1970s and Sue Savage-Rumbaugh in the 1980s and 1990s, who have attempted to communicate with apes by way of sign languages and lexigrams. The general inconclusiveness of such experiments, and the failure thus far of apes to converse with humans in any spontaneous or creative manner as infants come to do, may appear to reaffirm Tyson's perspective of the great gulf that the human capacity for linguistically representational culture establishes between our species and apes. But while Tyson attributed this difference to humankind's unique soul, physical anthropologists and primatologists today more characteristically ascribe the origins of language to differences in neurological evolution together with the development of the human sublaryngeal vocal tract.

Tyson died in London on 1 August 1708.

Robert Wokler

See also African Apes; Asian Apes; Blumenbach, Johann Friedrich; Buffon, (Compte) Georges-Louis Leclerc; Chain of Being; Greco-Roman Anthropology; Monboddo, Lord (James Burnett); Rousseau, Jean-Jacques; Tulp, Nicolaas

Bibliography
SELECTED WORKS

An anatomical observation of four ureters in an infant, and some remarks on the Glandulae Renales, made by the same ingenious person. *Philosophical Transactions of the Royal Society* 12:1039–1040, 1678; *Phocaena; or, The anatomy of a porpess . . . with a preliminary discourse concerning anatomy, and a natural history of animals.* London: Tooke, 1680; Vipera Caudi-Sona Americana; or, The anatomy of a rattlesnake dissected at the Repository of the Royal Society in January 1682–1683. *Philosophical Transactions of the Royal Society* 13:25–58, 1682–1683; Carigueya, seu Marsupiale Americanum; or, The anatomy of an opossum, dissected at Gresham College. *Philosophical Transactions of the Royal Society* 20:105–164, 1698; *Orang-Outang, sive Homo Sylvestris; or, The anatomy of a pygmie compared with that of a monkey, an ape, and a man. To which is added, a philological essay concerning the pygmies, the cynocephali, the satyrs, and sphinges of the antients. Wherein it will appear that they are all either apes or monkeys, and not men, as formerly pretended.* London: Bennet, 1699.

ARCHIVAL SOURCES

E. Tyson (Manuscripts and Drawings): Library, Royal College of Physicians of London, 11 St. Andrew's Place, Regent's Park, London NW1, England.

PRIMARY AND SECONDARY SOURCES

R. Descartes: *Traité de l'homme.* Paris: Angot, 1664; F.A. Montagu: *Edward Tyson, M.D., F.R.S., 1650–1708, and the rise of human and comparative anatomy in England: A study in the history of science.* Philadelphia: American Philosophical Society, 1943; C. Perrault: *Suite des mémoires.* Paris: Imprimerie royale, 1676; F. Tinland: *L'Homme sauvage: Homo ferus et homo sylvestris, de l'animal à l'homme.* Paris: Payot, 1968; N. Tulp: *Observationum medicarum libri tres.* Amsterdam: Elzevirium, 1641; R. Wokler: Tyson and Buffon on the orangutan. *Studies on Voltaire and the Eighteenth Century* 151–155: 2301–2319, 1976.

'Ubeidiya (Israel)

The site of 'Ubeidiya lies in the Jordan Valley about 3 km south of Lake Tiberias (the Sea of Galilee) just to the west of the Jordan River. It consists of a series of lakeshore deposits that have been extensively folded and then eroded by tectonic activities in the rift valley system of the Jordan Valley.

The archeological and paleontological levels were fortuitously discovered in 1959 and recognized as important by Moshe Stekelis (1898–1967) of Hebrew University in Jerusalem. He conducted excavations at the site from 1960 to 1967. The excavations were continued until 1974 by Ofer Bar-Yosef and Eitan Tchernov (Bar-Yosef 1974; Tchernov 1988b; Bar-Yosef & Goren Inbar 1993) and further fieldwork was undertaken in 1988 by a Franco-Israeli team directed by C. Guérin, Bar-Yosef, and Tchernov (Debard et al. 1989). During the Stekelis excavations, five pieces of hominid were discovered, including two parietal pieces, a temporal piece, an upper molar (M3), and an incisor (I_{1-2}) crown (Tobias 1966). However, only the incisor was found *in situ,* and the other remains may be more recent (Bar-Yosef, personal communication). All of the pieces were attributed to *Homo,* although the portions preserved did not permit specific attribution.

These pieces of hominid (or at least the incisor) are of particular interest in light of reassessments of the chronological position of the site based primarily on faunal considerations (e.g., Tchernov 1987, 1988a, 1988b), which place it ca. 1.4 my BP. Even if the 'Ubeidiya hominids prove to be slightly more recent than the biostratigraphic analyses of Tchernov would indicate, they would still be the oldest, or among the oldest, known hominid remains in Eurasia, outside the sub-Saharan African hominid homeland. Given this age and morphology, at least the incisor would be best attributed to *Homo erectus.*

Erik Trinkaus

See also Homo erectus; Israel

Bibliography
O. Bar-Yosef: 'Ubeidiya: A Lower Palaeolithic site in the Jordan Valley, Israel. In: A.K. Ghosh (ed) *Perspectives in palaeoanthropology* (D. Sen Festschrift). Calcutta: Mukhopadhyay, 1974, pp. 185–198; O. Bar-Yosef & N. Goren-Inbar: *The lithic assemblages of 'Ubeidiya: A Lower Palaeolithic site in the Jordan Valley.* Monograph No. 34. Hebrew University Institute of Archaeology, 1993; E. Debard et al.: Nouvelle mission archéologique et paléontologique d'Oubéidiyeh (Israël): Premiers résultats. *Paléorient* 15:231–237, 1989; E. Tchernov: The age of the 'Ubeidiya Formation, an Early Pleistocene hominid site in the Jordan Valley, Israel. *Israel Journal of Earth Sciences* 36:3–30, 1987; E. Tchernov: The age of 'Ubeidiya Formation (Jordan Valley, Israel) and the earliest hominids in the Levant. *Paléorient* 14:63–65, 1988a; E. Tchernov: La biochronologie du site de 'Ubeidiya (Valée du Jourain) et les plus anciens hominidés du Levant. *L'Anthropologie* 92:839–861, 1988b; P.V. Tobias: Fossil hominid remains from 'Ubeidiya, Israel. *Nature* 211:130–133, 1966.

UNESCO Statement on Race

In 1949, following in the wake of World War II, an invitation was issued by Arthur Ramos of the Social Science Department of UNESCO (United Nations Educational, Scientific and Cultural Organization) to a group of international social scientists to serve on a committee charged with formulating a statement on "race problems." Shortly after these invitations were issued, Ramos died. He was replaced by Robert C. Angell (United States), who subsequently served as chairman of the committee, which met in Paris in December 1949. This committee consisted of: Ernest Beaglehole (New Zealand), Juan Comas (Mexico), Jan Czekanowski (Poland), Franklin Frazier (United States), Morris Ginsberg (United Kingdom), Humayun Kabir (India), Claude Levi-Straus (France), Ashley Montagu (United States), L.A. Costa Pinto (Brazil), and Joseph Sköld (Sweden). After three days of deliberation, a draft of the committee's "Statement" was signed by all participants. Copies of the draft were then distributed to the following scientists for comment: Julian Huxley (United Kingdom), Joseph Needham (United Kingdom), L.C. Dunn (United States), Theodosius Dobzhansky (United States), Otto Klineberg (United States), Gunnar Dahlberg (Sweden), and Gunnar Myrdal (Sweden). On receipt of these comments, a revised draft was prepared and circulated for comment from Hadley Cantril (United States), Edwin G. Conklin (United States), Theodosius Dobzhansky (United States), L.C. Dunn (United States), Donald Hager (United States), Julian Huxley (United Kingdom), Otto Klineberg (United States), Wilbert Moore (United States), H.J. Muller (United States), Curt Stern (United States), Earl Planty (United States), and Richard Wood (United States). Following further amendments, the committee's statement on race was formally published on 18 July 1950 (cf. Montagu 1951).

In rejecting the existence of racial hierarchies and the notion of pure races, the UNESCO Statement stressed that the mental capacities of the races are similar and that there was no scientific evidence that miscegenation resulted in biological deterioration. It also insisted that there was no correlation between temperament, personality, and character and race, nationality, or religious affiliation, and it concluded that "race is not so much a biological phenomenon as a social myth" (cf. Montagu 1951:116).

Not unexpectedly, the UNESCO Statement's publication created quite a stir, and its contents were immediately challenged by other experts. In reponse to this, a panel of physical anthropologists and geneticists was invited to the UNESCO headquarters in Paris (4–8 June 1951) to prepare a revised statement. This panel included: R.A.M. Bergman (The Netherlands), Gunnar Dahlberg (Sweden), L.C. Dunn (United States), J.B.S. Haldane (United Kingdom), Ashley Montagu (United States), A.E. Mourant (United Kingdom), Hans Nachtsheim (Germany), Eugène Schreider (France), Harry Lionel Shapiro (United States), J.C. Trevor (United Kingdom), Henri V. Vallois (France), and Solly Zuckerman (United Kingdom). Although the conclusions of this panel were not essentially different from the first in the rejection of racial hierarchies and the notion of pure races, the panel did advocate the retention of the term "race" as a biological entity, and it left open the possibility that human races manifested innate differences with regard to their intellectual and emotional capacities. The text of the 1951 "Statement on the Nature of Races and Race Differences by Physical Anthropologists and Geneticists" can be found in Montagu (1951:176–182). (For further background information on the UNESCO statement and developing views on race and racial issues during the second half of the twentieth century, see Shipman 1994.)

Frank Spencer

See also Comas, Juan; Czekanowski, Jan; Dobzhansky, Theodosius; Eugenics; Montagu, Ashley; Race Concept; Rassenhygiene and Rassenkunde; Schreider, Eugène; Shapiro, Harry Lionel; Vallois, Henri Victor; Zuckerman, Solly (Lord)

Bibliography
A. Montagu: *Statement on race.* New York: Schuman, 1951; P. Shipman: *The evolution of racism: Human differences and the use and abuse of science.* New York: Simon & Schuster, 1994.

Uniformitarianism

The term "uniformitarianism" is used to denote the belief that the historical development of the Earth and its inhabitants has been characterized by slow, gradual change (as opposed to "catastrophism," in which change is episodic and sudden). The term came into use in the mid-nineteenth century in association with the English geologist Charles Lyell's (1797–1875) geological theories. There are, however, some conceptual ambiguities associated with the use of the term. Continental geologists often speak of "actualism": the claim that the Earth's past history has been shaped only by forces that can still be observed in operation today. Lyell was certainly an actualist, but in addition he insisted that only observable causes *operating at present-day intensities* should be used to explain the past. He thus ruled out not only catastrophes based on nonobserved causes (e.g., an asteroid impact), but also those that might have been the result of observable causes operating at greater intensity than anything experienced during human history (e.g., massive eartquakes).

Modern geologists assume that the introduction of Lyell's uniformitarianism marks a major step forward in their discipline's move toward scientific status. Catastrophists are branded as conservative thinkers who tried to retain a role for the Noachian Flood and other supernatural events. In fact, the debate between Lyell and the catastrophists was by no means so obviously resolved in favor of Lyell's position. In order to sustain an absolute uniformitarianism, Lyell had to argue that observable causes are adequate to explain geological change however far back in time one looks. In principle, the geologist could not invoke a "primeval" period when things had been significantly different from what they are today. Lyell was thus forced to adopt a "steady-state" view of the Earth, in which the planet has always been more or less the same.

The catastrophists justified their belief that earlier geological changes had been more intensive than those of today by adopting a "directionalist" viewpoint, in which the Earth has changed systematically in the course of time. Noting that the interior of the Earth was very hot, they assumed that the planet must have been gradually cooling down through geological time. This was a perfectly reasonable assumption, and even modern geologists accept that the Earth had a beginning and that conditions during its early history would have been significantly different from those we experience today. Lyell's gradualism was a step forward, but his steady-state theory went too far.

The complete uniformitarian/steady-state position was first outlined by the Scottish geologist James Hutton (1726–1797) in his two-volume *Theory of the Earth* (1795). Hutton had little interest in establishing the sequence in which the formations of the Earth's crust had been laid down, but this became a primary objective of the early-nineteenth-century geologists. It was Lyell who adapted the uniformitarian position to this concern for historical geology in his three-volume *Principles of Geology* (1830–1833). Having originally absorbed the catastrophists' viewpoint in the 1820s, Lyell studied the structure of Mt. Etna and became convinced that it could be explained not as the product of a catastrophic upheaval, but as the result of a long sequence of small volcanic eruptions. He now became concerned about the extent to which some British catastrophists such as William Buckland (1784–1856) identified the last great geological discontinuity with the biblical flood (although, in fact, this was never a crucial part of catastrophist dogma, and there was never any suggestion that the flood had been caused by anything other than natural causes). The *Principles* presented much evidence to show the extent of the changes that could be produced by modern causes and argued that such causes were adequate to explain all of the formations observed by the geologist. Earth movements created new land, and erosion destroyed the existing surface, but the creative and destructive processes were perfectly balanced so that the overall ratio of land to sea remained always the same. For Lyell, it was unscientific to speculate about causes other than those observable today, even when seeking to explain the most ancient formations.

The second volume of the *Principles* extended the argument to the succession of species revealed by the fossil record, although Lyell could not bring himself to accept the theory of evolution. To explain the apparent progressive development of life revealed by the fossil record, Lyell argued that the "Age of Reptiles" had occurred when earth movements had changed the distribution of land and sea to create on overall climate more suitable to reptiles than to mammals. There was no true progression, and a new age of reptiles might occur in the future if the same kind of conditions were re-created by the slow but constant interchange between land and sea.

In the long run, Lyell was successful in forcing geologists to reduce the scale of their hypothetical catastrophes, and by the early twentieth century uniformitarianism was accepted to the extent that all recent geological changes were explained in gradualistic terms. But hardly anyone accepted the full steady-state position, not even Charles Darwin (1809–1882), who was Lyell's greatest supporter. Many continued to believe that there were episodes when the rate of mountain-building was much more rapid than any earth movements observed today. The theory that the Earth was gradually cooling down remained popular and received support from the physicist Lord Kelvin's (1824–1907) arguments based on thermodynamics. Kelvin pointed out that if the Earth was hot, then it must have been gradually cooling down, and he tried to estimate its age. Kelvin's arguments were found to be erroneous in the early twentieth century when it was shown that radioactivity could provide a very long-term source of energy to maintain the Earth's central heat. But the very fact that radioactivity eventually provided a means of estimating the Earth's total age (4.5 billion years) confirmed that Lyell's refusal to allow scientific geology to discuss the concept of a beginning was unreasonable.

Modern geologists are uniformitarians when it comes to explaining the changes to which the Earth has been subject in the more recent geological periods, but they do not accept a steady-state view of the Earth's history. During the second half of the twentieth century, catastrophism has been revived in the form of the theory that asteroid impacts are responsible for some of the "punctuations" in the sequence of formations. Thus, even the gradualist aspect of Lyell's position has become controversial once again, although the disruptions are attributed to an external cause that leaves the uniformity of internal geological processes untouched.

Peter J. Bowler

See also Buckland, William; Catastrophism; Cuvier, Georges Léopold Chrétien Fréderic Dagobert (Baron); Darwin, Charles Robert; Kelvin, William Thomson (Lord); Lyell, (Sir) Charles

Bibliography
S.J. Gould: *Time's arrow, time's cycle: Myth and metaphor in the discovery of geological time.* Cambridge, Massachusetts: Harvard University Press, 1987; A. Hallam: *Great geological controversies.* Oxford: Oxford University Press, 1983; R. Hooykaas: *Natural law and divine miracle: The principle of uniformity in geology, biology, and history.* Leiden: Brill, 1959; J. Hutton: *Theory of the Earth, with proofs and illustrations.* 2 vols. Edinburgh: Cadell & Davis, 1795; C. Lyell: *Principles of geology: Being an attempt to explain the former changes of the Earth's surface by reference to causes now in operation.* 3 vols. London: Murray, 1830–1833. Reprint, with introduction by M.J.S. Rudwick. 3 vols.

Chicago: University of Chicago Press, 1991; M.J.S. Rudwick: Uniformity and progression. In: D.H.D. Roller (ed) *Perspective in the history of science and technology.* Norman: University of Oklahoma Press, 1971, pp. 209–227.

United Kingdom[1]

The history of British physical anthropology is extensive. Its tentative beginnings can be seen in such medieval texts as the influential encyclopedia *De proprietatibus rerum* (On the Properties of Things), compiled by the Franciscan Bartholomaeus Anglicus (fl. ca. 1220–1240), who lectured on divinity for a time at the University of Paris (cf. Steele 1924). However, it was not until the sixteenth century, in the decades immediately following Christopher Columbus' return from the New World, that anthropological inquiries finally took off with an urgency that was to continue to the present day. Obviously, it is not possible in the restricted limits of this entry to do justice to the accumulated scholarship of 500 years. Hence what follows is not so much an analytical history, as a simple chronological outline, in which some of the major intellectual and institutional developments occurring in British physical anthropology (from the sixteenth century to the second half of the twentieth century) are characterized through the activities of representative scholars, many of whom have separate biographical entries in this volume. For further details relating to the history of British physical anthropology, see Barkan (1992), Kuklick (1991), Stepan (1982), and Weiner (1982).

From the Elizabethans to the Georgians: 1485–1836
The demise of Richard III at Bosworth Field on 22 August 1485, marks the collapse of the Plantagenets and the beginning of the Tudor dynasty, which lasted until the death of Elizabeth I in 1603. During this period, the shroud of medievalism was slowly lifted in Britian as scholars such as Thomas Linacre (ca. 1460–1524), who studied medicine at the University of Padua, absorbed the spirit of the Italian Renaissance. From this beachhead, subsequent advances in the study of the natural world were made using the scientific methods advocated by Francis Bacon (1561–1626) in his celebrated *Novum Organum* (1620). Although, as represented by Linacre's activities, this revival in England had involved a promotion of the study of Greek medical classics, there were

other forces that contributed to the shredding of the medieval shroud—not least the impulse of rising commercial capitalism, which had promoted among Englishmen a desire to colonize the "Lord's vineyard" and to "seek new worlds" in search of gold as well as glory.

Although as islanders the British peoples had long been associated with the sea, it was not until 1497, when the Italian navigator Giovanni Caboto (more commonly known as John Cabot) (1450–1498) sailed from Bristol in search of the Northwest Passage to China, that they finally ventured far beyond their "scept'red isle." Among the many who followed in Cabot's wake were Martin Frobisher (ca. 1535–1594), John Hawkins (1532–1595), Francis Drake (ca. 1540–1596), and Walter Raleigh (ca. 1552–1618), whose legendary exploits were recorded for posterity by the Elizabethan scholar-diplomat Richard Hakluyt (ca. 1552–1616). Besides becoming a treasury of national pride, Hakluyt's *The Principal Navigations, Voiages, Traffiques, and Discoveries of the English Nation* (1589) also documents a developing break with traditional medieval cosmography and the emergence of the modern view of the world.

This burgeoning travel literature also prompted a reexamination of traditional notions regarding human natural history. The flowering of anthropology, however, unlike many other nascent sciences, continued to be handicapped by the influence of religion. Furthermore, despite the mounting self-confidence and willingness of scholars in the late sixteenth and early seventeenth centuries to challenge the authority of both medieval and classical scholarship, the anthropological literature from this period continued to be haunted by fables, as can be readily seen from Edward Topsell's (1572–1625) *The Historie of Foure-Footed Beastes* (first published in 1607). Inspired by the German natural historian Konrad von Gesner's (1516–1565) *Historia animalium* (1551–1558), which enjoyed considerable popularity in Britain well into the seventeenth century, Topsell's compendium is, like its prototype, a peculiar mix of new facts and old fabulous lore. By the mid-seventeenth century, however, interest in tales of fabulous human monsters went into a sharp decline, a trend hastened in part by the founding of the Royal Society of London (ca. 1660), which stressed the need for research based solely on experiment and accurate observation. Until the nineteenth century, this society's *Transactions* was a major conduit for the publication of research in all branches of science, includ-

ing anthropology. Another early organization germane to the history of British anthropology is the Society of Antiquaries, whose origin can be traced to an Academy for the Study of Antiquity and History founded in 1572. After 1604, however, this academy became inactive until it was revived in the early 1700s. In 1751, it was incorporated as the Society of Antiquaries, London, and in 1770 it began publishing its journal, *Archaeologia*.

From the accumulating anthropological literature of the sixteenth and seventeenth centuries, two primary issues can be identified that are germane to this narrative: (1) the developing debate on the origins and significance of the inhabitants of the New World, and (2) the problem of explaining the overt physical (and cultural) differences of humankind.

Initially, the debate on the origins and significance of the Indians of the Americas had been confined to Spanish and Portugese scholars and, as their literature reveals, opinions were widely divergent. In fact, by the close of the sixteenth century it is possible to identify four competing hypotheses to account for the origins of the American Indians. In a nutshell, the Indians were viewed as descendants of either: (1) the Lost Tribes of Israel, (2) the survivors of the fabled and fated continent of Atlantis, (3) shipwrecked Carthagenian explorers, or (4) immigrants from Asia (cf. Huddleston 1967). With the shifting balance of maritime power during the late sixteenth century, however, northern European scholars began to take a more active interest in this debate, and from all indications the first English scholar to address this issue was Edward Brerewood (also known as Bryerwood) (ca. 1565–1613), a mathematician and the first professor of astronomy at Gresham College, London. In his book *Enquiries Touching the Diversity of Languages and Religions through the Chief Parts of the World* (1614), which is also widely regarded as a landmark in the history of comparative linguistics, Brerewood reached the same conclusion José de Acosta (1539–1600) had in his *Historia natural y moral de las Indias* (1590; the first English translation was published in 1604), namely, that the Indians were in all probability the offspring of the "Tartars" in Asia. While this essentially modern conclusion continued to be debated to the beginning of the twentieth century, it appears that the Acosta-Brerewood thesis has been a viewpoint shared by later British scholars.

Of all of the books produced during the seventeenth century dealing with the issue of the origin of the New World's inhabitants, there is little question that *Prae-Adamitae*, written by the French Calvinist scholar Isaac La Peyrère (1596–1676), was the most provocative. Translated into English and published in London in 1665, *Men before Adam*, unleashed a controversy that was unparalleled at that time. Although the Neapolitan heretic-philosopher Giordano Bruno (1548–1600), who had spent a short time in England (1583–1585), had argued in his *De innumerabilibus sive de immenso* (1591) that the African Negro was of a different "protoplast," this view had not stirred opinion to the same extent as La Peyrère's *Prae-Adamitae*. In England, as on the Continent, its frankly polygenistic intentions led to an avalanche of refutations that included the posthumous work *The Primitive Origination of Mankind* (1677) by the legal scholar Matthew Hale (1609–1676).

Although the most popular and enduring explanation of racial diversity was the environmental (climate) hypothesis whose intellectual roots extended into classical antiquity, there were a number of Elizabethans, such as the mariner-geographer George Best (d. 1584), who were clearly troubled by this hypothesis. In Best's case he conjectured that the blackness of the African Negro proceeded "from some naturall infection"—an idea that was later resuscitated by the American physician Benjamin Rush (1745–1813) at the close of the eighteenth century (cf. Rush 1799). What had troubled Best and continued to perplex scholars into the eighteenth century was that contrary to expectations the transportation of African slaves from equatorial latitudes to the more temperate climes of North America had not brought about a change in the Negro's complexion; similarly, the complexion of the Europeans living near the equator appeared unchanged. The Padua-trained physician Thomas Browne (1605–1682), ruminating on this troubling observation in his *Pseudodoxia epidemica* (1646), ventured that the differences in racial skin color were innate and permanent. To those who found the polygenistic inference of this conclusion too daring for comfort, a simple solution was to fall back on the authority of the Genesis story of Noah's curse on his son Ham, as the historian Peter Heylyn (1600–1662) had done in his *Microcosmus* (1621). Alternatively, rather than ignore the plurality hinted at by Browne, it occurred to William Petty (1623–1687), a physician-economist and founding member of the Royal Society, that the African Negro, along with other sorts

of men and to say nothing of "Gyants and Pigmyes," might, in fact, represent a graded series that connected with a similar gradation among the "Beastes" on down to the "smallest worm" (cf. Lansdowne 1927, Vol. 2:26–31). The advantage of this approach was that it allowed for the view that the human family was composed of discrete entities that could be ranked according to their degree of "perfection," while still retaining a monogenetic perspective. How much of this Petty aired in his 1676 lecture at the Royal College of Physicians in Dublin is not known, and what influence, if any, it had had on subsequent developments is far from clear. But whatever Petty's role may have been in the history of this scheme, the fact remains that during the last decades of the seventeenth century the application of the Aristotelian concept of the *scala naturae* (Chain of Being) to the problem of racial diversity became an increasingly attractive idea. Indeed, it was destined to dominate anthropological thinking until well into the latter half of the nineteenth century.

As Petty's correspondence reveals, he had also toyed with the idea of using physiognomic traits to separate and rank the human races. The first attempts along this line were taken by the French savant François Bernier (1620–1688), who presented in an anonymous communication published in the *Journal des Sçavans* (1684; see Bendyshe 1864:360–364 for an English translation) a simple racial classification based primarily on skin color, hair type, and pigmentation. The first Englishman to attempt a similar classification was the Cambridge naturalist Richard Bradley (d. 1732) (1721). While both declined to rank the races they had identified, it is evident from others such as John Ovington (1653–1731), author of *A Voyage to Surat in the Year 1689*, that the African Negro, and in particular the "Hottentots," had by this time been assigned to the bottom rung of the *scala naturae*. "If there's any medium between a rational Animal and a Beast," Ovington declared, "the Hotantot [sic] lays the fairest claim to that Species" (Ovington 1696). Soon thereafter, this lowly assignment was consolidated by the anatomist Edward Tyson (1650–1708), who in presenting the results of his dissection of an Angolan chimpanzee to the Royal Society in June 1698 provided compelling evidence for the hierarchical relationship between humans and the anthropoid apes. Dismissing earlier folklore about such animals being half-human, Tyson declared his creature "to be wholly a Brute, tho' in the formation of the body . . .it may be more resembling a Man." All told, Tyson catalogued forty-eight anatomical features that his Angolan "Pygmie" shared with humans, and thirty-four it had in common with "Apes and monkey-kind"—all of which served to convince him and several generations to follow that these creatures were an intermediate link between the most degenerate form of humanity and the apes (Tyson 1699).

While these ideas continued to receive sporadic consideration during the first half of the eighteenth century, it was not until the mid-1770s and the appearance of the Scottish jurist and philosopher Henry Home's (Lord Kames) (1696–1782) *Sketches of the History of Man* (1774) and Edward Long's (1734–1813) *The History of Jamaica* (1774) that the monogenist–polygenist debate took on a renewed intensity.

Among the first to respond to the overt polygenist stance of Kames et al. was John Hunter (ca. 1752–1809) (1775), not to be confused with the London anatomist-surgeon John Hunter (1728–1793). Like his counterpart at Göttingen University, Johann Friedrich Blumenbach (1752–1840) (1775), Hunter endeavored in his Edinburgh M.D. thesis to defend monogenism and explain human variation in terms of the traditional environmental thesis (a translation of both Hunter's thesis *Quaedum de hominum varietatibus* and Blumenbach's *De generis humani varietate nativa* can be found in Bendyshe 1865). Another notable defense of the traditional monogenist thesis was mounted by the Scottish historian William Robertson (1721–1793) (1777).

Coinciding with this surge in the monogenist literature was the introduction of the facial angle by the Dutch physician Petrus Camper (1722–1789), which provided, so it seemed, irrefutable evidence for the reality of the Great Chain of Being. However, it is important to underline the fact that while this development greatly enhanced the authority of the polygenists' cause and sanctioned such treatises as *An Account of the Regular Gradation of Man* (1799), written by the Manchester surgeon Charles White (1728–1813), adherence to this hierarchical concept did not necessarily imply an allegiance to polygenism. For example, the London anatomist-surgeon John Hunter (cf. Hunter 1861) and the Scottish naturalist William Smellie (1740–1795) (1790) were both declared monogenists yet resolute enthusiasts of the Great Chain of

Being. The same can be said of the anatomist William Lawrence (1783–1867) (1822). There were, however, many British monogenists, such as James Cowles Prichard (1786–1848) (1813), who followed Blumenbach in his rejection of the chain concept and supported in some form or another the traditional environmental hypothesis. In Prichard's case, he believed that racial variation was more likely the result of the process of civilization rather than simple climatic conditions. But as subsequent editions of his *Researches into the Physical History of Man* (1826, 1836–1847) suggest, the validity of this idea and monogenism per se had been seriously undermined by the evidence supplied through the comparative study and measurement of human crania (*vide infra*). For example, the study conducted by the American physician Samuel George Morton (1799–1851) (1844) in Philadelphia on ancient Egyptian crania seemed to support the view that human physical diversity had been coeval with the primitive dispersion of the human species that had followed the Creation, and that, since this diaspora, the racial types had remained essentially unchanged. Viewed from this perspective, it appeared to many that the single-origin hypothesis could not be reasonably accommodated within biblical chronology, which left the monogenists with two options: Either changes in human morphology had occurred rapidly, soon after the Creation, or biblical chronology was incorrect and human beings had existed long before the 6,000 years stipulated in the Pentateuch. Reluctant to challenge the authority of the latter, Prichard and his followers were for the time being obliged to embrace the former proposition (e.g., William B. Carpenter's [1813–1885] [1848] review of the third edition of Prichard's *Researches*).

Although there were those who still continued to operate within the limits of a literalistic exegesis of Genesis, claiming, as the Archbishop of Amargh James Ussher (1581–1636) had, that the Earth and its inhabitants were created upon "the twenty-third day of October" in the year 4004 B.C., there were, in fact, few scientific geologists at the commencement of the nineteenth century who seriously applied this date to the age and natural history of the Earth. However, as indicated by Prichard's stance, Ussher's date was still widely regarded as the boundary of human history, which in geological terms was then thought to be represented by the superficial gravels of the Tertiary formations. During the opening decades of the nineteenth century, these superficial gravels were generally viewed as evidence of the Noachian Flood. Later, during the 1840s, this interpretation was rapidly replaced by the glacial hypothesis (*vide infra*).

Although in the meantime the French savants Georges Cuvier (1769–1832) and Alexandre Brongniart (1770–1847) were the first to employ index fossils in their study of the Paris Basin (1808), the English surveyor William Smith (1769–1839) (cf. Smith 1816) is nevertheless generally acknowledged as being the first to recognize the utility of fossil fauna in identifying geological strata and their succession—a step that contributed significantly not only to the development of geochronology, but also to the ultimate recognition of human antiquity.

From the close of the eighteenth century to the mid-nineteenth century there had been sporadic reports of flint artifacts being found in these gravels, and often in direct association with the remains of extinct mammalian fauna, such as the discoveries made by the Essex antiquarian John Frere (1740–1807) (1808) at Hoxne in Suffolk. However, it was not until 1859 that the barrier of biblical chronology was finally breached and the reality of the greater antiquity of the human species finally accepted—an event that was largely achieved through the efforts of a small group of British scientists (*vide infra*).

From the Victorians to the Edwardians: 1837–1936
The years between 1837 and 1936 (i.e., from the crowning of Queen Victoria to the abdication of Edward VIII) witnessed the emergence of Britain as one of the leading industrial nations of Europe and the creator of an unrivaled colonial empire. It is in this general context that the modern contours of British anthropology were slowly established. Following a description of the emerging institutional framework, the developments in the steadily diversifying discipline of anthropology will be briefly considered under the broad headings of comparative primate anatomy, paleoprimatology, and primate behavior, human paleontology and paleoanthropology, craniology, and human biology.

INSTITUTIONAL FRAMEWORK. Even though academic programs in anthropology emerged at Oxford and Cambridge Universities toward the middle of this period, initially this development had only a marginal impact on physical anthropology, which until World War II continued to be dominated by researchers trained and employed in other fields. As in the preceding period, this community was composed largely of individuals trained in the medical sciences, and in many cases anthropological research conducted in this quarter tended to be a peripheral activity, though there were exceptions, such as Richard Owen (1804–1892), William H. Flower (1831–1899), and Arthur Keith (1866–1955), who, as conservators at the Royal College of Surgeons, London, were able to devote significant amounts of time to the pursuit of physical anthropology. The remainder of the community was composed of individuals trained in the natural sciences who held either full-time museum or academic positions, along with a significant amateur contingent. This latter group, particularly during the early phase of this period, was dominated by what might be called gentleman-scientists (those of independent means), though as the century wore on they were slowly replaced by individuals who earned their living in either business or one of the "new" professions. As this suggests, throughout much of this period the "amateur" continued to enjoy a respected status in British scientific circles—a situation in marked contrast to that of the United States where the "amateur" was stigmatized by a rapidly evolving professionalized community.

The growing interest in anthropology among early Victorians is clearly reflected in the creation of the Ethnological Society of London (ESL) in 1843. From its inception, however, the ESL was concerned more with philology, history, and geography, than human biology. As such, in the early 1860s, a number of dissatisfied ESL members, led by James Hunt (1833–1869), broke away to form the Anthropological Society of London (ASL). And it is interesting to note that it was Hunt who was responsible for securing anthropology's present location in Section H of the British Association for the Advancement of Science (BAAS). Initially, Hunt had endeavored to affiliate his group of "anthropologicals" with the biologists in Section D in an effort to underscore the differences between the ASL and the "ethnologicals" who, from the outset had been associated with geography in Section E. As this indicates, the BAAS (founded in 1831), was a major arena for airing the results of anthropological research throughout much of the nineteenth and early twentieth centuries.

During the ASL's brief existence (1863–1870), its *Memoirs* and *Anthropological Review* became important outlets for articles pertaining to paleoanthropological issues and other aspects of physical anthropology. Following Hunt's death, a merger between the ASL and the ESL was brokered by Thomas Henry Huxley (1825–1895) that resulted in the establishment of the Anthropological Institute of Great Britain and Ireland in 1871 (the institute received its royal charter in 1907). Although from the outset an effort was made to balance the needs of both physical and cultural anthropology, the latter tended to dominate the pages of both the institute's official organ, the *Journal of the Anthropological Institute of Great Britain and Ireland* (1872–) and its supplementary publication, *Man* ("a monthly record of anthropological science"), which began publication in 1901. But be that as it may, physical anthropology faired well in this new institutional setting (see Table 1), and since Huxley's installation as the institute's first president there have been a number of physical anthropologists who have presided over this august body. In addition to the Anthropological Institute (and its precursors), there were a host of other scientific societies that were congenial to the needs of physical anthropologists. For example, the Geological Society of London (GSL), founded in 1807, became an important outlet for paleontological research. Like the Royal Society *(vide ante)*, the GSL's *Transactions* (1811–) and *Proceedings* (1827–), are vital sources in the history of human paleontology. Another is the Zoological Society of London (AZL), founded in 1826. In the case of the AZL's *Transactions* and *Proceedings*, they became important conduits for primatological research throughout the period under discussion and beyond.

Finally, this period also witnessed the emergence of two major research museums that figure prominently in the history of Victorian physical anthropology, namely, the museum of the Royal College of Surgeons of London (later the Royal College of Surgeons of England) and the Natural History Museum, London. The former museum was initially created in 1813 to house the vast natural history collection made by the London surgeon John Hunter (1728–1793); whereas the Natural History Museum (NHM), located in South Kensington, had been conceived as an extension of the British Museum that was established in Bloomsbury in the early 1750s to house the library and art collection of Hans Sloane (1660–1753). Specifically, the NHM was built in 1881 to house the Natural History Department, formerly located in the Bloomsbury establishment. Although formal separation of these two institutions occurred in 1963, the NHM is still frequently referred to as the British Museum of Natural History

COMPARATIVE PRIMATE ANATOMY. Despite the absence of any reference to the issue of human origins and our relationship to anthropoid apes in Charles Darwin's (1809–1882) revolutionary work *On the Origin of Species* (1859), the relevance and implication of his evolutionary theory was not lost, least of all to Huxley. Besides becoming an influential advocate of evolutionary studies, Huxley made his own contribution to this burgeoning field. His book *Evidence as to Man's Place in Nature* (1863) represents the beginnings of modern comparative anatomy—though it is important not to overlook the prior contributions to this field by such workers as Richard Owen (e.g., Owen 1855).

Among the host of workers who immediately followed Huxley into this domain was St. George Jackson Mivart (1827–1900), whose definition of the order Primates (1873) is still largely valid. Subsequent developments in this field on through into the first quarter of the twentieth century can be conveniently traced via the work of Arthur Keith, Grafton Elliot Smith (1871–1937), Frederic Wood Jones (1879–1954), and Wilfrid Edward Le Gros Clark (1895–1971). Their collective work represents the first major attempt at a functional understanding of primate anatomy and evolution.

Both Keith and Smith developed influential hypotheses to account for human origins. In Keith's case, he viewed this evolutionary process from an essentially locomotory viewpoint. He was convinced that the specific arboreal locomotive postures of apes revealed important clues to the manner in which humans had acquired orthograde posture. In 1903, he outlined a four-stage hypothesis, which he developed further in 1923. Smith (e.g., 1902, 1912), on the other hand, focused his attention on the development of cerebral functions, claiming that the early adaptation of the primates to an arboreal mode of life was the key to the development of the brain and (contra Keith) that erect posture was not a crucial event in human evolution.

By contrast, Jones refused to identify the primary instigating forces leading to the emergence of the Hominidae, though he believed, like Smith, that too much emphasis

TABLE 1. Huxley Memorial Lectures, 1900–1995

Date	Lecturer	Topic
1900	Lord Avebury (John Lubbock)	Huxley: The Man and His Work
1901	Francis Galton*	Possible Improvement of the Human Breed under the Existing Conditions of Law and Sentiment
1902	D.J. Cunningham	Right-Handedness and Left-Brainedness
1903	Karl Pearson	On the Inheritance of the Mental and Moral Characters in Man
1904	Joseph Deniker	Les six races composant la population actuelle de l'Europe
1905	John Beddoe*	Colour and Race
1906	W.M. Flinders Petrie	Migrations
1907	Edward B. Tylor	No lecture
1908	William Z. Ripley	The European Population of the United States
1909	Magnus Gustaf Retzius*	The So-Called North European Race of Mankind
1910	William Boyd Dawkins*	The Arrival of Man in Britain in the Pleistocene Age
1911	Felix von Luschan*	The Early Inhabitants of Western Asia
1912	William Gowland	Metals in Antiquity
1913	William J. Sollas*	Paviland Cave: An Aurignacian Station in Wales
1914		No lecture
1915	Émile Cartailhac*	No lecture
1916	James G. Frazer	Ancient Stories of a Great Flood
1917		No lecture
1918		No lecture
1919		No lecture
1920	A.C. Haddon*	Migrations of Culture in British New Guinea
1921	Henry Balfour	The Archer's Bow in Homeric Poems
1922	Marcellin Boule*	L'oeuvre anthropologique du prince Albert 1e de Monaco et les récentes progrès de la paléontologie humaine en France[2]
1923	E.S. Hartland	No lecture
1924	René Verneau*	La race de Néanderthal et la race de Grimaldi: Leur rôle dans l'humanité
1925	Arthur Evans	The Early Nilotic Libyan, and Egyptian Relations with Minoan Crete
1926	William Ridgeway	No lecture
1927	Aleš Hrdlička*	The Neanderthal Phase of Man
1928	Arthur Keith*	The Evolution of the Human Races
1929	Erlan Nordenskiold	The American Indian As an Inventor
1930	A.H. Sayce	The Antiquity of Civilized Man
1931	Georg Thilenius	On Some Biological Viewpoints in Ethnology
1932	C.G. Seligman	Anthropological Perspective and Psychological Theory
1933	J.K. Myers	The Cretan Labyrinth: A Retrospect for Aegean Research
1934	Aurel Stein	The Indo-Iranian Borderlands: Their Prehistory in the Light of Geography and of Recent Explorations
1935	Grafton Elliot Smith*	The Place of Thomas Henry Huxley in Anthropology
1936	Edward Westermarck	Methods in Social Anthropology
1937	H.J. Fleure	Racial Evolution and Archaeology
1938	Marcel Mauss	Une categorie de l'esprit humaine: La notion de personne, celle de "moi"
1939	R.R. Marett	Charity and the Struggle for Existence
1940	H.J.E. Peake	The Study of Prehistoric Times
1941	Henri Breuil*	Découverte de l'antiquité de l'homme et quelques unes de ses evidences
1942	Leonard Woolley	North Syria As Cultural Link in the Ancient World
1943	F.C. Bartlett	Anthropology in Reconstruction
1944	V. Gordon Childe	Archaeological Ages As Technological Stages
1945	Alfred Louis Kroeber	The Ancient Oikumenê As an Historic Culture Aggregate
1946	G. Caton-Thompson	The Aterian Industry: Its Place and Significance in the Palaeolithic World
1947	W.L.H. Duckworth*	Some Complexities of Human Structure
1948	Robert H. Lowie	Some Aspects of Political Organization among the American Aborigines
1949	James Hornell	No lecture

1950	Julian S. Huxley	New Bottles for New Wines: Ideology and Scientific Knowledge
1951	A.R. Radcliffe Brown	The Comparative Method in Social Anthropology
1952	Peter Buck (Te Rangi Hiroa)*	No lecture
	Kaj Birket-Smith	The History of Ethnology in Denmark
1953	M. Ginsberg	On the Diversity of Morals
1954	Ralph Linton	No lecture
	Henri V. Vallois*	Neanderthals and Praesapiens
1955	F.W. Jones*	No lecture
	Robert Redfield	Societies and Cultures As Natural Systems
1956	J.B.S. Haldane	The Argument from Animals to Men: An Examination of Its Validity for Anthropologists
1957	J.E. Sigvold Linné	Technical Secrets of American Indians
1958	Wilfrid E. Le Gros Clark*	Bones of Contention
1959	Raymond Firth	Problems and Assumptions in an Anthropological Study of Religion
1960	Samuel K. Lothrop	Early Migrations to Central and South America
1961	A.E. Mourant	Evolution, Genetics, and Anthropology
1962	Dorothy A.E. Garrod	The Middle Palaeolithic of the Near East and the Problem of Mount Carmel Man
1963	E.E. Evans Pritchard	The Azande State
1964	G.H.R. von Koenigswald*	Early Man: Facts and Fantasy
1965	Claude Lévi-Strauss	The Future of Kinship Studies
1966	J.E.S. Thompson	The Maya Central Area
1967	Sherwood L. Washburn*	Behaviour and the Origin of Man
1968	Georges H. Rivière	My Experience at the Musée d'Ethnologie
1969	I. Schapera	The Crime of Sorcery
1970	C. Daryll Forde	Ecology of the Social Structure
1971	C. Peter Murdock	Anthropology's Mythology
1972	L. Cavalli-Sforza	Human Races: Their Origin and Differentiation
1973	K. Wacksmann	Spencer to Hood: A Changing View of Non-European Music
1974	J. Desmond Clark	Africa in Prehistory: Peripheral or Paramount?
1975	G. Reichel	Cosmology As Ecological Analysis: A View from the Rain Forest
1976	M.N. Srinivas	The Changing Position of Indian Women
1977	Meyer Fortes	Sacrifice; or, Was Your Fieldwork Really Necessary?
1978	Joseph S. Weiner*	Beyond Physical Anthropology
1979	Gordon Willey	Toward a Holistic View of Ancient Maya Civilizations
1980	Edmund R. Leach	Why Did Moses Have a Sister?
1981	Fei Hsiao-tung	Some Observations on the Transformation of Rural China
1982	Paul T. Baker*	Adaptive Limits of Human Populations
1983	Clifford Geertz	Culture and Change: The Indonesian Case
1984	Junichiro Itani	The Evolution of Primate Social Structure
1985	Louis Dumont	Are Cultures Living Beings? German Identity in Interaction
1986	Lewis Binford	Data, Relativism, and Archaeological Science: Looking at, Thinking about, and Inferring the Past
1987	G. Ainsworth Harrison	Social Heterogeneity and Biological Variation
1988	Carleton Gajdusek	New Plagues-Old Scourges: Epidemics of Brain Disease in Population Isolates in the Twentieth Century
1989	Frederik Barth	Transmission and the Shaping of Culture in Asia and Melanesia
1990	Robert Hinde	A Biologist Looks at Anthropology
1991	Colin Renfrew	Archaeology, Genetics and Linguistic Diversity: A New Synthesis?
1992	Mary Douglas	The Talking Donkey: Balsam's story on the Book of Numbers (Chapters 22–24)
1993	George Stocking Jr.	Reading the *Palimpsest of Enquiry*: "Notes and Queries" and the History of British Social Anthropology
1994	Sidney W. Mintz	Enduring Substances and Trying Theories: The Caribbean Region As Oikumenê
1995	Zack Goody	A kernel of doubt: agnosticism in cultural and cross-cultural perspective

*Denotes a biographical entry in the encyclopedia.

had been placed on the acquisition of erect posture in human evolution. Furthermore, in contrast to Keith and to some extent Smith, Jones was more interested in primate origins. It was from this perspective that Jones developed his controversial tarsoid hypothesis, in which he endeavored to show that hominid characters could be traced to this basal primate stock (cf. Jones 1916, 1929).

In many respects, Clark's contributions built on Smith's legacy, and although his activites spill over into the recent modern period, his *Early Forerunners of Man* (1934, later republished in 1962 under the title *Antecedants of Man*), which is widely regarded as a landmark publication in modern primatology, serves to characterize this subdiscipline at the close of the Edwardian period.

PALEOPRIMATOLOGY. Following the pioneering description of a Siwalik fossil primate by William E. Baker (1808–1881) and Henry Durand (1812–1871) in the mid-1830s, the next major British contribution to the field of paleoprimatology was not made until the last quarter of the nineteenth century, when Richard Lydekker (1849–1915) undertook at the NHM in London a summary of fossil primate material recovered during the interim from the Siwaliks and associated deposits. During the first quarter of the twentieth century, this work was further advanced by Guy Ellock Pilgrim (1875–1943). It was also during the later phases of this period that Arthur Tindell Hopwood at the NHM (1897–1969) provided the first description of *Proconsul africanus*, the remains of an African dryopithecine that had been recovered from Miocene deposits at Koru, Kenya, in the mid-1920s (cf. Hopwood 1933).

PRIMATE BEHAVIOR. In the same way that Hopwood's study signals a mounting interest in African paleontology, so the publication of the book *The Social Life of Monkeys and Apes* (1932) by Solly Zuckerman (1902–1993) reflects an emerging interest in the cognate field of primate behavior. Although the relevance of such studies is clearly reflected in Darwin's *The Expression of Emotions in Man and Animals* (1872), as well as in George Romanes' (1848–1894) *Mental Evolution in Animals* (1883), it was not until after World War II that a concerted effort was launched to study primate ecology and behavior.

HUMAN PALEONTOLOGY AND PALEOANTHROPOLOGY. Along with Darwin's *Origin*, pub-lished in November 1859, the establishment of human antiquity in the spring of 1859 ranks as one of the primary landmarks in the history of anthropology. The major players in this latter drama were Hugh Falconer (1808–1865) and Joseph Prestwich (1812–1896). Their involvement in the excavations at Brixham Cave (1858–1859) in Devon led to a general acceptance of the artifacts found there, and more particularly those collected in the 1840s by the French antiquarian Jacques Boucher de Perthes (1788–1868) in the Somme River Valley in northwest France, as *prima facie* evidence for extending human antiquity into the Pleistocene.

Following the events of 1859, there was a mounting interest in the problem of determining the extent of human antiquity and the task of establishing a reliable framework of relative chronology into which both ancient human skeletal and cultural remains could be fitted. Prominent among these early efforts was Prestwich's (1863) practical classification of the river terrace gravels, which continued to be used (with refinement) well into the next century. Another was the synthesis of the evidence for multiple glaciations in Scotland and northern England by James Geikie (1839–1915) (1874, 1877), which provided a new perspective on Pleistocene geology. The correlation of Geikie's scheme with the cultural subdivisions of the Paleolithic—a term coined by John Lubbock (1834–1913) in his *Prehistoric Times* (1865)—devised by Continental workers such as Édouard Lartet (1801–1871) and Gabriel de Mortillet (1821–1898) furnished late-nineteenth-century workers with an essentially modern chronological framework.

The status of the European human fossil record in the 1860s and the then current British views on the evolutionary significance of these materials can be gleaned from Lyell's *The Geological Evidences of the Antiquity of Man* (1863). This work also contains an account of Huxley's examination of the celebrated Neandertal skull (though its phylogenetic significance was not recognized at the time) found in 1865 near Düsseldorf, Germany, and later described by the Bonn anatomist Hermann Schaaffhausen (1816–1893). A translation of Schaaffhausen's historic paper by the anatomist William Busk (1807–1886) was published in the *Natural History Review* in 1861. Busk was also responsible for providing the first description of the Gibraltar cranium (1865). Much later, the Oxford geologist William J. Sollas (1849–1936)

(1908) submitted this specimen to an exacting study, from which he concluded that it was a member of the then recognized Neandertal group.

With the probable exception of a molar tooth found (and since lost) in association with Mousterian-like artifacts at Pontnewydd, Wales, in the early 1870s (cf. Hughes & Thomas 1874), British workers were deprived of hominid fossils akin to those found in abundance on the Continent. Whether it was this deprivation, or simply the compelling logic of the argument made by the French prehistorian Gabriel de Mortillet for the existence of the "Eolithique"—the dawn of human industrial development—the fact remains that British workers, or at least many of them, became enthusiastic converts to this idea in the late nineteenth century. Indeed, it was largely this eolithic movement, compounded with the changing expectations of scholars concerning the evolutionary route via which the modern human form emerged, that provided the platform from which the now infamous Piltdown assemblage was launched in 1912. The authority of this spurious fossil, which continued well into the early 1950s, not only delayed recognition of the evolutionary significance of the australopithecine material found in South Africa between the two World Wars, but also served to obscure the importance of the early hominid fossil recovered at Swanscombe, in West Kent, England, in the mid-1930s by Alvan T. Marston (1889–1971).

During this same time period, British workers were also intimately involved in the discovery of important hominid fossils overseas, namely at Gibraltar (cf. Garrod et al. 1928) and Mount Carmel in the Middle East (cf. Garrod & Bate 1937). The skeletal remains from the latter site formed the basis of the now classic volume published on the eve of World War II by the American Theodore D. McCown (1908–1969) and Arthur Keith (McCown & Keith 1939).

Running parallel with these latter events was the protracted biometric study of Paleolithic crania by Geoffrey M. Morant (1899–1964) in Karl Pearson's (1857–1936) Galton Laboratory at University College, London. Aside from its contribution to the perennial debate on the evolutionary significance of the Neandertals and the origin of modern humans, Morant's study (cf. Morant 1926, 1927, 1928, 1930–1931) is important in that it reflects a trend away from the more traditional craniometric methodologies established in the nineteenth century and toward the progressive application of more-elaborate statistical techniques after World War II.

CRANIOLOGY. Although Thomas Browne (*vide ante*) had noted in his *Hydriotaphia* (1658) that the skull of the Negro could be distinguished from an Englishman by its shape, it was not until the early nineteenth century that British workers began to take an active interest in the then nascent field of craniology. Similarly, while the naturalist and president of the Royal Society (1778–1820) Joseph Banks (1743–1820) had taken an interest in the work of Blumenbach and had significantly enriched his craniological collections at Göttingen, from all indications it was the Scottish anatomist Charles Bell (1774–1842) at Edinburgh University who was among the first scientists in the United Kingdom to investigate the scientific possibilities of Blumenbach's comparative method (cf. Bell 1824).

Further impulse to the study of human crania in Britain was provided by the emergence of the abortive phrenological movement, fostered by George Combe (1788–1858) and James Straton (d. 1856), among others. Straton's *Contributions to the Mathematics of Phrenology* (1845) is of particular interest since it provides a convenient summary of the status of craniometric methodology at mid-century. Likewise, the work of Joseph Barnard Davis (1801–1881) mirrors both the ethos and the intellectual objectives of craniology at this juncture. In many respects, Davis can be viewed as the British equivalent to Samuel George Morton in Philadelphia. In addition to his impressive compendium *Thesaurus Craniorum* (1867), Davis also produced in collaboration with John Thurnam (1810–1873) a major synthetic work, the two-volume *Crania Britannica* (1865), in which they endeavored to reconstruct the racial history of Britain from early Saxon times to their present.

Further developments during the second half of the nineteenth century can be tracked through the catalogs and miscellaneous publications of such workers as William H. Flower at the Royal College of Surgeons in London and William Turner (1832–1916) in Edinburgh. In fact, it was Turner who was largely responsible for describing the wealth of cranial skeletal material collected during the voyage of HMS *Challenger* during the early 1870s (cf. Turner 1884–1886).

HUMAN BIOLOGY. Closely tied in with these

craniological pursuits was a burgeoning concern with the diversity of modern human populations and an effort to understand their inherent biological relationships. Employing a wide variety of anthropometric methods, British workers such as John Beddoe (1826–1911) were as energetic as their Continental and American counterparts in measuring and describing the human form. And as was the scientific fashion of the period, their raw comparative data provided the basis for grand classificatory schemes, such as those produced by Huxley (1870) and Flower (1885). Although this activity continued well into the second quarter of the twentieth century, for example, the schemes presented in Herbert J. Fleure's (1877–1969) *The Peoples of Europe* (1922) and A.C. Haddon's (1855–1940) *The Races of Man* (1925), the sterility of mere data collection was beginning to be recognized (cf. Haddon et al. 1935). (For insights into this incipient transition, see Stepan 1982 and Barkan 1992.)

While workers such as Beddoe (1885) and others were endeavoring to characterize the racial composition of Britain, there were others busy studying the comparative growth and development of British children. At first, these studies were driven in part by the changing sociopolitical climate in early Victorian England, and subsequently by the Darwinian conviction that the study of human growth would provide evolutionary insights.

As vividly portrayed in the novels of Charles Dickens, the conditions of the poor, and especially their children, in early Victorian England were wretched. This deplorable situation began to change with the passage of the Factories Regulation Act in 1833—the first in a series of radical social reforms—which prohibited the employment of children under nine years of age. It was against the backdrop of this act that Leonard Horner (1785–1864), one of four government inspectors of factories appointed at the time, produced the first large-scale survey on record of the heights of British children (cf. Tanner 1981:153–161). Further developments along this line occurred in 1873, when the biometrician Francis Galton (1822–1911) began a program of body measurements on schoolchildren sponsored by the newly created Anthropological Institute (cf. Galton 1873, 1874, 1875)—which led others in Europe and the United States, such as the physiologist Henry Pickering Bowditch (1840–1911) in Boston, to follow suit. However, for reasons not entirely clear, there was a palpable decline in the tempo of growth-and-development research in Britain until after World War II. Despite this apparent shift in focus, the decades prior to World War II were not completely devoid of significant activity. In addition to Karl Pearson and the anthropological wing of his biometric school (that included such workers as Miriam L. Tildesley) at University College, London, which spearheaded the development of modern population statistics, there were also the protracted efforts of J. Arthur Thomson (1861–1933) to introduce a functional perspective to the study of human variation (e.g., Thomson 1908). Later, during the 1920s, Thomson in collaboration with L.H. Dudley Buxton (1889–1939) published an important study in which they demonstrated, using statistical methods, a correlation between the nasal index and climate (Thomson & Buxton 1923). Another important contribution was D'Arcy Wentworth Thompson's (1860–1948) *On Growth and Form* (1917).

The New Elizabethans: Post–World War II Developments

The decades immediately following World War II witnessed a gradual break-up of the British Empire and a resulting change in the nation's identity as a major world power. The "winds of change" that began to blow through the kingdom in the early 1950s, however, were not limited to just sociopolitical and economic spheres of activity. At this time, as elsewhere, British physical anthropology began to undergo a dramatic transformation as workers absorbed the theoretical implications of the new synthetic theory of evolution that had been formulated largely by an informal group of American and British biologists and geneticists during the 1930s and early 1940s. Prominent among the British contributors to this synthesis were Julian S. Huxley (1887–1975) (1940, 1942), J.B.S. Haldane (1892–1964) (1932), and Ronald A. Fisher (1890–1962) (1930). It was largely the absorption of this new synthesis that led to the almost sudden appearance of populational and adaptational thinking among both human biologists and paleontologists. Coinciding with this event, and adding inestimably to the momentum of the neo-Darwinian movement, was the announcement in 1953 of the Watson-Crick model of DNA (deoxyribonucleic acid), which as it happened was also the product of Anglo-American cooperation. This elegant model opened the door onto a new vista of bioevolutionary research. Where a decade earlier the interplay between mutation and selection had been an abstract and largely speculative venture, these concepts were now grounded in a molecular landscape that was readily accessible to experimental study.

Another event that serves to capture the scientific ethos of the new Elizabethan Age was the debunking of the Piltdown remains in 1953 by Joseph Sidney Weiner (1915–1982) and his colleagues at Oxford (including Wilfrid Edward Le Gros Clark) and at the Natural History Museum (in particular, Kenneth Page Oakley [1911–1981]) (cf. Weiner, Oakley, & Clark 1953). The unmasking of the Piltdown forgery set the stage for an en masse acceptance of the long-neglected South African australopithecines into the hominid fold and the creation of a more favorable climate for the commencement of a general reassessment of other major fossil hominids that had been pruned from the human evolutionary tree as a consequence of Piltdown's arrival. As in the preceding period, British involvement in human paleontological research unfolded simultaneously on several overlapping fronts that embrace three major geologic-time segments: the Miocene, the Pliocene, and the Pleistocene.

In Miocene hominoid research, a convenient starting point is Clark's work on the East African Rusinga material (Clark & Leakey 1951). From Clark, it is possible to trace the development of this field through the subsequent activities of John R. Napier (1917–1987) and a new generation of workers that emerged during the 1960s and 1970s that includes, among others, Leslie Aiello, Peter Andrews, M.J. Bishop, R.D. Martin, David Pilbeam, Ian Tattersall, and Alan C. Walker. With few exceptions, many of the above workers, along with others such as the anatomists Michael H. Day (Natural History Museum) and Bernard A. Wood (University of Liverpool), have made significant contributions to Pliocene hominid research as well (e.g., Day 1986; Wood 1991).

Although during the 1960s and 1970s the discoveries in East Africa served to draw scientific attention away from the later stages of human evolution, Pleistocene hominid research continued to attract British workers—particularly the perennial debate on the evolutionary significance of the European Neandertals to the origins of modern humans. Most notable among the earlier contributors to the modern debates were Weiner and the physical anthropologist Bernard Campbell (cf. Weiner 1958; Weiner & Campbell 1964). It is also pertinent to note that Campbell is the author of two widely adopted introductory textbooks dealing with human evolution (cf. Campbell 1966, 1976). Later contributors to this debate and related issues include Chris B. Stringer of the Natural History Museum (e.g., Stringer 1989; Stringer & Mckie 1996) and Robert Foley at the University of Cambridge (e.g., Foley 1987, 1991).

The cognate field of primate behavior also underwent rapid development during the late 1950s and early 1960s. In large part, this impulse was derived from the activities of K.R.L. Hall (1917–1965), who, following a short stint (1955–1959) as chairman of the Psychology Department at the University of Cape Town, South Africa, established at Bristol University an important research environment for the study of primate behavior. Although Hall's career was cut short by an untimely death, his impact is clearly reflected in the subsequent work of his students and colleagues at Bristol—in particular, John H. Crook, P. Aldrich-Blake, J.S. Gartlan, and Vernon and Frances Reynolds. Among many others who have contributed to this field are Clifford Jolly and John F. Oates (both trained at the University of London), Richard W. Wrangham (trained at Cambridge), and Louis Leakey's protégé, Jane Goodall.

As in paleoanthropology, the study of human variation in the 1950s and 1960s adopted the perspective of the "new" anthropology, which is clearly mirrored in the highly successful textbook *Human Biology* (1964), authored by Geoffrey A. Harrison, Weiner, James M. Tanner (1920–), and N.A. Barnicott. In fact, several of these authors were also intimately involved in a movement that had led to the founding of the Society for the Study of Human Biology (SSHB) in 1958, the first society founded in the United Kingdom devoted exclusively to physical anthropology. Other prominent founding members of the SSHB included Arthur E. Mourant (1904–), E.H. Ashton from Birmingham University, and J.C. Trevor (1908–1967) from Cambridge. Although at this juncture the SSHB did not have its own journal, this deficiency was rectified in 1973, when the *Annals of Human Biology* was inaugurated. In the meantime, much of the work produced by the SSHB membership tended to be published overseas, primarily in American journals such as *Human Biology* and the *American Journal of Physical Anthropology*.

The research produced in human biology during this period can be separated into two main (but interrelated) categories: (1) those studies manifesting an essentially adaptive and ecological orientation and (2) those primarly concerned with determining genetic structure. Among some early and notable studies from the first category are Derek F. Roberts' (1953) demonstration of the applicability of the Bergmann and Allen rules to the human condition, and the commencement of the Harpenden Growth Study under the control of Tanner and R.H. Whitehouse in 1948. (For a detailed summary of post-1950 British contributions to research in growth and development, see Tanner 1981.) In the second category, the genetic studies of workers such as A.C. Allison (1957) and G.A. Harrison (e.g., Harrison 1961, Harrison & Owen 1964) at Oxford are notable earlier examples.

Subsequent research development in the sphere of human biology was further enhanced during the 1960s and 1970s by the International Biological Programme (IBP), which was organized by the International Council of Scientific Unions (ICSU) in 1964. The activities of the IBP, which lasted until 1974, were coordinated in London by Weiner. Emerging from the founding of the IBP was the establishment in 1967 of the International Association for Human Biologists.

As this brief survey indicates, the second half of the twentieth century is characterized by the rapid emergence of a fully professionalized community that is supported by both academic and other professional institutions. As of the mid-1990s the major academic centers for post-graduate training and research in the United Kingdom include the Universities of Cambridge, London, Newcastle, Oxford, and Liverpool. Futhermore, since the foundation of the European Anthropological Association in 1975, British workers have become increasingly involved in European research and training agendas—while at the same time nurturing and maintaining their long and intimate connections with their transatlantic counterparts in North America (cf. Harrison 1982:470–471).

Frank Spencer

Endnote

1. The term "United Kingdom" embraces Great Britain (the island consisting of England, Scotland, and Wales), Northern Ireland (the six counties of Antrim, Down, Armagh, Tyrone, Fermanagh, and Londonderry, also known as Ulster), plus several smaller islands. The term United Kingdom

was officially adopted following the union with Ireland in 1801. Prior to this, the term Great Britain (sometimes shortened to Britain, from the Latin *Britannia*) had been in use since the Act of Union in 1707. Although the word English is often used by foreigners as a synonym for the inclusive term British, it correctly applies only to those people native to England.

See also Acosta, José de; Allen's Rule; Beddoe, John; Bipedalism; Blumenbach, Johann Friedrich; Bowditch, Henry Pickering; Bradley, Richard; Brixham Cave; Busk, George; Camper, Petrus; Chain of Being; Clark, (Sir) Wilfrid Edward Le Gros; Cuvier, Georges Léopold Chrétien Fréderic Dagobert (Baron); Darwin, Charles Robert; European Anthropological Association; Falconer, Hugh; Flower, (Sir) William Henry; Galton, (Sir) Francis; Geikie, James; Gibraltar; Gregory, William King; Haddon, A(lfred) C(ort); Hakluyt, Richard; Hale, (Sir) Matthew; Hall, Kenneth Ronald Lambert; Hunt, James; Huxley, Thomas Henry; International Association of Human Biologists; International Biological Programme (Human Adaptability Section); Jones, Frederic Wood; Keith, (Sir) Arthur; Kent's Cavern; La Peyrère, Isaac; Lartet, Édouard (Armand Isidore Hippolyte); Lubbock, (Sir) John; Lydekker, Richard; Lyell, (Sir) Charles; McCown, Theodore D(oney); Malthus, (Reverend) Thomas Robert; Mivart, St. George Jackson; Modern Human Origins; Morton, Samuel George; Mount Carmel (Israel); Napier, John Russell; Owen, (Sir) Richard; Pilgrim, Guy Ellock; Piltdown; Polygenism; Prestwich, (Sir) Joseph; Prichard, James Cowles; Primate Field Studies; Ray, John; Schaaffhausen, Hermann; Skin Color; Smith, (Sir) Grafton Elliot; Sollas, William Johnson; Swanscombe; Tanner, James Mourilyan; Tyson, Edward; Weiner, Joseph Sidney; Woodward, (Sir) Arthur Smith; Zuckerman, Solly (Lord)

Bibliography
J. de Acosta: *Historia natural y moral de las Indias.* Seville, 1590. Translated by E. Grimston: *The natural and moral history of the East and West Indies.* London: Blout & Aspley, 1604; A.C. Allison: Malaria in carriers of the sickle-cell trait and in newborn children. *Experimental Parasitology* 6:418–477, 1957; F. Bacon: *Novum organum.* In: *Instauratio magna.* Londini: Billium, 1620; E. Barkan: *The retreat of scientific racism.* New York: Cambridge University

Press, 1992; J. Beddoe: *The races of Europe.* London: Trubner, 1885.

C. Bell: *Essays on the anatomy and philosophy of expression.* 2d ed. London: Murray, 1824; T. Bendyshe: The history of anthropology. *Memoirs of the Anthropological Society of London* 1:335–420, 1864; T. Bendyshe: *The anthropological treatises of Johann Friedrich Blumenbach.* London: Longman, Green, Longman, Roberts & Green, 1865.

R. Bradley: A *philosophical account of the works of nature, endeavouring to set forth the several gradations remarkable in the mineral, vegetable, and animal parts of creation, tending to the composition of a scale of nature.* London: Mears, 1721; E. Brerewood: *Enquiries touching the diversity of languages and religions through the chief parts of the world.* London: Bill, 1614; T. Browne: *Pseudodoxia epidemica; or, Enquiries into very many tenants and commonly presumed truths.* London: Dod, 1646; T. Browne: *Hydriotaphia urne-buriall; or, A discourse on the sepulchrall urnes lately found in Norfolk.* London: Brome, 1658; G. Busk: On the crania of the most ancient races of man. *Natural History Review* 2:155–176, 1861.

G. Busk: On a very ancient human cranium from Gibraltar. In: *Report of the British Association for the Advancement of Science* (thirty-fourth meeting, Bath, England, 1864). London: Murray, 1865, pp. 91–92; W. Busk: On the crania of the most ancient races of man. *Natural History Review* 2:158–176, 1861. English translation of H. Schaaffhausen: Zur Kenntniss der ältesten Rassenschädel. *Archiv für Anatomie* 5:453–478, 1858; B.G. Campbell: *Human Evolution: An introduction to man's adaptions.* Chicago: Aldine, 1966 (3d ed:1985); B.G. Campbell: *Humankind emerging.* Boston: Little, Brown, 1976 (7th ed: 1996); W.B. Carpenter: Review of Prichard's *Researches into the Physical History of Man* (1843). *Edinburgh Review* 88:429–487, 1848; W.E. Le Gros Clark: *Early foreunners of man.* London: Baillière, Tindall & Cox, 1934.

W.E. Le Gros Clark & L.S.B. Leakey: *The Miocene Hominoidea of East Africa.* London: British Museum (Natural History), 1951; G. Cuvier & A. Brongniart: Essai sur la géographie minéralogique des environs de Paris. *Journal des Mines* 23:421–458, 1808; C.R. Darwin: *On the origin of species by means of natural selection, or the preservation of favoured races in the struggle for life.* London: Murray, 1859; C.R. Darwin: *The expression of emotions in man and animals.* London: Murray, 1872; J.B. Davis: *Thesaurus craniorum: Catalogue of the skulls of the various races of man.* London: privately printed, 1867; J.B. Davis & J. Thurnam: *Crania Britannica: Delineations and descriptions of the skulls of the Aboriginal and early inhabitants of the British Isles.* 2 vols. London: privately printed, 1865.

M.H. Day: *Guide to fossil man.* 4th ed. Chicago: University of Chicago Press, 1986; R.A. Fisher: *The genetical theory of natural selection.* Oxford: Clarendon Press, 1930; H.J. Fleure: *The peoples of Europe.* London: Oxford University Press, 1922; W.H. Flower: On the classification of the varieties of the human species. *Journal of the Anthropological Institute* 14:378–393, 1885; R. Foley: Hominid species and stone tool assemblages. How are they related? *Antiquity* 61:380–392, 1987; R. Foley: *Origin of human behaviour.* London: Unwin, 1991; J. Frere: Account of flint weapons discovered at Hoxne in Suffolk. *Archaeologia* 13:204–205, 1808; F. Galton: Proposal to apply for anthropological statistics from schools. *Journal of the Anthropological Institute* 3:308–311, 1873; F. Galton: Notes on the Marlborough School statistics. *Journal of the Anthropological Institute* 4:130–135, 1874; F. Galton: On the height and weight of boys aged fourteen years in town and country public schools. *Journal of the Anthropological Institute* 5:174–181, 1875; D.A.E. Garrod & D.M.A. Bate: *The Stone Age of Mount Carmel. I: Excavations at the Wadi el-Mughara.* Oxford: Clarendon Press, 1937.

D.A.E. Garrod et al.: The excavation of a Mousterian rockshelter at Devil's Tower, Gibraltar. *Journal of the Royal Anthropological Institute* 48:33–113, 1928; J. Geikie: *The great Ice Age and its relation to the antiquity of man.* London: Isbister, 1874. (2d ed.: London: Stanford, 1877); K. Gesner: *Historia animalium.* 4 vols. Tiguri: Froschoverum, 1551–1558; D.K. Grayson: *The establishment of human antiquity.* New York: Academic Press, 1983; A.C. Haddon: *The races of man and their distribution.* London: Macmillan, 1925; A.C. Haddon et al.: *We Europeans: Survey of racial problems.* London: Cape, 1935; R. Hakluyt: *The principal navigations, voiages, traffiques, and discoveries of the English nation.* London: Bishop & Newberie, 1589.

J.B.S. Haldane: *The causes of evolution.* London: Longmans, Green, 1932; M. Hale: *The primitive origination of mankind, considered and examined according to the light of nature.* London: Godbid, 1677; G.A. Harrison: Pigmentation. In: G.A. Harrison (ed): *Genetical variation in human populations.* Oxford: Pergamon, 1961; G.A. Harrison: The past fifty years of human population biology in North America: An outsider's view. In: F. Spencer (ed) *A history of American physical anthropology, 1930–1980.* New York: Academic Press, 1982, pp. 467–472; G.A. Harrison & J.J.T. Owen: Studies on the inheritance of human skin color. *Annals of Human Genetics* 28:27–37, 1964.

G.A. Harrison, J.S. Weiner, J.M. Tanner, & N.A. Barnicott: *Human biology: An introduction to human evolution, growth, and ecology.* London: Oxford University Press, 1964; P. Heylyn: *Microcosmus: A little description of the great world.* Oxford: Lichfield, 1621; H. Home (Lord Kames): *Sketches of the history of man.* 4 vols. Edinburgh: Creech, 1774; A.T. Hopwood: *Miocene primates from Kenya. Journal of the Linnean Society of London* 38:437–464, 1933; L.E. Huddleston: *Origins of the American Indians: European concepts, 1492–1729.* Austin: University of Texas Press, 1967.

T.M. Hughes & D.R. Thomas: On the occurrence of felstone implements of the Le Moustier type in Pontnewydd Cave, near Cefn. *Journal of the Anthropological Institute* 3:387–392, 1874; J. Hunter: *Disputatio inauguralis: Quaedam de hominum varietatibus.* Edinburgh: Balfour & Smellie, 1775. English translation in T. Bendyshe: *The anthropological treatises of Johann Friedrich Blumenbach.* London: Longman, Green, Longman, Roberts & Green, 1865, pp. 357–394; J. Hunter: *Essays and observations on human anatomy, psychology, and geology.* 2 vols. Reprint, edited by R. Owen. London: Taylor & Francis, 1861; J.S. Huxley: *The new systematics.* London: Oxford University Press, 1940; J.S. Huxley: *Evolution: The modern synthesis.* London: Unwin & Allen, 1942.

T.H. Huxley: *Evidence as to man's place in nature.* London: Williams & Norgate, 1863; T.H. Huxley: On the geographical distribution of the chief modifications of mankind. *Journal of the Ethnological Society of London* 2 (n.s.):404–412, 1870; F.W. Jones: *Arboreal man.* London: Arnold, 1916; F.W. Jones: *Man's place among the mammals.* London: Arnold, 1929; A. Keith: The extent to which the posterior segments of the body have been transmuted and suppressed in the evolution of man and allied primates. *Journal of Anatomy and Physiology* 37:18–40, 1903; A. Keith: Man's posture: Its evolution and disorders. *British Medical Journal* 1:451–454, 499–502, 545–548, 624–626, 669–672, 1923; H. Kuklick: *The savage within: The social history of British anthropology, 1885–1945.* New York: Cambridge University Press, 1991.

H.W. Lansdowne (ed): *The Petty papers: Some unpublished writings of Sir William Petty.* 2 vols. London: Constable, 1927; I. La Peyrère: *Men before Adam* and *A theological system upon that presupposition that men were before Adam.* London, 1655; W. Lawrence: *Lectures on comparative anatomy, physiology, zoology, and the natural history of man.* London: Smith, 1822; E. Long: *The history of Jamaica; or, A general survey of the antient and modern state of that island.* 3 vols. London: Lowndes, 1774; J. Lubbock: *Prehistoric times, as illustrated by ancient remains and the manners and customs of modern savages.* London: Williams & Norgate, 1865; C. Lyell: *The geological evidences of the antiquity of man, with remarks on the theories of the origin of species by variation.* London: Murray, 1863.

T.D. McCown & A. Keith: *The Stone Age of Mount Carmel. II: The fossil human remains from the Levalloiso-Mousterian.* Oxford: Clarendon Press, 1939; St. G.J. Mivart: On *Lepilemur* and *Cheirogaleus* and the zoological rank of the Lemuroidea. *Proceedings of the Zoological Society of London* 41:484–510, 1873; G.M. Morant: Studies of Palaeolithic man. I. The Chancelade skull and its relation to the modern Eskimo. *Annals of Eugenics* 1:257–276, 1926; G.M. Morant: Studies of Palaeolithic man. II. A biometrical study of Neanderthal skulls and their relationships to modern racial types. *Annals of Eugenics* 2:318–381, 1927.

G.M. Morant: Studies of Palaeolithic man. III. The Rhodesian skull and its relations to Neanderthaloid and modern types. *Annals of Eugenics* 3:337–360, 1928; G.M. Morant: Studies of Palaeolithic man. IV. A biometric study of the Upper Palaeolithic skulls of Europe and their relationship to earlier and later types. *Annals of Eugenics* 4:109–214, 1930–1931; S.G. Morton: *Crania Aegyptiaca.* Philadelphia: Pennington, 1844; J. Ovington: *A voyage to Surat in the year 1689.* London: Towson, 1696. Reprint edited by H.G. Rawlinson. London: Oxford University Press, 1929.

R. Owen: *The principal forms of the skeleton and the teeth as the basis for a system of natural history and comparative anatomy.*

London: Orr, 1855; J. Prestwich: Theoretical considerations on the conditions under which the drift deposits containing the remains of extinct mammalia and flint implements were accumulated; and their geological age. *Proceedings of the Royal Society of London* 12:38–62, 1863; J.C. Prichard: *Researches into the physical history of man.* London: Arch, 1813 (2d ed.: 1826, 3d ed.: 1836–1847); D.F. Roberts: Body weight, race, and climate. *American Journal of Physical Anthropology* 11:533–558, 1953; W. Robertson: *The history of America.* 2 vols. London: Strahan, 1777.

G.J. Romanes: *Mental evolution in animals with a posthumous essay on instinct by C. Darwin.* London: Kegan Paul, Trench, 1883; B. Rush: Observations intended to favour a supposition that the black colour (as it is called) of the Negroes is derived from the Leprosy. *Transactions of the American Philosophical Society* 4:289–297, 1799; W. Smellie: *The philosophy of natural history.* 2 vols. Edinburgh: Elliot, 1790; G.E. Smith: On the morphology of the brain in the Mammalia, with special reference to that of the lemurs, recent and extinct. *Transactions of the Linnean Society* 8 (2d ser.):319–432, 1902.

G.E. Smith: Presidential address to the Anthropological Section. In: *Reports of the British Association for the Advancement of Science (Dundee 1912).* London: Murray, 1912, pp. 575–598. Reprinted in *Nature* 90:118–126, 1912; W. Smith: *Strata identified by organized fossils, containing prints on coloured paper of the most characteristic specimens in each stratum.* London: Arding, 1816; W.J. Sollas: On the cranial and facial characters of the Neandertal race. *Philosophical Transactions of the Royal Society of London* 190:281–339, 1908.

R. Steele: *Mediaeval lore from Bartholomew Anglicus.* London: Chatto & Windus, 1924; N. Stepan: *The idea of race in science: Great Britain, 1860–1960.* London: Macmillan, 1982; J. Straton: *Contributions to the mathematics of phrenology; chiefly to aid students.* Aberdeen: Russel, 1845; C.B. Stringer: Documenting the origin of modern humans. In: E. Trinkaus (ed) *The emergence of modern humans.* Cambridge: Cambridge University Press, 1989, pp. 67–96; C.B. Stringer & R. Mckie: *African exodus: The origins of modern humanity.* London: Cape, 1996; J.M. Tanner: *A history of the study of human growth.* London: Cambridge University Press, 1981; D'A.W. Thompson: *On growth and form.* London:

Cambridge University Press, 1917; J.A. Thomson: *Heredity.* London: Murray, 1908; J.A. Thomson & L.H.D. Buxton: Man's nasal index in relation to certain climatic conditions. *Journal of the Royal Anthropological Institute* 53:92–122, 1923; E. Topsell: *The historie of foure-footed beastes.* London: Jaggard, 1607.

W. Turner: Report on the human crania and other bones of the skeletons collected during the voyage of HMS *Challenger* in the years 1873–1876. I. Crania. II. Bones of the skeleton. In: *Report of the scientific results of the voyage of HMS Challenger during the years 1873–1876* (Zoology). Vol. 16. London: Longmans, 1884–1886, pp. 1–136; E. Tyson: *Orang-Outang, sive Homo sylvestris; or, The anatomy of a pygmie compared with that of a monkey, an ape, and a man.* London: Bennet, 1699. J.S. Weiner: The pattern of evolutionary development of the genus *Homo. South African Journal of Medical Science* 23:111–120, 1958.

J.S. Weiner & B.G. Campbell: The taxonomic status of the Swanscombe skull. In: C.D. Ovey (ed) *The Swanscombe skull.* London: Royal Anthropological Institute, 1964, pp. 175–201; J.S. Weiner, K.P. Oakley, & W.E. Le Gros Clark: The solution to the Piltdown problem. *Bulletin of the British Museum (Natural History)* 2:141–146, 1953; C. White: *An account of the regular gradation of man, and in different animals and vegetables; and from the former to the latter.* London: Dilly, 1799; B.A. Wood: *Koobi Fora Research Project.* Vol. 4, *Hominid cranial remains.* Oxford: Clarendon Press, 1991; S. Zuckerman: *The social life of monkeys and apes.* New York: Harcourt, Brace, 1932.

United States of America

Almost seventy-five years before the publication of Charles Darwin's (1809–1882) revolutionary *On the Origin of Species* (1859), physical anthropology in the United States was being founded in the debates surrounding the nature and origins of racial variation. For example, in 1787, Samuel Stanhope Smith's (1750–1819) *Essay on the Causes of the Variety of Complexion and Figure in the Human Species* argued that all modern peoples were a single species whose physical differences developed anew in each generation mainly through the influence of climatic and other environmental factors. This widely read and commented upon work was criticized by proslavery scholars, such as the physician-anthropologist Charles Caldwell (1772–1853), who noted that environmental influences like climate could produce only limited effects on individuals, and that the distinctive features of the various human races were firmly fixed, perhaps originating with the Creation (cf. Caldwell 1814). Others, like the physician Samuel Latham Mitchill (1764–1831), though agreeing with Smith that all modern humans belonged to a single species, also believed that hereditary factors, the "generative influence," were the primary powers responsible for the physical appearance of people (Mitchill 1820).

This debate was significantly broadened by the work of Samuel George Morton (1799–1851), a Philadelphia physician, who is often regarded as the founder of physical anthropology in the United States (Brace 1982). Becoming interested in craniology, Morton was eventually to amass one of the largest collections of its time of human skulls of peoples from many parts of the world ("the American Golgotha" as it was known; it is now curated in the University of Pennsylvania Museum). In 1839 he published *Crania Americana*; in 1844, *Crania Aegyptiaca*. In these volumes, in which more than a dozen measurements for each skull were recorded, often including the cranial capacity, Morton documented distinctive differences in the crania of the various peoples in his collection. These variations in shape and size must have been of great antiquity, Morton argued, because he could find no differences between the skulls of ancient Egyptians (then regarded as the most ancient human remains) and modern Europeans. After Morton's death in 1851, others, like George R. Gliddon (1809–1857) and Josiah Clark Nott (1804–1873), used these conclusions in books such as *Types of Mankind* (1854) and *Indigenous Races of the Earth* (1857) to promote their brand of polygenism. In the years immediately before the Civil War, these arguments were often used to support the institution of slavery.

Morton's quantitative approach, like that of Anders Adolf Retzius (1796–1860) in Europe, as well as his use of a time depth in his analyses, offered persuasive evidence to many scholars of the day, and until the recognition that Darwinian evolutionary theory provided mechanisms to explain how human differences arose over time, Morton's work remained a generally accepted view of human variation and development.

The subsequent developments that mark the emergence of paleoanthropology and modern human biology are described in separate subsections that reflect current research specializations. For much of nineteenth and early twentieth centuries, however, this is a somewhat artificial division since many researchers actively pursued research in both human biology and its evolutionary development. Furthermore, while much of the discipline's history in the second half of the twentieth century unfolded in academia, from the nineteenth century through the second quarter of the twentieth century the traditional institutional context of physical anthropological research was museums and learned societies. During this latter period, several major academic foci (see Table 1) were established that provided the foundations for the dramatic expansion of academic departments supporting graduate programs in physical anthropology that occurred during the 1950s and 1960s. Also intrinsic to the rapid professionalization of the discipline was the founding the *American Journal of Physical Anthropology* in 1918, followed by the American Association of Physical Anthropologists in 1930. (For pertinent details relating to the rise of academic physical anthropology in the United States, see Darnell 1969 and Spencer 1981.)

Human Biology

In the United States, human biology is characterized not so much by a single organized body of theory and method, but by a focus on human variability and its relationship to issues of evolution, health, and ecological interactions. As a biological science, human biology has been shaped, even driven, by advancements in its cognate disciplines. As a part of anthropology, it has also been responsive to the development of techniques for analyzing interactions with culture and with behavior. And, because of its eclectic mix, those who identify themselves as human biologists have, in their research, collaborated with colleagues in related disciplines as least as often as with colleagues from anthropology and human biology. Early in its history, physical anthropology, including human biology, located itself within university departments of anthropology, where it has remained until the present day. The affiliation with degree-granting institutions has established a direct intellectual link between the research interests of senior anthropologists and the training of students, leading to academic pedigrees and the continuity of orientations and approaches. Furthermore, the American university tradition of Faculties of Arts and Sciences has created the atmosphere for greater interchanges of ideas, especially between the social and the biological sciences, than has generally been the case outside of the Western Hemisphere.

The leaders of American human biology, in its early stages of development—the late nineteenth and early twentieth centuries—also played a major role in channeling the field along the directions it has followed. These early leaders, typified by Franz Boas (1858–1942), were not experimental biologists. Rather, their research was conducted more in the style of natural scientists, with a clear emphasis on field studies of particular societies and groups, and oriented toward a holistic approach to the study of humankind.

Throughout its development, human biology has been caught in a dynamic tension between a holistic, population-centered approach, with an emphasis on fieldwork, synthesis, and questions of population dynamics, and a more overtly biological approach, emphasizing experimentation, reductionism, and questions whose answers depend upon the methodology of the biological and the physical sciences. In some periods, advancements came mainly from field studies, while in others the reverse was true.

Human biology in the United States has also been shaped by developments in anthropology as a whole, and, even more broadly, in the social and biological sciences. A number of key conceptual, methodological, and technological advancements have had enormous impacts on human biology. Among them are:

(1) the development of population biology and population genetics, including the new evolutionary synthesis that emerged after World War II; (2) ecology and ecosystem analysis; (3) computers and quantitative methods; and (4) the integration of biological, medical, social, and behavioral sciences in the formation of a biomedical perspective. While it is difficult, perhaps impossible, to construct a taxonomy of research themes in any discipline, it is particularly hard to do for human biology. Nonetheless, it is useful, if nothing else than in a heuristic sense, for a brief review such as this. Given such a caveat, the major themes and perspectives that have engaged human biologists in the United States include human variation, human adaptability, human biology, anthropological genetics, human growth and development, and biomedical anthropology (health and disease).

HUMAN VARIATION. Among the earliest research in American human biology were descriptive studies of population variation, carried out within the context of race and racial taxonomy. Earnest A. Hooton (1887–1954), who began his career at Harvard University in 1913, was among the first. While Hooton's breadth of interests and research spread throughout the subject matter of physical anthropology, his contributions to the systematics of human biological variation are especially noteworthy. He developed the concept of primary and secondary races to resolve the dilemma over the relationship between the "major racial stocks"

TABLE 1. Major Academic Foci in Physical Anthropology in the United States Prior to 1960

Institution (founded)	Anthropology Department established	Physical Anthropology Program established	Associated individuals
U Pennsylvania (1740)	1886	late 1940s	Wilton Marion Krogman[1]
Harvard U (1636)	1887	late 1920s	Earnest Albert Hooton[2]
U Chicago (1892)	1892	late 1940s	Sherwood L. Washburn[3]
U California, Berkeley (1873)	1901	1940s	Theodore D. McCown[4]

1. Krogman joined the Department at the University of Pennsylvania in 1947. Between 1950 and 1970, he produced a crop of Ph.D.s. For further details, see University of Pennsylvania in this volume.

2. Prior to Hooton's appointment in 1913, Harvard's graduate program focused mainly on archeology, though a few doctorates in physical anthropology were produced, most notably W.C. Farabee in 1903. Hooton's graduate program was not launched until the mid-1920s. It subsequently became the major source prior to 1960. For a complete listing of Hooton's Ph.D. students, see Hooton in this volume.

3. Before Krogman's arrival, physical anthropology at Chicago in the 1920s was taught by Fay Cooper Cole. After Krogman's departure for Pennsylvania in 1947, physical anthropology at Chicago was developed by Washburn (a former Hooton student). Washburn remained at Chicago until 1958. During this time Washburn produced four Ph.D.s. See Washburn, in this volume for further details.

4. McCown created the program in physical anthropology at Berkeley in the 1940s. Later, in 1958, when Washburn joined the department, the program was expanded. During the second half of the twentieth century, Berkeley became a major source of Ph.D.'s in physical anthropology.

and the smaller units that had arisen through admixture and other local phenomena. At the level of the individual, Hooton's interests in body form and physique led to research into the behavioral correlates of constitutional variation.

The description and analysis of variation in constitution, or physique, has advanced significantly since the earlier excesses of interpretation by the constitutional psychologist William H. Sheldon (1898–1977). The assessment of the somatotype and its relationship to performance and to disease is now accepted widely and used in many disciplines (cf. Carter & Heath 1990). American human biologists are not as widely involved in this work as they once were, or as are their colleagues elsewhere. Nonetheless, those whose work interacts with physicians, exercise physiologists, and physical educators, as well as those involved with the comparative morphology of populations, frequently utilize somatotype ratings in their research.

The purpose of much of the descriptive work on human variation in early human biology was the construction of racial taxonomy, both as an aid to the systematization of variability and as a device to understand historical relationships among populations. Prior to the 1950s, morphological data were utilized. The first major challenge to this approach came from the geneticist William C. Boyd (1903–1983), whose landmark *Genetics and the Races of Man* (1950), advocated the use of gene frequencies rather than morphological traits, which were argued to be of unknown genetic basis and hence subject to environmental pressures.

The American human biologist most identified with racial classification was Carleton S. Coon (1904–1981). A former student of Hooton, Coon was very much the field-worker, who cataloged and classified variability in living and in skeletal populations with an energy and enthusiasm unequaled by his peers and certainly by subsequent generations of human biologists. Unfortunately, in Coon's later years, racial classification lost its appeal as a scientific topic, while, at the same time, his views on the interpretation of differences between taxa became highly controversial and politicized (cf. Coon 1963). His book *The Living Races of Man* (1965) may be the last major work on racial taxonomy in *Homo sapiens* that will appear.

HUMAN ADAPTABILITY. The central place of racial taxonomy began to disappear in American human biology in the years following World War II. The development of population biology struck typology a death blow, and the new evolutionary synthesis brought together population genetics, natural selection, and evolution into a testable, mechanistic model. Human variability became increasingly interpreted as essentially adaptive, and population differences were seen as reflecting adaptive gradients rather than historical events. Leading figures in promoting this adaptive view were Coon, Sherwood L. Washburn (1911–), Stanley M. Garn (1922–), and Joseph B. Birdsell (1908–1994)—all, incidentally, Hooton students. Boyd's book had moved the emphasis from morphology to genetics, while physical chemists and immunologists began to develop analytic techniques permitting the examination of a wider segment of the human genome. Finally, the concept of the genetic polymorphism and of its maintenance by balancing selection, advanced in particular by E.B. Ford (1901–), a British geneticist, led human biology in the 1960s to concentrate on genetic polymorphisms in their search for evidence for natural selection (cf. Ford 1945).

Among the many human biologists who studied genetic polymorphisms was Frank B. Livingstone (1928–), whose classic work on hemoglobin polymorphism and malaria, especially sickle-cell hemoglobin, still is a masterful demonstration of population-centered human biology at its best (cf. Livingstone 1958). Other investigators also carried out research into the detection of biochemical polymorphisms and their possible selective value. Among these individuals were B.S. Blumberg, Alice M. Brues (1913–), John Buettner-Janusch (1924–1992), Frederick S. Hulse (1906–1990), A.J. Kelso, N. Morton, James Neel, William S. Pollitzer, James N. Spuhler (1917–1992), and Peter L. Workman.

However, the biggest boost to whole-population studies of human adaptability came from the International Biological Programme (IBP), in particular its Human Adaptability Section (HAS), established by the International Council of Scientific Unions and lasting from 1964 to 1974. This massive worldwide program was the largest coordinated effort ever to study human biology in an ecological setting and led to the formation of the International Association of Human Biologists (IAHB), the primary international organization of individuals and national societies that share its legacy and its interests.

Three major research programs were begun under the IBP-HAS, all focused on eliciting adaptive responses of populations living under environmental stress. The program in the biology of human populations at high altitude dealt initially with the Peruvian Andes, and later with the Himalayas, and was directed by Paul T. Baker (1927–). The study of circumpolar peoples included major research programs among Aleuts, directed by William S. Laughlin (1919–), and Eskimos, directed by F.A. Milan. The third focused on the genetic structure of South American Indians. It was directed by J.V. Neel and involved projects among the Xavante of southern Brazil and the Yanomama of Venezuela.

These projects generated enormous amounts of data and led, as well, to the formulation of important theoretical models of the interaction of biology, culture, and the environment in the adaptive process (e.g., R.B. Thomas 1975). Perhaps their most important contribution was as a training ground for a generation of American human biologists and physical anthropologists who, as graduate students, participated in the research and, by so doing, had their theoretical orientations, methodological skills, and professional interests shaped and molded by their experiences. As they have moved through their own careers, they have carried these orientations and skills with them, in areas ranging from environmental physiology to nutritional ecology to genetic epidemiology. Furthermore, these once-students have themselves trained scores of graduate students, establishing a lineage of ecologically oriented human biologists and stamping the discipline, for the foreseeable future, as one that is ecological and adaptive in its perspective.

While many persons were involved in the IBP, in the United States the leader was Baker, whose career was spent primarily at Pennsylvania State University. Not only was he the intellectual and organizational leader of the human-adaptability movement in American human biology, he was also a tireless teacher and mentor, whose students have passed through the sequence leading from graduate student to junior colleague to established independent investigator.

As noted above, Baker's research as part of the IBP was carried out in the extreme highlands of Peru, India, and Nepal. However, subsequent to that program, he has continued his ecological studies with another major project, this time among the intensively modernizing Samoans of Oceania. While the orientation has continued to be ecological and adaptive, the particular situation in Samoa led to a focus on the health aspects of modernization, as seen in Samoa, American Samoa, and the United States itself. Overall, this work, especially as carried on by Baker's students, has led to important findings of relevance to obesity, hypertension, and other chronic disease.

ANTHROPOLOGICAL GENETICS. In addition to studies of the adaptive value of genetic polymorphisms, human biologists interested in population genetics have also carried out research into the genetic structure of human populations. While not ignoring selection as a force, the primary focus of this research has been the movement of genes across space and time. In some instances, the emphasis was on the gene pool; in others, on the demographic structure; while in still others, a broad ecological design was followed. The term genetic structure refers not only to the gene pool itself, but also to the demographic, behavioral, and cultural processes by which genes are transmitted within and among populations. Involved in this research is the examination of the social and cultural processes constraining the flow of genes, of migration and admixture, of inbreeding, of mutation, and of genetic drift.

Some investigators studied discrete semiisolated groups in South America (e.g., Neel 1970), in Southern Africa (cf. Pennington & Harpending 1993), and in Papua New Guinea, while others dealt with larger and demographically more complex societies, such as the research of Albert Damon (1914–1973) and Jonathan Friedlaender in the Solomon Islands (cf. Friedlaender 1987). Often the research dealt with a specific component of genetic structure, as in Spuhler's (1953) calculation of the coefficient of inbreeding among the Ramah Navaho (cf. Spuhler & Kluckhohn 1953), R.B. Reid's examination of the biocultural interactions leading to inbreeding in south India, or the studies by Michael Crawford and his students of migration and gene flow in the highlands of Mexico.

Because of the complexity of human population genetic structure, other researchers devised innovative methods for their studies. Gabriel W. Lasker (1912–), one of the leading figures in American human biology, is widely known for his refinement of isonomy, a technique for assessing inbreeding from the analysis of surnames clustering between spouses.

Demographic processes have also been used in studying natural selection, such as James Crow's Index of Selection Potential from the analysis of variance in mortality and fertility. Another example is Blumberg and Peter Workman's use of estimates of the degree of admixture as evidence for the possible action of natural selection.

In contrast to studies of polymorphism and selection, research into genetic structure has continued to flourish (cf. Mielke & Crawford 1980). This work has become increasingly quantitative, formal, and theoretical, relying to a greater and greater degree on mathematical models and computer simulation, and can be seen, among human biologists, in publications by researchers such as K. Weiss, J. Friedlaender, H. Harpending, and J. Relethford.

Interestingly, the movement in anthropological genetics away from natural selection as a prime focus of research represents a return to the theoretical orientations of the first half of the twentieth century. Even while limited to external morphology and a typological approach, patterns of population similarities and differences were, at that time, interpreted as evidence of historical relationships. The rise of neo-Darwinism and the human-adaptability movement shifted the emphasis to selection, with population patterns reflecting adaptive responses to similar or to different environments. Since the mid-1970s, even newer developments have moved the field back to a historical perspective, though employing the methods and perspectives of modern population biology. This is seen in studies of genetic distance by researchers such as Emöke Szathmary (Kirk & Szathmary 1985).

HUMAN GROWTH AND DEVELOPMENT. The role of human biologists and physical anthropologists has been central to the study of human growth. Franz Boas was one of the most important figures in growth research whose academic career largely unfolded at Columbia University in New York City during the first three decades of the twentieth century. He is responsible for the refinement of techniques for studying the phases of growth, as well as for the establishment of a huge data-base on the growth of Native American children measured in the earlier part of the twentieth century.

Of equal importance was Boas' research into the effects of the environment on human form, a major focus of his work even before he came to the United States. His studies on changes in size and shape of the offspring of migrants has been the impetus for a wide range of research interests grouped under the term "human plasticity" (cf. Boas 1912). While many researchers have carried out their studies on adults, his most important work had been on children, examining the ways in which the growth process is shaped by the environment within which it is expressed. Subsequent work on human plasticity by Gabriel Lasker, William A. Stini, and others builds directly on a foundation laid by Boas.

Though Boas is important in the history of growth studies for his appreciation of the role of the environment, the father of the study of growth in American human biology is Wilton Marion Krogman (1903–1987), a physical anthropologist who was trained at the University of Chicago and at Western Reserve University in 1930s, and who spent most of his professional career at the University of Pennsylvania. Krogman's influence has been through his research but even more through his students, almost all of whom have gone on to carry out research into the process of development.

The third major figure in the history of growth studies by American human biologists is Stanley Garn, who was trained by Hooton at Harvard and who spent his career largely at the Fels Research Institute in Ohio and at the University of Michigan. As with Krogman, Garn's influence has been widespread outside of human biology, especially among the biomedical sciences.

It is convenient to identify three approaches in growth studies. The first is the description and analysis of the growth process itself, of its relationship to other features of human development, and of deviations resulting from specific clinical factors (cf. Roche et al. 1988). This theme is characteristic of much of the research by Krogman, Garn, E.E. Hunt Jr. (1922–1991), and the Australian Alex F. Roche (1921–), who has spent his American career at the Fels Institute. It also characterizes the work on developing mathematical models of the process, on saltatory growth, and on relationships between growth and performance.

The second approach deals with the evolution of the growth process. Much of this work focuses on the study of fossils and is not covered in this section. However, another component comes from the study of primate growth and development from a comparative perspective. While this represents one of the oldest themes in American human biology (Krogman's Ph.D. (1929) dissertation dealt with the subject), it has not been represented overall by as much work. However, the contributions of James Gavan, Elizabeth Watts, and Barry Bogin have been especially important.

The third approach is the study of growth within an ecological context—the sensitivity of the process to the surrounding environment. Often these studies have an adaptive emphasis, as seen, for example, in the work of Phyllis Eveleth, Roberto Frisancho, and Jere Haas in South America; Michael A. Little and Peter Workman in Africa; Cynthia Beall in South Asia; and James Bindon and Babette S. Zemel in Oceania. Other studies have focused more on public-health issues, as in the use of growth as an index of community health status by Reynaldo Martorell and John Himes in Latin America and by Lawrence Schell in the United States. Growth patterns of prehistoric populations have been reconstructed from skeletal studies and used as indicators of health status.

BIOMEDICAL ANTHROPOLOGY. Biomedical anthropology is conceptualized best not as a separate field, but rather as an application of the work of human biologists to issues of clinical and public-health relevance. Given the focus of anthropology upon variability, the relevance to issues of health and disease is obvious. Many human biologists are physicians and dentists by training; many others have carried out their research in schools of medicine, dentistry, public health, and the allied health professions; and still others apply their work to health issues and problems. In other words, all of the themes discussed here have a biomedical component.

Among the earliest to apply their work as human biologists directly to medical problems were Krogman and C. Wesley Dupertuis at Case Western Reserve University, Damon and Carl C. Seltzer at Harvard, William Montague Cobb (1904–1990) at Howard, nad Garn at the Fels Institute. The development of an ecological perspective led to a systemic approach, emphasizing the interactions among biology, behavior, culture, and the environment.

Prominent in the role of human biology in biomedical science has been the development of the concept of body composition and of methods to analyze fat, bone, lean body mass, and body water. In the United States, the concept and importance of body-composition studies were introduced almost single-handedly into human biology by the Czech-American psychobiologist Josef Brozek in the 1950s and 1960s (cf. Brozek 1956). His contributions have been supplemented by the appearance of new models and methods, the results applied to a broad range of problems of biomedical relevance. While body compo-

sition is important in all of the areas discussed so far, it is especially relevant in issues related to nutrition and nutritional status.

Finally, anthropological genetics has been increasingly identified with genetic epidemiology, seen in research into areas such as variation in genes related to histocompatibility.

Paleoanthropology

ESTABLISHMENT OF AMERICAN PALEOANTHROPOLOGY: 1900s–1940s. Through the latter third of the nineteenth and the beginning decades of the twentieth centuries, fossil evidence documenting human evolution was discovered at sites scattered across Eurasia and was excavated and described by European scholars. Only gradually did Americans become involved in this scholarly inquiry. Initially, their role was limited to the evaluation of the significance of previously discovered finds, and only later were they to take a direct part in the actual discovery and description of the fossils. Indeed, the paleontologist Othniel C. Marsh's (1831–1899) 1896 assessment of the *Pithecanthropus erectus* finds from Trinil, Java, might be reasonably said to mark the commencement of American paleoanthropological research. Marsh traveled in September 1895 to Leiden for the International Zoological Congress, where he was permitted by the Dutch physician Eugène Dubois (1858–1940) to examine the original fossils. Marsh noted that Dubois "has proved to science the existence of a new prehistoric anthropoid form, not human indeed, but in size, brain power, and erect posture, much nearer man than any animal hitherto discovered, living or extinct" (1896: 482).

At that time, however, there were still many scholars who believed that major phases of human evolution had taken place in North and South America, and considerable effort was expended in the search for fossilized remains that could establish this. The scientist primarily responsible for documenting that human evolution had *not* occurred in the New World, thus concentrating the attention of Americans on the discoveries abroad, was Aleš Hrdlička (1869–1943), who also established human evolutionary studies in the United States. In 1909 and 1912, while undertaking research trips to Egypt, Siberia, and Mongolia, he managed brief stopovers in Europe to review the European hominid fossil record, which he summarized in "The Most Ancient Skeletal Remains of Man" (1914). The publication was much in demand, and a second edition was issued in 1916.

During the next decade, Hrdlička journeyed to Europe, Asia, Australia, Java, and South Africa, visiting many of the original hominid fossil sites, often interviewing quarry workers or others who were involved in the discovery of the specimens. In the case of locales far removed from the centers of research in Europe, such as Kabwe in Zambia (at that time, Broken Hill in Northern Rhodesia), Trinil in Java, and Taung in South Africa, where few European scientists had traveled, he made discoveries that materially enhanced our knowledge of these sites. The information he gathered in these later trips was incorporated into a greatly expanded reissuing of the 1914 publication, which appeared in 1930 under the title *The Skeletal Remains of Early Man*—the first comprehensive synthesis of the fossil evidence for human evolution by an American. In concept and coverage, it ranks with the major contributions published around the same time in Europe, such as Marcellin Boule's (1861–1942) *L'homme fossiles* (1923) and Arthur Keith's (1866–1955) *The Antiquity of Man* (1915; 1925). Hrdlička was also a major critic of the controversial Piltdown remains, and evidently it was he who had prompted the study of them by Gerrit S. Miller (1869–1956), a mammalogist and colleague at the National Museum of Natural History at the Smithsonian Institution, Washington, D.C. Both had argued that the cranial fragments and mandible belonged to separate creatures, with Miller (1915) claiming chimpanzee affinities for the jaw.

Another major figure was William King Gregory (1876–1970) at the American Museum of Natural History (AMNH) in New York. Gregory joined the Department of Vertebrate Paleontology at the AMNH in 1911 and published his first article on primate evolution in 1916. Over the next three decades, he made many contributions to the study of human evolution, such as his widely cited and influential analysis of the hominid affinities of the *Australopithecus* dental sample (Gregory & Hellman 1939).

Gregory's mentor—or, as he preferred, "my *fidus Achates*"—at the AMNH had been Henry Fairfield Osborn (1857–1935), who had more than a passing interest in paleoanthropology. Indeed, through his *Men of the Old Stone Age* (1915) and his administration of the AMNH he did much to popularize paleoanthropology in America between the two World Wars. A leading advocate of the idea that central Asia was the cradleland for the human genus, Osborn was instrumental in organizing the Central Asiatic Expedition (CAE) in the early 1920s. Led by naturalist-explorer Roy Chapman Andrews (1884–1960), this expedition traveled through Mongolia and north China in an ultimately futile search for evidence of humans' Asian origins (Andrews 1926). The CAE marks the initial effort by an American institution to explore parts of the Old World for traces of our ancestors.

In 1922, there was one final attempt to place events in human evolution in the New World. *Hesperopithecus haroldcookii*, the name given to a single tooth discovered in Tertiary deposits in Nebraska, was initially identified as "the first anthropoid primate found in America" (Osborn 1922). Further discoveries, however, led to the recognition that the tooth was from an extinct form related to modern peccaries (Gregory 1927).

In 1927, Henry Field, a curator at the Chicago Museum of Natural History, purchased the Magdalenian-age female skeleton discovered in 1911 at the Cap Blanc abri (Dordogne, France). Exhibited for many years in the museum (it is no longer on public view), this specimen was the first human fossil to be permanently housed in the United States.

In 1929, excavations began at several caves and rockshelters in the Wadi el-Mughara on Mount Carmel in what is now northern Israel. A joint project of the British Museum of Natural History (now the Natural History Museum) and the American School of Prehistoric Research, it was directed by the British archeologist Dorothy A.E. Garrod (1892–1968). A major role in the excavations at Mugharet es-Skhul Cave was performed by American paleoanthropologist Theodore D. McCown (1908–1969), who had trained in Britain under Arthur Keith at the Royal College of Surgeons of England, London, and who was given responsibility for describing the hominid skeletal materials. The descriptive monograph (1939) dealing with the Skhūl and Tabūn remains, written in collaboration with Keith, marked the initial contribution of an American to the excavation of fossil specimens and their monographic description. These specimens continue to play a central role in theories of Upper Pleistocene human evolution, and the McCown and Keith volume remains a widely used reference.

At the completion of the skeletal analysis, the hominid fossils were distributed among the Rockefeller Museum in Jerusalem, the Natural History Museum in London, and the Harvard Peabody Museum in Cambridge, Massachusetts, with the latter obtaining Skhūl 2, 3, 5–8 and Tabūn B1 and B4 for permanent curation. In 1938, McCown obtained an academic position in the Department of Anthropology at the University of California, Berkeley, thereby becoming the first paleoanthropologist in the United States to have a university appointment.

While Hrdlička was the most influential scientist in the establishment of paleoanthropology in the United States and a dominant force during the interwar years, his position at the National Museum was not conducive to the training of students. Hooton (*vide ante*), who began teaching at Harvard in 1913, was responsible for training a whole generation of professional physical anthropologists that included William W. Howells (1908–) and Washburn, who, in turn, trained many of the paleoanthropologists active in the field in the 1990s. Although Hooton himself did not engage in any original paleoanthropological research, his widely used textbook, *Up from the Ape*, first published in 1931, contained major sections detailing the fossil evidence for human evolution.

In 1932, the Yale–North India Paleontological Expedition, under the geologist G.E. Lewis, began work in the Miocene deposits of the Siwaliks, an area that had already yielded numerous hominoid fossil finds. Near the village of Haritalyangar, Lewis found a portion of a maxilla (Yale Peabody Museum No. 13799), which he placed in the new taxon *Ramapithecus brevirostris*, noting that some of its morphological features would be those expected on a very early human ancestor. This suggestion, however, was vigorously opposed by Hrdlička. Later, in the early 1960s, the paleoprimatologist Elwyn Simons (along with David Pilbeam) resuscitated Lewis' proposal, establishing *Ramapithecus*, now including several other fossil fragments, as an early member of Hominidae, where it remained until additional discoveries indicated more reasonable affinities with the *Pongo* lineage.

In the spring of 1941, German-born anatomist-paleoanthropologist Franz Weidenreich (1873–1948) arrived at the American Museum of Natural History, where he remained until his death in 1948. An experienced researcher on hominid fossils who had already produced a major monograph on the Ehringsdorf (Germany) finds (cf. Weidenreich 1928), in 1934 Weidenreich was appointed to succeed the Canadian anatomist Davidson Black (1884–1934) at the Peking Union Medical College, where he extended Black's former involvement with the excavations of the cave site at Zhoukoudian (formally Choukoutien), just outside of Peking (now Beijing). The results of his anatomical investigations of the Zhoukoudian *Homo erectus* specimens were presented in a series of now classic illustrated monographs that described the mandibles and teeth, postcrania, and skulls in great detail (cf. Weidenreich 1937, 1941, 1943). These volumes, in addition to a superb set of primary casts of virtually all of the Zhoukoudian fossils (which he brought with him to the American Museum of Natural History in New York), are all that remain of this original material, which was lost at the beginning of World War II (Mann 1981).

MATURATION OF AMERICAN PALEOANTHROPOLOGY: 1950s–1990s

The end of World War II marked a crucial turning point in the development of American paleoanthropology. A major synthesis of Darwinian evolutionary theory and genetics had been presented in the late 1930s and early 1940s, but concentration on the war effort limited the dissemination of this work in American science. In 1947, an international conference on "Genetics, Paleontology, and Evolution" was held at Princeton, New Jersey. Papers presented at this conference and published in book form (Jepsen, Mayr, & Simpson 1949), along with George Gaylord Simpson's (1902–1984) *The Meaning of Evolution* (1949), did much to communicate details of the synthetic theory, and its application to the fossil record, to paleoanthropologists.

This enhanced appreciation of evolutionary mechanisms was further developed at an international conference held at Cold Spring Harbor, Long Island, New York, in the summer of 1950. The program of this conference, entitled "The Origin and Evolution of Man," was organized by the geneticist Theodosius Dobzhansky (1900–1975) and the physical anthropologist Washburn (*vide ante*). The papers presented at this conference—anthropologists, geneticists, and evolutionary biologists—broadly examined the ways by which human evolution could be understood within a neo-Darwinian framework.

In 1951, Washburn summarized this approach as "the new physical anthropology," emphasizing the need to utilize a variety of evolutionarily based approaches to paleoanthropological research, especially a consideration of the importance of behavior. As Washburn later observed: "Evolution is the history of adaptation, in which reproductive success depends on behavior. Without an appreciation of the significance of behaviors, there can be no understanding of evolution" (1968:193–194). Many of Washburn's students, trained in the 1950s and 1960s, utilized this emphasis in their own research, thereby launching a major trend in human evolutionary studies (cf. Haraway 1988).

The growth of the U.S. academic community beginning in the late 1950s can also be seen in the dramatic increase in the number of paleoanthropologists who began their professional careers after 1960 (Spencer 1981). For example, the 1953 membership of the American Association of Physical Anthropologists numbered twenty scholars who could be broadly considered paleoanthropologists on the basis of their research. Most also published on other subject areas in physical anthropology, reflecting the relatively unspecialized nature of physical anthropology at that time. In 1993, the American Anthropological Association's *Guide to Departments* listed 183 scholars who were professionally involved in paleoanthropological research and/or teaching; 61 in primate evolution; 9 in genetic studies directly dealing with questions in human evolution; and 18 who described themselves as being concerned with evolutionary theory in general. This growth has resulted in an enormous increase in the number of scholarly papers being published each year, and this, along with the variety of subjects being examined and the increasing sample of hominid fossils, has inevitably led to a narrowing of research specializations. The result is that there are few individual paleoanthropologists who deal with the entire hominid fossil record; the majority focus their research on a limited time zone of the human evolutionary continuum and/or on a particular aspect of the anatomy of the fossils.

These modern scholars have a range of academic backgrounds. While the majority were trained by students of Hooton, or by students of students of Hooton, there has also been a significant influx of British paleoanthropologists who have taken up professional posts in the United States. Finally, a number of American students have studied at foreign institutions—for example, with Phillip V. Tobias (1925–) at the University of the Witwatersrand in Johannesburg, South Africa.

There has also been a marked diversification in both the kinds of studies that have been undertaken and the perception of the research itself. For example, in the main, American-trained paleoanthropologists continue to utilize an anthropological perspective in their research, while British-trained scientists often emphasize aspects of anatomy or geology.

In 1967, paleoanthropology itself underwent an expansion of vision with contributions from comparisons of the proteins and DNA (nuclear and mitochondrial) of living peoples, and the African apes, being employed to construct phylogenetic trees and provide a set of time scales for the divergence of major and minor taxa (Goodman & Cronin 1982).

AMERICAN PALEOANTHROPOLOGICAL FIELDWORK
In the years after World War II, Americans increasingly participated in field research, especially in Africa. Two expeditions from the University of California, Berkeley, in 1947 and 1948, worked at several sites in South Africa, but without discovering hominid specimens (Camp 1948). The major American emphasis would focus on the Rift Valley of East Africa. At Olduvai Gorge, research by geologist R.L. Hay on the stratigraphy began in 1962, and later a date of 1.76 my for the layer in which *Zinjanthropus boisei* was found was determined using the potassium-argon dating technique (cf. Evernden & Curtis 1965).

In 1951, F. Clark Howell (1925–), a student of Washburn, produced the first of a series of papers on the evolutionary relationships of the Neandertals to early modern humans. Howell's work emphasized the importance in paleoanthropological investigations of understanding not only the anatomy of fossil bones, but also the geological, archeological, and temporal contexts as well. This interdisciplinary approach to the study of human evolution characterized the joint Franco-American-Kenyan Expedition, organized in 1967 by Howell and Yves Coppens of the Museé de l'Homme, Paris, to the Omo River Basin in southern Ethiopia. Over nine seasons, more than 225 hominid fossil specimens were recovered, virtually all belonging to various species of *Australopithecus*. Just as important, aspects of the stratigraphy, vertebrate paleontology, sedimentology, palynology, and archeology were also studied, providing a more integrative context within which to place the hominid fossils. This model of organization has been widely followed, especially by two of Howell's students, Noel Boaz and Donald Johanson. The latter jointly organized an expedition with French geologist M. Taieb, beginning in 1973, to the Hadar region of north-central Ethiopia (cf. Johanson & Edey 1981). This work, which has continued intermittently into the 1990s, has resulted in a remarkable series of hominid fossil discoveries, including the partial skeleton of a female australopithecine (A.L. 288).

There have also been successful American-led expeditions to other parts of the Old World. From 1951 through 1960, the Columbia University archeologist Ralph S. Solecki excavated Shanidar Cave in Kurdistan in northern Iraq, ultimately discovering the remains of nine Neandertals associated with Mousterian tools (Solecki 1971; Trinkaus 1983).

The volumes detailing the Shanidar Neandertals, as well as the publications on the Omo and the Hadar fossils (cf. *American Journal of Physical Anthropology*, Vol. 57. No. 4, 1982, which is devoted exclusively to the "Pliocene Hominid Fossils from Hadar, Ethiopia"; and Howell & Coppens 1974, 1976; Howell, Haessaerts, & de Heinzelin 1987), are some of a small number of primary descriptions of fossil hominids that have been prepared by Americans or by Americans working jointly with other scholars. Others include the description of the Narmada calotte from India (Kennedy et al. 1991) and specific chapters describing aspects of the *Homo erectus* youth discovered in the early 1990s by a team from the Kenya National Museum at Nariokotome, west of Lake Turkana (Walker & Leakey 1993).

In this same region, beginning in the early 1970s, David Pilbeam at Yale, and later Harvard, initiated (in conjunction with the Geological Survey of Pakistan) an ongoing program of research in the Potwar Plateau region that has led to the subsequent recovery of important Miocene hominoid fossils (e.g., Pilbeam et al. 1980).

Apart from these examples, however, post–World War II American paleoanthropology continues to be focused on the examination and evaluation of hominid fossils discovered and initially described by others.

Francis E. Johnson
Alan Mann

Authors' Note
American physical anthropologists have also played a major role in the development of primate field studies and paleoprimatology. The development of these and related areas of specialization can be found in the following separate entries: African Apes; African Monkeys; Asian Apes; Asian Monkeys; Malagasy Primates; New World Primate Studies; Paleoprimatology; and Primate Field Studies.

See also Academy of Natural Sciences (Philadelphia); Adaptation; American Anthropological Association; American Association of Physical Anthropologists; American Philosophical Society; Americas: Paleoanthropology; Andrews, Roy Chapman; Anthropometry; Anthropometry in Physical Education and Sports Sciences; Asian Paleoanthropology; Australopithecines; Baker, Paul Thornell; Black, Davidson; Boas, Franz; Body-Composition Studies; Buettner-Janusch, John; Caldwell, Charles; Child-Growth Studies; Cobb, William Montague; Coon, Carleton S(tevens); Damon, Albert; Dobzhansky, Theodosius; Fels Research Institute; Garn, Stanley M.; Gregory, William King; Growth Studies; Harvard University; Health and Disease; Hooton, E(arnest) A(lbert); Howells, William White; Hrdlička, Aleš; Hulse, Frederick Seymour; International Biological Programme (Human Adaptability Section); Keith, (Sir) Arthur; Krogman, Wilton Marion; Lasker, Gabriel Ward; Laughlin, William S.; McCown, Theodore D(oney); Molecular Anthropology; Morton, Samuel George; Mount Carmel (Israel); Multidisciplinary Research of Human Biology and Behavior; Neandertals; Neo-Darwinism; Nott, Josiah Clark; Oceania; Olduvai Gorge; Omo; Osborn, Henry Fairfield; Paleopathology; Pennsylvania, University of; Piltdown; *Ramapithecus;* Shanidar (Iraq); Sheldon, William H(erbert); Simpson, George Gaylord; Siwaliks; Skhūl, Mughâret es- (Israel); Smith, Samuel Stanhope; Spuhler, J(ames) N(orman); Tabūn, Mughâret et- (Israel); Tobias, Phillip V(allentine); Washburn, Sherwood L.; Weidenreich, Franz; Zhoukoudian

Bibliography
R.C. Andrews: *On the trail of ancient man.* New York: Putnam, 1926; P.T. Baker & J.S. Weiner (eds): *The biology of human adaptability.* Oxford: Clarendon Press, 1966; F. Boas: *Changes in bodily form of descendants of immigrants.* New York: Columbia University Press, 1912; M. Boule. *L'homme fossiles. Éléments de paléontologie humaine.* Paris: Masson, 1923; W.C. Boyd: *Genetics and the races of man.* Boston: Heath, 1950; C.L. Brace: The roots of the race concept in American physical anthropology. In: F. Spencer (ed) *A history of American physical anthropology, 1930–1980.* New York: Academic Press, 1982, pp. 11–29; J. Brozek

(ed): *Body measurement and human nutrition*. Detroit: Wayne State University Press, 1956.

C. Caldwell: An essay on the causes of the variety of complexion and figure in the human species. *Port-Folio* (ser. 3) 4:8–33, 148–163, 252–271, 447–457, 1814; C.L. Camp: University of California Expedition—southern section. *Science* 108:550–552, 1948; J.E.L. Carter & B.H. Heath: *Somatotyping: Development and applications*. London: Cambridge University Press, 1990; C.S. Coon: *The origin of races*. New York: Knopf, 1963; C.S. Coon: *The living races of man*. New York: Knopf, 1965; R. Darnell: The development of American anthropology, 1879–1920: From the Bureau of American Ethnology to Franz Boas. Ph.D. Thesis. University of Pennsylvania, 1969; J.F. Evernden & G.H. Curtis: The potassium argon dating of Late Cenozoic rocks in East Africa and Italy. *Current Anthropology* 6:343–364, 1965; E.B. Ford: Polymorphism. *Biological Reviews of the Cambridge Philosophical Society* 20:73–88, 1945.

J. Friedlaender: *The Solomon Islands Project: A long-term study of health, human biology, and cultural change*. Oxford: Clarendon Press, 1987; M. Goodman & J.E. Cronin: Molecular Anthropology: Its development and current directions. In: F. Spencer (ed) *A history of American physical anthropology, 1930–1980*. New York: Academic Press, 1982, pp. 105–146; W.K. Gregory: Studies in the evolution of the primates. II. Phylogeny of recent and extinct anthropoids, with special reference to the origin of man. *Bulletin of the American Museum of Natural History* 35:258–355, 1916; W.K. Gregory: Hesperopithecus apparently not an ape nor a man. *Science* 66:579–581, 1927; W.K. Gregory & M. Hellman: The South African fossil man-apes and the origin of the human dentition. *Journal of the American Dental Association* 26:558–564, 1939.

D.J. Haraway: Remodelling the human way of life: Sherwood Washburn and the new physical anthropology, 1950–1980. In: G.W. Stocking Jr. (ed) *Bone, bodies, behavior*. Madison: University of Wisconsin Press, 1988, pp. 206–259; R.L. Hay: *Geology of the Olduvai Gorge*. Berkeley: University of California Press, 1976; E.A. Hooton: *Up from the ape*. New York: Macmillan, 1931; F.C. Howell: The place of Neanderthal man in human evolution. *American Journal of Physical Anthropology* 9:379–416, 1951; F.C. Howell: Pleistocene glacial ecology and the evolution of "classic Neanderthal" man. *Southwestern Journal of Anthropology* 8:377–410, 1952.

F.C. Howell: The evolutionary significance of variation and varieties of "Neanderthal" man. *Quarterly Review of Biology* 32:330–347, 1957; F.C. Howell & Y. Coppens: The inventory of remains of Hominidae from Pliocene formations of the Lower Omo basin, Ethiopia (1967–1972). *American Journal of Physical Anthropology* 40:1–16, 1974; F.C. Howell & Y. Coppens: An overview of Hominidae from the Omo Succession, Ethiopia. In: Y. Coppens et al. (eds) *Earliest man and environments in the Lake Rudolf Basin*. Chicago: University of Chicago Press, 1976, pp. 522–532; F.C. Howell, P. Haesaerts & J. de Heinzelin: Depositional environments, archaeological occurrences, and hominids from Members E and F of the Shungura Formation (Omo basin, Ethiopia). *Journal of Human Evolution* 16:665–700, 1987; A. Hrdlička: Skeletal remains suggesting or attributed to early man in North America. *Bulletin of the Bureau of American Ethnology* 33:1–113, 1907.

A. Hrdlička: The most ancient skeletal remains of man. *Smithsonian Institution Annual Reports for 1913*. Washington, D.C.: Government Printing Office, 1914, pp. 491–552; A. Hrdlička: *The skeletal remains of early man*. Smithsonian Miscellaneous Collections. Vol. 83. Washington, D.C.: Smithsonian Institution, 1930; J. Huxley: Evolution: The modern synthesis. London: Harper, 1942; G.L. Jepsen, E. Mayr, & G.G. Simpson (eds): *Genetics, paleontology, and evolution*. Princeton, New Jersey: Princeton University Press, 1949; D. Johanson & M. Edey: *Lucy and the beginnings of humankind*. New York: Simon & Schuster, 1981; A. Keith: *The antiquity of man*. London: Williams & Norgate, 1915; A. Keith: *The antiquity of man*. 2 vols. London: Williams & Norgate, 1925.

K.A.R. Kennedy et al.: Is the Narmada hominid an Indian *Homo erectus*? *American Journal of Physical Anthropology* 64:105–118, 1991; R. Kirk & E. Szathmary (ed): *Out of Asia: Peopling of the Americas and the Pacific*. Canberra: ACT, 1985; F.B. Livingstone: Anthropological implications of the sickle-cell gene distribution in West Africa. *American Anthropologist* 60:533–562, 1958; T.D. McCown & A. Keith: *The Stone Age of Mount Carmel II: The fossil human remains* from the Levalloiso Mousterian. Oxford: Clarendon Press, 1939; A.E. Mann: The significance of the Sinanthropus casts and some paleodemographic notes. In: B.A. Sigmon & J.S. Cybulski (eds) Homo erectus: Papers in honor of Davidson Black. Toronto: University of Toronto Press, 1981, pp. 41–62; O.C. Marsh: On the Pithecanthropus erectus from the Tertiary of Java. American Journal of Science 1:475–482, 1896.

J.H. Mielke & M.H. Crawford (eds): Current developments in anthropological genetics. New York: Plenum, 1980; G.S. Miller: The jaw of "Piltdown Man." Smithsonian Miscellaneous Contributions 65:1–31, 1915; S.L. Mitchill: The original inhabitants of America shown to be the same family and lineage as those of Asia, by a process of reasoning not hitherto advanced. Archaeologia Americana 1:225–232, 1820; S.G. Morton: Crania Americana. Philadelphia: Dobson, 1839; S.G. Morton: Crania Aegyptiaca. Philadelphia: Penington, 1844; J.V. Neel: Lessons from a primitive people. Science 170:815–822, 1970; J.C. Nott & G.R. Gliddon (eds): Types of mankind. Philadelphia: Lippincott, Grambo, 1854; J.C. Nott & J.R. Gliddon (eds): Indigenous races of the earth; or, New chapters of ethnological enquiry. Philadelphia: Lippincott, 1857.

H.F. Osborn: Men of the Old Stone Age. New York: Scribner's, 1915; H.F. Osborn: Hesperopithecus, the first anthroid primate found in America. American Museum Novitates (April) 1922; R. Pennington & H. Harpending: The structure of an African pastoralist community: Demography, history, and ecology of the Ngamiland Herero. Oxford: Clarendon Press, 1993; D. Pilbeam et al.: Miocene hominoids from Pakistan. Postillo 181:1–94, 1980; A.F. Roche et al.: Assessing the skeletal maturity of the hand-wrist: Fels method. Springfield, Illinois: Thomas, 1988; G.G. Simpson: The meaning of evolution. New Haven, Connecticut: Yale University Press, 1949; S.S. Smith: An essay on the causes of the variety of the complexion and figure in the human species. Philadelphia: Aitken, 1787; R.S. Solecki: Shanidar, the first flower people. New York: Knopf, 1971.

F. Spencer: The rise of academic physical anthropology in the United States, 1880–1980: A historical overview. American Journal of Physical Anthropology 56:353–364, 1981; J.N. Spuhler & C. Kluckhohn: Inbreeding coefficients of the Ramah Navaho population. Human Biology 25:295–317, 1953; R.B. Thomas: The ecology of work. In: A. Damon (ed) Physiological anthropology. New York: Oxford University Press, 1975, pp. 59–79; E. Trinkaus: The Shanidar Neandertals. New York: Academic Press, 1983; A. Walker & R.E.F. Leakey (eds): The Nariokotome Homo erectus skeleton. Cambridge, Massachusetts: Harvard University Press, 1993.

S.L. Washburn: The new physical anthropology. Transactions of the New York Academy of Science 13:298–304, 1951. S.L. Washburn: Speculations on the problem of man's coming to the ground. In: B. Rothblatt (ed) Changing perspectives on man. Chicago: University of Chicago Press, 1968, pp. 191–206; F. Weidenreich: Der Schädelfund von Weimar-Ehringsdorf. Jena: Fischer, 1928; F. Weidenreich: The mandibles of Sinanthropus pekinensis: A comparative study. Palaeontologica Sinica. (ser. D) 7(3), 1936; F. Weidenreich: The dentition of Sinanthropus pekinensis: A comparative odontography of the hominids. Palaeontologica Sinica, (n.s. D) No. 1, 1937; F. Weidenreich: The extremity bones of Sinanthropus pekinensis. Palaeontologica Sinica. (ser. D) No. 5, 1941; F. Weidenreich: The skull of Sinanthropus pekinensis: A comparative study on a primitive hominid skull. Palaeontologica Sinica. (ser.D) No. 10, 1943; K.M. Weiss & Ballonoff (ed): Demographic genetics. Stroudsberg, Pennsylvania: Dowden, Hutchinson & Ross, 1975.

Uruguay

Compared with other Latin American countries, physical anthropology developed late in Uruguay. In fact, the discipline was not formally recognized until the mid-1970s. However, it is possible to find antecedents in the work of José H. Figueira (1860–1946) at the end of the nineteenth century. Essentially, Figueira's research was limited to the study of archeological sites in the eastern part of the country, where he described human burials and the physical characteristics of recovered skeletal material (Figueira 1892, 1900). Later, the Argentine researcher Luis María Torres (1878–1937) included data about the human remains described by Figueira in his book on the ancient inhabitants of the Delta del Paraná (Torres 1911).

During the first half of the twentieth century, this interest in Uruguayan prehistory was further promoted by the French anthropologist Paul Rivet (1876–1958) with his 1930 study of the remains of four Uruguayan Indians (Charruas) that were taken to Paris in

1832. This same time period also witnessed a number of publications dealing with the cranial anatomy and other physical traits of Uruguay's prehistoric inhabitants (cf. Seijo 1923, 1930). Between 1950 and 1975, this field of inquiry was developed further, most notably by the biologist Juan Ignacio Muñoa (1925–1960). In 1954, he published a complete study of human skeletal remains that embodied the theoretical concepts of the time. Two other significant publications from this period include the general work on Uruguayan prehistory by Rodolfo Maruca Sosa (1957), who was a self-taught anthropologist, and the medical study of children in prehistoric Uruguay by the physician M. Jaureguy et al. (1956).

Although prior to 1950 there had been sporadic publications dealing with the biology of the contemporary Uruguayan population (e.g., Rovira 1911), it was not until the second half of the century that this area of physical anthropology began to receive increasing attention. Much of the work was performed by faculty members of the School of Humanities and Sciences at the Universidad de la República (URM) in Montevideo. The primary focus of this effort was the study of dermatoglyphics (e.g., Kolski & Scazzocchio 1961; Lázaro et al. 1961) and blood groups (e.g., Caragna et al. 1950; Seuánez et al. 1973). Other related subjects that attracted attention included the frequency of consanguineous marriages (Holcman 1970), miscellaneous morphological traits (e.g., Kolski 1955), and the age of menarche (Sprechmann 1973). During this same time period and at the same institution, studies were begun on human and primate behavior (Tálice 1978).

In 1976, an undergraduate degree program (Licenciatura) in anthropology (involving courses in physical anthropology) was established in the School of Humanities and Sciences at the URM, the first of its kind in the country. At the same time, there were a number of research studies published that documented the continuing development of the study of the modern Uruguayan population. These studies covered a wide variety of subjects, ranging from dermatoglyphics (e.g., Dei-Cas 1975; Oyhenart-Perera 1976, 1979) to fecundity (Oyhenart-Perera 1980), to the HLA system (Alvarez et al. 1993). The 1980s also saw the emergence of forensic anthropology, which is now a discrete area of inquiry (e.g., Soiza 1989; Solla 1989), as well as work connected with the archeological salvage work at Salto Grande (e.g., Pereira 1989; Oliver 1989).

In 1991, the School of Humanities and Sciences at the URM was reorganized, resulting in the separation of the humanities and the sciences, with anthropology (including physical anthropology) being grouped with the former rather than the latter. A Section of Physical Anthropology (SAP) was created in the School of Humanities and Educational Sciences, which has permitted a continuing dedication to this field of interest.

Although by the mid-1990s there was no formal postgraduate program in physical anthropology at the URM, graduate research, particularly in the area of human genetics, was being fostered through the graduate program in biology. In the meantime, however, faculty associated with the SAP have developed an active research agenda directed primarily to the study of prehistoric human remains (e.g., Sans 1988, 1989) and the study of human genetics. Work in the latter field is being developed in conjunction with other research units within the URM, as well as the Universidade Federal do Rio Grande do Sul, Brazil (e.g., Alvarez et al., 1993; Sans et al. 1993). Further impulse was given to the development of physical anthropology in Uruguay with the meeting of the First Congress of the Latin American Association of Biological Anthropology in Montevideo in 1990.

Monica Sans

See also Brazil; Molecular Anthropology; Muñoa, Juan Ignacio; New World Primate Studies; Oyhenart-Perera, Martín; Rivet, Paul

Bibliography
I. Alvarez et al.: *Taller Latinoamericano de histocompatibilidad*. Montevideo: Banco Nacional de Organos y Tejidos, 1983; I. Alvarez et al.: HLA gene and haplotype frequencies in Uruguay. *International Journal of Anthropology*, 8:163–168, 1993; H. Caragna et al.: Distribución de los grupos sanguíneos en 11704 dadores voluntarios de sangre. *Archivos Uruguayos de Medicina, Cirugía, y Especialidades* 37:41–43, 1950; E. Dei-Cas: Dermatoglifos palmares en una muestra normal de la población de Montevideo. *Revista Uruguaya de Patología Clínica y Microbiología* 13:30–39, 1975; J.H. Figueira: Los primitivos habitantes del Uruguay. In: *El Uruguay en la exposición histórico-americana de Madrid*. Montevideo: Artistica de Dornaleche y Reyes, 1892, pp. 121–221; J.H. Figueira: Paraderos: In: Diccionario geográfico del Uruguay. *Boletín*

Histórico del Estado Mayor General del Ejército 104–105, 1900.

B. Holcman: Nivel de consanguinidad en la población del Uruguay. *Revista Uruguaya de Patología Clínica* 8:128–133, 1970; M. Jaureguy et al.: Estudio médico del niño indígeno del Uruguay. *Archivos de Pediatría del Uruguay* 37:293–301, 1956; R. Kolski: Estudio de 11 genealogías en los que aparece el carácter lóbulo adherente. *Revista de la Facultad de Humanidades y Ciencias* 14:321–328, 1955; R. Kolski & C. Scazzocchio: *Estudio de frecuencia de caracteres dermopapilares en nuestra población.* Montevideo: Facultad de Humanidades y Ciencias, Laboratorio de Genética, 1961; C. Lázaro et al.: Study on dermatoglyphics in 200 pedigrees. In: *Proceedings, II International Congress of Human Genetics*. Rome: Edizioni Istituto "G. Mendel," 1961, pp. 1497–1502; R. Maruca Sosa: *La Nación Charrúa*. Montevideo, 1957; J. Muñoa: Contribuciones a la antropología física del Uruguay. I. Los primitivos pobladores del Este. *Anales del Museo de Historia Natural de Montevideo* 6 (2d ser.):1–19, 1954.

R. Oliver: Estudio odontológico de los restos humanos. In: *Misión de rescate arqueológico Salto Grande*. Primera parte. Montevideo: Ministerio de Educación y Cultura, 1989, pp. 401–426; M. Oyhenart-Perera: Los estudios dermatoglíficos en el Uruguay. *Revista Uruguaya de Patología Clínica y Microbiología* 14:10–23, 1976; M. Oyhenart-Perera: Contribución al estudio de los dermatoglíficos digitales de la población de Montevideo (Uruguay). II. Caracteres cuantitativos. *Revista de Biología del Uruguay* 7:65–76, 1979; M. Oyhenart-Perara: Variación mensual del número de nacimientos en la población de Montevideo (Uruguay). *Revista Española de Pediatría* 36:309–310, 1980.

M. Pereira: Estudio del material óseo. In: *Misión de rescate arqueológico Salto Grande*. Primera parte. Montevideo: Ministerio de Educación y Cultura, 1989, pp. 346–400; P. Rivet: Les derniers Charruas. *Revista Sociedad "Amigos de la Arqueología"* 4:5–117, 1930; T. Rovira: Sobre la mancha azul mongólica congénita. *Archivos Latinoamericanos de Pediatría* 1:174–186, 1911; M. Sans: *Las poblaciones prehistóricas del Uruguay.* Montevideo: Facultad de Humanidades y Ciencias, Universidad de la República, 1988; M. Sans: Extracción e identificación de restos óseos humanos: Un ejemplo arqueológico. *Ciencias Forenses (Anales de la Sociedad Uruguaya de Ciencias Forenses)* 1:32–35, 1989; M. Sans et al.: Blood-group frequencies and the question of race admixture in Uruguay. *Interciencia* 18:29–32, 1993.

C. Seijo: De prehistoria. *Revista Histórica* 11:1491–1508, 1923; C. Seijo: Cráneo con fragmentos de un collar. *Revista Sociedad "Amigos de la Arqueología"* 4:183–195, 1930; H. Seuánez et al.: Proporción sexual secundaria y grupos sanguíneos A-B-O. *Revista de Biología del Uruguay* 1:51–56, 1973; A. Soiza: Un sepultamiento colectivo en el Montevideo colonial: Estudio antropológico e histórico. *Anales del 6o. Encuentro Nacional y 4o. Regional de Historia, Montevideo* 1:85–90, 1989; H. Solla: Antropología forense. *Investigación Criminal (Revista del Instituto Técnico Forense)* 1:34, 1989; P. Sprechmann: Nuevos datos para la edad de la menarca en Montevideo, Uruguay. *Revista de Biología del Uruguay* 1:57–72, 1973; R. Tálice: *Comportamiento sexual humano*. Montevideo: Arca, 1978; L.M. Torres: *Los primitivos habitantes del delta del Paraná*. Buenos Aires: Universidad de La Plata Biblioteca Centenario, 1911.

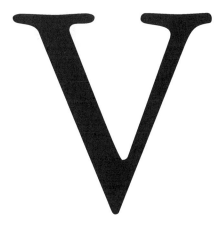

V

Vallois, Henri Victor (1889–1981)

Born in Nancy, France, Vallois was trained as a physician and a naturalist in Montpellier and Paris. At Montpellier in 1914, he defended a thesis in medicine on the knee of the primates; at Paris in 1922, a thesis in natural history entitled "Les transformations de la musclature de l'épisome chez les Vertébrés" (Vallois 1922). From 1922 to 1941, he taught anatomy and zoology in the Faculty of Medicine at Toulouse. During his tenure at Toulouse, he increasingly focused on physical anthropology and human paleontology. He had regular contacts with the anatomist Raoul Anthony (1874–1941) and physical anthropologist Léonce Manouvrier (1850–1927) and was deeply influenced by the views of the paleoanthropologist Marcellin Boule (1861–1942). In 1937, he moved to Paris, where he became professor and director (1938–1960) of the Laboratoire d'Anthropologie of the École Pratique des Hautes Études. In 1941, he was also installed at the Museum National d'Histoire Naturelle, where, until his retirement in 1960, he occupied the Chaire d'ethnologie et d'anthropologie des hommes actuels et des hommes fossiles (*vide infra*), which was formerly the "Chaire d'anatomie et d'anthropologie" of Etienne Serres (1780–1862) and Armand de Quatrefages (1810–1892).

One of the most striking aspects of Vallois' career was the central and exceptionally influential position he gradually managed to reach in the French institutional structure. To name only the most important positions he held during his career: director of the Institut de Paléontologie Humaine (1942–1971), director of the Musée de l'Homme

(1941–1945 and 1950–1960), and president of the Centre National de la Recherche Scientifique committee in charge of supervising anthropology (1949–1966). He was also president of the Société d'Anthropologie de Paris in 1932, and its general secretary from 1938 until 1969. Last, but not least, he served as editor of the three main French serial publications in physical anthropology: *L'Anthropologie,* the *Bulletins et Mémoires de la Société d'Anthropologie de Paris,* and the *Archives de l'Institut de Paléontologie Humaine.* His exceptionally strong scientific and institutional position is also revealed by his contributions to primary reference works such as the *Traité d'anatomie humaine,* for which he wrote the volume *Arthrologie* (1926), and the volume on primates in the Grasse *Traité de zoologie* (1955). After Boule's death, he was responsible for revising the third and fourth editions of *Les hommes fossiles* (Vallois & Boule 1946, 1952). He also coauthored with the Harvard geologist Hallam Movius (1907–1987) the *Catalogue des hommes fossiles* (1953).

Vallois' bibliography is composed of 439 references. He studied and published on an impressive number of prehistoric human remains, ranging from the the Lower Paleolithic to protohistoric times. Among his main works are studies of the Mesolithic and Epipaleolithic—see particularly his "Les mésolithiques de France" (Vallois & de Félice 1977). He also reexamined the Upper Paleolithic remains of Chancelade (1946) and Cro-Magnon (Vallois & Billy 1965). In the field of Lower Paleolithic studies, he described a number of important specimens such as the Montmaurin mandible (1956; Billy & Vallois 1977), the Fontéchevade specimens (1958), and the Rabat hominid (1960; Thoma & Vallois 1977).

He was an outstanding anatomist who provided extremely detailed osteological studies. For example, his analysis of the Neandertal temporal (1969) is still a standard reference work. Another interesting aspect of Vallois' approach in paleoanthropology was his attempt to deal with some paleobiological aspects rather than confine himself exclusively to purely taxonomic discussions. In this way, he published general studies on the longevity (1937) and the paleopathology of the fossil hominids (1934, 1948, 1949). His main contributions to paleoanthropology, however, were theoretical. He defended the monophyletic origin of humans in various papers (1927, 1929, 1952) and was opposed to the view propounded by such workers as the American physical anthropologist Aleš Hrdlička (1869–1943) and the German paleoanthropologist Franz Weidenreich (1873–1948) that the Neandertals were either antecedants of, or closely related to, modern humans. In accordance with the earlier work of Boule, he consistently supported the evolutionary discontinuity between Neandertals and Upper Paleolithic hominids. Moreover, his name is primarily associated with the pre-sapiens concept. After the discovery of the Fontéchevade cranial remains in 1947, he began promoting a biphyletic model that sorted the European Pleistocene fossil hominids into two groups. In the conclusion of his monograph on the Fontéchevade remains (1958), he clearly delineated the then three competing hypotheses on the origin of modern humans: the Neandertal hypothesis (modern humans derived from Neandertals), the pre-Neandertal hypothesis (modern humans derived from pre-Neandertals), and the pre-sapiens hypothesis (modern humans derived from a special lineage). Vallois strongly rejected the first and second hypotheses. In his view, a series of European specimens (which included Piltdown, Swanscombe, and the Fontéchevade remains), representing the origin of anatomically modern Europeans, had evolved alongside the lineage leading to the Neandertals. Even after Piltdown was demonstrated to be a forgery in 1953, this model survived and deeply influenced most of the studies in European paleoanthropology until the 1970s, at which time the "pre-sapiens" nature of pre-Würmian specimens like Swanscombe was strongly refuted (cf. Hublin 1978, 1982; Santa-Luca 1978). Interestingly, the European pre-sapiens were considered by Vallois as emissaries of a Western Asian stock penetrating into Europe during an interglacial period. Viewed from this perspective, the pre-sapiens hypothesis can be regarded as a forerunner of the modern "replacement model" (the "Garden of Eden" hypothesis), which also excludes the Neandertals and other contemporaneous archaic populations from the ancestry of modern humans. The pre-sapiens model was subsequently rejected, mainly for its Eurocentric orientation.

Vallois was also interested in living populations, and especially undertook field studies of the African pygmies. In contrast to the French anthropologist Joseph Deniker (1852–1918), who believed that the Oceanic Negritos were related to the African pygmies, Vallois contended that they were two independent groups (Vallois 1938). Between 1929 and 1946, he also made a special study of the human scapula. In his book *Les races humaines* (1944, 1948) he proposed a classification of humankind consisting of twenty-seven races divided into four major subgroups: White (nine races), Black (seven races), Yellow (eight races), and Australoid (two races). In the intense debates surrounding eugenics and the concept of race before World War II, he kept a median position, in contrast to other French workers such as Etienne Patte and Henri Neuville who fought courageously against racism and raciology (cf. Bocquet-Appel 1989). This neutral stance was likely the reason that he was the preferred choice to occupy the Chair of Ethnology and Anthropology at the Muséum National d'Histoire Naturelle after Paul Rivet (1876–1958), the director of the Museé de l'Homme, was fired in 1940 by the Vichy government (Bocquet-Appel 1989). Vallois remained, until the 1960s, a supporter of typological classifications of the human races, even though this question was never a major preoccupation. Similarly, although between 1940 and 1960 he developed a line of research on human blood groups, he remained essentially an anatomist and did not really discern the revolutionary impact genetics had in the field of physical anthropology.

Jean-Jacques Hublin

See also Anthony, Raoul; Boule, Marcellin; France; Hrdlička, Aleš; Manouvrier, Léonce-Pierre; Neandertals; Paleoanthropology Theory; Piltdown; Quatrefages, (de Breau), Jean Louis Armand de; Société d'Anthropologie de Paris; Swanscombe; Weidenreich, Franz

Bibliography
SELECTED WORKS

Les transformations de la musculature de l'épisome chez les Vertébrés (Thèse de Doctorat ès Sciences Naturelles, Paris). *Archives de Morphologie Générale et Expérimentale* 14:1–538, 1922; *Arthrologie.* Vol. 2 of: Poirier, Charpy & Nicolas (eds) *Traité d'anatomie humain.* Paris: Masson, 1926; Y a-t-il plusieurs souches humaines? *Revue Générale des Sciences* 37:201–209, 1927; Les preuves anatomiques de l'origine monophyletique de l'Homme. *L'Anthropologie* 39:77–101, 1929; Les maladies de l'homme préhistorique. *Revue Scientifique* 72:666–678, 1934; La durée de la vie chez l'homme fossile. *L'Anthropologie* 47:499–532, 1937; Les Pygmées et l'origine de l'homme. *Revue Scientifique* 76:227–236, 1938.

Les races humaines. Paris: P.U.F., 1944 (2d ed.1948); Nouvelles recherches sur le squelette de Chancelade. *L'Anthropologie* 50:165–202, 1946; Les maladies de nos ancêtres. *La Clinique* 43:7–13, 1948; The Fontéchevade fossil man. *American Journal of Physical Anthropology* n.s. 7:339–362, 1949; Monophyletism and polyphyletism in man. *South African Journal of Science* 48:1–16, 1952; Ordre des Primates. In: P.P. Grasse: *Traité de Zoologie.* Vol. 2. Paris: Masson, 1955, pp. 1854–2206; The pre-Mousterian mandible from Montmaurin. *American Journal of Physical Anthropology* 14:319–323, 1956; La grotte de Fontéchevade. I. Anthropologie. *Archives de l'Institut de Paléontologie Humaine* 29:7–164, 1958; L'homme de Rabat. *Bulletin d'Archéologie Marocaine* 3:87–91, 1960.

Le temporale néandertalien H27 de La Quina: Étude Anthropologique. *L'Anthropologie* 73:524–544, 1969; (with G. Billy) Nouvelles recherches sur les hommes fossile de l'abri de Cro-Magnon. *L'Anthropologie* 69:608–613, 1965; (with G. Billy) La mandibule pré-rissienne de Montmaurin. *L'Anthropologie* 81:273–312, 411–458, 1977; (with M. Boule) *Les hommes fossiles; éléments de paléontologie humaine.* 3d ed. Paris: Masson, 1946 (4th ed.: 1952); (with S. de Félice) Les mésolithiques de France. *Archives de l'Institut de Paléontologie Humaine* 37:1–194, 1977; (with H.L. Movius) *Catalogue des hommes fossiles.* Algeria: Publication of the Nineteenth International Geological Congress, 1953; (with A. Thoma) Les dents de l'homme de Rabat. *Bulletins et Mémoires de la Société d'Anthropologie de Paris* 1:31–58, 1977.

PRIMARY AND SECONDARY SOURCES

J.P. Bocquet-Appel: L'Anthropologie physique en France et ses origines institutionelles. *Gradhiva* 6:23–34, 1989; J.-J. Hublin: Quelques caractères apomorphes du crâne néandertalien et leur interprétation phylogénétique. *Comptes-rendus hebdomadaires des séances de l'Académie des Sciences de Paris* D 287:923–926, 1978; J.-J.Hublin: Les anténéandertaliens: Présapiens ou prénéandertaliens? *Geobios* 6:345–357, 1982; A.P. Santa-Luca: A reexamination of presumed Neandertal-like fossils. *Journal of Human Evolution* 7:619–636, 1978; [Special issue on H.V. Vallois, with papers by P. Huard, M.C. Chamla, A. Delmas, Y. Coppens, J.L. Heim, plus an exhaustive bibliography]. *Bulletins et Mémoires de la Société d'Anthropologie de Paris* 9 (13th ser.) 1982.

Venezuela

Physical anthropology has a relatively recent formal history in Venezuela. The first references to this area of inquiry can be found in the publications of travelers, such as the observations of Venezuelan aborigines made in the eighteenth century by the Spanish cleric Joseph Gumilla (d. 1750) in his book, *El Orinoco ilustrado* (1745), and in the early nineteenth century by the German naturalist Alexander von Humboldt (1769–1859).

Venezuelan anthropology, and more specifically physical anthropology, has been greatly influenced by the development of the discipline in the United States, particularly during the twentieth century. However, prior to this, it appears that the European anthropologists also had a significant influence on the initial development of the field in Venezuela. For example, in 1870, the German naturalist and ethnologist Adolf Ernst (1832–1899) began publishing a series of brief articles in local and foreign journals dealing almost exclusively with descriptions of crania collections housed in the Museum of Natural Sciences, Caracas, of which he was the founder (e.g., Ernst 1870, 1885, 1889). This effort was subsequently reinforced by the work of Gaspar Marcano (1850–1910). Marcano, a physician who had received training in anthropology in Paris, was the first Venezuelan-born investigator to carry out important studies within this discipline, specifically in the fields of craniometry and osteology. Marcano studied the craniometric characteristics of pre-Colombian inhabitants from various regions of Venezuela—though his findings were published mainly in France (Marcano 1889–1891, 1891). This traditional preoccupation with descriptive studies in craniometry and osteometry continued in Venezuela well into the fourth decade of the twentieth century (cf. Barras de Aragón 1932; Jahn 1932).

However, the interest awakened by Marcano's craniometric studies resulted in the establishment of the first Chair of Physical Anthropology in Venezuela in 1896 by the Venezuelan physician Rafael Villa-Vicencio (1832–1920), who was an ardent supporter of Darwinian evolution. This incentive led directly to the appearance of *Antropología General de Venezuela Precolombina* (General Anthropology of Pre-Colombian Venezuela) (1906) written by another Venezuelan doctor, Elia Toro (1871–1918)—the first book of its kind to be published in Venezuela. Toro was also the author of a number of articles in which he defended the evolutionary synthesis, while at the same time dealing with the question of human origins in the Americas (e.g., Toro 1898, 1900). This latter interest was subsequently developed by a number of Venezuelan workers during the first half of the twentieth century (e.g., Díaz Sánchez 1938; Febres Cordero 1946).

Running parallel with these studies, and perhaps influenced by an incipient interest in the racial definition of the Venezuelan population, were several biotypic studies, which among other things were conducted in an effort to establish normal weight and height values for Venezuelan children (e.g., Sánchez Carvajal 1939). Medical practitioners also became involved in the study of the normal population, and some papers were published at that time on serological characteristics (e.g., Lima Gómez & Carbonell 1946). This latter study is of particular interest since it mentioned for the first time in Venezuela the presence of sickle-cell anemia in Negroes. This discovery marked the first step in the research of abnormal hemoglobin, which was later further covered by other authors. During that same year, López Ramírez (1946) published the first bibliographical compilation of physical anthropology in Venezuela.

The Department of Sociology and Anthropology of the Central University of Venezuela, Caracas (Universidad Central de Venezuela), was created in 1953, under the influence of American anthropology. This was an important step in the formal development of anthropology in Venzuela, and the department later became the School of Sociology and Anthropology, the only one in the country where degrees for those disciplines are granted. In the early 1960s, American anthropologists arrived to study Venezuelan Indian communities. Among them was the American geneticist James V. Neel's interdisciplinary group, which did much to change the orientation of physical anthropology in the country away from the traditional craniometric focus to an increasing interest in the study of the biological characteristics of living populations. Leading figures in this emerging intellectual shift were the anthropologist Adelaida Díaz Ungría (1913–), who had received her training in Spain, and two medical practitioners, Miguel Layrisse and Tulio Arends. Díaz Ungría started her research in the 1950s, using anthropometric techniques to sketch the physical type of the Venezuelan Indian (e.g., Díaz Ungría 1953).

Further impetus was given to these developments in 1954 with the discovery of the "Diego" blood factor in a Venezuelan Indian family, which prompted a search for this new blood factor among other Venezuelan Aborigines (e.g., Layrisse et al. 1955). This effort was carried out mainly by Venezuelan investigators associated with the Venezuelan Institute for Scientific Research (IVIC) in Caracas.

The search for the Diego factor also motivated an interest in the genetic characterization of the Venezuelan population. Since the mid-1950s, many studies have been made to determine the frequencies of blood groups and other seroproteins, with work mostly carried out by medical doctors on Indian populations. As this suggests, the orientation of these studies has been more often than not clinical rather than anthropological, though there have been a number of notable exceptions (e.g., Layrisse & Wilbert 1966; Layrisse et al. 1972; Arends et al. 1978).

Parallel to the genetic studies initiated at the IVIC, a group of young Venezuelan physical anthropologists trained by Díaz Ungría and working at the Department of Human Biology of the Institute of Economic and Social Research of the Central University of Venezuela started to study the physical characteristics of Venezuelan Indians based on anthropometric techniques. By the end of the 1960s, this group had published a significant number of genetic and anthropometric papers on Indian groups from various areas of Venezuela: the Guajiros living in the Peninsula of Guajira, which borders with Colombia (e.g., Nuñez Montiel & Nuñez Montiel 1957; Díaz Ungría 1966); the Guarao Indians living in the Orinoco delta (cf. Díaz Ungría 1966); the Yaruro Indians in the southern plains of the Apure State (cf. Díaz Ungría 1966); the Guahibo of the plains (cf. Díaz Ungría 1966); the Kariña Indians living on the left shore of the Orinoco River (e.g., Kohn & Méndez 1972), and the Yanomama Indians in the Amazon (e.g., Brewer Carías et al. 1976).

Apart from anthropometry, other areas of anthropology have also been studied by several researchers, including dental anthropology (e.g., Brewer Carías 1964; Castillo 1973; Méndez de P. 1975), dermatoglyphics (e.g., Laurrauri & Rodríguez 1984; Díaz Ungría & Martín 1985), growth and development (e.g., Farid-Coupal 1981; Arechabaleta 1985), and population genetics (Díaz Ungría & Díaz 1986).

At the beginning of 1970, the Laboratory of Forensic Anthropology of the Technical Body of the Judicial Police Force was created, under the guidance of the Venezuelan physical anthropologist Maritza Garicochea, who has been largely responsible for developing this subdisciplinary interest in Venezuela.

In 1972, Project Venezuela was launched. The primary objective of this project was to establish the normal growth and development patterns for Venezuelans. This interdisciplinary project, although physical anthropologists were not actively engaged in its planning, did provide anthropology students with a source of work in this area, which up to that time had been conducted by the Department of Human Biology of the Central University of Venezuela.

The School of Sociology and Anthropology of the Central University of Venezuela was divided in 1984, thereby creating the country's only School of Anthropology. Although this event greatly improved the professional education of the candidates for a degree in anthropology, this school remains a limited source of practitioners, due in part to its limited faculty and corresponding research potential. However, efforts have been made to improve this situation—as indicated by the work of Betty Méndez de Pérez, who has developed a line of research using anthropometric techniques in the evaluation of the anthropometric profile of the Venezuelan population and the state of nutrition (e.g., Méndez de P. 1986). Indeed, with these efforts, anthropometric techniques have been instituted in the area of public health, together with the already existing ones proposed by A. Rodríguez & S. Arias (1980).

During the mid-1970s, the Laboratory of Human Genetics of the IVIC started serious study of the genetic and matrimonial structure of Venezuelan populations. This line of research was initiated by Juan Pinto Cisternas with his studies of endogamy and consanguinity in the Venezuelan population (e.g., Pinto et al. 1981; Pinto et al. 1985). This initiative was followed by the study of certain anthropometric characteristics of Venezuelan Blacks (e.g., Champin et al. 1982). In 1987, under the guidance of anthropologist Dinorah Castro de Guerra, this work was extended to incorporate the genetic and anthropologic characteristics of the Black Venezuelan population, including such factors as isolation, endogamy, and consanquinity (e.g., Castro de Guerra et al. 1990; Castro de Guerra 1992).

By the mid-1990s, research continued to be limited to three centers: the Department of Physical Anthropology of the School of Anthropology of the Central University of Venezuela; the Department of Human Biology of the Central University of Venezuela; and the Center of Experimental Medicine of the Venezuelan Institute for Scientific Research. As this indicates, the field of physical anthropology in Venezuela continues to be a fertile and relatively underexplored area, particularly in its application and relevance to public health, genetic counseling, and the outlining and classification of diseases.

Dinorah Castro de Guerra

See also Diaz-Ungria, Adelaida

Bibliography
G. Arechabaleta: Talla y peso en una muestra de escolares de Caracas, Venezuela. *IV Congreso Español de Antropología Biológica.* Barcelona, España, 1985; T. Arends et al.: Tapipa: A Negroid Venezuelan isolate. In: *Evolutionary models and studies in human diversity.* The Hague: Mouton, 1978, pp. 201–214; F. Barras de Aragón: Estudio de los cráneos de indios Coajiros, existentes en el Museo de Historia Natural de Caracas, Venezuela. *Sociedad Española de Antropología, Etnología y Prehistoria, Actas y Memorias* 96:69–119, 1932; C.H. Brewer Carías: *Algunos aspectos sobre antropología dental de los Indios Soto y otras experiencias en La Guayana Venezolana.* Caracas: Grafos, 1964; C.H. Brewer Carías et al.: Genetic structure of a tribal population: The Yanomama Indians. XIII. Dental microdifferentiation. *American Journal of Physical Anthropology* 4:5–14,

1976; H. Castillo: *Odontometria y morfología dental de los Goajiros*. Serie de Biología Humana. Caracas: Instituto de Investigaciones Económicas y Sociales, Universidad Central de Venezuela, 1973.

D. Castro de Guerra: *Factores condicionantes de la Estructura genética en dos poblaciones negras venezolanas*. Ph.D. Thesis. Instituto Venezolano de Investigaciones Cientificas, 1992; D. Castro de Guerra et al.: Inbreeding as measured by isonomy in two Venezuelan populations and its relationship to other variables. *Human Biology* 2:269–278, 1990; J. Champin et al.: Some variables of the craniofacial complex in Venezuelan populations of Negroid ancestry. *American Journal of Physical Anthropology* 59:9–19, 1982; R. Díaz Sánchez: *Ambito y acento: Para una teoría de la venezolanidad*. No. 22. Caracas: Cuadernos Literarios de la Asociación de escritores Venezolanos, 1938; A. Díaz Ungría: El tetraedro facial y su aplicación al grupo étnico Motilón. *Memorias de la Sociedad de Ciencias Naturales de la Salle* 13:57–77, 1953.

A. Díaz Ungría: *Estudio comparativo de las características serológicas y morfológicas correspondientes a la poblaciones Guajiro, Guahibo, Guarao y Yaruro*. Colección Esquemas, Ediciones Facultad de Economía. Caracas: Universidad Central de Venezuela, 1966; A. Díaz Ungría & J. Díaz: *Consanguinidad entre los aborígenes Yukpa*. Sociedad Venezolana de Antropología Biológica Publicaciones ocasionales. No. 1. Caracas: Sociedad Venezolana de Antropología Biológica, 1986; A. Díaz Ungría & J. Martín: Quantitative dermatoglyphic traits in Venezuelan Yukpa natives. *Dermatoglyphics, Bulletin of the International Dermatoglyphics Association,* 1–2:21–38, 1985; A. Ernst: Anthropological remarks on the population of Venezuela. *Journal of the Anthropological Society of London* 3:274–287, 1870.

A. Ernst: Heber die reste de Ureinwohner in den Gegirgen von Mérida. *Zeitschrift für Ethnologie* 190–197, 1885; A. Ernst: Un cráneo Motilón. *Revista Científica de la Universidad Central de Venezuela* (Caracas) 1:119–124, 1889; N. Farid-Coupal: The age of menarche in Caracas, Venezuela. *Annals of Human Biology* 3:283–288, 1981; T. Febres Cordero: Algunas teorías sobre procedencia del hombre americano. In: *Panorama histórico de Venezuela*. Maturin, 1946, pp. 20–32; J.

Gumilla: *El Orinoco ilustrado, y defendido, historia natural y civil y geografía de este gran río y de sus caudalosas vertientes, gobiernos, usos y costumbres de los indios*. Madrid: Fernandez, 1745; A. Jahn: Los cráneos deformados de los aborígenes de los Valles de Aragua: Observaciones antropológicas. *Boletín de la Sociedad Venezolana de Ciencias Naturales* 1(8):205–308, 1932.

B.F. de Kohn & P.B. de Méndez: *Antropometría de los Indios Cariña*. Facultad de Ciencias Económicas y Sociales, División de Publicaciones, Caracas: Universidad Central de Venezuela, 1972; S. Laurrauri & A. Rodríguez: Dermatoglifos en una muestra de población Venezolana. *Acta Científica de Venezuela* 35:253–264, 1984; M. Layrisse & J. Wilbert: *Indian societies of Venezuela: Their blood group types*. Publication No. 13. Caracas: Instituto Caribe de Antropología y Sociología, 1966; M. Layrisse et al.: Nuevo grupo sanguíneo encontrado en descendientes de indios. *Acta Medica Venezolana* 33, 1955; M. Layrisse et al.: Study of the HLA system in the Warao population. In: J. Dausset & J. Colombani (eds) *Histocompatibility testing*. Copenhagen: Munksgaard, 1972, pp. 337–385; L. Lima Gomez & L. Carbonell: Drepanocitos en Venezuela. *Memorias de la Sociedad de Ciencias Naturales de la Salle* 15:80–82, 1946.

T. López Ramírez: Materiales para la bibliografía de antropología fisica Venezolana. *Acta Venezolana* 1(4):445–458, 1946; G. Marcano: *Ethnographie precolombienne du Venezuela. Valles d'Aragua et de Caracas*. 3 vols. Vol. 1, *Région des raudas de l'orenoque;* Vol. 2, *Indiens Piaroas, Guahibos, Goajires, Cuicas et Timotes;* Vol. 3, *Vallées d' Aragua et de Caracas*. Paris: Hennuyer, 1889–1891; B. Méndez de P.: *Odontología y morfología dental de los Yukpa*. División de Publicaciones. Caracas: Universidad Central de Venezuela, 1975; J. Nuñez Montiel & A. Nuñez Montiel: El factor Diego y otros sistemas Rh, Hr, ABO, MN en los indios Rionegrinos. *Acta Científica de Venezuela* 8–9: 134–136, 1957.

J. Pinto et al.: La consanguinidad en la parroquia de Los Teques, Venezuela, desde 1790 a 1869. *Acta Científica de Venezuela* 32:262–268, 1981; J. Pinto et al.: Estimation of inbreeding by isonimy in Ibero-american populations: An extension of the method of Crow and Mange. *American Journal of Human Genetics* 37:373–385, 1985; A. Rodríguez & S. Arias: Ecuaciones de regresión para estimar la edad por la longitud de los huesos largos de la mano en la población venezolana en crecimiento. *Acta Científica de Venezuela* 31:468–474, 1980; M. Sánchez Carvajal: El peso y la talla del escolar Venezolano. *Boletín del Ministerio de Sanidad y Asistencia Social* (Caracas) 4(5):1939; E. Toro: Crónica científica: Antiguedad del hombre. Erroneas interpretaciones de los libros santos. *El cojo Ilustrado* 146: 1898; E. Toro: Crónica científica: El Hombre primitivo en América. *El cojo Ilustrado* 195: 1900; E. Toro: *Antropología general de Venezuela Precolombina.* Caracas: Tipografía Herrera Irigoyen, 1906.

Verneau, René (Pierre) (1852–1938)

Born in La Chapelle-sur-Loire (Touraine), France, Verneau received his medical training in Paris, where he took courses from Armand de Quatrefages (1810–1892) and Théodore Hamy (1842–1908). Impressed by Verneau's ability, Quatrefages appointed him as an instructor in his laboratory at the Muséum National d'Histoire Naturelle (MNHN) in 1870, and it was here that Verneau spent the remainder of his career. Following his promotion to the status of assistant in 1892, Verneau subsequently succeeded Hamy to the Chair of Anthropology in 1909 (as well his position as keeper at the Musée d'Ethnographie du Trocadéro)— which he occupied until his retirement in 1927. In addition to Hamy, the paleoanthropologist Marcellin Boule (1861–1942) also had a strong influence on Verneau. From 1894 to 1930, Verneau assisted Boule in his editorial management of *L'Anthropologie.*

Like his primary mentors Hamy and Quatrefages, Verneau had a strong interest in ethnology, and early in his tenure at the MNHN he was attracted to the subject of the Guanches of the Canary Islands, where he led several scientific expeditions in the 1880s (cf. Verneau 1891). This work essentially confirmed the earlier studies of Quatrefages and Gregorio Chil y Naranjo (1831–1901), a former student of Paul Broca (1824–1880), that the aboriginal population of the island appeared to represent a survival of Cro-Magnon man. In 1901, in collaboration with Émile Cartailhac (1845–1921) and Boule, Verneau was responsible for the systematic excavation of the Grotte des Enfants (Grimaldi) site at Ponte San Luigi, Liguria, close to the French border. The skeletal materials recovered during the course of this work were initially attributed by Verneau to the Mousterian,

but later it was shown that they were, in fact, intrusive burials. In the meantime, however, this dating, together with the fact that these skeletons were morphologically modern, served to reinforce Boule's growing conviction that the *sapiens* lineage was an ancient one and that Neandertals had not been a precursor.

The interpretations of the Grimaldi materials were further confounded by Verneau's claim that some of the skeletons displayed Negroid characteristics. This latter view was later shown to be the product of an erroneous reconstruction of the remains.

In addition to his work on the Grimaldi skeletons, Verneau also published works on crania collections drawn from such diverse sources as Patagonia, Pho-Binh-Gia (China), and Beni-Segoual (Algeria), as well as numerous studies dealing with a range of subjects in ethnography and prehistory.

In 1924, he was the recipient of the Huxley Medal of the Royal Anthropological Institute. The subject he chose for his lecture was the controversial issue of the Neandertals and their phylogenetic relationship with modern humans. As this paper (1924b) reveals, Verneau was among the few workers at that time who openly supported the idea of the Neandertals being the antecedants of modern humans. According to Verneau's scheme, the Neandertals were the progenitors of the primitive Negroid Grimaldi race from which the various modern racial types were ultimately derived.

Verneau died in Paris on 7 January 1938.

Frank Spencer

See also Cro-Magnon; Grimaldi; Hamy, Jules Ernest Théodore; Neandertals; Quatrefages, (de Breau), Jean Louis Armand de; Rivet, Paul

Bibliography
SELECTED WORKS
La race de Cro-Magnon. *Revue d'Anthropologie* 1 (3d ser.):10–24, 1886; *Les races humaines.* Paris: Baillière, 1890; *Cinq années de séjour aux îles Canaries.* Paris: Hennuyer, 1891; *Crânes préhistoriques de Patagonie. L'Anthropologie* 5:420–450, 1894; *Les anciens Patagons; contribution à l'étude des races précolumbiennes de l'Amérique du Sud.* Monaco: Imprimerie de Monaco, 1903; *Les Grottes de Grimaldi (Baoussé-Roussé).* Vol. 2, *Anthropologie.* Monaco: Imprimerie de Monaco, 1906; *Crânes d'Indiens de la Colombie: L'élément Papoua en Amérique. L'Anthropologie* 34:353–386, 1924a; Le race de Néanderthal et la race de Grimaldi:

Leurs role dans l'humanité. *Journal of the
Royal Anthropological Institute of Great Britain
and Ireland* 54:211–230, 1924b; *Les origines
de l'humanité.* Paris: Rieder, 1926; (with M.
Boule & H.V. Vallois): *Les grottes
paléolithique des Beni-Segoual* (Algérie). Part
2. Paris: Archives de l'Institut de
Paléontologie humaine, 1934; (with P.
Rivet) *Ethnographie ancienne de l'Equateur.* 2
vols. Paris: Gauthier-Villars, 1912–1922.

Vesalius, Andreas (1514–1564)

Born in Brussels, Belgium, Vesalius completed his primary education at the University of Louvain before going on to study
medicine at the Universities of Paris (1533–
1536) and Padua. On receiving his M.D. degree at Padua in 1537, he was immediately
installed there as professor of surgery and
anatomy, and it was in Padua that he produced
his first anatomical work, *Tabulae anatomicae
sex* (1538). Five years later, he published his
magnum opus, the massive *De humani corporis
fabrica,* plus a student edition called *Epitome.*
The *De fabrica* was dedicated to the Holy
Roman Emperor Charles V, who engaged
Vesalius as his personal physician—a position
he retained from 1543 through 1556. In
1559, he went to Spain, where he had been

appointed physician to the court of Phillip II,
Charles V's son. He remained in Spain until
1563, when he received permission to make
a pilgrimage to the Holy Land. Little is
known of this trip and his motives for undertaking such a journey. It has been suggested
that he was looking for an excuse to extricate
himself from the Spanish court, but, whatever
the reasons, Vesalius died on the return journey from Jerusalem and was buried on the
Greek island of Zakinthos. The date and circumstances of his death are not known.

What makes the *De fabrica* so important
is that both its text and illustrations were
grounded in the empirical method—namely,
the dissection of human cadavers. Prior to
Vesalius' time, human dissection had been
either forbidden or severely restricted, and the
art of anatomical illustration did not exist in
the Vesalian sense. Where Vesalius' illustrations were detailed and naturalistic renditions
of the body's anatomy (see Fig. 1), earlier
anatomical texts were illustrated, if at all, with
crude diagrams (see Fig. 2). Besides revolution-
izing the medical textbook, Vesalius' *De fabrica*
also served to undermine the traditional authority of Galenic anatomy. Not surprising,
there was some initial resistance to the Vesalian
revolution as indicated by the works of Jacques
Dubois (also known as Jacobus Sylvius) (1478–
1555) (1555) and Realdo Colombo (ca. 1516–
ca. 1559) (1559), but it amounted to little
more than a rearguard action.

The *De fabrica* is divided into seven
books (consisting of 663 pages, illustrated
with 203 woodcuts): Book 1, Bones and Cartilage; Book 2, Ligaments and Muscles; Book
3, Blood Vessels; Book 4, Nerves; Book 5,
Abdominal Organs; Book 6, Thoracic Organs;
and Book 7, Brain. The *Epitome,* given its intended audience, is about one-sixth the length
of the parental volume. It consists of six chapters, illustrated with nine full-page woodcuts.
In 1555, Vesalius' publisher, Oporinus of
Basel, published a more sumptuous second
edition of the *De fabrica,* which was followed
by a number of pirated (though much abbreviated) editions such as Thomas Geminus'
(ca. 1510–1562) *Compendiosa totius anatomie
delineatio* published in London in 1545. Similarly, the *Epitome* went through a number of
editions and was translated into German in
1543 and Dutch in 1569. From all indications,
the *De fabrica* has never been translated in its
entirety into English.

Frank Spencer

See also Belgium; Galen

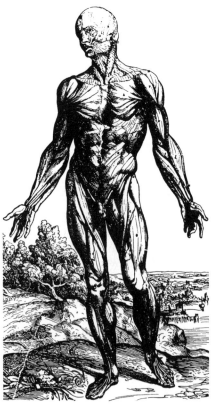

*Fig. 1. A woodcut illustrating
human muscles from Andreas
Vesalius'* De humani
corporis fabrica *(1543).*

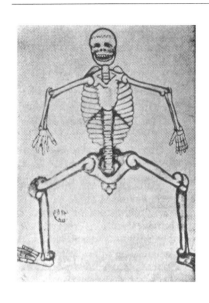

a

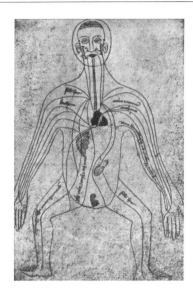

b

Fig. 2. Early anatomic illustrations. A: Human skeleton from 14th-century German manuscript; B: Arterial system, from 14th-century manuscript; C: Nervous system, from 14th-century manuscript; D: Gravida, from 15th-century German manuscript.

c

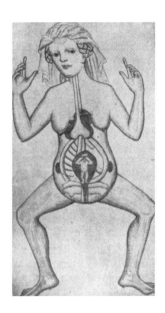

d

Bibliography

SELECTED WORKS

Tabulae anatomicae sex. Venetiis, 1538; *De humani corporis fabrica libri septem.* Basel: Oporinus, 1543a (2d ed.: 1555); *Epitome.* Basel: Oporinus, 1543b; *Epitome anatomica.* Basel: Oporinus, 1543c. See: *The Epitome of Andreas Vesalius.* Translated from the Latin, with a preface and introduction by L.R. Lind. With anatomical notes by C.W. Asling. New York: Macmillan, 1949; *Epistola, rationem modumque propinandi radicis Chynae decocti . . . pertractans.* Basel: Oporinus, 1546.

PRIMARY SOURCES

R. Colombo: *De re anatomica.* Libri XV. Venetiis: Bevilacquae, 1559; J. Dubois (Sylvius): *In Hippocratis et Galeni physiologiae partem anatomicam isagoge.* Parisiis: Hulpeau, 1555.

SECONDARY SOURCES

C.D. O'Malley: *Andreas Vesalius of Brussels.* Berkeley, University of California Press, 1964; C.D. O'Malley & J.B. de C.M. Saunders: *The illustrations of the works of Andreas Vesalius of Brussels.* Cleveland: World Publishing, 1950.

Viking Fund Medal

The Viking Fund Medal was established in 1946 by the Wenner-Gren Foundation for Anthropological Research to honor distinguished contributions to physical anthropology. The medal was given annually until 1960. The first recipient was Franz Weidenreich (1873–1948) in 1946, followed by Earnest A. Hooton (1887–1954) in 1947; Adolph Hans Schultz (1891–1976) in 1948; William King Gregory (1876–1970) in 1949; Wilton Marion Krogman (1903–1987) in 1950; Carleton S. Coon (1904–1981) in 1951; William L. Straus (1900–1981) in 1952; T. Dale Stewart (1901–) in 1953; William White Howells (1908–) in 1954; Wilfrid Edward Le Gros Clark (1895–1971) in 1955; Mildred Trotter (1899–1991) in 1956; Raymond A. Dart (1893–1988) in 1957; Henri Victor Vallois (1889–1981) in 1958; William W. Greulich (1899–1986) in 1959; and Sherwood L. Washburn (1911–) in 1960.

Frank Spencer

See also Wenner-Gren Foundation for Anthropological Research

Bibliography
J. Comas: *Historia sumaria de la Asociación Americana de Antropólogos Físicos, 1928–1968.* Mexico: Instituto Nacional de Antropologia e Historia, 1969, pp. 61–62.

Virchow, Rudolf (1821–1902)

Born in Schivelbein, Germany, Virchow entered the Friedrich-Wilhelms Institut at the University of Berlin in 1839 and there came under the influence of the experimental physiologist-anatomist Johannes Müller (1801–1858). Virchow completed his medical studies in 1843 with a doctoral dissertation on the corneal manifestations of rheumatic disease. Three years later, he received an appointment as privatdocent, under Müller, at the University of Berlin. That same year, assisted by a colleague, Benno Reinhardt, he founded the *Archiv für pathologische Anatomie und Physiologie, und für die klinische Medizin* (often referred to as "Virchow's Archiv"), which became an influential journal during the second half of the nineteenth century.

During the upheavals of the 1848 revolution, Virchow's social consciousness was raised by a visit to Upper Silesia. He had originally gone there to report on a typhus epidemic, but the poverty and misery he saw so distressed him that he was led on his return to Berlin to recommend sweeping social and economic reforms for the region. As this indicates, Virchow was not only an energetic scientist but also a medical activist who throughout his career campaigned for medical and social reforms (cf. Virchow 1879).

In 1849, he accepted the newly created Chair of Pathological Anatomy at the University of Würzburg, where he remained until 1856. During this period, he taught a number of notable students, such as Ernst Haeckel (1834–1919), and in 1854 initiated under his editorship the publication of the six-volume *Handbuch der speziellen Pathologie und Therapie.* After only seven years at Würzburg, however, he returned to Berlin as professor of pathological anatomy and director of the newly created Pathological Institute—positions he retained until his retirement. Under his direction, this institute became an important training center for German and foreign pathologists. Although Virchow is best remembered in medical circles for such works as his *Die Cellularpathologie* (1858) and his three-volume *Die krankhaften Geschwülste* (1863–1867), his name is also closely associated with German anthropology: He did much to promote the discipline during the last quarter of the nineteenth century. In particular, he took a leading role in the creation of Berliner Gesellschaft für Anthropologie (BGA) in 1869 and of the Deutsche Anthropologische Gesellschaft the following year. The BGA, over which Virchow presided until his death, also provided invaluable assistance in developing the collections of the Berlin Museum für Volkerkunde. Besides conducting his own excavations in Pomerania, he also took an interest in the archeological work of Heinrich Schliemann (1822–1890), and in 1879 he traveled with him to Hisarlik, Turkey, which Schliemann had identified as the Homeric city of Troy. Virchow was also instrumental in the founding of the Berlin Museum für Volkstrachten in 1888. Throughout his presidency of the BGA, Virchow also served as the editor of its journal, *Zeitschrift für Ethnologie.*

Unlike his former student Haeckel, who became an ardent convert to Darwinism (via the work of the British biologist Thomas Henry Huxley), Virchow remained resistant to this thesis. His position is clearly revealed in his efforts to derail the case for the evolutionary significance of the Feldhofer skeleton, found in the Neander Valley near Düsseldorf in 1856, by claiming that its morphology could be accounted for as a pathology (cf. Virchow 1872). Later (1874), he documented a number of extraordinarily low "chamaecephalous" skulls from northwestern Germany, which he used to reinforce his case. He used a similar argument in the early 1880s to counter a movement supporting the antiquity of the Šipka mandible. Virchow also argued that the Feldhofer cranium's degree of suture closure indicated that it had reached too advanced an age to have lived in a "primitive" society. Not unexpectedly, he also refused to accept Eugène Dubois' (1858–1940) finds from Trinil, Java, in the early 1890s, as evidence for human evolution. In addition to arguing for the disassociation of the Javan femur from the calotte, Virchow claimed that the latter was not human but rather from an extinct giant gibbon (Virchow 1895b) and that the femur, which manifested a pathology (a myostitis ossificans on the medial aspect of the proximal half of the femoral shaft), belonged to a human and not an ape (1895a). In addition to these excursions into human paleontology, he also published numerous studies of European crania (e.g., Virchow 1876). Also worthy of mention are his *Menschen und Affenschädel* (1870) and *Crania Ethnica Americana* (1892).

Virchow died in Berlin on 5 September 1902.

Fred H. Smith

See also Deutsche Anthropologische Gesellschaft; Dubois, (Marie) Eugène (François Thomas); Haeckel, Ernst Heinrich Phillip August; Jones, Joseph; Neandertal (Feldhofer Grotte); Neandertals; Paleopathology

Bibliography
SELECTED WORKS
(ed. and contrib.) *Handbuch der speziellen Pathologie und Therapie*. Erlangen: Enke, 1854–1865; *Die Cellularpathologie in ihrer Begründung auf physiologische und pathologische Gewebelehre*. Berlin: Hirschwald, 1858; *Die krankhaften Geschwülste*. 3 vols. Berlin: Hirschwald, 1863–1867; *Menschen und Affenschädel*. Berlin: Hirschwald, 1870; Untersuchung des Neanderthal-schädels. *Zeitschrift für Ethnologie* 4:157–165, 1872; Über eine niedrige Schädelform in Norddeutschland. *Zeitschrift für Ethnologie* 6:239–251, 1874; *Beiträg zur physische Anthropologie der Deutschen mit besonderer Berücksichtigung der Friesen*. Berlin: Akademie der Wissenschaften, 1876. *Gesemmelte Abhandlungen aus dem Gebiete offentlichen Medizin und der Seuchenlehre*. 2 vols. Berlin: Hirschwald, 1879; Der Kiefer aus der Schipka-Höhle und der Kiefer von la Naulette. *Zeitschrift für Ethnologie* 14:277–310, 1882; *Crania ethnica americana, Sammlung auserlesener amerikanischer Schädeltypen*. Berlin: Asher, 1892; The place of pathology among the biological sciences. (Croonian Lecture). *Proceedings of the Royal Society of London* 53:114–129, 1893; Exostosen und Hyperstosen von Extremitätenknochen des Menschen, in Hinblick auf den den *Pithecanthropus*. *Zeitschrift für Ethnologie* 27:787–793, 1895a; Weitere Mittheilungen über den *Pithecanthropus erectus* Dubois. *Zeitschrift für Ethnologie* 27:648–656, 744–747, 1895b.

SECONDARY SOURCES
E.H. Ackerknecht: *Rudolf Virchow: Doctor, statesman, anthropologist*. Madison: University of Wisconsin Press, 1953; F. Boas: Rudolf Virchow's anthropological work. *Science* 16:441–445, 1902; F. Boenheim: *Virchow, Werk und Wirking*. Berlin: Rütten & Loening, 1957; H.M. Koelbing: Rudolf Virchow und die moderne Pathologie. *Münchener medizinische Wochenschrift* 110:349–354, 1968; L.J. Rather: Rudolf Virchow's views on pathology, pathological anatomy, and cellular pathology. *Archives of Pathology* 82:197–204, 1966; J. Schwalbe: *Virchow Bibliographie, 1843–1901*. Berlin: Reimer, 1901; F. Semon: Rudolf Virchow. *British Medical Journal* 2:795–802, 1902.

Vrolik, Gerardus (1775–1859)

Born in Leiden, Vrolik studied medicine at the University of Leiden. In February 1795, just before his twentieth birthday, he defended his academic paper, *De Homini ad Statum Gressumque Erectum per Corporis Fabricam Disposito* (On the Predetermined Construction of the Body of Man to Have an Erected Gait). The subject of the thesis was at that time a controversial one, particularly because Vrolik pointed out, contrary to other investigators, that the erect posture of human beings is predetermined by their morphology. In 1796, he was appointed professor of botanics at the Athenaeum Illustre (AI) of Amsterdam even before he defended his M.D. thesis, *Observationes de Defoliatione Vegetabilium et de Viribus Plantarum* (Observations on the Falling of Leaves and on Green Plants), which he did on 10 December 1796. He presented his inaugural address, *De Eo, quod Amstelaedamensis ad Rem Botanicum Exornandam Contulerunt* (On the Contribution of the People of Amsterdam to the Expansion of Botanics), 3 April 1797. On 5 November 1798, he received an additional appointment to the Chair of Anatomy and Physiology, while later that year he also was named to the Chair of Theoretical and Clinical Obstetrics. For that occasion, the title of his inaugural address was *De Viribus Vitalibus in Omni Corpore Organico Observandis, Iisque Constantibus* (On the Observation that the Whole Organic Body in Living Man Is Unchangeable). For his obstetrical tasks, Vrolik was given a special ward in the St. Pietersgasthuis (City Hospital). In 1819, as a member of the Board charged with the supervision of medical care in Holland, he published the standing orders *(Reglement van Orde voor de Provinciale Commissie van Geneeskundig Onderzoek en Toezicht in Holland)*. He continued to teach botanics, anatomy, physiology, and obstetrics until 1820. In that year, he quit teaching anatomy and physiology, followed by obstetrics in 1828, and botanics in 1842. From that time onward, he taught only theoretical obstetrics. He died on 10 November 1859.

Vrolik was an active member of many scientific societies in The Netherlands. In particular, as secretary of the first section of the Koninklijke Nederlandsche Akademie van Wetenschappen (Royal Netherlands Academy of Arts and Sciences), a position to which he was appointed when the Academy was founded in 1808, he was familiar with many scientific subjects. He published numerous scientific articles in the fields of botany, comparative anatomy, human pathology, and patho-physiology, as well as physical anthropology. Many of his publications were on botanical topics. In 1804, he published a list of the medicinal plants in the Hortus Botanicus of Amsterdam (*Naamlijst der Geneesrijke Plantgewassen in den Amsterdamschen Kruidtuin*). In 1805, he coauthored with S.J. Brugmans, P. Driessen, and J.R. Deiman the *Pharmacopoea Batave,* while that same year his *Catalogus Plantarum Medicinalium in Pharmacopoea Batava Memoratarum* was published. This was followed in 1825 by the *Catalogus Plantarum Medicinalium in Pharmacopoea Belgica Enumeratorum.* Among his comparative anatomical studies were an examination of a shark in 1826 and of a mole cricket in 1857. Many of Vrolik's publications focused on pathology and congenital malformations, and case studies of his medical practice. He also gave lectures on a wide range of topics in medicine. For example, in 1806 he lectured on inocula-

tion with smallpox according to the findings of the English physician Edward Jenner (1749–1823); in 1827 he published a paper dealing with the impression of the rope in the neck of a hanged person being an uncertain sign of the cause of death; and in 1831 he introduced the therapeutic utility of ammonia in cholera cases.

Vrolik's work in physical anthropology was mainly based on topics related to obstetrics and topics he came across as secretary of the Academy of Sciences. In 1804, he introduced to The Netherlands the doctrine of the German physician Franz Joseph Gall (1758–1828) concerning the shape of the brain and skull (i.e., phrenology) by giving a lecture to the Society Felix Meritis titled "The System of Franz Joseph Gall Outlined and Interpreted," which was published later in that year (cf. Vrolik 1804a). In 1826, he published a paper dealing with the differences in the pelvises of several ethnographic groups. For this particular study, Vrolik used pelvic specimens from his collections, which were well known as the Museum Vrolikianum. In contrast to the extreme opinion of one of his predecessors at the AI, Petrus Camper (1722–1789), who had dissected the body of a Black Angolese boy before his students in order to refute notions about the inferiority of the Negro, Vrolik's study was more objective and concerned the morphology and measurements of the pelvic specimens he studied. In 1830, he wrote a letter to Moritz Weber (1795–1875) criticizing his book on the variability of skulls and pelvises of man all over the world (*Ur- und Raschenformen der Schaedel und Becken des Menschen*); in 1851, he published a paper about how to take measurements of the human female pelvis, still demonstrating his interest in this subject. However, because he published no monographs or handbooks in the field of physical anthropology, his impact on the field was largely indirect.

Bob Baljet
Trinette S. Constandse-Westermann

See also Camper, Petrus; Phrenology

Bibliography
SELECTED WORKS
     Dissertatio academica de homine ad statum gressumque erectum per corporis fabricam disposito. Lugdunum Batavorum, 1795; *Dissertatio medico-botanica sistens observationes de defoliatione vegetabilium, nec non de viribus plantarum ex principiis botanicis dijudicandis.* Lugdunum Batavorum, 1796; *Oratio de eo*

quod Amstelaedamensis ad rem botanicam exornandam contulerunt. Amsterdam, 1797; *Oratio de viribus vitalibus in omni corpore organico observandis, iisque constantibus.* Amstelaedami, 1799; *Het leerstelsel van Franz Joseph Gall Geschetst en Opgehelderd.* Amsterdam, 1804a; *Naamlijst der geneesrijke plantgewassen in den Amsterdamschen kruidtuin.* Amsterdam, 1804b.

Catalogus plantarum medicinalium in pharmacopoea batave memoratarum: accedit de studio botanico recte instituendo. Amsterdam, 1805; *Reglement van orde voor de provinciale commissie van geneeskundig onderzoek en toezicht in Holland, zitting houdende te Amsterdam.* Amsterdam, 1819; *Pharmacopoea Belgica.* The Hague, 1823; *Catalogus plantarum medicinalium in pharmacopoea Belgica enumeratorum; accedit introductio ad studium botanicum.* Amsterdam, 1825; Ontleed- en natuurkundige aantekeningen over den Haai. *Bijdragen tot de Natuurkundige Wetenschappen* 1:304–315, 1826.

Beschouwing over het Verschil der Bekkens in Onderscheidene Volksstammen. Amsterdam, 1826; Het indruksel, dat door het koord bij gehangenen verwekt wordt, als onzeker kenteeken van den aangebragten dood beschouwd. Bijdragen tot de Regtsgeleerdheid, van den Tex en van Hall, 1827; *Schreiben an Dr. M.J. Weber über dessen Lehre von den Ur- und Raschenformen der Schaedel und Becken des Menschen.* Amsterdam, 1830; *Brief aan Bernard over de Ammonia als geneesmiddel tegen de cholera.* Amsterdam, 1831; *Hoe Men Zich de Doormetingen aan het Vrouwelijk Bekken bij de Mensch Behoort Voor te Stellen.* Amsterdam, 1851; (with S.J. Brugmans, P. Driessen, & J.R. Deiman) *Pharmacopoea Batave.* Amsterdam, 1805; (with S.J. Brugmans, P. Driessen, & J.R. Deiman) *Bataafsche Apotheek.* Amsterdam, 1807.

ARCHIVAL SOURCES
1. Gerardus Vrolik Correspondence: Municipal Archives Amsterdam (Archief College van Curatoren van het Athenaeum Illustre, Archief van het College van Rector en Assessoren van het Athenaeum Illustre Archief Openbare Werken) Gemeentelijke Archiefdienst, Amstelkade 67, 1078 AK Amsterdam, The Netherlands; 2. Gerardus Vrolik Correspondence: University of Amsterdam, Universiteitsmuseum "De Agnietenkapel," Oudezijds Voorburgwal 231, 1012 EZ Amsterdam, The Netherlands; 3. Gerardus Vrolik Correspondence:

University of Amsterdam, Department of Anatomy and Embryology and Museum Vrolik, Meibergdreef 15, 1105 AZ Amsterdam, The Netherlands.

SECONDARY SOURCES
B. Baljet: The Vrolik Collection. In: P. Blom & T. van den Berg (eds) *Out and about in Amsterdam.* Amsterdam: Nederlands Theater Instituut, 1985, pp. 40–47; B. Baljet: Museum Vrolik. In: C. Habrich & J.C. Wilmanns (eds) *Actes du 3ième Colloque des Conservateurs des Musées d'Histoire des Sciences médicales.* Lyon: Fondation Marcel Mérieux, 1988, pp. 241–253; B. Baljet: Uit de geschiedenis van het Museum Vrolik, de Snijkamer en het Theatrum Anatomicum te Amsterdam. In: B. Baljet (ed) *Gids voor het Museum Vrolik.* Amsterdam: Universiteit van Amsterdam, 1990, pp. 7–24; B. Baljet: Veterinary specimens of congenital malformations of the Vrolik Collection. *Historia Medicinae Veterinariae* 8:1–21, 1993; J. van der Hoeven: Levensberigt van Gerardus Vrolik. *Jaarboek der Koninklijke Akademie van Wetenschappen* 116–134, 1859.

Vrolik, Willem (1801–1863)

Vrolik was born in Amsterdam, the son of Gerardus Vrolik (1775–1859), who was professor of anatomy and physiology at the Athenaeum Illustre (AI), the predecessor of the University of Amsterdam. Young Vrolik entered this institution as a student in 1817. After two years, he continued his studies at the Utrecht Hoogeschool. Toward the end of his years at Utrecht (1822–1823), he spent six months in Paris, where he visited several well-known hospitals and naturalists. Two months after his return from Paris, he defended his Ph.D. thesis in Utrecht on 10 June 1823.

After six years as a general practitioner in Amsterdam, in 1829 he was appointed professor of anatomy and physiology at the Groningen Hoogeschool. After an interval of about one-and-a-half years, he was appointed professor of anatomy, physiology, natural history, and theoretical surgery at the AI in Amsterdam. At that time, his father, Gerardus, still held the position of professor in botany and obstetrics at the AI. During his years in Amsterdam, Willem Vrolik was an active member of several Dutch and foreign scientific societies. From 1851 until his death on 20 December 1863, he was general secretary of the Koninklijke Nederlandsche Akademie van Wetenschappen (Royal Netherlands Academy of Arts and Sciences).

Two main lines of research can be observed in Vrolik's work. First was his never-fading interest in (comparative) zoology. As a student, in 1821 he already had published a prize-winning study on the auditory organ in humans and animals, followed a year later by a publication, illustrated with drawings from his hand, concerning two seals (*Phoca vitulina*) sent to him from the Dutch province of Zeeland, which he studied alive for several months. During the more than thirty years of his Amsterdam professorship, Vrolik remained active in this field. This was made possible by the connections he and his father maintained with the overseas areas then owned by The Netherlands on the one hand, and by his relations with the learned society Natura Artis Magistra on the other. Indicative of this continuing interest is his fascinating account (1837–1838) of the dissection of a Nordic whale (*Balaenoptera rostrata*) in 1835 on the beach of a small Dutch coastal village, Wijk aan Zee. Still later (1841), he published a monograph on chimpanzees, and in 1844 he became involved in a scientific discussion with J.L.C. Schroeder van der Kolk (1797–1862) on certain anatomical characteristics of *Stenops d'Illiger* (cf. Vrolik 1844). In the last decade of his life, he worked on a study in three parts, in which he gave an account of the current state of affairs in the zoology of the vertebrates.

Vrolik's other field of interest was human pathology. The first work in which he showed this interest was his 1823 Ph.D. thesis, *De Mutatio Vasorum Sanguiferorum Decursu in Scoliosi et Cyphosi*, in which he discussed the change in the course of the blood vessels in patients with scoliosis and kyphosis. During the year and a half of his professorship in Groningen, he studied the collection of the Groningen Hoogeschool, to which the contents of the Kabinet (cabinet) of the Dutch anatomist Petrus Camper (1722–1789) had recently been added. The latter collection contained specimens of a large number of congenital malformations. In later years, he also published on cyclopia (1834), based on Camper's specimens, those in the collection of his father (*vide infra*), and those published in the literature. His work resulted in a definition of cyclopia and a subdivision of this malformation, still useful to date.

Also in other respects Vrolik was preoccupied with classification and the assessment of regularities. In 1840, he published a classification of Siamese twins, based on the literature and his own research (Vrolik 1840a).

In that same year, he published the first part of his handbook on pathological anatomy, in which he makes a clear distinction between the regular and the irregular development of the human embryo/fetus (Vrolik 1840b). In 1842, a second part followed. However, he did not achieve his goal of completing this work with several other parts—primarily because he had other ambitions, one of which was the composition of an illustrative companion to his handbook. This work, which appeared in several installments (Vrolik 1844–1849), brought him international fame and, in 1850, an award from the Académie des Sciences in Paris. In the later years of his life, Vrolik continued to publish on pathology and teratology.

A last aspect of Vrolik's work is the private collection of the osteological specimens, dried and alcoholic preparations, plaster masks, and the like that was brought together by him and his father, Gerardus. It covers many aspects of human and animal anatomy, including osteological differences between individuals of various ethnic origins, ontogenetic development, pathology, and teratology. Toward the end of his life, Vrolik started cataloguing the collection. After he died, this work was completed by J.L. Dusseau (1864).

During his life, Willem Vrolik displayed an encyclopedic knowledge, which was supported by a huge and valuable library. Most of his publications go beyond description and pertain to the classification of the described phenomena and their etiology. His many studies of teratology and zoology led him to the insight that many congenital malformations represent earlier developmental stages, which are also to be found in the animal world. He also noticed that usually restrained development is not the only cause of birth defects, but that the embryo/fetus shows a further development in a deviant direction which ultimately leads to the birth of the injured individual. Many of his insights remain valid.

Bob Baljet
Trinette S.Constandse-Westermann

See also Camper, Petrus

Bibliography
SELECTED WORKS
    Specimen anatomico-zoölogicum de Phocis, Speciatim de Phoca vitulina. Utrecht van Paddenburg, 1822; *De Mutatio vasorum Sanguiferorum Decursu in Scoliosi et Cyphosi*. Utrecht: 1823; Over den aard en oorsprong der cyclopie. *Nieuwe Verhandelingen der Eerste Klasse van het Koninklijk Nederlandsch*

Instituut 5:25–112, 1834; Ontleedkundige aanmerkingen over den Noordschen Vinvis (*Balaenoptera rostrata*) in de maand September des jaars 1835 te Wijk aan Zee gestrand. *Tijdschrift voor Natuurlijke Geschiedenis en Physiologie* 4:1–24, 1837–1838; Over dubbele misgeboorten. *Nieuwe Verhandelingen der Eerste Klasse van het Koninklijk Nederlandsch Instituut* 9:1–232, 1840a.

Handboek der Ziektekundige Ontleedkunde. Vol. 1. Amsterdam: Sulpke, 1840b; *Recherches d'Anatomie comparée sur le Chimpansé*. Amsterdam: Muller, 1841; *Handboek der Ziektekundige Ontleedkunde.* Vol. 2. Amsterdam: Sulpke, 1842; Brief van W. Vrolik aan den Hoogleraar Schroeder van der Kolk, over het vermeend verschil in inwendig maaksel tussen den *Stenops javanicus* en den *Stenops tardigradus*. Het Instituut: 147–250, 1844; *Tabulae ad Illustrandam Embryogenesis Hominis et Mammalium tam Naturalem quam Abnormen.* Amsterdam: Londonck, 1844–1849; *Het Leven en Maaksel der Dieren*. Amsterdam, 1853–1860; *Musée Vrolik: Catalogue de la Collection d'Anatomie humaine, comparée et pathologique de M.M. Ger. et W. Vrolik*. Vol. A, *Partie ethnographique*. Amsterdam: Roever Kröber, 1864.

ARCHIVAL SOURCES

1. Willem Vrolik Correspondence: Municipal Archives Amsterdam (Archief College van Curatoren van het Athenaeum Illustre, Archief van het College van Rector en Assessoren van het Athenaeum Illustre, Archief Openbare Werken), Gemeentelijke Archiefdienst, Amstelkade 67, 1078 AK Amsterdam, The Netherlands; 2. Willem Vrolik Correspondence: University of Amsterdam, Universiteitsmuseum "De Agnietenkapel," Oudezijds Voorburgwal 231, 1012 EZ Amsterdam, The Netherlands; 3. Willem Vrolik Correspondence: University of Amsterdam, Department of Anatomy and Embryology and Museum Vrolik, Meibergdreef 15, 1105 AZ Amsterdam, The Netherlands.

SECONDARY SOURCES

B. Baljet: Willem Vrolik als zoöloog. *Vakblad voor Biologen* 63:214–217, 1983; B. Baljet: Willem Vrolik als teratoloog. *Nederlands Tijdschrift voor Geneeskunde* 128:1530–1534, 1984; B. Baljet: Uit de geschiedenis van het Museum Vrolik, de Snijkamer en het Theatrum Anatomicum te Amsterdam. In: B. Baljet (ed) *Gids voor het Museum Vrolik*. Amsterdam: Universiteit van Amsterdam, 1990, pp. 7–24; B. Baljet, F. van der Werf & A.J. Otto: Willem Vrolik on cyclopia. *Documenta Ophtalmologica* 77:355–368, 1991; J.L. Dusseau: *Musée Vrolik: Catalogue de la Collection d'Anatomie humaine, comparée et pathologique de M.M. Ger. et W. Vrolik*. Vol. B, *Partie ostéologique;* Vol. C, *Partie splanchnologique;* Vol. D, *Partie pathologique;* Vol. E, *Partie tératologique*. Amsterdam: Roever Kröber, 1864.

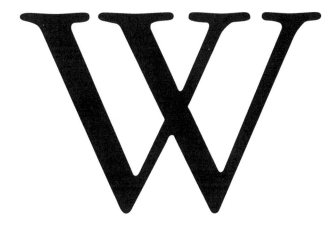

Wallace, Alfred Russel (1823–1913)

Born in Usk, Monmouthshire, Wales, Wallace had no formal scientific education. His interest in natural history was evidently awakened in the late 1830s while he was working for his brother, who was a surveyor. In 1844, due to a decline in his brother's business, Wallace moved to Leicester (England) to become a schoolteacher, and it was there that he met Henry Walter Bates (1825–1892), another amateur naturalist. Evolving out of his friendship with Bates was an ambitious plan to mount an expedition to the Amazon Basin, where they proposed to support their explorations through the sale of natural history specimens and, at the same time, establish their scientific reputations. The four years Wallace spent exploring and collecting in South America (1848–1853) served as his scientific apprenticeship, and an account of his adventures there can be found in his *A Narrative of Travels on the Amazon and Rio Negro* (1853a), published soon after his return to London. Although this book was far from the commercial success he had hoped for, it did (along with a small book on *Palm Trees of the Amazon* published the same year) bring him to the attention of the London scientific establishment—in particular, the Royal Geographical Society. On hearing of his ambition to explore the islands of the Malay Archipelago, the society agreed to fund him.

Among the many interesting discoveries he made while on this protracted expedition (1854–1862) was that the region could be divided zoologically into two quite distinct regions, marked by a line (subsequently known as the "Wallace Line") extending from the Indian Ocean through Selat Lombok (between the islands of Bali and Lombok) northward through the Makassar Strait (between Borneo and the Celebes) and then eastward into the Philippine Sea. To the west of this line, fauna appeared to be characteristically "Oriental," whereas east of the line it was essentially Australasian. Emerging from this and related observations was a two-volume work, entitled *The Geographical Distribution of Animals* (1876), which became a cornerstone of modern biogeography.

It was also during the course of this work that Wallace became one of the cofounders of modern evolutionary biology. Since 1845, when he first read *Vestiges of the Natural History of Creation* (1844) by the Scottish publisher and author Robert Chambers (1802–1871), he had been ruminating on the question of how new species are formed, but it was not until after his arrival in the Far East that he began speculating publicly on the subject. Although still at a loss to explain the divergence mechanism, it was abundantly clear from his paper "On the Law Which Has Regulated the Introduction of New Species" (1855), published by the Linnean Society, that he was on the right track. Indeed, the appearance of this paper so impressed the geologist Charles Lyell (1797–1875) that he brought it to the immediate attention of Charles Darwin (1809–1882), who since the mid-1840s had been working intermittently on his masterwork, eventually published as *On the Origin of Species* (1859). Fearing that Darwin might be pipped at the post, Lyell urged the reticent Darwin to publish his solution to the species problem as soon as possible. In the meantime, while Darwin was contemplating a course of action, Wallace was on his way to Ternate in the Moloccas, the Spice Islands, between New Guinea and Borneo. No sooner had he arrived (early in January 1858) than he began suffering from an intermittent fever, probably malaria. It was during one of these attacks, Wallace later recalled, that the idea of natural selection as the solution to the species puzzle came to him in a serendipitous flash. Sometime during the next month (February), Wallace committed his theory to paper, a copy of which he sent to Darwin for comment. Darwin was stunned by Wallace's communication. "I never saw a more striking coincidence," he later confessed to Lyell. In fact, he went on: "If Wallace had my manuscript sketch written out in 1844, he could not have made a better short abstract!" (Darwin to Lyell, 18 June 1858, in F. Darwin, Vol. 1, 1887:473). As Darwin's correspondence reveals, he was clearly undecided what he should do. In due course, however, Darwin was rescued from his dilemma by his two closest confidants, Lyell and Joseph Hooker (1817–1911). Through them, it was arranged that Wallace's paper, along with an extract from Darwin's manuscript and a copy of a letter from Darwin to the Harvard botanist Asa Gray (1810–1888), confirming his earlier recognition of the principle of divergence, were all read before the Linnean Society of London on 1 July 1858 and published the following month. During the next year, Darwin completed his long awaited *Origin*, which was published in November 1859. Although Wallace was not consulted on the Lyell-Hooker arrangement, there is not the slightest hint in his correspondence of either resentment or disagreement with it. Indeed, when Darwin's *Origin* appeared, Wallace wrote Bates that he was relieved that Darwin, and not he, had been called upon to set forth the theory in detail.

On returning to England in 1862, Wallace devoted the next decade primarily to writing. Most notable among the books he produced during this time were *Contributions to the Theory of Natural Selection* (1870), a collection of evolutionary essays, and his monumental *The Geographical Distribution of Animals* (1876). These were followed by *Island Life* (1880), in which he applied evolutionary concepts to insular flora and fauna. Although, as these publications reveal, Wallace became a forceful and effective promoter of the evolutionary thesis, this conviction did not carry over into his anthropology. Indeed, beginning

in the early 1860s, Wallace (1864, 1870) registered increasing doubts about the role of natural selection in human evolution. He became convinced that once they had differentiated from their apish kin, human beings had been progressively partitioned from the whims of natural selection. The subsequent development of the human intellect and moral nature was guided, so he believed, by a higher supernatural force. Precisely what had led Wallace to this surprising conclusion is not clear, but it is significant that this modification in his evolutionary views coincided with a developing and sustained interest in spiritualism (cf. Wallace 1874; Kottler 1974).

In 1886, he spent a year lecturing in the United States on evolutionary theory, an experience that led to his reflective volume *Darwinism* (1889). During the 1890s and early 1900s, he devoted himself largely to writing articles on a variety of social and scientific subjects, a summation of the scientific progress in the nineteenth century titled *The Wonderful Century* (1898), and his autobiography, *My Life* (1905).

Among the many awards and honors Wallace received during his lifetime were the Royal Medal of the Royal Society in 1868, the Darwin Medal of the Royal Society in 1890, and the Gold Medal of the Linnean Society in 1892. He was made a Fellow of the Royal Society in 1893.

Wallace died at his home in Broadstone, Dorset, England, on 7 November 1913.

Frank Spencer

See also Biogeography; Chambers, Robert; Darwin, Charles Robert; Evolutionary Theory; Lyell, (Sir) Charles; Paleoanthropology Theory

Bibliography
SELECTED WORKS

A narrative of travels on the Amazon and Rio Negro. London: Reeve, 1853a; *Palm trees of the Amazon and their use*. London: Van Voorst, 1853b; On the law which has regulated the introduction of new species. *Annals and Magazine of Natural History* 16:184–196, 1855; Note on the theory of permanent and geographical varieties. *Zoologist* 16:5887–5888, 1858; The origin of human races and the antiquity of man deduced from the "theory of natural selection." *Journal of the Anthropological Society of London* 2:clvii–clxxxvii, 1864; *The Malay Archipelago: the land of the Orang-Utan and the bird of paradise: A narrative of travel with studies of man and nature*.

London: Macmillan, 1869; *Contributions to the theory of natural selection*. London: Macmillan, 1870 (2d ed.: 1871); *A defence of modern spiritualism*. Boston: Colby & Rich, 1874.

The geographical distribution of animals. 2 vols. London: Macmillan, 1876; *Island life; or, The phenomena and causes of insular faunas: Including a discussion and an attempted solution to the problem of geological climates*. London: Macmillan, 1880 (2d ed.: 1892); *Darwinism: An exposition of the theory of natural selection with some of its applications*. London: Macmillan, 1889 (3d ed.: 1912); *The wonderful century*. London: Sonnenshein, 1898; *My life: A record of events and opinions*. 2 vols. London: Chapman & Hall, 1905 (2d ed.: 1908); (with C. Darwin) On the tendency of species to form varieties; and on the perpetuation of varieties and species by natural means of selection. *Journal of the Proceedings of the Linnean Society* 3:44–62, 1858.

ARCHIVAL SOURCES

1. A.R. Wallace Correspondence: Department of Manuscripts, British Library, Great Russell Street, London WC1B 3DG, England; 2. A.R. Wallace Papers: Library, Linnean Society of London, Burlington House, Picadilly, London WIV OLQ, England; 3. A.R. Wallace Miscellanous Collection of Letters: Library, University of Oxford, University Museum, Parks Road, Oxford OX1 3PW, England.

PRIMARY AND SECONDARY SOURCES

A.C. Brackman: *A delicate arrangement: The strange case of Charles Darwin and Alfred Russel Wallace*. New York: Times Books, 1980; R. Chambers: *Vestiges of the natural history of creation*. London: Churchill, 1844; F. Darwin (ed): *The life and letters of Charles Darwin, including an autobiographical chapter*. 2 vols. New York: Appleton, 1887; W. George: *Biologist-philosopher: A study of the life and writings of Alfred Russel Wallace*. London: Schuman, 1964; M.J. Kottler: Alfred Russel Wallace: The origins of man and spiritualism. *Isis* 65:145–192, 1974; H.L. McKinney: *Wallace and natural selection*. New Haven, Connecticut: Yale University Press, 1972; J. Marchant (ed): *Alfred Russel Wallace: Letters and reminiscences*. London: Cassell, 1916; R. Smith: Alfred Russel Wallace: Philosophy of nature and man. *British Journal for the History of Science* 6:178–199, 1972.

Warren, John Collins (1778–1856)

Born in Boston, Massachusetts, Warren followed his father, John Warren (1753–1815), who was the first professor of anatomy and surgery at Harvard Medical School, into medicine. The younger Warren received his formal medical education at the University of Edinburgh, Scotland, where he studied under the neuroanatomist Charles Bell (1764–1842). On receiving his M.D. degree in 1801, Warren spent some time in Paris before returning to Boston, where he subsequently succeeded his father at Harvard in 1815. He remained at the university until his death in 1856.

During his career, Warren made a number of significant contributions to the development of the medical sciences. In particular, he was responsible for introducing ether anesthesia in surgery and for pioneering a number of surgical techniques, including the excision of bones and joints such as the hyoid in 1804 and the elbow in 1834. He was also founder in 1811 of the Massachusetts General Hospital. In addition to these contributions, Warren is important to the development of American physical anthropology primarily because he was one of the first Americans to concern himself with, and promote, the work and "system of craniognomy" (cf. E. Warren 1860, Vol. 2:10–13) devised by the German physician Franz Gall (1758–1828). From all accounts, Warren first became interested in the work of Gall when he visited Paris in 1802 and was further stimulated by the appearance of Gall's book *Anatomie et physiologie du système nerveux* (1810). Like others at that time, Warren was impressed by Gall's phrenological system because it appeared not only to explain developmental aspects of the anatomy and physiology of the nervous system, but also (through the study of the conformation of the human skull) to understand the degree of intellectual power possessed by individuals. Although Gall was unquestionably the primary influence, it is conjectured that Charles Bell in Edinburgh, who is known to have been an early student of craniology, might also have contributed to Warren's developing interest in this field of inquiry.

A product of Warren's interest in phrenological research was his book *A comparative view of the sensorial and nervous system in man and animals* (1822). As this work reveals, Warren did not absorb all of the theoretical inferences implicit in Gall's system, in particular its racial determinism. Warren attributed the differences in the "races of men" to environmental rather than innate biological factors. As such, his anthropological interpretations are decidedly more optimistic than those of other contemporary American phrenologists. This is particularly evident in his comments on Africans born in America:

{T}heir appearance alters for the better; the features expand, and assume a milder character; the body becomes more upright. In one of the New England States, where slavery was retained, in a mitigated form, longer than in the rest, it has been distinctly noticed that the children of Africans born in this country, and brought up with those of Whites, as occasionally happened in large estates, were as intelligent, as gay, as ready to imbibe the rudiments of learning, as the Whites; and if their education had kept pace with that of the latter, they might have continued on the same level through life. (cf. Warren 1822)

Unfortunately, with the exception of a couple of craniological publications, Warren appears to have made no further contribution to anthropology after 1838.

Frank Spencer

See also Phrenology; Polygenism

Bibliography
SELECTED WORKS

   A comparative view of the sensorial and nervous system in man and animals. Boston: Ingraham, 1822; Some remarks on the crania of the Mound Indians of the interior of North America. *Boston Medical and Surgical Journal* 17:249–253, 1838.

PRIMARY AND SECONDARY SOURCES

   F.J. Gall: *Anatomie et physiologie du système nerveux en générale, et du cerveau en particulière avec observations sur la possibilité de reconnoitre plusiers dispositions intellectuelles et morales de l'homme et des animaux par la configuration de leur têtes.* 4 vols. Paris: Schoell, 1810; J.A. Meigs: On the measurement of the skull. *North American Medico-Chirurgical Review* 5:853, 1861; E. Warren: *The life of John Collins Warren: Compiled chiefly from his autobiography and journals.* 2 vols. Boston: Ticknor & Fields, 1860.

Washburn, Sherwood L. (1911–)

Born in Cambridge, Massachusetts, Washburn attended Groton School from 1926 to 1931 before going on to Harvard University. There, after receiving his B.A. degree in 1935, he entered the graduate program in physical anthropology, which was then under the direction of Earnest A. Hooton (1887–1954). He became interested in anthropology as an undergraduate through Alfred M. Tozzer's (1877–1954) introductory course and Hooton's lectures and seminars. Given his burgeoning interest in comparative primate anatomy, he spent the winter semester of 1936 in Ann Arbor, where he took an anatomy course at the University of Michigan that prepared him for a comparable medical anatomy course offered later that year by Wilfrid E. Le Gros Clark (1895–1971) at Oxford University. In 1937, he was invited to join an expedition sponsored by Harvard, Columbia, and Johns Hopkins Universities to study and collect primates from Thailand and Borneo. He completed the requirements for his Ph.D. degree in anthropology at Harvard with a thesis entitled *A Preliminary Metrical Study of the Skeleton of Langurs and Macaques* in 1940 (cf. Washburn 1942).

   In 1939, just prior to receiving his doctorate, he was appointed instructor in anatomy at Columbia University Medical School (CUMS). It was there that he came under the influence of the experimental embryologist Samuel R. Detwiler (1890–1957) and added a developmental and experimental approach to his functional comparative anatomy. It was also while at Columbia that he met the geneticist Theodosius Dobzhansky (1900–1975), from whom he learned of the new evolutionary synthesis. Later, Dobzhansky and Washburn were responsible for organizing the influential international symposium on the "Origin and Evolution of Man" held at Cold Spring Harbor, Long Island, New York, in the summer of 1950, which served as a platform from which Washburn launched his campaign for the "new" anthropology. In a series of papers published in the early 1950s (cf. Washburn 1951a, 1951b), he underlined the distinction between the strategies of the "new" and the "old" anthropology. Where the latter was essentially descriptive and static, the former was envisioned as a dynamic amalgam of functional, populational, and behavioral approaches whose collective aim was the understanding of human biocultural history as a "history of genetic systems" manifest as "a sequence of more effective behavior systems" (Washburn 1953:718–719).

   Washburn remained at Columbia until 1947, when he moved to the University of Chicago (UC) to occupy the position formerly held by Wilton Marion Krogman (1903–1987) in the Department of Anthropology. At Chicago between 1947 and 1958, he rose from

TABLE 1. Washburn's Doctoral Students (incomplete)

Degree Date	Name	Primary Research Interest
1953	James A. Gavan[1,2]	Comparative primate anatomy
	F. Clark Howell[1]	Paleoanthropology, human paleontology
1962	Irven DeVore[1]	Primate behavior, evolutionary studies
1963	Phyllis C. Jay (now Dolhinow[1])	Primate behavior, ecology
	Paul E. Simonds	Primate behavior
1964	Theodore I. Grand[3]	
	Ralph Holloway	Comparative neuroanatomy
	Mary W. Marzke	Comparative primate anatomy, paleoanthropology
1965	Richard B. Lee	Human ecology
	Russell H. Tuttle	Primatology, paleoanthropology
1966	Donald S. Sade	Primate and animal behavior
1967	Claud A. Bramblett	Primatology
	John O. Ellefson	Primate behavior
	Jane B. Lancaster	Primate behavior
	Vincent M. Sarich	Molecular anthropology, mammalian systematics
	Judith Shirek-Ellefson[2]	Primate behavior
	Adrienne L. Zihlman	Primate behavior, comparative primate anatomy
1968	Michael H. Roberts[3]	
	Alan E. Mann	Paleoanthropology, primatology
	Jack M. Whitehead	Biological anthropology
1969	Richard N. Van Horn[3]	
	Mark L. Weiss	Molecular anthropology
1970	Suzanne Chevalier-Skolnikoff	Primate behavior
	Kathleen R. Gibson	Biological anthropology
	Stephen F. Holtzman[2]	History of physical anthropology
1971	James D. Cadien	Biological anthropology
	Glenn E. King	Primate and animal behavior
	Lewis L. Klein	Primate behavior
1972	Alan J. Almquist	Primatology, paleoanthropology
	Mary E. Morbeck	Primate evolution, functional morphology
1973	Philip G. Grant[3]	
	Robert S.O. Harding	Primate evolution, human evolution
	Donald A. Symons	Evolutionary psychology
1974	Horst D. Steklis	Primatology, primate behavior
	Brian L. O'Conner	Comparative primate anatomy

1. Degree from University of Chicago—all others from University of California, Berkeley; 2. Deceased; 3. Specialization unkown

the rank of associate to full professor and served briefly (1953–1955) as chairman of the department. In 1958, he accepted a professorhip in anthropology at the University of California, Berkeley (UCB), and it was there that the remainder of his academic career unfolded. Since his retirement in 1978, he has held the position of University Professor Emeritus at UCB.

In addition to being a central figure in the codification of the new evolutionary synthesis in American physical anthropology, Washburn was also highly influential in establishing primate studies as an integral feature of the academic curriculum in anthropology and in promoting primate field research. (For a discussion and analysis of Washburn's impact on American anthropology during the period 1950–1980, see Haraway 1988.)

As was the case with his former mentor at Harvard, Hooton, Washburn was a dedicated teacher, and between 1947 and 1978 he produced an important crop of Ph.D.'s (see Table 1 for an incomplete list).

He is a member of the National Academy of Sciences, and a recipient of the Viking Fund Medal of the Wenner-Gren Foundation for Anthropological Research in 1960, the Ciba Foundation Annual Lecture Medal in 1965, and the Huxley Memorial Medal of the Royal Anthropological Institute of Great Britain in 1967. He has also held offices in several societies, including the American

Association of Physical Anthropologists, which he served as secretary/treasurer (1943–1947), president (1951), and Executive Board member (1956–1960); and the American Anthropological Association, which he served as president (1961). In addition, he was editor of the *American Journal of Physical Anthropology* (1955–1957) and *Viking Fund Publications in Anthropology* (1956–1960).

Frank Spencer

See also African Apes; Bipedalism; Clark, (Sir) Wilfrid Edward Le Gros; Dobzhansky, Theodosius; Harvard University; Hooton, E(arnest) A(lbert); Krogman, Wilton Marion; McCown, Theodore D(oney); Neo-Darwinism; Primate Field Studies

Bibliography
SELECTED WORKS

Skeletal proportions of adult langurs and macaques. *Human Biology* 14:444–472, 1942; The analysis of primate evolution, with particular reference to the origin of man. *Cold Spring Harbor Symposia of Quantitative Biology* 15:67–78, 1951a; The new physical anthropology. *Transactions of the New York Academy of Science* 13 (2d ser.):298–304, 1951b; The strategy of physical anthropology. In: A.L. Kroeber (ed) *Anthropology today: An encyclopedic inventory.* Chicago: University of Chicago Press, 1953, pp. 714–727; (ed) *Classification and human evolution.* New York: Viking Fund, 1963; Evolution of a teacher. *Annual Review of Anthropology* 12:1–24, 1983; (with I. DeVore) Social behavior of baboons and early man. In: S.L. Washburn (ed) *The social life of early man.* New York: Viking Fund, 1961, pp. 91–319; (with D.A. Hamburg) The study of primate behavior. In: I. DeVore (ed) *Primate behavior: Field studies of monkeys and apes.* New York: Holt, Rinehart & Winston, 1965, pp. 1–13.

SECONDARY SOURCES

D.J. Haraway: Remodelling the human way of life: Sherwood Washburn and the new physical anthropology, 1950–1980. In: G.W. Stocking Jr. (ed) *Bones, bodies, behavior: Essays on biological anthropology.* Madison: University of Wisconsin Press, 1988, pp. 206–259.

Weidenreich, Franz (1873–1948)

Born in Edenkoben of the Palatinate, Germany, Weidenreich studied medicine at the Universities of Munich, Kiel, and Berlin be-fore completing his M.D. at the University of Strassburg[1] in 1899 with an inaugural dissertation titled *Zur Anatomie der zentralen Kleinhirnkerne der Säuger.* This work on the central nucleus of the mammalian cerebellum was followed two years later by the completion of his *Habilitationschrift,* an important professional qualifying publication, on the secretory system of human milk (cf. Weidenreich 1901b). During this same time period, he also published a series of papers summarizing his study of the human spleen, and other elements of the reticulo-endothelial system (cf. Weidenreich 1900, 1901b, 1901c). Also important from the standpoint of his future career was that during his two years at Strassburg (1899–1901) he worked under Gustav Schwalbe (1844–1916), a leading German anatomist-anthropologist and a leading proponent of the idea that Neandertals were directly ancestral to modern humans.

After a brief hiatus (1901–1902), when he worked with the immunologist Paul Ehrlich (1854–1915) in Frankfurt am Main, Weidenreich returned to Strassburg, where he remained until 1918. Returning as prosector in 1902, he was subsequently promoted to the rank of professor in 1904. By 1914, he had published fifty-five scientific papers, mostly in the area of hematology. His interest in human morphology is apparent from two papers published in 1904, one of which was on the development of the human chin and its functional significance for speech (cf. Weidenreich 1904a) and the other on primate posterior limb morphology in relation to upright posture and locomotion (Weidenreich 1904b).

The outbreak of World War I marked the first of what would be several major disruptions in Weidenreich's professional and personal life. During the war years (1914–1918), he served as a member of the municipal council of Strassburg and was responsible for producing a pamphlet on wartime food rationing; this area of his civic responsibility was one that he took so seriously that his own family cook wrote a letter of complaint about the rigor of his policies.

Following Germany's defeat in 1918, the provinces of Alsace and Lorraine were ceded to France, which resulted in Weidenreich's dismissal as professor of anatomy at the University of Strassburg, and it was not until 1921 that he finally succeeded in finding a new position at the University of Heidelberg. His departure from Strassburg affected the pattern of his subsequent research: He wrote less on cytology and more on skeletal morphology, with particular reference to human evolution. This trend is clearly revealed in his influential 1921 paper on the human foot and its origin, which undoubtedly led to the invitation to describe the hominid skull found at Weimar-Ehringsdorf in 1925 (cf. Weidenreich 1928).

During this same time period, Weidenreich began publishing papers on modern human variation, beginning with a paper on "Rasse und Konstitution" (1926), which appeared in the journal of the fledgling Deutsche Gesellschaft für Physische Anthropologie (DGPA). Weidenreich was a founding member of this society, which later became an important vehicle for the more extreme aspects of the Rassenhygiene and Rassenkunde movements that flourished in Germany after the Nazis came to power in 1933.

In the meantime, at Heidelberg he was promoted to the rank of professor in (physical) anthropology—a position he retained, technically, until 1935. During this period, his objective research on human variation, past and present (compounded with the fact that he was a Jew), placed his career on a collision course with Nazi racialist doctrines and jeopardized his safety and that of his family. Fortunately, his professional talents led to a timely invitation in 1934 to serve as visiting professor of anatomy at the University of Chicago. In the following year, he moved to China, where he had been appointed to succeed Davidson Black (1884–1934) as professor of anatomy at the Peking Union Medical College (PUMC) and as honorary director of the Cenozoic Research Laboratory. While extending the pioneering investigations begun by Black, Weidenreich worked in collaboration with a number of notable Chinese anthropologists, including Pei Wenzhong (1904–1982). The outcome of Weidenreich's work in China was a magnificent set of monographs on the Zhoukoudian hominid material, then known as *Sinanthropus pekinensis* (now *Homo erectus*) (cf. Weidenreich 1936a, 1936b, 1937, 1943).

Although perhaps best known for his descriptive anatomical research, Weidenreich also made some major theoretical contributions. For example, his "polycentric theory" of human origins anticipated the "multiregional theory" of modern human origins that is one of several present explanations for existing human specific unity in the face of regional genetic diversity. Also of particular

historical interest is his rejection of the monistic interpretation of the now infamous Piltdown skull—maintaining that the lower jaw was not human but that of an ape.

In 1941, he returned to the United States, where he spent his remaining years at the American Museum of Natural History in New York City. Among the many works he completed during this time is his book *Apes, Giants, and Man* (1946), which essentially summarizes his views on human evolution. Many of Weidenreich's views remain valid, although work on *Gigantopithecus* in the 1980s has shown it to be an ape and not an early hominid as he had supposed.

Weidenreich died in New York City on 11 July 1948.

Robert Eckhardt

Editor's Note

1. Prior to the Franco-Prussian War of 1870–1871, the provinces of Alsace and Lorraine had been French territory. In 1871 these provinces became a part of Germany until 1919, when they were returned to France. Thereafter Strassburg became Strasbourg—as it had been before 1871.

See also Asian Paleoanthropology; Black, Davidson; China; Germany; *Gigantopithecus*; Java; Koenigswald, (Gustav Heinrich) Ralph von; Modern Human Origins; Pei Wenzhong; Rassenhygiene and Rassenkunde; Schwalbe, Gustav; Zhoukoudian

Bibliography
SELECTED WORKS

Zur Anatomie der zentralen Kleinhirnkerne der Säuger. *Zeitschrift für Morphologie und Anthropologie* 1:259–312, 1899; Ueber Blutlymphdrüsen. Die Bedeutung der eosinophilen Leucocyten, über Phagocytose und die Entstehung von. Riesenzellen. *Anatomischer Anzeiger* 20:203–206, 1900; Weitere Mitteilungen über den Bau der Hornschicht der menschlichen Epidermis und ihren sog. *Archiv für Mikroskopische Anatomie* (Bonn) 57:583–622, 1901a; Das Gefässystem der menschlichen Milz. (Zugleich Habilitationsschrift). *Archiv für Mikroskopische Anatomie* (Bonn) 58:247–376, 1901b; Nochmals geschlossne oder offene Blutbahn der Milz. *Anatomischer Anzeiger* 22:203–206, 1901c.

Die Bildung des Kinns und seine angebliche Beziehung zur Sprache. *Anatomischer Anzeiger* 24:545–555, 1904a; Zur Kinnbildung beim Menschen.

Anatomischer Anzeiger 25:314–319, 1904b; Der Menschenfuss. *Zeitschrift für Morphologie und Anthropologie* 22:51–282, 1921; Rasse und Konstitution. *Verhandlungen der Deutschen Gesellschaft für Physische Anthropologie* 1:56–57, 1926; Der Schädel von Weimar-Ehringsdorf. *Verhandlungen der Deutschen Gesellschaft für Physische Anthropologie* 2:34–41, 1927; *Der Schädelfund von Weimar-Ehringsdorf*. Jena: Fischer, 1928.

The mandibles of *Sinanthropus pekinensis*: A comparative study. *Palaeontologia Sinica* 7 (ser. D):1–162, 1936a; Observations on the form and proportions of the endocranial casts of *Sinanthropus pekinensis* and other hominiods, and the great apes: A comparative study of brain size. *Palaeontologia Sinica* 7 (ser. D):1–50, 1936b; The dentition of *Sinanthropus pekinensis*: A comparative odontography of the hominids. *Palaeontologia Sinica* 1 (n.s. D):1–180, 1937; The skull of *Sinanthropus pekinensis*: A comparative study on a primitive hominid skull. *Palaeontologia Sinica* 5 (n.s. D):1–150, 1943; *Apes, giants, and man*. Chicago: University of Chicago Press, 1946; Facts and speculations concerning the origin of *Homo sapiens*. *American Anthropologist* 49:187–203, 1947.

ARCHIVAL SOURCES

F. Weidenreich Papers: Archives, Pattee Library, Pennsylvania State University, University Park, Pennsylvania 16802-3902.

SECONDARY SOURCES

A.M. Boring: In memoriam: Franz Weidenreich, 1873–1948. *Peking Natural History Bulletin* 17:i–ii, 1948–1949; H. von Eggeling: Franz Weidenreich, 1873–1948. *Anatomische Nachrichten* 1(9–12):149–168, 1950; L.C. Eiseley: Franz Weidenreich, 1873–1948. *American Journal of Physical Anthropology* (n.s.) 7:241–253, 1949; W.K. Gregory: Franz Weidenreich, 1873–1948. *American Anthropologist* 51:85–90, 1949; W.W. Howells: Franz Weidenreich, 1873–1948. *American Journal of Physical Anthropology* 56:407–410, 1981; S.L. Washburn & D. Wolffson (eds): *The shorter anthropological papers of Franz Weidenreich published in the period 1939–1948*. New York: Viking Fund, 1949.

Weiner, Joseph Sidney (1915–1982)

Born in Pretoria, South Africa, Weiner was educated in his native city at the Boys' High School, and then the University of the Witwatersrand, Johannesburg, where he read physiology, anatomy, and anthropology, receiving his B.Sc. in 1934 at the early age of 19, and then his M.Sc. in physiology in 1936. In 1937, he moved to Britain, where he made his home, though he retained links with his South African colleagues and the large family of which he was a member. In 1940–1941, he was demonstrator in the Department of Applied Physiology at the London School of Hygiene and Tropical Medicine; from 1942 to 1946, he was a scientific officer of the Medical Research Council staff. In 1946, he received a Ph.D. from the University of London, followed a year later by the Licentiate of the Royal College of Physicians (L.R.C.P.) and membership of the Royal College of Surgeons (M.R.C.S.) at St. George's Hospital, London, and went on later to be elected MRCP (1973) and FRCP (1978) and to receive a D.Sc. in the University of Oxford (1971). Meanwhile, in 1946, he was invited by Wilfrid Edward Le Gros Clark (1895–1971), professor of human anatomy at Oxford University, to join him. The established readership in physical anthropology in that department had been vacant since the death of L.H. Dudley Buxton (1889–1939), and Weiner's views on the aims and content of physical anthropology coincided with those of Clark. Both recognized the decayed state of the subject at that time. The majority of its practitioners had dropped out of the scientific mainstream; the trivial issues to which they devoted their attention could no longer be considered as part of the intellectual climate of the moment. To this charnel house, the arrival of Weiner brought a gale of fresh air. With his schooling in the biological and medical sciences, his early exposure to the ideas of the South African anatomist-anthropologist Raymond A. Dart (1893–1988), and his strong awareness of recent developments in biology, he saw physical anthropology as a living discipline that was very relevant to modern scientific problems. He saw human communities as dynamic functional entities displaying adaptive responses to the demands and stresses of the environment, as well as of day-to-day events. The efficiency of those responses could be characterized in genetic, physiological, nutritional, biomedical, developmental, demographic, and cultural terms. As such, Weiner is considered to have played a major role in establishing the intellectual contours of the discipline during the second half of the twentieth century.

He held his readership in Oxford for seventeen years. On Clark's retirement in 1962, Weiner succeeded him as director of the Medical Research Council Environmental Physiology Unit and moved it to London. Three years later (1965), he was appointed professor of environmental physiology. He held the positions of director and professor until his retirement in 1980. During his Oxford years, he helped develop the diploma in anthropology there, supervised the research of many who have since gone on to make their names in various universities and research establishments, and ensured that his colleagues were not so overburdened by teaching requirements that they were prevented from pursuing their researches. At the University of London, he was instrumental in establishing the degree of M.Sc. in ergonomics.

His own researches were primarily experimental, mainly in the laboratory, where he made many fundamental contributions to applied physiology, and in particular the physiology of climatic adaptation. But he also appreciated the value of fieldwork, and he led two expeditions to South and Southwest Africa. His experimental approach provided him with the material that led to the exposure in 1953 of the Piltdown forgery. His modest book describing this (Weiner 1955) was the first of fifteen books he wrote himself or in collaboration with others. In addition, he was the author or coauthor of 300 scientific publications.

He was largely responsible for founding in 1958 the Society for the Study of Human Biology, and later the International Association of Human Biologists in 1967. His influence led eventually to the development of the subject in a number of universities throughout the United Kingdom, as in the establishment in 1976 of the Department of Biological Anthropology at Oxford as a separate administrative entity, and similarly at Cambridge. He was also the architect of the Human Adaptability Section of the International Biological Programme (1964–1974), which permitted for the first time a coordinated worldwide comparative study of human population biology. The research agenda of the Human Adaptability Section included studying communities ranging from the very simple to the highly industrialized, applying standard methods drawn from all relevant fields. Weiner played a critically important part in this, taking the responsibility for drawing together and publishing handbooks on recommended techniques, planning, and for participating in review conferences all over the world. The result of all of this activity was an unprecedented contribution to our knowledge of the human species.

Among the various honors and distinctions he received were the Vernon Medal (1956), the Rivers Memorial Medal (1969), and the Darwin and Huxley Lectureships (1978). He was president of the Royal Anthropological Institute from 1962 to 1964, honorary secretary (1958–1963) and chairman (1968–1973) of the Society for the Study of Human Biology, and president (1977–1982) of the International Association of Human Biologists. He was active in many learned societies and organizations, including the Oxford-based Ergonomics Research Society (of which he was cofounder in 1949), the Physiological Society of Great Britain, the Royal Society, the Royal Society of Medicine, and the Scientific Committee for Problems of the Environment in Paris.

Derek F. Roberts

See also Clark, Wilfrid Edward Le Gros; Dart, Raymond A(rthur); International Association of Human Biologists; International Biological Programme (Human Adaptability Section); Piltdown; Society for the Study of Human Biology; South Africa

Bibliography
SELECTED WORKS
   The Piltdown forgery. London: Oxford University Press, 1955; *A guide to human adaptability proposals.* International Biological Programme Handbook. No. 1. Oxford: Blackwell, 1965 (2d ed.: 1969); *The natural history of man.* London: Weidenfeld & Nicolson, 1971. Translated into French, Spanish, German, and Italian; *Physiological variation and its genetic basis. Society for the Study of Human Biology.* Symposium. No. 17. London: Taylor & Francis, 1977; (with P.T. Baker) *The biology of human adaptability.* London: Oxford University Press, 1966; (with B.G. Campbell) *The taxonomic status of the Swanscombe skull.* London: Royal Anthropological Institute, 1964.
   (with K.J. Collins) *Human adaptability: A history and compendium of research in the International Biological Programme.* London: Taylor & Francis, 1977; (with O.G. Edholm) *Principles and practice of human physiology.* London: Academic Press, 1981; (with G.A. Harrison, J.M. Tanner, & N.A. Barnicot) *Human biology: An introduction to human evolution, variation, and growth.* London: Oxford University Press, 1964

(2d ed.: 1977); (with J. Huizinga) *The assessment of affinities between human populations.* London: Oxford University Press, 1972.

(with J.A. Lourie) *Human biology: A guide to field methods. International Biological Programme Handbook.* No. 9. Oxford: Blackwell, 1969; (with J.A. Lourie) *Practical human biology.* London: Academic Press, 1981; (with H.G. Maule) *Case studies in ergonomic practice.* Vol. 1, *Human factors in work design and production.* London: Taylor & Francis, 1977; (with H.G. Maule) *Case studies in ergonomic practice.* Vol. 2, *Design for work and use.* London: Taylor & Francis, 1981; (with G.T. Nurse & T. Jenkins) *Peoples of southern Africa and their affinities.* London: Oxford University Press, 1985; (with D.F. Roberts) *The scope of physical anthropology and its place in academic studies.* London: Society for the Study of Human Biology, 1958.

ARCHIVAL SOURCES

J.S. Weiner Papers: Archives, Library of Palaeontology, Natural History Museum, Cromwell Road, London SW7 5BD, England.

SECONDARY SOURCES

G.A. Harrison: J.S. Weiner and the exposure of the Piltdown forgery. *Antiquity* 57:46–48, 1983; G.A. Harrison & K. Collins: Joseph Sidney Weiner, 1915–1982. *Annals of Human Biology* 9:583–592, 1982.

Weinert, Hans (1887–1967)

Born in Braunschweig, Germany, Weinert received his scientific training in medicine and anthropology at the Universities of Göttingen, Leipzig, and Berlin. From 1926 to 1935, he held the positions of privatdocent (lecturer) then *professor extraordinarius* (1932) at the University of Berlin. During this same time period, he was an assistant professor at the University of Munich, as well as a member of the Kaiser Wilhelm Institut für Anthropologie, menschliche Erblehre und Eugenik in Berlin (1927–1935). In 1935, he moved to the University of Kiel, where he remained until his retirement, holding the positions of *professor ordinarius* and director of the Kiel Institut für Anthropologie. During the course of his career, Weinert published 250 papers and monographs dealing with human evolution, racial biology, and human genetics.

In the area of human paleontology, he contributed several notable publications, such as his detailed accounts of the Le Moustier

skull (1925) and the Steinheim calvaria (1936), and his reconstruction and evaluation of the hominid crania discovered by the German Ludwig Kohl-Larsen in East Africa in the 1930s. He dubbed these latter remains *Africanthropus njarensis* (Weinert 1939), which he considered to be morphologically similar to the Asian pithecanthropines (i.e., *Homo erectus*)—a proposition that was subsequently attacked by Franz Weidenreich (1873–1948) (1943). Also of historical interest is the work he did in the early 1930s on the now infamous Piltdown remains (cf. Weinert 1933). Based on his examination of the original remains at the Natural History Museum in Kensington, London, he essentially endorsed Arthur Smith Woodward's (1864–1944) monistic reconstruction of the Piltdown remains, but while generally supportive of Piltdown as hominid precursor—in contradistinction to other German workers of the period, such as Weidenreich and Gustav Schwalbe (1844–1916) (cf. Brace 1964)—he questioned the validity of the Piltdown II remains, which he believed belonged to Piltdown I (cf. Weinert 1944:233, 1951; Weinert to K.P. Oakley, 19 September 1951, in: Spencer 1990:193–194).

As for his views on race and racial classification, they are generally representative of the period. He recognized four major branches of the human family: Australoid, Europoid, Mongoloid, and Negroid, each divided into a number of subraces or groups based on physical attributes he considered to be evolutionary criteria (cf. Weinert 1939).

Weinert served as editor of the *Zeitschrift für Morphologie und Anthropologie (ZMA)* from 1949 through 1957. Prior to this, the editorship of the *ZMA*, which was founded by Gustav Schwalbe in 1899, had been in the hands of the German geneticist-anthropologist Eugen Fischer (1874–1964) from 1916 to 1948.

Ursula Zängl-Kumpf

See also Fischer, Eugen; Neandertals; Piltdown; Schwalbe, Gustav; Weidenreich, Franz

Bibliography
SELECTED WORKS

Der Schädel des eiszeitlichen Menschen von le Moustier, in neuer Zusammensetzung. Berlin: Springer, 1925; Das Problem des *Eoanthropus* von Piltdown. *Zeitschrift für Morphologie und Anthropologie* 32:1–76, 1933; Der Urmenschen-Schädel von Steinheim. *Zeitschrift für Morphologie und Anthropologie* 35:463–518, 1936; Entstehung *der Menschenrassen.* Stuttgart: Enke, 1938. French translation: *L'homme préhistorique, des préhumains aux races actuelles.* Paris: Payot, 1939; *Africanthropus njarensis. Zeitschrift für Morphologie und Anthropologie* 37:18–24, 1939; *Ursprung der Menschheit: Über den engeren Anschluss des Menschengeschlects an die Menschenaffen.* Stuttgart: Enke, 1944; *Stammesentwicklung der Menschheit.* Braunschweig: Vieweg, 1951.

PRIMARY AND SECONDARY SOURCES

F. Berktau & G. Oestreich (eds): *Kürschners Deutscher Gelehrten-Kalendar 1950.* Berlin: Gruyter, 1950, p. 2226; C.L. Brace: The fate of the "classic" Neanderthals: A consideration of hominid catastrophism. *Current Anthropology* 5:3–43, 1964; W. Habel (ed): *Wer ist wer? Das Deutsche Who's Who.* Vol. 1. Berlin, 1965, p. 2131; F. Spencer: *The Piltdown papers, 1908–1955: The correspondence and other documents relating to the Piltdown forgery.* London: Oxford University Press, 1990, pp. 193–194. F. Weidenreich: The skull of *Sinanthropus pekinensis:* A comparative study on a primitive hominid skull. *Palaeontologia Sinica* 5 (n.s. D):1–150, 1943.

Weninger, Josef (1886–1959)

Born in Salzburg, Austria, Weninger attended the local Technical College, where he studied buildings and road construction. His introduction to physical anthropology, ethnology, and prehistory came from one of the teachers there, Moritz Hoernes (1852–1917), a pioneer in the study of prehistoric archeology in Vienna. Weninger received his training in anthropology at the Institute for Anthropology and Ethnography, which had been established in Vienna by Rudolf Pöch (1870–1921) in 1913. He eventually became an assistant and gradually a close coworker of Pöch. Since the institute did not provide a regular salaried position for an assistant, Weninger worked as a scientific officer at the Staatsdenkmalamt in Vienna, where he took charge of the preservation of monuments in the area of prehistory, ethnology, and art history. The results of his scientific activity during this period (1915–1926) include several publications in prehistoric and physical anthropology (cf. Weninger 1920, 1924). In 1926, he received an appointment as a lecturer at the University of Vienna. The title of his inaugural dissertation was *Morphologische Studien an westafrikanischen Negern* (Morphological Studies of West African Negroes). In 1927, he was elevated to the rank of professor and entrusted with the directorship of the Institute for Anthropology and Ethnography in Vienna. In 1938, however, his career came to an abrupt halt. Because of his anthropologist wife Margarete's Jewish descent, he was released from his position and prohibited from working. However, after the war, in 1945, his professorial chair was returned to him along with the directorship of the institute. He retained these positions until his retirement.

The focus of Weninger's research was the development of scientific methods in the study of human morphology. As early as 1924, he published "Leitlinien zur Beobachtung der somatischen Merkmale des Kopfes und des Gesichts am Menschen" (Guidelines for the Observation of the Somatic Features of the Head and Face). The inclusion of fine morphological characteristics was an essential part of his inaugural dissertation on West African Negroes (1927), as well as of his later monographs about the Albanians (1934a), the Armenians (1951), the Mingrels (1955), and the Georgians (1959). His morphological methodology also addressed problems in applied human genetics, like twin-diagnosis and the appraisal of disputed paternity (1932). He also published several works on the structure of the iris (cf. Weninger 1934b, 1954). Weninger's contribution to the geneticist Günter Just's (1892–1950) *Handbuch der Erbbiologie des Menschen* (1940) is an excellent summary of his morphological method.

Weninger received numerous honors in his country and abroad. He was a member and president of the Austrian Academy of Science; (Österreichischen Akademie der Wissenschaften); honorary president of the Österreichischen Vereins für Völkskunde in Vienna; honorary member of the Deutsche Gesellschaft für Anthropologie; member of the Permanent Council of the International Congress for Anthropological and Ethnological Sciences; member of the Comitato Internazionale for l'Unificazione dei Metodi di Antropologia e Eugenia; and an Honorary Fellow of the Royal Anthropological Institute of Great Britain.

Weninger died in Vienna on 29 March 1959.

G. Ziegelmayer

See also Pöch, Rudolf; Weninger, Margarete

Bibliography
SELECTED WORKS

Die physisch-anthropologischen Merkmale der vorderasiatischen Rasse und ihre geographische Verbreitung. *Mitteilungen der Geographischen Gesellschaft in Wien* 63:13–37, 1920; Leitlinien zur Beobachtung der somatischen Merkmale des Kopfes und des Gesichtes am Menschen. *Mitteilungen der Geographischen Gesellschaft in Wien* 54:232–270, 1924; Über die Weichteile der Augenregion bei erbgleichen Zwillingen. *Anthropologischer Anzeiger* 9:57–67, 1932; *Rassenkundliche Untersuchungen an Albanern: Ein Beitrag zum Problem der dinarischen Rasse.* Wien: Anthropologische Gesellschaft in Wien, 1934a; Irisstruktur und Vererbung. *Zeitschrift für Morphologie und Anthropologie* 34:469–492, 1934b.

Zur Vererbung der "blauen" Irisfarbe. *Mitteilungen der Geographischen Gesellschaft in Wien* 68:206–219, 1938; Die anthropologischen Methoden der menschlichen Erbforschung. In: G. Just (ed) *Handbuch der Erbbiologie des Menschen.* Vol. 3. Berlin: Springer, 1940, pp. 1–52; *Armenier: Ein Beitrage zur Anthropologie der Kaukasusvölker.* Wien: Rohrer, 1951; Variabiltät der Struktur der menschlichen Iris. *Homo* 5:137–142, 1954; *Die Mingrelier aus dem Kaukasus in ihrer anthropologischen Stellung.* Wien: Rohrer, 1955; (with M. Weninger) *Anthropologische Beobachtungen an Georgiern.* Wien: Rohrer, 1959.

SECONDARY SOURCES

E. Breitinger: In memoriam Josef Weninger, 1886–1959. *Anthropologischer Anzeiger* 23:236–238, 1959; E. Ehgartner: Josef Weninger. *Mitteilungen der Anthropologischen Gesellschaft in Wien.* 88–89:1959.

Weninger, Margarete (1896–1987)

Born in Wien (Vienna), Austria, Margarete entered the University of Vienna in 1915, initially studying Latin, and later Greek and German. Her interest in anthropology of the so-called *Naturvölker* was stimulated by Rudolf Pöch (1870–1921), and in 1921 she graduated with a degree in geography and anthropology. For a long time, she was active in the Anthropological Institute of Vienna. Her scientific activity, however, was interrupted during the period of National Socialism in Austria (1938–1945). Being of Jewish descent, she was forbidden, along with her husband, Josef Weninger (1886–1959), also an anthropologist, from entering the institute, but after the war the Weningers were reinstated.

After her husband's death, she participated in three successful expeditions: to the Canary Islands in 1962, Angola in 1964, and Mozambique in 1971. The morphometric and morphognostic data collected on these trips formed the bases of numerous publications.

Her international reputation, however, was based on her dermatoglyphic studies, which amount to 100 publications. Apart from her many publications on dermatoglyphics in European and non-European populations (e.g., 1951, 1971, 1974, 1975), she wrote about the heredity of these patterns, and especially during the period 1966–1976 she did research work on the formation of papillar patterns in relation to hereditary anomalies and nonhereditary diseases.

Weninger was a member of scientific societies in Austria, Germany, Slovakia, and Spain; a board member of the European Society of Human Genetics; a member of the Permanent Council of the International Congress of Anthropological and Ethnological Sciences; an Honorary Fellow of the Royal Anthropological Institute of Great Britain; and honorary president of the International Dermatoglyphics Association.

Weninger died in Vienna on 14 October 1987.

G. Ziegelmayer

See also Dermatoglyphics; Pöch, Rudolf; Weninger, Josef

Bibliography
SELECTED WORKS

Die Papillarmuster der Fingerbeeren, das Leistenrelief der Palma und die Handlinien der Zwillinge. In: H. Hartmann & F. Stumpf (ed) Pyschosen bei eineiigen Zwillinген. *Zeitschrift ges Neur Psych* 123:290–298, 1930; *Fingerabdrücke von zentralafrikanischen Batwa-Pygmoiden des Kivu-Gebietes.* Wien: Anthropologischen Gesellschaft in Wien, 1937; Zur Verebung der Hautleistenmuster am Hypothenar der menschlichen Hand. *Mitteilungen der Anthropologischen Gesellschaft in Wien* 73–77:55–82, 1947; Das Hautleistensystem der Negrito. In: P. Schebesta (ed) *Die Pygmäenvölker der Erde II: Die Negrito Asiens.* Wien-Mödling: St. Gabriel, 1951, pp. 259–298; *Physischen-anthropologische Untersuchungen an einigen Stämmen Zentralindiens.* Wien: Herold, 1952.

Der Beitrag des Hautleistensystems zum Pygmäenproblem. *Zeitschrift für Morphologie und Anthropologie* 45:207–234, 1953; Hautleistenbefunde bei Thyroiditis lymphomatosa Hashimoto. *Humangenetik*

1:676–680, 1965; Hautleisten und Krankheiten außerhalb chromosomaler Aberrationen. In: W. Hirsch (ed) *Kolloquium Hautleisten und Krankheiten* (Berlin, 1970). Berlin: Grosse, 1971, pp. 133–157; Hautleisten- und Handfurchenuntersuchungen zur Frage der Heterogenität des ideopathischen Diabetes mellitus. *Humangenetik* 22:45–58, 1974; Fingerbeerenmuster von 500 Mittelschülern aus Mödling bei Wien. *Mitteilungen der Anthropologischen Gesellschaft in Wien* 105:111–117, 1975; Die Rassengeschichte Österreichs. In: K. Saller & I. Schwidetzky (eds) *Rassengeschichte der Menschheit*. Vol 5. München-Wien: Oldenburg, 1978, pp. 7–33.

SECONDARY SOURCES

G. Hauser: In memoriam Frau Professor Dr. Margarete Weninger. *Anthropologischer Anzeiger* 46:277, 1988; W. Hirschberg: Prof. Dr. Margarete Weninger 80 Jahre, 1896–1976. *Mitteilungen der Anthropologischen Gesellschaft in Wien* 107:1–7, 1977.

Wenner-Gren Foundation for Anthropological Research

The Wenner-Gren Foundation for Anthropological Research in New York City is the only philanthropic organization that is dedicated completely to the support of anthropology in the world. The foundation's beginnings date to 1941, when the Swedish industrialist Axel Wenner-Gren (1881–1961) created the Viking Fund, with Paul Fejos (1897–1963) as its first director. That the fund was directed toward anthropology and not toward some other discipline is attributed to Fejos' influence on Wenner-Gren. The size of the fund itself—just under $2 million worth of stock in the U.S. Electrolux Corporation that had been established in the 1920s by Wenner-Gren—restricted the kinds of research that could be undertaken. Fortunately, anthropological investigations could be conducted at relatively modest cost. The fund's (and later the foundation's) goals were to promote cultural, historical, and biological perspectives in anthropology. Its small endowment would be used by distributing small grants to promising individuals, by supporting ventures that brought new techniques and methods from other disciplines into anthropology, and by enhancing rapid communication among all members of the discipline (Dodds 1973). Although many factors are responsible for the growth and character of anthropology since

World War II, there is no doubt that the Wenner-Gren Foundation is responsible for facilitating the directions in which the discipline moved. After Fejos' death, his widow, Lita Fejos (now Lita Osmundsen), directed the foundation until 1986 and developed its interdisciplinary and international focus. Since 1987, the former City University of New York anthropologist Sydel Silverman has continued support for basic research and seeks to enhance the discipline's international focus and to extend its frontiers. The Wenner-Gren Foundation's impact on physical (biological) anthropology alone is easily demonstrable in four areas: (1) theoretical transformation, (2) enhanced communication, (3) infrastructure support for subdisciplinary growth, and (4) small grants to individual researchers.

Theoretical Transformation

Although physical anthropology is now conceptualized as the biological study of the human species, including its antecedents and its collateral relatives in form and function, this unified perspective is a departure from what existed in the first half of the twentieth century. At that time, American physical anthropology seemed to comprise two solitudes: one with "anatomical" interests; the other, with "biological" interests (Goldstein 1940). The backgrounds of researchers in these two areas differed; they were often located in different academic departments; and they tended to publish in different journals—the *American Journal of Physical Anthropology (AJPA)* on the one hand, and *Human Biology (HB)* on the other. In neither camp was there an articulated theory that bound together the researchers who focused on aspects of group biology and those who focused on the comparative study of anatomical structure and function (Goldstein 1940). This basic division of interest, albeit with some modification (e.g., primatology is part of the discipline), continues to characterize physical anthropology at the end of the twentieth century. However, there is one fundamental difference with the past: All physical anthropologists recognize that their subject is fundamentally biological, and that its ultimate unifying theory is evolutionary theory. Evolutionary principles and mechanisms are expounded in all introductory textbooks, and only after such exposure do students focus on paleoanthropology, primatology, human genetic diversity, and human adaptability.

This incorporation of the methods and theories of evolutionary biology represents the "new" physical anthropology. It does not seem "new" to us because all practicing physical anthropologists were either trained in this paradigm or participated in its formulation in the 1950s–1960s. In contrast to research that explained observations through static evolutionary schemes (e.g., early, middle, late) and was otherwise preoccupied with perfection of measurement (Hunt 1981), the "new" physical anthropology emphasized (1) understanding process rather than just classifying differences, (2) testing hypotheses arising from underlying theory rather than ignoring theory, (3) reducing emphasis on perfection of measurements as an end in itself, and (4) interpreting evidence arising from testable hypotheses about the process and course of human evolution (Washburn 1953).

How did this change come about? Intellectual transformations of a body of knowledge often involve many people; thus, it should not be surprising that the new perspective was "based heavily on the discussions which have been held at the Wenner-Gren summer seminars for physical anthropologists, and those reading only current American physical anthropology would get little idea of the size or importance of those changes" (Washburn 1953: 715–716). There were eight such seminars in the period 1946–1955, with the last held at the Smithsonian Institution, Washington, D.C. The seminars fostered an engagement with new ideas that is imperative for research advances, and they made possible the transformation of a discipline. While the shift might have come about by itself, there was risk that delay in incorporating ideas from mainstream biology would quickly make physical anthropology intellectually irrelevant. The foundation trusted the conviction of "junior" scientists that infusion of new ideas was imperative, and it provided the financial means to hold the summer seminars. The foundation also disseminated the results by aiding publication of seminar discussions in the *Yearbook of Physical Anthropology* and by supporting an international symposium of new developments and publishing the papers as a book (Kroeber 1953). Notions of the "new" physical anthropology were, therefore, quickly accessible to the community at large.

Enhanced International Communication of Ideas
The principal vehicle through which the Wenner-Gren Foundation has encouraged scholarly discourse is its international symposia. These began in 1952 and continue to this day. Characteristically, the symposia are restricted to twenty or fewer participants; they

exclude individuals who are not actively involved in the discussion; and they are held in secluded locations that ensure that participants focus their attention on the symposium theme. Books edited by symposium organizers are the products of these meetings, virtually all of which have produced "state of the art" perspectives.

In the area of biological anthropology, in addition to chapters in texts that focused on anthropology (Kroeber 1953) or physical anthropology (Washburn 1964) as a whole, three books since the 1960s have had singular impact: *The Biology of Human Adaptability* (Baker & Weiner 1964), *The Assessment of Population Affinities in Man* (Weiner & Huizinga 1972), and *The Structure of Human Populations* (Harrison & Boyce 1972). These three defined the themes of human population biology and articulated the research directions that very many biological anthropologists have pursued since their appearance. Other international symposia have elaborated methods to assess children's nutritional status through measurements that document their growth and development (Roche & Falkner 1974), or have marked the culmination of interest in evidence for natural selection in human populations (Salzano 1975), or have noted the growing utility of molecular biology for elucidating phylogenetic relationship within the Order Primates (Goodman & Tashian 1976). The study of the biology of populations residing on specific continents has received support (e.g., Laughlin & Harper 1979; Salzano 1970), as has the study of biocultural factors—be they food use or disease—that affect the health status of populations and may contribute to evolutionary changes (Harris & Ross 1987; Swedlund & Armelagos 1990). Symposia that explore the biological bases of human behavior, from its first serious articulation in evolutionary terms (Spuhler 1967) to current sociobiological exposition (Hausfater & Hrdy 1984), have also been funded. The foundation has also organized symposia that focused on the behavior, ecology, and biological history of nonhuman primates (Szathmary 1991), and it has been critically important in sponsoring developments in hominid paleontology (Howell 1991).

Infrastructure Support and the Small-Grants Program
Assisting intellectual developments through a variety of means is a major achievement of the Wenner-Gren Foundation. However, ensuring that intellectual advances have a lasting impact on a discipline also requires

direction of funds to allow structural developments that cut across university, national, and international boundaries. The foundation has provided financial support for more than fifteen conferences between 1945 and 1985. The themes reflect traditional areas of interest, including growth and development, regional adaptations, genetic structure of isolate populations, demography and population structure, culture change and stress, the impact of stress on health and physiological function, and sociobiology. Infrastructural assistance has included small subventions to assist student attendance at conferences, funds for at least initial publication of national and international newsletters (e.g., of International Association of Human Biologists and the Canadian Association for Physical Anthropology), and even funds to allow the publication of a full volume of professional journals, such as *Human Biology* (1953) and *The Yearbook of Physical Anthropology* in the periods 1945–1951 and 1962–1963. These kinds of assistance allowed fledgling publications and professional associations to develop until their own revenues were sufficient to handle the costs of communication among professionals. Befitting a foundation that understands anthropology, the Wenner-Gren Foundation has also provided funds for celebration. Thus, the fiftieth-anniversary celebrations of the American Association of Physical Anthropologists were made possible largely through the support of the foundation (cf. the special issue of the *American Journal of Physical Anthropology* Vol. 56, 1981).

With reference to aid to scholarship at the grass-roots level, the small-grants program has served a critical function by providing seed money for pilot projects. If these are successful, then application to larger government funding agencies is warranted. The list of biological anthropologists who have received support from the foundation reads like a who's who of the discipline (cf. Szathmary 1991) and includes a Nobel Laureate, individual recipients in more than eighteen countries, and scores of students engaged in doctoral research. Many have also received financial assistance for publishing books, so that the foundation can justly claim a role in fostering the primary-research enterprise as well as making available its outcome to the larger scholarly community.

Conclusions

The Wenner-Gren Foundation has been instrumental in the development of biological anthropology, given its role in fostering a new understanding about the evolutionary process and its operation in human biological history, and its influence on how biological anthropologists conceptualize, analyze, and interpret information. The foundation has never been passive, but neither has it been directive, for its aim has been to identify biological anthropologists with insights into the research needs of their discipline. It has traditionally bet on young scholars who otherwise might not have received start-up funds for risky projects. By bringing together young and established scholars in various international symposia, conferences, and other meetings, the foundation has enhanced intensive exchange of ideas. By assisting with the publication of the results, it has informed a wide readership about new developments. The foundation provided what was needed at critical times in the history of biological anthropology and continues to support research on themes that expand understanding of the biocultural nature of humanity.

Emöke J.E. Szathmary

See also Viking Fund Medal

Bibliography
P.T. Baker & J.S. Weiner (eds): *The biology of human adaptability*. Oxford: Clarendon Press, 1964; J.W. Dodds: *The several lives of Paul Fejos*. New York: Wenner-Gren Foundation, 1973; M.S. Goldstein: Recent trends in physical anthropology. *American Journal of Physical Anthropology* 26:191–390, 1940; M. Goodman & R. Tashian (eds): *Molecular anthropology: Molecular evolution in the ascent of the primates*. New York: Plenum Press, 1976; M. Harris & E.B. Ross (eds): *Food and evolution*. Philadelphia: Temple University Press, 1987; G.A. Harrison & A.J. Boyce (eds): *The structure of human populations*. London: Oxford University Press, 1972; G. Hausfater & S.B. Hrdy (eds): *Infanticide*. Hawthorne, New York: Aldine, 1984; F.C. Howell: Paleoanthropology: Reflections on fifty years of anthropology and the role of the Wenner-Gren Foundation. In: *Report for 1990 and 1991* (Fiftieth Anniversary Issue). New York: Wenner-Gren Foundation, 1991, pp. 6–17.
E. Hunt Jr.: The old physical anthropology. *American Journal of Physical Anthropology* 56:339–346, 1981; A.L. Kroeber (ed): *Anthropology today: An encyclopedic inventory*. Chicago: University of Chicago Press, 1953; W.S. Laughlin & A.B. Harper (eds): *The first Americans: Origins,*

affinities, and adaptations. New York: Fischer, 1979; A.F. Roche & F. Falkner (eds): *Nutrition and malnutrition: Identification and measurements*. New York: Plenum Press, 1974; F. Salzano (ed): *The ongoing evolution of Latin American populations*. Springfield, Illinois: Thomas, 1970; F. Salzano (ed): *The role of natural selection in human evolution*. Amsterdam: North-Holland, 1975; J.S. Spuhler (ed): *Genetic diversity and human behavior*. Chicago: Aldine, 1967.

A. Swedlund & G. Armelagos (eds): *Disease in populations in transition*. New York: Bergin & Garvey, 1990; E.J.E. Szathmary: Biological anthropology: Reflections on fifty years of anthropology and the role of the Wenner-Gren Foundation. In: *Report for 1990 and 1991*. (Fiftieth anniversary issue). New York: Wenner-Gren Foundation, 1991, pp. 18–30; S.L. Washburn: The strategy of physical anthropology. In: A.L. Kroeber (ed) *Anthropology today: An encyclopedic inventory*. Chicago: University of Chicago Press, 1953, pp. 714–727; S.L. Washburn (ed): *Classification and human evolution*. London: Methuen, 1964; J.S. Weiner & J. Huizinga (eds): *The assessment of population affinities in man*. Oxford: Clarendon Press, 1972.

Wistar Institute of Anatomy and Biology
During his tenure (1808–1818) as professor of anatomy at the University of Pennsylvania, Caspar Wistar (1761–1818) founded a museum of anatomical specimens modeled along the lines of the English anatomist John Hunter's (1728–1793) collection in London. After his death, Wistar's collection was presented to the University of Pennsylvania, where it was fostered by the surgeon Philip Syng Physick (1768–1837) and subsequently enlarged by his successor, William Edmonds Horner (1793–1853). Later, in 1891, Wistar's grandnephew Isaac Jones Wistar (1827–1905) provided an endowment for the construction and maintenance of a building to house the Wistar-Horner Collection and a research facility that was henceforth to be known as the Wistar Institute. Although part of the University of Pennsylvania, the institute's charter ensured its financial and administrative independence; it was incorporated in 1892 and formally opened in 1893, with Harrison Allen (1841–1897) installed as its first director. Allen, however, resigned the following year and was replaced by Horace W. Jayne (1857–1911), who served until 1905, when the assistant director, Milton J. Greenman

(1866–1937), was promoted to director. Following his death in 1937, the directorship passed to Edmond J. Farris (1907–1958), who served until 1957, whereupon the office passed to Hilary Koprowski (1917–). Like Greenman, her tenure spanned the better part of three decades (1957–1991). Since her departure, the director has been Giovanni Rovera (1940–).

The institute became an important center for biological research and also the publisher of several major scientific journals: the *Journal of Morphology*, founded by Charles Otis Whitman (1842–1910) in 1887 and assigned to the institute in 1908; the *Journal of Comparative Neurology*, founded by C. Judson Herrick (1860–1960) in 1901 and assigned to the institute in 1908; the *American Journal of Anatomy* and the *Anatomical Record*, founded in 1901 and 1906, respectively, by members of the American Association of Anatomists and assigned to the institute in 1920; the *Journal of Experimental Zoology*, acquired by the institute in 1932; and the *American Journal of Physical Anthropology*, founded by Aleš Hrdlička (1869–1943) in 1918, acquired by the institute in 1928, and subsequently adopted by the American Association of Physical Anthropologists as its official organ. However, in 1980, the Wistar Press was disbanded, and the publication rights for all of the "Wistar journals" were acquired by the New York publishing firm of Alan R. Liss Inc., which later in the decade became a division (Wiley-Liss) of the New York publisher John Wiley & Sons.

Frank Spencer

See also Allen, Harrison; American Association of Physical Anthropologists; Hrdlička, Aleš

Bibliography
A. Hrdlička: *Physical anthropology: Its scope and aims; its history and present status in United States*. Philadelphia: Wistar Institute of Anatomy & Biology, 1919, pp. 110–111; N.A. Michels: For the advancement of anatomical science. In: J.E. Pauly (ed) *The American Association of Anatomists, 1888–1987: Essays on the history of anatomy in America and a report on the membership past and present*. Baltimore: Williams & Wilkins, 1987, pp. 25–29.

Woodward, (Sir) Arthur Smith (1864–1944)
Born in Macclesfield, Cheshire, England, Woodward entered Owen's College of the then newly established Victoria University of

Manchester (now Manchester University) in 1880, studying geology and paleontology under William Boyd Dawkins (1837–1929). However, in 1882 (prior to completing his degree and with the full approval of Dawkins), he successfully competed for a vacant position in the Department of Geology of the Natural History Museum (NHM), also called the British Museum of Natural History, in South Kensington, London. Woodward began working at the NHM in August 1882; ten years later he was promoted to assistant keeper, and in 1901 he succeeded Henry Woodward (1832–1921) as keeper—a position he retained until his retirement in 1923. (It was while working under Henry Woodward, that he became generally known as "Smith Woodward," which served to differentiate him from his boss.)

Woodward's scientific reputation was founded primarily on his work on Paleozoic and Mesozoic fish. In fact, by the early 1900s he had several hundred publications to his credit, many of which represent the product of fieldwork conducted in Europe and North America. He had also accrued by that time a number of prestigious awards, including the Wollaston (1889) and Lyell (1896) Medals of the Geological Society of London, an honorary doctorate from Glasgow University (1900), and a coveted Fellowship of the Royal Society (1901).

Although by the early 1900s he was known primarily as a paleoichthyologist, Woodward had also produced a number of studies of higher vertebrates; a notable example is *A Catalogue of British Fossil Vertebrata* (1890). Also worthy of note is his popular textbook *Outlines of Vertebrate Palaeontology* (1898). This latter work is of some importance since it reveals a latent interest in paleoanthropology, and more particularly a sympathetic inclination to eolithic theory.[1] It is likely it was this latter predisposition that led to his involvement in the excavations at Piltdown (1912–1916) and the subsequent decision to take on the responsibility of reconstructing the cranial fragments found there (cf. Dawson & Woodward 1913). These highly controversial remains became the focus of an intense international debate that continued to rage into the 1920s and 1930s. Throughout this protracted debate Woodward remained loyal to his original interpretation of the Piltdown remains and reconstruction (cf. Dawson & Woodward 1913), which he dubbed *Eoanthropus,* or "Dawn Man." As this name indicates, Woodward regarded the Piltdown

remains as an early ancestor of modern humans. However, in 1953, long after Woodward's death, the entire assemblage at Piltdown was shown to be bogus. Although this finding initially cast a shadow of suspicion over Woodward, there is, in fact, every reason to suppose that he had been the unwitting dupe of Charles Dawson (1864–1916), the discoverer of the Piltdown site (cf. Spencer 1990).

During the years immediately preceding his retirement in 1923, Woodward received a number of additional awards, which included the Royal Medal from the Royal Society (1917) and the Prix Cuvier from the Académie Français (1918). He received his knighthood in 1924 and spent the remaining years of his life at Hayward's Heath in East Sussex. Just prior to his death in 1944 he completed a small book titled *The Earliest Englishman* that summarized his work at Piltdown. This book was published in 1948 with a Foreword by Arthur Keith (1866–1955), his main antagonist in the earlier Piltdown debates.

Woodward died at his home in Hayward's Heath on 2 September 1944.

Frank Spencer

Endnote

1. Following the acceptance of evidence demonstrating the contemporaneity of human artifacts with the remains of extinct quadrupeds in 1859, there was a growing conviction among scientists such as the French prehistorian Abbé Louis Bourgeois (1819–1878) that the stone tools of the earliest humans (i.e., the hypothesized form that stood between the apes and man) would have been crudely manufactured and quite distinct from the tool types associated with the Paleolithic (cf. Bourgeois 1873). Early in the 1880s, the French prehistorian Gabriel de Mortillet (1821–1898) gave further impetus to this movement when he proposed the term "Eolithique" or "Dawn Stone Age" to characterize this early-transitional tool industry (cf. Mortillet 1880). Despite the fact that many scientists vigorously rejected eoliths as nothing more than natural objects, the movement continued to prosper. During the last quarter of the nineteenth century, the eolithic movement was advanced in Britain principally through the work of the Oxford geologist Joseph Prestwich (1812–1896) and the amateur archeologist Benjamin Harrison (1837–1921). Their work attracted the

attention of Woodward. For further details on the British eolithic movement, see Spencer 1988.

See also Dawkins, (Sir) William Boyd; Keith, (Sir) Arthur; Paleoanthropology Theory; Piltdown

Bibliography
SELECTED WORKS
Catalogue of the fossil fishes in the British Museum (Natural History). 4 vols. London: British Museum (Natural History), 1889–1901; *Outlines of vertebrate palaeontology for students of zoology.* Cambridge University Press, 1898; On the jaw of an anthropoid ape (*Dryopithecus*) from the Upper Pliocene of Lérida (Spain). *Quarterly Journal of the Geological Society of London* 70:316–320, 1914; On a bone implement from Piltdown (Sussex). *Quarterly Journal of the Geological Society of London* 71:144–149, 1915; Fourth note on the Piltdown gravel, with evidence of a second skull of *Eoanthropus dawsonii. Quarterly Journal of the Geological Society of London* 73:1–10, 1918a; *A guide to the fossil remains of man in the Department of Geology and Palaeontology in the British Museum (Natural History).* London: British Museum (Natural History), 1918b.
A new cave man from Rhodesia. *Nature* 108:371–372, 1921; *The earliest Englishman.* London: Watts, 1948; (with C. Dawson) On the discovery of a Palaeolithic human skull and mandible in a flint-bearing gravel overlying the Wealden (Hastings Beds) at Piltdown, Fletching (Sussex). *Quarterly Journal of the Geological Society of London* 69:117–144, 1913; (with C. Dawson) Supplementary note on the discovery of a Palaeolithic human skull and mandible at Piltdown (Sussex). *Quarterly Journal of the Geological Society of London* 70:82–99, 1914; (with C.D. Sherborn) *A catalogue of British fossil vertebrata.* London: British Museum (Natural History), 1890.

ARCHIVAL SOURCES
1. A.S. Woodward Correspondence: Archives of the Department of Palaeontology, Natural History Museum, Cromwell Road, London SW7 5BD, England; 2. A.S. Woodward Papers: D.M.S. Watson Library, University College London, Gower Street, London WC1E 6BT, England.

PRIMARY AND SECONDARY SOURCES
L. Bourgeois: Sur les silex considérées comme portant les marques d'un travail humain et découvertes dans le terrain miocène de Thenay. In: *Comptes rendus du Congrès International d'Anthropologie et d'Archéologie Préhistorique (Bruxelles 1872).* Bruxelles: Murquardt, 1873, pp. 81–92; C. Forster Cooper: Arthur Smith Woodward, 1864–1944. *Obituary Notices of Fellows of the Royal Society* 5:79–112, 1945–1948; G. de Mortillet: *Le préhistique: Antiquité de l'homme.* Paris: Reinwald, 1880; F. Spencer: Prologue to a scientific forgery. The British eolithic movement—from Abbeville to Piltdown. In: G.W. Stocking, Jr. (ed) *Bones, bodies, behavior: Essays on biological anthropology.* Madison: University of Wisconsin, 1988, pp. 84–116; F. Spencer: *Piltdown: A scientific forgery.* London: Oxford University Press, 1990; W.T. Stearn: *The Natural History Museum at South Kensington: A history of the British Museum (Natural History), 1753–1980.* London: Heinemann, 1981, pp. 235–237.

Wu Rukang (1916–)

Born in Wujin County, Jiangsu Province, China, Wu Rukang (also known as Woo Ju-Kang) received a B.A. from the National Central University, Nanking, in 1940. After graduation, he worked with Wu Dingliang (1894–1969) (also known as Woo Ting-Lian) in the Section of Ethnology and Anthropology of the National Research Institute of History and Philology (IHP), Academia Sinica, in Sichuan. Under Wu Dingliang, who had received his training in London, principally under the statistician-anthropologist Geoffrey M. Morant (1899–1964), Wu was introduced to a broad range of anthropological research. Although the outbreak of the Sino-Japanese War in 1937 seriously hampered Wu Dingliang's research agenda, a modest amount of fieldwork was achieved during this period (1937–1945). For example, in 1941, Wu Rukang assisted his mentor in a number of field surveys conducted on different ethnic communities in Guizhou Province, which led to the publication of his first scientific paper (cf. Wu 1941b).
In 1946, following the Japanese retreat from China, the IHP was transferred to Taiwan. At this juncture, Wu Dingliang moved to Zhejiang University in Hangzhou, while Wu Rukang embarked for the United States, where arrangements had been made for him to study and work on a doctorate in physical

anthropology at Washington University Medical School in St. Louis, Missouri. His thesis adviser was Mildred Trotter (1899–1991). During his sojourn (1947–1949) in the United States, Wu Rukang spent the summer of 1948 studying paleoanthropology under the direction of T. Dale Stewart (1901–) at the National Museum of Natural History, Smithsonian Institution, Washington, D.C. The following summer, he received his Ph.D. degree and returned to China, where he was appointed professor of anatomy at Dalian Medical College (DMC) in Liaoning Province. Then, in 1956, he accepted the position of research professor at the Institute of Vertebrate Paleontology and Paleoanthropology (IVPP) of the Academia Sinica in Beijing—a position he continues to occupy. During the period of reconstruction that followed the establishment of the People's Republic of China in 1949, he played a vital role in resuscitating anthropological research, particularly in the areas of human paleontology, paleoanthropology, and paleoprimatology.

It was principally his energy and vision that led to a protracted, and successful, search for early hominid sites in the eastern and southern provinces of China during the next three decades. The material recovered spans much of the Pleistocene and ranges from *Homo erectus* (e.g., Hexian, Anhui Province), early archaic *Homo sapiens* (e.g., Mapa, Kwangtung Province), and late archaic *Homo sapiens* (e.g., Liujiang, Guangxi) to early modern *Homo sapiens* (cf. Wu Rukang 1982). It was from the perspective of this emerging assemblage that Wu Rukang and Wu Xinzhi became ardent supporters of the hypothesis of multiregional continuity as an explanation for the origin of modern *Homo sapiens* (cf. Wolpoff, Wu Xinzhi, & Thorne 1984). In addition to this work, he was also instrumental in organizing a new excavation and comprehensive study of the Zhoukoudian site in the 1970s. The result of this work provided a series of chronometric data for the different layers of the deposits in the cave and showed that the indigenous *H. erectus* had probably occupied the site for at least 200 ky (cf. Wang Linghong 1989).

In the late 1950s, Wu Rukang made a detailed study of *Gigantopithecus*, which was published as a monograph in 1962. This work is regarded as a classic work in Chinese paleoanthropology. During the 1970s, extensive excavations were conducted in Lufeng County in Yunnan Province by Wu Rukang and his associates at the IVPP, which yielded a wealth of fossil hominoid material. Initially,

Wu Rukang and his team separated the Lufeng assemblage into two genera: *Sivapithecus* and *Ramapithecus* (cf. Etler 1984; Wu Rukang, Xu Qinghua, & Lu Qingwu 1986), but later studies led Wu Rukang (1987) to the proposition of collapsing the two groups into a new and single genus *Lufengpithecus*—a move generally endorsed by the international community. But whatever the systematic position of this taxon may be, it is clear that the Lufeng material has provided crucial insights into the complex and tantalizing evolutionary history of the Miocene Hominoidea in Asia.

During the 1980s, Wu Rukang also worked on the anthropology of Chinese minority groups. It was in the context of this interest in contemporary human biology that he introduced the term "neoanthropology" to embrace all of the subfields of biological anthropology. Succinctly, he defines this umbrella term as the "study of the process and changes of physical characteristics of [modern] humankind as a whole" (Wu Rukang 1988:268; 1991). The term is an attractive one, though it remains to be seen whether it will be adopted by the international community.

In addition to his own scientific research agenda, Wu Rukang, in spite of imposed government restrictions, has worked tirelessly to sustain and promote anthropology in China as both an academic and a practical discipline. Furthermore, during the early period of reconstruction, when the country was essentially insulated from the rest of the world, he came to represent an important link with the international community, providing a regular flow of information from the IVPP on Chinese research efforts and discoveries. Since the early 1980s, many of the earlier restrictions have been lifted, resulting in a sudden florescence of academic departments of anthropology throughout the country. Responding to these changes, he founded in 1982 the anthropological journal *Acta Anthropologica Sinica*. Although Wu Dingliang had established a similar journal in the 1930s, only two numbers were issued before it ceased publication. Wu Rukang's journal, which continues to be published, serves a national and an international audience. Besides being honorary president of the Chinese Association of Anatomical Sciences, he is also a member of the Chinese Academy of Sciences.

Frank Spencer

See also Asian Paleoanthropology; China; *Gigantopithecus*; Stewart, T(homas) Dale; Trotter, Mildred; Zhoukoudian

Bibliography
SELECTED WORKS

The atlas and axis in Chinese. *Anthropological Journal* (Academia Sinica) 2:47–57, 1941a; Notes on the vertex whorl of the Chinese and two other racial groups in Kweichow, China. *Anthropological Journal* (Academia Sinica) 2:43–46, 1941b; Anterior and posterior mediopalatine bones. *American Journal of Physical Anthropology* 6 (n.s.):209–224, 1948; New discoveries about *Sinanthropus pekinensis* in Choukoutien. *Scientia Sinica* 3:335–351, 1954; *Dryopithecus* teeth from Keiyuan, Yunnan Province. *Vertebrata PalAsiatica* 1:25–32, 1957; Tzeyang Paleolithic man: Earliest representative of modern man in China. *American Journal of Physical Anthropology* 16:459–471, 1958.

Fossil human skull of early paleoanthropic stage found at Mapa, Shaoquan, Kwangtung Province. *Vertebrata PalAsiatica* 4:176–183, 1959; The mandibles and dentition of *Gigantopithecus*. *Palaeontologia Sinica* (n.s.). No. 11. Beijing: Science Press, 1962; Discovery of the mandible of *Sinanthropus lantianensis* in Shensi Province, China. *Current Anthropology* 5:98–101, 1964; Fossil finds: The skull of Lantian man. *Current Anthropology* 7:83–86, 1966a; The hominid skull of Lantian, Shensi. *Vertebrata PalAsiatica* 10:1–22, 1966b.

Paleoanthropology in the new China. In: L-K. Königsson (ed) *Current argument on early man*. Report from a Nobel Symposium. London: Pergamon, 1980, pp. 182–206; Paleoanthropology in China, 1949–1979. *Current Anthropology* 23:473–477, 1982; (ed) *Multidisciplinary study of the Peking Man site at Zhoukoudian*. Beijing: Science Press, 1985; A revision of the classification of the Lufeng geat apes. *Acta Anthropologica Sinica* 6:265–271, 1987; Paleoanthropology and neoanthropology. *International Social Science Journal* 116:265–270, 1988; *Neoanthropology*. Anhui: Science & Technology Press, 1991; On the classification of subspecies of *Homo*. *Acta Anthropologica Sinica* 11:109–111, 1992.

(with Dong Xingren) Preliminary study of *Homo erectus* remains from Hexian, Anhui. *Acta Anthropologica Sinica* 1:2–13, 1982; (with Lin Shenglong) Peking Man. *Scientific American* 248:78–86, 1983; (with J.W. Olsen [eds]) *Palaeoanthropology and Palaeolithic archaeology in the People's Republic of China*. Orlando, Florida: Academic Press, 1985; (with Xu Qinghua & Lu Qingwu): Morphological features of *Ramapithecus* and *Sivapithecus* and their phylogenetic relationships: Morphology and comparison of the crania. *Acta Anthropologica Sinica* 2:1–10, 1983; (with Xu Qinghua & Lu Qingwu): Relationship between Lufeng *Sivapithecus* and *Ramapithecus* and their phylogenetic position. *Acta Anthropologica Sinica* 5:1–30, 1986; (with M. Wu & S. Zhang [eds]) *Early humankind in China*. Beijing Science Press, 1989.

SECONDARY SOURCES

D. Etler: The fossil hominoids of Lufeng, Yunnan Province, the People's Republic of China: A series of translations. *Yearbook of Physical Anthropology* 27:1–55, 1984; Wang Linghong: New progress in chronology in Chinese paleoanthropology. In: Wu Rukang et al. (eds) *Early humankind in China*. Beijing: Science Press, 1989, pp. 392–431; M.H. Wolpoff, Wu Xinzhi, & A.G. Thorne: Modern *Homo sapiens* origins: A general theory of hominid evolution involving the fossil evidence from east Asia. In: F. Smith & F. Spencer (eds) *The origins of modern humans: A world survey of the fossil evidence*. New York: Liss, 1984, pp. 411–483.

Wyman, Jeffries (1814–1874)

Born in Chelmsford, Massachusetts, Wyman entered Harvard University to study medicine in 1833. On receiving his M.D. in 1837, he became an assistant to his former anatomy professor, John Collins Warren (1778–1856), and soon thereafter curator of the Lowell Institute. In the summer of 1841, he made the first of many trips to Europe. On this occasion, after a short stay in Paris, he went to London, where he worked on the osteological collections housed in the Royal College of Surgeons of England, and became acquainted with the British paleontologist Richard Owen (1804–1892). From 1843 to 1848, he was professor of anatomy at the Hampden-Sydney Medical College in Richmond, Virginia. Thereafter, the remainder of his career unfolded at Harvard, where he succeeded Warren to the Hersey Professorship.

While modern biologists and physiologists might associate Wyman's name with mid-nineteenth century experiments on "spontaneous generation" (cf. Droesch 1962) and perhaps even remember that he was a correspondent of Charles Darwin (1809–1882) (cf. Dupree 1951, 1953), among anthropologists he is perhaps best remembered for his participation in the Webster-Parkman murder trial and for providing the first scientific description of the gorilla.

Following the first report in British geographer Richard Hakluyt's sixteenth-century compendium *The Principal Navigations* (1589), there had been repeated stories of a ferocious African ape (seemingly quite different from that of the chimpanzee), but it was not until the American missionary-physician Thomas Staughton Savage (1804–1880) brought the remains of such an animal to Boston that its existence was finally verified (cf. Savage 1847). Through his comparative studies, Wyman correctly determined that Savage's specimen was quite different from published accounts of both the African chimpanzee and the Asian orangutan. Contrary to Wyman, who believed the gorilla's skeleton deviated significantly from the human condition, Owen (based on drawings sent him by Savage) claimed that the animal had a greater affinity with Homo (cf. Owen 1848).

Following close on the heels of these events, Wyman was invited, along with the Harvard anatomist Oliver Wendell Holmes (1809–1894), to be an expert witness for the prosecution of John W. Webster, a chemist at Harvard, who had been charged with the murder of George Parkman in 1849. While Wyman's forensic analysis of the charred remains of Parkman's body was inconclusive, Webster was subsequently found guilty. (For further details of this trial and Wyman's involvement, see Bemis 1850.)

In 1866, when the Peabody Museum was founded as a result of a bequest to Harvard, Wyman was installed as its first director—a position he held until his death in 1874. In this capacity, he continued to make modest anthropological contributions, such as his anatomical evaluation of the celebrated Calaveras skull (in Whitney 1879) and his analysis of the freshwater shell mounds of Florida (1875).

Wyman died in Cambridge, Massachusetts, on 4 September 1874.

Frank Spencer

See also African Apes; Calaveras Skull; Hakluyt, Richard; Harvard University; Owen, (Sir) Richard; Warren, John Collins

Bibliography

SELECTED WORKS

A description of two additional crania of the "Engéena" (*Troglodytes gorilla*, Savage), from Gaboon, Africa. *American Journal of Science and Arts* 9:34–45, 1850; Observations on crania. *Proceedings of the Boston Society of Natural History* 11:440–462, 1868; Observations on crania and other parts of the skeleton. *Fourth Annual Report of the Peabody Museum*, pp. 10–24, 1871; *Freshwater shell mounds of the St. John's River, Florida.* Fourth Memoir of the Peabody Academy of Science. Salem, Masssachusetts: Peabody Academy, 1875; [Report on Calaveras skull]. In: J.D. Whitney: Auriferous gravels of the Sierra Nevada. *Memoirs of the Harvard Museum of Comparative Anatomy* 6:258–288, 1879; (with T.S. Savage) Notice of the external characters and habits of *Troglodytes gorilla*, a new species of orang from the Gaboon River, Africa. *Boston Journal of Natural History* 5:417–442, 1847.

PRIMARY SOURCES

R. Hakluyt: *The principal navigations, voiages, traffiques, and discoveries of the English nation.* London: Bishop & Newberie, 1589; R. Owen: Osteological contributions to the natural history of the chimpanzees (*Troglodytes*, Geoffroy) including the description of the skull of a large species (*Troglodytes gorilla*, Savage) discovered by Thomas S. Savage, M.D., in the Gaboon country, West Africa. *Transactions of the Zoological Society of London* 3:381–422, 1848; T.S. Savage: Notice of the external characters and habits of a new species of *Troglodytes* (*T. gorilla*, Savage) recently discovered by Dr. Savage near the River Gaboon, Africa. *Proceedings of the Boston Society of Natural History* 2:245–247, 1847.

SECONDARY SOURCES

G. Bemis: *Report of the case of John Webster, indicted for the murder of George Parkman.* Boston: Little, Brown, 1850; R.N. Droesch: Early American experiments on "spontaneous generation" by Jeffries Wyman, 1814–1874. *Journal of the History of Medicine and Allied Sciences* 17:326–332, 1962; A.H. Dupree: Some letters from Charles Darwin to Jeffries Wyman. *Isis* 42:104–110, 1951; A.H. Dupree: Jeffries Wyman's views on evolution. *Isis* 44:243–246, 1953; A. Gray: Jeffries Wyman. *Proceedings of the Boston Society of Natural History* 17:96–124, 1874; A.S. Packard: Memoir of Jeffries Wyman, 1814–1874. *National Academy of Sciences, Biographical Memoirs* 2:75–126, 1878; B.G. Wilder: Sketch of Dr. Jeffries Wyman. *Popular Science Monthly* 6:355–360, 1875.

Yarkho, Arkady Isaakovich (1903–1935)

Russian physical anthropologist Yarkho studied anthropology at Moscow University. He was secretary in chief of the *Journal of Anthropology*, which he reorganized and controlled from 1932 to 1935. He was also head of the Department of Racial Studies at the Museum of Anthropology at Moscow University. Although an ardent Marxist, he was not dogmatic, and as such he did much to modernize Soviet physical anthropology. His principal writings were leveled against archaic racial typologies. Indeed, many of his ideas are much in line with later cladistic reasoning in which he stressed the importance of assigning different taxonomic weight to various somatic characters. Besides studying the racial affinities of various ethnic populations of the USSR (mainly Turkish-speaking groups), Yarkho also studied growth and demography. His principal monograph, a study of a small Siberian town, was published posthumously in 1947.

Alexander G. Kozintsev

See also Russia

Bibliography
Selected Works
   The Altai-Sayan Turks. Abakan: Khakassian Regional Publication, 1947.

Young, Robert Burns (1874–1949)

Born in Perth, Scotland, Young was educated at the Universities of Glasgow and Edinburgh. He went to South Africa in 1903. After a spell at the South African College, Cape Town, he became assistant professor of geology in 1904 at the Transvaal Technical Institute, forerunner of the South African School of Mines and Technology and then of the University of the Witwatersrand (UW) in Johannesburg. He filled the Chair of geology at UW from 1922 to 1934 and contributed an important work on the gold-bearing rocks of the Witwatersrand (Young 1917). He later researched the South African dolomite. Among Young's other writings was a biography of the pioneer geologist George W. Stow, who first made careful and systematic copies of protohistoric rock paintings in the caves of the southeastern Orange Free State and the northeastern Cape Colony in the nineteenth century (Young 1908).

Young was the professor of geology at UW, when the Taung skull came to light in November 1924, and he contributed importantly to the recovery of that skull. A fossil baboon cranium that had been recovered from the Buxton Limeworks in 1924 was removed to Johannesburg by E.G. Izod, a director of the Northern Lime Company. It was shown by his son to Josephine E. Salmons, a member in 1924 of the first Bachelor of "Medical" Science class, who in turn showed it to her professor, R.A. Dart (1893–1988) in the Anatomy Department of the UW Medical School. Dart enlisted the cooperation of Young who happened to be a consultant to the Northern Lime Company. Young requested A.F. Campbell, the General Manager of the Northern Lime Company, to arrange for any further specimens of fossil bones to be kept for Dart. Coincidentally, Young had been asked to investigate the lime deposits at Thoming, about 10 km south of Buxton, and at Boetsap further south along the Campbell Rand. Young agreed that, during his inspection of these sites, he would call on A.E. Spiers, the Works Manager of the Buxton Limeworks, to look out for further fossils.

On his visit in November 1924, Young inspected the site of the discovery. He examined a number of chunks of breccia which had been assembled in Spier's office, including a large endocranial cast which M. de Bruyn had blasted out a week or two earlier. Impressed by this specimen, Young selected it and a related piece of bone-bearing breccia to bring back to Dart and, indeed, these proved to be the parts of the famous hominid child. Young also chose some other fragments containing baboon bones for Dart. The larger pieces were handed to Dart on 28 November 1924.

It is clear that history should assign a greater role to Young in the chain of discovery of *Australopithecus* than has hitherto been recognized (Tobias 1984, 1990). Not only did he, as Dart said at the beginning, select the hominid and other remains which were to come to Dart, but he brought the *Australopithecus* skull back with him to Johannesburg and, jointly with Dart, manipulated the endocast and a piece containing the front of the calvaria and the face into perfect alignment with each other, as Dart acknowledged in a press interview on 4 February 1925.

Following the revelation of the high importance of the Taung child skull, Young made a study and took photographs of the tufa deposits and of the fossiliferous cave-earth of Buxton, Thoming, and Boetsap in February 1925. He presented a paper on his results to the Geological Society of South Africa on 20 April 1925 and stated that he had identified the very spot from which M. de Buyn had recovered the type skull of *Australopithecus africanus* (Young 1925). His paper included a careful description of the site, including the provenience of the skull *A. africanus*.

Young died in Johannesburg on 21 April 1949.

Phillip V. Tobias

See also Dart, Raymond A.; South Africa; Taung (formerly Taungs)

SELECTED WORKS

The life and work of George William Stow. London: Longmans, Green, 1908; *The Banket: a study of the auriferous conglomerates of the Witwatersrand, and associated rocks*. London: Gurney & Jackson, 1917; The calcareous tufa deposits of the Campbell Rand, from Boetsap to Taungs native reserve. *Transactions of the Geological Society of South Africa* 28:55–67, 1925.

PRIMARY AND SECONDARY SOURCES

Anon: Obituary of Professor R.B. Young. *The Star*, Johannesburg, 22 April 1949; R.A. Dart: *Australopithecus africanus, the man-ape of South Africa*. *Nature* 115:195–199, 1925; R.A. Dart & D. Craig: *Adventures with the missing link*. New York: Harper, 1959; *Dictionary of South African Biography*. Vol. 1. Pretoria: Human Sciences Research Council, 1968, pp. 892–893; B.K. Murray: *Wits: The early years*. Johannesburg: Witwatersrand University Press, 1982; P.V. Tobias: *Dart, Taung, and the 'missing link': an essay on the life and work of emeritus professor Raymond Dart*. Johannesburg: Witwatersrand University Press and Institute for the Study of Man in Africa, 1984; P.V. Tobias: When and by whom was the Taung skull discovered? In: L. Lara-Tapia (ed) *Para Conocer el Hombre*. Mexico, D.F.: Universidad Nacional Autónoma Mexico, 1990, pp.207–213.

Zhoukoudian

Located 48 km southwest of Beijing, the more than 50 m. thick karst deposits of Zhoukoudian (Choukoutien) have yielded what is still the world's single largest sample of *Homo erectus*. The Locality 1 site (see Fig. 1) of this fissure-cave complex was the site of the first truly multidisciplinary paleoanthropological investigation.

Begun originally as part of a wider paleontological exploration of northern China, excavations in the 1920s soon evolved into an international research effort. This began essentially with the activities of the Swedish geologist Johan Gunnar Andersson (1874–1960), who was informed by local villagers of

the existence of "Chicken Bone Hill." Acting on this information, Andersson organized a preliminary excavation of the site (1921–1923), which was carried out under the leadership of the Austrian geologist Otto Zdansky, who recovered an "anthropoid" tooth and quartz fragments that Andersson believed were artifacts. This led him to continue his search, which yielded another "anthropoid" tooth. In 1927, the Canadian anatomist Davidson Black (1884–1934) of the Peking Union Medical College recognized these as hominid teeth, which he attributed to a new genus and species, *Sinanthropus pekinensis*. This announcement led to a protracted investigation of Locality 1 (1927–1937). Although

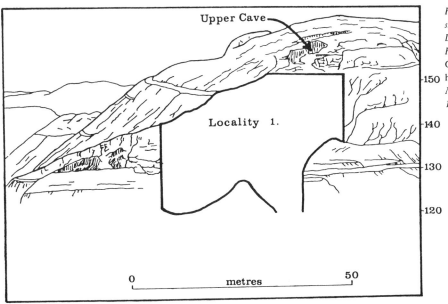

Fig. 1. Zhoukoudian site, showing positions of Locality 1 and Upper Cave. From K.P. Oakley et al.: Catalogue of fossil hominids. London: British Museum (Natural History), 1975.

Fig. 2. Section of fissure-fill deposits (Zhoukoudian), showing relative positions of hominid loci, layers, and levels. From K.P. Oakley et al.: Catalogue of fossil hominids. London: British Museum (Natural History), 1975.

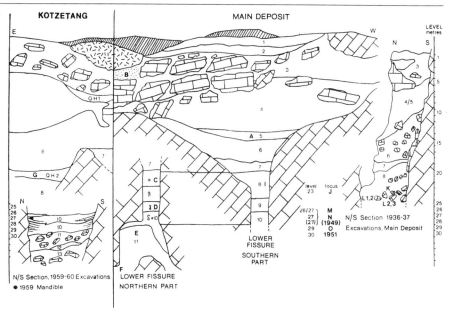

officially under the leadership of Black from 1927 to 1934, and then the German anatomist Franz Weidenreich (1873–1948) from 1935 to 1937, along with codirector Weng Wenhao of the Cenozoic Research Laboratory (CRL), the initial fieldwork was done largely under the supervision of Yang Zhongjian (also known as C.C. Young) (1897–1979), who was followed by Pei Wenzhong (also known as W.C. Pei) (1904–1982) from 1929 to 1934, and by Jia Lanpo from 1935 to 1937. The CRL was founded in 1927 under the auspices of the Geological Survey of China, and later, in 1953, it was reorganized as the Institute of Vertebrate Palaeontology of the Academia Sinica, which was renamed in 1959 the Institute of Vertebrate Paleontology and Paleoanthropology.

Prior to 1929, little attention had been given to the recovery of cultural remains. It was at this juncture that Pei and the French paleontologist Pierre Teilhard de Chardin (1881–1955) began a conscientious survey of Locality 1 deposits with dramatic results (Pei 1931; Teilhard de Chardin & Pei 1932). In 1936, Jia was responsible for introducing a grid system, which ensured a more systematic and scientifically controlled excavation. Jia's system involved laying out meter squares and working in units of 1 m depth, known as levels (*vide infra*).

In addition to Locality 1, other sites in the Zhoukoudian area were identified. These localities were also given a number (1–24), which in most cases was correlated with a particular stratigraphic unit at Locality 1, which had been divided into a system of "Layers," "Levels," and "Loci."

The Layers referred to natural lithostratigraphic units and were originally grouped into 10 layers, which in turn were grouped into three loosely defined units that have produced the majority of the evidence for a hominid presence at Zhoukoudian. Almost all of the paleoanthropological material derives from Layers 1–10: with Layers 1–3 containing hominid fossils, artifacts, and indications of fire; Layers 4–10 essentially the same as 1–3; and Layers 11–13 containing only artifacts and mammalian fossils. With the resumption of excavations at Zhoukoudian after World War II, the number of Layers was increased to 17 or 18. The Levels refer to twenty-nine arbitrary 1 m thick units that were used to subdivide the Layers. A lettered Locus (A–F) designated areas where hominid remains were relatively abundant or complete. In retrospect, this latter system proved to be confusing, since the first relatively complete skull was found at Locus E, while a similarly well-preserved cranium had been found earlier at Locus D but remained unrecognized until laboratory preparation began. By 1937, when work was brought to a halt, the excavations had reached the bottom of Level 29, in Layer 10. All of the material found up to that point is listed in Weidenreich (1936, 1937, 1941a, 1943). (See Table 1 for a summary of the chronology of events and discoveries at Zhoukoudian.)

The first major discovery of hominid remains—namely, a relatively complete skullcap, was made by Pei in 1929. Eventually, more than forty individuals were recovered from Locality 1. In 1930, excavations were

TABLE 1. Chronology of Events Associated with Research at Zhoukoudian

Date	Event
960–1274	Song Dynasty lime kiln operations at Zhoukoudian.
1900	The German physician K.A. Haberer purchases "Dragon Bones" from Beijing area drug stores.
1903	Haberer returns to Germany and donates fossils to the paleontologist Max Schlosser. Schlosser identifies lower M3 as that of an "ape-man."
1918	J.G. Andersson (director of the Geological Survey of Sweden) assumes position as a mining adviser to the Chinese Department of Agriculture and Commerce in Beijing, and begins inquiries about possible fossiliferous sites in China.
1919	The Canadian anatomist Davidson Black begins his tenure at the Peking Union Medical College.
1921	The Austrian paleontologist Otto Zdansky arrives in China. At the urging of Andersson, he conducts preliminary excavations at Zhoukoudian. Walter Granger, attached to the Third Asiatic Expedition of the American Museum of Natural History, visits Andersson and Zdansky.
1923	Zdansky returns to Sweden and publishes a description of Jigu Shan fauna. Although he notes the quartz artifacts found by Andersson, he omits to mention the "anthropoid" teeth recovered at Zhoukoudian.
	Pierre Teilhard de Chardin arrives in China and begins a survey in Inner Mongolia (Ordos) with Emile Licent.
1926	Davidson Black announces the earlier discovery of the Zhoukoudian hominid teeth at a meeting of the Geological Survey of China in Beijing. Black also publishes a paper reaffirming his support for the idea that Central Asia is the most likely geographic origin of hominids.
1927	The Chinese geologist Li Jie and the Swedish paleontologist Birger Bohlin arrive at Zhoukoudian.
	Black assigns the Zhoukoudian hominid teeth to *Sinanthropus pekinensis*.
	An agreement is signed between Chinese and foreign workers to establish the Cenozoic Research Laboratory.
	Organized fieldwork begins at Zhoukoudian.
	Black leaves China for a two-year trip to North America and Europe, raising money and support for his new taxon and research at Zhoukoudian.
1928	C.C. Young (Yang Zhongjian) returns from graduate studies with Schlosser in Munich. He replaces Li Jie as leader of excavations at Zhoukoudian.
1929	Teilhard de Chardin and Young establish the first ten levels of Locality 1.
	W.C. Pei is appointed to direct excavations at Locality 1.
	Pei discovers a calotte in Layer 9 (Locus E).
1930	A calotte recovered at the boundary between Layers 8 and 9 (Locus D) is recognized in the laboratory.
	Excavation of the Upper Cave begins.
1931	Jia Lanpo arrives at Locality 1.
	2 "quartz" horizons excavated in Pigeon Hall.
	Henri Breuil attends conference hosted by Geological Survey of China and examines the Zhoukoudian fossils and declares the presence of stone artifacts.
1932	Systematic trenching and daily photographic records are implemented at Jia Lanpo's recommendation.
	Locality 15 is discovered.
1933	Pulley basket system is introduced at Locality 1.
	"Old Man" (Skull 1 cranium: Ckn.UC.101) is discovered in the Upper Cave. Eventually six individuals are recovered.
	Excavation begins at Locality 13, which is determined to be older than Locality 1.
1934	Work is concentrated at Locality 1 to the exclusion of all other localities.
	Davidson Black dies at his desk on March 15.
	Franz Weidenreich (then occupying a visiting professor position at the University of Chicago) is selected as Black's replacement.
1935	Excavation begins at Locality 15. At Locality 1 excavations reach Layer 6.
	Locality 18 (Huiyu) is discovered by Jia.
	Weidenreich arrives at Zhoukoudian.

TABLE 1. continued	*Date* *Event*

Date	Event
1936	Complete mandible discovered at Locality 1. Layers 7, 8, and 9 are excavated revealing teeth, mandibulae, and a skull of *Macaca robustus*, plus cranial fragments of three individuals and flake artifacts.
	Weidenreich is reported to have been so excited by the find of L1 cranial fragment that he "put his pants on inside out" (Jia & Huang 1990).
1937	Cranial fragments of at least two individuals recovered from Layers 8 and 9.
	Japanese troops begin to occupy northern China.
	Japanese troops arrive at Locality 1.
1939	G.H.R. von Koenigswald arrives with Sangiran specimens and spends two months in Beijing.
	Breuil publishes his paper on "Bone and Antler Industry of Choukoutien" after a second trip to China.
1940	Weidenreich publishes paper maintaining that the paucity of post-cranial hominid remains at Zhoukoudian may indicate cannibalism.
1941	Analysis of ash discovered from "Quartz Horizon" (Layers 3 and 4) proves to be the result of fire. Weidenreich orders casts to be made of the Zhoukoudian fossils. Jia smuggles copies of the excavation grids of Locality 1 out of the Cenozoic Research Laboratory, which is now under Japanese occupation. Weidenreich leaves China having made arrangements for shipment of the original Zhoukoudian hominid material to the United States. This shipment never arrived.
1945	Weidenreich publishes his book *Apes*, *Giants*, *and Man*
1948	Weidenreich dies at his desk while preparing his monograph of the Solo hominids.
1949	Excavations resume at Zhoukoudian. Layers 11–13 recognized at Locality 1.
	A Communist government established in mainland China.
1952–1957	Excavations at Zhoukoudian suspended.
1953	Exhibition Hall opened at Zhoukoudian.
1955	The Zhoukoudian Exhibition Hall expanded.
1958	Excavations at Pigeon Hall are resumed under Jia.
1959	Pigeon Hall excavations recover an "old female" mandible from Layer 10.
	Debate emerges between Jia and Pei over the antiquity and interpretation of the Zhoukoudian artifacts—which continues to 1960.
1966	Pei commences new excavations at Locality 1 and discovers a tooth and frontal and occipital belonging to fragments of an individual found in 1934 and 1936 (now designated Skull 5).
1967	Locality 4 (New Cave) discovered. Excavation yields quartz artifacts and burnt bones.
1972–1973	Excavations at New Cave continue.
	Displays in the Exhibition Hall at Zhoukoudian arranged to fit ideology of the Cultural Revolution.
1978	Plan drawn up for new program of excavations (1978–1984).
	Exhibition Hall restructured to reflect a scientific rather than political perspective.
1980	Harry L. Shapiro of the American Museum of Natural History visits Beijing in an effort to reconstruct events relating to the disappearance of the Zhoukoudian hominid fossils.
1993	The Zhoukoudian International Palaeoanthropological Research Centre is established with the task of organizing future research at Zhoukoudian and other localities in northern China.

extended to an adjacent site (in the hill above Locality 1) called Upper Cave. There, at least seven anatomically modern *H. sapiens* individuals were discovered in association with bone artifacts. Weidenreich (1941b) later described three of the more complete crania as representatives of Mongolian, Eskimo, and Melanesian "racial" groups. Subsequent discussion of the Upper Cave finds has focused on their disputed dating and whether or not they represent a burial ground perhaps result-ing from intertribal conflict. Subsequent re-study of the Upper cave has downplayed a direct relationship between the skulls and extant populations.

Perhaps more than anyone else, Weidenreich was responsible for establishing the paleoanthropological importance of the Zhoukoudian site. His monographs on the dentitions, crania, and postcrania material have become classic works and still serve as the primary reference resource on the Zhoukoudian hominids. It is often overlooked that Weidenreich treated the entire 40 m sequence of hominids at this site as if it were a single synchronic sample. Furthermore, his collaboration with the paleontologist G.H.R. von Koenigswald (1902–1982) also established the essential similarities and presumed synchroneity of the Javanese and Chinese hominid fossils. Decades after his death, the Zhoukoudian and most of the Javanese hominids continue to be used to support the argument affirming stasis.

Although plans had apparently been made to secure the Zhoukoudian hominid fossils and to transport them to the United States for safekeeping, during the chaotic months following the Japanese attack on Pearl Harbor in 1941 these precious remains disappeared. Despite numerous attempts to reconstruct events, the fate of these fossils remains a mystery (cf. Shapiro 1974). But while the originals have been lost, there is an excellent collection of casts made by Weidenreich's Chinese assistants prior to the outbreak of the war and sent to the American Museum of Natural History in New York. Copies of these casts and of Weidenreich's reconstructions have since been widely distributed throughout the world.

After World War II (ca. 1949), work resumed at Zhoukoudian under the sole direction of Chinese investigators. A few new finds were made, and the stratigraphy was refined and extended to include three additional lower layers, as well as new areas of excavation at Pigeon Hall and New Cave.

During the 1950s, an exhibition facility was opened at Zhoukoudian. In addition to associated fossil mammals, Paleolithic artifacts were also displayed as evidence of the daily activities of the Zhoukoudian hominids. The displays of bone and stone artifacts served as a springboard for a debate over the antiquity and interpretation of the artifacts. For example, Pei Wenzhong took the position that the Zhoukoudian artifacts were among the oldest in the world, whereas Jia Lanpo and his then student Wang Jian argued that not only were they relatively recent, they also were more advanced than the Paleolithic industries from elsewhere in Asia and Africa. This debate, while curious in retrospect, actually emerged in the context of a growing acceptance of the South African australopithecines as hominids and the mounting evidence for the great antiquity of hominid evolution in Africa. As the twentieth century draws to a close, no Chinese scholars view Zhoukoudian as the oldest or most primitive evidence of Paleolithic culture, but many still believe that hominids may be more than 2.5 my old in China. In the early 1970s, a more political and much less publicized debate erupted over the use to which the Zhoukoudian evidence was to be put in the context of China's Cultural Revolution. During that period, the exhibits at Zhoukoudian, were first arranged to reflect Communist interpretations of the evolution of human society. Jia, however, who was by then the *de facto* head of scientific work at Zhoukoudian, eventually succeeded in having the exhibition arranged to reflect an emphasis on scientific, rather than political, considerations.

In 1993, the Zhoukoudian International Palaeoanthropological Research Centre was established and charged with conducting further research at Zhoukoudian and surrounding areas in northern China.

Geoffrey G. Pope

See also Andersson, Johan Gunnar; Asian Paleoanthropology; Australopithecines; Black, Davidson; China; *Homo erectus;* Koenigswald, (Gustav Heinrich) Ralph von; Pei Wenzhong; Teilhard de Chardin, Pierre; Weidenreich, Franz

Bibliography
J.G. Andersson: *Children of the yellow earth.* London: Macmillan, 1934; D. Black et al.: Fossil man in China: The Choukoutien Cave deposits with a synopsis of our present knowledge of the Late Cenozoic of China. *Memoir of the Geological Survey of China* 11:1–166, 1933; L.P. Jia & W.W. Huang: *The story of Peking Man.* London/New York: Beijing Foreign Languages Press & Oxford University Press, 1990; W.C. Pei: Notice of the discovery of quartz and other stone artifacts in the Lower Pleistocene hominid-bearing sediments of the Choukoutien Cave deposit. *Bulletin of the Geological Survey of China* 11:112, 1931; H.L. Shapiro: *Peking man.* New York: Simon & Schuster, 1974; P. Teilhard de Chardin & W.C. Pei: The lithic industry of the Sinanthropus deposits in Choukoutien. *Bulletin of the Geological Society of China* 11:315–364, 1932.

F. Weidenreich: The mandibles of *Sinanthropus pekinensis*: A comparative study. *Palaeontologia Sinica* 7 (Ser. D):1–162, 1936; F. Weidenreich: The denitition of *Sinanthropus pekinensis*: A comparative odontography of the hominids. *Palaeontologia Sinica* 1(n.s. D):1–121, 1937; F. Weidenreich: The extremity bones of *Sinanthropus pekinensis*. *Palaeontologia Sinica* 115 (n.s. D):1–150, 1941a; The Upper Palaeolithic man of the Upper Cave of Choukoutien and his bearing on the problem of the provenance of the American Indians. *Proceedings of the Sixth Pacific Science Congress* (1939) 4:165–168, 1941b; F. Weidenreich: The skull of *Sinanthropus pekinensis*: A comparative study on a primitive hominid skull. *Paleontologia Sinica* 10 (n.s. D):1–484, 1943; Wu Rukang & J.W. Olsen (eds): *Palaeoanthropology and Palaeolithic archaeology in the People's Republic of China*. Orlando, Florida, Academic Press, 1985.

Zuckerman, Solly (Lord) (1904–1993)

Born in Cape Town, South Africa, to eastern European Jewish parents who had fled Tsarist oppression in eastern Europe, Zuckerman received his B.A. in 1923 and his M.A. in 1925 from the University of Cape Town before leaving South Africa to complete the clinical part of his medical degree at University College Hospital, London. He then settled in England with an undeclared resolve never to return to South Africa. From 1928 to 1932, he served as anatomist to the Zoological Society of London and demonstrator in anatomy at University College, London. After a year (1933–1934) at Yale University in New Haven, Connecticut, he joined Wilfrid Edward Le Gros Clark's (1895–1971) department of anatomy at Oxford University, where he remained until his appointment in anatomy at the University of Birmingham (UB) (1945). During World War II, he served as scientific adviser to the Royal Air Force and the Allied Forces in the Mediterranean. In 1960, he was appointed chief scientific adviser to the British Ministry of Defence, a position he retained until his formal retirement in 1971. Following his retirement from the UB in 1968, he became professor-at-large at the University of East Anglia (1969–1993).

As this abbreviated review suggests, his long career involved not only doing science, but also a personal understanding of what science is about—that is, its application and the relationship between science and public affairs and between scientists and the machinery of government.

His scientific career had many different facets. From his start with the behavior and anatomy of the Cape baboons leading to extensive investigations of the anatomy, behavior, and evolution of the primates in general, he carried out, largely in parallel, an array of other scientific studies. These spanned a series of spectra, from mammalian egg cells to contraceptives; from the hormones of the endocrine system to the then new field of hormonal secretions of the brain; from the anatomy of the living primates to the then (and now) contentious story of human evolution as viewed from the fossils; and from highly applied work on the effect of blast upon organisms to warfare, disarmament, and the nuclear deterrent. Perhaps most potent of all, and certainly influencing all of his work in every field, was the introduction of measurement and statistical analysis, especially into those biological areas from which it had been, up to then, largely missing.

His contributions to anthropology were not to a narrow world of anthropological description, but to an enormously broad world of the study of humans through an understanding of their underlying biology and the ways in which that biology interacts in a wide range of related fields. That breadth was evident in his earlier activities working in Clark's department at Oxford (and was part of the reason for the sad break between them).

That breadth was later especially reflected in the remarkable developments in anatomy at the UB, through a career move that started in the offer of appointment before World War II, but was not completed until its end. The war interruption saw Zuckerman utilize the anthropological method for a wider topic: "the macabre and fascinating world of [human] destruction." He made an enormous contribution to the Allied war effort and was involved in bitter disputes about the value of strategic bombing and the uselessness of the bombing of civilian targets (his view later admitted to be correct by General Gerd von Rundstedt at one time overall commander of the German Western Front). As for so many of his generation, the war was a key stage in his life. On returning to the UB, his wider views prevailed.

Of his many scientific contributions, perhaps three summarize his career. The first relates to the mammalian oocyte. The conventional wisdom had been that every female mammal is born with a finite stock of germ cells. But a group of American anatomists had proposed that this was not so, that new oocytes could be produced in the adult animal. In a career-long series of studies, Zuckerman eventually found evidence, much of it based upon careful quantitative investigation with many colleagues and students, supporting the older hypothesis, which is now generally acknowledged as correct.

A second major problem upon which he worked was the pituitary gland. The idea had gained currency that the brain controlled the pituitary, at least in part, through substances produced in the hypothalamus and transported to the anterior pituitary in the bloodstream through a special local set of blood vessels passing between the two. He challenged this view, but, in this case, it was Zuckerman who eventually had to change his mind.

A third major problem in which he was interested related to the views of human evolution current during much of the twentieth century. In particular, he took issue not only with the idea that the South African australopithecines were bipedal in the human manner, but also with the selective presentation of data for corroboration, with the use of the unsupported anecdote, and with the often unreservedly anthropomorphic nature of many human evolutionary studies themselves.

In this third case, his studies and those of his colleagues and students have generally been ignored, even denigrated. However, since the late 1980s assessments remove the South African australopithecines from a direct place on the human lineage—though there are still those who disagree. The new views do not utilize Zuckerman's work. Though they do not support the old idea of the South African australopithecines as simply human, neither do they mark them as simply apes. They are seen as functionally and uniquely different from both. But though it is the new work that is quoted as general support for this view, it is the old work of Zuckerman and his colleagues that first provided the evidence. It is of special interest that studies in the 1990s of these fossil postcranial remains by Zuckerman's students, and by Zuckerman's students' students (e.g., Oxnard & Hoyland-Wilks 1994; Kidd, O'Higgins, & Oxnard 1994; Kidd 1995), using what have been styled as the new morphometrics and biomechanics—techniques of which he himself was not aware—are starting to indicate in some detail just what were the unique functional adaptations of those ancient fossils. Even those of contrary view are now starting to discover that much anatomical evidence, for example from fossil foot fragments found long ago but described only in 1995, show that the australopithecine "while bipedal, was equipped to include arboreal, climbing activities in its locomotor repertoire. Its foot has departed to only a small degree from that of the chimpanzee. It is becoming clear that *Australopithecus* [*africanus*] was likely not an obligate terrestrial biped,

but rather a facultative biped and climber" (Clarke & Tobias 1995). This conclusion is further supported by new studies of a 4.0 my old hominid tibia from Kenya, which show that a much older species (*Australopithecus anamensis*) was bipedal (Leakey et al. 1995). This new Kanapoi tibia was therefore more like humans than *africanus* and this confirms what Patterson and Howells (1967) already knew about the humeral fragment discovered at Kanapoi in the late 1960s—that it is almost indistinguishable in shape from many modern human humeri. It thus preempted *africanus* humeri, which are quite different (cf. Oxnard 1975a). Zuckerman would not have been surprised at the 1995 conclusions; he knew many years ago that this is what the older evidence had always indicated, if only people would be willing to look (e.g., Oxnard 1975b). Thus, it would appear that in this case, Zuckerman was neither entirely right nor entirely wrong. But as time passes it seems more and more likely that he was more right than wrong. In either case, the doubts that he tried to engender have led to a new level of complexity of human evolutionary studies.

Zuckerman's eminence in the combined worlds of science and public affairs was recognized by many scientific societies, universities, and governments throughout the world. He was knighted in 1956, and then elevated to life peerage in 1971. His list of publications is staggering, with more than 1,000 individual papers up to 1990.

He died in London of a heart attack on 1 April 1993.

Charles E. Oxnard

See also Australopithecines; Bipedalism; Clark, (Sir) Wilfrid Edward Le Gros; Primate Field Studies

Bibliography
SELECTED WORKS
Growth changes in the skull of the baboon. *Proceedings of the Zoological Society of London* 55:843–873, 1926; Age changes in the chimpanzee, with special reference to growth of brain, eruption of teeth, and estimation of age; with a note on the Taungs ape. *Proceedings of the Zoological Society of London* pp. 1–42, 1928; The social life of the primates. *Realist* 1:72–88, 1929; *The social life of monkeys and apes.* London: Kegan Paul, 1932; *Functional affinities of man, monkeys, and apes.* London: Kegan Paul, 1933; Taxonomy and human evolution. *Biological Reviews* 25:435–485, 1950; An ape or the ape?

Journal of the Royal Anthropological Institute of Great Britain and Ireland 81:57–68, 1952.

Correlation of change in evolution of higher primates. In: J. Huxley, A.C. Hardy, & E.B. Ford (eds) *Evolution as a process.* London: Allen & Unwin, 1954, pp. 300–352; *A new system of anatomy.* London: Oxford University Press, 1961; *The ovary.* 2 vols. London: Academic Press, 1962; *Scientists and war.* London: Hamish Hamilton, 1966; *Beyond the ivory tower.* London: Weidenfeld & Nicolson, 1970; (ed) *The concepts of evolution.* Symposia of the Zoological Society of London. No. 33. London: Academic Press, 1973; *From apes to warlords.* London: Hamish Hamilton, 1978; *Nuclear illusion and reality.* London: Collins, 1982; *A system of practical anatomy for dental students.* Oxford: Oxford University Press, 1986; *Monkeys, men, and missiles.* London: Collins, 1988; *Six men out of the ordinary.* London: Owen, 1992.

ARCHIVAL SOURCES

Zuckerman Archive: Library, University of East Anglia, Norwich, Norfolk NR4 7TJ, England.

PRIMARY AND SECONDARY SOURCES

R.J. Clarke & P.V. Tobias: Sterkfontein Member 2 foot bones of the oldest South African hominid. *Science* 269:521–524, 1995; R. Kidd: *An investigation into the patterns of morphological variation in the proximal tarsus of selected human groups, apes, and fossils: A morphometric analysis.* Ph.D. Thesis. University of Western Australia, 1995; R. Kidd, P. O'Higgins, & C.E. Oxnard: The OH 8 foot: A reappraisal of the hindfoot utilising a multivariate analysis. *Perspectives in Human Biology* 4:72–73, 1994; M.G. Leakey et al.: New four-million-year-old hominid species from Kanapoi and Allia Bay. *Nature* 376:565–571, 1995; C.E. Oxnard: *Uniqueness and diversity in human evolution.* Chicago: University of Chicago Press, 1975a; C.E. Oxnard: The place of the australopithecines in human evolution: Grounds for doubt? *Nature* 258:389–395, 1975b; C.E. Oxnard & C. Hoyland-Wilks: Hominid bipedalism or bipedalisms? The pelvic evidence. *Perspectives in Human Biology* 4:13–14, 1994; B. Patterson & W.W. Howells: Hominid humeral fragment from the early Pleistocene of northwestern Kenya. *Science* 156:64–66, 1967.

Zuttiyeh, Mugharet el- (Israel)

In 1925, following a previous archeological survey by P. Karge, Francis A.J. Turville-Petre (1901–1942) surveyed the area of the Wadi Amud to the west of Lake Tiberias (the Sea of Galilee) for Paleolithic sites of interest. He ended by excavating in two of those sites, Mugharet el-Emireh and Mugharet el-Zuttiyeh (Turville-Petre 1927). The former became the type site for the Middle to Upper Paleolithic transitional industry (the Emiran), and the latter yielded the first reasonably complete archaic human fossil from western Asia, the Zuttiyeh 1, or Galilee fossil.

The Zuttiyeh fossil, a frontal, zygomatic, and sphenoidal piece of a young adult and rather small individual, was found at the bottom of a Paleolithic level, which was in turn sealed below a layer of rockfall within the limestone cave. The archeological material was considered by Turville-Petre to be Middle Paleolithic, despite the presence in the collection of *coup-de-poing* bifaces. The human remains were turned over to the anatomist-anthropologist Arthur Keith (1866–1955) in London, who produced a detailed description of the fossil, comparing it primarily to an "Australian" (Keith 1927), and then gave a more general interpretation in his subsequent book (Keith 1931). There Keith concluded that "the ancient Galilean was of the Neanderthal type, and apparently a racial variant of that type" (1931:191).

This general view of a Neandertal-like fossil associated with a Middle Paleolithic industry was reinforced by the American paleoanthropologist Theodore D. McCown (1908–1969) and Keith in their Mount Carmel volume (1939), in which they noted its similarities to the Tabūn 1 Neandertal skeleton from Mount Carmel. Nonetheless, there were already indications that it might represent an earlier hominid group than the Neandertals. The British archeologists Dorothy Garrod and Dorothea M.A. Bate (1937), on the basis of their excavations at Tabūn, had noted that the industry probably represented the earlier late Acheulean of Yabrudian facies, thereby predating the Mousterian-associated Neandertals. A similar conclusion was reached by A. Rust (1950) at Yabrud in Syria (cf. Rust 1950).

Subsequent interpretations of the Zuttiyeh fossil largely maintained that it was a Near Eastern archaic human, generally related to the Neandertals but preceeding them in time (e.g., Howell 1957; Trinkaus 1983, 1984). This was reinforced by the reexcavation of the site by the Israeli archeologists I. Gisis and O. Bar-Yosef in 1973

(Gisis & Bar-Yosef 1974), which confirmed the Yabudian nature of the industry. Further confirmation of the early age for Zuttiyeh was provided by the dating of a travertine above the deposits to the end of the Middle Pleistocene by H.P. Schwarcz (1980). In particular, the American paleoanthropologist Erik Trinkaus (1983) noted the fossil's similarities to the Tabūn frontal, highlighted previously by McCown and Keith (1939), and the resemblance between its zygomatic region and those of the earlier (and probably last interglacial) Shanidar 2 and 4 specimens.

This view was challenged in 1981 by the French paleoanthropologist Bernard Vandermeersch, who suggested that the Zuttiyeh fossil represented the oldest known representative of a lineage leading solely to the early modern human Qafzeh and Skhūl samples, already distinct from the lineage resulting in the Near Eastern late archaic humans from Amud, Tabūn, and Shanidar (Vandermeersch 1981, 1989). In this, he used primarily the shape of the orbits, the horizontal angulation of the zygomatic bone, and the (supposedly) high angle of the frontal bone. In response, Trinkaus (1988) pointed out the generally archaic nature of the Zuttiyeh specimen and the absence of any clearly derived Neandertal or modern human feature on the specimen. This latter view was generally supported by other reanalyses of the specimen (e.g., Simmons et al. 1991; Sohn & Wolpoff 1993) and the highlighting of its similarities to east Asian late *Homo erectus* as well as to some Near Eastern archaic humans (Sohn & Wolpoff 1993). The morphophylogenetic affinities of the specimen thus remain in limbo, with the majority view being that it documents a later Middle Pleistocene hominid, the oldest hominid cranial remains from the Near East (matched or exceeded in age only by the Tabūn Layer E femur and tooth, the Gesher-Benot-Ya'acov femora, and the 'Ubeidiya incisor), representing a population that could be ancestral to the later Near East Neandertals and/or early modern humans.

Erik Trinkaus

See also Gesher-Benot-Ya'acov (Israel); Israel; Keith, (Sir) Arthur; McCown, Theodore D(oney); Mount Carmel (Israel); Neandertals; Qafzeh (Jebel) (Israel); Shanidar (Iraq); Tabūn, Mughared et- (Israel); 'Ubeidiya (Israel)

Bibliography
D.A.E. Garrod & D.M.A. Bate: *The Stone Age of Mount Carmel I: Excavations at the Wadi el-Mughara.* Oxford: Clarendon Press, 1937; I. Gisis & O. Bar-Josef: New excavation in Zuttiyeh Cave, Wadi Amud, Israel. *Paléorient* 2:175–180, 1974; F.C. Howell: The evolutionary significance of variation and varieties of "Neanderthal" man. *Quarterly Review of Biology* 32:330–347, 1957; A. Keith: A report on the Galilee skull. In: F. Turville-Petre (ed) *Researches in prehistoric Galilee.* Jerusalem: British School of Archaeology in Jerusalem, 1927, pp. 53–106; A. Keith: *New discoveries relating to the antiquity of man.* London: Norton, 1931.

T.D. McCown & A. Keith: *The Stone Age of Mount Carmel II: The fossil human remains from the Levalloiso-Mousterian.* Oxford: Clarendon Press, 1939; A. Rust: *Die Höhlenfunde von Jabrud (Syrien).* Neumünster: Wachholtz Verlag, 1950; H.P. Schwarcz: Absolute age determinations of archaeological sites by uranium-series dating of travertines. *Archaeometry* 22:3–24, 1980; T. Simmons et al.: Frontal bone morphometrics of southwest Asian Pleistocene hominids. *Journal of Human Evolution* 20:249–269, 1991; S. Sohn & M.H. Wolpoff: Zuttiyeh face, a view from the east. *American Journal of Physical Anthropology* 91:325–347, 1993; E. Trinkaus: *The Shanidar Neandertals.* New York: Academic Press, 1983.

E. Trinkaus: Western Asia. In: F.H. Smith & F. Spencer (eds) *The origins of modern humans: A world survey of the fossil evidence.* New York: Liss, 1984, pp. 251–293; E. Trinkaus: The evolutionary origins of the Neandertals; or, Why were there Neandertals? In: E. Trinkaus (ed) L'Homme de Néandertal 3: L'Anatomie. *Etudes et Recherches Archéologiques de l'Université de Liège* 30:11–29, 1988; F. Turville-Petre: *Researches in prehistoric Galilee.* Jerusalem: British School of Archaeology in Jerusalem, 1927; B. Vandermeersch: Les premiers *Homo sapiens* au proche-Orient. In D. Ferembach (ed): *Les processus de l'hominisation.* Paris: CNRS, 1981, pp. 97–100; B. Vandermeersch: The evolution of modern humans: Recent evidence from southwest Asia. In: P. Mellars & C.B. Stringer (eds) *The human revolution.* Edinburgh: University of Edinburgh Press, 1989, pp. 155–164.

Name Index

Subject Index